# ENCYCLOPEDIA OF
# SOCIAL WORK

20TH EDITION

# Encyclopedia of

# Social Work

20TH EDITION

Terry Mizrahi
Larry E. Davis

*Editors in Chief*

VOLUME 4
S–Y
Biographies
Index

NASW PRESS

OXFORD
UNIVERSITY PRESS

2008

# NASW PRESS

The NASW Press is a leading scholarly press in the social sciences. It serves faculty, practitioners, agencies, libraries, clinicians, and researchers throughout the United States and abroad. Known for attracting expert authors, the NASW Press delivers professional information to more than 250,000 readers through its scholarly journals, books, and reference works.

## OXFORD
### UNIVERSITY PRESS

Oxford University Press, Inc., publishes works that further
Oxford University's objective of excellence
in research, scholarship, and education.

Oxford New York
Auckland   Cape Town   Dar es Salaam   Hong Kong   Karachi
Kuala Lumpur   Madrid   Melbourne   Mexico City   Nairobi
New Delhi   Shanghai   Taipei   Toronto

With offices in
Argentina   Austria   Brazil   Chile   Czech Republic   France   Greece
Guatemala   Hungary   Italy   Japan   Poland   Portugal   Singapore
South Korea   Switzerland   Thailand   Turkey   Ukraine   Vietnam

Copyright © 2008 by NASW Press and Oxford University Press, Inc.

Published by

NASW Press
750 First Street, NE • Suite 700 • Washington, DC 20002-4241
http://www.socialworkers.org/

and

Oxford University Press, Inc.
198 Madison Avenue, New York, New York, 10016
http://www.oup.com

Oxford is a registered trademark of Oxford University Press

ISSN 0071-0237

ISBN 978-0-19-530661-3 (hardcover)
ISBN 978-0-19-531036-8 (paperback)

# ENCYCLOPEDIA OF
# SOCIAL WORK

20TH EDITION

# S

## SCALES AND INDICES

**ABSTRACT:** This entry reviews the uses of scales and instruments in social work practice, including scales and instruments for diagnosis and evidencing treatment necessity, as methods for monitoring client progress, and as outcomes measures of clinical significance. A resource list for locating scales and instruments is provided.

**KEY WORDS:** measurement tools; instruments and scales; practice evaluation single system design; quantitative methods

Standardized instruments have been part of social work practice since its beginning. The very notion of "scientific charity," characteristic of the Charity Organization Society in the late 1870s, had an "emphasis on the need for hard data" (Trattner, 1999, p. 95), an emphasis furthered with Mary Richmond's advocacy for "social research" (Zimbalist, 1977, p. 21). Significant advancement in the use of measurements resulted from the call for accountability (Briar, 1973), the introduction of behavioral interventions (Fischer & Gochros, 1975), and the need to demonstrate treatment effectiveness (Bloom, Fischer, & Orme, 2006).

The routine use of instruments and scales by practitioners, however, had to wait until a sufficient number were developed on a wide range of client conditions. The first major effort was Hudson's *Clinical Measurement Package* (1982). Subsequently, Corcoran and Fischer (1987) published the first compendium with over 125 rapid assessment tools for couple, family, children, and adult conditions. After 20 years the number of scales and instruments has grown expedientially, with thousands available with a simple Google search and over 500 reprinted in Fischer and Corcoran (2007a, 2007b). The number of compendiums providing reprinted instruments has also flourished (Fischer & Corcoran, 2007a).

Just as the number of instruments and scales have increased, so too has their use in social work practice. Although once chiefly the domain of problem identification and diagnosis, instruments and scales are also useful for evidencing the need for treatment in managed care settings (Corcoran & Boyer-Quick, 2002; Corcoran & Vandiver, 1996), monitoring the

treatment effectiveness throughout clinical services (Bloom, Fischer, & Orme, 2006), and establishing clinical significance (Jacobson & Truax, 1991). This entry will review these uses of instruments and scales.

### Essential Features of Instruments and Scales

Instruments and scales are designed to quantitatively ascertain some "thing." In social work practice, this "thing" is likely a client's behaviors, thoughts, and feelings, and the interaction of clients with others in the social environment. The "thing" may be considered in terms of the problem presented for clinical attention or the goal of the intervention.

As standardized measurements, instruments and scales assign a number to the different attributes of the thing being assessed. The attributes are ascertained in terms of their magnitude, frequency, or duration. As a consequence of having numbers as referent points for the attributes, scores may be compared by using the arithmetic operations of addition, subtraction, multiplication, and division—an advantage not afford by qualitative accounts.

The data from instruments and scales also provide information that is designed to be consistent and accurate. Consistency is estimated with reliability procedures and accuracy is estimated with validity procedures; both enable the social worker to estimate how much error is actually involved in the scores (Corcoran, 1995).

In summary, the essential features of instruments and scales are that the scores provide quantitative referent points of the attributes of some topic of interest. The numeric referents are intended to tap magnitudes, frequency, or duration of that topic with consistency and accuracy. Moreover, scores may be compared with addition, subtraction, multiplication, and division. As such, there are four major ways social workers can use instruments and scales in practice.

### Instruments and Scales for Problem Identification and Diagnosis

Instruments and scales have traditionally been used to identify clinical problems and for diagnostic purposes. Instruments and scales allow the clinician to narrow the wide range of client concerns and complaints into a formulated case description with a diagnostic summary. The outcome of this use is that the social worker narrows the focus and purpose which guides the selection of the intervention.

A major advantage of an instrument and scale is that the score not only helps determine the clinical condition, for example, depression, but also affords an assessment of the severity of the condition, typically in terms of its magnitude. The practitioner is thus able to understand the severity level of a client's condition and then compare this severity with other scores, particularly clinical norms and the general population.

## Instruments and Scales
## to Establish Treatment Necessity

By comparing a client's score with normative data, the social worker is able to use instruments and scales to establish treatment necessity. This is a frequent prerequisite to services in managed care setting. By comparing the client's score with a clinical sample, one is able to determine how similar the client is with individuals already receiving services. Such a situation would persuasively suggest that services are warranted. Similarly, treatment necessity may be shown by determining how different a client's score is from the general population. Being distinguishable from the typical or average person evidences a need for services. In addition, simple procedures are available to calculate the percentage of others who are more and less severe in the symptoms (Corcoran & Boyer-Quick, 2002).

## Instruments and Scales
## to Monitor Client Progress

One of the more common uses of instruments and scales is to monitor a client's condition before, during, and after services (Bloom, Fischer, & Orme, 2006). Instruments and scales may be used to monitor a client by observing the decrease in the problem, clinical condition, or symptoms, and by assessing the obtainment of treatment goals. A more informative use of instruments and scales is to collect observation of both the problem and the obtainment of the goals.

The practical values of these data are greatly enhanced by plotting the scores on a graph to form a simple, single system design. This allows the social worker to visually determine whether the problems decreased and whether the goals were obtained.

## Instrument and Scales
## to Establish Clinical Significance

Another use of instruments and scales is to establish a definition of "clinical significance," the obtainment of which is itself a treatment goal (Jacobson & Truax, 1991). Clinical significance is defined as an accurate score on an instrument or scale, which at the end of treatment, is similar to the general population and distinguishable from the clinical sample. Clinical significance is, in fact, the mirror opposite of the use of scores for establishing treatment necessity based on having scores similar to a clinical sample but distinguishable from the general population.

In essence, by comparing a client's scores to norms after treatment the social worker has another indication of treatment outcomes. Moreover, by being able to say that the client is no longer similar to those in treatment and is now like the "average," "typical," or "normal" individual is probative evidence of treatment effectiveness, which is afforded only by the use of instruments and scales in social work practice.

In conclusion, the short history of using scales and instruments in social work practice has accompanied the advancement in the field. From a humble beginning or assessing client progress with a limited number of instruments, the field had witnessed huge growth in the number and variety of available instruments. Moreover, the use of scales and instruments has expanded to include diagnostic purposes, evidencing treatment necessity and even illustrating clinical significance. One can only hope that the future witnesses similar growth in the effort to help clients change.

## REFERENCES

Bloom, M., Fischer, J., & Orme, J. (2006). *Evaluating practice: Guidelines for the accountable professional*. Boston: Allyn & Bacon.

Briar, S. (1973). Effective social work intervention in direct practice: Implications for education. In S. Briar et al. (Eds.), *Facing the challenge*. Plenary session papers from the 19th Annual Program Meeting. Alexandria, VA: Counsel on Social Work Education.

Corcoran, K. (1995). Psychometrics in social work. In R. Edwards et al. (Eds.), *Encyclopedia of social work* (19th ed., pp. 1942–1947). Silver Spring, MD: NASW Press.

Corcoran, K., & Boyer-Quick, J. (2002). How clinicians can effectively use assessment tools to evidence medical necessity and throughout the treatment process. In A. R. Roberts & G. J. Greene (Eds.), *Social work desk reference*. New York: Oxford University Press.

Corcoran, K., & Fischer, J. (1987). *Measures for clinical practice: A sourcebook*. New York: Free Press.

Corcoran, K., & Vandiver, V. (1996). *Maneuvering the maze of managed care*. New York: Free Press.

Fischer, J., & Corcoran, K. (2007a). *Measures for clinical practice and research: A sourcebook*, Vol. 1: Couples, families and children. New York: Oxford University Press.

Fischer, J., & Corcoran, K. (2007b). *Measures for clinical practice and research: A sourcebook*, Vol. 2: Adults. New York: Oxford University Press.

Fischer J., & Gochros, H. (1975). *Planned Behavior Change: Behavior Modification in Social Work*. NY: Free Press.

Hudson, W. W. (1982). *The clinical measurement package: A field manual*. Chicago: Dorsey Press.

Jacobson, N. S., & Truax, P. (1991). *Clinical significance: A statistical approach to defining meaningful change in psychotherapy research. Journal of Consulting and Clinical Psychology, 59,* 12–19.

Trattner, W. I. (1999). *From poor laws to welfare state: A history of social welfare in America*. New York: Free Press.

Zimbalist, S. E. (1977). *Historic themes and landmarks in social welfare research*. New York: Harper.

—KEVIN CORCORAN

**SCHOOLS.** *See* Education Policy.

## SCHOOL SOCIAL WORK

**ABSTRACT:** School social work has recently celebrated 100 years as a vibrant profession. This entry details the genesis and development of this particular specialization to the modern day, exploring the history of the profession including policy and legislation that has either resulted from or affected schools on a national level. Additionally, the entry explains the knowledge-base of school social work, examines the regulation and standards for both practice and practitioners, and considers future trends for the field.

**KEY WORDS:** schools; education; children and adolescents; public education; service delivery

In 2006, school social work celebrated its existence for 100 years as a vibrant profession (School Social Work Association of America, 2005a). As practitioners and scholars alike continue to seek solutions and interventions for ever-changing social problems, school social work will continue to be defined by research and new knowledge developments in social work and related fields.

School social workers started as and remain an integral link between school, home, and community. Those who choose this particular field of social work provide direct services, as well as specialized services such as mental health intervention, crisis management and intervention, and facilitating community involvement in the schools. Working as an interdisciplinary team member, school social workers not only continue to provide services to school children and their families, but also continue to evaluate their role and consequently modify it to meet organizational or contextual needs and changes in policies and practice.

School social work as a discipline continues to develop in relation to social issues, school systems, continuing education, and evolving research, perhaps more so than other school-based disciplines. Statistics indicate a recent upswing in the number of school social workers or social work services in schools. As a result, at the date of the last Substance Abuse and Mental Health Services Report, school social workers are engaged in 44% of all school districts (Foster et al., 2005).

In the next century, practitioners will face evolving definitions of personhood and family, economics and health will continue to affect how children learn and function in a school environment, and schools will remain one of the most practical arenas in which to assess and provide social services. Through it all school social work will continue to change, thrive, and provide evidence-based solutions for children and families. Before discussing more fully the current trends and issues that are impacting, or have the potential to impact, school social work practice, it is vital to revisit and examine its historical evolution.

### History

Social work in schools began between 1906 and 1907, (Allen-Meares, 2006), with initial development outside the school system, as private agencies and civic organizations took on the work (Costin, 1969). It was not until 1913 that the first Board of Education initiated and financed a formal visiting teacher program, placing visiting teachers in special departments of the school under the administration and direction of the superintendent of schools.

EARLY INFLUENCES As the school social work movement gained momentum, the early twentieth century proved to be a fruitful period in its development. Several important influences included the following:

1. *The passage of compulsory school attendance laws:* Concern regarding the illiteracy of youth brought attention to a child's right to receive a minimum education and the states' responsibility for providing it. This attention led to support for the enactment of compulsory attendance statutes, and by 1918 each state had passed its own version. The lack of effective enforcement led to the idea that school attendance officers were needed, and Abbott and Breckinridge (1917) held that this

responsibility should be assigned to the school social worker.

2. *Knowledge of individual differences:* As the scope of compulsory education laws expanded, states were required to provide an educational experience for a variety of children. At the same time, new knowledge about individual differences among children began to emerge. Previous to this there had been no real concern about whether children had different learning needs; those who presented a challenge were simply not enrolled.

EXPANSION During the 1920s the number and the influence of school social workers increased, largely as a result of a series of demonstrations held over three years, organized and funded by the Commonwealth Fund of New York (Oppenheimer, 1925), which provided financial support to the National Committee of Visiting Teachers and increased experimentation in the field of school social work.

The 1920s were also the beginning of a therapeutic role for school social workers in public schools. According to Costin (1978), the increasing recognition of individual differences among children and interest on the part of the mental hygienists in understanding behavior problems led to an effort on the part of visiting teachers to develop techniques for the prevention of social maladjustment.

SHIFTING GOALS The development of social work service was greatly hindered during the Depression, with services either abolished or reduced in volume (Areson, 1923). As the Depression worsened the social work activity that did take place centered on ensuring that people's basic needs were met. During this time, visiting teachers began viewing their role in a different way, with their early responsibilities as attendance officers being replaced by the burgeoning role of social caseworker.

EMPHASIS ON SOCIAL CASEWORK By 1940, the shift to social caseworker was complete. No longer were social change and neighborhood conditions seen as the sole points of intervention. Instead, the profession was beginning to build its clinical base, with the personality needs of the individual child taking primary attention.

CHANGING GOALS AND METHODS Public schools came under attack in many different ways during the 1960s. There were those who argued that public

education was not sufficient. Several studies documented adverse school policies, and claimed that inequality in educational opportunity existed as a result of racial segregation. There was considerable discussion about the need for change, including change in the practices of both social workers and guidance counselors.

During this time, group work, which had previously been introduced to the school system, was becoming a prominent method. In a research progress report, Robert Vinter and Rosemary Sarri described the effective use of group work in dealing with such school problems as high school dropouts, underachievement, and academic failure (Vinter & Sarri, 1965).

CHANGING DEMOGRAPHICS AND INCREASED RECOGNITION IN EDUCATIONAL LEGISLATION During the 1970s the number of school social workers increased and at the same time more emphasis was being placed on family, community, teaming with workers in other school-related disciplines, and the education of handicapped pupils.

In 1975, Congress passed The Education for All Handicapped Children Act (EAHC), which had "impacted social work services in schools profoundly," as "[s]ocial workers were named specifically as one of the related services required to help individuals with disabilities benefit from special education" (Atkins-Burnett, 2006). This would be the first time, but not the last, that the importance of school social workers was recognized and codified.

Educational legislation continues to play a major role in the definition and function of school social workers and shaping and expanding the services they provide. In the 1980s school social workers were included as "qualified personnel" in Part H of the Education of the Handicapped Act Amendments of 1986, the Early Intervention for Handicapped Infants and Toddlers; and in the Elementary and Secondary School Improvement Amendments of 1988.

The 1990s brought with them many more changes. National organizations grew and offered added support to the specialty. Codified standards for school social workers were edited and tailored for relevance, and states themselves began to take an active role in what it means to be a school social worker.

In 1994 school social workers were once again included in a major piece of legislation—the American Education Act, which included eight national goals, of which the major objectives were research promotion, consensus building, and systemic change, to ensure equality of educational opportunities for all students.

Additionally, two key pieces of legislation have influenced the job and roles of school social workers. In 1990, the Individuals with Disabilities Education.

Act (IDEA) was authorized. Amended several times, IDEA further refined services, eligibility, parent involvement, assessment and testing, and learning opportunities for students with disabilities or special needs.

In 2002, President George W. Bush signed into law a comprehensive and controversial piece of federal legislation titled the No Child Left Behind Act (NCLB). Reauthorized in 2006, NCLB was conceived as a way to hold school systems and students accountable for learning, and includes standards for those with special needs.

### Knowledge Base of School Social Work

As school social work evolved, so too did different practice models. A practice model may be defined as "a coherent set of directives which state how a given kind of treatment is to be carried out.... It usually states what a practitioner is expected to do or what practitioners customarily do under given conditions" (Reid & Epstein, 1972, pp. 7–8).

Alderson (1972) offered four models of school social work practice: the traditional clinical model, the school change model, the community school model and the social interaction model.

TRADITIONAL CLINICAL MODEL The best-known and most widely used is the traditional clinical model, which focuses on individual students with social and emotional problems that interfere with their potential to learn. The model's primary base is psychoanalytic and ego psychology. The model's major assumption is that the individual child or the family is experiencing difficult times or dysfunction. As a result, the school social worker's role is that of a direct caseworker—providing services to the child or the family and not focusing on the school itself. School personnel are only involved as a source of information about the child's behavior.

SCHOOL CHANGE MODEL In contrast, the school change model's target is, in fact, the school and changing any institutional policies, conditions, and practices that were seen as causing student dysfunction or malperformance. The school itself is considered the client, and school personnel are involved in discussion, identification, and change.

COMMUNITY SCHOOL MODEL The community school model focuses primarily on communities with limited social and economic resources. The social worker's role is to educate these communities about the school's offerings, organize support for the school's programs, and explain to school officials the dynamics and societal factors affecting the community. This model assumes that school personnel require ongoing and up-to-date information about social problems and their effects on school children in order to have a complete understanding.

SOCIAL INTERACTION The social interaction model emphasizes reciprocal influences of the acts of individuals and groups. The target of intervention is the type and the quality of exchanges between parties (the child, groups of children, families, the school, and the community). The school social worker takes on the role of mediator and facilitator with the goal of seeking common ground and common solutions.

COSTIN'S MODEL Another important model grew out of a demonstration project of a multi-university consortium for planned change in pupil personnel services. An amalgamation of several methods, Lela B. Costin's school-community-pupil relations model (Costin, 1973) emphasized the complexity of the interactions among students, the school, and the community. Especially relevant in today's schools, its primary goal serves to bring about change in the interaction of this triad and thus, to modify to some extent harmful institutional practices and policies of the school.

### Demographics and Standards

STATE-BY-STATE REGULATION AND REQUIREMENTS Since the early 1970s, the number of state associations of school social workers has risen. These organizations play an important part in heightening this field's visibility, and regulate the profession. A state-by-state list of specific requirements for school social workers may be found at http://www.sswaa.org/links/statedoe.html (School Social Work Association of America, 2005b).

EDUCATIONAL REQUIREMENTS In most states a Masters of Social Work (MSW) is required. However, some states allow certification at the entry level with a Bachelor's Degree (School Social Work Association of America, 2005c).

STANDARDS FOR SOCIAL WORK SERVICES IN SCHOOLS In 1976, the National Association of Social Workers (NASW) developed the first standards for school social work services, which were grouped into three areas: attainment of competence; organization and administration; and professional practice. NASW continues to provide guidelines, standards, and a Code of Ethics (1994) for the social work community, as well as specific standards for school social workers (NASW, 2002).

RESOURCES FOR SCHOOL SOCIAL WORKERS In addition to its specific standards for school social work, the NASW offers specialized certification as a Certified School Social Work Specialist (C-SSWS), as well as a dedicated specialty practice section.

In 1994, spearheaded by the school social work leadership, School Social Work Association of America (SSWAA) was formed, independent of the NASW (National Association of Social Workers Commission on Education, 1991). There are also several regional councils supporting school social work.

In addition, important journals supported by major organizations such as Children and Schools (NASW) and the School Social Work Journal (Lyceum Books) provide research, theoretical practice, and policy information.

## Trends and Directions
NEW STRUCTURES, NEW PARTNERS As we look into the future of school social work, concerns about the quality and cost of education, student learning outcomes, accountability, increased demand to serve more diverse student populations, and increased social problems among children and families, will challenge the profession to think creatively and differently about their services and how to organize them for greater effectiveness and efficiency. What does this mean for school social work services?

Current trends indicate that school systems are implementing new organizational structures and creating new partnerships. Some districts are contracting with external mental health service providers or other agencies in what they believe to be a cost-efficient way to serve their students. Schools have also formed relevant partnerships, termed *school-linked* or *integrated services*, with organizations such as health providers, which provide their services through the school system (Franklin, 2004).

Among its most pressing issues, this field of practice will be facing a myriad of changes and issues, including:
1. Increased global competition and educational excellence. School social workers will need to empirically demonstrate their contributions to the national focus on performance measures and standardized tests, and warn the school system about misuse and problems facing vulnerable pupils.
2. Social, economic, and educational policy and its impact on education. School social workers must be knowledgeable of those policies and advocate for those that are just, and lobby for the elimination of those that are problematic.
3. Technological advances. The gap between those who are technologically literate and those who are not will have an effect on poverty and unemployment rates. Working with other relevant school personnel, school social workers must also make others aware of these inequities.
4. Growing diversity and new immigrant populations. Multicultural competency, including knowledge about new immigrants, will challenge our public schools and consequently the profession. In response, school social workers will need to increase their knowledge to remain effective assessors, advisors, and advocate for these students.
5. The focus on evidence-based interventions. Practitioners will need to keep abreast of and incorporate evidence-based interventions, new problem-solving approaches, and innovative partnership to address the needs of all students.

## Conclusion
The American public education system is an institution subject to numerous criticisms and challenges. Yet it is has proven to be resilient and essential to the core values of our democracy. As adaptations or new innovations develop, the profession of social work must not only respond, but be proactive in shaping the future. School social workers provide crucial social services in one of the most accessible settings, playing an integral role in prevention, intervention, and positive change for school-aged children and their families.

## REFERENCES
Abbott, E., & Breckinridge, S. (1917). *Truancy and non-attendance in the Chicago schools: A study of the social aspects of the compulsory education and child labor legislation of Illinois.* Chicago: University of Chicago Press.

Alderson, J. J. (1972). Models of school social work practice. In R. Sarri & F. Maple (Eds.), *The school in the community* (pp. 151–160). Washington, DC: NASW.

Allen-Meares, P. (2006, Summer). One Hundred Years: A Historical Analysis of Social Work Services in Schools. *School Social Work Journal*, Special Issue, 24–43.

Areson, C. W. (1923). Status of children's work in the United States. *Proceedings of the national conference of social work* (p. 398). Chicago: University of Chicago Press.

Atkins-Burnett, S. (2006). Children with disabilities. In C. Franklin, M. B. Harris, & P. Allen-Meares (Eds.), *The school services sourcebook: A guide for school-based professionals.* New York: Oxford University Press.

Costin, L. B. (1969). An analysis of the tasks in school social work. *Social Service Review, 43,* 274–285.

Costin, L. B. (1973). School social work practice: A new model. *Social Work, 20,* 135–139.

Costin, L. B. (1978). *Social work services in schools: Historical perspectives and current directions. Continuing education series* #8 (pp. 1–34). Washington, DC: NASW.

Education for All Handicapped Children Act. (1975). Federal Register (P.L. 94–142 41:46977).

Foster, S., Rollefson, M., Doksum, T., Noonan, D., Robinson, G., Teich, J. (2005). *School Mental Health Services in the United States, 2002–2003.* DHHS Pub. No. (SMA) 05-4068. Rockville, MD: Center for Mental Health Services, Substance Abuse and Mental Health Services Administration.

Franklin, C. (2004). The delivery of school social work services. In P. A. Meares (Ed.), *Social work services in the school* (4th ed.) (pp. 295–326). Boston: Allyn & Bacon.

Individuals with Disabilities Education Act (IDEA). (1991). Congressional Information Service Annual Legislative Histories for U.S. Public Laws (P.L. 101–476).

Individuals with Disabilities Education Improvement Act of 2004. H. R. 1350.

National Association of Social Workers. (1994). *NASW code of ethics.* Washington, DC: Author.

National Association of Social Workers. (2002). *Standards for school social work services.* Washington, DC: Author.

National Association of Social Workers Commission on Education. (1991). *Fact sheet-School social work and NASW* (pp. 1–7). Washington, DC: NASW.

No Child Left Behind Act. P.L. 107–110.

Oppenheimer, J. (1925). *The visiting teacher movement, with special reference to administrative relationships (2nd ed.)* (p. 5). New York: Joint Committee on Methods of Preventing Delinquency.

Reid, W., & Epstein, L. (1972). *Task-centered casework.* New York: Columbia University Press.

School Social Work Association of America (2005a). Publications and Resources. Retrieved September 27, 2007 from http://www.sswaa.org/members/career.html

School Social Work Association of America (2005b). Publications and Resources. Retrieved October 4, 2006 from http://www.sswaa.org/links/statedoe.html

School Social Work Association of America (2005c). Publications and Resources. Retrieved October 4, 2006 from http://www.sswaa.org/about/career.html

Vinter, R., & Sarri, R. (1965). Malperformance in the public school: A group work approach. *Social Work, 10,* 38–48.

—PAULA ALLEN-MEARES

# SCHOOL VIOLENCE

**ABSTRACT:** Research suggests that school violence victims may experience physical harm, psychological trauma such as anxiety, depression, loneliness, low self-esteem, poor academic outcomes, low school attendance, suicidal ideation, and in rare cases, extreme outbursts of lethal aggression. One of the most common definitions had emphasized school bullying, defined by most researchers as an aggressive repetitive behavior emanating from a perpetrator who is larger and stronger than the victim. Currently there is a fairly strong consensus in academia that the term "school violence" includes a wide range of intentional behaviors that aim to physically and emotionally harm students, staff, and property, on or around school grounds. These acts vary in severity and frequency, and include behaviors such as social isolation, threats, and intimidation (including through electronic communications), school fights, possession and use of weapons, property theft and vandalism, sexual harassment and assault, abuse from school staff, gang violence, and hate crimes.

**KEY WORDS:** school violence; monitoring; mapping; interventions

School violence has deleterious consequences for children and schools. Research suggests that victims may experience physical harm, psychological trauma such as anxiety, depression, loneliness, low self-esteem, poor academic outcomes, low school attendance, suicidal ideation, and in rare cases, extreme outbursts of lethal aggression (Juvonen & Graham, 2001; Limber, 2006; Olweus, 1993; Rigby, 1996; Smith & Brain, 2000; Vossekuil, Fein, Reddy, Borum, & Modzeleski, 2002).

Definitions of school violence have varied considerably over the past 40 years. One of the most common emphases was on school bullying, defined by most researchers as an aggressive repetitive behavior emanating from a perpetrator who is larger and stronger than the victim (Olweus, 1993). Currently there is a fairly strong consensus in academia that the term "school violence" includes a wide range of intentional behaviors that aim to physically and emotionally harm students, staff, and property, on or around school grounds. These acts vary in severity and frequency, and include behaviors such as social isolation, threats, and intimidation (including through electronic communications), school fights, possession and use of weapons, property theft and vandalism, sexual harassment and assault, abuse from school staff, gang violence, and hate crimes.

In the global arena, the work of Olweus in 1970s has had the greatest impact on practice and research.

Olweus (1993) designed large-scale school-based interventions in Scandinavia, which were later emulated by many countries around the world, including England, Japan, New Zealand, Israel, and Australia. Public interest in school violence emerged in the United States only after a series of highly publicized fatal school shootings in the late 1990s. These acts prompted significant national, state, and local efforts to increase school safety through changes in legislation, policy, intervention, large-scale funding, and research (for example, Osher & Dwyer, 2005; Gun Free School Act of 1994).

The shootings also led to an array of zero tolerance policies that mandated expulsion for possession of weapons, and a range of draconian measures such as security guards, metal detectors, and video surveillance cameras. On the whole, research suggests that these kinds of interventions are less effective, discriminate against students of color, and often create the perception that school is "prison like" (Astor, Meyer, & Behre, 1999; Skiba et al., 2006). However, educational and community-oriented, evidence-based programs also emerged from this post-Columbine national effort that have positive effects without the negative side effects of Zero Tolerance measures (Derzon, 2006).

## Theoretical Models:
### Causes and Multiple Ecological Influences
Multiple disciplines (for example, social work, education, psychology, criminology, public health, medicine) have studied why school violence occurs from many theoretical perspectives. Many of these theories employ social systems-ecological frameworks that focus on the interplay between individual students and the contexts in which they are embedded—school, family, neighborhood or community, and culture (Astor, Benbenishty, Marachi, & Meyer, 2006; Benbenishty & Astor, 2005; Bronfenbrenner, 1979; Fraser, 1996; Garbarino, 2001; Swearer & Espelage, 2004). For instance, Benbenishty and Astor (2005) emphasize how school policies and climate could mediate effects of negative external influences (for example, community poverty and crime) and reduce victimization rates on school grounds. These theories address why school violence occurs and have direct relevance to practice and interventions as they help identify risk and protective factors associated with the individual student, family, school, peer-group, and community.

In contrast with prior ecological theories on youth violence, gangs, and juvenile delinquency, newer theories of school violence emphasize the practical and theoretical values of including the "school" in "school violence." These emerging theories focus on establishing a deeper understanding of school organizational and social dynamics as they pertain to external contexts and acts of violence on school grounds. This research suggests that different forms of school violence are influenced by specific and multiple levels of the social ecology. For example, a negative school climate has a strong association with levels of bullying, whereas the use of weapons in school is predicted by a combination of family, school, and community factors (for examples, see Benbenishty & Astor, 2005).

### Cultural and Ethical and Social Justice Issues
School violence occurs in all social, cultural, and economic settings, but overall more severe forms of violence are more associated with urban school environments. Within the United States, high school violence rates are associated with academically underperforming schools, high drop out rates, economically underfunded schools, high teacher turnover rates, transient student populations, high community gang activity, and schools that lack strong administrative leadership. Since race, ethnicity, poverty, and underfunded schools are so confounded in the United States, a social justice approach targeting poor and disadvantaged communities can help reduce high levels of school violence and improve academic attainment in these communities.

## Exemplars of
## Demographics and Victimization Trends
Prevalence of school violence varies according to the type of violent acts (more extreme violent behaviors are very rare), the characteristics of schools and students involved, and the timeframe considered. In the United States, there was less than 1 homicide or suicide of a school-age youth at school per million students enrolled during the 2001–02 school year. The rate of students reported being victims of serious violence on school grounds was 0.6%. In 2003, about 6% of students in grades 9–12 reported that they had carried a weapon on school property. Physical fights and bullying are more common. For example, 13% of U.S. students said that they had been in a fight on school property during the preceding 12 months (DeVoe et al., 2004). As for bullying, 10.6% said they were victims of bullying, 13% bullied others, and 6.3% were bullies and victims (Nansel et al., 2001).

Gender and age differences are consistent across many studies. Males have higher rates of victimization and perpetration of physical violence (Espelage, Mebane, & Swearer, 2004). For instance, in the United States the prevalence of physical fights among males (17%) is double than that of females (8%). These

TABLE 1

*Model Violence Prevention Programs and Evaluating Sources*

| PROGRAM (AUTHORS) | GRADE | PARTICIPANTS | PROGRAM COMPONENTS | OUTCOME MEASURES | RESULTS |
|---|---|---|---|---|---|
| *Bullying Prevention Program* (Olweus, 1993) www.clemson.edu/olweus | 4th–7th grades | 2,500 students in 42 primary and secondary schools in Norway. (The program is now international and is being applied in 15 countries. The materials are translated into more than 12 languages.) | Core components of the program are implemented at the school level, the class level, and the individual level. Components include the following:<br>• Distribution of anonymous student questionnaire assessing the nature and prevalence of bullying<br>• Development of positive and negative consequences for students' behavior<br>• Establishment of a supervisory system<br>• Reinforcement of schoolwide rules against bullying<br>• Classroom workshops with video and discussions to increase knowledge and empathy<br>• Interventions with perpetrators and victims of bullying<br>• Discussions with parents | Student self-report measures collected at introduction of the program, 4 months after introduction, 1-year follow-up, and 2-year follow-up.<br>• Reports of bullying and victimization incidents<br>• Scale of general youth antisocial behavior<br>• Assessment of school climate—order and discipline<br>• Measure of social relationships and attitude toward school | The results show a 33–64% reduction in the levels of bully incidents. The author found a 30–70% reduction in aggregated peer rating variables. In addition, there was no displacement of bullying to before or after school. There was also a significant reduction in antisocial behavior such as fighting, theft, and truancy. The school climate showed marked improvement, with students reporting an increased satisfaction with school in general, positive social relationships, and positive attitude toward schoolwork and school. Rated effective—1, 2, 3, 4, 6, 7, 8, 9 |
| *Child Development Project* (Battistich, Schaps, Watson, & Solomon, 1996) www.devstu.org | 3rd–6th grades | 4,500 students in 24 elementary schools from 6 diverse districts throughout the United States. | This is a comprehensive model focused on creating a cooperative and supportive school environment. Classroom components include the following:<br>• Staff training in cooperative learning<br>• Implementation of a model that fosters cross-grade "buddying" activities<br>• A developmental approach to discipline that fosters self-control<br>• A model to engage students in classroom norm-setting and decision-making | Data were collected after 1 year and 2 years of intervention. Teachers were assessed through four 90-minute observations and annual teacher questionnaires. Student assessments were self-report surveys of drug use and delinquent behavior. | Results showed that students experienced a stronger sense of community and more motivation to be helpful, better conflict-resolution skills, greater acceptance of people who are different, higher self-esteem, stronger feelings of social competence, less loneliness in school, and fewer delinquent acts. Statistically significant decreases were found for marijuana use, vehicle theft, and weapons. By the second year of the program, students in schools showed significantly lower rates of skipping school, carrying weapons, and stealing vehicles ($p$'s $< .01$). Rated effective—3, 4, 5, 6, 7, 9 |

(cont.)

TABLE 1
(cont.)

| PROGRAM (AUTHORS) | GRADE | PARTICIPANTS | PROGRAM COMPONENTS | OUTCOME MEASURES | RESULTS |
|---|---|---|---|---|---|
| FAST Track-Families and Schools Together (Conduct Problems Prevention Research Group) www.fasttrackproject.org | Three cohorts of students. Grade 1–10. (Still ongoing) | At-risk kindergartners identified based on combined teacher and parent ratings of behavior (CBCL). Highest 10% recruited for study. N = 445 intervention children. N = 446 control group children. | Schoolwide community-building activities are used to promote school bonding and parent involvement activities such as interactive homework assignments that reinforce the family–school partnership. Long-term program. Weekly enrichment program for high-risk children and their parents. Students placed in "friendship groups" of 5–6 students each. Discussions, modeling stories and films, role-plays. Sessions focused on reviewing and practicing skills in emotional understanding and communication, friendship building, self-control, and social problem-solving. Parents meet in groups led by family coordinators to discuss parenting strategies, then 30-min parent–child cooperative activity time; biweekly home visits. Academic tutoring provided by trained tutors in 30-min sessions 3× a week. | • Externalizing Scale of CBCL—*oppositional, aggressive, and delinquent* behaviors <br> • *Parent Daily Report*—degree to which child engaged in aggressive and oppositional behaviors during previous 24 hr (given 3×) <br> • Child behavior change <br> • Teacher assessment of acting out behaviors in school (Teacher Report Form, Achenbach 1991) <br> • Scale from the TOCA-R (Teacher Observation of Classroom Adaptation–Revised) <br> • Authority Acceptance Scale <br> • Peer rating of aggressive and hyperactive-disruptive behaviors | Intervention group had higher scores on emotion recognition, emotion coping, and social problem-solving, compared with control group. It also had lower rates of aggressive retaliation when compared with control group. Direct observation results: <br> • Intervention group spent more time in positive peer interaction than did the control group. <br> • Intervention group received higher peer social preference scores than did control group. <br> • Intervention group had higher language arts grades than did control group. Rated effective—2, 3, 6, 8, 9, 11 |
| PATHS curriculum (Component of FAST Track) | 1st–5th grades over three cohorts (Results from Grade 1 findings only are reviewed here) | 198 intervention classrooms 180 control classrooms matched by school size, achievement levels, poverty, and ethnic diversity 7,560 total students | Quality of implementation was assessed by observer rating of teacher's <br> • Skill in teaching PATHS concepts <br> • Management of the classroom <br> • Modeling and generalizing PATHS throughout day <br> • Openness to consultation | 1. Teachers were interviewed about behavior of each child in class (fall/spring of first grade) <br> 2. Sociometric assessments (peer nominations made by students) collected to assess the following: | Hierarchical Linear Modeling (accounting for gender, site, cohort, and intervention) Intervention classrooms had lower ratings of hyperactivity/disruptive behavior, aggression, and more favorable observer ratings of classroom atmosphere. |

845 students were in high-risk intervention or control conditions (6,715 students non-high-risk children).

- Peer aggression
- Peer hyperactivity/disruptiveness
- Peer social status
3. Quality of classroom atmosphere was assessed by observer ratings assessing the following:
- Level of disruption
- Ability to handle transitions
- Ability to follow rules
- Level of cooperation
- Use of problem-solving skills
- Ability to express feelings
- Ability to stay focused on task
- Criticism vs. supportiveness

Three cohorts of intervention, and so teachers administered curriculum once, twice, or thrice. When teacher experience was included in analyses, teachers who taught more cohorts had higher classroom atmosphere ratings (by neutral observer). Teacher skill in program implementation was also related to positive outcomes. Rated effective—2, 3, 6, 9, 11

CBCL, child behavior checklist. Adapted from "Evidence-based violence prevention program and best implementation practices," by R. A. Astor, M. Rosemond, R. O. Pitner, R. Marachi, & R. Benenishty, In C. Franklin, M. B. Harris, & P. Allen-Meares (Eds.), *The school services sourcebook: A guide for school-based professionals* (pp. 423–442), 2006, New York: Oxford University Press.
Evaluating sources:
1. American Youth Policy Forum. See R. A. Mendel (2000). *Less hype, more help: Reducing juvenile crime, what works and what doesn't.* Washington, DC: American Youth Policy Forum. Programs are categorized as *Effective* (refer to www.aypf.org).
2. Blueprints for Violence Prevention. Programs are divided into *Model and Promising* (refer to www.colorado.edu/cspv/blueprints).
3. Center for Mental Health Services, U.S. Department of Health and Human Services, Prevention Research Center for the Promotion of Human Development. Programs are divided into *Effective and Promising* (refer to www.prevention.psu.edu).
4. Center for Substance Abuse Prevention, Substance Abuse and Mental Health Services Administration, Department of Health and Human Services, National Registry of Effective Programs. Programs are divided into *Model, Promising, and Effective* (refer to www.modelprograms.samhsa.gov).
5. Department of Education, Safe and Drug Free Schools. Programs are divided into *Exemplary and Promising* (refer to www.ed.gov/about/offices/list/osdfs/index.html?src=mr).
6. Communities that Care. See R. Posey, S. Wong, R. Catalano, D. Hawkins, L. Dusenbury, & P. Chappell (2000). *Communities that care prevention strategies: A research guide to what works.* Programs are categorized as *Effective* (refer to http://www.channing-bete.com/prevention-programs/communities-that-care.php).
7. Sherman et al. (1998). *Preventing crime: What works, what doesn't, what's promising* (NCJ 165366). University of Maryland, Department of Criminology and Criminal Justice. Programs are categorized as *Effective* (refer to http://www.ncjrs.org/works/).
8. *Youth violence: A report of the Surgeon General.* Programs are divided into *Model and Promising: Level 1—Violence prevention; Level 2—Risk prevention* (refer to www.surgeongeneral.gov/library/youthviolence).
9. Title, V. (OJJDP). *Effective and promising programs guide.* Washington, DC: Office of Juvenile Justice and Delinquency Prevention, Office of Justice Programs, U.S. Department of Justice. Programs are divided into *Exemplary, Effective, and Promising* (refer to www.dsgonline.com).
10. Centers for Disease Control: National Center for Injury Prevention and Control—Division of Violence Prevention. *Best practices of youth violence prevention: A sourcebook for community action 2002.* Programs are categorized as *Effective* (refer to www.cdc.gov/ncipc/dvp/bestpractices.htm).
11. Hamilton Fish Institute on School and Community Violence. Programs are divided into *Effective and Noteworthy* (refer to www.hamfish.org/programs/).

differences are much smaller with regard to verbal and relational aggression, and in some studies females were more involved in such types of school violence than were males (Bjorkqvist, 1994). Younger students tend to report more victimization than older ones, especially with regard to more moderate types of physical violence (Benbenishty & Astor, 2005; Smith, Madsen, & Moody, 1999). Approximately 18% of ninth graders in the United States reported being involved in a physical fight in the past year, compared with only 7% of 12th graders (DeVoe et al., 2004).

There are considerable variations in prevalence and characteristics of school violence across nations and cultural groups (for example, Astor, Benbenishty, & Marachi, 2006; Smith, 2003; Smith, Morita, et al., 1999). African-American and Latino or Latina students (17%) were significantly more likely than White students (10%) to report involvement in a physical fight on school grounds during the 12 months prior to the survey. Native-American students (24%) were more likely than White (10%) and Asian-American students (13%) to report physical fights on school grounds (DeVoe et al., 2004). Students in schools located in poor neighborhoods with high community violence tend to report more victimization (Gottfredson & Gottfredson, 1985; Herrenkohl, Chung, & Catalano, 2004). Students in schools with positive school climate and consistent and fair practices of discipline report less victimization than students in other schools (Gottfredson, Gottfredson, Payne, & Gottfredson, 2005).

U.S. national data indicate steady declines in rates of school violence since the mid-1990s, with a 56% decline in overall school crime victimization between 1992 and 2003 (DeVoe et al., 2004). Empirical evidence suggests that U.S. schools have seen a 47% reduction in violent deaths on school grounds from 1992/1993 to 2001 (see DeVoe et al., Table 1.1 for details). Similarly, between 1993 and 2003, the percentage of students who reported carrying a weapon to school generally declined from 12% to 6%, a 50% nationwide reduction. However, annual rates of fights on school grounds for students in 9th to 12th grade from 1993 to 2003 have shown only a slight decline from 16% to 13% (DeVoe et al.).

### Best Practices and Evidence-Based Intervention Programs

Since the mid-1990s there has been a steady increase in the number of school safety programs that are evidence-based. Table 1 represents examples of model evidence-based programs. It includes web-based sources, research that backs the use of the program, and national organizations that have examined, evaluated, and endorsed each program.

According to a current analysis, successful school-wide intervention programs have the following core implementation characteristics (Astor, Marachi, & Benbenishty, 2006):

- Raise the awareness and responsibility of students, teachers, staff, and parents regarding the types of violence in their schools (for example, sexual harassment, fighting, and weapon use).
- Create clear guidelines and rules for the entire school.
- Target the various social systems in the school and clearly communicate to the entire school community the procedures that should be followed before, during, and after violent events.
- Focus on getting the school staff, students, and parents involved in the program, and utilize them in the school setting in order to plan, implement, and sustain the program.
- Fit easily into the normal flow and mission of the school setting.
- Increase monitoring and supervision in nonclassroom areas.
- Are culturally sensitive, culturally competent, and immersed within the community/culture of the students.

### Monitoring and Mapping, Evidence-Based Practice, and Empowerment: Implications for Social Work

When evidence-based practices (EBPs) are not adapted to the specific characteristics of the district or local school level they often fail (Astor, Benbenishty, Marachi, & Meyer, 2006). This stems from the practice of adopting a program (for example, an anti-bullying program) without accurate local or regional data on the nature of the violence problem. Astor, Marachi, and Benbenishty (2006) endorse the practice of using local school data as the basis for adaptation of EBP, planning, interventions, and their subsequent evaluations.

This data-based approach assumes that locally successful programs stem out of the following beliefs and assumptions: (a) the efforts to "fit" a program to a school requires grassroots participation, (b) students and teachers in the school must be empowered to deal with the problem, (c) democracy is at the core of a good evidence-based violence program, and (d) schools should demonstrate a proactive vision surrounding the violence problem in their school. This embodies traditional social work beliefs about empowerment and helps better implement programs in a way that best fits each community and school.

Utilizing this approach would also help social workers better connect issues of school safety with academic attainment in schools. Currently, under the No Child Left Behind laws, both academic standards and school safety data reports are required (Olweus, 1993; Skiba, Ritter, Simmons, Peterson, & Miller, 2006). This law was designed with the acknowledgment that students cannot perform well in academic environments that are persistently dangerous. Regardless, the vast majority of schools collect academic information only. Even in those states where school safety data is collected, very few schools know how to use it to adapt interventions (Astor & Benbenishty, 2005). Consequently, many students may be attending school in fear due to substandard safety environments, yet are expected to meet the same academic standards as those students attending safe schools.

This means that future social work interventions surrounding school safety need to connect more with the academic mission of the school. Sustainable models of school safety are more similar in structure and goals to school reform efforts that impact the entire school organization (including the student, teacher, parent, and community constituents of the school). Effective social work school safety interventions need to go beyond familiarity and selection of evidence-based programs. New programs should engage in both empowerment and a data-driven process that match, monitor, and connect the specific school's violence issues to interventions geared toward those forms of violence and the academic outcomes. Future school safety interventions should attempt to utilize multiple layers of ecological environment.

## REFERENCES

Astor, R. A., & Benbenishty, R. (2005). Zero tolerance for zero knowledge [Commentary]. *Education Week*, *24*(43), 52.

Astor, R., Benbenishty, R., & Marachi, R. (2006). Making the case for an international perspective on school violence: Implications for theory, research, policy and assessment. In S. R. Jimerson & M. J. Furlong (Eds.), *Handbook of school violence and school safety: From research to practice* (chap. 17). Mahwah, NJ: Earlbaum.

Astor, R. A., Benbenishty, R., Marachi, R., & Meyer, H. A. (2006). The social context of schools: Monitoring and mapping student victimization in schools. In S. R. Jimerson & M. J. Furlong (Eds.), *Handbook of school violence and school safety: From research to practice* (pp. 221–233). Mahwah, NJ: Erlbaum.

Astor, R. A., Marachi, R., & Benbenishty, R. (2006). Violence in schools. In P. A. Mearesm (Ed.), *Social work services in schools* (5th ed., pp. 145–181). Boston: Allyn & Bacon.

Astor, R. A., Meyer, H. A., & Behre, W. J. (1999). Unowned places and times: Maps and interviews about violence in high schools. *American Educational Research Journal*, *36*(1), 3–42.

Astor, R. A., Rosemond, M., Pitner, R. O., Marachi, R., & Benbenishty, R. (2006). Evidence-based violence prevention program and best implementation practices. In C. Franklin, M. B. Harris, & P. Allen-Meares (Eds.), *The school services sourcebook: A guide for school-based professionals* (pp. 423–442). New York: Oxford University Press.

Benbenishty, R., & Astor, R. A. (2005). *School violence in context: Culture, neighborhood, family, school, and gender.* New York: Oxford University Press.

Bjorkqvist, K. (1994). Sex-differences in physical, verbal, and indirect aggression: A review of recent research. *Sex Roles*, *30*(3/4), 177–188.

Bronfenbrenner, U. (1979). *The ecology of human development: Experiments by nature and design.* Cambridge, MA: Harvard University Press.

Derzon, J. (2006). How effective are school-based violence prevention programs in preventing and reducing violence and other antisocial behaviors? A meta-analysis. In S. R. Jimerson & M. J. Furlong (Eds.), *Handbook of school violence and school safety: From research to practice* (pp. 429–441). Mahwah, NJ: Erlbaum.

DeVoe, J. F., Peter, K., Kaufman, P., Miller, A., Noonan, M., Snyder, T. D., et al. (2004). *Indicators of school crime and safety: 2004* (NCES 2005-002/NCS 205290). U.S. Departments of Education and Justice. Washington, DC: U.S. Government Printing Office.

Espelage, D., L., Mebane, S. E., & Swearer, S. M. (2004). Gender differences in bullying: Moving beyond mean level differences. In D. L. Espelage & S. M. Swearer (Eds.), *Bullying in American schools: A social-ecological perspective on prevention and intervention* (pp. 15–36). Mahwah, NJ: Erlbaum.

Fraser, M. W. (1996). Aggressive behavior in childhood and early adolescence: An ecological-developmental perspective in youth violence. *Social Work*, *41*(4), 347–361.

Garbarino, J. (2001). An ecological perspective on the effects of violence on children. *Journal of Community Psychology*, *29*(3), 361–378.

Gottfredson, G. D., & Gottfredson, D. C. (1985). *Victimization in schools.* New York: Plenum Press.

Gottfredson, G. D., Gottfredson, D. C., Payne, A. A., & Gottfredson, N. C. (2005). School climate predictors of school disorder: Results from a national study of delinquency prevention in schools. *Journal of Research in Crime and Delinquency*, *42*(4), 412–444.

Gun Free School Act of 1994, 20 U.S.C. chap. 70, § 8921 Gun-free requirements (1994).

Herrenkohl, T. I., Chung, I., & Catalano, R. F. (2004). Review of research on the prediction of youth violence and school-based and community-based prevention approaches.

In P. Allen-Mears & M. F. Fraser (Eds.), *Intervention with children and adolescents: An interdisciplinary perspective* (pp. 449–476). Boston: Pearson.

Juvonen, J., & Graham, S. (Eds.). (2001). *Peer harassment in school: The plight of the vulnerable and victimized*. New York: Guilford Press.

Limber, S. P. (2006). The Olweus Bullying Prevention Program: An overview of its implementation and research basis. In S. R. Jimerson & M. J. Furlong (Eds.), *Handbook of school violence and school safety: From research to practice* (pp. 293–307). Mahwah, NJ: Erlbaum.

Nansel, T., Overpeck, M., Pilla, R., Ruan, W., Simons-Morton, B., & Scheidt, P. (2001). Bullying behaviors among U.S. youth: Prevalence and association with psychosocial adjustment. *Journal of the American Medical Association, 285*, 2094–2100.

Olweus, D. (1993). *Bullying at school: What we know and what we can do*. Malden, MA: Blackwell.

Osher, D., & Dwyer, K. (2005). *Safeguarding our children: An action guide revised and expanded*. Longmont, CO: Sopris West.

Rigby, K. (1996). *Bullying in schools: And what to do about it*. Bristol, PA: Jessica Kingsley.

Skiba, R., Ritter, S., Simmons, A., Peterson, R., & Miller, C. (2006). The safe and responsive schools project: A school reform model for implementing best practices in violence prevention. In S. R. Jimerson & M. J. Furlong (Eds.), *Handbook of school violence and school safety: From research to practice* (pp. 631–650). Mahwah, NJ: Erlbaum.

Skiba, R., Reynolds, C. R., Graham, S., Sheras, P., Conoley, J. C., & Garcia-Vazquez, E. (2006). *Are zero tolerance policies effective in the schools? An evidentiary review and recommendations*. A report by the American Psychological Association Zero Tolerance Task Force.

Smith, P. K. (2003). *Violence in schools: The response in Europe*. London: Routledge Falmer.

Smith, P. K., & Brain, P. (2000). Bullying in schools: Lessons from two decades of research. *Aggressive Behavior, 26*, 1–9.

Smith, P. K., Madsen, K., & Moody, J. (1999). What causes the age decline in reports of being bullied at school? Towards a developmental analysis of risks of being bullied. *Educational Research, 41*(3), 267–285.

Smith, P. K., Morita, Y., Junger-Tass, J., Olweus, D., Catalano, R., & Slee, P. (Eds.). (1999). *The nature of school bullying: A cross-national perspective*. New York: Routledge.

Swearer, S. M., & Espelage, D. L. (2004). Introduction: A social-ecological framework of bullying among youth. In D. L. Espelage & S. M. Swearer (Eds.), *Bullying in American schools: A social-ecological perspective on prevention and intervention* (pp. 1–12). Mahwah, NJ: Erlbaum.

Vossekuil, B., Fein, R. A., Reddy, M., Borum, R., & Modzeleski, W. (2002). *The final report and findings of the Safe School Initiative: Implications for the prevention of school attacks in the United States*. Washington, DC: U.S. Secret Service and U.S. Department of Education.

—RON A. ASTOR, RAMI BENBENISHTY, AND JOEY NUÑEZ ESTRADA

**SECTARIAN AGENCIES.** *See* Faith-based Agencies and Social Work.

# SELF-HELP GROUPS

ABSTRACT: Self-help groups facilitate mutual assistance. They offer a vehicle for people with a common problem to gain support and recognition, obtain information on, advocate on behalf of, address issues associated with, and take control of the circumstances that bring about, perpetuate, and provide solutions to their shared concern. Self-help groups may be small informal groups, confined to interactive support for their members, or differentiated and structured multiservice agencies. They empower members through shared example and modeled success. Spread throughout the world they are a major resource to social workers seeking to help their clients to help themselves.

## Self-Help Groups

Self-help groups facilitate mutual assistance. (*Alcoholics Anonymous*, 1976; Low, 1950). They offer a vehicle for people with a common problem to gain support and recognition, obtain information on, advocate on behalf of, address issues associated with, and take control of the circumstances that bring about, perpetuate, and provide solutions to their shared concern. It is the shared problem that binds a group together and the belief that having experienced the problem gives one a special understanding of how to address its solution. Self-help groups may be small informal groups, confined to interactive support for their members, or differentiated and structured multiservice agencies. Small groups frequently affiliate with national organizations that facilitate the promotion of their philosophy and method and enable the formation of new affiliates by providing support, expertise, and referrals.

## Scope

The American Self Help Group Clearing House provides a key-word-searchable database of over 1,100 national, international, model, and online self-help support groups and agencies covering ~433 separate problems involving addictions, bereavement, health, mental health, disabilities, abuse, parenting, caregiver concerns, and other stressful life situations. The single listing of one of the oldest surviving groups—Alcoholics Anonymous World Services, Inc., founded in 1935—alone includes 106,202 Alcoholics Anonymous (AA) groups in 180 countries worldwide. A few listings in the mental health area include Recovery, Inc., with over 700 affiliate groups, Schizophrenics Anonymous, Inc., with 130 groups and Grow, Inc., with 143 groups worldwide.

### Philosophy, Method, and Objectives

The small free-standing self-help group shares much with the multifunction self-help agency in philosophy and method yet varies in the breadth of its functional objectives.

Both organization types attempt to empower people to change their own lives and provide them a loving, safe, nonjudgmental place where they can find community, information, and support. The group's purpose is to pursue personal growth and change. Everyone in the group is a peer. There is sharing or interaction or both between members. Decisions about the group are made by the group. Group leadership is nonprofessional. Any leadership positions in the group are shared or rotated. Each member of the group could become a leader with minimal training. The group is not dependent on a particular person for its continued existence. Each member of the group has a right to due process in disputes with the group. Dues and fees are nominal, reflecting group expenses (www.shareselfhelp. org; *Alcoholics Anonymous*, 1976; Low, 1950). The self-help agency, usually incorporated as a nonprofit, with a lay board looks from the outside very much like a traditional community-based nonprofit multiservice agency. It differs in that it is run by and for the service user. Its director, a majority of its governing board, and its staff are current or former service users. Like in the small free standing self help group the expertise underlying the recovery or helping process derives from personal experience with the problem. Self-help agencies serving people with mental illness include independent living programs that help members access material resources and gain practical skills, and drop-in community centers that provide a place for members to socialize, build a supportive community, and get advocacy and a gamut of independent living services (Zinman, 1987).

The program of the free-standing-small-self-help group generally is embodied in a written text and constitutes a structured *philosophy of life and a psychology of mental health for the ordinary person*. This document is often born out of the founders' resolve to record, and share what worked in their own recovery or the recovery of others they are familiar with. The continued development of the structure and philosophy of the groups are ensured by the leaders and the groups' umbrella organizations over the years.

Large numbers of self help groups are modeled on the AA philosophy and method contained in their 12 step—12 traditions approach discussed in *Alcoholics Anonymous*, and adapted in such places as Grow's "Blue Book," or Dual Recovery Anonymous' *The twelve steps and dual disorders*. Important elements in these 12-step groups include the recognition that the problem is out of control, the member wants to deal with it, and deal with it in a spiritual framework.

AA describes itself as a fellowship of men and women who share their experience, strength, and hope with each other that they may solve their common problem and help others to recover from alcoholism. The only requirement for membership is a desire to stop drinking. There are no dues or fees for AA membership; they are self-supporting through their own contributions. AA is not allied with any sect, denomination, politics, organization, or institution; does not wish to engage in any controversy, neither endorses nor opposes any causes. Their primary purpose is to stay sober and help other alcoholics to achieve sobriety (www.aa.org). Their 12 steps and traditions are included in the following text box:

### Empowerment

Self-help is about empowerment, the investment of power in a member to overcome a problem. According to *The compact edition of the Oxford English dictionary* (1971), "to empower" implies a formal investment of power. Power over the inner self so that one may take control of one's impulses to abuse drugs, food, gambling, or other substances or activities; formal power to cope with one's inner emotions in grief, in gaining control over one's internal voices or demons, and power over one's social and political context so as to create accommodation of disability, direct one's own care, and overcome social stigma, poverty, homelessness, and other structural impediments to solving one's problem. The self-help group in its written principles and by the examples of its members who have actually taken control of their situations, exercised control over their problem, provides a supportive testing ground for the individual to take control of theirs—as power is rarely given it is taken. Power can be formally invested but must be exercised. The 12-step group legitimizes and supports the member's appeal to a higher authority to help provide the internal strength to exercise such power (*Alcoholics Anonymous*, 1976; Low, 1950).

| THE 12 STEPS OF ALCOHOLICS ANONYMOUS | THE 12 TRADITIONS OF ALCOHOLICS ANONYMOUS |
| --- | --- |
| 1. We admitted we were powerless over alcohol—that our lives had become unmanageable. | 1. Our common welfare should come first; personal recovery depends upon AA unity. |
| 2. Came to believe that a Power greater than ourselves could restore us to sanity. | 2. For our group purpose there is but one ultimate authority—a loving God as He may express Himself in our group conscience. Our leaders are but trusted servants; they do not govern. |
| 3. Made a decision to turn our will and our lives over to the care of God *as we understood Him.* | 3. The only requirement for AA membership is a desire to stop drinking. |
| 4. Made a searching and fearless moral inventory of ourselves. | 4. Each group should be autonomous except in matters affecting other groups or AA as a whole. |
| 5. Admitted to God, to ourselves, and to another human being the exact nature of our wrongs. | 5. Each group has but one primary purpose—to carry its message to the alcoholic who still suffers. |
| 6. Were entirely ready to have God remove all these defects of character. | 6. An AA group ought never endorse, finance, or lend the AA name to any related facility or outside enterprise, lest problems of money, property, and prestige divert us from our primary purpose. |
| 7. Humbly asked Him to remove our shortcomings. | 7. Every AA group ought to be fully self-supporting, declining outside contributions. |
| 8. Made a list of all persons we had harmed, and became willing to make amends to them all. | 8. AA should remain forever nonprofessional, but our service centers may employ special workers. |
| 9. Made direct amends to such people wherever possible, except when to do so would injure them or others. | 9. AA, as such, ought never be organized; but we may create service boards or committees directly responsible to those they serve. |
| 10. Continued to take personal inventory and when we were wrong promptly admitted it. | 10. AA has no opinion on outside issues; hence the AA name ought never be drawn into public controversy. |
| 11. Sought through prayer and meditation to improve our conscious contact with God, *as we understood Him,* praying only for knowledge of His will for us and the power to carry that out. | 11. Our public relations policy is based on attraction rather than promotion; we need to always maintain personal anonymity at the level of press, radio, and films. |
| 12. Having had a spiritual awakening as the result of these steps, we tried to carry this message to alcoholics, and to practice these principles in all our affairs. | 12. Anonymity is the spiritual foundation of all our traditions, ever reminding us to place principles before personalities. |

While many self-help groups originate to deal with an internal issue and are nonpolitical, others come from dissatisfaction with external conditions and their seeming lack of power to do anything about these conditions—such is the case of those groups coming out of the disability rights movement and the antipsychiatry movement. Disability rights advocates banded together to empower themselves to force society to accommodate their disabilities, antipsychiatry consumers to empower themselves to have a voice in the design and implementation of mental health services and their own care and to stop what many described as patient abuse—their current motto: "Nothing About Us Without Us!" These newer self-help groups address issues of personal, organizational, and extra organizational empowerment of their members through the following related activities:

1. Individuals are directly provided or helped to gain access to resources and skills necessary to reach desired goals, and alternative models are provided to counter stigma.

2. Organizations are structured to give clients access to roles that permit them to take responsibility for and exercise discretion over policies that affect them collectively within the agencies.

3. Changes are sought in the larger society that both better the condition of people with disabilities as a class and empower them to participate in making decisions concerning policies that affect them. (Segal, Silverman, & Temkin, 1995)

People who use the services run them, making all the decisions; service providers and recipients are one and the same. The groups strive to share power, responsibility, and skills and seek a nonhierarchical structure in which people reach across to each other, rather than up and down. They are based on choice; they are totally voluntary.... And finally, they address the real economic, social, and cultural needs of suffering people (Zinman, 1986).

### Implications and Trends for Social Work
Social work's contribution is to help people to help themselves, to empower them. Thus engaging their

clients with self-groups is one important tool social workers have to do. Recognition of the origin of some self-help initiatives in dissatisfaction with traditional helping interventions that some self-helpers find dissempowering is a challenge for social work. Social work must consider in the development of its interventions distinctions between treating the patient and enabling the client and how it is possible to create empowering interventions that do not do for the client but empower the client to do for themselves.

## REFERENCES

*Alcoholics Anonymous* (3rd ed.). (1976). New York: Ancoholics Anonymous World Services.

Low, A. (1950). *Mental health through will-training. A system of self-help in psychotherapy as practiced by recovery, incorporated* (336 pp.). Boston, MA.: Christopher Publishing (present publisher: Glencoe, IL.: Willett Publishing).

*The compact edition of the Oxford English dictionary.* (1971). New York: Oxford University Press.

Segal, S. P., Silverman, C., & Temkin, T. (1995). Measuring empowerment in client-run self-help agencies. *Community Mental Health Journal, 31*(3), 215–227.

Zinman, S. (1986). Self-help: The wave of the future. *Hospital and Community Psychiatry, 37*(3), 213.

Zinman, S. (1987). Definition of self-help groups. In H. Zinman, H. Harp, & S. Budd (Eds.), *Reaching across: Mental health clients helping each other.* Sacramento, CA: California Network of Mental Health Clients.

## SUGGESTED LINKS

Alcoholics Anonymous.
  *www.aa.org*
The American Self Help Group Clearing House.
  *www.selfhelpgroups.org;*
  *http://mentalhelp.net/selfhelp/*
Dual RecoveryAnonymous.
  *www.draonline.org*
Self-Help and Recovery Exchange.
  *www.shareselfhelp.org*

—STEVEN P. SEGAL

**SENTENCING.** *See* Criminal Justice: Corrections.

# SETTLEMENTS AND NEIGHBORHOOD CENTERS

**ABSTRACT:** Settlement houses are a prism though which the turbulent history of social work can be viewed. This article specifically examines the genesis of social settlements over the past century. It describes the early work of the settlements in spearheading social reform and building community solidarity. It explores the relationship between historic shifts in the political economy and the changed work of settlements, particularly the development of neighborhood houses. Finally, it emphasizes the dynamic interplay in the past twenty years between corporatization of not-for-profit culture, shrinking government funding, and the redefinition of settlement services.

**KEY WORDS:** social settlements; neighborhood houses; corporatization of social services; community building; history of social welfare; and neoliberalism

## A Brief Introduction to the History of Settlement Houses

The very mention of social settlements evokes a time when settlements and settlement leaders were at the center of a national movement for social welfare reform and the origins of the social work profession. But settlements and neighborhood centers are not mere historical artifacts. Contemporary settlements are very different from their ancestors. Today, they are nonprofit multiservice centers heavily tied to centralized structures of programming and support; they can no longer claim to be unique social welfare or neighborhood institutions. Nevertheless, the early work of the settlement houses and their leaders still serves as a reference point for progressive social service principles and practices: the interconnection between the betterment of the individual and the betterment of society; a collaborative practice that builds alliances between settlement workers and neighborhood residents; the importance of community and community building; and a willingness to organize and advocate for social, political, and economic justice.

The settlement house idea originated in Great Britain in 1884 with the founding of Toynbee Hall in the East End of London, where students could reside, provide social services to the poor, and publicize the oppressive conditions of industrial capitalism. The settlement house idea flourished, however, in the United States, beginning in New York City in 1886 with the founding of Neighborhood Guild (later University Settlement) on the Lower East Side by Stanton Coit (Coit, 1974; Kendall, 2000; Skocpol, 1992). Shortly thereafter, what were to become the most prominent houses emerged: Hull-House in Chicago and Henry Street Settlement in New York City, founded respectively by Jane Addams and Lillian Wald, two of the many distinguished settlement leaders of the era (Addams, 1910; Wald, 1915). By 1910, there were as many as 400 settlement houses nationwide. Nowhere was this expansion of houses more evident than in New York City and Chicago (Kraus, 1980), which were not only the sites of some of the most important social innovations of the era, but also at the confluence of the massive social challenges of the time—immigration, urbanization, and industrialization. Settlement leader Vida Scudder saw the turn-of-the-century city as a "cleavage of classes, cleavage of races, cleavage of faiths: an inextricable confusion" (cited in Shapiro, 1978, p. 215).

In response and in contrast to the Charity Organization Societies, the other historic arm of the social work profession, the founders of settlements helped develop a communitarian counterideology and social movement which argued that (a) society, not simply individuals, was responsible for social conditions; and (b) the environment, not simply one's personal characteristics, heavily shaped life experience (Quandt, 1970): "charity workers emphasized the individual causes of poverty while settlement workers stressed the social and economic conditions that made people poor....The settlement workers tried desperately to disassociate their movement from charity in the public mind" (Davis, 1967, pp. 18–19). In this way, settlements differed from the approach of Charity Organization Societies, then the dominant approach to serving poor communities and individuals.

## Core Practice Principles: Collaboration, Community Building, and Social Action

Settlement house workers came to understand that it was not possible to alter slum neighborhoods without transforming urban life, as well. Building on their sense of the interconnectedness between individual problems and social betterment, their practice method included three core elements: (a) an integrated collaborative practice that intervened at the individual as well as the community level and sought to develop solidarity between settlement workers and neighborhood residents; (b) a sense of the essential importance of community and community building; and (c) a willingness to organize and advocate for social, political, and economic justice (Fabricant & Fisher, 2002).

First, in terms of collaborative practice, as Simon (1998) puts it, "The settlement house movement gave to...the emergent social work profession a core principle of practice, that of the indispensability of

collaborative give and take alliances between settlement workers and neighbors in the larger endeavor to build enduring communities" (p. 3). Second, they saw neighborhoods as the natural, organic scale of intervention and community building—that is, increasing social cohesion and social solidarity in these communities—as central to all their work. Finally, because settlement leaders understood that the causes of most community problems resided outside of the neighborhood, they promoted social action to tackle larger social problems and conditions. Vida Scudder, one of the founders of College Settlement in New York City, emphasized the importance of social action to settlement work: "Unless settlements continue to hold and foster this attitude of protest, their highest possibilities will be forfeited. Only as they cling to an impassioned, rational discontent with existing conditions, only as they resist the seductive encroachments of social fatalism and remain full of hope that never wavers, are they true to their initial impulse and to their best ideal" (as cited in Pacey, 1950, p. 72).

Settlement houses organized to improve local health conditions, develop small parks and public recreation, reform municipal politics, upgrade public schools, promote political candidates, occasionally run for office themselves, conduct social research, and participate in broad campaigns for tenement house reform, defense of labor unions, and the rights of workers, women, and children. The larger settlement houses, especially in New York and Chicago, tended to be more involved in social action. Although the daily program of daycare, medical care, recreation, and education gave all settlements viability and permanence (Rothman, 1973), it was the combination of collaborative practice, community building, and social action that signified their practice at the time and for later generations.

These core concepts aside, settlement houses were a diverse lot. They reflected a range of ideologies and political perspectives from advocates of Americanization, to the social feminism of Jane Addams, and the socialism of Florence Kelley (Chambers, 1886; Shapiro, 1978; Sklar, 1995). The settlement movement was full of contradictions—compassion and protection, reform and coercion, noble goals, well-intentioned interventions, and lamentable failures (Crocker, 1992). Nevertheless, they had their critics. Francis Hackett observed in 1915 that for many people the social settlement suggests images "of young ladies with weak eyes and young gentleman with weak chins fluttering confusedly among heterogeneous foreigners, offering cocoa and sponge cake as a sort of dessert for the factory system they deplore" (Rose, 1994, p. 4). On the other hand, the most recent biographer of Jane Addams remarked how the settlements dramatically changed the lives of residents, both those in the neighborhood and those, like Addams, residing in the settlement houses (Knight, 2006).

## From Settlement Houses to Neighborhood Centers

One way to understand and evaluate settlements as more than historical artifact is to use a widely adopted social reform model of social welfare history. In short, it proposes that the dominant political economy and historical events of each era help shape and profoundly influence social provision and social change. In more liberal or public eras, activism on the "Left" increases, as does the importance of social welfare and social investment for reform efforts. Settlement houses achieved initial prominence during the first two decades of the 20th century, the 1930s, and the 1960s, when funding and innovation moved along progressive lines and settlements. For the most part, they were able to operationalize the three dimensions of their work: community building, social action, and collaboration. For example, to strengthen their social action and policy advocacy dimension, settlement leaders formed the National Federation of Settlements in 1911. During the New Deal of the 1930s, many former social workers and allies—including Eleanor Roosevelt, Harry Hopkins, and Frances Perkins—achieved national prominence as social welfare advocates in the Roosevelt Administration. In the 1960s, while settlements were maligned as outdated by community organizers such as Saul Alinsky and by some architects of the Great Society programs, neighborhood centers captured significant funding to continue the era's long-term agenda of community building and social action (Alinsky, 1946; Trolander, 1987).

On the other hand, in more conservative or private eras—such as the 1920s, 1950s, and the years following 1975—conservative policy and "Right-wing" movements dominated, and business and more individualist prerogatives were asserted with greater openness. Social welfare systems became increasingly privatized and timid, which continue to constrain practice, reduce interest in, and narrow funding for settlement houses and neighborhood centers. As settlement houses were transformed in the 20th century into nonresidential service centers, they became (a) more focused on individual needs than on social needs, (b) more bureaucratic and professional-oriented, (c) less tied to a single neighborhood building objective or to broader social action, and (d) increasingly dependent on centralized sources of funding. Over time, this shift and these services were more likely to be defined by programming initiated by those outside the neighborhood center, whether the local Community Chest in the 1920s or public sector contractors in the past generation. Since 1980, these once privately funded nonprofit organizations receive an increasingly high percentage of their funding—on average 85%—from public sector contracts, which furthers the process of formalization, bureaucratization, and corporatization of neighborhood center role and program (Kraus & Chaudry, 1995). This captures the cyclical history of settlement houses since their initial founding.

## The Conservative Context Today

As the political climate has become increasingly conservative since the 1980s during the past twenty-five years, settlement houses have experienced a sea of change in their circumstance. These changes have also affected the culture of agencies. The settlements' increasing reliance on state contracts to finance services has resulted in even more restricted forms of funding and accountability. As Smith and Lipsky (1993) noted, "Not-for-profit agencies are being asked to, and their own inclinations toward altruism dictate that they cushion state fiscal crises by treating more and more clients and more difficult clients with without compensating reimbursement. . . . Asking providers to do more and more with less and seeing many providers sink under budget reductions do not bode well for public policy in the long run." Critically, these trends have intensified for settlement houses since the 1990s. These new fiscal realities have been part of a larger political intention to "shrink" social service funding at every level of government and recast them in the image of market or private sector institutions. This agenda is not politically neutral but rather deeply embedded in an ascendant conservative ideology during the historic cycle of the past 25 years. Importantly, change in the settlements' contracting environment has contributed to a decline in their physical plants, infrastructure, and administrative supports. The work environment of settlement staff is also affected by new demands for productivity. An even more industrialized model of efficient, productive service delivery has created the basis for producing quantitative, measurable outputs. Critically, many recent reports on settlement houses indicate that although reconfigured contracts may produce more output, they contradictorily erode the conditions necessary for promoting either individual or communal change (Fabricant & Fisher, 2002).

The more rapid, circumscribed, and often discontinuous contacts that characterize the settlement service experience tend to commodify it. The more the number of clients processed, the more the revenue generated. Clearly, the logic and experience of the marketplace is being imposed on a growing number of settlements, and more generally, on nonmarket institutions through the financing mechanism of contracting. This has also been accomplished through the increased hiring of MBA's and or managers with a market orientation. As Newfield (1998) has remarked, "Financial culture tends to view labor as a cost, as a site of potential savings. From this perspective, better means cheaper, growth means restriction, productivity means discipline and knowledge means regulation". In response to these efforts to reinvent nonmarket institutions, such as settlements, Peter Drucker argues, "We are learning the belief that the free market is all it takes to have a functioning economy is pure delusion...For any time period longer than five years, a functioning civil society...is needed for the market to function in its market role" (Newfield, 1998). These changes are occurring at the very moment when an increasing number of policy makers are calling for community building initiatives that recall an earlier era of settlement house accomplishment. As Fisher and Karger (1997) note, "Increasing globalization requires the building and rebuilding of communities to provide a basis of stability and identity in a global context that challenges both." However, the structure of state contracts has made it especially difficult for settlements to promote a social solidarity capable of addressing the myriad social problems and even crises of many communities. Deborah Mott warned that a fundamental conflict may exist between contract logic and the dynamics of building social relationships: "Reducing all relations to short-term calculation can witlessly provide the mechanics to undermine the normative core of many relationships. To reduce relations to nothing more than contracts is to destroy their special nature."

## The Theory and Practice of
## Social Capital and Community Building

The impact of strong and extended social network on the well-being of individuals and communities is well documented. Some of the outcomes include (a) the creation of opportunity structures (Naperstack & Dooley, 1998), (b) maintaining health (Bloomberg, Meyers, & Bravernman, 1994), (c) educational attainment (de Souza Briggs, Mueller, & Sullivan, 1997), and (d) local economic development (Putnam, 2000,

Fabricant 2008). Historically, settlements understood the importance of social capital or solidarity through the provision of social services. Some part of their work linked services and activities in ways that concretely addressed the needs of individuals while amplifying the neighborhood residents' voices in the house, the community, and the larger political arena (Mulroy & Cragin, 1994). Although in the social service literature, the terms for this objective may have shifted from social solidarity, to collective empowerment, to social capital formation or community building, the underlying intention has remained constant (Fabricant & Fisher, 2002, Fabricant, 2008). The objective of agencies engaged in such work is to promote deepened and extended forms of affiliation among service users that, over time, will cohere into a political power that can benefit the community. This is precisely the historic record and contemporary commitment of many social settlements.

The work of rebuilding community through social service work grounded in social work principles and practice, although both complex and often thwarted by contracting policy, remains a central part of both the work and aspiration of settlements. Many of the most interesting experiments in community building have been incubated by settlements. The New Settlement Apartments, for example, played an instrumental role in helping to organize neighborhood residents to improve local schools. Their program Parents Action Committee (PAC) built strong bonds between local parents that produced a widening circle of participation and collaboration in education reform within the school district. This initiative yielded concrete reforms and investment in local schools, which have since been replicated throughout the city of New York (Fabricant, 2008). University Settlement, founded in 1886, recently created a program, Women As Resources Against Poverty (WAR). WAR originated as a self-selected group to discuss common problems. Over time, the group has grown in both the number of participants and the ambition of its agenda (Brown & Barnes, 2001). Recently, WAR members have planned domestic violence trainings, cosponsored rallies, written a child welfare bill of rights and responsibilities, and spoken before legislative bodies on welfare reform, homelessness, domestic violence, and economic development. What has remained constant for members, however, is the often strong bond of friendship that draws new members to the group and expands its influence to a larger political and social arena.

An especially inventive program was developed by the United Community Centers (UCC), a settlement house, which implemented an HIV prevention project in a 10-block area of East New York. The program established a relationship with an independent taxi association and trained drivers to promote awareness of HIV and AIDS throughout the targeted area. This example is unique because it suggests that an agency's organizing projects can build partnerships with small business groups. Over time, new forms of collaboration evolved between the taxi drivers and UCC, which contributed to crime prevention (Hirota, Brown, & Richman, 1997). Importantly, the association provided a new conduit to parts of the neighborhood that were not easily reached by UCC. These are but three examples of the many innovative programming experiments in community building currently being developed and implemented by settlements.

## Challenges and Trends

The project of community building has both historic and contemporary significance for settlements. This is an age dominated by a highly conservative credo of corporatization that emphasizes privatization and disinvestment in poor communities (Harvey, 2006) Settlements are faced with the dilemma of gaining support for community work oriented to political mobilization for social investment. Creating the internal and external resources for such initiatives, although increasingly difficult, remains possible. Only in this way can settlements contribute to the renewal of poor communities. Settlements and United Neighborhood Houses will also need to participate in a larger community reimagining of a public life that includes greater access to resources. Only in this way can settlements in particular and social work in general fulfill part of their early promise and hope: service provision and social activism as gifts to and foundations of a just community (Fabricant & Fisher, 2002).

## REFERENCES

Addams, J. (1910). *Twenty years at hull-house*. New York: Macmillan.

Alinsky, S. (1946). *Reveille for Radicals* New York: Vintage.

Bloomberg, L., Meyers, J., & Bravernman, M. T. (1994). The importance of social interaction: A new perspective on social epidemiology and social risk factors and social health. *Social Health Quarterly*, 4, 447–463.

Brown, P., & Barnes, K. (2001). *Connecting neighbors: The role of settlement houses in building bonds within communities*. Chicago, IL: Chapin Hall.

Chambers, C. (1986). "Women in the creation of the social work profession." *Social Service Review*, 60/1, 1–33.

Coit, S. (1974, reprint). *Neighbourhood guilds: An instrument of social reform*. New York: Arno.

Crocker, R. H. (1992). *Social work and social order: The settlement movement in two industrial cities, 1889–1930*. Urbana: University of Illinois Press.

Davis, A. F. (1967). *Spearheads for reform: The social settlements and the progressive movement. 1890–1914*. New Brunswick, NJ: Rutgers University Press.

de Souza Briggs, X., Mueller, E., & Sullivan, M. (1997). *From neighborhood to community: Evidence on the social effects of community development*. New York: Community Development Research Center, New School for Social Research.

Fabricant, M., & Fisher, R. (2002). *Settlement houses under siege: The struggle to sustain community organizations in New York City*. New York: Columbia University Press.

Fabricant, M. (2008). *Organizing Hope to Revive Public Schools: CC9's Campaign for Parent Led Educational Justice in the South Bronx* (in press).

Fisher, R., & Karger, H. (1997). *Social work and community in a private world: Getting out in public*. New York: Longman.

Harvey, David (2006). *A Brief History of Neoliberalism*. New York: Oxford University Press.

Hirota, J., Brown, P., Mollard, W., & Richman, H. (1997). *Pathways to change: Settlement houses and the strengthening of community*. Chicago, IL: Chapin Hall.

Kendall, K. (2000). *Social work education: Its origins in Europe*. Alexandria, VA: Council on Social Work Education.

Knight, L. W. (2006). *Jane Addams and the struggle for democracy*. Chicago: University of Chicago Press.

Kraus, A. (1980). *The settlement house movement in New York City, 1886–1914*. New York: Arno.

Kraus, A., & Chaudry, A. (1995). The settlement house initiative: Merging head start and day care in New York. *Public Welfare*, 53(4), 34–43, 52.

Mulroy, E., & Cragin, J. (1994). Training future community based managers: The politics of collaboration in a turbulent urban environment. *Journal of Teaching in Social Work*, 9, 17–35.

Naperstack, A., & Dooley, D. (1998). Countering urban disinvestment through community building initiative. In P. Ewalt, et al. (Eds.), *Community building: Renewal, well being, and shared responsibility* (pp. 6–16). Washington, DC: NASW Press.

Newfield, C. (1998). Recapturing academic business. In R. Martin (Ed.), *Chalk lines: The politics of work in the managed university* (pp. 69–102). Durham, NC: Duke University Press.

Pacey, L. (Ed.). (1950). *Readings in the development of settlement work*. New York: Association Press.

Putnam, R. (2000). *Bowling alone revisited: The collapse and revival of American community*. New York: Simon and Shuster.

Quandt, J. (1970). *From the small town to the great community*. New Brunswick, NJ: Rutgers University Press.

Rose, E. (1994). From sponge cake to hamantashen: Jewish identity in a Jewish settlement house, 1885–1952. *Journal of American Ethnic History*, 13, 3–23.

Rothman, S. (1973, Winter). Other people's children: The day care experience in America. *The Public Interest*, 30, 11–27.

Shapiro, E. S. (1978). Robert A. Woods and the settlement house impulse. *Social Service Review, 52*, 215–226.

Simon, B. (1998). *CUSSW and settlement houses: Yesterday, today, and tomorrow.* Unpublished presentation, Columbia University School of Social Work, July 12.

Sklar, K. (1995). *Florence Kelley and the nation's work.* New Haven, CT: Yale University Press.

Skocpol, T. (1992). *Protecting soldiers and mothers: The political origins of social policy in the United States.* Cambridge, MA: Harvard University Press.

Smith, S., & Lipsky, M. (1993). *Non profits for hire: The welfare state in the age of contracting.* Cambridge: Harvard University Press.

Trolander, J. (1987). *Professionalism and Social Change: From the settlement house movement to neighborhood centers, 1886-present.* New York: Columbia University Press.

Wald, L. (1915). *The house on Henry street.* New York: Dover.

—MIKE FABRICANT AND ROBERT FISHER

## SEXUAL ASSAULT

ABSTRACT: Sexual assault or rape affects millions of women and men in the United States; however, it is only in the last 30 years that it is being considered a social problem. During this period, many policies at the state and federal levels have attempted to address sexual assault and provide legal remedies for victims. However, sexual assaults are still the most underreported crime in the United States and are accompanied by bias and misinformation that plague our response. Social workers play a crucial role in offering services to survivors and advocating for more education and awareness in our communities and universities.

KEY WORDS: rape; violence against women; sexual abuse; sexual violence

The rape (or sexual assault) of women is not a new phenomenon; indeed, rape was found in court documents in England as early as 1736 (Gavey, 2005). However, as late as the 1980s, most policy makers and researchers believed that rape was a rare event, usually "occurring at the hands of a psychopathic stranger terrorizing women on the streets or breaking into their homes in the middle of the night" (Gavey, 2005, p. 62). The emergence of rape as a social problem coincided with the emergence of the first rape crisis centers in the 1970s as part of the radical feminist women's movement (Campbell & Martin, 2001) and with some ground breaking and controversial research (Gilbert, 1997; Muehlenhard, Highby, Phelps, & Sympson,

1997). Research conducted by Koss and Russell (1987) demonstrated that rape was more common than once thought, perpetrators were primarily someone known (for example, dates, boyfriends, or husbands), and victims seldom report their victimization to the police.

Since the mid 1970s, understanding of sexual assault or rape through research has increased significantly. Empirical studies reveal that perpetrators come from all walks of life, are usually someone known to the victim, and are not antisocial, psychopathic men, living on the edge of society as once believed (Brownmiller, 1975). However, sexual assaults are still the most underreported crime in the United States, and, even with rape reform laws, are accompanied by bias and misinformation that plague the response by the criminal justice and human services systems (Tjaden & Thoennes, 2006; Rennison, 2002).

### Definitions

Rape was redefined as sexual assault as part of the rape reform laws so as to be similar to other assaults in which the victim's consent is not an issue (Russell & Bolen, 2000). Sexual assault is viewed as a series of sexually aggressive acts which range from the nonviolent (obscene phone calls, verbal harassment, or indecent exposure) to violent acts or attempted acts within intimate or familial relationships (date rape, marital rape, sexual abuse, incest, or statutory rape) as well as violent acts outside intimate relationships (gang rape, stranger rape, sexual homicide, ritual abuse) (Edward & Macleod, 1999).

The previous entry in the Social Work Encyclopedia differentiated between rape and sexual assault (Byington, 1995); that distinction has somewhat blurred since then. However, these terms vary depending on individual state laws, with some states using generic terms while others use distinct terms, for example, aggravated, simple, or forcible rape (Clay-Warner & Burt, 2005).

### Prevalence

In the most recent nationally representative study, the National Violence Against Women Survey (NVAWS) reports that 17.7 million women (or 17.6%) and 2.8 million men (or 3%) in the United States were forcibly raped at some point in their lives (Tjaden & Thoennes, 2006). Nonrepresentative studies report the prevalence of rape among females in the United States from as little as 2% reporting rape at some point in their lifetime (Gordon & Riger, 1989) to 44% (Russell & Bolen, 2000) to 56% (Goodman, 1991) to a high of 67% in a study that included women from prison (Postmus &

Severson, 2006). Additional studies on college campuses reveal prevalence rates of 25% of women who had experienced rape or attempted rape in their lifetimes (Koss, Gidycz, & Wisniewski, 1987). The variation in these nonrepresentative samples suggests that different data collection methodologies will generate different results.

Research is much more limited regarding the prevalence of rape in different ethnic groups. Factors surrounding historical treatment of ethnic groups, patriarchal family structures, values placed on sexual chastity before marriage and faithfulness afterward, the fear of racism, and the need to keep family matters private may create seemingly insurmountable barriers for rape survivors to report their victimization (Lee & Law, 2001; Low & Organista, 2000; Neville & Pugh, 1997; Washington, 2001; Wyatt, 1992). Results from NVAWS reveal that 34% of Native American women were raped at some point in their lifetime compared to 24% women of mixed race, 19% of African Americans, 12% of Latinas, and 18% of non-Hispanic Whites (Tjaden & Thoennes, 2006). The study was unable to estimate the percentage of women from Asian or Pacific Island ethnicities because there were too few rape victims identified.

### Policy Responses

With more attention brought to rape and sexual assault by women's organizations, state policy makers responded by passing rape reform laws beginning in the mid 1970s. Although differences exist between state laws, the primary focus of the reforms has been to shift the attention away from the victim and instead, focus on the perpetrator's behavior (Clay-Warner & Burt, 2005). The most significant changes to state statutes included expanding the definition of rape to include various forms of sexual assault, marital rape, and all types of penetration (that is, vaginal, oral, and anal). A second important change was that the laws altered evidentiary requirements by removing the requirement that victims must have corroborating evidence—a requirement steeped in the notion that victims fabricated their victimization and hence, needed an additional source to verify the rape. A third major shift in rape reform included the modification of resistance requirements; thus, victims no longer have to prove that they resisted the rape as evidence of not giving consent to the sexual act. Finally, the most controversial reform included the creation of rape shield laws, which prevent the victim's past sexual history and reputation being discussed in cross examination (Clay-Warner & Burt, 2005).

In 1994, a federal policy, Violence Against Women Act (VAWA), was enacted, which provided new legal remedies for victims of sexual assault or other forms of violence against women. The goals of VAWA include enhancing the ability of law enforcement departments, prosecutors, and victim assistance programs to increase services for women victims of violence, to better assure victim safety, and to increase offender accountability (Chaiken, Boland, Maltz, Martin, & Targonski, 2001). VAWA was reauthorized in 2000 and again in 2006, each time adding funding for services specifically geared towards sexual assault survivors, addressing trafficking, and amending violence against women to include dating violence and stalking (Legal Momentum, 2005).

Since the rape reform laws, rape is more likely to be reported; however, aggravated rapes (that is, if committed by a stranger or multiple perpetrators, if physical force or weapons were used, or if an injury occurred) are more likely to be reported than simple rapes regardless of when the rape occurred (Bachman, 1993; Clay-Warner & Burt, 2005; Du Mont, & Myhr, 2003).

**CURRENT CHALLENGES AND CONTROVERSIES** Institutions, including the criminal justice system, erect barriers that discourage victims from reporting their victimization to law enforcement. Researchers have used terms such as secondary rape or secondary victimization to describe these institutional barriers as causing additional trauma and problems for victims (Campbell, Sefl, Barnes, Ahrens, Wasco, & Zaragoza-Diesfeld, 1999; Frohmann, 1991; Madigan & Gamble, 1991; Martin & Powell, 1994; Matoesian, 1993). In one study, 40% of rape survivors who had contact with legal or medical services experienced secondary victimization from the helping professionals because their stories of rape were considered unbelievable or not serious enough to pursue in court (Campbell et al., 1999).

Not only do institutions erect barriers to discourage reporting, but society as a whole seems to continue blaming the victim because of deeply embedded beliefs about the role of women during the sexual assault (McMahon, unpublished). These beliefs stem from policies, prior to the 1970s, whose goals were to protect the alleged rapist from being falsely accused (Bohmer, 1991; Cuklanz, 1996). For example, in New Jersey, from 1576 to 1978, conviction on a rape charge required proof that women did not give consent by strongly resisting and that force was used (Oppenheim, 1995). Hence, while rape reform laws removed the non-consent language, "the myths that the rape occurred because she failed to resist enough, she was drinking, she wore certain clothes, or she secretly fantasized about it" continue to date (McMahon, unpublished). Hence more education and awareness that challenge these long-standing myths and beliefs are needed at all levels from individuals to communities and institutions to policies.

## Implications for Social Work

Social workers often play a crucial role in the services created for and offered to rape survivors, whether involved with rape crisis centers in communities or participating with sexual assault services on university campuses. Services usually include 24-hour crisis hotlines, counseling with individuals, groups, and families, and advocacy with legal and medical services. Part of the work focuses on preventing secondary victimization; hence, advocates strive to promote Macro level strategies including the education of providers and community groups in an effort to change organizational practices, influence policies and legislation, or to foster coalitions and networks (Campbell & Martin, 2001; Davis, Parks, & Cohen, 2006).

Social workers can continue to advocate for more education for helping professionals, including other social workers, as well as more evaluation of the effectiveness of treatment services for sexual assault survivors. While some have suggested that rape crisis centers in the community and on college campuses show some success (Bachar & Koss, 2001; Campbell & Martin, 2001), little research is available that identifies "best" practices when working with survivors. The sexual assault field needs more social work researchers evaluating programs and services, identifying effective practices with survivors, and educating more social workers to continue the work.

### REFERENCES

Bachar, K., & Koss, M. P. (2001). From prevalence to prevention: Closing the gap between what we know about rape and what we do. In C. M. Renzetti, J. L. Edleson, & R. K. Bergen (Eds.), Sourcebook on violence against women. Thousand Oaks, CA: Sage.

Bachman, R. (1993). Predicting the reporting of rape victimizations: Have rape reforms made a difference? Criminal Justice and Behavior, 20(3), 254–270.

Bohmer, C. (1991). Rape and the law. In A. Parrot & L. Bechhofer (Eds.), Acquaintance Rape: The Hidden Crime (pp. 317–333). New York: John Wiley & Sons, Inc.

Brownmiller, S. (1975). Against our will: Men, women and rape. New York: Simon & Schuster.

Byington, D. B. (1995). Sexual assault. In R. L. Edwards & J. G. Hopps (Eds.), Encyclopedia of Social Work (19 ed., pp. 2136–2141). Washington, DC: NASW Press.

Campbell, R., Sefl, T., Barnes, H. E., Ahrens, C., Wasco, S. M., & Zaragoza-Diesfeld, Y. (1999). Community services

for rape survivors: Enhancing psychological well-being or increasing trauma? Journal of Consulting and Clinical Psychology, 67(6), 847–858.

Campbell, R., & Martin, P. Y. (2001). Services for sexual assault survivors: The role of rape crisis centers. In C. M. Renzetti, J. L. Edleson, & R. K. Bergen (Eds.), Sourcebook on Violence Against Women. Thousand Oaks, CA: Sage.

Chaiken, M. R., Boland, B., Maltz, M. D., Martin, S., & Targonski, J. (2001). State and local change and the violence against women act. Washington, DC: U.S. Dept. of Justice.

Clay-Warner, J., & Burt, C. H. (2005). Rape reporting after reforms: Have times really changed? Violence Against Women, 11(2), 150–176.

Cuklanz, L. M. (1996). Rape on Trial: How the Mass Media Construct Legal Reform & Social Change. Philadelphia: University of Pennsylvania Press.

Davis, R., Parks, L. F., & Cohen, L. (2006). Sexual violence and the spectrum of prevention: Towards a community solution. Enola, PA: National Sexual Violence Resource Center.

Du Mont, J., Karen-Lee, M., & Myhr, T. L. (2003). The role of "real rape" and "real victim" stereotypes in the police reporting practices of sexually assaulted women. Violence Against Women, 9(4), 466–486.

Edward, K. E., & Macleod, M. D. (1999). The reality and myth of rape: Implications for the criminal justice system. Expert Evidence, 7, 37–58.

Frohmann, L. (1991). Discrediting victims' allegations of sexual assault: Prosecutorial accounts of case rejections. Social Problems, 38, 213–226.

Gavey, N. (2005). Just sex? The cultural scaffolding of rape. London: Routledge.

Gilbert, N. (1997). Advocacy research exaggerates rape statistics. In M. R. Walsh (Ed.), Women, men, and gender: ongoing debates. New Haven, CT: Yale University Press.

Goodman, L. A. (1991). The prevalence of abuse among homeless and housed poor mothers: A comparison study. American Journal of Orthopsychiatry, 61, 163–169.

Gordon, M. T., & Riger, S. (1989). The female fear. New York: Macmillan.

Koss, M. P., Gidycz, C., & Wisniewski, N. (1987). The scope of rape: Incidence and prevalence of sexual aggression and victimization in a national sample of higher education students. Journal of Consulting and Clinical Psychology, 55, 162–170.

Lee, M. Y., & Law, P. F. M. (2001). Perception of sexual violence against women in Asian American Communities. Journal of Ethic & Cultural Diversity in Social Work, 10(2), 3–25.

Legal Momentum. (2005). The Violence Against Women Act: Reauthorization 2005. Washington, DC: National Task-Force to End Sexual and Domestic Violence Against Women.

Low, G., & Organista, K. C. (2000). Latinas and sexual assault: Towards culturally sensitive assessment and intervention. *Journal of Multicultural Social Work* 8(1/2), 131–157.

Madigan, L., & Gamble, N. (1991). *The second rape: Society's continued betrayal of the victim.* New York: Lexington Books.

Martin, P. Y., & Powell, M. R. (1994). Accounting for the "second assault": Legal organizations' framing of rape victims. *Law and Social Inquiry, 19,* 853–890.

Matoesian, G. M. (1993). *Reproducing rape: Domination through talk in the courtroom.* Chicago: University of Chicago Press.

McMahon, S. (unpublished). Tracing the roots of victim-blaming.

Muehlenhard, C. L., Highby, B. J., Phelps, J. L., & Sympson, S. C. (1997). Rape statistics are not exaggerated. In M. R. Walsh (Ed.), *Women, men, and gender: Ongoing debates.* New Haven, CT: Yale University Press.

Neville, H. A., & Pugh, A. O. (1997). General and culture-specific factors influencing African American women's reporting patterns and perceived social support following sexual assault. *Violence Against Women, 3*(4), 361–381.

Oppenheim, J. (1995). Revising rape law: From property to people. In C. Carter (Ed.), *The Other Side of Silence* (pp. 85–92). Gilsim, NH: Avocus Publications, Inc.

Postmus, J. L., & Severson, M. (2006). Violence and victimization: Exploring women's histories of survival. Washington, DC: Dept. of Justice, Office of Justice Programs, National Crime Justice Reference Service.

Rennison, C. M. (2002). *Rape and sexual assault: reporting to police and medical attention, 1992–2000.* Washington, DC: U.S. Dept. of Justice, Office of Justice Programs, Bureau of Justice Statistics.

Russell, D. E. H., & Bolen, R. M. (2000). *The Epidemic of rape and child sexual abuse in the United States.* Thousand Oaks, CA: Sage.

Tjaden, P., & Thoennes, N. (2006). Extent nature, and consequences of rape victimization: Findings from the National Violence Against Women Survey. National Institute of Justice.

Washington, P. A. (2001). Disclosure patterns of Black female sexual assault survivors. *Violence Against Women, 7*(11), 1254–1283.

Wyatt, G. E. (1992). The sociocultural context of African American and White American women's rape. *Journal of Social Issues, 48*(1), 77–91.

### SUGGESTED LINKS

National Sexual Violence Resource Center.
*http://www.nsvrc.org/*
Office of Violence Against Women.
*http://www.usdoj.gov/ovw/*
Office for Victims of Crime.
*http://www.ojp.usdoj.gov/ovc/*
Pennsylvania Coalition Against Rape.
*http://pcar.org/*
Rape, Abuse, and Incest National Network.
*http://www.rainn.org/*

Sexual Assault Nurse Examiner/Sexual Assault Response Team (SANE/SART).
*http://www.sane-sart.com/*
Center on Violence against Women & Children (Rutgers, School of Social Work).
*http://vawc.rutgers.edu*

—JUDY L. POSTMUS

## SEXUAL HARASSMENT

**ABSTRACT:** Sexual harassment is a form of discrimination as well as a complex social issue with psychological implications for both those who are harassed and those who perpetrate the harassment. Women continue to be primary targets, although men, youths and sexual minorities are increasingly pursued. Legally prohibited in the workplace and educational institutions, it persists in personal interactions as well as by electronic means despite prevention efforts such as education programs and zero tolerance policies. This entry will define sexual harassment, provide an overview of its prevalence, and describe approaches for its remedy.

**KEY WORDS:** sexual harassment; discrimination; civil rights; women; equality

### History

Title VII of the Civil Rights Act of 1964 set the legal foundation for a claim of sexual harassment in the workplace. It protected employees in private companies with 25 or more workers from discrimination based on "race, color, religion, *sex*, or national origin." It was extended in 1972 to cover local, state, and federal offices, businesses with 15 or more employees, and educational institutions (Gutman, 2000). In 1976, sexual harassment was first legally recognized under Title VII as a form of sex discrimination in a federal court decision (*Williams v. Saxbe*).

In 1985, the Equal Employment Opportunity Commission (EEOC), the federal agency responsible for enforcing Title VII, defined sexual harassment as:

Unwelcome sexual advances, requests for sexual favors, and other verbal or physical conduct of a sexual nature constitute sexual harassment when:

1. submission to such conduct is made either explicitly or implicitly a term or condition of an individual's employment,

2. submission to or rejection of such conduct by an individual is used as the basis for employment decisions affecting such individual, or

3. such conduct has the purpose or effect of unreasonably interfering with an individual's work performance or creating an intimidating, hostile or offensive working environment (Singer, 1995, p. 2149).

The following year, the Supreme Court rendered its first decision on sexual harassment in the 1986 *Meritor v. Vinson* case. The Court concluded that there must be either an implicit or explicit *quid pro quo* situation (conditions 1 or 2) or a *hostile environment* (condition 3) in sexual harassment cases (Chan, 1994). Subsequent Supreme Court cases considered issues of how to determine a hostile environment (*Harris v. Forklift Systems*, 1993), same-sex harassment (*Oncale v. Sundowner*, 1998), employer liability (*Burlington v. Ellerth*, 1998; *Faragher v. City of Boca Raton*, 1998), and expanding guidelines to protect claimants from retaliation (*Burlington Northern & Sante Fe Railway Co v. White*, 2006).

Title IX of the Education Amendment of 1972 prohibits sex discrimination in educational environments receiving federal assistance. The Department of Education, Office of Civil Rights (ORC) responsible for enforcing sexual harassment laws defines it as:

> Unwelcome sexual advances, requests for sexual favors and other verbal, nonverbal, or physical conduct of a sexual nature by an employee, by another student, or by a third party, which is sufficiently severe, persistent, or pervasive to limit a student's ability to participate in or benefit from an education program or activity, or to create a hostile or abusive educational environment (Strauss, 2003, p. 107).

Notable Supreme Court rulings include the following: schools can be held liable for punitive damages (*Franklin v. Gwinnet County Public Schools*, 1992), school districts can be liable if a school official with authority acted with indifference to a report (*Gebster v. Lago Vista Independent School District*, 1998), and recognizing *peer*-to-peer student harassment under Title IX (*Davis v. Monroe County*, 1999).

Despite increased legislation prohibiting sexual harassment in various settings, public attention to this issue increased dramatically during the October, 1991 Supreme Court confirmation hearings of Clarence Thomas, an African-American. During these sessions, testimony from Anita Hill, an African-American law professor, revealed that Mr. Thomas sexually harassed her while she was working as his assistant. These statements were vehemently denied by Mr. Thomas who was later confirmed by an all-male Senate Committee for a seat in the Supreme Court. The hearing process was carried by various media outlets and highlighted the multifaceted issues involved in sexual harassment cases, such as power differentials, gender solidarity, time relevance, reluctant witnesses, and race politics. This helped to ignite a public discourse about the complex issue of sexual harassment. When later cases of alleged sexual harassment by powerful men such as Senator Bob Packwood, and former Governor and later President Bill Clinton were reported by the media, these cases received increased scrutiny and public outrage (Black & Allen, 2001). The way these cases were resolved can be traced back to the Hill/Thomas hearings (Gould, 2000; Hartman, 1992).

### Theories of Sexual Harassment

Theories to explain sexual harassment are varied and continue to emerge. Power theory (Powell, 1986), differences in the formal and informal power structures in organizations (Lundberg-Love & Marmion, 2003), and the interaction of gender, race and class (Rospena, Richman, & Nawyn, 1998) are often cited. Male-dominated occupations, such as the military, machinists, police and firefighters, and work environments that condone unprofessional behaviors have been linked to higher levels of harassment (Gruber, 2003; Lundberg-Love & Marmion, 2003). Social workers and social work students are not immune from harassment on the job or in field settings (Anderson & Kreuger, 2005; Fogel & Ellison, 1998; Fogel, Ellison & Morrow, 2001; Maypole, 1986; Risley-Curtiss & Hudson, 1998; Valentine, Gandy, Burry & Ginsberg, 1994).

### Prevalence of Sexual Harassment As a Social Problem

Anyone can experience sexual harassment. It can be subtle as well as overt, occurring in both public and private settings. Statistics available through the EEOC (www.eeoc.gov) indicate that since 1997, the overall number of complaints of sexual harassment or discrimination has decreased by approximately 24%. However, the number of complaints filed by men has jumped by 3.8% in nine years. Approximately 99% of all claims filed to the EEOC in 2006 were investigated and resolved, although almost half of all cases filed, 47.5 percent, were found to be without cause. This suggests the continued difficulty of establishing proof that the offending behavior or incident(s) constitutes sexual harassment.

Characteristics of perpetrators who are male include holding conventional attitudes about women (Zalk, 1996) and conforming to and displaying stereotyped male behaviors (Doyle & Paludi, 1998). Prior research findings suggest that demographic characteristics such as age, marital status, or occupation, do not predict the likelihood that a male will enagage in sexual harassment behaviors (Lundberg-Love & Marmion, 2003). There is, at this time, scant information regarding women who harass or harassment by same-sex individuals.

Studies of sexual harassment in educational institutions from elementary school through university indicate it is prevalent (American Association of University Women Educational Foundation, 2001; Fineran & Bennett, 1998; Stein, 1995; Till, 1980). While the scenario of teacher/faculty to student has been well documented, (Dziech & Weiner, 1990), peer-to-peer student harassment, including targeting of sexual minorities (Fineran, 2002; Fineran & Bennett, 1999; Fineran & Bolen, 2006), and student-to-teacher, including harassment of teachers who are gay or lesbian (Human Rights Watch, 2001), is growing.

The internet provides another venue for sexual harassment to occur at work, school, or even in the privacy of one's home (Barak, 2005; Finn, 2004; Finn & Banach, 2000). Unwanted emails, unsolicited pornographic materials, and cyberstalking are common methods used to harass through the internet. The extent and harm caused by such activities is unknown; however, it is acknowledged that internet harassment is growing (Barak, 2005; Cooper, Safir, & Rosenmann, 2006).

## The Effects of Sexual Harassment

There are many reactions to experiencing sexual harassment. For youth, symptoms may include changes in appetite, sleep patterns, or interest in daily activities, decline in attention to school work or participation in school activities, and increased expressions of sadness, anger, or isolation (Fineran, 2002). Youth who are sexual minorities and harassed, particularly through the internet, may also be at greater risk for suicide (Fineran, 2002; Finn, 2004).

Among adults, sexual harassment can cause emotional and physical problems similar to those of PTSD (Avina & O'Donohue, 2002; McDermut, Haaga, & Krik, 2000), and reduced self-esteem, fear, anxiety, depression, and disillusionment (Lundberg-Love & Marmion, 2003). Victims may demonstrate learned helplessness, exhibit conditioned responses, and changes in their world view and social relationships; their job performance may suffer as well (Avina & O'Donohue, 2002; Gould, 2000; Lundberg-Love & Marmion, 2003; MacKinnon, 1979). Recent research suggests that many victims do not seek professional services, but rather rely on informal support systems such as friends and family for help (Rospenda, Richman, & Shannon, 2006).

## Best Policies and Practices

A zero-tolerance policy toward sexual harassment is recommended for organizations and educational institutions (Rose, 2004); however, questions remain regarding the effectiveness of this strategy (Stockdale, Bisom-Rapp, O'Connor, & Gutek, 2003). At a minimum, policies should include a clear definition and guidelines on what constitutes sexual harassment, how to report it, grievance procedures, and training programs to educate all employees, faculty, students and those in management as to what sexual harassment is. Gender-specific programs are recommended in order to clarify perceptions of behaviors that can be interpreted as sexual harassment (Antecol & Cobb-Clark, 2003). Education and training programs such as assertiveness and conflict resolution training should extend to youth in schools and colleges to reduce peer-to-peer harassment as well. Appropriate mental health treatment for the individual as well as the family may be needed to address the psychological impact of experiencing sexual harassment (Woody & Perry, 1993).

Given the increase in the use of the internet as a means of engaging in sexual harassment, it is also critical to educate users of technology in practices that protect their identity online such as creating a screen name that does not reveal gender or age, using different screen names for different purposes, and sharing information only on secure web-sites (Barak, 2005; Finn, 2004). Furthermore, organizations and educational institutions should limit access to employee and student information (Cooper, Safir, & Rosenmann, 2006; Finn, 2004).

At a minimum, employers need to inform employees that all emails transmitted on company email system networks can be reviewed (Finn, 2004). This, as well as the other prevention strategies listed above, can create an environment where workers are challenged to be authentic in their daily interactions and in email communications. It is critical that trainings on this topic be repeated often in the work place or educational setting so that all workers are informed as to what constitutes harassment. In addition, supervisors must remain attuned to the interaction subtleties among employees within the work environment.

## Implications for Social Work

It is critical for social workers to be aware that sexual harassment continues despite legal and organizational policies to prevent its occurrence in the workplace, educational settings and over the internet. Social work roles are vital at the micro and macro levels. Emerging issues on this topic include understanding how age, race, culture, gender, sexual orientation, and the socio-economic status of the individuals involved are factors in the event, as well as an understanding of the offending behavior (Berdahl & Moore, 2006). Additional research focusing on the cases that are deemed "without reasonable cause" by the EEOC should also provide useful information about what is legally interpreted as sexual harassment.

Finally, further legislative and advocacy efforts are needed to encourage reporting and to protect those who report from retaliation. Social workers are bound by the Code of Ethics and professional mission to act to prevent discrimination (Gould, 2000; Hartman, 1992). Sexual harassment is a discriminatory practice that needs continued attention in our clinical, employment, and educational settings in order to provide appropriate education and other interventions to victims and perpetrators and decrease its frequency. Social work managers can set the appropriate climate and culture for a caring yet careful environment.

## REFERENCES

American Association of University Women Educational Foundation. (2001). *Hostile hallways: Bullying, teasing, and sexual harassment.* Washington, DC: Harris Interactive Research.

Anderson, K. M., & Kreuger, L. W. (2005, February). *Toward a better understanding of sexual harassment among female social workers.* Annual Program Meeting for Council on Social Work Education, New York, New York.

Antecol, H., & Cobb-Clark, D. (2003). Does sexual harassment training change attitudes? A view from the federal level. *Social Science Quarterly, 84*(4), 826–842.

Avina, C., & O'Donohue, W. (2002). Sexual harassment and PTSD: Is sexual harassment diagnosable trauma? *Journal of Traumatic Stress, 15*(1), 69–75.

Barak, A. (2005). Sexual harassment on the Internet. *Social Science Computer Review, 23*(1), 77–92.

Berdahl, J., & Moore, C. (2006). Workplace harassment: Double jeopardy for minority women. *Journal of Applied Psychology, 9*(2), 426–436.

Black, A. E., & Allen, J. L. (2001). Tracing the legacy of Anita Hill: The Thomas/Hill Hearings and media coverage of sexual harassment. *Gender Issues, 19*(1), 33–52.

*Burlington Industries, Inc. v. Ellerth,* 118 S.Ct. 2257 (1998).

*Burlington Northern & Santa Fe Railway Co v. White,* 126 S.Ct. 2405 (2006).

Chan, A. A. (1994). *Women and sexual harassment.* Binghamton, NY: Haworth Press.

Cooper, A., Safir, M. P., & Rosenmann, A. (2006). Workplace worries: A preliminary look at online sexual activities at the office—Emerging issues for clinicians and employers. *CyberPsychology & Behavior, 9*(1), 22.

*Davis v. Monroe County Board of Education,* 119 S.Ct. 1661 (1999).

Doyle, J., & Paludi, M. A. (1998). *Sex and gender: The human experience* (4th ed.). Dubuque, IA: William C. Brown/ Benchmark.

Dziech, B. W., & Weiner, L. (1990). *The lecherous professor: Sexual harassment on campus* (2nd ed.). Boston: Beacon Press.

Fineran, S. (2002). Sexual harassment between same-sex peers: Intersection of mental health, homophobia, and sexual violence in schools. *Social Work, 47*(1), 65–74.

Fineran, S., & Bennett, L. (1998). Teenage peer sexual harassment: Implications for social work practice in education. *Social Work, 43*(1), 55–64.

Fineran, S., & Bennett, L. (1999). Gender and power issues of peer sexual harassment among teenagers. *Journal of Interpersonal Violence, 14*(6), 626–641.

Fineran, S., & Bolen, R. M. (2006). Risk factors for peer sexual harassment in schools. *Journal of Interpersonal Violence, 21*(9), 1169–1190.

Finn, J. (2004). A survey of online harassment at a university campus. *Journal of Interpersonal Violence, 19*(4), 468–483.

Finn, J., & Banach, M. (2000). Victimization online: The down side of seeking human services fro women on the internet. *CyberPsychology & Behavior, 3*(2), 243–254.

Fogel, S. J., & Ellison, M. E. (1998). Sexual harassment of BSW field students: Is it a problem?. *Journal of Baccalaureate Social Work, 3*(2), 17–29.

Fogel, S. J., Ellison, M. E., & Morrow, D. F. (2001). BSW graduates respond: Is sexual harassment a problem in field placement? *Journal of Baccalaureate Social Work, 7*(1), 79–93.

*Franklin v. Gwinnett County Public Schools,* 505 U.S. 60 (1992).

Gould, K. H. (2000). Beyond *Jones v. Clinton:* Sexual harassment law and social work. *Social Work, 45*(3), 237–248.

Gruber, J. (2003). Sexual harassment in the public sector. In M. Paludi & C. A. Paludi, Jr. (Eds.), *Academic and workplace sexual harassment: A handbook of cultural, social science, management, and legal perspectives* (pp. 49–75). Westport, CT: Praeger Publisher.

Gutman, A. (2000). *EEO law and personnel practices* (2nd ed.). Thousand Oaks, CA: Sage Publications.

*Harris v. Forklift Systems,* 510 U.S. 17 (1993).

Hartman, A. (1992). It was not our finest hour. *Social Work, 37*(1), 3–4.

Human Rights Watch. (2001). *Hatred in the hallways: Violence and discrimination against lesbian, gay, bisexual and transgender students in US schools.* St Paul, MN: Author.

Lundberg-Love, P., & Marmion, S. (2003). Sexual harassment in the private sector. In M. Paludi & C. A. Paludi, Jr. (Eds.), *Academic and workplace sexual harassment: A handbook of cultural, social science, management, and legal perspectives* (pp. 77–101). Westport, CT: Praeger Publisher.

MacKinnon, C. A. (1979). *Sexual harassment of working women: A case of sex discrimination.* New Haven, CT: Yale University Press.

McDermut, J. F., Haaga, D. A. F., & Kirk, L. (2000). An evaluation of stress symptoms associated with academic sexual harassment. *Journal of Traumatic Stress, 13*(3), 397–411.

Maypole, D. E. (1986). Sexual harassment of social workers at work: Injustice within? *Social Work, 31*(1), 29–34.

*Oncale v. Sundowner Offshore Services,* 118 S.Ct. 998 (1998).

Powell, G. N. (1986). Effects of sex-role identity and sex on definitions of sexual harassment. *Sex Roles*, 14(1/2), 9–19.

Risley-Curtiss, C., & Hudson, W. W. (1998). Sexual harassment of social work students. *Affilia: Journal of Women and Social Work*, 13(2), 190–111.

Rose, K. J. (2004). "Zero tolerance" for sexual harassment by supervisors in the workplace: Employers don't have a real choice. *Journal of Forensic Psychology Practice*, 4(1), 57–64.

Rospena, K. M., Richman, J. A., & Nawyn, S. (1998). Doing power: The confluence of gender, race, and class in contrapower sexual harassment. *Gender & Society*, 12(1), 40–60.

Rospenda, K. M., Richman, J. A., & Shannon, C. A. (2006). Patterns of workplace harassment, gender, and use of services: An update. *Journal of Occupational Health Psychology*, 11(4), 379–393.

Singer, T. L. (1995). Sexual harassment. In R. Edwards (Ed.), *Encyclopedia of Social Work*, (19th ed., vol. 3. pp. 2148–2156). Washington, DC: National Association of Social Workers.

Stein, N. (1995). Sexual harassment in school: The public performance of gendered violence. *Harvard Educational Preview*, 65, 145–162.

Stockdale, M. S., Bisom-Rapp, S., O'Connor, M., & Gutek, B. (2003). Coming to terms with zero tolerance sexual harassment policies. *Journal of Forensic Psychology Practice*, 4(1), 65–78.

Strauss, S. (2003). Sexual harassment in K-12. In M. Paludi & C. A. Paludi, Jr. (Eds.), *Academic and workplace sexual harassment: A handbook of cultural, social science, management, and legal perspectives* (pp. 105–145). Westport, CT: Praeger Publisher.

Till, F. (1980). *Sexual harassment: A report on the sexual harassment of students*. Washington, DC: National Advisory Council on Women's Educational Programs.

Valentine D., Gandy, J., Burry, C., & Ginsberg, L. (1994). Sexual harassment in social work field placement. In M. O. Weil, M. Hughes, & N. R. Hooyman (Eds.), *Sexual harassment and schools of social work: Issues, costs, and strategic responses* (pp. 39–53). Washington, DC: Council on Social Work Education, Inc.

Woody, R. H., & Perry, N. W. (1993). Sexual harassment victims: Psycholegal and family therapy considerations. *The American Journal of Family Therapy*, 23(2), 136–144.

Zalk, S. R. (1996). Psychological profiles of men who harass. In M. S. Paludi (Ed.), *Sexual harassment on college campuses: Abusing the ivory power*. Albany, NY: SUNY Press.

### FURTHER READING

Education Amendments of 1972, P.L. 92–318, 86, Stat.235.

*Faragher v. City of Boca Raton*, 118 S.Ct. 2275, (1998).

*Gebster v. Lago Vista Independent School District*, 118. S.Ct. 1989 (1990).

*Meritor Savings Bank v. Vinson*, 106 S.Ct. 2399 (1986).

*Williams v. Saxbe*, 413 F. Supp. 645 (D.C. Cir. 1976).

—SONDRA J. FOGEL

# SINGLE PARENTS

**ABSTRACT:** Between 1990 and 2003, the single-parent family continued to emerge as a major family form in the United States. Individuals come to single parenthood through different routes (divorce, separation, birth outside of marriage, widowhood, and adoption). And most of them are women. Intervention implications are framed in terms of primary, secondary, and tertiary strategies. Increasing family benefits and child care provisions are highlighted as well as strategies for preventing teen pregnancy, increasing access to educational and entry to the work force for low-income women, and identifying mothers early on in the process of marital disruption.

**KEY WORDS:** single mothers; teen pregnancy; workforce entry; homeless and abused women; mothers in child welfare

## Demographics

From 1970 until 1990, the single-parent family emerged as a major family form in the United States, and from 1990 to 2003, the single-parent family remained a major family form, due to increasing birth rates in never-married women and increasing divorce rates through the 1990s. Families headed by single mothers accounted for 26% of all family households by 2003, while families headed by fathers alone accounted for 5% of all family households. The 10 million families maintained by women were twice as likely as the 2 million families headed by men to have family incomes below the poverty level (32% compared with 16%) (U.S. Bureau of the census fields, 2003).

The breakdown by race and ethnicity of single-parent families in 2003 is shown in Table 1.

## U.S. Social Context

Single parents have unique needs that are quite varied (Weinraub, Horvath, & Gringlas, 2002), and risks to these families and children are heightened because of the stress of lower socioeconomic resources and the cumulative effect of multiple family transitions and family relationships often characterized by negativity and conflict (Carlson & Trepani, 2006). Individuals come to single parenthood through different routes (divorce, separation, birth outside of marriage, widowhood, and adoption). And most of them are women.

Single mothers have lower income than do single fathers (U.S. Bureau of the Census Fields, 2003). A recent study of the level of assets and debt of single mothers revealed that the net worth of these mothers is

TABLE 1

*Type of Family Household by Ethnicity and Gender of Head of Household, 2003*

| HEAD OF HOUSEHOLD | NUMBER OF FAMILY HOUSEHOLDS (IN THOUSANDS) | PERCENTAGE OF TOTAL NUMBER OF FAMILY HOUSEHOLDS |
|---|---|---|
| Total family households | 79,210 | |
| Total family households with children | 64,186 | |
| White | | |
| Married couples | 50,865 | 78 |
| Female | 15,623 | 16 |
| Male | 5,001 | 6 |
| Black | | |
| Married couples | 4,264 | 44 |
| Female | 4,534 | 47 |
| Male | 830 | 9 |
| Hispanic | | |
| Married couples | 6,583 | 66 |
| Female | 2,479 | 25 |
| Male | 975 | 9 |
| Asian or Pacific | | |
| Married couples | 2,454 | 80 |
| Female | 393 | 13 |
| Male | 236 | 7 |

significantly less than that of married-couple households and male-headed households (Ozawa & Lee, 2006). The single mother is vulnerable to role strain, including shortage of time for personal care activities, sleep, and rest and, if employed, less time for children and child care, household tasks, and volunteer work (Atwood & Genovese, 2006).

## International Comparisons

MacBlain and MacBlain (2004) note that the number of children from lone-parent households is increasing worldwide. Single-parent families have become a more significant family form in European countries, and out-of-wedlock births and divorce are typically the route to single parenthood (Hampden-Thomas & Pong, 2005). The relative economic status of single mothers is lower in the United States than in most other Western industrialized countries (Herd 2006; Ozawa, 2004). The performance gap in single parents providing education for their children is also higher in countries with strong family and welfare policies than that in countries (such as the United States) that tend to leave family welfare to the market economy (Hampden-Thompson & Pong, 2005; Marks, 2006). Adolescent

child-bearing is more common in the United States than in other developed countries (Darroch, Singh, & Frost, 2001; Finer & Henshaw, 2006).

## Basic Principles of Intervention

The prevention paradigm offers a useful framework for organizing strategies for intervention with single parents.

PRIMARY PREVENTION: LEGISLATIVE AND COMMUNITY ORGANIZATION Primary prevention strategies are designed to help avert a condition or to strengthen protective factors that already exist. In the United States, linking family benefits to parenthood, as opposed to marriage, adversely affects women (and primarily poor and Black women) (Herd, 2006); adolescent child rearing is higher in the United States than in other developed countries, and school achievement is positively associated with social democratic regimes in Europe (Hampden-Thompson & Pong, 2005). This underscores the need for policy reform in the United States to address the social constraints faced by many single parents. Adolescent parents in particular lack many material resources (Mollborn, 2007).

High child care costs and low wages are particularly problematic for single women (Ford, 1996). As single parents move transition from welfare to work, the critical need for child care subsidies as well as available, quality day care has become apparent. Single mothers are far more likely to work and to work more hours when states offset child care costs (Crawford, 2006).

SECONDARY PREVENTION: IDENTIFICATION AND INTERVENTION WITH HIGH-RISK SINGLE PARENTS Single-parent families vary by gender of the head of household, age, race–ethnicity and education, and all these characteristics shape how much single parents experience positive or negative outcomes in terms of psychological well-being, health, and parent–child relationships (Amato, 2000). Preventing teen pregnancy, increasing access to education and entry to the work force for low-income women, and identifying mothers early on in the process of marital disruption are groups that could be targeted for early intervention.

A meta-analysis of 16 secondary pregnancy prevention programs suggest that these programs are effective in reducing pregnancy, at least for a year and a half after completion of the program (Corcoran & Pilaio, 2007). Women moving from welfare to work have been found to experience a myriad of problems, including unreliable child care. For single parents, factors that lead to a better work-family fit include support from the workplace as well as other community sources (DeBord, Canu, & Kerpelman, 2000).

A third population at risk is women facing marital disruptions. Ozawa and Yoon (2003) found that from 6 months before marital disruption to 6 months after, children's economic well-being declined significantly. Research has also suggested that single parenthood represents a risk for children's development (DeKlyen, Brooks-Gunn, McLanahan, & Knab, 2006; Fombey & Cherlin, 2007; Kesner & McKenry, 2001). The level of education for the divorced or separated mother will be critical for maintaining the living standard of children (Ozawa & Yoon, 2003).

**TERTIARY PREVENTION: CLINICAL INTERVENTIONS WITH SINGLE PARENTS** Prevention strategies at the tertiary level involve those designed to help women who are already single parents. Research illustrates that the higher levels of psychological distress suffered by single parents is more strongly related to their greater exposure to stress and strain than to personal deficits (Avison, 1999). Although single parents interface with multiple personal social service delivery systems, there are several situations in which social workers encounter single parents who are among the most stressed and are vulnerable in child welfare (Mills, 2000; Wulczyn, Barth, Yuan, Harden, & Landsverk, 2005), in services to victims of intimate partner violence (Kali, Tolman, Rosen, & Gruber, 2003), and in homeless service delivery system (Roditti, 2005). Vulnerability is heightened when these parents have very young children.

Clinical interventions with single parents include crisis intervention, engagement in therapy, recognizing and mobilizing strengths, dealing with both ex- and live-in partners, and building on natural connections (Anderson, 2003; Peeble-Wilkins, 2003). The latter may be especially important for women involved in the service delivery systems noted above and for women with very young children (Davey, 2004; Letiecq, Anderson, & Koblinsky, 1998; Phillips, DeChillo, Kronenfeld, & Middleton-Jeter, 1988; Roditti, 2005).

### Emerging Directions and Challenges

The need to develop evidence-based, outcome-oriented services is increasing. The personal social services face the challenge of developing service delivery systems that better fit the needs of single parents, including the recruitment of diverse staff that represents the populations served and more home-based services. At the policy level, family–friendly benefit systems and reimbursement systems designed to support the development of staff trained in evidence based and single-parent family-centered approaches are among the challenges faced by the profession.

### REFERENCES

Amato, P. R. (2000). Diversity within single parent families. In D. H. Demo, K. R. Allen, & M. A. Fine (Eds.), *Handbook of family diversity* (pp. 149–172). New York: Oxford University Press.

Anderson, C. (2003). The diversity, strength and challenges of single-parent households. In F. Walsh (Ed.), *Normal family processes: Growing diversity and complexity*. New York: Guilford Press.

Atwood, J. D., & Genovese, F. (2006). *Therapy with single parents: A social constructionist approach*. New York: Haworth Press.

Avison, W. (1999). Family structures and processes. In A. V. Horwitz & T. L. Scheid (Eds.), *A handbook for the study of mental health: Social contexts, theories and systems*. New York: Cambridge University Press.

Carlson, C., & Trepani, J. N. (2006). Single parenting and stepparenting. In G. Bear & K. N. Minke (Eds.), *Children's needs III: Development, preventions, and intervention*. Washington, DC: National Association of School Psychologists.

Corcoran, J., & Pilaio, V. K. (2007). Effectiveness of secondary pregnancy prevention programs: A meta-analysis. *Research on Social Work Practice, 17*(1), 5–18.

Crawford, A. (2006). The impact of child care subsidies on single mothers. *Review of Policy Research, 23*(3), 699–712.

Darroch, J. E., Singh, S., & Frost, J. J. (2001). Differences in teenage pregnancy rates among five developed countries: The roles of sexual activity and contraceptive use. *Family Planning Perspectives, 33*(6), 244–251.

Davey, T. A. (2004). A multiple family group intervention for homeless families: The week-end retreat. *Health and Social Work, 29*(4), 326–329.

DeBord, K., Canu, R. F., & Kerpelman, J. (2000). Understanding a work-family fit for single parents moving from welfare to work. *Social Work, 45*(4), 313–324.

DeKlyen, M., Brooks-Gunn, J., McLanahan, S., & Knab, J. (2006). The mental health of married, cohabiting and non-cohabiting parents with infants. *American Journal of Public Health, 96*(10), 18–36.

Finer, L. B., & Henshaw, S. K. (2006). Disparities in rates of unintended pregnancy in the United States, 1994 and 2001. *Perspectives on Sexual and Reproductive Health, 38*(2), 90–96.

Fombey, P., & Cherlin, A. J. (2007). Family instability and child well-being. *American Sociological Review, 72*(2), 181–208.

Ford, R. (1996). *Children in the balance*. London: Policy Studies Institute.

Hampden-Thompson, G., & Pong, S. L. (2005). Does family policy environment moderate the effect of single parenthood on children's academic achievement? A study of 14 European countries. *Journal of Contemporary Family Studies, 36*(2), 224–252.

Herd, P. (2006). Crediting care or marriage? Reforming social security benefits. *The Journal of Gerontology, 61B*(1), 524–534.

Kali, A., Tolman, R., Rosen, D., & Gruber, G. (2003). Domestic violence and children's behavior in low-income families. *Journal of Emotional Abuse, 3*(1/2), 75–101.

Kesner, J. E., & McKenry, P. C. (2001). Single parenthood and social competence in children of color. *Families in Society, 82*(2), 135–143.

Letiecq, B. I., Anderson, E. A., & Koblinsky, S. A. (1998). Social support of homeless and housed mothers: A comparison of temporary and permanent housing arrangements. *Family Relations, 47*(4), 415–421.

MacBlain, S. P., & MacBlain, M. S. (2004). Is there a role for school social workers in addressing the longer-term needs of children from lone-parent households? *Journal of School Social Work, 13*(2), 59–73.

Marks, G. (2006). Family size, family type and student achievement: Cross-national differences and the role of socioeconomic and school factors. *Journal of Contemporary Family Studies, 37*(1), 1–27.

Mills, L. G. (2000). Women abuse and child protection: A tumultuous marriage (Part I). *Children and Youth Services Review, 22* (entire issue), 199–205.

Mollborn, S. (2007). Making the best of a bad situation: Material resources and teenage parenthood. *Journal of Marriage and Family, 69*(1), 92–105.

Ozawa, M. (2004). Social welfare spending on family benefits in the United States and Sweden: A comparative study. *Family Relations, 53*(3), 301–310.

Ozawa, M., & Lee, Y. (2006). The net worth of female-headed households: A comparison to other types of households. *Family Relations, 55*(1), 132–144.

Ozawa, M., & Yoon, H. S. (2003). Economic impact of marital disruption on children. *Children and Youth Services Review, 25*(8), 611–632.

Peeble-Wilkins, W. (2003). Support networks and well-being. *Children and Schools, 25*(2), 67–68.

Phillips, M., DeChillo, N., Kronenfeld, D., & Middleton-Jeter, V. (1988). Homeless families: Services makes a difference. *Social Casework, 69*(1), 46–53.

Roditti, M. G. (2005). Understanding communities of neglectful parents: Child caregiving networks and child neglect. *Child Welfare, 84*(2), 277–298.

U.S. Bureau of the Census Fields. (2003). *America's families and living arrangements: 2003; Population characteristics. Current population reports.* US Department of Commerce, Economic and Statistics Administration, US Census Bureau.

Weinraub, M., Horvath, D. L., & Gringlas, M. B. (2002). Single parenthood. In M. Bornstein (Ed.), *Handbook of parenting, Vol 3: Being and becoming a parent* (2nd ed.). Mahwah, NJ: Lawrence Erlbaum.

Wulczyn, F., Barth, R., Yuan, Y. Y., Harden, B. J., & Landsverk, J. (2005). *Beyond common sense.* New York: Adline Transaction.

### SUGGESTED LINKS

Census Bureau data.
*http://www.census.gov/acs/www/*

—VIRGINIA C. STRAND

## SINGLE-SYSTEM DESIGNS

**ABSTRACT:** Single-system designs (SSDs) are a family of user-friendly empirical procedures that can be used to help professionals to monitor and evaluate the effectiveness of the services they provide to clients and to guide practice. SSDs can be used to evaluate interventions based on any theory or approach. Repeated measurement of the target(s) of intervention is an intrinsic and key element of SSDs. Dozens of SSDs exist, and each has its own strengths and limitations. The most basic and most widely used design is the A-B design. Data from SSDs are analyzed visually, using simple, descriptive or inferential statistics, or using criteria for practical or clinical significance.

**KEY WORDS:** single-system designs; single-subject designs; N = 1 designs; practice evaluation

Practice research provides important guidance for helping professionals when selecting effective intervention strategies (Roberts & Yeager, 2004; see also Evidence-Based Practice; Best Practices; Practice Interventions and Research; Intervention Research). However, interventions shown to be effective in research may not be effective when used in practice with some clients, and problems presented by some clients may not have interventions with known effectiveness. Given this uncertainty in the application of practice knowledge, and increasing pressure to evaluate and document the effectiveness of services, it is important that helping professionals have practical tools they can use to evaluate and document the effectiveness of the services they provide to individual clients.

Single-system designs (SSDs) are a family of user-friendly empirical procedures that can be used to help professionals to monitor and evaluate the effectiveness of the services they provide to clients and client/systems and to guide practice. SSDs are known by a number of different names: *single N or N = 1 designs, single-subject designs,* and *time-series designs,* among others. We prefer *single-system design* because it emphasizes the person-in-environment and it refers to evaluating practice-virtually all potential clients and systems, including individuals and groups, such as families, agencies, classrooms and entire communities. The basic characteristics of SSDs are described in the subsequent text.

### Measurement

Repeated measurement of the target(s) of intervention is an intrinsic and key element of SSDs. The amount of some identified target is measured repeatedly over time with, say, higher scores indicating more depression on a standardized depression scale. Through repeated measurement, an ongoing picture of the target is created. This moving picture can be used to guide decisions about whether an intervention should be implemented, continued, changed, replaced, or discontinued, so that it can guide the ongoing course of practice with client systems toward more effective, evidence-based, accountable practice.

Target information can be provided by the various parties involved, such as clients, helping professionals or relevant others, as suitable. Different measurement methods can be used, such as standardized scales and indices (see also Scales and Indices and Fischer & Corcoran, 2006a, b), individualized rating scales, self-monitoring, or direct behavioral observation (Bloom, Fischer, & Orme, 2006). The quality of measures (see also Psychometrics) is very important because information from them is used to make practice decisions, and measures should be easy to use and directly relevant to intervention planning.

## Designs

With most SSDs the target is measured on a continuing basis before intervention (baseline, designated by A), during intervention (designated by some letter other than A) and, sometimes, after intervention is complete to check the staying power of the results. Time periods during which different events occur are known as *phases*.

Baseline typically is used as the frame of reference for changes during intervention. For example, the pattern of changes in the target during intervention is compared to the pattern during baseline to determine if the target has improved, deteriorated, or remained unchanged relative to baseline. In this way the single-system acts as its own *control group*.

Dozens of designs are detailed in Bloom et al. (2006), and each has its own strengths and limitations that make it suitable for specific situations. For example, the A-B design, consisting of a single baseline phase (A) followed by an intervention phase (B) is the basic single-system design that can be used with virtually all cases. Alternately, an A-B-C design might be used if the first intervention (B) was unsuccessful and it was necessary to try a second (C). In these and all situations, the design ultimately used for evaluation is shaped by the pattern of change and practice priorities rather than being immutably fixed at the outset.

Most SSDs, such as the A-B design, described above, can be used to determine if a target changed for better or worse, or did not change at all. To determine whether an intervention *caused* a change requires an arrangement of phases and a pattern of results that let you conclude logically that the intervention, not something else for example, some change over time in the client's environment), caused the change. For instance, the A-B-A-B design starts with a baseline, introduces an intervention, removes it, and then reintroduces it. If the target improves during intervention and deteriorates during baseline then you are in a better position to conclude that the intervention caused the change. The multiple baseline design also can provide causal information but without removing the intervention. Instead, in the multiple baseline design, more than one problem is assessed during baseline; after the intervention is introduced with the first problem, the same intervention is introduced sequentially with the second problem. However, introduction of the intervention with the second problem occurs only *after* the intervention produces change in the first problem. This sequential introduction of the intervention allows the practitioner to see if change occurs only when the intervention is introduced and thus infer causality.

Many other even more complex designs are available to assist the practitioner in making causal inferences (Bloom et al., 2006). Of course, sometimes it is difficult to use these designs, and there are ethical reasons for considering carefully the effects on clients of such actions as temporarily removing apparently effective interventions as in the A-B-A-B design, but these designs are relatively powerful in establishing causality.

## Interventions

SSDs can be used to evaluate interventions based on any theory or approach, from psychodynamic practice (Dean & Reinherz, 1986) to cognitive behavior therapy (Bradshaw & Roseborough, 2004). Any method of practice, from primary prevention through treatment and rehabilitation, can employ SSDs. All that is required is that the practitioner define the intervention clearly enough to be able to specify precisely when the intervention begins and when it ends.

## Analysis

To determine whether change occurred, target data during one phase (for example, intervention) are compared to target data during another phase (for example, baseline). Descriptive and inferential statistics can be used to add to the visual analysis of graphed data, and computer programs such as SINGWIN and Microsoft

Excel can be used to reduce the amount of work-time needed to graph and analyze data (Bloom et al., 2006).

To determine whether sufficient change occurred, cultural norms or values, theories of human development and psychopathology, subjective impressions of clients or significant others, and intervention goals should be considered.

## Conclusion

SSDs are practical tools that can be integrated into practice to provide immediate ongoing feedback to guide practice with individual client systems toward more effective, evidence-based, accountable practice. SSDs can provide evidence that the targets of intervention have changed and, to some extent, depending on the design, that these changes may be caused by the intervention. These designs represent a high level of ethically appropriate practice since they appear to meet the NASW Code of Ethics standards that state that practitioners should evaluate their practice (NASW, 1996). It is likely that the future will see the refinement of computer programs that currently are available to make them more accessible to practitioners using SSDs. As these designs and other methods of evaluation become taught in more schools of social work, it is likely also that a higher percentage of practitioners will be using them in a wider variety of practice situations.

### REFERENCES

Bloom, M., Fischer, J., & Orme, J. (2006). *Evaluating practice: Guidelines for the accountable professional* (5th ed.). Boston: Allyn & Bacon.

Bradshaw, W., & Roseborough, D. (2004). Evaluating the effectiveness of cognitive-behavioral treatment of residual symptoms and impairment in schizophrenia. *Research on Social Work Practice, 14,* 112–120.

Dean, R. G., & Reinherz, H. (1986). Psychodynamic practice and single system design: The odd couple. *Journal of Social Work Education, 22,* 71–81.

Fischer, J., & Corcoran, K. (2006a). Measures for clinical practice and research: A sourcebook (4th ed.). Volume I: *Couples, families, and children.* Oxford: Oxford University Press.

Fischer, J., & Corcoran, K. (2006b). Measures for clinical practice and research: A sourcebook (4th ed.). Volume II: *Adults.* Oxford: Oxford University Press.

NASW. (1996). *NASW code of ethics.* Washington, DC: NASW.

Roberts, A. R., & Yeager, K. R. (2004). *Evidence-based practice Manual:* Research *and outcome measures in health and human services.* New York: Oxford University Press.

—JOEL FISCHER AND JOHN G. ORME

## SOCIAL CAPITAL

**ABSTRACT:** In social work, social capital is linked to both the prevention and treatment of mental and physical health. This concept has also been incorporated in the development of empowering interventions with marginalized minorities. The capacity-based and the youth development models of intervention, both call on social service organizations to work interdependently around meeting the needs for the human and social capital growth of youth (Morrison, Alcorn, & Nelums, 1997). Social capital is also a feature of empowering interventions in neighborhoods and community development, as is collective efficacy, which is a measure of working trust that exists among residents and has been popularized as a way to stop youth high-risk behavior.

**KEY WORDS:** social support; empowerment; capacity-based interventions; collective efficacy; micro- and macro-practice; integrative and leverage bridges; social networks; community organizing; community building; settlement houses

### History

Modern use of the term *social capital* can be traced to Jane Jacobs, the urban planner and critic who linked it to the value of social networks while writing about communities in the 1960s (Jacobs, 1961). Bourdieu (1985) was the first to provide a cohesive definition, expanding the economic concept of "capital" to include social, cultural, symbolic, as well as economic resources. He defined social capital as "the aggregate of the actual or potential resources which are linked to possession of a durable network of more or less institutionalized relationships of mutual acquaintance or recognition" (p. 248). His term has gained popularity as a tool for understanding the stratification process at individual and aggregate levels, consistent with the micro and macro social work practices. As it has gained popularity, some scholars have used it to explain racial disparities and inequality, albeit with different terms. For example, the economist Glenn Loury (1977) highlighted social capital as a potential explanatory variable when assessing the economic performance of minorities who had unequal access to the benefits of informal ties. James Coleman (1988) adopted Loury's definition of social capital to the study of its relation to the development of human capital.

Social capital is built on the concept of social networks studied by social workers among others (Naparstek, Biegel, & Spiro, 1982). Social networks can vary in size, geographical location, and location of ties in the social structure. Depending on their makeup, social networks differ in what they yield. Small, homogeneous networks can help to conserve existing resources and provide social support, particularly in small, insular communities (Stack, 1974). Large, dispersed, and heterogeneous (interclass) social networks increase the opportunity structure of individuals (Burt, 1987). Homogenous social networks recycle the same type of information. This is problematic for low-income populations who lack access to different ideas and opportunities; homogeneity in social relationships is also negative for insular communities such as high-income populations who lack knowledge of other people's realities and cannot act with an informed understanding when supporting or opposing social welfare policies. These policies could increase services provided by social workers and improve the opportunity structure of marginalized communities, such as the mentally ill, of concern to social work.

Social capital became well known more broadly with the publication of *Bowling Alone* by Robert Putnam (2000), who found that the level of civic participation was decreasing in the United States. From another standpoint, William J. Wilson (1987) encouraged more analysis of the relationship between social capital and socioeconomic outcomes by highlighting the importance of structural dynamics related to deindustrialization and unemployment in central cities. By focusing on low-income neighborhoods, Wilson spearheaded the argument that people who live segregated in concentrated areas of poverty are socially isolated and thereby lack the social ties to working and middle-class individuals that serve as key sources of information to access employment. As Briggs (2002) points out, "Differential coping or mobility chances are explained directly by access to social connections, net of education, income, and other factors" (p. 34).

### Social Capital and Microlevel Interventions

At the micro-practice level, social capital explains how social ties linked to networks and associations promote social support and status attainment (Briggs, 1998). This level of social capital closely fits Portes's (1998) definition as the "ability of actors to secure benefits by virtue of membership in social networks or other social structures" (p. 3). Social support is linked to both the prevention and the treatment of mental and physical health. Social support is most often associated with "strong" ties, which tend to be made of kin, neighbors, and intimate friends. Ties that offer *social support* help individuals to "get by" or cope with the demands of everyday life and other stresses. These ties generally provide individuals with emotional and expressive support; informational support that contain guidance and access to services; as well as certain forms of instrumental help such as rides, small emergency loans, and a place to stay in case of emergency (Briggs, 1998). Help with these basic needs are particularly significant for people who are suffering from symptoms related to mental health problems such as depression and others.

Social support is known to be essential in the maintenance of a balanced life by reducing stress in everyday life. As a preventive measure, adequate social support helps people to balance the intricate needs of survival, as well as those of balancing work and family. It has been linked to the prevention of problems in childhood, adolescence, adulthood, and senescence, including high-risk behaviors and relapses in addiction, and physical and mental illnesses. As a preventive measure, social support reduces the need for formal mental health treatment (McKensie, Patel, & Araya, 2004).

As a major component in treatment, social capital in the form of support has been found to be helpful in the recovery processes of physical and mentally ill people. In certain conditions such as addictions, violence, or other risky behaviors closely related to peer influence, a change of one's social network is necessary in order to cease the condition (Beal, Ausiello, & Perrin, 2001). This is particularly the case in forensic settings and in mandated addiction- and violence-related services where it is necessary for clients to be able to remove themselves from their peers who enabled participation in risky behaviors. In these situations, social workers should consider the ways in which networks can be changed to foster supportive ties that help to avoid relapse and reoffending. These peer networks that enable participation in risky behavior are examples of negative or draining types of ties, which are also prevalent in the social capital literature. Draining ties are those which demand too much without reciprocating. Draining ties are particularly an issue for low-income people because of the structural limitations and lack of opportunity structures available in contexts of poverty. One thing that social workers can do is to help clients do an inventory of their ties and look for alternatives for the ones that drain resources away from them. The ability to set limits on ties that do not reciprocate is necessary for people who are suffering from mental health problems. At the same time, mental and physical illnesses reduce the networks of those affected, as people shy away from "unpleasant" situations and demonstrate a temporary symptom-based inability to reciprocate.

## Social Capital and Macrolevel Interventions

At the macro-practice level, social capital has been used to study neighborhood social organization (Sampson, Raudenbush, & Earls, 1997), as well as civic and economic regional performance (Putnam, 2000). An increased focus on the macro level is exemplified by its use by the World Bank with regard to economic and societal development (Dasgupta & Serageldin, 2000).

While in macro-practice social capital is a defining feature of empowering interventions in neighborhoods and community development, it is also essential for the development of tightly knit and connected communities that foster positive youth development by offering opportunities for training and employment through institutional linkages. Indeed, in tightly knit communities, the "strength of strong ties" can be manifested in the development of "enforceable trust" and "bounded solidarity." Enforceable trust is created when someone extends a favor to a fellow member in expectation of both guaranteed repayment and group approval (Portes, 1998). Bounded solidarity can be understood as the mechanism by which network ties are turned into sources of social capital (Portes, 1998). Bounded solidarity consists of the sentiments of solidarity derived from the common experience of discrimination or exclusion by a group, while enforceable trust entails the internal sanctioning capacity of the community. While such strong ties are an important ingredient in the strategies families develop to survive and advance, these aspects of community life are often linked to the view of social capital as a source of social control as observed in gang and mafia activity (MacDonald, 2000; Patillo, 1999).

Another theoretical construct relevant to macro social work practice is *collective efficacy*, which merges social organization theories with social capital (Sampson, Raudenbush, & Earls, 1997). Collective efficacy is the capacity of a neighborhood to intervene when a problem arises. It is based on a measure of working trust among residents with shared expectations. The concept of collective efficacy has been popularized as a way to stop youth high-risk behavior and decrease criminal activity and violence (Sampson et al., 1997).

## Trends in Social Capital and Social Work

Social capital has also been incorporated in *empowering interventions* with marginalized minorities (Gutierrez & Lewis, 1999). As a model of practice, empowerment has three components: the understanding of power and powerlessness, the psychological transformation encompassing the development of a critical consciousness, and self-efficacy through connection with social networks to foster their development (Gutierrez &

Lewis, 1999). The development of critical consciousness includes the understanding of power distribution in society and how that distribution affects the opportunities and constraints available to individuals, influencing their perceptions and experiences. Self-efficacy results from the identification of skills and interventions that build on these skills. Connection involves the development of social networks that offer support as well as leverage that increases life chances. Empowerment-based interventions are specially suited to social workers, who work with minority-excluded populations. *Capacity-based* paradigms in social work also rely heavily on social capital in the form of linkages among service organizations (Glicken, 2004). The capacity-based paradigm (also known as assets and strengths) rose out of a concern for the overutilization of a deficit-based, pathology-focused paradigm that further stigmatizes minorities and low-income people (Saleebey, 1992). The deficit-based perspective focuses on problem-solving solely from an individual perspective, while the capacity-based modality relies on the identification of strengths and the development of organizational linkages to implement their further development. These linkages among community resources are also prevalent on the *youth development* model of intervention, which calls on social service organizations to organize interdependently around meeting the needs of human and social capital growth of youth, especially in low-income areas. The youth development model is now implemented in many youth organizations, including the Boys and Girls Clubs of America.

Another aspect of social capital, which is vital in individual treatment and community development, is *bridges* (Briggs, 2004). Bridges are ties among socially dissimilar persons (bridging ties), which play a vital role in the social, economic, and political life of diverse societies. Bridges expand identities, open up insular communities, and contain ethnic and other intergroup conflicts. In this way, bridges reduce intergroup inequalities. Bridges have been identified in the literature as integrative and leverage-producing (Domínguez, 2005). *Integrative bridges* are individuals that act as bridges connecting two ethnically differentiated populations that exist in a given neighborhood or community. Often, these integrative bridges rise from outreach efforts that community-based organizations make to immigrant and minority populations in an effort to integrate them into the community's service delivery system and incorporating them into the larger society. *Leverage bridges* are also connecting two different populations but in this case across social class. Leverage bridges open up leverage-producing opportunities to individuals, giving them access to resources normally outside of their context. In turn, these bridges become integrated into the minority individuals' social networks. As such, bridges provide a link between two populations that may be differentiated by race, ethnicity, or class, therefore increasing the heterogeneity of ties in social networks of the individuals and integrating them further into the neighborhood, community, and society.

Social capital is a core concept in business, economics, organizational behavior, political science, public health, and sociology (Portes, 1998). Social work has gained the most understanding and application of social capital from sociology and public health (Winkler, 2004). Sociological studies of neighborhoods, social mobility, and the integration of immigrants have shed light on the positive and negative aspects of social networks. Public Health has illuminated the power of social support as it relates to physical and mental health.

## Roles for Social Workers

Social work is well positioned to implement, through micro- and macro-practices, theory research and practice of social capital. Many agencies, community centers, and service providers have become the sole sources of support to low-income, isolated clients whose families are nonexistent, are working multiple jobs, or have become stressful (Dominguez & Watkins, 2003). Therefore practitioners and students are in a prime position to foster the development of leverage and integrative bridges among future professionals. Challenges remain in that micro-practice in social work has fully embraced the medical model of decease and pathology in the last 30 years, limiting applications for social capital. Noteworthy exceptions have been psycho-educational and psycho-social interventions that focus on developing of alternatives to combat problems and the development of social relationships for support in club-houses. Meanwhile, empowerment and capacity-based perspectives that rely heavily on social capital need to be incorporated more widely into school curricula and agency-based medical and psychiatric services. In this case, it is macro-practice in social work that more readily uses the development of social capital in its interventions and the challenge is for micro-practice to catch up by incorporating the identified aspects of social capital in their interventions.

## REFERENCES

Beal, A. C., Ausiello, J., & Perrin, J. M. (2001). Social influences on health-risk behaviors among minority middle school students. *Jounal of Adolescent Health, 28*(6), 474–480.

Bourdieu, P. (1985). The forms of capital. In J. G. Richardson (Ed.), *Handbook of theory and research for the sociology of education* (pp. 241–258). New York: Greenwood.

Briggs, X. S. (1998). Brown kids in white suburbs: Housing mobility and the many faces of social capital. *Housing Policy Debate, 9*(1), 177–221.

Briggs, X. S. (2002). *Social capital and segregation: Race, connections, and inequality in America.* Unpublished paper, John F. Kennedy School of Government, Harvard University.

Briggs, X. S. (2004). *Who bridges? Race, friendships, and segregation in American communities.* John F. Kennedy School of Government, Harvard University.

Burt, R. S. (1987). Social contagion and innovation: Cohesion vs. structural equivalence. *American Journal of Sociology, 92*(6), 1287–1335.

Coleman, J. S. (1988). Social capital in the creation of human capital. *American Journal of Sociology, 94,* S95–S121.

Dasgupta, P., & Serageldin, I. (Ed.). (2000). *Social capital: A multifaceted perspective.* Washington, DC: World Bank. (Book preview except pp. 217–401, 403–425).

Domínguez, S. (2005). *Latina immigrants in public housing: Race relations, social networks, and access to services.* Ph.D. Dissertation, Boston University.

Domínguez, S., & Watkins, C. (2003). Creating networks for survival and mobility among African-American and Latin-American low-income mothers. *Social Problems, 50*(1), 111–135.

Glicken, M. D. (2004). *Using the strengths perspective in social work practice.* Boston: Pearson.

Gutierrez, L. M., & Lewis, E. A. (1999). *Empowering women of color.* New York: Columbia University Press.

Jacobs, J. (1961). *The death and life of great American cities.* New York: Random House.

Loury, G. C. (1977). A dynamic theory of racial income differences. In P. A. Wallace & A. L. Mund (Eds.), *Women, minorities, and employment discrimination* (pp. 153–186). Lexington, MA: Heath.

MacDonald, Michael P. (2000). *All Souls: A family Story from Southie.* New York: Random House

McKenzie K., Patel V., & Araya R. (2004). Learning from low-income countries: mental health. *British Medical Journal, 329:* 1138–1140.

Morrison, J. D., Alcorn, S., & Nelums, M. (1997). Empowering community-based programs for youth development: Is social work education interested? *Journal of Social Work Education, 33*(2), 321–333.

Naparstek, A., Biegel, D. E., & Spiro, H. R. (1982). *Neighborhood networks for humane mental health.* New York: Plenum.

Pattillo, M. (1999). *Black picket fences: Privilege and peril among the black middle class.* Chicago: University of Chicago Press.

Portes, A. (1998). Social capital: Its origins and applications in modern sociology. *Annual Review of Sociology, 24,* 1–24.

Putnam, R. D. (2000). *Bowling alone: The collapse and revival of American community.* New York: Simon & Schuster.

Saleebey, D. (1992). *The strengths perspective in social work practice.* New York: Longman.

Sampson, R. J., Raudenbush, S., & Earls, F. (1997). Neighbor-hoods and violent crime: A multi-level study of collective efficacy. *Science, 277*, 918–924.

Stack, C. B. (1974). *All our kin: Strategies for survival in a black community.* New York: Harper and Row.

Wilson, W. J. (1987). *The truly disadvantaged: The inner city, the underclass, and public policy.* Chicago: University of Chicago Press.

Winkler, M. (Ed.). (2004). *Community building and community organizing for health.* Brunswick, NJ: Rutgers University Press.

### SUGGESTED LINKS

Boys and Girls Clubs of America.
  *http://www.bgca.org/whoweare/special.asp*

The University of Edinburgh, school of social & political studies.
  *http://www.socialwork.ed.ac.uk/Social/index.htm*

Website of the National association of Social Workers.
  *http://www.socialworkers.org/sections/credentials/cultural_comp.asp*
  *www.soc.washington.edu/users/matsueda/Notes%20Lecture%20Social%20Capital.pdf*

—SILVIA DOMINGUEZ

# SOCIAL DEVELOPMENT

ABSTRACT: Social development is an all-inclusive concept connoting the well-being of the people, the community, and the society. The term gained popularity in the 1920s when it began as a mass literacy campaign under British rule in Africa; it was later called *community development*. In 1954, the British government officially adopted the term *social development* to include community development and remedial social services. With the Universal Declaration of Human Rights in 1948, the United Nations assumed the role of promoting social development globally. Social development strategies have been classified as *enterprise, communitarian*, and *statist* (Midgley, 1995; Lowe, 1995) based on their ideological orientations. An institutional approach to social development provides a pragmatic synthesis of these and emphasizes a balanced social development strategy. The current microcredit and microenterprise initiatives constitute a movement in the direction in which free market, private initiatives, and government support play key roles in social development, poverty alleviation, and promoting world peace.

KEY WORDS: social development; microcredit and microfinance; community development; Copenhagen Declaration; Millennium Development Goals

### Definitions

Generally, social workers define social development as a comprehensive, all-inclusive concept (Khinduka, 1987; Midgley, 1995). Gary Lowe (1995) defines it as an encompassing concept that refers to a dual-focused, holistic, systematic, ecologically oriented approach to seeking social advancement of individuals as well as broad-scale societal institutions (p. 2168). Midgley (1995) maintains that it is a process of planned social change designed to promote the well-being of the population as a whole in conjunction with a dynamic process of economic development (p. 25). Other notable social workers have provided compatible definitions of the social development concept (Billups, 1994; Meinert & Kohn, 1986; Paiva, 1982; Panday, 1981). The underlying notion of social development assumes progress and welfare of the people leading to their overall well-being. Similar definitions of social development are also available on the following websites: envision.ca/templates/profile.asp; (www.polity.org.za/html/govdocs/white_papers/social97gloss.html).

### History of Social Development

The social development perspective emerged with the popularization of the term by L.T. Hobhouse in the 1920s. The early emphasis on social development was propelled by the British initiative in West Africa in the 1940s, which was directed primarily toward mass literacy that included efforts toward economic development, increased literacy, poverty eradication, generating employment, and gender equity, among others, to help promote welfare for individuals, the community, and the society.

Since the writings of L.T. Hobhouse, the term *social development* has signified all efforts directed toward improving the conditions of the poor and disadvantaged. From the 1920s to the 1940s, especially after World War I, the British government faced heightened agitation from all the colonies against their alleged exploitation of the natural resources of their countries and impoverishing the people. The economic depression of the 1930s and the increased demand for independence by the colonies propelled the British government to direct its urgent attention toward economic development in the colonies. According to Midgley (1995), the British efforts for social development first began in Africa in the late 1920s and then spread to other British colonies. A more systematic approach to social development emerged in West Africa in the 1940s, when colonial administrators introduced the policy of *mass education* (Brokensha & Hodge, 1969; Lowe, 1995) that included instruction in the English language, agricultural production, road building, and other matters having practical utility. However, the scope of mass education was so broad that a concept like community development was introduced to capture the essence of all the efforts initiated under it. Community development activities also included the establishment of health centers, small family enterprises, schools, and infrastructure such as bridges, roads, and sanitation and irrigation systems. In 1954, the term *social development* was officially adopted by the British government; it included community development and remedial social welfare services (Lowe, 1995; Midgley, 1995).

By the 1950s, as the British Empire's influence over the newly independent states waned substantially, its role in social development was taken over by the United Nations. With the Universal Declaration of Human Rights by the General Assembly on December 10, 1948, the United Nations committed itself deeply to ensure fundamental human rights encompassing the well-being of individuals and the society. In the 1960s, the United Nations initiated a large-scale campaign for social development. It emphasized the need for national development planning and committed resources and technical assistance for its member states for expanding their activities in the health, education, agriculture, housing, and social welfare sectors. They were encouraged to establish central planning ministries and extend training opportunities for administrators, planners, and other professionals. A number of UN-sponsored short-term training programs were organized for government functionaries. While a new momentum picked up in the 1960s for central planning and administration of the social development programs, by the 1970s it became clear that the benefits of these programs were reaped mainly by a privileged class living in the urban areas. Consequently, a phenomenon called distorted development (Midgley, 1995) appeared in the social welfare arena, and was perpetuated by government corruption, bribery, bureaucratic red tape, favoritism, administrative mismanagement, and a large-scale neglect of the needs of women, children, and the common people.

The failure of the community development programs under statist management gave rise to a critical approach known as *community action* or *community participation* programs. This approach called for more active participation of local people, the opinion leaders, and non-governmental organizations in funding, planning, and implementing the programs independently. Meanwhile, the enforcement of the Structural Adjustment programs by the IMF and the World Bank forced many countries to incur huge debts from their past loans. This adversely affected many governments' ability to keep up with the social welfare services for their citizens and had a crippling effect on the UN

and governmental social welfare programs that faced massive cuts in their budgets. Consequently, the UN officials, experts, and consultants gradually diverted their energies to more income-generating projects funded by NGOs (non-governmental organizations), including that of micro-enterprise and micro-finance initiatives.

During the 1980s, the advanced industrial countries, especially the United States and the United Kingdom, witnessed an ascendancy of neo-liberal ideology in their political fronts. Consequently, the governments in these countries cut many social welfare programs drastically. The UN at this time was almost compelled to redirect its social development efforts toward a statist strategy. In March 1995, at the World Summit in Copenhagen, the UN, in an unprecedented bid, obligated its 117 member countries to ten binding commitments. These included eradication of poverty; the support of full employment; the promotion of social integration including the protection of all human rights; the achievement of gender equality and equity; enhancement of development of the LDCs including Africa; inclusion of social development goals in the structural adjustment programs; increasing the resource allocation to social development; creation of a social, political, cultural, economic, and legal environment to facilitate social development; promotion of the universal and equitable access to primary health care and education; and the strengthening of cooperation for social development through the UN. (The Copenhagen Declaration, United Nations/Division for Social Policy and Development: 1999; http://www.visionoffice.com/socdev/wssd.htm). The Copenhagen Declaration thus set the tone for statist social policy planning and implementation at a global level.

In 2005, 10 years after the Copenhagen Declaration, another World Summit, held in New York, renewed its commitment for social development by offering a comprehensive policy framework based on equity and equality (United Nations, 2005). This Summit concentrated on poverty eradication, employment, and social integration as core issues, and recognized that social development basically requires a multifaceted approach that should be socially, culturally, and environmentally sustainable. The UN also advanced another lofty set of goals in 2005, known as the United Nations Millennium Declaration and the Millennium Development Goals (MDG's) that addressed social concerns like poverty and hunger, infant and child mortality, health, and literacy. The MDG goals were mandated to be attained by member countries by 2015. This statist initiative also met with failure due to centralized bureaucratic red tape, increased corruption, and inefficient management.

It also created a chilling gap between the rich and the poor. A sharp criticism of this approach generated overwhelming support for the small-scale, autonomous, free-market strategies for micro-finance and micro-credit initiatives. The success of the "Grameen Bank" approach, which was conceptualized, designed, and implemented by 2006 Nobel Peace Laureate Professor Muhammad Yunus and involved micro-lending to the poorest of the poor women in Bangladesh, added a new significance to micro-finance activities as a social and economic enterprise. Within a span of twelve years (1974–1986), the "Grameen Bank" microcredit concept had developed into a global movement and received worldwide support and acceptance (Miah, 2003; Mizan, 1994; Yunus, 1995, 2003).

## Approaches to Social Development

Tracing its ideological groundings in Western political thought, Midgley (1993, 1995, 1997) classifies social development strategy into three types: enterprise, communitarian, and statist (Lowe, 1995). Enterprise strategies emphasize individual entrepreneurship in maximizing the welfare of the people. This approach calls for minimum government involvement in developmental activities and maximum involvement of informal sectors, including small business development, to promote healthy income generation and rising standards of living. Statist strategies call for a total control of social development activities by the government, including planning, financing, and implementing. This requires a vast bureaucracy to plan, deliver, and administer the programs. The third approach, communitarian strategies (Midgley, 1997), grew out of severe criticism of the statist regimes for their unbridled corruption, wasting of scarce resources, bureaucratic red-tapism, and a lack of involvement of the local people in the development process. This strategy requires grass-roots participation of the local community in planning, designing, and implementing all social development programs.

Since each of the approaches mentioned above appear to be diametrically opposed to the others, Midgley (1995, 1997) proposed a fourth strategy of social development known as the institutional approach. Under this approach, the positive sides of all three approaches are underscored and a synthesis of all three is proposed as a coherent and integrated whole. It promotes maximum participation of the community, the market, and the people. The institutional approach requires the government to play an active role in the management and coordination of development activities that Midgley (1997) calls "managed pluralism" (Miah & Tracy, 2001).

A plethora of studies on social development have shown that the statist strategies disproportionately benefited the privileged class and helped increase the extent of poverty in a society (Birdsall, 1993; Haque, 1999; UN, 2004). The statist model generated a phenomenon called "distorted development" (Midgley, 1995), which became quite conspicuous in the context of social development worldwide. The "trickle down" theory of economic growth did not translate into reality was originally envisioned. Many unintended negative consequences followed from it that adversely affected peoples' well-being and living conditions (UN, 2004).

Irma Adelman and Cynthia Morris (1973) opined that the advance of capitalism in an uncontrolled fashion allowed the privileged class to amass huge wealth and, thus, poverty continued to grow unabated. Wolfgang Sachs (1992) stated: "The idea of development stands like a ruin in the intellectual landscape. Delusion and disappointment, failures and crimes, have been the steady companions of development and they tell a common story: it did not work" (p. 1). A number of other scholars offer similar critiques on the failure of social development initiatives in developing countries (Alavi, 1972; Amin, 1990; Preston, 1985).

## Assessment and Future Trends

The microcredit and microfinance initiatives worldwide constitute a signal move toward the synthesis proposed by Midgley (1997) as the institutional approach to social development. The award of the 2006 Nobel Peace Prize to Dr. Muhammad Yunus and his Grameen Bank testifies to the fact that social development should be conceived and delivered as a social enterprise at the grass-roots level supported by the people, the market, and the legal framework provided by the government.

As the world faces more and more cultural, ethnic, religious, political, economic, and other conflicts, including widespread human rights violations, social development may seem more of a "distorted development" than a movement toward progressive development (Haque, 1999; Midgley, 1997). All these are resulting in pervasive violence and deep-rooted hatred, heightened political and social unrest, and profound destabilization of the economic and social fiber in many parts of the world, necessitating unfettered promotion of peace as an essential, ingredient for social development (Yunus & Jolis, 2003).

In this regard, Yunus's clarion call for world peace and the end of poverty globally (during the 2006 Global Microcredit Summit held in Halifax, Nova Scotia, November 12–15, 2006) and Midgley's (1997) unequivocal advocacy of peace as "a prerequisite for the attainment of social development goals" (p. 11) should be given priority attention by social work educators, policy makers, and the practice community. This will certainly advance the cause of a global society that will not divide, but will peacefully unite and bind together the Global North and the Global South.

An integrated policy for social development that is pro-people, pro-government, pro-market, and pro-community is fundamentally needed as the institutionalized arrangement in a society for balanced functioning and equilibrium at the economic, political, social, and cultural levels. *Managed pluralism*, as advanced by Midgley (1995), or *engaged governance*, as advocated by the United Nations Department of Economic and Social Affairs (UNDESA), that will involve NGOs and civil society in states' decision making, should be the policy for effective social development strategies (UNDESA, 2004, p. 27, New York: UN). Although social development cannot be construed as a panacea for all problems in the world, Midgley's (1997) insightful observation "it [social development] does provide a comprehensive, pragmatic, and workable approach to social welfare that deserves to be more widely adopted" (p. 202) is quite instructive and logically coherent, and clearly sets the tone for the future of social work education, policy, and practice in a global context.

## REFERENCES

Alavi, H. (1972). The state in post-Colonial societies: Pakistan and Bangladesh. *New Left Review, 74*, 59–81.

Amin, S. (1990). *Maldevelopment: Anatomy of a global failure.* Tokyo: United Nations University Press.

Birdsall, N. (1993). *Social development is economic development.* World Bank: Policy Research Department, WPS–1123.

Haque, M. S. (1999). *Restructuring development theories and policies.* Albany: State University of New York Press.

Khinduka, S. K. (1987). Development and peace: The complex nexus. *Social Development Issues, 10*(3), 19–30.

Lowe, G. R. (1995). Social development. In *Encyclopedia of social work* (19th ed., pp. 2168–2173). National Association of Social Workers, Washington, DC: NASW Press.

Meinert, R., & Kohn, E. (1986, August). Towards operationalization of social development concepts. Paper presented at the fourth international symposium on international development. Hachioji: Tokyo.

Miah, M. R. (2003). Empowerment zone, microenterprise, and asset building. In *Encyclopedia of social work* (19th ed., Supplement, pp. 38–47). Washington, DC: National Association of Social Workers.

Miah, M. R., & Martin B. Tracy (2001). The institutional approach to social development. *Social Development Issues, 23*(1), 58–64.

Mizan, A. (1994). *In quest of empowerment: The grameen bank impact on women's power and status.* Dhaka: The University Press Limited.

Midgley, J. (1997). *Social welfare in global context.* Thousand Oaks, CA: Sage Publications.

Midgley, J. (1995). *Social development: The developmental perspective in social welfare.* Thousand Oaks, CA: Sage Publications.

Midgley, J. (1993). Ideological roots of social development strategies. *Social Development Issues, 15*(1), 1–14.

Paiva, F. J. (1982). The dynamics of social development and social work. In D. S. Sanders (Ed.), *The developmental perspective in social work* (pp. 1–11). Manoa: University of Hawaii Press.

Pandey, R. (1981). Strategies for social development: An international approach. In J. Jones & R. Pandey (Eds.), *Social development: Conceptual, methodological and policy issues* (pp. 33–49). New York: St. Martin's Press.

Preston, P. W. (1985). *New trends in development theory.* London: Routledge & Kegan Paul.

Sachs, W. (1992). Introduction. In W. Sachs (Ed.), *Ten Years Later.* New York: Department of Economic and Social Affairs.

United Nations. (2004). Report on the follow-up of the World Summit for Social Development: State and Globalization, Challenges for Human Development, Bangkok, 17–19 December, 2003.

United Nations. (2005). *The social summit: Ten years later.* New York: Department of Economic and Social Affairs.

Yunus, M., & Jolis, A. (2003). *Banker to the poor: Microlending and the battle against world poverty.* New York: Public Affairs.

Yunus, M. (1995). Grameen Bank: Experiences and Reflections. *Impact, 30*(3/4), 13–25.

## SUGGESTED LINKS

*www.u.org/esa/socdev/.icony.op.org/gossary.html*
*http://1wweb18.worldbank.org/ESSD/sdvext.nsf/gobydocname/ socialdevelopment home*
*http://www.imf.org/external/np/exr/facts/social.htm*
*http://www.sdc.admin.ca/index/php?nanID=64957&landID=1&*

—MIZANUR R. MIAH

# SOCIAL IMPACT ASSESSMENT

**ABSTRACT:** Social impact assessment (SIA) is the process of analyzing (predicting, evaluating and reflecting) and managing the intended and unintended consequences on the human environment of planned interventions (policies, programs, plans, and projects) and any social change processes brought into play by those interventions so as to bring about a more sustainable and equitable biophysical and human environment (Vanclay, 2002). This subfield of impact assessment attempts to identify future consequences of a current or proposed action related to individuals, organizations and social macro-systems. SIA is policy-oriented social research often referred to as ex-ante evaluation, which involves pre-testing actions/interventions, or analyzing consequences.

KEY WORDS: assessment indicators; ecological; well-being; social justice; sustainability; indigenous

## Broadened SIA Definition

Social impact assessment first appeared as a working concept in the 1969 U.S. National Environmental Policy Act (Inter-organizational Committee on Guidelines and Principles, 1994). Debatably, predicting and assessing consequences of change on societies can be traced back to early cultural practices which utilized prediction to avert disaster. In the modern era, SIAs are conducted with the intent of sustaining the well-being of people within their environment. Becker (1997) defined SIA as a process of "identifying the future consequences of a current or proposed action . . . related to individuals, organizations and social macro-systems." Vanclay's (2002) broadened definition included the analysis and management of intended and unintended consequences and social change with the goal of increasing sustainable, equitable human and environmental well-being.

## Value-Based SIA Practice

SIA practitioners work from a strong social justice value base and commitment to accountability, equity, human rights, inclusive participation, scientific integrity, sustainability, and transparency. SIA has the potential to serve beyond the prediction of adverse impacts to advocate for empowerment of local people, enhance the position of women, minority groups and disadvantaged populations, develop capacity building, alleviate all forms of dependency, increase equity, and aid in poverty reduction (Vanclay, 2003).

Earlier SIAs were confined to developed countries and a specific regulatory context. This focus on small groups and individual property rights could not effectively capture the cultural contexts of developing and non-Western countries. In those contexts, the emphasis needs to be on the impact of changes such as land development or other profit-driven endeavors on the life-ways and livelihoods of diverse cultural and socio-economic groups.

Current conceptual and methodological advances in SIA include the use of local and cultural knowledge, longitudinal research, examining social change processes, ecological models, geographic information systems, public participation and other culturally appropriate, creative approaches (Becker & Vanclay, 2003), which can capture the complex and dynamic processes of societal change and well-being.

## Culturally Relevant SIAs

SIAs conducted in the context of developing countries, non-Western cultures, indigenous cultures, or subcultures within a predominant Western culture, should consider the culturally distinct properties associated with well-being. SIAs are an important means of determining unanticipated impacts of land development on people in the context of social systems. They provide planners and decision-makers with a basis for deciding whether to approve development proposals and ways to mitigate negative social impacts. Conventional SIAs omitted factors such as spirituality, subsistence practices and indigenous economies, collective and mutual social patterns, sense of place, and "ways of knowing" as indicators of well-being. However, as development encroaches more on pristine ecological and cultural areas, it poses greater threats to the life ways of indigenous people who draw their existence from the elements of nature.

As SIAs evolve in scope and method, many cultural phenomena need to be considered as potential receptors of impacts related to proposed development. Viewing cultural phenomena from the person-in-environment context represents a marked departure from Western social constructions; however, it may serve in understanding the etiology of social pathos resulting from disruptions to customary and traditional land-use patterns in indigenous rural communities.

An ecological model is useful in conceptualizing how human systems interact (McGregor, Morelli, Matsuoka, & Minerbi, 2003). The model assumes that individuals, families and their communities can reciprocally affect each other. Changes to the environment and land can influence changes in families, communities and governance.

A comprehensive SIA would assess impacts on natural and cultural resources utilized by indigenous peoples for subsistence, cultural, and spiritual purposes. Impacts to be assessed include changes in the condition, integrity, use, access to, boundaries of, ownership of, and quality of experience with, natural and cultural resources.

In indigenous cultures, for example, social structures and systems emerged from the local economy, and cultural beliefs and spirituality support and promote human well-being. Communities live in habitats that have critical effects on human behavior. From that perspective, economic development and formal jobs are not necessarily analogous to human well-being. For example, the benefits derived from subsistence economies are not adequately valued because they cannot be enumerated. Subsistence provides a regimen of physical activity that binds practitioners to the land, enhances a nature-based spirituality, produces healthy food products for family consumption, cultivates social cohesion in the community through the sharing and exchange of resources, and promotes social welfare as younger practitioners share resources with older, less ambulatory residents. Such activities reduce the likelihood of less healthy behaviors (for example, listlessness leading to obesity or substance abuse) that are often associated with having too much discretionary time.

The following are examples of indicators that may be considered when conducting SIAs with indigenous communities:

- Change in adequacy of social and cultural infrastructure to accommodate community needs related to quality;
- Disruption in the natural course of community development, continuity, and family permanence;
- Change in activities and attributes that constitute life style or life ways and the persistence of indigenous economies;
- Increase in rate, type, and severity of crimes with indigenous perpetrators;
- Increase in rate of substance abuse and type of substance; its influence on behavior and related problems (e.g., crime);
- Change in rate, patterns and severity of domestic violence, and family and community response;
- Change in educational achievement and aptitude, delinquency (for example substance abuse, crime, and status offences), socio-emotional issues or family supports, and educational, employment, and recreational opportunities;
- Change in social cohesion, degree of social and racial integration or conflict, and changes in community leadership;
- Change in number and types of events or activities, participation rates, relevance to traditional and contemporary conditions, and decision-making power;
- Change in levels of community or cultural identity, and personal sense of connection and pride in belonging to a locale, and related to genealogical and intergenerational ties.

In non-Western cultures, human well-being is often synonymous with the health and vitality of natural resources in addition to the perpetuation of cultural traditions and a communal identity (McGregor, Minerbi, & Matsuoka, 1998; Papa Ola Lokahi, 1992).

Culturally relevant SIAs require understanding of indigenous cultural ways such as the nature of relationships, values, beliefs, interactions, processes, and traditions that form the foundation of a harmonious family life. Family resilience and well-being indicators may include the following:

- Family belief systems: Utilizing relationally based strengths, finding meaning in adversity, a positive outlook, transcendence, and spirituality;
- Organizational patterns: Flexibility, connectedness, mutual support, and social and economic resources;
- Communication processes: Clarity, open emotional expression, and collaborative problem solving.

SIAs can provide information critical to the interrelated survival of diverse populations and life forms on this planet, and therefore, should reflect the complexities and subtleties of people within the context of their culture and environment as well as the tangible and intangible aspects of their life experiences in order to preserve, sustain and plan for viable, future well-being.

### REFERENCES

Becker, H. A. (1997). *Social impact assessment*. London: University of London Press.

Becker, H. A., & Vanclay, F. (2003). *The international handbook of social impact assessment: Conceptual and methodological advances*. Cheltenham, UK: Edward Elgar.

Interorganizational Committee on Guidelines and Principles. (1994). Guidelines and principles for social impact assessment. *Impact Assessment, 12*(2), 107–152.

McGregor, D., Minerbi, L., & Matsuoka, J. (1998). A holistic assessment method of health and well-being for native Hawaiian communities. *Pacific Health Dialogue, 5*(2), 361–369.

McGregor, D., Morelli, P. T., Matsuoka, J. K., & Minerbi, L. (2003). An ecological model of wellbeing. In H. A. Becker & F. Vanclay (Eds.), *The international handbook of social impact assessment: Conceptual and methodological advances* (pp. 108–126). Cheltenham, UK: Edward Elgar.

Papa Ola Lokahi. (1992). *Native Hawaiian health data book*. Honolulu: Papa Ola Lokahi.

Vanclay, F. (2002). Social impact assessment In M. Tolba (Ed.), *Responding to global environmental change* (In T. Munn (Ed.), *Encyclopedia of global environmental change* vol. 4, pp. 387–393). Chichester, UK: Wiley.

Vanclay, F. (2003). Conceptual and methodological advances in social impact assessment In H. A. Becker & F. Vanclay (Eds.), *The international handbook of social impact assessment: Conceptual and methodological advances* (pp. 1–9). Cheltenham, UK: Edward Elgar.

—PAULA T. T. MORELLI AND JON KEI MATSUOKA

# SOCIAL JUSTICE

**ABSTRACT:** This entry examines the concept of social justice and its significance as a core value of social work. Diverse conceptualizations of social justice and their historical and philosophical underpinnings are examined. The influence of John Rawls' perspectives on social justice is addressed as are alternative conceptualizations, such as the capabilities perspective. The roots of social justice are traced through social work history, from the Settlement House Movement to the Rank and Film Movement, Civil Rights Movement, and contemporary struggles in the context of globalization. Challenges for social justice-oriented practice in the 21st century are address. The discussion concludes with concrete example of ways in which social workers are translating principles of social justice into concrete practices.

**KEY WORDS:** social justice; distributive justice; John Rawls; capabilities perspective, Settlement House Movement; participatory democracy; globalization

Social justice is one of the core values guiding social work, a hallmark of its uniqueness among the helping professions. It is a concept deeply rooted in social work history. The *Social Work Dictionary* defines social justice as:

> ... an ideal condition in which all members of a society have the same rights, protections, opportunities, obligations, and social benefits. Implicit in this concept is the notion that historical inequalities should be acknowledged and remedied through specific measures. A key social work value, social justice entails advocacy to confront discrimination, oppression, and institutional inequities. (Barker, 2003, p. 405).

The concept of social justice draws attention to institutional arrangements and systemic inequities that further the interests of some groups at the expense of others in the distribution of material goods, social benefits, rights, protections, and opportunities (Delaney, 2005; Dewees, 2006). Social justice can be thought of as a perspective through which social workers recognize and address the connection between personal struggles and structural arrangements of society (Fisher & Karger, 1997). It can also be conceived as a goal for an equitable, sustainable society.

The NASW Code of Ethics mandates social workers to work toward social justice with all people but particularly with those marginalized from full participation in society because of discrimination, poverty, or other forms of social, political, and economic inequality. It emphasizes that social workers need to develop an understanding of oppression and cultural and ethnic diversity. It highlights a fundamental principle of social justice: the promotion of participatory processes to enable all people to engage in decision making that affects their lives (NASW, 1999). However, as indicated by Banerjee (2005), while the NASW Code of Ethics refers to a practice informed by social justice, it does not provide a clear definition of the term.

## Meanings of Social Justice

The meanings of social justice are far reaching and ambiguous; translation into concrete practice is fraught with challenges. Social justice is a contextually bound and historically driven concept, and as such it has been a subject of ongoing debate in social work (Banerjee, 2005; Caputo, 2002; McGrath Morris, 2002; Miller, 1999; Pelton, 2001; Reisch, 2002; Saleebey, 1990; Scanlon & Longres, 2001; Van Soest, 1995; Van Soest & Garcia, 2003). Political theorists, philosophers, and social workers alike have explored what it means to be in "right relationship" between and among persons, communities, states, and nations. As McCormick (2003) notes, "There is not even agreement about whether liberty, equality, solidarity or the common good is the primary cornerstone on which the edifice of justice is to be constructed" (p. 8).

Understandings of social justice in U.S. social work are largely derived from Western philosophy and political theory and Judeo-Christian religious tradition. Conceptions of justice are abstract ideals that overlap with beliefs about what is right, good, desirable, and moral. Notions of social justice generally embrace values such as the equal worth of all citizens, their equal right to meet their basic needs, the need to spread opportunity and life chances as widely as possible, and finally, the requirement that we reduce and, where possible, eliminate unjustified inequalities. As Caputo (2002) remarks, the concept of social justice invoked by social work has largely been one steeped in liberalism, which may serve to maintain the status quo. However, Caputo also contends that social justice remains relevant as a value and goal of social work.

Some students of social justice consider its meaning in terms of the *tensions* between individual liberty and common social good, arguing that social justice is promoted to the degree that we can promote collective good without infringing upon basic individual freedoms. Some argue that social justice reflects a concept of *fairness* in the assignment of fundamental rights and duties, economic opportunities, and social conditions (Miller, 1976, p. 22, as cited in Reisch, 1998). Others frame the concept in terms of three components – legal justice, which is concerned with what people owe society; commutative justice, which addresses what people owe each other; and distributive justice, or what society owes the person (Reichert, 2003, p. 12; U.S. Catholic Bishops, 1986; Van Soest, 1995, p. 1811). From a distributive perspective, the one most often referenced by social workers, social justice entails not only approaches to societal choices regarding the distribution of goods and resources, but also consideration of the structuring of societal institutions to guarantee human rights and dignity and ensure opportunities for free and meaningful social participation.

Discussions of social justice in the context of social work generally address the differing philosophical approaches used to inform societal decisions about the distribution or allocation of resources. These discussions refer to three dominant theories of resource distribution: *Utilitarian, libertarian* and *egalitarian*.

*Utilitarian* theories emphasize actions that bring about the greatest good and least harm for the greatest number. From this perspective, individual rights can be infringed upon if so doing helps meet the interests and needs of the majority (McCormick, 2003; Van Soest, 1994). *Libertarian* theories reject obligations for equal and equitable distribution of resources, contending instead that each individual is entitled to any and all resources that he or she has legally acquired (Nozick, 1974). They emphasize individual autonomy and the fundamental right to choose; they seek to protect individual freedom from encroachment by others. Proponents support minimal state responsibility for protecting the security of individuals pursuing their own separate interests (McCormick, 2003). *Egalitarian* theories contend that every member of society should be guaranteed the same rights, opportunities, and access to goods and resources. From this theoretical perspective the *redistribution* of societal resources should be to the advantage of the most vulnerable members of society. Thus, redistribution is a moral imperative to ensure that unmet needs are redressed (e.g., Rawls, 1971). However, as Reichert (2003) notes, the idea of social justice, expressed variously in these theories, remains elusive, especially in terms of concrete applicability to practice.

A number of social workers concerned about questions of social justice have turned to the work of the political philosopher John Rawls (1971), whose theory of justice is grounded in the egalitarian approach addressed above. Drawing from liberal thought, Rawls critiqued utilitarian and libertarian conceptualizations of social justice for their justification of personal hardships in lieu of a greater common good (Swenson, 1998). Rawls' theory asks, what would be the characteristics of a just society in which basic human needs are met, unnecessary stress is reduced, the competence of each person is maximized, and threats to well-being are minimized? For Rawls, distributive justice denotes "the value of each person getting a fair share of the benefits and burdens resulting from social cooperation," both in terms of material goods and services and also in terms of nonmaterial social goods, such as opportunity and power (Wakefield, 1988, p. 193). In *Justice as Fairness: A Restatement*, Rawls (2001) provides two basic principles of social justice, modified from his earlier work:

a. Each person has the same indefeasible claim to a fully adequate scheme of equal basic liberties, which scheme is compatible with the same scheme of liberties for all; and

b. Social and economic inequalities are to satisfy two conditions: first, they are to be attached to offices and positions open to all under conditions of fair equality of opportunity; and second, they are to be to the greatest benefit of the least-advantaged members of society (the difference principle). (pp. 42–43)

Jerome Wakefield (1988) argues that Rawls' notion of distributive justice is the organizing value of social work. He proposes that a Rawlsian perspective helps social work integrate its micro and macro practice divide and that it contains "the power to make sense of the social work profession and its disparate activities" (p. 194). Michael Reisch (1998) draws on Rawls' principle of "redress," that is, to compensate for inequalities and to shift the balance of contingencies in the direction of equality, in articulating the relationship between social work and social justice. He argues that a social justice framework for social work and social welfare policy would "hold the most vulnerable populations harmless in the distribution of societal resources, particularly when those resources are finite. Unequal distribution of resources would be justified only if it served to advance the least advantaged groups in the community" (Reisch, 1998, p. 20). Banerjee (2005), following a thorough review of the literature, claims that social work scholars and practitioners most often refer to Rawls' theory of social justice primarily because of its emphasis on egalitarianism, attention to distributive principles, and potential to bridge micro and macro levels of practice.

The concept of distributive justice is central to a number of discussions of social justice and social work. For example, according to Dorothy Van Soest and Betty Garcia (2003, p. 44), "Our conception of social justice is premised on the concept of distributive justice, which emphasizes society's accountability to the individual.

What principles guide the distribution of goods and resources?" Van Soest and Garcia address five perspectives on distributive justice that help us grasp the complexity of the concept. Three of these perspectives, addressed previously—utilitarian, libertarian, and egalitarian—are prescriptive in nature, speaking of what social justice should be. A fourth, the racial contract perspective, offers a description of the current state of society and the unequal system of privilege and racism therein. The racial contract perspective argues that the notion of the "social contract" as the basis of Western democratic society is a myth. The contract did not extend beyond white society. Thus white privilege is a constitutive part of the "social contract" and must be dismantled in the struggle for social justice. A fifth view, the human rights perspective, makes human rights central to the discussion of social justice (p. 45). From this perspective, social justice encompasses meeting basic human needs, equitable distribution of resources, and recognition of the inalienable rights of all persons, without discrimination.

Stanley Witkin (1998), Jim Ife (1997, 2001), and Elizabeth Reichert (2003) have argued for the possibilities of the Universal Declaration of Human Rights as a conceptual frame for social work practice. Reichert contends that a human rights approach encompasses "a more comprehensive and defined set of guidelines for social work practice than social justice" (2003, p. 13). As Catherine MacDonald claims (2006, p. 176), "Social work practice can be seen as promoting a universalist view of social justice balanced by and expressed through a relativist view of human needs, varying from person to person, context to context." She suggests that a human rights-based practice has a moral and political clarity that can provide social work with legitimacy for action, something lacking in more ambiguous constructions of social justice.

The work of Iris Marion Young (1990, 2001) on processual justice has also influenced social work thought and practice (Caputo, 2002). Processual justice "refers to the decision-making processes that lead to decisions about the distribution [of social goods and resources] and to the relationships between dominant and subordinate groups, such as racial majorities and people of color, that affect decisions about distribution" (Longres & Scanlon, 2001, p. 448). In sum, Young argues that distributive issues are important, but that "the scope of justice extends beyond them to include the political as such, that is, all aspects of institutional organization insofar as they are potentially subject to collective decision" (1990, p. 8). In contrast to Rawls, Young's view of social justice is grounded in an explicit critique of capitalism and its inherently unjust social and economic relations. Her approach calls for participatory processes in decision making regarding issues of social allocation and distribution, rather than focusing solely on outcomes.

Patricia McGrath Morris (2002) calls social workers' attention to another approach to social justice—the capabilities perspective. This perspective addresses the limitations of the Rawlsian perspective, the foundation for which is grounded on fairness in the distribution of liberties and social primary goods. The capabilities perspective builds on the work of economist Amartya Sen; it focuses "on the fair distribution of capabilities—the resources and power to exercise self-determination—to achieve well being" (p. 368). It goes beyond the importance of securing social primary goods and sees these as an essential part of a process toward achieving social justice but not the ultimate goal: "Capability is based on what a person wants to achieve and what power she or he has to convert primary goods to reach her or his desired goals" (p. 368). Whereas the Rawlsian perspective of social justice defines societal principles, the capabilities perspective begins at the individual level and imagines what a person is capable of doing and of becoming (Nussbaum, 2002). Martha Nussbaum (2002, 2004) has generated a list of capabilities, such as bodily health, affiliation, and play, that can be changed and expanded in congruence with social and cultural context. Thus, the list is suggestive and meant to facilitate discussion and decision making by providing "a focus for quality of life assessment and for political planning." (Nussbaum, 2002, p. 131). In addition, Nussbaum (2004) presents a cogent argument for the structural inadequacies of Rawlsian-influenced perspectives when applied to a global context. She argues that solutions to problems of global justice cannot be addressed through an approach that denies the fundamental inequalities of nations and views them as equals in terms of power and resources. Instead, she advocates for a perspective that resurrects "the richer ideas of human fellowship that we find in Grotius and other exponents of the natural law tradition" (p. 4). Nussbaum views the capabilities perspective as emergent and calls for it to be further informed by the perspectives of those whose lived experiences makes them experts in the day-to-day struggles to achieve a modicum of justice in what Reisch (2002, p. 343) refers to as a "socially unjust world."

McGrath Morris (2002) advocates for the capabilities perspective because it expands on a distributive justice perspective commonly referred to in social work and includes and emphasizes the importance of other social work values such as self-determination, well-being, and human dignity. She highlights the compatibility of the capabilities framework with the underlying principles set forth in social work's dominant theoretical approaches that focus on strengths, person-in-environment, and empowerment. Banerjee (2005) also notes the need to rethink social work's emphasis on Rawls' view of social justice and to more thoroughly critique its application to social work practice. He contends that drawing on other justice theorists such as Nussbaum guides practice toward advocacy, especially "when society and life's circumstances outside of one's control do not permit some people, especially people of color and particularly women, to develop their capabilities" (p. 53).

### Historical Perspective

In claiming the roots of social justice in social work history, the early settlement house movement has generally served as a starting point (See entry on Settlement houses). Through the movement, social workers were developing a critical consciousness about dramatically changing social, economic, and political conditions and their differential impacts in the lives of poor and vulnerable groups, particularly immigrants. Settlement house workers located their work in contrast to the "charity" approach to social work gaining prominence in the late 19th century. They began to make the connections between individual misery and societal arrangements and to address both the logic and the impacts of structural inequalities. Citing the National Conference on Charities and Corrections in 1909, McGrath Morris (2002) evokes the fervor of the time when social workers were challenged to "dare to repeat the creed of the Hebrew prophet – justice, justice shalt thou pursue... We have had the age of chivalry, the age of generosity, and the age of mercy, and now we need the age of justice" (Wise, 1909, p. 29 as cited in McGrath Morris, 2002, p. 365).

As Eleanor Stebner (1997) notes, the concept of the "social" was acquiring new power at the turn of the 20th century. Settlement houses were experiments in social democracy; their residents were advocates of social reform, and often, followers of the social gospel. When Jane Addams made the decision to cast her lot with the poor she embraced a concept of social justice. In her presidential address to the 1910 National Conference on Charities and Corrections, Addams spoke directly of the limits of charity and the challenges of social justice (Addams, 1960, pp. 85–87). However, as Sharon Berlin (2005, p. 490) notes, Addams' efforts were also "constrained by her own ideological blind spots," which kept her from finding common cause with early 20th century African American women reformers whose activism against racism and segregation was also shaped by a strong spiritual commitment (Carlton-LaNey, 1999).

Other noted Hull House residents, such as Florence Kelly, engaged in trenchant critiques of industrial capitalism and its relationship to the lived experience of the urban poor. Their work in documenting exploitative labor practices, unsafe housing conditions, and the vulnerability of women and children, made explicit links between personal struggles and public issues. While invoking the language of social reform and social democracy, they modeled a philosophy and practice of social justice that called for them to see the world from the vantage point of the less powerful; to invite participation of those affected in the understanding and resolution of social problems; to construct new forms of social life grounded in belonging, respect, and participation; and to hold to a vision of a just world.

"Groups were the primary modus operandi from which the settlement house agenda was to be achieved," and were, therefore, a vehicle of social justice (Jacobson & Rugeley, in press). Group work theory and practice were firmly embedded in democratic principles that embodied humanitarian concerns, social responsibility, human relationships, and social justice (Andrews, 2001; Lee, 1986, 1992; Schwartz, 1986). Addams envisioned the group as a means for learning about democracy as people engaged in democratic group processes. She emphasized the need to exchange "the music of isolated voices [for] the volume and strength of the chorus" (as cited in Schwartz, 1986, p. 12). Throughout social work's history, organizing efforts to combat social injustice were forged through the development of groups. For example, in the midst of the Great Depression of the 1930s, the Rank and File Movement arose from within service organizations, provoked by unfair labor conditions, oppressive bureaucratic structures, and an economic system that favored corporate interests over human need. Bertha Capen Reynolds, a leader of the movement, helped form unions, and she illustrated through her work "a justice-oriented social work practice" (Reisch, 2002, p. 348). Reynolds' principles of practice emphasized belonging, mutuality, power sharing, and "forming and joining coalitions with clients, community groups, and like-minded colleagues from all disciplines" (Reynolds, 1963, pp. 173–175). She recognized groups as arenas and relations through which social justice principles and aims can play out on the broader landscape.

As the emphasis on group work within social work waxed and waned through the 1940s and 1950s so did the profession's attention to issues of social justice. One of the most damaging impacts to the profession's concern for social justice and participatory democracy came by way of McCarthyism: "By the 1940s, particularly after the War, many activities engaged in by social workers, especially the practice and ideology of group workers, came under attack by anti-Communists" (Andrews, 2001, p. 52). As cited in Andrews' historical analysis of group work, Harold Lewis believed that group work was a significant casualty of the post-WWII period:

> This was a serious loss, since this method was the most democratic in the profession. The core concept of group work and the goal of its major proponents was participatory democracy....What survived was the method's narrower function, therapeutic aid. (Lewis, 1992, pp. 41–42, as cited in Andrews, 2001, pp. 52–53)

The powerful social and political movements of the 1960s pressed the social work profession to further examine its commitment to social justice. The civil rights movement, poor people's and welfare rights movements, women's movement, and anti-war movement demanded public and professional attention to deeply embedded social and economic inequalities and to the workings of structural as well as physical forms of violence. In 1973 NASW published an edited volume titled *Social Work Practice and Social Justice* that grappled with stark examples of racism and inequality as manifest in correctional, health, education, and welfare systems; the complicity of social work and social workers in perpetuating systemic injustices; and the responsibility of the profession to advocate for justice-oriented social change. The contributors critiqued the dominance of individual pathology approaches to theory and practice, which tended to bracket attention to social structures. They argued that social work had failed to live up to its professed values of human dignity, worth, and self-determination by ignoring social structures, failing to identify basic social problems and participate in their resolutions, and claiming a stance of professional neutrality regarding issues that are fundamentally political. Bess Dana (1973) challenged social workers to advocate for health care as a right. She argued that social justice honors knowledge that illuminates human possibility, values respect for others, and demonstrates a willingness to give up power and prestige. She called for a practice of social justice based on partnership, collaborative action, promotion of rights, pursuit of new knowledge, and advocacy. The contributors advocated for the right to a minimum standard of living for all and for the right to involvement in the issues that affect one's life.

As Bernard Ross concluded (1973, p. 152), "Social justice is concerned not just with the equitable distribution of goods and services but with the right and power of persons and groups to obtain their fair share. Thus social workers necessarily accept as a goal the redistribution of goods, services, and power." However, despite the evocation of a language of rights and calls for a rights-based practice, general knowledge of human rights and specific attention to human-rights based practice have not played a dominant role in social work in the United States. Questions of power, on the other hand, have become central to emergent theoretical directions of late 20th century social work, where empowerment perspectives, envisioned as a route toward social-justice-oriented practice, have gained prominence.

## Social Work and Social Justice in a Global Context

Each year the United Nations completes a Human Development Report documenting global disparities that highlight life expectancies, access to material and social goods, and inequalities based on gender, race, age, and other markers of difference. The report points to the growing divide between those with an abundance of resources and those with little or no access to basic necessities. These issues raise questions of social justice. As Nussbaum (2004) indicates, "Any theory of justice that proposes political principles defining basic human entitlements ought to be able to confront these inequalities and the challenge they pose, in a world in which the power of the global market and of multinational corporations has considerably eroded the power and autonomy of nations" (pp. 3–4). The global economy and its penetration into every aspect of human existence link people through what Polack (2004) refers to as "a complex web of economic relationships" (p. 281). Therefore, social workers need to locate and understand many domestic social justice issues within a larger global context.

Lynne Healy (2001) argues for the need to pay simultaneous attention to global interdependence and social exclusion, or the forces of social and economic marginalization that deny whole populations the right to participate in opportunities available in society. Karen Lyons (1999) argues that attention to social justice on a global scale requires critical thinking and action to address poverty, migration, disasters, and their global impacts (1999, p. 14). Polack (2004) notes that the NASW *Code of Ethics* puts forth a global mandate for the promotion of social justice. In making explicit that the ethical responsibilities of social workers extend beyond national boundaries, NASW challenges social workers to broaden and deepen their knowledge base.

Polack argues that, in order to address the structures of privilege and inequality in the global economy, social workers need a critical understanding of colonialism and its legacies; the global structuring of debt; the logic and function of structural adjustment programs; and shifting forms of labor and movements of labor forces.

Echoing Polack's concerns, Caputo (2002) argues that a commitment to social justice and the "ethics of care" are critical counter forces for social change in the context of the ascendancy of neoliberalism and the infiltration of market principles in all aspects of social life. These conceptualizations of justice speak of broad societal responsibilities that cannot be readily confined to the concerns and obligations of particular states or nations. If social workers limit their focus to the situation of social justice within a given state, they miss fundamental inequalities among states and the transnational policies and practices that maintain and justify them. As Lyons (1999) notes, citizenship as it is conceptualized and practiced at the national level is inherently exclusionary when we consider the differences in power and access to resources among states.

Social workers in both the United States and abroad have reported on the insidious impacts of marketization, managerialism, and fragmentation of social welfare systems and social work practices in the era of neoliberal globalization (Clarke, Gewirtz, & McLaughlin, 2000; Harris, 2005; Jones; 2005). Healy (2005, p. 220) warns of the trend toward "reprivatization of public concerns, such as poverty" and the implications for a justice-oriented practice of social work. In this new environment of marketization and managerialism, Healy (2001) expresses concern that increasing demands by funding agencies and service managers for cost-effectiveness and evidence of service outputs may constrain practice grounded in the profession's core values. Similarly, Dominelli (1996) has expressed concern over the "commodification of social work" that moves the focus of practice away from concern about people and relationships toward a "product that is being purchased from a contractor" (pp. 163–164). Rossiter (2005) challenges social workers to think specifically about the clinical, legal, and ethical implications of social work within the neoliberal global order. She asks: "Can we picture our current students working for a private child protection service owned by an American multinational?" (p. 190). If social workers take principles of social justice seriously then they have to develop an international or transnational perspective of the obligations of both citizenship and the profession. These are fundamental challenges for social work in the 21st century.

## Linking Social Justice and Social Work Practice

The meaningful incorporation of social justice principles into social work practice calls for an ongoing examination of the questions of difference, power, and oppression (Saleebey, 2006). As Beth Glover Reed and colleagues (Reed, Newman, Suarez, & Lewis, 1997, p. 46) argue, "recognizing and building on people's differences is important and necessary, but not sufficient for a practice that has social justice as a primary goal." For social justice-oriented practice, "both *difference* and *dominance* dimensions must be recognized and addressed. Developing and using individual and collective critical consciousness are primary tools for understanding differences, recognizing injustice, and beginning to envision a more just society" (Reed et al., 1997, p. 46). Translating the value of social justice into practice requires that social workers align themselves with those who have experienced the world from positions of oppression and challenge the practices and conditions that reproduce inequality. Social work becomes a transformative process in which both social conditions and participants, including the social worker, are changed in the pursuit of a just world (Adams, Domenelli, & Payne, 2005; Witkin, 1998).

Social workers are translating the principle of social justice into concrete practices. For example, Lynn Parker (2003) argues that a social justice perspective informed by feminism calls attention to questions of power, privilege, and oppression in all aspects of social work, including clinical practice. Lorraine Gutiérrez and Edith Lewis (1999) have drawn from the experiences of women of color to promote social justice through an empowerment-based model of practice (Gutiérrez & Lewis, 1999). Janet Finn and Maxine Jacobson (2007) have put forth the "just practice framework," as a guide to social justice-oriented practice. The framework brings together five interrelated concepts—meaning, context, power, history, and possibility—as a basis for critical inquiry and action. Advocacy practice provides another direction for social justice-oriented social work. Richard Hoefer (2006, p. 8) defines advocacy practice as "that part of social work practice where the social worker takes action in a systematic and purposeful way to defend, represent, or otherwise advance the cause of one or more clients at the individual, group, organizational, or community level in order to promote social justice."

Charles Waldegrave and colleagues at the Family Centre in Wellington, New Zealand, have developed a model for "Just Therapy," which makes social justice the heart of direct practice (Waldegrave, 2000).

The approach is characterized by three main concepts: *belonging, sacredness,* and *liberation.* Waldegrave describes the emergence of Just Therapy in a "reflective environment" in which diverse stakeholders came together and critically examined the ways in which helping systems and demands of help seeking have served to reproduce inequalities and experiences of marginalization. Waldegrave describes Just Therapy as a demystifying approach that involves a wide range of practitioners in addressing the deep social pain experienced by people who have been systematically marginalized.

Elizabeth Mulroy (2004) presents a framework for thinking about organizational and community practice in an increasingly complex context of "shifting resources and constraints." It highlights social justice as a core principle of macro-level practice and the need to "understand how the forces of oppression operate across a metropolitan landscape in order to devise strategies capable of bringing about lasting change" (p. 81). Mulroy emphasizes the need for environmental surveillance in order to stay alert to a rapidly changing social environment where organizational survival is predicated on mobilizing power through inter-organizational collaboration, gaining legitimacy by reaching out to the community and maintaining relationships, and sustaining vertical and horizontal linkages to economic resources.

Using a social justice lens helps organizations to reframe issues generally viewed as individual in origin to include broader social, political, economic, and cultural understandings. These open up possibilities for new solutions. The examples cited here are but a few of social workers' efforts to translate the principles of social justice to a practice level. Efforts along these lines continue to grow stronger as social, economic, and political disparities increase. They signal that a commitment to social justice remains an imperative of the profession and a core value guiding social work into the 21st century.

## REFERENCES

Adams, R., Domenelli, L., & Payne, M. (Eds.). (2005). *Social work futures: Crossing boundaries and transforming practice.* New York: Palgrave/MacMillan.

Addams, J. (1960). *A centennial reader.* New York: MacMillan.

Andrews, J. (2001). Group work's place in social work: A historical analysis. *Journal of Sociology and Social Welfare, 28*(4), 45–65.

Banerjee, M. (2005). Apply Rawlsian social justice to welfare reform: An unexpected finding for social work. *Journal of Sociology and Social Welfare, 32*(2), 35–57.

Barker, R. (2003). *The social work dictionary* (5th ed.). Washington, DC: NASW Press.

Berlin, S. (2005). The value of acceptance in social work direct practice: A historical and contemporary view. *Social Service Review, 79*(3), 482–510.

Caputo, R. (2002). Social justice, the ethics of care, and market economies. *Families in Society, 83*(4), 355–364.

Carlton-LaNey, I. (1999). African American social work pioneers' response to need. *Social Work, 44*(4), 311–321.

Clarke, J., Gewirtz, S., & McLaughlin, E. (2000). *New managerialism, new welfare?* London: Sage.

Dana, B. (1973). Health, social work, and social justice. In B. Ross & C. Shireman (Eds.), *Social work practice and social justice* (pp. 111–128). Washington, DC: NASW.

Delaney, R. (2005). Social justice. In Francis J. Turner (Ed.), *Encyclopedia of Canadian Social Work* (pp. ??). Waterloo, Ontario: Wilfred Laurier University Press.

Dewees, M. (2006). *Contemporary social work practice.* Boston: McGraw-Hill.

Dominelli, L. (1996). Deprofessionalizing social work: Anti-oppressive practice, competencies and post-modernism. *British Journal of Social Work, 26,* 153–157.

Finn, J., & Jacobson, M. (2007). *Just practice: A social justice approach to social work* (2nd ed.). Peosta, IA: Eddie Bowers Publishing, Inc.

Fisher, R., & Karger, H. (1997). *Social work and community in a private world.* New York: Longman.

Gutiérrez, L., & Lewis, E. (1999). *Empowering women of color.* Columbia University Press.

Harris, J. (2005). Globalisation, neo-liberal managerialism and UK social work. In I. Ferguson, M. Lavalette, & E. Whitmore (Eds.), *Globalisation, global justice and social work* (pp. 81–93). New York: Routledge.

Healy, K. (2005). Under reconstruction: Renewing critical social work practices. In S. Hick, J. Fook, & R. Pozzuto (Eds.), *Social work: A critical turn* (pp. 219–229). Toronto: Thompson Educational Publishing, Inc.

Healy, L. (2001). *International social work: Professional action in an interdependent world.* New York: Oxford University Press.

Hoefer, R. (2006). *Advocacy practice for social justice.* Chicago: Lyceum Press.

Ife, J. (1997). *Rethinking social work: Towards critical practice.* Melbourne: Longman.

Ife, J. (2001). *Human rights and social work: Towards rights-based practice.* Cambridge, UK: Cambridge University Press.

Jacobson, M., & Rugeley, C. (in press). Community-based participatory research: Group work for social justice and community change. *Social Work with Groups, 30*(4).

Jones, C. (2005). The neo-liberal assault: Voices from the front line of British state social work. In I. Ferguson, M. Lavalette, & E. Whitmore (Eds.), *Globalisation, global justice and social work* (pp. 97–109). New York: Routledge.

Lee, J. A. B. (1986). Seeing it whole: Social work with groups within an integrative perspective. *Social Work with Groups, 8*(4), 39–49.

Lee, J. A. B. (1992). Jane Addams in Boston: Intersecting time and space. In J. Garland (Ed.), *Group work reaching out: People, places and power* (pp. 7–21). New York: Haworth Press.

Lewis, H. (1992). Some thoughts on my forty years in social work education. *Journal of Progressive Human Services, 3*(1), 39–51.

Longres, J., & Scanlon, E. (2001). Social justice and the research curriculum. *Journal of Social Work Education, 37*(3), 447–463.

McCormick, P. (2003). Whose justice? An examination of nine models of justice. *Social Thought, 22*(2/3), 7–25.

McDonald, C. (2006). *Challenging social work: The institutional context of practice.* New York: Palgrave.

McGrath Morris, P. (2002). The capabilities perspective: A framework for social justice. *Families in Society, 83*(4), 365–373.

Miller, D. (1976). *Social justice.* Oxford: Clarendon Press.

Miller, D. (1999). *Principles of social justice.* Cambridge, MA: Harvard University Press.

Mulroy, E. (2004). Theoretical perspectives on the social environment to guide management and community practice: An organization-in-environment approach. *Administration in Social Work, 28*(1), 77–96.

National Association of Social Workers. (1999). *Code of ethics of the national association of social workers.* Washington, DC: Author.

Nozick, R. (1974). *Anarchy, state, and utopia.* New York: Basic Books.

Nussbaum, M. (2002). Capabilities and social justice. *International Studies Review, 4*(2), 123–135.

Nussbaum, M. (2004). Beyond the social contract: Capabilities and global justice. *Oxford Development Studies, 32*(1), 3–18.

Parker, L. (2003). A social justice model for clinical social work practice. *Affilia, 18*(3), 272–288.

Polack, R. (2004). Social justice and the global economy: New challenges for social work in the 21st century. *Social Work, 49*(2), 281–290.

Rawls, J. (1971/1995). *A Theory of justice* (1st & 2nd eds.). Cambridge, MA: Harvard University Press.

Rawls, J. (2001). *Justice as fairness: A restatement.* Cambridge, MA: Belknap Press of Harvard University Press.

Reed, B. G., Newman, P., Suarez, Z., & Lewis, E. (1997). Interpersonal practice beyond diversity and toward social justice: The importance of critical consciousness. In C. Garvin & B. Seabury (Eds.), *Interpersonal practice in social work: Promoting competence and social justice* (2nd ed., pp. 44–78). Boston: Allyn and Bacon.

Reichert, E. (2003). *Social work and human rights: A foundation for policy and practice.* New York: Columbia University Press.

Reisch, M. (1998). *Economic globalization and the future of the welfare state. Welfare reform and social justice visiting scholars program.* Ann Arbor: The University of Michigan School of Social Work.

Reisch, M. (2002). Defining social justice in a socially unjust world. *Families in Society, 83*(4), 343–354.

Reynolds, B. (1963). *An uncharted journey.* Washington, DC: NASW Press.

Ross, B. (1973). Professional dilemmas. In B. Ross & C. Shireman (Eds.), *Social work practice and social justice* (pp. 147–152). Washington, DC: NASW Press.

Rossiter, A. (2005). Where in the world are we? Notes on the need for a social work response to global power. In S. Hick, J. Fook, & R. Pozzuto (Eds.), *Social work: A critical turn* (pp. 189–202). Toronto: Thompson Educational Publishing, Inc.

Saleebey, D. (1990). Philosophical disputes in social work: Social justice denied. *Journal of Sociology and Social Welfare, 17*(2), 29–40.

Saleebey, D. (Ed.). (2006). *The strengths perspective in social work practice* (4th ed.). Boston: Pearson Education, Inc.

Schwartz, W. (1986). The group work tradition and social work practice. *Social Work with Groups, 8*(4), 7–27.

Stebner, E. (1997). *The women of hull house: Study in spirituality, vocation, and friendship.* Albany: State University of New York Press.

Swenson, C. (1998). Clinical social work's contribution to a social justice perspective. *Social Work, 43*(6), 527–537.

United States Catholic Bishops. (1986). *Economic justice for all: Pastoral letter on Catholic social teaching and the U.S. economy.* Washington, DC: National Conference of Catholic Bishops.

Van Soest, D. (1994). Strange bedfellow. A call for reordering national priorities from three social justice perspectives. *Social Work, 39*(6), 710–717.

Van Soest, D., & Garcia, B. (2003). *Diversity education for social justice: Mastering teaching skills.* Alexandria, VA: Council on Social Work Education.

Wakefield, J. (1988). Psychotherapy, distributive justice and social work: Part I – Distributive justice as a conceptual framework for social work. *Social Service Review, 62*(2), 187–210.

Waldegrave, C. (2000). Just therapy with families and communities. In G. Burford & J. Hudson (Eds.), *Family group conferencing: New directions in community-centered child and family practice* (pp. 153–163). New York: Aldine de Gruyter.

Wise, S. (1909). The conference sermon. Charity versus justice. *Proceedings of the National Conference of Charities and Corrections, 36,* 20–29.

Witkin, S. (1998). Human rights and social work. *Social Work, 43*(3), 197–201.

Young, I. M. (1990). *Justice and the politics of difference.* Princeton, NJ: Princeton University Press.

Young, I. M. (2001). Equality for whom? Social groups and judgments of injustice. *The Journal of Political Philosophy, 9*(1), 1–18.

## FURTHER READING

Council on Social Work Education. (1994). *Handbook of accreditation standards and procedures.* Alexandria, VA: Author.

Dominelli, L. (2002). *Anti-oppressive social work theory and practice.* London: Macmillan.

Ferguson, I., Lavalette, M., & Whitmore, E. (2005). *Globalisation, global justice and social work.* New York: Routledge.

Harvey, D. (1989). *The condition of postmodernity: An enquiry into the origins of cultural change.* Oxford, UK: Basil Blackwell, Ltd.

Reisch, M. (2005). American exceptionalism and critical social work: A retrospective and prospective analysis. In I. Ferguson, M. Lavalette, & E. Whitmore (Eds.), *Globalisation, global justice and social work* (pp. 157–172). New York: Routledge.

Reisch, M., & Andrews, J. (2001). *The road not taken: a history of radical social work in the United States.* New York: Brunner/Routledge.

Ross, B., & Shireman, C. (Eds.). (1973). *Social work practice and social justice.* Washington, DC: NASW Press.

—JANET L. FINN AND MAXINE JACOBSON

**SOCIAL LEGISLATION.** *See* Social Policy: Overview.

# SOCIAL MOVEMENTS

ABSTRACT: Since the 19th century, social movements have provided U.S. social work with its intellectual and theoretical foundations and many of its leaders. Social workers were among the founders of the Progressive movement and have played important roles in the labor, feminist, civil rights, welfare rights, and peace movements for over a century. More recently, social workers have been active in New Social Movements (NSMs), which have focused on issues of identity, self-esteem, critical consciousness, and human rights, and in international movements which have emerged in response to economic globalization, environmental degradation, and major population shifts, including mass immigration.

KEY WORDS: collective action; progressive movement; labor movement; populism; New Social Movements; resource mobilization theory; feminism; civil rights; pacifism; Socialism, Rank and File Movement

Since the 19th century social movements have significantly influenced the development of U.S. social work (Day, 2000). They have provided its intellectual and theoretical foundations and goals, and most of its strongest allies. Many social workers have held leadership positions in national and international social movements (Reisch & Andrews, 2001). Although fewer social workers play such roles today, social movements continue to have an important impact on social work theory and practice.

## The Nature of Social Movements

Modern social movements have used a variety of sustained, organized, and public activities to advance their goals and to portray their members as worthy, unified, numerous, and committed to specific changes (Tilly, 2004). Most social movements share several common traits. As "collective challenges based on common purposes," they assert particular claims on society for tangible resources, recognition, and status. They consist of groups of actors who share common goals yet compete over tactics, resources, and distribution of benefits. Although they usually emerge locally, social movements eventually become established on a regional, national, or international basis and, as a result, become dependent on the support of external sponsors.

Theorists of social movements focus on the following issues:

- Tensions between structure and spontaneity;
- Origins of movements;
- How movements articulate goals, frame their message, mobilize members, cultivate collective consciousness or identity, obtain and utilize resources, develop and implement strategies, and take advantage of opportunities.

Today, the term "social movement" is often mistakenly applied to all forms of collective action, even those without clear political goals (D'Arcus, 2006). Social movements, interest groups, or parties are frequently equated. A movement's collective action is often conflated with actions undertaken by the organizations within it; these entities are sometimes identified with the movement itself. Discussions of social movements frequently assume internal unity, overlooking their dynamic internal relationships.

The beginnings of most social movements often go unnoticed (Mansbridge & Morris, 2001). They emerge within preexisting networks or homogeneous communities, whose members adopt its ideology and goals. An unanticipated crisis or the deliberate, planned interventions of individuals or small groups usually crystallizes these conditions into a movement and establishes its legitimacy among constituents, other political actors, and the general public.

A social movement generally takes one of three structural forms. *Segmented* movements are constantly changing coalitions of diverse groups. *Polycentric* movements incorporate two or more competing organizations into *ad hoc* alliances around common goals. *Reticulate* movements create loosely integrated networks with multiple formal and informal connections (Zald & McCarthy, 1987).

Many social movements focus on the pursuit of social justice, although their definitions of social justice have varied depending on the historical context in which they emerged and the demographic composition of their members. Social movements have influenced public policy by addressing its substance and goals, the structures through which it is developed, and the processes that determine and implement societal priorities. Often, the "window of opportunity" for movements to shape policy is limited, although some movements have maintained long-term involvement in the policymaking process by building institutions which are compatible with existing political structures.

Different theoretical models proffer varying explanations for the failure of social movements. The classical model attributes their decline to tendencies toward oligarchy and conservatism, or the institutionalization of the movement's values and goals into the dominant culture. Resource mobilization theorists emphasize the loss of critical assets, particularly from key external supporters. Theorists who focus on political processes stress changes in "opportunity structures" and the ways in which allies, neutrals, and opponents respond to the challenges movements present. Their studies conclude that the environmental "set" is often as significant as the strategic choices of movements in determining their success or failure. Finally, some theorists analyze the internal dynamics of movement organizations and attribute their decline to inflexible structures, failure to accommodate new members, gaps between members' and leaders' goals, and a misdirection of energy and resources toward internal disputes, rather than external enemies.

While previous research focused on the compatibility of movement goals and strategies with dominant values and institutions, scholars have recently examined how governments or mass media deliberately suppress movements through such means as resource depletion, stigmatization, disruption, intimidation, and marginalization. States engage in direct violence, prosecute and harass movement leaders, blacklist movement members, conduct surveillance against movement organizations, infiltrate groups to promote factionalism and spread disinformation, and adopt a variety of repressive laws. The media shape the perception of social movements, often in negative ways, and distort public awareness of their values, goals, and activities.

### Social Movements and the Emergence of Social Work

During the formative years of U.S. social work, social movements arose in reaction to rapid socioeconomic changes produced by industrialization, urbanization, and mass immigration. Inspired by secular and religious ideologies, they challenged institutional discrimination and sought to correct prevailing inequalities in the distribution of resources, rights, power, opportunities, and status. While some of these movements reflected strong anti-egalitarian biases against non-native born Americans, especially Catholics, Jews, and immigrants of color, others sought to diminish growing social tensions by recreating a pre-modern "organic community" comparable to efforts by the contemporary communitarian movement.

Industrial workers organized trade unions in large numbers, often influenced by European ideas such as socialism and anarcho-syndicalism. Many clients of early social service organizations belonged to these unions. Their problems—low wages, terrible working conditions, slum housing—inevitably came to the attention of social workers who were compelled to take a stance on "the Social Question."

Other movements also shaped the character of social work. An unprecedented multiracial coalition of agricultural workers, small farmers, small business owners, and industrial workers created populism, a unique form of American radicalism. Before racial divisions led to the movement's demise, populists challenged the growing dominance of trusts and banks and the concentration of wealth and power among the elite.

The "first wave" of American feminism and the beginnings of the modern civil rights movement also had major impacts on social work. Many social work leaders, such as Florence Kelley, Lillian Wald, Ellen Gates Starr, Ida Wells-Barnett, and Jane Addams, played active roles in feminist organizations around issues such as suffrage, industrial exploitation, and public health. They helped found civil rights organizations, such as the National Association for the Advancement of Colored People and the National Urban League and joined anti-lynching crusades. While participation in such movements was not without conflict, the involvement of white, middle and upper class social workers with African Americans, immigrants, and ethnically and religiously diverse trade unionists broadened their understanding of social conditions and sharpened their interest in social justice.

### Progressivism and the Settlement House Movement

Not all social movements of this era, however, emerged from disadvantaged segments of society. Many well-educated middle and upper class men and women became increasingly dissatisfied with the nation's direction and their future roles within it. Under the banner of Progressivism they organized a movement to redirect the country from its heedless pursuit of material wealth and to address the serious social consequences of the new political-economic environment.

Progressivism thrived in the generation before World War I (Davis, 1967). Its ranks included such diverse figures as philosophers John Dewey and William James, journalists Herbert Crowley and Walter Lippman, politicians Theodore Roosevelt and Woodrow Wilson, and social workers like Jane Addams. Its future-oriented goals, which focused on education, child welfare, the amelioration of urban and industrial conditions, the assimilation of immigrants, and the expansion of democracy, were well-suited for the emerging field of social work (Lubove, 1965). Many reforms advocated by social workers—the establishment of the juvenile court, the expansion of state-funded education and recreation, the eradication of child labor, and the promotion of public health measures—originated within the Progressive movement (Axinn & Stern, 2008). Progressivism also appealed to many social workers because it promised reform without violent social conflict or a dramatic transformation of the nation's class structure or culture (Wenocur & Reisch, 1989).

### Social Work and the Labor Movement
The organization of individual trade unions in the late 19th and early 20th centuries took on the character of a social movement due to the sheer size of this phenomenon, the emergence of powerful leaders, and the infusion of unifying ideologies, including socialism and anarcho-syndicalism. While its goals reflected serious political and ideological divisions, the movement as a whole called increased attention to poverty and socioeconomic inequality and their consequences for human health and well-being.

The relationship of organized social work with the labor movement reflected the ambiguities and tensions of class differences. Some social workers, such as Florence Kelley, Lillian Wald, Ellen Gates Starr and, later, Mary van Kleeck and Bertha Reynolds, helped organize trade unions, particularly among women, investigated industrial conditions, developed programs that served working families, and advocated for policies abolishing child labor and establishing better wages and working conditions. Although many others sympathized with industrial workers and their families, only a minority supported the labor movement's more radical goals.

### Feminism, Pacifism, and Socialism
In the era before World War I some social workers were drawn to more radical social movements, which sought not merely to reform but to transform U.S. society. The Socialist movement was particularly influential among urban social workers, especially those from immigrant families. Florence Kelley, the head of the National Consumers League, was a leading Socialist who corresponded with Friedrich Engels and produced the first

American translation of his work. Lillian Wald, the founder of public health nursing and director of the Henry Street Settlement, was also an active Socialist, as was Ellen Gates Starr, who co-founded Hull House with Jane Addams. Through the socialist movement, they had contact with radicals like Emma Goldman and Crystal Eastman, whose ideas shaped their views on issues from income support to reproductive rights.

Social workers held leadership positions in the National Women's Party and helped organize the Women's Trade Union League. Mary van Kleeck conducted the first investigations of factory conditions affecting women and girls, such as those leading to the tragic 1911 Triangle fire (Karger, 1988). Many social workers, however, disagreed with other feminists over issues such as contraception and the Equal Rights Amendment. Addams was reluctant to support birth control advocate Margaret Sanger, due to a combination of residual Victorian morality and fear of alienating Catholic supporters. Kelley opposed the Equal Rights Amendment because she thought its passage would undercut efforts to improve the conditions of women. She favored a "maternalist" strategy to provide the "wedge" to expand social benefits for all Americans (Sklar, 1995).

The outbreak of World War I united social workers with diverse allies within the pacifist movement. Some, like Addams, opposed war on religious or moral grounds; others like Wald and Kelley linked their opposition to domestic policy concerns (Reisch & Andrews, 2001). Their outspoken critiques of American militarism prompted scathing attacks on their patriotism which persisted into the 1920s and seriously undermined public support for the causes they espoused.

### The Rank and File Movement
After a period of political quiescence, the Great Depression spurred the growth of new social movements and revived others of a radical nature. The Socialist and Communist movements attracted many converts and sympathizers, particularly among urban immigrants and social workers. Beginning in 1931, activist social workers organized discussion clubs and unions, ultimately leading to the formation of the Rank and File Movement, which included such notable social workers as Bertha Reynolds, Mary van Kleeck, Jacob Fisher, and Harry Lurie. By 1936, it had more members than the American Association of Social Workers and developed close ties with left-wing political parties and organized labor, particularly the Congress of Industrial Organizations. Until it dissolved in the early 1940s, the Rank and File Movement pressured the Roosevelt administration to adopt more sweeping reforms in social welfare and industrial policy.

## Civil Rights, Welfare Rights, and the War on Poverty

The anti-Communist crusades of the postwar McCarthy period seriously diminished the size, scope, and influence of social justice-oriented movements in the United States. Left-wing unions, including social work unions, were broken up, progressive social workers were investigated by legislative committees, and many social workers were fired because of their political beliefs. This climate produced a general decline in social activism within the United States and the social work field (Schrecker, 1998).

One exception was the resurgence of the civil rights movement among African Americans, whose participation in military and defense industries during World War II strengthened their commitment to social equality. Inspired by the 1954 *Brown* decision and the courage displayed by civil rights activists in the 1955–1956 Montgomery bus boycott, the freedom rides of the early 1960s, Southern voting rights campaigns, and protests against the war in Vietnam, a new generation of activists arose. Although few social workers led civil rights or anti-war organizations, many joined movement-based groups. Social workers, however, played significant roles as strategists and organizers in the welfare rights movement. As in the 1930s, considerable conflict erupted between supporters of these movements and their more mainstream, reform-minded colleagues (Nadasen, 2005).

## Identity-Based Social Movements

The nature of social movements changed dramatically in the 1960s and early 1970s. New social movements (NSMs) among women, gays and lesbians, people of color, and the disabled appeared, which differed substantially from past social movements in their missions, actions, and structure. They combined anti-government and anti-institutional goals with attempts to acquire legal protections and tangible resources from the state. They challenged prevailing hierarchies and privileges and emphasized egalitarian behavioral norms and organizational structures. They replaced or augmented class-based, often Marxist-oriented worldviews with a focus on identity politics and the roles of experience and positionality (Freeman & Johnson, 1999).

These changes prompted a revision in the theoretical frameworks used to analyze social movements. Resource mobilization theorists challenged prevailing paradigms which looked at social movements and collective behavior through the lens of irrationality. Instead, they emphasized the rationality of collective action and focused primarily on an assessment of social movements' response to environmental threats, risks, and opportunities. New social movement theory stressed the subjective, nonrational experiences of oppression, identity, autonomy, and culture, and the ways in which NSMs consciously reject dominant institutions and their "integrating rationalities," including meta-analyses of history and society. Other theorists looked at a combination of resource, institutional, and ecological factors, including the roles of informal networks, local grassroots groups, spatiality, and personal relationships (Kelly, 2001).

During the 21st century, it is likely that social movements will continue to reflect a variety of new organizational, strategic, and ideological trends. These include a greater likelihood of trans-national alliances which focus on both global issues and their local manifestations; the growing linkage of social and environmental concerns; the emergence of movement coalitions that transcend various identity boundaries; and the increased use of the internet and cellular technology for purposes of intra-organizational and inter-organizational communication, recruitment, planning, research, and information sharing (Hamel, Lustiger-Thaler, Pieterse, & Roseneil, 2001).

## Globalization, NSMs, and Social Work

During the past several decades economic globalization has significantly affected the distribution of income and wealth within and between nations, transformed the character of work and labor-management relations, heightened inter-generational tensions, and altered the nature of property and property relations. It spurred the emergence of new communication technologies which have contributed to the globalization process itself and speeded the flow of information about its consequences. Globalization promoted the consolidation of corporate power, the growth of supra-national international financial institutions such as the World Bank and International Monetary Fund, and the emergence of new conflicts between these institutions and increasingly anachronistic national governments. NSMs responded to these developments by changing their structure, scope, and strategies.

NSMs no longer function solely within national boundaries or even cross-nationally as movements did in the past. Increasingly, they attempt to combine a complex array of global, local, and personal/identity factors in a dynamic, interactive relationship. From one perspective, the core issues facing NSMs involve the democratization of institutions; from another, they reflect the challenge of new demographic patterns, the merger of local and global cultures, and the advent of cross-cutting issues such as global warming and the relationship between humans and nature.

NSMs are more loosely structured than traditional social movements and are more likely to address local as well as international concerns. Although they tend to emphasize identity and personal equality to a greater extent, they are—paradoxically—less driven by narrow ideologies. At least in theory, they reflect the reduced importance of formal organizations, which increases the opportunity for resource-deprived groups to influence developments. In response to the rapidity of change, their strategies are more fluid and their action campaigns less segmented, with increased roles for symbolic and virtual politics.

A consistent thread connecting NSMs with social work is that both are linked, philosophically and practically, to the expansion of democracy and the promotion of social justice globally. To realize these lofty goals, social workers will have to revise long-standing assumptions about their constituents and clients, their relationship with the state, and their strategies of personal and social intervention. As participants in the global social justice movements of the 21st century, social workers can help expose the consequences of globalization and develop viable alternatives to existing institutional arrangements. This will require greater imagination, flexibility, and adaptability in defining and addressing new and persistent social issues. It will also require social workers to clarify the meaning of social justice in an increasingly globalized and multicultural environment.

## REFERENCES

Axinn, J., & Stern, M. J. (2008). *Social welfare: A history of the American response to need* (7th ed.). Boston: Allyn and Bacon.

D'Arcus, B. (2006). *Boundaries of dissent: Protest and state power in the media age.* New York: Routledge.

Davis, A. F. (1967). *Spearheads for reform: Social settlements and the progressive movement, 1890–1914,* New York: Oxford University Press.

Day, P. J. (2000). *A new history of welfare* (3rd ed.). Boston: Allyn and Bacon.

Freeman, J., & Johnson, V. (Eds.). (1999). *Wave of protests: Social movements since the sixties.* New York: Rowman and Littlefield.

Hamel, P., Lustiger-Thaler, H., Pieterse, J. N., & Roseneil, S. (Eds.). (2001). *Globalization and social movements.* New York: Palgrave.

Karger, H. J. (1988). *Social workers and labor unions.* New York: Greenwood Press.

Kelly, C. A. (2001). *Tangled up in red, white, & blue: New social movements in America.* New York: Rowman and Littlefield.

Lubove, R. (1965). *The professional altruist: The emergence of social work as a career, 1880–1930,* Cambridge, MA: Harvard University Press.

Mansbridge, J., & Morris, A. D. (Eds.). (2001). *Oppositional consciousness: The subjective roots of social protest,* Chicago: University of Chicago Press.

Nadasen, P. (2005). *Welfare warriors: The welfare rights movement in the U.S.,* New York: Routledge.

Reisch, M., & Andrews, J. L. (2001). *The road not taken: A history of radical social work in the United States.* Philadelphia: Brunner-Routledge.

Schrecker, E. (1998). *Many are the crimes: McCarthyism in America,* Boston: Little, Brown.

Sklar, K. K. (1995). *Florence Kelley and the nation's work,* New Haven, CT: Yale University Press.

Tilly, C. (2004). *Social movements, 1768–2004.* Boulder, CO: Paradigm Publishers.

Wenocur, S., & Reisch, M. (1989). *From charity to enterprise: The development of American social work in a market economy,* Urbana: University of Illinois Press.

Zald, M. N., & McCarthy, J. D. (Eds.). (1987). *Social movements in an organizational society: Collected essays,* New Brunswick, NJ: Transaction Books.

## FURTHER READING

Anner, J. (Ed.). (1996). *Beyond identity politics: Emerging social justice movements in communities of color.* Boston: South End Press.

Berg, J. C. (Ed.). (2003). *Teamsters and turtles? U.S. progressive political movements in the 21st century.* New York: Rowman and Littlefield.

Boykoff, J. (2006). *The suppression of dissent: How the state and mass media squelch American social movements.* New York: Routledge.

Daniels, R. V. (2006). *The fourth revolution: Transformations in American society from the sixties to the present.* New York: Routledge.

Kaplan, T. (1997). *Crazy for democracy: Women in grassroots movements.* New York: Routledge.

Meyer, D. S., Jenness, V., & Ingram, H. (Eds.). (2005). *Routing the opposition: Social movements, public policy, and democracy.* Minneapolis: University of Minnesota Press.

Minkoff, D. C. (1995). *Organizing for equality: The evolution of women's and racial-ethnic organizations in America, 1955–1985.* New Brunswick, NJ: Rutgers University Press.

Pope, D. (Ed.). (2001). *American radicalism.* Malden, MA: Blackwell Publishers.

—Michael Reisch

# SOCIAL PLANNING

**Abstract:** Social planning emphasizes the application of rational problem-solving techniques and data-driven approaches to identify, determine, and help coordinate services for target populations. Social planning is carried out by a myriad of organizations—from federal agencies to community organizations—attempting to solve problems ranging from child welfare to aging. The advantages and disadvantages of this empirically objective data-driven approach, including different forms, will be discussed along with past, current, and future trends within the field of social work.

KEY WORDS: social planning; planning councils; comprehensive rational planning; incrementalism; decision-making; rational problem-solving; geographic information systems; spatial mismatch; sustainable development

## Social Planning

Prototypical social planning is the application of rational problem-solving techniques and data-driven methodologies to conceiving, developing, coordinating, and delivering human services. Social planning occurs in federal, state, county, and city bureaus, and in the voluntary sector, including community councils, United Ways, Area Agencies on Aging, voluntary associations, and faith-based organizations. Planning can be carried out locally, regionally, nationally, or internationally, and addresses such problems as poverty, child and family welfare, aging, housing, crime, delinquency, mental health, and so forth. Social planners function in a variety of disciplines, including social work, urban planning, public administration, health care, and public policy.

The social planning rubric has been broadly applied to encompass an array of activities, from technical experts systematically analyzing data to facilitators incorporating input from participating citizens. Nevertheless, Rothman (in press) forthcoming states that prototypical social planning emphasizes data-driven and carefully calibrated change grounded in social science principles and empirical objectivity. The approach is viewed as evidenced-based and technocratic, and rationality is the dominant ideal.

## Historical Trends in Social Planning

The origins of modern social planning can be traced to the urban transformation inspired by the industrial revolution in late 19th century. Through rational planning, charity organizations and settlement movements attempted to avoid duplicating services, indiscriminate spending, and fraud. In 1908 in Pittsburgh, the first community welfare and social agency councils were formed. They attempted to centralize social planning in order to improve service coordination, efficiency, and quality. With the advent of World War I, centralized agencies developed war chests to efficiently coordinate services. After the war, these agencies and war chests became community chests and councils. They were the harbinger of raising and overseeing welfare funds and engaging in large-scale community planning. These community chests and councils were the predecessors of organizations such as the United Way, and sought to rationally allocate funds among a number of social agencies providing various services. The New Deal of 1930s and 1940s ushered in important changes, as voluntary agencies, which had been dominant in social planning, were supplanted, and social planning expanded, by federal, state, and local agencies. The federal government became more active and consolidated social planning, applying it across large groups of people.

The 1950s arrived on a wave of American affluence. For first time in the history of the world, the majority of a nation's population began to live above a minimum poverty level. With the advent of the liberal Presidents Kennedy and Johnson, gains in civil rights and concomitant changes in legislation provided momentum and optimism for the effectiveness of social planning into the 1960s. The Johnson administration declared a War on Poverty in which it promoted equality of opportunity, with massive sums of money having been allocated to solve numerous social problems The Johnson administration declared a war on poverty, promoting equal opportunity and allocating massive sums of money to solve numerous problems. Major federal social programs were initiated in health, housing, preschool (Head Start), elementary and secondary education, urban renewal, poverty, and unemployment. Typically, these initiatives mandated citizen and client participation to complement technocratic planning. However, soon programs such as the Federal Model Cities shifted greater power and responsibility back to city mayors, councils, and managers. The 1968 Comprehensive Health Planning Act provided funds to involve all the stakeholders, including providers and consumers, to examine health needs and resources for the first time in U.S. history, and strengthened it in 1974 with the Health Care Resource, Planning and Development Act mandating 60% consumer involvement.

Nevertheless, with the advent of the Nixon Administration optimism for the benefits of social planning began to erode. The Vietnam War, the oil shock of the early 1970s, a mild recession and later inflation culminated with the Nixon administration attempting to cut spending and rollback progressive legislation and transfer responsibility back to the States. The 1980s entailed an attack on social programs and welfare by the Reagan and Bush I administrations. Funds devoted to social problems were significantly reduced, taxes were cut, and military spending soared, while supply-side economists proclaimed that market forces would resolve social issues. As the 20th century ended, the Clinton administration attempted to achieve liberal ends by conservative means. The Personal Responsibility and Work Opportunity Reconciliation Act of 1996 now funded state programs with federal block grants and state resources. Temporary Assistance for Needy Families (TANF) grants ceded most authority to states, but restricted states from reducing welfare by more than 20%. Receiving welfare was now contingent on clients going to work or undertaking activities, such as education or training.

At the dawn of the 21st century, the Bush II administration incurred tremendous expense and trillions of dollars of deficit due to large trade imbalances, a war on terrorism, and the costly war in Iraq. Social planners now face the dubious task of devoting scarcer resources to increasingly complex and systemic social problems.

## The Foundations of Social Planning

Social planning is rooted in the philosophy of logical positivism. Positivism assumes social phenomena, which like physical phenomena, exist in a scientifically ordered world that functions according to knowable and discernable laws. This approach to social planning is currently known as comprehensive rational planning. This is not to be confused with comprehensive social planning, which pertains to large-scale, national-level planning, such as social security. Comprehensive rational planning assumes that social problems can be defined and the root causes identified. Complete information can be gathered, and the resulting plans are based on facts, data, and logical calculations. Moreover, such rationality is universal—all plans and decisions can be completely informed, factual, and logical regardless of culture, context, or individual differences (Morcol, 2007). Few social planners believe that these assumptions are true, but they can serve as reasonable approximations. Therefore, the aggregation of rational choices, somewhat like a mean or central tendency of rational choices, can result in a collective rationality.

Herbert Simon (1955) convincingly reasoned that human rationality was bounded by the limits of human intelligence, psychosocial experience, socialization, language, culture, and context. Hence, planners in practice typically satisfied choosing an acceptable alternative, rather than optimizing and choosing the best possible alternative.

An alternative to comprehensive rational planning was Charles Lindblom's (1959) incrementalism or disjointed incrementalism, sometimes referred to as the "science of muddling through." Lindblom contended that rational planning could only occur under the most

ideal conditions. In contrast, incrementalism eschewed the pretense of an underlying order and pure objectivity. Instead, social planners focused on concrete problems and actual conditions, typically localized. By having success and failure in specific situations, social planners could identify what worked under specific circumstances, and discard programs, services, and approaches that performed poorly. By making adjustments, these small incremental improvements would theoretically culminate in better and better solutions.

## Roles and Functions of Social Planners

Social planners enact various roles and engage in various functions. They plan, identify key issues, set priorities, and advocate for certain social policies. They conduct research and gather data about human needs and resources. They serve as a resource, providing technical assistance for planning, developing, and improving programs and services. Planners advise public, private, federal, state, and local agencies. They develop new resources and seek new sources of funding. They organize people and agencies and mobilize resources to improve services and interagency cooperation.

Such activities are often perceived to have more in common with other professions (for example, city or public health planners) than with social workers for whom process and direct practice are perceived to be incongruent with technocratic orientations. Gilbert and Specht (1977) observed that besides contrasting activities, there are discrepant views concerning the central purpose of social planning. The first, *Integration and capacity building objectives*, is consistent with the process and direct practice orientation, while the other, *program development and social reform objectives*, is supported by technical and analytical scrutiny. Rothman (in press) helps clarify and reconcile these apparent discrepancies by explaining the mixing and phasing of models of community intervention. While one may be able to find distinct instances of prototypical social planning, they are just as likely to find mixed models. For example, The Children's Defense Fund combines social action and planning by vigorous advocacy and the effective use of research data. Hardina (2002) emphasizes the analytical skills for the macrolevel social worker which include technical as well as political considerations. Effective social planning requires a flexible and multiskilled practitioner.

## Criticisms and Limits of Social Planning

Criticisms of prototypical social planning are that it assumes a unified view of the public interest and a consensus on goals or means to solve problems. Davidoff (1965) points out that such planning is typically top-down and unitary, meaning only one agency in a community is responsible for comprehensive planning. Davidoff advocates pluralistic planning by involving other community agencies and citizens. He further notes that social planning is not devoid of values and that these should be clear to the planners as well as citizens. In pluralistic planning, advocacy is practiced by professional planners on behalf of clients and communities, compelling planners to deal with political considerations.

Another criticism involves the methodology of social planning. Collecting and analyzing data consumes time and resources. Using data to reflect a social problem requires a frame of reference, and planners may view the same data and come to divergent conclusions about the data as well as the situation. Moreover, having a plan does not necessarily mean it will be implemented.

Social planning is decontextualized. It takes place within contexts, such as public management networks. As these networks share information, build capacity, develop strategies, formulate policy, and modify programs, social planning becomes less straightforward and more politicized. The *Garbage Can Model of Decision Making*, described by March and Olsen (1976), points out how decisions are influenced by a variety of stakeholders and interest groups (for example, neighborhood councils, community groups, business associations, other agencies from various government entities), whose input arrives at different times, affecting saliency, and profoundly impacting decisions. These nontechnical factors preclude rationality in the planning process.

Moreover, Rittel and Webber (1973) point out that social planning typically addresses "wicked problems." Wicked problems are ill-defined, unique, intractable, and never solved, and resolutions repeatedly emanate from furtive political reasoning. Furthermore, wicked problems are usually symptoms of other problems and confounded by the systemic nature of society, its complexity, and increasing pluralism.

## Methods of Social Planners

The fundamental methods of social planning are rational and data-related. There are numerous approaches to rational problem-solving, but all basically begin with identifying the issue or problem, setting priorities, analyzing the problem or situation, setting objectives, developing alternatives to achieve the objectives, anticipating obstacles and adverse consequences associated with alternatives, and choosing the best alternatives to achieve the optimum solution.

As part of this rational problem-solving process, social planners employ need assessments, systems analyses,

linear programming, integer programming, evaluation, experiments, and quasi-experimental designs, queuing theory, Markov chains, simulations, gaming theory, Monte Carlo techniques, cost-benefit analyses, Delphi and Nominal Group techniques, Q methodology, P sets, repertory grids, and panoplies of statistical applications (see Morcol, 2007).

### Participation and Social Planning

Participatory planning is an important value of social work and requires a "strong commitment to plan with rather than for people in communities" (Weil, 2005, p. 219). However, social planning typically originates from bureaucracies with formal rules, chains of command, professional cadres, and a penchant for efficiency. Chaskin (2005) documents the inherent tension in bringing together bureaucratic sponsoring organizations such as foundations and formal service agencies, on one hand, and citizens and voluntary groups, on the other. Nevertheless, the advantages of incorporating participation in the social planning process include a deeper and often different understanding of the nature of a community or target population, as well as their definition and framing of the problem and views concerning solutions.

### Current Trends in Social Planning

One of the interesting trends in contemporary social planning is geographic information systems (GIS). GIS has emerged as a widespread approach for managing information, and for storing and interpreting data. According to the department of the interior, 97% of local governments with populations greater than 100,000 and 88% of those with populations between 50,000 and 100,000 use GIS (Haque, 2007). It is so important that the federal government has created the National Spatial Data Infrastructure and the Federal Geographic Information Committee.

The application of GIS technology permits digital mapping and multidimensional graphs of social, political, economic, and physical phenomena. For example, GIS maps can reveal shifting demographics, growth trends, socioeconomic status, crime rates, and susceptibility to earthquakes, floods, fires, environmental hazards, pollution, harmful landfills, and transportation availability in relation to job opportunities and so on. With GIS social planners can study racial, ethnic, and economic factors in a specific area, or study the proximity of crime, drug use, HIV clients, and employment opportunities in a particular city, state, region, country, continent, or any part of the world (Haque, 2007).

GIS spatial mapping helps the planner improve social service delivery systems, evaluate programs, locate service areas, and organize service delivery. GIS is typically used in target-based intervention planning, such as identifying the most deficient neighborhoods of school children by age and nutrition.

Because so many governments are so enthralled with and rely on GIS, practitioners have developed collaborative practices and actively seek community involvement. A new methodology known as public participation geographic information systems (PPGIS) has been used to allow local community members to participate in decisions that affect them. Such involvement may involve the scale of analysis, identification of needs, access to information, and influencing how the GIS information is compiled, presented, and used (Haque, 2007).

Spatial mismatch is an area of social planning that tends to focus on the segregation of racial, ethnic, sexual, age, occupational, and poverty sectors or segments that emerge from a lack of opportunities in urban areas due to the spatial distribution of people (Poon, Button, & Nijkamp, 2006). The spatial distribution of various groups (for example, racial, ethnic, elderly) affects economic opportunities through spatial mobility, as well as through social relationships in social networks.

Sustainable development (SD) is another advance in social planning. Sustainable development involves the recognition that social conditions affect the ecological and socioeconomic sustainability of urban areas, communities, and regions. In SD, social planners attempt to address issues such as the desirability of urban sprawl in contrast to compact cities or the benefits of economic growth versus the costs of environmental degradation. Other areas of interest in SD involve poverty, international trade, agriculture, and so forth. In practice, there is little consensus about what SD means; the strategies to achieve SD are often contradictory, and the impact appears to serve political expediency, rather than thoughtful, rigorous interventions (Lele, 2006).

The social organization approach attempts to examine regional and urban concerns that constrain or support social opportunities (Poon et al., 2006). Here, the focus is on how social and human capital shape urban social infrastructure. As regions and cities become more complex, social planning needs to become more inclusive of diverse social groupings, as well as expand the social categories by which a society is understood and programs and services planned.

## Implications for Social Work

With the growing interest in GIS, spatial mismatch, and other advances in social planning technologies, the need for social workers who engage in social planning has become increasingly important. However, the number of social workers engaged in all phases of social service administration is declining drastically (Wuenschel, 2006). Without social workers, the current resurgence of social planning is dominated by individuals from disciplines that may or may not share social work values.

Organizations such as the Association for Community Organization and Social Administration (www.acosa.org) and Planners Network (www.plannersnetwork.org) are promoting the participatory and political dimensions of planning as part of social work and urban planning respectively.

### REFERENCES

Chaskin, R. J. (2005). Democracy and bureaucracy in a community planning process. *Journal of Planning, Education and Research, 24,* 408–419.

Davidoff, P. (1965). Advocacy and pluralism in planning. *Journal of the American Institute of Planners, 31,* 331–337.

Gilbert, N., & Specht, H. (1977). *Planning for social welfare: Issues, models and tasks.* Englewood Cliffs, NJ: Prentice-Hall.

Haque, A. (2007). Decision making in geographic information systems. In G. Morcol (Ed.), *Handbook of decision making* (pp. 525–536). New York: CRC Press, Taylor & Francis Group.

Hardina, D. (2002) *Analytical skills for community organizing practice.* New York: Columbia University Press.

Lele, S. M. (2006). Sustainable development: A critical review. In J. P. H. Poon, K. Button, & P. Nijkamp (Eds.), *Social planning* (pp. 139–153). Northampton, MA: Edward Elgar.

Lindblom, C. E. (1959). The science of "muddling through." *Public Administration Review, 19*(2), 79–88.

March, J. G., & Olsen, J. P. (1976). *Ambiguity and choice in organizations.* Bergen, Norway: Universitetsforlaget.

Morcol, G. (Ed.). (2007). *Handbook of decision making.* New York: CRC Press, Taylor & Francis Group.

Poon, J. P. H., Button, K., & Nijkamp, P. (Eds.). (2006). *Social planning.* Northampton, MA: Edward Elgar.

Rittel, W. J., & Webber, M. M. (1973). Dilemmas in a general theory of planning. *Policy Sciences, 4*(2), 155–169.

Rothman, J. (in press). Multi models of community intervention. In J. Rothman, J. L. Erlich, & J. E. Tropman (Eds.), *Strategies of community intervention* (7th ed.). Peosta, IA: Eddie Bowers.

Simon, H. A. (1955). A behavioral model of rational choice. *Quarterly Journal of Economics, 69,* 99–118.

Weil, M. (2005). Social planning with communities: Theory and practice. In M. Weil (Ed.), *The handbook of community practice* (pp. 215–243). Thousand Oaks, CA: Sage.

Wuenschel, P. C. (2006). The diminishing role of social work administrators in social service agencies: Issues for consideration. *Administration in Social Work, 30*(4), 5–18.

SUGGESTED LINKS

American Planning Association.
  *http://www.planning.org/*
Association of Collegiate School of Planning.
  *http://www.acsp.org/*
Cyburbia Forums.
  *http://www.cyburbia.org/*
The National Association of Planning Councils.
  *http://www.communityplanning.org*
Urban Planning Research.
  *http://planningresearch.blogspot.com/*
Planners Network.
  *http://www.plannersnetwork.org/*

—JON SIMON SAGER

**SOCIAL POLICY.** [*This entry contains five subentries:* Overview; History (Colonial Times to 1900); History (1900–1950); History (1950–1980); History (1980 to Present).]

## OVERVIEW

ABSTRACT: Social policy may be defined as any formal government enactment that affects the well-being of people, including laws, regulations, executive orders, and court decisions. In the United States, with its federal tradition of shared government, social policies are made by governments at many levels—local, state, and national. A broad view of social policy recognizes that corporations and nonprofit and for-profit social service agencies also develop policies that affect customers and those they serve and therefore have social implications. Social policies affect society and human behavior, and their importance for social work practice has long been understood by the social work profession. Modern social welfare policies have changed dramatically since their introduction in the New Deal of the 1930s. Today, the idea that the state should guarantee the welfare and well-being of its citizens through a progressive welfare state has few adherents among policymakers. The complex social realities of the globalized marketplace, escalating budget deficits, an intractable war in Iraq, threats to national security from terrorism, and a resurgence of beliefs that the solution to poverty lies in changing the behaviors of the poor, requiring work for short-term assistance, are reflected in our social policies. Social workers, long committed to the ideal of social justice for all, are obligated to understand how policies affect their practice as well as the lives of those they serve and to advocate for policies that will improve social well-being.

KEY WORDS: social policy; welfare; globalization

### Definitions

Social policies are created and function in dynamic social, economic, and cultural environments. In the postindustrial society, ideas and interests continually emerge about what kinds of policies are needed to address social problems and human needs.

The concept *social welfare* refers broadly to what is needed to provide people with resources and opportunities to lead satisfying and productive lives (Midgley, Tracy, & Livermore, 2000). A broad array of economic and social policies affect social welfare, ranging from tax policy to educational policy. More narrowly, students of social policy have often focused on policies and programs that provide income assistance and social services to people in need. Conservatives have generally supported "residual" time-limited social welfare policies and services while liberals have argued for "universal" or "institutional" social welfare policies that provide assistance to citizens as communal rights. Institutional social welfare polices adopted by European "welfare states" never received much political support in the United States, where residual programs providing limited assistance to those seen as having genuine needs were favored (Patterson, 2000). Poverty, unemployment, dependent children, family instability, inadequate health care, and the needs of the elderly have been targets of social welfare policies.

Socially constructed family and gender norms influence social policy and the lives of beneficiaries. Traditions of public debate and discourse encourage interest groups to lobby for policies that will advantage their members. Some critics argue that the corporate and business sectors have become so powerful that they dominate policymaking, making government less responsive to social needs (Rauch, 1995). Sometimes policies enacted to benefit special interests produce disastrous social results. For example, opening public lands to the oil, timber, and mineral corporations has harmed people and the environment (Gore, 2007). Foreign policy also has social impact. During the Cold War in the second half of the 20th century, social policy enforced family norms and supported growth of a strong workforce that would enable the United States to compete for international economic hegemony. In the early 21st century, in the wake of the terrorist attacks on the United States on September 11, 2001, the expansion of homeland security and the controversial and inconclusive war in Iraq have consumed resources that might have been used to develop or expand social welfare programs such as access to health care for the millions of Americans without health insurance. The escalating U.S. national debt and the demands of the competitive, globalized marketplace have adversely affected the industrial U.S. workforce, as U.S. corporations seek cheaper labor and land outside the United States (Blau, 1999). After the terrorist attacks of 9/11, the federal government enacted new security policies that gave government officials the right to curtail civil liberties, which some believe have abrogated constitutional freedoms. Given the range and relative importance of policy choices, social policies must compete with economic, political, and defense policies for attention and resources. At least since the presidency of the Republican conservative Ronald Reagan, government policies and programs directed at public social welfare provision have been attacked as ineffectual and inappropriate interferences in the marketplace. Social policies that transferred and redistributed income from the wealthy to the poor, such as programs assisting poor women with families, were harshly criticized. Efforts have been made to privatize social services and the Social Security system, our most universal social welfare program. Our political parties continue to debate how our nation can promote economic growth and social well-being while recognizing that human need and poverty must be addressed.

## Philosophical Underpinnings of U.S. Social Policy

The notion of citizenship carries specific rights and obligations. Individualism, personal liberty, and the rights of persons to pursue activities freely and without excessive governmental intrusion are hallmarks of U.S. political philosophy, and they inform policymaking. Political and social conservatives generally support limited government and private activities to promote social well-being or social welfare, while liberals, recognizing that social conditions often limit people's ability to be self-sufficient, have supported the use of government authority (Ginsberg, 1998). The radical left and progressive critics generally reject both conservative and liberal social policy perspectives because they believe that social inequality and social problems can be resolved most effectively by active social planning and government redistribution of wealth (Roth, 2002).

## Social Policy Development

During the Progressive Era, Jane Addams and other reformers argued that government had obligations to protect poor women and children who were seen as victims of industrialization. Despite opposition from business and from organized labor, "maternalist" reform achieved some success. Many states enacted mothers' pensions that provided limited cash support to women and children in dire economic need (Gordon, 1994), as well as categorical assistance programs targeted at

specific groups—the elderly and the blind. These programs were administered locally with few consistent standards used to determine eligibility or payment levels, allowing local prejudices and biases about who were "worthy" recipients (Abramovitz, 1996).

Skocpol (1998) has argued that social policy analysis must recognize how political and institutional forces influence policy choices and the administration of services and benefits as evidenced by mothers' pensions and contemporary social welfare programs. Progressive Era Workers' Compensation laws provided income support to injured workers and were supported by conservative businessmen who realized that it was better that the state aid injured workers than to subject business to the uncertainties of injured workers' negligence lawsuits and unpredictable jury verdicts.

Modern social welfare policy began with the New Deal enacted in the 1930s during the administration of the liberal Democrat Franklin D. Roosevelt in response to the Great Depression and unprecedented unemployment and social unrest. Policymakers understood that private charities, voluntary organizations, and local and state governments were unable to provide enough economic assistance to address the needs of millions of people who were unemployed. Nearly one third of private social service agencies ceased operations between 1919 and 1932 (Trattner, 1999). The federal government assumed unprecedented authority to intervene in the economy, resulting in controversy and opposition from conservatives who felt New Deal policy innovations were unwarranted intrusions by government into the lives of Americans. The most sweeping New Deal social welfare legislation, the Social Security Act of 1935, created new social insurance and public assistance programs. Social insurance included unemployment insurance and the Social Security pension program and Old Age, Survivors, and Disability Insurance financed by payroll taxes on employees and employers. Public assistance (or welfare) was limited to the most needy and was administered by local governments, which often denied benefits to persons of color.

Progressive and radical critics, including some social workers, felt that the liberal reforms of the New Deal did not go far enough in addressing social inequality and the needs of working Americans and argued for national planning and an institutional welfare state to distribute national wealth and end poverty (Reynolds, 1951; Selmi, 2005).

American social welfare grew incrementally, subject to political pressures and changing priorities, and never adopted the progressive vision. While the Social Security pension program expanded over the years to include agricultural workers and others not originally covered, many of whom were people of color living in the South, it was influenced by contemporary gender and racial norms. Although it has provided a measure of economic security for retired workers who earned high incomes for many years, it disadvantaged women workers, who because of home and family responsibilities were unable to work outside the home for extended periods, resulting in smaller contributions to Social Security and reduced pensions (Abramovitz, 1996).

Social welfare policy and programs were expanded in liberal President Johnson's Great Society of the 1960s. Medicare and Medicaid provided health insurance for retired workers and medical assistance for the poor. Although the Social Security pension system has been successful in reducing poverty among elderly workers and has widespread public support, its public assistance or welfare programs have been controversial. Both the New Deal Aid to Dependent Children program, which assisted children, and its successor, Aid to Families with Dependent Children (AFDC), which began in 1962, offered residual "means tested" cash assistance to the poor, financed by the federal government and the states, and administered locally. Between 1960 and 1967, welfare roles doubled, encouraging critics to argue that welfare was being abused by "cheats" and "unworthy" recipients, many of whom were people of color. A Work Incentive program, WIN, which required work from AFDC recipients, began a long retreat from support for dependent women and families. Conservatives went on the offensive against liberal welfare policies. Public opinion was galvanized against social welfare programs by using gender and racial stereotypes to stigmatize welfare recipients as indolent and irresponsible. Single African American mothers receiving AFDC assistance were denigrated and called "welfare queens" (Gilons, 1994; Quadagno, 1994). In 1995, President Clinton, a Democrat, campaigned to "end welfare as we know it" (Rector, 1997) and collaborated with the conservative Republican legislators who took control of Congress in 1994, to pass The Personal Responsibility and Work Opportunity Reconciliation Act (PRWORA) of 1996, abolishing AFDC and ending the federal entitlement to public assistance that had existed since the New Deal. In its place, the new Temporary Assistance to Needy Families program gave states "block grants" to establish welfare assistance programs consistent with changing social priorities. New rules required work from recipients and limited cash assistance to 5 years. The 1998 Workforce Investment Act required welfare recipients to seek work before receiving social services which was criticized by social workers as ignoring the needs of women and children who needed long-term assistance and supportive services. By 2005, the number of persons receiving public assistance was half of what it had been in the 1990s. Although it is certain that many single mothers and others left the welfare roles, whether or not they have achieved economic and social self-sufficiency is debatable. Securing employment with employers who provide low wages and few, if any, benefits, such as health insurance, does not provide a decent standard of living or good job security. There is clear evidence of large increases in the numbers of those receiving Medicaid and Food Stamps since 1996, supporting the argument that former welfare recipients have joined the ranks of the working poor, struggling to obtain decent housing, medical care, and food for their families (Shipler, 2004). Policymakers face ongoing dilemmas as they attempt to promote work, decrease dependency, and alleviate need among the most needy members of American society (Grogger & Karoly, 2005).

Research shows that for the poor to become self-sufficient they need support that will provide for their basic needs so that they can engage in learning to acquire skills to obtain good jobs (Andersson, Holzer, & Lane, 2005; Austin, 2004) Today, there are many training and temporary assistance programs offered by social workers and others working in government, nonprofit, and for-profit agencies that can assist those transitioning from welfare to work by matching them to supportive programs, including medical assistance, housing, and child care (Popple & Leighninger, 2001). A "pluralist" model of social welfare provision that integrates government programs with nonprofit and for-profit agencies and community resources has evolved. Funded from many sources, including federal and local governments, foundations, philanthropists, and private citizens, today's social services offer assistance targeted to meet specific needs, reminiscent of "residual" models of social welfare.

Assaults on Social Security, our most large-scale and institutional social welfare program, have continued under the administration of President George W. Bush, a conservative Republican. He proposed privatizing Social Security, a market solution by giving workers options to invest in individual retirement accounts that could allow greater financial returns than those promised by Social Security (Herrick & Midgley, 2002). President Bush favored state and charitable solutions rather than federal social welfare programs. He proposed the faith-based and community initiative that would permit federal funding for faith-based community services, based on the premise that local service providers can deliver the most humane and cost-effective human services. Although the Initiative was not enacted by Congress, he used his executive authority to fund an array of nonprofit faith-based social services (Smith, 2007), illustrating how a socially conservative administration can devolve responsibility for human services to religious institutions in keeping with his belief on the impact of faith on behavior.

## The Future of U.S. Social Policy

Ongoing attempts by conservatives to alter Social Security, our most basic and universal social welfare program, reflect the strength of belief that the free market, unfettered by constrictive social welfare policies, can best respond to human needs by offering short-term assistance when necessary and more important, opportunities to acquire the skills necessary to succeed in the globalized marketplace. American history has been replete with examples of the collision of market-oriented values and policies with policies supportive of liberal welfare state programs. Today's globalized marketplace, with its emphasis on technological innovation, requires a nimble and skilled workforce as the United States downsizes industries where it has lost economic advantage and outsources jobs to reduce labor costs. Labor unions, once a powerful force supporting progressive social policies, have lost membership and influence (Polzin, 2005).

The traditional liberal response to unemployment has been to provide education and training programs to promote job readiness but these efforts do not produce immediate results, leaving laid-off workers with uncertainties. As the labor market changes, residual social policy responses do not address increasing inequality in the United States (Krugman, 1999). Low-income jobs, often taken by single women with children, once supported by welfare, contribute to the wage gender gap (Kuttner, 2002). In the United States, the gap between the rich and the rest of its citizens is growing. CEOs of major corporations earn hundreds of times more than their workers (Anderson, Cavanagh, Collins, Pizzigati, & Lapham, 2007). Furthermore, the share of total national income earned by an increasingly smaller percentage of persons is growing. In 2005, the top 1% of Americans received 21.2% of all U.S. income (Inequality.org, 2007). Tax policies have provided some relief to the working poor through the Earned Income Tax Credit but the middle class and the wealthy have benefited far more under the tax code as income has been redistributed upward in a social sense.

Globalization has exacerbated social inequalities worldwide (Chomsky, 2000).The United Nations University, World Institute for Development Economics Research (2005) found that in 2000 1% of the world's population owned 40% of global assets and that half of the world's adults owned only 1% of its wealth.

Some argue for progressive policies that alter social structures to reduce social, racial, and gender inequalities by giving people more power and control over government decision-making (Bates, 2007; Chomsky, 2000) Others support pushback from the rush toward globalization, pointing out that although it has produced immense wealth for some nations and individuals, millions of others in the United States and worldwide have been left behind and their needs cannot be ignored (Bates, 2007).

## Roles of Social Workers

Social workers, concerned about social justice, may find that this inequality is not supportive of long-term social welfare and international peace. International social work is addressing these needs with innovative policies and programs, including social development strategies such as microcredit enterprises that have enabled the poor to become economically self-sufficient. These programs may serve as models for innovative and effective service delivery in the United States (Midgley, 1995).There are many promising signs that social work will continue to work for sound social policies and creative approaches to service delivery (Social Work Speaks, 2006).

Across the country, social workers have been elected to local, state, and federal positions, including the U.S. House of representatives and the Senate. The National Association of Social Workers both nationally and through its state chapters engages in lobbying to influence social policy development and sharing knowledge of how current policies respond to human needs. Social work educators, students, and practitioners engage in advocacy for social policies to assist women, children, AIDS victims, prisoners reentering society, victims of abuse, the homeless, and others in need. Social workers have the knowledge, skills, and values to be strong advocates for the poor (Marsh, 2005; Schneider, 2000), continuing the social action begun long ago by social work pioneers such as Jane Addams, Bertha Reynolds, and Whitney Young. As the debate continues about the privatization of public goods such as public social services and programs, social workers will be challenged to continue their dedication to reduction of social injustice and social inequality.

### REFERENCES

Abramovitz, M. (1996). *Regulating the lives of women: Social welfare policy from colonial times to the present* (rev. ed.). Boston: South End Press.

Anderson, S., Cavanagh, J., Collins, C., Pizzigati, S., & Lapham, M. (2007). *Executive excess 2007: The staggering cost of U.S. business leadership.* Washington, DC, and

Boston: Institute for policy Studies and United for a Fair Economy.

Andersson, F., Holzer, H., & Lane, J. (2005). *Moving up or moving on: Who advances in the low wage labor market.* New York: Russell Sage Foundation.

Austin, M. (2004). *Changing welfare services: Case studies in local welfare reform programs.* Binghamton, NY: Haworth Press.

Bates, J. (2000). *Globalization, poverty and inequality.* Washington, DC: Progressive Policy Institute.

Blau, J. (1999). *Illusions of prosperity: America's working families in an age of economic insecurity.* New York: Oxford University Press.

Chomsky, N. (2000). *Profit over people: Neoliberalism and global order.* New York: Seven Stories Press.

Gilons, M. (1994). "Race coding" and white opposition to welfare. *American Political Science Review, 90,* 593–604.

Ginsberg, L. (2002). *Conservative social welfare policy: A description and analysis.* Chicago: Nelson-Hall.

Gordon, L. (1994). *Pitied but not forgotten: Single mothers and the history of welfare.* New York: Free Press.

Gore, A. (2007). *The assault on reason.* New York: Penguin.

Grogger, J., & Karoly, L. (2005). *Welfare reform: Effects of a decade of change.* Cambridge, MA: Harvard University Press.

Herrick, J., & Midgley, J. (2002). The United States. In J. Dixon & R. Scheurell (Eds.), *The state of social welfare: The twentieth century in cross-national review* (pp. 187–216). Westport, CT: Praeger.

Krugman, P. (1999). *The return of Depression economics.* New York: Norton.

Kuttner, R. (Ed.). (2002). *Making work pay: America after Welfare.* New York: The New Press.

Marsh, J. (2005). Social justice: Social work's organizing value. *Social Work, 50*(4), 293–294.

Midgley, J. (1995). *Social development: The developmental perspective in social welfare.* Thousand Oaks, CA: Sage.

Midgley, J., Tracy, M., & Livermore, M. (Eds.). (2000). *The handbook of social policy.* Thousand Oaks, CA: Sage.

Patterson, J. (2000). *America's struggle against poverty in the twentieth century.* Cambridge, MA: Harvard University Press.

Polzin, M. (2005). Labor movement and social welfare (United States). In J. Herrick & P. Stuart (Eds.), *The encyclopedia of social welfare history in North America* (pp. 213–216). Thousand Oaks, CA: Sage.

Popple, P., & Leighninger, L. (2001). *Social work, social welfare, and American society* (5th ed.). Boston: Allyn & Bacon.

Quadagno, J. (1994). *The color of welfare.* New York: Oxford University Press.

Rauch, J. (1995). *Demosclerosis: The silent killer of American government.* New York: Three Rivers Press.

Rector, R. (1997). Welfare reform is necessary. In D. Bender et al. (Eds.), *Welfare reform* (pp. 45–80). San Diego: Greenhaven Press.

Reynolds, B. (1951). *Social work and social living: Explorations in philosophy and practice.* New York: Citadel.

Roth, W. (2002). *The assault on social policy.* New York: Columbia University Press.

Schneider, R. (2000). *Social work advocacy.* New York: Wadsworth.

Selmi, P. (2005). Mary van Kleeck. In J. Herrick & P. Stuart (Eds.), *Encyclopedia of social welfare history* (pp. 413–415). Thousand Oaks, CA: Sage.

Shipler, D. (2004). *The working poor, invisible in America.* New York: Alfred A. Knopf.

Smith, S. (2007). Social services and social policy. *Society, 44*(3), 54–59.

*Social work speaks* (7th ed.). (2006). Washington, DC: National Association of Social Workers.

Trattner, W. (1999). *From Poor Law to the welfare state: A history of social welfare in America* (6th ed.). New York: The Free Press.

United Nations University, World Institute for Development Economics Research. (2005). World economic income inequality database. http://www.wider.unu.edu/wiid/wiid.htm

## FURTHER READING

Beland, D. (2005). *Social security: History and politics from the New Deal to the privatization debates.* Lawrence: University Press of Kansas.

Etzioni, A., & Marsh, J. (Eds.). (2003). *Rights vs. public safety after 9/11: America in the age of terrorism.* Lanham, MD: Rowman and Littlefield.

Funigiello, P. (2005). *Chronic politics: Health care security from FDR to George W. Bush.* Lawrence: University Press of Kansas.

Gilbert, N. (2004). *Transformation of the Welfare State: The silent surrender of public responsibility.* New York: Oxford University Press.

Kilty, K., & Segal, E. (Eds.). (2003). *Rediscovering the other America: The continuing crisis of poverty and inequality in the United States.* New York: Haworth.

Middlestadt, J. (2005). *From welfare to workfare: the Unintended consequences of liberal reform, 1945–1965.* Chapel Hill: University of North Carolina Press.

Mullaly, B. (1997). *Structural social work: Ideology, theory, and practice* (2nd ed.). New York: Oxford University Press.

Noble, C. (1997). *Welfare as we knew it.* New York: Oxford University Press.

Pimpare, S. (2004). *The new Victorians: Poverty, politics and propaganda in two Gilded Ages.* New York: The New Press.

Quadagno, J. (2005). *One nation uninsured: Why the U.S. has no national health insurance.* New York: Oxford University Press.

Skocpol, T. (1998). The limits of the New Deal system and the roots of contemporary welfare dilemmas. In M. Weir, A. Orloff, & T. Skocpol (Eds.), *The politics of social policy in the United States* (pp. 293–312). Princeton, NJ: Princeton University Press.

Sosin, M., & Smith, S. (2006). New responsibilities for faith-related agencies. *The Policies Studies Journal, 34*(4), 533–562.

Stoesz, D. (1996). *Small change: Domestic policy under the Clinton presidency.* White Plains, NY: Longman.

Stoesz, D. (2005). *Quixote's ghost: The right, the liberati, and the future of social policy.* New York: Oxford University Press.

U.S. Census Bureau. (2006). *Income, poverty and health insurance coverage in the United States: 2005.* Washington, DC: Government Printing Office.

### SUGGESTED LINKS

Center for Law and Social Policy.
  *http://www.clasp.org/*
The Urban Institute.
  *http://www.urban.org/*
Center for Social policy, Poverty and Homelessness Research at the John W. McCormack Graduate School of policy Studies, University of Massachusetts, Boston.
  *http://www.mccormack.umb.edu/csp/index.jsp*
Progressive Policy Institute.
  *http://www.ppionline.org*
Weiner Center for Social Policy, John F. Kennedy School of Government, Harvard University. Research on social problems and social policy.
  *http://www.ksg.harvard.edu/socpol/*
The Association for Policy Analysis and Management.
  *http://www.appam.org*
Conservative social welfare policy. www.intellectualconservative.com, for an article by Bruce Thyer, a conservative Professor of Social Work at the University of Florida.
U.S. Government Sites: the Social Security Administration.
  *www.ssa.gov/; the Census Bureau,*
  *www.census.gov/*
National Association of Social Workers.
  *http://www.socialworkersa.org*

—JOHN M. HERRICK

## HISTORY (COLONIAL TIMES TO 1900)

ABSTRACT: American social welfare began in the colonial period with the adoption of the Elizabethan Poor Laws as the basis for treatment of society's poor and deviant. By the beginning of the Progressive Era (1900), immigration, the Women's Movement, scientific investigation of social problems, and societal growth produced significant innovations in both public and private perceptions, programs, and treatment in such areas as poor relief, mental and physical health, and corrections, and led to the beginnings of professionalization of social work.

KEY WORDS: Charity Organization Society; Child-Saving Movement; Elizabethan Poor Laws; friendly visitors; protestant work ethic; Settlement House Movement

### Colonial Social Welfare: 1607–1776

The few French and Spanish settlements of colonial America followed the European Catholic charity traditions of aiding the poor through almsgiving, shelter, health care, and so on, while English colonists imported the harsher Elizabethan Poor Laws and the Protestant Work Ethic, which equated work with morality and deemed the poor immoral, denying them any kind of charity unless they worked in return.

As early as 1632, town authorities assigned "overseers of the poor" to investigate poverty and problems such as physical and mental disabilities, crime, or vagrancy. Their tasks were to assess need, collect and distribute funds (from a combination of taxes, private donations, church collections), and decide the fates of needy or deviant townspeople (Day, 2006, pp. 144–146). Work was required of all, and so almsgiving (poor relief) was meager, since people believed that it discouraged work and contributed to immorality. War veterans were exceptions: from as early as 1616, they, their survivors, and their dependents were allotted pensions, and by 1777 almost every colony had veterans' benefits (Compton, 1980, p. 198).

The Poor Laws categorized public dependents as worthy or impotent poor (aged or mentally or physically impaired) and perhaps deserving of aid; unworthy poor (sturdy beggars—able-bodied adults in poverty); and dependent children—poor, unwanted, abandoned, or orphaned. Laws requiring family and local responsibility for public dependents were passed in 1662 and 1675, respectively. The Law of Settlement (1662) required towns to supply food, firewood, clothing, and household essentials for their poor. But alternatives were also used for penalties, which ranged from stocks and pillory to whippings and tar and feathering; "warning out," which warned strangers that they could expect no help if they entered town, and warned residents that if they had no incomes they could be indentured or forced from the community to other towns or to die in the forests; auctioning whole families or individuals to work for their keep; placing them in prisons, workhouses, or almshouses; and hanging. Dependent children usually shared their parents' fates, though they may also be placed in almshouses, orphanages, or apprenticeship; or auctioned off ("sold") to families, work schools, and factories. Some work was demanded of children as young as 3 years (Grob, 1976, p. 6–7).

The most popular solution was for the local authorities to place all public dependents (those who had no means to support themselves or their children and so had to depend on local governments for food, shelter, clothing, and so forth) in institutions, which included almshouses, workhouses, orphanages, asylums, and prisons, as soon as they could afford them. All emphasized work rehabilitation, but their purposes were primarily to control or warehouse society's unwanted. Inmates were not segregated based on sex, age, or reason for incarceration—crime, poverty, insanity, age, or physical disability. Local administrators were paid "by the head," and care and sustenance depended on keepers' largesse, inmates' ability to pay, or kindness from other inmates. Thousands died from a combination of starvation, freezing, epidemics, lack of medical care, and violent deaths, but this was acceptable because it rid towns of "social burdens" (Grob, 1976, pp. 6–7, 48–53).

### Policies Concerning Poverty and Dependency

Institutionalization ("indoor relief"), meager poor relief, and individual responsibility for subsistence remained unchanged well into the 1700s. Toward mid-century, the Enlightenment and evangelical religious movements (1730–1750) aroused interest in the causes and remedies of social problems, especially poverty. The Revolutionary War had little effect on attitudes and policies toward the poor, but the Enlightenment that accompanied it brought attention to their needs, especially for children. Catholic charities and Quakers began to open orphanages both for children without parents and unwanted children, including African American children, and expanded charitable work into local work in communities. Philanthropists founded schools for blind and deaf children and began to investigate lack of employment, drunkenness, ill health, and other causes for public dependency. Mill work, especially in the South, became placements for women and poor children, and more poorhouses and old age homes were opened. Although the poor were still blamed for not overcoming their poverty through work, for the first time critics looked at sociostructural problems as causative.

In 1818, a report by the Society for the Prevention of Pauperism blamed these problems on drunkenness and work immorality, the belief that not working was in itself immoral. This position was reiterated in an 1824 report by New York's Secretary of State John V. N. Yates (see Yates, 1900) and again in 1832 by John Tuckerman, who began a ministry to the poor in that era. Each report generally condemned outdoor relief and made several recommendations: division of cities into wards for welfare administration; community-wide planned giving through a central agency; private rather than public charities for temporary poor relief distribution; and trained "friendly visitors" (later to become social workers) to investigate need and distribute alms, advice, and moral support. The reports also recommended employment bureaus, savings banks, mutual aid societies, and insurance programs to address employment hazards (a forerunner of today's later workers' compensation programs) (Compton, 1980, p. 236).

### Other Social Welfare Policy Areas

Physical and public health problems, mental illness, crime and delinquency, and the need for public education were areas that states and localities began to tackle along with private charity. All these were aggravated by the growing immigrant population that arrived during different periods in the 18th and 19th centuries.

As early as 1647, Massachusetts legislated public schools, and free schools proliferated in the 1700s. By 1802 some states ordered overseers of the poor to set up free education for poor children, and the Catholic Church opened free schools beginning in 1809. New York legislated a 3 months' school year in 1812, and Massachusetts increased its school year to 9 months in 1852. Drs. John Sanford and T. Gallaudet, among others, began work with blind and deaf children as early as 1817, and this led John Fisher and Samuel Howe to establish in 1819 what would become Perkins Institute. In 1846 Perkins expanded to offer treatment and education for developmentally disabled children.

Compulsory education was one solution to the growing numbers of unsupervised and undisciplined children who contributed to the crime and chaos in many cities. Another solution was the Reformatory movement, led by the Society for Reformation for Juvenile Delinquents, which in 1825 opened the House of Refuge, a combined prison, factory, and school. These institutions emerged throughout the states, with reformatories for boys opened in 1847, and a cottage system for girls opening in 1854. With new research, the emphasis on work and education rather than punishment as rehabilitation made New York's Elmira Reformatory, established in 1870, a model for others (Platt, 1977, p. 73). Along with elements of prevention of cruelty to children, the child-saving movement was derived from the belief that poverty was genetic but that children could be saved if taken from bad environments and placed in homes where they could learn the value of hard work. Child-savers took children from parents whom they deemed "bad," often because they were poor, or even kidnapped them from city streets and put them on trains to the West. At each stop, some were chosen by local people to work on farms, often to death, though some found happy homes. The reformatory and child-saving movements both worked for children's legal rights, and one result was that in 1869, state agents were appointed to ensure fair court trials of delinquents and take responsibility for children's probation.

For adults, colonial workhouses were the original prisons. Boston built the first House of Correction in 1660 for criminals and the able-bodied poor, and over the next century they spread throughout the colonies, evolving into prisons. Not until 1776 did the workhouse concept change, as Quakers theorized that penitence for deviance could be achieved through silence and solitary confinement. Their belief led them to open penitentiaries, where the able-bodied poor, debtors, and vagrants, as well as criminals, would work hard, pray, and meditate on the error of their ways, and receive rehabilitation rather than punishment. Their first penitentiary opened in 1823, and their innovations appeared in later institutions such as Sing Sing (New York, 1825) and San Quentin (California, 1852). In the last half of the century, new architectural designs provided more efficient supervision, and rehabilitation became the treatment goal. Probation for those convicted of lesser crimes began in 1852, under Isaac Hopper, who informally helped discharged prisoners, and Boston's John Augustus, who, in agreement with the courts, supervised people who committed minor offenses, and posted their bail rather than see them imprisoned. With his own money he provided rehabilitation for them, and became a model for social workers in the field of probation.

Mental and physical illness, including public health issues, became humanitarian concerns before and after the country was founded. Though in 1676 Massachusetts enacted a law instructing towns to provide care and protect the public, for the next century most mentally ill people had little or no care, whether left with their families or placed in almshouses. Disturbed by such inhumane treatment, in 1755 Thomas Bond and Benjamin Franklin secured room for the mentally ill in the cellar of the Philadelphia hospital they founded. The first colony-wide mental hospital opened in Virginia in 1769, and in 1783, Dr. Benjamin Rush developed "moral treatment" for the insane, which became the prototype for future asylums (Compton, 1980, p. 76). The Marine Hospitals Service (later the Department of Public Health) opened the first medical school (1765) and first federal public health program (1789) (Day, 2006, p. 235). As early as 1791 in New York's general hospitals often had areas set aside for the mentally ill. Not until 1870 did the first state hospital open (Willard). When Bellevue opened in 1906, it developed a medical social work unit to help patients and outpatients, including the mentally ill.

IMMIGRATION AND SOCIAL WELFARE Massive immigration in the mid-19th century brought vast numbers of the ill, unemployed, and destitute to the United States and overwhelmed local almshouses. Most of them came from Ireland after the potato famines of the 1850s. New York City turned the whole of Ward's Island into a hospital, refuge for the unemployable, and nursery and school for orphans and unwanted children

(Compton, 1980, p. 226). As thousands crowded into tenements and cellars, public health concerns grew (Hymowitz & Weissman, 1980, p. 195), and lack of sanitation, crowding, inability to find work, crime, delinquency, epidemics, and starvation killed thousands. The Association for Improving the Condition of the Poor, organized in 1843 by Robert Hartley, opposed to almsgiving; it eventually changed its stand in response to the time's enormous human difficulties and by 1877 became a major private poor relief agency.

RACIAL AND ETHNIC MINORITIES Ethnic groups, including those of African descent, Finns, Poles, and Chinese, began mutual aid and insurance societies (Seller, 1984, p. 179). To give support to young people, Jewish centers for boys and girls opened in the 1840s, and Protestant groups opened young men's Christian associations beginning in 1851 and young women's Christian associations in 1866. Numerous private agencies concerned with child care, drunkenness, moral reform, employment, and health care were created, including the Salvation Army, Volunteers of America, Florence Crittenton Homes, and Boys and Girls Clubs. The Catholic Church built orphanages, schools, and hospitals and instituted highly effective outdoor relief programs through Catholic Charities, St. Vincent de Paul Societies, and Sisters of Charity.

With the exception of concern for children's education, neither public nor private agencies gave aid to people of color. Until the Civil War, slaves were subject to plantation rule and freed persons had access to help only from their churches and mutual aid societies. Later, this "race work," which is defined as African Americans aiding other African Americans, laid the foundations of African American social work (Schiele, 2000). Native Americans did not have citizenship, and following their banishment to reservations, received no government aid except meager allotments often stolen by Indian agents appointed by the federal government. Native American children were sent to boarding schools, less to educate them than to take away their languages and cultures. People of color had some access to Catholic charities but were denied mainline assistance. Asian immigrants, mainly from Philippines and China, who were brought to United States to build railroads, could rely only on their mutual aid societies.

After the Civil War, the Freeman's Bureau (1865–1872) was a federally funded agency designed to aid former slaves, but it evolved into a full service agency for all. It provided finances, land, counsel and advice, education, community action, and children and family services. Though extremely successful and a model of state and federal cooperation, it was eliminated by the

Reconstruction Congress in 1876, which feared federal encroachment on states' rights as White politicians regained control of the South.

## WOMEN AND THE BEGINNING OF SOCIAL WORK

Although men continued to control social welfare throughout the 1800s, women from middle and upper economic classes influenced new humanitarian movements, first in women's rights and antislavery movements and then in other social concerns. Among early women leaders were Emma Willard, who opened the Troy Seminary for Women in 1821; Angelina and Sarah Grimke, avid abolitionists; women's rights leaders Lucretia Mott, Elizabeth Cady Stanton, and Susan B. Anthony. Dorothea Dix in 1843 convinced the Massachusetts legislature of its moral obligation to the mentally ill. This resulted in her Ten Million Acre Bill, proposed to the United States Congress in 1848 to provide treatment for the indigent insane. This was a milestone for women's status in social welfare, even though President Franklin Pierce vetoed the bill. Drs. Elizabeth and Emily Blackwell and Dr. Marie Zakrzewska set a new benchmark for women in medicine by establishing health centers for poor women (Seller, 1984, pp. 97–98).

During the Civil War, women developed essential services for the Union. Drs. Blackwell and Zakrewska, along with Clara Barton and Dorothea Dix, formed the Women's Central Association of Relief on the Battlefield, which became the U.S. Sanitary Commission. The Commission trained nurses for battlefield duty, set up a mobile hospital on the railroad, provided medical and health services, staffed field hospitals, and provided social services, including informing relatives of war deaths, transporting the wounded, distributing relief to dependents, and counseling soldiers and their families. Women's societies in the North gathered the food and clothing distributed by the Commission (Jacobs, 1976, p. 98). For poorer women, the Civil War meant new opportunities for better-paid employment previously reserved for men, as nurses, teachers, secretaries, and workers in the expanding field of social services.

### Social Welfare: The Progressive Era

There were several trends that were evident during the last half of the 19th century that influenced early 20th social welfare and social work. These were the movement from state to federal organization and the divergence of private and public charities, as private charities moved toward reforming individual clients and public bureaucracies toward provision of money, and specifically, (a) the child welfare ("child-saving")

movement, (b) the Charity Organization Society (COS), and (c) the Settlement House Movement. Child-saving developed from the Reformatory and orphanage movements that removed juveniles from almshouses and adult prisons to become child rights advocacy programs. It was spurred by the Mary Ellen child abuse case in 1875. The movement aided in promoting new protective legislation, research in child psychology, and charities oriented to child and family counseling. Its first Children's Aid Societies opened in New York in 1853 and Boston in 1864, and the movement evolved into Child and Family Services in the mid-1900s.

Charity Organization Societies (COSs), first organized in Buffalo in 1877, developed centralized community cooperative agencies and central client registries, and trained friendly visitors (caseworkers). COSs promoted the coordination services of and private fundraising for private agencies at both local and national levels, which became the United Way organizations of the mid-1900s. In 1882, Josephine Shaw Lowell established New York's COS, and in 1876 she became the first woman member of the New York State Board of Charities (Coll, 1971, p. 61).

Finally, in the last decade of the 1800s, the Settlement House Movement led by Lillian Wald in New York's Henry Street Settlement, and, in Chicago, Jane Addams and the women of Hull House (established in 1887) became a reality in America. On the basis of a model from Toynbee Hall in London, England, their goals were to provide safe houses where women, particularly immigrants, could become educated for citizenship and become employable. Settlement houses became centers for social action and client-oriented practices from which developed group work, community practice, and policy advocacy promoting new legislation for children, women, and workers.

As social welfare moved to state and national levels, State Boards of Charities and Corrections began, first in New York (1858) and Massachusetts (1863). Other states soon adopted their model, charged with the goal of inspecting asylums, hospitals, almshouses, industrial schools, and publicly supported charities. In 1865 state boards organized nationally in the American Social Science Association (1865), which later became the National Conference on Social Welfare. In 1874, the National Conference of Boards and Public Charities formed, evolving into State Departments of Public Welfare that supported poor relief through county boards of supervisors. By the 1890s, most public funding had been withdrawn from private agencies except those for the aged, and the government assumed responsibility for income maintenance, care for the aged, disabilities and deaths related to employment, public health, and corrections.

## The Beginning of the Profession

In 1882, Pennsylvania's Children's Aid Society became the first to train friendly visitors, the predecessors of professional social workers. In 1893, Boston Associated Charities began to pay workers to learn COS techniques developed under the leadership of Mary Richmond, who conducted a series of conferences defining the meaning and practice of casework and the importance of person-in-situation counseling. In 1897, Richmond developed a curriculum for a philanthropic school (Day, 2005, pp. 237–238), and in 1898, with the cooperation of the New York COS, sponsored a course in applied philanthropy that evolved into the New York School of Philanthropy in 1901. At the same time, the Chicago School of Civics and Philanthropy opened to train caseworkers and administrators of social agencies, becoming the Institution of Social Sciences in 1903–1904 and later the Chicago School of Social Service Administration.

## Overview

From the colonial period to the Progressive Era, social welfare's roots remained firmly embedded in the Elizabethan Poor Laws. They dictated that poverty and deviance were personal rather than societal problems, with hard work rather than public aid the cure. Throughout the 17th and 18th centuries, family and local responsibilities, categorization of poor, and institutional placement provided the solution to social problems. In the 1700s new humanitarian and scientific interests began to differentiate social needs, leading to new perspectives and programs in the 1800s. The women's movement, massive immigration, and the Civil War led to the divergence of private and public care systems and the proliferation and diversification of social welfare agencies organized at the state and then the national level, and training for caseworkers and administrations led to social work as a profession steeped in the dual approaches of casework and community organization, of work with individuals and families, and advocacy and policy change.

### REFERENCES

Coll, B. (1971). *Perspectives in public welfare: A history*. Washington, DC: Government Printing Office.

Compton, B. R. (1980). *Introduction to social welfare: Structure, function, and process*. Homewood, IL: The Dorsey Press.

Day, P. J. (2006). *A new history of social welfare* (5th ed.). Boston: Allyn & Bacon.

Grob, G. N. (1976). *The state and public welfare in nineteenth century America*. New York: Arno Press.

Hymowitz, C., & Weissman, M. (1980). *A history of women in America*. New York: Bantam Books.

Jacobs, W. J. (1976). *Women in American history*. Encino, CA: Glencoe.

Platt, A. B. (1977). *The child-savers: The invention of delinquency* (2nd ed.). Chicago: University of Chicago Press.

Schiele, J. (2000). *Human services and the Afrocentric paradigm*. New York: Haworth Press.

Seller, M. (1984). *Immigrant women*. Philadelphia: Temple University Press.

Yates, J. V. N. (1900). Report of the Secretary of State in 1824 on the relief and settlement of the poor. Reprinted in the 34th *Annual Report of the State Board of Charities of the State of New York* (Vol. 1, pp. 939–963).

—PHYLLIS J. DAY

## HISTORY (1900–1950)

**ABSTRACT:** This entry traces American social welfare development from the 1890s to 1950. It also includes social work's participation and response to need during two critical times in American history: the Progressive Era and the New Deal. Social reformers were instrumental in the development of social legislation, including the establishment of the Children's Bureau as well as the development of a public welfare system at the state level. America's response to human suffering left many groups, such American Indians, African Americans, and Asians, marginalized. In response, African Americans established a parallel system of private relief through organizations such as the National Urban League, unlike the other racial groups.

**KEY WORDS:** social welfare; history; Social Security Act; Progressive Era; New Deal

### Progressive Era Social Welfare Policy

During the Progressive Era, the period from about 1890 to 1920, reformers made concerted efforts to address the many critical social problems that resulted in human deprivation. The period saw the development of an array of services and programs designed to meet the needs of many suffering Americans; however, others, particularly people of color, continued to be ignored and marginalized from government policy. Progressive Era social welfare was dominated by the private sector, meaning charitable giving, as few states had instituted any measures to address social welfare needs. In addition, funding for social services on the federal level was virtually nonexistent.

The Charity Organization Society and the social settlement houses funded by sectarian and nonsectarian giving had both begun a movement to respond to overwhelming need during the preceding decades. Other private efforts that influenced social welfare included mutual aid and benevolent societies and a proliferation of women's clubs among African American and White women. These segregated women's groups—the white General Federation of Women's Clubs formed in 1890 and the black National Association of Colored Women founded in 1896—embraced the social reform movements of the day and became a constant force for legislative change and mutual help. The formal institutionalization of these women's clubs ensured their influence well into the Progressive Era and beyond (Martin & Martin, 1985; Neverdon-Morton, 1989).

The Progressive Era was marked by economic, social, and political changes. This time period saw a steady movement toward economic prosperity, reforms in women's rights, social services, health care, and education. A tremendous belief in social and economic justice was also characteristic of this era. It was believed that both individuals and social systems could be altered for the greater good. Emigrants from eastern Europe and migrants from southern rural communities filled the cities of the Northeast and Midwest in search of a better life with opportunities for employment, education, and recreation. The United States experienced tremendous industrialization and changed from a rural agrarian society to an urban society.

Life was, however, not progressive for all. The filth, overcrowding, crime, and disease of urban communities extracted a heavy toll. These social problems ushered in an era of social welfare development. Unionization was an important component of the Progressive Era, and employment opportunities were tightly guarded and controlled. The depressions that occurred during this period were accompanied by strikes and labor riots. Despite the danger inherent in labor organizing, women were very active labor organizers. The International Ladies' Garment Workers Union grew out of the depression of 1897–1908 (Day, 2006). Despite the protections that labor unions provided, or purported to provide, demands were sometimes ignored. The 1911 Triangle Shirt Waist Factory fire, in New York's Tribeca, revealed a lack of attention to issues of health and safety resulting in a major labor disaster. Such labor issues magnified the degree of human suffering and the level of individual need among the poor. Simultaneously, the definition of private troubles expanded, bringing more attention to the need for public involvement and governmental responsibility. The awareness of the impact that environmental and structural forces had on individuals, families, and communities led to even more agitation for change.

The expansion of social welfare from the private sector to a state regulated system became part of the Progressive Era agenda. Noted social workers, including Henry Street Settlement founder Lillian Wald and child labor reform advocate Florence Kelley, solicited input from New York City settlement houses to discuss the troubling issue of child labor. Owing to their initiative, in 1904, the National Child Labor Committee was formed as a clearinghouse against child labor. This led President Theodore Roosevelt to call social workers and child welfare workers to Washington to participate in the first White House Conference on Dependent Children in 1909. This conference moved responsibility for child welfare from the private and local levels to the public and federal arena. After nearly a decade of National Child Labor Committee lobbying, Congress passed legislation that established the Children's Bureau in 1912. Similar to the 1909 White House Conference that failed to acknowledge the needs of African American children, the advocates and framers of the Children's Bureau sacrificed African American children and their families in their zeal to move the Bureau's agenda forward. The Children's Bureau, nonetheless, was a landmark in federal involvement in children's issues (Day, 2006; McRoy, 2004; Trattner, 1999.

These social reformers were passionate and strategic in their campaign to have a woman lead the Children's Bureau. Sympathetic to their request and finding no legal barriers, in 1912, President Taft appointed Julia Lathrop, a prominent Hull House resident, as the Bureau's first chief. Lathrop lobbied vigorously for the establishment of public health clinics and hospitals, which resulted in the Sheppard-Towner Act in 1921. This legislation was effective in establishing children and maternal health centers in 45 states which eventually served thousands of women and children. Subsequently, both infant and maternal mortality dropped precipitously.

Similarly the first mothers' pension law was enacted in Missouri in 1911, followed two months later by Illinois. This legislation moved state government into the domain of out-door relief, marking a major breach in the American orthodoxy of private charity and indoor relief. By 1919, 39 states had some type of mother's pension in place. The mother's pension program was not a universally embraced welfare program. The idea that needy widowed mothers were "worthy" and should have the right to stay at home and raise their children was controversial. Some social workers, for example, were opposed to this legislation, fearing that it would eventually develop a populace who demanded relief as a right, while others believed that raising children was a valuable service to society and should be supplemented (Martin & Martin, 1985). Operating with low appropriations and long waiting lists, the mother's pension programs varied from state to state and served very few. Immigrants were generally ineligible for assistance based on residency and citizenship requirements. Moreover, the values and discretion of the local field investigators, along with common local practices, restricted pensions to Whites only (Day, 2006; Jansson, 2004).

These social programs grew, but African American and Mexican American children and families continued to be denied access because of racial discrimination. In response, a parallel system of social services was established in the African American community and a system of mutual aid grew in many other communities of color. Individuals and organizations, such as the National Urban League (NUL) founded in 1910 by social worker George Edmund Haynes and wealthy New Englander Ruth Baldwin, responded to these unmet needs. Through a number of programs, including the NUL Fellowship Program, designed to secure and train, educate, and prepare African American social workers to direct services such as housing referrals and employment counseling, the NUL became synonymous with social work in the African American community by 1916.

The NUL's focus on individuals migrating from the rural south to urban centers resulted in the development of many of the same programs and services that settlement houses provided to immigrants. African American social reformers also developed a range of services under the aegis of "self-help," including orphanages, old folks homes, day nurseries, burial societies, schools, homes for wayward boys and girls, and others. Ida B. Wells-Barnett's Negro Fellowship League and Reading Room in Chicago, Janie Porter Barrett's Locust Street Settlement in Hampton, Virginia, Lugenia Burns Hope's Atlanta Neighborhood Union, Maggie Lena Walker's St. Luke Penny Savings Bank in Richmond, Marcus Garvey's Universal Negro Improvement Association, and Edna Jane Hunter's Phillis Wheatley Homes for women, all testify to African Americans' response to need during the Progressive Era (Carlton-LaNey, 1999, 2001).

The Virginia Industrial School for Wayward Girls founded by Janie Porter Barrett and Charlotte Hawkins Brown's Efland Home for Girls in North Carolina provided models for developing services for girls identified as delinquents. Providing health care for these inmates produced a challenge, especially when sexually transmitted diseases were prevalent. These diseases were a serious health problem for many of these girls, as sexual exploration, rape, promiscuity, and prostitution exposed them to venereal diseases. Furthermore, both inside and outside of institutions, poverty, ignorance, and the desire for affection left many girls and women of this era victimized by sexist norms and an unresponsive health care system (Brice, 2005; Carlton-LaNey, 2001).

Progressive Era reformists' concern for maternal and child health logically included women's sexual health. Margaret Sanger, founder of Planned Parenthood, was at the center of a movement to address this issue. In 1916, she opened the Brownsville Clinic in Brooklyn, New York, to share her knowledge of contraception. She was arrested and her clinic closed under Comstock Act violations, which labeled any communication about birth control a federal offense. The following year, after opening her second clinic, physicians provided medically needy women diaphragms smuggled from Europe. Others, usually middle and upper class women, found help from understanding doctors. Yet, it remained illegal for physicians to dispense contraceptives to women until 1936.

Social insurance also developed as a major issue. A general disinclination of government to become involved in individual problems and industrial issues contributed to America's resistance to social insurance. However, Isaac Rubinow, Jane Addams, Paul Kellogg, and other social workers and their allies, including the American Association for Labor Legislation, led the fight for social insurance. Rapid U.S. industrialization and resulting industrial accidents, along with pressure from scholars and reformers, led to the enactment of workers' compensation legislation. By 1920, nearly all states had enacted some form of workers' compensation (DiNitto, 2007). Although jealously guarding their right to advocate for workers' welfare, labor union leaders generally opposed workers' compensation, claiming that workers could get greater compensation awards through the courts. Eventually Workers' Compensation would become part of the New Deal legislation.

With the focus on World War I from 1914, less attention was paid to the domestic agenda. The Russian revolution in 1917 brought a wave of "nativism" and antiprogressive sentiment in the country. As World War I drew to a close and the economy took an upturn, interest in societal responsibility diminished, and people were again expected to meet their needs through the market economy. Nevertheless, many social welfare and social work pioneers and other reformers were undaunted and continued to engage in and advocate for change strategies that embraced governmental responsibility for meeting the needs of the citizenry (Chambers, 1963). Social workers, however, were not united in their beliefs. For example, radical social workers such as Florence Kelley used cities as laboratories to research the causes of societal ills and to design possible service solutions. While these social workers were pushing for structural change, others believed that the friendly visitors represented an antidote to socialism. Mary Richmond and other Charity Organization Society leaders regarded social work professionalization as a way "to create necessary changes in social service work without promoting a dramatic restructuring of society and its institutions (Reisch & Andrews, 2001, p. 22; Simon, 1994). The concepts of worthy versus unworthy poor adopted during the colonial era in many ways illustrated these divergent strategies and continues to influence attitudes, values, and practices today (Crewe, 2004).

## New Deal Social Welfare

In response to the Great Depression, which began long before the economic collapse in 1929, an era of emergency reforms began. Economic and social conditions during the depression years created rampant poverty among a new group of American citizens. The people who were poor before the depression remained in poverty, but the middle classes, who embraced the idea of rugged individualism and hard work, suddenly found themselves poor. They were not able to maintain their homes, farms, and other businesses. Personal shame, suicide, and mobility were characteristic of the depression years. From an unemployment level of nearly 3 million in May 1929, the number skyrocketed to more than 5 million by September 1930. By the following spring, more than 8 million people had joined the jobless ranks. When 1932 was ushered in, 1 in every 4 persons was jobless (Day, 2006). Some counties experienced 90% unemployment while the GNP went from an all-time high of $103 billion in 1929 to $55.6 billion in 1933 (Day, 2006).

Unlike many of his predecessors, President Franklin Roosevelt believed that the federal government was obliged to help those in distress. With the aid of trusted advisors, Roosevelt pushed through a barrage of social legislation within the first 100 days of his administration, unprecedented in U.S. history (Day, 2006; Trattner, 1999).

These emergency responses included the Federal Emergency Relief Administration (FERA); the Works Progress Administration (WPA); the National Youth Administration (NYA); the Civilian Conservation Corps (CCC); and the Tennessee Valley Authority, which brought electricity to rural America. FERA was one of the first responses to the nation's economic crisis. Under the direction of noted social worker Harry Hopkins, FERA required that states establish emergency relief authorities to receive and disburse the funds. Many social workers and others remained uncomfortable with

public relief and made their feelings known (Day, 2006). Hopkins, on the other hand, was sure that he was responding to the immediacy of human suffering and expressed indifference toward his critics. States were encouraged to include racial minorities as recipients, but were not mandated to do so. Southern states in particular engaged in discriminatory practices, generally denying resources completely or changing the rules to reduce benefits because of race.

The WPA, which superseded the FERA, paid wages directly to employees. Although the WPA paid less than regular employment, it paid more than relief. The WPA had a nondiscriminatory policy, and under Harry Hopkins' vigilance, it provided jobs to African American workers that exceeded their population proportion. Women however were systematically excluded from participation in these work programs because mother-only families were designated unemployable, ensuring that men had exclusive access (Trattner, 1999).

The CCC was one of two national youth programs. Operating under the Department of Agriculture, the CCC initially employed young men aged 18–25 years, but in response to criticisms of gender discrimination began to employ unemployed young women as well. One of the most popular programs of the Roosevelt Administration, the CCC placed enrollees in camps run by the Army to engage in reforestation, fire prevention, and flood control. Except for a few camps in New England, CCC camps were racially segregated. About 10% of the CCC's enrollees were African American (Cole, 2003; Jansson, 2004).

Mexican Americans were equally excluded from many New Deal programs. Housing and labor programs ignored both Mexican Americans and African Americans. In 1935 the National Labor Relations Act was passed, which gave workers the right to bargain and to legally join unions. The American Federation of Labor ignored this legislation and, without governmental sanction, continued to discriminate against minorities of color for the next 20 years. Yet many Mexicans and African Americans were used as strike-breakers during the labor movement era (Day, 2006).

The National Housing Act of 1934 facilitated home ownership for working families but simultaneously led to redlining—excluding certain neighborhoods from mortgage loan eligibility. This trend reserved White neighborhoods without integration and left minorities of color isolated in ghettos without access to safe and affordable housing (Figueira-McDonough, 2007).

The NYA, another youth program of the New Deal, was designed to give high school and college students employment to ensure they remained in school.

The NYA included a Negro Division headed by Mary McLeod Bethune, founder of Bethune-Cookman College and the only female member of President Roosevelt's Black Cabinet. Through the NYA, thousands of African American youth remained in school. Ten percent of all youth in the NYA were African American; and thousands who were not enrolled in school were given the opportunity to develop skilled trades via the NYA (Carlton-LaNey, 2005).

The federal government's involvement with Native Peoples' welfare has been largely through the Bureau of Indian Affairs housed in the Department of Interior, founded after the establishment of reservations based on treaties with tribes (Davis & Iron Cloud-Two Dogs, 2004). In 1932, social reformer and Indian affairs activist John Collier became director of the Commission of Indian Affairs and through his efforts established the Indian Civilian Conservation Corps (CCC). The Indian New Deal was introduced with the enactment of the Wheeler-Howard (Indian Reorganization) Act of 1934. Touted as the most influential and lasting federal Indian policy, this legislation reversed the Dawes Acts' privatization of common holdings and returned Native people to local tribal self-governance and communal Indian land-holdings (Davis & Iron Cloud-Two Dogs, 2004). Although Collier worked as an advocate for Indian people, he was not an Indian, and as such, was criticized for his shortsightedness and his underestimation of the diversity of Indian life (Davis & Iron Cloud-Two Dogs, 2004).

Mexican Americans, who were largely landless, were devastated by the depression. Of the more than 2 million Mexicans who were residents of the United States, nearly a forth of these families were returned to Mexico at the behest of local officials. This 1929 repatriation effort was in response to welfare administrators' need to show some tangible way to deal with the onslaught of poor applicants seeking aid. Of those repatriated, half were Mexican Americans. The individuals who remained in the United States as farm labors found that they were not protected under the Social Security Act because the legislation did not cover farm laborers. They were not accorded the right to organize because the Wagner Act of 1936 excluded them. They were, therefore, left without protection and subject to the demands of employers (Figueira-McDonough, 2007).

In 1934, President Roosevelt instructed the Committee on Economic Security to develop a "Grand Design" to ensure that all American citizens were properly housed, clothed, and fed. The Social Security Act (SSA) became law in 1936. This, the most enduring of the Roosevelt administration's legislation, was made up of two systems: federal social insurance and federal or state public assistance. The SSA provided two social insurance programs for persons with work histories: Old Age and Survivors Insurance and Unemployment Compensation. The three public assistance programs were Old Age Assistance, Aid to the Blind, and Aid to Dependent Children which became Aid to Families with Dependent Children in 1950.These public assistance programs were based on economic need known as means-tested, while the social insurance programs were based on work history with contributions in the form of taxes taken from workers and employers (Day, 2006; Jansson, 2004).

Jane Hoey, a graduate of the New York School of Philanthropy (later renamed the Columbia School of Social Work), brought national attention to the social work profession during her term as director of the Bureau of Public Assistance from 1936 to 1953. Through this federal agency, Hoey was charged with implementing the SSA and establishing the state organizations needed to carry out the program. Trattner (1999) notes that Hoey and other social workers provided the professional skills of development, management, and administration that helped craft the nation's response to the Great Depression.

The SSA was fraught with controversy. It was criticized by progressive and radical left critics for not doing enough and by conservatives and the far right for doing to much (Reisch & Andrews, 2001). Nevertheless, the SSA was a landmark in liberal response to the welfare of its needy. Aid to Dependent Children became the most controversial of the public assistance programs. Benefits were not standardized, and states were allowed to determine their own subsistence level and to limit eligibility based on their resources, which was also true of Old Age Assistance and Aid to the Blind. Many of President Roosevelt's reforms were deemed unconstitutional by the U.S. Supreme Court, but the SSA endured and formed the foundation for a major federal involvement in social welfare.

The Rank and File Movement, led by radicals such as Mary van Kleeck of the Russell Sage Foundation, Harry Lurie of the Council of Jewish Federations and Welfare Funds, and Smith College professor Bertha Capen Reynolds expressed resolute dissatisfaction with the New Deal legislation. These social workers attacked the New Deal's bent toward political compromise, ties to business, and overt racism. In their social agencies, the Rank and File Movement's members experienced deprivation and inadequacies that heightened their consciousness and made the sharp contradictions between their work and the capitalist system apparent. Their charge to distribute funds and to alleviate human suffering within the confines of underfunded, restrictive, and abusive welfare agencies radicalized the social work profession. Through Rank and File discussion clubs, social workers addressed and debated critical issues, including the function of public welfare, race relations, and clinical versus community practice (Reisch & Andrews, 2001).

In 1940, as President Roosevelt was elected to a third term, the reform momentum began to wane, the economy improved, and the United States entered World War II. Attention was focused on Europe and Japan. Japanese Americans, who faced discrimination and persecution during the turn of the century "Yellow Peril," were victimized by the Oriental Exclusion Act of 1880. Although this law referred primarily to Chinese, Japanese were also included and faced continued racism and harassment during World War II. Pursuant to Executive Order 9066 issued in 1942 and the Violations of Military Orders Act, which reinforced this executive order, 126,000 Japanese immigrants and citizens were forced to relocate to concentration or internment camps in several states. They remained interned until 1946. The Japanese were perceived to be an internal threat to the war effort. However, Italians and Germans living in America were not targeted for internment and consequently did not suffer the same spiritual, psychological, and real property losses as did their fellow Americans of Japanese origin (Davis, Kim, & Romero, 2004).

Large-scale agriculture began on the Colorado River Indian Reservation after the Poston Japanese Internment camp opened there in 1942. Forced to "volunteer" their labor, the more than 17,000 Japanese internees were very productive laborers with highly valued horticulture skills. Poston was the largest internment camp and was constructed on the reservation against the Tribal Council's objection. After the camp closed in 1945, the Navajo and Hopi were relocated from other reservations and became occupants of the Indian River Reservation (Hoxie, 1996).

Civil rights for people of color were not an integral part of the New Deal legislation, and legally segregated facilities and public accommodations remained in effect. In 1945, Vice-President Truman assumed the office of President after Roosevelt's death. He then won the 1948 Presidential race with a surprising victory over Dewey. President Truman issued Executive Order 8802 in 1941, which stated that there would be no discrimination in defense industries or Government because of race, creed, color, or national origin, ultimately providing jobs for African Americans and Native Americans which were unprecedented.

In 1948, President Truman issued Executive Order 9981, which desegregated the Armed Forces, allowing these groups to advance in military positions.

Also during the Truman era, several notable pieces of social legislation were enacted during the late 1940s, including the National Mental Health Act of 1946, the National School Lunch Program of 1946, the Full employment Act of 1946, the Housing Act of 1949, and the 1946 Hospital Survey and Reconstruction Act known as the Hill-Burton Act (Trattner, 1999). The Servicemen's Readjustment Act of 1944 or the GI Bill created great opportunities for the upward mobility of millions of Veterans and their family. In addition to providing educational opportunities, the GI Bill also helped servicemen to become homeowners. Essentially, the bill promoted the gradual reintegration of servicemen into society.

After the war, people began to migrate from the South to the North in an effort to access greater educational and economic opportunities. Some entered the migration stream to escape the South's veneration for past traditions and institutions that had not served them well. One of the major noneconomic reasons that African American men migrated to the North was to avoid lynching.

By the time of the election of President Eisenhower in 1952, the United States had made significant strides toward becoming a welfare state, albeit an imperfect and a reluctant one (Jansson, 2004).

## REFERENCES

Brice, T. (2005). Disease and delinquency know no color: Syphilis and African American female delinquency. *Affilia*, 20, 300–315.

Carlton-LaNey, I. (1999). African American social work pioneers response to need. *Social Work*, 44, 311–322.

Carlton-LaNey, I. (Ed.). (2001). *African American leadership: An empowerment tradition in social welfare history*. Washington, DC: NASW Press.

Carlton-LaNey, I. (2005). African American social welfare. In J. Herrick & P. Stuart (Eds.), *Encyclopedia of social welfare history in North America* (pp. 15–18). Thousand Oaks, CA: Sage.

Chambers, C. (1963). *Seedtime of reform: American social service and social action, 1918–1933*. Minneapolis: University of Minnesota Press.

Cole, O. (2003). *The African-American experience in the civilian conservation corps*. Gainsville: University Press of Florida.

Crewe. S. (2004). African Americans and welfare reform: Success or failure? In K. Davis & Bent-Goodley (Eds.), *The color of social policy* (pp. 185–202). Alexandria, VA: CSWE Press.

Davis, K., & Iron Cloud-Two Dogs, E. (2004). The color of social policy: Oppression of indigenous tribal populations and Africans in America. In K. Davis & T. Bent-Goodley (Eds.), *The color of social policy* (pp. 3–19). Alexandria, VA: CSWE.

Davis, K., Kim, E., & Romero, J. (2004). The color of social policy: Mexicans, Chinese, and Japanese in America. In K. Davis & T. Bent-Goodley (Eds.), *The color of social policy* (pp. 21–36). Alexandria, VA: CSWE.

Day, P. (2006). *A new history of social welfare* (5th ed.). Boston: Allyn and Bacon.

DiNitto, D. (2007). *Social welfare: Politics and public policy* (7th ed.). Boston: Allyn and Bacon.

Figueira-McDonough, J. (2007). *The welfare state and social work: Pursuing social justice.* Thousand Oaks, CA: Sage.

Hoxie, F. (1996). *Encyclopedia of North American Indians.* Boston: Houghton Mifflin Company.

Jansson, B. (2004). *The reluctant welfare state* (5th ed.). Belmont, CA: Wadsworth.

Martin, E., & Martin, J. (1985). *The helping tradition in the Black family and community.* Silver Spring, MD: NASW Press.

McRoy, R. (2004). The color of child welfare. In K. Davis & T. Bent-Goodley (Eds.), *The color of social policy* (pp. 37–63). Alexandria, VA: Council on Social Work Education.

Neverdon-Morton, C. (1989). *Afro-American women of the South and the advancement of the race, 1895–1925.* Knoxville: University of Tennessee Press.

Reisch, M., & Andrews, J. (2001). *The road not taken: A history of radical social work in the United States.* New York: Brunner-Routledge.

Simon, B. (1994). *The empowerment tradition in American social work: A History.* New York: Columbia University Press.

Trattner, W. (1999). *From poor law to welfare state: A history of social welfare in America* (4th ed.). New York: The Free Press.

### SUGGESTED LINKS

Howard University Archives.
*http://www.founders.howard.edu/moorland-spingarn/*
Social Welfare History Archives.
*http://special.lib.umn.edu/swha/s*
NASW Archives.
*http://www.naswfoundation.org/messagefromNancyPerlman.asp#*

—IRIS CARLTON-LANEY

## HISTORY (1950–1980)

Between 1950 and 1980, the United States developed a welfare state that in many ways was comparable to those of other advanced industrial nations. Building on its New Deal roots, the Social Security system came to provide a "social wage" to older Americans, people with disability, and the dependents of deceased workers. It created a health-care insurance system for the elderly, the disabled, and the poor. Using the tax system in innovative ways, the government encouraged the expansion of pension and health-care protection for a majority of workers and their families. By 1980, some Americans could argue that their identification as a "laggard" in the field of social provision was no longer justified.

### Toward a Welfare State

The 1950 amendments to the Social Security Act—signed into law by President Truman in August of that year—marked a notable "modernization" of federal social welfare programs. The amendments dramatically expanded the number of workers covered by old age and survivors' insurance by adding most self-employed, domestic, and agricultural workers and by expanding benefits. In addition, survivors' benefits became more gender-neutral with the addition of benefits for widowers and their children. The expansion of coverage to women and African Americans (who had been disproportionately excluded from the system because of the restrictions on domestic and agricultural workers) began a steady process of benefits and coverage expansion that would continue for the next 3 decades. The amendments changed public assistance as well, most notably by adding benefits for the permanently and temporarily disabled and by providing benefits for parents or other caretakers under Aid to Dependent Children (ADC).

Although historical memory of the 1950s under Republican President Eisenhower usually focuses on the role of capitalism in fueling consumerism and "traditional" family life, public policy and shifts in personal life were critical to the social history of the era. Poverty declined dramatically during the 1950s, falling from about a third to a fifth of the population, but rising wages were only part of the story. Women's labor force participation—although little noted at the time—expanded from and had a decisive role in the decline in poverty. At the same time, social insurance protection for the older Americans, the unemployed, and the people with disabilities was critical to the decline in poverty. Taken together, women's work and social insurance account for about two thirds of the decline in poverty during the decade.

The other significant sociodemographic event of the era was the internal migration of African Americans. In the years between World War II and the 1960s, the African American population shifted from the rural South to the urban North. The postwar African American migration had two important impacts on social welfare. First, because of the almost universal disenfranchisement of black Southerners, the migration turned African Americans into a significant voting bloc for the first time since Reconstruction. Second, the discrimination Blacks experienced in the North assured that they would become a disproportionate share of the urban poor. Within a decade African Americans became a significant proportion of the public assistance population. Combined with the exit of widows and their children from ADC because of survivors' benefits in the Social Security program, the Black migration effectively *racialized* public assistance by the 1960s.

Between 1950 and 1965, the American welfare state continued to expand. Guided by the leadership of the Social Security Administration, and with the support of organized labor, Congress added new groups and programs. Although the effort to add disability insurance to old age and survivors' benefits was thwarted in 1950, by 1956 the program had won Congressional approval. Over the next decade, the major objective of social insurance advocates was the enactment of medical coverage for the elderly and the poor (Medicare and Medicaid in 1965).

The late 1950s and early 1960s marked the zenith of the social work profession's influence in social welfare policy. The expansion of income support programs reduced the role of "charity" in social workers' interaction with clients. Increasingly, social workers focused their professional engagement on the provision of services. Two emerging social problems contributed to social work's increasing influence. First, changes in urban labor markets and the life-course led to the emergence of *juvenile delinquency* as a social problem. Second, the number of ADC recipients rose from 2.2 million in 1955 to 3.7 million in 1962. As these social problems emerged in the late 1950s, they both were framed around issues of human development and psychology. Policy makers turned to social workers to develop programs that would address the counseling and service needs of these populations. In response to the ADC increase, Congress renamed the program Aid to Families with Dependent Children (AFDC) and enacted the Public Welfare Amendments of 1962, which provided funding for expanded services and training for welfare recipients. Policy development to address juvenile delinquency eventually led to an expansion of youth services, incorporated into the Economic Opportunity Act of 1964—the major legislation of President Johnson administration's War on Poverty.

The Public Welfare amendments led to a vast expansion of services for welfare recipients but failed to produce the promised reduction in welfare rolls. Indeed, the "uptake" rate—the proportion of eligible persons who actually apply for benefits—increased during the 1960s as welfare lost some of its historical stigma. The number of AFDC recipients rose from 3.7 million in 1962 to 8.4 million in 1970. Although a conservative reaction led to Congressional adoption of a "welfare freeze" in 1967, social work and public welfare advocates continued to wield influence. Congress's decision to separate benefits or determining eligibility from services completed the transformation of the relationship between social workers and clients by the early 1970s.

While casework advocates influenced the transformation of public assistance during these years, another branch of social work—group workers and community organizers—showed more commitment to a part of Johnson's War on Poverty—community action. Community action had its origins in a psychological perspective on poverty. Influenced heavily by Lloyd Ohlin and Richard Cloward's study of delinquency, *Delinquency and Opportunity: A Theory of Delinquent Gangs* (1960), President Kennedy's Committee on Juvenile Delinquency established several pilot projects to test the theory that providing legitimate opportunities for urban youth would reduce the attraction of delinquency. The original intent of community action was to allow the poor to move away from apathy and powerlessness that hampered their ability to take advantage of opportunities.

After President Kennedy's assassination in November 1963, the political and social contexts of the War on Poverty changed profoundly. Originally conceived as a top-down effort to increase the consumption capacity of "islands of poverty" in isolated rural areas and declining cities, the War on Poverty emerged as a melding of a traditional "services" strategy with a new belief that involving the poor in creating and overseeing programs could overcome the inertia of unresponsive bureaucracies. At the same time, the civil rights movement had a catalytic impact on both poor African Americans and community organizers, resulting in the passage of the Voting Rights and Civil Rights Act by the mid-1960s. Finally, President Johnson's unwillingness to support the tax increase necessary to pay for the expanded jobs program advocated by the Department of Labor led the new Office of Economic Opportunity to turn to the community action program as its primary mechanism for engaging poor neighborhoods. The War on Poverty also included several other major pieces of social legislation to foster or promote equality of opportunity, including Head Start for early childhood enhancement, Neighborhood and migrant health centers, rural and urban health initiatives, and the legal services program to provide access to attorneys for poor people in the civil courts for the first time in American history.

In this dynamic context, the meaning of community action seemed to change. From a small program focused on improving the social functioning of the poor, it became a major insurgent social movement to shake up existing public bureaucracies. At the same time, the welfare rights movement pursued both a community organizing and legal strategy to expand the involvement of and due process protection of welfare recipients. Many landmark 1970 *Goldberg v. Kelly* decision.

By 1966, controversies associated with community action programs; riots in Los Angeles, Detroit, Newark, and other cities; and the opposition of local officials brought much of the War on Poverty to a halt. Within a few years, the Nixon administration's call for "law and order" rather than ending poverty became the dominant theme in domestic politics. The eclipse of the War on Poverty represented as well the end of social work's broad influence over social welfare policy.

Although the War on Poverty has a significant place in political history, it created relatively few programs that outlived it, relatively few long-lasting programs. Rather, the expansion of social welfare during the Nixon and Ford administrations established the lasting American welfare state. Supplemental Security Income (1972) federalized assistance for the aged and people with disability. Food Stamps expanded nutritional assistance for poor families and individuals. The Rehabilitation Act greatly expanded services and the civil rights of people with disabilities. The largest public employment program of the postwar years—the Comprehensive Employment and Training Act (CETA)—created a variety of work training programs as well as provided federal funding for public service employment. The Community Development Block Grant program and the Community Reinvestment Act channeled new federal funding to America's ailing cities.

In terms of social services and benefits, expanded spending for social services led to the addition of Title XX providing federal funding for social services. The most far-reaching and expensive expansion, however, was the increase in benefit levels of Old Age, Survivors, and Disability Insurance. Between 1969 and 1972 benefit levels increased by over 60%, and in 1974 benefits were indexed to protect them from inflation. Taken together, these efforts caused a historic shift in the nature of government spending. In 1968, the year Nixon was elected, the federal government spent more than twice as much on defense as it did on social welfare. The year Ford left office, the proportions had been reversed.

Certainly by one measure—the poverty rate—social welfare policy between 1960 and the mid-1970s was a success. In 1959, the first year for which an "official" poverty rate was calculated, poverty stood at 21%. Fifteen years later, the rate stood at only 11.1%, the lowest figure in history. The success of these years

demonstrated that poverty had no single cause. Only a set of policies that targeted different elements of the problem—old age, disability, joblessness, lack of work skills, and geographic concentration, could bring the overall rate of poverty down.

Yet, as welfare expanded, a conservative critique of public policy gained momentum. Two failed efforts of the 1970s were emblematic of the rising tide of conservatism. First, Nixon's proposal for a Family Assistance Program, which would have replaced AFDC with a federalized program. It failed because of conservative opposition, its cost, concerns about its effect on work incentives, and fears of the increasing number of female-headed families, particularly among African Americans. Nixon also proposed what would have amounted to a universal health-care coverage by expanding Medicaid and Medicare to cover all Americans. At the same time, Nixon vetoed the Comprehensive Child Development Act of 1971, which would have professionalized early childhood education; Nixon's veto message warned that child care was a threat to the American family as an example of communist-type Soviet influence.

Less noticed than the expansion of direct public spending on social welfare, but no less important, was the expansion of employer-provided benefits. Three trends sparked this expansion. First, beginning with the Revenue Act of 1942, the Federal government provided tax incentives to corporations for providing these benefits. In 1948, the Supreme Court ruled (*Inland Steel v. NLRB*) that unions could negotiate benefits. Finally, the significant organizing setbacks for labor unions after the War, especially "Operation Dixie"—a failed attempt to expand unionization in the South, convinced many unions that it was wiser to push for employer-based systems for health care and pensions than to count on the expansion of the Social Security system.

The importance of private health and pension benefits expanded during the 1970s. The Employee Retirement Income Security Act of 1974 established Individual Retirement Accounts for workers who did not have employer-provided pensions. In 1978, the revisions of the Internal Revenue Code established 401(k) plans—defined contribution pension plans—that soon became the most common form of employer-provided retirement benefit. The flaw of employer-based approaches to social was that they disproportionately help higher-income groups. As a result, this aspect of social welfare expansion may have accelerated economic inequality by the late 1970s.

The program expansions of the 1970s did not require tax increases because of the decline in spending on the Vietnam War. However, by the late 1970s, the true costs of the new programs began to exert new pressures of social welfare spending. The recession of the mid-1970s slowed the expansion of projected revenue in the Social Security trust accounts at the same time as inflation increased benefit outlays. Between 1974 and 1980, the combined OASI and DI trust funds fell from just under $46 billion to $26.4 billion. Congress made some minor revisions to benefit formulas and accelerated tax increases in 1978, but it was not until the more sweeping reforms of 1983 that the decline in the trust funds was reversed.

By the late 1970s under President Carter, the wave of welfare expansion that had gathered strength during the 1950s and crested during the 1960s was ebbing. The Carter administration's efforts at welfare reform failed. Efforts to develop a national family policy that may bridge the emerging cultural gaps in American society only exacerbated them. Even the title of the White House conference on family policy created divisions as conservatives demanded a conference on the "American family" while liberals advocated one for the "nation's families". His Human Rights agenda for conducting foreign policy was attacked by the growing right wing politicians. The election of 1980 brought to power President Ronald Reagan and a conservative coalition with an antientitlement and social spending point of view.

In spite of these successes, by 1980, American social welfare programs found themselves increasingly vulnerable. The economic costs of social welfare programs provided grist for the mill of those who advocated reducing taxes. At the same time, the real and imagined impacts of social welfare on family life made it a target of social conservatives who saw government action as undermining the traditional family. As a result, social welfare, and especially public assistance, was a central means through which the two wings of American conservatism—fiscal and social conservatives—were able to fuse their beliefs into a single program, one that would be the nation's dominant ideological force for the years to come.

In the end, the history of social welfare between 1950 and 1980 was one of institutional success and political failure. By the end of the Carter administration, social welfare programs provided greatly expanded aid to a variety of needy groups. At the same time, the pressure those programs placed on the federal budget and the opposition they sparked among many conservative Americans placed them squarely in the site of an ascendant conservative movement in the last years of the 20th century.

—MARK STERN

## HISTORY (1980 TO PRESENT)

**ABSTRACT:** With the election of President Ronald Reagan in 1980 the United States entered an era of social policy development shaped in large measure by themes associated with political conservatism: privatization, federalism, work-linked benefits, personal responsibility, and "family values." These themes have resulted in changes to the basic structure of American social welfare that will persist into the 21st century.

**KEY WORDS:** social welfare history; social welfare policy; privatization; social welfare expenditures; welfare reform

### The American Social Welfare Model
The distinctiveness of the American model is often described in negative comparative terms: The United States does not have a European style welfare state and is usually described as an example of an "individualist/market" model of welfare provision (Esping-Anderson, 1990). The United States is far less generous to the poor in terms of social benefits, far less protective of low-wage workers, does not have a comprehensive public structure for health finance or social services, has less progressive taxation overall, and has somewhat higher levels of inequality and poverty (and most certainly severe poverty). The Organization for Economic Cooperation and Development analysis of net social expenditure demonstrated that the United States in 2003 spent 31.1% of its net national disposable income on social welfare, a figure far above the average expenditure of 28.5% by most industrialized countries and ranking the United States in total social expenditure about on the same level as the United Kingdom and the Netherlands, two countries normally placed in the "welfare state" category (http://www.oecd.org/dataoecd/14/23/38143827.xls). As Hacker (2002, p. 7) points out, American social provision does not stand out in international comparison in regard to "...the level of spending but the source" of that spending.

In the United States, then, a large share of the social welfare expenditure shouldered by the governments of most industrialized countries is instead the responsibility of the private sector, both corporate and nonprofit.

More than half of that cost is accounted for by employer spending for health insurance. The remainder is largely employer-based pension programs, employer-matched IRAs, and sickness, accident, and disability payments. Taking out these mostly work-linked private social welfare expenditures leaves the United States as one of the lower ranking nations in regard to public social welfare expenditure per capita, along with

Australia and New Zealand. But consider as well that the great bulk of those public expenditures in the United States funds an effectively "work based" benefit structure, with Social Security retirement, Medicare, and Medicaid benefits alone accounting for nearly 90% of total public spending. It is this direction of spending toward the working and middle classes that reduces the antipoverty effect of U.S. social welfare dollars.

In general then, the United States has moved since 1980 even further away from the "welfare state" and toward what Gilbert dubs the "enabling state," a system of social welfare with a primary focus on "public support for private responsibility" (Gilbert, 2004, p. 43), meaning promoting work rather than protecting labor, privatization rather than public provision, and selectivity rather than universal entitlement.

## The Social and Political Context of Reagan Era Policy

Reagan came into office after two decades that witnessed what Patterson (2000, p. 153) called the "unsung revolution": a dramatic decrease in the numbers and proportion of the poor and a "stunning enlargement" of social welfare programs and expenditures. In 1961 nearly 40 million Americans fell below the Census Bureau defined poverty standard, 22% of the population; by 1976, there were 24.6 million Americans in poverty, about 12% of the total population. Liberals also liked to point to the fact that the poverty measure did not take into account "income" from in-kind programs such as Food Stamps and Medicaid, both of which grew substantially in this period, and counting these programs as cash benefits the poverty rate could be reduced by an additional one third or more. But this decline in poverty had a price. Expenditures in social benefit programs increased in these years from about 8% of GNP in 1960 to nearly 17% in 1974. Social Security retirement benefits and Medicare led the way, but there were also dramatic cost increases in Medicaid, Food Stamps, and Aid to Families with Dependent Children. The "old welfare" of social benefit transfer payments had finally struck and it was effective and costly, but not soul satisfying. America wanted to reduce poverty through the "new welfare," promised in the Kennedy and Johnson years in the 1960s. What America had in mind was something more akin to that envisioned by the "War on Poverty," the reduction of poverty through increased opportunity and human investment. The old welfare had brought a level of poverty reduction unimaginable to earlier reformers, but it submitted a sizable financial and cultural bill.

Despite the hostility expressed toward governmental social welfare in general, the Reagan administration did recognize the need for "a safety net for the truly needy" and did not, in the end, make a frontal assault on the basic structure of social welfare. The administration had the opportunity to do so in the early 1080s when the Social Security system was faced with dire predictions based on income and payouts to the various trust funds in the Social Insurance system. Older persons had increased as a percentage of the population, the post-WWII baby-boom wave was on the way, and low birth rates suggested proportionally far fewer workers making FICA contributions in the future. The social security system was said to be facing "bankruptcy," and President Reagan, who had more than once characterized social security as a "pyramid scheme," seemed to have a once-in-a-century political opportunity. But a recession was on, the Republican Party counted on older voters, and preliminary efforts to cut benefits in Social Security and Medicare had been rebuffed. So, in 1981 the President appointed the bipartisan Greenspan commission to study Social Security (http://www.ssa.gov/history/reports/gspan.html). The commission recommended that the retirement age be moved, in increments, to 67, that benefits of persons with incomes above a certain specified level be taxed, and that COLA adjustments be delayed. Together, these changes, adopted in 1983, substantially shored up the system, producing a large surplus in the retirement trust account by the early 1990s. President Reagan, perhaps the most ideologically conservative U.S. president in the century, had, ironically, strengthened the center piece of the American welfare system.

The administration succeeded in 1981 in passing the Omnibus Budget Reconciliation Act, a comprehensive piece of legislation that substantially cut funding for social services, generally tightened eligibility requirements in a number of federal benefit programs in order to focus on the "truly needy," and created seven block grant areas to states greatly increasing state governmental latitude. OMBRA was a piece of an overall strategy of creating budgetary shortages through popular tax reductions that would then force congress into cuts.

In regard to "welfare," popularly identified entirely with AFDC, the White House Policy Office concluded that work incentives had had little impact on labor force participation of AFDC adult recipients and, so, sought to encourage states to implement "workfare" requirements that would exchange work, however modest in hours and type, for benefits. In addition, the administration promoted state experimentation through granting waivers from federal regulation a policy that would come to have great impact in the following administration of George H. W. Bush. Consistent with the administration's "individual responsibility" theme, the White House strongly supported child support enforcement, producing higher levels of federal support and cooperation with states (Patterson, 2000, p. 234).

Total federal outlays for social welfare continued to increase under President Reagan, but the rate of increase was down to an annual 5–6% from the 10% typical of the previous decade. As federal expenditures slowed, however, state and local governmental costs continued to rise, and many states and localities found that their share of various social programs, often in the form of mandated expenditure levels, required substantial increases in taxes and reduced budgetary flexibility (Katz, 1986, p. 274).

The human and social service sector, overall, grew substantially in the 1980s, much of this growth occurring in the voluntary and for-profit sectors. Title XX of the Social Security Act had allowed rapid expansion of contracting with private providers for services in the 1970s and 80s, and despite caps on spending and effective cuts in allocations in the Reagan era, the private sector, overall, grew in numbers of agencies and organizations, employees and budgets.

On the for-profit side human service corporations in hospitals, nursing homes, home health care, and day care emerged as major actors in service delivery and management. The Reagan administration supported "privatization" with considerable rhetoric, the appointment of a privatization commission, and some operational and policy decisions (President's Commission on Privatization, 1988). In the United States privatization most often refers to use of market forces to deliver publicly funded services in a way that provides for choice, competition, and cost constraint, and diminishes state investment in permanent facilities, services, and personnel. The postal services, garbage collection, park management, data management, air traffic control, weather information, housing finance, and similar others have all been the target of privatization efforts. Conservatives, having a great deal of faith in the ability of economic markets and little faith in planning and administration, have also proposed vouchers in education, health-care, housing, and social services. In some areas, notably food programs, special education, and housing, vouchers have become more widely utilized, and as noted earlier, private provision is the norm in health services.

In the last months of his presidency, Ronald Reagan signed the Family Support Act of 1988. This legislation authored primarily by Democratic Sen. Daniel Moynihan and supported more vigorously by Democrats than by Republicans, incorporated all of the Reagan era themes in regard to assistance to the poor: work, family, and personal accountability. In signing the act the President said that despite the "best of intentions" the Federal Government had in the past "usurped" parental responsibilities and had "reinforced dependency" and separated welfare recipients from the "mainstream" of society.

The Family Support Act, heralded as a major welfare reform, required states to meet progressive targets in the participation of AFDC adult recipients in "job opportunity and basic skills" (JOBS), linked Medicaid eligibility to AFDC, provided transitional Medicaid for those leaving AFDC rolls, increased federal support for child care where necessary to support JOBS participation, and, yet again, strengthened child support enforcement. The Act in retrospect was doomed by the late 1980s recession, which created huge deficits in state budgets and prevented many of them from funding the JOBS and associated child care programs. AFDC rolls rather than decreasing rose precipitously in 1989–1991, causing federal expenditures to reach record levels—$23 billions in 1992.

The Reagan years, then, witnessed a rather persistent and effective political attack on "welfare state" ideology, a significant reduction of federal, and to a degree state, funding in the social services, and an increased importance of the voluntary and for-profit sectors. The Reagan years established very clearly the policy preference for work-based programs and the linking of eligibility to "worthiness" measured by work participation.

### Policy Developments of George H. W. Bush

George Bush became President in 1988, after eight years as Vice President, promising a "kinder and gentler" America, which many understood to be a mild criticism of the previous administration. Bush strongly voiced support for the private nonprofit sector in social welfare and introduced the term "thousand points of light" in his inaugural address. On the public expenditure side, the tax reductions of the mid-1980s combined with Gramm-Rudman-Hollings deficit controls and the President's campaign pledge of no new taxes kept a firm grip on even the most modest of program intentions. The administration did have success in shaping a new Civil Rights Act of 1991, which expanded somewhat the rights of those discriminated against to seek relief.

But the most notable of the social policy developments in the G. H. W. Bush years was the passage of the Americans with Disabilities Act of 1990, which dramatically increased protection from discrimination in housing, work, and public accommodation for the disabled. Overall, however, the thawing of the cold war, the collapse of the Soviet Union, the overthrow of Noriega in Panama, and the first Iraq war would give the Bush administration a strong foreign policy flavor. In the meantime, the economy slipped into recession, and the Los Angeles riots, after the first Rodney King arrest and beating case was tried in 1992, reminded everyone that the problems of race and poverty were very much with us.

## The Clinton Years

President Bill Clinton, elected in 1992, had campaigned on a promise to reform the nation's health-care system and to "end welfare as we know it," and as former Governor of Arkansas he had direct experience with many domestic social welfare problems. He appointed a more diverse, and decidedly more domestically oriented, cabinet, and with his wife Hillary at his side, sought to tackle a number of social matters. In the first year of the Clinton administration the most evident of these was Health Care. Emphasizing basic principles, including universality of coverage and cost control, the administration proposed a far-reaching health scheme that would enroll all Americans in a "health alliance" that would seek provider bids on a basic insurance package. For the first time, it would have created a genuinely national health-care structure within the American government. As a result of strong opposition, the effort was not achieved (Mizrahi, 1997).

The Clinton administration supported a major expansion of the EITC, the Earned Income Tax Credit, a policy dating back to the Nixon administration, which allowed lower income workers to credit selected work-related expenses against the federal tax obligation. If the credit exceeds the tax obligation the credit is "refundable." The administration, continuing the policy of the Republican years to allow state waivers, granted permission to Wisconsin to implement a bipartisan "Wisconsin Works" program complete with benefit time limits and detailed work requirements. The expansion of EITC and the emergence of state reforms such as Wisconsin's would anticipate the architecture of the coming major welfare reform.

## Reforming Welfare

The Clinton administration would work diligently with the conservative Republican majority elected to the House of Representatives in 1994, which had, under the leadership of House Speaker Newt Gingrich, crafted a guiding policy document called "The Contract with America". After considerable effort, Congress would pass in 1996 and the President would sign the Personal Responsibility and Work Opportunity Act, which would create the Temporary Assistance to Needy Families (TANF) program. The new program incorporated work requirements and time limits. The time

limits allowed 2 years of benefits prior to work as defined by the legislation and a 5-year lifetime maximum of benefits. States are allowed a 20% caseload exemption from time limits, but at this writing no state has utilized this provision.

The act is usually regarded as a great political success, with both political parties claiming credit for the dramatic decline in welfare caseload and the associated increase on labor force participation. As policy the program represents a radical shift from the original Aid to Dependent Children construct that was, after all, a child welfare provision designed clearly to keep women out of the labor market and at home in a parental role.

The success of welfare reform for the great bulk of the poor depends upon an effective system of work support that would "make work pay." The most important of these programs are the minimum wage, the Earned Income Tax Credit, the child tax credit, income supplement programs conducted by states, food stamps, health insurance, child support enforcement, and child care. A recent study by the Congressional Budget Office (2007) showed that numerous expansions of these programs since the mid-1980s have increased by a factor of more than 8 the value of federal work support benefits now being paid to working families. If American social policy for the poor is going to be work-based in character these programs will continue to play the critical role in maintaining work incentives and in supplementing earned income so that working families can provide a minimum living standard for their children.

Another important element in the Clinton administration's efforts was creation of The State Children's Health Insurance Program (SCHIP), included in the Balanced Budget Act of 1997. Title XXI of the Social Security Act had allocated about $20 billion over 5 years to help states insure more children. SCHIP continues to receive considerable attention as states implement or continue to expand and refine their initial SCHIP plans. SCHIP plans have been approved in all 50 states, the District of Columbia, and 5 territories (http://www.cms.hhs.gov/home/schip.asp).

## The George W. Bush Years

Bush, the son of the 41st President came into office after a controversial election against Al Gore because Gore won the popular vote and the Supreme Court stopped the recount (*Bush v. Gore*, 531 U.S. 98, 2000). He promised Compassionate Conservatism, a doctrine supporting sensitivity to social issues but a nonstatist response to them emphasizing private, community-based action most especially from faith-based, charitable organizations.

Just 8 months into the new presidency, the events of September 11, 2001, gave the administration a focus and urgency in international matters. Afghanistan, and then Iraq, would come to represent the administration's central focus in combating radical Islamic actions and "remodeling" the Middle East. This would prove to be the context for many of the most controversial elements of administration policy and operations, from reorganizing the armed services to contracting with Halliburton, and would overshadow for the entire period of the Bush presidency domestic policy matters.

President George Bush's 2003 tax proposals offered a sweeping package of tax cuts and incentives primarily of benefit to higher income brackets. There was some tax relief for married couples and an increase in the tax deduction for families with children, but $364 billion out of the $674 billion "economic stimulus" tax plan would be devoted to eliminating the tax on dividends when the poorest fifth of Americans have an average of $25 in dividend income.

The Bush administration addressed the problem of Americans not seeming to be competitive in public education with other high GDP nations and persistent racial and socioeconomic gaps in tested school performance in supporting the No Child Left Behind legislation, passed with considerable bipartisan support in late 2001 (http://www.ed.gov/policy/elsec/leg/esea02/index.html). The act provides increased federal funding for schools in return for states to establish mandatory testing by subject and a public rating system on school performance. It gives parents the option to transfer their children from low-performing schools. Although the policy is hailed by many as moving the United States finally toward the sort of national educational standards typical in other countries, the state variations in testing and the general resistance to standard outcome measures by teacher groups combined with lower levels of funding than originally promised have plagued the policy from the beginning.

In early 2002 the President established the New Freedom Commission on mental health. The report of that commission (www.mentalhealthcommission.gov) recommends far more extensive screening for mental illness and emotional disturbance, especially for children and with a focus on schools and institutions and generally supports the privatization of mental health services.

The Medicare Prescription Drug Improvement and Modernization Act of 2003 created a prescription drug benefit beginning January 2006. Some 44 million seniors and disabled persons would participate notwithstanding a complex system of coverage with limits at different points, which from a liberal perspective was not considered generous (although future cost projections through 2016 exceed $500 billion). There is specific provision against the Medicare administration "negotiating" for favorable pharmaceutical prices (as does the Veteran's Administration for example); nevertheless, the history of social welfare policy suggests that benefits provided to a substantial portion of a politically active aging population may expand over time.

Despite these domestic initiatives, the election of 2004 against Democratic opponent John Kerry became one dominated by national security, with few substantive issues of national policy, foreign or domestic, dividing them. There were undercurrents of "moral" issues (gay marriage bans were on the ballot in 11 states) and "character" (Kerry and the Swift Boat and Bush and his National Guard experience) but the relatively close election (51% to Kerry's 48%) seemed to turn on security issues.

If 9/11 and its aftermath provided a context for the Bush White House to develop a focus, identity, and considerable early public support, it would be another disaster (again just months after the election) that would come to define the second term. Hurricane Katrina, in August of 2005, devastated New Orleans and the Gulf Coast and would provide the lowest moment in the administration's domestic political life. Katrina proved to be a public administrative disaster, with state and federal agencies, as well as local governments, proving unable to communicate and coordinate. But more than that it was a political disaster, with the White House appearing both confused and disinterested. Quite in contrast to the 9/11 George Bush who was visibly "in charge" and whose policy development (however unsuccessful in some aspects) was both rapid and clear, this time the President and his administration seemed deaf to political reality. The impact of Katrina, combined with the declining fortunes in Iraq, has created a circumstance that has not allowed the Bush administration to pursue aggressively any major policy developments in social welfare.

An example of the administration's political incapacity is Social Security Reform. In December 2001, an administration commission charged with addressing the long-term financing problems of the Social Security program introduced three possible plans for privatizing the existing federal Old Age, Survivors, and Disability Insurance. The administration supported the report's recommendation which would cut benefits compared to current law by replacing "wage indexing" with "price indexing," resulting in a benefit cut that would save billions over time presuming the official inflation index would be lower than earnings increases over time. The report also recommended the creation of private investment accounts financed by diverting a relatively small portion of a worker's Social Security payroll taxes into a private account managed, within limits, as one may manage an IRA. There are potential long-term public cost savings to this plan and potential increase in retirement support for long-term contributors to this scheme but the short-term volatility of financial markets also creates the possibility for reducing the very thing promised in 1935, security. Nevertheless, the political opposition and his own unpopularity due in part to a continuing and costly (in terms of lives and money) war in Iraq and Afghanistan have kept any proposals from moving forward.

Another example of administrative reform intention that has not developed political gravity is immigration reform. The Bush White House has, from the beginning, sought some sort of resolution to the current contradiction of having strict immigration controls in the context of rather porous borders and a demand for labor in the United States that greatly exceeds that in Mexico and Latin America. President Bush called for legislation strengthening security along the U.S.–Mexico border, involving both an increase in Border Patrol agents and the building of a wall in a lengthy section of the border, combined with a renewed and expanded guest-worker program and a process that would allow some of the more than 11 million illegal immigrants already in the United States to work their way toward citizenship, by paying fines and back taxes, working in a job "for a number of years," and learning English. But the administration and supporters of "comprehensive immigration reform" were stymied in Congress in the summer of 2007.

The reauthorization of the TANF provision of the 1996 welfare reform occurred in the 2005 Deficit Reduction Act which keeps the principal elements of TANF intact. It does provide $200 million in new federal funding for child care and, in a central element of political compromise, increases the "charitable choice" faith-based initiatives associated with TANF-related social services and work placement and support. In an immigration related aspect of the law individuals are required to present documentation of citizenship or nationality when they apply for Medicaid benefits.

## Conclusion

What we know from the history of American social welfare is that although there have been moments of dramatic political departure, those swings usually produce far less, in a policy sense, than may be expected either right or left. The basic elements of what Wilensky and Lebaux (1958) labeled the "culture of capitalism" are still with us, meaning a pervasive and strong belief in the United States as a society of opportunity and individual initiative and responsibility. The new economy, being postindustrial, has washed away many of the labor structural factors that create class identity and politics, and the new politics of "identity" (race, gender, sexual orientation) tend to cut across economic interests and undermine a traditional welfare state agenda. In addition, the increasing population diversity of the United States combined with the continuing effects of a federal governmental structure all suggest that we will not see an American version of a recognizable "welfare state" no matter which party occupies the White House or controls Congress.

Work-based social benefits and privatization of public and social services, while associated with the Reagan Republican political era that may be in decline, are so based on elements of American culture, governmental and economic organization that they will still be very much with us. There is reason to believe that the United States will move toward some sort of national health policy and structure, but one can be assured that it will incorporate both a financing and delivery system that keeps the private provision of health services and the private, usually occupationally based, system of health finance largely intact. So powerful is the health industry and its critical actors in the United States that we can be assured, as well, that social services will be both increasingly defined in terms of "health" and that the delivery and financing structures will look very much like the physical health industry.

Lord Beveridge observed in the 1940s that the object of social welfare (and government more broadly) was not the "glory of rulers or of races" but the "happiness of the common man." Perhaps this is a point on which to end this consideration of the recent decades of American social welfare development. Social policy is ultimately an expression of a positive ideal of a decent society providing opportunity for human meaning and satisfaction. Social policy is an expression of the search for that ideal and the fierce competition over definitions, means, and winners and losers. That competition rests on the differential values of security and humanitarianism on the one hand and self-reliance and competitiveness on the other. The continuous compromise between these two that is American social welfare will, no doubt, persist.

## REFERENCES

Congressional Budget Office. (2007). *Changes in the economic resources of low-income households with children*. Washington, DC.

Esping-Anderson, G. (1990). *Three worlds of welfare capitalism*. Princeton, NJ: Princeton University Press.

Hacker, J. (2002). *The divided welfare state: The battle over public and private social benefits in the United States.* Cambridge, UK: Cambridge University Press.

Gilbert, N. (2004). *Transformation of the welfare state: The silent surrender of public responsibility.* New York: Oxford University Press.

Katz, M. (1986). *In the shadow of the Poorhouse: A social history of welfare in America.* New York: Basic Books.

Mizrahi, T. (1997). Health care policy. *Encyclopedia of social work* (19th ed., supplement). Washington, DC: NASW Press.

Patterson, J. (2000). *America's struggle against poverty in the 20th century.* Cambridge, MA: Harvard University Press.

President's Commission on Privatization. (1988). *Privatization: Toward more effective government.* Washington, DC: U.S. Government Printing Office.

Wilensky, H. L., & Lebaux, C. (1958). *Industrial society and social welfare.* New York: Russell Sage Foundation.

—P. NELSON REID

# SOCIAL PROBLEMS

**ABSTRACT:** Societies greatly vary in how social ills or conditions are framed and addressed. What is socially problematic and why specific societal responses are developed depends on competing social values in social, political, and historic context. Social constructionists examine how some social behaviors and conditions come to be publicly viewed as social problems. Recent studies document two contemporary trends—the medicalizing and criminalizing of behavior for labeling problems and subjecting them to institutions of social control. Analyses of social problems allow social workers to consider how power, politics, fears, prejudices, and values "create" what is problematic about a variety of social conditions.

**KEY WORDS:** social construction; medicalization; criminalization

## Definition

Social workers come into contact with many *social problems* and work in programs and settings designed to ameliorate or prevent them. How do the private woes of an individual or group become widely recognized as a social problem? How are social problems defined, and with what consequences for how a society attempts to correct or address them?

Social welfare historians and sociologists have documented many different patterns in how societies frame and address problems such as juvenile crime, mental illness, and alcohol and drug addiction. Note that what is socially problematic, that is, what makes it necessary to develop a societal or institutional solution, and often, a particular approach to social services, depends on assessments of competing social values and ideology, and social, political, and historic context. Whether we see some constellation of behaviors as posing a "social problem" depends on social processes including which definitional claims become prominent in the culture and which organizational responses are developed to address them.

A review of prominent social welfare policy textbooks commonly used in foundation courses reveals that surprisingly few authors define the term social problem. Nonetheless the texts provide long lists of social ills, such as homelessness, crime, poverty, child abuse, discrimination, et cetera, which social workers are expected to address through social service provision in one or more institutional contexts such as the educational, health care, criminal justice, or social welfare systems. Throughout the history of American social welfare, we have changed the definition and treatment of such social ills in most every era and we often find competing definitions of these problems in the public discourse. However, dominant "causal" explanations come to be accepted or believed and these influence changes in policies, programs, and services (institutional responses).

For example, assumptions that vice and lack of moral guidance are root causes of a "problem" such as homosexual behavior may be supplanted by medical or biologically-based assumptions. Medical or psychiatric claims and cures in the 20th century of homosexuality as a pathology or psychiatric disorder came to dominate analyses of the behavior in the social sciences and fields of professional practice, in part because of the comparative social power and authority of scientific explanations—particularly those made by physicians—over religious reason (Kirk & Kutchins, 2003). However, both moral and medical analyses have continued as competing ways to "problematize" the social construction of homosexuality. It was not until 2003 that the United States Supreme Court struck down a criminal sodomy law in *Lawrence v. Texas*, 539 U.S. 558 (2003) that had been justified on moral grounds but was found to be an unconstitutional violation of individual's 14th Amendment liberty interests.

## History of the Study of Social Problems

There is a long and distinguished sociological literature on the topic of social problems. One school of thought, *structural functionalism,* dominated discussions in the 1950s and 1960s. Theorists such as Robert Merton believed that objective social conditions existed independently from interpretation and social values; given sufficiently rigorous scientific study, some social conditions would be determined to be social problems. Merton and Nisbet (1971) defined social problems as "a substantial discrepancy between widely shared social standards and actual conditions of social life."

Other theorists, such as Fuller, Myers, Becker, and Blumer advanced a "value-conflict approach" to social problems. For example, in 1941 Fuller and Myers defined social problems as, "a condition which is defined by a considerable number of persons as a deviation from some social norm which they cherish" (Fuller & Meyers, 1941, p. 320). For these theorists, the objective social condition and value judgments about social norms were necessary prerequisites for establishing a social problem. Both structural functionalists and conflict-theorists shared a common focus on the *social condition*, which under some circumstances will constitute a "social problem."

In the 1970s, in reaction to both the structural functionalists and the value-conflict approaches, Kitsuse and Spector (1973) among others produced seminal work that inspired a fundamental and significant shift in thinking about the sociology of social problems. They argued that earlier theorists who focused on *social conditions* failed to appreciate the political aspect and processes associated with formulating *social problems* (See also Spector & Kitsuse, 2000).

They challenged the notion that social problems were the product of objective social conditions and argued instead that social problems were, in fact, created or constructed as the result of ongoing *social processes*. They initially defined social problems "as the activities of groups making assertions of grievances and claims with respect to some putative conditions." In short, this perspective examines the interpretative processes that determine which social conditions come to be seen in public opinion or debate as social problems.

The sociology of social problem construction has undergone considerable critique since the 1970s (Holstein & Miller, 1993; 2003). Nonetheless, in its basic form, it continues to dominate the discussion of what makes a problem *social*. A number of influential scholars have used this theoretical perspective to study problems to which social workers respond.

The participants in this process, known as "claims-makers," could include advocacy groups, politicians, journalists, experts such as doctors, clergy, and social workers, or any other interested parties who argue that certain social conditions are inherently immoral or unjust. Schneider (1985) notes that Kitsuse and Spector provided a comprehensive theory *of* social problems, as opposed to earlier writing that tended to be *guided by* theoretical approaches used in order to understand social problems. In doing so, the social constructionist approach to social problems resulted in a new wave of empirical studies. Social scientists could study the process by which social problems were constructed, produced, maintained or evolved over time by looking at how claims activities were made and supported.

These claims-makers play a role both in drawing attention to certain social conditions but also in shaping how the problem is defined. For example, claims-makers in the abortion debate, activists and theorists on both the pro- and anti-abortion ideological continuum have framed the act of abortion as a moral issue, a medical issue, a civil rights issue, a criminal issue, a gender issue, and even a mental health issue (see also Lee, 2003). Even examining the rhetoric associated with the debate, "pro-life" versus "pro-choice" illustrates the competing value frameworks utilized by advocates to shape public debate. The dominant cultural view or views will influence at any given historical moment the "social" responses to abortion. It is either resolved in private between a woman and her medical provider or it is publicly outlawed, thus subjecting persons who participate to criminal prosecution. Social constructionists analyze these types of issues regarding the abortion controversy, but not necessarily the factual basis for the causal claims or the changing demography or political economy of abortion.

While the social constructionist approach is only one theoretical lens for examining social problems, it provides a useful perspective for the question of why social workers define and treat certain behaviors and conditions in some ways at specific points in time and how social processes affect changes in the way social work approaches particular social conditions or ills.

## Trends

Two important themes in the literature on social problems focus on identifying recurrent patterns of framing and responding to problems in modern society. Studies of the medicalizing and the criminalizing of conditions or behavior problems examine how social behavior becomes stigmatized, labeled and subject to particular institutions of social control.

*Medicalizing social problems.* Some social scientists argue that there is a trend in modern society toward the "medicalization" of a number of social problems. Increasing numbers and types of behavioral or individual conditions are interpreted as being evidence of illness, sickness, or medical syndromes (Conrad, 2007; Conrad

& Schneider, 1992). The social condition is argued to then have individualized medical remedies or treatments. Conrad and others have noted that the range of "life problems" that receive medical diagnoses is expanding, despite the sometimes dubious nature of the scientific evidence. Ivan Illich popularized this argument of the "medicalization of life" and its negative consequences for health, attributing the sociocultural process to the monopolistic expansion of the medical profession (Illich, 1976).

Examples of where this might be problematic are medical diagnoses for male baldness, male erectile dysfunction, adult hyperactivity, human growth hormone treatment, and other enhancements such as breast implants (Conrad, 2007). In some cases, the medicalizing of a problem can lead to reduction of stigma and blaming individuals for their conditions, such as treating the biological basis of some forms of alcoholism, obesity, or ADHD. In some cases, it can lead to harm reduction, such as by encouraging providing preventive care for sexually-transmitted illnesses. With widening medicalization at the frontiers of human physical differences, however, the question becomes one of when society is "pathologizing" difference and when medical models of treatment result in narrowing conceptions of "normal." The women's health movement emerged in the 1970s and 1980s with a broad critique of medical control over the conceptualization of women's health issues that result in excessive surgical and pharmaceutical intervention (Ruzek, 1993; Bertin, 1993).

In another example, Horwitz and Wakefield (2007) have examined how once-separate domains of "sadness with cause" (appropriate sadness in response to obvious causes) and clinical depression—sadness without cause—have become conflated. The result is rapid diagnostic inflation of depressive disorders. The increasing medicalization of "sadness" has serious intervention and treatment implications.

*Criminalizing social problems.* Crime and criminality are critically important domains of social problems. What behaviors are deemed criminal, what constitutes a crime, how crimes are publicly portrayed, what trends are reported in the news, how we respond to or punish behavior deemed criminal, are questions of social problem construction. Joel Best (1999) refers to violence, victimization, and villainy. For example, rhetoric involving "innocent victims" (such as women and children) and "super predators" (such as sex fiends, pedophile priests, and gang members) and "brutal" or "random" attacks are ways of inciting public passion about criminal behavior and forcing a societal response. These social processes in turn can lead to changes in the criminal justice system (and in other social institutions such as family and school systems).

Furthermore, generalizing from individual "incidents" to "instances" of a purportedly large and growing trend ("crime wave") is one method of linking individual events and converting them into socially constructed public problems (Best, 1999; Fishman, 1998). Sometimes these efforts are short-lived, such as when several random shootings occurred on the LA freeway and led the media to claim a new trend or wave in highway shootings (Best, 1999). The attempt to turn these individual "incidents" into "instances" of a larger public problem failed, in part, because it was hard to establish that the problem was "getting worse" and because no advocates or experts stepped forward to claim "ownership" of the problem.

Best (1999) has referred to the "iron quadrangle" of players necessary to discover, interpret, and explain social problems. They are the media, activists, government, and experts. He argues that all these players are necessary for a social problem to have staying power. A classic example of activists converting individual incidents into instances of a social problem can be seen in the history of Mothers against Drunk Driving (MADD). Here a specific type of car accident (those involving a driver who had been drinking) was picked up as cause by activists and is now recognized as a specific form of *criminal* social problem (Best, 1999; Reinarman, 1998).

Many social science researchers have empirically studied the role of the media in constructing social problems (Potter & Kappeler, 1998; Sacco, 1998). One way that mass concern about a problem can become aroused through the use of media or other channels for spreading information is the creation of a "moral panic" (Goode & Ben-Yeduha, 1994). The phrase first coined in a classic study from the 1960s by Stanley Cohen of young British teenagers who were either portrayed as "mods" (modernist youth who listened to pop music and frequented discos) or "rockers" (youth who more were more classically "delinquent") and the clashes between them resulted in a public overreaction to otherwise relatively minor incidents (Cohen, 1980). Sociologists have studied how these periods of intense concern that frame an issue as a threat to society result from specific social forces and dynamics, how they may exaggerate or misplace the analysis of the threat, how they may divert attention from other important issues, and how they leave a legacy on the institutional order long after the moral panic subsides.

Social problem construction of the criminal use of drugs is illustrative of the ebb and flow of these moral panics. Claims of large and growing numbers (often unsubstantiated) supplied by activists fuel moral panics. According to Goode and Ben-Yehuda, moral panic led to the criminalization of marijuana use in the 1930s in the United States (153–154). Sensationalist media supported by "facts and figures" released by government officials facilitated the passage of anti-marijuana legislation to control the "drug menace." In the 1980s the discovery of the "crack epidemic" led to President Bush's declaration of a "War on Drugs (Reinarman & Levine, 1997); and more recently "ice" and "crystal methamphetamine" has joined the list of drugs receiving particular public attention (Jenkins, 1998).

These framings have significant institutional impact. For example, the "crack epidemic" has had a disparate impact on the arrest and incarceration of poor people of color (Beckett, Nyrop, Pfingst, & Bowen, 2005). Young women are especially vulnerable because they are subjected to both criminal sanctions and heightened scrutiny by child protective services for delivering "crack babies" (Toscano, 2005).

## Implications for Social Work

Social workers should be particularly attentive to their role as claims-makers in helping to construct social problems of importance to our work. It would seem that social work, as a profession, ought to be particularly concerned with and attuned to conditions that have not yet been problematized or received recognition as a social problem. After all, frontline social workers are apt to see serious social conditions—individual hardships on a large scale—affecting their clients before the public recognizes the problem. The increasing number of AIDS orphans is illustrative of a condition that social workers saw before it was conceptualized as a public problem (see for example, Roby & Shaw, 2006).

Perhaps some of our advocacy efforts should aim to increase the power of social work's "claims-making" expertise in order to shape social problem construction and societal responses. For example, the knowledge gleaned by social workers in assessing and treating child and family well-being does not typically carry weight in current policy discussions of educational reform. Were a social work ecological perspective to achieve greater dominance in public discourse, perhaps more institutional effort to increase parental involvement in children's learning would result.

Analyzing the construction of social problems allows social workers and others to consider the power, politics, fears, prejudices, values, and other factors that have gone into the process of "creating" what is deemed "problematic" about a variety of social conditions that advocates, journalists, politicians, and others address.

In addition, social constructionist theorists and other researchers would caution professionals and service practitioners of their susceptibility to the claims making of others who may work to advance their own position of social and ideological control over the best interests of our clientele. Social workers are in a unique position to utilize a social justice lens in public discussion of social problems.

Finally, social work historians have challenged the profession to guard against privileging some types of claims over others in defining and addressing social problems. For example, Reisch and Andrews (2001) and Specht and Courtney (1994) question the ascendance within the profession of interpersonal practice solutions over advocacy for social change in the broader societal environment to address social problems.

## REFERENCES

Beckett, K., Nyrop, K., Pfingst, L., & Bowen, M. (2005). Drug use, possession arrests, and the question of race: Lessons from Seattle. *Social Problems, 52,* 419–441.

Bertin, J. E. (1993). Pregnancy and social control. In B. K. Rothman (Ed.), *Encyclopedia of childbearing: Critical perspectives* (pp. 317–323). Phoenix, AZ: Oryx Press.

Best, J. (1999). *Random violence: How we talk about new crimes and victims.* Berkeley: University of California Press.

Cohen, S. (1980). *Folk devils and moral panics: The creation of the mods and rockers* (2nd ed.). New York: St. Martin's Press.

Conrad, P. (2007). *The medicalization of society.* Baltimore: Johns Hopkins University Press.

Conrad, P., & Schneider, J. W. (1992) *Deviance and medicalization.* (expanded ed.). New York: Mosby.

Fishman, M. (1998). Crime waves as ideology. In G. W. Potter & V. E. Kappeler (Eds.), *Constructing crime: Perspectives on making news and social problems* (pp. 53–69). Prospect Heights, IL: Waveland Press.

Fuller, R. C., & Myers, R. R. (1941). The natural history of a social problem. *American Sociological Review, 6,* 320–328.

Goode, E., & Ben-Yeduha, N. (1994). Moral panics: culture, politics, and social construction. *Annual Review of Sociology, 20,* 149–171.

Holstein, J. A., & Miller, G. (1993). *Reconsidering social constructionism: Debates in social problems theory.* New York: Aldine deGruyter.

Holstein, J. A., & Miller, G. (2003). *Challenges and choices: Constructionist perspectives on social problems.* New York: Aldine deGruyter.

Horwitz, A. V., & Wakefield, J. C. (2007). *The loss of sadness.* New York: Oxford University Press.

Illich, I. (1976). *Medical nemesis: The expropriation of health.* New York: Pantheon Books.

Jenkins, P. (1998). The ice age. In G. W. Potter & V. E. Kappeler (Eds.), *Constructing crime: Perspectives on making news and social problems* (pp. 137–160). Prospect Heights, IL: Waveland Press.

Kirk, S. A., & Kutchins, H. (2003). Psychiatrists construct homosexuality. In D. R. Loseke & J. Best (Eds.), *Social problems: Constructionist readings* (pp. 59–65). New York: Aldine deGruyter.

Kitsuse, J. I., & Spector, M. (1973). Toward a sociology of social problems: Social conditions, value-judgments, and social problems. *Social Problems, 20,* 407–419.

Lee, E. (2003). *Abortion, motherhood, and mental health: medicalizing reproduction in the United States and Great Britain.* New York: Aldine deGruyter.

Merton, R. K., & Nisbet, R. (1971). *Contemporary social problems.* New York: Harcourt Brace Jovanovich.

Potter, G. W. L., & Kappeler, V. E. (1998). *Constructing crime: Perspectives on making news and social problems.* Prospect Heights, IL: Waveland Press.

Reinarman, C. (1998). The social construction of an alcohol problem: The case of Mothers against Drunk Drivers and social control in the 1980s. In G. W. Potter & V. E. Kappeler (Eds.), *Constructing crime: Perspectives on making news and social problems* (pp. 193–220). Prospect Heights, IL: Waveland Press.

Reinarman, C., & Levine, H. G. (1997). *Crack in America: Demon drugs and social justice.* Berkeley: University of California Press.

Reisch, M., & Andrews, J. (2001). *The road not taken: A history of radical social work in the United States.* New York: Brunner-Routledge.

Roby, J. L., & Shaw, S. A. (2006). The African orphan crisis and international adoption. *Social Work, 51,* 199–210.

Ruzek, S. B. (1993). Women's health movement. In B. K. Rothman (Ed.), *Encyclopedia of childbearing: Critical perspectives* (pp. 423–425). Phoenix, AZ: Oryx Press.

Sacco, V. F. (1998). Media construction of crime. In G. W. Potter & V. E. Kappeler, *Constructing crime: Perspectives on making news and social problems* (pp. 37–51). Prospect Heights, IL: Waveland Press.

Schneider, J. W. (1985). Social problems theory: The constructionist view. *Annual Review of Sociology, 11,* 209–229.

Specht, H., & Courtney, M. E. (1994). *Unfaithful angels: How social work has abandoned its mission.* New York: Free Press.

Spector, M., & Kitsuse, J. I. (2000). *Constructing social problems.* New Brunswick, NJ: Transaction Publishers.

Toscano, V. (2005). Misguided retribution: Criminalization of pregnant women who take drugs. *Social and Legal Studies, 14,* 359–386.

—SANDRA K. DANZIGER AND KAREN M. STALLER

# SOCIAL SECURITY PROGRAM

ABSTRACT: After discussing the social insurance approach to economic security and the principles and values underlying Social Security, this entry reviews its history—beginning with the enactment of the Social Security Act of 1935, through its incremental development to the changed in the politics of Social Security since the mid-1990s. Next, program benefits and financing are described, and then contemporary challenges identified. The pros and cons of various means of addressing projected financing and related policy concerns are reviewed. The entry concludes by highlighting the importance of understanding Social Security as a program that strengthens families and community and gives expression to widely held values.

KEY WORDS: social security; social insurance; economic security; income maintenance; generational equity; aging policy

Enacted in 1935, today Social Security—the Old-Age, Survivors and Disability Insurance program (OASDI)—does more to prevent and reduce poverty than any other program, public or private. The nation's central retirement income policy is also its most important disability and life insurance program.

In the United States, "Social Security" commonly refers to the program that provides cash benefits to retired and disabled workers, their spouses and dependent children, and certain survivors of deceased workers. It is sometimes used to describe both the OASDI and Medicare programs. In other national contexts, "Social Security" is often referred to as a system of social insurance, public assistance (welfare), and related social interventions. "Social Security" also represents an ideal, a value to be achieved by a civilized society seeking to provide widespread basic protection against what Franklin D. Roosevelt called "the vicissitudes of life."

## The Social Insurance Approach

The social insurance approach to economic security protects against identifiable risks that could overwhelm the finances of individuals and families—loss of income due to death of a parent or spouse, disability, health care expenses, retirement, or workplace injury. Whereas welfare programs give immediate relief to extreme financial problems, social insurance programs in the United States—including Medicare, Social Security, Unemployment Insurance, and Worker's Compensation—seek to prevent financial distress. Built on the principle of universal coverage, social insurance provides a social means of pooling risks. Utilizing insurance principles, the costs and risks of coverage (for example, health insurance) are spread across a broad population (all working Americans). In exchange for modest work-related contributions over many years, social insurance provides a floor of protection against predictable risk (Ball, 2000).

Benefit receipt is tied to contributions made by an employee and/or employer. The right to a social insurance benefit is considered "earned". Eligibility does not require a means test. By providing benefits as an "earned right" while simultaneously protecting individuals and their families against economic insecurity, Social Security enhances the dignity of beneficiaries (Ball, 2000; Schulz & Binstock, 2006).

The concept of "social adequacy," which means that benefits meet the basic needs of the protected population, is the driving principle of social insurance and is consistent with the social goals of providing for the general welfare, maintaining dignity, and enhancing the stability of families and society. Absent a concern to provide widespread (ideally universal) adequate financial protection, there would be no reason for public social insurance (Hohaus, 1960). Protection against risks such as disability could be left to families, private savings, private pensions, private insurance, the vagaries of the economy and chance. But such mechanisms fall short of providing universal, adequate protection.

Commitment to "adequacy" is blended with concern for "individual equity"—the principle that dominates in private insurance that the more one contributes to a plan, the larger the benefit returns should be. Consequently, social insurance benefits bear some relationship to contributions made, with people who have worked consistently at higher wages, making larger payroll tax contributions and receiving larger monthly benefits. But reflecting the adequacy principle, people who have worked for many years at low or moderate wages receive proportionately larger benefits, relative to payroll tax contributions.

In order to both provide widespread adequate protection and maintain financial stability, participation must be compulsory. Of necessity, private insurance companies "cream off" the best risks and try to screen out expensive risks. But publically funded social insurance programs do not turn away "bad risks": for example, persons likely to require expensive surgery. Consequently, if the "good risks" are allowed to opt out, a social insurance system becomes financially unstable and costly. Moreover, some who opt out might eventually have to be rescued by taxpayer-financed welfare (Ball, 2000; Schulz & Binstock, 2006).

Social insurance programs reflect taxpayer and politician concern for stable financing. In most instances, payroll tax contributions and other revenues flow to dedicated trust funds earmarked to pay for benefits and administration. Safeguards assure stable financing. Legislative oversight and review by program officials, actuaries and independent experts, provide an early warning

system for financing problems that arise periodically. The authority and taxing power of government as well as the self-interest of political leaders to maintain the program for current and future generations, guarantee the continuity and financial integrity of these programs. As J. Douglas Brown, a Princeton economist, eloquently observed, an implied covenant, arising from a deeply embedded sense of mutual responsibility, reinforces and underlies "the fundamental obligations of the government and citizens of one time and the government and citizens of another to maintain a contributory social insurance system" (1977, 31–32).

Social insurance programs give concrete expression to widely held and time-honored liberal American commitments. They are grounded in values of shared responsibility and concern for all members of society. They reflect an understanding of the social compact which suggests that, as citizens and human beings, we all share certain risks and vulnerabilities; and we all have a stake in advancing practical mechanisms of self- and mutual support. They are based on the belief that government can and should uphold these values by providing practical, dignified, secure, and efficient means to protect Americans and their families against risks they all face (Cornman, Kingson, & Butts, 2005).

## History

Faced with unprecedented economic dislocation, President Roosevelt and the New Deal reformers saw the need and opportunity for an economic security bill to address unemployment and old age insecurity. In 1934 Roosevelt established the Committee on Economic Security (CES), chaired by social worker and the first woman cabinet officer, Secretary of Labor Frances Perkins, and including social worker and federal relief administrator, Harry Hopkins. Two young professionals on the CES staff, Eveline Burns and Wilbur Cohen, became prominent social work educators. At Columbia University, Burns distinguished herself as a social insurance scholar. Cohen, the first Social Security employee, would later be a social work professor at the University of Michigan, a Johnson administration cabinet officer and the person generally credited with launching the Medicare legislative strategy (Berkowitz, 1995).

The CES report provided the basis for the Social Security Act of 1935. In a January 17, 1935 message to Congress, Roosevelt commends the CES proposals as a plan that "is at once a measure of prevention and a method of alleviation" (Roosevelt, 1935).

We can never insure one hundred percent of the population against one hundred percent of the hazards and vicissitudes of life, but we have tried to

frame a law that will give some measure of protection to the average citizen and his family...
(Roosevelt, 1935)

Signed into law on August 14, the Act initiated two social insurance programs, three public assistance programs (means-tested welfare programs) and several public health and social service programs.

**INCREMENTAL EXPANSION (1935 TO 1975)** Incremental expansion characterized the development of Social Security from 1939 through the mid-1970s. Benefits were extended in 1939 to wives of retired workers and surviving wives and children of deceased workers (and to men, in 1950). The 1950 Social Security Amendments established social insurance as the nation's dominant means of protecting older Americans against loss of income in retirement. Coverage was extended to regularly employed domestic and farm workers and benefits increased, making Social Security more available and more valuable than benefits provided through the federal-state Old Age Assistance program, the welfare program funded under the Social Security Act.

In 1956, disability insurance protections for permanently and severely disabled workers aged 50 to 64 were added, then extended to all workers under 65 in 1960. The 1956 Amendments also gave women the right to accept permanently reduced retired workers benefits between ages 62 and 64, an option extended to men in 1961. The high poverty rate among the old—an estimated 39% of persons over 65 in 1959—combined with a growing economy provided political rationale for substantial benefits increases from 1965 through 1972. In 1972, the automatic cost-of-living allowance (COLA) was incorporated into the law, assuring that, once received, benefits would maintain their purchasing power no matter how long a beneficiary lived. While critically important for helping stabilize the incomes of the old, disabled and surviving family members, this provision is expensive and made the financing of the program more sensitive to economic change (Berkowitz, 2007).

**FINANCING PROBLEMS EMERGE (1975–1990)** By the mid-1970s, the pattern of incremental expansion halted as attention turned to program financing. Unanticipated economic changes (high inflation, slow economic growth, and lower than anticipated wage growth) created short-term financing problems in the mid-1970s and again in the early 1980s. Demographic changes (e.g., declining birth rates, increased life expectancies, and the anticipated aging of 76 million

baby boomers) fueled long-term financing problems. Legislation passed in 1977 and 1983 addressed these problems through a combination of modest benefit reductions and tax increases, spreading the pain of reform across many constituencies: working persons, employers, current and future beneficiaries (Altman, 2005; Berkowitz, 2007). By the mid-1980s, when the federal government was running large annual deficits in general revenues, the Social Security program began accumulating large yearly surpluses, a trend expected to continue through about 2020.

**ATTEMPTS TO PRIVATIZE AND REFORM (1990S TO PRESENT)** Except for a few doctrinaire conservatives, the voices favoring means-testing and privatizing Social Security were quiet until the early 1990s. But persistent claims that Social Security is unfair, false claims that it is unsustainable (see, for example, Peterson, 1996), a soaring stock market, and growing skepticism about whether the program will continue, combined with the deficit politics of the 1980s and 1990s to undermine faith in the program, especially among young adults (Altman, 2005; Herd & Kingson, 2005; Schulz & Binstock, 2006; White, 2001).

By the late 1990s proposals to partially privatize Social Security were being advanced in many quarters—conservative think tanks (for example, the Cato Institute), conservative advocacy groups (for example, The National Taxpayers Association), the Republican congressional leadership and some neoliberal Democrats. With support from many business groups—including the National Association of Manufacturers, Business Roundtable and Security Industry Association—advocacy helped advance privatization as a possible solution to a projected financing problem (Dreyfuss, 1999).

George W. Bush seized on these concerns in the 2000 presidential election, proposing that a portion of payroll taxes be diverted to individual accounts. Aware that the elimination of Social Security, and its payroll tax, was unlikely, conservatives proposed "partial privatization." Some hoped it might be the first step to a fully privatized system, and sought to "sell a market approach as a 'solution' to Social Security's financing troubles. Individual accounts would not only cure Social Security's bankruptcy blues, they would allow Americans more choice, increased savings, and bigger returns on their retirement investments—all while making the program more equitable for women and minorities" (Herd & Kingson, 2005).

Senior organizations, unions and Democratic Party leadership mounted a campaign opposing privatization.

Advocates, moderate and liberal think tanks, and analysts highlighted policy options that could address the projected shortfall without undermining the traditional program. They observed that partial privatization would actually make the projected shortfall much worse (Altman, 2005; Diamond & Orszag, 2005; Schulz & Binstock, 2006). Furman and Greenstein (2005) analyzed the impact of a plan similar to one the president was favoring, to divert four percentage points of a worker's payroll tax to private accounts without tax increases or benefit reductions for older workers and today's beneficiaries. By 2028, federal debt would increase by $4.9 trillion (about 14% of GDP in that year). The Bush administration "proposal" required very large reductions in benefits for young workers by changing how benefits are computed—from "wage-indexing" to "price-indexing" in determining initial benefits—greatly reducing guaranteed benefits, especially for the very young. For example, the projected average retirement benefits, including anticipated returns from private accounts, of future workers who are age 15 in 2005, would be $13,104, compared to $23,300 under the current system.

Many organizations expressed concern that partial privatization would pull a critical source of economic security out from under their constituents. In a January 27, 2005 letter to President Bush, NAACP Chairman Julian Bond and NOW President Kim Gandy wrote:

> Without Social Security benefits, the poverty rate among older African Americans would more than double, pushing most African American seniors into poverty. And more than half of all elderly women would be poor. (http://www.now.org/issues/economic/social/012805lett0er.html)

Public education, a stagnant stock market, a growing federal debt, and the Bush administration's declining approval ratings all combined to shift the politics of Social Security. As of 2007, proposals to partially privatize Social Security do not seem to be politically viable.

### Program Structure

Social Security affects virtually all Americans, as taxpayers and as beneficiaries. About 163 million people—over 95% of working persons—made payroll tax payments in 2007. In December 2006, 49 million people received benefits—including 4.5 million aged widow(er)s, 3.2 million children under age 19, 6.8 million disabled workers, 31 million retired workers, 2.5 million spouses of retired workers, 777,000 severely disabled dependent adult children, 156,000 spouses of disabled workers, and 171,000 spouses of deceased workers caring for dependent children (Social Security Administration, 2007).

FINANCING Retirement, survivors and disability protection and benefits are earned through payment of payroll taxes—"payroll tax contributions"—by workers and their employers, which serve as the basis for future eligibility and benefit decisions. The Social Security Administration (SSA) maintains a record of the earnings on which workers make payroll tax payments. Current benefits are funded largely from the taxes paid by current workers, with the promise—held together by the taxing power of the federal government—that current workers will themselves receive benefits when they become eligible. Additional revenues come from treating a portion of Social Security benefits as taxable income and from the interest earned from investing the growing OASDI trust fund assets in government bonds. Less than one percent (0.9%) of expenditures is spent on administration.

Employed persons contribute 6.2% of their earnings (with an equal employer match) up to a maximum taxable ceiling ($97,500 in 2007) into two trust funds: the Old-Age and Survivors Insurance (OASI) and the Disability Insurance (DI), or what is more conveniently called the combined OASDI trust fund. Self-employed persons make contributions equivalent to those made by regular employees and their employers. The maximum taxable ceiling is adjusted each year for changes in average wages. The goal is for Social Security to receive a constant share of national earnings. Another 1.45% payroll tax on all earnings goes to Medicare's Hospital Insurance (HI) trust fund.

In calendar year 2007, the combined OASDI trust fund received $780 billion dollars from all sources—$652 billion from payroll tax revenues, $17 billion from treating Social Security benefits as taxable income, and $101 billion in interest payments for treasury bonds and other federal securities held by Social Security. In turn, $591 billion were expended—$582 billion on Social Security benefit payments, $3.9 billion on the portion of the railroad retirement program integrated with Social Security, and $5.5 billion on administrative expenses (see Board of Trustees, 2006).

### Future Trends

Through 2027, Social Security is, under commonly accepted projections, expected to take in more funds than it expends. In 2007, it collected $189 billion more than was paid out in benefits or administrative expenses. This excess—the "surplus"—is deposited in the OASDI trust fund, swelling the fund's assets to over $2.2 trillion in 2007. Invested in federal government obligations, these funds are essentially loaned to the federal treasury, which uses them to offset the federal debt. Without borrowing from the OASDI trust fund, the federal treasury would need to fund the national debt with additional borrowing from the domestic private sector or from international sources. As with other holders of federal obligations, the treasury makes regular interest payments: as noted, $109 billion in 2007 to the OASDI trust funds (see Board of Trustees, 2006).

The Social Security trustees—the secretaries of the Treasury, Labor, and Health and Human Services, the commissioner of Social Security and two publicly—appointed members—issue an annual report on the program's financial status. Ongoing analysis by the Office of the Actuary, an independent and professional office within SSA, serves as the basis for the trustees report, and as an early warning system and means of assessing the scope and types of changes that may be needed periodically.

**BENEFITS** Because Social Security provides very substantial protections to children, persons with disabilities and older Americans, social workers need a basic understanding of its benefits.

It is useful to differentiate between Social Security and Supplemental Security Income (SSI). SSI—an important means-tested program administered by SSA—provided cash benefits to roughly 7.2 million low-income, severely disabled, blind or aged (65 and over) people in January 2007 (see the "Supplemental Security Income" entry and www.ssa.gov for additional information).

Social Security provides cash benefits to retired and disabled persons and, under certain conditions, to spouses, dependent children, and occasionally financially dependent grandchildren. In 2007, the maximum monthly benefit for persons first retiring at full retirement age is $2,116. Average monthly benefits in January 2007 were as follows:

| | |
|---|---|
| All retired workers | $1,044 |
| Aged couple with both receiving benefits | $1,713 |
| Widowed mother and two children | $2,167 |
| Aged widow(er) alone | $1,008 |
| All disabled workers | $ 979 |
| Disabled worker, spouse and one or more children | $1,646 |

Special rules link employee contributions to benefits they receive. Persons who have worked for ten years or more in covered employment (that is, earned credit for forty quarters) are almost always eligible to receive retirement benefits at age 62 or later, and their survivorship protections are in force. In 2007, credit for a quarter of coverage is earned during each quarter, as soon as payroll tax contributions are made on $1,000 of earnings. Additionally, for disability protections, workers usually need to have worked for five out of the past ten years. There are exceptions: for example, younger workers are subject to far less restrictive eligibility requirements for survivorship and disability protections.

The benefit formula assures that long-term, low-wage workers receive a proportionately larger benefit (relative to their contributions) than high-wage workers. The payroll tax contributions of high-wage workers are recognized by a larger monthly benefit, but such workers receive a proportionately smaller benefit. For workers retiring at the full retirement age in January 2007 (65 years and 8 months), Social Security replaces about 29% of earnings for those with earnings consistently at the maximum taxable earnings ceiling, compared to about 56% for those with earnings at 45% of median wages, and 41% for average earners.

Nearly all covered workers are eligible for full benefits at the full retirement age. Full retirement age, 66 for workers born from 1943 to 1954, is scheduled to gradually increase to age 67 for workers born in 1960 or later. Covered workers may accept retirement benefits beginning on the first month that they turn 62. However, if accepted at the earliest age, monthly retirement benefit amounts are permanently reduced, for example, by 25% for workers born from 1943 to 1954 and by 30% for workers born in 1960 or later. Workers receive credits that permanently increase the value of their monthly benefits, for each month benefit receipt is postponed past the full retirement age, up to age 70. The surviving spouses of retired workers may receive reduced survivor benefits at age 60 (or age 50 if severely disabled) or full benefits at full retirement age or later. Severely disabled workers are also eligible to receive monthly benefits if their condition meets disability eligibility criteria. Other dependents of retired, deceased or disabled workers, including financially dependent grandchildren or adult children who were disabled prior to age nineteen, may be eligible for monthly benefits.

When covered workers become severely disabled, they may be eligible, after a five-month waiting period, to receive monthly disability benefits. After 24 months of entitlement to disability benefits, disabled workers (as well as disabled widow(er)s aged 50 through 64), and adult disabled children are eligible for all Medicare benefits. Medicare does not, however, cover other family members, except for an aged spouse (see Social Security Administration, 2007).

To be considered disabled, in 2007 a person must be unable to earn $900 a month ($1,500 for blind people) because of a physical or mental impairment that is expected to last at least a year or result in death. A worker does not actually have to earn this amount, just be able to earn it. A worker must be unable to do any kind of job that exists in significant numbers in the national economy. The local or regional availability of jobs is not taken into consideration, although age, education, and previous work experience are.

Social Security disability and life insurance cover the great majority of the nation's families, including 73 million children under 18. In 2003, without Social Security benefits, the poverty rate of families with a disabled worker would have tripled, from 18.5% to 55% for all disabled workers; from 31.1% to 68% for African American families, and from 26.4% to 65.3% for Hispanic families (Beedon & Nawrocki, 2003).

In each state, SSA contracts with that state's disability determination service, to review disability applications and make initial eligibility decisions. If denied, claimants may request that the disability determination service reconsider their application. Claimants have the right to sequentially pursue three other levels of appeal: a hearing before an SSA administrative law judge, a hearing before the SSA Appeals council, and a lawsuit filed in a U.S. district court. Claims initially rejected are often accepted on appeal.

IMPACT ACROSS GENERATIONS The only pension protection available to six out of ten working persons in the private sector, Social Security is the foundation of the nation's retirement income system. More than 70% of the income going to aged households in the bottom 60% of the elderly income distribution comes from Social Security (see Table 1). Only for those in the highest 20% of the elderly income distribution, do other sources of income (i.e., assets income) equal or surpass (Social Security in relative contribution to household income. Occupational pensions make significant contributions to the aggregate incomes going to households in the three highest quintiles, but generally fall short of Social Security.

Although the economic status of today's older Americans has greatly improved, many remain at significant financial risk. Adjusted for inflation, the median income of elderly households increased from $13,670 in 1960 to $26,036 in 2005. Poverty rates declined precipitously from 35.2% in 1959 to 14.6% in 1974, and have since declined more slowly to 10.1% in 2005. Without Social Security, the poverty rate among the aged would jump from 10% to nearly 50%;

TABLE 1

*Importance of Various Sources of Income to Elderly Households (Aged Units), 2004* [*] (All Members over Age 65)*

| | ALL AGED UNITS | QUINTILES UNITS UNDER $10,399 (Q1) | $10,399–$16,363 (Q2) | $16,363–$25,587 (Q3) | $25,587–$44,129 (Q4) | $44,129 AND OVER (Q5) |
|---|---|---|---|---|---|---|
| Number of Units (in millions) | 27.0 | 5.3 | 5.5 | 5.4 | 5.4 | 5.4 |
| Percent of Total Income From: [**] | | | | | | |
| Social security (OASDI) | 38.6 | 82.6 | 83.4 | 66.6 | 47.5 | 18.9 |
| Railroad Retirement | 0.5 | 0.3 | 0.4 | 0.6 | 1.0 | 0.3 |
| Government employee pension | 9.0 | 0.8 | 2.1 | 5.5 | 10.4 | 9.9 |
| Private pension/annuity | 10.2 | 0.7 | 2.2 | 6.0 | 10.1 | 10.9 |
| Income from assets | 12.6 | 2.3 | 3.8 | 6.0 | 8.4 | 17.8 |
| Earnings | 26.3 | 1.2 | 2.8 | 7.1 | 15.7 | 40.1 |
| Public assistance (welfare) | 0.6 | 8.4 | 1.6 | 0.9 | 0.2 | 0.1 |
| Other | 2.4 | 2.0 | 1.5 | 2.7 | 2.6 | 1.9 |

[*] All members of households are 65 or over. Aged units are married couple living together–at least one of whom is 65– and non-married persons 65 or older.

[**] Details may not sum to totals due to rounding error.

US Department of Health and Human Services, Social Security Administration, Office of Policy Office of Research, Evaluation and Statistics, *Income of the Population 55 and Over* (Washington, DC: 2006), pp. 139, 143 (http://www.ssa.gov/policy/docs/statcomps/income_pop55/2004/incpop04.pdf).

from 15% to 58% for unmarried aged beneficiaries, and from 24% to 75% for African American seniors (Cornman, Kingson, & Butts, 2005).

For a covered 27-year-old married couple with two children under age four, Social Security is the equivalent of a term life insurance policy in excess of $400,000 and a disability policy in excess of $350,000. Ten million people *under age 60* receive Social Security benefits each month. Benefits received by these surviving family members, severely-disabled workers, spouses, children and some adopted grandchildren living in a grandparent's home, go a long way towards enabling families to maintain their living standards. In addition to the over 4.1 million children receiving Social Security checks each month, another 2.2 million children under 18, while not receiving benefits themselves, live with relatives who do. Social Security is the largest and most substantial source of public cash benefits going to 2.4 million grandparent-headed households responsible for 4.5 million children under 18, and Social Security lifts one-million children from poverty (Cornman, Kingson, & Butts, 2005).

### Contemporary Challenges

Barring extraordinary circumstances (for example, economic collapse) Social Security will not face a short-term shortfall within the next 20 years as it did in the early 1980s (Altman, 2005; Diamond & Orszag, 2005; Schulz & Binstock, 2006). However, a significant shortfall exists.

THE PROJECTED FINANCING PROBLEM The most commonly accepted estimates suggest that OASDI has sufficient funds to meet all obligations until 2040. Outlays are projected to exceed tax revenues (payroll tax receipts and taxes on benefits) in 2017. However, income from all sources, including interest on trust fund investment, is projected to exceed expenditures through 2027. After that, timely payment of benefits will require drawing down the OASDI assets, depleting them in 2040. Trust fund depletion does not mean that Social Security will be "bankrupt" or "unsustainable." It is politically inconceivable that future Congresses would not act before 2040. Even if they failed to act, Social Security's dedicated stream of income after 2040 is sufficient to pay about 74 cents of every dollar promised over the remaining 75-year estimating period. Of course, the size of the actual problem could grow or shrink, depending on economic and demographic changes (Board of Trustees, 2006).

Theoretically, the financing problem could be addressed immediately by raising the Social Security payroll tax on employers and employees from 6.2% to 7.2% or by immediately reducing all future benefits by about 14%. While this reflects the size of the problem, no one seriously advocates either approach but it does provide a very rough indication of the size of the financing problem.

MEANS-TESTING Means-testing is sometimes considered as a solution. Some, from across the political spectrum, have suggested it is preferable to reduce or eliminate the benefits of well-off beneficiaries rather than increase taxes of moderate-income workers or cut the benefits of low- and moderate-income persons. Means-testing can reasonably be viewed as an equitable reform, but it would also place political support for the program at risk and undermine beneficiaries' dignity. Means-testing potentially moves so far from individual equity that it would segment political support, creating a strong incentive for higher-income people—including many opinion leaders—to oppose the program. Ironically, by "punishing" the thrifty and rewarding those who do not save, means-testing would also introduce significant savings disincentives (Kingson & Schulz, 1997).

REFORM OPTIONS For the past decade, addressing the projected long-term shortfall has been the paramount Social Security policy concern. With the debate over privatization subsiding, attention will likely turn to how best to address the financing problems within the structure of the existing program.

*Increasing Revenues.* Modest changes can increase revenues (see Reno & Lavery, 2005). For example, traditionally and following the enactment of the 1983 financing amendments, about 90% of national employment earnings were subject to the Social Security payroll tax. As income became more unevenly distributed, the payroll tax base eroded, so that today only 83% of earnings are taxed. Returning the ceiling to 90% of payroll, gradually over 10 years, would address about 40% of the problem. Covering all newly hired state and local employees would bring the last large group of workers not covered into the program, addressing 10% of the problem. Increasing the payroll tax by 0.50% on both the employer and employee, in 2020, could address 25% of the problem. Rather than eliminating the estate tax after 2010 as proposed by President Bush, directing revenues into Social Security from taxing estates worth $3.5 million or more would address 27% of the problem. Diversifying trust fund investments by allowing for a small portion of trust fund assets to be invested by an independent board in a broad selection of private equities could help improve rates of return, reducing the projected deficit by an estimated 25% if one-fifth of the trust fund is so invested (see Altman, 2005; Ball, 2007; Diamond & Orszag, 2005; Steuerle & Bakija, 1994).

**Reducing Expenditures.** Modest benefit changes can reduce program expenditures (see Reno & Lavery, 2005). For example, cutting benefits by 3% for those starting them in 2008 would address about 20% of the projected problem, as would lowering the annual COLA by 0.25 percentage points each year. Accelerating the increase in the full retirement age to 67 for persons born in 1949 or later and then gradually increasing it to 68 for those born in 1973 or later would address 28% of the financing problem. Gradually phasing in a change in the benefit formula resulting in modest benefit reductions, mostly among future beneficiaries with the largest monthly benefits and longest life expectancies, would address 9% of the projected deficit (see Altman, 2005, Ball, 2007; Diamond & Orszag, 2005; Steuerle & Bakija, 1994).

Reasonable people may disagree about benefit reductions or revenue increases. Some argue that given the increase in life expectancies, further increases in the age of eligibility for full benefits are needed. Others point out that retirement age increases and COLA cuts are especially deleterious for low- and moderate-income persons who depend more on Social Security as a source of income. Some raise concern about the federal government investing a portion of the trust fund in private equities, fearing it may lead to an attempt to manipulate markets. Some argue that raising the payroll tax ceiling is a just mechanism for addressing the financing problem; others term it costly to business and workers. Bringing all new state and local workers into Social Security will be resisted by some government employee unions as undermining their occupational pension systems. Others will observe that in 1983 new federal workers were brought in and they have fared well (Herd & Kingson, 2005).

Robert Ball, who has dedicated his life to Social Security (Berkowitz, 2004), offers the wisdom of a long and distinguished career, beginning as a SSA field office representative in 1939, serving as its principal administrator and commissioner for over two decades, and then founding the National Academy of Social Insurance (see www.nasi.org). Ball issued a three-point plan that addresses the financing problem by restoring the maximum taxable ceiling to 90% of earnings, earmarking the estate tax, and investing a portion of the trust funds in private equities. He reasons that the problem should be addressed through revenue increases, not benefit cuts: retirement age increases are already resulting in benefit cuts; moreover, reducing benefits is not a good idea because of the uncertain future of private pensions and retiree health insurance protections (Ball, 2006; also see www.robertball.org).

SOCIAL JUSTICE ISSUES OF ADEQUACY AND EQUITY The next round of Social Security reform, though focused on financing concerns, will provide opportunity to improve benefits for persons at financial risk. African American and Hispanic elders are more likely to be poor or near poor than White elders, as are nonmarried elders of all races and ethnicities and women, especially the very old (see United States Census Bureau, 2006).

Differences in income and poverty of various groups are tied to labor force participation, earnings histories, and occupational pension coverage of these groups. Women's employment histories tend to be interrupted by caregiving responsibilities to children and other family members. The economic costs of caregiving— lost opportunity for employment advancement, less wage growth and fewer years of coverage under Social Security—are not adjusted for in the Social Security benefit calculus. The cost of divorce regarding lost Social Security pension income also falls more heavily on women. Older heterosexual couples are well protected but very old widowed women are not. Neither are people in committed gay or lesbian relationships since, unlike married heterosexual couples, survivorship benefits do not accrue to same-sex partners. Very significantly, as retirement ages increase, the permanent reduction in benefits will increase for persons first accepting Social Security benefits before full retirement age. While not problematic for those who choose to leave work, those compelled to stop working before full retirement age—disproportionately low-income and minority persons—face financial risk. In short, beyond financing reforms, much remains to be done to address Social Security adequacy and equity concerns (see also Tracy & Ozawa, 1995).

CONCLUSION An institution that social workers Harry Hopkins, Francis Perkins, Wilbur Cohen and others helped to nurture, Social Security is the nation's most successful social policy. As policy discussions advance about future reforms, it will be important for new generations of social workers to help advance an understanding of the full range of benefits provided and the moral dimensions of the program.

### Acknowledgments

The author wishes to acknowledge with appreciation Diana Biro, Coordinator of Research Development in Syracuse University's College Human Ecology, who assisted in editing this entry.

## REFERENCES

Altman, N. J. (2005). *The battle for social security: From FDR's vision to Bush's gamble.* Hoboken, NJ: John Wiley and Sons.

Ball, R. M. (2000). *Ensuring the essentials.* New York: The Century Foundation Press.

Ball, R. M. (2006, December). Meeting Social Security's Long-Range Shortfall: A Golden Opportunity for the New Congress. Accessed from www.robertball.org.

Beedon, L., & Nawrocki, H. (2003, February). Social Security Disability Insurance: Some Facts. AARP Public Policy Institute. Accessed from http://www.aarp.org/research/social security/ssdi/aresearch-import-364-FS92.html#SEVENTH

Berkowitz, E. D. (1995). *Mr. Social Security: The life of Wilbur J. Cohen.* Lawrence: University Press of Kansas.

Berkowitz, E. D. (2004). *Robert Ball and the politics of social security.* Madison: University of Wisconsin Press.

Berkowitz, E. D. (2007). The historical development of social security in the United States. In E. R. Kingson & J. H. Schulz (Eds.), *Social security in the 21st century.* New York: Oxford University Press.

Board of Trustees, Federal Old Age and Survivors Insurance and Disability Insurance Trust Funds. (2006). *2006 Annual Report of the Trustees of the Federal Old-Age and Survivors Insurance and Disability Insurance Trust Funds.* Washington, DC: U.S. Government Printing Office.

Bond, J., & Gandy, K. (2005, January 27). Letter from NOW and NAACP to George W. Bush Regarding a "Separate but Equal" Privatized Social Security System. Accessed from http://www.now.org/issues/economic/social/012805letter.html

Brown, J. D. (1977). *Essays on social security.* Princeton, NJ: Princeton University Press.

Cornman, J. C., Kingson, E. R., & Butts, D. (2005, May/June). Should we be our neighbors' keeper? Church and Society, *Journal of the Presbyterian Church USA* (*Special Issue on the Social Compact*), 34–41.

Diamond, P. A., & Orszag, P. R. (2005). *Saving social security: A balanced approach.* Washington, DC: Brookings Institution Press.

Dreyfuss, R. (1999, February 8). The Real Threat to Social Security. *The Nation* Accessed from http://www.ourfuture.org/issues_and_campaigns/socialsecurity/key_issues/money_trail_and_wall_street/readarticle50.cfm

Furman, J., & Greenstein, R. (2005, February 7). An Overview of Issues Raised by the Administration's Social Security. Center for Budget and Policy Priorities Accessed from http://www.cbpp.org/2-2-05socsec4.htm

Herd, P., & Kingson, E. R. (2005). Selling social security reform: A story of framing and reform. In R. B. Hudson (Ed.), *Age based public policy in the 21st century.* Baltimore: Johns Hopkins University Press

Hohaus, R. A. (1960). Equity, adequacy and related factors in old age security. In W. Haber & W. J. Cohen (Eds.), *Social security programs, problems and policies.* Homewood, IL: Richard D. Irwin, Inc.

Kingson, E. R., & Schulz, J. H. (1997). Should Social Security be means-tested? In E. R. Kingson & J. H. Schulz (Eds.), *Social security in the 21st century.* New York: Oxford University Press.

Peterson, P. G. (1996). *Will America grow up before it grows old?* New York: Random House.

Reno, V. P., & Lavery, J. (2005, February). Options to Balance Social Security Funds Over the Next 75 Years. *Brief* No. 18 Accessed from http://www.nasi.org/usr_doc/SS_Brief_18.pdf.

Roosevelt, F. D. (1935, August 15). Presidential Statement signing the Social Security Act.

Schulz, J. H., & Binstock, R. H. (2006). *Aging Nation: The Economics and politics of growing older in America.* Westport, CT: Praeger Publishers.

Social Security Administration, Office of Policy, Office of Research, Evaluation and Statistics (2007). Annual Statistical Supplment. Washington, DC: Social Security Administration http://www.ssa.gov/policy/docs/statcomps/supplement/2007/

Social Security Administration, Office of Policy, Office of Research, Evaluation and Statistics (2005). Income of the Population 55 and Over. Washington, DC: Social Security Administration, pp. 120, 123 http://www.ssa.gov/statistics/incpop55/1998

Steuerle, C. E., & Bakija, J. M. (1994). *Retooling social security for the twenty-first century.* Washington, DC: Urban Institute Press.

Tracy, M. B., & Ozawa, M. N. (1995). Social security. *Encyclopedia of social work.* Silver Spring, MD: National Association of Social Workers.

United States Census Bureau (2006). Age and Sex of All People, Family Members and Unrelated Individuals Iterated by Income-to-Poverty Ratio and Race: 2005 Below 100% of Poverty. Accessed from http://pubdb3.census.gov/macro/032006/pov/new01_100_06.htm.

White, J. (2001). *False alarm.* New York: The Century Foundation Press.

## SUGGESTED LINKS

Center on Budget & Policy Priorities.
*http://www.cbpp.org/pubs/socsec.htm*

Fact Sheet: The Stake of Children and Youth in Social Security.
*http://www.socialsecurity4youth.org/Portals/1/GU-StakeChildrenSSFactSheet.pdf*

National Academy of Social Insurance (February 2005). "Options to Balance Social Security Funds Over the Next 75 Years,".
*http://www.nasi.org/publications2763/publications_show.htm?doc_id=263184*

Social Security Administration.
*www.ssa.gov*

Students for Social Security.
*http://www.studentsforsocialsecurity.org/*

The Century Foundation (2005). The Basics: Social Security Reform.
*http://www.tcf.org/list.asp?type=PB&pubid=509*

The Social Security Network.
*http://www.socsec.org*

—ERIC R. KINGSON

# SOCIAL SERVICES

ABSTRACT: Formal or institutional social services began in the United States in the late 19th century as a response to problems that were rapidly increasing as a result of modernization. These services were almost entirely private until the Great Depression in the 1930s when the government became involved via provisions of the Social Security Act. Services expanded greatly, beginning in the 1960s when the federal government developed a system wherein services were supported by public funds but provided through contracts with private agencies. This trend has continued and expanded, resulting in a uniquely American system wherein private agencies serve as vehicles for government social service policy.

KEY WORDS: Charity Organization Society; contracting; Omnibus Budget Reconciliation Act; Personal Responsibility and Work Opportunity Reconciliation Act; Social Security Act; social service funding; Title XX

## Definitions and Background

The social welfare system can be roughly divided into two components. The first is social provision, which is the provision of income and income equivalents (food stamps, public housing, Medicaid, and the like) serving the purpose of elevating people's material level of living up to some minimum point. The second is social services, sometimes (especially in Europe) referred to as personal social services, which comprise "the activities of human services personnel in promoting the health and well-being of people and in helping people become more self-sufficient; preventing dependency; strengthening family relationships; and restoring individuals, families, groups, or communities to successful social functioning" (Barker, 2003, p. 407). These services generally include daycare, counseling, job training, child protection, foster care, residential treatment, homemaker services, rehabilitation, and sheltered workshops (Kramer, 1987, p. 240). Social services to both the poor and the nonpoor have experienced tremendous growth over the past century with provision evolving from almost entirely private charitable funding, to a dual system of public and private nonprofit services, sometimes referred to as the voluntary sector, to the present complex system wherein the majority of services are provided by private nonprofit and for-profit agencies, mostly funded by public sources, and carrying out the policies of government.

THE BEGINNING OF SOCIAL SERVICES Prior to the second half of the 19th century, an era characterized by the beginning of the evolution of American society from rural to urban and from agricultural to industrial, there was little, in fact little need for, social services. Following the Civil War, the massive changes in the country, mainly rapidly increasing urbanization, industrialization, and immigration, led to correspondently increasing problems of poverty, crime, and public health. In response to these problems three major social movements developed that, together, constitute the beginning of social services in this country—the Charity Organization Society (COS) Movement (also known as scientific charity), the Settlement House Movement, and several loosely related developments, notably the Children's Aid Society and the Society for the Prevention of Cruelty to Children, that together formed the basic elements of a child welfare movement (Trattner, 1999, pp. 77–107). These movements were nearly entirely privately funded and managed, and they pursued objectives that were primarily nongovernmental.

Although the settlements and the early child welfare agencies eventually made important contributions to the development of social services in the United States, it was the COS agencies that were primarily responsible for the development of technical methods of social services and the development of a social work profession. This movement began in Buffalo, New York, in 1877 with the general goal of assisting the poor (Lewis, 1954, pp. 10–24). Although programs to aid the poor have been in existence since nearly the beginning of human society, the COS movement represented a new approach. Its main purpose was not to provide material aid (in fact, in the beginning, the COS provided no aid) but to understand and cure poverty and family disorganization. The COS was the first organization to propose that one person, using only his or her own self, could bring about a change and improvement in the life of another person. This was the beginning of the concept of social services. The COS worker, forerunner of today's social worker, was called a "friendly visitor"; and the agency quickly developed a methodology for these persons to apply. The 1887 annual report of the COS stated:

> Marvelous indeed it is to find in how many cases some cause of poverty and want exists which you can remove!...You go in the full strength and joy and fire of life; full of cheer and courage; with a far wider knowledge of affairs; and it would be indeed a wonder if you could not often see why the needy family does not succeed, and how to help them up. (quoted in Lubove, 1965, pp. 12–13)

What technical skills the early friendly visitors possessed consisted mainly of personal attributes such as "all possible sympathy, tact, patience, cheer, and wise advice (Lubove, 1965, p. 13).

Those involved in the COS believed that it was not enough to relieve want and suffering with the provision of material assistance, but that it was possible actually to remediate the causes of dependence through the medium of social services. It did not take long for COS staff to realize that a cheerful nature, a willing spirit, and a good example were not enough to solve the problems that client families presented to the agency. What they often found was not families in need of moral guidance, but families of "exemplary piety" and diligence who were overwhelmed by circumstances beyond their control. This discovery led, by the end of the 19th century, to a movement to research the causes of dependency and to develop technical methods that could be used to remedy the discovered problems. A critical event in this effort was the establishment, in 1898, of the New York School of Philanthropy, the first school of professional social work in the world.

GOVERNMENT BECOMES INVOLVED The private provision of social services, however, flowered following the turn of the century with the addition of medical social services, social services in mental hospitals and clinics, school social services, juvenile court services, and the gradual evolution of the work of the COS agencies into what we now think of as family services. Shortly after the entry of the United States into the First World War, the Red Cross began the development of psychiatric social work, and supported the establishment of the Smith College School for Psychiatric Social Workers. All of these developments shared the common goal of developing social services to mediate the effects of the environment on the mission of various institutions (Lubove, 1965, pp. 78–83).

Prior to the Great Depression and the Social Security Act of 1935, social services were provided almost entirely by voluntary nonprofit agencies, were financed by private contributions and bequests, and were only coincidentally agents of public policy. There was a small amount of government involvement in social provision, mainly in the form of widow's pensions, veteran's benefits, and care in various institutions such as special schools and state hospitals, but there was virtually no federal government involvement in social services.

In 1929 the country entered a depression that was to be the longest and deepest in its history. The Great Depression had an immediate and profound effect on social services. Prior to this time, the social welfare system, social provision as well as social services, had been almost entirely private. The development of a public social welfare system had been vigorously opposed by most social workers who felt that private services were superior to public services because public agencies were thought to be corrupt and inefficient

and therefore not settings conducive to high-quality services (Leiby, 1978, pp. 178–179). After the election of Franklin D. Roosevelt in 1933, this situation changed rapidly. The Social Security Act, passed in 1935, moved financial assistance, as well as much of public health and child welfare, to the public sector. However, the passage of this act did not have any profound, immediate effect on the provision of social services. The majority of the 40,000 social service personnel hired to work in the new public welfare programs were untrained, were not accepted by the profession of social work as full-fledged colleagues, and were mainly involved in determination of client eligibility for welfare benefits. Those services generally considered to be social services, with the exception of a relatively small number of public employees engaged in child welfare, continued to be provided by the social workers employed in private settings, and these agencies continued to operate independently of public funding, and largely independent of public policy (Jansson, 2005, pp. 165–224).

The social service system in this country has never moved very far from the original Charity Organization Society goal of reducing dependency. It is this goal that led to the growth of public social services beginning in the 1950s. Amendments to the Social Security Act for the first 22 years of its existence consisted mainly of changes in eligibility and benefit levels. The 1956 amendments began the process of adding other services. As reported by Jay Roney, Director of the Bureau of Public Assistance, the bureau found that the major factors contributing to dependency had changed since the passage of social security from mass unemployment to disability, chronic illness, advanced age, and family disruption. The 1956 amendments allowed federal sharing in vendor payments for medical services and provided funds to support "... planning by federal, state, and local agencies and other interested groups to coordinate medical, social, vocational, and other services with financial assistance to provide a broad range of services to help needy persons increase their capacity for self-care or self-support, and to maintain or strengthen family life." (Roney, 1960, p. 467). The amendment also called for funds to train state public assistance personnel to provide social services, but these funds were never actually provided.

The social services hinted at in the 1956 amendments to the Social Security Act were made real in Pub. L. No. 87-543, the Public Welfare Amendments of 1962, often referred to as the Social Service Amendments. Following the reports of an Ad Hoc Committee on Public Welfare, and of independent consultant George K. Wyman, the amendments signaled a fundamental shift in the approach to public assistance. This new approach was summarized in the statement of the

Ad Hoc Committee's report that "financial assistance to meet people's basic needs for food, shelter, and clothing is essential, but alone is not enough. Expenditures for assistance not accompanied by rehabilitation services may actually increase dependency." The committee was convinced that by providing social services public welfare could become a "positive wealth-producing force in society" by contributing to an "attack on such problems as dependency, juvenile delinquency, family breakdown, illegitimacy, ill health, and disability" (quoted in Axinn & Stern, 2008, p. 250). The 1962 amendments followed the advice of the committee by recommending that states provide social services to welfare recipients to promote self-care and self-support. In order to facilitate this new approach, the federal share of the cost of these services was set at 75% of expenditures for services to reduce dependency and for training staff carrying out the intent of the law. These amendments also heralded a new era in the relationship between public and private agencies by providing a purchase-of-services mechanism that made federal funds available for contracting of services provided by private nonprofit agencies (Popple, 1995, p. 2288).

THE PUBLIC–PRIVATE PARTNERSHIP The belief of Congress when it passed the 1962 social service amendments was that providing social services to welfare recipients, especially services provided by trained social workers, would result in declining welfare rolls. The fact that welfare rolls did not decline, but in fact increased at a faster rate than ever, caused Congress to become quickly disillusioned with the theory that social services can reduce dependency (Steiner, 1971, p. 57). As a result, the next round of Social Security Act amendments, passed in 1967, completely separated social services from income assistance in favor of a "hard services" approach initially in the form of the Work Incentive Program, (hard services are those services that lead or directly support entry into employment, such as job training and child care, as opposed to soft services that address, generally through some form of casework or counseling, personal problems that are viewed as the underlying causes of poverty and unemployment) and a new formula for computing benefits that allowed recipients to retain a portion of any earned income. However, Congress did not so much lose faith in social services as it lost faith in the ability of government to directly provide these. While it moved to reduce social services directly provided by state social service departments, Congress developed new mechanisms and greatly increased funding for states to purchase social services from private providers. As a result, between 1971 and 1978 the percentage of social service funding

under the Social Security Act that was dispersed through purchase-of-service contracting increased from 25 to 54% (Kramer & Grossman, 1987, p. 33).

In 1975 Congress once again expanded mechanisms and funding for service contracting through the passage of Title XX of the Social Security Act, which was amended in 1981 by the Omnibus Budget Reconciliation Act to establish a program to provide block grants to states for the provision of social services. This is a capped block grant that was partially a response to fear of the runaway growth of spending under the 1967 uncapped entitlement program, under which spending had increased from $242 million in 1967 to $1.688 billion in 1972 (Lynn, 2002, p. 63). The grant called for $2.5 billion per year for states to purchase social services directed toward one of five hierarchal goals. These goals are as follows: achieving or maintaining economic self-support; achieving or maintaining self-sufficiency; preventing or reducing neglect, abuse, or exploitation; preventing or reducing inappropriate institutional care; and securing referral or admission for institutional care when appropriate (Committee on Ways and Means, 2006, p. 10–17). The Title XX act also widened the scope of government-funded social services by reducing the number of service recipients who had to be eligible for financial assistance from 90% to 50%. States currently spend the largest amount of Title XX funds on child protective services (11.8%), foster care services (10.1%), disability services (8.3%), protection or intervention services (7.7%), home-based services (7.6%), and child day care (7.6%) (Committee on Ways and Means, 2006, p. 10–19).

The 1996 Personal Responsibility and Work Opportunity Reconciliation Act (the TANF program) has further strengthened the position of the federal government as the primary funding source of social services whether provided by public, voluntary, or for-profit organizations. The act has done this in two ways. The first is a provision in the act that authorizes states to transfer up to 30% of their TANF allotments to Title XX or to the Child Care and Development Block Grant. This has greatly expanded the amount of funds states have in excess of the $2.5 billion cap. The second is the expansion of the number of agencies eligible to contract for services through the charitable choice provisions that authorize states to administer and provide TANF and Supplementary Security Income services through contracts with charitable, religious, or private (including for-profit) organizations (Lynn, 2002, pp. 58–59). Private corporations that have taken advantage of government social service contracts include the $12.2 billion Electronic Data Systems and the $30 billion Lockheed Martin Corporation.

With Title XX the government tentatively began to assert social services as a right, but this quickly engendered Congressional opposition and a funding cap. However, legislators have managed to do what Smith refers to as an "end run" around the Social Services Block Grant cap and expanded federal funding of social services by making technical changes to existing laws by, for example, greatly expanding Supplemental Security Income and Medicaid coverage, creating new programs targeted at specific problems such as child welfare and drug abuse treatment, and by reclassifying certain social services as long-term care or health care (Smith, 2002, p. 180).

The American system of social services has created a greatly expanded system of services, but one that is highly unstable because modest changes to existing laws can have major negative repercussions on funding, the restrictiveness of existing laws create difficulties for agencies to respond to changes, and the increasing competition between nonprofits and for-profits make the survival of smaller, traditionally more flexible, organizations questionable.

### Trends and International Comparisons

In Europe social services have come to be regarded as an essential right of every citizen and are championed by major political parties. As a result, extensive networks of government-provided services exist. This has never been the situation in the United States, where social services have been considered the province of private charity. The Federal Government has increasingly entered the picture in the past half-century but, rather than developing an extensive network of European-style government-provided services, has relied on the American tradition of private charity but has, through the provision of funding, made these agencies instruments of government policy.

#### REFERENCES

Axinn, J., & Stern, M. J. (2008). *Social welfare: A history of the American response to need* (6th ed.). Boston: Allyn & Bacon.

Barker, R. L. (2003). *The social work dictionary* (5th ed.). Washington, DC: NASW Press.

Committee on Ways and Means. (2006). *2004 Green book: Background material and data on the programs within the jurisdiction of the Committee on Ways and Means*. Washington, DC: U.S. Government Printing Office.

Jansson, B. S. (2005). *The reluctant welfare state—American social welfare policies: Past, present, and future* (5th ed.). Belmont, CA: Brooks/Cole.

Kramer, R. M. (1987). Voluntary agencies and the personal social services. In W. W. Powell (Ed.), *The nonprofit sector: A research handbook*. New Haven, CT: Yale University Press.

Kramer, R. M., & Grossman, B. (1987). Contracting for social services: Process management and resource dependencies. *Social Service Review, 61*(1), 32–53.

Leiby, J. (1978). *A history of social welfare and social work in the United States*. New York: Columbia University Press.

Lewis, V. S. (1954). *The development of the Charity Organization Movement in the United States 1875–1900: Its principles and methods*. Unpublished Ph.D. Dissertation, Case Western Reserve University, Cleveland.

Lubove, R. (1965). *The professional altruist: The emergence of social work as a career*. Cambridge, MA: Harvard University Press.

Lynn, L. E., Jr. (2002). Social services and the state: The public appropriation of private charity. *Social Service Review, 76*(2), 58–82.

Popple, P. R. (1995). Social work profession: History. In R. L. Edwards (Ed.), *Encyclopedia of social work* (19th ed., pp. 2282–2292). Washington, DC: NASW Press.

Roney, J. L. (1960). Public assistance. In R. L. Kurtz (Ed.), *Social work yearbook, 1960: A description of organized activities in social work and related fields* (pp. 460–470). New York: National Association of Social Workers.

Smith, S. R. (2002). Social services. In L. M. Salamon (Ed.), *The state of nonprofit America* (pp. 149–186). Washington, DC: Brookings Institution Press.

Steiner, G. Y. (1971). *The State of welfare*. Washington, DC: The Brookings Institution.

Trattner, W. I. (1999). *From poor law to welfare state: A history of social welfare in America* (6th ed.). New York: Free Press.

—PHILIP R. POPPLE

## SOCIAL WELFARE EXPENDITURES

**ABSTRACT:** Understanding both public and private welfare expenditures is necessary to appreciate the full scope of a social welfare system. This entry examines spending in four major areas of social welfare policy (health, medical, and nutrition; retirement and disability insurance; income maintenance and welfare; and education), comparing the public and private sectors. While expenditures for both sectors are increasing, private expenditures are not increasing as a percentage of total costs, despite efforts to privatize social welfare. This may change in the future if military costs continue to siphon governmental costs away from social welfare expenditures.

**KEY WORDS:** social welfare; expenditures; health; nutrition; income maintenance; education; welfare; retirement

Social welfare in the United States has always operated under a mixture of public (governmental) and private auspices. Public expenditures, particularly at the national level, began to increase during the Great Depression of the 1930s with the advent of the New Deal era. Programs that are mainstays of social welfare today, such as Social Security pensions and Temporary Assistance for Needy Families (the successor to Aid to Families with Dependent Children), began with the passage of the Social Security Act of 1935. Public expenditures again rose significantly in the 1960s, as programs associated with President Johnson's War on Poverty were begun (for example, Medicare and Medicaid).

While most attention by policy scholars is given to public expenditures, as these are paid from taxes, private expenditures for social welfare functions are also important. As Kerns (1994) argued, knowledge of both public and private expenditures is needed to fully understand social welfare spending.

## Definitions and Measures of Social Welfare Expenditures

The term *social welfare* is often thought of as a synonym for human services directed towards the poor, or means-tested programs. Some authors use a broader definition to include governmental expenditures and tax breaks for the middle and upper classes. Adopting this broader definition shows that the poor receive only a small percentage of public social welfare expenditures (Abramovitz, 2001; Hoefer & Colby, 1997).

Given the level of ambiguity of the term *social welfare*, it is no surprise that difficulty exists in determining how much is spent on social welfare in the United States. Thus, different researchers, with different definitions, will develop different estimates of total social welfare expenditures.

Expenditure estimates by governmental bodies are relatively easy to track, because of their public nature. Still, public spending estimates usually lag by 1 or 2 years and sometimes cost figures undergo revisions that make previously published data incompatible with current estimates. Private expenditures are even more difficult to identify with precision. Most data for this entry are taken from *The 2007 Statistical Abstract of the United States*, a compendium of government-collected information published by the U.S. Census Bureau.

## Health, Medical, and Nutrition Expenditures

While most industrialized countries have national health systems that are mainly funded by government sources, the United States utilizes a broader mixture of public and private spending. Costs for both sectors have risen quickly since mid-1990s. Table 1 provides information comparing private and public expenditures for health, for selected years from 1960 and projections for 2010. Private expenditures are divided into *consumer out of pocket* and *insurance* subcategories. Public expenditures are divided into *federal* and *state and local* subcategories.

Most striking about these numbers is the increase in medical and health costs. Total costs were 72 times higher in 2005 (projected) than in 1960. Total expenditures after 2005 were projected to continue to increase rapidly. Private expenditures were 52 times higher in 2005 than in 1960, compared with the nearly 130-fold increase in public costs over those same years.

Looking only at the last decade, four points are important. First, the private and public shares of total health costs are holding steady, at around 55%, with public costs accounting for about 45% of total costs. Second, within the private expenditures category, consumer out-of-pocket costs, while rising rapidly, are falling as a percent of total private health costs. In 1960, out-of-pocket costs were 62%, but fell to 26% in 1995 and 2000. They dipped slightly again by 2005, to 23%. Third, within the public expenditures category, federal costs, while rising from 43% in 1960, have hovered at about 70% of governmental costs since 1995. Finally, the rate of increase in health expenditures since mid-1990s was similar for private and public sources. Between 1995 and 2005 total health expenditures increased 98%; private health expenditures increased 99%; and public health expenditures rose 96%.

In addition to the private health expenditures shown in Table 1, private philanthropy provided $12.6 billon in 1995, increasing to $22.0 billion in 2004, an increase of 75% (U.S. Census Bureau, 2006, Table 567, p. 366).

The United States government and private citizens and organizations spend an increasingly large share of their income on medical expenses. Yet, the United States has generally dismal rates of infant mortality, death due to preventable diseases, low birth weight, and other markers of poor health compared with other industrialized countries that spend much less on healthcare on a per capita basis but have publicly funded universal health care programs (Reinhardt, Hussey, & Anderson, 2004).

NUTRITION Adequate and proper food intake is clearly related to staying healthy and avoiding medical problems due to malnourishment, obesity, diabetes, and other nutrition-related problems. Federal government programs to provide adequate nutrition include Food Stamps; the Nutrition Assistance Program for Puerto Rico; the National School Lunch Program; the School Breakfast Program; the Women, Infants and Children Supplemental Food program (WIC); the Child and Adult Care program, and the Commodities program. The federal cost for these programs was $34.1 billion in 1995, compared with $45.9 billion in 2005, a 35% increase (U.S. Census Bureau, 2006, Table 556, p. 362).

TABLE 1

*Private and Public Expenditures for Health, United States, (Selected Years, in Billions of Dollars)*

| YEAR | TOTAL HEALTH EXPENDITURES[a] | PRIVATE EXPENDITURES TOTAL[b] PRIVATE AND PERCENT OF TOTAL HEALTH EXPENDITURES | OUT OF POCKET | INSURANCE | PUBLIC EXPENDITURES TOTAL PUBLIC AND PERCENT OF TOTAL HEALTH EXPENDITURES | FEDERAL | STATE AND LOCAL |
|---|---|---|---|---|---|---|---|
| 1960 | 28 | 21 (75%) | 13 | 6 | 7 (25%) | 3 | 4 |
| 1995 | 1,020 | 554 (54%) | 146 | 327 | 467 (46%) | 325 | 141 |
| 2000 | 1,359 | 756 (56%) | 193 | 455 | 602 (44%) | 418 | 184 |
| 2005 (proj.) | 2,016 | 1,101 (55%) | 249 | 706 | 915 (45%) | 646 | 269 |
| 2010 (proj.) | 2,879 | 1,545 (54%) | 316 | 1,018 | 1,335 (46%) | 971 | 371 |

The complete table showing years 1960–2004 and projections 2005–2015 is available from Table 120, p. 95, of *Statistical Abstract of the United States: 2007*, by U.S. Census Bureau, 2006, Washington, DC: Author. Percentage calculations have been done by the author.

[a]Includes medical research and medical structures and equipment, not shown separately.

[b]Includes other private expenditures, not shown separately.

Private expenditures for food (purchased for off-premise consumption, that is, food that must be prepared in some way before being ready to eat) and purchased meals and beverages (this includes restaurant and take out food ready to eat) totaled $915.5 billion in 2000, compared with $1,123.3 billion in 2004, an increase of 23% (U.S. Census Bureau, 2006, Table 656, p. 435). Food costs, as a percentage of personal consumption spending, have decreased in recent years. In 1990, average food costs were 15.1% of total expenditures; in 1995, 14.0%; in 2000, 13.6%; and, in 2004, 13.3% (U.S. Census Bureau, 2006, Table 665, p. 442). Expenditures by other private sources, such as food banks, are unavailable, despite the large numbers of people served by such organizations. Ohls and Saleem-Ismail (2002) report that in 2002, about 5,300 emergency kitchens provide more than 173 million meals a year, and 32,700 food pantries distribute about 2.9 billion pounds of food a year (roughly 2,200 million meals) (p. 1).

Despite this level of public and private spending, Americans' nutritional needs are not fully met. Food insecurity and hunger continue to be problems in the United States. Households affected by food insecurity are defined as households with limited or uncertain ability to acquire acceptable foods in socially acceptable ways (U.S. Census Bureau, 2006, Table 200, p. 132). Food insecure households increased from 11,101,000 in 2000 (10.5% of all households) to 13,494,000 in 2004 (11.9% of all households), an increase of 22%. This number of households represents 20,336,000 adults and 12,896,000 children in 2000 and 24,328,000 adults and 13,868,000 children in 2004 (U.S. Census Bureau, 2006, Table 200, p. 132). Of these, in 2004, 7,382,000 adults and 545,000 children experienced hunger due to food insecurity (U.S. Census Bureau, 2006, Table 200, p. 132).

## Retirement and Disability Insurance Expenditures

Replacement of income in the event of retirement or disability is a major aim of social welfare systems. Components of this category of expenditures include Old Age, Survivors and Disability Insurance (OASDI more commonly called Social Security); Railroad retirement and disability; federal and state worker's compensation payments; and other government disability insurance and retirement programs, such as temporary disability payments, pension benefit guaranty payments, and black lung payments. In 1995, the sum of such expenditures was $350.3 billion. This rose to $517.8 billion in 2004, a 48% increase (U.S. Census Bureau, 2007, Table 526, p. 346). Most of these cost increases were due to the growing number of retirees. The number of cases

receiving payments in 1995 was 43,387,000 but grew to 48,434,000 in 2005, an increase of almost 12% (U.S. Census Bureau, 2006, Table 533, p. 351). The average benefit to worker and wife, 62 years and above, increased from $1,565 per month in 1995 to $1,660 per month in 2005, an increase of only 6% (U.S. Census Bureau, 2006, Table 533, p. 351). Because Social Security is adjusted for inflation only after prices have risen, it is always somewhat behind the inflation curve. Thus, these increases leave retirees somewhat worse off because of inflation.

The private expenditures side of retirement and disability payments has not only increased in dollar amounts, it has also changed radically in structure. Defined benefit plans are decreasing in number, defined contribution plans are increasing, and participation in any type of plan is declining (Parent, 2006). Defined benefit plans provide retired persons a pension of a definite size, generally based on how long they worked for a company and the amount they were paid during their tenure. Defined contribution plans (collectively known as 401(k) plans) provide employees the opportunity to invest a certain amount of funds (contributed by the employer, and, often, added to by the employee). The amount of pension received during retirement depends on the amount of money set aside and how well the investments perform.

The speed of this shift in private retirement plan structure is remarkable. In 1988, 63% of full-time employees in establishments with 100 or more workers participated in a defined benefit plan compared with only 34% in 2004 (Parent, 2006, Table 1, p. 2). This drop was not compensated for by an increase in workers in defined contribution plans. In 1988, 45% of full-time employees in establishments with 100 or more workers participated in a defined contribution plan compared with 53% in 2004 (Parent, 2006, Table 1, p. 2). The net effect of these two changes is that fewer people were receiving any type of company-sponsored pension. In 1988, 80% of full-time employees in establishments with 100 or more workers participated in at least one retirement plan compared with only 67% in 2004 (Parent, 2006, Table 1, p. 2).

Another option for privately funded retirement is the ownership of an Individual Retirement Account (IRA). There are two major types of IRAs (traditional and Roth), which have different requirements and tax benefits at withdrawal. If Americans were increasingly contributing to IRAs, then the decreasing percentage of employees with pension plans might not be so important. The data show, however, that IRAs are not much more common in 2004 than they were in 2002. U.S. Census Bureau (2006, Table 542, p. 356) data show that 39.5% of Americans had an IRA of any type in 2002,

41.4% in 2003, 40.4% in 2004, and 41.4% in 2005. Private pensions have also been the subject of various scandals as employers have taken out most of the money in a pension fund in order to fund lavish corporate perks for top-level management. This further decreased access to pensions and a secure retirement for workers.

The benefits of these private retirement programs are not evenly spread across the population. In 1999, 10% of poor people of retirement age (65 years or older) had at least one retirement account, compared with 29% of nonpoor elderly people (Parent, 2006, Table 2, p. 4). The prospects for the future look similar. In 1999, 13% of poor people of working age (18–64 years of age) had at least one retirement account, compared with 42% of nonpoor working-age people (Parent, 2006, Table 2, p. 4). Lower income retirees rely more heavily on Social Security benefits to replace lost wages, while high-income retirees receive the largest portion of their replacement income from 401(k) savings (Martin, 2003/2004, p. 24).

### Income Maintenance and Welfare Expenditures

In industrialized countries, most people work for wages to provide for themselves and their families. The American public assistance (often called "welfare") system is designed to provide temporary and generally low levels of assistance through various programs to certain categories of people deemed eligible for aid due to low income or poverty.

Government spending on income maintenance and unemployment insurance vacillated between 1995 and 2004, rising, falling, then rising again (U.S. Census Bureau, 2006, Table 525, p. 346) (see Table 2). Two factors help explain this pattern: The major policy change from the Aid to Families with Dependent Children program to the Temporary Assistance to Needy Families program and a very strong economy during the late 1990s that provided jobs to people who previously were unemployed or employed for short periods.

Most Americans meet their needs using personal income (see Table 2). Table 2 also shows that this form of "income maintenance" grew 58% between 1995 and 2004, increasing from $6,152.3 billion to $9,713.3 billion (U.S. Census Bureau, 2006, Table 657, p. 436). Comparing governmental spending for income maintenance and unemployment insurance benefits to private earnings shows that government expenditures historically range between 1.5 and 2%.

### Education Expenditures

Primary and secondary education (kindergarten through high school, known as K-12) is a local and state responsibility, although private secular and religious schools also are important provider of primary and secondary education. Higher education is a mix of state-supported and private colleges and universities, with limited direct federal funding.

KINDERGARTEN THROUGH TWELFTH GRADE (K-12) Spending on primary and secondary education rose since mid-1990s with public funds accounting for around 92% of all expenditures. In constant 2003–2004 dollars, public expenditures rose from $345,193 million in 1995 to $419,731 in 2000 and $475,500 million in 2004, an increase of 38% from 1995 to 2004. Private expenditures grew from $29 billion in 1995 to $33 billion in 2000, to $36 billion in 2004. Private expenditures grew 23% rate since 1995; though considerable, they are less than 10% of all K-12 education expenditures and have grown more slowly than public costs (U.S. Census Bureau, 2006, Table 205, p. 137). Private expenditures come largely from individuals with some additional amount coming from other sponsors (such as businesses or nonprofits) of scholarships.

HIGHER EDUCATION AND WORK-RELATED TRAINING The public and private sectors also share the costs of higher education. Since mid-1990s, the public sector financed approximately almost two-thirds of total higher education costs, with private spending accounting for about one-third of all costs. In constant 2003–2004 dollars, public expenditures grew from $143 billion in 1995 to $167 billion in 2000, to $200 billion in 2004. This represents a total growth of 40%. Private expenditures for higher education changed from $83,519 million in 1995 to $92,841 million in 2000 and $115,300 million in 2004, an increase of 38% (U.S. Census Bureau, 2006, Table 205, p. 137).

Employers also contributed to higher education and other work-related educational costs. Types of support include financial support (such as for tuition, books, and materials); the program being offered at the worksite; the program being offered during regular working hours, and the employee being paid while in classes (O'Donnell, 2006). Private philanthropy accounted for $17.6 billon in educational expenditures in 1995, rising to $33.8 billion in 2004, an increase of 92% (U.S. Census Bureau, 2006, Table 567, p. 366). Even with the combined public and private spending on education in the United States, there is concern over the ability of students to keep up with graduates from other countries. Math and science test results still lag the results of most other countries and concern exists for the health of American industry with a population that does not possess the job skills desired and needed by the science and technology sector.

TABLE 2

Government Income Maintenance and Unemployment Insurance Costs and Personal Income (in Billions of Dollars) and Federal Expenditures as a Percent of Personal Income (Selected Years, 1990–2004)

| Year | Total, Government Income Maintenance, and Unemployment Insurance Benefits | Income Maintenance Benefits | Unemployment Insurance Benefits | Personal Income | Federal Expenditures as Percent of Personal Income |
|---|---|---|---|---|---|
| 1990 | 81.7 | 63.5 | 18.2 | 4,878.6 | 1.67 |
| 1994 | 119.6 | 96.6 | 24.0 | n/a | n/a |
| 1995 | 122.2 | 100.4 | 21.8 | 6,152.3 | 1.98 |
| 1996 | 125.0 | 102.6 | 22.4 | n/a | n/a |
| 1997 | 120.8 | 100.5 | 20.3 | n/a | n/a |
| 1998 | 120.0 | 101.1 | 19.9 | n/a | n/a |
| 1999 | 125.6 | 104.8 | 20.8 | n/a | n/a |
| 2000 | 127.3 | 106.6 | 20.7 | 8,429.7 | 1.51 |
| 2001 | 141.6 | 109.4 | 32.2 | 8,724.1 | 1.62 |
| 2002 | 173.4 | 119.7 | 53.7 | 8,881.9 | 1.95 |
| 2003 | 184.8 | 131.2 | 53.6 | 9,169.1 | 2.01 |
| 2004 | 178.6 | 141.5 | 37.1 | 9,713.3 | 1.84 |

From Tables 525 (p. 346) and 657 (p. 436) of Statistical Abstract of the United States: 2007, by U.S. Census Bureau, 2006, Washington, DC: Author. Percentage calculations were done by the author.

n/a, not available.

## Future Issues

The American social welfare system continues to operate with a mix of public and private funding. Although the data are not always readily available to make comparisons, the pendulum seems to be swinging to a greater share of health, retirement, income maintenance, and education costs being borne by public sources. Even though more services are being provided by private entities, many of them are being paid for with public funds.

Public and private social welfare expenditures in the United States do not always result in the desired outcomes, especially compared with other countries, and the have nots continue to have worse outcomes than the haves. Herein lies the greatest danger, that those with adequate income, health, retirement accounts, and education will apply a "bootstrap mentality" to both public and private expenditures. Demanding that recipients lift themselves out of their own situation may become even more common than today, particularly as competing demands for public funds (such as for supporting and rebuilding the military) grow. If this occurs, then we can expect the percentage of social welfare costs paid by government to stabilize or decrease, the percentage of total costs paid by private social welfare expenditures to increase, and inequality to grow.

While it is important to know that social welfare expenditures are increasing, funding nonetheless appears to lag behind need. Social workers at all levels should work to ensure that a fair share of resources is available to overcome social problems and to allow all of us to have an equitable chance for receiving adequate health care, living a secure retirement, earning an adequate income and accessing information and knowledge. If this does not occur, then social workers at the micro level will find themselves working with more people in poor health and living in low-income situations. Macro social workers, on the other hand, will find themselves constantly advocating for more resources and trying to run programs without necessary resources.

### REFERENCES

Abramovitz, M. (2001). Everyone is still on welfare: The role of redistribution in social policy. *Social Work*, 46(4), 297–308.

Hoefer, R., & Colby, I. (1997). Social welfare expenditures: Private. *Encyclopedia of social work* (19th ed., pp. 274–281, Supplement). Washington, DC: NASW Press.

Kerns, W. (1994). Private social welfare expenditures: 1972–91. *Social Security Bulletin*, 57, 87–95.

Martin, P. (2003/2004). Comparing replacement rates under private and federal retirement systems. *Social Security Bulletin*, 65(1), 17–25.

O'Donnell, K. (2006). *Adult education participation, 2004–2005*. Washington, DC: National Center for Education Statistics, United States Department of Education. Retrieved February 2, 2007, from http://nces.ed.gov/pub search/pubsinfo.asp?pubid=2006077

Ohls, J., & Saleem-Ismail, F. (2002, October). *The emergency food assistance system: Findings from the provider survey, Vol. 1: Executive summary. Food assistance and nutrition research report* (FANRR16–1). Washington, DC: U.S. Department of Agriculture.

Parent, R. (2006, March). *Defined contribution pension plans and the supplemental security income program. Policy Brief 2006-01* (SSA Publication No. 13-11702). Washington, DC: Social Security Administration.

Reinhardt, U., Hussey, P., & Anderson, G. (2004). U.S. health care spending in an international context. *Health Affairs*, 23(3), 10–25.

U.S. Census Bureau. (2006). *Statistical abstract of the United States: 2007*. Washington, DC: Author.

### FURTHER READING

Besharov, D., & Higney, C. (2006). Federal and state child care expenditures (1997–2003): Rapid growth followed by steady spending. Retrieved February 2, 2007, from www.welfareacademy.org/pubs/childcare/childcarespending.pdf

Boyd, D. (2006, April). *2006 Rockefeller reports on state and local government finances: The 2001 recession continues to affect state budgets*. Albany, NY: Rockefeller Institute of Government. Retrieved February 2, 2007, from http://rfs.rockinst.org/exhibit/9054/Full%20Text/GovtFinancesBrief2001Recession.pdf

—RICHARD HOEFER

**SOCIAL WELFARE LEGISLATION.** See Social Policy: Overview.

**SOCIAL WORK EDUCATION.** [*This entry contains eight subentries:* Overview; Doctoral; Electronic Technologies; Field Work; Human Behavior and Social Environment; Multiculturalism; Research; Social Welfare Policy.]

### OVERVIEW

**ABSTRACT:** Education in social work has seen considerable growth over the course of the 20th century. Social work education in the United States began with only a few training programs established in partnership with charitable organizations at the end of the 19th century (Austin, 1997), and has grown to 641 accredited baccalaureate and master's programs at of the February, 2007 Commission on Accreditation meeting, and over 70 doctoral programs (Group for the Advancement of Doctoral Education, 2007). These programs represent over 7,000 faculty and administrators and over 60,000 students at the baccalaureate and master's level (Council on Social Education, 2007). Social work education is available at the baccalaureate, master's, and doctoral level with at least one level of program represented in each of the states, as well as in the United States' Territories of Puerto Rico and Guam. Concentrations and specializations are offered in programs in many areas from practice levels (for example, direct practice, policy analysis) or areas of interest (for example, child welfare, medical social work, housing policy). Current trends in social work education include the use of distance education, the call for more accountability from accrediting bodies and social work programs (Watkins & Pierce, 2005), and work toward unification in social work professional organizations (Hoffman, 2006).

KEY WORDS: accreditation; Council on Social Work Education; education; Educational Policy and Accreditation Standards (EPAS)

## History

Prior to the late 19th century, education for social work was primarily conducted on an informal basis. Those early social workers, including family visitors and case workers, were, for the most part, trained by fellow workers (Austin, 1997; McCrea, 1911). Education for social workers occurred under an apprenticeship model wherein current social workers would train new social workers on the skills needed to perform basic job functions (Bernard, 1977; McCrea, 1911). However, as the field of social work professionalized and grew in scope and purpose the apprenticeship model failed to keep pace with the needs of the growing field (Frumpkin & Lloyd, 1995; McCrea, 1911). Growing charitable organization staff size, specialization within the field, and the need for professionalization compounded the failure of the apprenticeship model and led to interest in movement to a more formal education system in social work (McCrea, 1911). Philanthropic or charitable organizations were some of the first to respond to this need for a formalized education. Some of the first professional schools in social work were started by philanthropic organizations in the late 1800s, beginning with short training programs (Austin, 1997; Bernard, 1977; Frumpkin & Lloyd, 1995).

The first classes in social work were primarily led by teachers who were seasoned workers, recruited from the practice field (Austin, 1997; McCrea, 1911). As the classes grew, programs realized that they would need to further formalize the system with full-time faculty and structured course offerings to limit overlap in content being offered. The programs began by hiring social science faculty to fill positions in schools of social work (McCrea, 1911). The National Conference on Charities and Corrections provided a venue for national discussion of the emerging profession of social work and the need for appropriate training of new workers, and advanced training and specialization for senior workers (Austin, 1997). Students in these early schools had widely varying interests for pursuing classes, from an entry level "family visitor," to advanced training in leadership of nonprofit organizations (McCrea, 1911).

The development of schools of social work and corresponding classes opened a new discussion about the knowledge and skills necessary for practice of social work. One aspect of social work education, which became a crucial element from the very beginning, was field education (Austin, 1997; McCrea, 1911). Field education is meant to give students an opportunity to apply the techniques and theories of social work in practice under the guidance of a supervisor and mentor and to "reinforce students' identification with the purposes, values, and ethics of the profession" (CSWE, 2001). As schools of social work grew and changed in administrative structure, the focus became one of defining and teaching the specialized knowledge unique to social work (Frumpkin & Lloyd, 1995).

ACCREDITATION OF SCHOOLS OF SOCIAL WORK In 1919, the AASSW was developed in 1919 to accredit schools of social work. Many of the first social work programs were graduate programs started and supported by private philanthropic organizations (Bernard, 1977; Kendall, 2002). The majority of these early schools, as discussed more in-depth in earlier text, were administratively located in a university (two-thirds by 1932) and the remaining were still independently administered through philanthropic organizations (Bernard, 1977). The primary constituency of AASSW was graduate schools of social work located in urban areas. In the 1930s, AASSW determined to make it the organization's policy to only accredit graduate programs in social work (Kendall, 2002).

Concurrent to the policy development of AASSW to accredit only graduate programs, two trends led to the development in 1943 of a second accrediting body in social work, the NASSA (Kendall, 2002). First, the AASSW decision to only accredit graduate programs had disenfranchised a number of undergraduate programs in social work; many schools reacted by suggesting the establishment of a second accrediting body (Austin, 1997). Second, the U.S. federal government became interested in social work programs emphasizing the training of students for public positions, such as those being established in child welfare and public administration. New public service initiatives in the 30s led to the establishment of new positions for social workers. The government supported the establishment of undergraduate social work programs, especially those in public universities, or in rural areas to meet this need (Kendall, 2002).

## NEED FOR CONSISTENCY AND LESS FRACTURING IN THE DEVELOPMENT OF FIELD

The coexistence of two accrediting bodies in social work, the AASSW, and NASSA, caused difficulties for several reasons, including that two organizations were promoting different directions and purposes for education (Kendall, 2002), and were causing confusion for students, faculty, and employers. This confusion was further exacerbated when the two groups determined to accredit similar programs (5 year program by NASSA, 1 year graduate program by AASSW) with different degrees. The federal government intervened through the Committee on Accrediting to give an ultimatum to the two groups, stating that they should resolve their issues or both would be refused accrediting status (Kendall, 2002). An interim committee for education in social work was convened by stakeholders in social work education, and included representatives of AASSW, NASSA, federal government agencies, and other private organizations (Austin, 1997; Kendall, 2002).

The interim committee commissioned a comprehensive research study of social work education, curriculum, and the relationship between graduate and undergraduate education, which was to be carried out by a newly formed National Council on Social Work Education (NCSWE). The NCSWE brought together stakeholders for the design and administration of the study on social work education (Kendall, 2002). Social work organizations, social work program representatives, private foundations, and federal government representatives were involved in the work, which was partially funded by the Carnegie Foundation and managed in part by the National Education Association. The resulting Hollis–Taylor report set the stage for the future direction of professional education, particularly with accreditation (Frumpkin & Lloyd, 1995; Kendall, 2002). The report specifically recommended that accreditation be limited to two-year graduate programs,

that the purposes for social work be expanded, and that a new organization be formed, which could meet the needs of the social work education community for accreditation (Kendall, 2002).

In 1952, the recommendation from the Hollis–Taylor report was taken up and the Council on Social Work Education (CSWE) was formed as the sole accrediting body in social work (Frumpkin & Lloyd, 1995; Kendall, 2002). The purpose of CSWE initially outlined in the by-laws was the "development of sound programs of social work education" (Kendall, 2002, p. 109). This purpose was later expanded to include specific activities under the purview of CSWE, including accreditation, consultation, research, and publishing (Kendall, 2002). In line with the recommendations of the Hollis–Taylor report, the CSWE began to accredit only two-year graduate programs; the exclusion of baccalaureate programs from accreditation was changed only in the 1970s (Austin, 1997; Kendall, 2002) (see "The Educational Continuum" section for more information). Currently, CSWE's mission is phrased as follows:

> CSWE aims to promote and strengthen the quality of social work education through preparation of competent social work professionals by providing national leadership and a forum for collective action. CSWE pursues this mission through setting and maintaining policy and program standards, accrediting bachelor's and master's degree programs in social work, promoting research and faculty development, and advocating for social work education (CSWE, n.d.).

### CSWE Standards and Policy Changes

The CSWE by-laws state that the Commission on Curriculum and Educational Innovation (COCEI) will develop "a statement of social work educational policy to encourage excellence and innovation in the preparation of social work practitioners in educational programs" (CSWE, 2005, p. 8). The policy statement is used by the Commission on Accreditation (COA) for development of accreditation standards. The policy statement and a statement of standards combine to form the document titled Educational Policy and Accreditation Standards (EPAS), which is used by the COA to make accreditation determinations. (See "Accreditation Process" section for further information.) As mandated by CSWE by-laws the EPAS must undergo review and revision every seven years with a final draft presented to the CSWE Board of Directors for approval (CSWE, 2005). The EPAS outlines the requirements for social work program curriculum, faculty, and institutional resources (CSWE, 2002).

**EPAS CHANGES** The educational policy and corresponding accreditation standards that guide the accreditation of social work programs have gone through many different iterations. In fact, as stated previously, the policy and standards are mandated by CSWE by-laws to undergo revision at least every seven years in order to ensure that the policy and standards are reflective of innovations in the field (CSWE, 2005). Past changes to the policy and accreditation standards have included the addition of standards for baccalaureate social work programs (Austin, 1997; Kendall, 2002), and a general movement towards a less prescriptive set of standards regarding social work curriculum (Frumpkin & Lloyd, 1995).

The most recent iteration, EPAS, is currently being revised by the COCEI and the COA for review by the CSWE Board of Directors in 2008. Drafts of the new EPAS by the COCEI and COA seem to indicate a continuation of that trend, as well as a concern with competency-based education. While the EPAS revision is currently in draft form, the move to a competency-based EPAS is reflective of a growing concern with the social work education community (and education as a whole) that students not just *taught* content, but that they are also *able to apply* those things which they are supposed to learn (See "Trends" section for more information) (Hoffman, 2006). The COCEI and COA are holding public meetings at the CSWE Annual Program Meeting to discuss the direction and timeline of the EPAS revisions.

### The Educational Continuum

Currently, there are three major levels of social work education: baccalaureate, master's, and doctoral. CSWE accredits programs at the baccalaureate and master's programs. Doctoral programs in social work are not accredited; however, many of the social work doctoral programs belong to the Group for the Advancement of Doctoral Education (GADE), which offers *Guidelines for Quality in Social Work Doctoral Programs* ("Guidelines") for the development and review of doctoral programs (GADE, 2003). Continuing education programs are also available under many auspices, and indeed, continuing education is mandated in many states for the maintenance of licensure (Association of Social Work Boards [ASWB], n.d.).

Following the establishment of CSWE as the sole accrediting body in social work in 1952, there was some confusion regarding the educational continuum. The two organizations that had previously accredited, AASSW and NASSA, had very different ideas about the purposes and needs for education in social work at the baccalaureate and master's level (Kendall, 2002). As a result of the pre-CSWE study conducted by the NCSWE, baccalaureate programs in social work could seek "approval" rather than accreditation (Bernard, 1977; Kendall, 2002; Witte, 1966), which remained the case until 1974. The admission of baccalaureate programs into accreditation was a long process, which required first convincing the practice community that there was a purpose for social work practitioners at the baccalaureate level. In 1962, because of the proliferation of baccalaureate level programs, CSWE published a "guide" for baccalaureate programs (Bernard, 1977; Kendall, 2002). Baccalaureate social workers were then first recognized and permitted as members in the National Association of Social Workers (NASW) in 1970. After this CSWE began to seek approval from the Department of Education, which then recognized CSWE for accreditation purposes, to begin accrediting at the baccalaureate level (Bernard, 1977; Frumpkin & Lloyd, 1995; Kendall, 2002).

Accrediting both baccalaureate and master's programs did not solve the issues of the continuum in social work, rather, in many ways it exacerbated the issues. Disagreements regarding the continuum have stemmed from a couple issues: the purposes for education at each level and the curriculum provided at each level (Kendall, 2002). Some efforts have been made to resolve these difficulties in the continuum (Austin, 1997). The EPAS mandates that, "In those foundation curriculum areas where students demonstrate required knowledge and skills, the program describes how it ensures that students do not repeat that content" (CSWE, 2001, p. 16). The EPAS also outlines that programs are to be, "differentiated according to (a) conceptualization and design, (b) content, (c) program objectives, and (d) depth, breadth, and specificity of knowledge and skills" (CSWE, 2001, p. 6).

One of the most obvious cooperative steps has been the inclusion of "advanced standing" in many programs. Advanced standing students are master's students who have had some of the hours earned at the baccalaureate social work level credited toward their master's degree coursework (CSWE, 2001).

**BACCALAUREATE SOCIAL WORK PROGRAMS** The purposes for education at the baccalaureate level are preparation for generalist social work practice (Bernard, 1977; CSWE, 2001; Frumpkin & Lloyd, 1995). Baccalaureate programs are housed in a college or university, and typically are two years long, consisting of the junior and senior years of a four-year program (CSWE, 2001; Frumpkin & Lloyd, 1995). Baccalaureate curriculum is foundational and generalist in nature. Additionally, at the baccalaureate level students are required to complete at least 400 hr of field education (CSWE, 2001).

In 1971, just before CSWE first began accrediting baccalaureate social work programs, there were 158 approved baccalaureate social work programs (Stamm, 1972). As of the February 2007 COA meeting, there were 459 accredited baccalaureate social work programs located in the United States, Puerto Rico, and Guam. Of those, 131 are located in "combined programs," that is in an institution with both baccalaureate and master's social work programs. In 2004, there were over 28,000 full-time baccalaureate social work students of which 88.1% were female and 35.4% were racial or ethnic minority. There were an additional 4,500 part-time students. In 2003–2004 period, 9,889 baccalaureate degrees in social work were awarded (CSWE, 2007).

## MASTER'S SOCIAL WORK PROGRAMS

At the master's level the purpose for education is the preparation of students for "advanced professional practice in an area of concentration" (CSWE, 2001, p. 6; Frumpkin & Lloyd, 1995). The programs are typically two years in length, with the first year devoted to foundation curriculum and the second to advanced curriculum in an area of concentration (Frumpkin & Lloyd, 1995). The EPAS mandates little for the concentrations; the concentration topic and curriculum is decided largely at the discretion of the program. At the master's level students are required to complete at least 900 hr of field education (CSWE, 2001).

As of the February 2007 COA meeting, there are 182 master's of social work programs in the United States and Puerto Rico; 131 of those programs are "combined programs." In 2004, there were nearly 23,000 full-time master's students of which 86.1% were female and 29.1% were racial or ethnic minority. An additional 13,539 were in a master's program part-time. The master's programs tend to be much larger than the baccalaureate programs in terms of number of students per program. In 2003–2004, 15,473 master's degrees were awarded. Programs reported that the largest number (14,671) of master's students were in concentration that focused on direct or clinical practice in combination with a field of practice or social problem (for example, aging/gerontological social work, child welfare, school social work, etc.). Direct practice (without a combination with field of practice or social problem) made up the second largest category (5,307). Together the direct practice concentrations consist of 54.8% of master's concentration students (CSWE, 2007).

## DOCTORAL SOCIAL WORK PROGRAMS

According the GADE Guidelines the purpose of doctoral education in social work is to prepare students to be "scholars and researchers" in social work (GADE, 2003). Prior to the 1950s doctoral degrees in social work were rare; only two doctoral social work programs existed at Bryn Mawr College and the University of Chicago. Most students who were interested in education beyond the master's degree engaged in "third year programs" (Frumpkin & Lloyd, 1995), which were primarily focused on advanced practice preparation (Kendall, 2002). However, as schools of social work sought more recognition within their academic institutional settings, more social work faculty members began to seek a doctoral degree in social work (Austin, 1997). Demand grew for doctoral degrees and third year programs closed in favor of the development of doctoral programs (Bernard, 1977). Doctoral degrees in social work have been provided as either a DSW or Ph.D. Now almost all social work doctoral programs have converted to the Ph.D. (Thyer & Arnold, 2003).

In 2006–2007 there are 74 doctoral programs in social work in the United States that are members of GADE (GADE, n.d.). The CSWE (2007) reports that in 2004 there were approximately 1,800 full-time doctoral students of which 76.7% were female and 34% were racial or ethnic minority. Although the number of doctoral programs in social work has been increasing significantly, the number of degrees awarded has increased at a slower rate—313 in 2004 (CSWE, 2007; Watkins & Pierce, 2005). Concurrently, demand for doctoral degree holders is expected to continue to rise as many social work programs move to require a doctoral degree for social work faculty (Watkins & Pierce, 2005).

A few significant initiatives have been developed to address the need for more doctoral trained social workers. The CSWE Minority Fellowship Program (MFP) has been providing funding for racial or ethnic minority doctoral students in social work since 1974. The MFP is funded by the National Institute for Mental Health and the Substance Abuse and Mental Health Services Administration and has supported over 500 doctoral students over the course of the program (CSWE, n.d.). The John A. Hartford Foundation has also been providing funding since 2001 to social work doctoral students who are completing dissertations in the area of gerontology (Geriatric Social Work Initiative, n.d.). The need to fully address the issues in doctoral social work education prompted a meeting of stakeholders in doctoral education in 2006. The Task Force on Doctoral Education in Social Work met to discuss issues of purpose, structure, recruitment, retention, mentoring, and funding (Hoffman, 2006) (See "Cooperative Ventures" for more information).

## Social Work Faculty

In 2004, social work programs reported 6,857 faculty members. Graduate and combined programs accounted for 5,457 of faculty members, with 62.5% being female and 22.4% reported as racial or ethnic minority. Baccalaureate faculty members were 63.6% female and 23.9% racial or ethnic minority. Median salary in graduate and combined programs for 2004 was $81,153 for a full-time Professor, $61,047 for a full-time Associate Professor, and $50,804 for a full-time Assistant Professor (CSWE, 2007).

The EPAS requires that baccalaureate programs have a minimum of two full-time faculty members with master's of social work degrees (doctoral degree preferred,) and that master's programs have at least six full-time faculty with master's social work degrees, with the majority holding master's and doctoral degrees. Additionally, faculty who teach practice courses at either level must have a master's degree in social work and two years practice experience (CSWE, 2001). Because of these standards, in part, the majority of social work faculty at all levels hold a master's degree in social work (CSWE, 2007).

Doctoral degree attainment for faculty members became increasingly desired as social work programs located in academic institutions (rather than with private social service organizations) (Austin, 1997). A doctoral degree in social work is not mandatory, but remains a topic of on-going discussion in social work education venues. In 2004, responding programs reported that 43% of graduate social work faculty held a doctorate in social work and 57.8% held a doctoral degree in another discipline. Looking at "combined program" faculty, 37.7% held a doctoral degree in social work and 51.4% a doctoral degree in some area. And at the baccalaureate level, 25.7% of faculty held a doctoral degree in social work and 39.9% held a doctoral degree in some area (CSWE, 2007).

## Accreditation Process

The CSWE is recognized by the Council for Higher Education Accreditation (CHEA) as the sole accrediting body in social work. In its by-laws, the CSWE Board of Directors has given the COA the authority to accredit social work schools. Specifically, the COA has the authority to "accredit, impose conditional accredited status, to deny accreditation to or to withdraw accreditation of master's and baccalaureate degree programs in social work" (CSWE, 2005, p. 8). A minimum of 25 commissioners, consisting of volunteer representatives from the social work education and practice community and two public members, are appointed to positions on the COA by the President of CSWE. The

majority of the commissioners (20) must hold full-time positions at an accredited school of social work (CSWE, 2005).

The COA outlines the standards for accreditation at the baccalaureate and master's level, and along with the educational policy laid out by the COCEI, develop the EPAS. The EPAS is revised every seven years and is approved by the CSWE Board of Directors (CSWE, 2005). The structure of the accreditation process at the outset of CSWE as the accrediting body in social work and that used currently by CSWE had several of the elements used for the review of programs in common—the development of a "self-study" by the program under review, receiving a "site visit" during the process, and the COA reaching an accreditation decision as a result of the previous two elements (Kendall, 2002).

## Trends

One of the rising trends, not only in social work education, but in the wider education and funding community, is the call for more accountability. This call for accountability can be seen in federal, state, and private organizations requirements for more information on outcomes, emphasis on evaluation, and discussion of need for comparability. Social work education is also responding to this growing trend by considering a new framework for the EPAS revision, which will emphasize competencies in social work and on-going evaluation for social work programs (Hoffman, 2006; Watkins & Pierce, 2005).

Distance Education as a means for providing social work courses is also a developing area in social work. There are already some distance education and online programs in social work being provided at the baccalaureate, master's, and doctoral levels. The EPAS does not specify the methods for providing course content to students (CSWE, 2001), so distance education programs are evaluated in exactly the same manner that any other program is under accreditation standards. Because of the growing interest in the field, the CSWE will be holding a Distance Education Summit during the 2007 Annual Program Meeting. The Summit will include the results from a survey conducted by CSWE of the distance education offerings in social work programs.

## Cooperative Ventures between Social Work Organizations

Recent trends have led to a proliferation of social work organizations; at least 50 social work organizations now exist to represent various aspects of education, research, and practice. Many of those organizations are focused specifically on social work education (Hoffman, 2006). In an effort to coordinate initiatives and activities taking place in these disparate organizations, a Leadership Roundtable was commissioned in 2004 from some of the most prominent of those organizations with a vested interest in education. Leadership Roundtable representatives from the Council on Social Work Education (CSWE), National Association of Social Workers (NASW), National Association of Deans and Directors (NADD), Association of Baccalaureate Program Directors (BPD), Group for the Advancement of Doctoral Education (GADE), Society for Social Work Research (SSWR), the St. Louis Group, the Institute for the Advancement of Social Work Research (IASWR), and the Association of Social Work Boards (ASWB) meet at least once a year to discuss priorities for social work education and currently initiatives in the organizations.

In 2006, a landmark meeting was convened on doctoral education in social work. This meeting was a collaborative activity supported by the Leadership Roundtable and the first such discussion of the purposes and needs of doctoral education in social work. The Task Force on Doctoral Education in Social Work brought together leaders from many different backgrounds to discuss purpose, recruitment, retention, funding, and future directions for doctoral education (Hoffman, 2006). Strategies and activities were identified during the meeting, and have now been delegated to the individual organizations in the Leadership Roundtable for completion.

The Leadership Roundtable will be continuing their discussions in 2007 with a conference sponsored by the Johnson Foundation on the potential for unification in the profession. Unifying initiatives in education, research, and practice is imperative to the continued health of the profession and for the improvement of services social workers are able to provide to their clients. The conference, *Social Work: Future of the Profession*, will continue the discussion of how the purposes and activities of the various social work organizations can be better integrated and complemented in order for the organizations to ultimately provide better service to their constituencies (Hoffman & Godenzi, 2007).

## REFERENCES

Association of Social Work Boards (ASWB). (n.d.). *Social work laws & regulations online comparison guide*. Retrieved May 24, 2007, from http://www.aswbdata.powerlynxhosting.net/

Austin, D. M. (1997). The institutional development of social work education: The first 100 years—And beyond. *Journal of Social Work Education, 33*(3), 599–612.

Bernard, L. D. (1977). Education for social work. In *Encyclopedia of social work* (17th ed., pp. 290–300). Washington, DC: National Association of Social Workers.

Council on Social Work Education (CSWE). (2001). *Educational policy and accreditation standards*. Alexandria, VA: Author. Retrieved May 23, 2007, from http://www.cswe.org/NR/rdonlyres/111833A0-C4F5-475C-8FEB-EA740FF4D9F1/0/EPAS.pdf

Council on Social Work Education (CSWE). (2005). *By-laws.* Alexandria, VA: Author. Retrieved May 23, 2007, from http://www.cswe.org/NR/rdonlyres/09F835FE-DEDA-4B76-8BD8-85022BC18B72/0/BylawsforWinter07golive.doc

Council on Social Work Education (CSWE). (2007). *Statistics on social work education in the United States: 2004.* Alexandria, VA: Author.

Council on Social Work Education (CSWE). (n.d.) *Council on social work education (website)*. Retrieved May 24, 2007, from http://www.cswe.org/CSWE/

Frumpkin, M., & Lloyd, G. A. (1995). Social work education. In *Encyclopedia of social work* (19th ed., pp. 2238–2246). Washington, DC: NASW Press.

Geriatric Social Work Initiative. (n.d.) *Hartford doctoral fellows program in geriatric social work*. Retrieved May 24, 2007, from http://www.gswi.org/programs/hdf.html#aboutdoc

Group for the Advancement of Doctoral Education. (2003). *Guidelines for quality in social work doctoral programs* (Revised). Retrieved May 23, 2007, from http://web.uconn.edu/gade/gadeguidelines.pdf

Group for the Advancement of Doctoral Education. (n.d.) *Purpose of GADE*. Retrieved May 24, 2007, from http://web.uconn.edu/gade/

Hoffman, K. (2006). *CSWE and social work education's joint agenda (Remarks based on the President's Address at the 2006 CSWE Annual Program Meeting: Chicago, IL)*. Retrieved May 24, 2007, from http://www.cswe.org/CSWE/research/research/reports/

Hoffman, K., & Godenzi, A. (2007). Guest editorial—Increasing our impact through unification. *Journal of Social Work Education, 43*(2), 181–185.

Kendall, K. (2002). *Council on social work education: Its antecedents and first twenty years.* Alexandria, VA: Council on Social Work Education.

McCrea, R. C. (1911). The professional school for social workers, its aims and methods. In A. Johnson (Ed.), *Proceedings of the national Conference of Charities and Correction*. Fort Wayne, IN: The Fort Wayne Printing Company.

Stamm, A. (1972). *An analysis of undergraduate social work programs approved by CSWE, 1971.* New York: Council on Social Work Education.

Thyer, B. A., & Arnold, T. G. (2003). *A program guide to doctoral study in social work.* Alexandria, VA: Council on Social Work Education.

Watkins, J. M., & Pierce, D. (2005). Social work education: A future of strength or peril. *Advances in Social Work, 6*(1), 17–23.

Witte, E. F. (1966). The purposes of undergraduate education for social welfare. *Journal of Education for Social Work, 1*(2), 53–60.

## FURTHER READING

Boehm, W. W. (1959). Objectives of the social work curriculum of the future. *The comprehensive report of the curriculum* study (Vol. 1). New York: Council on Social Work Education.

Council on Social Work Education. (2006). *Focusing on our future (annual report)*. Alexandria, VA: Author.

Kendall, K. (1966). Issues and problems in social work education. *Social Work Education Reporter, 14*(1), 15, 34–38, 48.

Leighninger, L. (2000). *Creating a new profession: The beginnings of social work education in the United States*. Alexandria, VA: Council on Social Work Education.

United States Department of Labor. (2006). *Social workers occupational outlook handbook*. Retrieved June 8, 2006, from www.bls.gov/oco/ocos060.htm

## SUGGESTED LINKS

*www.cswe.org*
*http://web.uconn.edu/gade/*
*http://www.bpdonline.org/*
*http://www.naddssw.org/*
*http://www.iaswresearch.org/*

—KAY S. HOFFMAN

## DOCTORAL

**ABSTRACT:** Social work doctoral education in the U.S. commenced almost 100 years ago. Although initial growth was slow, the number of universities offering doctoral degrees in social work has rapidly grown over the last 25 years. During this time, the Group to Advance Doctoral Education (GADE) in social work has fostered excellence. There is considerable variation in program emphasis. Financial support for doctoral education in social work appears to be growing along with employment opportunities for graduates. Emerging trends and issues will pose major challenges for doctoral education in social work.

**KEY WORDS:** doctoral education; GADE; research doctorates; practice doctorates

## History

The first PhD in social work was awarded by Bryn Mawr College in 1920 (Thyer & Arnold, 2003). Four years later, the University of Chicago awarded its first doctorate in social work. However the severe economic conditions of the Great Depression followed by those associated with World War II greatly slowed the development of new doctoral programs in all fields of study and social work was no exception. At the start of the 1950s, there were only eight social work doctoral programs in the U.S. The greatest growth in doctoral education in most disciplines took place in the 1960s and 1970s, largely due to new national policies that

were in reaction to the Soviet Union's early lead in the race for outer space (NSF, 2006). This brought a large infusion of federal investment designed to increase the number of research universities and subsequently a large increase in the production of research scholars in all scientific disciplines.

The increase in social work doctoral programs echoed these national trends. Seven new doctoral programs in social work were added in the 1960s and another 13 were added in the 1970s. There were 14 more programs developed in the 1980s and 15 in the1990s (Thyer & Arnold, 2003). Presently, there are 73 social work doctoral programs in the United States, listed on the Group to Advance Doctoral Education (GADE) in the social work website. The National Opinion Research Center's annual survey of recipients of doctorates in the United States reported that there were 325 doctorates awarded in social work in 2005 (Hoffer et al., 2006). This represents a 27% increase over the number reported a decade earlier, suggesting that the growth in the number of doctoral programs is generating a corresponding increase in the number of degrees awarded.

Social work doctoral programs are not evenly distributed across the country. Many more programs are located in the eastern part of the United States than in the west. There are over 30 social work programs located on the East Coast, whereas there are only 5 on the West Coast. Looking at the two most populated states on both coasts further illustrates differences in geographic distribution. Whereas there are 10 social work doctoral programs in New York, there are only 3 in California, despite great similarities between these two large states regarding the need for social work.

Historically, social work doctoral education has primarily been housed in research universities and emphasizes the acquisition of advanced research skills. In keeping with this emphasis, the doctoral degree that is presently awarded by all social work doctoral programs is the PhD As recently as 25 years ago, a number of social work doctoral programs awarded a DSW (Doctor of Social Work) instead of the PhD In the last 15 years, however, there has been a significant increase in the proportion of social work doctoral programs located in non-research universities. This can be illustrated using the 2005 Carnegie Foundation classification system for institutions of higher education. This classification system also distinguishes among research universities rated as *Very High Research (VHR)* universities and those rated as *High Research (HR)* universities (McCormick & Zhao, 2005). As shown in Table 1, only one out of eight doctoral programs was located in a non-research university prior to 1990. This proportion more than

TABLE 1
*Doctoral Program Establishment Date by University Type*

|  | NUMBER | VHR UNIVERSITY | HR UNIVERSITY | NON-RESEARCH |
|---|---|---|---|---|
| Prior to 1990 | 48 | 67% | 21% | 12% |
| 1990 or later | 25 | 52% | 20% | 28% |
| Total | 73 | 62% | 21% | 18% |

doubled after 1990, while the proportion of social work doctoral programs housed in a VHR university dropped from 67% to 52%.

## Demographics
The 2005 NORC survey showed differences between social work doctoral recipients and the national averages for all fields of study. Women constituted a large majority (73%) of social work doctorate recipients, whereas women comprised less than half (45%) of recipients of doctorates awarded in all fields of study in 2005. Social work also differed from overall norms in terms of foreign students. A larger proportion of social work degree recipients (91%) were U.S. citizens compared to the averages for all fields of study (82%).

## The Role of GADE in Promoting Excellence
The Group to Advance Doctoral Education (GADE) in social work is the primary external organization that attempts to foster quality in doctoral education. GADE is essentially a self-help organization consisting of the chairs of all social work doctoral programs in the United States and Canada, along with those from a few other international programs. GADE has no paid staff and it does not conduct reviews of individual programs. Its influence over the quality of doctoral education is through a listserv directed at doctoral chairs; a website, where it publishes relevant information on doctoral education in social work; and an annual meeting, where key topics relevant to doctoral education are addressed. An orientation for new doctoral chairs is also provided at the annual GADE meeting.

Some key publications have also been developed by GADE. One is a compendium of descriptions of individual doctoral programs facilitating a side by side comparison (Thyer & Arnold, 2003). Another is a set of guidelines designed to promote excellence in social work doctoral programs. This document was updated in 2003 and is available for downloading on the GADE website. The guidelines provide suggestions for governance and structure of a social work doctoral program within the institutional context of a given university. The guidelines also recommend that a minimum of two years be spent on course work prior to dissertation research. Suggested courses include social behavioral theory, social welfare policy, research methods, statistics, and philosophy of science. The GADE guidelines also recommend that students should be given individualized opportunities to hone the writing and analytic skills essential for high quality scholarship.

The capstone experience of a research-orientated doctoral program is the dissertation in which the student demonstrates a capacity for independent scholarship. The GADE guidelines define a dissertation as "a student generated work of independent research and scholarship addressing significant, professionally relevant, theoretically grounded questions or hypotheses." The dissertation is supervised by a faculty committee. The size of this committee generally ranges from three to five members. The chair of the committee is most often chosen from the ranks of social work tenure-track faculty at the student's chosen university. In most universities there is a requirement that at least one of the dissertation committee members come from outside the school or department of social work.

The GADE guidelines call for periodic reviews of the doctoral program ensuring that the curriculum remains relevant to emerging needs and that the graduates secure a high quality doctoral education. GADE offers the following set of indicators to measure program quality:

- Number, range, rigor, depth, and currency of courses
- Opportunities for students to participate in research, teaching, and other practicum experiences with faculty mentorship
- Quality of dissertation proposals and completed dissertations
- Student publications and conference presentations
- Records of accomplishments of doctoral graduates.

Unlike BSW and MSW programs, social work doctoral education is not accredited by the Council on Social Work Education (CSWE) or any other national organization. Formal external reviews of any given social work doctoral program are generally limited to evaluations conducted by the university at which the program resides. There is considerable variation among the universities regarding the nature of such reviews and how often they are conducted. In general, these programmatic reviews reflect the cultural norms of a given university and generally compare the merits of the social work doctoral program with those of comparable doctoral programs across that campus. In some cases, national experts may be hired as consultants to facilitate the campus evaluation of its social work doctoral program. Through this periodic review process the university's academic culture necessarily shapes the general content and quality of social work doctoral education on that particular campus.

### Variations in Program Emphasis

An examination of the websites for the 73 GADE programs suggests considerable variation in program emphasis. One of the major differences among social work doctoral programs concerns the extent to which other disciplines are involved. Some programs appear relatively insular from other academic units on their campus whereas others have interdisciplinary exposure built into the program. The most common forms of interdisciplinary involvement are requirements for students to take part of their formal coursework from other academic units and to include members from other academic disciplines on dissertation committees. Some social work doctoral programs offer a joint degree with another academic discipline, such as the University of Michigan School of Social Work.

The curriculum offered by social work doctoral programs is greatly influenced by the academic environment in which the program is housed. Those programs housed in more research intensive universities tend to place a greater emphasis on research training, capitalizing on a rich array of research resources available throughout their campuses. Although it is possible to identify many exemplars of social work doctoral programs situated in research intensive universities, UCLA's PhD program in particular illustrates how a program might wish to leverage the vast array of resources available at a major research university. Those programs housed at a university not considered to be research intensive by the Carnegie classification often construct very different types of research experiences for students. These programs tend to place greater emphasis on advanced practice skills than programs housed in research intensive universities. Smith College is an example of this type of program.

Doctoral programs also vary with respect to whether they require students to be full- or part-time. For most programs it is an issue of limited financial resources available for students. Some universities have deliberately chosen to offer a part time program to reach a different market than would be available if the program offered only a full time course study (Biegel, Singer, Hokenstad, & Guo, 2006). Universities with limited resources organize their curriculum around an assumption that doctoral students will need to be employed off campus in order to self-finance their education.

### Financing Doctoral Education

Doctoral programs are expensive to operate. GADE guidelines outline some of the institutional resources required for quality doctoral programs, most critically, the faculty resources both committed to and qualified to mentor doctoral students. Another key resource is an adequate base of financial support for students, particularly in the early stage of their doctoral programs. The strength of a doctoral program is often determined by how well it is able to exploit not only the resources of the academic unit in which it is housed, but also the resources of the whole university and the local community. Exploitation of external resources requires strong faculty and administrative leadership.

Financing doctoral education is also expensive from a student's perspective. The typical program requires a commitment of a minimum of 4 to 5 years of full time work. Those offering a joint degree require even higher time commitments. Thus, the opportunity costs are quite high given loss of earnings during this 4 to 5 year period. Part time employment is often used as a solution to the loss of income. However, this creates additional problems, given that the time to finish the degree is inevitably lengthened. The preferred solution is extensive financial assistance either directly from the student's university or from outside sources.

Many universities now offer multiyear financial aid packages to incoming students. Generally these packages cover tuition for the first 2 to 3 years of the doctoral program, along with a modest stipend to cover other costs. Those programs located in research universities often have the capacity to support doctoral students working on externally funded research grants. Some universities offer part time teaching opportunities to advanced doctoral students. Many programs also encourage students to apply to external sources to fund their dissertation research. The Institute for Social Work Research (IASWR) website publishes a roster of a vast array of funding opportunities for doctoral students. IASWR also sponsors a series of pre-conference workshops for doctoral students at the annual meeting of the Society for Social Work Research (SSWR), whose website also includes a roster of funding opportunities. The largest private source of dissertation support for social work doctoral work is funded by the John A. Hartford Foundation (Lubben & Harooytan, 2002). The Hartford Doctoral Fellows program was established in 2000, and has so far awarded 68 dissertation grants to students whose research examines aspects of health and aging.

For more than 30 years CSWE has sponsored a Minority Fellows Program designed to help ethnic minorities complete their doctoral dissertations. Over the years, more than 500 individuals have received support from this program.

## Employment Opportunities for Doctoral Graduates

Although the number of academic job openings is approximately equal to the number of new doctorates awarded in social work, it does not imply market equilibrium. While there are approximately 250 openings for junior faculty appointments in social work, and most of these require a doctorate (Anastas, 2006), many social work doctoral degrees awarded each year are to individuals who do not seek a full-time faculty appointment. As a result, there is a growing shortage of qualified candidates for junior faculty appointments in social work (Zastrow & Bremner, 2004).

Those doctoral graduates who do not seek full time faculty appointments often pursue a clinical practice career path. A number also build upon the skills developed in their doctoral programs to pursue a career in social research, policy analysis, or administration. Some of these graduates eventually contribute to social work education through part time teaching or supervision of B.S.W and M.S.W. students in practice settings. Some also mentor social work doctoral students and create research opportunities for them.

## Emerging Trends and Issues

Shanti Khinduka gave the keynote address at the annual GADE meeting in 2001 in which he identified five emerging issues in social work doctoral education (Khinduka, 2002). These were promoting interdisciplinary preparation; strengthening the quality of the social work faculty; balancing rigorous research with effective teaching; developing postdoctoral social work education; and fashioning an institutional culture supportive of excellence in social work education. All five of these issues remain vital for social work educators at all levels.

Another emerging issue concerns whether the M.S.W. should remain the terminal practice degree for social work or whether a practice doctorate should be created. This is being driven by the expansion of professional doctorates in other fields (Chronicle of Higher Education, 2007). Recently the University of Pennsylvania resurrected the D.S.W. as a practice doctorate to be offered in addition to a research-based PhD. Other GADE programs have also reported exploring the development of a professional doctorate. Obviously this emerging issue will receive considerable attention over the next decade.

### REFERENCES

Anastas, J. W. (2006). Employment opportunities in social work education: A study of jobs for doctoral graduates. *Journal of Social Work Education, 42,* 195–209.

Biegel, D. E., Singer, M. I., Hokenstad, M. C., & Guo, S. (2006). One's school's experience in reconceptualizing part-time doctoral education in social work. *Journal of Social Work Education, 42,* 231–247.

Chronicle of Higher Education. (2007, June 22). *Credential Creep.* http://chronicle.com/weekly/v53/i42/42a01001.htm

Hoffer, T. B. et al. (2006). *Doctorate recipients from United States universities: Summary report 2005.* Chicago: National Opinion Research Center.

Khinduka, S. (2002). Musings on doctoral education in social work. *Research on Social Work Practice, 12,* 684–694.

Lubben, J., & Harooytan, L. K. (2002). Strengthening geriatric social work through a doctoral fellowship program. *Journal of Gerontological Social Work, 39,* 145–156.

McCormick, A. C., & Zhao, C. M. (2005). Rethinking and reframing the Carnegie classification. *Change, 37,* 51–57.

National Science Foundation, Division of Science Resources Statistics. (2006). *U.S. Doctorates in the 20th Century,* NSF 06–319. Arlington, VA: author.

Thyer, B. A., & Arnold, T. G., (Eds.). (2003). *A program guide to doctoral study in social work.* Alexandria, VA: Council on Social Work Education.

Zastrow, C., & Bremner, J. (2004). Social work education responds to the shortage of persons with both a doctorate and a professional social work degree. *Journal of Social Work Education, 40,* 351–358.

### SUGGESTED LINKS

GADE.
  *http://web.uconn.edu/gade/*
Carnegie Classifications.
  *http://www.carnegiefoundation.org/classifications/index.asp*
NORC.
  *http://www.norc.uchicago.edu/issues/docdata.htm*
IASWR.
  *http://www.iaswresearch.org/*
SSWR.
  *http://www.sswr.org/*
Hartford Doctoral Fellows.
  *http://www.gswi.org/*
CSWE Minority Fellowships.
  *http://www.cswe.org/CSWE/scholarships/fellowship/JSA 35 minutes*

—JAMES E. LUBBEN

## ELECTRONIC TECHNOLOGIES

ABSTRACT: The growth in technological advances in recent years has revolutionized the way we teach, the way we learn, and the way we practice social work. Due to increases in educational costs and the need for students to maintain family and work responsibilities, an increasing number of social work programs have turned to today's advances in technology to deliver their courses and programs. This has resulted in the creative use of new multimedia tools and online pedagogical strategies to offer distance education programming. With increases in technology-supported programs, recent research studies have identified a number of areas needing further investigation to ensure that quality distance education programs are developed.

KEY WORDS: technology; e-learning strategies; simulations; assessment; educational paradigms

With the continuing globalization of our profession, one of the biggest changes social work education has seen has been the technological revolution. We currently have a new generation of social work students who are well versed in the use of computer technology and advanced communication networks as evidenced by the steady growth of distance technologies in social work programs (Siegel, Jennings, Conklin, & Flynn, 2000). The growth in technological advances in recent years has revolutionized the way we teach, the way we learn, and the way we practice social work. The integration of technology for teaching the social work curriculum has the potential to make social work education, and ultimately direct practice, more effective, more widespread, and less expensive.

In the last 20 years the needs of students have changed, due in part to the rise of technology, increased educational costs, and the need for students to maintain family and work responsibilities as they pursue their educational goals. Studies have indicated that students would not have been able to pursue their degree without distance education opportunities (Coe & Gandy, 1999). As a result, an increasing number of social work programs, both undergraduate and graduate, have engaged in the development and implementation of technology-supported courses and programs (Raymond, 2005). A recent distance education survey conducted by the Council for Social Work Education Commission on Accreditation found that 41% of the respondents of BSW programs and 52% of the respondents from graduate programs deliver courses using some form of technology (Vernon, 2006). In the last 10 years, the integration of technology to deliver courses has included two-way video classrooms (Ostendorf, 1994), and cluded two-way video classrooms (Ostendorf, 1994), and

television (Petracchi & Patchner, 2000), and computers (Blakely, 1994). In the last 5 years, the continued enhancement in course management software systems, improved access to broadband computer networks, and the creative use of a number of new multimedia tools—such as Micromedia Flash animations, streaming video, and Web-based audio-video presentations—has provided educators with a variety of new tools to offer distance education programming to students (Coe, 2005).

Although concerns still permeate the field with respect to negative faculty attitudes toward distance education (Freddolino, 1996; Haga & Heitkamp, 2000), recent studies have revealed that technology-supported instruction and programs are comparable to, if not better in some cases than, traditional face-to-face instructional formats (Macy, Rooney, Hollister & Freddolino, 2001). Even practice courses, which have been viewed as being the least amenable to the electronic medium, have been found to have no significant difference as to learning outcomes when taught using a technology-supported environment as compared to traditional classroom-based instructional formats (Coe & Elliot, 1999; Ouellette, Westhuis, Marshall, & Chang, 2006).

As computer technology and communication networks continue to improve, so do the growth and quality of e-learning opportunities and strategies. With the advent of more powerful processors, high-end graphics cards, and animation tools, computer-assisted and Web-based simulations have become powerful new instructional e-learning tools for teaching and learning a variety of skills such as leadership (Aldrich, 2004) and basic counseling skills (Seabury, 2003). The continued development and inclusion of simulations in online instructional environments have the potential of improving the quality and outcomes of e-learning (Thomas, 2001).

As technology tools become easier, new challenges for social work educators in the coming years will be two-fold: (1) a shift in educational paradigms and (2) the assessment of processes and the outcomes of this shift. This new educational era evokes new roles and educational paradigms for social work educators. As the use of electronic technologies for teaching and learning expands, the role of the educator moves from being the sole provider or source of information to students to one in which the educator acts more as a facilitator and enabler in the learning process. In a technology-supported learning environment, students take on a more proactive role assuming increasing responsibility for their own learning. As a result, the teacher-student relationship becomes more egalitarian (Ouellette & Rank, 2000).

The second challenge for educators is the need for increased research to adequately assess the processes and learning outcomes for students acquiring their training in a technology-supported instructional environment. In recent years, researchers have identified a number of areas needing further investigation. Some have suggested that future research should take into account variables such as the specific technology being used, specific learner characteristics of students, faculty concerns and characteristics, pedagogical strategies, content areas of courses, and administrative and broader community issues. (Westhuis, Ouellette, & Pfahler, in press). Others have discussed the importance of forming a community of learners and how it can affect student satisfaction, retention, and learning (Gabelnick, MacGregor, Matthews, & Smith, 1990; Johansen & Ouellette, in press). Brown (2001) suggests the instructor build in opportunities for students to learn about each other and discover commonalities. Additional research needs to be done to determine how pedagogical processes such as discussion forums and group assignments impact learning outcomes. Other studies have suggested the following pedagogical strategies as the important elements impacting effective online instruction: the instructor's visibility to the students; the instructor's modeling of how the electronic discussion model works; frequent, consistent, and timely feedback by the instructor; instructor evaluation of student discussion processes; providing a template to students on how to give feedback; presenting course content in an orderly and consistent manner; and assisting students who encounter technical issues related to hardware and software (Bischoff, 2000). Additional research needs to be directed at determining what the optimal elements are for student learning for each pedagogical strategy and determine if what Bischoff suggests is valid. Further research should explore what needs to be done to determine how much instructor visibility is needed. What technology should the instructor use to create that visibility? What technology-supported format (audio, written, or video) should the instructor be using to optimize student learning?

Potts (2005) has provided a conceptual framework for evaluating distance learning that includes inputs, throughputs, and outcomes and recommends a number of issues for further investigation. Specifically, there is a need to evaluate how institutional infrastructure impacts the success of distance education (DE) programs. What are the characteristics of effective DE faculty? What training is needed for distance educators? How do the Council of Social Work Education standards contribute to or hinder DE programs? What type of student recruitment efforts are effective in helping students determine if they are appropriate for DE programs? What needs to be provided to students during the orientation process of a DE program to increase the probability for their success?

## Future Trends

The increasing use of technology for teaching and learning, coupled with profound technological advances, will continue to challenge not only what we know about what constitutes good teaching and learning but also provide exciting new opportunities for social work education.

## REFERENCES

Aldrich, C. (2004). Simulations and the future of learning. An innovative (and perhaps) revolutionary approach to e-learning. San Francisco: Pfeiffer.

Bischoff, A. (2000). The Elements of Effective Online Teaching. In K. W. White & B. H. Weight (Eds.), The online teaching guide: A handbook of attitudes, strategies, and techniques for the virtual classroom (pp. 57–72). Boston: Allyn and Bacon.

Blakely, T. J. (1994). Strategies for distance learning. Journal of Continuing Social Work Education, 6, 4–6.

Brown, R. (2001). The process of community-building in distance learning classes. Journal of Asynchronous Learning Networks, 5(2), 18–35.

Coe, J. R. (2005). Faculty issues in distance education. In Paul Abels (Ed.), Distance education in social work: planning, teaching, and learning (pp. 119–139). New York: Springer Publishing Company.

Coe, J. R., & Elliot, D. (1999). An evaluation of teaching direct practice courses in a distance education program for rural settings. Journal of Social Work Education, 35, 353–365.

Coe, J. R., & Gandy, J. (1999). Perspectives from Consumers (Students) in a Distance Education Program. Journal of Technology in Human Services, 16(2/3), 161–174.

Freddolino, P. P. (1996). Maintaining quality in graduate social work programs delivered to distant sites using electronic instruction technology. In E. T. Reck (Ed.), Modes of professional education II: The electronic social work curriculum in the twenty-first century, Tulane Studies in Social Welfare, 20. New Orleans: Tulane University.

Gabelnick, F., MacGregor, J., Matthews, R. S., & Smith, B. L. (1990). Students in learning communities: Engaging with self, others, and the college community. New Directions for Teaching and Learning, 41, 39–51.

Haga, M., & Heitkamp, T. L. (2000). Bringing social work education to the prairie. Journal of Social Work Education, 36, 309–324.

Johansen, P., & Ouellette, P. (in press) Integrating learning community strategies for enhancing academic and social agency partnerships in social work education. Advances in Social Work, 7(2), 101–114.

Macy, J. A., Rooney, R. H., Hollister, C. D., & Freddolino, P. P. (2001). Evaluation of distance education programs in social work. *Journal of Technology in Human Services, 18*, 63–84.

Ostendorf, V. A. (1994). *The two-way video classroom.* Littleton, CO: Author.

Ouellette, P., & Rank, M. (2000). Transitioning from teaching to life-long learning: Towards yet another paradigm shift. *Journal of Family Social Work, 5*, 57–73.

Ouellette, P., Westhuis, D., Marshall, E., & Chang, V. (2006). The acquisition of social work interviewing skills in a Web-based and classroom instructional environment: Results of a study. *Journal of Technology and Human Services, 24*, 53–76.

Petracchi, H., & Patchner, M. (2000). Social work students and their learning environment: A comparison of interactive television, face-to-face instruction and the traditional classroom. *Journal of Social Work Education, 36*, 335–346.

Potts, M. (2005). Measuring distance education: evaluation of distance education in social work. In Paul Abels (Ed.), *Distance education in social work: planning, teaching, and learning* (pp. 97–118). New York: Springer Publishing Company.

Raymond, Frank. B. (2005). The history of distance education in social work and the evolution of distance education modalities. In Paul Abels (Ed.), *Distance education in social work: planning, teaching, and learning* (pp. 23–40). New York: Springer Publishing Company.

Seabury, B. (2003). On-line, computer-based, interactive simulations: Bridging classroom and field. *Journal of Technology in Human Services, 22*, 29–48.

Siegel, E., Conklin, J., Jennings, J., & Flynn, S. (2000, February). The present status of distance learning in social work education: an update. Paper presented at the Annual Program Meeting of the Council on Social Work Education, New York, NY.

Thomas, R. (2001). Interactivity & Simulations in e-Learning. Retrieved October 9, 2007, from http://elearning.typepad.com/thelearnedman/files/Interactivity_Simulations_in_eLearning.pdf

Vernon, B. (2006). CSWE-Commission on Accreditation: Distance Education Survey. Unpublished manuscript.

Westhuis, D., Ouellette, P., & Pfahler, C. (2005). A comparative analysis of two class formats for teaching and learning social work research. *Advances in Social Work, 7*(2), 84–100.

—PHILIP M. OUELLETTE AND DAVID WESTHUIS

## FIELD WORK

**ABSTRACT:** Field education has played a significant role in the professional development of social workers since the beginning of the last century. Although the apprenticeship model of training continues to play a significant role, variations on this theme have been explored and continue to be developed in response to political, academic, and economic challenges. Technological advances will enable programs to expand field education into new communities, both nationally and internationally. In addition, changes in educational policy and accreditation guidelines have the potential to revitalize the role of field education and increase research efforts devoted to this important component of professional education.

**KEY WORDS:** field education; Council on Social Work Education; Education Policy and Accreditation Standards; Edith Abbott; Bertha Capen Reynolds

Field education plays a prominent, challenging, and somewhat perplexing role in social work education. From the establishment of the Amsterdam Institute for Social Work Training in 1899—the first, full-time school of social work—to the present, academic programs and agencies have struggled to define their roles and responsibilities in the process that many graduates define as their most valuable and memorable educational experience. Transported back in time, today's student would readily recognize field education as described in this century-old program:

Field work in the first year included visits to various social institutions, agencies, and factories, and introduced all students to the activities suggested by the classes and lecture. . . . The second year of field work included regular supervision in the practice setting selected by the student (Kendall, 2000, p. 63).

However, much has changed to challenge the field education mission, goals, and objectives at the bachelor's (BSW) and master's (MSW) levels of social work education, such as the restructuring of higher education, modified service delivery patterns, managed care, student demographics, diminishing funding sources, devolution of governmental roles and responsibilities, immigration and population trends, and critical shortages of resources for those served. Each of these challenges has, in different ways, changed the academic–agency relationship, reduced field instructor time and availability, narrowed the range of student experiences, and restricted options for placements in the field.

## Council on Social Work
## Education Policy and Accreditation Standards
The Council on Social Work Education (CSWE), social work education's national accrediting body, establishes basic requirements for BSW and MSW programs. Doctoral programs in social work are not accredited by this organization. Balancing local program flexibility with national program requirements, the Council's *Educational Policy and Accreditation Standards* (EPAS; Council on Social Work Education, 2004) attempts to

establish minimal criteria for the existing 670 BSW and MSW programs, as well as for those that develop in the future. Currently, few mandates are stated, and instead programs are directed to create a classroom and field curriculum that is consistent with their institutional and program missions, goals, and objectives. EPAS is currently being modified, and new directions will shape field education in the future.

Students working toward a BSW degree are required to complete a minimum of 400 clock hours of field experience; MSW students need a minimum of 900 hours. Field settings are to ". . .reinforce students' identification with the purposes, values, and ethics of the profession; foster the integration of empirical and practice-based knowledge; promote the development of professional competence" (EPAS, 10–11), and "model understanding of and respect for diversity" (EPAS, 17). Field instructors in BSW programs must hold a CSWE-accredited BSW or MSW degree and MSW field instructors must hold an MSW degree. Although no practice experience is required of field instructors, many programs require their field instructors to have a minimum of 2 years of postprofessional degree experience. When these minimal instructor requirements cannot be met, the programs must provide instruction that reinforces the social work perspective.

Field directors must hold a CSWE-accredited MSW degree and earn 2 years of postbaccalaureate or post master's practice experience before being employed in this capacity. Field directors must provide administrative leadership and devote at least 25% of their time in BSW programs and 50% of their time in MSW programs to their field responsibilities. These are EPAS requirements. If a citation is needed here it would be (EPAS, 14).

As increasing numbers of graduate and undergraduate students require employment during their matriculation, they often seek practicum placements in their employing agencies. EPAS recognizes this, and requires BSW and MSW programs to establish policies for such placements that ensure the responsibilities and experiences of the placement differ from the student's job, have assignments that develop different skills, and have supervision that differs from that required by their employer.

## Field Education Leadership

Field education program directors play a critical role in the development and maintenance of practicum programs. Many are experienced practitioners, but this role is often marginalized in academia (Wayne, Bogo, & Raskin, 2006). A study by Morrow and Fogel (2001) found that most directors in graduate programs were Caucasian

(more than 75%), women (84%), held an MSW degree (68%), and employed in nontenure track positions (more than 60%). More than two thirds of MSW field program directors had less than 6 years of director experience, vacancy rates approached 10%, and turnover was high. Similar patterns held for BSW programs except 75% of director positions were tenure line and slightly more men were employed. Morrow and Fogel noted other studies which argued that "compared to tenure-track faculty, non-tenure-track faculty have lower salaries, fewer fringe benefits, less job security, and less power in making curriculum decisions" and that women in nontenured positions may be in double jeopardy in academia because of sexism (2001, p. 84).

## Innovations and New Opportunities

New designs or renewed designs enter the field practicum arena periodically, but the predominant pattern of assignment remains a single placement with one or two students assigned to an agency practicum instructor. The practicality of block placements, typically 4 or 5 days per week in field, was recognized by Smith College in the 1930s, based on their rather remote location. Similarly, in the 1960s as the University of Illinois at Urbana-Champaign's program grew in size and practicums had to be planned statewide, block formats became the primary pattern for its field instruction. Today, concurrent patterns, rotating days of class and field, and block options are frequently used at the graduate level, while B.S.W. programs have found that the block alternative and their class scheduling needs often work best.

Rotational models, where students gain field education experiences in several related practicum sites, are being employed by the gerontology programs currently supported by the John A. Hartford Foundation of New York City. The rotations permit students to experience a greater breadth of programs and services than provided in the traditional model. This structuring of social work field practicums is being well received, but it is not a new approach. Edith Abbott strongly advocated for this model at the University of Chicago in the 1930s (Abbott, 1942; Ivry, Lawrance, Damron-Rodriguez, & Robbins, 2005).

Recognizing that agency staff have diminished time and availability, some current Title VI-E Child Welfare Collaboratives have placed full-time faculty in public welfare agencies as field instructors, another of the innovations supported by Abbott. In the 1960s Kindelsperger and Cassidy (1966) employed the training center concept to maximize the use of both traditional and atypical field placements. Such centers structured learning opportunities that closely supplement the classroom curriculum in collaboration with supporting field agencies. Social service centers, which are analogous to education's laboratory schools or medicine's university teaching hospitals, employ group field instruction as first developed in the 1960s and 1970s (Brieland, 1969), and are again being explored (Poulin, Silver, & Kauffman, 2006).

The full impact of the development of the World Wide Web and virtual education has not yet been experienced in social work education, but rapid change is expected. A 2006 survey by CSWE found one B.S.W. program and a few MSW programs that provide the majority of their curriculum though online courses (personal communication with Lisa Weidekamp, CSWE, December 13, 2006). Florida State University's online advanced standing, part-time clinical program is perhaps the best documented (Wilke & Vinton, 2006). Advances in the use of video conferencing, computer-based and hybrid classrooms, and computer-assisted instruction will continue to grow as technological options develop (Birkenmaier et al., 2005). Field supervision and training of distance education students using Webcams is expanding rapidly as this alternative becomes more economical. Travel costs and time in transit are reduced significantly using this option, and programs' geographical boundaries broaden, effectively increasing the available options for qualified practicum placements, and providing a much needed benefit as training sites decline.

## National and International Placements

Most students are placed within reasonable driving distances of their educational institutions. However, the technological innovations noted earlier are making it possible for students to be placed nationally and even internationally. Online libraries, economical or free telecommunications, discussion boards, e-mail, and websites enable students to be placed in distant agencies and still complete field assignments, participate in integrative seminars, and remain in touch with their classmates and faculty.

International educational and social service opportunities for BSW and MSW students are challenging social work programs to globalize their classroom and practicum training. EPAS encourages this expansion by stating that one purpose of social work education is "to develop and apply practice in the context of diverse cultures" (EPAS, EP Sec. 1.0) by "preparing social workers to recognize the global context of social work practice" (EPAS, EP Sec. 1.2). Panos, Pettys, Cox, and Jones-Hart (2004) found that 21% of CSWE-accredited programs placed an MSW or BSW student in 55 different

countries between 1997 and 2002. Although these students were placed primarily in English- or Spanish-speaking countries, the demand for bilingual and multilingual students is increasing, and schools will need to identify ways that students can incorporate language and cultural studies into their classes and practicum placements. Improved and inexpensive communication options are making these placements easier to plan, monitor, and supervise; however, ongoing efforts to integrate these opportunities into the curriculum and to establish well-supported and coordinated efforts in the host countries rather than individualistic and sporadic learning opportunities need to continue.

## Empirical Evidence for Field Practice Effectiveness

Another requirement of EPAS states that "field education is systemically designed, supervised, coordinated, and evaluated on the basis of criteria by which students demonstrate the achievement of program objectives" (EPAS, 11). Abbott observed the need for field assessment and research more than 65 years ago. She declared that "our great problem has been, and still is, to make fieldwork truly educational. Its importance is accepted by all of us; but few attempts have been made to analyze carefully its educational content and the methods of securing proper educational results" (1942, p. 57). Forty years later Jenkins and Sheafor wrote, "Social work education has been unable or unwilling to submit the field instruction process to disciplined evaluation and, therefore, it has not generated an adequate literature to become an appropriately creditable part of higher education" (1982, p. 3–4).

Although between 20 and 30% of the professional social work curriculum is typically devoted to field education at the BSW and MSW level, the research base is thin. Alfred Kadushin noted that between 1981 and 1989 only 45 of the 13,000 articles cited in *Social Work Abstracts* addressed field education (Schneck, Grossman, & Glassman, 1991); and while updating this study, Lager and Robbins (2004) found that of the almost 14,000 articles cited between 1995 and 2004, only 118 were field-related, and even fewer were research-based.

All programs provide field instructor orientations to introduce field faculty to the various roles and responsibilities of the parties involved in the field education endeavor. Class and field curricula are distributed, former field instructors and students share their practice wisdom, and requirements and forms are reviewed. Ongoing relations with field instructors are carried out by program field liaisons using personal contacts, websites, e-mail correspondence, and mailings. However, student evaluation is given insufficient attention (Jenkins & Sheafor, 1982, and Wayne, Bogo & Raskin, 2006). Much of field education is evaluated by using field instructors' and students' self-reports. Direct observation of students' interventions by school faculty or field instructors is minimal. One study (Knight, 2001) of 500 BSWs and MSWs in field placements found that two thirds of the respondents had field instructors who never provided live supervision and never used audio or videotape recordings of student performance. In addition, 40% of the students did not receive weekly supervision. Field instructors, in this and related studies of field supervision, were rated most favorably when frequent supervision was provided along with live supervision. Some argue that to do otherwise is unethical (Haynes, Corey, & Moulton, 2003). Currently, field instructor assessment of student performance and field effectiveness remains questionable and will require a significant research emphasis going forward (Regehr, Bogo, Regehr, & Power, 2007).

### Challenges

Reynolds (1942) identified field instruction issues that academia and the profession continue to debate today. How can we better stress the importance of field teaching within the curriculum? Why field instruction is not valued the same as classroom instruction and staffed with equally well-qualified faculty? When should field education start? How much time should be devoted to field instruction? When should classes meet? How can we select agencies that will give our students broad social work skills rather than apprenticeship training for potential employment in the field agency? Should we establish training centers rather than place students individually in field agencies? How can we better prepare field instructors? What can colleges and universities do to help overburdened field instructors and agencies? Should experienced practitioners be challenged with a different and more advanced curriculum or perhaps spend less time in school? Must graduate education take 2 years? How can we better integrate class and field?

Challenges that Reynolds did not foresee also exist. Social work's emphasis on evidenced-based practice as well as the increased use of scripted interventions that yield greater intervention fidelity and effectiveness will require significant modifications in the way practitioners are trained and how they think and act (Gambrill, 2003). The revised EPAS will emphasize field education as a "signature pedagogy," of the profession, the way "novices are instructed in critical aspects of the three fundamental dimensions of professional work—to think, to perform, and to act with integrity" (Shulman, 2005, p. 134). This change is an attempt to rebalance and strengthen the relationship between class and field education and to emphasize the importance of field education in the attainment and assessment of students' acquired professional knowledge, values, and skills. Such rebalancing between class and field, in the past, has not been successful, perhaps because of the multiple demands of academia and the emphasis on doctoral studies and grant acquisition. The incorporation of technology and distant education modalities, while welcome, will also challenge present field educators with new ethical dilemmas and change.

New BSW and MSW programs continue to develop not only in underserved areas but also in communities well addressed by existing programs, thus placing even greater strains on available field instructors and sponsoring placement agencies. More collaborative state and regional coalitions similar to that of the Greater New York Metropolitan Area Directors of Field Instruction will be needed to share resources and faculty, train and certify field instructors, and prepare agencies for future curricula innovations. The training and support provided by the Association of Baccalaureate Program Directors (Buchan et al., 2004) and the CSWE will be of increasing importance to those programs that may lack the internal resources to meet the growing, rigorous demands of future professional social work education and practice.

### Past, Present, and Future

Field education, primarily employing an apprenticeship model, has played a significant role in the professional development of social workers since the beginning of the last century. Typically, a student is assigned to one field instructor who supervises the student, assigns cases, and evaluates outcomes guided by criteria established by the cooperating educational institution. Variations on this theme have been explored and continue to be developed in response to political, academic, and economic challenges that have narrowed field education opportunities and the range of student experiences. Although slow to adopt technological advances, field education is beginning to embrace an array of technological options that will enable field education programs to expand into new communities both nationally and internationally. In addition, changes in CSWE EPAS guidelines have the potential to revitalize the role of field education and increase the amount of research devoted to this important component of professional education.

## REFERENCES

Abbott, E. (1942). *Social welfare and professional education.* Chicago: University of Chicago Press. Original work published 1931.

Birkenmaier, J., Wernet, S. P., Berg-Weger, M., Wilson, J. R., Banks, R., Olliges, R., et al. (2005). Weaving a web: The use of internet technology in field education. In R. L. Beaulaurier, & M. Haffey (Eds.), *Technology in social work education and curriculum: The high tech, high touch social work educator* (pp. 3–19). New York: The Haworth Social Work Practice Press.

Brieland, D. (1969). A social services center for a multi-problem community. In B. L. Jones (Ed.), *Current patterns in field instruction in graduate school work education* (pp. 61–64). New York: Council on Social Work Education.

Buchan, V., Rodenhiser, R., Hull, G., Smith, M., Rogers, J., Pike, C., et al. (2004). Evaluating an assessment tool for undergraduate social work education: Analysis of the baccalaureate educational assessment package. *Journal of Social Work Education, 40,* 239–253.

Council on Social Work Education. (2004). *Educational policy and accreditation standards.* Alexandria, VA: Author.

Gambrill, E. D. (2003). Evidence-based practice: Sea change or the emperor's new clothes? *Journal of Social Work Education, 39,* 3–23.

Haynes, R., Corey, G., & Moulton, P. (2003). *Clinical supervision in the helping professions: A practical guide.* Pacific Grove, CA: Books/Cole-Thomson Learning.

Ivry, J., Lawrance, F. P., Damron-Rodriguez, J., & Robbins, V. C. (2005). Fieldwork rotation: A model for educating social work students for geriatric social work practice. *Journal of Social Work Education, 41,* 407–425.

Jenkins, L. E., & Sheafor, B. (1982). An overview of social work field instruction. In B. W. Sheafor & L. E. Jenkins (Eds.), *Quality field instruction in social work* (pp. 3–20). New York: Longman.

Kendall, K. A. (2000). *Social work education: Its origins in Europe.* Alexandria, VA: Council on Social Work Education.

Kindelsperger, W. L., & Cassidy, H. (1966). *Social work training centers: Tentative analysis of the structure and learning environment.* New Orleans: Tulane University, School of Social Work.

Knight, C. (2001). The process of field instruction: BSW and MSW students' views of effective field supervision. *Journal of Social Work Education, 37,* 357–379.

Lager, P. B., & Robbins, V. C. (2004). Field education: Exploring the future, expanding the vision. *Journal of Social Work Education, 40,* 3–11.

Morrow, D. F., & Fogel, S. J. (2001). Staffing patterns of field directors in social work programs. *Arete, 25,* 78–86.

Panos, P. T., Pettys, G., Cox, S. E., & Jones-Hart, E. (2004). Survey of international field education placements of accredited social work education programs. *Journal of Social Work Education, 40,* 467–478.

Poulin, J., Silver, P., & Kauffman, S. (2006). Serving the community and training social workers: Service outputs and student outcomes. *Journal of Social Work Education, 42,* 171–184.

Regehr, G., Bogo, M., Regehr, C., & Power, R. (2007). Can we build a better mousetrap? Improving the measures of practice performance in the field practicum. *Journal of Social Work Education, 43,* 327–342.

Reynolds, B. C. (1942). *Learning and teaching in the practice of social work.* New York: J. J. Little and Ives.

Schneck, D., Grossman, B., & Glassman, U. (1991). *Field education in social work: Contemporary issues and trends.* Dubuque, IA: Kendall/Hunt.

Shulman, L. S. (2005). Signature pedagogies in the professions. *Daedalus, 134,* 52–59.

Wayne, J., Bogo, M., & Raskin, M. (2006). The need for radical change in field education. *Journal of Social Work Education, 42,* 161–169.

Wilke, D., & Vinton, L. (2006). Evaluation of the first Web-based advanced standing MSW program. *Journal of Social Work Education, 42,* 607–620.

## FURTHER READING

Panos, P. T., Panos, A., Cox, S. E., Roby, J. L., & Matheson, K. (2002). Ethical issues concerning the use of videoconferencing to supervise international social work field practicum students. *Journal of Social Work Education, 38,* 421–437.

—GARY L. SHAFFER

## HUMAN BEHAVIOR AND SOCIAL ENVIRONMENT

**ABSTRACT:** This entry provides a brief history of social work's changing knowledge base about human behavior and identifies the current knowledge base as multidimensional, multispherical, multicultural, multidirectional, multidisciplinary, and multitheoretical. It provides an overview of eight broad theoretical perspectives currently used in social work: systems, conflict, rational choice, social constructionist, psychodynamic, developmental, social behavioral, and humanistic perspectives. Each perspective is analyzed in terms of its central ideas, practice implications, and empirical evidence. The entry ends with a brief discussion of trends and directions.

**KEY WORDS:** systems perspective; conflict perspective; rational choice perspective; social constructionist perspective; psychodynamic perspective; developmental perspective; social behavioral perspective; humanistic perspective

### Introduction and History

From its beginning in the late 19th century, social work has sought to base its practice on the best available knowledge of human behavior. Social work scholars have searched for useful frameworks for organizing social and behavioral science knowledge to support multiple social work roles. In the earliest days, sociological knowledge was the primary source of information about the social problems that social workers sought to ameliorate. By the 1920s, social work sought psychiatric and medical knowledge, and began to draw heavily on the psychodynamic approach. Beginning in the 1950s, the Council on Social Work Education (CSWE) recommended a sequence of courses on human behavior in social work education programs. In 1962, this sequence was named Human Behavior and the Social Environment (HBSE) and every CSWE curriculum policy statement since then has mandated HBSE content (Germain, 1994).

Since the beginning of social work as a profession, the knowledge base for practice has been dynamic. Social work roles have shifted over time and a vast multidisciplinary literature about human behavior has grown at a fast pace, leading to different emphases in the HBSE curriculum. Today, there is general agreement that a multidimensional, multispherical, multicultural, multidirectional, multidisciplinary, and multitheoretical focus on human behavior is essential to guide contemporary practice. Human behavior is multidimensional, occurring along biological, psychological, spiritual, and social dimensions. It is multispherical, occurring in families, small groups, communities, formal organizations, social institutions, and social movements. It is multicultural, constantly enacted and negotiated in diverse cultural contexts. It is multidirectional, with mutual influences flowing between multiple dimensions and spheres. Knowledge of human behavior relevant to social work practice is currently dispersed over more than thirty disciplines, and multidisciplinary theory and empirical research form the base of current HBSE knowledge (see Kirk & Reid, 2002). Theory provides a conceptual way of explaining the relationships between aspects of our world, and empirical research examines those relationships with careful, purposeful, and systematic observation. Multiple theories, and the empirical research related to them, are necessary to account for the complexities of human behavior.

### Theories of Human Behavior

Theorists from a number of disciplines have attempted to provide conceptual tools for understanding human behavior, and social workers make use of many of these different theories. Some of these theories are narrow in scope and some are more broad-based. In the contemporary era, eight broad theoretical perspectives are widely used by social workers and other professionals: systems, conflict, rational choice, social constructionist, psychodynamic, developmental, social behavioral,

and humanistic. Each of these perspectives has been reconceptualized and extended over time to more adequately cover diversity in social life, and each comprises a number of different theories. Each has a wide range of application across multiple dimensions and multiple spheres of human behavior. Each has received some empirical support, some only in a narrow range of behaviors and circumstances and some more broadly. These eight perspectives come primarily from the disciplines of psychology and sociology, but several have interdisciplinary roots and all are increasingly being used across disciplinary lines. In addition, there is much recent evidence of conceptual synthesizing across theoretical lines, and the boundaries between theories are becoming blurred.

SYSTEMS  The systems perspective sees human behavior as the outcome of reciprocal interactions between people and their environments, focusing on the interconnectedness of all life. A variety of disciplines were involved in the early development of the systems perspective, including physics, mathematics, engineering, biology, psychology, cultural anthropology, economics, and sociology. Some systems theories emphasize the mechanisms by which social systems maintain stability over time, and others emphasize the dynamic nature of social systems. Some see systems as relatively closed to their external environments and others see them as very open.

Interest in the social systems perspective has waxed and waned since it first emerged in the 1940s and 1950s. In recent years, however, the systems perspective, in the form of ecological theory, has become very popular in the social and behavioral sciences and in professions like social work.

Ecological theory focuses on the dynamic and reciprocal interaction between organisms and their multiple environments. It pays particular attention to how people and other organisms adapt to the contexts of their lives and how their adaptations in turn help to shape those contexts. Researchers in the fields of developmental and clinical psychology, psychiatry, and behavior genetics have used an ecological multidimensional risk and protection approach to understand the multiple systems of influence that lead to psychological resilience or psychopathology. They have identified risk factors that both increase the probability of developing and maintaining problem conditions and protective factors that decrease the probability of problem conditions. Researchers in the field of epidemiology have used the same approach to understand health disparities and patterns of disease across population groups (see Fraser, 2004). There is growing empirical support for ecological theory, with strong evidence that human behavior is influenced by factors in multiple dimensions and spheres. The growing evidence regarding risk and protective factors has implications for targeting interventions to reduce risk and, or, increase protection. Ecological theory is recently being used to understand the impact of economic and cultural globalization on human behavior of groups around the globe.

*Conflict.* The conflict perspective sees conflict as a central feature of society and focuses on power and inequalities in social life, and on the role of conflict in generating social change. Theories in the conflict perspective typically look for sources of conflict and causes of human behavior in the economic and political spheres, and also, recently, in the cultural sphere. The roots of contemporary conflict theory can be traced to the late 19th century work of Karl Marx and Friedrich Engels who were concerned about the class system generated by economic capitalism, a system they saw as based on exploitation of workers and natural resources. More recently, ImmanuelWallerstein (1979) has focused on international inequality created by economic globalization. Critical theorists have argued that, in advanced stages of capitalism, people are dominated by the culture industry, with the advertising industry exploiting consumers to work harder and harder in order to shop (Habermas, 1987). According to conflict theorists, oppression of non-dominant groups leads to alienation, indifference, and hostility.

Early settlement house social workers recognized social conflict and social inequality and focused on eliminating oppression of immigrants, women, and children. Over time social workers have not made consistent use of the conflict perspective, but, in the recent past, the social work profession has renewed its public commitment to social justice and has begun to draw more heavily on conflict theories. Feminist theories that focus on male domination and present a vision of a more just world have been influential in this renewal. Social workers have used the conflict perspective to develop practice-oriented empowerment theories, which call attention to processes of oppression and propose action strategies to increase power among members of non-dominant groups (Lee, 2001). The conflict perspective has empirical support from historical research, naturalistic inquiry, and experimental studies of reactions to coercive power. It is essential for a profession committed to pursuing social justice.

*Rational Choice.* The rational choice perspective sees human behavior as based on self-interest and rational choices about effective ways to accomplish goals. The perspective is interdisciplinary, with strong roots in utilitarian philosophy, economics, and social behaviorism. Social workers are most familiar with social exchange theory, rational choice models of organizations, public choice theory in political science, and the emerging social network theory. Social exchange theory, which proposes that social behavior is based on the desire to maximize benefits and minimize costs in social relationships, has been used to understand partner relationships and family dynamics. The rational choice perspective has also been used to make policy recommendations about using financial and other types of incentives to encourage pro-social behavior and social solidarity (Coleman, 1990). It has been used to understand health behaviors and to develop public health prevention strategies for a wide range of health problems. In addition, it is currently being used to assess the reciprocity of exchange in social networks. The empirical evidence for the rational choice perspective is mixed, and there is much disagreement among theorists about the limits of rationality.

***Social Constructionist.*** The social constructionist perspective focuses on how people learn—through their interactions with each other—to classify the world and their place in it. Human understanding is seen as both the product and the driving force of social interaction. Humans are social beings who interact with each other on the basis of a shared understanding about the world, which is itself developed in social interaction. The roots of the social constructionist perspective can be traced to philosophical phenomenology and symbolic interaction theory. To social constructionists, there is no singular objective reality that exists outside people's perceptions. Rather there are multiple social and cultural realities. Radical social constructionists believe there is no objective reality. More moderate social constructionists believe there are "real objects" in the world, but those objects are never known objectively, but only through the subjective interpretations of individuals and groups.

In recent years, social workers have been drawn to the social constructionist perspective because of its ability to accommodate diversity. Those versions of the perspective that recognize power differentials in meaning making have been particularly useful for considering mechanisms of oppression (Laird, 1998). The current interest in solution-focused, narrative and storytelling therapies is based on the social constructionist perspective. These approaches can be used with individuals, as well as with families, groups, communities, and organizations. Social constructionism has stimulated a trend in the behavioral sciences to use a mix of quantitative and qualitative research methodologies to accommodate both objective and subjective reality.

*Pyschodynamic.* The psychodynamic perspective is concerned with how internal processes such as needs, drives, and emotions motivate human behavior. The perspective has evolved over the years, moving from the classical emphasis on innate drives and unconscious processes toward greater emphasis on the adaptive capacities of individuals and their interactions with the environment. The origins of the perspective are in the classical psychoanalytic approach of Sigmund Freud, but social workers make greater use of the more recent formulations found in ego psychology, object relations, and self psychology theories. Ego psychology gives primary attention to the rational part of the mind and the human capacity for adaptation. It recognizes conscious as well as unconscious attempts to cope. Object relations theory studies how people develop attitudes toward others and how those attitudes affect social relationships and the view of the self. Self psychology focuses on the individual need to organize the personality into a cohesive sense of self and to build relationships that support it.

All versions of the perspective have the following implications for direct social work practice: the paramount role of the professional–client relationship, the curative value of expression of emotional conflicts and understanding past events, and the goals of self-awareness and self-control. All versions of the perspective also emphasize the importance of early life experiences, and, indeed, recent long-term longitudinal research confirms the importance of childhood experiences, but also indicates that personality continues to develop throughout life. There is growing evidence of the supremely important role that early attachment plays in healthy brain development (Applegate & Shapiro, 2005).

*Developmental.* The developmental perspective focuses on how human behavior changes and stays the same across the life course. Human development is seen as a complex interaction of biological, psychological, and social processes, which occur in defined stages. There are two streams of the developmental perspective. The life span or life cycle theory, based in psychology, focuses on inner life during age-related stages. Erik Erikson is the best known theorist in this tradition. The life course perspective, based in sociology, focuses on the human life course as a social phenomenon that is influenced by shared social and historical contexts. In its current state, there are six major themes in the life course perspective: the interplay of human lives and historical time; biological, psychological, and social timing of human lives; linked or interdependent lives; human capacity for choice-making; diversity in life course trajectories; and developmental risk and protection (Hutchison, 2008). There is a great deal of empirical support for the developmental perspective, but much of the early research masked the diversity of life course trajectories. For the past several decades, large-scale longitudinal studies have found support for the idea that events in one stage of life have impacts down the developmental line (Werner & Smith, 2001). This research, which also chronicles the self-righting capacities of humans and diversity in life course trajectories, has numerous implications for social work interventions at every stage of the life course.

*Social Behavioral.* The social behavioral perspective sees human behavior as learned as individuals interact with their environments. Different social behavioral theories focus on the different ways in which learning occurs. There are three main approaches: classical conditioning, operant conditioning, and cognitive social learning theory. Classical conditioning theory sees behavior as learned through association, when a naturally satisfying stimulus (unconditioned stimulus) is paired with a neutral stimulus (conditioned stimulus). Operant conditioning theory sees behavior as the result of reinforcement. Cognitive social learning theory suggests that behavior is also learned by imitation, observation, beliefs, and expectations. According to the social behavioral perspective, all human problems of living can be defined in terms of undesirable behaviors, and all behaviors can be defined, measured, and changed. All streams of the social behavioral perspective have a relatively high degree of empirical support. A major strength of the perspective is the ease with which principles of behavior modification can be extrapolated, and social behavioral principles are frequently used in social work practice. It is important to note, however, that the professional behavior modifier can easily use social behavioral principles in a coercive manner to accomplish oppressive ends if the principles are applied outside the professional code of ethics.

*Humanistic.* The humanistic perspective emphasizes the human capacity for directing one's own life and the human desire for growth, personal meaning, competence, and connectedness with others. It was developed in reaction to the determinism found in early versions of both the psychodynamic and behavioral perspectives. Social workers make use of Maslow's theory of hierarchy of needs and Rogers' core conditions of the therapeutic process (empathy, warmth, and genuineness), both of which are humanistic theories.

There is much empirical evidence that empathy, warmth, and genuineness are necessary conditions of therapeutic relationships. The long-held social work adage "begin where the client is" comes from social work's historical involvement in the development of humanistic theory. More recently, the humanistic perspective has been the cornerstone of the strengths perspective on social work practice, and of the growing interest in spiritual dimensions of human behavior among social workers. The humanistic perspective has been used to understand organizations as well as individuals.

## Trends and Directions

The multidimensionality and multidirectionality of human behavior is increasingly clear. Knowledge of genetic and neurological contributions to human behavior is expanding rapidly. At the same time, we are learning more and more about the impact of social and economic conditions, as well as the physical environment, on gene expression, the brain, and the immune system. Research on spiritual mechanisms of protection, in its early stages, is providing useful insights. Social workers will need to keep up with these trends in behavioral science theory and research. In addition, the social work commitment to social justice compels us to understand the mechanisms of oppression at home and around the globe.

## REFERENCES

Applegate, J., & Shapiro, J. (2005). *Neurobiology for clinical social work*. New York: W. W. Norton & Company.

Fraser, M. (Ed.). (2004) *Risk and resilience in childhood: An ecological perspective* (2nd ed.). Washington, DC: NASW Press.

Germain, C. (1994). Human behavior and the social environment. In F. Reamer (Ed.), *The foundations of social work knowledge* (pp. 88–121). New York: Columbia University Press.

Habermas, J. (1987). *The theory of communicative action: Vol. 2. Lifeworld and system: A critique of functionalist reason* (T. McCarthy, Trans.). Boston: Beacon Press.

Hutchison, E. (2008). A life course perspective. In E. Hutchison (Ed.), *Dimensions of human behavior: The changing life course* (3rd ed.). Thousand Oaks, CA: Sage.

Kirk, S., & Reid, W. (2002). *Science and social work: A critical appraisal*. New York: Columbia University Press.

Laird, J. (1998). Theorizing culture: Narrative ideas and practice principles. In M. McGoldrick (Ed.), *Revisioning family therapy* (pp. 20–36). New York: Guilford.

Lee, J. (2001). *The empowerment approach to social work practice* (2nd ed.). New York: Columbia University Press.

Wallerstein, I. (1979). *The capitalist world economy*. London: Cambridge University Press.

Werner, E. E., & Smith, R. S. (2001). *Journeys from childhood to midlife*. Ithaca, NY: Cornell University Press.

## SUGGESTED LINKS

Conflict Theory(ies).
    *www.umsl.edu/~rkeel/200/conflict.html*
Humanistic Psychology.
    *www.ahpweb.org/aboutahp/whatis.html*
Personality Theories.
    *www.ship.edu/~cgboeree/perscontents.html*
Sociological Theories and Perspectives.
    *www.sociosite.net/topics/theory.php*
William Alanson White Institute.
    *www.wawhite.org*

—ELIZABETH D. HUTCHISON

## MULTICULTURALISM

ABSTRACT: Despite many debates about the meaning and implications of multiculturalism, it remains an important concept within social work and other professional and academic disciplines. The basic idea of multiculturalism in social work education is that social work students need to learn to work effectively with people from many different cultures, and that this will have a positive impact on their social work practice and on outcomes for those with whom they work. It has been linked to issues of power, oppression, and social change. Future directions include focus on intersectionality and continued development of the implementation and implications of multiculturalism within social work education.

KEY WORDS: multiculturalism; cultural competence; social work education; diversity; race; ethnicity; sexual orientation; social change; empowerment

The basic idea of multiculturalism in social work education is that social work students need to learn to work effectively with people from many different cultures, and that this will have a positive impact on their social work practice and on outcomes for those with whom they work. Many sources and educators agree that the steps involved in multicultural social work education include developing self-awareness and self-knowledge with regard to culture, acquiring knowledge about the culture(s) of others in specific groups or categories, and learning how to translate this knowledge into effective practice with people of various cultures.

Multiculturalism has been an important concept within social work education since the early 1980s. After much focus on the concepts and discussion about implementation, the National Association of Social Workers developed and disseminated its Standards for Cultural Competence in Social Work Practice in 2001.

This work was taken into account by the Council on Social Work Education, the accrediting body for schools of social work, in the Educational Policy and Accreditation Standards it implemented in 2002.

Disciplines other than social work have also included multiculturalism as a focus for teaching and practice. For example, the concept is studied and taught in the fields of psychology, nursing, and education. The American Psychological Association was an early leader in this area, adopting standards for professional cultural competence in 1980.

Debates about multiculturalism have centered on its meaning and its implications. There is no consensus among social workers or social work educators as to the definition of multiculturalism. Some include a variety of groups who can be said to share at least some aspects of culture, and who also share a history of and vulnerability to oppression within mainstream society. Proponents of this approach typically focus not only on racial and ethnic identity, but on all or some of the following: national origin, religion or spirituality, sex, gender, sexual orientation, mental and physical (dis-)ability, age, and socioeconomic status or class. This may also include a focus on the intersectionality among and across identities or characteristics. Others believe that it is important and preferable to limit the interpretation exclusively to culture as shared within a specified racial or ethnic group. However, this may cluster people into groups—for example, Asian Americans— that actually encompass many cultural differences. Finally, some limit discussions of multiculturalism to *people of color*– those whose racial and ethnic heritage is not purely or primarily Caucasian. One drawback to this is that it excludes from consideration whites or European Americans, who embody many cultural differences.

Another important debate about multiculturalism is what relationship, if any, it should have to concepts and goals of social change, social justice, and even social transformation. At the two extremes, some people do not feel that these enter into the equation at all, while others think that they are central to the concept and its implementation. Those in the latter group believe that the incorporation of power and oppression is a necessary and significant aspect of a multicultural paradigm; many people then link that paradigm to an empowerment framework.

With regard to implications, concerns focus on the important questions of whether multiculturalism is essentially a perspective or a principle, or whether it can be expressed as knowledge and/or a defined skill set. In addition, various groups of people of color have taken exception to the term multiculturalism and to the impact of use of the term on attention paid to and services provided to specific ethnic and racial minorities. The concerns have been twofold: (a) that multiculturalism may be used as a proxy for assimilation and may ignore some challenging realities and differences; and (b) that it may detract from both ongoing needs and hard-won gains of specific groups (for example, African Americans), by clustering them with other ethnic or racial groups.

Dilemmas about definitions and implementation extend also to other concepts related to multiculturalism. For example, many think the term *cultural competence* is inaccurate and misleading, extending a false promise of reaching a state of mastery—that is to say interacting competently and effectively with all individuals from all cultures. Another concern about this term is that it may actually lead to the stereotyping it seeks to eradicate, if social work students (and, later, practitioners) interpret and apply their learning about other cultures very narrowly. Other terms that have been proposed and utilized—sometimes in conjunction with cultural competence, and other times as alternatives—include ethnic competence, cultural appropriateness, cultural humility, cultural relevance, cultural proficiency, and cultural sensitivity.

Further challenges have come from conservatives who contend that multiculturalism and its associated concepts and practices reflect liberal ideology, rather than professional best practices or knowledge and skills. Concern from these sectors has led to challenges as to the utility, appropriateness, and legality of curricula, teaching, and accreditation standards framed in terms of multiculturalism.

Despite these debates and challenges, multiculturalism remains a significant concept within social work education. Students can be assured that it is important to learn as much as possible about the culture of different groups, while recognizing that generalized information about group norms, beliefs, and behaviors may not apply to a specific member of that group. This approach makes it more likely that the student/practitioner will not make practice mistakes based on faulty assumptions or ignorance about the realm of possibilities.

Recent trends in multiculturalism have included both focus on a broader interpretation of the term, and increasing emphasis on intersectionality in social work theory and practice. This implies that students working with individuals, groups, or communities need to take into account simultaneous, multiple, and complex aspects of diversity. These may include race and ethnicity, sex, gender, sexual orientation, (dis-)ability status, national origin, religion, age, and socioeconomic status.

The debates about the language to use, the scope of interpretation, and the methods of teaching and practice to use with regard to multiculturalism and social work education will no doubt continue into and well beyond the foreseeable future. The directions and outcomes of these important debates will influence social work theory, practice, and policy and have implications for consumers of social work services currently and for the generations to follow.

## FURTHER READING

Atherton, C. R., & Bollard, K. A. (1997). The multiculturalism debate and social work education: A response to Dorothy Van Soest. *Journal of Social Work Education*, 33(1), 143–150.

Feld, P. (2000). Revisiting multiculturalism in social work. *Journal of Social Work Education*, 36(2), 261–278.

Fong, R., & Furuto, S. (Eds.). (2001). *Culturally competent practice: Skills, interventions, and evaluations.* Needham Heights, MA: Allyn & Bacon.

Gutiérrez, L., & Alvarez, A. R. (2000). Educating students for multicultural community practice. *Journal of Community Practice*, 7(1), 39–56.

Gutiérrez, L., Zuñiga, M. E., & Lum, D. (2004). *Education for multicultural social work practice: Critical viewpoints and future directions.* Alexandria, VA: Council of Social Work Education.

Schlesinger, E. (2004). Historical perspectives on education for ethnic sensitive and multicultural practice. In L. Gutiérrez, M. E. Zuñiga, & D. Lum, (Eds.), *Education for multicultural social work practice: Critical viewpoints and future directions* (pp. 31–52). Alexandria, VA: Council of Social Work Education.

Weaver, H. N. (2000). Culture and professional education: The experiences of Native American social workers. *Journal of Social Work Education*, 36(3), 415–428.

## SUGGESTED LINKS

Council on Social Work Education.
*www.cswe.org*
National Association of Social Workers.
*www.socialworkers.org*

—ANN ROSEGRANT ALVAREZ

# RESEARCH

**ABSTRACT:** Research education on the Bachelors and Masters levels has attempted to address concerns related to student's purported lack of interest in research courses and graduates failure to conduct research as practitioners. Research education on the doctoral level has benefitted from a significant increase in the number of faculty members with federally funded research grants, though quality of doctoral research training across programs is uneven. A continuum of specific objectives for research curricula on baccalaureate, masters and doctoral levels is needed leading to clearer specifications of research knowledge and skills that should be taught in all schools of social work.

**KEY WORDS:** empirical; research and practice; evidence-based practice

The role of research in social work education can only be understood in the context of the role of research in social work. The function and importance of empirical research in social work has been a source of contention and debate in the profession for a considerable period of time, with concerns expressed about the gap between research and practice and the degree to which science has been integrated into the social work profession (Kirk, 1999; Kirk & Reid, 2001). Issues have been raised historically about the complexity of issues affecting the relationship between research and practice, the value and usefulness of social work research to practitioners, and gaps in practitioner's ability to conduct research and or to assess research studies (Jensen, 2005; Lindsey & Kirk, 1992; Reinherz, Regan, & Anastas, 1983). As Dunlap (1993) notes, the role of the research curriculum in bachelors and masters level social work education has waxed and waned over the years in terms of expectations of graduates, perhaps paralleling, to a degree, the role of research in the social work profession. Unlike sister professions, such as psychology, the empirical basis of social work has not been a prominent fixture of the profession, and prior to the 1990s, for example, relatively few social workers engaged in empirical research studies funded through federal research grants.

The 1991 report of the Task Force on Social Work Research, funded by the National Institute of Mental Health, identified a crisis in the current development of research resources in social work. The report criticized research education on the bachelors and masters level for the lack of connection between the teaching of research methods and practice methods, and also identified as a problem the lack of opportunities for students to participate in practice-related research. Research training on the doctoral level in social work was criticized for the unevenness in training among programs and lack of opportunities for students to participate in research activities prior to their dissertation research (Task Force on Social Work Research, 1991). The growth of interest in evidence-based practice in social work has led to recent calls by some for significant changes in the research curricula on all levels of social work education (Howard & Allen-Meares, 2006; Thyer, 2001).

## Research Education on the Bachelors and Masters Levels

The Educational Policy and Accreditation Standards of the Council of Social Work Education (2001) pertaining to foundational research content states that

> "Qualitative and quantitative research content provides understanding of a scientific, analytic, and ethical approach to building knowledge for practice. The content prepares students to develop, use, and effectively communicate empirically based knowledge, including evidence-based interventions. Research knowledge is used by students to provide high quality services; to initiate change; to improve practice, policy, and service delivery; and to evaluate their own practice (p. 10)."

As with other areas of curriculum focus, it is left to individual schools to determine advanced content in the research curriculum area. In addition, individual schools are also free to determine how to integrate research content with practice courses and field settings. It is not surprising therefore, to find considerable variations in research curricula across schools (Howard & Allen-Meares, 2006; Fraser & Lewis, 1993). To the degree that research and practice integration is not widely implemented in schools of social work, problems concerning the relationship between research and practice and value of research to practitioners will continue to be major concerns.

The role of research in social work education on the bachelors and masters levels has been influenced by concerns pertaining to students' purported lack of interest in research courses, graduates' failure to conduct research as practitioners, the relationship between research courses and the rest of the curriculum, and a gap between empirically-based knowledge and the use of such knowledge in practice (Austin, 1986, 2003; Cournoyer & Powers, 2002; Kirk & Reid, 2001; Task Force on Social Work Research, 1991).

It is generally believed by faculty, with some empirical support, that bachelors and masters students in social work approach research courses with high levels of anxiety, lack of interest, and they often have difficulty seeing the relevance of research to social work practice (Epstein, 1987; Green, Bretzin, Leininger, & Stauffer, 2001). As a result, since 1980s there have been a number of strategies suggested for reducing student anxiety and increasing student interest in research courses. These suggestions have included linking research courses and assignments to field placement responsibilities, creating ties between research and practice courses, and providing students with opportunities to engage in the research process through service learning approaches involving them as active participants in community-based research projects (Grossman, 1980; Kapp, 2006; Rubin, 1981; Wells, 2006).

## Research Education on the Doctoral Level

In the decade and one-half since the publication of the report of the Task Force on Social Work Research, there have been a number of research developments, as follows, that have had a positive impact on the research training of doctoral students: 15 social work research development centers funded by NIMH and NIDA have provided opportunities for doctoral students in 14 schools of social work to have hands-on, multi-year research training opportunities; there has been a large increase in the number of individual faculty members at schools of social work who have received federal research grants, which can provide research training support for doctoral students (about 50 schools of social work had faculty with NIH grants during the 1993–2005 period); NIMH-funded quality guidelines for social work doctoral education were published by the Group for the Advancement of Doctoral Education in 1992 and revised in 2003; the Institute for the Advancement of Social Work Research has offered well-attended methodological skills training and dissertation proposal workshops for doctoral students on a regular basis at pre-conference sessions of the Society for Social Work and Research's annual meetings; large numbers of doctoral students participate at the annual meetings of the Society for Social Work and Research; there has been an increase in social work doctoral students who have received federal or national foundation funding for dissertation grants; and doctoral research curricula in many schools now incorporate more sophisticated methodological and statistical training (Austin, 1998; Group for the Advancement of Doctoral Education in Social Work, 2003; Institute for the Advancement of Social Work Research, 2005).

While the above developments are quite positive, there is tremendous variation in the quality of doctoral education in research among the large and growing numbers of doctoral programs in social work, which have increased in number from 35 doctoral programs in 1977 to 62 doctoral programs by 1999 (Lennon, 2001; Wittman, 1979).

A number of concerns raised since [the]-1980s about the quality of doctoral programs in social work, such as the need to strengthen the research productivity of graduates, the limited publication records and involvement in funded research by doctoral program faculty at some schools, and the limitations of part-time doctoral education in producing research scholars, are still valid today (Austin, 1999; Briar,

1982; Proctor & Snowden, 1991; Reisch, 2002; Rubin, 2000). In regard to this last point, data compiled by the Council on Social Work Education indicate that beginning in 1984, a significant percentage of doctoral students were part-time students. This percentage ranged from 42 to 53% of enrolled doctoral students during the 1990s. Data pertaining to students enrolled in 2000, separated for the first time by students taking coursework or in the dissertation stage, indicate that 36% of all doctoral students were taking coursework on a part-time basis, while 46% of students who had completed coursework were part-time students (Lennon, 2001). An important aspect of doctoral education in research is the opportunity for students to gain research experience under faculty mentorship through an applied research experience prior to completion of the doctoral dissertation. Such experience, however, is extremely difficult to integrate into part-time doctoral education.

## The Future of Research Education in Social Work

As noted above, a number of problems remain in the teaching of research on bachelors, masters, and doctoral levels. Since [the]1990s there have been calls for the establishment of a continuum of specific objectives for research curricula on baccalaureate, masters, and doctoral levels that will lead to clearer specifications of research knowledge and skills that should be taught in all schools of social work (Fraser & Lewis, 2003; Henley & Dunlap, 1995/1996). More recently, on the graduate level in particular, the scientist–practitioner model underlying masters level research curricula has been called into question by some as being ineffective because of the few masters graduates that go on to doctoral education or conduct research in their professional practices. Recommendations have been made that traditional masters level research courses should be replaced by courses that strengthen student competencies as evidence-based practitioners (Howard & Allen-Meares, 2006; Jensen, 2006; Shlonsky & Stern, 2006).

### REFERENCES

Austin, D. M. (1986). A history of social work education. In J. Otis, D. M. Austin, & A. Rubin (Eds.), *Social work education monograph series*. Austin: School of Social Work, University of Texas at Austin.

Austin, D. M. (1998). *A report on progress in the development of research resources in social work*. Washington, DC: IASWR.

Austin, D. M. (1999). A report on progress in the development of research resources in social work. *Research on Social Work Practice, 9*(6), 673–707.

Austin, D. M. (2003). History of research in social work. In R. A. English (Ed. In Chief), *Encyclopedia of social work*

(19th ed., 2003 Supplement, pp. 81–94). Washington, DC: NASW Press.

Briar, S. (1982). Major trends and issues affecting the future of doctoral education in social work and social welfare. In A. Rosen & J. J. Stretch (Eds.), *Doctoral education in social work: Issues, perspectives and evaluation* (pp. 251–257). St. Louis, MO: Group for the Advancement of Doctoral Education in Social Work.

Council on Social Work Education. (2001). *Educational policy and accreditation standards*. New York: Council on Social Work Education.

Cournoyer, B. R., & Powers, G. T. (2002). Evidence-based social work: The quiet revolution continues. In A. R. Roberts & G. J. Greene (Eds.), *Social workers desk reference*. New York: Oxford University Press.

Dunlap, K. M. (1993). A history of research in social work education: 1915–1991. *Journal of Social Work Education, 29*(3), 293–301.

Epstein, I. (1987). Pedagogy of the disturbed: Teaching research to the reluctant. *Journal of Teaching in Social Work, 1*(1), 71–89.

Fraser, M. W., & Lewis, R. E. (1993). Research education in M.S.W. programs: Four competing perspectives. *Journal of Social Services Research, 17*(3/4), 71–90.

Green, R. C., Bretzin, A., Leininger, C., & Stauffer, R. (2001). Research learning attributes of graduate students in social work, psychology, and business. *Journal of Social Work Education, 37*(2), 333–341.

Grossman, B. (1980). Teaching research in the field practicum. *Social Work, 36*–39.

Group for the Advancement of Doctoral Education in Social Work. (2003). *Guidelines for quality in social work doctoral programs* (Revised).

Henley, H. C. Jr., & Dunlap, K. M. (1995/1996). Policies and performance in the MSW research curriculum. *Arete, 20*(2), 16–23.

Howard, M. O., & Allen-Meares, P. (2006, October). Teaching evidence-based practice: Strategic and pedagogical recommendations for schools of social work. Paper presented at the Improving the Teaching of Evidence-Based Practice Symposium, University of Texas at Austin, Austin, Texas.

Institute for the Advancement of Social Work Research. (2005). *Directory of Social Work Research Grants awarded by the National Institutes of Health, 1993–2005*. Washington, DC: IASWR.

Jensen, J. M. (2005). Connecting science to intervention: Advances, challenges, and the promise of evidence-based practice. *Social Work Research, 29*(3), 131–135.

Jensen, J. M. (2006, October). Evidence-based practice and the reform of social work education: A response to Gambrill and Howard and Allen-Meares. Paper presented at the Improving the Teaching of Evidence-Based Practice Symposium, University of Texas at Austin, Austin, Texas.

Kapp, S. A. (2006). Bringing the agency to the classroom: Using service-learning to teach research to BSW students. *The Journal of Baccalaureate Social Work, 12*(1), 56–70.

Kirk, S. A. (1999). Good intentions are not enough: Practice guidelines for social work. *Research on Social Work Practice*, 9(3), 302–310.

Kirk, S. A., & Reid, W. J. (2001). *Science and social work: A critical appraisal*. New York: Columbia University Press.

Lennon, T. M. (2001). *Statistics on social work education in the United States: 2000*. Alexandria, VA: Council on Social Work Education.

Lindsey, D., & Kirk, S. A. (1992). The continuing crisis in social work research: Conundrum or solvable problem? An essay review. *Journal of Social Work Education*, 28(3), 370–382.

Proctor, E. K., & Snowden, L. R. (1991). Resources for doctoral education in social work. *Arete*, 16(1), 12–22.

Reinherz, H., Regan, J. M., & Anastas, J. W. (1983). A research curriculum for future clinicians: A multimodal strategy. *Journal of Education for Social Work*, 19(2), 35–41.

Reisch, M. (2002). The future of doctoral social work education in the United States: Questions, issues and persistent dilemmas. *Arete*, 26(2), 57–71.

Rubin, A. (1981). Integrating practice and research curricula: A synthesis of four regional conferences. In S. Briar, H. Weissman, & A. Rubin (Eds.), *Research utilization in social work education* (pp. 48–58). New York: Council on Social Work Education.

Rubin, A. (2000). Editorial: Social work research at the turn of the millennium: Progress and challenges. *Research on Social Work Practice*, 10(1), 9–14.

Shlonsky, A., & Stern, S. B. (2006, October). Reflections on the teaching of EBP. Paper presented at the Improving the Teaching of Evidence-Based Practice Symposium, University of Texas at Austin, Austin, Texas.

Task Force on Social Work Research. (1991). *Building social work knowledge for effective services and policies: A plan for research development*. Austin: School of Social Work, University of Texas at Austin.

Thyer, B. A. (2001). Guidelines for research training in Social Work doctoral education. *Arete*, 25 (1), 39–52.

Wells, M. (2006). Teaching notes. Making statistics "real" for social work students. *Journal of Social Work Education*, 42(2), 397–404.

Wittman, M. (1979). Feast or famine: The future of doctoral education in social work. *Journal of Education for Social Work*, 15(1), 110–115.

## FURTHER READING

Mullen, E. J., Bostwick, G. J., Jr., & Ryg, B. (1980). Toward an integration of research and practice in the social work curriculum: A description and evaluation of a one-quarter course. In R. W. Weinbach & A. Rubin (Eds.), *Teaching social work research: Alternative programs and strategies* (pp. 30–41). New York: Council on Social Work Education.

Rabin, C. (1985). Matching the research seminar to meet practice needs: A method for integrating research and practice. *Journal of Social Work Education*, 21(1), 5–12.

—DAVID E. BIEGEL

## SOCIAL WELFARE POLICY

**ABSTRACT:** The educational imperative to study social welfare policy has remained a constant throughout the history of social work education. While specific policies and social issues may change over time, the need to advocate for and create humane, justice-based social policy remains paramount. The study of welfare policy contributes to the effectiveness of practitioners who are knowledgeable and skilled in analysis, advocacy, and the crafting of justice based social welfare policies. In addition to traditional policy content areas, students should develop knowledge and skills in critical thinking, understand a range of justice theories, and recognize the direct interaction between globalization and national and local policy matters.

**KEY WORDS:** accreditation; critical thinking; educational policy and accreditation standards; globalization; justice theories; social welfare policy; social work education

### Studying Social Policy: A History

Social welfare policy is a required foundation area of study in the Council on Social Work Education's (CSWE) accredited social work programs. The study of social welfare is not a recent innovation, as its antecedents can be traced to the late 1890s and early 1900s. Mary Richmond, in her 1897 address during the National Conference of Charities and Corrections, identified the need for a "training school in applied philanthropy" (cited in Haggerty, 1931, p. 40). Within 10 years of Richmond's speech four schools of social work were organized including the New York School of Philanthropy, the Chicago School of Civics and Philanthropy, the St. Louis School of Social Economy, and the School of Social Workers of Boston (Haggerty, pp 42–44). While accreditation and other forms of curriculum regulation were non-existent, all programs did include the study of welfare history and policy matters (Haggerty, p. 45).

The need to study welfare policy was aggressively supported by Edith Abbott in 1928 when she argued "there are no more fundamental or basic subjects of study for our profession than public welfare administration, social legislation..." (cited in Kendall, 2002, p. 17). By 1944, social welfare policy was identified by the American Association of Schools of Social Work as one of the "basic eight" areas of study (Kendall, p. 151) and was included in CSWE's original accreditation standards in 1952 (Frumkin & Lloyd, 1995, p. 2239). Subsequent accreditation revisions (for example, see CSWE 1974; CSWE 1988; CSWE 1991; CSWE 1994) and the current 2002 Educational Policy and Accreditation Standards (EPAS) include social welfare policy content as part of the required foundation curriculum (CSWE, 2002, p. 10).

Inclusion of social welfare policy in education extends to social work programs around the world. Canadian social work education, for example, requires the study of Canadian welfare policy in accredited social work programs (Canadian Association of Social Work, 2004, p. 9); an "accredited social worker" in Australia must have knowledge and ability for analysis of and impact with policy development (Australian Association of Social Workers, 2004, p. 3); and in 2004, the International Association of Schools of Social Work and the International Federation of Social Workers adopted the "Global Standards for the Education and Training of the Social Work Profession," which include social policy as a core area of study (Global Standards, n.d., p. 7).

Worldwide, the promotion, development, and cultivation of effective policy in micro and macro arenas cross geographic borders and cultural divides. Social welfare policy is envisioned to be a powerful tool that can realize the aspirations of an entire society, as well as the dreams and ideals embraced by a local community, group, family, or individual.

Macro social welfare policy provides a framework and means to strengthen larger communities. As an instrument of change, social welfare policy can reduce or eliminate a particular issue that impacts at-risk and marginalized population groups such as children, families, seniors, and people of color. Conversely, social policy may exacerbate or penalize a particular population group.

Micro social welfare policy directly influences the scope of work provided by the practitioner. Program eligibility, the form of services provided, a program's delivery structure, and funding mechanisms are outcomes of micro social welfare policy. Ineffective social policy creates frustrating practice obstacles. Typical of the barriers created by policy are eligibility criteria that limit client access to services, regulations that do not allow for case advocacy, and increased caseloads supported with minimal resources and capped time limits.

## Social Welfare Policy Defined

In its most basic form, social policy incorporates five core characteristics. First, policy is the formal expression of a community's values, principles, and beliefs. Second, these values, principles, and beliefs become

reality through a program and its resulting services. Third, policy provides legitimacy and sanctions an organization to provide a particular program or service. Fourth, policy offers a roadmap for an organization to realize its mission. Fifth, policy creates the broad structural framework that guides the practitioner in his or her professional role.

Though social welfare policy is not specifically defined in the Social Work Dictionary (Barker, 2003), conceptually, it is best thought of as a subset of the larger social policy arena. Policy has been formally defined as "the explicit or implicit standing plan that an organization or government uses as a guide for action" (Barker, p. 330). Policy establishes a specific set of program procedures (Baumheier & Schorr, 1977, p. 1453), includes all public activities (Zimmermann, 1979, p. 487), and considers resource distribution and its affect on "peoples' social well-being" (Dear, 1995, p. 2227). While policy creates a plan of action, it also, as Titmuss (1966) writes, directs attention to "definite problems" (p. 68). Countering the preciseness of policy, Rohrlich (1977) finds it to be often vague and imprecise (p. 1463).

Policies, as outgrowths of values, beliefs, and principles, vary in their commitments and range of services. For example, the primary public assistance program targeting poor families, Temporary Assistance to Needy Families (TANF), is time-limited and does not include full, comprehensive services. Social Security benefits, on the other hand, provide monthly retirement income based on the worker's life-long financial contributions through payroll deductions. Essentially, TANF reflects the centuries old belief that the poor are the cause of their life situation and public assistance only reinforces their dependence on others. Retirees, on the other hand, who worked and contributed to the greater good through their payroll taxes, are able to make a just claim for retirement benefits.

Wilensky and Lebeaux, in their classic work Industrial Society and Social Welfare (1965), provide a framework that captures the differences in social policies. Their model includes two perspectives, residual and institutional.

A residual framework conceptualizes social welfare in narrow terms, typically restricted to public assistance or policies related to the poor. Residual services carry a stigma, are time-limited, means-tested, emergency based, and are generally provided when all other forms of assistance are unavailable. Welfare services come into play only when all other systems have broken down or prove to be inadequate. Public assistance programs reflect the residual descriptions and include among others TANF, Food Stamps, Supplemental Security Income, General Assistance, and Medicaid.

Institutional welfare, according to the Wilensky and Lebeaux model, is a normal function of a society that supports the interests of the broader community in a non-stigmatizing manner. Services are available to all persons and are universal and comprehensive in nature. They are designed to both prevent and address issues. Social insurance programs, veterans programs, public education, food and drug regulations, and Medicare are institutional by nature.

## Social Welfare Policy: An Educational Imperative

Throughout the first half of the 20th century, social work education struggled to organize curricula in a systematic fashion. Competing educational and professional membership associations hindered academic consensus and created division within the profession (Kendall, 2002). It was not until 1952, with the organization of the Council on Social Work Education, that curricula became unified and systemized under one educational umbrella. The inclusion of social welfare policy in curriculum has remained steadfast since CSWE's initial Curriculum Policy Statement (CPS), which was written in 1952, with subsequent CPS and EPAS revisions continuing to include policy as a core or foundation area of learning (Frumkin & Lloyd, 1995, p. 2239). The 2002 EPAS notes that baccalaureate and masters social work programs, while differing in "design, structure, and objectives," will prepare "social workers to formulate and influence social policies and social work services in diverse contexts (CSWE, 2002, p. 7). EPAS defines social welfare policy and services as follows.

> Programs provide content about the history of social work, the history and current structures of social welfare services, and the role of policy in service delivery, social work practice, and attainment of individual and social well-being. Course content provides students with knowledge and skills to understand major policies that form the foundation of social welfare; analyze organizational, local, state, national, and international issues in social welfare policy and service delivery; analyze and apply the results of policy research relevant to social service delivery; understand and demonstrate the policy practice skills in regard to economic, political, and organizational systems, and use them to influence, formulate, and advocate for policy consistent with social work values; and identify

financial organizational, administrative, and planning processes required to deliver social services follows (CSWE, 2002, p. 11).

The 2002 EPAS statement is prescriptive with its requirements of curricula areas and twelve specific foundation educational objectives, two of which— "understand and interpret the history of the social work profession and its contemporary structures and issues" and "analyze, formulate, and influence social policies" (CSWE, 2002, p. 9)—relate to social policy. EPAS provides educational programs the flexibility to determine how these outcomes are achieved by encouraging curricula that reflect the unique characteristics of the college, university, and region.

Acquiring knowledge and skills in the social welfare policy fosters the application of "analytic skills to social and economic policies with reference to social justice" (Ewalt, 1983, p. 40). While specific content, such as social welfare history, knowledge of current welfare legislation, and understanding the dynamics of the policy process, are traditional areas of study, the mastery of knowledge and skills in three spheres are essential: critical thinking, theories of justice, and globalization.

### Critical Thinking and Social Welfare Policy

Successful policy work requires critical thinking, which Ennis defines as "reasonable and reflective thinking focused on deciding what to believe or do" (Fisher, 2001, p. 7). The development of critical thinkers, as Bok (2006) writes, is one of the central purposes of the college experience (p. 67).

Critical thinking requires the ability to analyze and organize facts, develop opinions based on the facts, argue the position, and evaluate alternatives, all of which lead to the solution of specific problems. A rational and structured thinking process is important in organizing and distilling facts from myth, and allows clear, objective solutions to emerge. Even so, critical thinking must also allow for creative thinking, which is a dynamic, vibrant, and intuitive process. Creative thinking enables a free flow of ideas while recognizing that some biases are impossible to disregard or subordinate in policy work.

The World Wide Web revolutionized critical thinking by opening the doors to a variety of data, information, and analyses of issues. The advantages, while many, can be overshadowed by the enticement of readily available information, and if left unattended will result in faulty policy work. First and foremost, the reliability and validity of Web sources must always be questioned—just because information is posted on a

Web page does not mean it is legitimate. A second issue deals with information overload. The ease of information accessibility can be overwhelming. For example, performing a Web search using the phrase "social welfare policies in Texas" resulted in 1.12 million sites collected in .25 seconds (www.google.com). Critical thinking requires disciplined analysis of the Web, the ability to discern good information from bad, and ensuring that creativity is applied while seeking accurate and useful information.

### Justice and Social Welfare Policy

Social welfare policy is rooted in the principles and theories of justice. Effective policy practice requires identification, understanding, and assessment of the various justice theories that interact with and influence the development of a policy position. Justice theories are varied and reflect different perspectives on the human condition. For example, Rawls (1971) believes that birth, status, and family are matters of chance, which should not influence or bias the benefits one accrues, and true justice allows a society to rectify its inequities with the end result yielding fairness to all its members. Conversely, Nozick (1974) argues a free-market libertarian model that advocates for individuals to be able to keep what they earn. For Nozick (1974) "the less government approach" is the best model and he asks, "If the state did not exist would it be necessary to invent it? Would one be needed, and would it have to be invented?" (p. 3). Other justice theorists include Dworkin (2001) who presents resource-based principles, Miller (1976) who represents the just desert-based principle, and works by Pateman (1988) and Tong (1993) who set forth feminist principles that examine the difference that gender makes in the execution of justice and policy.

Policy incorporates a justice theory through one of four models, (Maiese, 2003b): distributive, procedural, retributive, and restorative. *Distributive* justice refers to a fair share model that expresses its concern for the welfare of a community's members; ideas of equity, equality, and need are central in distributive discussions (Maiese, 2003a). *Procedural* justice considers processes in which decisions are made and recognizes that people feel vindicated if the proceedings result in fair treatment no matter the outcome (Deutsch, 2000, p. 45). *Retributive* justice, commonly referred to as the "just dessert" approach, suggests that people should be treated in a similar manner as they treat others with the response proportional to the originating act (Maiese, 2004). The focus of *restorative* justice is multifaceted, with a focus on the victim, the offender, and the community, though the emphasis rests with the victim (Maiese, 2003c).

Justice theories offer various perspectives of how people or social issues are viewed. Reflecting an individual, group, or organization's values and beliefs, justice theories create a rationale to support particular policy initiatives. Recognizing and understanding the various, often competing justice theories, is central in policy practice. In creating a successful policy change strategy, such understanding requires the social work profession, as Morris (1986) writes "to take into account not only its own beliefs and values, but those held by a large number of other nonadvocate citizens" (p. 678).

### Changing Global Environment

The convergence of key unrelated, global social, political, economic, and technological events that began in the 1980s and continue into the new millennium require a global perspective in policy matters. *New York Times* writer Thomas L. Friedman (2005) contends a new "flattened" world order emerged at the outset of the 21st century and reshaped the lives and relationships between people in all economic and social spheres. In less than a decade, global experiences have dramatically changed to a more open world with fewer borders to separate or stifle collaborations and interactions.

Concurrent with the world's "flattening" has been global growth and change. Depending on the information source, there are 191,192, or 193 nations with the world's population fast approaching 6.6 billion people (www.cia.gov, n.d.). This growth will be trumped in the future as the world population is estimated to double in size by the year 2060 (http://www.audubon.org, n.d.).

New nations will continue to be added as existing countries divide and create new states. Between 1900 and 1950, approximately 1.2 countries were created each year; from 1950–1990, 2.2 nations were born each year; and in the 1990s, the number of new nations created jumped to 3.1 annually (Enriquez, 2005). The physical and political makeup of the world that existed in 2000 was very different from the world's composition in 2007. One must assume that global geo-, socio-, and political changes will continue in the future. Understanding and recognizing the consequences of the shifting dynamics in the global community will be critical in the development of effective social policies.

### Summary Comments

The educational imperative to study social welfare policy has remained a constant throughout the history of social work education. There is no indication or reason to believe that its emphasis will diminish in the future, nor should it. Social welfare policy offers a mechanism to realize opportunities that promote equality, improve the individual's social position, and address institutional and societal prejudices. While specific policies and social issues may change over time, the need to advocate for and write humane, justice-based social policy remains paramount. Sound policy analysis, supported by critical thinking, building on justice theories, and reflecting the changing global and local communities, creates the capacity and opportunity for the social work profession to influence the scope and design of social welfare policy.

## REFERENCES

Australian Association of Social Workers. (2004). *Continuing professional educational policy.* Retrieved December 2, 2006 from http://www.aasw.asn.au/adobe/profdev/CPE_policy_2006.pdf.

Barker, R. L. (2003). *The social work dictionary* (5th ed.). Washington, DC: NASW Press.

Baumheier, E. C., & Schorr, A. L. (1977). Social policy. In J. Turner, (Ed.), *Encyclopedia of social work* (17th ed., pp. 1453–1463). Washington, DC: NASW Press.

Bok, D. (2006) *Our underachieving colleges, a candid look at how much students learn and why they should be learning more.* Princeton, NJ: Princeton University Press.

Canadian Association of Schools of Social Work. (2004). *CASSW standards for accreditation.* Ottawa, Ontario: Author.

Council on Social Work Education. (2002). *Educational policy and accreditation standards.* Alexandria, VA: Author.

Council on Social Work Education. (1988). *Handbook of accreditation standards and procedures.* Alexandria, VA: Author.

Council on Social Work Education. (1991). *Handbook of accreditation standards and procedures.* Alexandria, VA: Author.

Council on Social Work Education. (1994). *Handbook of accreditation standards and procedures.* Alexandria, VA: Author.

Council on Social Work Education. (1971). *Manual of accrediting standards for graduate professional schools of social work.* New York: Author.

Dear, R. B. (1995). Social welfare policy. In R. L. Edwards & J. G. Hobbs. *Encyclopedia of Social Work* (19th ed., vol. 3, pp. 2226–2237). Washington, DC: NASW Press.

Deutsch, M. (2000). Justice and conflict. In M. Deutsch & P. T. Coleman (Eds.), *The Handbook of conflict resolution: theory and practice.* San Francisco: Jossey-Bass Inc. Publishers.

Dworkin, R. (2001). *Sovereign virtue.* Cambridge, MA: Harvard University Press.

Enriquez, J. (2005). *The United States of America: Polarization, fracturing, and our future.* New York: Crown.

Ewalt, P. (1983). *Curriculum design and development for graduate social work education.* New York: Council on Social Work Education.

Fisher, A. (2001). *Critical thinking: an introduction.* New York: Cambridge University Press

Friedman, T. L. (2005). *The world is flat: a brief history of the twenty-first century.* New York: Farrar, Straus ands Giroux.

Frumkin, M., & Lloyd, G. (1995). Social work education. In R. L. Edwards & J. G. Hobbs (Eds.), *Encyclopedia of Social Work* (*19th ed*). (pp. 2238–2247). Washington, DC: NASW Press.

Global Standards for the education and training for the social work profession. Retrieved December 1, 2006. from http://www.iassw-aiets.org

Haggerty, J. (1931). *The training of social workers.* New York: McGraw-Hill Book Company.

Kendall, K. (2002). *Council on social work education, its antecedents and first twenty years.* Alexandria, VA: Council on Social Work Education.

Maiese, M. (2003a). *Distributive justice.* Retrieved January 20, 2007 from http://www.beyondintractability.org/essay/distributive_justice/

Maiese, M. (July 2003b). *Types of Justice.* Retrieved January 20, 2006 from http://www.beyondintractability.org/essay/types_of_justice/

Maiese, M. (October 2003c). *Restorative justice.* Retrieved January 20, 2007 from http://www.beyondintractability.org/essay/restorative_justice/

Maiese, M. (May 2004). *Retributive Justice.* Retrieved January 20, 2007 from http://www.beyondintractability.org/essay/distributive_justice/.

Miller, J. (1976). *Social justice.* Oxford: Clarendon Press.

Morris, R. (1986). Social welfare policy: trends and issues. In A. Minahan (Ed.), *Encyclopedia of Social Work* (18th ed., vol. 2, pp. 664–681). Silver Spring, MD: National Association of Social Workers.

Nozick, R. (1974). *Anarchy, state, and utopia.* NY: Basic Books.

Pateman, C. (1988). *The sexual contract.* Stanford, CA: Stanford University Press.

Rawls, J. (1971). *Theory of justice.* Harvard, MA: Harvard University Press.

Rohrlich, G. (1977). Social policy and income distribution. In J. Turner (Ed.), *Encyclopedia of Social Work* (17th ed., vol. 2). Washington, DC: NASW Press.

Titmuss, R. (1966). The relationship between schools of social work, social research, and social policy. *Journal of Education for Social Work. Spring.* (1), 68–75.

Tong, R. (1993). *Feminine and feminist ethics.* Belmont, CA: Wadsworth Publishing Company.

Wilensky, H., & Lebeaux, C. (1965). *Industrial society and social welfare.* New York: Free Press.

Zimmerman, S. L. (1979). Policy, social policy, and family policy. *Journal of Marriage and the Family. 41,* 467–495.

## SUGGESTED LINKS

*http://www.audubon.org/campaign/population_habitat/why html/www.cia.gov/cia/publications/factbook/print/xx.html*

—IRA C. COLBY

**SOCIAL WORK PRACTICE.** [*This entry contains two subentries:* History and Evolution; Theoretical Base.]

## HISTORY AND EVOLUTION

ABSTRACT: Social work is a profession that began its life as a call to help the poor, the destitute and the disenfranchised of a rapidly changing social order. It continues today still pursuing that quest, perhaps with some occasional deviations of direction from the original spirit.

Social work practice is the primary means of achieving the profession's ends. It is impossible to overstate the centrality or the importance of social work practice to the profession of social work. Much of what is important about the history of the profession is the history of social work practice.

Social work is a profession that began its life as a call to help the poor, the destitute and the disenfranchised of a rapidly changing social order. It continues today still pursuing that quest, perhaps with some occasional deviations of direction from the original spirit.

Social work practice is the primary means of achieving the profession's ends. It is impossible to overstate the centrality or the importance of social work practice to the profession of social work. Much of what is important about the history of the profession is the history of social work practice.

We must consider both social work practice per se (the knowledge base, practice theories and techniques) and the context for social work practice. The context of practice includes the agency setting, the policy framework and the large social system in which practice takes place.

Social work practice is created within a political, social, cultural and economic matrix that shapes the assumptions of practice, the problems that practice must deal with and the preferred outcomes of practice. Over time, the base forces that create practice and create the context for practice, change. Midgley (1981) correctly notes that practice created in one social order is often inappropriate for work in another social order. Since the social order changes over time, practice created at one point in time may no longer be appropriate in the future.

KEY WORDS: social work history; social work practice; social work profession social work organizations

### The Profession Develops

Social work, in the United States, is largely a product of the same industrial revolution that created the welfare state and industrial society. As Garvin and Cox (2001) note, industrialization led to the factory system, with its need for large numbers of concentrated workers, and subsequently created mass immigration, urbanization, and a host of consequent problems. Social work was a response to many urban problems such as mass poverty, disease, illiteracy, starvation, and mental health challenges.

Both the Charities Organization Society and the Settlement House Movement were responses to these problems. Both movements were imported from Great Britain and supplemented the efforts of religious groups and other associations, as well local and state governments in dealing with the problems of urbanization and industrialization. The Charities Organization Society and the Settlement Houses were important forces in shaping the development of American social work practice and the professionalization of social work.

The Charities Organization Society (COS) represented the cause of scientific charity, which sought to introduce more rational methods to charity and philanthropy (Trattner, 2004). The direct services component consisted of paid investigators, who worked for the COS, and "Friendly Visitors," who were volunteers that visited the clients. There were also Councils of Social Agencies, which coordinated the efforts of social services agencies. It can be argued that the paid investigators were probably the precursors of caseworkers while the Councils of Social Agencies gave rise to social planning in community practice. The United Way Movement, which credits its founding to the Denver COS, was another product of this group. Richmond's (1917) very important contribution was *Social Diagnosis*, which presented her observations on the nature of social casework. Perhaps the final contribution made to social work practice by the COS was the mark it made on social work education through its role in creation of the New York School of Philanthropy. As Austin (1986) notes, the scholar practitioner model, where faculty come from a social work practice (as opposed to a traditional academic model), is our prevailing mode of preparing social workers today.

The Settlement House Movement aimed at the inner-city and created houses as community centers in urban area. This was a completely different approach from that used by the COS. The settlement house workers used social group work to help socialize new immigrants to the city. They offered adult education for their urban neighbors and provided help and advice. They worked on community problems together with the other residents of poor urban neighborhoods. The Settlement House Movement is often most thought of for its social action efforts (Trattner, 2004). Working in conjunction with organized labor and other community activists, the settlement house workers were instrumental in the creation of the juvenile court, mother's pensions, child labor laws, and workplace protections. This is often seen as the touchstone of social work's involvement in social action and policy practice. Jane Addams was well known in this regard. Because many of the Settlement house workers were social scientists who worked in conjunction with university-based academic social scientists, they began important research into urban problems.

Between these two movements lies the foundation of much of the practice we see today, accounting for casework, social group work, community development, social planning, and social action. The beginning of research supporting social policy is also here.

The development of fields of practice began to occur with the development of psychiatric social work and medical social work (Dolgoff & Feldstein, 1980; Lubove, 1969). These new specialties allowed the creation of practice methodology refined for certain populations.

All of this occurred during the process of professionalization described by Lubove (1969). This included the creation of professional organizations, a code of ethics, professional agencies, and the creation of professional schools and a knowledge base.

In 1915 Abraham Flexner questioned whether social work was actually a profession because of what he saw as the lack of a scientific knowledge base. This created an underlying theme in the profession that has occasionally led to unfortunate results (Austin, 1983; Eherenreich, 1985). Social workers, in response to this criticism, worked to find a knowledge base that would satisfy Flexner's critique. This quest continues to this day.

As the profession developed and changed, so did society. As America became more conservative, social action activities decreased. This was especially true during the first three decades of the 20th century. Eherenreich (1985) observes that the rediscovery of poverty and the changing national mood toward social programs created a crisis for the profession. It did not, on balance, lead to much in the way of changes in social work practice.

Freud and psychoanalysis became very influential in social work from the early part of the 20th century until the sixties. This period, often called the Psychoanalytical Deluge, saw social workers eagerly adopting psychoanalysis as a means to solve several of the profession's needs. While social work created its own variants that brought more social factors into the mix (ego psychology and psychosocial treatment), psychodynamic treatment became fashionable. Psychoanalysis

was popular with psychiatrists, which facilitated the creation of strong bonds with the medical profession and the emerging mental health movement (see Eherenreich, 1985). Although, it is not completely clear whether the profession as a whole endorsed Freud or just its leadership (see Alexander, 1972). The impact of psychoanalysis cannot be discounted. The individually centered nature of psychodynamic theory also served to push the profession further from social action. Although one can debate whether psychoanalysis was the cause or consequence of a disengagement from social action and the poor, it is clear that this extraordinarily individualistic practice method closed off many avenues of engagement. Casework was the dominant practice method, a trend that can be seen throughout the history of the professional, and this was, perhaps, its most individualistic form.

The Milford Conference (1923–1929) came to an agreement on the importance of casework to the profession (Eherenreich, 1985). The Lane Report in 1939 argued that community organizers deserved equal status to caseworkers and social groupworkers (Dolgoff & Feldstein, 1980).

There were dissenting voices in direct practice however. A group of social workers formed the Functionalist School, providing a challenge to psychoanalysis. Functionalist theory, based on the work of Otto Rank, advocated an agency-based view of practice, which was different from the psychodynamically based diagnostic school. The Functional-Diagnostic Debate continued, with the more psychodynamically based diagnostic school maintaining the upper hand.

There were also social workers who bucked both the more conservative national mood and the conservative orientation of the social work profession and engaged in social action. Perhaps the best known were Bertha Capen Reynolds and Mary Van Kleek who led a group called the Rank and File Movement during the Depression years. They advocated more progressive politics and a movement away from casework (Eherenreich, 1985). The response of the profession was less than positive and the conservative mood that characterized social work reflected a conservative political mood.

Until the end of the 1950s, social work was a far more unified profession. Disagreements had been worked out and the profession presented a singular face to the world. That was about to change as the nation and the profession encountered the 1960s.

## The Profession Changes in the Sixties
The sixties changed the social policy, and the forces changing the context of practice changed the nature of

professional social work practice and ultimately the profession. The politically and culturally conservative fifties gave way to a new national mood and a series of social movements that changed the political agenda for a nation. Poverty was part of the national debate in a way that it had not been since the Depression. This time, the results were different for social work and social work practice.

There were major changes in social work practice during the 1960s. Those changes continued at least for the next four decades and will likely continue into the future. The most momentous change was the erosion of the psychodynamic influence in social casework. There are many possible explanations for this situation, but it is important to note this as a major change in the profession's view of practices. This does not mean that social workers no longer do psychodynamic practice, nor does it mean that social work schools no longer teach psychodynamic practice theory. The hold that Freudian and neo-Freudian approach had on social casework was, however, broken.

In the macro area, politically oriented community action reemerged. Certainly the War on Poverty and the Ford Foundation's Gray Areas project helped this to occur. Involvement in social planning was facilitated by the Model Cities Program and the regional planning agencies such as the Appalachian Regional Commission. Rothman's (1969) influential approach to community organization theory helped define and organize the field. This was less than 10 years before the Lurie, writing in the Boehm Report, had questioned the lack of integration in the field.

It is fair to say that the 1960s began a pattern of fundamental change in the profession and within social work practice. This change continues even today.

### The Changing Face of Social Work Practice
In the three decades that followed the 1960s there were a great many changes in the way that social work practice was described, conducted, and taught. This reflected an adaptation to changes in the context of practice, as well as the efforts of social workers to move beyond the older agreement.

Micro practice has taken advantage of models and approaches from the social sciences and from other helping groups. While some practitioners still use psychodynamic approaches, social workers also use behavioral and phenomenological approaches. Theories such as task-centered treatment, cognitive behavioral approaches, reality therapy, and so forth provide options for the social work micro practitioner. New approaches that look at social networks and other sets of relationships are also used. Turner (1996) and Payne

(2005) describe a vast variety of clinical approaches that move beyond the single theory approach of the profession prior to 1960.

Macro practice has matured since the 1960s and will continue to develop as time goes forth. Community practice has developed new approaches that encompass a wide variety of strategies and techniques. Political organizing, locality development, and social planning have matured and developed. Administration once had an unclear place in social work practice, but is now clearly established as a method of social work practice. This began with a series of reports and projects in the 1970s and evolved into eventual recognition of the approach. Recognition of policy practice as a practice field is also established in most of the profession. This brings in policy analysis and policy change (advocacy, lobbying, and so forth) together in a single social work role. These are developments that would have been unthinkable in the past.

Going beyond the macro–micro divisions, the growth of generalist practice theory is noteworthy. Generalist social work means using an essentially constant set of approaches at multiple levels. Generalist practice has developed a robust set of theories and approaches to inform this perspective.

Ecological systems theory and the Life Model, the Strengths Perspective and Empowerment practice, as well as Feminist Social Work Practice Theory, provide explanations at multiple levels that can encompass several types of techniques. These are, in many ways, recognition of the limitations of earlier approaches.

Evidence-based practice (O'Hare, 2005) is a likely paradigm shift in social work, judging from the impact of evidence-based approaches on medicine, public health, and nursing. The use of research findings to guide practice is an attractive theory and one that promises further improvement in the quality of practice.

Also important are the developments inx technology-based practice, including e-therapy, telemedicine, electronic advocacy, and other techniques that use high technology. These are likely to grow in importance as the technology evolves and experience and research push the development of practice toward further refinement.

### What Is Next?
We are now in midst of a new transition, one that began in the 1970s and continues today. This transition will create an information economy that will be as different from our industrial economy as it was from the agricultural society that preceded it. It is already changing the nature of society in many profound ways and changing the environment of practice. Friedman (2005)

identifies major changes in the political economy of the near future, including global competition, outsourcing, more technology, and so forth. This will have major impacts on policies, agencies, and clients. The profession will have to adapt, much in the way that social workers in the 1800s adapted.

## The History of Social Work Practice Considered

There are a number of lessons that can be gleaned from this discussion of social work practice. It is undeniable that direct services/casework is the primary practice orientation in social work. The orientation of social work practice often conflicts with its concerns for social justice and systems change. When Specht and Courtney (1994) called social workers "Unfaithful Angels," there was significant evidence to back up that charge. Social work has evolved into a conservative profession that has a hard time resolving the conflict between its social justice values and its choice of primary practice methodologies. It often seems that whatever the problem is, casework or psychotherapy is often our primary answer. That does not mean that it is the correct answer.

Social work practice will face a number of challenges in the future. The change in political economy, coupled with other changes in culture and social organization, will create the need for new practice methods and make others less viable. Social workers must resist the temptation to hold on to the past when the future is at our door.

### REFERENCES

Alexander, L. B. (1972). Social work's Freudian deluge: Myth or reality? *Social Service Review, 46,* 517–538.

Austin, D. M. (1983). The Flexner Myth and the History of Social Work. *Social Service Review, 57,* 357–377.

Austin, D. M. (1986). *A History of social work education* (Monograph No. 1). Austin: University of Texas School of Social Work.

Dolgoff, R., & Feldstein, D. (1980). *Understanding social welfare.* New York: Harper & Row.

Eherenreich, P. (1985). *Altruistic imagination: A history of social work and social policy in the United States.* Ithaca, NY: Cornell.

Flexner, A. (1915). Is social work a profession? In *National Conference of Charities and Corrections, Proceedings of the National Conference of Charities and Corrections at the 42nd Annual Session, Baltimore, Maryland, May 12–19.* Chicago: Hildmann, pp. 581, 584–588, 590.

Friedman, T. L. (2005). *The world is flat: A brief history of the twenty-first century.* New York: Farrar, Straus and Giroux.

Garvin, C., & Cox, F. (2001). A history of community organization since the Civil War with special reference to oppressed communities. In J. Rothman, J. Erlich, & J. Tropman (Eds.), *Strategies of community intervention* (pp. 65–100). Itasca, MN: Peacock.

Lubove, R. (1969). *Professional altruist: The emergence of social work as a career 1880–1930.* New York: Macmillian.

Midgley, J. (1981). *Professional imperialism: Social work in the third world.* London: Heinemann.

O'Hare, T. (2005). *Evidence-based practices for social workers: An interdisciplinary approach.* Chicago: Lyceum Books.

Payne, M. (2005). *Modern social work theory* (3rd ed.). Chicago: Lyceum Books.

Richmond, M. (1917). *Social diagnosis.* New York: Russell Sage Foundation.

Rothman, J. (1969). Three models of community organization practice. In *Social work practice 1968* (pp. 16–47). New York: Columbia University Press.

Specht, H., & Courtney, M. (1994). *Unfaithful angels: How social work has abandoned its mission.* New York: Free Press.

Trattner, W. J. (2004). *From poor law to welfare state: A history of social welfare in America* (6th ed.). New York: The Free Press.

Turner, F. J. (Ed.). (1996). *Social work treatment: Interlocking theoretical approaches* (4th ed.). New York: The Free Press.

—JOHN MCNUTT

## THEORETICAL BASE

**ABSTRACT:** This essay broadly examines theory, practice, and the role of theory in practice. Theory has an abstract and philosophical side and a concrete, empirical, or practice side. Theories need practitioners to activate their power, which is to name the attributes, qualities, limits, and potentials of client and social work realities. No theory is so powerful it knows or explains everything, thus practitioners must use their in vivo perceptual skills to fit the best theory to the level of practice reality that confronts them. This essay broadly examines the role of theory in social work practice. To do so, one must answer three related questions: what is theory?, what is practice?, and, what is the role of theory in practice? In answering the first question, it is useful to examine the etymology of the word theory, identify its various meanings, and specify which meanings are relevant to a discussion of the role of theory in practice, and second, it is useful to understand the philosophical assumptions that inevitably influence the process of theory building and application.

**KEY WORDS:** theory practice; reflective practitioner; philosophy of social science

### Theory

As a noun, the word theory can be traced to the last part of the sixteenth century. At that time, theory referenced two related ideas: (a) the idea of a mental scheme or conception and (b) the idea of contemplation, speculation, a looking at, or things looked at ("theory," Online Etymology Dictionary. Douglas Harper, Historian. 02 Mar. 2007. Dictionary.com http://dictionary.reference.com/browse/theory). And from about 1638, theory became specifically associated with scientific explanations based on observation and reasoning. The 20th-century "evidenced-based practice" conceptualization of theory is very similar to the 1638 definition, yet for the purpose of this essay, theory is best understood when discussing it in the context of its scientific meanings and its broader meanings of "looking at" and "contemplation." For example, numerous scholars and practitioners have argued that intuitive, practical, or situated knowledge (that is, knowledge gained from practice) is a form of knowledge that does not conform to standard scientific rules but is, nevertheless, a type of theory that guides how social workers look at, reflect upon, or view clients, social problems, or institutions (Zeira & Rosen, 2000). If practical intuition were excluded from an overall definition of theory, and only the scientific meanings included (that is, rules of observation, testing, sampling, and deductive reasoning), then all nonscientific derived theories would be regarded as atheoretical and shelved as not relevant to any discussion on theory. Thus, although different rules (for example, scientific vs pragmatism) for what constitutes a valid theory are applied to the actual work of creating a theory, across all definitions and in its broadest sense, theory is the product of the mind and its work in social work is to create abstract or symbolic representations of social and client realities. It is the latter general meaning of theory that is applied in this essay.

Second, theories are the products of interconnected philosophical inquiries that question the nature of (a) what constitutes a social work knowledge claim (that is, epistemology) and (b) what constitutes the nature of social work reality (that is, ontology). These two philosophical questions have been at the center of social science debates for nearly two centuries, and since the 1960s, at the center of the qualitative/quantitative research and evidenced-based/interpretive practice debates (Gambrill, 2003; Gilgun, 2006). A detailed rendering of these controversies (Sayer, 2000) is outside the focus of this essay, but nevertheless, it is relevant for a discussion of theory to point out that absolute closure on which epistemological and ontological assumptions are true and which are false is not yet possible. No single philosophical viewpoint and corresponding theory can account for all that is uncertain about the meaning of life and history; nor for that matter, be used to predict how the future will unfold. Thus, in this essay, the place of theory in social work is conceptualized as standing somewhere between the practitioner's philosophical assumptions and their social work action; theory is an intermediate concept situated with one foot in philosophy (that is, the most abstract moment) and one foot in practice (that is, the most concrete and empirical moment). In other words, theory lies in a restless tension between the universal and the particular; indeed, critics of a particular theory will often attack it for being too general or too specific.

Because client and community "facts" do not speak for themselves, theory, by definition, names the attributes, powers, and characteristics of reality (for example, client or community) that are not readily transparent; if theory did not do this work, then practitioners would have to find some other means to see things about their clients or communities that are not readily apparent. Social workers take action in real time and space and it is in the immediacy of taking action that practitioners inevitably see how theory works. For practitioners, theory makes it possible to see and understand the universal and the particular of a client's sense of self or being (that is, knowing, feeling, seeing, and acting self) or a community's sociocultural structure (that is, economic, political, and cultural). Without theory, a practitioner would either become endlessly immobilized by philosophical discussions about life and society, or they would be inclined to assume (that is, take for granted) that facts speak for themselves without any intermediate work on the part of the practitioner to use theory to understand clients and communities.

Practitioners are social beings and they *learn* theories through life experience, including educational pursuits and professional training programs. In other words, practitioners do not have intrinsic perceptual capacities that can be used to automatically recognize and make sense of clients and their social environments; instead, they require theory to do this work. Theory, on the other hand, does not have a mind, a brain, and a nervous and skeletal system with which it could perceive and take action (that is, these features define what is uniquely called human agency). Social work practitioners and theory are, therefore, in a mutually dependent and interactive relationship.

Indeed, a trained practitioner would not be necessary if, in fact, theory saw everything and could do everything. In short, theories provide the practitioner with the flexibility to see clients, social problems, organizations, or institutions with multiple points of view, allowing the practitioner to take into account the immediacy of the present reality and then weigh its specifics against what we know about the general. It follows, then, that theories can be wrong, or practitioners can make mistakes in applying theory. Thus, there is no standpoint where theory might rest and be assured of getting social reality "exactly" right. Practitioners, thus, must cope with the restless position of theory and learn how to respect its limitations and appreciate its potential.

### Practice

Up to this point, theory has been examined in this essay. The next question is what is practice? As a verb, practice has origins in the late 16th and early 17th centuries. Practice was defined as action: to do, to act, to perform in a habitual manner. Indeed, "practicing," in 1625, became associated with the professions about the same time that theory became associated with science (Practice, Online Etymology Dictionary. Retrieved March 14, 2007, from Dictionary.com website: http://dictionary.reference.com/browse/practice).    A key point about the verb "to practice" is that a social worker has to put into action the skill of comparing and contrasting the facts (or empirical data) of a social work reality with a theory of that same reality; theory, in and of itself, does nothing, it is an inert force that requires a human agent to activate. In short, a professional social worker is a worker that applies theory to reality and takes (inter)action on that reality.

Practitioners, acting within the limits and potential of their own personal agency and history, apply their perceptual/action capabilities to client and community realties. Social workers have the perceptual and linguistic powers to ask, to observe, to listen, and to read symbolic systems, including all forms of language and life: oral, written, and images. The perceptual skill that a practitioner would use at any given instance depends largely on their targeted level of practice: micro, mezzo, or macro. Someone who studies the history of social welfare policy may depend heavily on reading legislative and organizational documents and use these data to derive a theory of social welfare. Another may read the hundreds of memos and manuals associated with a particular welfare office and with these data, theorize how welfare policies are organizationally implemented. Still, other practitioners are engaged in front line work; they listen, ask, and observe the clients who seek welfare support and determine (that is, take action) the type of assistance to be given. Thus, social work is *the act of using perceptual capacities* to gather, through our senses (for example, seeing, hearing, thinking, touching, and feeling), the relevant practice data.

At the micro level, practitioners see, feel, hear, and think about a specific client's reaction, for example, to the death of a loved one. At the mezzo level, administrative decisions to terminate a mental health service requires practitioners to think and feel about how a community might be affected. And, at the macro level, policy makers collect and analyze data to demonstrate that a national government is spending less on mental health services and relying more on business sector solutions to mental health funding. At each level of practice, practitioners study the empirical world that is served up to them, and then, hopefully, they use theory to guide action upon that world. In the micro example mentioned earlier, social workers would use various theories of grief and mourning to assist the client in naming their experience and in living through that experience; in the mezzo example, theories of how government organizations secure public monies might be used to help a community mental agency reorganize and advocate for services; and in the macro illustration, theories of the welfare state would be deployed to assist various groups to advocate for government sponsored social and mental health services. Practice, in sum, is our human capacity to perceive the environment and with these perceptions take action upon the world. And, of course, it is the perception/action interaction that allows for change and history. Thus, practitioners are both the byproducts of their environment, but also makers of their practice environment.

### The Role of Theory in Practice

With theory and practice defined, the role of theory in practice, the third question, is now ready for examination. As mentioned earlier, theory holds a restless position between the abstract (that is, philosophical assumptions) and the concrete (that is, practice reality). Yet, there is another reason why theory holds such a restless position. Since practitioners, researchers, and scholars make up theories that are used to view reality, theories are never totally independent of the theorist. In other words, the practitioner is part of the world that their theory attempts to understand. This fact can make the work of theory-building and practice a very nervous and restless activity because it may appear that one cannot separate their theoretical constructions of reality from the actual reality that theory is attempting to represent; the latter assumption is a social constructivist view, a philosophical position that asserts that social workers construct reality (Greene & Lee, 2002). Restless because social work realities could have infinite theories to represent them, and nervous because, as a practitioner, no theory reveals truth; indeed, the social constructionist position is that all theories are more or less correct.

Fortunately, the social constructivist conundrum is only related to the philosophical side of theory, that side of theory that assumes what something "is" (that is, ontology) and what criteria establish a knowledge claim (that is, epistemology). The practice side to theory, on the other hand, brings an immediate reality to the worker; for example, a client who has just experienced the death of a loved one, an administrator reducing services, and a government that has reduced taxes and social service spending. In each of these hypothetical illustrations, no amount of social work theory will make the "actual" realities disappear, or become something the worker wishes or theorizes them to be. In other words, there may be *competing theories* about grief and grieving clients, the decline of social service spending, and the role of government, but those *competing theories* reference *a reality* that a particular practitioner, in a specific time and space, has had to come face-to-face with. In short, theories compete to "represent" reality not to "create" reality. Practice realities present themselves to practitioners and theory is deployed to understand those realities (Floersch, 2004).

Consequently, the immediacy of reality, its here and now component, bumps up against the practitioner's theory of it and sets up the context for the "role of theory in practice." The practitioner is constantly testing theory against a specific reality, searching for the best, or good enough fit. Good enough or best, because no theory can see everything about a given social reality. The lack of an all-knowing theory means that practitioners must stay "actively" and "reflectively" engaged with clients or communities in applying theory to any given practice reality (Schön, 1983). To be complacent, and assume that theory does all the work without one's in vivo, reflective input, is to assume that some omniscient social scientist, or guru, has "the" theory and the role of the practitioner is to simply apply "the" theory, regardless of the context.

### REFERENCES

Floersch J. (2004). A method for investigating practitioner use of theory in practice. *Qualitative Social Work, 3*(2), 161–177.

Gambrill, E. (2003). *Evidence based practice: Implications for knowledge development and use in social work.* In A. Rosen & E. K. Proctor (Eds.), *Developing practice guidelines for social work interventions: Issues, methods and research agenda* (pp. 37–58). New York: Columbia University Press.

Gilgun, J. (2006). The four cornerstones of qualitative research. *Qualitative Health Research, 16*(3), 436–443.

Greene, G., & Lee, M. (2002). Using social constructivism in social work practice, In A. R. Roberts & G. J. Greene (Eds.),

*Social workers' desk reference* (pp. 143–149). New York: Oxford University Press.

Sayer, A. (2000). *Realism and social science.* Thousand Oaks, CA: Sage.

Schön, D. (1983). *The reflective practitioner: How professionals think action.* New York: Basic Books.

Zeira, A., & Rosen, A. (2000). Unraveling 'tacit knowledge': What social workers do and why they do it. *Social Service Review, 74*(1), 103–123.

—JERRY FLOERSCH

## SOCIAL WORK PROFESSION. [*This entry contains three subentries:* Overview; History; Workforce.]

### OVERVIEW

**ABSTRACT:** As social work enters the twenty-first century, we look back at the changing landscape that gave shape and form to this contextual profession in the twentieth century. Together with the unprecedented global strife of two World Wars, several conflicts, and current instability of the changing world, this era has witnessed extremes of economic depression and expansion; waves of immigration and in-migration; unprecedented recognition of human and civil rights; intervention in old human problems and awareness of new ones and recognition of the need for ongoing knowledge and skill advancement; and rapidly changing technological advances that have added new meaning and urgency to the meaning of "global." Thus, the social work profession has been transformed by internal and external conditions that have both challenged and embraced its role among professionals. As the social work profession ended its first professional century, there is renewed hope for growth in a more positive, socioeconomic-political context for practice.

### The Profession

This 20th-century profession recently celebrated it first centennial. Social work was established to address a panoply of social concerns associated with industrial growth and turmoil, poverty, child welfare, family relations, malnutrition and health care, infant mortality, waves of new immigrants and internal migration and other maladies associated with terrible slums in rapidly expanding cities and urban areas (Austin, 2000; Glicken, 2007). Before the American Revolution, help for children, the poor, and the mentally ill had been available, based on the ideology embodied in the historical legacies of the British Elizabethan Poor Laws. By the 1800s, aid was provided at local levels through town and county offices. Recognizing the limitations of these efforts, benevolent and faith-based societies and business leaders supplemented the early, often limited, public initiatives. The revivalist movement ushered in the age of enlightenment that undergirded a belief in the values of justice, rational thinking in approaches to human suffering, and the capacity of people to proceed with work for the "improvability" of men, women, and society (Karger & Stoesz, 2002, Katz, 1986).

In the last half of the 19th century, economic crisis, racism and social subordination, and immigration prompted the need for even stronger social programs and led to the organizing paradigm of scientific charity (Glicken, 2007). The profession grew largely in response to northern industrial growth; however, the South was also challenged by the depth and magnitude of human suffering (Wisner, 1970; Lowe & Hopps, in press). The slave question dominated thought in the South and later, a large segment of national society, as the Union became more divided over the immensely varied, complex dynamic of individual and collective white control and black slave resistance (Lowe, 2006; Wood, 1978). The level of care for this population however was shockingly divergent, not necessarily based on human standards available to men and whites but rather, sub-human ideals owing to beliefs in scientific sexism and racism, respectively, that held sway, as well as the insidious discrimination generated by social scientists (Abramovitz, 1998; Byrd & Clayton, 2000).

Friendly visitors, settlement house workers, muckrakers, social activists, and union organizers generated the enthusiasm and energy of this nascent profession, which was largely an informal, fragmented, and volunteer-led initiative to organize and distribute charitable acts, goods, and services. These leaders envisioned a more structured, systemic approach to unfathomable social ills, ignorance, poverty, disease, and human suffering that were endemic to the new industrial nation, based on the welfare capitalism (Austin, 2000) that was emerging at the end of the 1800s and the dawn of the 20th century. Even then, with modest ideals, but unbridled hope, this emerging profession envisioned that society's worst conditions could be relieved if individuals could be helped to move up and eventually out of the engulfing vortex of personal maladies and slum conditions through improvement of their own moral and physical capacities, with the aid of helpers. At the same time, other volunteers worked along with the poor to teach and help empower them to take matters in their own hands to improve personal and neighborhood circumstances through groups and collective

actions. Although different in conception and organizational ideas, these parallel efforts (that is, the former being micro-change and the latter macro-change) were largely mutually supportive (Morris, 2000), but there were times of struggle and contest (Abramovitz, 1998; Drew, 1983, as cited by Figueira-McDonough, 2007). Both approaches incorporated concepts of care and social control (Day, 2003; Figueira-McDonough, 2007; Piven & Cloward, 1971) though the latter is not often acknowledged.

These humble ideals became the basis for a profession that advanced the notion that national society was responsible for addressing the impact that a fast changing and evolving industrial world had on human lives; that a system's wide response, via agencies, would be needed to achieve the national purpose; that a part-time, lay person's responsibility would have to be replaced by professional responsibility, and that an emerging profession would need to direct attention to the intersection of psychological development and educational growth of individuals and the socio-political-economic world in which they lived and were hopefully nurtured (Morris, 2000).

## The Origins
EARLY VOLUNTARY AND MUTUAL AID SOCIETIES EFFORTS As a natural response to local needs, voluntary–mutual aid organizations, including benefit and burial societies, relief associations and faith-based groups (that is, missionaries) that created collective networks for different immigrant and racial group and communities dotted the nation's landscape (Katz, 1986; Sabbath, 1994). Among early self-help and relief organizations were the Scot Charitable Society of New York (1744), African Masonic Lodge of Boston (1784), Philadelphia Free African Society (1787), New York Society for the Relief of Poor Widows with Small Children (1798), Samaritan Society of New York (1805), and the Children's Aid Society (1853) to name a few (Curry, 1981; Frazier, 1932; Katz, 1986; Lincoln & Mamiya, 1990). As a benefit society, the Philadelphia Society was organized to provide insurance benefits for widows and children, and later established branches in Charleston, South Carolina, Boston, and New York. In the meantime, many churches, synagogues, and other groups mobilized to organize orphanages and hospitals. As relief to the poor, in conjunction with blacks and members of the Abolition Society, the Society of Friends established in 1822 the Shelter for Colored Orphans in Philadelphia (Dolgoff & Feldstein, 2007). Despite these, and many other notable efforts, more organized efforts were necessary to address access and funding limitations, and to reduce service fragmentation. Similarly, in the

Southwest, early Latinos provided social welfare services through the auspices of the Catholic Church (Dolgoff & Feldstein, 2007). Missions, churches, schools, hospitals, convents, and missionaries provided some social services. Although Catholic priests and nuns provided social services, it has been reported, however, that similar to the attitudes of early protestant benefactors, there were traces of altruism, egalitarians, racism, and class-based condescension (Anderson, 2000; Trevino, 2003).

THE FREEDMEN'S BUREAU: THE FIRST FEDERAL SOCIAL WELFARE AGENCY In 1865, at the end of the Civil War, some four million formerly enslaved African Americans, never the recipients of basic human and civil rights, ravaged and poor, unlearned and unlettered, though skilled and with a demonstrated work ethic, were granted freedom. What meaning did freedom have in the face of abject poverty, lack of voting rights, property ownership, housing, health care, and education? What was life like for whites accustomed to a structure supported largely by slave labor? What was the nation's responsibility? The national response was the passage of the Freedmen Bureau of Refugees, Freedmen and Abandon Land Act of 1865 that established America's first federal welfare agency, commonly called the Freedmen's Bureau.

The Freedmen Bureau, a source of federal relief and the nation's first federal social welfare agency, provided a broad range of services, such as food, social and child welfare, and medical, educational, banking, and contract services at the individual and community levels (Olds, 1963). For example, the agency supervised labor contracts between newly freed slaves and the southern elite (that is, the planters' class) in an effort to prevent further exploitation and enforce provisions of contracts. One significant empowerment act accomplished with the aid of newly elected blacks and northern philanthropists during Reconstruction was the establishment of universal, free education for both blacks and whites in the South (Anderson, 1988; Hopps, 2006). Early leadership for emerging black self-help, church, and social service initiatives that paralleled primarily Euro-American settlements and social service organizations were aided by the educational and other iniatives of the Bureau (Burwell, 1994; Carlton-LeNay & Hodges, 1994; Lerner, 1974; Pollard, 1978).

CHARITY ORGANIZATION SOCIETIES: EMERGENCE OF SCIENTIFIC PHILANTHROPY The Charity Organization Societies (COS) facilitated both the professionalization and bureaucratization of social work by advancing the concept of scientific charity in the late 1800s. Philanthropists combined prudence with dedication in helping

and fueled the reorganization of COS. They adopted a systemic, organized approach to identify and determine needs (case evaluation), and to deliver services effectively. Their ideas about efficiency and functional specialization were based on those of the business/industrial world (Lubove, 1965). Based on social Darwinism, these ideals were also intended to facilitate principles of social stratification and the maintenance of social control (Day, 2003).

Although the thrust toward professionalization grew out of the reorganization of COS in the context of scientific charity (Larson, 1977), the professionalization movement was aided and accelerated by caseworkers who asserted that they had the "beginning of a scientific knowledge base, as well as specialized skill, technique and function that differentiated them from the layman or volunteer" (Larson, 1977, p. 182). In the push for professionalization, the leadership of caseworkers led to their subsequent dominance in the profession. Specializations were developed in social casework, child welfare, medical, and psychiatric work, and others facilitating the establishment of a program of study offered by the New York Charity Organization and Columbia University in 1897; several other schools followed in rather rapid succession. These specialties developed their individual associations and each operated with their own unique organizational culture. This phenomenon, compounded by religious and secular orientations, would make later negotiation and development of a unified profession more difficult to achieve (Hopps & Lowe, in press).

PROGRESSIVES AND THE SETTLEMENT MOVEMENT Settlements and the Progressive Reform movement joined together to tackle and improve the neglected urban infrastructure and poor sanitary conditions; deplorable, unsafe housing; exploitative employment; ignorance; poor educational opportunities; restrictive, if available recreation; police brutality and malpractice, as well as other quality of life concerns for immigrants and other poor people in cities, who were often isolated owing to language, cultural and/or resource limitations. Women reformers, usually well-heeled financially, who became settlement leaders, came from a number of disciplines and believed that opportunities for informal pedagogy could be instrumental in helping individuals improve their own human capital and competencies as well as the social capital of their environment via the group approach. They implemented this vision through their work, which was heavily influenced by thinker, philosopher, and activist John Dewey (Garvin, 1981). By the end of the first decade of the 20th century, there were over 400 settlements. Important work was accomplished: The seeds for the founding of the Children's Bureau (1912) germinated at Hull House. Women's suffrage, labor, civil rights, and peace were among the movements that were led and/or assisted by settlement activists. These effective initiatives led to the development of many national, social welfare and social change-oriented organizations. In contrast to the COS, relief was not the focus of settlements—reform was the goal. Progressives advocated social insurance instead of charitable aid, which was eventually enacted following the Depression (DiNitto, 2007).

An important challenge to the Progressive's record was the lack of demonstrated concern about the plight of African Americans. Parenthetically, the conditions of white tenant farmers and their families in the southern states were also not targeted (Austin, 2000). There is evidence also of "social negligence" as the young social work profession did not show early support and commitment to service for people of color, which eventually forced the creation of a parallel system of aid for African Americans by African Americans, among others (Austin, 2000; Carlton-LeNay & Hodges, 2004; Hopps & Lowe, in press; Pollard, 1978). This separate system was severely underresourced, even when eventually given ideological support and encouragement by social reformer and iconoclast Jane Addams. For all of its fame and historical contributions, Hull House and its leadership are tainted because of the unwillingness to serve all Americans and most particularly African Americans and other people of color (Duster, 1970). In essence, a system of service apartheid (apartness) based on race was established in the social service delivery system. Vestiges of these 19th- and early 20th-century policies and services continue to challenge the field (Lowe, 2006).

Ida B. Wells-Barnett, an African American, spearheaded the establishment of a settlement house for her people in Chicago under the auspices of the Negro Fellowship League. In the South, Margaret Washington, the wife of Tuskegee Institute's founder and a leading American political figure, organized settlement efforts in the rural community of Tuskegee, Alabama. In the meantime, Eugenia Hope, wife of John Hope, the first African American President of Morehouse College, established the Wheat Street Settlement in urban Atlanta, Georgia.

## Professionalism Develops in a New Century
It has been argued that there were many opportunities for the profession to continue and build upon the convictions that social work would develop expertise in understanding the behavior of individuals in their social, political, and economic context. In order to develop this mission well, there was expectation that

contributions from cognate disciplines including economics, sociology, psychology, political science, and later, science and technology, would be sought out and integrated into the profession. This ambitious ideal was undercut by the need to provide services to individuals often within the context of medical and mental health protocols (Morris, 2000). The emphasis on studying, understanding, and helping individuals on a case-by-case approach (Mary Richmond, *Social Diagnosis*, 1917), minimized the view that indigent and victimized people suffered from social and economic circumstances that could be changed by joint organizational and collective efforts and structural change (for example, the neighborhood Guild in New York, about 1886 and Jane Addams and Ellen Star, Hull House in Chicago, about 1889).

Over the 20th century, these initial positions were modified through choices relative to how the profession would simultaneously address the goal of improving the lives of individuals and family, and change societal conditions (Morris, 2000). Regardless of the reasons, at particular times in history, the profession made choices that limited its capacity to address structural change and to improve major societal problems and conditions. These decisions resulted in consequences that had a bearing on the status of the profession at the dawn of the 21st century. Morris (2000) summarized the profession thus:

- The tradition was initially a part of a much wider interest in social change and human needs that had been expressed since 1860 through the National Conference of Charities and Corrections and the American Social Science Association.
- The movement became a part of the later Progressive movement.
- The early participants were multidisciplined, drawn from sociologists, nascent economists, other social scientists, lay community leaders, clergy, and workers in agencies.
- Social work as a distinctive vocation soon concentrated on developing its position as a profession, with the apparatus of a social science: academic training to combine learning and practical experience and professional associations with accrediting authority.
- The twin aims of providing individual care and changing social conditions have been retained in the expressed aims of the field, but after 1935, the Great Depression and World War II forced the field to reconsider its future.
- A series of choices, some taken almost unwittingly, were reinforced by the popularity of new mental health thinking and the compatibility of

psychological theory with social casework, along with the great social and economic changes following the Depression.

- By 1990, the field was primarily involved in interpersonal and mental health careers, while work to change conditions remained at the rhetorical level rather than providing jobs and institutional opportunities to work for change.
- At the same time, social work as a profession was identified mainly with counseling help to individuals or as adjunct staff for organizations, rather than becoming "the profession" associated with any one service system (Morris, 2000, p. 44–45).

**SCOPE OF THE PROFESSION** The scope of social work over the latter part of the 19th and 20th centuries has evolved as a result of many ensuing internal and external forces that gave rise to this contextual profession. External forces, both positive and negative, have played a stronger hand in defining the field than the former, since practice is defined by the profession's position in the geo-socio-eco-political environment at a particular period of time (Gibelman, 1999; Hopps & Lowe, in press). The social work profession has long been acknowledged for its breadth of practice, while concurrently criticized for its lack of sufficient depth, fragmentation, and inadequate conceptual framework (Hopps & Collins, 1995; Hopps & Lowe, in press). Relevant are the words of noted social work educator, the late Carol H. Meyer: "Whereas other professional specialists become expert by narrowing their knowledge parameters, social workers have had to increase theirs" (Meyer, 1976, p. 21).

**THE BOUNDARY CONUNDRUM** With knowledge created by the profession, from its own research enterprise and theory testing, practice intervention and monitoring for effectiveness, and stronger interest and expectations from universities for improved scholarship, the question is: What content is most relevant, verifiable and organized into a taxonomy, and is also useful for the profession?" (Hopps & Lowe, in press). Acknowledging the challenges regarding ever-expanding boundaries, the core issue can be narrowed to one of focus.

Do the lack of a cohesive organizing framework and the reality of fragmented approaches to both knowledge development and knowledge application cast a shadow over the profession (Gambrill, 2003; Hopps & Lowe, in press; Tucker, 2000)? If this is the case, it seems imperative that the profession should continue to address inquiry relevant to its purpose and identity, as well as a unifying, coherent conceptual framework and

supporting theories. Two decades ago Scott Briar (1977) asked: What is common to the activities of social work (Brieland & Korr, 2000)? What then is the field's "problematic" (Tucker, 2000)? That is an "integrated framework of concepts, propositions, and practices that together define the central intellectual problems of a field" (p. 239).

For social work, the unit of analysis is the interaction of person and environment. The goal is to have as strong, robust, and positive an interaction as possible between these two systems. A weakness however, is the proclivity of the profession to minimize or become overwhelmed by conditions that emanate from the geopolitical-economic environment, which most assuredly has an impact on human functioning (Morris, 2000; Tucker, 2000; Pinderhughes, 1995; 2001). Solomon's (2002) argument that the profession prefers to discuss "individual variables" over "system variables" holds currency; however, the Curriculum Policy Statement has given more thought and emphasis to this area of concern vis-a vis its stance on social justice.

Without a consensus-driven working definition, conceptual clarity, and, or, a cohesive element, the profession must continue to struggle with the tendency of generating many theories, technologies, methodologies, and interventional strategies that both invite and enhance tendencies toward eclecticism (Hopps & Lowe, in press). However, it is argued that eclecticism is not a "free good" (Tucker, 2000), but rather, one which extracts a premium that relegates social work to a comparative disadvantage in relation to disciplines where there is evidence of higher paradigm development. Consequently, social work is less proficient in grasping and holding on to resources and assets; in the pace at which knowledge is developed and disseminated; the degree of power and autonomy it has amassed; and in the capacity for collaborative study and research (Hopps & Lowe, in press; Tucker, 2000). New questions regarding intellectual property may well compound this phenomenon. Although the profession has not yet developed as strong a "problematic" and a more cohesive conceptual framework as it might desire, it would be an enormous oversight if the contributions of many scholars, and the profession's own initiatives toward a common base and working definition to advance social work conceptually, were not acknowledged. Examples include Bartlett's (1958) definition and Gordon's (1962) critical assessment of it, along with contributions from others working for a unified, common base (Bartlett, 1970; Boehm, 1959) and those acknowledging practice at various system levels and size (Pincus & Minahan, 1977; Schwartz, 1961; Siporin, 1975). Briar's (1977) challenge, that "it is not good when the profession cannot clearly and simply articulate what is common to the activities of all social workers" is still relevant (Brieland & Korr, 2000, p.130). Certainly, practitioners recognize that vague constructs make goal setting and measurement complicated (Hopps & Lowe, in press). Others helped move the profession to broader views, leading to the use of the generic term "social work practice." Several new perspectives were developed including the generalist perspective (Baer & Frederio, 1979), strength based (Saleeby, 2002), ethnic sensitive (Devore & Schlesginger, 1999; Schiele, 2000), policy practice (Jannson, 1990), and political advocacy (Haynes & Mickelson, 2003).

NATIONAL ORGANIZATIONS  In an effort to enhance professionalization and status, a major restructuring and consolidation of professional organizations took place in the 1950s with the formation of the Council on Social Work Education (CSWE) (1952) and the National Association of Social Workers (NASW) (1956) (Austin, 1997; Austin, 2000). The former spearheaded needed oversight of the enterprise which educated and socialized members, while the latter provided the structure for organizational unity to a former, fragmented set of methods- and program-based associations. Developing unity was hard to achieve initially, and hard to sustain over time, as several specific interest groups formed separate associations (that is, National Association of Black Social Workers and the North American Association of Christian Social Workers). One committee supported by NASW is Political Action for Candidate Election (PACE), which encourages social workers to help elect individuals who support social justice, a theme which was given great emphasis in the 2003 NASW Policy Statement.

## Contempopary Context of Social Welfare

SOCIO-POLITICAL ENVIRONMENT  Several major events had a seismic influence on the country's approach to social welfare: The aftermath of the Civil War when the Union government took on major responsibilities for restoring order, providing food, shelter, and services to large areas of the country (Day, 2003); President Roosevelt's response to the 1929 economic crisis and financial depression, which held sway for over half a century when the welfare state, social services, and the profession grew; the Kennedy-Johnson 1960s civil rights, war on poverty, and buildup in domestic policies where social welfare and social security surpassed national defense in federal spending (DiNitto, 2007); and, the conservative revolt, which attempted to move government responsibility back to pre-depression, 1929 ideology known as Reagonomics

(after former California governor Ronald Reagan who became president).

Reagan successfully galvanized the elites, corporate America, and middle America with an anti-government, anti-welfare theme resulting in Republican control, based on supply-side economics. Tax policy favoring wealthy and affluent Americans and business, deregulation of industry, massive reductions and cuts in government support for social service and return to reliance on the private sector, severe attacks and reversals on civil rights gains and massive buildup of the federal deficit (some $925 billion) (Day, 2003; DiNitto, 2007; & Figueira-McDonough, 2007), and the appointment of conservative minds to the federal courts, including the U.S. Supreme Court, were outcomes of the dominant party and its leadership. The Reagan agenda was continued by President George H. W. Bush who served as his Vice President, but lost after one term because of problems related to economic disarray, a heavy federal deficit, and a tax increase he pledged not to support during his campaign, but, reversing his position, signed into law (Day, 2003; DiNitto, 2007; Figueira-McDonough, 2007).

Still enamored by supply-side economics, the country nonetheless voted in a more centrist, in contrast to liberal, ideology with the election of William Jefferson Clinton in 1992. The new president and his team tried to pull away from supply-side economics. Emphasizing the economy and infrastructure improvement, Clinton pushed through a cut in taxation, a Stimulus Program, and reduced the deficit (Figueira-McDonough, 2007). But the administration's big push for universal health care led by then first lady Hillary Rodham Clinton failed after attack by Republicans, although the majority of Americans favored the plan (Figueira-McDonough, 2007). Most of all, there was the regeneration of a vibrant economy which created many new jobs, about 22.5 million, mostly in the private sector. Technology boomed, expanding the information age. The minimum wage was raised to $5.15 per hour after debate (during roughly the same timeframe, the CEO of Disney earned $78,000 per hour) (Day, 2003), a fact that highlights the perennial wealth and inequality problem in this society (Korr & Brieland, 2000) and around the globe (Iatridis, 2000).

During Clinton's first term, the Democrats lost control of Congress to the Republicans who started building a "conservative opportunity society" under the leadership of House Speaker Newt Gingrich. A conservative manifesto, *Contract with America*, became an influential document, with a major focus on reducing welfare and strengthening some families while at the same time punishing other families economically. This document influenced conservative thought and had a role in ending "welfare as we knew it." Facing an election, President Clinton finally supported the Personal Responsibility and Work Opportunity Reconciliation Act of 1996, which focused on stiffer work requirements and limitation on time recipients could receive financial (or welfare) benefits (Day, 2003; DiNitto, 2007; Karger & Stoesz, 2002). The passage of the new law was not unrelated to public perceptions relative to racial stereotypes about AFDC (Aid to Families and Dependent Children) recipients (Gillens, 1999, as reported in Figueira-McDonough, 2007). When Clinton became president, he inherited a deficit from the first Bush presidency, but left a surplus.

George W. Bush narrowly won the election in 2000 over former Vice-President Al Gore in a contested election where the Supreme Court played an unusual role by calling off recounting of ballots in Florida (DiNitto, 2007). What this election meant was a return to Reagan philosophy, including but not limited to, supply-side economics (cuts in taxes that benefited the highest income earners and corporations, at the expense of the middle class); an expanded inclusion of the faith community into social service delivery via the signing of the Faith and Community-Based Act (the new president's first executive action); expanded privatization of social service and continued devolution of government responsibility to the states; appointment of conservative federal judges and most especially to the Supreme Court. The 2000 and 2004 elections represented a stronger coalescing of big business and corporations, the religious right, and the elite classes than the country had seen since Reagan. Although President Bush inherited a budget surplus from President Clinton, he created a $317 billon deficit by 2005, owing to the tax cut, cost of the Iraq War, and natural disasters (that is, hurricanes Katrina and Rita), among other expenditures. To offset revenue downfall from the tax cuts and major additional spending, the 2005 Deficit Reduction Act (DRA) was enacted and social welfare programs were targeted for cuts (DiNitto, 2007). However, the political scene changed.

The 2006 Congressional election resulted in a victory for Democrats, a defeat for the Republicans, and a strong rebuke of the Bush Agenda, largely because of the unpopular Iraq War and the response to the victims of Hurricane Katrina. Correlative to the war question per se and loss of American lives (Hopps & Lowe, in press; See, 2001), is the escalating cost of the conflict contributing to the national debt and stagnation in domestic and nondefense policies and programs. At the same time that some Americans were making more money across income categories above $50,000 (Wall Street Journal, 2006), many were struggling and the middle class declining (Glicken, 2007; Ragland, 2006).

It is not clear that the 2006 election was a clarion call or mandate for the return to a more expansive social welfare philosophy; however, it did throw cold water on the 30-year spell of conservatism (Kilpatrick & Parle, 2006). Within the 110th Congress, many new leaders have demonstrated a strong history of support for public aid; namely Speaker of the U.S. House of Representatives Nancy Peolosi (D-CA), the first woman to hold this position and Chairman of the powerful Ways and Means Committee Charles Rangel (D-NY), and John Conyers, Chairman of the Judiciary Committee (D-MI). The three represent more liberal congressional districts. These changes in leadership in the U.S. House of Representatives are especially important because all tax proposals must be initiated in that legislative body.

CLASSIFICATION AND DECLASSIFICATION A pressing threat to the credibility, status, cohesion, and unity of the profession has grown out of the effort to meet human needs in a fast-changing, complex society, often resulting in declassification and deprofessionalization. Workers from various educational backgrounds were recruited to the multiplying positions (especially those in the public sector) that were created by the new Great Society programs and the Social Security amendments of 1961 (P.L. 87–543). These new practitioners were identified equally in the public mind as social workers; and their inclusion meant that the profession was differentiated not only into higher levels of education and skill beyond the professional Master of Social Work (MSW) degree, but also into lower levels (high school or GED). The media is particularly influential in the declassification question due to the tendency to refer to all human service workers, regardless of education or rank, as social workers. Additionally, the media often emphasizes mistakes, popularizes failures, and ignores successes, thereby helping to create a poor public perception of practitioners (Ellett & Leighninger, 2007). There has been, however, some movement to help strengthen the profession and also protect or shield the title of social worker. The U.S. Supreme Court in *Jaffe v. Redmond* (1996) ruled that in federal courts, social workers have rights of privileged communication with their clients (Barker, 2003). In Hawaii, government employees who possess a professional BSW, MSW, and, or, PhD are referred to as social workers; others are called human service professionals (Pace, 2005, p. 9).

*Classification.* In an effort to provide some order to the reigning confusion about functional parameters and to meet the demand for accountability in relation to them decades ago, in 1973, the National Association of Social Workers (NASW) came up with the following classification:

**Preprofessional Level**
- Social work aide (high school diploma)
- Social services technician (associate degree)

**Professional Level**
- Social worker (Bachelor of Social Work [BSW] accredited)
- Certified social worker or member of the Academy of Certified Social Workers (ACSW; requires two years of post-MSW experience and passing an examination)
- Social work fellow (advanced practice).

In 1990 and 2006, specializations in School Social Work and Aging were created, respectively, by NASW.

Theoretically, each level should reflect certain responsibilities that presumably become more complex as one moves up the career ladder. In practice, however, the lines of classification are not neatly drawn or clearly compartmentalized. In the pubic child welfare sector, for example, civil service requirements demonstrate limited differentiation of tasks and credentials at any structural level, unclear career paths, and questions related to qualifications for high-level appointments. These concerns are in addition to those related to non-social work degree holders or to those who have only attained a high school diploma or GED (Ellett, Ellett, & Rugutt, 2003, as cited in Ellett & Leighninger, 2007).

For positions in mental health, an MSW is required. This area of practice vastly expanded employment opportunities in response to federal funding of mental health centers in the 1960s and 1970s. An additional attraction to mental health was the possibility of moving into private practice of clinical social work (Ellett & Leighninger, 2007; Helfgott, 1990). Increasingly, a doctoral degree is required for academic, administrative, research, and practice leadership positions.

*Declassification.* Declassification can be considered similar to deprofessionalization, an assumption that the "interchangeability of baccalaureate degrees, the reorganization of jobs to reduce educational requirement, the substitution of experience for education, the non-recognition of the exclusivity of bachelor's and master's degrees in social work" (Costin, Karger, & Stoesz, 1996, p. 158). Many states that have enacted legislation to regulate practice have incorporated the

various levels as outlined in the 1973 NASW Policy Statement (NASW, 1973). Under declassification, job qualifications and standards of performance were reviewed, revised, and rewritten with the recommendation that educational requirements be lowered and length of professional training shortened (NASW, 1981). There, however, is evidence that practitioners with a professional social work education are better prepared for child welfare as well as other areas of practice. Specifically, they score higher regarding knowledge of child welfare and do better on job rating from their supervisor, and in expression of intent to stay in the field (Booze-Allen & Hamilton, 1987; Ellett, Ellett, & Rugutt, 2003; Fox, Miller, & Barbee, 2003) and in offering professional care and supervision to carers in service to overwhelmed clients (Hopps, Pinderhughes, & Shankar, 1995).

**LEGAL REGULATION OF PRACTICE** In response to the need for professional regulation and certification, the NASW in 1961 took the lead by establishing the National Academy of Certified Social Workers (ACSW) credential for master's level practitioners. Similarly, at the bachelor's level of practice, the Academy of Certified Baccalaureate Social Workers (ACBSW) was established in 1991. All states at the current time have some form of legal regulation. Licensing means that because of state law, only those people who have attained certain educational requirements, including completing an appropriate educational program, and even postgraduate program, can have a certain title. Social workers are licensed at the associate's, bachelor's (that is, LSW), and master's levels (that is, LMSW, BCSW, LCSW, LICSW). Regulations, in general, address a number of critical concerns for the profession, clients, and the public. They provide legal sanction that affords the professional social workers needed authority. More importantly, they help provide a measure of professional competence by requiring a minimum level of education and licensure. Finally, legal regulation protects the public interest by creating quality control and oversight of the profession as well as providing a process for appeal when professional malfeasance occurs (Hardcastle, 1981).

**PRACTICE LIABILITY** Liability is another important issue for social workers, especially in the nation's increasingly litigious environment. NASW monitors this important area. For example, in 2003, the Legal Defense Fund filed a supporting document in a California case that extended liability relative to threats noted to third parities regarding clients. Specifically, the California Supreme Court was asked to review a lower court's ruling in *Ewing v. Goldstein*. NASW pointed out that "the ruling imposes a burden on psychotherapists and jeopardizes the confidential relationship between a therapist and a patient ..." (Fred, 2005). In general, malpractice involves violation of the profession's ethical responsibilities. The Code of Ethics & Standards developed by NASW serves as a guide in civil, criminal, and ethical issues concerning professional practice.

### The 21st-Century Social Worker

Although poised to make a significant impact in response to cultural transformation and a fast growing population, with much greater racial and ethnic diversity due in part to the 1960s immigration reforms, there are concerns related to the social work profession's workforce in the 21st century. The National Association of Social Workers (NASW) commissioned a national survey of over 4,500 licensed social workers in 2004 with the Center for Workforce Health Studies (CWHS). The findings of the report, *Assuring the Sufficiency of Frontline Workforce: A National Study of Licensed Social Workers*, reflected ongoing practice and demographic trends and the emergence of new trends (NASW, 2006; Stoesen & Moss, 2006). Caution is warranted largely because this national sample of over 240,000 licensed professional social workers represented only 63 percent of the 460,000 social workers reported by the Bureau of Labor Statistics (BLS, 2006). Still, this sample represents an important profile of professional social workers as follows.

EMPLOYMENT  Seventy-five percent of licensed social workers reported full-time employment, while another 13 percent recorded part-time employment. Thirty-seven percent reported employment under private, not-for-profit auspices; 29 percent reported employment under private, for-profit auspices (that is, private practice and organizations); and 16 percent reported employment in local or federal government auspices. However, social work's low involvement in the public sector suggests a decline in employment standards in that area owing to declassification, signaling an ongoing and major challenge to the profession. In the meantime, NASW membership has shown an upward drift toward private practice: Roughly 11% in 1982 reported active involvement, while 20% in 1995 reported similar practice (Gibelman & Schervish, 1997). The majority of the respondents were employed in direct service practice roles, which highlights the ongoing strength of clinical as the dominant sector in the scope of practice (Gibelman & Schervish, 1997). There are indications

that this drift is continuing as practitioners carry cases on a contract basis, if they are certified and eligible for third-party payment from profit and nonprofit service providers.

Among new trends, social workers are increasingly looking toward international, nongovernmental organizations (NGOs) for opportunities. In a randomly selected sample of 20 NGOs registered with the United Nations, Clairborne (2004) found that almost 16,600 (or 37%) of their 44,600 full-time positions were held by social workers (that is, BSW, MSW, PhD/DSW), who served mostly as program directors. This is no doubt associated with forces of globalization, interdependence, and socioeconomics, integration found across other industries and the pace of international immigration, space innovations, and urbanization facilitated by the mass media, new computing and communication technology (Iatridis, 2002). Globalization means opening up societies, not only economics, and is therefore a social and political construct (p. 210). Social work, like business, is going to have to get used to the idea that thinking about the world in terms of national boundaries, rather than as a single system, is "old fashioned" (p. 211), since what takes place in one geopolitical system has an impact across the world.

Facilitating this global thrust is the increasing utilization of international and cross-cultural credit courses offered by colleges, universities, and schools of social work that expose students to experiential opportunities in other countries. Similarly, as international fieldwork placements are offered, both faculty and students become open to and less intimidated with new and varied employment vistas, settings, and different people. The increasing awareness of interglobal dependence will lead to recognition of the need for more in-depth knowledge of other cultures and languages across countries and continents. This acknowledges professional participation beyond current cross-cultural or ethnic- sensitive practice curriculum offerings (Glicken, 2007). It also forces schools to grapple with content on American, global, and regional economics, political structures, and welfare systems (Morris, 2000, Iatridis, 2002).

A small, but growing, number of social workers seek careers in politics as elected officials at all levels of government. At least six social workers have been serving in the U.S. Congress, while more can be found across the country as mayors, commissioners, and in state legislative bodies. Increasingly, policies that affect the lives of clients, for example, health, same sex marriage, and allocations for TANF, are addressed by legislation enacted at the state level. Nonetheless, more social workers are desired at all levels of government to help advocate for old, unsolved problems, and new groups of needful populations.

GENDER, RACE, AND ETHNICITY Demographic data from a 2004 workforce study of licensed social workers found similar rates (81% compared to 79%) to the 1995 membership study, confirming that the profession remains predominantly female (NASW, 2006). Regarding settings, women were almost twice as likely to practice in health service and aging, than men. Conversely, male social workers were slightly more likely to practice in mental health service and more than twice as likely to practice in addiction service. With regard to practice roles, women were more likely to be found in direct service and private practice, while men were more likely to be carrying out responsibilities in supervision, administration, and education. Salaries are generally higher in these latter areas.

Licensed social workers in general report higher salaries than their nonlicensed colleagues. In fact, licensed male social workers in the NASW commissioned study reported median income of over $61,000, compared to over $48,000 for female colleagues (NASW, 2006). This pattern has existed over many decades and continues in spite of professional dialogue and voiced interest in women being appointed to more equitable paying positions. Going forward, given demographic changes, a substantially more diverse group of social workers, particularly women not from middle class backgrounds, will provide increased leadership in social work education and practice for the profession; one that serves a predominately female clientele by female employees (Austin, 2000).

Social work, as with other health service professions, is less reflective of the nation's racial and ethnic profile. The majority (84.5%) of licensed social workers report being European American (NASW, 2006); and the remaining 15.5% are composed of African Americans (6.8%), Hispanic and Latino Americans (4.3%), Asian Americans (1.4%), and Native Americans (0.5%) and others (1.4%). However, the 2001 Current Population Survey, which is a self-reporting census, found a different racial and ethnic profile of professional social workers. That survey found that almost two-thirds (64.6%) of the respondents were European American, while African-Americans were 23% and Hispanic Americans made up 8.3%. These findings demonstrate different racial and ethnic profiles of the social work workforce. Still, both findings suggest expanding diversity, as compared to the Gibelman and Schervish (1993) report. Nonetheless, the profession continues to be largely composed of persons of European descendent. In light of demographic trends, the profession, as others, will need to continue to pursue a diverse workforce that is more reflective of the nation's population.

SUPPLY, DEMAND, AND AREAS OF PRACTICE From all projections, social workers will be in demand for years to come. The Bureau of Labor's *Occupational Outlook Handbook* projects a 40% increase in demand for professional social work into the next decade (BLS, 2000). In fact, among the major findings from the NASW (2006) workforce study among licensed social workers are that (1) the number of new practitioners servicing older adults is decreasing; (2) the supply of practitioners in agencies serving children and families is insufficient; (3) growing caseloads and shrinking resources impede practitioners' retention; and agencies are struggling to fill existing vacancies. This information signals an increased demand for social workers in new and old fields of service.

Because of the profession's and the public's growing demand for interest in effective service, evidence- or empirically-based social work practice is positioned to move to the forefront in an effort to address the nation's social problems. This trend has already emerged in the mental health sector. The assumption is that effective services are, in the long run, more cost-effective. This alone is a motivation for the profession to continue the movement toward evidence-based expectations (Hopps et al., 1995; O'Hare, 2005; Reid, 1997; Thyer, 2004).

In keeping with the profession's renewed emphasis on social justice, professional social workers are found in many fields, serving many new and traditional populations, and serving different roles. Of the most reported fields of practice among NASW members and licensed social workers across the nation are mental health, child welfare, health and school social work (U.S. Department of Health and Human Services, 1998; NASW, 2006). In these fields, practitioners serve diverse populations with many pressing, ever-challenging needs (Hopps & Lowe, in press).

This discussion on areas and methods is not exhaustive, but is, rather, a notation of common areas of social work practice: advocacy (personal and political), environmental justice, criminal justice, legislative and policy practice, school, children, youth, gerontology, gender, families, couples and singles, physical, behavioral, and developmental health, vocational rehabilitation, employee assistance, research and evaluation, immigrant and refugee work, emergency and disaster services (that is, the Hurricane Katrina in 2005 and the tsunami in Southeast Asia in 2004). Most organize practice into the methods of casework, group work, community organization, and policy practice (Figueria-McDonough,

1993; Pincus & Minahan, 1977). In the context of micro practice, casework (that is, generalist or advanced), social workers may serve individual or family client systems as direct practitioners. In terms of group work, practitioners serve individuals in therapeutic, task, support, and empowerment groups with different goals and objectives. On the macro practice scene, community organization practitioners can be found mobilizing neighborhoods and communities, among others. Some emphasis has been seen on policy planning, policy practice, advocacy, and administration. New computing and mass communication technologies have also had major impact on all practice approaches (Boland, Barton, & McNutt, 2002; Hopps & Lowe, in press).

## Future Trends

The profession will not only continue to address issues it faced in its first century, but will also be challenged with new ones. Paramount among the influences will be the geo-political-economic context. Although the geo-political context may be more subject to immediate change than the latter, both turbulence and hope are anticipated. The election of a Democratic Congress, the 110th, might indicate a more hopeful environment for positive change toward social welfare programs and a decline in negativism toward the field.

Nonetheless, the 2005 Social Work Congress, which included key social work associations and stakeholders, developed 12 "imperatives" (Stoesen, 2006) that speak to: excel in services for aging; participate in politics and policy; guarantee quality services to children; demonstrate leadership in advocacy for universal health care; enhance the public's understanding of efficiency and cost-effectiveness of social work in health care; deal with racism, oppression, and social injustice and human rights violations; strengthen the profession's capacity to influence the political and corporate landscape; improve the quality of social work education; mobilize the profession for participation in politics, policy and social action; confront racism at all levels; utilize cultural competence social work interventions and research methodology; and develop research and practice partnerships.

## Special Thanks

We wish to thank Kareema Gray, MSW, and Keith Brown, MSW Candidate for their research assistances at the University of Georgia; and Drs. Ollie Christian, Professor, Southern University and Lee See, Professor Emerita, University of Georgia, for their consultation.

## REFERENCES

Abramovitz, M. (1998). Social work and social reform: An arena of struggle. *Social Work, 43*(6), 512–526.

Anderson, J. D. (1988). *The education of blacks in the South, 1860–1935.* Chapel Hill: The University of North Carolina Press.

Anderson, M. C. (2000). Catholic nuns and the intervention of social work: The sisters of the Santa Maria Institute of Cincinnati, Ohio, 1897 through the 1920's. *Journal of women's history, 12*(1).

Austin, D. (2000). Greeting the second century: A forward look for a historical perspective in social pedagogy in informal learning. In J. Hopps & R. Morris (Eds.), *Social work at the millennium: Critical reflections on the future of the profession.* (pp. 18–41). New York: Free Press.

Austin, D. M. (1997). The institutional development of social work education: The first 100 years – and beyond. *Journal of Social Work Education, 33*(3), 599–614.

Barker, R. L. (2003). Milestones in the development of social work and social welfare. In R. L. Barker (Ed.), *The social work dictionary* (5th ed., pp. 473–493).

Bartlett, H. M. (1958). Toward clarification. *Clinical Social Work, 5,* 363–366.

Bartlett, H. M. (1970). *Common Base of Social Work Practice.* Washington, DC: NASW.

Boehm, W. (1959). *Objective of the social work curriculum of the future.* New York: Council of Social Work Education.

Boland, K., Barton, J., & McNutt, J. (2002). Social work advocacy and the internet knowledge base. In S. Hick & J. McNutt (Eds.), *Advocacy, activism and the internet: Community organization and social policy* (pp. 19–31). Chicago: Lyceum.

Booze, A., & Hamilton, I. (1987). *The Maryland social work service job analysis and personnel qualification study.* Silver Springs, MD: National Association of Social Work.

Briar, S. (1977). In summary. *Social Work, 22*(5), 415–416.

Brieland, D., & Korr, W. S. (2000). Social work: Conceptual frameworks revisited. In J. G. Hopps & R. Morris (Eds.), *Social Work at the millennium: Critical reflections on the future of the profession* (pp. 123–137). New York: Free Press.

Bureau of Labor Statistics. (2000). *The occupational outlook handbook.* Washington, DC: Department of Labor. Retrieved November 2006, from www.bls.gov

Burwell, Y. (1994). North Carolina public welfare institutes for Negroes. *Journal of Sociology and Social Welfare, 21*(1), 55–65.

Byrd, M. W., & Clayton, F. (2000). *An American health dilemma: A medical history of African American and the problem of race, beginning to 1900.* New York, NY: Routledge.

Carlton-LeNay, L., & Hodges, V. (1994). The career of bridge of Henriette Haynes, a pioneer settlement house worker. *Social Service Review, 68,* 254–273.

Carlton-LeNay, L., & Hodges, V. (2004). African American reformers' mission: Caring for our girls and women. *AFFILIA, 19*(3), 257–272.

Costin, L., Karger, H., & Stoesz, D. (1996). *The politics of child abuse and neglect in America.* New York: Oxford University Press.

Curry, L. P. (1981). The poor you have always with you: Black poverty and urban welfare. *The free black in urban America 1800–1850.* Chicago: The University of Chicago Press.

Day, P. J. (2003). *A new history of social welfare* (4th ed.). Boston: Allyn & Bacon.

Devore, W., & Schlesginger, E. G. (1999). *Ethnic-sensitive social work practice* (5th ed.). Boston: Allyn & Bacon.

DiNitto, D. M. (2007). *Social welfare: Politics and public policy.* New York: Pearson Education, Inc.

Dolgoff, R., & Feldstein, C. (2007). *Understanding social welfare: A search for social justice* (7th ed.). Boston: Allyn and Bacon

Drew, P. (1983). *A longer view: The Mary Richmond legacy.* Baltimore: University of Maryland Press.

Duster, A. (Ed.). (1970). *Crusade for justice: The autobiography of Ida B. Wells. Negro American biographies and autobiographies.* Chicago: University of Chicago Press.

Ellett, A. J., Ellett, C. D., & Rugutt, J. K. (2003). *A study of personal and organizational factors contributing to employee retention and turnover in child welfare in Georgia.* Athens: University of Georgia.

Ellett, A. J., & Leighninger, L. (2007). What happened? An historical analysis of the de-professionalization of child welfare with implications for policy and practice. *Journal of Public Child Welfare, 1*(1), 3–34.

Figueria-McDonough, J. (1993). Policy practice: The neglected side of social work intervention. *Social Work, 38*(2), 179–188.

Figueira-McDonough, J. (2007). *The welfare state and social work: Pursuing social justice.* Thousand Oaks, CA: Sage.

Fox, S. R., Miller, V. P., & Barbee, A. P. (2003). Finding and keeping children welfare workers: Effective use of training and professional development. *Journal of Human Behavior of the Social Environment, 7*(1/2), 67–81.

Frazier, E. F. (1932). *The negro family in Chicago.* Chicago: University of Chicago Press.

Fred, S. (2005, November). Review of liability expansion sought, *NASW News,* p. 5.

Gambrill, E. (2003). Evidence-based practice: Implications for knowledge development and use in social works. In A. Rosen & E. Proctor (Eds.), *Developing practice guidelines for social work practice: Issues, methods and interventions* (pp. 37–58). New York: Columbia University Press.

Garvin, C. (1981). *Contemporary group work.* Englewood Cliffs, NJ: Prentice Hall.

Gibelman, M. (1999). The search for identity: Defining social work – past, present, and future. *Social Work, 44*(4), 298–307.

Gibelman, M., & Schervish, P. H. (1993). *Who we are: The social work labor force as reflected in the NASW membership.* Washington, DC: NASW Press.

Gibelman, M., & Schervish, P. H. (1997). *Who we are: The social work labor force as reflected in the NASW membership.* Washington, DC: NASW Press.

Gillens, M. (1999). *Why Americans hate welfare: Race, media and the politics of antipoverty policy.* Chicago: University of Chicago Press.

Glicken, M. D. (2007). *Social work in the 21st century.* Thousand Oaks, CA: Sage.

Gordon, W. E. (1962). A critique of the working definition, *Social Work, 7,* 3–13.

Hardcastle, D. (1981). The profession: Professional organizations, licensuring, and private practice. In N. Gilbert & H. Specht (Eds.), *Handbook of the social services* (p. 677). Englewood Cliffs: NJ: Prentice Hall.

Haynes, K. S., & Mickelson, J. S. (2003). *Affecting change: Social workers in the political arena* (5th ed.). Boston: Allyn & Bacon.

Helfgott, K. (1990). *Staffing the child welfare agency: Recruitment and retention.* Washington, DC: Child Welfare League of America, Inc.

Hopps, J. G. (2006). *Still striving: Challenges for board of trustees of historically black college.* Atlanta, GA: Southern Education Foundation.

Hopps, J. G., & Collins, P. M. (1995). Social work profession overview. In R. L. Edward (Ed.), *Encyclopedia of social work* (19th ed.). pp. 2266–2282. Washington, DC: NASW Press.

Hopps, J. G., & Lowe, T. B. (In press). Scope of social work practice. In B. White (Ed.), *The hand book of social work practice.* New York: Haworth Press.

Hopps, J. G., Pinderhughes, E., & Shankar, R. (1995). *The power to care: Clinical practice effectiveness with overwhelmed clients.* New York: Free Press.

Iatridis, C. (2000). State social welfare: Global perspective. In J. S. Hopps & R. Morris (Eds.), *Critical reflections on the future on the profession social work at the millennium.* pp. 207–221. New York: Free Press.

Jannson, B. (1990). *Social welfare policy: From theory to practice.* Belmont, CA: Wadsworth.

Karger, H., & Stoesz, D. (2002). *American social welfare policy: A pluralist approach* (4th ed.). Boston: Allyn & Bacon

Katz, M. G. (1986). In the shadow of the poorhouse: A social history of welfare in America (10th ed.). New York: Harper Collins Publishers.

Kilpatrick, D., & Parle, D. (2006, November 12). For conservatives its back to basis. Week in Review. Sunday, *New York Times,* Sec. 4, p. 11.

Korr, W., & Brieland, D. (2000). Social justice, human rights and welfare reform. In J. G. Hopps & R. Morris (Ed.), *Social work at the millennium.* New York: Free Press.

Larson, M. S. (1977). *The rise of professionalization: A sociological analysis.* Berkeley: University of California Press.

Lerner, G. (1974). Early community work of black club women. *The Journal of Negro History, 59*(2), 158–167.

Lincoln, C. E., & Mamiya, L. H. (1990). *The black church in African American experience.* Durham, NC: Duke University Press.

Lowe, T. B. (2006). Nineteenth century review of mental health care to African Americans: A legacy of service and policy barriers. *Journal of Sociology and Social Welfare, 234* pp. 7–27.

Lowe, T. B., & Hopps, J. G. (In press). African American's response to their social environment: A macro perspective.

In L. See (Ed.), *Human behavior in the social environment from an African American perspectives* (2nd ed.). New York: Haworth Press.

Lubove, R. (1965). *The professional altruist: The emergence of social work as a career, 1880–1930*. Cambridge, MA: Harvard University Press.

Meyer, C. H. (1976). *Social work practice* (2nd ed.). New York: Free Press.

Morris, R. (2000). Social work's century of evolution as a profession: Choices made, opportunities lost. From the individual and society to the individual. In J. G. Hopps & R. Morris (Eds.), *Social work at the millennium* (pp. 42–70).

National Association Social Workers. (1973). *Standards for social service manpower*. Washington, DC: Author.

National Association Social Workers (1981). *NASW code of ethics*. Washington, DC: Author.

National Association Social Workers (2006). Landmark study warns of impending labor force shortages for social work profession. Retrieved January 5, 2007, from http://www.workforce.socialworkers.org

O'Hare, T. (2005). *Evidence-based practices for social workers: An interdisciplinary approach*. Chicago, IL: Lyceum Books, Inc.

Olds, V. (1963). The Freedmen's Bureau: A nineteenth-century federal welfare agency. *Social Casework, 44*(5), 247–254.

Pace, P. (November, 2005) Hawaii shields title. *NASW News*, p. 9.

Pincus, A., & Minahan, A. (1977). Conceptual frameworks for social work practice. *Social Work, 22*, 347–352.

Pinderhughes, E. (1995). Direct practice overview. In R. L. Edward (Ed.), *Encyclopedia of social work* (19th ed., pp. 740–751). Washington, DC: NASW Press.

Piven, F. F., & Cloward, R. A. (1971). *Regulating the poor: The functions of welfare*. New York: Pantheon.

Pollard, W. (1978). *A study of black self-help*. San Francisco: R & E Research Associates, Inc.

Ragland, L. (2006, July 29). Homeownership up among blacks. *Atlanta Journal and Constitution*, E4.

Reid, W. J. (1997). Long-term trends in clinical social work. *Social Service Review, 71*(2), 200–213.

Sabbath, T. F. (1994). Social work services and social work training for African Americans in Philadelphia, Pennsylvania 1900–1930. *Journal of Sociology & Social Welfare, 21*(1), 83–95.

Saleeby, D. (2002). *The strengths perspective in social work practice* (3rd ed.). Boston: Allyn & Bacon.

Schiele, J. H. (2000). *Human services and the Afrocentric paradigm*. New York: Haworth Press.

Schwartz, W. (1961). The social worker in the group. *The New Perspective on service to group: Theory, Organization, and Practice*, pp. 7–340, New York: NASW.

See, L. A. (Ed.). (2001). *Violence as seen through a prism of color*. New York: Haworth Press.

Siporin, M. (1975). *Introduction to social work practice*. New York: Macmillian.

Solomon, B. B. (2002). Social work practice with African Americans. In A. T. Morales & B. W. Sheafor (Eds.), *The many faces of social work clients* (pp. 295–315). Boston: Allyn and Bacon.

Stoesen, L. (2006). Social work congress report issued, *NASW News, 51*(4), p. 1.

Stoesen, L., & Moss, S. (2006). Workforce study results released, *NASW News, 51*(4), p. 1.

Thyer, B. A. (2004). Science and evidence-based social work practice. In H. E. Briggs & T. L. Rzepnicki (Eds.), *Using evidence in social work practice: Behavioral perspectives* (pp. 54–65). Chicago: Lyceum Books.

Trevino, R. R. (2003). Facing Jim crow: Catholic sisters and the "Mexican problem" in Texas. *The Western Historical Quarterly, 34*(2), 139–164.

Tucker, D. J. (2000). Eclecticism is not a free good: Barriers to knowledge development in social work. In J. G. Hopps & R. Morris (Eds.), *Critical reflections on the future of the profession: Social work at the millennium* (pp. 225–248). New York: Free Press.

U.S. Department of Health and Human Services. (1998). *Mental Health, United States, 1998* (Publication No. 99–3285). Washington, DC: Substance Abuse and Mental Service Health Administration.

*Wall Street Journal*. (2006, December 20). The top 1% pay 35% [Editorial]. p. A.18.

Wisner, E. (1970). *Social welfare in the south: From the colonial times to world war I*. Baton Rouge: Louisiana State University Press.

Wood, P. H. (1978). Black resistance: The stono uprising and its consequences. In J. K. Martin (Ed.), *Interpreting colonial American: Selected readings* (2nd ed.). New York: Harper & Row Publisher, Inc.

—JUNE GARY HOPPS AND TONY B. LOWE

## HISTORY

**ABSTRACT:** The social work profession originated in volunteer efforts to address the "social question," the paradox of increasing poverty in an increasingly productive and prosperous economy, in Europe and North America during the late nineteenth century. By 1900, working for social betterment had become an occupation and social work achieved professional status by 1930. By 1920, social workers could be found in hospitals and public schools, as well as in child welfare agencies, family agencies, and settlement hoses. During the next decade, social work focused on the problems of children and families. As a result of efforts to conceptualize social work method, expand social work education programs, and develop a stable funding base for voluntary social service programs, social work achieved professional status by the 1930s. The Great Depression and World War II refocused professional concerns, as the crises of depression and war demanded the attention of social workers. After the war, mental health concerns became important as programs for veterans and the general public emphasized the provision of inpatient and outpatient mental health services. In the 1960s, social workers again confronted the problem of poverty. Since then, the number of social workers has grown even as the profession's influence on social welfare policy has waned.

**KEY WORDS:** social work; profession; professionalization; personal service; social services

Originating in volunteer efforts for social betterment in the late 19th century in Europe and North America, social work became an occupation by the turn of the 20th century and achieved professional status by the 1920s. Social work began as one of several attempts to address the "social question," the paradox of increasing poverty in an increasingly productive and prosperous economy. Social workers focused on the problems of children and families in the 1920s, achieving professional status as a personal service profession by the 1930s, as a result of the growth of professional organizations, educational programs, and publications (Walker, 1933). But depression and war refocused professional concerns, as the crises of the Great Depression and World War II demanded the attention of social workers. After the war, mental health concerns became important as programs for veterans and the general public emphasized the provision of inpatient and outpatient mental health services. In the 1960s, social workers again confronted the problem of poverty and continued to grow as a profession, so that by the 21st century social work was licensed in all 50 states. Since then, the number of social workers has grown even as the profession's influence on social welfare policy has waned.

### The Emergence of the Social Question

During the late 19th century, industrialization created an urban society in a globalizing economy. Steam power fueled an expansion of industrial production and revolutionized transportation, resulting in expedited communication and the worldwide movement of capital, manufactured goods, and people. Cities in the industrializing societies of Europe and North America grew larger and social problems seemed to reach a critical level, as industrial economies produced new problems—unemployment, neglected and abandoned children, chronic disability, and poverty in the midst of unprecedented wealth. While the United States remained a predominantly rural society, big cities seemed to portend the future, and many reacted with horror to the apparent misery of the urban poor—and to their potential for disruption (Bremner, 1956; Rodgers, 1998).

In the United States, interest in the social question, as concern with urban problems and the consequences of industrialization came to be known, had both religious and rationalistic roots. The sentimental reformism that had informed antislavery efforts before the Civil War turned to the problems of the poor, particularly children. In charity organization, child saving, and the settlements, religious people campaigned for reform in assistance to the poor. Later, Protestant ministers professed a Social Gospel, proclaiming that Christians had a duty to campaign for social reform. Roman Catholic reformers heeded Pope Leo XIII's encyclical *Rerum Novarum* (1891), which called for justice in the relations between capital and labor. Jews in Germany and the United States embraced a reform movement that emphasized social justice. But the development of big business and its increasing reliance on technology and new models of formal organization also suggested directions for reform: modern charity work would be scientific and would borrow organizational structures from the emerging corporate world.

Boards of Charity, composed of prominent citizens who served without pay, attempted to rationalize state residential institutions created before the Civil War. Rational administration meant careful budgeting, civil service rules, and the collection of data on the performance of state institutions. Board members visited and inspected state institutions—mental hospitals, prisons, orphanages, and schools for persons with a variety of disabilities—and made recommendations for more efficient management. Beginning with Massachusetts in 1862, most states established boards of charities during the last third of the 19th century. Most boards had an advisory function, while others (usually called Boards of Control) had administrative oversight over state institutions.

In the nation's large cities, child saving movements sought to improve the lives of orphans and poor children. Protestant minister Charles Loring Brace founded the New York Children's Aid Society (CAS) in 1853. Over the next half century, the CAS initiated a variety of child saving measures, notably the orphan trains, which placed poor New York children with Christian farm families in the Midwest. The orphan train movement stimulated the development of Jewish and Catholic orphanages and the child saving movement soon outgrew its origins. Orphanage care of children increased during the late 19th century as states attempted to end the practice of placing children in poorhouses. By the turn of the century, reformers contemplated a mixed system of care for dependent children, involving both public and private institutions, community placement as well as institutional care, and preventive legislation, including laws regulating or prohibiting child labor and requiring school attendance.

In the 1880s, two new institutions were created that would be formative in creating a new occupation to provide assistance to the poor. Most large American cities, beginning in Buffalo in 1877, established charity organization societies (COS), modeled on the London Charity Organisation Society. Charity organization emphasized a controlled form of love extended to the poor. An organization of voluntary charities rather than a provider of direct material assistance, the COS organized a city's voluntary relief associations on a rational basis. District agents, paid COS employees, interviewed applicants for relief, determined appropriate assistance, and arranged for friendly visits by volunteers. The visitors provided good advice and an example of caring, while the district agents curbed potential abuse. During the 1880s, most COS work was done by volunteers called "friendly visitors." By the 1890s, however, paid employees supplanted volunteers (Lubove, 1965). COS also became increasingly active in environmental work. In 1898, the New York COS established the Summer School of Applied Philanthropy, which later became the New York School of Philanthropy (1904). The school was renamed the New York School of Social Work in 1919 and became part of Columbia University in 1940, becoming the Columbia University School of Social Work in 1963.

Settlement houses, also based on an English model, were established in large cities in the United States during the 1880s. Jane Addams and Ellen Gates Starr founded Chicago's Hull House, the most famous settlement in the United States, in 1889 after a visit to London's Toynbee Hall, the first settlement house. Settlement workers were middle-class and affluent volunteers who "settled" in the immigrant districts of large cities. The settlements have provided a vital service, Addams believed, both for the volunteer residents, who needed a purpose in life, and for the society at large, by building needed bridges between the classes in an increasingly stratified and fragmented society (Addams, 1893).

Members of the existing state boards of charities members began to meet in 1874 as a section of the American Social Science Association. In 1879, the group formed its own organization, the Conference of Boards of Public Charities, which became the National Conference of Charities and Correction in 1880 and the National Conference of Social Work in 1917. Although the conference was initially an annual gathering of the members of state boards, child savers, COS workers, and settlement house residents, many others interested in the social question, became active in the organization. For much of the 20th century, the National Conference was the major meeting place for social workers (Bruno, 1957).

## Social Work as an Occupation

By the first decade of the 20th century, a separate occupational status for charity workers had emerged. Schools of charity or philanthropy in five cities provided training to members of the new occupation. COS visitors, child care workers, and settlement house residents were joined by social workers in new settings—big city general hospitals, public schools, psychiatric clinics, and juvenile courts. Although the methods to be used by the new occupation were hardly defined, the emerging methods and techniques were applied to new populations in these new settings. The decade also saw the beginnings of investment in the new occupation, with the founding of the Russell Sage Foundation in 1907. For its first 40 years, the foundation supported the development of a profession of social work.

Career COS administrator Mary Richmond joined the new Russell Sage Foundation in 1908 as director of its Charity Organization Department. During the next 20 years, she and fellow staff member Francis McLean transformed charity organization. They worked on two fronts—the organizational and the conceptual. McLean worked with COS to form a new national organization, the National Association of Societies for Organizing Charity, in 1911. Richmond worked to develop the conceptual base for social case work, which would become the primary method for social work practice with individuals and families. The foundation published Richmond's *Social Diagnosis*, which quickly became an authoritative text, in 1917; in 1919, the National Association of Societies for Organizing Charity changed its name to the American Association for Organizing Family Social Work and in 1930 to the Family Welfare Association of America.

In addition to its efforts in charity organization, the Russell Sage Foundation supported the developing field of child welfare. A Child Welfare Department, headed by Hastings Hart, consulted with states on legislation and services for children. Campaigns for the codification of state laws on children, the Children's Code, energized child savers on the state level, as states codified the laws on children, adding or strengthening provisions regulating child labor, requiring school attendance, establishing juvenile courts, and providing payments for children in single parent households. In 1909, President Theodore Roosevelt called the first White House Conference on Dependent Children. The conference called for the creation of a Children's

Bureau in the federal government "to investigate and report... upon all matters pertaining to the welfare of children." Congress established the Children's Bureau in 1912. Eight years later, in 1920, child welfare agency executives founded the Child Welfare League of America.

World War I, the United States' first European war, resulted in an expansion of the social work profession both in numbers and in scope. The Red Cross's Home Service provided linkage between soldiers and other service personnel and their families. Richmond was involved in training home service workers, who provided social case work services to rural and small town families for the first time. Other war-related charities also expanded, as did the Army Medical Corps. Faced with a variety of psychological and neurological problems, the army used social workers, many of whom were Red Cross personnel detailed to army units in the field. Smith College established its School for Social Work in 1918 as a wartime measure. Graduates provided services to soldiers and veterans suffering from shell shock and other psychiatric disabilities. The war also resulted in an increase in social planning. Social worker Mary van Kleeck temporarily left the Russell Sage Foundation to help set up the Women in Industry Service in the U.S. Department of Labor.

### From Occupation to Profession

Social work education programs expanded during the years 1913–1919 and more rapidly during the next decade, as a result of changes in charity organization and the expansion of hospital social work, school social work, and child welfare. Educator Abraham Flexner's conclusion in a paper read at the National Conference of Charities and Correction in 1915 that social work was not a profession because it lacked original jurisdiction and an educationally transmissible technique stimulated the development of social work theory. During the 15 years following the delivery of the paper, professional education flourished. Schools of social work were established in the South and the West as well as in the Northeast and Midwest. Professional organizations and national federations of agencies were established and engaged in explorations of social work practice theory.

Perhaps the most important development of the 1920s was the expansion of federated fundraising. Before World War I, most social work agencies had survived by soliciting subscriptions and contributions from wealthy donors. Such financing was often unreliable, and fluctuations in agency budgets were not unusual. During World War I, a united "War Chest" raised money for war-related charities in many American

cities. After the war, these war chests were converted to Community Chests, local agencies that raised money for the community's social work agencies, usually through an annual campaign that solicited funds from middle-class and working people as well as the wealthy. With its annual campaign targeted on a broad base of potential donors, incremental budgeting, and generally successful fund drives, the community chest provided voluntary agencies with financial stability during the 1920s. Although some social workers objected to the "stereotyped social work" that resulted from the budgeting process, most cities had adopted the Community Chest idea by the end of the decade.

Public social services had expanded enough by 1923 that a prominent social welfare administrator could write about a transformation "from charities and correction to public welfare" (Kelso, 1923). Most professional social work, however, was practiced in voluntary agencies. Social workers did practice in some correctional agencies, particularly in juvenile corrections and in law enforcement, during the 1920s. State hospitals and outpatient programs employed social workers as well. The Commonwealth Fund supported child guidance clinics, new children's mental health clinics staffed by social workers and other professionals, and school social work demonstration projects. The federal Sheppard-Towner Act of 1921 established a maternal and child health program of grants to the states administered by social workers in the Children's Bureau. State children's code campaigns resulted in the creation of statewide child welfare and public assistance programs in many states during the decade.

By the end of the decade, voluntary social work had a stable financial base, social workers had created a number of professional organizations, and public social services had expanded. In his 1929 presidential address to the National Conference of Social Work, social work educator Porter R. Lee could say that social work "once a cause" had become "a function of a well-ordered society." The project of professionalization now seemed complete, although Lee worried about how to maintain zeal in an increasingly routinized profession. The 1930 Census, which classified social work as a profession for the first time, enumerated over 30,000 social workers in the United States, but only 5,600 of them were members of the American Association of Social Workers, the largest professional organization of social workers (Walker, 1933).

### The Great Depression:
### A Crisis for the New Profession

The worldwide economic contraction that began in 1929 resulted in economic and social crises as the demand for products slackened, workers lost their jobs, and political unrest toppled established governments around the world. In Europe, a fascist takeover of the German government led to the emigration of many, including leading social workers like Maida Solomon, to the United States and elsewhere. Ultimately, the worldwide depression of the 1930s resulted in a World War II, which began in 1939 with the German invasion of Poland.

In the United States, voluntary and state-supported social welfare services contracted in response to reductions in funding. Community Chest donations declined in the early years of the Great Depression, and over one-third of the nation's voluntary social service agencies closed. Other agencies contracted with local governments to provide relief to the swelling ranks of the unemployed. The slowing economy resulted in declining tax receipts for property and sales taxes, making it difficult for state and local governments to meet increasing demands for unemployment relief. Cities that had resisted the Community Chest movement, notably Boston, Chicago, and New York, turned to federated fund raising to broaden the pool of potential donors. The federal government began to support state and local relief efforts, first with loans to the states beginning in 1932 during the Hoover administration and then with grants for unemployment relief during the Roosevelt administration.

Herbert Hoover, who served as president in the early years of the depression (1929–1933), increased the federal budget but wanted states and the voluntary sector to take the lead in relief. In contrast, the Roosevelt administration, while it enlisted state governments, favored a strong federal role. President Franklin D. Roosevelt took office in 1933, promising a "New Deal" for the American people—a more vigorous federal government and renewed experimentation in recovery efforts. Roosevelt's Federal Emergency Relief administrator, Harry Hopkins, a social worker with a background in the administration of both public and voluntary agencies, required that states receiving federal grants for unemployment relief establish public agencies to administer the relief program, ending the practice of contracting with voluntary agencies (Trattner, 1999). In response, the general director of the Family Welfare Association of America charted a new course for private social work. Public agencies should provide relief to the unemployed while voluntary family agencies should concentrate on casework services for "disorganized families"(Swift, 1934).

The Social Security Act (1935) established a federal old age insurance program and state programs, supervised and partially funded by the federal government of unemployment insurance, public assistance, and social services. States pressed new employees, most of them without social work experience, into service in the rapidly expanding state welfare systems. States established training programs and many state universities introduced undergraduate social work education programs. The established schools of social work, concentrated in urban areas and often in private universities, increasingly emphasized graduate education. Two social work education organizations, the American Association of Schools of Social Work (AASSW) and the National Association of Schools of Social Administration (NASSA), representing the two movements in social work education, attempted to represent education for the new profession.

While NASSA supported undergraduate education, the AASSW emphasized graduate education; in 1939, AASSW restricted membership to graduate programs. During the next few years, the master of social work (MSW) became the standard professional degree. To some in social work education, it appeared that two social work professions were emerging, a graduate profession based on the MSW degree and a baccalaureate profession based on the acquisition of a baccalaureate degree. While many MSWs continued to work in the voluntary social service sector, opportunities for public employment increased during the 1930s, as states implemented the services titles of the Social Security Act.

Social workers developed new conceptualizations of social work practice methods during the 1930s. Different branches of psychoanalytic casework, influenced by psychiatrists Otto Rank and Sigmund Freud, contested for dominance in social case work. Group workers and community organizers attempted to conceptualize their methods by sponsoring special sessions at the National Conference of Social Work in 1935 and 1939. The 1935 group work sessions resulted in the creation of a new group work organization, the Association for the Study of Group Work, and the 1939 session on community organization eventually led to another new organization, the Association for the Study of Community Organization.

## Maturation

The United States entered the World War II in December 1941 after an attack on Pearl Harbor in Hawaii by the Japanese Navy. By then the war was already being fought worldwide and some refugees from Hitler's Europe found sanctuary in the United States. Some, like Werner Boehm, had not been social workers in Europe but would become leaders in social work practice and education after the war. The growth of army camps and war-related industries ended the depression and disrupted community life even before the United States entered the war. Congress passed the Lanham Act of 1940 to provide assistance for war-impacted communities. Veteran social workers like Bertha Reynolds, who worked for the Personal Service Department of the National Maritime Union, devoted themselves to war work even as she challenged the direction of the profession. New social workers were recruited to war-related social work services.

Wars bring about psychological crises for service members whether they are called shell shock (World War I), battlefield neurosis (World War II), or posttraumatic stress disorder (Vietnam and Iraq wars). During World War II, the Army Medical Corps developed psychiatric social work as a service for service men and women suffering from war-related psychological trauma. In 1944, Congress enacted the Servicemen's Readjustment Act, or G.I. Bill, which provided health care, home and business loans, and postsecondary education loans for veterans of World War II. The Act, which some hailed as "completing the New Deal," created the postwar middle class by making home ownership and college education available to veterans. The G.I. Bill also resulted in an expansion of the Veterans Administration (VA) hospital system. Social work was an important part of the VA health care system, which planners hoped would model an efficient public health system for the nation.

Congress enacted new social legislation after World War II. The National Mental Health Act (1946) created the National Institute of Mental Health (NIMH). Opportunities for social workers in health and mental health expanded as a result of the Hill-Burton Hospital Construction Act of 1946, the creation of NIMH, and the expansion of the VA Hospital System. The United States signed the charter of the United Nations in 1945, creating an international body that provided an arena for international exchange. Social workers in the United States were eager to share their expertise with development programs in war-ravaged Europe and Asia and later with developing nations in an era of decolonization. Unfortunately, the models were sometimes based on what was effective in the United States, with little effort to adapt to local conditions (Midgley, 2005). Social work in the late 1940s was a fragmented profession. Practitioners working in different fields of practice emphasized the special skills and knowledge needed by specialists, so that graduate education emphasized specialized rather than generic content. Separate education organizations accredited undergraduate and graduate programs. Many believed that the social work profession needed to speak with one voice.

A movement for generic casework practice, initiated at the University of Chicago by Charlotte Towle, appeared to have promise for unifying social work practice. Social work practice organizations and social work education organizations amalgamated. In 1947, NASSA and AASSW formed a National Council on Social Work Education to explore professional unification. A study of social work education was commissioned, conducted by adult educator Ernest W. Hollis and social work educator Alice Taylor. The Hollis–Taylor Report, as the study was known, appeared in 1951; the following year, NASSA and AASSW merged to form the Council on Social Work Education (CSWE). CSWE moved quickly to require graduate status and university affiliation for institutional membership—social work would be a graduate profession.

Social work practitioner organizations presented a more confusing picture. The American Association of Social Workers (AASW), organized in 1921, attempted to represent all social workers, but specialized practitioner organizations existed for medical social workers (organized in 1918), school social workers (1919), psychiatric social workers (1926), group workers (1936), community organizers (1946), and researchers (1949). Several interorganizational committees met during the early 1950s to develop an agreement for a single social work practitioner organization. Although the early committees included the AASSW as a nonvoting member, consolidation of the education and practitioner organizations was not pursued. In 1955, the 7 practitioner and researcher organizations joined to form the National Association of Social Workers (NASW), which had 22,000 members after the merger.

In 1958, an NASW Commission on Social Work Practice issued a Working Definition of Social Work Practice to provide a generic definition of social work practice (Bartlett, 1958). CSWE commissioned a comprehensive study of the social work curriculum, directed by Werner Boehm. Published in 1959, the 13 volume *Curriculum Study* included volumes on undergraduate education; specialized practice methods—administration, community organization, group work, and casework; fields of practice—corrections, public social services, and rehabilitation; and curriculum areas—human growth and behavior, research, social welfare policy and services, and values and ethics (Boehm, 1959). The intent of both efforts was to unify social work by providing a common set of concepts and educational experiences.

### The Profession Broadens
In 1955, the Mental Health Study Act (PL 84–182) created the Joint Commission on Mental Illness and

Health. The commission issued *Action for Mental Health* (1961), a report that called for renewed investment in mental health. The new liberal Kennedy administration in 1961 proposed an expansion in community mental health, based on the report and California's experience with community mental health centers. The Community Mental Health Centers Act (PL 88–164), enacted by Congress in 1963, provided grants-in-aid, dministered by NIMH, to states for local Community Mental Health Centers that would serve mentally ill persons outside of state facilities. By the end of the decade, social workers provided the majority of mental health care in the United States.

The Kennedy administration initiated other projects, notably in public welfare and delinquency prevention. After Kennedy delivered a special message on Public Welfare, Congress enacted the Public Welfare Amendments of 1963 (PL 87–543) to the Social Security Act, which provided funds to the states for training social workers to work in state public welfare programs. The act increased opportunities for public welfare personnel to enter MSW programs and resulted in expanded opportunities in public welfare programs for professional social workers. Two years later, a federal task force projected increased need for social work personnel and called for additional investment in social work education, including the development of undergraduate education for social work (U. S. Task Force on Social Work Education and Manpower, 1965).

President Kennedy's Committee on Juvenile Delinquency provided demonstration grants for antidelinquency programs. The example of the President's Committee led the new Johnson administration to propose a War on Poverty in 1964. A vigorous antipoverty program would be directed by quasi-public entities. Some social workers were involved in the design of the program, while others looked askance at its nonprofessional, some thought antiprofessional, approach to solving the problem of poverty. Voluntary social service agencies found new opportunities for contracting to provide services to the poor, from community organization to family counseling. Under President Johnson, a federal health insurance program for the elderly, Medicare, and a health assistance program for the poor, Medicaid, which was to be state administered, were passed by Congress as Titles XVIII and XIX of the Social Security Act, along with the Older Americans Act (PL 89–73) in 1965.

The effect of the expansion of government social welfare services during the Great Depression and after World War II was to shift the most important source of funding and practice for social work from the voluntary, nonprofit sector to the public sector,

particularly toward health and mental health programs. Other sectors, such as corrections and child welfare, medicalized their approaches, as talk of treatment for offenders and dependent children began to dominate professional discourse in these areas.

The increasing complexity of the emerging welfare state resulted in an increasing emphasis on of policy, planning, and administration in social work curricula and in practice. Many programs in the Kennedy–Johnson era, from the antidelinquency programs of the Kennedy years to the community action, older Americans, and Model Cities programs of the Johnson administration, relied on increasingly complex federal relationships with state and local governments managed by community planners, many with social work credentials. If the decade was contentious, the social work profession seemed vibrant during the 1960s. In 1966, the membership of NASW reached nearly 46,000, doubling its membership in its first decade.

### Social Work in a Conservative Era

In 1969, NASW, which had previously required the MSW for full membership, opened full membership to individuals with a baccalaureate degree from programs approved by CSWE. In doing so, NASW endorsed the conclusion of the Task Force on Social Work Education and Manpower that baccalaureate social work education was needed to fill the many social work positions created by the expansion of social welfare programs in the 1960s. CSWE subsequently developed standards and accreditation procedures for undergraduate social work programs. It seemed that the goal of NASSA for recognition of the undergraduate degree had been achieved. However, some believed that recognition of the BSW had "deprofessionalized" social work.

Federal spending for social welfare increased during the 1970s, but employment for social workers stagnated as a result of several related trends (Patterson, 2000). Congress and the Nixon administration favored "hard" services, such as material provisions, over such "soft" services as counseling. Hard services could be provided by anyone, many believed, resulting in reduced demand for MSWs and even BSWs. State public welfare departments separated social services from public assistance payments, reversing the logic of the 1963 Public Welfare Amendments. State and local public social service agencies reclassified jobs to require a BSW rather than an MSW—and sometimes any or no baccalaureate degree rather than a BSW. Often justified as cost-saving measures, these changes, which were particularly important in public child welfare services, limited employment opportunities for professional social workers even as they reduced the quality of services for client. By the 1970s, many social services were provided by private or quasi-public agencies or by private practitioners under contract to public authorities rather than by public agency employees.

These trends were exacerbated during the 1980s as the Reagan administration used the block grant mechanism to "return power to the states" while reducing federal commitments for social service spending. Many conservatives around Reagan were suspicious of social workers, whom they viewed as misguided philanthropists, harming poor people even as they attempted to assist them. In response, social work practitioner organizations lobbied for legal regulation. Licensing by the state, accomplished to varying degrees in all of the states by the 1990s, would assure the public of quality social services while increasing the demand for licensed social workers, advocates believed. Licensing also facilitated the growth of private practice, as in many states it provided standards for independent practice. In 1988, the Director of NIMH appointed a Task Force on Social Work Research to study the status of research and research training in social work. The Task Force Report, published in 1991, recommended the creation of an Institute for the Advancement of Social Work (IASWR) and increased attention to social work research by NIMH, CSWE, and NASW (Task Force on Social Work Research, 1991).

Despite a new democratic administration in Washington, the trends of the 1980s continued during the Clinton administration—growth in government contracting with nonprofit and for profit organizations, increasing reliance on third-party payments, and privatization of social services. In spite of the creation of IASWR in 1993 and of a new national organization for social work researchers, the Society for Social Work and Research (SSWR) in 1994, social work was largely ignored when Congress enacted the Personal Responsibility and Work Opportunity Reconciliation Act of 1996 (PL 104–193), eliminating the 40-year-old entitlement aid to families with dependent children, and instead imposed work requirements and time limits for the receipt of public assistance now known as TANF (temporary aid for needy families).

As the 21st century began, new organizations of practitioners, educators, and researchers had arisen to complement CSWE and NASW, creating a situation reminiscent of the 1940s. Research, increasingly emphasized by social work educators, did not seem to influence social work practice, signaling a potentially dangerous division between academics and practitioners. NASW held a Social Work Summit in 2002 bringing together 43 different social work organizations to begin discussing coalitions and collaborative undertakings, and a Social Work Congress in 2005 to identify common goals for the next 10 years.

## Challenges and Trends

Although the social work profession seemed fragmented, a number of organizations of practitioners and educators were able to work together on interorganizational projects to promote social work research and focus the profession's political advocacy activities. The number of social work education programs at the BSW and MSW levels grew during the last decade of the 20th century and continue in early 21st century. By 2004, there were nearly 400 social work education programs in the United States, including 239 baccalaureate programs, 47 masters programs, and 111 combined (baccalaureate and masters) programs (Council on Social Work Education, 2007). Over 800,000 people in the United States identified themselves as social workers. However, many of those employed as social workers were not professionally educated. Of over 400,000 licensed social workers, less than half belong to NASW. The Bureau of Labor Statistics predicted that the number of positions would increase more rapidly than the average for all occupations, particularly as the population aged. During the first decade of the 21st century, social workers were uncertain about the profession's mission and its relationship to the welfare state. Fragmentation, together with privatization, deprofessionalization, and competition with other professions in a shrinking human service arena, provided challenges for the profession.

### REFERENCES

Addams, J. (1893). *Philanthropy and Social Progress.* New York: T. Y. Crowell.

Bartlett, H. M. (1958). Toward clarification and improvement of social work practice. *Social Work, 3*(2), 3–9.

Boehm, W. W. (Ed.). (1959). *The curriculum study* (Vols. 1–13). New York: Council on Social Work Education.

Council on Social Work Education. (2007). *Statistics on Social Work Education in the United States: 2004.* Alexandria, VA: CSWE.

Hollis, E. V., & Taylor, A. L. (1951). *Social work education in the United States: The report of a study made for the national council on social work education.* New York: Columbia University Press.

Joint Commission on Mental Illness and Health. (1961). *Action for mental health: Final report.* New York: Basic Books.

Kelso, R. W. (1923). The transition from charities and correction to public welfare. *Annals of the American Academy of Political and Social Science, 105,* 21–25.

Lee, P. R. (1929). Social work: Cause and function. National conference of social work, *Proceedings, 56,* 3–20.

Midgley, J. (2006). International social welfare. In *Encyclopedia of Social Welfare History in North America,* edited by

J. M. Herrick and P. H. Stuart. (pp. 198–203.) Thousand Oaks, CA: Sage Publications.

Richmond, M. E. (1917). *Social diagnosis*. New York: Russell Sage Foundation.

Swift, Linton B. (1934). *New Alignments between Public and Private Agencies in a Community Family Welfare and Relief Program*. New York: Family Welfare Association of America.

Task Force on Social Work Research. (1991). *Building Social Work Knowledge for Effective Services and Policies: A Plan for Research Development*. Austin, TX: Task Force on Social Work Research.

Trattner, W. I. (1999). *From Poor Law to Welfare State*, 6th edition. New York: Free Press.

U.S. Task Force on Social Work Education and Manpower. (1965). *Closing the gap in social work manpower: Report of the departmental task force on social work education and manpower*. Washington, DC: U.S. Government Printing Office.

### FURTHER READING

Huff, D. (n.d.). *The social work history station*. Retrieved November 18, 2097, from http://www.boisiestate.edu/socialwork/dhuff/central/core.htm. Leiby, J. (1978). *A history of social welfare and social work in the United States*. New York: Columbia University Press.

Leighninger, L. (1988). *Social work: Search for identity*. Westport, CT: Greenwood Press.

Lubove, R. (1965). *The professional Altruist: The emergence of social work as a career, 1880–1930*. Cambridge, MA: Harvard University Press.

Maas, H. S. (1951). *Adventure in mental health: Psychiatric social work with the armed forces during world war II*. New York: Columbia University Press.

National Conference on Social Welfare. (1874–1982). *Proceedings* [Electronic resource]. Retrieved November 18, 2007, from http://www.quod.lib.umich.edu/n/ncosw/ (Also called: Conference of Boards of Public Charities, 1874; Conference of Charities, 1875–1879; Conference of Charities and Correction, 1880–1881; National Conference of Charities and Correction, 1882–1916; National Conference of Social Work, 1917–1956; National Conference on Social Welfare, 1957–1982.).

National Institutes of Health. (2005). *NIH history* [Electronic resource]. Retrieved November 18, 2007, from http://www.nih.gov/about/history.htm

Odum, H. W. (1933). Public welfare activities. In *Recent social trends in the United States: Report of the president's research committee on social trends* (Vol. 2, pp. 1224–1273). New York: McGraw-Hill.

Reynolds, B. C. (1971). *Social work and social living: Explorations in philosophy and practice. NASW classics series*. Washington, DC: National Association of Social Workers (originally published 1951).

Social Security Administration. (2007). *Social security online: Social security history* [Electronic resource]. Retrieved November 18, 2007, from http://www.ssa.gov/history/history.html.

Trattner, W. I. (1999). *From poor law to welfare state: A history of social welfare in America* (6th ed.). New York: The Free Press.

Walker, S. H. (1933). Privately supported social work. In *Recent social trends in the United States: Report of the president's research committee on social trends* (vol. 2, pp. 1168–1223). New York: McGraw-Hill.

Wenocur, S., & Reisch, M. (1989). *From charity to enterprise: The development of American social work in a market economy*. Urbana: University of Illinois Press.

—PAUL H. STUART

## WORKFORCE

**ABSTRACT:** A profession's ability to identify and predict its workforce capacity depends largely upon its understanding of labor market trends and emerging service delivery systems. Concerns about the adequacy of the future supply of the social work workforce are being driven by a number of factors, including trends in social work education and demographic shifts in the country. The stability and continuity of a social work workforce depends on the profession's ability to attract new workers; agencies' abilities to retain their staff; and the larger society's investment in this pool of workers, and the clients they serve.

**KEY WORDS:** workforce; labor force; trends; shortage; retiring; recruiting; retention

### Background Overview

A profession's *labor force* includes people who are both employed and unemployed, whereas the *workforce* refers only to the actual number of workers, excluding those who are unemployed. As defined by the profession, the social work labor force is composed of individuals who have undergraduate or graduate degrees from programs accredited by the Council on Social Work Education. This council maintains educational policy standards and provides accreditation of professional social work education programs in the United States. The National Association of Social Workers (NASW) promulgates standards for professional practice in many areas of social work, offers credentials and certifications that define areas of expertise, and establishes a code of ethics to guide practitioners in their work with individuals, families, and communities. Educational policy and practice standards serve as foundation documents for the profession that explicate core knowledge, skills, and values as well as elaborate the roles, functions, and scope of practice according to education and experience (Council on Social Work Education, 2001; National Association of Social Workers [NASW], 2007a).

The nature of social work practice and the actual tasks performed by social workers have been extensively described and documented by examining traditional fields of social work practice (Gibelman, 2005) and by actual task studies (Teare & Sheafor, 1995). Despite the diversity of practice settings and roles, social work tasks have been clustered under four primary functions: (a) enhance problem-solving, coping, and development of capacities of people; (b) link people with systems that provide resources, services, and opportunities; (c) promote effective and humane operations of systems; and (d) develop and improve social policy (NASW, 1981). These functions are carried out within a values framework that is articulated in the NASW's *Code of Ethics*. Social work practice, like other professions, is legally regulated by all state jurisdictions as well as the District of Columbia by the Association of Social Work Boards.

Although the study of social work practitioners is complex because of the many areas of specialization, levels of practice, and settings in which social work services are provided, several studies of sectors within the profession provide a detailed and fairly consistent description of social work practice and the evolving role of the profession in the provision of human services. Several descriptive studies have also been conducted using the entire NASW membership database (Gibelman and Schervish, 1993, 1997; NASW, 1987).

In some cases, the study has been of the entire NASW membership, and in other cases, it has been of subsets of the membership in order to examine fields of practice such as child welfare, behavioral health, or aging. Variations in study methodologies do not permit precise trend analyses; however, these studies have provided useful insights into practitioner demographics, practice settings, roles, and compensation, and have revealed clear indications of changing dynamics in service delivery systems and within practice specializations. Significant themes include the following:

- The movement of social workers from public agency auspice to private, nonprofit auspice
- The increasing numbers of social workers in private practice, either part-time or full-time
- The lack of sufficient progress in the recruitment of a more racially diverse workforce
- Enduring salary inequities between women and men, despite the profession's increased female dominance
- Increasing identification of behavioral health and mental health as practice specialization.

## Characteristics of Workforce

Extensive detailed information is collected by the U.S. Census Bureau with its Current Population Studies (CPS) used by many researchers to analyze economic and social conditions. However, a major limitation of CPS data is that individual respondents define their occupation. Among those who say that their occupation is social work, almost 30% do not have a college degree and 10% have received no college instruction (Barth, 2003). CPS data from 2000 report 845,000 persons who declare social work as their occupation. Previous investigators have pointed to these gaps in data sources that complicate attempts by the profession and workforce planners to accurately forecast the supply and demand of social workers (Barth, 2003).

The U.S. Department of Labor's Bureau of Labor Statistics provides the most current data on persons employed in social work positions as well as occupational forecasts. The limitations of these data are as follows: (a) not all persons employed in positions titled "social worker" may be professionally trained, and (b) social workers who are self-employed are not included. Despite these limitations, Bureau of Labor Statistics data represent a useful overview of the active workforce and an analysis of trends for future employment. Table 1 shows the estimates of social workers employed in May 2005 and their mean annual salary according to the Occupational Employment Statistics (http://www.bls.gov/oes/current/oes211021.htm).

TRENDS IN SOCIAL WORK EDUCATION Despite the continued growth of the number of social work educational programs, the number of students graduating from these programs has fluctuated in recent years, thus raising concern about the supply of trained professionals available to meet an anticipated increased workforce need (Lennon, 2007, pp. 52–53). See Table 2.

Social work graduates continue to be predominately female and white at both the BSW level (88.3%) and the MSW level (86.6%). The number of ethnic and racial minority graduates has increased slightly. Among 2002 social work graduates, 33.1% were persons of color in B.S.W. programs, and 28.4% in M.S.W. programs.

2004 BENCHMARK STUDY OF LICENSED SOCIAL WORKERS To better predict the adequacy and sufficiency of the frontline social work labor force to meet the changing needs of society, the NASW, in partnership with the Center for Health Workforce Studies, School of Public Health, University at Albany, conducted a benchmark national survey of licensed social workers in 2004 (Whitaker, Weismiller, & Clark, 2006). A random sample of 10,000 licensed social

TABLE 1
Social Work Employment and Median Salary in May 2005

|  | NUMBER EMPLOYED | MEAN ANNUAL SALARY ($) |
|---|---|---|
| Children, family, and school social workers | 256,430 | 38,780 |
| Medical and public health social workers | 112,220 | 42,690 |
| Mental health and substance abuse social workers | 120,140 | 36,920 |
| Social worker, all others | 60,940 | 42,720 |
| Total | 549,730 |  |

TABLE 2
Highlights of Recent Trends in Baccalaureate and Graduate Social Work Education

|  | 1998 | 1999 | 2000 | 2001 | 2002 | 2003 | 2004 |
|---|---|---|---|---|---|---|---|
| B.S.W. degrees awarded | 11,435 | 12,798 | 11,773 | 10,009 | 9,363 | 9,889 | 11,159 |
| M.S.W. degrees awarded | 13,600 | 15,061 | 15,016 | 13,524 | 13,339 | 15,473 | 14,482 |

workers from across the country was surveyed to learn more about their demographic characteristics, practice settings and work locations, their activities and tasks, their access to and satisfaction with formal education and continuing education, their compensation and benefits, their attitudes about the profession and their work, and their perceptions about the current and future job market. Data from the study provided important qualitative information about job satisfaction and contextual factors within practice settings that affect service provision. The study took an in-depth look at the four major areas of social work practice: social work with older adults, social work with children and families; social work in health-care settings, and social work in behavioral health-care settings. The findings from the survey revealed much about the characteristics of licensed social workers, their clients, and their perspectives on social work. The study also identified a range of factors pointing to a shortage of social workers in the coming decades. To ensure a sufficient supply of social workers in the future, the study recommended that the profession begin to address three challenges: (a) the replacement of retiring social workers, (b) the recruitment of a more diverse pool of professionals, and (c) the improvement of workplace conditions to retain social workers.

## Challenges

RETIREMENT The study identified a number of factors indicating a significant number of social workers will leave the profession because of retirement. Social work has been identified by the Bureau of Labor Statistics as one of the occupations most affected by baby boomer

retirements. The retirement replacement needs for social workers are estimated to reach 95,000 between 2003 and 2008. The study also identified an older workforce compared with the civilian workforce. Licensed social workers were significantly more likely to be in older age groups than were the U.S. civilian labor force. Also, the predominance of women in the profession adds to the retirement dilemma. Occupations dominated by women, such as social work, are especially vulnerable with an aging workforce since women's level of workforce participation is lower than men's as they approach retirement age.

Another finding was the trend of people entering the field of social work later in life. The mean age of entry into the licensed social work profession increased from 26.3 years old for those who entered prior to 1960, to 34.2 years old for those who entered between 2000 and 2004, resulting in shorter careers for licensed social workers than for most major health professions. In addition to the anticipated loss of frontline workers, community service organizations are also in the midst of a crisis in succession planning as many agency executives retire.

RECRUITMENT The study identified a range of concerns about the profession's ability to recruit a sufficient workforce. Study respondents' reports of the increased use of nonsocial workers to fill vacant social work positions as well as increased outsourcing of social work tasks indicate that more professional social workers are needed to meet agency and client needs. The study also encouraged broader recruitment of men and people of color into the profession to keep pace with the increasing diversity of client populations.

RETENTION The study also identified factors that impede retention of professional social workers. In addition to those planning to leave the profession because of retirement, almost 5% of the respondents planned to leave the profession for other reasons. Personal safety issues were reported by 44% of the respondents. Social workers also described increases in paperwork, severity of client problems, caseload size, and assignment of nonsocial work tasks as well as decreases in job security, staffing levels, and levels of reimbursement.

In public child welfare, a field led by social work, the factors affecting the recruitment and retention of workers have generated considerable interest among researchers. A systematic review of the research on this topic was conducted by the Institute for the Advancement of Social Work Research (2005). Their synthesis of qualitative findings indicated that there are both personal factors and organizational factors that contribute to staff retention. Among the personal factors are professional commitment to children and families, previous work experience, education, job satisfaction, efficacy, and personal characteristics such as age and bilingual skills. The most important organizational factors that impact staff turnover are better salary, supervisory support, reasonable workload, coworker support, opportunities for advancement, and organizational commitment and valuing of employees. The review also discussed the attributes of staff burnout which involve emotional exhaustion as well as role overload and role conflict. Although these factors were documented in the child welfare practice setting, it is reasonable to suggest that they may be applicable across other frontline service settings.

TRENDS AND FUTURE DIRECTIONS Shifts in the demographic landscape are prompting critical review of the composition, capacity, and development needs of the current and future U.S. labor force. Projected growth in minority populations, children, the number of immigrants, and the aging of the baby boom generation are major catalysts fueling increased attention to projections of labor force professionals to meet the demands for services in the coming decades.

Demographic shifts will combine to result in a population increasingly characterized by its diversity in race, ethnicity, and age with implications for members of the labor force and well as for recipients of services. As this diversified labor force emerges, several professions have begun to examine the future sufficiency and capacity of their workforces and found evidence of current or looming shortages. Professional workforce shortages are predicted for a range of professions, including nursing, dentistry, pharmacy, medicine, allied health, social work, public health (Association of

Academic Health Centers, 2003; Whitaker et al., 2006). In addition, concerns about the capacity of professionals to meet the needs of vulnerable populations have fueled a flurry of activity among governmental and philanthropic groups to study the current workforce and professional training pipelines of many occupations, including social work. This interest has helped social work education launch several faculty development, curricula enhancement, research and training initiatives to better prepare students for future practice realities.

With the aging of the baby boom cohort and the continued lengthening of the average life span, the number and proportion of older Americans is quickly rising. By 2030, the United States will have roughly 70 million people over the age of 65—more than double the amount in 2000. Also, the cohort of workers nearing retirement age is increasing, while the number of workers in the "middle-age" cohort poised as replacements is declining (Dohm, 2000; Toosi, 2004, 2005). These factors are converging to put pressure both on demands for services and the available pool of workers.

Estimates from the National Institute on Aging project that 60,000 to 70,000 social workers will be needed by 2010 to provide services for the baby boomer cohort that will begin turning 65. For specific community services serving the elderly, such as long-term care, the need for social workers is expected to nearly triple (U.S. Department of Health and Human Services, 2006). Another sector of the health-care system expected to face increased service demands is the behavioral health arena. There is strong speculation that the current supply of the behavioral health-care workforce is inadequate to provide services to all who currently need them (McRee et al., 2003), much less to meet a significantly increased demand.

Employment of social workers is expected to increase faster than the average for all occupations through 2014, according to government sources (Bureau of Labor Statistics, 2006). Growth in demand is expected in service sectors serving the elderly, agencies providing substance abuse treatment, and in organizations serving children. While competition for jobs will continue in urban and suburban areas, there will continue to be a high demand for social workers in rural areas.

Several action initiatives are underway to strengthen the profession so that it may continue to provide vital frontline services. NASW launched a public education campaign in 2005, which targets national media to build awareness of the contribution of social workers to the well-being of individuals, families, and communities (NASW, 2005). Recently, the Social

Work Reinvestment Initiative, a coalition effort throughout the profession, began efforts to advance policy changes at both the state and federal levels to support social work education, research, and practice (NASW, 2007b).

In order to better serve vulnerable populations, social work must continue to study and analyze workforce trends and emerging service delivery systems. Understanding and advocating for the value of social work services is central to the vitality and relevance of the profession in improving social conditions for all persons.

The stability and continuity of a social work workforce depends on the profession's ability to attract new workers; agencies' abilities to retain their staff; and the larger society's investment in this pool of workers, and the clients they serve. Public policy decisions about the role and value of social work are integral to the continued viability of the profession. In turbulent and fast-growing practice environments such as health care, recommended strategies to sustain the workforce include the increased use of technology, new models of care, more cross-discipline teams, and better career ladders within a teaching and learning organization. The challenge for social work is to be knowledgeable about workplace issues and actively engage in leading organizational change that will improve services to clients.

## REFERENCES

Association of Academic Health Centers. (2003). *Fact sheet: Workforce shortages compromise access to health care.* Retrieved January 2, 2007, from http://www.aahcdc.org/pdf/workforce_shortages.pdf

Barth, M. (2003). Social work labor market: A first look. *Social Work*, 48(1), 9–19.

Bureau of Labor Statistics. (2006). *Occupational outlook handbook, 2006–2007.* Retrieved January 30, 2007, from http://www.bls.gov/oco/ocos060.htm

Council on Social Work Education. (2001). *Educational policy and accreditation standards.* Retrieved October 2007, from http://www.cswe.org/NR/rdonlyres/111833A0-C4F5-475C-8FEB-EA740FF4D9F1/0/EPAS.pdf

Dohm, A. (July 2000). Gauging the labor force effects of retiring baby-boomers. *Monthly Labor Review*, 123, 17–25.

Gibelman, M. & Schervish, P. (1993). *Who we are: The social work labor force as reflected in the NASW membership.* Washington, DC: NASW Press.

Gibelman, M., & Schervish, P. (1997). *Who we are: A second look.* Washington, DC: NASW Press.

Gibelman, M., (2005). *What social workers do* (2nd ed.). Washington, DC: NASW Press.

Institute for the Advancement of Social Work Research. (2005). *Factors influencing retention of child welfare staff: A systematic review of research.* Washington, DC: Author.

Lennon, T. (2004). *Statistics on social work education in the United States, 2002.* Alexandria, VA: Council on Social Work Education.

McRee, T., Dower, C., Briggance, B., Vance, J., Keane, D., & O'Neil, E. (2003). *The mental health workforce: Who's meeting California's needs?* San Francisco: California Workforce Initiative, University of California, San Francisco Center for the Health Professions.

National Association of Social Workers. (1981). *Standards for the classification of social work practice: A policy statement.* Silver Spring, MD: Author.

National Association of Social Workers. (1987). *Salaries in social work: A summary report on the salaries of NASW Members, June 1986 – July 1987.* Washington, DC: Author.

National Association of Social Workers. (2005). *Social work public education campaign.* Retrieved October 2007, from http://www.naswfoundation.org/imageCampaign/default.asp

National Association of Social Workers. (2007a). Social work practice standards. Retrieved October 2007, from http://www.socialworkers.org/practice/default.asp

National Association of Social Workers. (2007b). Social work reinvestment initiative. Retrieved October 2007, from http://www.socialworkreinvestment.org/

Teare, R., & Sheafor, B. (1995). *Practice-sensitive social work education.* Alexandria, VA: Council on Social Work Education.

Toosi, M. (2004). Labor force projections to 2012: The graying of the U.S. workforce. *Monthly Labor Review*, 127(2), 37–57.

Toosi, M. (November 2005). Labor force projections to 2014: Retiring boomers. *Monthly Labor Review*, 128, 25–44.

U.S. Department of Health and Human Services, Assistant Secretary for Planning and Evaluation, Office of Disability, Aging and Long-Term Care Policy. (2006). *The supply and demand of professional social workers providing long-term care services: A report to congress.* Washington, DC: Government Printing Office.

Whitaker, T., Weismiller, T., & Clark, E. (2006). *Assuring the sufficiency of a frontline workforce: A national study of licensed social workers. Executive summary.* Washington, DC: National Association of Social Workers.

## SUGGESTED LINKS

National Association of Social Workers.
*http://workforce.socialworkers.org/studies/natstudy.asp*
Institute for the Advancement of Social Work Research.
*http://www.iaswresearch.org/*

—TOBY WEISMILLER AND TRACY WHITAKER

**SOUTH ASIANS.** *See* Asian Americans: South Asians.

**SOUTHEAST ASIANS.** *See* Asian Americans: Southeast Asians.

**SPOUSE ABUSE.** *See* Intimate Partner Violence.

# STRATEGIC PLANNING

ABSTRACT: Strategic planning is a key management process in nonprofit organizations and a collaborative methodology for addressing complex community needs. This entry presents an overview of strategic planning, with dual emphasis on the content and format of the final product. It highlights phases and steps in the planning process, along with trends and directions for such planning in the future. Despite its increased use, however, confusion and skepticism about the value of strategic planning remain. Therefore, we describe specific approaches that have yielded good results.

KEY WORDS: planning; strategic planning; decision making; nonprofit management

## Perspectives and Practices

Bryson (2004) defined strategic planning as "a disciplined effort to produce fundamental decisions and actions that shape and guide what an organization (or other entity) is, what it does, and why it does it" (p. 6). Known as the "critical issues" approach, the Bryson model is consistent with social work values and is particularly suited for social service agencies. This approach assumes that strategic planning is simultaneously a dynamic, inclusive, and analytical process designed to help organizations "fulfill their missions, meet their mandates, satisfy their constituents, and create public value" (p. xii). Strategic planning is different from long-range and tactical planning. A strategic plan focuses on the near future (3–5 years) and assumes that an organization's environment is in flux. A long-range plan encompasses 10–20 years and works in an organization that operates in a relatively stable environment. In contrast, a tactical (or operational) plan translates the broad goals and objectives in a strategic plan into an annual plan.

Strategic planning builds social capital. Social capital refers to the "features of social organizations, such as trust, norms, and networks, that can improve the efficiency of society by facilitating coordinated actions" (Putnam, 1993, p. 167). Theorists argue that nonprofit organizations are important sources of social capital because they stimulate the voluntary mobilization of citizens to achieve civic purposes not attainable through individual action.

Bryson identified the following benefits of strategic planning. The first benefit is the promotion of strategic thinking, acting, and learning through forward-looking conversations among key actors. The second is improved organizational decision-making. Strategic planning gives organizational leaders a coherent and defensible basis to justify their decisions. The third benefit is enhanced organizational effectiveness. Strategic planning links resource allocations to outputs and outcomes. The fourth is that strategic planning directly benefits the people involved by producing results or services they need or desire.

In addition, strategic planning yields the following seven benefits by

1. providing a common purpose for future organizational development,
2. building teamwork and expertise,
3. promoting responsiveness to community needs,
4. enhancing employee morale and commitment to the organizational mission,
5. directing fundraising efforts,
6. educating stakeholders (and the larger community) about the organization, and
7. improving communications and public relations, creating a positive organizational image.

While strategic planning is generally viewed as a "smart practice," it is not a panacea. Thus, social work managers and administrators must understand the "readiness" of their organizations to engage in strategic planning. Three situations make an organization unready. One situation is if the organization is in a crisis because of a cash-flow crunch, a vacancy in a key leadership position, or a lack of skills, resources, or commitment to the strategic planning process.

How should strategic planning be done? Bryson's critical issues approach has three distinct phases— (a) planning-to-plan, (b) analytic, and (c) committee deliberation.

PLANNING-TO-PLAN PHASE The "planning to plan" phase clarifies the main planning tasks, the roles and responsibilities of decision makers, the expected outcomes, and the time line for implementation. Among the questions addressed in this phase are the following:

1. Why is the organization engaging in strategic planning?
2. What is the level of commitment to the process?
3. Who will lead (or serve to chair) the Strategic Planning Committee?
4. Who are the key stakeholders? A stakeholder refers to any person or group that can make a claim on the organization's resources, attention, or output, or is affected by its output.

5. Which of these stakeholders will serve on the Strategic Planning Committee?
6. How will the stakeholders not on the Strategic Planning Committee be engaged?
7. What are the specific steps and timetable for the overall effort?
8. What staff will be available to support the planning process?
9. How will the organization use outside consultants? Will a consultant facilitate the entire process, or will content experts be used for a specific task?

Answers to these questions will result in an initial strategic planning agreement. A carefully crafted agreement gives participants a sense of how they fit—and their importance—in the collective effort. This phase can be completed in a month.

ANALYTIC PHASE  The second phase involves an analysis of the organization's internal and external environments. Data are drawn from (a) a perceptual analysis, (b) a mandate analysis, and (c) an environmental scan. In the perceptual analysis, stakeholders, including the entire board, provide their perspective concerning the critical issues facing the organization, such as the following:

1. Programming and services
2. Financial stability and fundraising
3. Image, visibility, and community relations
4. Human resources (board-and-staff relations)
5. Facilities and technologies

The mandate analysis examines the multiple controls that underpin the organization, both formal and informal. Formal mandates relate to bylaws, incorporation requirements, legal commitments, funding obligations, and professional certification or accreditation. Informal mandates may be based on organizational traditions or mythology. An environmental scan provides information about the social, demographic, political, legal, economic, funding, and technological factors affecting the organization's capacity to fulfill its mission. Trends within a particular subsector (such as child welfare) are also scanned. Most social service organizations allocate 3 months for this phase.

COMMITTEE DELIBERATION PHASE  Apart from weaving the information strands together, the Strategic Planning Committee's deliberations shape the following tasks:

- Developing or renewing the organization's mission, vision, and core values

- Conducting the baseline assessment (the SWOT analysis—This is an assessment of the organization's strengths, weaknesses, opportunities, and threats. This analysis provides an understanding of the organization's internal resources and capacity and the external forces that affect its future [Barry, 1997, pp. 44–49].)
- Identifying and prioritizing critical issues
- Setting goals and strategies to address these critical issues
- Drafting and adopting the strategic plan
- Refining and finalizing the plan
- Presenting the plan to the board for approval

The deliberation phase typically spans 4–5 months. Typically, the Committee uses a process facilitator to gather input from internal and external stakeholders in a series of meetings and small group sessions. If the organization has professional staff, they should be involved in the committee's deliberations because of their responsibility to implement the plan. Techniques and sample documents for carrying out this process are found in Allison and Kaye (1997, chap. 3).

### Strategic Planning Steps
SETTING DIRECTION AND CREATING PUBLIC VALUE  To set direction, the organization must clarify its mission and the values and vision that influence it. The mission statement is a concise action-oriented expression of the organization's reason to exist—its unique purpose. This statement should address *what* the organization does best for the community. The organizational mission must be aligned with its mandates. Values express *how* the organization treats its internal and external stakeholders—its guiding philosophy. The statement of core values expresses timeless principles, such as integrity, compassion, innovation, and accountability. Describing the organization under ideal conditions, the vision statement is a source of inspiration and aspiration. The organizational vision may be for a longer period than the 3–5 years typical of a strategic plan.

Social service organizations create public value in one of three ways. The first way is for the organization to achieve tax-exempt status under Section 501(c)(3) of the Internal Revenue Service Code. Tax exemptions are permitted if the organization operates for one or more of the following public purposes: religious, charitable, scientific, public safety, literary, educational, and the prevention of cruelty to animals or children (Wilbur & Associates, 2000, p. 331). A second way is by promoting a sense of individual and collective identity, affiliation, recognition, and security for organizational stakeholders. A third way is by building social capital through the mobilization of citizens on behalf of the most vulnerable persons in society.

## IDENTIFYING AND FRAMING STRATEGIC ISSUES

The identification of strategic issues includes an assessment of the organization's environment—the Strengths, Weaknesses, Opportunities, and Threats. Strategic planners who fail to conduct the SWOT analysis in the beginning of the process may misidentify issues as strategic (Jackson, 2007, p. 99).

An effective SWOT analysis uncovers the organization's critical success factors (CSFs). The critical success factors are what the organization must do or the criteria it must meet for stakeholders to consider it a success. A discussion of the organization's CSFs will lead to a review of its distinctive competencies. Competencies refer to the set of actions, skills, or strategies at which the organization is particularly good. If the organization has any distinctive competency, then replicating it should be difficult for others. Having distinctive competencies gives the organization an enduring advantage in a changing environment. A set of core competencies is necessary for the organization to perform successfully. A distinctive core competency allows the organization to add more public value than can alternate providers (Bryson, 2004, pp. 124–128).

The SWOT analysis is the basis for framing the organization's strategic issues. The framing process yields information on how stakeholders define their interests, the potential costs and benefits of alternative strategies, and whether specific strategies are likely to gain supporters or foes. Bryson (2004) found that three types of strategic issues are likely to emerge during the framing process:

1. Issues that require immediate attention because they affect how the organization carries out its mission
2. Issues that require action in the future but that the organization can handle as part of the regular planning cycle
3. Issues that require no action yet need continuous monitoring (p. 155)

Some operational or tactical issues are likely to emerge as well. Capturing these issues is important for three reasons. First, the operational issues are, for most people, the ones that affect their day-to-day lives. Therefore, they will want to see that the organization takes some action on them. Second, such action creates energy for strategic planning because it demonstrates the organization's commitment to the process. Third, operational actions often remove some barriers that affect the organization's strategic issues. By framing strategic issues carefully, the committee will produce a politically acceptable and technically workable plan.

## DEVELOPING, EVALUATING, AND SELECTING STRATEGIC ALTERNATIVES

During this step, the Strategic Planning Committee breaks into work groups. These groups develop goals and strategies that address the organization's strategic issues. Key stakeholders with expertise in specific issue areas should be added to these work groups. Bryson identified two methods to select strategic alternatives—"the 5-part process" and oval mapping.

Bryson's 5-part process answers the following questions about each strategic issue (pp. 199–200).

1. What are the practical alternatives that may be pursued to address this strategic issue?
2. What are the barriers precluding the realization of these alternatives?
3. What major proposals could be pursued to achieve these alternatives directly or to overcome the barriers to their realization?
4. What major actions with existing staff must be undertaken to implement these proposals?
5. What specific steps must be taken within the next 6 months to implement the major proposals, and who is responsible for each step?

Oval mapping, Bryson's second method, is a facilitated process that engages participants in the creation of word-and-arrow diagrams about the organization's potential strategic actions. Participants (a) envision possible actions and write them on oval-shaped post-it notes, (b) arrange these actions according to similar themes, and (c) cluster which actions cause which effects. The result is a map of the action-to-outcome relationships (pp. 163–164, 205–206). Important clusters of potential actions indicate strategic issues. According to Bryson, oval mapping is useful under the following three conditions.

1. The participants are having trouble making sense out of complex issue areas.
2. Time is short, and the organization must act immediately.
3. The commitment of those involved is particularly important (p. 164).

No matter which method is applied, the committee must establish clear standards for the groups to select a strategic issue. The United Way of America (1986) and Eadie (2006, pp. 381–383) suggest the following factors for selecting strategies:

1. Suitability: Are there some sustainable advantages?
2. Validity: Are the assumptions realistic?
3. Feasibility: Does the organization have the necessary skills, resources, and commitments?
4. Consistency: Is the strategy externally and internally consistent?
5. Vulnerability: What are the risks and contingencies?
6. Timing: When must the organization act, and when will it benefit?
7. Adaptability: Can the organization retain its flexibility?
8. Uniqueness: What makes this strategy distinctly different from others?
9. Usability: Can the organization readily implement the strategy?
10. Cost: What are the direct and indirect costs (including financial, human, and reputational) the organization must bear if it chooses not to move forward?
11. Impact: Can the organization have the desired positive impact within the resource constraints?

PREPARING, REVIEWING, AND ADOPTING THE STRATEGIC PLAN After selecting the strategic alternatives, the committee must prepare the first draft of the strategic plan. The committee reviews this draft and makes modifications until achieving a consensus on the content. Once the organization's board adopts the strategic plan, the process transitions from strategic planning to strategic management. At this point, attention focuses on the implementation challenges, such as organizational commitment, the allocation of resources, and the process for monitoring and updating the strategic plan. The committee must also decide who will assume responsibility for translating the strategic plan into an operational or tactical plan. The organization must be willing to shift resources to match its strategic priorities for it to be successfully implemented.

## Trends and Directions
### Impacting Strategic Planning

Six trends in the nonprofit sector significantly impact strategic planning. One trend is the increasing diversity of the larger community. This diversity affects strategic planning by increasing the number of stakeholder groups to consider. According to Bryson, this diversification "complicate(s) the quest for public value, governance, service design and delivery, and workforce recruitment, retention, training, and management" (pp. 132–133). On the other hand, strategic planning provides opportunities to engage diverse groups through membership on the Strategic Planning Committee and in the workgroups.

Another trend is that strategic planning has become the smart social work practice. Financial challenges, turnover in small organizations, and the need to plan for succession are critical issues readily addressed through strategic planning. A third trend concerns the dramatic growth of the nonprofit sector since the mid-1970s. Fueled in part by the devolution of the federal government, this growth has increased the competition for scarce resources among social service providers. Furthermore, governments and funding agencies are encouraging strategic alliances, collaborations, and partnerships among social work organizations that serve the same clientele or address the same community need. These alliances may take many forms, from information sharing to organizational mergers, and all add levels of complexity to the planning process (Bailey & Koney, 2000; Yankey & Willen, 2005). Also, social work leaders need to pay more attention to these interorganizational relationships that can shape their agency's future direction.

Two additional trends are clear. Although the ideal strategic plan covers 3–5 years, the greater uncertainty in the external environment is prompting some social service organizations to adopt shorter time horizons, 1–2 years. Also, business practices have been introduced into the implementation process and the reporting of planning outcomes, most notably, the balanced scorecard and dashboard indicators (Kaplan, 2001).

## Strategic Planning Challenges

No guarantee exists that strategic planning can provide all these benefits. Moreover, critics raise important reservations about strategic planning. One concern is that the process is time-consuming. Given that the world changes rapidly, a strategic plan may become obsolete by the time the organization develops it. A second concern is that such planning is too remote from the day-to-day operations such that staff may view it as a distraction from their real work. According to Bryson, strategic planning "should take no more than 10 percent of the ordinary work time" (p. 14). A third concern is that many organizations do not implement their strategic plans. The failure to implement may lead to cynicism and disillusionment about the value of planning.

Strategic planning has become the standard practice of nonprofit organizations. Implementation since the mid-1970s has produced knowledge about why strategic planning efforts may yield less-than-expected results. Problems are bound to happen when

1. strategic planning was delegated to other professionals in the organization.
2. the plan failed to incorporate political considerations.

3. the process failed to build ownership of the plan among those who were responsible for implementing it.
4. the organization did not allocate sufficient time for a meaningful planning process.
5. the planners overestimated the organization's capacity.
6. no contingency plans existed for funding shortfalls, rapid staff turnover, technology failures, or environmental catastrophes, such as Hurricane Katrina.
7. the organization did not transition from strategic planning to operational planning.
8. the strategic plan became outdated.
9. the plan was never implemented.

For social work organizations attentive to these pitfalls, strategic planning provides the roadmap to achieve their desired future. To fail to plan strategically is to plan to fail strategically.

Social workers practice in increasingly complex and constantly changing environments. Such environments require a well-designed and facilitated strategic planning process to manage the inevitable change. This planning is an organizational, political, and rational activity. It is planning that requires analysis, critical thinking, judgment, and creativity. While social work values such as diversity, inclusiveness, and integrity serve as a strong foundation upon which to plan for and facilitate strategic planning, macrolevel social work practitioners must develop the knowledge and skills necessary to conduct organizational analyses, think critically, engage multiple constituencies, offer creative solutions, facilitate meetings, and demonstrate sound political and economic judgment.

### REFERENCES

Allison, M., & Kaye, J. (1997). *Strategic planning for non-profit organizations: A practical guide and workbook.* New York: Wiley & Support Center for Nonprofit Management.

Bailey, D., & Koney, K. M. (2000). *Strategic alliances among health and human services organizations: From affiliations to consolidations.* Thousand Oaks, CA: Sage.

Barry, B. W. (1997). *Strategic planning workbook for nonprofit organizations.* St. Paul, MN: Amherst H. Wilder Foundation.

Bryson, J. M. (2004). *Strategic planning for public and nonprofit organizations* (3rd ed.). San Francisco: Jossey-Bass.

Eadie, D. C. (2006). Planning and managing strategically. In R. L. Edwards & J. A. Yankey (Eds.), *Effectively managing nonprofit organizations* (chap. 17, pp. 375–390). Washington, DC: NASW Press.

Jackson, P. M. (2007). *Nonprofit strategic planning: Leveraging Sarbannes-Oxley best practices.* Hoboken, NJ: Wiley.

Kaplan, R. S. (2001). Strategic performance measurement and management in nonprofit organizations. *Nonprofit Management and Leadership, 11*(3), 353–370.

Putnam, R. D. (1993). *Making democracy work.* Princeton, NJ: Princeton University Press.

United Way of America. (1986). *Strategic management and the United Way.* Alexandria, VA: J. A. Yankey.

Wilbur, R. H. & Associates (Eds.). (2000). Knowing important legal requirements (chap. 14). In *The complete guide to nonprofit management* (2nd ed., pp. 327–345). New York: Wiley, and Smith, Bucklin & Associates.

Yankey, J. A., & Willen, C. K. (2005). Strategic alliances (chap. 11). In R. D. Herman & Associates (Eds.), *Handbook of nonprofit leadership and management* (2nd ed., pp. 254–276). San Francisco: Jossey-Bass.

### SUGGESTED LINKS

Association for Research on Nonprofit & Voluntary Organization.
*www.arnova.org*
Board Source (formerly the National Center for Nonprofit Boards).
*www.boardsource.org*
Fieldstone Alliance (formerly Wilder Publishing Center).
*www.fieldstonealliance.org*
The Independent Sector.
*www.independentsector.org*
Maxine Goodman Levin College of Urban Affairs, Center for Nonprofit Policy & Practice, Cleveland State University.
*http://urban.csuohio.edu/nonprofit/*
Mandel Center for Nonprofit Organizations, Case Western Reserve University.
*www.case.edu/mandelcenter/strategicplanning*

—JOHN A. YANKEY AND VERA VOGELSANG-COOMBS

## STRENGTHS-BASED FRAMEWORK

**ABSTRACT:** The strengths perspective is a paradigmatic shift away from problem-focused approaches to social work practice. The strengths perspective focuses not on the defectiveness of the client system in an attempt to undo these problems but on the inherent strengths, competencies, and resiliency that are the building blocks of a better future. It does not ignore pain and suffering but asks how people make it under such difficult times and builds on those amazing capacities. It assumes the expertise of the client and privileges client knowledge and capabilities. Diversity, self-determination, empowerment, and social justice are inherent in this practice.

**KEY WORDS:** strengths; resilience; empowerment; social justice; diversity; communities; group work; practice organizations; self-determination; social policy

The strengths perspective represents a fundamental change or paradigm shift in social work practice at all levels of engagement. It represents a major change in how social workers think and practice by shifting from viewing individuals, families, groups, agencies, organizations, and communities as defective or deficient to recognizing, appreciating, and working with the strengths and capacities available at all systemic levels of practice. Although social work literature has increasingly appeared to embrace the idea of strengths, often suggesting statements about people's strengths be included in assessments as an example, this is a very small part of what the strengths perspective means in terms of social work practice. Saleebey (2006) poignantly makes this point:

> The strengths perspective is a dramatic departure from conventional social work practice. Practicing from a strengths orientation means this-everything you do as a social worker will be predicated, in some way, on helping to discover and embellish, explore and exploit client's strengths and resources in the service of assisting them to achieve their goals, realize their dreams, and shed the irons of their own inhibitions and misgivings, and society's domination. (p. 1).

Integrating the strengths perspective into practice requires a change in attitude and the manner by which social work is practiced (Blundo, 2006). From the strengths perspective, all client systems are viewed as experts on their own situation. Any system is understood as doing the best it can at the time, given its resources and life context, though not without possible pain, difficulties, setbacks, and suffering (Saleebey, 2006). The strengths perspective does not ignore the problem. The problem or issues are acknowledged, understood, and appreciated by the worker as described by the client or client system. The shift comes as the collaboration then looks toward what goals or desired outcomes the clients or client system wants that are of benefit to them and others. The client-identified problems are considered the starting point for change, and finding a new direction built of client strengths, resiliency, and hope is the collaborative work to be done.

The strengths perspective takes the viewpoint that people, organizations, and communities are always in a state of change which has the potential to lead to more satisfying conditions. The traditional model of deficit-based problem focused practice can blind the social worker from "noticing and appreciating people's, organizations, and communities strengths and the capacity to find their own solutions" (McCashen, 2005, p. 9). The strengths perspective's fundamental shift to an intention to noticing and working with people's strengths

contrasts with the traditional attempts to locate the problem, usually within the person, organization, or community; identifying the cause of the problem from the expert's perspective and prescribing an intervention to fix the problem. This expert position of possessing a special knowledge to assess, diagnose, and prescribe a treatment is viewed as disingenuous from the strengths perspective in terms of the social work values of self-determination, empowerment, respecting diversity, and social justice.

### Empowerment
The strengths perspective conceives of empowerment as "power with" rather than "power over" as is the position of expertise that the traditional pathology-based models espouse (McCashen, 2005). The idea that a trained professional knows what is best for a person, family, group, or community is an obvious "power over" that is rationalized by the idea that professionals possess special and privileged knowledge unavailable to the "client." The strengths perspective is focused on knowledge and skills that enable the professional worker to be a collaborator who privileges "client" knowledge, strengths, resiliency, and goals. Reflective of this shift is the significant effort to recognize that those with whom we are collaborating are not the diagnoses or multiple diagnoses ascribed to them. From a strengths perspective, those people most often referred to as "clients" or by their "diagnosis" are "people, just like you and me who are striving for the same things we are" (Rapp & Goscha, 2006, p. xix).

### Diversity
Respect for and the inclusion of diversity is inherent in the strengths perspective and the work that follows from that position. The fact that the strengths perspective requires the worker to be a collaborator and to view the clients as the expert on their own lives privileges the world of the clients. The cultural, ethnic, racial, spiritual, socioeconomic, gender, age, and sexual preference of the client are all present in the narrative the person provides the worker. The strengths and resiliency reflect the life of the client within his or her complex social world. Saleebey (2006) describes the strengths-based worker functioning as of an ethnographer, trying to learn the world views of the client. Importantly, diversity is also understood in terms of the unique perspective of this or that particular client. In this way, the complexity of diversity is understood in terms of the personal life experiences and not as fitting into a generalized version of a "culture" or "ethnicity." Both diversity and uniqueness are central elements of strengths-based practice.

## Social Justice

Social justice in practice requires that social workers deal with power differentials inherent in social systems and professional relationships. Power-over has been the hallmark of professional practice given the professionalism and adherence to the "medical model" of expert diagnosing and prescribing interventions. It privileges the knowledge base of the dominate culture, gender, race, sexual orientation, and socioeconomic position. McCashen (2005) describes "power-over" as "occurring when individual, group or institution assumes the right to control or colonize others" (p. 20). Obviously, social work would not assume to be doing this; yet, the traditional model of practice assumes a position of professional "expertise" with a knowledge base that reflects values, attitudes, and beliefs of the dominate groups in society. The strengths perspective positions the worker in terms of "power-with" or "values, beliefs and actions that do not colonize" (McCashen, 2005, p. 31). From this position, the strengths-based worker assumes power-with through privileging the expertise of the client and the client's goals and solutions. The worker's expertise is in assisting in creating this collaborative mutual learning process. In addition, it is important to recognize the commonalities we all share, such as "we all make mistakes, we all have regrets," "we are all trying to make it some way in the world," and so on (McCashen, 2005, p. 32). This collaborative power-with position reduces power differentials between the social worker and clients as much as possible given the nature of professional agencies, directives, and practice. Obviously, the worker can engage in social action and community organizational practice to address the larger societal issues faced by oppressed and disadvantaged groups.

## Self-Determination

A long-standing social work maxim asserts client self-determination. This social work value or principle is a central theme of the strengths perspective. This value compels the strengths-based worker to collaborate with clients in a manner that turns over real choices and direction of our work to the client. McCashen (2005) describes this collaboration as clients having ownership. It is the client's "right to take an active lead in the service delivery process... [it] is they who decide on, and participate in, action to address their concerns and interests" (McCashen, 2005, p. 36). This position is one of sharing power with the client or client system. The client is expert and the work is client-directed.

## Individuals and Families

The strengths approach to practice asks the social worker to listen closely to the story of those with whom they are engaging. The task is to listen intently to the reality of the person in the moment and "honor their story" (Saleebey, 2006, p. 88). Importantly, it is the ability to listen for the evidence of resiliency, will, knowledge, and hope that may appear hidden in the anguished story that initiates a strengths-based process. The fact that a person is engaging you at the moment and sharing his or her struggle with you, even if traditionally seen as "resistance," demonstrates the capacity to struggle and to seek a change or meaning in his or her life. The social worker takes a stance of awe, respectful curiosity, acute listening, and openness to learning about the personal reality of this person. Through unique questions, the social worker further collaborates in a manner to "stimulate constructive discourse and narratives of resilience and strength" (Saleebey, 2006, p. 88). The use of constructive questions, that is, questions designed not to gather further information but to "generate new experiences about potential solutions and the strengths and capabilities of the [person]" promotes integrating strengths with establishing personal goals and potential solutions to what appear as vexing "problems" (Sharry, 2001, p. 33). This is the point where persons engage their strengths and capacities to take the first small steps toward well-formed outcomes or goals established by the collaboration. The use of personal, family, and community resources is always a central factor in these first small steps.

## Group Work

The extension of the basic strengths-based practice to working with groups for the purpose of individual growth and enhancement of the quality of life assumes the same basic constructs. The individual members as well as the group as a whole are viewed as having strengths, capabilities, and potentials for creating more meaningful lives. Sharry (2001) describes group work as focusing "on the client's strengths rather than weakness, on their resources rather than their deficits, on their competencies and skills rather than their areas of weakness" (p. 23). It is the client's strengths and resiliency that will be the road to recovery and growth, not their deficits and weaknesses (Metcalf, 1998; Sharry, 2001).

The use of the strengths perspective is fundamental to the point that the very names we give to various therapeutic groups are important to consider. For example, rather than referring to a group as a "divorce support group," using the title "New Beginnings" sets the tone for a different group experience, one focused on how members can let go of the past and move on in life. It is looking at the present and future, to the goals and possibilities that is distinctive about strengths-based therapeutic groups. It assumes potential and possibilities even in the title of the group.

## Communities and Organizations

Macro practice is focused on considering the larger context of social systems and socioeconomic conditions as potential areas for change. The strengths perspective shifts the practitioner away from assessing what is wrong, lacking, and defective to being alert to the assets and resources that are often unrecognized to meet desired outcomes and changes that will enhance the organization, neighborhood, community, or society. Saleebey (2006) emphasizes the importance of engaging members of organizations, neighborhoods, and communities in conversations that "ask questions about survival, support [resources], positive times, interests, dreams, goals, and pride" (p. 217). Strengths-based macro practice is focused on collaborative relationships "to strengthen and maximize opportunities for people at the organizational, community, societal, and global levels" (Long, Tice, & Morrison, 2006, p. 3).

*Community* level practice follows the same basic principles as does the strengths perspective at all other levels. Members of neighborhoods and larger communities are considered as experts in the context in which they function, and their direct involvement as collaborators is the first principle in the process. This is followed by members taking on the roles of leadership and defining directions with other members of the group. The resources found within the group and the larger community are seen as allies in creating the potential goals. Cultivating these resources and the strengths of members is the focus of a strengths-based macro practitioner. Forming alliances and cooperative relationships with the various resources within a neighborhood's larger context or community's larger context is an important part of building communities of any size. Saleebey (2006) describes community building and community work as dependent on "establishing a respectful, collaborative, light-hearted relationship with residents—a relationship that sees clients as equals and as having the potential for insight, change, and growth—[as] essential" (p. 255).

*Organizational* level work, both structurally and functionally, such as management and supervision, is considered from the point of what is "working well" and what are the resources and potentials of the clients and staff that can be supported by management and supervisors (McKergow & Clarke, 2005). The strengths perspective suggests that the agency or organizations exist to support the "client system" it is intended to serve. The usual top-down structure with director, management, and the supervisors setting the culture of the agency is turned on its head (Rapp & Goscha, 2006). From a strengths perspective the client system is understood as the reason for the agency's existence and the work of the members of the agency. It is recognizing this relationship that then directs the work of the agency down through the line worker, supervisor, and management to the agency director at the base of the flow chart. It is the director's responsibility to be responsive to the needs of those the agency serves by responding to that directive through a respectful and collaborative flow of responsibility from the client system. Rather than the usual agency profile as representing the bureaucrat expectations of the mandating body charged to the director, who charges the management, supervisors, down to the line workers and final implementation on the "client system," the strengths-based practice would reverse this top-down system to enable resources to be responsive to the human needs of those intended to be served.

*Social planning* from a strengths perspective "seeks ways to utilize existing strengths in organizations, communities, and society to enrich the environment and create opportunities for people" (Long et al., 2006, p. 150). Social advocacy, collaboration with consumers, building coalitions, emphasizing prevention, resiliency enhancement, and taking the perspective that human services and social programs are investments rather than costs are significant elements of a strengths-based policy effort (Long et al., 2006).

## Conclusion

Every successful change in the direction of a better life can only take place when founded on people's strengths, hopes, and aspirations. The strengths perspective takes this to heart and builds a manner of working with others on this principle of transforming lives within the context of a unique world of a client or client system. People are doing the best they can at the moment and with the resources they have available to them. This is not without pain and anguish. Yet, people are amazingly "self-righting" and resilient in the face of a great deal of difficulty. The strengths perspective recognizes the problem and the pain but importantly recognizes that people survive and change based on their strengths, will, hope, and resources. The social work practice done from the strengths perspective recognizes this, collaborates and shares power-with clients in the work to be done.

## REFERENCES

Blundo, R. (2006). Shifting our habits of mind: Learning to practice from a strengths perspective. In D. Saleebey (Ed.),

*The strengths perspective in social work practice* (4th ed., pp. 25–45). Boston: Allyn & Bacon.

Long, D. D., Tice, C. J., & Morrison, J. D. (2006). *Macro social work practice: A strengths perspective.* Belmont, CA: Thompson Brooks/Cole.

McCashen, W. (2005). *The strengths approach.* Bendigo, Australia: St. Luke's Innovative Resources.

McKergow, M., & Clarke, J. (Eds.). (2005). *Positive approaches to change: Applications of solution focus and appreciative inquiry at work.* Cheltenham, UK: SolutionsBook.

Metcalf, L. (1998). *Solution-focused group therapy: Ideas for groups in private practice, schools, agencies, and treatment programs.* New York: Free Press.

Rapp, C. A., & Goscha, R. J. (2006). *The strengths model: Case management with people with psychiatric disabilities.* (2nd ed.). New York: Oxford University Press.

Saleebey, D. (2006). The strengths approach to practice. In D. Saleebey (Ed.), *The strengths perspective in social work practice* (4th ed., pp. 1–24). Boston: Allyn & Bacon.

Sharry, J. (2001). *Solution-focused groupwork.* London: Sage.

## FURTHER READING

Beilharz, L. (2002). *Building community: The shared action experience.* Bendigo, Australia: St. Luke's Innovative Resources.

DeJong, P., & Berg, I. K. (2008). *Interviewing for solutions.* (3rd ed.) Belmont, CA: Thompson.

Saleebey, D. (2001). *Human behavior and the social environment: A biopsychosocial approach.* New York: Columbia University Press.

Saleebey, D. (Ed.). (2006). *The strengths perspective in social work practice* (4th ed.). Boston: Allyn & Bacon.

Turnell, A., & Essex, S. (2006). *Working with 'denied' child abuse. A resolution approach.* Berkshire, UK: Open University Press.

—ROBERT BLUNDO

# STRENGTHS PERSPECTIVE

**ABSTRACT:** In social work practice, the strengths perspective has emerged as an alternative to the more common pathology-oriented approach to helping clients. Instead of focusing on clients' problems and deficits, the strengths perspective centers on clients' abilities, talents, and resources. The social worker practicing from this approach concentrates wholly on identifying and eliciting the client's strengths and assets in assisting them with their problems and goals (Saleebey, 2006). This entry discusses the historical development of the strengths perspective, practice techniques, current applications, and philosophical distinctiveness.

**KEY WORDS:** strengths perspective; strength-based case management; strengths-based practice; strengths

## History

Although the profession of social work has a long history of recognizing client strengths, most social workers tend to focus on clients' problems and their dysfunctions (Weick, Rapp, Sullivan, & Kisthardt, 1989). However, in 1982, the strengths perspective movement began to emerge from various faculty and staff members at the University of Kansas School of Social Welfare (Brun & Rapp, 2001; Rapp, 1998; Saleebey, 1996), which encouraged social workers to shift from this problemfocused approach to helping. At that time, the school was awarded a small grant to provide case management services to people with psychiatric disabilities. Spearheading this project were faculty member Charles Rapp and doctoral student Ronna Chamberlain, who together, decided to take a different approach to case management services by having case managers focus on their clients' strengths and clients' abilities to function successfully in the community (Brun & Rapp, 2001; Rapp, 1998). Results from this project were successful, and this "strength-based case management" approach was implemented the following year in three other mental health centers in Kansas (Rapp, 1998). From the success of these projects, the strength-based approach started to develop, and other faculty members from KU School of Social Welfare began to apply it to other areas of social work practice.

By the late 1980s, KU faculty member Dennis Saleebey, Dean Ann Weick, and others at the school began developing and writing the conceptual understanding of the strengths perspective (Rapp, 1998; Weick et al., 1989). This effort culminated in the article "A Strengths Perspective for Social Work Practice," published in the journal *Social Work* (Weick et al., 1989) and the book *The Strengths Perspective in Social Work Practice* by Saleebey (1992). These writings aided in spreading the word about the strengths perspective and helped popularized the approach in the social work field. Interest in the strengths perspective continues to grow each year and its application continues to expand into the many different aspects of social work practice.

## Definition

The strengths perspective is not so much a theory as it is a way of viewing clients that influences the social worker's approach to helping them. It is a set of principles and ideas that require social workers to help their clients identify and emphasize talents, skills, possibilities, and hopes. Cultural and personal narratives, along with family and community resources, are explored and drawn on to aid the clients (Saleebey, 1996).

The basic assumptions inherent in the strengths perspective address the clients' capabilities. One of the main assumptions is that all individuals possess talents and skills, some of which may be untapped, and that each therefore has the capacity to develop and improve. It is also assumed that growth is more likely to occur in the individual from focusing exclusively on clients' strengths rather than their deficits,. Finally, clients are viewed as equals and expected to help define the problem as well as its possible resolutions (Bell, 2003; Saleebey, 1992; Weick et al., 1989).

Saleebey (2006) recommends looking for clients' strengths and resources not only within individuals but also within their communities. The strengths perspective emphasizes knowledge gained from difficulties and struggles as well as from mentors and teachers. Realized strengths abound in all individuals when thinking about their various talents, virtues, personality traits, and spiritual beliefs. Strengths can be found in personal and cultural stories in addition to the various community resources that may be overlooked.

From these assumptions and ideas, Saleebey (2006) identifies six key principles of the strengths perspective which helped to further define this approach and serve as a guide. These principles include the following:

1. *Individual, family, and community strengths.* Social workers must view their clients as competent and possessing skills and strengths which may not be initially visible. In addition, clients may have family and community resources which need to be explored and utilized.

2. *Illnesses, abuses, and struggles can serve as opportunities.* Clients can not only overcome very difficult situations, but also learn new skills and develop positive protective factors. Individuals exposed to a variety of trauma are not always helpless victims or damaged beyond repair.

3. *Respect client aspirations and hold high expectations.* Too often professional "experts" hinder their clients' potential for growth by viewing clients' identified goals as unrealistic. Instead, social workers need to set high expectations for their clients so that the clients believe they can recover and that their hopes are tangible.

4. *Collaborate with clients.* Playing the role of expert or professional with all the answers does not allow social workers to appreciate their clients' strengths and resources. The strengths perspective emphasizes collaboration between the social worker and the client.

5. *Environmental resources.* Every community, regardless of how impoverished or disadvantaged, has something to offer in terms of knowledge, support, mentorship, and tangible resources. These resources go beyond the general social service agencies in the communities and can serve as a great resource for clients.

6. *Care for each other.* Strength perspective recognizes the importance of community and inclusion of all its members in society and working for social justice. This is built on the basic premise that caring for each other is a basic form of civic participation.

These key principles help guide social work practice from a strengths perspective. It should be noted, however, that these principles continue to evolve and be refined (Saleebey, 2006). What remains constant and central, though, is the strengths perspective's focus on clients' personal assets along with their environmental resources rather than on their pathology and limitations.

## Change Philosophy and Techniques

The strengths perspective contends that focusing on clients' pathology and incompetencies hinders clients' progress toward growth. In contrast, underlying the change process in the strengths perspective is the belief that focusing entirely on clients' strengths will help bring about positive changes in the clients (Holmes & Saleebey, 1993). This approach to practice provides a perspective from which to work with clients and has not developed specific techniques and skills to the same degree as in other practice models. However, Saleebey (2006) does identify some elements of strengths-based practice, namely, listening for and sharing client strengths, providing words and images that help identify client strengths, and collaboratively discovering client resources in their environment.

Besides Saleebey's (2006) elements of strengths-based practice, Rapp (1998) offers more concrete techniques to help social work case managers apply the strengths perspective framework to their practice. The strength-based case management model was developed in the early 1980s to work in community settings with people suffering from psychiatric disabilities (Rapp, 1998). It includes a set of practice methods based on the six strengths perspective principles described earlier. Rapp and Goscha (2006) identify five categories of practice methods which serve as a function of the strengths model for case management: (a) relationship building, (b) assessing client strengths, (c) planning client goals, (d) acquiring environmental resources, and (e) collaborating continuously with client.

Additionally, a review of the empirical studies on strengths-based case management by Staudt, Howard, and Drake (2001) identified and described how these studies defined strengths-based case management. These common themes included focusing on client strengths, providing services in community, focusing on client identified needs, helping clients acquire resources, letting clients determine goals and interventions.

Another tool to aid social workers practicing from a strengths perspective approach is to utilize a strengths assessment. Brun and Rapp (2001) recommend conducting a strengths assessment early on in the therapeutic work to help identify capabilities and resources the client can utilize. The focus of the assessment should be entirely on clients' abilities and assets, both personally as well as environmentally, which provides the foundation for a strengths-based practice. Information can be gathered on what clients want, what their current situation is like, and available resources and skills (Rapp & Goscha, 2006; Weick et al., 1989).

### Current Applications

Over the years, researchers and practitioners have applied the strengths perspective approach to a wide variety of client populations and problems both domestically and internationally. The strengths-based practice model has been studied and applied to substance use (Siegel et al., 1995), community practice (Itzhaky & Bustin, 2002), social policy development (Chapin, 1995), elderly (Chapin & Cox, 2001; Perkins & Tice, 1999; Yip, 2005), domestic violence (Bell, 2003), families (Allison et al., 2003; Early & GlenMaye, 2000; Werrbach, 1996), and adolescents (Yip, 2006).

One of the earliest and most studied applications of the strengths perspective is with case managers working with adults having psychiatric disabilities. Rapp and Goscha (2006) summarize nine studies (Barry, Zeber, Blow, & Valenstein, 2003; Kisthardt, 1993; Macias, Farley, Jackson, & Kinney, 1997; Macias, Kinney, Farley, Jackson, & Vos, 1994; Modrcin, Rapp, & Poertner, 1988; Rapp & Chamberlain, 1985; Rapp & Wintersteen, 1989; Ryan, Sherman, & Judd, 1994; Stanard, 1999) that examined the effectiveness of the strengths-based case management model on people with psychiatric disabilities. Overall the review found support for the strengths-based case management model, but concerns about the lack of rigorous research designs, types of measures used, and small sample sizes warranted caution regarding the conclusiveness of the studies' results (Chamberlain & Rapp, 1991; Rapp & Goscha, 2006; Staudt et al., 2001).

Despite the popularity of the strengths perspective approach to social work practice, research on its effectiveness as a practice model has not been fully answered. For example, the review of nine strengths-based case management studies by Staudt et al. (2001) found

similarities in how these studies operationalized and defined the techniques used in strengths-based case management practice, but noted that none of the studies provided examples of specific questions or protocols. The authors were critical of the lack of measurement of treatment fidelity in the studies they reviewed, noting that only three studies describe efforts to ensure adherence to treatment model. Furthermore the article questioned the uniqueness of the strengths-based case management practice model, citing similar features in other case management models. Subsequent books and articles (Rapp & Goscha, 2006; Saleebey, 2006; Yip, 2006) have been written to further elaborate and differentiate the practice model of strengths perspective as well as strengths-based case management. Additionally, efforts are under way to further operationalize and empirically test the effectiveness of the strengths-based case management approach through rigorous research designs, including the development of strengths-based case management fidelity measures (Green, McAllister, & Tarte, 2004; Rapp & Goscha, 2006).

### Distinctiveness

The strengths perspective is clearly distinct from a medical model approach to helping which has significantly influenced social work practice, especially within the mental health field. This approach views clients from an illness and pathological standpoint. The social worker attempts to diagnose the clients' problem, develops a treatment plan, and evaluates the outcome (Shulman, 2006). This traditional stance of helping assumes that clients have problems that they are unable or unwilling to resolve and therefore, they need professional services. Many times, this view assumes that the existence of the problem and the need for the client to seek professional help indicate deficits or flaws in clients (Weick et al., 1989). In addition, the emphasis on the problems in the client creates a wave of pessimistic expectations about the client's capabilities and environment. Clients may then believe that because they have these problems, they are somehow deficient or abnormal. This ignores the idea that clients have tremendous assets and potential that may not be recognized (Saleebey, 2006).

Strengths perspective, in contrast to the medical model, provides a different way of viewing clients and the helping process in social work practice. It balances out this problem-focused emphasis in social work practice and provides an alternative framework for working with clients. Instead of focusing mainly on the problems of the clients, the strengths perspective is goal oriented and focuses primarily on the strengths of the clients, looking for talents, knowledge, capacities, and resources. Practicing from this perspective means the social worker is always exploring and utilizing clients' strengths and resources, both within the person and their environment, in helping them with their problems or goals (Saleebey, 2006; Sullivan, 1992).

Another major influence in social work practice, containing both similar and differing elements of the strengths perspective, is generalist social work practice. Generalist social work practice assesses clients' problems, strengths, and abilities to develop an intervention plan (Boyle, Hull, Mather, Smith, & Farley, 2006). The distinction between the strengths-based interventions and traditional generalist social work practice is the concerted emphasis on clients' strengths and resources rather than their problems and dysfunctions. This emphasis creates a different context for the social-worker–client relationship whereby the discussions and questions being asked have less to do with their inabilities and symptoms but instead on their resiliencies and resources (Saleebey, 1996; Weick et al., 1989).

### Integration
The central idea of focusing on client strengths and assets emphasized in the strengths perspective has also been identified and discussed in other disciplines and practice models. For example, emerging from resiliency theory, resilience-based practice is another model in psychology and social work that explores protective factors, especially in at-risk adolescents (Saleebey, 2006). Resilience revolves around the idea of positive adaptive strategies clients use to overcome adverse situations or conditions (Greene, 2007). Similarly, empowerment-oriented practice also posits focusing on client strengths and environmental resources and shares many of the same commonalities as the strengths perspective (Chapin & Cox, 2001).

In psychology, the theory and practice of positive psychology has gained significant attention for its differing approach to working with clients. Snyder (2000) promoted hope as a core construct of positive psychology, acting as a motivator and key influence in client behavior. Similar to the strengths perspective, positive psychology centers on the ideas of optimism, resilience, hope, and motivation (Seligman & Csikszentmihalyi, 2000).

Other social work researchers and practitioners have also advocated incorporating the strengths perspective principles with their practice models as a way of expanding on the strengths-based approach. For example solution-focused brief therapy has been linked with the strengths perspective as a way to add specific practice techniques to build on clients' abilities and solutions to solve their problems (DeJong & Miller, 1995;

Lee, Uken, & Sebold, 2004). Both are grounded in the social worker working collaboratively with the client to look for client's abilities and to focus on client's goals, rather than dwelling on the problems (Weick, Kreider, & Chamberlain, 2006). The difference lies in the specific questions and interviewing techniques solution-focused brief therapy uses that allows the conversation with the client to center on identifying solutions to the problems. Weick, Kreider, and Chamberlain (2006) explain:

> The strengths perspective tends to emphasize goal-setting as the strategy for moving toward a new future and identifying the strengths that will help lead there. Solution-focused therapy emphasizes solution-finding through a strategy of purposeful questions that are intended to develop a detailed picture of a future beyond the problem. (p. 123)

Other social workers have suggested the use of integrative relational approach to enhance the strengths perspective approach to practice because of its similarities in therapeutic communication with both the strengths perspective and solution-focused brief therapy (Ornstein & Ganzer, 2000).

### REFERENCES
Allison, S., Stacey, K., Dadds, V., Roeger, L., Wood, A., & Martin, G. (2003). What the family brings: Gathering evidence for strengths-based work. *Journal of Family Therapy*, 25(3), 263–284.

Barry, K. L., Zeber, J. E., Blow, F. C., & Valenstein, M. (2003). Effect of strengths model versus assertive community treatment model on participant outcomes and utilization: Two year follow-up. *Psychiatric Rehabilitation Journal*, 26(3), 268–277.

Bell, H. (2003). Strengths and secondary trauma in family violence work. *Social Work*, 48(4), 513–522.

Boyle, S. W., Hull, G. H., Mather, J. H., Smith, L. L., & Farley, O. W. (2006). *Direct practice in social work*. Boston: Allyn and Bacon.

Brun, C., & Rapp, R. C. (2001). Strengths-based case management: Individuals' perspectives on strengths and the case manager relationship. *Social Work*, 46(3), 278–288.

Chamberlain, R., & Rapp, C. A. (1991). A decade of case management: A methodological review of outcome research. *Community Mental Health Journal*, 27(3), 171–188.

Chapin, R. (1995). Social policy development: The strengths perspective. *Social Work*, 40(4), 506–514.

Chapin, R., & Cox, E. O. (2001). Changing the paradigm: Strengths-based and empowerment-oriented social work with frail elders. *Journal of Gerontological Social Work*, 36, 165–179.

DeJong, P., & Miller, S. D. (1995). How to interview for client strengths. *Social Work*, 40(6), 729–736.

Early, T. J., & GlenMaye, L. F. (2000). Valuing families: Social work practice with families from a strengths perspective. *Social Work*, 45(2), 118–130.

Green, B. L., McAllister, C. L., & Tarte, J. M. (2004). The strengths-based practices inventory: A tool for measuring strengths-based service delivery in early childhood and family support programs. *Families in Society, 85*(3), 326–334.

Greene, R. R. (2007). *Social work practice: A risk and resilience perspective*. Belmont, CA: Thomson Brooks/Cole.

Holmes, G. E., & Saleebey, D. (1993). Empowerment, the medical model, and the politics of clienthood. *Journal of Progressive Human Services, 4*, 61–78.

Itzhaky, H., & Bustin, E. (2002). Strengths and pathological perspectives in community social work. *Journal of Community Practice, 10*(3), 61–73.

Kisthardt, W. (1993). The impact of the strengths model of case management from the consumer perspective. In M. Harris & H. Bergman (Eds.), *Case management: Theory and practice* (pp. 165–182). Washington, DC: American Psychiatric Association.

Lee, M. Y., Uken, A., & Sebold, J. (2004). Accountability for change: Solution-focused treatment with domestic violence offenders. *Families in Society, 85*(4), 463–476.

Macias, C., Farley, O. W., Jackson, R., & Kinney, R. (1997). Case management in the context of capitation financing: An evaluation of the strengths model. *Administration and Policy in Mental Health, 24*(6), 535–543.

Macias, C., Kinney, R., Farley, O. W., Jackson, R., & Vos, B. (1994). The role of case management within a community support system: Partnership with psychosocial rehabilitation. *Community Mental Health Journal, 30*(4), 323–339.

Modrcin, M., Rapp, C., & Poertner, J. (1988). The evaluation of case management services with the chronically mentally ill. *Evaluation and Program Planning, 11*, 307–314.

Ornstein, E. D., & Ganzer, C. (2000). Strengthening the strengths perspective: An integrative relational approach. *Psychoanalytic Social Work, 7*(3), 57–78.

Perkins, K., & Tice, C. (1999). Family treatment of older adults who misuse alcohol: A strengths perspective. *Journal of Gerontological Social Work, 31*(3/4), 169–185.

Rapp, C. A. (1998). *The strengths model: Case management with people suffering from severe and persistent mental illness*. New York: Oxford University Press.

Rapp, C. A., & Chamberlain, R. (1985). Case management services to the chronically mental ill. *Social Work, 30*(5), 417–422.

Rapp, C. A., & Goscha, R. J. (2006). *The strengths model: Case management with people with psychiatric disabilities* (2nd ed.). New York: Oxford University Press.

Rapp, C. A., & Wintersteen, R. (1989). The strengths model of case management: Results from twelve demonstrations. *Psychosocial Rehabilitation Journal, 13*(1), 23–32.

Ryan, C. S., Sherman, P. S., & Judd, C. M. (1994). Accounting for case management effects in the evaluation of mental health services. *Journal of Consulting and Clinical Psychology, 62*(5), 965–974.

Saleebey, D. (1992). *The strengths perspective in social work practice*. New York: Longman.

Saleebey, D. (1996). The strengths perspective in social work practice: Extensions and cautions. *Social Work, 41*(3), 296–305.

Saleebey, D. (2006). *The strengths perspective in social work practice* (4th ed.). Boston: Allyn and Bacon.

Seligman, M. P., & Csikszentmihalyi, M. (2000). Positive psychology. *American Psychologist, 55*, 5–14.

Shulman, L. (2006). *The skills of helping individuals, families, groups, and communities* (5th ed.). Belmont: Brooks/Cole.

Siegel, H. A., Fisher, J. H., Rapp, R. C., Kelliher, C. W., Wagner, J. H., O'Brien, W. F., et al. (1995). The strengths perspective of case management: A promising inpatient substance abuse treatment enhancement. *Journal of Psychoactive Drugs, 27*, 67–72.

Snyder, C. R. (2000). *Handbook of hope: Theory, measures, and applications*. San Diego: Academic Press.

Stanard, R. P. (1999). The effect of training in a strengths model of case management on outcomes in a community mental health center. *Community Mental Health Journal, 35*(2), 169–179.

Staudt, M., Howard, M. O., & Drake, B. (2001). The operationalization, implementation, and effectiveness of the strengths perspective: A review of empirical studies. *Journal of Social Service Research, 27*(3), 1–21.

Sullivan, W. P. (1992). Reclaiming the community: The strengths perspective and deinstitutionalization. *Social Work, 37*(3), 204–354.

Weick, A., Kreider, J., & Chamberlain, R. (2006). Solving problems from a strengths perspective. In D. Saleebey (Ed.), *The strengths perspective in social work practice* (4th ed., pp. 116–127). Boston: Allyn and Bacon.

Weick, A., Rapp, C., Sullivan, P., & Kisthardt, W. (1989). A strengths perspective for social work practice. *Social Work, 34*(4), 350–354.

Werrbach, G. B. (1996). Family-strengths-based intensive child case management. *Families in Society, 77*(4), 216–226.

Yip, K.-S. (2005). A strengths perspective in working with Alzheimer's disease. *The International Journal of Social Research and Practice, 4*(3), 434–441.

Yip, K.-S. (2006). A strengths perspective in working with an adolescent with self-cutting behaviors. *Child and Adolescent Social Work Journal, 23*(2), 134–146.

—Johnny S. Kim

# SUBSTANCE ABUSE. *See* Addictions; Alcohol and Drug Problems.

# SUICIDE

**Abstract:** Every year, more people in the world die from suicide than from homicide and wars combined. Efforts to reduce suicide have made several advances. Research has identified numerous suicide risk factors, and, though small in number, effective prevention and intervention strategies have been identified. Social workers are likely to encounter suicidal clients in their work, requiring suicide assessment and intervention skills.

KEY WORDS: suicide; attempted suicide; suicidal ideation; suicide prevention; treatment

Throughout history, people have struggled to understand suicide. Some historical and biblical figures portrayed suicide as an honorable act performed to save oneself from disgrace, servitude, or capture. Most religions condemned suicide. Many societies outlawed suicide. Philosophers such as Albert Camus opined that suicide is the only serious philosophical issue. Today, suicide is increasingly recognized as a tragic outcome of mental illness and life circumstances, and suicidality as a symptom to be treated, not scorned or stigmatized.

## Terminology

*Suicide* is self-inflicted, intentional death. A *suicide attempt* is a self-injurious act performed with the intent to end one's life. It is helpful to distinguish between true suicide attempts and *nonsuicidal self-injurious behaviors*, such as cutting oneself as a means to cope with or to signal distress to others. Researchers have used the term *parasuicide* to describe self-injury with or without suicidal intent, but the term has fallen out of favor due to its ambiguity. Thoughts of killing oneself, with or without the intent to do so, are referred to as *suicidal ideation*. Family members and others who are intimately affected by a person's suicide are called *suicide survivors*.

Many suicide prevention advocates use the phrase *completed suicide* to distinguish it from *attempted suicide*. Such terminology avoids the problematic language of "successful" and "failed" suicide, terms implying that someone who survives is a failure and that death equals success. However, the phrase "completed suicide" also elicits criticism, because incompletion generally has a negative meaning. Activists in the suicide prevention field discourage people from using the phrase "committed suicide," noting the term's stigmatizing connotations with committing a crime. Instead, many in the suicide prevention field prefer the term *died by suicide* (Suicide Prevention Resource Center, 2007).

"*Rational*" *suicide* occurs when, because of intolerable suffering caused by terminal illness, a person voluntarily ends his or her life (Werth & Holdwick, 2000). In *assisted suicide*, a physician or loved one acts on a terminally ill person's request to help him or her die. To many people, the topics of rational and assisted suicide fall more under the domain of end-of-life care than of suicide itself. For these reasons, clinicians and researchers often use the terms *hastened death*, *assisted death*, *aid in dying*, and *voluntary euthanasia* in lieu of suicide (Tucker & Steele, 2007).

## Demographics

Worldwide, approximately 900,000 million people die by suicide every year. The average suicide rate internationally is 15 per 100,000, and rates are three times higher in several eastern European countries. In 2004, when 32,439 people died by suicide in the United States, the U.S. rate was 11 out of 100,000. Suicide ranks as the 11th cause of death in the United States and the third leading cause among adolescents. Firearms account for slightly more than half of all suicides in the United States. Other common methods are suffocation (including hanging) and overdoses. Experts estimate that every suicide results in six suicide survivors, meaning that in a 10-year period, almost 2 million people in the United States are bereaved by suicide.

Suicide rates decreased in the United States and some western European countries in the 1990s (De Leo & Evans, 2004). For example, although suicides among young people in the United States had increased dramatically from 1950 to 1980, youth suicide rates fell by 20% from 1995 to 2003 (from 13 to 10 per 100,000) (Centers for Disease Control and Prevention, 2007). The reasons for the decline in youth's and adults' suicide rates are unknown, but cross-sectional studies indicate the drop is correlated with the rise in prescriptions of newer antidepressants such as selective serotonin reuptake inhibitors (for example, fluoxetine/ Prozac). Others have speculated that the decrease in number of suicides also coincides with decreases in substance use and with the widespread introduction of suicide prevention programs in schools.

For various reasons, suicide rates are estimated to be underreported by 10–50% (Maris, Berman, & Silverman, 2000). It may be difficult to determine whether a person actually intended to die, especially because only a minority of people who die by suicide leave a note. Suicide may be especially difficult to ascertain in cases of drowning and of recreational drug overdose (for example, opiates), because both can appear accidental. Coroners and medical examiners may avoid classifying a death as a suicide to spare the family any perceived stigma, guilt, and possible loss of insurance benefits.

In general, it is estimated that 18–36 suicide attempts occur for every completed suicide in the adult population, although estimates are much higher for adolescents (Crosby, Cheltenham, & Sacks, 1999; Moscicki, 2001). Up to 5% of adults and 10% of adolescents have reported ever attempting suicide. Researchers have not determined why a significant discrepancy exists between adolescent and adult reports of suicidal behavior. About 10–15% of individuals who make a nonfatal suicide attempt go on to later die by suicide.

## Cultural/Racial/Ethnic/Other Populations

Suicide rates vary considerably across age, gender, and racial groups (Table 1). On average, almost four times more men than women worldwide end their lives; the exception is China, where slightly more women than men die by suicide. Possible explanations for men's overall higher suicide rates concern their greater access to and familiarity with firearms and their lower rates of help seeking. Elderly white men die by suicide more than any group in the United States, with rates 3–5 times higher than average. Another high-risk group for suicide is American Indian/Alaska Native youth aged 15–24, whose suicide rate in 2004 was twice the average rate for youth (21 versus 10 per 100,000, respectively). In the United States, Black girls and women have the lowest suicide rates (1.8 per 100,000).

Age, gender, and racial differences also characterize suicide attempts. Unlike suicide, nonfatal suicide attempts occur far more frequently in girls and women than their male counterparts; the ratio is estimated to be 4 to 1. The highest risk for suicide attempts occurs from the late teens to early 20s. Latina adolescents are at particularly high risk for suicide attempts, with rates twice the national average for youth. American Indian adolescents also attempt suicide at disproportionately higher rates than other adolescents.

## Related Theory

Emile Durkheim is credited with beginning the sociological study of suicide. In his 1897 book *Le Suicide*, Durkheim (1951) contended that suicide rates reflect social dynamics, not individual pathology. He hypothesized that groups with sufficiently high levels of external regulation and social cohesion—what he termed "social integration"—generally had lower suicide rates than both less cohesive groups and excessively regulated groups. For example, Catholic communities had lower rates than Protestants, who more strongly encouraged individualism. Research has produced conflicting results about the merits of Durkheim's theories, and later sociological theories of suicidal behavior have focused on potentially causal factors in business cycles, social status, income, mobility, and societal attitudes toward suicide (Stack, 2000a, 2000b).

Numerous other theories of suicide have emerged from disciplines as diverse as epidemiology, biology, and economics, but the most influential theories center on psychology and biological psychiatry. The first major psychological theories of suicidal behavior emphasized unconscious psychological dynamics. The psychoanalyst Sigmund Freud (1957) suggested that suicidal thoughts actually represented hostile, unconscious wishes to kill another person. More recent psychological theories have stressed psychological pain and cognitive reactions. Edwin Shneidman, a psychologist who is considered the father of modern suicidology, notes that even though numerous risk factors exist for suicide, none is fatal unless there is also extreme psychological pain, what he calls "psychache" (1996). Such psychological pain arises from thwarted needs for nurturance, achievement, play, understanding, and other essentials for existence.

To the cognitive theorist, psychological pain is aggravated, or even fueled, by the ways individuals appraise themselves and their situations (Ellis, 2006). In the cognitive framework, thoughts determine feelings and behaviors. A distressed individual may fall prey to cognitive distortions about one's self, experiences with others, and future. Although the central focus in cognitive theories of suicide is on feelings of hopelessness,

TABLE 1
*Suicide Rates (Per 100,000) in the United States in 2004, by Age, Gender, and Race*

| AGE | 10–14 | 15–24 | 25–34 | 35–44 | 45–54 | 55–64 | 65–74 | 75+ | ALL AGES |
|---|---|---|---|---|---|---|---|---|---|
| Total | 1.3 | 10.4 | 12.7 | 15.1 | 16.6 | 13.8 | 12.3 | 16.4 | 11.0 |
| Gender | | | | | | | | | |
| Male | 1.7 | 16.8 | 20.4 | 23.0 | 24.8 | 22.1 | 22.5 | 37.2 | 17.7 |
| Female | 1.0 | 3.6 | 4.7 | 7.1 | 8.6 | 6.1 | 3.8 | 3.8 | 4.6 |
| Race/Ethnicity | | | | | | | | | |
| White (inc. Hispanic) | 1.3 | 11.0 | 13.6 | 16.9 | 18.6 | 15.1 | 13.4 | 17.5 | 12.3 |
| Black | 1.4 | 7.2 | 9.4 | 6.6 | 5.8 | 5.7 | 4.4 | 5.4 | 5.2 |
| American Indian/Alaska Native | 3.3* | 21.0 | 21.8 | 19.5 | 13.7 | 5.1* | 9.3* | 3.8* | 12.9 |
| Asian/Pacific Islander | 0.9* | 6.1 | 6.5 | 5.9 | 7.8 | 7.2 | 8.4 | 12.7 | 5.6 |

*Denotes an unreliable estimate, due to small populations in these age groups.
From Centers for Disease Control and Prevention, Web-Based Injury Statistics Query and Reporting System (WISQARS; http://www.cdc.gov/ncipc/wisqars/), 2007.

other problematic cognitions include negative myopia; black and white thinking; excessive self-blame; and the conviction that one is unlovable and helpless.

Theories of suicide in biological psychiatry implicate the roles of genetics; neurotransmitters, such as a serotonin; and impulsive and aggressive traits. In particular, a deficiency of serotonin, which may be genetically transmitted, is hypothesized to give rise to impulsivity and a vulnerability to suicide. The serotonin deficiency may also contribute to substance use, depression, and other risk factors for suicide. Although epidemiologic and twin studies (Joiner, Brown, & Wingate, 2005) have demonstrated that serotonin is associated with suicidal behavior, it is also understood that biological factors must intersect with psychological and social facets of living for suicidal behavior to eventuate.

## Risk and Protective Factors

Decades of research have identified numerous risk and protective factors for suicide and related behaviors (Maris et al., 2000). The most prominent risk factors are a prior suicide attempt and mental illness. Research indicates that 90–95% of people who die by suicide had at least one diagnosable mental disorder, particularly including depression, bipolar disorder, borderline personality disorder, and substance dependence or abuse. Other distal (that is, longstanding) risk factors include family history of suicidal behavior, exposure to suicide or suicidal behaviors in peers, disrupted family environment in childhood, and chronic illness. Proximal (that is, acute) risk factors include stressful life events (such as the recent loss of a loved one), intoxication, feelings of hopelessness, access to firearms, incarceration, and homelessness. Being gay, lesbian, or bisexual also relates to increased risk of suicide attempts (McDaniel, Purcell, & D'Augelli, 2001), but a relationship between sexual orientation and completed suicide has not been established.

Characteristics that may make individuals less likely to attempt or die by suicide are considered protective. Research has uncovered several protective factors that decrease suicide risk even in the face of major depression, including social support, spiritual and religious connections, moral objections to suicide, strong family ties (particularly feelings of responsibility to loved ones), emotional resilience, and academic and career achievements (Goldsmith, Pellmar, Kleinman, & Bunney, 2002).

Risk factors typically interact with each other to increase suicide risk and, as such, no one single cause of suicide exists. A person could have numerous suicide risk factors and not ever think about suicide, while another person could have only one risk factor and be severely suicidal. Despite numerous research findings about risk and protective factors, it still is impossible to predict whether a person will attempt suicide.

## Prevention

Primary prevention of suicide includes measures targeted at the general population. The *National Strategy for Suicide Prevention: Goals and Objectives for Action* (U.S. Dept. of Health and Human Services, 2001) calls for reducing access to lethal suicide methods. For example, some research shows that limiting access to firearms subsequently reduces suicide rates. Great Britain outlawed the sale of more than 16–32 over-the-counter analgesics (for example, acetaminophen) at any one time and required each pill to be individually wrapped. In the ensuing year, suicide by overdosing on these analgesics decreased by 22% (Hawton et al., 2004). Other primary prevention methods include screening people in nonclinical settings to detect suicide risk, improving access to mental health care services, and reducing stigma around suicide and mental illness.

## Treatment

Despite the gravity of suicide and related behaviors, little empirical evidence exists of effective interventions. One problem concerns the ethical and logistical difficulties inherent in conducting treatment effectiveness research with suicidal individuals. It simply is not possible to withhold treatment to people at risk for suicide in order to determine whether a comparison group receiving treatment improves at a superior rate. Consequently, studies investigating treatments with suicidal people have often excluded people at highest risk for suicide, had small numbers, and lacked a true comparison group (Hawton et al., 2003).

Nevertheless, several types of treatment have shown promise. In a randomized controlled trial (RCT), cognitive psychotherapy developed by the psychologist Aaron Beck reduced repetition of suicide attempts more effectively than "treatment as usual" or no treatment in the comparison group (Brown et al., 2005). Dialectical behavior therapy (DBT) also has demonstrated in randomized control trials its effectiveness at preventing or reducing repetition of suicide attempts in women with borderline personality disorder (Linehan, 2000), and it is becoming increasingly popular. DBT was developed by Marsha Linehan, a psychologist, and incorporates aspects of cognitive, behavioral, and skills training.

Treatment for suicidal people also may involve psychiatric medications prescribed by a physician. Lithium, a mood-stabilizing medication, has consistently shown evidence of preventing both suicide and suicide attempts in people with mood disorders.

However, lithium is toxic at high levels and requires regular blood testing. Although serotonin reuptake inhibitors (SSRIs) and other newer antidepressants correlate with recent declines in suicide rates, research indicates that a very small number of adolescents newly experience suicidal thoughts upon initiating SSRIs. This increased risk prompted the U.S. Food and Drug Administration in 2004 to issue "black box" warning, which requires that explicit warnings be placed on the medication's label and which stops one step short of prohibiting sales and use of the drug altogether for adolescents.

A common intervention, called "no-suicide contracts" or "safety agreements," involves having a suicidal client promise not to harm himself or herself within a specified period of time. However, no evidence has emerged that these agreements successfully prevent suicide. The use of the word "contract" can falsely imply that the document protects a social worker or other mental health professionals in the event of a lawsuit after a client death, which is not the case.

### Ethical Issues

A major ethical issue in working with suicidal individuals involves the right to self-determination. Although the social work profession promotes clients' entitlement to make and abide by their own decisions, the more important value of preserving life preempts self-determination. Consequently, social workers may need to take measures to involuntarily hospitalize someone whose suicidal plans place his or her life in imminent danger. It also may be necessary to violate a client's right to confidentiality (for example, by notifying authorities).

The need to protect people from their suicidal urges may be relative if a person has a terminal illness, lacks impaired judgment caused by mental illness, and acts without coercion. In their *Standards for Palliative and End of Life Care*, the National Association of Social Workers (2004) explicitly refrains from taking a moral stance on end-of-life issues such as assisted suicide. Physician-assisted death is legal in the Netherlands, Switzerland, and Belgium and in one U.S. state, Oregon, and almost 10% of U.S. physicians admit to having administered lethal overdoses or written a prescription for a lethal overdose to a terminally ill person regardless of the law (Meier et al., 1998).

### Roles and Implications for Social Work

When working with a client who may be at risk for suicide, social workers should conduct a thorough suicide risk assessment, asking at a minimum whether the client thinks about suicide, has a plan and the means to enact it, and intends to act on this plan. The social worker must ensure the client's safety, using hospitalization if the client is in imminent danger of harming himself or herself. All the while, social workers should routinely avail themselves of consultation and document all of these actions. Other steps to be taken include assessing the suicidal client's strengths and resources, and trying to limit access to a firearm or other lethal means.

Although social workers constitute the largest segment of mental health professionals in the United States, they have contributed very little to the development of theory, treatments, and research about suicide and related behaviors. A recent study determined that only 47 of 23,180 articles appearing in social work journals from 1980 to 2006 concerned empirical studies related to suicide (Joe & Niedermeier, 2006). Furthermore, the majority of social workers surveyed in a national study indicated that they received fewer than 2 hr of education related to suicide assessment and intervention during their graduate studies in social work (Feldman & Freedenthal, 2006).

Almost all social workers involved in direct practice, especially in mental health settings, will at one time or another work with a suicidal client. Other social work settings in which clientele may have elevated suicide risk include middle and high schools, jails and prisons, general medical hospitals, homeless shelters, sexual assault and domestic violence centers, and child welfare agencies. The very nature of social workers' jobs brings them in contact with people at elevated risk for suicide, making it essential that social workers have knowledge in suicide assessment and intervention.

### REFERENCES

Brown, G. K., Ten Have, T., Henriques, G. R., Xie, S. X., Hollander, J. E., & Beck, A. T. (2005). Cognitive therapy for the prevention of suicide attempts: A randomized controlled trial. JAMA: The Journal of the American Medical Association, 294, 563–570.

Centers for Disease Control and Prevention. (2007). Web-based injury statistics query and reporting system (WISQARS). Retrieved from www.cdc.gov/ncipc/wisqars

Crosby, A. E., Cheltenham, M. P., & Sacks, J. J. (1999). Incidence of suicidal ideation and behavior in the United States, 1994. Suicide and Life-Threatening Behavior, 29, 131–140.

De Leo, D., & Evans, R. (2004). International suicide rates and prevention strategies. Cambridge, MA: Hogrefe & Huber.

Durkheim, E. (1951). Suicide: A study in sociology (J. A. Spaulding & G. Simpson, Trans.). New York: Free Press (Original work published 1897).

Ellis, T. E. (Ed.). (2006). Cognition and suicide: Theory, research, and therapy. Washington, DC: American Psychological Association.

Feldman, B. N., & Freedenthal, S. (2006). Social work education in suicide intervention and prevention: An unmet need? *Suicide and Life-Threatening Behavior, 36*, 467–480.

Freud, S. (1957). Mourning and melancholia. In J. Strachey (Ed.), *The standard edition of the complete psychological works of Sigmund Freud* (Vol. 14, pp. 239–260). London: Hogarth Press (Originally published 1917).

Goldsmith, S. K., Pellmar, T. C., Kleinman, A. M., & Bunney, W. E. (2002). *Reducing suicide: A national imperative.* Washington, DC: National Academy Press.

Hawton, K., Simkin, S., Deeks, J., Cooper, J., Johnston, A., Waters, K., et al. (2004). UK legislation on analgesic packs: before and after study of long term effect on poisonings. *British Medical Journal, 329*, 1076–1080.

Hawton, K., Townsend, E., Arensman, E., Gunnell, D., Hazell, P., House, A., et al. (2003). Psychosocial and pharmacological treatments for deliberate self-harm (Cochrane Review). Retrieved from www.cochranelibrary.com

Joiner, T. E., Brown, J. S., & Wingate, L. R. (2005). The psychology and neurobiology of suicidal behavior. *Annual Review of Psychology, 56*, 287–314.

Joe, S., & Niedermeier, D. (2006). Preventing suicide: A neglected social work research agenda. *British Journal of Social Work*, Advance publication retrieved January 25, 2007, from http://bjsw.oxfordjournals.org/cgi/reprint/bcl353v1.pdf (doi:10.1093/bjsw/bcl353).

Linehan, M. M. (2000). The empirical basis of dialectical behavior therapy: Development of new treatments versus evaluation of existing treatments. *Clinical Psychology: Science and Practice, 7*, 113–119.

Maris, R. W., Berman, A. L., & Silverman, M. M. (2000). *Comprehensive textbook of suicidology.* New York: Guilford Press.

McDaniel, J. S., Purcell, D., & D'Augelli, A. R. (2001). The relationship between sexual orientation and risk for suicide: Research findings and future directions for research and prevention. *Suicide and Life-Threatening Behavior, 31* (Suppl.), 84–105.

Meier, D. E., Emmons, C. A., Wallenstein, S., Quill, T., Morrison, S., & Cassel, C. K. (1998). A national survey of physician-assisted suicide and euthanasia in the United States. *New England Journal of Medicine, 338*, 1193–1201.

Moscicki, E. K. (2001). Epidemiology of completed and attempted suicide: Toward a framework for prevention. *Clinical Neuroscience Research, 1*, 310–323.

National Association of Social Workers. (2004). *NASW standards for palliative and end of life care.* Washington, DC: Author.

Shneidman, E. S. (1996). *The suicidal mind.* Oxford: Oxford University Press.

Tucker, K. L., & Steele, F. B. (2007). Patient choice at end of life: Getting the language right. *Journal of Legal Medicine, 28*, 305–325.

Stack, S. (2000a). Suicide: A 15-year review of the sociological literature part I: Cultural and economic factors. *Suicide and Life-Threatening Behavior, 30*, 145–162.

Stack, S. (2000b). Suicide: A 15-year review of the sociological literature part II: Modernization and social integration perspectives. *Suicide and Life-Threatening Behavior, 30*, 163–176.

Suicide Prevention Resource Center. (2007). At a glance: Safe reporting on suicide. Retrieved November 9, 2007, from http://www.sprc.org/library/at_a_glance.pdf

U.S. Dept. of Health and Human Services. (2001). *The national strategy for suicide prevention: Goals and objectives for action.* Rockville, MD: Public Health Service.

Werth, J. L., Jr., & Holdwick, D. J., Jr. (2000). A primer on rational suicide and other forms of hastened death. *Counseling Psychologist, 28*, 511–539.

### FURTHER READING

Joiner, T. (2005). *Why people die by suicide.* Cambridge, MA: Harvard University Press.

Shea, S. C. (1999). *The practical art of suicide assessment: A guide for mental health professionals and substance abuse counselors.* New York: John Wiley.

### SUGGESTED LINKS

Web-Based Injury Statistics Query and Reporting System (WISQARS).
  *http://www.cdc.gov/ncipc/wisqars/*
Suicide Prevention and Resource Center.
  *http://www.sprc.org*
American Foundation for Suicide Prevention.
  *www.afsp.org*

—STACEY FREEDENTHAL

## SUPERVISION

**ABSTRACT:** Supervision of students and practitioners has been central to social work since its earliest evolution as a recognized profession. Central to the process is the idea of one professional with more knowledge, skill, and experience guiding the practice and development of another with less. The four content areas of supervision include direct practice, professional impact, job management, and continued learning. There are a number of supervision models, and most emphasize a positive supervisor–supervisee working relationship, a parallel process, and the importance of cultural competency. The contemporary context of social work supervision offers both opportunities and challenges to clinical supervision.

**KEY WORDS:** supervision; consultation; supervisor; supervisee; professional education; parallel process

## Definitions

Kadushin (1992) offered a definition of supervision in social work that combined the educational and administrative functions with an "expressive-supportive leadership" role (p. 20) as follows:

> A social work supervisor is an agency administrative staff member to whom authority is delegated to direct, coordinate, enhance, and evaluate on-the-job performance of the supervisees for whose work he (or she) is held accountable. In implementing this responsibility the supervisor performs administrative, educational and supportive functions in interaction with the supervisee in the context of a positive relationship. The supervisor's ultimate objective is to deliver to agency clients the best possible service, both quantitatively and qualitatively, in accordance with agency policies and procedures (p. 21).

In general, the content of social work supervision addresses four main areas (Kadushin & Harkness, 2002; Shulman, 1993): direct practice, professional impact, continued learning, and job management.

Supervision of direct practice refers to all activities designed to guide the social worker in assessment, intervention, and evaluation of client interventions. Such guidance usually involves regularly scheduled individual or group conferences with case presentations and process presentations. Case presentations address issues of assessment and treatment planning and can be opportunities for teaching the professional use of self. Process presentations involve analyzing records of interactions with clients, using media such as memory work (recalling the process from memory); process recording; observation; or audio- or video-taping.

Supervision of professional impact refers to all client-oriented activities designed to guide the social worker in dealing with other professionals (for example, psychiatrists, other social workers, and teachers), influencing policies and procedures in the professional environment, and affecting political systems whose policies have an impact on client interventions.

Supervision of continued learning involves working with the practitioner to help develop the skills required for life-long continued professional learning. This may include fostering professional use of self and self-scrutiny, tolerance for ambiguity, and openness to a variety of models and concepts. It may also include helping clinicians to articulate learning objectives and the steps for attaining them (see Caspi & Reid, 2002, for an elaboration in this area) and to use other sources of learning (that is, colleagues, group supervision, consultants, workshops, the literature) to enhance practice knowledge and skills.

Supervision of job management refers to guiding the supervisee in work-related issues, which create a frame for practice (Kadushin & Harkness, 2002; Munson, 2002; Shulman, 1993). Job management issues that can impact a supervisee's effectiveness with clients include record-keeping matters, handling of phone calls and missed sessions, timeliness, report-writing, and caseload management. Job management also refers to the supervisor's guidance relating to the supervisee's resolution of ethical issues, such as those arising from third-party matters (for example, managed-care requirements, insurance reimbursement) that can adversely affect service to clients.

IMPACT OF SUPERVISION ON SOCIAL WORK PRACTICE The nature of the supervisory relationship and the content and process of supervision can have a profound impact on the social worker's attitudes toward the practice setting (agency, school, hospital, and so forth) as well as on the social worker's direct practice and efforts toward professional impact. For example, in a large study of supervision and practice in a Canadian Provincial child welfare system, Shulman (1993) identified a parallel process in which the way supervisors related to their workers tended to impact the way workers related to their clients. The parallels also existed between managers and supervisors, with supervisors who reported having a positive relationship with their managers tending to have workers who reported a positive relationship with them. Positive relationship in this study was defined by items on questionnaires and included *rapport* (I get along with my supervisor), *trust* (I can tell my supervisor anything on my mind; I can share my mistakes as well as my failures), and *caring* (My supervisor cares as much about me as he cares about the clients; my supervisor is here to help me, not just to criticize me). Shulman points out that many of the skills needed to engage clients in order to develop a positive working relationship in the beginning phase of practice are the same skills as those needed in the supervision process (Shulman, 2006).

The important impact of supervision on practice can also be seen through its role in preparing BSW and MSW students for their roles as professional social workers. Bogo (2005), in a review of research studies on field education, defined this category of educational supervision as follows:

> Field education, also referred to as field practicum or field work, is the component of social work education where students learn to practice social

work through delivering social work services in agency and community settings. Field education is a required and integral component of the curriculum in all undergraduate and graduate programs in accredited schools of social work in the United States. It is organized in a systematic manner, directed by the university in partnership with a range of community organizations and settings, and evaluated in relation to the mission and goals of the academic program (pp. 163–164).

MODELS OF SOCIAL WORK SUPERVISION The supervision literature describes several models to guide the supervisor. Although assumptions and processes differ among the models, certain concepts are common to all. Most models emphasize "relationship" (Kadushin & Harkness, 2002; Munson, 2002; Shulman, 1993) and incorporate a developmental approach, in which supervision is dynamic in nature and evolves to meet the changing needs of the developing supervisee (Baker, Exum, & Tyler, 2002). Some models have addressed supervision and spirituality (Polanski, 2003) and Jungian psychology (Pajak, 2002). The theme of a "relational model" has been explored among trauma therapists (Wells, Trad, & Alves, 2003) and those whose AIDS clients are "in the shadow of death" (Ringel, 2001). Attempts have been made to integrate different models. Stoltenberg et al. draw upon elements of the following three models: The Elaboration Likelihood Model, The Interpersonal Influence Model, and The Integrated Developmental Model (Stoltenberg, McNeill, & Crethar, 1994). In addition, the growth of "evidence-based practice" has provoked discussion regarding models of practice and education.

Kadushin describes the *expressive-supportive leadership function*, in which supervisees are offered emotional support and given assistance when they have "job-related discouragements and discontents" (Kadushin & Harkness, 2002). Munson (1996) examines the *educational role*, the impact of different styles and approaches to supervision, and the skills needed to perform each supervisory function.

Building on the work of William Schwartz, Shulman identifies an *interactional model* in which the supervisor–supervisee relationship is examined against the back-drop of time phases: preliminary, beginning, middle, and ending and transition (Schwartz, 1960; Shulman, 2006). In this model, the supervisor mediates between the supervisee and the systems (that is, the client, the agency, or setting, and external professionals and systems) and describes educational supervision as mediating between the supervisee and the subject (that

is, assessment and practice knowledge, intervention skills, and so forth). Shulman (1978, 1981, 1993) also operationalized and researched the skills required to perform these functions. Most models have addressed the importance of integrating personal and professional, with special attention given to this issue by Aponte and Winter (2000) focusing on the "use of self."

### Contemporary Challenges

The model of social work supervision that integrates the administrative, educational, and emotional support functions of the supervisor is threatened by several trends and practices in today's service delivery environment. For example, as health-care delivery systems have "resized" their staff to decrease costs and improve efficiency (Berger & Mizrahi, 2001), clinical supervisors have been eliminated and clinical social workers are often left with "peer supervision" and supervision by other professionals (for example, director of nursing). A study of supervision models at 750 hospitals found that most clinical social workers were supervised by clinical social workers (the traditional model), but the use of that model has been decreasing since 1992. In some medical settings, supervision of practice has been shifted to the level of the interdisciplinary team, often resulting in the loss of centralized clinical supervision of clinical social workers by other clinical social workers (Berger & Mizrahi, 2001).

These trends represent a threat to traditional social work supervision, which presumes a strong professional relationship between supervisor and supervisee. Kaiser (1997) maintains what follows:

> Most would agree that a positive relationship between supervisor and supervisee is important if the supervision is to be effective. Although the tasks of supervision appear to follow common sense, those who have been either supervisors or supervisees observe that these tasks are often quite complicated in the real world. Two major blocks to the effective and smooth functioning of supervision are contextual issues, such as agency mission and funding restrictions, and relational issues. (p. 3)

The problems raised by employing professionals from other disciplines as supervisors of social workers mostly relate to the lack of understanding of the social work practice model and the wider functional role of the social work profession. For example, a supervisor from the nursing profession may not understand that the history of the social work profession calls for social workers to consider the hospital as the "second client." A nurse supervisor might not be supportive or helpful in supervision of the social worker's efforts to have professional impact on the system (for example, doctors, nurses, procedures, policies).

The dominant "managed-care" delivery system affects both the supervision model and the decision-making authority of the supervisor and the practitioner (Munson, 2002). Cost-containment measures may affect private practitioners as well as agency-based and organization-based clinicians, as when they are required to seek approval, often in a phone conversation with a managed-care employee who is not a clinical social worker, for continuation of service or referral to supplementary services. Munson highlighted this loss of professional autonomy as a growing threat that can adversely affect ethical decisions, practice relationships, fee setting, privacy and confidentiality, supervision issues, professional language, professional status, and professional organizations (Munson, 1996). Some forces damage clinical supervision, while others increase its importance: since clinical social workers constitute the largest group providing reimbursable mental-emotional health services, the need for skilled clinical supervision and consultation is growing. These often-conflicting contextual factors and pressure argue the need for clear criteria for effective supervision and standards of practice for supervision.

An effort to develop national standards for clinical supervision, undertaken by the American Board of Examiners in Clinical Social Work, included the publication of a position paper (American Board of Examiners in Clinical Social Work, 2004). (Some content in this entry is drawn from this position paper on clinical supervision developed by the American Board of Examiners in Clinical Social Work and drafted by me, with contributions from a committee of experts. See http://www.abecsw.org/diplomates/posit/d_abes_position.shtml.) The paper defines advanced clinical supervision practice, describes the domains of clinical supervision, and sets out behavioral standards. This position paper, and the approach to its development, has been recognized by the Annapolis Coalition, a private–public partnership backed by SAMHSA, as a model for others engaged in identifying practice competencies and best practices (see http://www.annapoliscoalition.org).

CULTURAL COMPETENCIES The importance of cultural competency is a theme that cuts across all other competencies required for supervision practice. Culture refers to ethnicity, race, age, class, gender, sexual orientation, religion, immigration status, mental or physical disability, and any other relevant characteristics. Cultural competence is generally defined as practice and supervision that are guided by an understanding of the impact of culture (Barker, 2003, p. 104).

A diagnosis or treatment plan that does not take culture into consideration will most often miss the mark. In terms of professional knowledge, the supervisor and supervisee need to understand how culture affects the client (that is, norms of behavior for a particular population).

Cultural competency includes an understanding of diversity within diversity (Kaiser, 1997; Shulman, 1993, 2006). The tendency to use general knowledge about a particular population leads to stereotyping, which is often a problem for beginning practitioners. No less important than understanding a group's culture is the appreciation of diversity within that group, and openness to the differences that make a client an individual. In particular, the supervisor needs to recognize that some students and practitioners have had experiences that led them to close off exploration of sensitive and taboo areas, including social work courses or training on oppression that were themselves oppressive. The supervisor needs to help these students and workers to feel safe, and needs to create conditions in which all supervisees can share what they really think and feel, rather than what they think the supervisor wants to hear. The impact of openness in the discussion of ethnic, gender, and sexual-orientation variables in supervision was studied by Gatmon et al. (2001), who reported that such openness resulted in supervisees' increased satisfaction with supervision (p. 102).

In addition to knowledge and skills in relation to particular cultures, both supervisor and supervisee need to address "interethnic" and "intraethnic" relationships. An interethic relationship may be one with an African-American supervisor and a white supervisee. An intraethnic example would be a Latino supervisor and a Latino supervisee. Gender relationships—such as a female supervisor with a male social worker—also need to be considered. Each instance offers potential barriers to effective supervision and opportunities to enhance supervision. Communication theorists have referred to this as developing a "third culture" that arises between supervisor and supervisee. Caspi and Reid (2002) address the issue of difference using this framework. The same societal taboos that make it difficult to address these issues in practice are paralleled in supervision. If the supervisor–supervisee pairing cannot even recognize either interethnic or intraethnic issues in their relationship, it makes it more difficult to discuss these issues in the social worker's practice. For example, an Asian-American social worker who experiences comments from a client that appear to be racist in nature may have difficulty even raising the issue with a white supervisor if their own interethnic relationship has never been identified.

## REFERENCES

American Board of Examiners in Clinical Social Work. (2004). *Clinical supervision: A practice specialty of clinical social work*. Salem, MA: Author.

Aponte, H. J., & Winter, J. E. (2000). The person and practice of the therapists: Treatment and training. In M. Baldwin (Ed.), *The use of self in therapy* (2nd ed.). New York: The Haworth Press.

Baker, S. B., Exum, H. A., & Tyler, R. E. (2002). The developmental process of clinical supervisors in training: An investigation of the supervisor complexity model. *Counselor Education and Supervision, 42*, 15–30.

Barker, R. L. (2003). *The social work dictionary*. Washington, DC: The NASW Press.

Berger, C., & Mizrahi, T. (2001). An evolving paradigm of supervision within a changing health care environment. *Social Work in Health Care, 32*(4), 1–18.

Bogo, M. (2005). Field instruction in social work: A review of the research literature. *The Clinical Supervisor, 24*(1/2), 163–193.

Caspi, J., & Reid, W. J. (2002). *Educational supervision in social work: A task-centered model of field instruction and staff development*. New York: Columbia University Press.

Gatmon, D., Jackson, D., Koshkarian, L., Martos-Perry, N., Molina, A., & Patel, N., et al. (2001). Exploring ethnic, gender, and sexual orientation variables in supervision: Do they really matter? *Journal of Multicultural Counseling and Development, 29*(2), 102–113.

Kadushin, A. (1992). *Supervision in social work* (3rd ed.). New York: Columbia University Press.

Kadushin, A., & Harkness, D. (2002). *Supervision in social work* (4th ed.). New York: Columbia University Press.

Kaiser, T. L. (1997). *Supervisory relationships: Exploring the human element*. Pacific Grove, CA: Brooks/Cole.

Munson, C. E. (1993). Clinical social work supervision, (2nd ed.). Binghamton, NY: Haworth Press.

Munson, C. E. (1996). Autonomy and managed care in clinical social work practice. *Smith College Studies in Social Work, 66*, 241–260.

Munson, C. E. (2002). *Handbook of clinical social work supervision* (3rd ed.). New York: Hawthorn Press.

Pajak, E. (2002). Clinical supervision and psychological functions: A new direction for theory and practice. *Journal of Curriculum and Supervision, 17*, 177–189.

Polanski, P. J. (2003). Spirituality in supervision. *Counseling and Values, 47*, 131–141.

Ringel, S. (2001). In the shadow of death: Relational paradigms in clinical supervision. *Clinical Social Work Journal, 29*(2), 171–179.

Schwartz, W. (1960). *Content and process in the educative experience*. Unpublished doctoral dissertation, Teachers College, Columbia University, New York.

Shulman, L. (1978). A study of practice skill. *Social Work, 23*, 274–281.

Shulman, L. (1981). *Identifying, measuring and teaching the helping skills*. New York: Council on Social Work Education and the Canadian Association of Schools of Social Work.

Shulman, L. (1993). *Interactional supervision*. Washington, DC: NASW Press.

Shulman, L. (2006). *The skills of helping individuals, families, groups and communities* (5th ed.). Belmont, CA: Thomson Brooks/Cole.

Stoltenberg, C. D., McNeill, B. W., & Crethar, H. C. (1994). Changes in supervision as counselors and therapists gain experience: A review. *Professional Psychology—Research and Practice, 25*, 416–449.

Wells, M., Trad, A., & Alves, M. (2003). Training beginning supervisors working with new trauma therapists: A relational model of supervision. *Journal of College Student Psychotherapy, 17*, 19–39.

## FURTHER READING

Hardy, K. V., & Laszloffy, T. A. (1992). Training racially sensitive family therapists: Context, content and contact. *Families in Society, 73*, 364–370.

Shulman, L. (1995). The clinical supervisor-practitioner working alliance: A parallel process. *The Clinical Supervisor, 24*(1/2), 23–48.

—LAWRENCE SHULMAN

# SUPPLEMENTAL SECURITY INCOME

**ABSTRACT:** This entry provides an overview of the federal Supplemental Security Income (SSI) program, including a discussion of who is eligible for benefits, benefit levels, and program administration. The history of the program is provided and the impact of the 1996 Welfare Reform Act on SSI is discussed. Current policy challenges and policy relevance to social work practitioners and educators are considered.

**KEY WORDS:** disability; older adults; income support; welfare

Supplemental Security Income (SSI) is a social welfare program in the United States established in the early 1970s as a part of the Federal War on Poverty program begun in 1964. SSI replaced many existing state programs in support of aged persons, the blind, and people with disabilities (Barusch, 2006). Because SSI is a federal program, the federal portion of benefits is consistent across states. In many states, SSI recipients receive a state supplement to SSI and the amount varies by state (Social Security Administration, 2006). Therefore, a person with a disability in Maryland may not receive the same benefits as someone with the same disability in California. Since SSI benefits are dependent not only upon meeting criteria of age or disability but upon income and assets, applicants must meet a "means test."

The work of Gilbert and Terrell (2005, p. 67) is used to evaluate four dimensions of SSI policy: *"what benefits are offered, to whom they are offered, how they are delivered, and how they are financed."*

## What Benefits Are Offered?

As of 2006 maximum SSI federal benefit levels are $603 a month for an individual and $904 for an eligible couple who both qualify for SSI benefits (Social Security Administration, 2006). Benefit levels are adjusted yearly according to formulas, incorporating cost of living increases. Some income is exempt when calculating benefit eligibility and levels, for instance the first $65 in earnings and unearned income such as food stamps or housing assistance are exempt. Resources counted in determining eligibility include assets and income. Assets may include savings and real estate investments. The allowable asset limits as of 2006 are $2,000 for an individual and $3,000 for a married couple (Social Security Administration). An individual's primary residence is not counted to determine eligibility. States may also supplement benefits and determine their supplement levels. For the 10 states that administer the SSI program, the application for the state supplement is included in the SSI application process. For the states that administer their own supplement program, the applicant must also apply for state benefits (Social Security Administration).

## Who Receives Benefits?

As of November 2006, there were over 7 million beneficiaries of SSI. To be eligible, applicants must be either over age 65, or have a disability that severely limits ability to work, and have no other income or resources to meet basic needs. The majority of recipients (~6 million) are adults with disabilities and over 1 million are children with disabilities.

## How Are They Delivered?

Though federally funded, benefits are often accessed and administered at the state level. The office of Disability Determination Services (DDS) processes claims for disability benefits through each state's disability determination service. Beneficiaries are subject to review to determine continued eligibility (Social Security Administration, 2006).

## How Are They Financed?

In the United States, programs requiring a means test are often described as welfare or assistance programs, while those based upon contributions in the form of earmarked taxes (that is, taxes for a particular purpose) are described as insurance programs. Assistance programs, including SSI, are financed through general revenues.

## Recent Changes and Trends

The Personal Responsibility and Work Opportunity Reconciliation Act of 1996 (PRWORA) is usually considered in association with the major shift from the Federal entitlement Aid to Families with Dependent Children (AFDC) program to the Temporary Assistance for Needy Families. However, it also had a profound effect upon SSI. For instance, many children with developmental disabilities were removed because disability criteria became more stringent, and many noncitizens were removed. Disabling conditions due to alcohol or drug addiction were also no longer eligible disabilities for benefit receipt. Some of these categories have been restored. For example, legal noncitizens (other than special categories) are currently able to apply for benefits after living in the country for 5 years, and many children have been returned to the roles following the 1997 Balanced Budget Act (Schmidt, 2004).

AFDC, although designed to serve a different population, was similar in some ways to SSI (Meyer, 1995) as it was a welfare entitlement program and means tested. Following the passage of PRWORA, AFDC was replaced with the Temporary Assistance to Needy Families (TANF) program. TANF programs vary from state to state but are not entitlement programs, and in addition to meeting needs or means tests, participants are subject to sanctions and time-limited benefits. In the past, SSI recipients who were caring for dependent children could also receive AFDC. Under the new TANF programs, this varies by state. Some states allow SSI recipients to receive TANF for their minor children with exemptions on work requirements and others have special programs for SSI recipients with dependent children.

## Current Challenges

More than a decade ago, Meyer (1995) identified the following problems and issues related to SSI: (a) benefits are inadequate, (b) benefits vary among states, (c) the program has built in disincentives to marriage, (d) the eligibility standards are outdated, (e) work incentives for disabled people are inconsistent, (f) many who appear eligible do not receive benefits, (g) the program discourages savings, and (h) the program may not adequately provide for individual needs. These issues continue to be present: benefits are still inadequate and many SSI recipients remain in poverty. Because of state supplements, benefits vary across states. The program discourages marriage by reducing benefits for married couples. Though slightly modified, the eligibility standards remain outdated and work incentives are inconsistent. Many older adults who are eligible still do not receive benefits. Beneficiaries are discouraged from saving by not being allowed to accumulate assets though there has been some progress in this area. For instance, at their discretion, states may specify the use of Individual Development Accounts (IDA) to promote saving for home ownership and disregard such savings as income in determining benefit eligibility (Sweeney, 2004). The number of potentially eligible who are not receiving benefits is hard to determine, however, some research suggests that up to 60% of individuals denied on the basis of disability were actually disabled (Szymendera, 2006). If we were to add in those that might be eligible but were denied or discouraged from applying due to asset limits, the numbers might be significant indeed.

## Implications for Social Work

Social workers need a working knowledge of the benefit system for older adults and people with disabilities of which SSI is a part. They need to be able to inform their clients about how to apply for SSI, which is a potential source of income and medical assistance; they need to have enough information to advocate with and for clients who are wrongly denied services. For instance, if initially denied benefits, a person with a disability has recourse to an appeals process. Navigation of the multi-layered appeal process can be arduous, with some cases even taking years. In response to criticisms and in an effort to reach some claimants that have been wrongly denied benefits in the past, new rules should soon go into effect nationally (Szymendera, 2006) that are argued to streamline the appeals process and increase accuracy of determination decisions. Social workers need to keep abreast of the policy issues that impact the people served, providing a relevant link to policy and practice. That not much has changed regarding SSI in the early 21st century, while discouraging, presents an opportunity for the engagement of social workers interested in social change and social justice issues. National groups with an interest in SSI advocacy, and represented by local chapters, include groups representing older Americans, the National Alliance on Mental Illness (NAMI), and Legal Aid Societies.

### REFERENCES

Barusch, A. S. (2006). *Foundations of social policy: Social justice in human perspective* (2nd ed.). Belmont, CA: Thompson Learning.

Gilbert, N., & Terrell, P. (2005). *Dimensions of social welfare policy* (6th ed.). Boston: Pearson Education.

Meyer, D. (1995). Supplemental security income, In *The encyclopedia of social work* (19th ed.). New York: Oxford University Press.

Schmidt, L. (2004). *Effects of welfare reform on the supplemental security (SSI) program.* National Poverty Center Policy Brief No. 4. Retrieved October 23, 2007, from http://npc.umich.edu/publications/policy_briefs/brief4/http://www.npc.umich.edu/publications/policy_briefs/brief4/brief4.pdf

Social Security Administration. (2006). SSI. Retrieved January 15, 2007, from http://www.ssa.gov/notices/supplemental-security-income/

Sweeney, E. P. (2004). *Moving in the right direction: Recent changes in benefit programs assist people with disabilities in building assets.* World Disability Institute. Retrieved October 24, 2007, from http://www.wid.org/programs/access-to-assets/equity/equity-e-newsletter-march-2004/moving-in-the-right-direction-recent-changes-in-benefit-programs-assist-individuals-with-disabilities-in-building-assets

Szymendera, S. (2006). *Social Security Disability Insurance (SSDI) and Supplemental Security Income (SSI): Proposed changes to the disability determination and appeals processes.* Congressional Research Service. Retrieved October 25, 2007, from http://opencrs.cdt.org/rpts/RL33179_20060424.pdf

—SANDY MAGAÑA AND SHAWN CASSIMAN

# SURVEY RESEARCH

**ABSTRACT:** Surveys have always been a popular social work research method. They are particularly applicable for portraying population characteristics on the basis of a sample. Two key methodological issues influencing the value of any survey are the representativeness of its respondents and the reliability and validity of its measures. Surveys can be administered by mail, online, or in face-to-face or telephone interviews. Each modality has advantages and disadvantages. Ultimately, which method to use will often depend on the purpose of the research, the nature of the research question, and feasibility considerations.

**KEY WORDS:** surveys; social survey movement; sampling; mailed surveys; online surveys; interview surveys; Pittsburgh Survey; nonresponse bias

A survey is a data-collection method that can be conducted to describe a population or test a hypothesis. Unlike data collection methods that rely on direct observation of behavior, surveys rely on what people say, rather than observing what they do. Typically, a sample of respondents is selected from a certain population. Ideally, the sample should represent that population. Depending on the sampling procedures used, some samples can be more safely assumed to be representative than others. The individuals constituting the sample are then interviewed or administered questionnaires. Surveys can be conducted at one point in time, and are thus deemed cross-sectional, or they can be conducted longitudinally to assess how populations change over time. When surveys are conducted in cross-sectional studies to test hypotheses, one of their chief disadvantages is that their findings are correlational only. They do not show which variable preceded which, and thus do not permit causal inferences. Longitudinal surveys, however, do reveal the chronological order of events and thus offer more of a basis for speculating about causal effects (Rubin & Babbie, 2008). But even longitudinal surveys—by definition—do not involve control groups, and thus are deemed to have less validity than do experiments when the research purpose is to ascertain causality, such as when we seek to evaluate the effectiveness of interventions, programs, or policies.

## Historical Roots

Despite their limitations, surveys have always been one of the most commonly used research methods in social work. The earliest surveys in social work typically were conducted to establish databases that could be used in advocating for social reform. According to Polansky (1975), perhaps the earliest surveys conducted for social reform purposes occurred mid-18th-century Europe. In some, the working poor were interviewed regarding their earnings and expenditures for the purpose of selecting appropriate levels of relief grants.

The most prominent early use of surveys in social work is associated with what was called the social survey movement (Rubin & Babbie, 2008). That movement emerged from the work of Charles Booth, a wealthy, conservative London shipowner who had worked his way out of poverty. In 1886 he set out to disprove an 1885 report by London Marxists claiming that one-fourth of the working class lived in severe poverty. Using more scientific and objective survey procedures, and funding the project himself, Booth and his assistants interviewed the residents of East London about their finances, living conditions, and other forces bearing on their lives (Rubin & Babbie, 2008). Their investigation, which also used participant observation and the analysis of available records, was reported in 17 volumes called *The Life and Labour of the People of London* (1891–1903/1970). Ironically, the conservative Booth concluded that the conditions of the working class were even worse than depicted by the

Marxists! He found that 30.7% of the population were living in poverty, and consequently wound up recommending some social welfare measures that he termed "limited socialism" (Polansky, 1975; Zimbalist, 1977).

Booth's work coincided with the emergence of the settlement house movement—an era commonly deemed to be the roots of the social reform component of social work. Settlement workers lived among the poor and working classes, served them in settlement houses in their neighborhoods, and thus learned about their living conditions. Some settlement workers published studies about what they learned. Most, however, lacked the time and other resources to carry out systematic research on the conditions of the poor. By the turn of the century, however, muckraking journalists and novelists began exposing urban squalor and exploitation that characterized the lives of the poor and working classes. Their works aroused public concern.

Among those aroused was a group of social workers and civic leaders in Pittsburgh, who raised funds to conduct a study of social conditions there. Their work became known as the famous *Pittsburgh Survey*, perhaps the most historically notable survey in social work (Zimbalist, 1977). Inspired by Booth's work, the Pittsburgh Survey was conducted from 1909 to 1914. It was published in a series of volumes covering a vast array of living and working conditions. Its major theme was "the grim omnipresence of the steel mills, whose impact on life and economy of this industrial center is seen on almost every page of the report" (Zimbalist, 1977, p. 125). This survey exposed the deplorable impact of the steel mills on the lives of the mill workers. It estimated that one-fourth of institutionalized children had diseases or accidents that were preventable (Zimbalist). Its findings stimulated social reforms, including the reduction of the work day to 8 hr and the abolition of the 7-day work week. Its success sparked the rapid spread of the Social Survey Movement during the second decade of the 20th century, as social workers in other cities emulated the Pittsburgh Survey.

The early social surveys covered all aspects of community life (industrial, economic, political, and social), and reported extensive statistics in diverse areas such as disease, crime, and income. Studying one community at a time and at one particular point in time, they did not aim to generalize beyond that community at that time (Zimbalist, 1977). Neither were they conducted in a balanced and objective manner. Rather than seeking truth, their aim was to amass data so that a compelling case could be made to arouse the community to take social action to achieve social reform. Although these surveys used research as a tool to galvanize facts, the facts sometimes were interpreted and reported in a partisan manner that struck some as propagandistic. The perception that they were biased is cited by Zimbalist (1977) as one reason why social surveys fell from grace during the 1920s. Other historical factors included the impact of World War I, the end of the social reform era, and the cost and time required by the broad scope of the surveys. Although depicting social surveys as a panacea that would dramatically alleviate all a city's ills initially seemed to justify their costs, those costs became less acceptable as the envisioned levels of social change were not achieved (Zimbalist, 1977).

The successes of the social survey movement also contributed to its decline. Local coordinating agencies and planning organizations during the late 1920s institutionalized survey data collection as a routine agency function. Narrower in scope than their social survey forerunners, the organizations focused their data collection on specific areas of social work needs and services. Their efforts yielded similar descriptive data from year to year and led to theoretical studies that attempted to answer specific research questions geared to bettering the ability to understand, explain, and alleviate specific problems in a particular area (for example, health or delinquency) (Polansky, 1975). The decline of the social survey movement did not, however, lead to decline in the use of survey methods in social work, which continue to be a prominent mode of inquiry for social work researchers. (Some may say "*too* prominent" in light of the need for more research on the effectiveness of social work interventions. More about that later.)

### Types of Social Work Surveys

Surveys can be conducted in various ways. Mailed surveys, for example, involve sending self-administered questionnaires for respondents to complete. Because they are one of the least costly and least time-consuming ways to collect data, mailed surveys are frequently used. More costly and time-consuming are interview surveys, which can be conducted face-to-face or over the telephone. Perhaps the most expedient way to conduct surveys is online. Although surveys typically involve collecting information from people, some surveys involve written materials, such as surveys of published articles to assess the characteristics of authors publishing different types of studies (Rubin & Babbie, 2008).

Surveys typically are associated with descriptive studies, but they can also be conducted for explanatory purposes. A common use of descriptive surveys in social work is to assess the service needs of a target population. Another common use is to assess consumer satisfaction with services. If a survey tests a hypothesis about something—such as the notion that recipients of one type of service will be more satisfied than recipients of a different type of service—then it goes beyond descriptive purposes and involves an explanatory purpose (Rubin & Babbie, 2008).

### Methodological Issues in Survey Research

One critical methodological issue that can influence a survey's validity is the representativeness of its respondents. Two key issues affecting the representativeness of survey respondents are the sampling methods employed and the degree of nonresponse bias. As to sampling, probability sampling methods are typically preferred to nonprobability methods in quantitative surveys. (In qualitative research, however, nonprobability methods are more commonly used and are generally less problematic [Rubin & Babbie, 2008].)

Probability, or random, sampling methods avoid selection bias—and thus are deemed more likely to accurately represent a population—by using random numbers to give every member of a population an equal chance of being selected for the sample. Many surveys in social work, however, use nonprobability sampling methods. The reasons for the frequent use of nonprobability methods pertain primarily to feasibility issues. It is very difficult, if not impossible, for example, to obtain a probability sample, of homeless people. In addition, nonprobability sampling methods are less time-consuming and are cheaper than probability sampling methods. Nonprobability sampling methods may involve the use of the researcher's own judgment in attempting to pick members who they think best represent a population. Relying on judgment can be risky. The researcher's judgment may be faulty, and may be biased. An even riskier alternative is to simply rely on individuals who are readily available (for example, surveying one's students or surveying clients who happen to be present at a particular time) (Rubin & Babbie, 2008).

Nonresponse bias can seriously impede the representativeness of a survey sample regardless of the sampling procedure used. If a questionnaire is mailed to a randomly selected list of potential respondents, for example, and a large proportion of them fail to respond, then there may be significant differences between the respondents and the nonrespondents regarding the survey topic. The respondents, for example, may feel more strongly, more positively, or more negatively about the topic than do the nonrespondents (Rubin & Babbie, 2008).

Another key methodological issue in survey research pertains to the validity of the survey's measurement procedures. For example, were questions administered in an unbiased fashion? Or was it biased, such as by cuing respondents as to which kinds of responses are desired. Bias is not the only form of invalidity in survey measurement. Another involves unreliability, which can result from the use of questionnaires or interview schedules that are too complex, cumbersome, fatiguing, or boring. Also, they may be culturally insensitive, such as by using language that some minority respondents do not understand or by using idiomatic phrases that do not have the same conceptual meaning in different cultures (for example, asking people to agree or disagree with the statement "The Encyclopedia of Social Work is so funny, it has me in stitches."). Steps that can be taken to avoid cultural insensitivity include translating and back-translating instruments, having a panel of experts from different cultures examine the back-translated versions to assess conceptual equivalence, using bilingual interviewers, sensitizing interviewers to cultural differences, conducting a series of pretest and revisions to debug survey instruments, and testing the reliability and validity of translated instruments in different cultures.

Each survey modality has advantages and disadvantages. Mailed surveys and online surveys, for example, are cheaper and less time-consuming to administer, and they provide respondents with complete anonymity, which is an important advantage when questions are asked about sensitive topics. Interviews, on the other hand, have the advantages of decreasing the likelihood of obtaining incomplete questionnaires, providing an opportunity to explain words or phrases that respondents do not understand, avoiding the discarding of questionnaires, and the providing the opportunity to observe and probe unexpected behaviors or comments.

Telephone interviews are cheaper and quicker than face-to-face interviews because there is no travel. They avoid the problem of how to dress. They may be safer for interviewers. Not having to face an interviewer may make it easier for respondents to answer sensitive questions candidly. Some respondents, however, may be wary when they cannot see the interviewer, and may be annoyed by intrusive survey calls that interfere with what they are doing at home. It is easy for them to abort the interview by simply hanging up.

In the past, telephone interviews were thought to be vulnerable to a class bias, because very poor people were less likely to be able to afford a telephone or because affluent people were more likely to have unlisted numbers. These concerns diminished as telephones became more widespread among the poor, and as random-digit dialing came into use rather than relying on selecting samples from listed telephone numbers. However, technological advances have led to new concerns about

class bias. One is the prevalence of answering machines. Another is the growth in popularity of cell phones.

New technologies also have increased the use of online surveys. For example, a questionnaire can be available at a Web site, and a very large number of potential respondents can be contacted at once via e-mail and asked to go to the website where they can anonymously complete the questionnaire and have their responses automatically submitted. This saves postage costs and the time it takes to stuff and address envelopes and to code and enter data for electronic processing. However, online surveys are particularly vulnerable to sampling bias. Internet users are more likely to be more affluent, younger, and better educated than nonusers. Over time, this may change, as was the case with the telephone.

### Conclusions and Future Trends

All social work research methods have their own advantages and disadvantages. For example, experimentation may be used to maximize internal validity, or qualitative methods may be used to maximize probing into the deeper meaning of a phenomenon or to observe actual behavior directly as it occurs in natural settings. When external validity is a priority, however, surveys may make the most sense. Surveys are a sensible choice when the priority is to portray a population accurately and objectively or to control statistically for a large number of variables.

Surveys have some special strengths. Assuming the use of proper sampling and measurement techniques, they make it feasible to gather data from a large sample and generalize to a large population. This in turn enables the use of multivariate analyses to control statistically for numerous exogenous variables. Even the best surveys, however, have some weaknesses that are virtually impossible to avoid. One such weakness is the need for standardization in soliciting responses, which limits idiosyncratic probing and observation to assess the deeper meanings and unique contexts of phenomena across diverse respondents. In addition, surveys are limited to assessing what people say; their words may not match their deeds.

Finally, the standardization and inflexibility of surveys—in addition to being a weakness—can also be a strength. By asking the same questions in the same manner to all respondents makes surveys less vulnerable to biases in observation and data collection than are some other research modalities.

Ultimately, decisions about which method to use will often depend on the purpose of the research, the nature of the research question, and feasibility considerations. These factors will influence the decision about what type of survey modality to use and whether to use some method other than a survey.

## REFERENCES

Booth, C. (1970). *The life and labor of the people of London*. New York: AMS Press. (Original work published 1891–1903)

Polansky, N. A. (1975). *Social work research*. Chicago: University of Chicago Press.

Rubin, A., & Babbie, E. (2008). *Research Methods for Social Work* (6th ed.). Belmont, CA: Thomson Brooks/Cole.

Zimbalist, S. (1977). *Historic themes and landmarks in social welfare research*. New York: Harper & Row.

## SUGGESTED LINKS

Online survey methods.
*www.websm.org/*
General Social Survey.
*http://gss.norc.org/*
Public opinion surveys.
*http://www.ciser.cornell.edu/info/polls.shtml*
United States Bureau of Census website.
*www.census.gov*
Survey research methods.
*http://gsociology.icaap.org/methods/surveys.htm*

—ALLEN RUBIN

# TASK-CENTERED PRACTICE

**ABSTRACT:** Task-centered practice is a social work technology designed to help clients and practitioners collaborate on specific, measurable, and achievable goals. It is designed to be brief (typically 8–12 sessions), and can be used with individuals, couples, families, and groups in a wide variety of social work practice contexts. With nearly 40 years of practice and research arguing for its effectiveness, task-centered practice can rightfully claim to be one of social work's original "evidence-based practices," though the relative paucity of research on its effectiveness in this decade suggests that the approach itself may have become increasingly integrated into other brief social work technologies.

**KEY WORDS:** brief treatment; case work; contracts; goal setting; task-centered

Task-centered practice (TCP) is now well into its fourth decade as a social work practice model, and has matured as a social work generalist practice tool that can empower clients to solve a wide variety of problems. Originally formulated by Laura Epstein (1914–1996) and William Reid (1928–2003) at the University of Chicago's School of Social Service Administration (SSA), the approach has been adopted by schools of social work and social work practitioners internationally, and the key textbooks for TCP have been translated into numerous languages. Many popular recent social work brief treatment approaches, such as narrative therapy and solution-focused brief treatment, have incorporated facets of TCP, and many key ideas of TCP are being taught in American schools of social work generalist practice courses. However, despite the seeming prevalence of the approach in multiple settings and its potential applicability to a wide variety of problems typically treated by social work practitioners, TCP struggles to gain the recognition and respect it deserves as a social work practice innovation.

## Definitions and Descriptions

TCP involves a four-step process that trains social work practitioners to work closely with clients to establish distinct and achievable goals based on an agreed-upon presenting problem, usually called the target problem. Under TCP, a maximum of three target problems are identified by the client and the social worker collaborates with the client on devising tasks to work on those target problems. The social worker and client cocreate a contract that contains the target problem, tasks to be implemented by both client and practitioner to address the target problem, and overall goals of the treatment. At all times through the process, TCP emphasizes client preferences by asking clients what they most want to work on to address their problems. Client priorities and strengths are interwoven into the entire TCP process. Most TCP involves working briefly with clients, typically 8–12 sessions over the course of a six-month period (Reid & Epstein, 1972).

The phases of TCP are both straightforward and flexible enough to be applied in almost any social work practice context (Marsh & Doel, 2005). After the target problem has been successfully defined (Step 1) and goals have been established to help deal successfully with the target problem (Step 2), a contract is created between the practitioner and the client that includes a schedule to help facilitate the intended changes (also Step 2). After several sessions in which clients and practitioners share the outcomes of the specific tasks they agreed to carry out (Step 3), the sessions turn to focusing on how well the overall goals have accomplished and whether another task-centered goal-setting process is necessary or whether the social work intervention has been successful enough to consider termination (Step 4) (Reid & Epstein, 1972). TCP developers Epstein and Reid acknowledged that these steps, while meant to be sequential, can often overlap and require that practitioners be trained to maximize the potential benefit of each step in the process when helping a client.

## Main Developers and Contributors

The TCP approach began with Epstein and Reid's work at SSA, with the major initial research and development of TCP taking place under their direction between 1970 and 1978. During that time, the SSA project had over 100 graduate students helping Reid, Epstein, and their research team test out TCP interventions in a variety of settings common to social work practice, for example, schools, child welfare agencies, and hospitals. Their initial findings demonstrated that TCP was a potentially effective and flexible modality to employ with a wide array of client populations and problems. Since that pioneering era of TCP, over 200 books, articles, and dissertations have been published describing the TCP approach and demonstrating its effects in a host of social work practice contexts. Reid and Epstein have continued to publish on TCP, and have been joined by Cynthia Bailey-Dempsey, Anne Fortune, Matthias Naleepa, Ronald Rooney, and Eleanor Tolson as major academic proponents of TCP (www.task-centered.com).

### Statistics and Demographics

TCP has become firmly ensconced in most generalist social work practice textbooks, and most students learn at least the rudiments of TCP in their introductory classes. Reid continued to write about TCP until his passing in 2003, and other TCP leaders continue to emphasize TCP's benefits in this new era of evidence-based practice. However, despite having TCP adherents in the academy, it is unclear what the perception is of TCP in the larger social work practitioner community. To some extent, TCP may be a victim of its own success in this respect. Many new social workers may just assume that the process of setting discreet measurable goals with clients on the basis of the clients' ideas about what they would like to change is simply good social work practice rather than being rooted in the principles of TCP.

Similarly, because advocates of TCP have always maintained that it is a social work technology that can be viewed as both a psychotherapeutic and a casework intervention, perhaps the other therapeutic techniques that many social workers favor today (solution-focused brief therapy, narrative therapy) are more prominent more because they emphasize the application of clinical skills over casework methods, and thus appeal to the desire of some social workers to be therapists first, and social workers second. Interestingly, these other brief therapy methods borrow heavily from the core concepts of TCP (respecting client views of the problem, helping the client set goals that they want to work on), though proponents of these approaches seldom explicitly acknowledge their debt to TCP, preferring instead to emphasize constructivist therapeutic ideas and the importance of cognitive-behavioral therapy research largely conducted in psychology.

The comparison with cognitive-behavioral therapy is particularly interesting, as it is slightly older as a treatment technology than is TCP but has been given far more attention from both researchers and practitioners in social work and other mental health fields. This may be another example of social work not being able to celebrate and further refine one of its own contributions to the knowledge base.

### Current Applications

Many social work practice settings are good fits for TCP. Hospital settings with the emphasis on brief treatment and discharge planning; schools, with the increasing emphasis on identifying specific behavioral and social/emotional goals for students to work on; private practice and community mental health settings wherein clients are encouraged to set concrete goals to fulfill the mandates of managed care and brief treatment; and gerontology settings wherein older clients and their families need help identifying target problems and marshalling their resources to address those problems in a step-by-step fashion are all good examples of settings wherein practitioners using TCP may be able to increase the effectiveness of their interventions with clients. Researchers have studied all these areas using TCP and have found that TCP bolsters client participations in treatment planning, increases prosocial behaviors, and empowers clients to accomplish the treatment goals they are most interested in achieving (Reid, 1997).

### Current Evidence on TCP and
### Its Connection to Evidence-Based Practice (EBP)

Like all models of casework and clinical practice, TCP cannot claim to be universally effective for all clients and all problems. However, given the over 200 published works on it, TCP stands as one of the most studied "home-grown" social work technologies in the profession's history. Sadly, with the death of Reid, it seems that interest in further establishing the research base for TCP's effectiveness has slowed considerably. Since 2000, there have been fewer than 10 published works on TCP, and those works have been mostly in the form of books, book chapters, and conceptual pieces rather than experimental studies of TCP's effectiveness. Though the early pioneers of TCP research have written consistently of the need for further refinement and adaptation of the model, few current researchers appear to be adding to the empirical research base of TCP.

A recent book chapter on TCP by Reid published posthumously (2004) correctly identified TCP as an "exemplar" of evidence-based practice. Indeed, TCP can claim to be one of social work's earliest examples of an evidence-based practice that was tested rigorously (including randomized controlled trials) and found to have modest but nonetheless consistently powerful effects for clients when compared with control groups (Reid, 1997). In this respect, supporters of TCP can rightfully claim that there is empirical support for TCP, though they would also readily acknowledge that much more study needs to be done on what clients and problems may benefit most from TCP. However, proponents of even more transparent approaches, for example, the kind of evidence-informed practice that Gambrill, Gibbs, and other EBP proponents favor, may chafe at the implication in TCP that while social workers using TCP make every effort to include clients in formulating the target problem to work on, they still maintain their authority as the director of the TCP process rather than being equal co-collaborators (Gambrill, 2006).

### Distinctiveness and Integrations of the TCP Model

Many of the central principles of TCP are now considered simply good social work practice; its influence has contributed to the theoretical move away by the profession from uniformly subscribing to a psychodynamic long-term treatment model embedded in the medical model to diagnose and treat clients. The client-centered qualities of TCP are congruent with social work's roots, in that TCP challenges social workers to start where the clients are and stay in that place until the clients feel their problem is solved. Experts in TCP freely acknowledge that TCP is less a stand-alone model than an approach that can be easily adapted into multiple social work practice frameworks and practice settings (Reid, 1992). This may ultimately be its major contribution to the field of social work practice: a sturdy yet flexible practice technology that contains enough rigor to be consistently effective but also enough space to be adapted creatively to an incredible number of social work practice contexts.

### REFERENCES

Gambrill, E. (2006). Evidence-based practice and policy: Choices ahead. *Research on Social Work Practice*, 16, 338–357.
Marsh, P., & Doel, M. (2005). *The task-centred book*. London: Routledge Books.
Reid, W. J. (1992). *Task strategies: An empirical approach to clinical social work*. New York: Columbia University Press.
Reid, W. J. (1997). Research on task-centered practice. *Research in Social Work*, 21, 132–137.
Reid, W. J., & Epstein, L. (1972). *Task-centered casework*. New York: Columbia University Press.

### FURTHER READING

Fortune, A. E. (1985). *Task-centered practice with families and groups*. New York: Springer.
Gibbons, J. S., Bow, I., Butler, J., & Powell, J. (1979). Clients' reactions to task-centered casework: A follow-up study. *British Journal of Social Work*, 9, 203–215.
Madden, L. L., Hicks-Coolick, A., & Kirk, A. B. (2002). An empowerment model for social welfare consumers. *Lippincott's Case Management*, 7, 129–136.
Rooney, R. H. (1992). *Strategies for work with involuntary clients*. New York: Columbia University Press.

### SUGGESTED LINKS

*http://www.task-centered.com/*
*http://www.ssa.uchicago.edu/aboutssa/history/tour1f.shtml*
*http://library.albany.edu/dewey/exhibits/current/reid.html*

—MICHAEL S. KELLY

## TEAMS

ABSTRACT: Teams maximize the coordinated expertise of various professionals. Social work skills used with clients, especially contracting, monitoring team processes, managing conflict, creating a climate of openness, and developing and supporting group cohesion, need to be purposefully utilized in practice with teams. Workers can improve team functioning by supporting families and clients as active team members, and by addressing ethical issues, including confidentiality and the competence and ethics of team members. Although there is some outcome-based research on teams, more is needed. Emerging trends in this field include embedding the notion of teams in a wider web of collaborative activities.

KEY WORDS: interdisciplinary; collaboration; interprofessional; teamwork; group; family

Although interdisciplinary teams first emerged in health care in the 1940s as a response to increased specialization, they did not become commonplace until the 1960s and 1970s (Julia & Thompson, 1994). Teams developed in U.S. industry in the 1970s in response to Japanese success with quality circles, in contrast to hierarchical management structures in their manufacturing systems (Levi, 2001). In health and mental health care, teams emerged to combine specialized knowledge to meet the range of needs of an individual. More recently, accreditation bodies and governmental and private funding sources have mandated collaborative approaches to human services in order to reduce duplication and promote coordinated service provision; as a result, teams have become commonplace in a range of settings (Payne, 2000; Proenca, 2000). Yet, as health care has shifted to a managed care structure with concomitant emphasis on cost containment, questions about the efficiency and effectiveness of team decision making are being raised. However, serious questioning of the use of interdisciplinary teams has been limited; despite the extensive personnel hours required, it remains at the center of service delivery in diverse settings. Therefore, social work practitioners need to understand principles and skills of interdisciplinary team practice to perform their functions effectively.

## Teams Defined

The term *team* was originally derived from Old English and was first used to refer to "a group of animals harnessed together to draw some vehicle" (Dingwall, 1980, p. 135). Various labels have been used to describe teams of professionals, including multidisciplinary, interprofessional, transdisciplinary, and interdisciplinary. Distinctions among them are not well articulated in the literature; here, the term interdisciplinary is used, primarily. It implies the following: a group of professionals from different disciplines; a common purpose; integration of various professional perspectives in decision making; interdependence, coordination, and interaction; integration of the client and family into team decision-making processes; active communication; role division based on expertise; a climate of collaboration (Abramson, 2002). A model for interdisciplinary teamwork among social workers and other professionals describes the following as components of this kind of collaboration: interdependence, newly created professional activities, flexibility, collective ownership of goals and reflection on process (Bronstein, 2002, 2003).

## Barriers to and Supports for Teamwork

Despite wide acceptance of teams as a mechanism of service delivery, the literature on teamwork primarily addresses obstacles to teamwork. Bronstein (2002, 2003), however, defines these barriers, in their inverse, as potential supports for teamwork; by understanding and addressing them, teamwork can be strengthened. The following are most often cited in the literature as potential barriers: structural characteristics (time and space for teamwork to occur; administrative support for teamwork; skilled team leadership, institutional value on diversity and equality); professional role (security in one's role; shared professional language and technologies; training for teamwork; dual affiliation with profession and team; role competition or blurring); personal characteristics (interactional styles; mutual respect; liking one's team mates; issues of color, culture, and gender); prior history with teamwork (Abramson, 2002; Bronstein & Abramson, 2003; Drinka & Streim, 1994; Lawson & Sailor, 2000; Bronstein, 2002).

The impact of distinct professional socialization processes on team functioning is profound and rarely well understood. Professional socialization shapes values, language, preferred roles, methods of problem solving, and establishment of priorities. As one becomes a social worker or other professional, perspectives particular to that profession become so integrated with a role that awareness of these perspectives diminishes, and thus, they remain unexamined for their impact on collaboration (Abramson, 2002). Yet, distinctions in

professional beliefs and approaches to treatment are often at the root of disagreements among team members, even if unrecognized as such (Abramson & Bronstein, 2004). In addition, professional education rarely teaches students about the contributions made by other professions or about the skills needed for teamwork. To compensate for the gaps in professional education, team members need to make systematic efforts to understand the socialization of other professionals.

## Skills in Teamwork

Although social work education, like other forms of professional training, rarely or only minimally teaches specific skills in teamwork, social work students do learn clinical and macro practice concepts and skills that can easily be adapted to work with teams. These include the following: careful listening; beginning where the client (team) is; respecting differences; maintaining a nonjudgmental stance; communicating empathically; reaching for feelings; assessing individuals, groups, and organizations, among others (Dana, 1983). Unfortunately, the relevance of these skills for teamwork is rarely articulated in the classroom or practice arena. Social workers do not sufficiently recognize or acknowledge that these skills are transferable to their work with colleagues; nor do they fully accept that strategic and thoughtful interventions are needed in their interactions with colleagues (Abramson & Bronstein, 2004).

Perhaps the most important social work skills for teamwork are those used in facilitating groups. Teams are unique among task groups in the direct connection between their performance, and the impact of their decisions on clients. Once social workers accept the need to address process issues in teams, they can draw on their group work knowledge base to assist teams in addressing these issues (Abramson & Bronstein, 2004).

It is a natural extension to apply contracting concepts used in group work to teamwork. Many of the difficulties faced by teams rest in unexamined assumptions and can be effectively addressed through a well-developed contracting discussion. Monitoring team processes is another critical team maintenance task for all team leaders and team members; yet, it is a responsibility often taken on reluctantly, if at all. Participants need to think simultaneously about treatment and team issues so that they are able to address team processes that obstruct the client-centered goals of the team. When working with client groups, social workers typically attend to interactions among clients while also addressing the topics being discussed; thus they can draw on similar skills in working with teams. In addition, their systems orientation can assist them in evaluating organizational factors that may impinge on team functioning.

Social workers can also play a key role in creating a team climate of openness, trust, and group cohesion. Cohesion has been identified as contributing to commitment to the team and to its effectiveness (Barrick, Stewart, Neubert, & Mount, 1998). Mutual support occurs when team members are "there" for one another as they deal with challenging patient or client or community circumstances and with the disappointments and struggles that are part of their daily work lives. Such support provides the cushion that then allows team participants to assert their expectations of each other (Abramson & Bronstein, 2004).

Teams that successfully manage conflict find their cohesion as a group greatly enhanced as well by their capacity to deal with differing points of view. The development of consensus in decision making and growth in team functioning often depend on the ability of group members to confront conflict within the group directly. The inability to deal with conflict within the team is perhaps the most critical obstacle to effective collaboration. A number of sources address strategies that can contribute to conflict resolution in teams (Abramson, 2002; Graham & Barter, 1999, Toseland & Rivas, 2005).

## Integrating Clients and Families into Teams

Effective teamwork is synonymous with an approach that views clients and families as critical team members when this is appropriate. For meaningful participation to take place, team professionals, clients, and their families need to engage jointly in the process of goal definition, attainment, and evaluation. Social workers can assure that clients and families are supported to find their own voices in team meetings.

The notion of families as collaborative team members has gone beyond the professional literature and is beginning to have a presence in the popular literature (Clemetson, 2006). As this occurs, it is likely that clients and families will demand increasing substantive involvement in decisions about their own and their loved ones' care. A December 16, 2006, *New York Times* article by Clemetson states that 21 states have adopted team approaches wherein family members involved with the foster care system help in "decisions about where endangered children should live . . . even families under scrutiny from state agencies can help make positive decisions for their children" (pp. A1, A13). Research studies, primarily in child welfare, are starting to evaluate the impact on service outcomes of participation by clients and families on teams. Results indicate benefits from their involvement through an array of structures including wraparound services and family group conferencing and indicate a positive trend related to improvement of child management skills by foster parents, greater sense of efficacy and improved perceptions of well-being by those involved as well as changes in child behavior (Ogles et al., 2006; Pennell & Anderson, 2005).

It is important, however, to recognize the challenges of fully involving clients and families as team members, especially in light of their time-limited involvement with the team and their perceived power-deficit. A recent literature review of the conceptual basis for interprofessional collaboration found no definitions of collaboration that either adequately reflect the patient or family's perspective or successfully conceptualize their role on the team (D'Amour, Ferrade-Videla, San Martin Rodriguez, & Beaulieu, 2005).

## Ethical Issues in Teamwork

The integration of client and family into the team is a key arena where ethical issues can arise in teamwork. Unfortunately, most professionals, including social workers, have been highly influenced by the medical model that emphasizes professional expertise and implicitly and often explicitly minimizes the role of clients and family in the decisions made about them (Opie, 2000; Freidson, 1984). How often does a team even share its assessment of the client's situation with the client and family, no less involve them as active participants in deciding what should be assessed or what options should be considered for addressing the problems identified?

Issues of confidentiality are embedded in the very nature of teamwork; a serious question is whether most clients understand that they are discussed in team meetings or that some professionals attend who are not directly involved in their care? How comfortable would clients and families be with team discussions if they were more aware of their existence? Information should be provided routinely to clients to explain the team approach, to communicate clearly how confidentiality is maintained, and to identify the contributions of interprofessional discussion to helping them meet their goals.

The ways that team members conduct themselves on the team can also raise ethical questions. Alliances among subgroups of team members or hierarchical or status issues can distort or dominate team decision-making as can personal relationships between or among team members. Unethical or incompetent behavior by a team member may be apparent to others on the team but remain unaddressed because of lack of clear accountability channels or discomfort in raising the concern. The codes of ethics of other professional groups (American Medical Association: http://www.ama-assn. org; American Psychiatry Association: http://www.psych.org/psych) are similar in warning of conflicts of interest and in spelling out professional responsibilities to perform competently and to report colleagues who are unethical or incompetent.

## Research on Team Effectiveness

Remarkably little empirical examination of the operating assumptions regarding teamwork has been undertaken. Interest in studying teamwork seems somewhat higher in United Kingdom, Australia, and New Zealand than in the United States, judging by the disproportionate number of studies originating in those countries. When research has been conducted, team processes have more often been evaluated than the impact of teamwork on client outcomes. Process evaluations focus on the interaction in a team (communication patterns, cohesion, norms, roles, leadership, level of investment), while outcome evaluation addresses the extent to which the team is effectively fulfilling its client care function (Toseland & Rivas, 2005). There are some studies that examine process for its impact on outcome. One such study evaluated the impact on patient outcomes by training health-care teams in continuous quality improvement methods (Irvine Doran et al., 2002). This study found that only 9 of 25 teams were successful in improving outcomes; the markers of these successful teams included success at problem-solving, more functional group interactions, and physician participation. Another study (Oliver, Bronstein, & Kurzejeski, 2005) found quality of hospice care related to effective management of conflict and referrals to social workers by other professionals.

More recently, enough research on team functioning and outcome has been published to allow for several review articles. Faulkner and Amodeo (1999) reviewed recent studies of teamwork effectiveness and found very few that met their design criteria. They identified substantial inconsistencies in definitions of the team across various studies, making comparisons of findings difficult and found none that looked directly at the relationship between these conditions and client outcomes. Schmitt (2001) reviewed studies over the previous 15 years and identified the methodological challenges of making the connection between teamwork and client outcomes. She notes the difficulties in integrating process variables with outcome variables, in developing conceptual clarity and valid measurement tools, in applying field experimental/control group multisite designs and in sifting out the impact of confounding factors. Both she and Lemieux-Charles and McGuire (2006), who reviewed the literature on health team effectiveness, note the research complexities posed by the multidimensionality of teamwork. Lemieux-Charles and McGuire did find evidence of positive teamwork on clinical outcomes and patient quality of life and satisfaction; impact on cost

factors was more mixed, although the longitudinal studies of geriatric evaluation teams in the Veterans' Administration, health care system have demonstrated significant reductions in costs of care (Englehardt, Toseland, Gao, & Banks, 2006).

It is essential that more empirical studies be conducted on the impact of teamwork on client outcomes; if not, this labor-intensive mechanism of service delivery may not have the future it deserves. However, even teams without research capacities can use a team assessment tool (see Bronstein, 2002, or Dattner Consulting, 2007, for exemplars) as part of a formal team evaluation process. It is possible to correlate team functioning with client outcomes through use of a brief checklist to evaluate various aspects of care in order to identify patterns in client outcomes that relate to team functioning.

## Emerging Trends in Teamwork

Emerging and critical trends in teamwork include an increase in research, greater emphasis on teamwork in professional education, a more expansive definition of collaboration, and greater inclusion of clients and family in teams.

As stated earlier, research on the work of interdisciplinary teams needs to be expanded and explicitly tied to client outcomes. The differences and similarities of teamwork in an array of settings need to be explored to develop generic models for practice as well as knowledge about how to shape particular teams to create the best fit with the needs of particular client populations and settings. Although there is much clinical wisdom and many case studies that guide this work, we need to increase efforts to develop evidence-based models to define and guide best practices. Many instruments exist in social work and related fields to assess teamwork, but they rely largely on self-report. Although research on teamwork has recently matured and expanded to include contextual factors, specific areas cited in the literature as influences on teamwork should be empirically examined for their impact on team processes and outcomes, that is, differential professional socialization, structural and organizational dimensions, contracting processes, the balance between task and process emphasis in teams, conflict management strategies, personal characteristics, and so forth.

In addition to further research efforts, social work educators can make more explicit linkages for students between their generic social work knowledge and skills, and their work on interdisciplinary teams (Howe et al., 2001). Outside the classroom, field instructors can also foster this linkage in their supervision of students in internship. For example, field instructors can require that students do process recordings of team meetings. If this aspect of their practice is elevated in importance to that given direct work with clients, and if students are evaluated on their performance in collaborative arenas, they will be eager to learn teamwork and collaborative skills. Field and classroom instructors should also articulate and consistently reinforce the connections between the group work skills students are using in their clinical work, and the skills needed as team members.

Last, it is critical to keep in mind that interdisciplinary teamwork is only one "type" of collaboration; it is not exercised in a void and is best achieved when interlocking with a number of other "types" of collaboration. These other forms of collaboration require many of the same skills necessary for interdisciplinary teamwork (Payne, 2000). Lawson (2008) categorizes these collaborative types as intraorganizational, interorganizational, or inter-agency and community-based, among others. The more we value and develop skills in each of these kinds of collaboration, the more we also develop our abilities in the others, and become more effective members and facilitators of interdisciplinary teams—a central component of quality social work practice and service delivery in the 21st century.

## REFERENCES

Abramson. (2002). Interdisciplinary team practice. In G. Greene & A. Roberts (Eds.), *Social work desk reference* (pp. 44–50). Oxford University Press.

Abramson, J. S., & Bronstein, L. R. (2004). Group process dynamics and skills in interdisciplinary teamwork. In C. Garvin, M. Galinsky, & L. Gutierrez (Eds.), *Handbook of social work with groups*. New York: Guilford.

Barrick, M., Stewart, G., Neubert, M., & Mount, M. (1998). Relating member ability and personality to work-team processes and team effectiveness. *Journal of Applied Psychology, 83*(3), 377–391.

Bronstein, L. R. (2002). Index of interdisciplinary collaboration. *Social Work Research, 26*(2), 113–126.

Bronstein, L. R. (2003). A model for interdisciplinary collaboration. *Social Work, 48*(3), 297–306.

Clemetson, L. (2006, December 16). Giving troubled families a say in what's best for the children. *New York Times,* pp. A1, A13.

D'Amour, D., Ferrade-Videla, M., San Martin Rodriguez, L., & Beaulieu, M. D. (2005). The conceptual basis for interprofessional collaboration: Core concepts and theoretical frameworks. *Journal of Interprofessional Care, 19*(Suppl. 1), 116–131.

Dana, B. (1983). The collaborative process. In R. Miller & H. Rehr (Eds.), *Social work issues in health care* (pp. 181–220). Englewood Cliffs, NJ: Prentice Hall.

Dattner Consulting 360 Feedback. Sample Leader. Feedback Report (2007). Dattner Consulting: www.dattnerconsulting.com

Dingwall, R. (1980). Problems of teamwork in primary care. In S. Lonsdale, A. Webb, & T. L. Briggs (Eds.), *Teamwork in the personal and social services and health care* (pp. 111–137). London: Personal Social Services Council.

Englehardt, J. B., Toseland, R. W., Gao, J., & Banks, S. (2006). Long term effects of outpatient geriatric evaluation and management on health care utilization and survival. *Research on Social Work Practice, 16*(1), 20–27.

Faulkner, S. R., & Amodeo, M. (1999). Interdisciplinary teams in health care and human services settings: Are they effective? *Health and Social Work, 24*(3), 210–219.

Freidson, E. (1984). The changing nature of professional control. *Annual Review of Sociology, 10*, 1–20.

Graham, J. R., & Barter, K. (1999). Collaboration: A social work practice method. *Families in Society, 80*(1), 6–13.

Howe, J. L., Schwartz, H. L., Hyer, K., Mellor, J., Lindemann, D. A., & Luptak, M. (2001). Educational approaches for preparing social work students for interdisciplinary teamwork on geriatric health care teams. *Social Work in Health Care, 32*(4), 19–42.

Julia, M. C., & Thompson, A. (1994). Group process and interprofessional teamwork. In R. M. Casto, M. C. Julia, L. Platt, G. Harbaugh, A. Thompson, T. Jost, et al. (Eds.), *Interprofessional care and collaborative practice* (pp. 35–41). Pacific Grove, CA: Brooks/Cole.

Irvine Doran, D. M., Baker, G. R., Murray, M., Bohnen, J., Zahn, C., Sidani, S., et al. (2002). Clinical improvement: An interdisciplinary intervention. *Health Care Management Review, 27*(4), 42–56.

Lawson, H. A. (2002). Pursuing and securing collaboration to improve results. In M. Brabeck & M. Walsh (Eds.), *The Contribution of interprofessional collaboration and comprehensive services to teaching and learning: The national society for the study of education yearbook 2002.* Chicago: University of Chicago Press.

Lawson, H. A. (2008). Collaborative practice. In T. Mizrahi & L. Davis (Eds.), *Encyclopedia of social work* (20th ed.). New York & Washington, DC: Oxford University Press & The National Association of Social Workers.

Lawson, H. A., & Sailor, W. (2000). Integrating services, collaborating and developing connections with schools. *Focus on exceptional children, 33*(2), 1–24.

Lemieux-Charles, L., & McGuire, W. (2006). What do we know about health care team effectiveness: A review of the literature. *Medical Care Research and Review, 63*(3), 263–300.

Levi, D. (2001). *Group dynamics for teams.* Thousand Oaks, CA: Sage.

Ogles, B. M., Carlston, D., Hatfield, D., Melendez, G., Dowell, K., & Fields, S. A. (2006). The role of fidelity and feedback in the wraparound approach. *Journal of Child and Family Studies, 15*(1), 115–129.

Oliver, D., Bronstein, L. R., & Kurzejeski, L. (2005). Examining variables related to successful collaboration on the hospice team. *Health and Social Work, 30*(4), 279–286.

Opie, A. (2000). *Thinking teams/thinking clients: Knowledge-based teamwork.* New York: Columbia University Press.

Payne, M. (2000). *Teamwork in multiprofessional care.* Chicago: Lyceum Books.

Pennell, J., & Anderson, G. (Eds.). (2005). *Widening the circle: The practice and evaluation of family group conferencing with children, youths and their families*. Washington, DC: NASW Press.

Proenca, E. J. (2000). Community orientation in hospitals: An institutional and resource dependence perspective. *Health Services Research*, 35(5), 210–218.

Schmitt, M. H. (2001). Collaboration improves the quality of care: Methodological challenges and evidence from US health care research. *Journal of Interprofessional Care*, 15(1), 47–66.

Toseland, R., & Rivas, R. (2005). *An introduction to group work practice* (5th ed.). Boston: Addison Wesley.

## FURTHER READING

Abramson, J. S., & Rosenthal, B. B. (1995). Interdisciplinary and interorganizational collaboration. In *Encyclopedia of Social Work* (19th ed., pp. 1479–1489). Washington, DC: NASW.

Bronstein, L. R., & Abramson, J. S. (2003). Understanding socialization of teachers and social workers: Groundwork for collaboration in the schools. *Families in Society*, 84(3), 1–8.

Bronstein, L. R., McCallion, P., & Kramer, E. (2006). Developing an aging prepared community: Collaboration among counties, consumers, professionals and organizations. *Journal of Gerontological Social Work*, 48(1/2), 193–202.

Bronstein, L. R., & Wright, K. (2006). The impact of prison hospice: Collaboration among social workers and other professionals in a criminal justice setting that promotes care for the dying. *Journal of Social Work in End-of-Life and Palliative Care*, 2(4), 85–102.

Cashman, S. B., Reidy, P., Cody, K., & Lemay, C. A. (2004). Developing and measuring progress toward collaborative, integrated, interdisciplinary health care teams. *Journal of Interprofessional Care*, 18(2), 183–196.

Drinka, T. J. K., & Clark, P. G. (2000). *Health care and teamwork: Interdisciplinary practice and teaching*. Westport, CT: Auburn House.

Fleming, J. L., & Monda-Amaya, L. (2001). Process variables critical for team effectiveness. *Remedial and Special Education*, 22(3), 158–172.

Garland, C., Frank, A., Buck, D., & Seklemian, P. (1995). *Skills inventory for teams*. Lightfoot, VA: Child Development Resources Training Center.

Kivimaki, M., Kuk, G., Elovainio, M., & Thomson, L. (1997). The team climate inventory (TCI)—Four or five factors? Testing the structure of TCI in samples of low and high complexity jobs. *Journal of Occupational and Organizational Psychology*, 70, 375–390.

Knox, K. S., & Roberts, A. R. (2005). Crisis intervention and crisis team models in schools. *Children and Schools*, 27(2), 93–100.

Mailick, M. D., & Ashley, A. A. (1981). Politics of interprofessional collaboration: Challenge to advocacy. *Social Casework: The Journal of Contemporary Social Work*, 62(3), 131–136.

Mizrahi, T., & Abramson, J. S. (1985). Sources of strain between physicians and social workers: Implications for social workers in health care settings. *Social Work in Health Care*, 10(3), 33–51.

Reese, D. J., & Sontag, M. A. (2001). Successful interprofessional collaboration on the hospice team. *Health and Social Work*, 26(3), 167–175.

Sands, R., Staffor, J., & McClelland, M. (1990). I beg to differ: Conflict in the interdisciplinary team. *Social Work in Health Care*, 14(3), 55–72.

Seaburn, D. B., Lorenz, A. D., Gunn, W. B., Gawinski, B. A., & Mauksch, L. B. (1996). *Models of collaboration*. New York: Basic Books.

Specht, H. (1985). The interpersonal interactions of professionals. *Social Work*, 30(3), 225–230.

Vinokur-Kaplan, D. (1995). Treatment teams that work (and those that don't): An application of Hackman's group effectiveness model to interdisciplinary teams in psychiatric hospitals. *The Journal of Applied Behavioral Science*, 31(3), 303–327.

Watson, W., Johnson, L., & Merritt, D. (1998). Team orientation, self-orientation and diversity in task groups. *Group and Organization Management*, 23, 161–188.

Waugaman, W. (1994). Professionalization and socialization in inter-professional collaboration. In R. M. Casto, M. C. Julia, L. Platt, G. Harbaugh, A. Thompson, T. Jost, et al. (Eds.), *Interprofessional care and collaborative practice* (pp. 23–31). Pacific Grove, CA: Brooks/Cole.

## SUGGESTED LINKS

American Medical Association Code of Ethics
  *http://www.ama-assn.org/ama/pub/category/2512.html*
American Psychiatry Association Code of Ethics
  *http://www.psych.org/psych_pract/ethics/ppaethics.cfm*
*www.dattnerconsulting.com*
*http://humanresources.about.com/od/involvementteams/a/team_culture.htm*
*http://www.hq.nasa.gov/office/hqlibrary/ppm/ppm5.htm*
*http://www.free-consumer-guide.com/team_building.htm?gclid=COnW-6en2IcCFRxSPgodkTpZoQ*
*http://www.tablegroup.com/store/index.php?main_page=product_info&products_id=4*
*http://www.officelookout.com/collaborative-workspaces.html*
*http://www.questia.com/library/health-care-teams.jsp*

—JULIE ABRAMSON AND LAURA BRONSTEIN

**TECHNOLOGY.** [*This entry contains five subentries:* Overview; Technology in Macro Practice; Technology in Micro Practice; Technology in Social Work Education; Tools and Applications of Technology.]

## OVERVIEW

**ABSTRACT:** Information technology (IT), which encompasses tools and prescribed actions, has begun to substantially impact social work, given 50 years of impressive developments. This entry looks at IT trends and their impact on society and social work. The trends covered concern rapid IT development, connectivity, globalization and outsourcing, intelligent applications and devices, centralization and distribution of power and control, and distance education. Issues and challenges for social work are also discussed.

**KEY WORDS:** technology; information technology; information and communication technology; computers; Internet; online education; online social work; digital divide

### Technology Definitions and Concepts

Technology refers to prescribed actions and tools directed toward goal achievement. Technology can be hard, involving tangible things, such as camcorders, computers, and other devices. Technology can also be soft, involving non-tangible processes, such as risk assessment systems and nonprofit accounting systems. This entry discusses electronic or digital information technology that is associated with computers and the Internet. The United Kingdom and Europe refer to this technology as information and communication technology, or ICT. In the United States, IT is the term most often used.

A useful concept in discussing human services IT is an application or software that solves user problems. Applications can be generic and address many types of user problems, for example, word processors, spreadsheets, or data management. Applications can also be specific to the problems of a narrow group of users, for example automated child welfare risk assessment systems. Applications can reside on one's computer, an agency network, or the Internet. An organization that provides Internet-based applications is called an application service provider, or ASP.

IT applications are expensive to design and maintain. Traditionally, human service applications have been management-focused, because management applications are easier to design and develop than clinical applications. Also, IT tools and processes from business and government management can be successfully applied to human services management. Since businesses and government do not have functions similar to social work practice with clients, many individual applications must be custom-designed and developed for the purpose.

Applications manipulate data, information, or knowledge. While these terms often overlap, data refers to characters (letters, numbers, and symbols), for example, the characters 76019–0129 consist of nine numbers and one symbol. Information is data within a context, for example, 76019–0129 is information when used as

the zip code for the University of Texas at Arlington School of Social Work. Knowledge is complex information, such as descriptions and relationships. For example, an application that guides one through an assessment can display the knowledge that alcohol is involved in 50% of similar domestic violence cases. Some knowledge applications are often said to be intelligent or smart, that is, they can learn and improve with use. For example, a risk prediction application might increase its prediction accuracy as it learns from more cases being entered (Schoech, 1999).

Little consensus exists on application types, resulting in a variety of confusing terms in the literature. Some application types are based on the terms data, information and knowledge, for example, database management systems, information systems, and knowledge systems. Other classifications are based on the tasks an application performs, for example, management information system, expert systems, performance support systems, or decision support systems. Most human services IT applications either manage information for reports, structure and assist with routine processes, or guide decision making.

This entry shows how IT trends affect society, the social work profession, social workers, and clients. Speculations on the future are also made. Specific applications will only be mentioned by type or services performed, since other encyclopedia entries will review technology tools and applications in micro and macro practice and education.

### Technology's Influence on Society and Social Work

Information technologies such as books and telephones have influenced family structure, work relations, politics, and human settlement patterns. This section will examine the influence of computer and communications technologies on society and social work by examining several major IT trends over the last 50 years. These trends are rapid IT development, connectivity, globalization and outsourcing, intelligent applications and devices, centralization and distribution of power and control, and distance education.

### Continued Rapid Pace of IT Development

**TRENDS** Moore's Law suggests that hardware capacity doubles and/or the price of hardware drops by about 50% every 18–24 months ("Moore's Law," n.d.). It continues to hold true for computers and other digital devices. Accompanying this increased capacity at reduced cost is miniaturization. Moore's Law does not apply to software, which can become more expensive as hardware capacities increase.

INFLUENCE ON SOCIETY The Internet-connected computer is merging with the television, smart cell phone, music player, and camera to produce a small, universal, wireless appliance that can be cheaply disseminated worldwide. The impact of smaller IT with increased capacity for less money is so gradual that it is often not noticed. However, over 10–30 years, these small trends have had a substantial impact that confounds even experts. For example, personal computers were predicted around the 1950s, but they were visualized as room size and used by only a small number of computer scientists (Rand, n.d.).

With hardware becoming increasing powerful, large companies like Microsoft continue to develop generic software that takes advantage of the increasing hardware capacity. The rule of thumb in application development is that hardware consumes approximately 10% of the budget, software and software development consume 40%, and training and implementation consume 50% (Neilson, 1985, p. 59).

INFLUENCE ON SOCIAL WORK Business IT can be linked to cost savings, increased competitiveness, and survival, but this is not the case in publicly funded human services. Current funding makes it difficult for agencies to devote resources to IT, thus agencies often reverse the 10–40–50 rule and spend 50% on hardware and only 10% on training and implementation (Eng, 2001). Consequently, many new applications require extra work and training by social workers over the 3–5 years required for their development and implementation. Another problem is that given the rapid pace of IT development, system maintenance and upgrades can require 5–15% of development costs each year (Bates, 2005). While still functional, older applications may feel bulky and outdated, given users experience with sophisticated IT features in computer operating systems and on the Internet.

Information systems are usually the first agency application experienced by social workers and many initial systems were custom built on low budgets. Their management rather than direct practice focus and their non-user-friendly interface have resulted in social workers not receiving useful system outputs, given that they may spend 50% of their time on data input. A common social work complaint about IT is, "We put a lot of information in the system, but can't get anything useful out." Where IT applications have been useful to social workers, they have been readily accepted (Monnickendam, 2000).

## Connectivity

Connectivity denotes how effortlessly information can be automatically and instantly pushed and pulled between networked computers given "need to know" authorizations. History tells us that connectivity provides a giant leap forward, for example, the linking of railroads, highways, and electric power. The Internet, which began linking personal computers globally in the late 1980s, is comparable to linking the U.S. railway networks in 1869 by driving the golden spike at Promontory, Utah.

TRENDS The Internet is connecting people globally at an astonishing rate. For example, 20 highly connected households in 2010 will generate more traffic than the entire Internet generated in 1995 (Giancarlo, 2007). However, 85% of the world's 6.5 billion people do not have Internet access. Most of the one billion with access reside in only 20 of the roughly 240 countries and territories worldwide. The United States has 4.6% of the world's population with roughly 76.6% having broadband Internet access. In contrast, South Asia has more than half of the world's population yet Internet access stands at 8.9%. While approximately 6% of the world speaks English, 68% of Web content is in English (The Bandwidth Report, n.d.; Haig, 2006).

Since 1996, the Internet2 consortium has been linking the research, academic, and business communities, using high speed and highly reliable networking. It has specific relevance for telehealth applications such as video consultations with clients, which require reliable high speed connectivity. However, low-speed smartphone connectivity is increasing faster than high-speed computer connectivity and is having a substantial impact. For example, African farmers can use smartphones to call a number to receive a RSS (Really Simple Syndication) message containing the current price and availability of vegetables that they plan to sell.

INFLUENCE ON SOCIETY The Internet has created new ways for people to communicate, work together, and socialize. We have online counterparts to most human activity, for example, writing notes (text messaging and e-mail), education (online universities) discussing in groups (bulletin boards, chat rooms, and listservs), keeping diaries (blogs), watching TV (YouTube), going to work (telecommuting), buying and selling (Amazon and eBay) going to the doctor (telehealth), social networking or hanging out (Second Life, MySpace, Facebook) dating (Friendster, eHarmony), and having fun (multi-user online games). Since human activity is increasingly taking place in the virtual world, social workers must practice in the virtual world just as they do in the physical world. The social work profession must not only become more adept at designing and using online intervention, but it must also address some of the new human service problems occurring in cyberspace, for example, cyberbullying and Internet addiction.

While Internet connectivity is what most people experience, an equally important connectivity is electronic data interchange (EDI). EDI is the automatic, seamless and instantaneous exchanging of information between separate organizations based on predetermined data definitions, standards, and protocols. XML (extensible markup language) and World Wide Web consortium (W3C) standards are integral to EDI (O'Looney, 2005).

Changes in banking over the last 20 years illustrate the importance and power of EDI. Twenty years ago, local banks manually sent checks and currencies around the world. Today, a global banking infrastructure exists with EDI that is protected by authentication, privacy, and confidentiality safeguards. People can pay bills using the Internet or obtain local currency using an ATM machine almost anywhere. Sophisticated computer programs, called agents or bots, analyze financial information for "unusual activity" and trigger the sending of alerts. For example, some banks have bots that analyze transactions and alert customers of large purchases from another country. Local banks, which chose not to connect to this global infrastructure, have gone out of business. This quiet revolution was spurred on by customers who gravitated to banks that offered convenient, reliable, and quick services.

INFLUENCE ON SOCIAL WORK The banking infrastructure illustrates changes EDI will bring to the human services over the next 20 years (Schoech, Fitch, MacFadden, & Schkade, 2002). Simply speaking, the three major components of the global banking infrastructure are: (A) local bank offices, (B) affiliations of local banks (Chase Banks), and (C) a global consortium for exchange and cooperation (International Monitory Fund or IMF). Three similar components of the global human services infrastructure (GHSI) will be (A) local agencies, (B) affiliations of local agencies (Red Cross), and (C) a global consortium for accumulating knowledge and developing protocols.

The GHSI is not an organizational or service structure, but an information sharing infrastructure. Throughout the GHSI, the extent of information sharing, the extent of adherence to protocols, and the latitude of agencies to "do their own thing" will be continually negotiated. These negotiations will occur between agency administrators, professional associations, funding sources, social workers, and community stakeholders including client advocates. The GHSI can perform many routine drudgery tasks, for example, scheduling meetings, sifting through volumes of information for knowledge, collecting evidence on client progress, keeping everyone informed, updating all appropriate records, conducting three and six month follow up, and documenting everything. With many routine tasks automated, social workers can concentrate on high-level tasks like those involving observation, sensing, working through what-if scenarios, and making complex judgments and cognitive leaps. Local social workers can also contribute to the global knowledge base by online involvement with global expert teams to research complex problems. While movement toward a GHSI will be slow due to the organizational and service changes required, it will have a profound influence on social work practice over the next 20 years.

### Globalization and Outsourcing

Globalization refers to the decline of local forces and the increase of global forces in people's lives. Outsourcing refers to transfer of functions from people inside to those outside an organization or to those in different geographic locations, typically for efficiency or effectiveness reasons.

TRENDS Wireless Wi-Fi and WiMAX technologies make it possible to quickly and inexpensively provide broadband Internet access to cities and countries. When countries develop 100% wireless coverage, information can flow as quickly and easily to a device anywhere in the globe as it does to a device in the same office. Outsourcing is predicted to grow substantially over the next five years. The easy and rapid connection of people and processes globally encourages the substitution of high-cost labor with lower-cost labor from anywhere in the world. Low-income countries with a highly educated work force benefit the most from globalization and outsourcing while countries with illiterate populations are left behind.

INFLUENCE ON SOCIETY Globalization and outsourcing are having major effects on societies. Where jobs are lost, community and family disintegration exist along with the loss of health insurance. Many of the jobs found after outsourcing pay low wages and do not have health care coverage, making individuals vulnerable to the host of human service problems associated with poverty and dislocation. In low-income countries where jobs are gained, disruption often occurs due to urbanization, family disintegration, and political instability. For example, females can perform IT jobs as well as males and often are paid less than males. Since outsourced IT jobs pay more than industrial or farm work, females may become the major wage earners in societies that are traditionally male-dominated and in which self-esteem is associated with earning power.

Similar disruptions exist where younger workers, who have more IT training, are making older workers less valued ("Anti-Globalization," n.d.).

**Influence on Social Work** As suggested above, globalization and outsourcing often increase individual, family and social problems such as substance abuse and violence. Communities devastated by outsourcing have fewer capacities to solve their problems. Organizations are negatively impacted because IT encourages rapid restructuring and shifting of costs between individuals, corporations, and governments. For examples, many financially troubled community hospitals were purchased by IT savvy chains that used automation and sophisticated management techniques to identify and discontinue unprofitable services and maximize profits. These changes were often devastating for hospital social workers whose jobs were restructured around cost savings rather than quality services. A similar impact concerns the outsourcing of social work jobs. Due to costs, health care is being outsourced to countries such as India and Thailand (Wachter, 2006). With the GHSI mentioned under connectivity, the outsourcing of services is possible and likely (see challenges below).

### Intelligent Applications and Devices

Intelligent applications were defined earlier as those that accumulate and manage knowledge and learn.

**Trends** Artificial intelligence (AI) is the IT field which builds applications that model human activities. Knowledge discovery and data mining are AI techniques for searching large volumes of data for patterns, trends, and predictions. Expert systems are AI applications that mimic the reasoning of human experts. Simulations are AI models that mimic phenomena and allow exploration and testing. Another AI area concerns building knowledge bases, for example, developing a computer chip containing the knowledge of a six year-old. Another form of AI uses small, wireless sensing devices that are woven into clothes, imbedded into skin, and implanted throughout one's environment. These sensors allow people and applications to continually interact with environments to improve quality of life, for example, heart monitors. A similar application involves robotics, or biomechanical devices capable of performing autonomous tasks. The most popular robots are humanoids, such as ASIMO who currently can walk, run, push carts, go up stairs, and perform basic office tasks. Another form of intelligence involves using global positioning systems (GPS) that provide geographically referenced information such as

the latitude and longitude. Applications that work with GPS coordinates are called geographic information systems (GIS). A final AI area involves working with knowledge in new formats, for example, being able to search for content in audio, pictures, animation, and video ("Artificial Intelligence," n.d.).

**Influence on Society** It is often said that we are drowning in information while being starved for knowledge. As more and more information becomes automated, intelligent tools are needed to allow humans to better use the information for tasks such as decision making. The phenomenal growth of Google illustrates the value of quickly providing specific information that meets people's decision making needs. Google also takes a multimedia approach to problem solving by capturing, storing, manipulating and displaying all forms of information including images, maps, and video ("More Google Products," n.d.).

**Influence on Social Work** Intelligent applications are important since social work is a knowledge based profession. Intelligent applications can help social workers by performing tasks such as informing, monitoring, guiding, suggesting, scheduling, and making routine decisions. For example, applications can alert relevant parties when a client's progress is predicted to fall below agency standards. A workload equalization application could present supervisors with caseloads, case severity, and time projections when assigning new cases. A database containing pictures of bruises could be searched to find medical reports for cases with bruises similar to a picture submitted by a child protective services worker.

Intelligent devices, GPS, and smart environments will be part of many new applications for social workers. Currently, sensing devices and environments, such as ankle bracelets to track probation or parolee movement, are the most familiar social work monitoring applications. However, with nanotechnology and miniaturization, smart clothes can be designed to monitor body temperature, smart buildings can monitor client movement and mood, and smart streets can monitor people's safety. For example sensors in a smart residential facility can monitor teens' anger symptoms, alert teens of potential outbursts via a smartphone, and walk angry teens through an appropriate anger reduction game using their smartphone. The large population of frail elderly can use intelligent applications such as smart pill boxes, smart environments that monitor health problems, video social networking, and even robots to help them live independently (Kawamoto, 2007; Olsen, 2007).

## Centralization and Distribution of Power and Control

Technology and information are continuing to have a strong influence on who has power and control as summarized by the popular phrase, "think globally, act locally."

TRENDS IT influenced power and control shifts are common, for example, mergers and the flattening of bureaucracies. In many societies, IT has also resulted in a vast centralization of resources, that is, moving power and control from the have-nots to the haves. For example, the wealthiest man in the world started out by selling the Microsoft operating system for personal computers in the 1980s. While this concentration of wealth has many negative impacts, becoming digital is still seen as an important step in raising the quality of life in low-income societies (Friedman, 2006).

Technologies that help distribute power and control through information are still being developed. One popular online collaborative content development tool, called a wiki, is a good example. A wiki is a content repository Web site that contains a variety of highly linked information that users can instantly change. The most familiar wiki is Wikipedia or the online version of the print encyclopedia. Wikis quickly accumulate quality information by allowing users to view and correct information in the wiki with monitoring by experts.

INFLUENCE ON SOCIETY The flattening of organizations due to increased span of control eliminates many middle level jobs, such as clerks. Social workers are expected to enter their information directly into a computer, browse the Internet for information, and to communicate with coworkers via e-mail. Customers are empowered through access to large amounts of organizational information. Governments see the Internet as an inexpensive way to provide information and involve citizens without increasing staff. This increased user access to information and control is changing the way many institutions operate. For example, the control of news is moving from a few large media giants to many smaller outlets. More teens today get information from the Internet than from newspapers and television (Geracl, Drath, Nagy, Burke, & Lynn, 2003). User generated news and entertainment, in the form of blogs and uploaded videos, now play an important role in society. These changes influence how news and entertainment are bought and sold, for example, via advertising. While newspapers are suffering from decreased advertising revenues, the user-driven IT model is making huge profits, for example, the profitability of Google.

INFLUENCE ON SOCIAL WORK Federal, state, and local hierarchies, which traditionally controlled the flow of government information and funds, are slowly being flattened. An information-rich IT infrastructure provides the workplace with the support needed to contract out social work jobs. For example, government agencies may contract with a national home-health chain for social workers to provide services to clients in their home. Client progress and satisfaction can be constantly monitored via computerized phone surveys to clients and the results analyzed and displayed for corporate management. Many new service models are being tried; some are very successful while some are failing (Puccio et al., 2006).

Social work is a profession that addresses numerous problems, each having substantial specialty knowledge. Given the difficulty of funding sophisticated IT in many human service agencies, clients may have better computers, faster Internet connections, and thus better information about their problems than the social workers trying to help them. The new, information-empowered client may be intimidating, but can also be beneficial to social work. The Internet can be viewed as an educational tool that provides the client with basic information, thus allowing the social worker to focus on more sophisticated tasks. However, clients have limited background and perspective and need help to analyze, synthesize, and place Internet information within a larger context. With IT, clients may also receive more agency contact, but that contact might be performed by IT tools or lower skilled staff with IT support. Clients are usually more receptive to IT than social workers.

## Distance Education, Learning Objects, and Learning Environments

To remain competitive in a global technological economy, a society must produce an educated workforce that can not only use, but develop, technology. With workers often changing jobs and careers, lifelong learning is considered essential. An IT-supported learning environment is an educational invention as important as the mass production of books. The academic tasks most impacted by IT are curriculum design, content delivery, course management, and research.

TRENDS IT frees educators from the semester and 1- to 3-hour class timeframes by using online, asynchronous content delivery to students' homes. A trend in education is to use course management applications such as Blackboard and its open source counterpart Moodle. Course management systems handle registration, authentication, attendance, assessment of student progress, and instructor-student communications. They also contain tools for constructing learning environments, for example, text, audio, or video chat, ways to upload and download content, and discussion forums.

One IT format for educational content delivery uses 10- to 15-minute learning modules linked together. Learning modules contain specific goals and objectives, training to achieve these objectives, and evaluation measures and strategies. The analogy of a course as a train, students as passengers, and learning modules as train cars can help one visualize this learning environment. Trains are designed in train yards where various cars heading in the same direction are linked together and then loaded with passengers. Similarly, instructors can link various learning modules together to form a course that moves students further towards their degree path. Learning modules may contain asynchronous online home-delivered content, simulations involving other online students, or face-to-face intensive exercises. With learning modules, instructors spend a lot of time in course design, monitoring, and continually improving the modules for use globally.

INFLUENCE ON SOCIETY IT disseminates the power and control that universities once held on education and research. Since large universities are often rigid bureaucracies, changes will occur most rapidly in private schools which can quickly adapt to customers' preferences, for example, the University of Phoenix and Walden University. Online learning environments change instructors' tasks from mostly classroom course delivery to online curriculum design and outcomes assessment. The instructor's role moves from being a "sage on the stage" to "a guide at the side." With tools like Google scholar and Wikipedia, students' tasks change from tracking down information to assessing, analyzing, synthesizing, critical thinking, and outcome evaluation. Students are spurring on these IT changes by preferring education and training that is flexible, low cost, effective, and convenient.

With courses and learning modules saved, education content can be more quickly transferred to developing countries. For example, OOPS (Opensource Opencourseware Prototype System) is an effort to translate the many courses in the Massachusetts Institute of Technology OpenCourseWare repository from English to various forms of Chinese, thus rapidly speeding up technology transfer. With wireless Internet access, people in rural areas can receive the education needed for teleworking, thus possibly stemming the mass rural-urban migration and associated social problems that have been occurring throughout the world.

INFLUENCE ON SOCIAL WORK Schools of social work have not embraced online learning as rapidly as some disciplines. The reason is that most current online tools focus on knowledge acquisition and testing rather than the development of professional skills, socialization, and values (Moore, 2005). However, as additional resources and tools become available, especially the video classroom, this reluctance may change.

The GHSI, discussed under Connectivity, will encourage these educational changes, since a key role of the global knowledge repository is research and training. Highly specialized academics will be needed to design the curriculum that teaches students to use the new knowledge that the GHSI accumulates. Researchers will be needed to conduct the studies and develop global standards, protocols, and tools with ways to customize them using local customs and practices. The evidence-based approach to social work practice will continue to gain momentum although the source of evidence will change from primarily research journal articles to intelligent GHSI applications (Schoech, Basham, & Fluke, 2006). Current online educational effort will looks crude and uncoordinated compared to what is possible once substantial electronic data interchange occurs throughout the GHSI.

## Challenges and Issues

Based on the previous discussion, the following challenges and issues face the social work profession.

### Researching Online Practice in the United States

Online social work practice continues to grow, given its popularity with consumers, its effectiveness, and the limited problems cited thus far in the literature. However, liability issues abound and a social worker violates professional ethics standards by providing online assistance to a client in a state in which the social worker is not licensed (NASW/ASWB, 2005). State licensing requirements are especially limiting in online self-help groups where social work group leaders must be licensed in every state in which group members reside. This requirement is impractical and denies social work guidance in online groups for clients with uncommon problems that draw several members from many states. To avoid the liability and ethical issues, those practicing online social work often call their services coaching, life skills development, and various non-professional terms. Thus, U.S. licensing and liability practices are restricting U.S. social workers from providing leadership and research into online social work and may be encouraging the future outsourcing of social work practice to human service professionals in countries without these restrictions.

Liability guidelines need to be developed and state licensing laws changed to allow large, controlled, multi-state studies on the effectiveness and efficiency of online social work practice. If clinical trials in other countries continue to find Internet-assisted and Internet-provided social work practice comparable to face-to-face practice, then consumers and insurance companies may outsource services to social workers in other countries who have developed the research, infrastructure, and applications. See for example, programs such as Fearfighter, Beating the Blues, or virtual reality therapies available on the Internet.

### Developing a Global Practice Infrastructure

In order for the GHSI infrastructure, discussed under Connectivity, to be controlled by the social work profession, much research needs to be conducted on a global basis. For example, XML taxonomies are needed to allow for electronic data interchange and standards and techniques are needed for client authentication, privacy and confidentiality. Work is beginning to be developed in this area, for example, by the child welfare XML Work Group. However, this work is underfunded and not global in nature. Global human services organizations capable of carrying out such research do not exist. In addition, most funding sources for human services IT are local rather than global. In the business sector, IT infrastructure research and development is funded by cost savings due to increased efficiency and productivity. However, the current funding of human services does not encourage global infrastructure changes based on efficiency and productivity.

### Capturing and Disseminating Accurate Knowledge for Social Workers and Clients

Given the imminent retirement of Baby Boomer social workers, efforts to retain the expertise they accumulated needs to be implemented before that expertise is lost forever. One approach might be to have the large agencies, governments, or associations such as NASW facilitate the accumulation of this expertise using IT tools such as wikis and drupals. These repositories should allow social workers, clients, and others to enter, verify, and add to knowledge repositories. These knowledge repositories are especially important as social workers are increasingly hired on a contract basis to perform diverse tasks with little training and technical support, for example, home-bound case management. These repositories are also important for Internet-savvy clients who have the capacity to search out information on their problem and its solution. A related issue concerns how accurate and reliable Internet Web sites are and how social workers and clients can be educated about assessing information accuracy (Vernon, & Lynch, 2003).

### Addressing the Digital Divide and Other Negative Impacts of IT

Often the potentials of IT are touted without any reference to IT's downside. The negative impacts of IT are often seen as a small price to pay for the benefits. For example, discussion of the digital divide and ways to overcome it are much more common in low-income countries than in high-income countries like the United States. Social work has a special role to play in addressing the negative influences of IT, since many social work clients are disadvantaged and often cannot speak for themselves due to vulnerabilities such as mental illness, hopelessness, and desperation. Also, client advocacy is required by the social work code of ethics. Responsible IT development and updating of laws can help eliminate IT problems such as Internet addiction and online porn, stalking, crime, and bullying. The disabilities community is a model to follow, since they passed legislation and worked with vendors to insure that computer accessibility was taken seriously. They also conducted studies to document that having IT accessible to those with disabilities was a win/win for software developers and all others involved. In addition, research is needed on how to preserve cultures and diverse communities as rapid globalization increases the blending and loss of cultures.

### Researching Virtual Learning Environments for Social Work Education

Online education of social work professionals is important because a shortage of social workers exists, especially in rural areas. IT can allow rural practitioners to receive an education while remaining in their communities. Currently, IT has proved more successful in knowledge dissemination than in the development of skills, values, and professional socialization. Current online social work education research typically concerns a single course or instructor. Thus, it suffers from evaluations based on small sample sizes. More coordinated effort needs to be sponsored by organizations like the Council on Social Work Education to ensure that large samples and sophisticated research designs are used to evaluate online learning.

### Assessment

Human services are adopting the information technology that has revolutionized other parts of society over the past 50 years. The automatic and instantaneous linking, storage, and analysis of human service delivery information is being accompanied by applications that guide, carry out, and monitor social work interventions. The implications of this transformation include globalization, organizational flattening, and the supplementation of highly skilled practitioners by lower skilled staff with extensive IT guidance and support. New tasks for social work academics and researchers concern developing a knowledge infrastructure along with the systems to deliver the knowledge when and where it is needed. While these changes will be gradual, over the next 20 years IT will revolutionize the way human services are provided. Although the IT adoption path will be rocky and difficult, human services with extensive IT support will be more effective and preferred by clients, practitioners, and educators.

## REFERENCES

Anti-globalization. (n.d.). Retrieved September 13, 2007, from http://en.wikipedia.org.

Artificial intelligence. (n.d.). Retrieved September 13, 2007, from http://en.wikipedia.org.

Bates, D. W. (2005). Physician and ambulatory electronic health records. *Health Affaris*, 24(5), 1180–89.

Eng, T. R. (2001). *The eHealth landscape: A terrain map of emerging information and communication technologies in health and health care*. Princeton, NJ: The Robert Wood Johnson Foundation. Retrieved September 13, 2007, from http://www.informatics-review.com/thoughts/rwjf.html.

Friedman, T. (2006). *The world is flat: A brief history of the twenty-first century*. New York: Farrar, Straus and Giroux.

Geracl, J., Drath, D., Nagy, J., Burke, J., & Lynn, M. (2003). Born to be wired. Retrieved September 13, 2007, from http://us.yimg.com/i/adv/btbw_execsum.pdf.

Giancarlo, C. H. (January 02, 2007). The Internet Accelerates While U.S. Trails Behind. *Government Technology*. Retrieved January 2, 2007, from http://www.govtech.net/digitalcommunities/story.php?id=103080.

Haig, W. (Dec 12, 2006). Using Technology to Fight Terror. Government Technology. Retrieved December 12, 2006, from http://www.govtech.net/digitalcommunities/story.php?id=102818.

Kawamoto, D. (2007). Videoconferencing ties seniors with families. Retrieved August 14, 2007, from http://www.news.com/Videoconferencing+ties+seniors+with+families/2100-1041-6202474.html?part=dht&tag=nl.e433.

Monnickendam, M. (2000). Computer systems that work: A review of variables associated with system use. *Journal of Social Service Research*, 26(2).

Moore, B. (2005). Faculty perceptions of the effectiveness of Web-Based instruction in social work education: A national study. *Journal of Technology in Human Services*, 23(1/2), 53–66.

Moore's law. (n.d.). Retrieved September 13, 2007, from http://en.wikipedia.org.

More Google products. (n.d.). Retrieved September 13, 2007, from http://www.google.com/intl/en/options/index.html.

NASW (National Association of Social Workers)/ASWB (Association of Social Work Boards). (2005). NASW & ASWB Standards for technology and social work practice. Retrieved on January 10, 2007, from http://www.socialworkers.org/practice/standards/NASWTechnologyStandards.pdf.

Neilson, R. E. (1985). The role of the federal government in social service systems development. *Computers in Human Services*, 1(2), 53–63.

O'Looney, J. (2005). Social work and the new semantic information revolution. *Administration in Social Work*, 29(4), 5–34.

Olsen, S. (2007). School uniforms to track kids. Retrieved August 22, 2007, from http://www.news.com/8301-10784_3-9764275-7.html?part=dht&tag=nl.e433.

Puccio, J., Belzer, M., Olson, J., Martinez, M., Salata, C., Tucker, D. et al. (2006). The use of cell phone reminder calls for assisting HIV-infected adolescents and young adults to adhere to highly active antiretroviral therapy: A pilot study. *ADIS Patient Care and STDs*, 20(6), 438–444.

Rand Corporation's 50 year prediction of the home computer (n.d.). Retrieved January 10, 2007, from http://www.data-backup-and-storage.com/home-computer.html.

Schoech, D. (1999). *Human Services Technology: Understanding, Designing, and Implementing Computer and Internet Applications in the Social Services*. New York: Haworth.

Schoech, D., Basham, R., & Fluke, J. (2006). A Technology Enhanced EBP Model. *Journal of Evidence Based Practice*, 3(3/4), 55–72.

Schoech, D., Fitch, D., MacFadden, R., & Schkade, L. L. (2002). From data to intelligence: Introducing the intelligent organization. *Administration in Social Work*, 26(1), 1–21.

The bandwidth report. (n.d.). Retrieved January 10, 2007, from http://www.websiteoptimization.com/bw/.

Vernon, R., & Lynch, D. (2003). Consumer Access to Agency Websites: Our Best Foot Forward? *Journal of Technology in Human Services*, 21/4, 37–51.

Wachter, R. M. (2006). The "dis-location" of U.S. medicine—The implications of medical outsourcing. *New England Journal of Medicine*, 354, 661–665.

## SUGGESTED LINKS

ASIMO humanoid robot.
   *http://asimo.honda.com/*
Child Welfare Extensible Markup Language (CW XML) Workgroup.
   *http://www.nrccwdt.org/xml/intro.html*
Drupal.
   *http://drupal.org/*
Internet2.
   *http://www.internet2.edu/*
MERLOT
   *http://MERLOT.com*
OOPS.
   *http://www.jhsph.edu/publichealthnews/articles/oops.html*

Scottish Institute for Excellence in Social Work Education (repository of social work learning modules).

*http://www.sieswe.org/learnx/*

Wiki.

*http://wiki.org/wiki.cgi?WhatIsWiki*

Stop cyberbullying.

*http://www.stopcyberbullying.org/*

—DICK SCHOECH

## TECHNOLOGY IN MACRO PRACTICE

**ABSTRACT:** Information technology has had a profound effect on social work practice with larger systems. This entry reviews the current use of technology in macro social work practice. It examines the role of technology in social administration, community practice, and social policy practice, and discusses current practice, tools, and challenges.

**KEY WORDS:** information technology; macro social work; social administration; community practice; social policy practice

Technology has been an important force in the recent development of macro social work practice. These tools improve traditional practice and allowed new forms of practice. This entry discusses the use of technology in social administration, community practice, and social policy practice, and challenges faced in the use of technology in macro practice.

### Administrative Practice

Technology has had a substantial impact on the way that agencies are managed, reflecting the growth of e-commerce and e-government. Most organizations have a series of databases that support their work and these developed into Management Information Systems (MIS) efforts (Schoech, 1999). These systems are intended to support management decision making by providing timely, decision-relevant information. Early MIS ran on Mainframe or Legacy systems that only the largest organizations could afford, but the growth of smaller computers and client–server configurations made these capabilities available to all. These systems were once relatively simple arrangements that collected, processed, and reported programmatic and financial data. They were often difficult for managers to use in guiding their organizations because the information provided was often not always what was needed for critical decisions. They have evolved into decision support systems that support management decision-making and eventually to Knowledge Management systems that can support organizational learning (Schoech, Fitch, MacFadden, & Schkade, 2002). These developments have tailored technology to the decision making environment and created ways to better use and preserve the information that the organization depends upon. Advanced statistical techniques, such as data mining, allow extraction of important information from large datasets created in the knowledge management process.

There are also efforts to bring together information from across organizations where individual units have data systems that cannot communicate with each other. This makes it difficult to provide strategic information to higher levels of management, and workers in complementary departments cannot have access to needed information. In response to this problem, organizations have developed Enterprise Resource Planning systems that combine many of the local systems into an organizational strategy. Internal communication is often facilitated through e-mail, wireless, and Intranet-based systems.

Technology also supports marketing, fund-raising, and financial management (Princeton Survey Research Associates, 2001). Organizational Web sites have become more important tools in promoting the agency in the community and many agencies have developed Content Management Systems to organize the information they provide. Some use technology to segment their market and develop messages that appeal to those segments. Marketing can also include e-mail newsletters, streaming video, and other appeals.

Web pages also provide a way to raise funds, solicit volunteers, and recruit employees. E-fund-raising has become an important source of funding for many agencies (Grobman & Grant, 2006). Some of the approaches include secure donation systems, shop for a cause approaches, and online charity auctions. Some organizations use e-mail to raise money. In addition to online systems, technology can be used to support more traditional fund-raising by facilitating prospect research. Spreadsheets and other forms of financial management software facilitate the management of money with an agency.

Larger agencies have information technology staff and may even have a department. Smaller organizations often rely on consultants or application service providers, which are organizations that provide all or part of the organization's technology on an outsourced basis (Grobman & Grant, 1998; Cortes & Rafter, 2007).

Finally, technology has facilitated the development of virtual organizations, which develop a network to perform the organization's work. Nearly every task is outsourced to another entity and work is coordinated through the network (Cooper & Muench, 2000).

## Community Practice

Community organization/development has also been influenced by new technology (Hick & McNutt, 2002). This not only makes current practice more effective, but allows community practitioners to extend their work into new areas, such as virtual communities.

Traditional social planning and community organizing/development have benefited from the growth of community data libraries, organizations that aggregate data on the community's situation, and the development of Geographic Information Systems. Geographic Information Systems provide the capacity to map data and a wealth of analytical facility with spatial statistics which can facilitate decision making (Queralt & Witte, 1998).

Some communities have Community Computer Networks, which provide access, resources, and a forum for community issues. Also important are Community Technology Centers, which address technology access and skills. These organizations not only reduce access disparities, but also create stronger communities.

Finally, there are the beginnings of work in virtual communities. There is accumulating evidence that you can build community in cyberspace. One example is virtual volunteering, which has grown in importance and represents an exciting new way for people to become involved. Virtual volunteers participate over the Internet doing things that traditional volunteers do.

## Social Policy Practice and Advocacy

The technological revolution in advocacy and political practice has matured into an accepted practice with a wide variety of available tactics and techniques (Hick & McNutt, 2002). While the use of technology for political advocacy emerged in the late 1980s, the last 10 or so years have seen it evolved into an important part of social movement efforts, political campaigning, and issue advocacy. Technology can assist advocates in gathering information, informing the public, organizing constituents, and applying pressure to decision makers. E-mail, Web sites, and discussion lists form the foundation of practice. These are being supplemented by newer techniques that reflected the Web 2.0 emphasis on social networking and user-generated content. These include wikis, blogs, social networking sites, online games, social bookmarking systems, and video/image sharing sites (Germany, 2006). An early social networking system, Meetup, was highly useful in the 2004 Dean campaign. One of the more significant developments in this area was the emergence of virtual advocacy organizations, such as MoveOn. These organizations, unlike many traditional social movement organizations, exist as virtual organizations almost totally in cyberspace. The question of effectiveness is difficult for any type of advocacy practice (McNutt, 2006), but recent findings suggest that decision makers are influenced by this technology (Congressional Management Foundation, 2005; Larsen & Rainie, 2002).

Technology has created new opportunities, capabilities, and challenges for macro social workers. It is a central force for improving the quality of macro social work practice and making life better for the people we serve.

Technology will become a more pervasive part of macro social work as time moves forward. It will become less a separate entity and more the way that practice is conducted.

## REFERENCES

Congressional Management Foundation. (2005). *Communicating with Congress: How capital hill is coping with the surge in citizen advocacy.* Washington, DC: Author.

Cooper, W. W., & Muench, M. L. (2000).Virtual organizations: Practice and the literature. *Journal of the organizational computing and electronic computing.* 10(3), 189–208.

Cortes, M., & Rafter, K (Eds.). (2007). *Information Technology Adoption in the Nonprofit Sector.* Chicago: Lyceum Books.

Germany, J. B. (Ed.). (2006). *Person to person to person: Harnessing the political power of on-line social networks and user generated content.* Washington, DC: The Institute for Politics, Democracy and the Internet, George Washington University.

Grobman, G., & Grant, G. (2006). *Fundraising online.* Harrisburg, PA: White Hat Communication.

Hick, S., & McNutt, J. G. (Eds.). (2002). *Advocacy and activism on the internet: Perspectives from community organization and social policy.* Chicago: Lyceum Books.

Larsen, E., & Rainie, L. (2002). *Digital town hall: How officials use the Internet and the civic benefits they cite from dealing with constituents on-line.* Washington, DC: Pew Internet and American Life Project.

McNutt, J. G. (2006). Building evidence based advocacy in cyberspace: A social work imperative for the new millennium. *Journal of Evidence Based Practice,* 3(2/3), 91–102.

Princeton Survey Research Associates. (2001). *Wired, willing and ready: nonprofit human services organizations' adoption of information technology.* Washington, DC: Independent Sector & Cisco Systems.

Queralt, M., & Witte, A. D. (1998). A map for you? Geographic Information Systems in the social services. *Social Work,* 43(5), 455–469.

Schoech, R. (1999). *Human services computing: concepts and applications* (2nd ed.). New York: Haworth Press.

Schoech, D., Fitch, D., MacFadden, R., & Schkade, L. L. (2002). From data to intelligence: Introducing the intelligent organization. *Administration in Social Work,* 26(1), 1–21.

—JOHN G. MCNUTT

# TECHNOLOGY IN MICRO PRACTICE

**ABSTRACT:** Online therapy is the delivery of supportive and therapeutic services over the Internet. Online therapy offers the advantages of convenience and increased access to services. Service delivery may be problematic due to ethical concerns and legal liability. Limited research supports the efficacy of online therapy for a variety of health and social concerns. Increased use of the Internet by consumers and human service agencies will likely see growing use of online therapy and require training for workers and development of new policies and procedures for online service delivery.

**KEY WORDS:** "online therapy"; Internet; psychotherapy; computer counseling

Online therapy is defined broadly as the delivery of psychotherapeutic and supportive services using Internet-based communications. These interventions are known by a variety of names, including online practice, etherapy, Internet therapy, online (psycho) therapy, Itherapy, Interapy, virtual therapy, online counseling, telehealth, cyberpsychology, therap-e, and others. Internet-based services are offered to individuals, couples, or groups through a variety of delivery systems, including asynchronous e-mail, electronic bulletin boards, real-time chat-based communication, Internet-based audio–video communication, and closed circuit video conferencing. Services are provided by professionals such as psychiatrists, social workers, psychologists, counselors, marriage and family therapists, and nurses. In addition, self-help groups with a therapeutic purpose and online supportive services using trained volunteers are offered on the Internet. Online therapy may be used as the sole intervention, as an adjunct to or follow-up to face-to-face interventions, or as part of a wait-list triage program. It is offered as private practice as well as through hospital and agency-based services. Some authors have used a more restricted definition of *etherapy* as the delivery of counseling, supportive, and psycho-educational services focused on specific problem-based or relationship issues that exclude diagnosis or treatment of mental disorders.

## Advantages and Disadvantages

Professionals debate online therapy's potential benefits and harm. Proponents describe the potential benefits of online therapy in terms of access, treatment modality, and cost. Online therapy is convenient, as services may be available at any time from any place. Internet-based services offer a stable source of support in an increasingly mobile society. In addition, services are available to those who might not otherwise seek services due to time constraints, geographic distance, caregiving responsibilities, lack of transportation, physical or social isolation, and physical or psychological disabilities. Online therapy may be more effective with some people since it uses a medium that promotes more open and disinhibited communication due the perceived anonymity and safety of online communications. Online therapy is also an option for those who might not otherwise seek such services in person due to fear of the unknown or stigma attached to seeking services. In addition, online therapy may also offer a source of culturally relevant information and services when they are not available in the local community. Finally, although costs vary greatly, online therapy may be less expensive since more consumers can be served in a shorter time with fewer overhead costs.

These advantages may be offset by a number of ethical and legal challenges. There is very limited empirically validated evidence related to models of online service delivery. Misunderstandings are more likely in online communications and cannot be immediately addressed in asynchronous modalities. Appropriate assessment is difficult (some argue impossible) due to lack of visual and verbal cues in text-only communications. Similarly, it may be difficult to know the true identity of the consumer or the practitioner in a strictly online environment. In addition, threats to privacy, security, and confidentiality of online communications require both technological safeguards from practitioners and education of consumers in safeguarding their own computers. Furthermore, ethical requirements to warn vulnerable third parties, to make appropriate referrals, to be available and intervene in emergency situations, and to consult with previous service providers may be difficult in online relationships. Finally, practitioners and consumers face unclear legal and liability standards surrounding the jurisdiction of online therapeutic services.

To enhance the effectiveness of online therapy and to protect consumers, the National Board for Certified Counselors (1998), the American Psychological Association (1998), and the International Society for Mental Health Online (2001) have developed ethical and practice standards related online therapy. The National Association of Social Workers (NASW) has not adopted a specific statement on the ethics of online practice. The NASW Code of Ethics has specified that social workers must take precautions to ensure the confidentiality of client records that are transmitted through electronic communications (NASW, 1996). They have also adopted *Standards for Technology and Social Work Practice* in conjunction with the Association of Social Work Board (ASWB). The standards state that, "Social workers should acquire adequate skills that use technology appropriately, and adapt traditional practice protocols to ensure competent and ethical practice" (ASWB, 2005).

There is general agreement in these codes of ethics that all ethical standards of face-to-face practice must be met in online therapy.

## Evidence of Effectiveness

There is a growing research literature that suggests that online therapy can be an effective treatment modality, although studies are limited in scope, sample size, duration, level of therapist experience, and outcome measures. Studies suggest that a therapeutic relationship can be established through online communications. The research includes numerous anecdotal reports, primarily showing positive outcomes of online services. In addition, a relatively small number of empirical studies have examined the effectiveness of online therapy with a variety of populations and social problems, including anxiety, depression, eating disorders, weight loss, panic disorder, substance abuse, caregiver stress, pediatric pain, cigarette addiction, grief, posttraumatic stress disorder, and recurrent headache. These studies generally find online therapy to be as effective as face-to-face interventions or more effective than wait-list control groups. In summary, online therapy is a promising but yet unproven intervention. Further research is needed to better determine for whom and under what circumstances online therapy is effective.

## Future Trends

It is estimated that in 2006, 73% of adults in the United States access the Internet and they are increasingly using it for support in social and health-related matters. Human service organizations will need to determine to what extent they will engage in online therapeutic and other services. For those who do offer online services, it will require use of secure computer systems, creating record-keeping procedures for online communications, training workers in online communication, creating policies regarding what services may be offered online by whom, developing policies for handling both expected and unsolicited e-mail, and evaluating the impact of their online services. In addition, legal issues related to online practice across state lines will need to be resolved. This may involve development of national standards and national licensure for online practice.

## REFERENCES

APA (American Psychological Association). (1998, August). Services by telephone, teleconferencing, and Internet. *Statement of the Ethics Committee of the APA*. Retrieved August 1998, from http://www.apa.org/ethics/stmnt01.html.

ASWB (Association of Social Work Boards). (2005). *National Association of Social Workers and Association of Social Work Boards Standards for Technology and Social Work Practice*. Retrieved October 4, 2007, from: http://www.aswb.org/TechnologySWPractice.pdf.

International Society for Mental Health Online. (2001). *Suggested principles for the online provision of mental health services*. Retrieved June 18, 2001, from http://www.ismho.org/suggestions.html.

NASW. (1996). (National Association of Social Workers). *Code of Ethics, 1.07(l)*. Retrieved October 4, 2007, from http://www.socialworkers.org/pubs/code/code.asp.

## FURTHER READING

Barak, A. (2001). *Online therapy outcome studies*. Retrieved July 24, 2001, from http://www.ismho.org/issues/cswf.htm.

Finn, J., & Banach, M. (2002). Risk management in online human services practice. *Journal of Technology and Human Services*, 20(1/2), 133–154.

Finn, J., & Holden, G. (Eds.). (2000). *Human Services Online: A new arena for service delivery*. New York: Haworth Press.

Grohol, J. M. (2000). *The insider's guide to mental health resources online*. New York: Guilford Press.

Mallen, M. J., Vogel, D. L., Rochlen, A. B., & Day, S. X. (2005). Online counseling: Reviewing the literature from a counseling psychology framework. *Counseling Psychologist*, 33(6), 819–871.

NBCC (National Board of Certified Counselors, Inc). (1998). *Standards for the ethical practice of web counseling*. Retrieved July 21, 2001, from http://www.nbcc.org/ethics/wcstandards.htm.

PEW Internet and American Life Project. (2006). Retrieved October 23, 2006, from http://www.pewinternet.org/.

Rochlen, A. B., Zack, J. S., & Speyer, C. (2004). Online therapy: Review of relevant definitions, debates, and current empirical support. *Journal of Clinical Psychology*, 60(3), 269–283.

Seuler, J. (2000). Psychotherapy in cyberspace: A 5-dimension model of online and computer-mediated psychotherapy. *Cyberpsychology and Behavior*, 3, 151–160.

Waldron, V., Lavitt, M., & Kelley, D. (2000). The nature and prevention of harm in technology-mediated self-help settings: Three exemplars. *Journal of Technology in Human Services*, 17(1–3), 267–294.

Zack, J. S. (2004). Technology of online counseling. In R. Kraus, J. Zack, & G. Stricker (Eds.), *Online counseling: A handbook for mental health professionals* (pp. 93–121). San Diego, CA: Elsevier Academic Press.

## SUGGESTED LINKS

Dr. Michael Fenichel's Current Topics in Psychology. *http://www.fenichel.com/OnlineTherapy.shtml*

Metanoia. ABCs of Internet Therapy. *http://www.metanoia.org/imhs/*

PsychCentral. Best Practices in Etherapy. *http://www.psychcentral.com/best/*

—JERRY FINN

# TECHNOLOGY IN SOCIAL WORK EDUCATION

ABSTRACT: The increased use of technology applications, particularly the Internet, has resulted in the rapid development of technology-supported learning environments to deliver higher education. This has begun to impact social work education as faculty struggle to meet the demands of their institutions to develop online courses, distance education programs, and distributed learning environments. This entry will provide an overview of current technology applications and how they are being used in social work education. Implications of using technology in social work education include educational quality issues, pedagogical, and philosophical concerns, as well as future trends and challenges will also be discussed.

KEY WORDS: distributed learning; distance education in social work education; technology-supported social work education; Web-based learning environments; synchronous, asynchronous, and hybrid learning

Technology has been used to deliver social work education, primarily through distance education modalities, since the early 1980s and is an accepted part of social work education (Raymond, 2005). The increased use of technology applications, computers, the Internet, and course management software systems has resulted in the rapid development of technology-supported learning environments in higher education institutions. Recent trends affecting technology-supported education are the advancement and convergence of these technologies, particularly through the Internet. Today's technology-supported social work education has dramatically shifted toward Web-based delivery. "Web-based learning environments" are characterized by the use of computers and the World Wide Web to deliver course work (Wilson, 1999). Web-based education is being used in a number of different social work program and course formats. Distance education programs in social work have typically used interactive compressed video systems to deliver coursework but Web-based courses are now the primary form of technology used to offer social work distance education courses (Raymond, 2005). The first entirely asynchronous, Web-based instruction only Advanced Standing Masters of Social Work (MSW) program is now offered. However, most other distance education programs use a hybrid or blended approach that combines a number of technology media such as videoconferencing, online as well as face-to-face instruction.

Various course formats that use Web-based learning are being developed by social work faculty. These formats range from providing all or some Web-supported/Web-enhanced courses for traditional face-to-face courses to totally online courses with Web instruction only. Hybrid courses are also being developed that combine traditional instruction with Web-based instruction. Distributed learning is a new term that is defined as an instructional model that involves using various information technologies to help students learn. Although the phrases "distributed learning" and "distance learning" are used interchangeably, distributed learning has a broader meaning. Distributed learning is based not only on new media but also on new pedagogy, whereas distance learning emphasizes the learning environment.

A primary characteristic of Web-based learning environments is whether they are synchronous, asynchronous, or a hybrid of the two. Synchronous learning environments involve the learner and other learners or instructors being online and communicating at the same time. Examples of these learning environments are video classrooms (done through computer conferencing systems), online chat rooms, and whiteboards. Communication in asynchronous learning environments takes place over elapsed periods of time, as opposed to real time. Learning environments in which students log on, view and read postings, submit assignments, and that do not use synchronous chat and whiteboard features are examples of asynchronous learning environments. These environments generally allow students the ability to access and download the course materials that allow for several advantages over their synchronous counterparts in that they do not require students to have to be online at the same time as other students or instructors. This allows students to perform their work at their own pace independent of time and place. Hybrid technologies allow for Web-based learning environments that use a combination of synchronous and asynchronous teaching and learning activities. Course Management Software systems (i.e., Blackboard/WebCT, eCollege) are software packages that bundle instructional technology tools such as e-mail, whiteboard, discussion/bulletin boards, virtual classroom via chat, and classroom management tools have helped to make it easier for faculty to use hybrid technologies in developing courses. These systems allow instructors to display the course content of their class to students such as grades, readings, and PowerPoint type presentations via a secure Web site. A new trend developing in hybrid technologies is the use of web conferencing software tools (i.e., Elluminate, Centra Symposium, Breeze) that provide audio and video delivered over the Internet and have features such as shared whiteboards, document sharing, presentations, instant polling, text, and sidebar chat that allow for most activities found in a traditional classroom with modifications for online but mostly synchronous activities. New technologies such as wireless, mobile laptop computing, personal digital assistants (PDAs), videoconferencing/video streaming on the Web, pod casting, virtual reality, and gaming environments are also influencing how social work education is being delivered.

The implications of using technology in social work education include educational quality issues, pedagogical, and philosophical concerns. There is much debate as to the effectiveness and practicality of technology-supported learning environments as well as resistance by social work educators. With a focus on human interaction and hands-on teaching of practice skills in social work education, technology-supported learning environments can seem incompatible with social work education. The recent developments in hybrid approaches and synchronous technologies for these learning environments can help to overcome concerns about lack of interaction and relationship building needed to teach social work practice skills. However, the amount of research done on these learning environments has not been adequately explored. There is a need to develop a coherent body of knowledge to support the delivery of teaching in technology-enhanced learning environments for future social work education. Furthermore, implications for students and faculty engaged in teaching and learning in these learning environments (i.e., increased surveillance by administrators, online assessment of courses) also needs to be explored. Web-based learning environments can allow for a class or entire course to be recorded and packaged in such a way so the instructor could be completely out of the picture. All of these issues need to be addressed as they have ominous aspects for the future of social work education.

Future trends in teaching through the use of technology indicate tremendous possibilities and changes for social work education. The use of cell phones, Ipods, and other technology media to access class lectures, the creation of virtual client systems, communities, and agencies through online digital worlds (i.e., *Second Life*) for field experiences, and the development of Web-based social work practice (i.e., Internet counseling) are examples of the current and future trends for social work education and practice. There is no doubt that new developments in technology will continue at a rapid pace that will make teaching with technology even more effective and widespread. However, it is important that these rapid developments in technology be tempered with careful planning, evaluation, and research as to the most effective and ethical methods for delivering this type of education that incorporates relevant theory, concepts, and methods for teaching in a technology-enhanced learning environment. Social work educators should be on the forefront of taking advantage of these technological developments to discover new and better ways of providing education to social work students and social workers.

[*See also* Social Work Education: Overview.]

## REFERENCES

Raymond, F. B. (2005). The history of distance education in social work and the evolution of distance education modalities. In P. Abels (Ed.), *Distance education in social work* (pp. 23–40). New York: Springer Publishing.

Wilson, S. (1999). Distance education and accreditation. *Journal of Social Work Education, 35*(3), 326–330.

## FURTHER READING

Abels, P. (2005). The way to distance education. In P. Abels (Ed.), *Distance education in social work: Planning, teaching, and learning* (pp. 3–22). New York: Springer Publishing.

Howell, S. L., Williams, P. B., & Lindsay, N. K. (2003). Thirty-two trends affecting distance education: An informed foundation for strategic planning. *Online Journal of Distance Learning Administration*. Retrieved October, 19, 2006, from http://www.westga.edu/~distance/ojdla/fall63/howell63.html.

Oblinger, D. G., Barone, C. A., & Hawkins, B. L. (2001). *Distributed education and its challenges: An overview*. Washington, DC: American Council on Education. Retrieved January 15, 2007, from http://www.acenet.edu/bookstore/pdf/distributed-learning/distributed-learning-01.pdf.

Pittinsky, M. S. (2003). *The wired tower: Perspectives on the impact of the internet on higher education*. Upper Saddle River, NJ: Prentice Hall.

Raymond, F. B., & Pike, C. K. (1995). Social work education: Electronic technologies. In R. L. Edwards (Ed.), *Encyclopedia of social work* (19th ed.). Washington, DC: NASW Press.

Verduin, J. R., & Clark, T. A. (1991). *Distance education: The foundations of effective practice*. San Francisco: Jossey-Bass.

Young, J. R. (2000). Scholar concludes that distance ed is as effective as traditional instruction. *Chronicle of higher education: Distance education*. Retrieved October 15, 2006, from http://chronicle.com/free/2000/02/2000021001u.htm.

—Jo Ann R. Coe Regan

## Tools and Applications of Technology

Abstract: Social workers across fields of practice now have a wide array of technology tools and applications for the conduct and augmentation of practice tasks. This entry is intended as a primer on information and communication technology computer hardware tools and software programs. It describes the essential features and practice utility of an array of information and communication technology hardware, including desktop and laptop computers, personal digital assistants, and smartphones. Software applications are described with a focus on their social work practice functionality in the capture or retrieval, analysis or synthesis, and presentation or dissemination of information. Described are many emerging Web-based applications with noteworthy practice significance.

KEY WORDS: databases; groupware; Hypertext Markup Language; information and communication technology; office application suites; open source; personal digital assistants; presentation software; server; smartphones; spreadsheets; Voice Over Internet Protocol

Social workers across fields of practice now have a wide array of technology tools and applications for the conduct and augmentation of practice tasks. This entry is intended as a primer on information and communication technology (ICT) hardware tools and software programs. In social work practice, ICT has three fundamental functions: (a) information capture, retrieval, or storage, (b) analysis or synthesis, and (c) presentation, dissemination, or communication

## Hardware

Hardware tools used by social workers include desktop computers and laptops, servers, data storage mediums, personal digital assistants (PDA) or wireless devices, and audio and visual digital capture tools. Desktops and laptops are typically personal computing devices used for information acquisition, computation, storage, and display. Their communication capabilities include e-mail, instant messaging, and more recently audio and video communications made possible by Voice over Internet Protocol software. Servers are computers on local networks or the Internet that perform specific network functions, including file storage, database queries, application hosting, or network management. Data storage mediums include diskettes, CD-ROMs, DVDs, flash drives, tape drives, file servers, and internal or external hard drives. PDAs are hand-held computing devices with an array of tools, including personal information management (PIM) software, calculator, spreadsheet, word processor, digital voice recording, photo and video storage or display, and wireless Web access. PDAs are linkable to personal computers to synchronize PIM calendars, contacts, tasks, e-mail, and other files. Wireless devices include cell phones and smartphones, though the distinction is increasingly blurred. In addition to telephone functions, smartphones offer numerous

PDA features, including PIM software, e-mail, text messaging, Web access, multimedia player, and camera. Audio and visual digital capture tools include wireless devices, paper scanners, digital sound recorders, and digital still and video cameras. Each device enables the creation of a digital representation for electronic storage, retrieval, and editing.

## Software

Computer software programs are sets of electronic instructions and procedures that give computer hardware function and utility. Fundamentally, there are two types of software, operating systems and applications. Operating systems such as Windows, Macintosh OS X, and Linux provide a complex set of instructions to run a computing device.

Software applications enable computer hardware to do specific tasks such as create text documents, calculate formulas, and search the Web. Software applications commonly used by social workers include word processors, spreadsheets, presentation software, and e-mail/PIM tools. When packaged together, these applications are commonly referred to as office suites. The functionality of word processing software extends beyond recording and organizing text. Expanded word processing functions useful to social workers include (a) the production of graphically rich documents such as flyers, booklets, and newsletters, (b) the production of collaborative documents in which changes made by multiple authors can be tracked and displayed, (c) the generation of mail merge documents, which combine unique individual information from a data file with a document template to produce individualized letters, and (d) the creation of Web pages. Spreadsheets are software applications that display a matrix of rows and columns of cells into which information, in the form of numbers, text, or formulas, is entered and shown. They are robust and highly flexible tools that can be used by social workers to (a) collect, store, and organize financial and practice data, (b) conduct a wide range of data analysis or statistical procedures, and (c) generate graphs and tables for summarization and presentation of information. This software is used to integrate text, graphics, animation, sound, and video into multimedia slide shows. Presentation software usually includes functions for creating, editing, arranging, and media enhancement of slides as well as a modality for displaying the resultant slide show. Slide presentations can be saved as Web pages and uploaded to the Web for broader dissemination. E-mail PIM tools are software applications that integrate the composition, sending, receipt, and storage of e-mail with scheduling calendars, address or contact databases, notes, and tasks. PIM tools are extremely useful for managing complex schedules, projects, and requisite communications.

There are many other categories of software applications with utility in social work practice. Database applications are used for data entry, storage, organization, query/selection, and report generation. Database software used by social workers range from single user database applications on the worker's personal computer to client databases running on agency networks to web-based databases linking multiple agency sites or multiple agencies. Statistical software applications are specialized tools for the collection, storage, and statistical analysis of data. HTML (hypertext markup language) editors are used for the creation of Web pages. Many HTML editors enable the creation of Web pages without having to write code and allow the creator review the page before uploading it to a Web file server. Digital editing tools are a broad category of applications used to modify digital files, including digital images, digital video, and digital sound recording. These digital editing tools are applicable in social work practice for the creation of training materials, presentations, and client education videos.

## Internet Tools

Historically, software applications were purchased for and run on an individual's computer. There are two noteworthy recent trends with significant implications for social work practice. First, open source software, cooperatively created and freely distributed, is available for operating systems and office application suites. For example, Ubuntu is a Linux-based operating system that includes a complete office application suite and other open source software. A second trend is the appearance of Web-based applications with the functionality of personal-computer-based software. For instance, Google.com now offers without charge a Google account that includes e-mail, scheduling calendar, word processor, spreadsheet, and a tool for digital photo editing or Web publication.

Finally, there are many Web-based applications with noteworthy social work practice utility. Web-based survey tools enable practitioners, administrators, and researchers to create surveys for the collection of information over the Web. Map databases such as Google Maps, MapQuest, and MapPoint make it possible to find and print maps of street addresses. Collaborative software, sometimes referred to as groupware, can be used by multiple users to (a) communicate by sending documents, files, or messages, (b) conference with each other through Internet forums, audio or video conferencing, and data or application sharing, and (c) collaborate with shared calendars, project tracking tools, and online spreadsheets.

## Future Trends

Three future trends in ICT are likely to affect social work practice. First, Web-accessible PDAs and smartphones will evolve with increased features and computing power, enabling them to become a vital link between practitioners and practice-critical information resources available through Web interface. Second, evidence-based practice will be aided by artificial intelligence based algorithms that will match best practices to users' practice context and population data. Third, centralized electronic health record databases developed and operated by third parties such as Google and Microsoft may revolutionize access and storage of client information. It is possible that in the future clients will request that all of the health and social service records be centrally stored, thereby allowing client-sanctioned access that transcends agency boundaries.

### REFERENCES

Coursen, D. (2006). An ecosystems approach to human service database design. *Journal of Technology in Human Services*, 24(1), 1–18.

Finn, J. (2006). An exploratory study of email use by direct service social workers. *Journal of Technology in Human Services*, 24(4), 1–20.

Patterson, D. A. (2000). *Personal computer applications in the social services*. Boston: Allyn and Bacon.

Patterson, D. A., & Basham, R. E. (2006). *Data analysis with spreadsheets*. Boston: Allyn and Bacon.

Schoech, D. (1999). *Human services technology: Understanding, designing, and implementing computer and internet applications in the social services*. New York: Haworth.

### SUGGESTED LINKS

Collaborative software.
  http://en.wikipedia.org/wiki/Collaborative_software
  http://www.phpgroupware.org/
  http://www.egroupware.org/
  http://en.wikipedia.org/wiki/Wiki
HTML Editors.
  http://www.w3.org/Amaya/
  http://www.mozilla.org/products/mozilla1.x/
  http://www.nvu.com/index.php
Map Databases.
  http://www.google.com/maps
  http://mappoint.msn.com
  http://www.mapquest.com/
Office Application Suites.
  http://www.openoffice.org/
  http://www.neooffice.org/
Spreadsheets.
  http://web.utk.edu/~dap/Random/Order/Start.htm
  http://www.usd.edu/trio/tut/excel/index.html
  http://www.csubak.edu/~jross/classes/GS390/Spreadsheets/
  ss_basics/ss_basics.html

Voice Over Internet Protocol.
  *http://www.voip-info.org/wiki/*
  *http://www.fcc.gov/voip/*
Web-based Survey Tools.
  *http://www.surveymonkey.com/*
  *http://info.zoomerang.com/*
  *http://www.questionpro.com/web-based-survey-software.html*

—David A. Patterson

# TECHNOLOGY TRANSFER

**Abstract:** The term *technology transfer* was first used widely during the Kennedy and Johnson administrations when the role of the United States in relation to developing countries was being formed. At that time, it meant knowledge transfer from the rich countries to the poor countries. In social work, the idea is important in efforts of community organization, community development, and social development. It is also an important idea in direct practice. Technology in these practice settings means the application of a basic social science toward facilitating one or more given ends that benefit human beings. Technology transfer means the passing on of such applied knowledge from one discipline or specialty to another. The application of technology transfer also requires understanding of the cultural setting where it originates as well as of the setting where it is imported for local use.

**Key Words:** technology transfer; community organization; community development; social development; international social work; culture; *DSM-IV*; strengths-based model

The term *technology transfer* was first used widely during the Kennedy and Johnson administrations when the role of the United States in relation to developing countries was being formed. At that time, it meant knowledge transfer from rich countries to poor countries. Since then, the idea has been imported in social work, where it means idea transfer in efforts of community organization, community development, and social development. It is also an important idea in direct practice. Technology in these practice settings means the application of a basic social science toward facilitating one or more given ends that benefit human beings. Technology transfer means the passing on of such applied knowledge from one discipline or specialty to another. The application of technology transfer also requires understanding of the cultural setting where it originates as well as of the setting where it is imported for local use.

In the social sciences, there seems to be a lack of agreement about what the term means (Arrow, 1969; Bozeman, 2000; Dosi, 1988; Foster, 1962; Johnson, 1970; Rogers, 1962, Rogers & Shoemaker, 1971; Service, 1971; Zhao & Reisman, 1992). In social work, Rothman, Erlich, and Teresa (1977) used the concept of diffusion of innovations to understand the process of technology transfer. We define it as having a two-step process. One, it requires conversion of knowledge in science into an applied science, which in turn produces artifacts useful to humans. The applied knowledge which builds these artifacts is called technology. Often creative expressions by human beings get added to this process, and are known as craft. Then, craft also may make a contribution to technology. Technology, thus, is a form of human knowledge that is founded on both science and art. Second, extended from this, technology transfer is defined as the exporting or importing of an applied knowledge-base from one human group to another.

Technology transfer occurs not only between nations but also within nations. Within nations, it may take place between disciplines, occupational groups, communities, and organizations (compare Chatterjee, 1995).

### An Example

The science of metallurgy, for example, can teach members of a human group how to do mining and then convert raw material from the mine into steel, and then into a sword. A knowledge system then arises about how a given type of sword may have a relative advantage in battle over other types of sword. The creative minds of the people who turn the steel into a sword, however, many inscribe various designs on the handle of the sword. These designs, then, are creative expressions which are crafted into the sword. Later, the knowledge base about how to construct a sword may get passed on to another group, community, or people, with or without the artwork on the handle.

### Intended and Unintended Consequences

Some examples of frequent applications of technology transfer in social work as well as in other disciplines are shown in Table 1.

In this table, knowledge is shown to be transferred from science to its application in several disciplines. It also creates intended and unintended consequences. For example, knowledge transfer about human behavior from psychiatry to social work may be used for illness management (or mental illness management) in a given society. The unintended consequence may be

TABLE 1
*Artifacts Derived From Science and Their Functions*

| SCIENCE | ARTIFACT IN APPLIED SCIENCE | FUNCTIONS |
| --- | --- | --- |
| Physics: Study of heat | Heat engine and automobile | Comfort |
| | | Transport |
| | | Status |
| | | (Several unintended consequences) |
| Information theory: Study of communications | Internet | Communication |
| | | Information storage |
| | | (Several unintended consequences) |
| Microbiology: Study of micro life form | Penicillin | Survival |
| | | Comfort |
| | | (Several unintended consequences) |
| Social Sciences: Study of human behavior in Psychology, Social Work, Management | Assessment tools | Illness management |
| | Diagnostic tools | Wellness pursuit |
| | Intervention | Standardizing work-related behavior |
| | Procedures | Deviance control |
| | Outcome standards | (Several unintended consequences) |

that the use of such medical metaphor may be used for status enhancement for the profession of social work.

## Models of Technology Transfer

Ruttan and Hayami (1973) described one form of agricultural technology transfer that has become an example of how to conceptualize the problem of technology transfer. They suggested that technology transfer involves three phases: *material transfer, design transfer, and capacity transfer*. Their study describes how the asexual reproductive nature of sugarcane was discovered independently in Java and Barbados during the 1880s. This discovery allowed the global export of a variety of seedlings, which, unfortunately, were highly susceptible to the diseases of the countries of destination. But experimental stations in India successfully developed interspecies hybrids that were both disease-resistant and suited to local conditions. After this breakthrough, different countries began experimenting with hybrids of imported and local seedlings. Today, although relatively little actual transfer of plants occurs, a great deal of information between countries is exchanged. In this example, material transfer involved the actual transfer of the plants; design transfer involved the transfer of knowledge about breeding sugarcane under local conditions; and capacity transfer involved the actual capacity for creating different strains under local conditions.

## Application to Social Work

The *DSM-IV* (*Diagnostic and Statistical Manual of Mental Disorders*, 4th ed.) model (Thakker & Ward, 1998) demonstrates the sequences of material, design,

and capacity transfer. This model is an assessment tool in the United States for diagnosing mental illnesses by mental health professionals. Material transfer of the model is embedded in the translation of terms and symptomology from the psychiatrist to the social worker. Design transfer is embedded in the transfer of roles and values in which the psychiatrist diagnoses the patient to that of the social work profession. The capacity is present if *DSM-IV* as a service delivery tool is supported by the health-care system and the social welfare system. However, an issue related to this model's effectiveness and reliability of diagnoses is that the perception of what is a disorder varies significantly across cultures (Thakker & Ward, 1998). Past models of the *DSM* recommended changes that clinicians respond with sensitivity to differences in behavior, values, and language as they vary across cultures (Thakker & Ward, 1998).

Considering the situation, culture, value, and social systems play a critical role in applying transferred technology to the field of social work in different countries (Ferguson, 2005; Jinchao, 1995; Nimmagadda & Cowger, 1999; Roan, 1980). For example, professional social work has been transferred from the developed world to the developing countries. However, the assumption about universalism in social work intervention did not fit many cases (Nimmagadda & Cowger, 1999). According to Ferguson (2005), the different perspectives on defining of social problems in each country as well as its "own political, economic, and social structures" intensify such discrepancy (p. 520).

Another example of cross-national transfer involves importing microlending technology of Muhammad Yunis in community and social development work, from Bangladesh to the United States (see Profile: *World banker to the poor*, extracted December 13, 2006, http://news.bbc.co.uk/2/hi/south_asia/6047234.stm). Some may argue that such a technology is not appropriate for importing into the United States. In that case, one would see an example of a politically problematic cross-national technology transfer.

[*See also* Clinical Social Work; Cognition and Social Cognitive Theory; Community; Community Development; Epistemology; Expert Systems; Health Services Systems Policy; Interdisciplinary and Interorganizational Collaboration; International and Comparative Social Welfare; International Social Welfare: Organizations and Activities; Planning and Management; Professions; Social Development; Social Work Profession Overview; Strategic Planning.]

### REFERENCES

Arrow, K. (1969). Classificatory notes on the production and transmission of technological knowledge. *American economic review, papers and proceedings, 59*(2), 29–35.

Bozeman, B. (2000). Technology transfer and public policy: A review of research and theory. *Research policy, 29,* 627–655.

Chatterjee, P. (1995). Technology transfer. In *Encyclopedia of Social Work* (Vol. 19, pp. 2393–2397). Washington, DC: NASW Press.

Dosi, G. (1988). The nature of the innovation process. In G. Dosi et al. (Eds.), *Technical change and economic theory.* London: Pinter.

Ferguson, K. M. (2005). Beyond indigenization and reconceptualization: Towards a global, multidirectional model of technology transfer. *International social work, 48*(5), 519–535.

Foster, G. (1962). *Traditional cultures and the impact of technological change.* New York: Harper.

Jinchao, Y. (1995). The developing model of social education in China. *International social work, 38,* 27–38.

Johnson, H. (1970). *The efficiency and welfare implications of the international corporation.* In C. Kindleger (Ed.), *International corporations.* Cambridge: Cambridge University Press.

Nimmagadda, J., & Cowger, C. D. (1999). Cross-cultural practice. Social worker ingenuity in the indigenization of practice knowledge. *International social work, 42*(3), 261–276.

Roan, S. (1980). Utilizing traditional elements in the Society in Casework practice. *International social work, 23,* 26–35.

Rogers, E. M. (1962). *Diffusion of innovations.* New York: The Free Press of Glencoe.

Rogers, E. M., & Shoemaker, F. F. (1971). *Communication of innovations:* A cross cultural approach. New York: Free Press.

Rothman, J., Erlich, J. L., & Teresa, J. (1977). Adding something new: Innovation. In E. M. Cox, J. L. Erlich, J. Rothman, & J. E. Tropman (Eds.), *Tactics and techniques of community practice* (pp. 157–166). Itasca, IL: F. E. Peacock.

Ruttan, V., & Hayami, Y. (1973). Technology transfer and economic development. *Technology and Culture, 14*(2), 119–150.

Service, E. (1971). *Cultural evolutionism.* New York: Holt, Rinehart, and Winston.

Thakker, J., & Ward, T. (1998). Culture and classification: The cross cultural application of the *DSM-IV. Clinical Psychology Review, 18*(5), 501–529.

Zhao, L. M., & Reisman, A. (1992). Toward meta research on technology-transfer. *IEEE Transaction on Engineering Management, 39*(1), 13–21.

### FURTHER READING

Aspinwall, L. G., & Staudinger, U. M. (2003). *A psychology of human strengths: Fundamental questions and future directions for a positive psychology.* Washington, DC: American Psychological Associations.

Barnett, H. (1953). *Innovation: The basis of cultural change.* New York: McGraw-Hill.

Batten, T. R. (1957). *Communities and their development.* London: Oxford University Press.

Beck, A. T. (1976). *Cognitive therapy and the emotional disorders.* New York: International Universities Press.

Berlin, S. B. (1982). Cognitive behavioral interventions for social work practice. *Social Work, 27,* 218–226.

Boseman, B. (2000). Technology transfer and public policy: A review of research and theory. *Research Policy, 29,* 627–655.

Bringham, R. P., & Saponaro, L. (2003, August). Social changes for 2025 and the role of counseling psychology. Paper presented at the annual convention of the American Psychological Association, Toronto, Ontario, Canada.

Burton, H. (1977). A note on the transfer of technology. *Economic Development and Cultural Change, 25*(4), S234–44 [Suppl.].

Chatterjee, P. (1990). *The transferability of social technology.* Lewiston, NY: E. Mellen.

Chatterjee, P., & Ireys, H. (1979). Technology transfer: Views from some social science disciplines. *Social Development Issues, 3,* 54–75.

Chatterjee, P., & Ireys, H. (1981). Technology transfer: Implications for social work practice and social work education. *International Social Work, 24,* 14–22.

Clark, M. D. (1999). *Strength-based practice: The ABC's of working with adolescents who don't want to work with you.* Retrieved February 28, 2001, from http://www.drugs.indiana.edu/prevention/assets/asset2.html.

Dube, S. (1958). *India's changing villages.* Ithaca, NY: Cornell University Press.

Ellis, A. (1962). *Reason and emotion in psychotherapy.* New York: Lyle Stuart.

Goodman, R. (1999). The extended version of the strengths and difficulties questionnaires as a guide to child psychiatric caseness and consequent burden. *Journal of Child Psychology and Psychiatry and Allied Disciplines*, 40, 791–799.

Gruber, W., & Marquis, D. (1969). *Factors in the transfer of technology*. Cambridge, MA: MIT Press.

Heller, T. (1971). [Book review]. *Technology and Culture*, 12, 370–372.

Hepworth, D. H., & Larsen, J. A. (1990). *Direct social work practice*. Belmont, CA: Wadsworth.

Kanfer, F. H., & Goldstein, A. P. (Eds.). *Helping people change* (pp. 390–422). Elmsford, NY: Pergamon.

Katz, M. (1997). *On playing a poor hand well*. New York: Norton.

Katz, E., Levin, M., & Hamilton, H. (1963). Traditions of research on the diffusion of innovation. *American Sociological Review*, 28, 237–252.

Kutner, S., & Kirsch, S. (1985). Clinical applications of SYMLOG: A graphic system of observing relationships. *Social Work*, 30, 497–503.

Lall, S. (1976). The patent system and the transfer of technology to less developed countries. *Journal of World Trade Law*, 10, 6–7.

Lerner, D. (1958). *The passing of traditional society*. New York: Free Press.

Martinez-Brawley, E. E. (with Delevan, S. M.) (Eds.). (1993). *Transferring technology in the personal social services*. Washington, DC: NASW Press.

Mason, E. (1955). *Promoting economic development*. Claremont, CA: Claremont College Press.

Mead, M. (1955). *Cultural patterns and technical change*. New York: UNESCO.

Meichenbaum, D., & Genest, M. (1980). Cognitive behavior modification: An integration of cognitive and behavioral methods. In K. H. Kanfer & A. D. Goldstein (Eds.), *Helping people change* (pp. 390–422). New York: Pergamon.

Merrill, R. (1972). The role of technology in cultural evolution. *Social biology*, 19(3), 246–256.

Mischel, W. (1973). Toward a cognitive social learning reconceptualization of personality. *Psychological Review*, 80, 252–283.

Mischel, W. (1979). On the interface of cognition and personality: Beyond the person-situation debate. *American Psychologist*, 34, 740–754.

Mischel, W., & Baker, N. (1975). Cognitive appraisals and transformation in delay behavior. *Journal of Personality and Social Psychology*, 31, 254–261.

National Science Foundation. (1966). *Proceedings of a conference on technology transfer and innovation*. Washington, DC: Author.

Owens-Kane, S., Smith, L., & Brinson, R. (2005). Transfer of child welfare research findings to the field: An internet-based training series. Professional development: *The International Journal of Continuing Social Work Education*, 8(1), 27–37.

Patel, S. (1974). The patent system and the third world. *World Development*, 2, 3–4.

Penrose, E. T. (1973). International patenting and the less developed countries. *Economic Journal*, 9, 777–780.

Polson, R. A. (1958). Theory and methods of training for community development. *Rural Sociology*, 23, 34–42.

Practicing Law Institute. (1970). *The local economic development corporation*. Washington, DC: U.S. Department of Commerce.

Roessner, J. D. (2000). Technology transfer. In C. Hill (Ed.), *Science and technology policy in the U.S.: A Time of Change*. London: Longman.

Rothman, J. (1968). *Three models of community organization practice: National Conference on Social Welfare, Social Work Practice, 1968*. New York: Columbia University Press.

Salin, E. (1967). The Schumpeterin theory and continental thought. In D. Spencer & A. Woroniak (Eds.), *The transfer of technologies to developing countries* (pp. 42–51). New York: Praeger.

Scheyett, A., Roberts, A., & Kirk, R. (2001). Social work practitioners and technology transfer. Professional Development. *The International Journal of Continuing Social Work Education*, 4(2), 42–53.

Seligman, M. E. (1998). The president's address. *American Psychologist*, 54, 559–562.

Sherrard, T. (1962). Community organization and community development. *Community Development Review*, 7, 11–20.

Smith, E. J. (2006). The strength-based counseling model. *The counseling psychologist*, 34(1), 13–79.

Spencer, D., & Woroniak, A. (1967). *The transfer of technology to developing countries*. New York: Praeger.

Spicer, E. (Ed.). (1952). *Human problems in technological change*. New York: Russell Sage Foundation.

Taylor, E. (1911). *Scientific management*. New York: Harper.

Thorpe, G. L., Hecker, J. E., Cavallaro, L. A., & Kulberg, G. E. (1987). Insight vs. rehearsal in cognitive-behavioral therapy. *Behavioral Psychotherapy*, 25(4), S234–44 [Suppl.].

Tonnies, F. (1957). *Community and society [Gemeinschaft und Gesellschaft]* (C. P. Loomis, Trans.). East Lansing, MI: The Michigan State University Press.

Tversky, A. (1977). Features of similarity. *Psychological Review*, 84, 327–352.

Twentieth Century Fund. (1971). *CDCs: New hope for the inner city*. New York: Author.

United Nations. (1955). *Social progress through community development*. New York: Author.

Walsh, W. B. (2004). *Counseling psychology and optimal human functioning*. New York: Erlbaum.

Weick, A., Rapp, C., Sullivan, W. P., & Kisthardt, W. (1989). A strengths perspective for social work practice. *Social Work*, 34, 350–354.

Weinstein, J., & Pillai, V. K. (1979). Appropriate technology versus appropriating technology. *Social Development Issues*, 3, 37–53.

## SUGGESTED LINKS

*http://news.bbc.co.uk/2/hi/south_asia/6047234.stm*
*http://www.drugs.indiana.edu/prevention/assets/asset2.html*
*http://www.spa.ucla.edu/dept.cfm?d = sw&s = home&f = aboutfield.cfm&sf = fieldagencies.cfm*
*http://www.cosw.sc.edu/field/agencies.html*

*http://socialwork.bc.edu/academics/masters/masters-field-education/*

*http://www.pitt.edu/~pittssw/hartford.html*

—Pranab Chatterjee,
Heehyul Moon, and Derrick Kranke

**TEENAGERS.** *See* Adolescents: Overview.

## TEMPORARY ASSISTANCE FOR NEEDY FAMILIES

**Abstract:** In 1996, The Personal Responsibility and Work Opportunity Reconciliation Act (PRWORA) repealed the 60-year-old national welfare program of Aid to Families with Dependant Children (AFDC) and replaced it with a new cash assistance program, Temporary Assistance for Needy Families (TANF). This law introduced a new generation of rules and regulations for delivering cash and other assistance to families who are poor and fundamentally changed the way the United States assists such families and their children. Opinions regarding the success of TANF and its impact on families vary; welfare caseloads have declined since TANF implementation, but economic self-sufficiency eludes many families.

Temporary Assistance for Needy Families (TANF), enacted as part of the Personal Responsibility and Work Opportunity Reconciliation Act of 1996, fundamentally transformed the nation's response to poor families and their children. TANF terminated the federal entitlement to cash assistance previously authorized under Aid to Families with Dependent Children (AFDC). In its place, states now are authorized to receive two block grants, one for TANF and the other for child care services under the Child Care and Development Block Grant. This block grant funding mechanism is the primary vehicle for achieving the main purpose of TANF, which is to increase state flexibility in operating welfare programs (42 U.S.C. sec. 601[a]). The legislation continues the traditional focus of AFDC with the goal of assisting "needy families so that child may be cared for in their own homes or in the homes of relatives" (42 U.S.C. sec 601[a] [1]). Additional goals are to reduce welfare dependence through job preparation, work, and marriage; prevent and reduce the incidence of nonmarital pregnancies; and encourage the formation of two-parent families.

**Key Words:** TANF; welfare; cash assistance; Aid to Families with Dependent Children (AFDC); The Personal Responsibility and Work Opportunity Reconciliation Act of 1996; Child Care and Development Block Grant

### Who Receives TANF?

TANF is a public assistance program for families with children who are poor. Under TANF, states have the authority to establish all eligibility requirements, and they are under no obligation to serve any particular type of family or any particular family. In general, however, financial eligibility is established through a means test, that is, families must demonstrate financial need for assistance according to standards set by each state. These standards include both income and asset limitations. In determining program eligibility, most states disregard some portion of a family's earned income and almost all states (48) disregard some portion of earned income when determining the family's actual benefit level (Rowe & Versteeg, 2005).

In FY 2003, approximately 5.5 million people received TANF benefits, including 4.1 million children. The average TANF family size is 2.5 people. In recent years, as the adult-headed caseload has declined, child-only cases in which no adult received benefits have increased proportionately, representing 37% of the TANF caseload in FY 2003. Ninety percent of the adult recipients are women and 23% of the adult recipients are employed (U.S. Department of Health and Human Services [HHS], 2005). African Americans represent 38% of the caseload; Whites, 32%; Hispanics, 25%; Asians, 2.2%; and Native Americans, 1.4% (HHS, 2004). In FY 2002, the average length of TANF assistance was 29 months (HHS, 2004). However, for one-half of those entering TANF between 2001 and 2003, the spells of TANF receipt lasted 4 months. Additionally, long-term welfare use has declined: "less than 4 percent of those with some AFDC/TANF assistance between 1991 and 2000 received assistance in nine or ten years of the period" (HHS, 2005, p. xiv).

**Work Requirements** TANF continues the practice begun in the late 1960s to replace welfare with work, and a work-based welfare program is the major feature of TANF. In other words, the emphasis is on a labor-force attachment approach rather than a human-capital investment one. In order to receive benefits, adult recipients must engage in work or work-related activities when the state indicates they are ready or after 2 years on assistance, whichever comes first. The law allows few exceptions to the work requirements.

If a recipient fails to comply with the work requirements, states may sanction the recipient by reducing or terminating benefits to the family. In the majority of states, sanctioning results in the termination of benefits to the entire family rather than a benefit reduction.

For all families, the average minimum hours of required work activity is 30 hr a week. The weekly requirement for two-parent families is 35 hr and the weekly requirement for single mothers with children under 6 years of age is 20 hr. Acceptable work activities include unsubsidized employment, subsidized private or public employment, work experience, community service, on-the-job training, job search, and job readiness. Vocational education is allowed but restricted to no more than 12 months. Although states emphasize this "work-first" approach, research suggests that a broader approach that focuses on work as well as skill building is more successful (Gueron & Hamilton, 2002).

DIVERSION PROGRAMS As part of the "work-first" strategy, most states have diversion programs that offer families a cash lump sum as an alternative to ongoing TANF assistance. In exchange, families agree not to reapply for cash assistance for a period of time. Some states' diversion programs include referrals to job search and job placement services as well as alternative assistance programs (HHS, 2004).

CASELOAD REDUCTIONS AND WELFARE LEAVERS Caseloads have declined by 56% since passage of TANF. Explaining the decline in caseloads is complex, given that TANF was implemented during a period of economic growth. In general, studies indicate that both economic conditions and welfare policy contributed to this dramatic decline in welfare caseloads (HHS, 2005). In view of the caseload declines, there are concerns about those who remain on welfare. Available administrative data show few significant changes in the caseload composition. However, several studies (for example, Danziger et al., 1999a; Hauan & Douglas, 2004) suggest that current welfare recipients have numerous barriers to employment, including low educational levels, limited or no work experience, limited job skills, and physical and mental health problems. Danziger et al. (1999a), in a study of women receiving welfare in Michigan, found that 37% had two or three barriers to work and 27% had four or more barriers. The more barriers a woman had, the less likely she was to be employed. For this group with multiple barriers, "work first" strategies will have limited effectiveness and other more comprehensive services are needed to have an impact (Danziger et al., 1999b).

Of those who leave welfare, three-fourths work at some point in the year after exiting welfare. However, only one-third work the entire year. Although they work a significant number of hours (35 hr each week), former recipients tend to earn low wages and only one-third have employer-sponsored health insurance. Their family income from all sources is near the poverty line, and studies suggest that it is not uncommon for leavers to experience material hardships such as hunger and housing problems (Acs, Loprest, & Roberts, 2001). Overall, approximately 30% return to TANF within a year (Acs, Loprest, & Roberts, 2001; Cancian, Meyer, & Wu, 2005).

### Benefits under TANF

The average monthly cash and cash-equivalent benefit for a TANF family is $355. This represents 61% of the benefits provided in the late 1970s. Cash benefits vary widely from state to state because each state establishes its benefit level. For example, in 2002, the maximum benefit for a family of three with no income was $164 in Alabama and $679 in California. Additionally, benefits may vary within a state by region, by urban or rural area, or by recipient status as exempt or not exempt from work participation requirements (HHS, 2004).

TIME LIMITS Under TANF, the federal legislation establishes a 5-year, lifetime limit for receiving assistance from federal TANF funds. However, states are free to use their own funds to support families after 5 years—and they are also free to establish shorter time limits for receiving benefits. State policies regarding time limits for the receipt of assistance vary greatly and some are complex. Most states have selected to use the federal 5-year time limit for receiving TANF benefits. However, in some of these states, there are intermittent time limits; that is, after a designated period, most commonly 24 months, benefits are either reduced or terminated for a period of time after which benefits are resumed. Eight states have established lifetime limits that are shorter than the federal limit, ranging from 21 to 48 months. Five states (MA, MI, NY, OR, and VT) have no lifetime limits, either because they have preexisting waivers or have chosen to use state funds if the 60-month limit for federal benefits is exceeded (HHS, 2004).

The most recent data suggest that case closures due to the federal time limits have been limited. If New York is excluded, less than 7,000 cases were closed under the federal time limits in FY 2002 (HHS, 2004). In New York, which accounted for 86,000 case closures due to the federal time limits, families were shifted to a state-funded program called

Safety Net Assistance. States are allowed to exempt up to 20% of their welfare caseloads from the 5-year time limit because of hardship or domestic violence. The hardship exemption has been exercised for a small proportion of TANF families—1.1% nationwide (HHS, 2004).

## Program Financing

Under the block grant, the federal funding for TANF is $16.6 billion, and each state receives a fixed amount of federal dollars for the TANF program. Supplementing the block grant is a contingency fund of $2 billion to assist states in the event of an economic downturn. Although there are no matching funds requirements, a "maintenance of effort" provision requires states to invest their own dollars in the TANF program. Combined federal and state expenditures for TANF in FY 2003 were $26.3 billion. Under TANF, funding has shifted from cash assistance to supportive services. In FY 2002, 41% of expenditures were for cash assistance and 25% for child care and work activities. This contrasts with FY 1997, in which 73% was allocated to cash assistance and 8% to child care and work activities (HHS, 2005). This pattern reflects the declining caseloads and the emphasis on labor force participation.

To receive full grant funding, states are required to have 50% of all adult recipients and 90% of two-parent households engaged in work activities. When TANF was reauthorized as part of the Deficit Reduction Act (Pub. L. No. 109-171 [DFA]) of 2005, increased demands were placed on states for work participation rates. The state's participation rate is based on families receiving TANF as well as families in state-funded programs included in the maintenance of effort spending. A state's work participation rate may be reduced if they have declines in their TANF caseload that occur after 2005. If states fail to meet the participation rates, their block grants may be reduced. Meeting these participation rates may prove challenging to some states; in FY 2002, 33.4% of those required to participate in work activities meet the work requirements.

## Family Violence Option

The potential vulnerability and needs of battered women are recognized through the Family Violence Option of the TANF legislation. Research suggests that between 15% and 56% of TANF recipients have been or are victims of domestic violence (GAO, 2005b). Under the Family Violence Option, states screen for domestic violence and are given flexibility in applying TANF rules to victims of domestic violence. States may waive time limits, family caps, work requirements, and child support enforcement requirements, if complying with them places clients at risk or unfairly penalizes them. Additionally, the Family Violence Option allows states to provide referrals for supportive and counseling services. Forty states have adopted the Family Violence Option; an additional seven states have developed comparable state policies for responding to victims of domestic violence. Findings on the implementation of the Family Violence Option indicate that relatively few recipients have obtained waivers and that notification and screening for domestic violence is frequently inadequate and needs improvement (GAO, 2005b; Lindhorst & Padgett, 2005).

## Child Care Provisions

As a block grant, the Child Care and Development Fund (CCDF) makes available $5 billion annually for child care services. Through matching funds and maintenance of effort provisions, states are required to invest their own funds in child care services as well. In FY 2003, a total of $12 billion was spent on child care services under CCDF, TANF, and state spending; this is almost a fourfold increase over the amount spent in FY 1997. CCDF serves approximately 1.75 million children (GAO, 2005a).

Under CCDF, states may provide child care subsidies to families earning up to 85% of the state median income and may transfer up to 30% of their TANF funds directly to child care services. States also have flexibility in determining income eligibility limits, provider reimbursement rates, and the use of copayments. Twenty states are not able to serve all eligible applicants. Seventeen of these states give priority to TANF families and 14 states have established waiting lists (GAO, 2005a).

## Family Structure Provisions

Several TANF provisions relate to the structure of families receiving TANF, including the birth of children, the number of parents, and parents' legal status. TANF relaxed work-related eligibility requirements for two-parent families. In addition, states are encouraged, although not required, to use TANF dollars to promote marriage and the formation of two-parent families. However, they are prohibited from using TANF funds to assist teen parents who are not in school and not living in an adult-supervised setting. In addition, states have explicit permission to deny payment increases for parents who have additional children while on welfare, a policy referred to as a family cap. Twenty-three states impose a full or partial family cap. The effectiveness of family caps in reducing out-of-wedlock births is difficult to determine, given limited research in this area (GAO, 2001).

In 2005, the DFA established a new marriage and fatherhood competitive grants program, with funding of $150 annually. Eligible applicants include state and local governments as well as various nonprofit organizations. Acceptable grant activities are wide ranging and include marriage and premarital education, marriage mentoring programs, and media campaigns.

## Child Support Enforcement

Under TANF, states are required to operate a child support enforcement program following federal requirements. TANF families must assign support rights to the states and cooperate in establishing paternity as a condition of eligibility. States have the option of either denying or reducing benefits for refusal to cooperate in paternity establishment or securing child support. In FY 2002, the Child Support Enforcement Program collected $2.9 billion in child support for families receiving TANF (HHS, 2004).

Under the DFA, the federal share of child support collections is waived if states pass through child support to TANF families and disregard child support of up to $100 for one child and up to $200 for two or more children in determining benefits. Additionally, TANF child support orders must be reviewed and adjusted in a 3-year cycle. DFA reduced the federal share of child support administrative spending, a change expected to result in decreased child support collections (CWLA, 2006).

## Roles and Implications for Social Work

Cash support to families living in poverty has been and remains a politically controversial and complex issue in the United States (Heclo, 1997; NASW, 2007). Some of the most contentious issues in TANF include the structure of work requirements for adults, the impact of program changes on child well-being, the funding and structure of marriage promotion activities and mechanisms that limit access to aid, including time limits, sanctions and diversion programs.

The challenges and opportunities under TANF require that social workers focus on accessing services to ensure that clients understand the time-limited nature of welfare benefits as well as the services to which they are entitled. The "delinking" of welfare benefits from Medicaid and food stamps requires that particular attention be given to accessing these services as well as child care subsidies and the earned income tax credit (EITC).

Additionally, social workers have a central role to play in the research, as well as the development and evaluation of new service models to assist clients with multiple barriers to employment and clients who interface with multiple service systems (Cancian, Meyers, & Wu, 2005; Danziger et al., 1999a, 1999b; Johnson, Chow, Ketch, & Austin, 2006; Lawrence, 2007; Lens & Vorsanger, 2005; Lindhorst & Padgett, 2005; Nam, 2005, Ozawa & Yoon, 2005).

Policy analysis must maintain a dual focus on national and state policies. Particular attention needs to be directed to the interaction and interrelatedness of various federal policies. Given the lack of federal oversight under TANF, ongoing monitoring of each state's program is mandatory. Based on these analyses, advocacy agendas can target both state and federal levels (Hagen, 1999).

## References

Acs, G., Loprest, P., & Roberts, T. (2001). *Final synthesis report of findings from ASPE's "leavers" grant.* Washington, DC: U.S. Department of Health and Human Services.

Cancian, M., Meyer, D. R., & Wu, C. (2005). After the revolution: Welfare patterns since TANF implementation. *Social Work Research, 29,* 119–214.

Child Welfare League of America. (2006). *Summary and analysis of child welfare provisions included in the Deficit Reduction Omnibus Reconciliation Act of 2005* (S. 1932). Washington, DC: Author. Retrieved from http://www.cwla.org/advocacy/fostercare060201.htm.

Danziger, S., Corcoran, M., Danziger, S., Heflin, C., Kalil, A., Levine, J., et al. (1999a). *Barriers to the employment of welfare recipients* (unpublished research report). Ann Arbor, MI: University of Michigan, Poverty Research and Training Center.

Danziger, S., Corcoran, M., Danziger, S., Heflin, C., Kalil, A., Levine, J., et al. (1999b). Barriers to work among welfare recipients. *Focus, 20,* 31–35.

Gueron, J., & Hamilton, G. (2002). *The role of education and training in welfare reform* (Welfare Reform & Beyond Policy Brief Series No. 20). Washington, DC: Brookings Institution.

Hagen, J. L. (1999). Public welfare and human services: New directions under TANF? *Families in Society 80*(1), 78–90.

Hauan, S., & Douglas, S. (2004). *Potential employment liabilities among TANF recipients: A synthesis of data from six state TANF caseload studies.* Washington, DC: U.S. Department of Health and Human Services. Retrieved from http://aspe.hhs.gov/hsp/leavers99/emp-liab04/.

Heclo, H. H. (1997). Values underpinning poverty programs for children. *The Future of Children, 7*(2), 141–148.

Johnson, M. A., Chow J., Ketch, V., & Austin, M. J. (2006). Implementing welfare-to-work services: A study of staff decision-making. *Families in Society 87*(3), 317–325.

Lawrence, C. K. (2007). State responses to the family formation goals of welfare. *Social Service Review 81*(1), 129–153.

Lens, V., & Vorsanger, S. E. (2005). Complaining after claiming: Fair hearings after welfare reform. *Social Service Review 79*(3), 430–453.

Lindhorst, T., & Padgett, J. D. (2005). Disjunctures for women and frontline workers: Implementation of the family violence option. *Social Service Review, 79,* 405–429.

National Association of Social Workers. (2007). *Issue Fact Sheets: Poverty*. Washington, D.C; Author. Retrieved from http://www.socialworkers.org/pressroom/features/issue/poverty.asp.

Nam, Y. (2005). The roles of employment barriers in welfare exits and reentries after welfare reform: Event history analyses. *Social Service Review* 79(2), 268–293.

Ozawa, M., & Yoon, H. (2005). "Leavers" after TANF and AFDC: How do they fare economically? *Social Work* 50(3), 239–249.

Rowe, G., & Versteeg, J. (2005). *Welfare rules databook: State TANF policies as of July 2003*. Washington, DC: The Urban Institute.

U.S. Department of Health and Human Services. (2004). *Temporary assistance for needy families: Sixth annual report to Congress*. Washington, DC: Author. Retrieved from http://www.acf.hhs.gov/programs/ofa/annualreport6/.

U.S. Department of Health and Human Services. (2005). *Indicators of welfare dependence: Annual report to Congress 2005*. Washington, DC: Author.

U.S. General Accounting Office. (2001). *Welfare reform: More research needed on TANF family caps and other policies for reducing out-of-wedlock births (GAO-01-924)*. Washington, DC: Author.

U.S. Government Accountability Office. (2005a). *Child care: Additional information is needed on working families receiving subsidies (GAO-05-667)*. Washington, DC: Author.

U.S. Government Accountability Office. (2005b). *TANF: State approaches to screening for domestic violence could benefit from HHS guidance (GAO-05-701)*. Washington, DC: Author.

### FURTHER READING

Congressional Budget Office. (2006). *Cost estimate: S. 1932 Deficit Reduction Act of 2005*. Washington, DC: Author. Retrieved from www.cbo.gov/ftpdocs/70xx/doc7028/s1932conf.pdf.

U.S. Government Accountability Office. (2006). *Welfare reform: Better information needed to understand trends in states' uses of the TANF block grant (GAO-06-414)*. Washington, DC: Author.

### SUGGESTED LINKS

Child Trends.
*www.childtrends.org*
Child Welfare League of America.
*www.cwla.org*
Congressional Budget Office.
*www.cbo.gov*
Economic Success Clearinghouse (formerly the Welfare Information Network).
*www.financeproject.org/irc/win.asp*
Institute for Poverty Research.
*www.irp.wisc.edu/*
National Poverty Center.
*www.npc.umich.edu/poverty/*
Urban Institute.
*www.urban.org*

U.S. Department of Health and Human Services, Administration for Children and Families Annual Welfare Research and Evaluation Conference.
*http://www.acf.hhs.gov/programs/opre/wrconference/prevMtgs.html*
U.S. Department of Health and Human Services, Assistant Secretary for Planning and Evaluation.
*http://aspe.hhs.gov*

—JAN L. HAGEN AND CATHERINE K. LAWRENCE

## TERMINAL ILLNESS

**ABSTRACT:** The ability of medical technology to prolong life over the past century has forced an examination of the experience and care of the dying. Many diseases that once were expected to follow a sloping illness trajectory with predictable deterioration and ultimately death are now more commonly experienced as chronic illnesses. They require more medical and other resources and challenge the family's ability to cope for much longer periods. The knowledge, value, and skill base of social work, and its broad range of practice sites make it uniquely suited to contribute to the movement to improve the care of the dying. The Social Work Hospice and Palliative Care Network were formed in 2007 to advance and give voice to social work's expertise in this area and to promote its development in practice, education, research, and policy.

**KEY WORDS:** health disparities; end of life care; hospice; palliative care

### A Century of Change

Table 1 reflects a century of change in America's experience of death as it compares conditions in the years 1900 and 2000. Owing to medical and technological advances, people are living longer; however, studies show that they are suffering from more disability, discomfort, and pain during an extended terminal illness. In 2004, the total number of deaths was 2,397,615, and life expectancy had increased to 77.8 years. Major causes of death continue to be heart disease, cancer, stroke, and chronic lower respiratory diseases, followed by accidents, diabetes, and Alzheimer's disease.

### Health Disparities

Recent studies have documented large ethnic and racial disparities in life expectancy. As a consequence, Health and Human Services has selected six focal areas

| TABLE 1 | | |
|---|---|---|
| *A Century of Change* | | |
| | 1900 | 2000 |
| Life expectancy (years) | 47 | 76 |
| Usual place of death | Home | Hospital |
| Most medical expenses | Paid by family | Paid by Medicare |
| Disability before death | Usually not much | 2 years, on average |

of health for program and research development. They are as follows:

- Infant mortality
- Cancer screening and management
- Cardiovascular disease
- Diabetes
- HIV and AIDS
- Immunizations

## Social Realities

In recent years, there has been increased attention to how people die in the United States on multiple levels. How end-of-life care is delivered has received particular attention in both Canada and the United States from public or consumer groups, popular media, health care professional organizations, and private foundations and organizations. In fact, the discussion and debate about how we define "dying well" often seems to permeate the newspapers and evening news, and shapes the plot lines of popular television series.

Social realities that influence this discussion include the following. (a) The aging of the "baby-boom generation" has increased the aging chronically ill population. (b) Physicians are finding it increasingly difficult to provide a prognosis, to know the dying trajectory? (c) Discussions of Medicare and Social Security are focused on the large number of individuals who will become eligible for those entitlements over the next 10 years and the smaller work force available to support such costs. (d) Entitlements will be used by an expanding population of individuals who confront a much longer trajectory of terminal illness. Family and community caregivers are shouldering an increasing burden of care for their family member's extended illness. (e) The number of uninsured increases as employers pull back from the rising costs of health care and benefits. Immigrants continue to be challenged by lack of health care. (f) There is increasing criticism of the care of the expanding aged, chronically ill, and dying population. (g) The debate about assisted suicide in high profile cases has increased attention to the realities of suffering at the end of life. (h) Increasing number of human-caused and natural disasters has made people more willing to discuss these hard issues.

## The Movement to Change the Culture of Care of the Seriously Ill and Dying

Several studies and a report of the Institute of Medicine gave particular momentum to the movement to change the culture of death and improve the care of the dying in America. The "Study to Understand Prognoses and Preferences for Outcomes and Risks of Treatments" (SUPPORT Study) conducted from 1989 to 1991 explored the actual experience of 4,301 U.S. hospitalized patients who were expected to survive 6 months or less. They found that the patients received much aggressive treatment, and that their wishes were not known; the patients did not have "do not resuscitate" orders until very late, and they experienced pain and spent time in the intensive care unit (SUPPORT Study). The second study conducted by American Health Decisions in 1997 (AHD, 1997) and funded by the Robert Wood Johnson Foundation studied Americans' views, hopes, and beliefs about the process of dying in America. They found that Americans feared reaching the end of their lives hooked up to machines. They did not believe that the current health-care system supported their concept of dying. They felt it was important to plan for death and dying but were uncomfortable with the topic and resisted taking action. The IOM report "Approaching Death: Improving Care at the End of Life," initiated by the Project on Death in America (PDIA) of the Open Society Institute, reviewed existing practice and research and developed expert consensus on recommendations to improve care of the dying (Field & Cassel, 1997). These included the following:

- Improve public dialogue and professional education
- Reestablish doctor–patient relationships
- Develop improved advance directives/care planning
- Overcome barriers to pain management
- Provide information to support informed decision-making
- Expand hospice-type services
- Respect cultural and religious differences

## Development of Social Work Hospice and Palliative Care Network

The Social Work Hospice and Palliative Care Network (SWHPN) was formally launched as an organization in July 2007. It emerged from the Social Work Leadership Development Awards program, which was supported by PDIA (Christ & Blacker, 2005). This program made a major contribution to improving the professional knowledge and skill base in end-of-life care through developing professional leaders in medicine, nursing, and social work. Participants were supported to create new models of service delivery and professional training, and to advance research within their discipline and across disciplinary boundaries. From 1999 to 2003 PDIA provided 2-year leadership development awards to 42 social workers to create innovative practice, research, and training programs in end-of-life care. Parallel with the concerns of medicine and nursing, social workers identified barriers to effective social work practice in this area: professional isolation, lack of visible leaders, and a fragmented knowledge base. The program aimed to develop a network of leaders, create new directions in education and training of social workers, and encourage evidence-based practice innovations.

The PDIA social work initiative vastly increased the number of social work publications, and education, research, and program grants obtained by social workers. This included, for example, the development of major social work textbooks (Berzoff & Silverman, 2004; Csikai & Chaitin, 2005; Hooyman & Kramer, 2006; Walsh-Burke, 2006), and the National Association of Social Workers initiative created practice standards in palliative and end-of-life care, a Web-based course, and a policy statement.

Despite remarkable accomplishments, there remained no single social work leadership organization with a primary focus on end-of-life care, palliative care, and grief work that could sustain and expand the capacity that had been developed. Social Work Hospice and Palliative Care Network was launched as a professional leadership structure that aims to advance the following:

- Formal participation in interdisciplinary policy and organizational initiatives
- Building consensus within the profession
- The creation of intraprofessional and interprofessional partnerships
- The further development of a social work specific knowledge and skill base within end-of-life and palliative care
- Dissemination of information
- Collaboration on program initiatives and resource-sharing
- Further development of capacity and advancement of the field

## Social Work Practice Roles and Unique Contribution in End-of-Life Care

The movement to improve care of patients and families living with chronic, life-threatening illness has gained tremendous momentum since the mid-1990s, and social work has made, and will make, important contributions to this improvement. Although social workers have long functioned as core team members providing essential services to dying individuals and their families, their contributions in education, research, administration, and advocacy have more recently emerged and become part of the debate in this expanding field.

All social workers, regardless of practice setting, will inevitably work with clients who are facing acute or long-term situations involving advanced chronic illness, dying, loss, death, grief, and bereavement. Care providers in nursing and medicine confront end-of-life care primarily in health settings; in the social work profession, however, the context and scope of practice relevant to palliative care and end-of-life care go beyond these settings. While social workers do have essential roles in the care of the dying and palliative care in a variety of health settings (for example, hospices, hospitals, nursing homes, long term care facilities, community-based clinics and services), they practice in many other arenas, and encounter individuals, families, groups, and communities affected by advanced chronic illness, dying and death in many profound ways.

Social work values are inherently consistent with the principles of palliative care, for example, client self-determination, the biopsychosocial perspective, the importance of family and social systems interventions, the right to access care, and commitment to ethnic and economic diversity, marginalized populations, and social justice. These values are integral to social work functioning in multiple methods of practice in palliative care, including clinical practice, advocacy/policy, research and education.

*Clinical practice.* Social workers possess expert knowledge and skills in navigating complex systems, developing programs to improve coordination and continuity of care, and identifying and solving problems around gaps in existing services. These include, for example, disease management, patient and care navigation programs. Social workers are experts in crisis intervention, individual and family counseling, patient and family education, reduction of psychosocial distress, grief, trauma, and loss, and intervention with the psychological, social, and cultural dimensions of symptoms related to illness. Social workers have advanced skills in communication, conflict resolution (for example, mediation around ethical dilemmas and interpersonal conflicts), ethnic and economic diversity, and interventions with populations that have been traumatized and bereaved from human-caused and natural disasters.

Social workers bring high levels of expertise that support leadership roles in working with the psychosocial needs of end-of-life patients and their caregivers, providing family-centered care, intervening with families and larger systems such as social networks, communities, and provider agencies (Blacker & Rainess-Jordan, 2004). They demonstrate administrative skills as they implement interventions to decrease the fragmentation in the system, as they seek to improve continuity and coordination of services and create a more nurturing environment in which services are provided to patients and families. Social workers also bring unique expertise in enabling the success of team-based care that is integral to effective end-of-life care.

*Advocacy/policy.* Social workers are skilled advocates both as "brokers" of services in direct practice and as advocates for system change at the institutional, community, public policy and legislative levels. They are the strongest consumer advocates, ever attuned to identifying unmet psychosocial needs and maladaptive service structures, policies, and procedures. They are increasingly encouraged to take leadership on ethics committees in health facilities to help address the perplexing new dilemmas around treatment efficacy, futility, and client self-determination.

*Research.* Social workers are increasingly active in developing ways to evaluate social work interventions and their effectiveness. They locate ways to obtain feedback from patients and families on a broad range of health services, identify at-risk individuals and groups, and suggest preventive interventions—for example, interventions for patients confronting chronic pain (Altilio, 2004), interventions for children and adolescents when a parent is dying (Christ et al., 2005), and disease management interventions.

Social workers conduct research that takes account of contextual factors such as ethnicity, culture, historical factors, life course issues, family relationships, and multiple concurrent stresses. They also participate in the dissemination of research knowledge and evidence-based interventions for patients, families, and larger systems in these rapidly changing areas (Kramer et al., 2005).

*Educator.* As educators, social workers in end-of-life care provide a broad range of education and training. They frequently educate other health-care professionals about psychosocial issues facing those with chronic, life-threatening illnesses. However, they are also effective team leaders in facilitating professional self-care, confronting vicarious traumatization, vicarious grief, and other reactions to daily encounters with highly stressed populations.

### Social Work Practice Sites in End-of-Life Care

There are few social work contexts in which practitioners do not interact with clients and their family members who are experiencing life-threatening illness,

loss, grief, or trauma in a family member or friend,. The context of palliative care, hospice, and grief work in social work is vast and has broad applicability to the profession in a number of settings. Examples of these settings include home health care, palliative care units or free standing hospice units associated with hospitals and skilled nursing facilities, the emergency room, intensive care units, and other acute care settings such as research hospitals, neonatal intensive care units, pediatric critical care units, pain clinics, community-based substance abuse and health agencies, and nursing homes. Mental health and gerontological social workers have important roles to play in enhancing well-being and working therapeutically with those coping with multiple losses, stressors, and chronic life-threatening illness as they age. Social workers in school settings must know their role in stress debriefing, suicide prevention, and bereavement support of children and teens who have experienced death of friends, family members, or teachers. Child welfare workers must understand their functions in addressing serious illness, loss, separation, anxiety, and bereavement in the child welfare system, and provide assessment and intervention to prevent child maltreatment fatalities. Hospice and hospital social workers are increasingly called upon to respond to human-caused and natural disasters and national crises such as those experienced in the Oklahoma City Bombing, the September 11, 2001, terrorist attacks, and the Katrina hurricane. Bereavement is often complicated for mourners when it is the result of violence, which is disproportionately experienced by families in poverty-stricken urban neighborhoods where social workers are committed to serve. Disparities in health require advocacy for health promotion and other preventive intervention. In summary, the scope of social work palliative, hospice, and end-of-life care extends across a broad range of practice sites and requires intervention at multiple system levels.

### REFERENCES

Altilio, T. (2004). Pain and symptom management: An essential role for social workers. In J. Berzoff & P. Silverman (Eds.), *Living with dying* (pp. 380–408). New York: Columbia University Press.

American Health Decisions. (1997). *The quest to die with dignity: An analysis of Americans' values, opinions, and attitudes concerning end-of-life care.* www.ahd.org/ahd/library/statements/quest.html.

Berzoff, J., & Silverman, P. (2004). *Living with dying.* New York: Columbia University Press.

Blacker, S., & Rainess-Jordan, A. (2004). Working with families facing life threatening illness in the medical setting. In J. Berzoff & P. Silverman (Eds.), *Living with dying* (pp. 548–571). New York: Columbia University Press.

Christ, G., & Blacker, S. (2005). Setting an agenda for social work in end-of-life and palliative care: Overview of leadership and organizational initiatives. *Social Work in End-of-Life and Palliative Care, 1*(1), 9–22.

Christ, G., Siegel, K., Raveis, V., Karus, D., & Christ, A. (2005). Evaluation of a bereavement intervention. *Social Work in End-of-Life and Palliative Care, 1*(3), 57–81.

Csikai, E., & Chaitin, E. (2005). *Ethics in end-of-life decisions in social work practice*. Chicago: Lyceum Books.

Hooyman, N., & Kramer, B. (2006). *Living through loss*. New York: Columbia University Press.

Field, M. J., & Cassel, C. K. (Eds.). (1997). *Approaching death: Improving care at the end of life*. Washington, DC: National Academy Press.

Kramer, B., Christ, G., Bern-Krug, M., & Francoeur, R. (2005). A national agenda for social work research in palliative and end-of-life care. *Journal of Palliative Medicine, 8*(2), 418–431.

SUPPORT Principal Investigators. (1995). A controlled trial to improve care for seriously ill hospitalized patients: The Study to Understand Prognoses and Preferences for Outcomes and Risk of Treatments (SUPPORT). *Journal of the American Medical Association, 274*, 1591–1598.

Walsh-Burke, K. (2006). *Grief and loss: Theories and skills for helping professionals*. Des Moines, IA: Allyn & Bacon.

### SUGGESTED LINKS

National Association of Social Workers, Standards for Palliative & End of Life Care.

    *https://www.socialworkers.org/practice/bereavement/standards/default.asp*

Social Work Hospice and Palliative Care Network (SWHPN).

    *www.swhpn.org*

Association of Oncology Social Workers.

    *www.aosw.org*

—GRACE CHRIST

# TERMINATION

ABSTRACT: The termination phase of clinical practice is an important component of the therapeutic process. The ending of the therapeutic relationship, whether planned or unplanned, can elicit feelings of loss, separation, and guilt, impacting both the client and the practitioner. The reasons for ending service and preparation for termination can affect the client's gains. Systematic research on the termination process and the maintenance of gains is needed to further determine variables for successful termination.

KEY WORDS: termination; endings; clinical practice

Unlike the other phases of clinical practice, the termination phase has not been examined as extensively in the social work literature (Mirabito, 2001). As a phase of intervention, termination is a concluding step between the client and the practitioner (Harrigan, Fauri, & Netting, 1998). Terminations, also referred to as endings, are a process of closure characterized by practitioners and clients (individuals, families, and small groups) completing their work in a mutually understood way and processing the experience (Walsh & Meyersohn, 2001). Together, they may review the successes and failures of their work, acknowledge feelings about the relationship, and attain a greater willingness to invest in future relationships (Walsh, 2007). Appropriate termination utilizes interventions to assist the client with retaining and extending the gains as well as transitioning from clinical services (Fortune, 1995).

While generally recognized as a vital part of the treatment process (Anthony & Pagano, 1998), termination is a frequently overlooked dimension of practice (Barton & Marshall, 1986; Gutheil, 1993; Walsh & Harrigan, 2003). Although practitioners recognize the importance of this phase and the issues of loss and separation inherent in termination (Levin, 1998), little time is spent planning and discussing termination with clients (Mirabito, 2001).

The termination phase of practice represents both an ending of the clinical relationship and the beginning of a new period without the assistance of the practitioner (Gutheil, 1993). Numerous factors like agency policy, financial and administrative concerns, situational constraints, and practitioner and client perception of success impact termination. Regardless of the impetus for ending, the significance of time and timing permeate the process and strongly shape the outcome (Webb, 1985).

Termination occurs as unplanned endings initiated by the client or practitioner or as planned endings. Unplanned termination generally occurs when the client decides to discontinue treatment (Mirabito, 2006). Client variables associated with early termination include level of distress, financial concerns, inability to establish trust with the practitioner, dissatisfaction with absence of perceived gains, and discomfort with the practitioner's personal characteristics (Ritter, 2003; Swett & Noones, 1989; Walsh, 2007). Practitioners may attribute these endings to resistance, perception of treatment as unbeneficial (Fieldsteel, 1996), or as a means for clients to assert control over the circumstances that originally led them to treatment (Hayes-Bautista, 1976).

Unplanned termination can also occur when the practitioner becomes ill, leaves an agency, or dies (Levin, 1998; Philip, 1994). Unplanned terminations initiated by practitioners may be attributed to a client's unwillingness to adhere to an intervention plan, to abuse of boundaries, or to displays of unacceptable behavior (Walsh, 2007). In such cases, lack of prepara- tion for termination, interruption of treatment, and the need to address the practitioner's personal life in the therapeutic context are issues that may arise (Siebold, 1991). Clients may feel rejected by the practitioner when treatment is abruptly terminated due to the ther- apeutic process being incomplete (Bembry & Ericson, 1999).

Planned termination may be the result of imposed time limitations such as with student internships in fieldwork, time-limited intervention modalities, or the expected death of a client (Walsh, 2007). Planned, mutually agreed-upon termination arises when the cli- ent has demonstrated changes in his or her behavior, achieved treatment goals, and demonstrated increased self-awareness (Fieldsteel, 1996). Planned termination is most likely to occur in short-term interventions (Mirabito, 2006), allowing for past losses to be exam- ined and coping skills for dealing with future losses to be discussed (Levin, 1998).

Clinical practice theories have unique features of the process of terminating; however, they share many common tasks for ending including deciding when to actively implement the ending phase; timing the announcement of one's own leaving; anticipating the client's and one's own reaction; appropriately spacing the remaining sessions; shifting the intervention focus from the context of practice to natural environments; reviewing intervention gains; generalizing interven- tion gains; planning for goal maintenance and relapse prevention; addressing the client's remaining needs; linking the client with social supports; resolving the clinical relationship; formally evaluating the interven- tion; and setting limits for future contact (Walsh, 2007, pp. 41–42).

During termination, the purpose and efficacy of the therapeutic process are evaluated (Fieldsteel, 1996). If termination is managed adequately by the practitioner, this phase of practice can be experienced as a time to review the gains made during therapy, thereby provid- ing closure to the therapeutic process (Gutheil, 1993). Termination also represents a period of transition for both the practitioner and the client, which can trigger feelings of loss and separation (Bembry & Ericson, 1999). Practitioners may experience guilt and am- bivalence about engaging in termination due to their past experiences with loss and separation (Anthony & Pagano, 1998; Baum, 2006). For clients, termination can trigger feelings of loss, abandonment, fear, and betrayal, especially when termination is not mutually agreed upon (Anthony & Pagano, 1998). Despite the loss and separa- tion, clients may experience as the therapeutic relation- ship ends, they can also celebrate the new skills and insights gained during the process (Gutheil, 1993). If managed properly, termination can increase a client's self-esteem and sense of competence (Levin, 1998).

There is an ample body of literature delineating client and practitioner reasons for and reactions to clinical endings (Baum, 2006). Historically, however, there have been few systematic attempts to study termination as it occurs in clinical practice (Mirabito, 2001). Empirical studies examining the efficacy of termination when coupled with such variables as length of the counseling relationship, theoretical modality used, existence of a predetermined termination date, initiation of termination by client versus practitioner, and client expectation of clinical practice are needed. Additionally, follow-up studies to assess whether clients who had terminated satisfactorily demonstrated the capacity to maintain gains and show improved coping skills should be conducted. The increasing use of short- term interventions and brief therapies based on varying clinical theories necessitates both an expanded view of termination and research on the efficacy of the termi- nation process and maintenance of future gains.

## REFERENCES

Anthony, S., & Pagano, G. (1998). The therapeutic potential for growth during the termination process. *Clinical Social Work Journal, 26*(3), 281–296.

Barton, B. R., & Marshall, A. S. (1986). Pivotal partings: Forced termination with a sexually abused boy. *Clinical Social Work Journal, 14*(21), 139–149.

Baum, N. (2006). End-of-year treatment termination: Res- ponses of social work student trainees. *The British Journal of Social Work, 36*(4), 639–656.

Bembry, J., & Ericson, C. (1999). Therapeutic termination with the early adolescent who has experienced multiple losses. *Child Adolescent Social Work Journal, 16*(3), 177–189.

Fieldsteel, N. D. (1996). The process of termination in long- term psychoanalytic group therapy. *International Journal of Group Psychotherapy, 46*(1), 25–39.

Fortune, A. E. (1995). Termination in direct practice. In R. L. Edwards (Ed.), *Encyclopedia of social work* (19th ed., vol. 3, pp. 2398–2404). Baltimore, MD: NASW Press.

Gutheil, I. A. (1993). Rituals and termination procedures. *Smith College Studies in Social Work, 63*(2), 163–176.

Hayes-Bautista, D. E. (1976). Termination of the patient- practitioner relationship: Divorce, patient style. *Journal of Health Social behavior, 17*(1), 12–21.

Levin, D. (1998). Unplanned termination: Pain and conse- quences. *Journal of Analytic Social Work, 5*(2), 35–46.

Mirabito, D. M. (2001). Mining treatment termination data in an adolescent mental health service: A quantitative study. *Social Work in Health Care, 33*(3/4), 71–90.

Mirabito, D. M. (2006). Revisiting unplanned termination: Clinicians' perceptions of termination from adolescent men- tal health treatment. *Families in Society, 87*(2), 171–180.

Philip, C. E. (1994). Letting go: Problems with termination when a therapist is seriously ill or dying. *Smith College Studies in Social Work*, 64(2), 169–179.

Ritter, R. S. (2003). Profile of some patients who prematurely terminate analysis. *Clinical Social Work Journal*, 31(4), 395–406.

Siebold, C. (1991). Termination: When the therapist leaves. *Clinical Social Work Journal*, 19(2), 191–204.

Swett, C., & Noones, J. (1989). Factors associated with premature termination from outpatient treatment. *Hospital Community Psychiatry*, 40(9), 946–947.

Walsh, J. (2007). *Endings in clinical practice: Effective closure in diverse settings* (2nd ed.). Chicago, IL: Lyceum Books.

Walsh, J., & Harrigan, M. (2003). The termination stage in Bowen's family systems theory. *Clinical Social Work Journal*, 31(4), 383–394.

Walsh, J., & Meyersohn, K. (2001). Ending clinical relationships with people with schizophrenia. *Health Social Work*, 26(3), 188–195.

Webb, N. B. (1985). A crisis intervention perspective on the termination process. *Clinical Social Work Journal*, 13(4), 329–340.

—Michelle S. Ballan and Maria S. Mera

# TERRORISM

ABSTRACT: Following the terrorist attacks of September 11, 2001, in the United States, social workers assumed a major role in providing services for people who were severely affected. A new literature was developed, relating to serving these individuals, families, organizations, and communities; responses of agencies and organizations to the needs of staff working with traumatized clients; and policy practice in response to restrictive government policies. Work with people affected by mass violence has emerged as a new field of practice within the profession.

KEY WORDS: communal bereavement; human rights violations; mass violence; organizational compassion; policy practice; September 11, 2001, attacks; social justice; social worker self-care; terrorism; trauma

Deriving from the word "terror," which in Latin refers to fear, "terrorism" is defined as "the systematic use of terror especially as a means of coercion" (Merriam-Webster Collegiate Dictionary, 2003). Terrorist acts are targeted against specific population groups and national symbols with the intention of creating fear and intimidation, as well as personal and environmental destruction (Kastenbaum, 2007). Fear of recurrent attacks causes hypervigilance and a heightened sense of vulnerability among potential targets (Miller, 2004; Webb, 2004). Terrorist acts often reflect a battle of political or religious ideologies; a group's terror actions may represent its own struggle for liberation or may be a reaction to the liberation tactics of another group. State-sponsored terrorism may result in the development of insurgent groups committed to conflicting ideologies (DiNitto, 2007; Holody, 2004).

While terrorism has a long history throughout the world, within the United States the first mass terrorist attack occurred in 1993 at the World Trade Center in New York City, followed by an attack on the Alfred Murrah federal building in Oklahoma City in 1996. However, it was not until the September 11, 2001, attacks on the World Trade Center and the Pentagon, and the plane crash in rural Pennsylvania, that there was public recognition, both nationally and worldwide, of terrorism in the United States. At this juncture, the social work profession was called on by both public and voluntary organizations to participate in providing services to those severely affected by the attacks. Agencies, particularly the American Red Cross, recruited hundreds of social workers to assist those affected by loss, psychological and physical trauma, and the social and economic dislocations created by what for many were life-changing events. In fact, social workers constituted the largest single group of mental health professionals responding to the events of September 11, 2001 (www.nasw.org).

With this new and urgent role, social workers turned to the literature for theoretical understanding, intervention strategies, and research approaches related to helping people impacted by terrorism. While the social work literature in the United States included related topics such as crisis intervention, trauma, and work with people affected by natural disasters, only the interdisciplinary and international literature addressed terrorism and mass violence in depth (Quota et al., 1995; Weine et al., 2001). During the ensuing years an expanded social work literature on terrorism, mass violence, and trauma was published in the United States. Social work with people affected by mass violence emerged as a new field of practice as schools of social work developed courses and specializations in this area. The new social work literature focused on the areas of direct client practice with people affected by terrorism and war; the impact of this practice on agencies and social workers, including the responses of social service agencies and organizations to the needs of staff and policy practice, was aimed at promoting social justice in times of repressive government policies.

## Direct Client Practice
In the aftermath of the terrorist attacks of September 11, 2001, the incidence of depression and posttraumatic stress disorder (PTSD) increased dramatically

(National Center for Posttraumatic Stress Disorder); in Manhattan, home of the World Trade Center, it doubled (Galea et al., 2002). With the nation's attention on the psychological effects of the attacks, there was a shift in the attitude of the public toward mental health services, leading to new funding from federal, state, city, and voluntary sources, and a destigmatization of services. The importance of providing services not only to individuals but also to families, organizations, and communities of those who lost their lives and those who were deeply affected by the events was broadly recognized (Rosenfeld et al., 2005). Extensive media coverage enlarged the affected group, and some proclaimed that "protecting the public's mental health must be a component of the national defense" (Susser et al., 2002, p. 70).

"First responders," including police, fire, medical and other personnel, were recognized as a new client group needing immediate clinical intervention. The public learned clinical terms and concepts important for social workers and other mental health professionals were brought to the public's attention. For example, the diagnosis of PTSD was broadly recognized in those severely affected by the attacks, including first responders (Danieli & Dingman, 2005).

In addition to traditional intervention strategies, "Critical Incident Stress Debriefing (CISD)," a first-step intervention to prevent and limit trauma symptoms, was found to be important immediately following the traumatic events (Mitchell, 1983). "Organizational bereavement" and "communal bereavement" were recognized as part of the healing process, as groups of people, whether in firehouses, police precincts, corporations, or other places of employment, and in schools, parks, or on the streets of affected communities, gathered to mourn together (Talbot, 2001; Zinner & Williams, 1999). Social workers also noted the role of spirituality and religious belief in the healing process for some clients (Gellman & Dane, 2004).

Intervention included response to "retraumatization," as repressed memories of earlier traumatic events were revived. "Survivors' guilt," common when one survives a tragedy in which family members, peers, colleagues, or others perish or are severely injured, affected all client groups (Castex, 2004). Other processes, such as "physiological responses to traumatic events" and "intergenerational transmission of trauma" also required the attention of the social work profession (Auerhahn & Laub, 1998; Elbert & Schauer, 2002).

These issues also apply to the military serving in unconventional warfare, such as in Iraq, where terrorism is common. Embedded and on-site journalists are also affected. In the light of the growing acknowledgment of the emotional toll of terrorism, mental health issues of military personnel and their families received increased media recognition. Social workers assumed a leadership role, both in battle areas and in military and veterans' hospitals (Hardaway, 2004). The need for intervention with veterans and their families became more pronounced with the ongoing war in Iraq, and military social work received more attention from the profession (DeAngelis, 2007).

## Social Work within Agencies and Organizations

When there are numerous agencies involved in recovery, a coordinated effort among agencies and federations is essential to establish an effective service network, both for individuals and families affected by the traumatic event and for rebuilding communities (Krauskopf, 2005). Policies reflecting organizational compassion are critical in agencies and organizations responding to the aftermath of terrorist attacks (Dutton et al., 2002). Social workers with ongoing exposure to traumatized clients are at risk for developing trauma-related responses. Among these are compassion fatigue, a consequence of continuous work with traumatized clients that leaves workers drained emotionally and susceptible to depression and exhaustion; secondary trauma, resulting from an indirect exposure to a traumatic event that produces symptoms in the helper similar to the clients'; and shared trauma, which can occur when the client and social worker have experienced the same traumatic event (Cunningham, 2003; Tosone & Bialkin, 2004). Social workers, as clients, are also vulnerable to retraumatization.

Agency administrators and supervisors can introduce innovative strategies reflecting organizational compassion. Strategies that can be useful in protecting and supporting individual staff members and staff morale include staff debriefings, balanced caseloads so that clients assigned to a worker are not all experiencing similarly high degrees and symptoms of trauma, an open-door policy for supervision, and specialized trainings and consultations. Social worker self-care is an important concern as it can minimize the risks of developing trauma-related responses that may arise when working with traumatized clients. Agency administrators and supervisors can provide opportunities for rest, recreation, and leisure activities for staff members, particularly during times of crisis.

## Social Welfare Policy and Advocacy

Terrorism leads to drastic national policy measures with far-reaching effects. Of great importance to social workers since the terrorist acts of September 11, 2001, has been the diversion of government funds from traditional domestic social welfare programs for populations-at-risk, not only to new services for people affected by the terrorist acts, but to antiterrorism and national security efforts. Restrictive government policies emerged following the development of the federal Department of Homeland Security and the USA PATRIOT Act (an acronym for Uniting and Strengthening America by Providing Appropriate Tools Required to Intercept and Obstruct Terrorism) as well as highly controversial government policies related to racial profiling, detentions, immigration, domestic surveillance, and involvements in war, which many social workers see as violations of the profession's core value of social justice. As a result, social workers and social work organizations have mobilized and taken action to combat policies challenging human rights and civil liberties (Mizrahi, 2003; Stoesen, 2004, 2007). The profession will continue to face serious challenges in the future as the nation struggles with controversial issues such as balancing security with privacy and other individual freedoms.

## REFERENCES

Auerhahn, N., & Laub, D. (1998). Intergenerational memory of the Holocaust. In Y. Danieli (Ed.), *International handbook of multigenerational legacies of trauma* (pp. 21–41). New York: Plenum.

Castex, G. M. (2004). Helping people retraumatized by mass violence. In S. L. A. Straussner & N. K. Phillips (Eds.), *Understanding mass violence: A social work perspective* (pp. 129–142). Boston: Allyn & Bacon.

Cunningham, M. (2003). The impact of trauma work on social work clinicians: Empirical findings. *Social Work, 48*(14), 451–459.

Danieli, Y., & Dingman, R. L. (Eds.). (2005). *On the ground after September 11: Mental health responses and practical knowledge gained.* Binghamton, NY: Haworth.

DeAngelis, T. (2007, Oct. 20). Social workers help military families. http://www.naswdc.org/pressroom.

DiNitto, D. M. (2007). *Social welfare: Politics and public policy,* 6th ed. Boston: Allyn & Bacon.

Dutton, J. E., Frost, P. J., Worline, M. C., Lilius, J. M., & Kanov, J. M. (2002). Leading in times of trauma. *Harvard Business Review, 80*(1), 55–61.

Elbert, E., & Schauer, M. (2002). Psychological trauma: Burnt into memory. *Nature, 419,* 883.

Galea, S., Ahern, J., Resnick, H., Kilpatrick, D., Bucuvalas, M., Gold, J., et al. (2002, March 28). Psychological sequelae of the September 11 terrorist attacks in New York City. *New England Journal of Medicine, 346*(13), 982–987.

Gellman, A., & Dane, B. (2004). The role of spirituality and religion in responding to mass violence. In S. L. A. Straussner & N. K. Phillips (Eds.), *Understanding mass violence: A social work perspective* (pp. 143–156). Boston: Allyn & Bacon.

Hardaway, T. (2004). Treatment of psychological trauma in children of military families. In M. B. Webb (Ed.), *Mass trauma and violence: Helping families and children cope* (pp. 259–282). New York: Guildford.

Holody, R. (2004). Social justice in times of mass violence. In S. L. A. Straussner & N. K. Phillips (Eds.), *Understanding mass violence: A social work perspective* (pp. 187–199). Boston: Allyn & Bacon.

Kastenbaum, R. J. (2007). *Death, society and human experience* (9th ed.). Boston: Allyn & Bacon.

Krauskopf, J. (2005). Assisting people after disaster: The role and impact of a social services network created for disaster response and recovery. In Y. Danieli & R. Dingman (Eds.), *On the ground after September 11: Mental health responses and practical knowledge gained* (pp. 445–453). Binghamton, NY: Haworth.

*Merriam-Webster Collegiate Dictionary* (11th ed.). (2003). Springfield, MA: Merriam-Webster, Inc.

Miller, M. (2004). Interventions with individuals and families affected by mass violence. In S. L. A. Straussner & N. K. Phillips (Eds.), *Understanding mass violence: A social work perspective* (pp. 23–40). Boston: Allyn & Bacon.

Mitchell, J. T. (1983). When disaster strikes: The critical incident stress debriefing process. *Journal of Emergency Medical Services, 8,* 36–39.

Mizrahi, T. (2003, April). In time of war, a legacy of peace. *NASW News,* p. 3.

National Center for Posttraumatic Stress Disorders. www.ncptsd.va.gov.

Susser, E. S., Herman, D. B., & Aaron, B. (2002). Combating the terror of terrorism. *Scientific American, 287,* 70–78.

Quota, S., Punamaki, R., & El Sarraj, E. (1995). The relations between traumatic experiences, activity, and cognitive and emotional responses among Palestinian children. *International Journal of Psychology, 30,* 289–304.

Rosenfeld, L. B., Caye, J. S., Ayalon, O., & Lahad, M. (2004). *When their world falls apart: Helping families and children manage the effects of disasters.* Washington, DC: NASW Press.

Stoesen, L. (2004, July). End to Iraq prisoner abuse demanded. *NASW News, 49*(7), 1.

Stoesen, L. (2007, February). Veterans aided with transition struggle. *NASW News, 52,* (4), p. 4.

Talbot, M. (2001, December 9). Communal bereavement. *New York Times Magazine,* 62.

Tosone, C., & Bialkin, L. (2004). Mass violence and secondary trauma: Issues for the clinician. In S. L. A. Straussner & N. K. Phillips (Eds.), *Understanding mass violence: A social work perspective* (pp. 157–168). Boston: Allyn & Bacon.

Webb, N. B. (Ed.). (2004). *Mass trauma and violence: Helping families and children cope.* New York: Guilford.

Weine, S., Kuc, G., Dzudza, E., Razzano, L., & Pavkovic, I. (2001). PTSD among Bosnian refugees: A survey of providers' knowledge, attitudes and service patterns. *Community Mental Health Journal, 37,* 261–271.

Zinner, E. S., & Williams, M. B. (Eds.). (1999). *When a community weeps: Case studies in group survivorship.* Philadelphia, PA: Brunner/Mazel.

## FURTHER READING

Greene, P., Kane, D., Christ, G., Lynch, S., & Corrigan, M. (2006). *FDNY crisis counseling: Innovative responses to 9/11 firefighters, families, and communities.* Hoboken, NJ: John Wiley.

Kaul, R. E. (2002). A social worker's account of 31 days responding to the Pentagon disaster: Crisis intervention training and self-care practices. *Brief Treatment and Crisis Intervention, 2,* 33–38.

Shalev, A. (2002). Treating survivors in the immediate aftermath of traumatic events. In R. Yehuda (Ed.), *Treating trauma survivors with PTSD.* Arlington, VA: American Psychiatric Press.

Schiff, M. (2006). Living in the shadow of terrorism: Psychological distress and alcohol use among religious and non-religious adolescents in Jerusalem. *Social Science and Medicine, 62,* 2301–2312.

Steele, W., & Raider, M. (2001). *Structured sensory intervention for children, adolescents, and parents (SITCAP).* New York: Mellen Press.

Straussner, S. L. A., & Phillips, N. K., (Eds.). (2004). *Understanding mass violence: A social work perspective.* Boston: Allyn & Bacon.

## SUGGESTED LINKS

*www.bt.cdc.gov/mentalhealth/*
*www.fema.gov/hazard/terrorism/index.shtm*
*www.NASW.org*
*www.ncptsd.va.gov*
*http://www.ncptsd.va.gov/ncmain/ncdocs/fact_shts/fs_self_ care_disaster.html*
*www.redcross.org/services/disaster*
*www.socialwelfareactionalliance.org/links.html*
*www.socialworkers.org/pace*

—NORMA KOLKO PHILLIPS

**THERAPY.** *See* Psychosocial and Psychiatric Rehabilitation.

**TOTAL QUALITY MANAGEMENT.** *See* Management: Quality Assurance.

# TRANSGENDER PEOPLE

**ABSTRACT:** In this entry, transgender is defined in the context of ethnomethodology and social construction of gender. A history of the role of transgender people in the gay, lesbian, and bisexual rights movement is presented, including tensions concerning the role of transgender people in this movement. Issues regarding social work practice related to transgender issues on the micro, mezzo, macro, and meta levels are discussed.

**KEY WORDS:** transgender civil rights; gay identity politics; lesbian feminism; bisexual; social construction

## Definitions and Meanings

Transgender is an evolving term used to describe people whose gender identity does not conform to that assigned at birth. Transgender people have existed throughout history and across cultures, with varying levels of acceptance from the societies in which they have lived (Feinberg, 1996).

Transgender can best be understood within the larger context of gender—one of the fundamental bases on which we organize our social relations. We attribute gender ("male" or "female") to every person we encounter, assuming that these are natural, rather than constructed, distinctions. Kessler and McKenna (1978) discussed how we create the social reality of a binary sexual dichotomy, ignoring or disregarding data that do not fit with it. Garfinkel (1967) posited the following as the "natural attitude" or social reality of gender. There are two, and only two, genders (male and female).

1. One's gender is invariant.
2. Genitals are the essential sign of gender.
3. Any exceptions to two genders are not to be taken seriously.
4. There are no transfers from one gender to another except ceremonial ones (for example, masquerades).
5. Everyone must be classified as a member of one gender or another.
6. The female and male dichotomy is a "natural" one (existing independently of anyone's criteria for maleness or femaleness).
7. Membership in one gender or another is "natural" (independent on anyone deciding what you are).

Transgender people transgress these fundamental assumptions (Meyerowitz, 2006). This explains why the emergence of transgender people has been controversial, and why they, like gay and lesbian people, have struggled to gain civil rights and public acceptance.

Using this framework as context, gender can thus be defined as follows:

> . . . a determination of maleness, femaleness or 'otherness', initially assigned at birth and then continuing throughout life. This assignment may be made according to genital or genetic type (often described as "sex") or according to hormonal balance, secondary characteristics, dress, behavior or other culturally specific signals (Gilbert & Zemsky, 1999).

Transgender can be defined as follows:

... an umbrella term used to describe people who in some major way defy the "natural attitude" concerning gender, or whose gender identity or presentation does not match that assigned to them at birth. For some, this nonconformity may be transient or intended to reveal the performative nature of gender. For others, it may take the form of a decision to change their actual assignment through legal records, appearance, pronoun usage or medical intervention (Gilbert & Zemsky, 1999).

Transsexuals is an inclusive term made up of diverse subgroups: those who may or may not pursue hormonal or surgical intervention to make their presentation more closely match their gender identity; cross-dressers who may have a gender identity in keeping with their assignment, but who express aspects of their personalities by wearing clothing not associated with their gender; drag kings and queens who cross gender boundaries for purposes of performance (highlighting the performative nature of gender itself); genderqueer people, who actively seek to transcend the system of binary gender in which "male" and "female" are the only, and mutually exclusive options (Nestle, Howell, & Wilkins, 2002, p. 15).

Not included in this category are intersex people who are born with physiological or hormonal attributes that do not conform to a binary system. They expose the limitations of the natural attitude toward gender. Babies born with healthy and well-functioning genitals that do not conform to male or female anatomy are routinely subjected to surgical interventions to force their bodies into conformity, often resulting in chronic pain or inability to experience sexual pleasure. In recent years, there has been activism on the part of these people to change this practice (Intersex Initiative, 2007).

**TRANSGENDER AND THE GAY, LESBIAN, BISEXUAL MOVEMENT** Transgender people have played a major role in the gay rights movement, and yet have struggled for recognition within it. Transgender people initiated the seminal event in the modern gay rights history, the Stonewall riot in 1969. They were active in organizing early gay rights organizations. The early gay and lesbian movements rejected transgender people, however, seeing them as a threat to wider acceptance (Brown, 1999). Transgender issues were seen as irrelevant to gay and lesbian people. In radical lesbian feminist circles, transgender people were sometimes castigated as reinforcing sexist stereotypes and threatening women's identity, having not been raised and socialized as women, and through the way in which the requirement that transsexuals seeking medical intervention were required to "live in the social role" of their desired sex, a role that was seen as defined and constrained by the view of a patriarchal society (Raymond, 1979). This view still persists in some feminist thought (Ruby, 2000). Transgender people were excluded from the historic 1993 march in Washington. Not until 2001 did the Human Rights Campaign, the largest gay and lesbian rights organization in the country, amend its mission to include transgender people, affirm that it will only support federal Employment Non-Discrimination Act legislation that is inclusive of transgender people. They also launched a number of initiatives related to transgender rights (National Gay and Lesbian Task Force, 2007). Uninformed health professionals may associate transgender with psychopathology, which can result in poor care, inappropriate referrals to mental health treatment, and medical records issues that can be damaging (Lev, 2004).

**TRANSGENDER AND SOCIAL WORK** An understanding of transgender people and issues is critical for social work on the micro, mezzo, macro, and meta levels. On the direct practice level, social workers work with transgender people across the life span. Transgender youth are at significant risk for harassment in school (Kosciw & Diaz, 2005), abuse, self-destructive behavior, and suicide (Brooks, 2005) as well as verbal and physical abuse in their families (Grossman, D'Augelli, Howell, & Hubbard, 2005). As adults, transgender people may require advocacy in getting their needs met with respect to health, mental health, and other social services. Aging transgender people have complex needs that have not been adequately studied (Witten, 2005). Social workers need to serve transgender people and their families in a manner that is informed, competent, empowering, and in keeping with the code of ethics.

On the mezzo level, schools, agencies, and social service organizations need to adopt policies and procedures that are sensitive to the needs of transgender people, including staff training, school dress codes, bathroom and other access issues. Risks include physical violence in schools (Kosciw & Diaz 2005), inability to access health-care services (Kenagy, 2005), and death, as in the case of Tyra Hunter, who died in 1995 from wounds suffered in a car accident when paramedics ceased treatment upon discovering she was a transwoman (Wright, 2001). On the macro level, transgender people are affected by a variety of legislative and policy issues. Six states currently have nondiscrimination statutes that explicitly protect transgender people (www.hrc.org). Beyond civil rights and employment protection, the ability to change birth certificates, driver's licenses, and school records can have a significant impact on quality of life and ability to obtain employment. Whether and how these changes can be made differs from state to state, and is often dependent on surgical status (Mottet, 2004). This can penalize individuals for whom surgery is not an option or a choice. There is also a significant risk of discrimination against transgender people in parenting and custody issues (Funatake, 2004). Serious barriers to health-care access among transgender people result in a number of risks, including the pursuit of black market hormones (Mottet, 2004), inability to meet basic needs, HIV infection, violence, and suicide (Kenagy, 2005). Transgender people in poverty face particular obstacles (Wright, 2001).

The inclusion of gender identity disorder in the *DSM* is seen by many transgender people as pathologizing, and the Harry Benjamin International Gender Dysphoria Association Standards of Care (Harry Benjamin International Gender Dysphoria Association, 2001), which are used by most professionals treating transsexuals, are seen by many as overly restrictive and paternalistic. (Lev, 2004, p. 49). The International Conference on Transgender Law and Employment Policy has proposed an alternative set of standards that emphasize self-determination of transgender people (International Conference on Transgender Law and Employment Policy, 2003).

### Challenges and Future Trends

Transgender people challenge social work theory related to group membership and identity politics (McPhail, 2004). The presence of transgender people in the culture and the questions they raise call into question other socially constructed categories such as race and ethnicity. This postmodern perspective can conflict with notions of social justice founded on collective action to address oppression based on group identification (McPhail, 2004). Social work is thus challenged to recognize the role of identity in both oppression and liberation, and to consider alternative paradigms of empowerment. In the future, social workers will have a major role to play on every systems level, standing with transgender people as they work to change the ways that they are viewed and treated in clinical, health-care, schools, and other institutional settings, and advocating for policy and legal changes that impact the civil rights and quality of life for transgender people. Social work as a profession should come to acknowledge how the struggle of transgender people for dignity and acceptance is part of the mandate to work for social justice.

### REFERENCES

Brooks, F. L. (2005). *Transgender behavior in boys: The social work response*. Doctoral dissertation, Simmons College School of Social Work.

Brown, K. (1999). *20th Century transgender history and experience*. Retrieved October 10, 2006, from http://jenelrose.com.

Feinberg, L. (1996). *Transgender warriors*. Boston, MA: Beacon Press.

Funatake, P. (2004). Transgender parents and custody. Retrieved April 19, 2007, from TransParentcy, http://transparentcy.org.

Garfinkel, H. (1967). *Studies in ethnomethodology*. Englewood Cliffs, NJ: Prentice Hall.

Gilbert, M. J., & Zemsky, B. (1999, October). *Transgender*. Training presented to Hennepin county social services, Minneapolis, MN.

Grossman, A. H., D'Augelli, A. R., Howell, T. J., & Hubbard, S. (2005). Parent's reactions to transgender youth's gender nonconforming expression and identity. *Journal of Gay and Lesbian Social Services, 18*(1), 3–16.

Harry Benjamin International Gender Dysphoria Association. (2001). *Standards of care* (6th version). Minneapolis, MN: World Professional Association for Transgender Health.

International Conference on Transgender Law and Employment Policy. (2003). *Health law standards of care for transsexualism*. Washington, DC: ICTCEP.

Intersex Initiative. (2007). *Intersex Frequently asked questions*. Retrieved April 19, 2007, from http://www.intersexinitiative.org/articles/intersex-faq.html.

Kenagy, G. P. (2005). Transgender health: Findings from two needs assessment studies in Philadelphia. *Health and Social Work, 30*(1), 19–26.

Kessler, S. J., & McKenna, W. (1978). *Gender: An ethnomethodological approach*. Chicago, IL: University of Chicago Press.

Kosciw, J. G., & Diaz, E. M. (2005). *The 2005 National School Climate Survey*. New York: Gay Lesbian and Straight Education Network.

Lev, A. I. (2004). *Transgender emergence: Therapeutic guidelines for working with gender-variant people and their families*. Binghampton, NY: Haworth Press.

McPhail, B. A. (2004). Questioning gender and sexuality binaries: What queer theorists, transgendered individuals, and sex researchers can teach social work. *Journal of Gay and Lesbian Social Services, 17*(1), 3–21.

Meyerowitz, J. (2006). Transforming sex: Christine Jorgensen in the postwar U.S. *OAH Magazine of History, 20*(2), 16–20.

Mottet, L. (2004). Education and policy needs of transgender individuals. *SIECUS Report, 32*(4), 35–39.

National Gay and Lesbian Task Force. (2007). *Transgender issues*. Retrieved April 19, 2007, from http://thetaskforce.org/issues/transgender.

Nestle, J., Howell, C., & Wilkins, R. (Eds.). (2002). *Genderqueer*. Los Angeles, CA: Alyson Books.

Raymond, J. (1979). *The transsexual empire*. Boston: Beacon Press.

Ruby, J. (2000). Men in ewes' clothing: The stealth politics of the transgender movement. *Off Our Backs, 30*(4), 5–9.

Witten, T. M. (2005). Aging and gender diversity. *Social Work Today, 4*(4), 28–32.

Wright, K. (2001). To be poor and transgender—Treatment and problems faced by transgender persons. *The Progressive, 65*(10), 21–25.

# TRAUMA

ABSTRACT: This entry summarizes the current state of knowledge about the nature of trauma and intervention with trauma reactions. It includes the history of traumatology, demographics, theory, research and best practices, controversies, and current trends as well as diversity issues and international and interdisciplinary perspectives.

KEY WORDS: trauma; posttraumatic stress disorder; disaster; abuse; stress; acute stress disorder

## History

The field of traumatology—the study of trauma—is relatively young; its current manifestation began in the 1980s. However, its roots date back to the 19th century.

As early as 1859, Briquet observed a connection between hysteria and childhood trauma, and in 1878, Tardieu and colleagues were among the first to document the sexual abuse of children. Shortly thereafter, Fournier suggested that some memories of incest were false. By 1887, Charcot had identified the hypnoid (dissociative) state as the key element of trauma reactions. Building on Charcot's work, Janet provided extensive case data demonstrating linkages between hysteria and trauma, and describing the phenomenon of dissociation and the fragmentation of traumatic memory. As a result, Freud proposed that childhood trauma, especially incest, caused hysteria. However, he subsequently abandoned this theory and postulated that memories of sexual abuse were, instead, fantasies resulting from psychosexual conflicts. Later, when confronted with World War I veterans' symptoms, Freud proposed two models of trauma: (a) unbearable situations (for example, war) and (b) unacceptable impulses (for example, fantasies of childhood sexual abuse). Thus, from its beginning, those interested in traumatology struggled with such issues as the nature of traumatic memories, false memories, and distinguishing between the trauma of war from the trauma that can occur in intimate relationships (van der Kolk, Weisaeth, & van der Hart, 1996).

Throughout most of the 20th century, the segregation of civilian and wartime trauma reactions continued, including observations of reactions to disasters such as the 1942 Cocoanut Grove nightclub fire in Boston and the 1972 Buffalo Creek flood in West Virginia, and Kardiner's 1940s descriptions of the traumatic neuroses of war. It was not until the mid-1970s that the separate threads were united to identify a common reaction to any trauma, in part as a result of political efforts by Vietnam veterans and others.

This, in combination with advocacy from professional mental health practitioners and researchers, culminated in the introduction of posttraumatic stress disorder (PTSD) as a diagnosis in 1980 in the third edition of the American Psychiatric Association's *Diagnostic and Statistical Manual of Mental Disorders* (*DSM-III*). At that time, trauma was defined as an event outside the range of normal experience. However, because later research indicated that exposure to a trauma was common, the diagnostic definition changed to experiencing or witnessing an event involving "actual or threatened death or serious injury, or a threat to physical integrity of self and other" (American Psychiatric Association, 2000, p. 467) in the *DSM-IV*. This definition encompasses a wide range of experiences, such as war, torture, natural disasters, terrorism, physical abuse, sexual abuse and rape, assaults, serious physical illness or injury, and death of a loved one.

DEMOGRAPHICS The 1995 National Comorbidity Survey reported prevalence rates for exposure to any trauma at 63% for men and 51% for women. The most common were witnessing someone being killed or badly hurt, involvement in a fire or natural disaster, and involvement in a life-threatening accident. Men reported experiencing each of these more frequently than did women, as well as combat, physical attacks, being threatened with a weapon, and being kidnapped. Women were more likely to report rape, sexual molestation, and childhood physical abuse or neglect.

Although exposure to traumatic events in the general population is widespread, the National Comorbidity Survey found the lifetime prevalence rate for PTSD to be 8% in the general population in the 1995 study, and 9% in the 2005 replication. The 1995 study found that women were twice as likely as men (10% versus 5%) to have PTSD during their lifetime. PTSD was more likely to result from exposure to some types of traumas over others. Among both men and women who experienced a trauma, rape was most likely to result in PTSD (65% of men, 46% of women), whereas childhood neglect was the least likely for women (28%), and childhood molestation the least for men (27%).

Within the U.S. general population, there appear to be no significant differences in lifetime PTSD rates among the major racial-ethnic groups—the National Comorbidity Survey 2005 Replication found that Hispanics report the lowest rates (5.9%), followed by non-Hispanic Whites (6.8%) and non-Hispanic Blacks (7.1%). However, the intersection of race-ethnicity and poverty can markedly increase vulnerability. Trauma and PTSD rates are likely to be higher among people living in high violence areas (for example, inner cities) than among the general population. Similarly, large-scale disasters such as hurricanes Katrina and Rita in 2005 have a greater impact on those with few resources—among displaced families almost half reported child mental health problems that were not present prior to those hurricanes (Abramson & Garfield, 2006).

## Assessment of Trauma

Increased understanding about trauma exposure has led to a more complex understanding of the range of psychological reactions to trauma. There are currently two psychiatric disorders that include trauma exposure at the core of their definition, acute stress disorder and posttraumatic stress disorder (PTSD). The former can begin within 4 weeks after exposure to the trauma. A disorder that lasts longer than 4 weeks is diagnosed as PTSD and can begin years after the onset of a trauma, although it is most likely to occur within the first 3 months. It is noteworthy that prior exposure to a trauma increases the risk of having PTSD after a subsequent traumatic event (Halligan & Yehuda, 2000).

It is now recognized that depression and anxiety disorders are also very common reactions to trauma. In addition, it is becoming clear that most people with dissociative disorders, substance use disorders, child disruptive behavior disorders, and borderline personality disorder have a history of some type of trauma exposure. As a result, some clinicians and researchers (for example, Ross, 2000) advocate that trauma is responsible for a large portion of mental and substance use disorders.

RELATED THEORY Many theories have played an important role in shaping understanding of the impact of and recovery from trauma. The specific theories and concepts discussed are information processing, Type I/Type II trauma, social cognitive theories, and disaster psychology. *Information processing theory* underlies much of what currently guides PTSD treatment and is based on the 1977 work of Lang. Simply stated, Lang proposed that fearful experiences are stored in the brain in emotionally charged images and related physiological, semantic, and behavioral responses; in order for new learning to occur, these networks must be activated and then emotionally processed or "digested."

Also key has been distinguishing between two major types of traumas, beginning with the work on childhood trauma by Lenore Terr (1991). Type I traumas are sudden and unexpected—such as the sudden death of a parent—and most typically result in the standard symptoms of PTSD. In contrast, Type II traumas are long-standing and repeated extreme events, such as ongoing violence exposure from war, physical abuse, or sexual abuse. Type II traumas more typically result in denial, psychic numbing, dissociation, and rage, although PTSD symptoms may also be present. Judith Herman's work added depth to understanding this latter type—she coined the term *complex trauma* to refer to Type II reactions and identified the following additional sequelae: affect regulation difficulties and pathological changes in relationships and in identity. She advocated conceptualizing many mental health problems, especially borderline personality disorder, as a consequence of trauma (Herman, 1992).

Critical to understanding the impact of trauma has been the work of several social-cognitive theorists (for example, Janoff-Bulman, 1992; McCann & Pearlman, 1990). Their theories focus on the importance of beliefs affected by trauma. Traumatic events can shatter a sense of safety and predictability, and can result in self-blame. And when trauma is caused by trusted others, as in the case of child abuse and family violence, it can result in subsequent trust problems in interpersonal relationships.

Finally, theories of disaster psychology and crisis intervention have guided understanding individual and community reactions and how best to intervene after a disaster. During the *Impact Phase*, when the disaster strikes, people need to focus on protecting themselves and others. Immediately following the disaster is the *Recoil and Rescue Phase*, when recovery and rescue efforts begin—intervention is directed at meeting practical and survival needs. People who are stunned and confused need to be both protected and compassionately directed to safe places. Following this, intervention focuses on connecting people with loved ones, obtaining accurate information, and establishing some sense of predictability. The *Recovery Phase* is the prolonged period of readjustment characterized by efforts to return to some stable day-to-day individual and community life; when damage and disruption have been significant, this phase can be lengthy. Often disillusionment sets in as the attention of others is directed elsewhere and many needs continue to be unmet. This is when significant emotional and mental health problems may arise and when people may need to receive more focused trauma treatment (Raphael, 2000).

**Latest Research and Best Practices** There has been an increased emphasis on empirically supported treatments as well as best practice guidelines. With regard to PTSD, professional associations such as the International Society for Traumatic Stress Studies (ISTSS; Foa, Keane, & Friedman, 2000) and organizations such as the Department of Veteran's Affairs/Department of Defense (2004) periodically review the literature and issue practice guidelines. The current PTSD practice guidelines for adults identify that trauma-focused cognitive-behavior therapy, stress inoculation therapy, and eye movement desensitization and reprocessing (EMDR) are the psychosocial treatment methods with strong research support. Cochrane Collaboration review of PTSD treatments recommends cognitive behavior therapy or EMDR for psychological treatments, and for pharmacological treatment, the selective serotonin reuptake inhibitors.

Current research has also focused on identifying risk factors for PTSD. Among the most accepted factors are prior traumatic or significant loss experiences, dissociation during the current traumatic event, severity and duration of the trauma, proximity to the trauma, lack of social support, prior psychiatric disorder, and heavy alcohol or drug use during the trauma (Halligan & Yehuda, 2000; Litz, Gray, Bryant, & Adler, 2007).

Research on PTSD treatment for children is still in its early stages; however, the intervention with the strongest support has been trauma-focused cognitive-behavior therapy. Research on acute stress disorder and early intervention is in its preliminary stages.

Because of a lack of large-scale research, treatment of people with more complex trauma reactions is guided by general practice standards. The consensus is that intervention with this population should follow a phase-oriented approach that focuses on establishing safety, stabilization, and developing coping skills prior to beginning any trauma-focused interventions (Chu, 1998; Herman, 1992).

**Diversity and Multicultural Content** Exposure to trauma varies widely among vulnerable and diverse populations. People living in high poverty communities often have the highest rates of exposure. Clearly, some populations by the nature of their circumstances, such as war refugees, have high trauma exposure rates. Because of the circumstances they are fleeing, refugees entering the United States often have high rates of trauma-related mental health problems. Understanding the cultural meaning of the trauma, as well as the cultural resources and spiritual traditions that can assist in healing, is essential to helping clients from diverse cultural backgrounds (Wilson, 2007).

Recent conceptualizations recognize the impact of historical trauma on multiple generations of disadvantaged or oppressed populations such as Native Americans and African Americans. The impact of trauma across generations has also been documented among Holocaust survivors and Japanese-American internment camp survivors, as well as within families experiencing multigenerational interpersonal violence (Danieli, 1998).

**International/Comparative Issues** The conceptualization of trauma and especially of PTSD as a unique area of study is relatively recent. Most published PTSD research has been done by researchers in developed countries, primarily the United States and Israel. However, trauma is clearly not an experience that is limited by national borders or experiences—global conflicts and natural disasters affect most nations. Mass violence and disasters affect entire communities and nations. As a result, recovery from trauma must be a community- and nationally based process that includes cultural and religious practices as keys to effective coping.

Global conflict has been a major cause of trauma exposure. The mental health consequences of war vary with many factors, including the severity of the trauma as well as the degree to which the violence affects the whole populace and disrupts social structures. It is not uncommon for more than half of a population to report psychiatric symptoms and for PTSD to be diagnosed at rates of 25% or more, with women and children having the highest rates (Murthy & Lakshminarayana, 2006).

**Interdisciplinary Connections** Recent research has shed important light on the impact of trauma on biology and neurobiology, especially in the early years of life when critical aspects of brain development are affected. In addition, cognitive sciences research has resulted in increased understanding about the nature of memory and traumatic memory. As a result, social workers working in the trauma field need to be knowledgeable about both of these areas. Planning and responding to disasters requires a wide range of professionals working together, including police, fire, paramedics and other rescue personnel (often called *first responders*), urban planners, medical and public health professionals, and engineers. But macrolevel social workers have a great deal of expertise in organizing and leading teams, and building partnerships and collaborations.

**Challenges** Since controversy has marked this field from the beginning, there are many challenges that social workers face in working with trauma survivors.

One of the most heated debates concerns trauma and memory and the question of amnesia for traumatic experiences, sometimes called *recovered memories* on one side of the debate, and *false memory syndrome* on the other. Of particular concern was whether practitioners could create false memories inadvertently through their interventions. This debate was most intense in the 1990s and culminated in efforts to come to a scientific consensus. In 1997 the ISTSS issued the following consensus points: there is evidence that memory is imperfect and reconstructive; there is evidence that people do forget traumatic memories and can later recall them with accuracy; traumatic memory may be different from normal memory (Roth & Friedman, 1997). More research is needed on this issue before there can be a scientific consensus. Memories are most likely to be recalled in situations where there are cues present that resemble the original trauma. It is possible to influence people such that they develop strongly believed false memories, and practitioners who do not follow accepted practices with trauma survivors may promote a false "recovered memory."

Other debates have focused on controversial treatments, most often EMDR and psychological debriefing. Although EMDR is now recognized as effective, the ISTSS PTSD practice guidelines note that the role of the eye movements in its efficacy remains controversial and unclear because of methodologically poor research. A recent Cochrane Collaboration review of psychological debriefing noted the lack of research support for its effectiveness; it also underscored the generally poor quality of the research. Overall, how best to intervene with trauma symptoms immediately following a trauma is a topic of much debate and current investigation.

## Trends and Directions

Trends and directions include identifying effective treatment of complex trauma reactions, including the co-occurring problems of PTSD and substance abuse; focusing on early intervention; improving disaster management; identifying and treating trauma reactions in children and adolescents; studying alternative trauma treatments (for example, yoga, art, and so forth); and exploring emotional abuse as a type of trauma. There has also been a growing interest in *vicarious traumatization*, that is, trauma symptoms that can occur in those who work with trauma survivors. Other new areas for research are on the potential negative psychiatric effects of media coverage of disasters on those who are exposed to it through watching or reading about it and identifying biological processes involved in trauma reactions. Finally, there has been increasing interest in posttraumatic growth and resilience.

## Implications for Social Work

Given the high prevalence rates of trauma exposure in many vulnerable and disadvantaged populations, social workers must understand the impact of trauma and how to identify the range of trauma reactions. Many social workers see a trauma perspective as congruent with the strengths perspective because much of what is traditionally considered as psychopathology (for example, client self-injury) can be seen as adaptive and meaningful within the context of the original traumatic situation. The person-in-environment perspective of social work is especially helpful in understanding and intervening in trauma-related problems. For macrolevel social workers, the concepts of community vulnerability and resilience come into play when working with neighborhoods, cities, regions, and the country. Social workers were the largest group of mental health volunteers working with the Red Cross post 9/11.

Trauma-informed policy and practice are very compatible with the values of social work in that the need to empower clients who have experienced trauma is considered essential. As a result, there is a critical need for social workers to advocate for trauma-informed policy and practice in all systems. Additional funds and resources are needed to train and mobilize first responders and to help build the infrastructure that could minimize the traumatic impact of large-scale disasters and the impact on populations of chronic threats of attack on everyday functioning.

The micro-, meso-, and macroperspectives of social work are ideally suited to the tasks of creating resilient communities and in working on disaster-preparedness. Within this latter context, social work has much to offer in ensuring that community evacuation planning incorporates the special needs of people with disabilities, children, and frail elders. Finally, social workers should play key roles within their own organizations to ensure that disaster preparedness plans are in place to provide service at times of service disruption.

## REFERENCES

Abramson, D., & Garfield, R. (2006). *On the edge: Children and families displaced by Hurricanes Katrina and Rita face a looming medical and mental health crisis.* Columbia University Mailman School of Public Health. www.ncdp.mailman.colum bia.edu/program_special.htm

American Psychiatric Association. (2000). *Diagnostic and statistical manual of mental disorders* (4th ed., text revision). Washington, DC: Author.

Chu, J. A. (1998). *Rebuilding shattered lives: The responsible treatment of complex post-traumatic and dissociative disorders.* New York: Wiley.

Danieli, Y. (Ed.). (1998). *International handbook of multigenerational legacies of trauma.* New York: Plenum.

Department of Veterans Affairs and Department of Defense. (2004). *VA/DoD clinical practice guideline for the management of post-traumatic stress*. Washington, DC. www.oqp.med.va.gov/cpg/PTSD/PTSD_cpg/frameset.htm

Foa, E. B., Keane, T. M., & Friedman, M. J. (Eds.). (2000). *Effective treatments for PTSD: Practice guidelines from the International Society for Traumatic Stress Studies*. New York: Guilford Press.

Halligan, S. L., & Yehuda, R. (2000). Risk factors for PTSD. *PTSD Research Quarterly, 11*(3), 1–8. www.ncptsd.va.gov/ncmain/nc_archives/rsch_qtly/V11N3.pdf?opm=1&rr=rr201&srt=d&echorr=true

Herman, J. (1992). *Trauma and recovery*. New York: Basic Books.

Janoff-Bulman, R. (1992). *Shattered assumptions*. New York: Free Press.

Litz, B., Gray, M., Bryant, R., & Adler, A. (2007). *Early intervention for trauma: Current status and future directions. National Center for PTSD Factsheet*. National Center for PTSD. www.ncptsd.va.gov/ncmain/ncdocs/fact_shts/fs_earlyint_disaster.html?opm=1&rr=rr64&srt=d&echorr=true

McCann, I. L., & Pearlman, L. A. (1990). *Psychological trauma and adult survivor theory*. New York: Brunner/Mazel.

Murthy, R. S., & Lakshminarayana, R. (2006). Mental health consequences of war: A brief review of research findings. *World Psychiatry, 5*, 25–30. www.pubmedcentral.nih.gov/articlerender.fcgi?artid=1472271

Raphael, B. (2000). *Phases of traumatic stress reactions in a disaster. National Center for PTSD Factsheet*. National Center for PTSD. http://www.ncptsd.va.gov/ncmain/ncdocs/fact_shts/fs_phases_disaster.html

Ross, C. A. (2000). *The trauma model*. Richardson, TX: Manitou Communications.

Roth, S., & Friedman, M. (Eds.). (1997). *Childhood trauma remembered: A report on the current scientific knowledge base and its applications*. Northbrook, IL: International Society for Traumatic Stress Studies. www.istss.org/publications/childhood_trauma.cfm

van der Kolk, B. A., Weisaeth, L., & van der Hart, O. (1996). The history of trauma in psychiatry. In B. A. van der Kolk, A. C. McFarlane, & L. Weisaeth (Eds.), *Traumatic stress* (pp. 47–74). New York: Guilford Press.

Wilson, J. P. (2007). The lens of culture: Theoretical and conceptual perspectives in the assessment and treatment of psychological trauma and PTSD. In J. P. Wilson & C. C. So-Kum Tang (Eds.), *Cross-cultural assessment of psychological trauma and PTSD* (pp. 3–30). New York: Springer.

### Further Reading

Horowitz, M. J. (Ed.). (1999). *Essential papers on post-traumatic stress disorder*. New York: New York University Press.

Kessler, R. C., Galea, S., Jones, R. T., & Parker, H. A. (2006). *Mental illness and suicidality after hurricane Katrina. Bulletin of the World Health Organization*. www.who.int/bulletin/volumes/84/10/06-033019.pdf

Kessler, R. C., Sonnega, A., Bromet, E., Huges, M., Nelson, C. B. (1995). Posttraumatic stress disorder in the National Comorbidity Survey. *Archives of General Psychiatry, 52*, 1048–1060.

Resick, P. A. (2001). *Stress and trauma*. New York: Taylor & Francis.

van der Kolk, B. A., McFarlane, A. C., & Weisaeth, L. (Eds.). (1996). *Traumatic stress*. New York: Guilford Press.

### Suggested Links

David Baldwin's Trauma Information Pages.
*www.trauma-pages.org*
National Center for PTSD.
*www.ncptsd.org*

—Nancy J. Smyth

## TREATMENTS FOR PEOPLE WITH SEVERE AND PERSISTENT MENTAL ILLNESS. *See* Mental Health: Practice Intervention.

# U

**UNDOCUMENTED ALIENS.** *See* Displaced People; Immigrants and Refugees; Immigration Policy; Migrant Workers.

**UNEMPLOYMENT.** *See* Human Needs: Work and Employment.

## UNEMPLOYMENT INSURANCE

ABSTRACT: In response to massive unemployment, in 1934 President Franklin Roosevelt charged members of the Committee on Economic Security to create a "cradle to grave" social security system. The resultant *Social Security Act* of 1935 had the Unemployment Insurance program as its cornerstone. While Congress and the general public were more interested in old age assistance, members of the Committee on Economic Security and their staff felt the unemployment insurance program was the most important element of the entire legislation. The program was designed to address unemployment caused by economic conditions and to regulate industrial employment. The Unemployment Insurance program, a federal-state partnership, has a number of critical coverage criteria. The importance of the Unemployment Insurance program and the complexity of interpreting both federal and state laws cannot be overstated.

KEY WORDS: unemployment; labor; history; coverage; benefits

### Unemployment Insurance

In 1934, President Franklin Roosevelt (FDR), motivated by a belief that the federal government should assume responsibility to assist the millions of individuals unemployed as a result of the Depression, charged members of the newly formed Committee on Economic Security (CES) to create an overall social security system aptly described as "cradle to grave" (Poole, 2006).

HISTORY In the early 1930s, with the country's unemployment rates as high as 30%, the members of the CES developed a plan. The CES counted two social workers among its total of five members: Frances Perkins, Secretary of Labor, and HarryHopkins, head of the Federal Emergency Relief Administrator. The distress of the country was so great and the number of people unemployed so alarming that FDR mandated the CES to complete their work in six months and report to the President's office by December, 1934 (Witte, 1962). Secretary Perkins filled key staff positions for the CES with members of the "Wisconsin Group," a small number of well-known policy innovators from Wisconsin. Edwin Witte was named CES executive director. Witte had played a major role in the development of a number of policy innovations in Wisconsin, such as an unemployment insurance plan, well before FDR's effort at a national level in 1934 (Poole, 2006). Witte's mentor John Commons, a major figure in American economics, theorized that unemployment had microeconomic impact on individuals and families, but also had macroeconomic impact, with sustained unemployment highlighting the importance of monetary policy designed to provide price stability (Rutherford & Samuels, 1996). For Commons, Witte, and others of the Wisconsin Group, unemployment insurance was the cornerstone of the entire social security legislation package (Witte, 1962). The Social Security Act, approved by the 74th Congress in 1935, included the Unemployment Insurance program, Title III (Poole, 2006), to offset the immediate economic crisis of the country's number of unemployed. In the spring of 1933, as the Depression passed its fourth winter, the unemployment rate approached 30% (Singleton, 2000).

#### Ideological Perspectives
The Act was hailed by most liberal policy makers and eventually by historians as the achievement of FDR's dream of a "cradle to grave" system. However, some groups voiced opposition. Ironically, these groups rested on the polar ends of the political spectrum: business interest groups on the one end and supporters of more radical political initiatives on the other (Poole, 2006).

This "cradle to grave" system, the so-called "Roosevelt Revolution," as embodied in the Unemployment Insurance program, was praised by liberal historians because it enhanced democracy, diminished the influence of big business on government and marked the end of a passive federal government. Other more radical historians viewed it as a failure to truly redistribute income and as a federal–state system that sanctioned racial segregation (Berstein, 1968), as agricultural and domestic workers, many of whom were African American, were excluded from unemployment insurance eligibility. Their coverage was not the intent of the program, which was to force industry to regulate industrial employment. The unemployment of these excluded workers was perceived as caused by their personal failure, whereas it was assumed that an imperfect economy caused the unemployment of white industrial workers (Poole, 2006). Opponents in business interest groups maintained their belief that private relief funded by voluntary organizations was the "American" way. They believed that federal intervention of the magnitude included in the Social Security Act was counterproductive to worker motivation and eventual economic recovery (Singleton, 2000).

EVOLVING PROGRAM DESIGN AND IMPLEMENTATION In 2007, the Employment and Training Administration (ETA) of the Department of Labor is responsible for the Unemployment Insurance program Additional descriptive and trend data and analyses are provided by the Bureau of Labor Statistics. As described in the U.S. federal government's own interpretation of federal unemployment insurance laws, the basic framework of the federal–state system of unemployment insurance in the year 2007 is congruent with the program design of 1935. The key elements remain as follows:

- allowance of a credit against the federal unemployment tax for taxes paid under a state law that meets federal unemployment law requirements,
- federal financing of administrative costs, and
- substantial state autonomy over all substantive elements of self-contained unemployment.

The Unemployment Insurance program is truly a federal–state partnership. Federal law sets wide parameters and each state is free to interpret and implement its own unemployment insurance program. Therefore, dramatic variations in state-implemented unemployment insurance programs exist. However, a primary question underpinning unemployment insurance coverage is ubiquitous: Are the services performed by a worker covered? Critical coverage criteria include: number of days or weeks a worker is employed, paid wages exceeding a certain dollar amount, and number of workers employed for specified periods of time in a calendar year. There have been incremental changes through the decades, mostly additions of new eligibility groups; for example., in 2007, agricultural and domestic workers are fully included. Additionally,

more specific definitions of what is work and who is a worker have been developed, which have both included and excluded individuals. Unemployment insurance payments provide temporary assistance to workers who meet the requirements of state law. Eligibility, benefit amounts, and the length of time benefits are paid are determined by state law. Applicants contact their state unemployment insurance agency. If determined eligible, it generally takes two to three weeks to receive a benefit check. Unemployment insurance benefits are based on a percentage of a worker's earnings over a recent 52 week period.

The general rule is that for workers to be eligible they must have lost their jobs through "no fault of their own" and must be able to work, available to work, and actively seeking work. The emphasis remains on unemployment caused by economic conditions. Extended benefits may be triggered by periods of high unemployment or by rising, sustained, or exceptional circumstances, for example, Hurricane Katrina. The duration of unemployment benefits is measured by the number of weeks, most commonly 26. The number of persons in the country in receipt of unemployment insurance benefits varies by season, region, and occupation. In January 2007, the four-week moving average for persons receiving benefits (sometimes referred to as the "insured unemployed") in the country was just under 310,000 and in October 2007 it was 324,750 persons per week (Employment and Training Administration, 2007).

Financing of unemployment insurance benefits remains almost unchanged since 1935. In 2007, a federal tax continues to finance the administrative costs and some benefit payments. The federal monies are housed in an Unemployment Trust Fund. State payroll taxes (contributions) finance the cost of most benefits. The amount of tax an employer pays depends on its number of employees, the state's taxable wages, and the contribution rate assigned the employer. Currently, the federal tax levied on covered employers is 6.2% of wages up to $7,000 a year paid to a worker.

LEGACY Unemployment insurance policy is influenced by, and influences, fiscal policy, labor policy, monetary policy, cash assistance (welfare) policy, food stamps policy, immigration policy, child support policy, disability policy, vocational and educational policy, and policy impacting particular populations, such as older persons and veterans. While no figure is more closely watched as a barometer of the country's economic condition than the unemployment rate, following close behind are the number of Unemployment Insurance program applicants and continuing recipients. If the positioning of work as the preferred solution to a host of social ills, including poverty, continues unabated, the Unemployment Insurance program will undoubtedly continue to grow in prominence. Implications for social work practice linked with possible changes in the Unemployment Insurance program need to be viewed from both a macro and micro perspective. From a macro perspective social workers need to be aware of the possible expansion of the Unemployment Insurance program, particularly as the eligibility for other social welfare benefits tightens, such as the limiting of eligibility caused by the inclusion of lifetime eligibility benefits in the Temporary Assistance for Needy Families program. To be effective in their roles as advocates for individuals and families, social workers need to be adept at understanding the federal–state complexities of the Unemployment Insurance program and the variances of eligibility and benefits by state.

## REFERENCES

Berstein, B. J. (1968). Towards a new past: Dissenting essays in American history. In B. J. Bernstein (Ed.), *The New Deal: The Conservative Achievements of Liberal Reform* (pp. 263–288). New York: Pantheon.

Employment and Training Administration, (2007). *Unemployment insurance weekly claims report* (DOL USDL 07-1626-NAT). Washington, DC: DOL, Office of Public Affairs.

Poole, M. (2006). *The segregated origins of Social Security: African Americans and the welfare state.* Chapel Hill: The University of North Carolina Press.

Rutherford, M., & Samuels, W. J. (1996). *John R. Commons: Selected essays.* V.1. New York: Routledge.

Singleton, J. (2000). *The American dole: Unemployment relief and the welfare state in the Great Depression.* Westport, CT: Greenwood Press.

Witte, E. (1962). *The development of the Social Security Act: A memorandum on the history of the Committee on Economic Security and drafting and legislative history of the Social Security Act—with a foreword by Frances Perkins.* Madison: The University of Wisconsin Press.

—LARRY NACKERUD

# UNIONS

**ABSTRACT:** This entry deals with the goals and tensions between professionalism and social work unionization. This entry addresses obstacles to the unionization of social workers, such as the mixed messages about unionization inherent in National Association of Social Workers' *Code of Ethics*, the incipient antiunion sentiment within social work (which partly explains the dearth of social work strikes when compared with teacher's strikes), the impact of privatized social services on unionization, and the chilling effects of a business union perspective on professional issues that concern social workers. The entry calls for a fusion between union and professional concerns.

**KEY WORDS:** business unionism; privatized social services; scope of bargaining

The Bureau of Labor Statistics (BLS) estimates that there were 562,000 U.S. social workers in 2004, a number that may be exaggerated in light of only 442 accredited bachelors and 148 master's degree programs in social work. BLS data is exaggerated since it does not depend on qualifications or degree, but on self-identification or job title. As such, it counts public welfare workers as social workers, even though they may lack any formal social work training. The BLS also estimates that 16.5% of community and social services occupations are unionized (Bureau of Labor Statistics, 2006).Despite BLS estimates, it is impossible to gauge the exact number of unionized social workers in the United States. First, the National Association of Social Workers (NASW) does not compile information on unionized social workers. Second, most social workers are ensconced in large bargaining units that are rarely broken down into discrete employee classifications. Third, the category of "social worker" is vague. For example, many states that license social workers mandate that only licensed social workers can use the title. (All told, there are 425,000 licensed social workers in the United States.) However, some of those states exempt public sector employees with social work titles from licensing requirements.

Social work's reliance on often rigid notions of professionalism has historically been an obstacle to unionization (Karger, 1987). For example, the NASW *Code of Ethics* contains contradictory messages. The Code states that "social workers may engage in organized action, including the formation of and participation in labor unions, to improve services to clients and working conditions." However, the Code also states that "the actions of social workers who are involved in labor-management disputes, job actions, or labor strikes should be guided by the profession's values, ethical principles, and ethical standards.... Social workers should carefully examine relevant issues and their possible impact on clients before deciding on a course of action" (National Association of Social Workers, 1996). Strikes will, by necessity, have a deleterious impact on clients, which means they must be carefully considered. NASW's ambivalence about professionalism stand in sharp contrast to the financial reality of social workers. For example, an AFSCME (American Federation of State and County Municipal Employees) salary study found that the salaries of social workers with a B.A. or B.S.W. ranged from $17,597 to $31,000, with most falling into the mid-20s (American Federation of State and County Municipal Employees, 2006). The study points out that in many agencies social workers seldom, if ever, approach the upper end of the salary scale. This extremely low salary structure is hardly congruous with a "profession" that requires a college degree and advanced training.

Despite the mixed messages in professionalism, large numbers of social workers have joined and are actively participating in union activities. For example, the union membership rate in the private sector fell from 25% in 1975 to 8.2% in 2004, while the unionization rate in the public sector increased to more than 35% in 2004 (Farber, 2005). Although there is no data to accurately pinpoint how many of these public sector union members are social workers, at least some are. One union actively organizing social workers as part of organizing health care sector workers is 1199 of the Service Employees International Union (SEIU).

Antiunion sentiments, combined with rigid notions of professionalism, may partly explain the dearth of reported social work strikes in the United States, which stands in stark contrast to the more frequent strikes or strike threats by social workers in European industrialized nations, such as the 2004 strike in Liverpool and the threatened strikes in Edinburgh and the Czech Republic, to name a few. There are, however, some exceptions. In Portland, Oregon, child welfare social workers in SEIU's Local 503 went on strike in 2004 to lower turnover rates, improve staffing ratios and working conditions, and for higher wages. The turnover rate for staff who worked with children was about 50%. College graduates working with vulnerable children earned $9.28 an hour with little possibility of raises. In contrast, a study by the Northwest Federation of Community Organizations found that a single person living in Oregon must earn $10.17 an hour to meet their basic needs. For those with a child, the minimum salary jumps to $17.60 an hour (Service Employees International Union, 2004). Ironically, child welfare workers working with impoverished children were themselves considered poor based on the standard of $17.60 an hour.

The opposition of management to an expanded scope of bargaining may partly explain why some observers view social work bargaining as less developed than teacher bargaining. (Scope of bargaining is the subject matter that employers and union representatives address in contract negotiations.) Teacher workloads, including periods of preparation and relief from extra curricular activities, are accepted as proper subjects for bargaining. Class size, once considered a policy issue, is now accepted as a working condition. Teacher consultation rights provide for a variety of labor management committees. Social service labor agreements, on the other hand, rarely specify maximum caseload size. Instead, work loads are subject to "reasonable standards," which if deemed unreasonable, must be challenged in the grievance process. In many agreements, joint labor-management committees are established for the specific purpose of evaluating staff caseloads.

## Trends and Challenges

A number of current trends may portend a stronger relationship between social workers and the labor movement. Primary among these is the proliferation of privatized, for-profit social services. Privatized social services (social services that operate on a for-profit basis) are being promoted as the public sector's answer to escalating costs, and their rapid growth is rooted in the desire of federal and state governments to offload their responsibility for delivering social welfare services (Karger & Stoesz, 2006). Consequently, the responsibility for service delivery is being increasingly carried out by subcontractors, most of whom provide little or no employee benefits and are hostile to anything resembling a labor union. In the end, privatization may lead to more disenfranchised social workers (Karger & Stoesz, 2006).

Addressing the challenge of privatization will require public sector unions to pursue a more aggressive policy of recruiting private sector social workers, many of whom are employed in small agencies. Unfortunately, this kind of small-scale organizing is not cost-effective and strains the fiscal resources of unions. Moreover, the reason that fewer trained and licensed social workers are unionized, compared to teachers, is that fewer of them work in the public sector. According to the BLS, public sector workers had a union membership rate nearly five times that of private sector employees. Workers in education, training, and library occupations had the highest unionization rate among all occupations, at 37% (BLS, 2007). Still another obstacle facing unionized social workers is that a social work strike is hardly a fearsome weapon. In fact, most social work strikes have been unsuccessful since managers, bureaucrats, and legislators seem not to fear them (Weber, 1969).

Still another obstacle to unionizing social workers is the emphasis on business unionism. (This relates to a bread-and-butter view of unionism that is mainly concerned with wages and benefits rather than professional issues like client caseloads.) Traditional beliefs about trade unionism fail to address many of the concerns of professional social workers. As such, union leadership must recognize that although bread-and-butter issues are important to social workers, this group is also concerned with professional issues that bear directly on their ability to serve clients. To be successful, unions must learn to better fuse traditional union concerns with the professional issues of social workers.

### REFERENCES

American Federation of State and County Municipal Employees [AFSCME]. (2006). *Salaries and qualifications.* Retrieved October 7, 2006, from http://www.afscme.org/publications/2746.cfm

Bureau of Labor Statistics. (2006). *Union members summary (USDL 06–99).* Retrieved January 20, 2006, from http://www.bls.gov/news.release/union2.nr0.htm

Bureau of Labor Statistics. (2007). *Union members summary (USDL 06–0113).* Retrieved September, 29, 2007, from http://www.bls.gov/news.release/union2.nr0.htm

Farber, H. (2005, September 19). Union membership in the United States (Working paper no. 503). Princeton University Industrial Relations Section.

Karger, H. (1987). *Social Workers and labor unions.* Westport, CT: Greenwood.

Karger, H., & Stoesz, D. (2006). *American social welfare policy* (5th ed.). Boston: Allyn&Bacon.

National Association of Social Workers [NASW]. (1996). *Code of ethics.* Approved 1996. Revised by the 1999 NASW Delegate Assembly. Silver Spring, MD: Author.

Service Employees International Union (SEIU) Local 503. (2004, November 18). *Go to college, care for children, live in poverty.* Retrieved February 14, 2006, from http://www.seiu503.org/ourlocal/bargaining/pnp/pcpoverty.cfm

Weber, A. (1969). Paradise lost: Or whatever happened to the Chicago social workers. *Industrial and Labor Relations Review, 22,* 330–343.

### FURTHER READING

Alexander, L., & Spiezman, M. (1980). The union movement in voluntary social work. *The Social Welfare Forum, 1979.* New York: Columbia University Press.

Chitnis, N., & Tigelaar, G. (1971). The impact of a strike on graduate students. *Social Work, 16,* 119–127.

Fisher, J. (1980). *The response of social work to the depression.* Rochester, VT: Schenkman.

Karger, H. (1989). Social service administration and the challenge of unionization. *Administration in Social Work, 13,* 199–217.

Kleingartner, A. (1973). Collective bargaining between salaried professionals and public sector management. *Public Administration Review, 33*(2), 165–172.

Lightman, E. (1978). An imbalance of powers. *Administration in Social Work, 2*(1), 75–84.

Oppenheimer, M. (1975). The unionization of the professional. *Social Policy, 5*(1), 34–40.

Shaffer, G. (1979 Winter). Labor relations and the unionization of professional social workers. *Journal of Education for Social Work,* 83–84.

Tambor, M. (1973). Unions and voluntary agencies. *Social Work, 18,* 41–47.

Tambor, M. (1979). The social worker as worker. *Administration in Social Work, 3*(3), 289–300.

### SUGGESTED LINKS

American Federation of State and County Municipal Employees (AFSCME)
  *www.afscme.org*
Bureau of Labor Statistics (BLS)
  *www.bls.gov*
National Association of Social Workers (NASW) *Code of Ethics*
  *www.naswdc.org/pubs/code/default.asp*
Service Employees International Union (SEIU)
  *www.seiu.org*

—HOWARD KARGER

## URBAN PRACTICE

**ABSTRACT:** Social work practice is best understood and practiced when taking into account the local context. The urban context of social work practice may share much with suburban and rural contexts but also brings with it unique problems and opportunities.

**KEY WORDS:** context; capacity enhancement; demographics; social and economic justice

### Background

The importance of grounding social work practice within a context is impossible to over stress, particularly as the profession continues to expand the social arenas and population groups it seeks to serve. This context is invariably characterized in terms of, among other things, the sociopolitical climate, history, sociodemographic patterns, and culture of a geographical area or population group. Contexts help inform assessment and intervention strategies. Further, conceptualizations of the context provide the theoretical and interactional terrain that helps minimize communication and collaborative barriers that have historically divided practitioners and academics, thereby aiding the profession (Delgado, 1999; 2000a, 2000b). However, this is not to say that the social work research and literature has kept pace with these developments.

The urban context is particularly vital to social work. It is impossible to talk about social work in the present without considering how this context shaped the birth of the profession (Fabricant & Fisher, 2002). Fabricant and Fisher (2002, p. 15), making reference to the settlement house movement, indirectly highlight the importance of an urban context to this movement: "While there is always a tendency to romanticize history by elaborating accomplishments or downplaying errors and failures, the interest in settlement history harks back to a glorious heyday when the leading houses served as free spaces of social activism and midwives of modern social services in the United States." Fabricant and Fisher rightly acknowledge the importance of the settlement house movement, which had urban roots, in shaping the social work profession. In fact, the profession generally developed and thrived in urban areas, where charity organization societies, juvenile courts, and other child-saving institutions, as well as hospital social work evolved.

Cities continue to shape and direct the profession in a manner that few social workers fully recognize, appreciate, and celebrate. True, there are other geographical areas in which social work is practiced and important work is accomplished. However, there is little dispute that social work is still primarily taught and practiced in cities across the United States. These urban contexts have a tremendous amount of influence over how social work gets conceptualized, researched, and practiced. Through scholarship, the implications of urban contexts find their way into social work curriculum.

There is hardly any question that urban centers have played an important role in the development of the nation in general. Historically, coastal cities such as Los Angeles (Sawhney, 2002; Waldinger & Bozorgmehr, 1997) and New York (Foner, 2000, 2001; Haslip-Viera & Baver, 1996), and Miami (Delgado, 2007) have been the port of entry of millions of newcomers from throughout the world (Segal, 2002). In circumstances where cities were not the primary point of entry into the United States, they eventually became one of the primary destinations once a newcomer entered the country, documented or undocumented. Consequently, cities have played an influential role in the lives of most newcomers to this country with the possible exception of Native Americans.

The United States historically has had a "love" and "hate" relationship with cities. This has continued into the present, and may well continue into the future. Cities represent opportunities for advancement and acceptance in this society. Cities have also been viewed as places where "deviance" is not only tolerated but celebrated, and thus are feared by Americans who are skeptical of diversity and fail to acknowledge and celebrate it. The antiurban bias, first described by

sociologists in the early 20th century (Parks, Burgess, & McKenzie, 1925) and critiqued in the classic work by Jane Jacobs in 1961, meant that solutions to urban problems were based on theories that sought to physically eliminate the "slums" through federal programs such as Urban Renewal, or to bring the country to the city with more open spaces, parks, malls—neither of which understood the dynamics of safe and thriving neighborhoods.

### Definition of Urban

Not surprisingly, there are numerous definitions of what constitutes a "city" or "urban area." The simplest definition is as follows: cities are defined as geographical entities with populations of over 50,000 and a local government. The mention of urban generally conjures up images of large metropolitan communities that are invariably located on either coast of the United States. This impression is largely the result of how the media has portrayed cities in the news and popular culture. In reality, cities vary in population size and also differ in such features as history, geographical location, and national reputations.

### Cities Worldwide

Urban centers have historically played a critical role in nation building internationally (Kirdar, 1997). Moreover, the world is becoming more urbanized every year. In 2003, 48% of the world's population lived in cities and this percentage is projected to increase to 50% by 2030 (United Nations, 2004). Further, it is estimated that between 2000 and 2030, urban populations will increase by a rate of 1.8% per year, which will result in a doubling of their population within 38 years (United Nations, 2004). Thus, the importance of urban areas can only be expected to continue to increase in the next half of this century.

### Demographics and Trends in the United States

The United States also is very much an urbanized society, with 79.2% of the population (almost 226 million people) residing in urban areas (U.S. Bureau of the Census, 2004). Over 58% of the nation's population resides in urbanized areas with populations over 200,000 (U.S. Bureau of the Census, 2004). The nation's cities, like cities worldwide, are not only growing but changing in racial and ethnic composition at an extremely rapid pace. Latinos in the United States, for example, accounted for 81% of the nation's growth in this country's 100 largest cities (United States Hispanic Leadership, 2004). Latinos now numerically outnumber African Americans in 6 of this country's largest cities and in 18 of the 25 most populous counties (Coleman,

2003). This shift in ethnic and racial composition has far wielding social, political, and economic consequences. The number of newcomers, documented and undocumented, is increasing in cities across the country, too (Delgado, Jones, & Rohani, 2005).

Some critics argue that this is happening at too great a pace, with deleterious consequences (Buchanan, 2006, 2007); advocates, in turn, argue that as cities grow so does the influence of a nation's most disenfranchised population groups, bringing with this increased presence the potential for positive social change. Concentration of marginalized people in urban areas can translate into concentrated political power through election of officials who embrace social and economic justice agendas. This concentration, however, does not necessarily translate into political power, but it certainly has the potential to do so and to bring national public attention on urban communities. However, regardless of one's point of view, demographic trends pertaining to cities must not be ignored by the social work profession in its attempts to better contextualize services, both asset and deficit-driven.

## The Complexity of Urban Life

Urban life, particularly for those who are newcomers to our country and city living, produces stressors. However, it would be foolhardy from a practice perspective to lose sight of the resources and experiences urban living can bring. Bernstein (2000) identifies 10 urban assets that are generally overlooked in any discussion concerning this nation's cities: (a) purchasing power (concentration of capital and markets), (b) concentration of workforce (availability), (c) mass transit systems (available and do not have to be created), (d) accessibility (general geographical accessibility facilitates development), (e) abandoned and underused land (open land and buildings are available for development), (f) underutilized infrastructure (available for upgrading where needed), (g) in-place infrastructure and underutilized carrying capacity (ready availability of utilities), (h) already assembled rights of way (incentives to establish new institutions and businesses), (i) efficient resource use (concentrated facilities), and (j) biodiversity and natural capital (availability of uncultivated land). Bernstein's list is heavily focused on physical capital. However, social capital, in the form of human diversity and cultural assets, also needs to be considered as an urban asset (Delgado, 2000b, 2007). A social work addendum to Bernstein's list represents an idea dimension by providing a balance between physical and social capital. Of course, the resources listed above are primary reasons why social work tended to develop in urban contexts.

## Context and Practice

Social workers quickly learn about the importance of "context" as both a backdrop and a shaper of how human behavior gets manifested. This context serves to influence all facets of an intervention starting with assessment, to actual intervention, to the final stage, evaluation. Further, the importance of context, in this case "urban" based, serves as a bridge between the clinical, macro, and mezzo worlds of practice social work is practiced. The sharing of an urban community context facilitates the collaboration between different branches of the profession in service to undervalued communities by providing practitioners with an important point of reference.

Urban social work practice may share many philosophical and practice principles with its suburban and rural cousins. However, how it is manifested or implemented on a daily basis results in substantial changes in perspective and operationalization. That is what is referred to as "urban practice." Urban social work practice is that practice that has specifically emerged to take into account a host of environmental (physical as well as social) factors in dictating how best to meet the needs of people who live in cities (Delgado, 2000a).

## Social Justice

The concentration of social problems in the nation's cities highlights social and economic injustices. Consequently, compelled by the NASW's *Code of Ethics*, it becomes imperative that urban social work practice incorporate the goals of eradicating these injustices as part of any social work intervention, micro or macrofocused. Oppression based upon ethnicity and race, gender, abilities, and sexual orientation, for example, is counter to our Code of Ethics that stresses equal opportunities and empowerment. Although social and economic justice issues are present in other geographical contexts, the issues take considerable prominence in urban social work practice because of the high concentration of marginalized groups residing in cities (Delgado & Staples, 2008).

The embrace of a community capacity enhancement paradigm for social work practice in urban areas necessitates a shift in perspectives. This shift focuses on identifying and mobilizing indigenous assets at all levels of social work practice. Assets such as murals, community gardens, community-built playgrounds, and sculptures, for example, typify the multitude of ways that urban assets can be conceptualized as unique forms of urban social work practice (Delgado, 2003). Urban social work practice utilizing a capacity enhancement paradigm is predicated on social workers being willing and able to identify the many advantages that urban areas bring as a context for practice. Vacant lots, for example, can be viewed as places where illegal activity can transpire within an urban community. However, they can also serve as places for cultivating community gardens that produce food for a community and can also serve as meeting places for residents.

### Challenges

Cities will continue to wield tremendous influence on the nation in the 21st century. Social work as a profession has continued to widen its influence into new areas and arenas for practice and will no doubt do so in the future. However, how social work is practiced in cities remains a central core of the profession; many social workers would agree that the key challenges facing the profession will be urban-based and urban-driven. Issues related to gentrification, political disenfranchisement, limited funding, and English as the Official Language movement, will continue to present the profession with obstacles in our pursuit of a social justice agenda.

Failure of the profession to actively and meaningfully address these challenges in the coming years will ultimately mean the marginalization of the profession within an urban context. Other helping professions, in turn, will fill that void. The political consequences of playing an active role in helping to shape public debate on these challenges will also open the door for the profession being criticized by the political right. Nevertheless, we cannot ignore these challenges for fear of being criticized.

### REFERENCES

Bernstein, S. (2000). *Using the hidden assets of America's communities and regions to ensure sustainable communities.* Symposium on the Future of Local Government in Midland, Michigan.

Buchanan, P. J. (2006). *State of emergency. How illegal immigration is destroying America.* New York: St.Martin's Press.

Buchanan, P. J. (2007). *State of emergency: The Third World invasion and conquest of America.* New York: St. Martin's Press.

Coleman, J. A. (2003, August 26). A changing landscape? *Si. America,* p. 5.

Delgado, M. (1999). *Social work practice in nontraditional urban settings.* New York: Oxford University Press.

Delgado, M. (2000a). *Community social work practice in an urban context: The potential of a capacity-enhancement perspective.* New York: Oxford University Press.

Delgado, M. (2000b). *New arenas for community social work practice with urban youth.* New York: Columbia University Press.

Delgado, M. (2003). *Death at an early age and the urban scene: The case for memorial murals and community healing.* Westport, CT: Praeger Press.

Delgado, M. (2007). *Social work practice with Latinos: A cultural assets paradigm.* New York: Oxford University Press.

Delgado, M., Jones, K., & Rohani, M. (2005). *Social work practice with immigrant and refugee youth.* Boston: Allyn & Bacon.

Delgado, M., & Staples, L. (2008). *Youth-led community organizing: Theory and action.* New York: Oxford University Press.

Fabricant, M. B., & Fisher, R. (2002). *Settlement houses under siege: The struggle to sustain community organizations in New York City.* New York: Columbia University Press.

Foner, N. (2000). *From Ellis Island to JFK: New York's two great waves of immigration.* New York: Columbia University Press.

Foner, N. (Ed.). (2001). *New immigrants in New York.* New York: Columbia University Press.

Haslip-Viera, G., & Baver, S. L. (1996). *Latinos in New York: Communities in transition.* Terre Haute, IN: University of Notre Dame Press.

Jacobs, J. (1961). *Death and life of great American cities.* New York: Vintage Books.

Kirdar, U. (Ed.). (1997). *Cities fit for people.* New York: United Nations.

Park, R., Burgess, E. W., & McKenzie, R. D. (1925). *The City.* Chicago: University of Chicago Press.

Sawhney, D. N. (Ed.). (2002). *Unmasking L.A.: Third worlds and the city.* New York: Palgrave.

Segal, U. A. (2002). *A framework for immigration: Asians in the United States.* New York: Columbia University Press.

United Nations. (2004). *UN Report says world urban population of 3 billion today expected to reach 5 billion by 2030.* New York: Author.

United States Hispanic Leadership. (2004). *Almanac of Latino politics.* Chicago: Author.

U.S. Bureau of Census. (2004). *U.S. population living in urban vs. rural areas.* Washington, DC: Author.

—MELVIN DELGADO

# V

## VETERAN SERVICES

**ABSTRACT:** The Department of Veterans Affairs (VA) operates the nation's largest health-care system, with 1,300 facilities providing health care to 5.6 million veterans. VA offers pension and compensation, vocational rehabilitation, education benefits, home loan guarantee, life insurance, and burial in national cemeteries. VA social workers have played key roles in the delivery of psychosocial and mental health services since 1926, creating seamless transition processes for combat veterans, care coordination programs for home health-care monitoring, and long-term case management for veterans with polytraumatic injuries. VA employs 4,500 M.S.W.s and trains 600–700 M.S.W. students each year.

**KEY WORDS:** Veterans Administration; Department of Veterans Affairs; veterans; veteran services

### Background

The U.S. Department of Veterans Affairs (VA) operates the largest health care system in the nation, with 1,300 health care facilities ranging from hospitals to outpatient clinics, and providing health care to more than 5.6 million veterans each year. The VA also provides pension and compensation, vocational rehabilitation, education benefits (GI Bill), home loan guarantee, life insurance, and burial in national cemeteries (Department of Veterans Affairs, 2006a).

As early as 1926, the Veterans Bureau began addressing the psychosocial needs of war veterans by hiring 36 hospital social workers. In 1930, when an Executive Order consolidated the Veterans Bureau, the Bureau of Pensions, and the National Homes for Disabled Volunteer Soldiers into the Veterans Administration, the number of social workers had grown to 97. The VA's mission was to provide medical services, disability compensation, and retirement pensions, with social workers offering restorative services to help veterans return to community living.

In 1989, Congress elevated the VA to Cabinet status, creating the Department of Veterans Affairs (Department of Veterans Affairs, 2006b). At that time, more than 3,000 social workers were providing psychosocial and mental health services in 175 VA hospitals (Manske, 2006).

By the 1990s, escalating health care costs and the VA's reputation as an inefficient system caused Congress to consider substituting health care vouchers for VA hospitals. Under Secretary for Health Kenneth Kizer responded by leading a transformation, using roadmaps such as the "Vision for Change: A Plan to Restructure the Veterans Health Administration"; "Prescription for Change: Healthcare Value Begins with VA"; and "Journey of Change." Dr. Kizer recognized that for VA to survive, the quality of and access to health care needed to improve dramatically. He urged Congress to pass the Veterans' Health Care Eligibility Reform Act of 1996, creating a VA health care benefits package, streamlining eligibility for services and focusing on outpatient versus inpatient care (Kizer, 1997).

Between 1995 and 2005, the number of inpatient beds decreased from 53,200 to 18,200, veterans were assigned to primary care providers, and more than 800 outpatient clinics were opened in rural and suburban areas. At the same time, the number of veterans treated increased from 2.9 million to 5.4 million (Department of Veterans Affairs, 2006b, 2006c, 2006d).

In today's VA, care is often delivered at home and in the community. Supportive services, such as homemakers and home health aides, adult day care, respite care, and home-based primary care, help veterans remain in their homes. Technology has assisted the move to home and community-based care, with telehealth equipment to monitor veterans with chronic diseases so as to reduce unnecessary outpatient visits and inpatient admissions. VA care coordination programs and social workers serving as care coordinators provided home-monitoring to more than 22,000 veterans in 2006 (Department of Veterans Affairs, 2006e).

### Roles of Social Workers

VA is the largest employer of master's-prepared social workers in the United States, with more than 4,500 on staff in 2006. Since federal law requires VA social workers to be licensed at the independent practice level, they function as Licensed Independent Practitioners. Their services are billable and they can be clinically privileged. Social workers also coordinate many of the major VA community programs, such as homeless programs, community nursing home contract programs, and care coordination programs (Manske, 2006).

To enhance health care delivery, VA has the largest medical and associated health training program in the country, affiliating with 107 medical schools and about 1,200 colleges and universities. Each year, more than 83,000 health professionals train in VA facilities, including 600–700 social work graduate students. More than 50% of all U.S. physicians have received VA training (Department of Veterans Affairs, 2006b).

As the wars in Iraq and Afghanistan escalated after 2001, injured active duty military members required rehabilitation and ongoing care. To meet their needs, VA social workers were assigned to military hospitals to facilitate transfers of care to VA hospitals. The seamless transition program included identifying case managers at each VA hospital, most of whom are social workers, to assure the health, mental health, and psychosocial needs of Operation Iraqi Freedom and Operation Enduring Freedom (OIF/OEF) veterans are addressed, including successful community reintegration (Department of Veterans Affairs, 2006b; Manske, 2006).

A number of OIF/OEF veterans suffered blast injuries, resulting in polytrauma, including traumatic brain injuries, spinal cord injuries, amputations, and hearing and vision loss. VA created four regional polytrauma rehabilitation centers, with social worker case managers at a ratio of one per six patients. VA polytrauma social workers provide long-term case management across the continuum of acute rehabilitation to community reintegration (Department of Veterans Affairs, 2006a; Manske, 2006).

## Current Challenges

One challenge facing the VA is a patient population significantly different from age-matched Americans. Veterans are older (49% older than 65 years) and sicker (with three additional nonmental health diagnoses and one additional mental health diagnosis). They are also poorer: 70% have annual incomes of less than $26,000 (Perlin, 2004). These veterans have great need for the psychosocial services of VA social workers, including case management.

In addition to meeting the needs of our newest generation of veterans, the VA has been challenged by the homeless veteran population. One-third of adult homeless men are veterans, and on any given night, more than 200,000 veterans are without permanent shelter. VA offers health and mental health services to more than 100,000 homeless veterans annually. To address homelessness, VA provides grants for transitional living, service centers, and transportation for outreach. The majority of homeless program coordinators are social workers, who develop community linkages and new community resources to help homeless veterans with transitional and permanent housing, vocational rehabilitation, and employment (Department of Veterans Affairs, 2006b, 2006f).

## Trends

Today, VA is recognized by the medical community and the media as a health care leader. Articles in the popular press laud VA's high-quality health care, high levels of patient satisfaction, high scores from accreditation bodies, and low costs. The transformation begun in the 1990s continues, and VA social workers are on the vanguard.

### REFERENCES

Department of Veterans Affairs. (2006a). *Strategic plan FY 2006–2011*. Washington, DC: Author.

Department of Veterans Affairs. (2006b). *History of the Department of Veterans Affairs*. Washington, DC. Electronic publication. http://www1.va.gov/opa/feature/history.

Department of Veterans Affairs. (2006c). *Veterans Health Administration Overview*. Washington, DC: Author.

Department of Veterans Affairs. (2006d). *Facts about the Department of Veterans Affairs*. Washington, DC: Author.

Department of Veterans Affairs. (2006e). *Care coordination in the Department of Veterans Affairs: Providing the right care in the right place at the right time*. Washington, DC: Author.

Department of Veterans Affairs. (2006f). *Fact sheet: VA programs for homeless veterans*. Washington, DC: Author.

Kizer, K. W. (1997). *Journey of change*. Washington, DC: Department of Veterans Affairs.

Manske, J. (2006). Social work in the Department of Veterans Affairs: Lessons learned. *Health and Social Work, 31*, 233–237.

Perlin, J. (2004). *Moving from strategy to action: 12 Priorities—12 months*. Washington, DC: Department of Veterans Affairs.

### FURTHER READING

Arnst, C. (2006, July 17). The best medical care in the U.S.: How Veterans Affairs transformed itself and what it means for the rest of us. *Business Week*, 50–56.

Department of Veterans Affairs. (2006). *Federal benefits for veterans and dependents, 2006*. Washington, DC: U.S. Government Printing Office.

Waller, D. (2006, August 27). How VA hospitals became the best. *Time Magazine*.

### SUGGESTED LINKS

U.S. Department of Veterans Affairs Internet Web page
  http://www.va.gov
U.S. Department of Veterans Affairs Internet Kids Web page
  http://www.va.gov/kids
U.S. Department of Veterans Affairs CARES Commission Internet Web page
  http://www.carescommission.va.gov
U.S. Government Printing Office Internet Web page.
  http://bookstore.gpo.gov

U.S. Government's official Web portal
  *http://www.firstgov.gov*
U.S. Census Bureau
  *http://www.census.gov/*

—Jill E. Manske

## VICTIM SERVICES

**Abstract:** Social workers provide services for crime victims and their families in a variety of settings, including law enforcement, the court systems, corrections, and parole or probation. This entry presents a historical overview of the types of victim services programs and models that have been developed over the past century. Social work roles and interventions in victim services programs are discussed. The need for specialized education and training in crisis intervention, domestic violence, and child abuse is addressed, along with recent challenges and innovations in the field of victim services.

**Key Words:** advocacy; victim services; victim and witness assistance; crisis intervention

In the aftermath of a crime, victims and their families often have to cope with the impacts of the traumatic incident, such as physical pain, acute stress, psychological trauma, phobias, fear, grief, loss, medical problems and expenses, financial needs, and legal proceedings (Knox & Roberts, 2007). This is a critical time for intervention, and social workers have unique opportunities to work with victims, survivors, and witnesses of family violence, child abuse, sexual assault, robbery, kidnapping, homicide, and other crimes. Across the country, social workers are employed by law enforcement agencies, court systems, and corrections departments in a variety of roles to meet the needs of these crime victims. As part of a team of first responders, victim services counselors in law enforcement also provide crisis intervention services to victims and survivors of disasters and terrorist attacks.

### History
The social work profession has a long history of working with police departments to provide victim services, beginning with the establishment of Women's Bureaus within police departments during the early 1900s (Roberts, 1997). There was a steady increase in the police social work movement over the next two decades; however, throughout this time period obstacles such as harassment, sexism, and stereotypes of women in law enforcement impacted negatively on this movement, which along with other problems, such as lack of funding and support from community leaders, led to a decline in victim services in law enforcement (Knox & Roberts, 2007).

It was not until the 1970s, when the battered women's and rape crisis movements became active, that the social work profession was focused again on crime victims. With the emerging crime victims' movement, federal legislation and funding established victim assistance programs in all states through the Federal Law Enforcement Assistance Administration (LEAA) and the Victims of Crime Act (VOCA) of 1984; by 1999, there were close to 10,000 victim and witness assistance, victim services, domestic violence, and sexual assault treatment programs nationwide (Brownell & Roberts, 2002; Roberts & Fisher, 1997).

### Programs and Models
The primary theoretical models used in victims services programs are crisis intervention, grief and bereavement therapy, brief or time-limited treatment, cognitive-behavioral approaches, family therapy, reality therapy, rational-emotive therapy, and eye-movement desensitization and reprocessing (Knox & Roberts, 2002). These models reflect the need for short-term treatment and a focus on immediate needs, not past issues or problems requiring long-term treatment.

Victim services programs in law enforcement offer crisis intervention on-the-scene or immediately following the crime or traumatic incident, short-term counseling, assistance and referrals for the victim's immediate needs, death notification to family members, and advocacy and assistance during the investigative process. Depending on other community resources, victim services workers may use a team approach with the local domestic violence shelter, rape crisis center, and mental health authorities.

Victim and witness assistance programs in the court systems try to minimize revictimization by the criminal justice system, and encourage cooperation of victims and witnesses during the court process. Revictimization can happen when victim and witnesses have negative experiences with the attorneys, prosecutors, and legal system that are insensitive, unfair, and provoke feelings of being victimized again, except by the legal system, not the offender. The primary objectives are to inform victims and witnesses of their legal rights, such as victims compensation and restitution benefits to which they are entitled, to provide information and notification on the court processes, and to offer court preparation, accompaniment, and crisis intervention during the court proceedings. Victim compensation is available in all

50 states and the District of Columbia, U.S. Virgin Islands, Puerto Rico, and Guam (Knox & Roberts, 2007). Victim compensation assists financially with medical expenses, lost wages, and counseling services.

Victim advocacy programs in corrections provide information on offender parole or probation status and release dates, opportunities to impact on parole board and probation hearings, and involvement with victim impact panels where survivors can confront and educate offenders on the effects and consequences of their violent crimes. Restorative justice programs focus on repairing the harm caused by offenders and include mediation and restitution services through which social workers advocate and mediate for victims and their families.

## Social Work Roles, Services, and Training

Microlevel practice and direct services and counseling roles start with crisis intervention and short-term counseling. The role of broker is essential as social workers make referrals to other community and social service agencies for long-term treatment. Basic needs services are provided through home visits, transportation services, and emergency assistance funds. Investigative services and roles include videotaping witness statements, hostage negotiation, and debriefing. At the macro level, the role of educator often involves victim services staff in providing public education and training for law enforcement personnel and community volunteers. The advocate role is an important one at both the micro and macro levels. At the case level, it is to ensure that the needs and rights of victims and their families are met during the investigative, court, and corrections processes. Also at the macro level, social workers engage in the roles of mediator, negotiator, and trainer in restitution programs, victim–offender mediation, and community services where offenders perform required community service as a condition of their probation or parole. Social workers also offer support and advocate for victims, survivors, and family members at court, probation, and parole hearings during victim impact statements and testimony. Victim impact statements are an opportunity for victims, survivors, and family members to tell the perpetrator and the judge and jury how the crime affected them and how the offender impacted their lives. It is also an opportunity to give their opinion and advocate during sentencing of the offender, so the victims and survivors have some input into what they consider a fair or just sentence to fit the crime.

Staffing patterns range from one-person programs to large programs with support staff and volunteers. Social workers are more frequently employed in victim services than are other counseling professionals (Knox & Roberts, 2002). Social workers in victim services are trained to work with a wide range of criminal offenses, mental health problems, family violence situations, child abuse and neglect, grief and loss, death, and drug- and alcohol-related offenses. Specialized knowledge of the dynamics and issues associated with these problem areas is essential, and can be provided by social work education programs, on-the-job training, and continuing education conferences and workshops. Opportunities for training and experience for social work student volunteers and internships are also available within victim services programs.

## Recent Challenges, Innovations, and Recommendations

Victim services programs must do a better job of educating the public and increasing awareness about their services. Recent research findings report that many victims who do not access services are unaware of and not informed about the services that are already available in their communities (Sims, Yost, & Abbott, 2005). Victim services programs also need to focus on those victims who are most likely to need and utilize services. Research findings show that those who experience more traumatic, serious offenses, those who are most vulnerable, and those who have the fewest resources are more likely to access services (Stohr, 2005).

Interagency coordination and cooperation between community victim service providers is necessary to meet the multiple needs of victims. Victim service providers should stress the importance of an interactive team approach in providing a continuum of services. Innovative programs have been implemented recently through the President's Family Justice Center Initiative (2003), which provides funding for comprehensive, collaborative, community-based domestic violence services, including medical care, counseling, law enforcement assistance, victim services, faith-based services, social services, employment assistance, and housing assistance. The Family Justice Centers are based on the "one-stop-shopping" model where multiple services and programs are housed in one central location, making them user-friendly.

Other opportunities to improve and coordinate victim services programs have been identified by a report from the Texas Crime Victims' Institute, which recommends establishing minimum basic service guidelines for victim services in criminal justice agencies and developing statewide certification or setting minimum standards for victim services providers (Office of the Attorney General, 1998). Evidence-based research in this field should guide best practices for training and education of victim services and criminal justice professionals.

With increasing opportunities for social workers to work with victims, witnesses, and family survivors, the profession must step up to the challenge to provide leadership and direction for victim services programs in the future.

## REFERENCES

Brownell, P., & Roberts, A. R. (2002). A century of social work in criminal justice and correctional settings. *Journal of Offender Rehabilitation, 35*, 1–17.

Knox, K. S., & Roberts, A. R. (2002). Police social work. In G. Greene & A. R. Roberts (Eds.), *Social workers' desk reference* (pp. 668–672). New York: Oxford University Press.

Knox, K. S., & Roberts, A. R. (2007). Forensic social work in law enforcement and victim service/victim assistance programs: National and local perspectives. In A. R. Roberts & D. W. Springer (Eds.), *Social work in juvenile and criminal justice settings* (pp. 113–123). Springfield, IL: Thomas.

Office of the Attorney General, State of Texas, Crime Victims' Institute. (1998). *The impact of crime on victims: A baseline study on program service delivery final report.* Retrieved November 20, 2006, from www.oag.state.tx.us/AG_Publications/pdfs/cvi_final_part2.pdf.

Roberts, A. R. (1997). The history and role of social work in law enforcement. In A. R. Roberts (Ed.), *Social work in juvenile and criminal justice settings* (pp. 105–115). Springfield, IL: Thomas.

Roberts, A. R., & Fisher, P. (1997). Service roles in victim/witness assistance programs. In A. McNeece & A. R. Roberts (Eds.), *Policy and practice in the justice system* (pp. 127–142). Chicago: Nelson-Hall.

Sims, B., Yost, B., & Abbott, C. (2005). Use and nonuse of victim service programs: Implications from a statewide survey of crime victims. *Criminology and Public Policy, 4*, 361–384.

Stohr, M. (2005). Victim services programming: If it is efficacious, they will come. *Criminology and Public Policy, 4*, 391–397.

## SUGGESTED LINKS

Crime Victims for a Just Society
*crimevictims.net/*

National Coalition of Homicide Survivors
*www.mivictims.org/nchs/*

National Crime Victim Bar Association
*www.victimbar.org/vb/Main.aspx*

National Organization for Victim Assistance
*www.trynova.org*

National Organization of Parents of Murdered Children
*www.pomc.org/*

Office for Victims of Crime
*www.ojp.usdoj.gov/ovc/welcome.html*

Restorative Justice Online
*www.restorativejustice.org/*

Victim Offender Mediation Association
*www.voma.org/*

Witness Justice
*www.witnessjustice.org/*

—KAREN S. KNOX

# VIOLENCE

**ABSTRACT:** Violence is a serious social issue that affects millions of individuals, families, and communities every year. It transcends across racial, age, gender, and socioeconomic groups, and is considered a significant public health burden in the United States. The purpose of this entry is to provide an overview of violence as a broad yet complicated concept. Definitional issues are discussed. Additional prevalence rates of select types of violence are presented in addition to risk and protective factors associated with violent behavior. The entry concludes with a summary of approaches to address violence in the context of prevention and intervention strategies.

**KEY WORDS:** crime; violence; risk factors; violence prevention

Violence is a global issue that directly causes injury to victims, and if widespread and severe can result in negative consequences for society at large. For example, a cross section of war, politics, and hate crimes has resulted in the violent mass murders (genocide) of hundreds of thousands of people in the region of Darfur in Sudan, resulting in an international debate and a call for humanitarian intervention efforts. In the United States, the murder rate has steadily declined since the mid-1990s from 9 per 100,000 persons in 1994 to 5.6 per 100,000 in 2005. However, an upward trend, or a 3.4% increase in the murder rate, was observed between 2004 and 2005, raising concerns, and the estimates for the first half of 2006 reflect an additional 1.4% increase (Department of Justice, 2006a, 2006b). Via its proximal and distal effects on millions of individuals, numerous families and communities, violence transcends across all racial, age, gender, socioeconomic, and geographical groups. No longer considered the epidemic it once was during the 1990s, violence continues to be a significant social issue and public health burden (National Center for Injury Prevention and Control [NCIPC], 2002).

## Definitions and Prevalence

There are many forms of violence, including everything from murder, homicide, genocide, rape, robbery, physical assault, hate crimes, to war and terrorism. In addition, the environmental contexts in which violence occurs broaden its scope—for example, violence may occur in homes, schools, the workplace, and in communities (urban, suburban, or rural). The relationship between a victim and a perpetrator can further expand the scope of violence. Still others call for the inclusion of acts such as stalking (Finch, 2002). Such a multitude of dimensions greatly broadens the concept of violence and complicates any effort to define it. Organizations committed to the prevention of violence, such as the National Center for Injury Prevention and Control and the Center for the Study and Prevention of Violence define violence differently, yet their definitions entail a common characteristic, that of *harm or injury*. Such harm or injury may be fatal or nonfatal, perpetrated or self-inflicted, and it may also be physical or psychological. Select forms of violence of interest to social work practitioners and researchers are discussed here.

VIOLENT CRIME Annually, the U.S Department of Justice conducts the National Crime Victimization Survey (NCVS), which allows for the monitoring of criminal victimization. According to the NCVS, "violent crimes include rape or sexual assault, robbery aggravated assault, and simple assault" (Catalano, 2006, p. 2). In 2005, among U.S. residents aged 12 and older, around 5.2 million violent crimes were reported. This 2005 violent crime rate of 21.4 per 1,000 persons represents a dramatic 10-year decline of 58%, from 50 per 1,000 persons in 1995. Specifically, between 1993 and 2005, declines were observed in the following categories: rape or sexual assault (down 69%), robbery (down 57%), and aggravated and simple assault (down 64% and 54%, respectively) (Catalano, 2006).

Although these significant reductions in violent crime rates since the mid-1990s are encouraging, specific groups continue to be particularly vulnerable to violence. Younger persons, males, and African Americans are victimized at higher rates than are persons older than 24 years, females, and whites. For example in 2005, rates of violent crime victimization for young people aged 12–15, 16–19, and 20–24 ranged from 44 to 46.9 per 1,000 persons. In contrast, these rates were significantly lower for older age groups, ranging from 2.4 per 1, 000 among persons 65 years or older to 23.6 per 1,000 among the 25–34 age group. Males are more likely to experience victimization than are females (25.5 versus 17.1 per 1,000); they are also more likely victimized by strangers (54% of all male victimizations) than are females, who are more likely to be victimized by nonstrangers (64% of all female victimizations). In 2003, the NCVS implemented new definitions for race and ethnicity which prevent long-term comparisons on the basis of race. This is significant in examining trends among African Americans because of the record high rates of violent crime involving this group in the early 1990s (Bureau of Justice Statistics, 1994). In 2005, violent victimization rates were higher for African Americans (27 per 1,000) than for whites (20.1 per 1,000) and

*persons of other races* (13.9 per 1,000), a category that includes American Indians, Alaska Natives, Asians, Native Hawaiians, and Pacific Islanders. However, the violence victimization rates for two other racial or ethic groups, in light of the new definitions, are noteworthy: Hispanic (25 per 1,000) and *two or more races* (83.6 per 1,000) (Catalano, 2006, p. 6).

FAMILY VIOLENCE AND CHILD ABUSE Family violence is defined by the U.S. Department of Justice as a violent crime committed by an offender who is related (biologically or legally) to the victim (Durose et al., 2005), and it accounts for about 1 in every 10 violent victimizations in the United States. Between 1998 and 2002, around 3.5 million violent crimes were committed against family members: the most common types of family violence were simple and aggravated assault (69.6% and 18.1%, respectively), while the least common was murder (0.3%). Sex offenses (3.6%) and robbery (8.4%) represent the remaining categories. Similar to the trends previously reported, the rate of family violence has also fallen: between 1993 and 2002, the rate declined from 5.4 to 2.1 victims per 1,000 persons 12 years and older. Because the family is a system, it is helpful to examine this type of violence by the relationship between the perpetrator and the victim. Between 1998 and 2002, approximately 49% were crimes committed against spouses, 47% against other family members, and 11% were committed by parents against their children. Family violence is most likely to take place in the home of the victim, a contextual factor associated with the underreporting of this type of violence. Most victims and perpetrators of family violence are white (74 and 79%, respectively), with 65% of victims ranging in age from 25 to 64. Females are disproportionately victimized by family violence in that 73% of victims are female, while almost 75% of family violence offenders are male. Violence perpetrated by one intimate partner (that is, spouse, partner, girl or boy friend) against the other is known as intimate partner violence. It often occurs in the context of family violence with women most likely victimized.

Children are also vulnerable to family violence. Specific types of child abuse may also be considered acts of family violence. For example, physical abuse, one type of child abuse, is characterized by beating, slapping, punching, biting, shaking, and burning—such acts depict violence. National victimization rates for child maltreatment are declining, from 15.3 to 12.3 per 1,000 children between 1993 and 2002. In 2002, child protective agencies substantiated around 906,000 cases (or 12.3 per 1,000 children) of child maltreatment, 18.6% of which were physical abuse cases. Of the

1,400 children who died as a result of child maltreatment that year, 28% of the deaths were caused by physical abuse (NCIPC, 2006b). Young children under age 4 are at the greatest risk for serious and fatal injury—this age group accounted for 76% of child maltreatment fatalities in 2002 (Child Welfare League of America, 2006).

SCHOOL VIOLENCE The scope of school violence is also quite broad, including acts of aggravated assault (fighting), bullying, rape, sexual assault, suicide, and homicide. Nonfatal incidents are the most prevalent types of school violence; however, since the late 1990s, an isolated group of highly publicized fatal school shootings has made the prevention of school violence a high priority for communities, law enforcement agencies, school districts, and parents alike. School shootings such as those that occurred in 1997 at Pearl High School in Pearl, Mississippi; in 1999 at Columbine High School in Littleton, Colorado; in 2005 at Red Lake Senior High School in Red Lake, Minnesota; in 2006 at the West Nickel Mines Amish School in Nickel Mines, Pennsylvania; and in 2007 at Virginia Tech university have generated heightened levels of public concern regarding school violence, when in fact school shootings are a rare occurrence.

According to the Centers for Disease Control, less than 1% of all homicides among school-age children happen at school (NCIPC, 2006a). The U.S. Department of Education's (2006) report on school crime and safety provides the most recent national level data available regarding school violence. Of the 54.9 million students enrolled in pre-Kindergarten through 12th grades during the 2004–2005 school year, 21 were victims of homicide and 7 committed suicide on school property: these incidents translate to a ratio of 1 homicide or suicide per 2 million students.

The numbers for nonfatal student victimization are far more excessive—in 2004, approximately 107,000 students aged between 12 and 18 were victims of serious violent crimes (rape, sexual assault, robbery, and aggravated assault) while at school; and 14% of high school students reported being involved in a fight on school property during the previous 12 months. In 2005, reports of being threatened or injured by a weapon while at school were most likely made by male (10%) versus female (6%) students, and males were twice as likely as females to report weapon possession at school during the previous 30 days. Contextual factors are also informative. For example, during the 2003–2004 school year, prevalence rates of violent crimes were higher in public schools than in private schools, and in public middle schools (53 per 1,000 students) versus public

primary or high schools (both 28 per 1,000 students) (U.S. Department of Education, 2006).

Bullying also occurs in the school environment, and has emerged as a social problem. (In fact, bullying has been associated with some of the school shooters who reportedly experienced teasing, isolation, and rejection by peers.) In 2005, among students aged 12–18 years, 28% reported being bullied within the past 6 months, and among those students bullied, 58% reported victimization once or twice during the 6-month survey period, while 24% reported physical injury as a result of being bullied (U.S. Department of Education, 2006). Such acts of school violence evoke fear in many students—6% of students aged 12–18 reported avoiding school activities because they feared being harmed; and Black and Hispanic students were more likely than their white counterparts to report fear for their safety while at school (U.S. Department of Education, 2006).

EFFECTS OF VIOLENCE As evidenced by these statistics, most violence is nonfatal; however, it does result in physical and psychological injury, mental health problems, public fear, and immense financial costs. In the year 2000 alone, nearly 1.9 million people were treated in emergency departments for violence-related injuries (Centers for Disease Control, 2001). Once exposed to violence, it is not uncommon for victims to experience traumatic stress reactions, particularly if the violent event was perceived as life-threatening or frightening (Fleisher & Kassam-Adams, 2006). The combination of physical and mental health treatments as a result of violence is very costly. For example, almost half of all intimate partner violence victimizations result in injury, with associated medical and mental health care costs totaling $4.1 billion annually (NCIPC, 2003). Societal costs are great as well, and can be partially evidenced by the expenses associated with incarcerating violent offenders. As an illustration, in the year 2003, around 667,000 inmates convicted of violent crimes were under the jurisdiction of state jails and federal prisons (Harrison & Beck, 2007). At an average annual operating cost of $22,600 per inmate (Stephan, 2004), taxpayers paid an estimated $15 billion in 2003 to incarcerate violent offenders.

## Risk and Protective Factors

According to the Centers for Disease Control (2007), a risk factor is a "characteristic that increases the likelihood of a person becoming a victim or perpetrator of violence," while a protective factor is a "characteristic that decreases the likelihood of a person becoming a victim or perpetrator of violence" (para. 7). Similarly, risk factors increase the chances a violent event will occur, or that violent behavior will develop, continue, or escalate. Alternatively, protective factors reduce or buffer the effects of risk factors. Both risk and protective factors may be personal characteristics or environmental conditions, and their *predictive value* varies by social context, timing, and circumstances (U.S. Surgeon General, 2001). For example, risk factors that predict the development of violent behavior for children may be irrelevant in predicting later onset among adults.

Through a growing body of research on risk and protection, a wide array of personal characteristics and environmental conditions have been identified, which may be grouped in four domains: individual, family, peer, and environmental, community, or societal (for comprehensive lists of risk and protective factors, see Fraser, 2004; Lipsey & Derzon, 1998). The National Institutes of Health (NIH) State-of-the-Science Conference Panel (2006) summarizes the following important risk factors: childhood fighting or aggression, victimization, substance abuse, criminal offenses, and school disengagement; familial conflict, inconsistent or harsh parenting practices; poor relationships with peers, and gang involvement; and neighborhood violence (pp. 459–460). The accumulation or clustering of multiple risk factors further increases risk when compared with the presence of a single risk factor. Understanding how identified risk and protective factors function has informed the development of violence prevention and intervention strategies. The development of some risk factors cannot be prevented; therefore, effective interventions are paramount. For example, physical aggression in childhood is often cited as a risk factor for violence; however, Tremblay (2006) argues that physical aggression is developmentally appropriate and questions why its development should be *prevented*. Instead, in this context, Tremblay proposes the notion of *corrective interventions* that teach self-regulation, prosocial negotiation with peers, and other alternatives to physical aggression.

## Approaches to Addressing Violence: Prevention and Intervention

The goal of preventive efforts is to preclude the occurrence of violence. Violence prevention efforts largely target children, adolescents, and families; however additional approaches include macro efforts at the community and policy levels, for example, neighborhood watch programs, drug- and gun-free zones, and community policing. Alternatively, interventions are delivered in situations when violence has already occurred, with the goal of preventing future violence. The public health approach to address violence involves reducing identified risk factors while increasing and strengthening protective factors through public awareness and program design and delivery. Prevention and intervention strategies should be guided by target risk factors, groups, and settings (Fraser, 1995).

Empirical evidence supports effectiveness of specific interventions that meet strict criteria and scientific rigor, including an ecological context that is multimodal and multidimensional, a focus on strong risk factors that are amicable to cognitive and behavioral strategies, developmental appropriateness, and a long-term clinical approach to treatment and treatment fidelity (NIH State-of-the-Science Conference Panel, 2006).

Social workers are and can be involved at all levels in the planning, intervention, and evaluation of programs to prevent, reduce, and treat violence. Specific characteristics of successful interventions at the individual and familial levels provide education and promote skills development (for example, problem solving, social competence, decision making, anger management, and self-control). They focus on effective parenting techniques, interpersonal communication and conflict-resolutions skills, and family management practices (Fraser & Williams, 2004; U.S. Surgeon General, 2001). Also, social workers work not only with victims of violence but also with the perpetrators in the criminal justice system.

Community-level approaches to violence prevention are not as abundant, nor have they been empirically validated as frequently as individual-focused strategies (NIH State-of-the-Science Conference Panel, 2006); however, promising approaches at this level collaboratively incorporate the resources, services, and expertise of various community entities such as law enforcement and juvenile justice, recreational facilities, child welfare agencies, social services departments, mental health agencies, schools, and churches (Gielen, Sleet, & Green, 2006).

A number of violence preventive and interventive programs have demonstrated effectiveness among select populations and communities, and the challenge now is to transition such effects "from demonstration projects to widespread implementation" so that the benefits are extended to the larger population (NIH State-of-the-Science Conference Panel, 2006, p. 464).

Since Fraser's 1995 overview of violence, overall rates of violence have decreased and significant scientific advances have improved the state of knowledge about the causes of violence, the associated risks and protective factors, and informed promising approaches to counter violence. Such improvements are encouraging, suggesting the desirable bridge between research and practice: advances in research on violence may be associated with the reductions in rates of violence.

While these improvements are encouraging, there are some indications that violence rates are on the rise again. In addition, specific groups continue to be at a greater risk for exposure to violence. Because violence varies by context, individual characteristics, and social and environmental conditions, it is a complex issue to address and resolve. Therefore, continued research with an emphasis on context and diversity is needed to improve the appropriateness and effectiveness of preventive and interventive strategies for diverse victims and perpetrators across various communities. Given the adverse consequences of violence for individuals, groups, and society at large, its prevention is imperative. The challenge is to prevent interpersonal and intergroup violence in a global climate currently characterized by suspicion, distrust, and vulnerability.

[*See also* School Violence; Terrorism.]

## REFERENCES

Bureau of Justice Statistics. (1994). *Violent crime* (NCJ 147186). Washington, DC: Government Printing Office.

Catalano, S. M. (2006, September). *National crime victimization survey: Criminal victimization, 2005 (NCJ214664)*. *Bureau of Justice Statistics Bulletin*. Washington, DC: U.S. Department of Justice, Office of Justice Programs, Bureau of Justice Statistics.

Centers for Disease Control. (2001). National estimates of non-fatal injuries treated in hospital emergency departments—United States, 2000. *MMWR Weekly*, 50(17), 340–346.

Centers for Disease Control. (2007). *The public health approach to violence prevention*. Retrieved September 28, 2007, from http://www.cdc.gov/ncipc/dvp/PublicHealthApproachTo_ViolencePrevention.htm.

Child Welfare League of America. (2006). *Child protection: Facts and figures*. Retrieved on January 15, 2007, at http://www.cwla.org/programs/childprotection/childprotectionfaq.htm#whatis.

Department of Justice. (2006a). *Crime in the United States 2005: Murder*. Washington, DC: Author, Federal Bureau of Investigation. Retrieved January 2, 2007, from http://www.fbi.gov/ucr/05cius/offenses/violent_crime/murder_homicide.html.

Department of Justice. (2006b). *2006 preliminary semiannual uniform crime report: January through June*. Washington, DC: Author, Federal Bureau of Investigation. Retrieved January 2, 2007, from http://www.fbi.gov.ucr/prelim06/table3.htm.

Durose, M. R., Harlow, C. W., Langan, P. A., Motivans, M., Rantala, R. R., & Smith, E. L. (2005, June). *Family violence statistics: Including statistics on strangers and acquaintances* (NCJ 207846). Washington, DC: U.S. Department of Justice, Office of Justice Programs, Bureau of Justice Statistics.

Finch, E. (2002). Stalking: A violent crime or a crime of violence? *The Howard Journal*, 41(5), 422–433.

Fleisher, C. L., & Kassam-Adams, N. (2006). Reducing post-traumatic stress after individual and mass trauma. In A. C. Gielen, D. A. Sleet, & R. J. DiClemente (Eds.), *Injury and violence prevention: Behavioral science theories, methods, and applications* (pp. 419–441). San Francisco: Jossey-Bass.

Fraser, M. W. (1995). Violence overview. In R. L. Edwards (Ed.), *Encyclopedia of social work* (19th ed., pp. 2453–2460). Washington, DC: NASW Press.

Fraser, M. W. (Ed.). (2004). *Risk and resilience in childhood: An ecological perspective*. Washington, DC: NASW Press.

Fraser, M. W., & Williams, S. A. (2004). Aggressive behavior. In L.A. Rapp-Paglicci, C. N. Dulmus, & J. S. Wodarski (Eds.), *Handbook of prevention interventions for children and adolescents* (pp. 100–129). Hoboken, NJ: Wiley & Sons.

Gielen, A. C., Sleet, D. A., & Green, L. W. (2006). Community models and approaches for interventions. In A. C. Gielen, D. A. Sleet, & R. J. DiClemente (Eds.), *Injury and violence prevention: Behavioral science theories, methods and applications* (pp. 65–82). San Francisco, CA: Jossey-Bass.

Harrison, P. M., & Beck, A. J. (2007, revised). Prisoners in 2005 (NCJ 215092). *Bureau of Justice Statistics Bulletin*, November 2006. Washington, DC: U.S. Department of Justice, Office of Justice Programs, Bureau of Justice Statistics. Retrieved October 7, 2007, from http://www.ojp.usdoj.gov/bjs/pub/pdf/p05.pdf.

Lipsey, M. W., & Derzon, J. H. (1998). Predictors of violent and serious delinquency in adolescence and early adulthood: A synthesis of longitudinal research. In R. Loeber & D. P. Farrington (Eds.), *Serious and violent juvenile offenders: Risk factors and successful interventions* (pp. 86–105). Thousand Oaks, CA: Sage.

National Center for Injury Prevention and Control [NCIPC]. (2002). CDC injury research agenda. Atlanta, GA Centers for Disease Control and Prevention. Retrieved November 6, 2007, from http://www.cdc.gov/ncipc/pub-res/research_agenda/Research%20Agenda.pdf.

National Center for Injury Prevention and Control [NCIPC]. (2003). *Costs of intimate partner violence against women in the United States*. Atlanta, GA: Centers for Disease Control and Prevention.

National Center for Injury Prevention and Control. [NCIPC]. (2004). *National violent death reporting system: Monitoring and tracking the causes of violence-related deaths*. Atlanta, GA: Centers for Disease Control and Prevention. Retrieved September 28, 2007, from http://www.cdc.gov/ncipc/pub-res/pubs.htm.

National Center for Injury Prevention and Control. [NCIPC]. (2006a). *CDC injury fact book*. Atlanta, GA: Centers for Disease Control and Prevention.

National Center for Injury Prevention and Control. [NCIPC]. (2006b). *Child maltreatment: Overview*. Atlanta, GA: Centers for Disease Control and Prevention. Retrieved January 27, 2007, from http://www.cdc.gov/ncipc/factsheets/cmoverview.htm.

National Institutes of Health State-of-the-Science Conference Panel. (2006). National Institutes of Health state-of-the-science conference statement: Preventing violence and related health-risking, social behaviors in adolescents, October 13–16, 2004. *Journal of Abnormal Child Psychology*, 34, 457–470.

Stephan, J. J. (2004). *Bureau of Justice Statistics special report: State prison expenditures, 2001* (NCJ 202949). Washington, DC: U.S. Department of Justice, Office of Justice Programs,

Bureau of Justice Statistics. Retrieved October 7, 2007, from http://www.ojp.usdoj.gov/bjs/pub/pdf/spe01.pdf.

Tremblay, R. E. (2006). Prevention of youth violence: Why not start at the beginning? *Journal of Abnormal Child Psychology, 34*, 481–487.

U.S. Department of Education. (2006). *Indicators of school crime and safety: 2006.* Washington, DC: Author, National Center for Education Statistics. Retrieved January 22, 2007, from http://nces.ed.gov/programs/crimeindicators/index.asp.

U.S. Surgeon General. (2001). *Youth violence: A report of the U.S. Surgeon General.* Retrieved January 25, 2007, at http://www.surgeongeneral.gov/library/youthviolence.

## SUGGESTED LINKS

Center for the Study and Prevention of Violence. *Blueprints for Violence Prevention.*
*www.colorado.edu/cspv/blueprints*
Federal Bureau of Investigation Uniform Crime Reports. *Crimes in the United States.*
*www.fbi.gov/ucr/ucr.htm*
National Center for Injury Prevention and Control (Centers for Disease Control).
*www.cdc.gov/ncipc/*
U.S. Department of Justice. Bureau of Justice Statistics. *Crime Characteristics.*
*www.ojp.usdoj.gov/bjs/cvict_c.htm*

—SHEARA A. WILLIAMS

## VIOLENCE AGAINST SOCIAL WORKERS.
*See* Client Violence.

## VOCATIONAL SERVICES

ABSTRACT: Vocational rehabilitation (VR) services, provided through a jointly funded state–federal rehabilitation system and available in each state, help people with disabilities prepare for, secure, and sustain employment. Since 1920, VR Programs have helped 10 million individuals with disabilities reach employment. Anyone with a mental or physical disability is eligible for VR services. While a range of services is provided, the services most consistent with VR goals are those, such as supported employment, that promote full integration into community life. Social workers are essential to community-based VR services; however, a challenge for the profession is to assume new roles to meet best practice vocational standards.

KEY WORDS: vocational services; employment; disabilities; Rehabilitation Act; supported employment

Vocational services for people with disabilities (PWD) are provided by federal legislative mandate through a jointly funded state–federal vocational rehabilitation system (VR Program). Administered by the Rehabilitation Services Administration (RSA), an agency of the U.S. Department of Education, the VR Program has the goal of making available in each state services that help PWD prepare for, secure, and sustain employment.

Initially designed to assist World War I veterans, the first VR Program was mandated by Civilian Vocational Rehabilitation Act of 1920. Continued legislation extended provisions to civilians and sanctioned improvements to, and expansion of, the Program scope and appropriations. However, the Rehabilitation Act of 1973, and its amendments (1978, 1984, 1986, and 1992), marked a major social policy shift toward the employment of PWD by introducing into the VR Program consumer empowerment, self-determination and civil rights in employment for PWD. The Workforce Investment Act (WIA) of 1998 reauthorized the Rehabilitation Act programs and, with the Ticket to Work and Work Incentives Improvement Act of 1999 (TWWIIA), marked another milestone in the development of VR Programs by integrating VR services with the state and local workforce development systems. TWWIIA mandated VR as a partner with One Stop Centers in the provision of services for those with disabilities seeking employment. TWWIIA included state VR Programs as employment network members through which "ticket" holders (PWD) can purchase vocational service.

### Eligibility and Services

Since 1920, VR Programs have supported 10 million individuals with disabilities reach employment. By 2004 VR Programs offered assistance to over 1.4 million individuals and, of these, 14.7% achieved employment (U.S. Department of Education, 2004). To be eligible for service an individual must have a mental, physical, or learning disability that interferes with the ability to work and must be able to benefit from services. Recipients of Supplemental Security Income (SSI) or Social Security Disability Insurance (SSDI) are presumed eligible. There are no federal requirements based on financial need. However, to respond to limited funds, states may choose to consider financial need as basis for determining order of selection for service (Hager, 2004).

Services are provided directly by the VR Program or purchased from community rehabilitation providers. They include any service described in an Individualized Plan for Employment (IPE) necessary to assist PWD achieve their vocational goals. Services cover assessment of vocational needs, development of the IPE that defines employment goals and services to achieve the goals, coordination of services to reach employment goals, and supports to help individuals secure and maintain work (for example, counseling, training, job coaching, transportation, referral, case management, advocacy, and access to assistive technologies or supports) (Hayward & Schimdt-Davis, 2003b).

Service delivery approaches include agency-based work, enclaves, and work crews. These approaches offer employment opportunities in a noncompetitive, supportive setting in which individuals engage in meaningful work at the agency where they receive rehabilitation services or as part of team that works in the community that is supervised by the provider. In these approaches, co-workers also tend to have disabilities and the provider is often the employer. Supported employment (SE) and transitional employment placements are provided in the community, where PWD work side-by-side with nondisabled co-workers. SE is an evidence-based approach for people with mental health conditions or mental retardation but has been applied more widely to those with other disabilities. SE helps individuals secure jobs that are permanent, pay at least minimum wage, and are obtained through a competitive hiring process. Transitional employment places individuals in jobs that are temporary, and are designated specifically for PWD. Services that promote full integration of PWD into community life are most consistent with VR Program goals (Stafford, 1995).

Evidence suggests that PWD who obtain employment by the time they exit VR Program services tend to be satisfied with the services received, and that PWD who exit into competitive employment are better off (in terms of integration into community life and self-sufficiency) than others (Hayward & Schmidt-Davis, 2003b). The likelihood of achieving employment, however, is dependent on the number of services and types of services received (for example, the quality of the relationship between the PWD and the counselor, flexibility in changing the IPE, job placement, and on-the-job-training or SE) (Hayward & Schmidt-Davis, 2005). In turn, the likelihood of receiving services is dependent upon characteristics of the PWD such as type of disability, benefit status, and work status at the time of receipt of services (Hayward & Schmidt-Davis, 2003a). For example, over time, people with severe physical disabilities have a statistically significantly greater likelihood of achieving competitive employment than those with psychiatric disabilities (Andrews et al., 1992).

## Challenges and Future Trends

The federal government continues to promote policy that supports employment for PWD through VR Programs and the integration of these programs with other initiatives. Significant challenges remain, however. Some providers as well as employers and families continue to question the ability of PWD to be productive workers. There is a lack of evidence-based vocational best practices to guide providers and a lack of community providers to which VR clients can be referred. There is a continued need for coordination among VR and other public systems that look to VR to serve their clients with disabilities. Finally, VR is not as effective in responding to the employment needs of people with mental disabilities as it is for those with physical disabilities and may not be equipped to respond to the vocational needs of the growing number of older Americans with disabilities who will be seeking or sustaining employment (Wadsworth & Kampfe, 2004).

## Roles of Social Workers

Social workers are essential to community-based vocational services at both the micro and macro levels. At the individual level, they provide vocational assessment, counseling and workplace support, partner with VR specialists, job developers and job coaches, and coordinate services to support PWD in employment. The social work role will become more important as agencies find that PWD request help with employment and that vocational service is increasingly a requirement for funding. Typically, however, social workers' formal training does not prepare them for their role. Some professionals hold the same misperception as do employers and families—that PWD cannot be productive workers. Social workers with a belief in human potential are needed to (a) help PWD understand the impact of work on benefits, (b) match PWD to jobs that best fit their needs, (c) assist PWD with disclosing their conditions at work and respond to possible stigma in the workplace, (d) negotiate with employers for accommodations, or (e) anticipate and respond to the nonvocational barriers to employment that may undermine successful outcomes (Akabas, Gates, & Oran-Sabia, 2006; Bond et al., 2001). Thus, to support PWD reach their vocational goals may require social workers to assume new roles that include career development, assessment of the challenges to employment, identifying, negotiating, and setting in place workplace accommodations, building relationships with employers responsive to hire PWD, and creating opportunities for mutual support and education to empower PWD in the employment process.

A challenge for the profession is to formalize the role of social workers in the provision of vocational services and be prepared to assume new roles in order to meet best practice vocational standards (Akabas & Kurzman, 2005).

## REFERENCES

Akabas, S. H., Gates, L. B., & Oran-Sabia, V. (2006). Work opportunities for rewarding careers: Insights from implementation of a best practice approach toward vocational services for mental health consumers. *Journal of Rehabilitation, 72*(1), 19–26.

Akabas, S. H., & Kurzman, P. (2005). *Work and the workplace: A resource for innovative policy and practice.* New York: Columbia University Press.

Andrews, H., Barker, J., Pittman, J., Mars, L., Struening, E., & LaRocca, N. (1992). National trends in vocational rehabilitation: A comparison of individuals with physical and psychiatric disabilities. *Journal of Rehabilitation 58*(1), 7–16.

Bond, G. R., Becker, D. R., Drake, R. E., Rapp, C. A., Meisler, N., Lehman, A. F., et al. (2001). Implementing supported employment as an evidence-based practice. *Psychiatric Services, 52*(3), 313–322.

Hager, R. (2004). *Policy and practice brief: Order of selection for vocational rehabilitation services: An option for state VR agencies who cannot serve all eligible individuals.* Ithaca, NY: Cornell University, Employment and Disability Institute, School of Industrial and Labor Relations.

Hayward, B. J., & Schmidt-Davis, H. (2003a). *Longitudinal study of the Vocational Rehabilitation Services program final report 1: How consumer characteristics affect access to, receipt of, and outcomes of VR services.* Washington, DC: U.S. Department of Education, Office of Special Education and Rehabilitative Services, Rehabilitation Services Administration.

Hayward, B. J., & Schmidt-Davis, H. (2003b). *Longitudinal study of the Vocational Rehabilitation Services program final report 2: VR services and outcomes.* Washington, DC: U.S. Department of Education, Office of Special Education and Rehabilitative Services, Rehabilitation Services Administration.

Hayward, B. J., & Schmidt-Davis, H. (2005). *Longitudinal study of the Vocational Rehabilitation Services program final report 3: The context of VR services.* Washington, DC: U.S. Department of Education, Office of Special Education and Rehabilitative Services, Rehabilitation Services Administration.

Stafford, B. J. (1995). A legislative perspective on the Rehabilitation Act. *American Rehabilitation, 21*(3), 37–41.

U.S. Department of Education. (2004). Rehabilitation Services Administration. Fiscal Year 2004 data tables. Retrieved February 13, 2007, from http://www.ed.gov/rschstat/eval/rehab/statistics.html.

Wadsworth, J., & Kampfe, C. M. (2004). The characteristics of senior applicants for vocational rehabilitation services. *Rehabilitation Counseling Bulletin, 47*(2), 104–111.

## FURTHER READING

Anonymous. (1995). Vocational rehabilitation: The first 50 years. *American Rehabilitation, 21,* 3, 43–52.

Cook, J. A. (2006). Employment barriers for persons with psychiatric disabilities: Update of a report for the President's Commission. *Psychiatric Services, 57*(10), 1391–1405.

Fesko, S., & Hamner, D. (2005). *Case studies of local boards and One-Stop career centers: Levels of involvement of state VR agencies with other One-Stop partners.* Boston: Institute for Community Inclusion, University of Massachusetts Boston.

Foley, S., & Woodring, J. (2005). *Employment services and outcomes of people receiving welfare benefits and vocational rehabilitation services.* Boston: Institute for Community Inclusion, University of Massachusetts Boston.

Landini, M. (1998). *Workforce Investment Act of 1998.* Washington, DC: U.S. Department of Labor, Employment and Training Administration.

Macro, B., Almandsmith, S., & Hague, M. (2003). *Creating partnerships for workforce investment: How services are provided under WIA: Revised final report for "Understanding the role of intermediaries under WIA."* Washington, DC: U.S. Department of Labor, Employment and Training Administration, Office of Policy and Research.

Metzle, D. S., Boeltzig, H., Butterworth, J., & Gilmore, D. S. (2004). *The national survey of community rehabilitation providers, FY2002–2003 Report 1: Overview of services and provider characteristics.* Boston: Institute for Community Inclusion, University of Massachusetts Boston.

Silverstein, R. (2001). *Provisions in the final regulations governing the state VR program describing the interplay with WIA and TWWIIA.* Boston: Institute for Community Inclusion, University of Massachusetts Boston.

Timmons, J. C., Schuster, J., Hamner, D., & Bose, J. (2001). *Characteristics of effective employment services: The consumers' perspective.* Boston: Institute for Community Inclusion/UAP.

—LAUREN B. GATES

## VOLUNTARISM

ABSTRACT: Voluntarism can be interpreted at the levels of values, structure, and ideology. In Western society, voluntarism rests heavily on secular and religious values originating in both Greco-Roman and Judeo-Christian traditions. Today the voluntary sector in the United States can be divided into five main types: social support networks, grassroots associations, nonprofit organizations, human service agencies, and private foundations. At the level of ideology, voluntarism can also be interpreted as "civil society."

KEY WORDS: community; civil society; independent sector; nonprofit; philanthropy; social network; mutual aid; grassroots; voluntary agency; voluntary association; voluntary sector; volunteerism

The term *voluntarism* can be interpreted from different levels, with profound implications for social welfare in general and social work in particular at each level

(Wilensky, 1981). Here we focus on three levels of interpretation—voluntarism as values, voluntarism as structure, and voluntarism as ideology.

## Voluntarism as Values

Voluntarism as a set of values derives meaning first from its Latin root *voluntas*. In philosophy, *voluntas* refers to the freedom of the will and its supremacy above all other human faculties. A voluntary action is one freely undertaken or chosen by an individual or group presumably without force or compulsion from, say, the government or "the state." Within the context of our discussion here, volunteers are people who choose to donate a portion of their time, talent, or resources, as individuals or in groups, to benefit others for some charitable, humanitarian, mutual aid, or public purpose.

Choosing to give or do good to others, voluntarily, rests on religious and secular values, as well as a mixture of human motives, both altruistic and narcissistic. Tracing the early evolution of caring concepts, Morris (1986) cites, for example, an early Egyptian inscription on philanthropy, which reads "When he is buried and joined to the earth his name is not wiped out on earth but he is remembered for goodness." Early Hebrew scripture enunciated obligations to give voluntarily to the needy, or risk punishment from God, as in the case of Sodom and Gomorrah. Christian scripture and tradition extended ancient beliefs about giving aid or help beyond members of one's family, tribe, or clan, to strangers elsewhere, as in the Good Samaritan parable, for example. The obligation to give charity is a key tenet of Islam as well.

In ancient Greece, the chief motivation for voluntarism was not altruism but secular values associated with reciprocity (givers expecting a gift, social recognition, cooperation, or a favor in return) and civil accord (givers distributing wealth to prevent social unrest or to maintain peaceful relations with the poor). The earliest usage of the Greek word *philanthropy* referred to benevolence between equals or friends. Later, the term evolved in meaning to gift-giving by the powerful or wealthy to their subjects or dependents.

Civic values linked with voluntarism—democracy, freedom of association, and citizenship—trace their origins to Greek culture as well. Aristotle's notion of civil society was founded on respect for different and multiple spheres of associations, as well as subordination of private interests voluntarily to the public good of the city-state. People voluntarily joined different associations to meet their basic needs or to gain some advantage for themselves. Civil society in this context was largely "organized around face-to-face relations of friends whose leisurely aristocratic benevolence

enabled them to discover and contribute to the public good" (Ehrenberg, 1999, p. xi).

Although ancient Rome adopted many Greek ideas about charity and philanthropy, it too made significant contributions to voluntarism (Morris, 1986). One contribution is the word *humanis*, the Latin root of humanitarianism. A secular and philosophical concept, *humanis* refers to the duty of the wealthy or powerful to express sympathy for the poor and the weak through humane treatment and assistance. The duty to promote social welfare is based on human rights, in contrast to religiously sanctioned values linked to justice and obligation.

As Republican and Imperial Rome expanded into a large impersonal empire, civic institutions had to accommodate the needs of diverse groups, races, and conquered peoples, lest Rome lose its worldwide hegemony. Civic values associated with democracy, pluralism, social integration, and civil society would, in time, have a lasting impact on the concept of voluntarism. The Romans, Ehrenberg explains (1999), "contributed a profoundly important view of civil society as a sphere of reason, justice, participation, and rights that sought a universal understanding of citizenship even if it recognized a powerful private centre of gravity" (p. x). Local, private, voluntary activity to sustain democracy and to promote benevolence was no longer the only way to understand civil society—and the functions of the state.

Voluntarism in modern Western society still rests heavily on religious values stemming from Judeo-Christian traditions, secular and civic values originating in Greco-Roman cultures, and a mixture of human dispositions toward both altruism and narcissism. These sets of values permeate literature on voluntarism today, and the role the voluntary sector plays to guard them in Western democratic societies (Hodgkinson & Foley, 2003; Kramer, 1981).

## Voluntarism as Structure

Voluntarism can also be interpreted at the level of structure. Brilliant (1995), who wrote the previous entry on this subject, divides American history into six major periods: community activity and mutual aid in the Colonial era (1601–1800); expansion of voluntary organizations (1800–1865); the rise of philanthropy and coordinating agencies (1865–1900); increased professionalization and policy reforms (1900–1932); emergent national government and voluntary partnerships (1932–1980); and a period of privatization (1980 to 1990s). Embedded within the chronicle is an array of voluntary structures (religious and secular) that emerged over time to meet the needs of vulnerable individuals and groups, usually in authorization rather than in conflict with the state.

Even though there is no generally accepted taxonomy of voluntary structures, they can be divided into five main types: social support networks, grassroots associations, nonprofit organizations, human service agencies, and private foundations. Here the focus is mainly on the first four types, given their historic roles in providing concrete services to vulnerable populations. Voluntary structures vary by degree of formalization, dependence on volunteers, and local control. They also vary by the amount of data available to count and assess them. Most databases on the voluntary sector in general and informal voluntary structures in particular are incomplete, unreliable, or biased (Grønbjerg, 2002).

One structural layer consists of *social support networks*. Social support networks are informal webs of relationships between friends, neighbors, peers, teachers, co-workers, and other people in the social environment of a vulnerable person that can serve as volunteer instruments of help, either face-to-face or through dispersed networks through the Internet (Zastrow, 2005). Social workers usually include social support networks in environmental assessments of resources available to people they serve. Although family members are typically included in such assessments, social support to one's immediate household or family is often viewed as outside the realm of voluntarism (Smith, 2000).

Voluntarism in social support networks can be in the form of material aid (money and goods), emotional support (encouragement, recognition, and affirmation), exchange of resources (child care and housing), ongoing support (activities of daily living and work-site assistance), or social capital (access to jobs and other resources through social connections) (Lin, 2001). Dramatic advances in supported employment and community inclusion of persons with disabilities, for example, owe much of their success to the utilization of social support networks in the workplace and in the community rather than professional supports alone (Wehman, McLaughlin, & Wehman, 2005).

Another structural layer in the voluntary sector consists of *grassroots associations* (Smith, 2000). They are defined here as informal, unincorporated, significantly autonomous local groups which rely on volunteer members to perform all or most of their activities or work. These social structures are usually formed on a voluntary basis by peers with similar needs, problems, concerns, or goals. They provide a vehicle for unified volition and action toward a common cause or purpose, ranging from mutual aid to public benefit.

Most grassroots associations take the form of mutual aid groups that provide direct services to help members deal with behavioral, emotional, or rehabilitative problems, such as alcoholism, compulsive gambling, parental abuse, and bereavement (Zastrow, 2005). Many of these associations (e.g., Alcoholics Anonymous) are loosely federated small groups clustered around formally incorporated general-service organizations that provide technical assistance and publications to local groups. Other grassroots associations take the form of unincorporated clubs or congregations, some consisting of immigrant associations with transnational affiliations (Poole & Negi, 2007). Still other grassroots associations operate as advocacy, political action, and social movement groups oriented toward social change (Chetkovich & Kunreuther, 2006)

Smith (2000) calls grassroots associations the "dark matter" of the voluntary universe. Small, informal organizations with revenues less than $5,000 (including churches, synagogues, and mosques) are not required to register with the U.S. Internal Revenue Service (IRS)—hence, they are hard to count. Smith's calculation of 30 grassroots associations per 1,000 population yields a rough estimate of 10 million grassroots associations, based on the current population base of 300 million residents in the United States. Despite being hard to count, grassroots associations merit attention by social workers, alongside larger service-providing voluntary agencies, due to the great array of services they deliver, and the historic roles many have played in social change and social justice.

The third structural layer of the voluntary sector consists of *nonprofit organizations*. They are defined here as formally incorporated, tax-exempt organizations governed by a volunteer board of directors, and legally required to return surplus funds to the corporation for public purposes—hence, the name "nonprofits." Registered under Section 501(c) of the IRS Code, these organizations do not have to pay federal income taxes, and are usually exempt from state and local taxes as well. Distributed across 27 major categories, they include an array of nonprofit organizations: service and fraternal organizations, religious and charitable societies, public trusts, social and recreational clubs, business leagues, war veterans' organizations, political parties, unions, cooperatives, and foundations. In 2006, 1,478,194 nonprofit organizations were registered in the master file of IRS, an increase of 36 percent in 10 years (National Center for Charitable Statistics, 2007).

About half of all exempt nonprofit organizations fall under the 501(c)(3) category of the IRS Code. As a group, they fall into two classes: public charities and private foundations. Some public charities focus on charitable activities related to poverty, others on religious, educational, scientific, literary, or other activities that serve broad public purposes. A substantial portion of the income of exempt nonprofit organizations must come from broad public support or from the government. The number of 501(c)(3) public charities in the United States increased dramatically over the last decade, from 535,930 in 1996 to 904,313 in 2006. Collectively they represent two-thirds of all tax-exempt nonprofit organizations (National Center for Charitable Statistics, 2007).

Most of the recent growth in nonprofit organizations can be traced to *human service agencies*, a substrata in the 501(c) (3) category of public charities of particular importance to social workers. These agencies are both nonprofit and governed by volunteer boards. They vary, however, by the extent to which they utilize volunteers in the delivery of services (versus professionals), and by the degree to which they are managed and controlled locally or by regional or national boards. Some of the prominent human service agencies in the United States are the American Red Cross, Boys and Girls Clubs, Catholic Charities, Community Action Agencies, Goodwill Industries, Habitat for Humanity, Planned Parenthood, and Salvation Army.

Human service agencies account for most of the dramatic escalation in public charity revenues over the past two decades. Annual revenues reported by public charities increased from $412 billion in 1987 to $665 billion in 2006. Most of the change was due to revenue through government fees and contracts (National Center for Charitable Statistics, 2007). These revenues are critically important to social workers, not merely because of the services they fund for client populations, but also the opportunities they create for professional employment. In the last quarter century, the number of employees in nonprofit organizations has doubled. Voluntary health and social service agencies have recorded the largest increases. The U.S. Bureau of Labor estimates that between 2000 and 2010 nonprofit health agencies will add 2.8 million jobs to the voluntary sector, and nonprofit social service agencies will contribute an additional 1.2 million jobs (available at http://www.bls.data). Most licensed social workers are employed by nonprofit health and social service agencies (National Association of Social Workers, 2006).

The last structural layer in the voluntary sector considered in this entry consists of *private foundations*. Another class of nonprofits under the 501(c)(3) tax-exempt category of the IRS Code, private foundations receive most of their income from investments and endowments. The number of private foundations nearly doubled in the last decade, from 58,774 in 1996 to 109,852 in 2006. Most of the $40.7 billion they distributed went to nonprofit organizations. The largest share went to tax-exempt educational organizations, while nonprofit service agencies received the largest percentage of grants (National Center for Charitable Statistics, 2007).

## Voluntarism as Ideology

Finally, voluntarism can be interpreted at the level of ideology. Ideology is defined here as a body of concepts, beliefs, or myths shared by a group about how society should function and be organized, how power should be distributed, and the ends to which it should be used. Since its main purpose in public affairs is to change or maintain the social order, ideology also includes views about what makes the best form of government, and how best to promote social welfare (Hofrichter, 2003).

The dominant ideology in voluntarism today is "civil society." Civil society, in contemporary parlance, is defined as social space between the market and the state occupied by voluntary structures such as social support networks, mutual aid groups, grassroots associations, nonprofit organizations, human service agencies, and private foundations. Despite great diversity, they share enough features in common to be viewed as a distinct social sector: specifically, they are private, nonprofit, self-governing, and voluntary. An array of terms are used to identify this sector—the voluntary sector, the nonprofit sector, the third sector, the independent sector, the nongovernmental sector, and most all-encompassing and ideologically laden, the civil society sector. Proponents claim that civil society serves "essentially public purposes" (Salamon, Sokolowski, & List, 2003, p. 1) and that it renews democracy through "politics of the third way" (Giddens, 1998, p. 78).

Hall (2006), in a historical overview of philanthropy, voluntary associations, and nonprofit organizations, divides U.S. history into six major periods, each well suited to the discussion of voluntarism as civil society. They include: charitable, educational, religious, and other nonproprietary activities (before 1750); revolution and republic (1750–1800); public and private charity associations (1800–1860); private institutions and the creation of the modern state (1860–1920); welfare capitalism, scientific management, and the "associative state" (1920–1945); the welfare state and the invention of the nonprofit sector (1945–2000).

The first two concepts that shape normative thought processes and ideological beliefs about voluntarism as civil society are "community" and "voluntary association." Sociologist Ferdinand Tönnies (1987), who coined the term voluntarism, was keenly interested in communities as social organisms for fostering an individual sense of belonging and a mutual bond of commitment and responsibility. These social benefits emerge through *Gemeinschaft*-type relationships, that is, through informal local gatherings of friends and neighbors, mutual aid, participation in local clubs and civic organizations, and other forms of voluntary association. When Alexis de Tocqueville visited the United States in the 1830s, he identified voluntary association as the distinguishing characteristic of American society (Tocqueville, 1990), an observation frequently noted in contemporary times by proponents of civil society (Putnam, 2000; Sandel, 1996).

Both civil society concepts—community and voluntary association—have been inextricably linked throughout American history to conservative and liberal causes alike: by volunteers and charity organization societies; community organizers and settlement house movements; Hoover and the associative state; Roosevelt and the New Deal; tax reformers and nonprofit deductions; civil rights activists and social movements; associational activism and the helping professions; Johnson and the model cities program; Reagan and devolution; Bush and the "thousand points of light" (each representing a voluntary community-based initiative serving the dependent and the disabled); Clinton and the National Community Trust Act; G. W. Bush and charitable choice (Hall, 2006; McConnell, 1996).

Three other fundamental concepts in the ideology of voluntarism as civil society are "social capital," "civic engagement," and "democracy." Robert Putnam examines empirical relationships between these three concepts, along with those of community and voluntary association. In *Making Democracy Work*, Putnam (1993) defines social capital as "features of social organization, such as trust, norms, and networks that can improve the efficiency of society by facilitating coordinated actions" (p. 167). His longitudinal study of social organizations in regions of Italy found that effective political institutions depend on a developed society of intermediate associations and a civic culture. Later, in *Bowling Alone*, Putnam (2000) reports that America's stock of social capital has declined. He attributes the decline to Americans becoming increasingly disconnected from family, friends, neighbors, and democratic structures. He concludes that the best way to restore the country's stock of social capital is for Americans to reconnect through greater associational life. Findings in both of Putnam's books have been challenged, as has his neo-Tocquevillean view of civil society "as a collection of spontaneous efforts detached from government and politics" (Skocpol, Ganz, & Munson, 2000, p. 542).

The next logical thread in the ideology of voluntarism as civil society is prescriptive. What makes the best form of government, and what is the best way to promote social welfare? The answer is decentralized government, with an emphasis on civic participation and on local voluntary associations (Putnam, 1993). This particular blueprint for action assumes that local citizens and local associations know better than central officials and public bureaucracies what local people need, how to coordinate resources to meet those needs, and how to customize services to fit local conditions (Poole, 2003).

Several arguments against such claims have been advanced. One is that the neo-Tocquevillean view of voluntarism is only one way to conceptualize civil society. A more ancient view of civil society emphasizes the role of the state in turning the pursuit of private interests through voluntary association toward the public good (Ehrenberg, 1999). McConnell (1966) warns "that the degree of power wielded by private groups is American democracy's great problem rather than its most important strength" (p. 6).

Critics also argue that the contemporary view of civil society often overlooks, or underestimates, the role of the state in creating fertile conditions for the growth of voluntarism in America (Hall, 2006; Nanetti, 1980; Skocpol, 1999; Skocpol, Ganz, & Munson, 2000), thus contributing to a false and rigid dichotomy between the state and civil society (that is, the "independent" sector). The tendency to overlook or underestimate the effects of economic forces on voluntarism has been cited as well, both in the economy at large (Curtis, Baer, & Graff, 2001; Ehrenberg, 1999) and in the influence of public fiscal incentives on economic and programmatic behaviors of nonprofits (Bielefeld & Scotch, 1998).

Another argument advanced against the claims of civil society is the downside of social capital (Portes, 2000; Portes & Landolt, 1996). Social capital can impede democracy and social justice just as easily as advance them. When local demands for conformity are excessive, local voluntary associations can work against the cause of freedom; when local networks of authorization exclude or marginalize certain groups, the cause of social justice can be compromised (Swanson, 2001). Local NIMBY (Not In My Backyard) opposition by neighborhood associations to something they consider undesirable, such as halfway houses and homeless shelters, keeps certain groups of people out as it protects and insulates social networks within (American Bar Association, 1999).

Also questioned is the assumption that local nonprofits have adequate capacity to accomplish broad public goals (Dickens & Ellwood, 2001; Poole, 2003; Salamon, 1997). When the public sector assumes the voluntary sector has more capacity than it does, a "disconnect" can occur in meeting human needs. Milward (1994) refer to this condition as the "hollow state" (p. 309). When the public sector transfers its responsibilities to the voluntary sector without adequate resources, nonprofits risk becoming part of what Grônberg (1992) calls an "organizational sink" for social problems (p. 95).

## Globalization

"A veritable 'global associational revolution' appears to be underway, a massive upsurge of organized private, voluntary activity in every region of the world" (Salamon et al., 2003, p. 1). Considerable thought and attention, therefore, must be given to potential constraints and opportunities. As nongovernmental organizations become increasingly important actors in social welfare, internal challenges (restricted focus, amateurism, fragmentation, parochialism, and inadequate resources for large-scale, long-term initiatives) and external challenges (accountability, state relations, cooptation, and foreign imperialism) must be addressed (Brown, 2006; Brown & Kalegaonkar, 1999). At the same time, the public sector must recognize and appreciate the critical roles nonprofit, nongovernmental organizations play in philanthropy, human security, empowerment, and sustainable development, to name a few (Michael, 2002; Nanetti, 1980; Salamon, Sokolowski, & List, 2003).

"Making nonprofits work" is generally accepted as part of the answer (Light, 2000). So too is providing technical support to help nonprofits scale-up for the job (Brown & Kalegaonkar, 1999; Poole, 2003). Collecting more empirical data on the scope, structure, contributions, and limitations of the voluntary sector in diverse societies throughout the world is a widely recognized need as well (Salamon, Sokolowski, & List, 2003).

There also appears to be growing recognition of the need to avoid "either and or" propositions—the market versus the state, the state versus the voluntary sector, the voluntary sector versus the market—in the provision of social goods and services (Brown, 2006; Hall, 2006; Kettl, 2000). The fundamental question now is one of shared responsibility (Moroney, 1986). What is the most desirable, efficient, and effective division of responsibility between the state, the market, and the voluntary sector to maximize social benefits and to create a vibrant democratic society? Successful reforms hinge on the degree of match between social allocations for collective tasks and the capacity of diverse public and private actors to carry them out.

## REFERENCES

American Bar Association (1999). *NIMBY: A primer for lawyers and advocates.* Chicago: Author.

Bielefeld, W., & Scotch, R. K. (1998). The decision-making context and its impact on local human service nonprofits. *Nonprofit Management and Leadership, 9,* 53–69.

Brilliant, E. (1995). Voluntarism. In R. Edwards (Eds.), *Encyclopedia of Social Work* (19th ed., pp. 2469–2482). Washington. DC: NASW Press.

Brown, L. D. (2006). *Civil society legitimacy and accountability: Issues and challenges.* (Working Paper #32). Cambridge, MA: The Hauser Institute for Nonprofit Management and The Kennedy School of Government, Harvard University.

Brown, L. D., & Kalegaonkar, A. (1999). *Addressing civil society's challenges: Support organizations as emerging institutions.* (IDR Reports #15). Boston, MA: Institute for Development Research.

Chetkovich, C., & Kunreuther, F. (2006). *From the ground up: Grassroots organizations making social change.* Ithaca, NY: Cornell University Press.

Curtis, J. E., Baer, D. E., & Graff, E. G. (2001). Nation of joiners: Explaining voluntary association membership in democratic societies. *American Sociological Review, 66,* 783–805.

Dickens, R., & Ellwood, D. T. (2001). *Whither poverty in Great Britain and the United States: Determinants of changing poverty and whether work will work.* Cambridge, MA: National Bureau of Economic Research.

Ehrenberg, J. (1999). *Civil society: The critical history of an idea.* New York: New York University Press.

Giddens, A. (1998). *The third way: The renewal of social democracy.* Cambridge, UK: Polity Press.

Grønbjerg, K. A. (2002). Evaluating nonprofit databases. *American Behavioral Scientist, 45,* 1741–1777.

Hall, P. D. (2006). A historical overview of philanthropy, voluntary associations, and nonprofit organizations in the United States, 1600–2000. In W. W. Powell & R. Steinberg (Eds.), *The nonprofit sector: A research handbook* (2nd ed., pp. 32–65). New Haven CT: Yale University Press.

Hodgkinson, V., & Foley, M. W. (Eds.). (2003). *The civil society reader.* Boston, MA: Tufts University Press.

Hofrichter, R. (Ed.). (2003). *Health & social justice: Politics, ideology, and inequality in the distribution of disease.* San Francisco, CA: Jossey-Bass.

Kettl, D. F. (2000). *The global public management revolution.* Washington, DC: Brookings Institution Press.

Kramer, R. (1981). *Voluntary agencies in the welfare state.* Berkeley, CA: University of California Press.

Light, P. (2000). *Making nonprofits work: A report on the tides of nonprofit management reform.* Washington, DC: Brookings Institution Press.

Lin, N. (2001). *Social capital.* Cambridge, UK: Cambridge University Press.

McConnell, G. (1966). *Private power and American democracy.* New York: Knopf.

Michael, S. (2002). *The role of NGOs in human security* (Working Paper #12). Cambridge, MA: The Hauser Center for

Nonprofit Organizations and The Kennedy School of Government, Harvard University.

Milward, H. (1994). Nonprofit contracting in the hollow state. *Public Administrative Review, 54,* 73–77.

Moroney, R. (1986). *Shared responsibility.* New York: Aldine.

Morris, R. (1986). *Rethinking social welfare: Why care for the stranger?* New York: Longman.

Nanetti, R. Y. (1980). From the top down: Government promoted citizen participation. *Journal of Voluntary Action Research, 9,* 149–164.

National Association of Social Workers. (2006). *Assuring sufficiency of a front-line workforce: A national study of licensed social workers.* Washington, DC: Center for Workforce Studies.

National Center for Charitable Statistics. (2007). Number of nonprofit organizations in the United States, 1996–2006. Retrieved August 2, 2007, from http://nccsdataweb.urbran.org.

Poole, D. L. (2003). Scaling up CBOs for second-order devolution in welfare reform. *Nonprofit Management & Leadership, 13,* 325–341.

Poole, D. L., & Negi, N. (2007). Transnational community enterprises for social welfare in global civil society. *International Journal of Social Welfare, 16,* Retrieved December 7, 2007.

Portes, A. (2000). The two meanings of social capital. *Sociological Forum, 15,* 1–12.

Portes, A., & Landolt, P. (1996). The downside of social capital. *American Prospect, 26,* 19–21.

Putnam, R. (1993). *Making democracy work: Civic traditions in modern Italy.* Princeton, NJ: Princeton University Press.

Putnam, R. (2000) *Bowling alone: The collapse and revival of American community.* New York: Simon & Schuster.

Salamon, L. M. (1997). *Holding the center: America's nonprofit sector at a crossroads.* New York: Nathan Cummings Foundation.

Salamon, L. M., Sokolowski, S. W., & List, R. (2003). *Global civil society: An overview.* Baltimore, MD: Center for Civil Society Studies, Johns Hopkins University.

Sandel, M. (1996). *Democracy's discontent: American in search of a public philosophy.* Cambridge, MA: Harvard University Press.

Skocpol, T. (1999). How Americans became civic. In T. Skocpol & M. Fiorina (Eds.), *Civic engagement in American democracy* (pp. 1–26). Washington, DC: Brookings Institution Press.

Skocpol, R., Ganz, M., & Munson, Z. (2000). A nation of organizers: The institutional origins of civic voluntarism in the United States. *American Political Science Review, 94,* 527–546.

Smith, D. H. (2000). *Grassroots associations.* Thousands Oak, CA: Sage.

Swanson, L. E. (2001). Rural policy and direct local participation: Democracy, inclusiveness, collective agency, and locality-based policy. *Rural Sociology, 66,* 1–21.

Tocqueville, A. D. (1990). *Democracy in America. 2 vols.* New York: Random House.

Tönnies, F. (1987). *Community and society* (Geminschaft und Gesellschaft). East Lansing, MI: Michigan State University.

Wehman, P., McLaughlin, P. J., & Wehman, T. (2005). *Intellectual and developmental disabilities: Toward full community inclusion.* (3rd ed.). Austin, TX: PRO-ED.

Wilensky, H. (1981). Foreword. In R. Kramer (Eds.), *Voluntary agencies in the welfare state* (pp. 14–22). New York: Free Press.

Zastrow, C. (2005). *Social work with groups: A comprehensive workbook* (6th ed.). Belmont, CA: Wadsworth.

—DENNIS L. POOLE

# VOTER EDUCATION

**ABSTRACT:** Scholars often refer to "American exceptionalism," meaning that unlike other rich, capitalist democracies, the United States has never had a strong working class political movement. One form of exceptionalism often overlooked in the academic literature on voting offers two strong explanations for this. Some scholars argue that the voting process has been encumbered by procedures that make actual voting difficult. Other scholars offer an alternative explanation that legal rights or not, the voters must be *mobilized* by political parties and other activist groups. This entry examines the dynamic interplay of electoral rules and political action to mobilize and demobilize the American electorate over the past 40 years.

**KEY WORDS:** politics; voter registration; voting

Scholars often refer to "American exceptionalism," meaning that unlike other rich, capitalist democracies, the United States has never had a strong working class political movement. Other differences seem to follow from this. The United States has a weaker welfare state, lower levels of unionism, and higher levels of inequality, and Americans are increasingly falling behind in earnings even while they also work longer hours than Europeans.

There still is another important difference. The United States has much lower levels of voter turnout (Jackman & Miller, 1995; Piven & Cloward, 2000; Powell, 1986). For example, between 1945 and 1999, the average turnout rate for national elections in the United States was 55.8%, compared to 74.6% in Canada, 76.4% in the United Kingdom, 76.7% in France, and 85.6% in Germany (Franklin, 2004, p. 11). Moreover, the class skew in the electorate toward the wealthiest segments of the population remains pronounced. Although 17 million more Americans voted for president in 2004 than in 2000, fewer than half of eligible voters with annual family incomes of $20,000 or less cast ballots, in contrast to 4 in 5 of those with family incomes of $100,000 or more (Holder, 2006, p. 4).

At first glance, this low voter participation seems anomalous. The legal right to vote has steadily expanded since the inception of the American republic. In the decades after the American Revolution the franchise was successively granted to unpropertied white men, then after the Civil War to African American men, and in 1920, to women. But parallel to this trend, there was another and reverse trend that began after Reconstruction in the closing decades of the 19th century. As the formal right to vote expanded, actual voter turnout as a percentage of that eligible population contracted.

The academic literature on voting offers two strong explanations of low voter turnout in the United States. Some scholars argue that, formal rights notwithstanding, the voting process has become encumbered by procedures that make actual voting difficult, including literacy tests, poll taxes, residence requirements, and a cumbersome and intimidating voter registration and balloting process (Piven & Cloward, 2000). Other scholars offer what is usually taken as an alternative explanation. Legal rights or not, the decision to vote is not automatic. Indeed, in a large polity where one vote cannot reasonably be thought to determine an election, it may not even be sensible to bother. Rather, the vote must be *mobilized*, and this task falls mainly on competing political parties (Rosenstone & Hansen, 1993; Schattschneider, 1960). Parties strive to win a majority of votes in order to control government. To this end, party operatives name the candidates and the programs, advance the cultural symbols, and then mount the advertising and door-knocking campaigns that they hope will draw a majority of voters to their line on the ballot.

Usually the role of procedural obstructions and mobilization efforts are treated as alternative explanations of nonvoting. In fact, obstructed access and partisan mobilization are closely interactive. People who are unlikely to vote because they are impeded and discouraged by the barriers created by registration and voting procedures are also unlikely to be targeted for mobilization by the parties. Moreover, if political events, such as successful reform efforts that liberalize voting procedures, or mobilization campaigns that successfully target those who are ordinarily less likely to vote, suddenly create the possibility that significant numbers of these people will in fact go to the polls, the opposing party that expects to be disadvantaged by these new voters is likely to try to introduce more restrictive procedures to encumber or reencumber the voting process, or to launch campaigns to demobilize rather than mobilize voters.

## The Origins of the Contemporary Conflict Over Election Procedures

The right to vote was a main rallying cry of the civil rights movement of the 1950s and 1960s, and the great achievement of the movement was the passage of the Voting Rights Act (VRA) of 1965. The pressures mounted by the movement included constitutional litigation, mass civil disobedience by African Americans in the South (and the mob violence by southern whites that the African American cause provoked), and protests and riots by African American northerners. Finally, the Congress removed the more obvious barriers to African American voting with the passage first in 1964 of the 24th Amendment outlawing poll taxes, and then in 1965, the VRA. Virtually overnight, millions of southern African Americans (as well as poor whites) became potential voters. In 1965, none of the majority African American counties in the South had majority African American electorates. The VRA authorized the use of federal registrars who were dispatched to the South to register African American voters. By 1968, nearly 40% of southern majority African American counties had majority African American electorates. By 1980, African American registration rates in the 11 states of the former confederacy were near equal to white rates (Alt, 1994).

At the same time, many African Americans were leaving the South for the cities of the North where they were generally eligible to vote. And so were growing numbers of Latinos migrating to these cities first from Puerto Rico, and then from Mexico and other Latin American countries. Demographic change combined with liberalized voting law and procedure to produce a huge and enlarging pool of potential voters. Changes were also occurring in voter mobilization. In fact, the events leading up to the passage of the VRA, and ensuring its implementation, included rising African American turnout, the result not of mobilization by either of the parties, but of the energy and passion of the civil rights movement and its local drives for the right to vote and get out the vote efforts.

As the VRA rapidly destroyed the legal foundation for a political system in the South that had at its core the purposeful disenfranchisement of African Americans, a new political system emerged in which African Americans were able to participate not only as voters but as candidates. There were fewer than 200 African American elected officials in the nation in 1965; since 2001, that number has increased to over 9,000 as a direct result of federal enforcement of the Act (Bositis, 2003; McDonald, 1992). The elimination of structural barriers to African American registration and voting was necessary and important in these gains.

But, the southern civil rights movement and the subsequent growth of African American politics — in the South and the rest of the nation — also stimulated a strong and effective conservative countermobilization. This movement began symbolically during the 1964 Goldwater campaign when then South Carolina Senator Strom Thurmond defected from the Democratic party. With the door closing on outright disenfranchisement, the movement of "massive resistance" to African American political equality shifted to what litigators refer to as "vote dilution" techniques designed to water down the inevitable gains in African American representation that structural reform would bring. These included the stepped up use of racial gerrymandering, the switch to at-large electoral schemes and to majority vote requirements from plurality-win rules, the conversion of elected to appointive offices, and changes in the qualification requirements for public office — all designed to thwart meaningful African American political representation (Parker, 1990).

### Mobilization in the Post–Civil Rights Era

As the civil rights movement waned, a countermobilization of voters was also inevitable, engineered in part by the resurgent Republican party. A Christian Right voter registration movement was undertaken, based mainly in Pentecostal and evangelical churches in the South and, to a lesser extent, in the Midwest, and led by white clergy members who wanted to reorient the Republican party. New religious–political organizations formed, such as the Moral Majority and the Religious Roundtable, which subsequently urged evangelical clergy members to adopt the tactics of the civil rights movement: make the church the staging area for political education, for voter registration drives, and for mass demonstrations and civil disobedience over issues such as reproductive rights (Guth, 1983; Liebman, 1983). The Moral Majority claimed that cooperating churches registered 4.4 to 8 million of these white evangelicals in the pre-1980 election period, although polls reported that they registered only between 1 and 2 million people (Piven & Cloward, 2000).

Competition for new voters intensified after the 1980 election, triggered in part by the recession of 1982. In the 1982 midterm election, a huge surge occurred in voting by African Americans, blue-collar workers, and the unemployed. In response to the highest unemployment since the Great Depression, midterm turnout rose for the first time in two decades, reaching 64 million, or 10 million more than in 1978, swelling the Democratic House vote by 6 million. The additional voters were mainly African American and unemployed people, and turnout was up most in the Midwest and South.

The sharp increase in blue-collar workers helped replace retiring Republican governors with Democrats in large industrial states such as Ohio, Michigan, New York, and Texas, as well as Wisconsin and New Mexico. At the same time, Republican incumbents were ousted in a number of economically hard-hit congressional districts, contributing to the Democrats' modest victory of 26 additional House seats (Edsall, 1984). Virtually every major political strategist began predicting that turnout would rise sharply in 1984, especially among "marginal groups" — poor people, people of color, and women. It was a time of "potentially historic significance" for the Democratic Party (Cook, 1983, p. 1503).

Christian Right leaders naturally worried that Reagan's prospects for victory in 1984 were endangered. Consequently, many of these leaders, including representatives of the Moral Majority and the Christian Voice, coalesced to launch a national umbrella organization, the American Coalition for Traditional Values. Its main goal was to register 2 million fundamentalist voters in 25 states. In a word, the largest voter registration mobilization in American history was forming in advance of the 1984 presidential election, whether measured by the money that would be spent, the number of organizations engaged, the variety of innovative approaches employed, or the number of people likely to be registered.

By election day 1984, 7 million new registrants had been added to the voter rolls. Still, more than 60 million remained unregistered (Human SERVE, 1990). This meant that the "hands-on" method of voter registration was not equal to the magnitude of the problem: too few volunteer canvassers, too many unregistered voters. Millions of unregistered low-income people and people of color could not be enrolled by volunteers. An institutional solution was needed.

### GOVERNMENT AGENCIES AS REGISTRATION SITES

The solution proposed was to permit people to register in a range of government agencies: Make voter registration a routine part of application procedures, whether in driver's license bureaus or food stamp offices. Government agencies could cope with the huge pool of unregistered voters; they could register all citizens regardless of race or income, thus overcoming class and racial skews; and they could reregister people after they moved.

In the fall of 1982, as ferment over voter registration spread, Frances Fox Piven and Richard A. Cloward formed Human SERVE (for Human Service Employees Registration and Voter Education) to promote this idea. Human SERVE found, despite the VRA, that powerful groups still opposed providing equal access to the vote by all citizens. Politicians were willing to make voter registration available in driver's license bureaus but not in public assistance offices where poor people and people of color were more likely to be found. By the late 1980s, Human SERVE had succeeded in winning motor voter programs in about 30 states.

The main opposition in the states and localities came from Republicans. They generally went along with motor voter initiatives but were adamantly opposed to human services voter registration. Public opinion surveys and exit polls strongly suggested that African American people were far and away the most Democratic (and the most progressive) constituency in the electorate, with Puerto Rican and Mexican American people not far behind. Many Democrats from White ethnic districts were also leery of registering welfare and food stamp recipients.

The federal government seemed the only hope, and Human SERVE campaigned for congressional legislation incorporating both motor voter and agency-based registration. That some state driver's license bureaus were already offering registration helped establish the precedent that government agencies should offer to register citizens to vote. Furthermore, this innovation originated at the state level, which meant that congressional opponents of reform could not argue that federal legislation would infringe on states' rights. In effect, federal legislation would simply nationalize a reform that had already spread widely among the states.

Human SERVE worked to get legislation introduced in both houses of Congress and helped mobilize a national coalition of civic, civil rights, labor, and kindred organizations, including those representing people with disabilities, to work for passage. Provisions for voter registration in human services agencies were the main stumbling block, and it was Republicans who were again in opposition. When a cloture motion finally survived in the spring of 1992, President George H. W. Bush vetoed the resulting bill—on the eve of Independence Day. A year later, however, after the bill survived another filibuster, this time for 11 days, Democratic president Bill Clinton signed the National Voter Registration Act (NVRA) of 1993 into law.

Following their takeover of the Congress in 1994, Republicans introduced bills to limit or defund the implementation of the Act. For example, on January 4, 1995, as the 104th Congress convened, Republicans introduced four bills to delay, repeal, or make the NVRA voluntary. Not surprisingly given the opposition, implementation of the agency-based provisions of the NVRA (Section 7) has been uneven at best. Immediately

following its passage, several states—including four big states outside the South, California, Illinois, Michigan, and Pennsylvania—resisted the new federal mandate to open up registration opportunities and challenged the law's constitutionality in court. Across the board, federal courts uniformly upheld the law, but have not gone further to establish mechanisms for monitoring compliance (U.S. General Accounting Office, 2001, pp. 5–7).

A recent study of Section 7 compliance found a huge fall-off in voter registration applications from public assistance agencies since the late 1990s (Kavanagh, Carbo, Mayo, & Slater, 2005). Compared to the first two years after the Act was implemented (1995–1996), applications from these agencies fell 60% by 2004, at the same time they increased 22% from all other NVRA-mandated sources. Although some proportion of the decline could be related to the rollback of welfare programs that began in 1996, the researchers' field work unearthed major failures in meeting federal mandates. For example, their report found public assistance agencies across the country failing to offer registration to clients changing their addresses, as required by NVRA; many did not offer registration to clients receiving services via phone, mail, or online; others were using inaccurate and outdated voter registration information and forms, jeopardizing their clients' registration status; some failed to offer bilingual registration applications and failed to use NVRA-mandated declination forms, and some were slow to process registration applications. Perhaps worse still are the widely reported problems in the processing of agency-based registration applications by state officials in time to qualify many low-income voters to participate in recent federal elections.

## Electoral Participation after the Contested 2000 Election

In the decade since Congress mandated full implementation, the hoped-for effects of NVRA are decidedly mixed. NVRA has had a discernible impact on voter registration, with the greatest effects in those states where there was no previous implementation of state motor voter programs (Brown & Wedeking, 2006; Martinez & Hill, 1999). However, to the dismay of reformers, NVRA has not met its goal of increasing voter turnout. This requires not only vigorous implementation of NVRA registration requirements, but that citizens go beyond registration to actually turnout on Election Day and that their votes are correctly counted. All of these issues surfaced during and after the contested 2000 election.

Advocates of voter registration reform in the 1970s and 1980s assumed, what a good deal of academic research confirmed, that "the registration laws in force throughout the United States are among the world's most demanding," and that "the restrictiveness of America's voter registration is one reason why voter turnout in the United States is near the bottom of the developed world" (Hansen, 2001, Part II, p. 3). By expanding registration opportunities, NVRA reduces registration "costs" to the voter, although full implementation of the Act would reduce costs far. The next step in this new "lower cost" political environment is to mobilize people to vote.

The last four federal elections demonstrate the growing importance of voter mobilization and demobilization for American politics. The 2000 election debacle in Florida revealed how parties, candidates, and their lawyers can demobilize voters, twisting and even defying electoral rules for partisan advantage (deHaven-Smith, 2005; Toobin, 2002; U.S. Commission on Civil Rights, 2001).

Since 2000, the policies of George W. Bush, who has been called "the most polarizing presidential candidate in modern political history" (Abramowitz & Stone, 2006, p. 142), helped drive up party competition, voter mobilization, and turnout in 2004 to the highest levels in nearly 40 years.

Turnout was also facilitated by groups of volunteers from both parties, armed with voter registration applications, walk lists, meet-up scripts, and handheld computers, who fanned out into the city streets, shopping malls, and church parking lots of America to register new voters and mobilize the base. Nonprofit and community-based organizations launched massive voter registration efforts claiming to sign up millions of new voters in anticipation of the election. The Republican strategy targeted 4 million evangelicals who were believed to have stayed home in 2000. The Democratic National Committee, led by former presidential candidate and grassroots Internet fund-raising innovator, Howard Dean, initiated a 50-state strategy to build get-out-the-vote operations across the country. Both parties relied on field-tested experimental research to design their outreach efforts. Both built sophisticated voter databases using data mining techniques borrowed from market research to link voters with their consumer profiles for pinpoint targeting campaigns (Balz & Edsall, 2004; Patterson, Monson, & Dennis, 2004).

Equally important was the stepped up use of vote suppression tactics by the Republicans, some familiar, others new, to demobilize minority and low-income voters (Davidson, Dunlap, Kenny, & Wise, 2004; Green, 2004). The use of these tactics expanded in the 2006 midterm elections and include race-based targeting of African American voter activists, misinformation campaigns and the distribution of erroneous election information in African American neighborhoods, the imposition of new restrictions on voter registration drives, strategically timed voter roll purges to cause confusion at the polls, and the widespread use of spurious voter fraud allegations to build support for the imposition of restrictive voter identification laws (Brennan Center for Justice, 2006; *The Long Shadow of Jim Crow*, n.d.). The new vote suppression continues the historical role of demobilization in the story of American democracy. The result today is an electorate that despite decades of structural reform continues to be one of the most unrepresentative among the advanced democracies.

## REFERENCES

Abramowitz, A. I., & Stone, W. J. (2006). The Bush effect: Polarization, turnout, and activism in the 2004 presidential election. *Presidential Studies Quarterly, 36*(2), 141–154.

Alt, J. E. (1994). The impact of the Voting Rights Act on black and white voter registration in the South. In C. Davidson & B. Grofman (Eds.), *Quiet revolution in the South: The impact of the Voting Rights Act, 1965–1990* (pp. 351–377). Princeton: Princeton University Press.

Balz, D., & Edsall, T. B. (2004, November 1). Unprecedented efforts to mobilize voters begin. *The Washington Post*, p. A1.

Bositis, D. A. (2003). *Black elected officials: A statistical summary, 2001*. Washington, DC: Joint Center for Political and Economic Studies. Available at http://www.jointcenter.org/publications1/publication-PDFs/BEO-pdfs/2001-BEO.pdf.

Brennan Center for Justice at NYU School of Law. (2006). *Cast out: New voter suppression strategies, 2006 and beyond*. Multimedia Presentation. Available at http://www.brennancenter.org/subpage.asp?key=413&tier3_key=38166.

Brown, R. D., & Wedeking, J. (2006). People who have their tickets but do not use them: "Motor Voter," registration, and turnout revisited. *American Politics Research, 34*(4), 279–504.

Cook, R. (1983, July 23). Reagan's legacy? "Have-not" surge to the polls: Major force in 1984 election. *Congressional Quarterly Weekly Report, 41*(29).

Davidson, C., Dunlap, T., Kenny, G., & Wise, B. (2004). *Republican ballot security programs: Vote protection or minority vote suppression—or both?* A Report to the Center for Voting Rights and Protection. Available at http://www.votelaw.com/blog/blogdocs/GOP_Ballot_Security_Programs.pdf.

deHaven-Smith, L. (2005). *The battle for Florida: an annotated compendium of materials from the 2000 presidential election*. Gainesville: University Press of Florida.

Edsall, T. B. (1984). *The new politics of inequality*. New York: Norton.

Franklin, M. N. (2004). *Voter turnout and the dynamics of electoral competition in established democracies since 1945*. New York: Cambridge University Press.

Green, J. (2004, October 29). DOJ actions on election law benefit republicans. *Southern Exposure*. Available at http://www.southernstudies.org/DOJVotingRights2.pdf.

Guth, J. L. (1983). Southern Baptist clergy: Vanguard of the Christian Right? In R. C. Liebman & R. Wuthnow (Eds.), *The new Christian Right: Mobilization and legitimation.* pp. 117–130. Hawthorne, NY: Aldine.

Hansen, J. M. (2001). Sizing the problem. Task force report. *To assure pride and confidence in the electoral process.* Washington, DC: National Commission on Election Reform.

Holder, K. (2006). *Voting and registration in the election of November 2004.* U.S. Census Bureau Current Population Reports. Washington, DC: U.S. Department of Commerce.

Human SERVE. (1990). Registration and voting. Human SERVE Fund Archives, Box 39, Folder 1842. New York: Columbia University, Rare Book and Manuscript Library.

Jackman, R. W., & Miller, R. A. (1995). Voter turnout in the industrial democracies during the 80s. *Comparative Political Studies, 27*(4), 467–492.

Kavanagh, B., Carbo, S., Mayo, L., & Slater, M. (2005 September). *Ten years later, a promise unfulfilled: The National Voter Registration Act in public assistance agencies, 1995–2005.* A Report by ACORN, Demos and Project Vote. Available at http://www.demos.org/pubs/NVRA91305.pdf.

Liebman, R. C. (1983). The making of the New Christian Right. In R. C. Liebman & R. Wuthnow (Eds.), *The new Christian Right: Mobilization and legitimation* (pp. 238–227). Hawthorne, NY: Aldine.

McDonald, L. (1992). The 1982 amendments of Section 2 and minority representation. In B. Grofman & C. Davidson (Eds.), *Controversies in minority voting: The Voting Rights Act in perspective.* Washington, DC: The Brookings Institution.

Martinez, M. D., & D. Hill. (1999). Did motor voter work? *American Politics Quarterly, 27*(3), 296–315.

Parker, F. R. (1990). *Black votes count: Political empowerment in Mississippi after 1965.* Chapel Hill: University of North Carolina Press.

Patterson, K. D., Monson, J. Q., & Dennis, J. M. (2004 Fall/Winter). A new politics for the new century? *Know Magazine, 1*(2). Available at http://www.knowledgenetworks.com/know/2004/fall/article7.pdf.

Piven, F. F., & Cloward, R. A. (2000). *Why Americans still don't vote, and why politicians want it that way.* Boston: Beacon Press.

Powell, G. B. (1986). American voter turnout in comparative perspective. *American Political Science Review, 80*(1), 17–43.

Rosenstone, S. J., & Hansen, J. M. (1993). *Mobilization, participation, and democracy in America.* New York: Macmillan.

Schattschneider, E. E. (1960). *The semisovereign people.* New York: Holt, Rinehart & Winston.

*The long shadow of Jim Crow: Voter intimidation and suppression in America today.* (n.d.). Special report of people for the American Way and the NAACP. Available at http://www.pfaw.org/pfaw/dfiles/file_462.pdf.

Toobin, J. (2002). *Too close to call: the thirty-six-day battle to decide the 2000 election.* New York: Random House.

U.S. Commission on Civil Rights. (2001). *Voting irregularities in Florida during the 2000 presidential election.* Washington, DC.

U.S. General Accounting Office. (2001 March). *Elections: The scope of Congressional authority in election administration* (GAO-01-047). Report to the Congress.

## SUGGESTED LINKS

Advancement Project.
*http://www.advancementproject.org*
American Civil Liberties Union Voting Rights Project.
*http://www.votingrights.org/*
Brennan Center for Justice at NYU School of Law.
*http://www.brennancenter.org*
Dēmos: A Network for Ideas and Action.
*http://www.demos.org*
Joint Center for Political and Economic Studies.
*http://jointcenter.org*
Lawyers Committee for Civil Rights Under Law.
*http://www.lawyerscommittee.org*
Leadership Conference on Civil Rights.
*http://www.civilrights.org*
NAACP Legal Defense Fund.
*http://www.naacpldf.org*
People For the American Way.
*http://www.pfaw.org*
Project Vote.
*http://www.projectvote.org*
U.S. Department of Justice, Civil Rights Division, Voting Section.
*http://www.usdoj.gov/crt/voting/index.htm*

—FRANCES FOX PIVEN AND LORRAINE C. MINNITE

# W

**WAGES.** *See* Employment and Unemployment; Human Needs; Work and Employment.

# WHITE ETHNIC GROUPS

**ABSTRACT:** Research on White ethnics is lacking in the diversity literature; when included, they are used as the comparison for other ethnic groups. Diversity exists among White ethnics; consequences of ignoring these differences include culturally insensitive and inappropriate treatment, misunderstanding clients, and poor therapeutic alliances. The heterogeneity within the White ethnic population and strategies for gaining cultural information and demonstrating cross-cultural effectiveness are discussed.

**KEY WORDS:** white ethnic; optional ethnicity; cultural values; acculturation; ethnic identity

Much of the diversity research ignores the heterogeneity in the White ethnic group by comparing other racial groups to "Whites," thus assuming all White ethnics are alike or ignoring them altogether (Alessandria, 2002; Moodley, 2007). Using Whites as a base group for comparisons in racial or ethnic identity research is problematic because of a lack of consensus on the definition of "White," the socioeconomic and cultural diversity among "Whites" and a varying range of privileges experienced by "Whites" (McDermott & Samson, 2005). The term White ethnic usually refers to people of European descent; however people of Middle Eastern and North African descent also belong to this group. Each White ethnic group has a unique set of values, traditions, religions, and languages. Although the experiences of White ethnics are qualitatively different from those of other ethnic minorities, the vast diversity within this group can influence attitudes toward practitioners and services (Ponterotto et al., 2001). Research has consistently indicated that ethnic identity continues to be salient and ethnicity related values persist beyond the first generation born in the United States (Carter & Parks, 1992; Papajohn, 1999; Ponterotto et al., 2001). The purpose of this entry is to build on Guzzetta's (1997) comprehensive description of White

ethnics by identifying contemporary issues and implications for culturally sensitive social work.

Waters's (1990; 2001) "Optional Ethnicity" concept suggests White ethnics can choose whether and when they want to identify with their ethnic group(s). Factors that influence and limit these choices include knowledge about ancestors, surname, socioeconomic status and education, information passed down through the family, recentness of immigration, resemblance to stereotypical ethnic characteristics, assumptions others make about ethnicity, and societal rankings of their group(s). Individuals' chosen affiliations may change over time and be more salient at different life stages. Identity development traditionally occurs during late adolescence/early adulthood; during this process individuals gain increased awareness of their ethnicity, particularly when transitioning from living in parents' homes to living on their own in ethnically heterogeneous environments (for example, dormitories or apartments). Ethnicity is salient when young couples have children and make conscious decisions about what children will be told about their heritage. A sense of knowing oneself ethnically has been noted to become more important as people age. The passing away of a loved one is another period when cultural traditions and beliefs are important. Often families draw on customs and values from the original and current cultures to provide a map for ceremonies (for example, funerals) and the grieving process as a whole (Safonte-Strumolo & Balaguer Dunn, 2000).

Although clients' issues are not necessarily caused by their cultural values, these values influence their experience of mental health issues, symptom expression (Papajohn, 1999), and willingness to trust mental health professionals (Baruth & Manning, 2003). White ethnics attitudes toward treatment are influenced by levels of acculturation, generation of immigration, language proficiency, age of immigration, gender, and socioeconomic status. Besides normal developmental issues, White ethnics may experience conflict between desires to maintain cultural values and pressure to adopt the majority culture's values and belief system. Acknowledging and exploring these values while incorporating clients' worldviews in treatment planning is critical in successfully addressing clients' concerns. Less acculturated individuals may have stronger preferences for ethnically similar counselors, particularly those of Italian and Greek descent (Ponterotto et al., 2001).

Clinicians working with families or couples need to understand the family's structure and should attend to intergenerational differences in values, reactions, and observances of cultural traditions to "design interventions . . . congruent with the relational and cultural values of the family" (Safonte-Strumolo & Balaguer Dunn, 2000, p. 339). Intracultural conflicts may occur because of different family of origin migration patterns and clients' resulting perceptions of their ethnic group's values (Softas-Nall & Baldo, 2000). For example, a Greek-American man whose parents immigrated in the 1920s and maintained traditional Greek values may have a different view of what it means to be Greek than his wife who was raised in contemporary Greece with modern values and traditions. These differences in cultural values may result in miscommunication and conflict within the couple or family. Cultural Genograms are a useful tool for understanding and conceptualizing clients' issues; intercultural relationships and each person's cultural background are identified to exemplify and clarify the influence of culture on the family system (Hardy & Laszloffy, 1995).

Jewish Americans are another population conceptualized as White ethnics. "[M]any nonobservant Jews still carry a strong sense of being outside mainstream American culture. . . . [D]espite appearances, Jews experience themselves as members of a minority culture" (Langman, 1995, p. 222). Practice suggestions include (a) examining one's own attitudes and feelings towards Jews, (b) understanding the basic subgroupings (that is, geographic origination such as Ashkenazic or Sephardic, and religious denominations such as Reform, Conservative, or Orthodox) and associated characteristics, and (c) learning about historic as well as current examples of anti-Semitism. Anecdotal reports indicate Jewish Americans tend to respond well to insight-oriented and group therapies. Research suggests that many Jews struggle with self-identification, difficulty with the integration of religious and cultural observances into their often secular lifestyles, feeling marginalized and experiencing discrimination; knowledge and sensitivity regarding these issues are necessary for culturally competent treatment (Friedman, Friedlander, & Blustein, 2005).

To assess the role of ethnicity and cultural values in presenting issues, competent practitioners must be able to: (a) hypothesize about client issues without making assumptions; (b) apply general characteristics of client cultures appropriately while acknowledging their individuality and avoiding stereotyping; (c) and understand the social, historical, and political contexts that led to clients' presence in the United States, and their experiences in their settlement areas (Arredondo et al., 1996; Hays, 2001), especially when clients have recently immigrated (Alessandria, 2002; Richmond, 2003). Questions to access this information include: (a) Who immigrated? When? Why?, (b) Where did they settle?, (c) What has life been like for the client's cultural group in the new country? In the country of origin?, (d) What has life been like for this particular individual or family?

Hays' (2001) ADDRESSING (Age and generational influences, Developmental and acquired Disabilities, Religion and spiritual orientation, Ethnicity, Socioeconomic status, Sexual orientation, Indigenous heritage, National origin, and Gender, p. 16) framework is an effective tool for gathering information and understanding clients in their unique social and historical contexts. These characteristics provide insight into the cultural influences in clients' lives, their worldviews, and their effects on clients' presenting problems. Information from multiple sources should be gathered to effectively assess client issues (for example, schools, parents, family members, healthcare providers, client's age, and development in relation to historical events, et cetera). Timelines of significant events in the client's life related to culture and of the immigration process provide useful information. When language barriers are present interpreters should be employed. Clients' culturally related strengths and support systems should be incorporated into treatment.

Although many White ethnic clients can choose to "pass" as members of the majority, the significance of ethnicity in clients' lives cannot be determined by appearances alone. In learning about each client's unique story it is suggested that practitioners be particularly diligent in exploring the role of ethnic and cultural values in presenting problems. Building a strong therapeutic relationship through empathy, genuineness, unconditional positive regard, and respect is imperative for culturally sensitive treatment (Alessandria, 2002).

## REFERENCES

Alessandria, K. P. (2002). Acknowledging white ethnic groups in multicultural counseling. *The Family Journal: Counseling and Therapy for Couples and Families, 10*(1), 57–60.

Arredondo, P., Toporek, R., Brown, S. P., Jones, J., Locke, D. C., Sanchez, J., et al. (1996). Operationalization of the multicultural counseling competencies. *Journal of Multicultural Counseling and Development, 24*, 42–48.

Baruth, L. G., & Manning, M. L. (2003). *Multicultural counseling and psychotherapy: A lifespan perspective* (3rd ed.). Upper Saddle River, NJ: Merrill Prentice Hall.

Carter, R. T., & Parks, E. E. (1992). White ethnic group membership and cultural value preferences. *Journal of College Student Development, 33*, 499–506.

Friedman, M. L., Friedlander, M. L., & Blustein, D. L. (2005). Toward an understanding of Jewish identity: A phenomenological study. *Journal of Counseling Psychology, 52,* 77–83.

Guzzetta, C. (1997). White ethnic groups. In R. L. Edwards & J. G. Hopps (Eds.), *Encyclopedia of social work supplement* (19th ed.). Washington, DC: National Association of Social Workers Press. Retrieved July 12, 2007 from The Social Work Reference Library CD-Rom.

Hardy, K. V., & Laszloffy, T. A. (1995). The cultural genogram: Key to training culturally competent family therapists. *Journal of Marital and Family Therapy, 21,* 227–237.

Hays, P. A. (2001). *Addressing cultural complexities in practice.* Washington, DC: American Psychological Association.

Langman, P. F. (1995). Including jews in multiculturalism. *Journal of Multicultural Counseling and Development, 23,* 222–236.

McDermott, M., & Samson, F. L. (2005). White racial and ethnic identity in the United States. *Annual Review of Sociology, 31,* 245–261.

Moodley, R. (2007). (Re)placing multiculturalism in counseling and psychotherapy (Electronic version). *British Journal of Guidance and Counselling, 35,* 1–22.

Papajohn, J. C. (1999). *The hyphenated American: The hidden injuries of culture.* Westport, CT: Greenwood Press.

Ponterotto, J. G., Rao, V., Zweig, J., Rieger, B. P., Schaefer, K., Michelakou, S., et al. (2001). The relationship of acculturation and gender to attitudes toward counseling in Italian and Greek American college students (Electronic version). *Cultural Diversity and Ethnic Minority Psychology, 7,* 362–375.

Richmond, L. J. (2003). Counseling European Americans. In F. D. Harper & J. McFadden (Eds.), *Culture and counseling: New approaches* (pp. 133–146). New York: Allyn & Bacon.

Safonte-Strumolo, N., & Balaguer Dunn, A. (2000). Consideration of cultural and relational issues in bereavement: The case of an Italian American family *The Family Journal: Counseling and Therapy for Couples and Families, 8,* 334–340.

Softas-Nall, B. C., & Baldo, T. D. (2000). Dialogues within a Greek family: Multicultural stories of a couple revisited. *The Family Journal: Counseling and Therapy for Couples and Families, 8,* 396–398.

Waters, M. C. (1990). *Ethnic options: Choosing identities in America.* Berkeley, CA: University of California Press.

Waters, M. C. (2001). Optional ethnicities: For whites only? In M. L. Andersen & P. H. Collins (Eds.), *Race class and gender: An anthology* (pp. 430–439). Belmont, CA: Wadsworth/Thompson Learning.

### SUGGESTED LINKS

Fort Gordon Equal Opportunity Office: White American Experience.
*http://www.gordon.army.mil/eoo/white.htm*
SAMHSA Office of Applied Studies.
*http://www.oas.samhsa.gov/race.htm*
Surgeon General's Report—Mental Health: Culture, Race, Ethnicity.
*http://mentalhealth.samhsa.gov/cre/default.asp*

—KATHRYN P. ALESSANDRIA

**WOMEN.** [*This entry contains three subentries:* Overview; Practice Interventions; Health Care.]

### OVERVIEW

**ABSTRACT:** This overview entry introduces the topic of women, beginning with general demographic information. The section on poverty and inequality, which follows, describes the gender differences and delineates some reasons why women are poor and unequal. Issues of childcare, welfare, and education are explored. Domestic violence and sexual assault are discussed, followed by a discussion of health and mental health issues affecting women. The role of women in politics is briefly explored. The entry concludes with a discussion of current trends and challenges, including implications for social justice.

**KEY WORDS:** abortion; abstinence education; domestic violence; feminism; feminization of poverty; marriage promotion; patriarchy; rape; temporary assistance for needy families

Because women comprise 51% of the United States population, all issues—war and peace, foreign aid and international development, environment and global warming, civil liberties and constitutional separation of powers—are of concern to women, as they are to men. This entry on *women's issues,* however, focuses on those issues that concern women most directly and that male-dominated policymaking bodies have frequently neglected or considered of secondary importance. As House Speaker Pelosi said recently, ". . . regarding those issues usually identified with women...I guess they're called women's issues because if women did not focus on them there really wouldn't be any chance of [getting something done]." (Coco, 2007, p. 37). Only recently, for example, has the National Institute of Health required researchers to include women as subjects in testing new drugs and other medical interventions.

"Women" are not a monolithic group. Differences in race, ethnicity, class, age, and sexual orientation are often as important as gender differences. Many women's issues have implications for social justice, a key value for social workers, including inequality, economic and sexual exploitation, violence, lack of choice, and powerlessness.

### General Demographics

The total population of the United States in 2005 was 288,378,137, with a female population of 147,103,173 and a male population of 141,274,964 (U.S. Census Bureau, 2005a). The sex ratio of males to females is 96; that is, for every 100 women in the United States there were a little over 96 men. However, the gender ratio varies considerably over the life cycle. More male than female children are born. For children under 5 years, boys represent 7.3% of the population in comparison with 6.7% for girls. This difference diminishes and the two sexes are about equal in early adulthood and midlife, until age 50, when the male population begins to decline in comparison to females. Between ages 5 and 14, 13.4% are girls and 14.6% are boys. But by 75 years and over, women represent 6.8% of the total population to only 5.7% for men, a difference of over 3 million more women than men (U.S. Census Bureau, 2005a).

This ratio varies by race and ethnicity. For African Americans in 2000 with a total population of 34,658,190, the male to female ratio was only 90.5; for Asians, with a total population of 10,242,998, it was 93.5; for American Indians and Alaska Natives it was 99.4, but for Latinos and Latinas, with a total 2000 population of 35,305,818, the male to female ratio was 105.9 (U.S. Census, 2000). These numbers exclude those who identify with more than one race.

### Poverty and Inequality

Women continue to suffer from economic inequality. The term *feminization of poverty*, introduced in the late 1970s, identified the phenomenon that poverty was increasingly a problem for women—that there was an increasing disparity in income for women and men (Pearce & McAdoo, 1981). Although the gap between men's and women's earnings has decreased since 1970, when the National Organization for Women distributed buttons emblazoned with "59 cents," the average median annual earnings ratio of women working full-time, full-year, compared with $1 earned by men, women are still paid less. Now they earn 77 cents for every dollar earned by men. In 2006 women working full-time, full year earned $31,800 annually compared with men's earnings of $41,300 (Institute for Women's Policy Research News, 2006). The Federal Equal Pay Law passed in 1963 requires equal pay for equal work, but most women are confined to "pink collar jobs," that is, jobs in a gender-segregated labor market. These include not only low-skilled jobs such as waitresses, cashiers, and retail clerks, but also professional jobs such as teachers and social workers. The 2004 average salary of social workers who were NASW (National Association of Social Workers) members (most of whom had an MSW) was $51,192. The proportion of women in NASW has consistently increased, and by 2004, was 81% of all members. Jobs and professions in which women predominate are consistently lower paid than those in which men predominate. But even within these "female" professions, women are consistently paid

less than men. The difference in average salaries for men and women social workers in 2004 was over $12,000; women earned an average of $48,995 and men earned $61,040. Even after controlling for various factors, the gender gap was 14% (Center for Workforce Studies, 2006, pp. 3–4).

Divorce rates have leveled off since the 1979s and 1980s, but almost 18% of all families in the United States, 14,018,712 families, are headed by women, with an average of 2 children (U.S. Census Bureau, 2005b). Between 1990 and 2000, there was a 25% increase in female-headed families. In 2000, for the first time, lesbian and gay households were enumerated and between 2 and 5% of all households were of same-sex partners. In households headed by lesbian couples, 23% included a child under age 18 (Seager, 2003, p. 20).

In 2005, 10.2% of all families fell below the poverty level. For married couples that figure was only 5%, but for female-headed families it was 29.4% and for those with children under 18 years it was 37.7% (as compared with 6.9% for married-couples with children under 18. The disparity is even greater for families of color. Over 37% of African American female-headed families fell below the poverty level, as did 38.9% of Latina families, and over 38% of American Indian and Alaska Native female-headed families. Asian female-headed families did slightly better at 19.7%, but still far below that of two-parent families (U.S. Census Bureau, 2005c, S1702).

CHILDCARE An important factor affecting women's earnings is that women have primary responsibility for the care of children. Women who bear children may take time from paid work, but an ever greater number return to the labor market when their children are young, many working part-time. The longer women are out of the labor force, the lower their lifetime earnings are likely to be. Because the United States is the only developed nation that has no state-sponsored childcare, women who cannot afford childcare either cannot join the labor market or do so during hours when their children are in school. In 2001, 23.6% of mothers with infants worked full-time and 15.7% worked part-time year-round. The figure was higher for nonpoor mothers and considerably lower for poor mothers (Lovell, 2003).

Limited federal funds are available for childcare under the Childcare and Development Fund, which merged funding streams from the Child Development Block Grant, Aid to Families with Dependent Children, and Transitional and At-Risk Child Care into the Personal Responsibility and Work Opportunity Reconciliation Act (PRWORA) of 1996. In the past, under the Family Support Act of 1988, women on welfare who were required to work were guaranteed childcare. Funding was also available through the Title XX Block Grant, but that funding has decreased since the era of President Reagan. Under the Childcare and Development Fund, which provides for childcare for poor women, for women on welfare and for those transitioning off welfare, the total annual amount is $5 billion. The amount of funding is grossly inadequate to meet the need. Not only are more women and women with younger children required to work under the new welfare provisions, but since the passage of the PRWORA of 1996, there has been no increase in childcare funding, even to keep up with inflation. At the same time, Title XX funding was decreased with the provision that some of the funding for Temporary Assistance to Needy Families (TANF) could be used for childcare instead of solely for financial aid to welfare recipients.

In two-partner families, which tend to have higher incomes, one of the parents may be available for childcare or the family may be more likely able to afford to pay for childcare. The percentage of mothers working full-time increases with the age of the youngest child. School often becomes the "babysitter" for school-age children. If the children are sick or disabled, women may lose their jobs when they take time off to care for them. Although the National Family Leave Act of 1993 provides parents the right to family leave for the birth, adoption, or illness of a child or other family member, it does not provide paid leave, and the Act does not cover companies with fewer than 50 employees, where many low-paid women work.

## TEMPORARY ASSISTANCE FOR NEEDY FAMILIES

Because female-headed families have one, rather than two earners, they usually must fill the dual roles of the sole caregiver as well as provider. In 1996, AFDC was eliminated and replaced by Temporary Assistance for Needy Families (TANF), Title I of the PRWORA. This legislation represents the culmination of a major shift in our nation's ideology regarding the role of mothers. TANF explicitly promotes self-sufficiency, marriage, and the reduction of unwed pregnancies, and emphasizes a "work first" strategy.

Recently, a trend seems to have developed for many educated, higher income mothers in two-parent families to choose to opt out of the workforce while their children are young. The popular literature has emphasized the importance of good childrearing and intellectual stimulation for the healthy early development of children. Yet, the national attitude, which has always stigmatized women on welfare, does not acknowledge the need for mothers on welfare to stay at home to raise their young children. TANF legislation requires mothers with infants as young as 3 months to "work first," up to 30 hours a week, as though caring for an infant is not work. A 5-year lifetime maximum on aid, work or work-seeking activities required after 3 months, and financial sanctions to states administering the program that do not meet the required percentages of participants in work activities, all push mothers with very young children into the workplace and off TANF.

Between 1994 and 2005 the caseload on welfare decreased by over 50%, but not all those mothers leaving TANF improved their lives. Among those who obtained jobs, the average hourly pay was slightly over $7, not enough to bring a family of three up to the poverty level. Not all former recipients obtained work. And even among those who did, many of the jobs were temporary. One study found that over 50% of TANF leavers who were employed were living below the poverty line (Peterson, Song, & Jones-DeWeaver, 2002). Food banks around the country are now finding that larger proportions of those seeking food are employed.

Over one quarter of all low-income families have at least one child with a disability, but the more stringent rules in the reauthorized 2005 TANF legislation make it more difficult for mothers of such children to receive waivers from work requirements or from the 5-year lifetime limit, and more stringent Supplemental Security Income guidelines for disabled children make it more difficult to receive financial aid from that source.

Although the child support provisions in the PRWORA have increased child support payments, no support collections have been collected for almost half of mothers who have sought support through the federal Office of Child Support Enforcement. Over $102 billion is owed to custodial parents, and about 25% of those not receiving child support to which they are entitled are poor. If TANF recipients refuse to cooperate by naming the father and providing information as to his whereabouts, they may be deemed ineligible for assistance (U.S. Department of Health and Human Services, 2006). Marriage promotion is one of the most contentious features of TANF. In the 1995 TANF Reauthorization $150 million was set aside for Healthy Marriage Promotion grants to the states and Demonstration Project grants to public and private groups, including religious entities. This legislation may have the effect of coercing women to marry and may stigmatize and discriminate against lesbians and other women who do not seek to marry. Because no new dollars were added to the 2005 Reauthorization, funds for these marriage promotion initiatives are being diverted from other services available through TANF such as financial assistance, childcare, training, or case management. Most disturbingly, it legitimates a specific ideological agenda by imposing these promarriage values on vulnerable, poor women. Linked to "healthy marriage" promotion is the promotion of abstinence for unmarried women. States have the initiative of requiring instruction for welfare recipients in abstinence, healthy marriage, and premarital and marital counseling.

One of the options states can implement is the "family cap." Under this provision, states may eliminate any increase in aid if a woman has another child while receiving TANF. The rationale for this is that if a woman cannot afford to support another child, she should not have one. In reality the assistance she receives, already meager, now has to stretch to cover an additional member of the household.

EDUCATION Traditionally, education has been a source of mobility for Americans. Those with a high school education earn more than those who have not completed high school, those with college earn more and those with a graduate degree earn substantially more. People of color (except Asians) are less likely than Whites to have college degrees. Nevertheless, TANF, since its inception in 1996, consistent with its "work first" approach, first prohibited higher education and then limited it to one year, and only for a small proportion of those on state TANF rolls.

Despite these restrictions, a few states developed creative ways to enable women to obtain a college education. One of the most innovative of these was the Maine "Parents as Scholars" program, which used the state's matching funds to provide continuing financial assistance for recipients attending college after the first year allowable under TANF funding.

In the 2005 TANF Reauthorization, higher education for a maximum of 1 year is allowable, after 20 hours of other "core" work activities. For many mothers of young children with childcare and transportation problems, this is not feasible. Moreover, any educational activities require daily supervision, which may pose administrative difficulties for the local welfare offices. These new federal regulations also put additional restrictions on the use of state matching funds, putting the Parents as Scholars program in jeopardy. Rationally, it would seem that government policy would encourage more education for welfare recipients, as the higher a woman's education level, the higher her earning, the less likely her need for welfare, or if on welfare, the shorter her stay on it, and once off, the less likely her return (Brandwein, 1999).

It is particularly important for women to achieve a higher educational level because of disparities in earning levels between men and women. Males without a high school degree earned a median income in 2005 of $22,138, compared with only $13,076 for females; for those with high school degrees the comparable figures were $31,683 for males and $20,179 for females, one-third less. With a bachelors degree men earned $53,693 as compared with $36,250 for women. A woman needs a college degree to earn slightly more than a man with a high school degree (U.S. Census Bureau, 2005d). Inequality also exists among different groups of women. White women with a four-year college degree earn a median annual income of $37,600, Asian women $39,000, African American women $35,000, Latina women $34,000, and Native American women only $31,00 (Werschkul, 2005).

AGING AND SOCIAL SECURITY Women who were poor when young will be poor when they are old. The average median income for women over 65 years in 1998–2000 from earnings was $8450, compared with $14,780 for men. Twelve percent of female household heads over 65 years lived below the poverty level. Because women earn less and tend to work fewer years because of childrearing responsibilities when they are younger, when they retire their Social Security payments are less; women receive an average of $7,750 annually, compared with $11,040 for men (U.S. Census Bureau, 2005c; Hartmann & Lee, 2003). Moreover, women are less likely to have worked for employers providing pensions, or have not worked long enough or enough hours to be eligible for a pension, so that more women rely on Social Security as their only or primary source of retirement income. Because women have a longer life span, whatever savings or investments they may have accrued must last longer. Therefore, many women over 65 years remain in the labor force. Some prefer to, but many find they must continue to be employed in order to supplement their often meager Social Security income. Because of continued age as well as sex discrimination, women over 50 frequently find it difficult to find employment except in low-paid, low-skilled jobs.

**Sexual Assault and Domestic Violence**

In 1994 Congress passed the Violence Against Women Act, for the first time providing recognition and funding for sexual assault, domestic violence, and stalking against women. Since then the Act has been reauthorized and strengthened twice. It funds training for police officers and court officials, for battered women's shelters, rape crisis clinics, elder abuse, and a myriad of other services, including prevention and education. It has also strengthened laws regarding interstate stalking, provides for refugee status for undocumented immigrants who are domestic violence victims, and provides special funding to combat domestic violence, sexual assault, and stalking on Native American tribal lands.

**RAPE** Many states have now substituted the term *sexual assault* for *rape*. In 2005 there were 191,670 reported cases of rape (or sexual assault) or attempted rape in the United States (U.S. Bureau of Justice Statistics, 2005). These are the reported cases, but this crime is still underreported because of stigma or an all-too-often well-founded fear of "blaming the victim."

Rape is any coerced sexual act, including but not limited to sexual intercourse, even between married couples. It has been only since the second wave of the women's movement that marital rape has been recognized as a crime. Date rape, which has also been recognized as rape only recently, is sexual assault by someone known to the victim.

It is estimated that 1 of 4 girls is a victim of sexual abuse, which includes fondling and exposure to pornographic material as well as intercourse. Girls who have been victimized in this way may experience both short- and long-term effects. Among the long-term effects may be posttraumatic stress disorder, sexual acting out and promiscuity (which can result in teen pregnancy), and a higher risk for being a victim of domestic violence.

**DOMESTIC VIOLENCE** Domestic violence, also called intimate partner violence, is defined as actions causing deliberate harm to an intimate partner. The National Crime Survey, which records only physical violence that has been reported to police, reports that over 2 million women each year are victims of abuse by intimate partners. These figures do not include psychological or emotional abuse, which usually precedes and almost always accompanies physical abuse, nor do they include financial abuse. Other sources have estimated that as many as 3–4 million women are abused annually and that half of all women will experience some form of domestic violence at least once in their lifetime (Wallace, 2005). Stalking has only recently been recognized as a crime, and if committed by an intimate partner it is another form of domestic violence. Sexual abuse, especially marital rape, is often unreported. Women still may be stigmatized or blamed when reporting rape, and despite the fact that marital rape can be criminally prosecuted, many women may be unaware of that (Wallace, 2005).

In adjudicating cases of domestic violence, most courts define it only to cover those married, related by blood, or having a child in common. This excludes dating couples, cohabiting homosexual and heterosexual couples, and childless divorced couples. Many reasons have been offered for why women stay in abusive relationships but the most compelling ones are economic dependence and fear. Three quarters of all murders by intimate partners occur after women leave relationships or seek restraining orders. Thirty percent of all female homicides are committed by their intimate partners (U.S. Department of Justice, 2001).

Although domestic violence occurs in all racial, ethnic, age, and income groups, abuse and the most severe violence are more prevalent among the poor. In the late 1990s, simultaneously with the passage of TANF legislation, a spate of research documented the link between domestic violence, poverty, and the use of welfare. Welfare can provide the economic support for women leaving a domestic violence situation. One survey found that 60% of women on public assistance reported sexual and physical abuse by intimate partners. A study in another state found that over 57% had experienced physical abuse. Another study on a random sample of recipients in still another state found that 19.5% were currently in abuse situations, with 64% having experienced intimate partner violence as adults (Albelda & Withorn, 2002; Allard et.al., 1997; Brandwein, 1999; Curcio, 1997; Raphael, 1996; Raphael & Tolman, 1997).

A majority of states have chosen the Domestic Violence Option, a provision of TANF legislation that allows applicants and recipients to identify themselves as domestic violence victims. This makes them eligible for screening, referrals, and the possibility of obtaining waivers for the work requirement, the time limit for assistance, and child custody reporting requirements if they or their children are found to be at risk. The number of women identifying themselves has been considerably less than what the data show to be victims. This may be due to the reluctance of women to so identify, fearing they may be at risk of losing custody of their children In March 2002 a federal judge found, in the Nicholson lawsuit, that New York City should not remove children from parents because the parent was a victim of domestic abuse or could not prevent her child from witnessing the abuse (Kaufman, 2003). Another explanation for the underuse of the Domestic Violence Option may be the reluctance of some welfare staff to encourage its use, believing women will use it as a ploy to evade TANF requirements.

**MENTAL HEALTH** Survivors of domestic violence, as well as child abuse, and particularly sexual abuse, have been found to be at risk for both mental and physical health problems. Post-traumatic stress disorder, a *DSM-IV* diagnosis, was originally found in survivors of war. Women living for years in domestic violence situations, as well as children victimized by sexual abuse, are in similar situations. Girls who have experienced sexual abuse, especially over a long period, by a close family member or accompanied by violence are most likely to suffer a variety of symptoms, including depression, eating disorders, and sexual acting out. Sexually acting-out girls are more likely to be promiscuous, and are at risk of becoming unwed mothers in adolescence. They may be more likely to enter into a domestic violence situation with a boyfriend or husband. There is also a high incidence of child and domestic abuse occurring simultaneously within the same family.

Women survivors of domestic violence often suffer from depression, a lack of self-esteem, isolation from support systems, and a feeling of helplessness, resulting from the coercive control by their partners. Until recently such women were often misdiagnosed with other mental illnesses.

The majority of mental health clients are women, but this may be because women are more likely to seek help than are men. Recently, feminist researchers have begun to empirically explore the efficacy of different approaches to treatment for women and men. Feminist therapy, utilizing feminist principles of egalitarian relationships and the importance of developing a trusting relationship between therapist and client are consistent with social work values.

## Health

Health is an issue for women of all ages and ethnicities. Young women have the need for reproductive health choices, and prenatal and postnatal care. One of nine American women will face breast cancer in their lifetime. Regular breast examinations and mammograms, as well as regular pap smears to test for uterine cancer, are important preventive measures for all women. Although more White than African American women are diagnosed with breast cancer (116 versus 12 per 100,000), African American women have a higher death rate (31 versus 24 per 100,000) (American Cancer Society, 2002). Older women are at increased risk for other cancers as well as breast cancer, heart disease, and osteoporosis. Type II diabetes, previously known as adult-onset diabetes, is reaching epidemic proportions, especially among the Native American, Latino and Latina, and African American communities. It is particularly associated with poverty.

The use of contraceptives for the spacing of births is healthier for both mothers and infants, and condoms are also effective in preventing AIDS and other sexually transmitted diseases. At its onset in the United States, AIDS was predominantly found in the White, male, gay, and bisexual population. Now, the proportion of women with AIDS, especially women of color, has dramatically increased. Of all American women with AIDS, 60% are African American, as opposed to 22% who are White. In contrast, 34% of men with AIDS are African American and 49% are White (U.S. Department of Health and Human Services, 2000). Despite these health concerns, the federal government, in 2006, spent $176 million for abstinence-only education and the law prohibits programs accepting these funds from advocating contraceptive use.

Abortion becomes a health issue if legal abortions are unavailable. Currently half of all pregnancies in the United States are unintended and 40% of these end in abortion. Economically disadvantaged women account for 57% of all abortions in the nation. By the age of 18, 60% of all teenage women have had sexual intercourse, 750,000 become pregnant, and a fourth of these pregnancies end in abortion (Boonstra, 2007).

A majority of those on Medicaid are women; over 70% of those over 15 years are women. Nevertheless, only 15% of low-income women are covered by Medicaid (Kaiser Family Foundation, 2006). Almost all recipients of TANF, who are also Medicaid-eligible, are women with young children. The poor elderly, the majority of whom are women, are also Medicaid-eligible, as are the disabled who qualify for Supplemental Security Insurance. Medicaid covers 70% of all nursing home care. When poor seniors are discussed, more often these seniors are women. Medicare, the federal health insurance program for those over 65 years, also covers more women, as their life expectancy is longer than men's.

The number of Americans without health care continues to rise. Women who are poorer and tend to work in jobs without benefits are less likely to have employment-related health insurance. African Americans and Latinos and Latinas are 2–3 times as likely to be without health insurance as are non-Latino or Latina Whites (19.7%, 32.7%, and 11.3%, respectively) (Center for Budget and Policy Priorities, 2005).

## Policies and Politics

Political progress for women has been a mixed picture.

RECENT AND PENDING LEGISLATION The Family and Medical Leave Act was first passed by Congress but vetoed by the first President Bush. This was one of the first bills signed by President Clinton when he took office. The bill provides for up to 3 months of unpaid leave for either parent for the birth, adoption, or care of a child or other family member. It only applies to workplaces with 50 or more employees. It guarantees the same or similar job upon return from leave. Although this is an important first step, it is of little help to poorer families, particularly female-headed ones, and for those working for small firms. In contrast, most developed nations provide for paid family leave of up to 1 year.

In 1996, the federal entitlement of aid to poor mothers was eliminated and replaced with TANF. This is a block grant, which has been capped since 1996 and can be used for services as well as financial assistance. While few would argue with the concept that fathers should take responsibility for their families, The Responsible Fatherhood Act of 2003 supports the conservative agenda of using the federal government to promote one particular type of family—the traditional two-parent, patriarchal heterosexual family. This approach was reinforced in the TANF reauthorization with its funding for "healthy marriage promotion."

Recently, a few states have recognized either same sex marriage or same sex civil unions. In reaction, attempts are being made in Congress to pass a Constitutional amendment that would prohibit such laws, and several states now have such exclusionary legislation. The federal Defense of Marriage Act, passed in 1996, stipulates that such unions in one state may not be recognized in others. Many lesbians are in long-term, stable relationships but without legal protections for health decisions, inheritance, or Social Security benefits. These are but a few of the many rights denied to same-sex couples.

After considerable controversy, a law making RU486, a nonsurgical abortifacent, available in the United States was passed in 2000, enabling women easier access for terminating pregnancies. A woman's right to abortion was confirmed in the *Planned Parenthood v. Casey* decision, but the current Supreme Court may support further challenges, chipping away at *Roe v. Wade*.

WOMEN IN GOVERNMENT Women continue to make progress in elected and appointed governmental offices on the local, state, and national levels. The most historic development occurred in 2006, when with a new Democratic majority in the House of Representatives, Nancy Pelosi was named the first woman Speaker of the House in our nation's history. This is particularly significant as that office is second in line, after the Vice President, to succeed the President. In early 2007, Hillary Clinton declared that she was a candidate for President in the 2008 election. If nominated, she will be the first woman from a major political party to be a Presidential candidate. Three states, California,

Maine, and Washington, currently have two women Senators each. After the 2006 election, the total number of women in the Senate was 16 and 71 in the House of Representatives. Although these numbers represent major gains for women, they are only 16% of the Senate and only 18% of the House, in contrast to 51% of the total population. At the local level, women were mayors in 21% of cities with populations over 30,000 (Center for American Women and Politics, 2006). As of 2005, there were six female social workers in Congress, two of them in the Senate. A total of 109 female social workers held elective office at the federal, state, or local levels (National Association of Social Workers, 2007).

A number of women's organizations have been active in politics. Emily's List has provided millions for prochoice women candidates for public office. The National Organization for Women, Planned Parenthood, and other organizations advocating for women have political action committees, and NASW—four fifth of whose members are women—has made electing social workers a priority and has an active political action committee.

### Trends and Challenges

Women's issues are not the same as feminist issues, and currently there are several approaches to feminism. The second wave of feminism emerged in the 1960s with the publication of Friedan's *The Feminine Mystique* in 1963 and the creation of the National Organization for Women in 1960 (the first wave was the 19th-century suffragists). Liberal feminists sought equality of opportunity before the law. These feminists claimed that women and men were inherently equal and fought for women's equality, especially in education and employment. Radical feminists began with the concept of patriarchy, believing that women are oppressed as a group. They promoted a separate women's culture and lesbian rights. Social feminists linked class and racial oppression with sexual oppression (Jagger & Struhl, 1978). The third wave of feminists, emerging in the 1990s, criticized second wave feminists as "essentialists," that is, assuming a universal feminist identity. It has integrated postmodernist theory, queer theory, and "womanism," maintaining that different feminisms apply to different groups of women. Applied to social policy and social work practice, this approach deconstructs meaning, focuses on the social and cultural context, and uses a feminist lens to understand women's "reality" (Van Den Bergh, 1995).

Since the Reagan era of the 1980s, the conservative social agenda has challenged many of the rights women fought for during the second wave of the women's movement in the 1960s and 1970s. Affirmative action has been limited by the Supreme Court in certain cases. A women's right to choose an abortion continues to be challenged with limitations on late term abortion, requirements of parental consent and sanctions for anyone but a parent taking a minor over state lines for the purpose of obtaining an abortion. The principle of privacy underlying *Roe v. Wade* is itself being challenged. Marriage promotion and "responsible fatherhood" challenge women's rights to live and raise their children independently. The "abstinence only" policies of the Bush administration, limiting aid for family planning within the United States and in foreign aid is a further assault to women's rights to make their own sexual decisions. It deprives women of information about other means of contraception, endangering their physical and mental health. Recent studies have found that abstinence education is not effective in preventing sexual activity or pregnancy (Boonstra, 2007).

Over the last few decades lesbians, as well as gay men, bisexuals, and transgendered people, have gained more recognition and acceptance. The media, both film and television, have presented positive images of these groups. By 1999, 52% of the U.S. population considered homosexuality "an acceptable lifestyle," up from 38% just 7 years earlier (Seager, 2003, p. 25). The movement for same sex marriage emerged, but conversely, pressure for a constitutional amendment declaring that marriage be limited to one man and one woman continues.

In addition to these very real and continuing challenges to women's freedom and equality, a noteworthy value issue is emerging that presents both philosophical and structural challenges. The "third wave" of feminism focuses not on the similarities between women and men underlying the arguments for equal rights, but on the special and different qualities of women. Most prominent is the work of feminist ethicists, philosophers, and psychiatrists in promoting the value of caring, interdependence, and the importance of relationships, in contrast to the "male" values of independence, autonomy, and personal responsibility.

Women continue to have primary responsibility for the caring and rearing of children. Although many professional and highly educated women enjoy fulfilling careers, increasing economic pressures and welfare laws are forcing poorer and less-educated women into paid employment. These jobs are often low-paid, arduous, and not personally fulfilling. Many women must work overtime or at two jobs to make ends meet. While some would argue that women should be able to stay home and care for their children, others fear that this marks a return to the separate and unequal traditional gender roles of the past. The key is whether women have the choice to work outside the home or are forced by punitive welfare laws or economic necessity.

If women are to maintain both roles, and many women want that choice, then the occupational structure needs to be more family-friendly. Quality, accessible childcare should be available as a right. The minimum wage should be automatically increased, based on the cost of living increases, as is Social Security. Family leave should be paid. Increasingly, technology is making it possible for more women, as well as for men, to work from home. This also has its limitations, as well as benefits. In the coming years, efforts to achieve a balance between work and family can be expected to continue to challenge women and our society.

This has particular relevance for social workers. Not only are most of them women, but so are most of their clients, many of whom may be survivors of child or intimate partner abuse. Whether working at the micro, mezzo, or macro levels, social workers need to use a feminist lens to understand and advocate for women. Feminist therapy sues feminist principles of egalitarian relationships. Caring and building trusting relationships, and social justice are central to social work values and practice and are consistent with feminist principles.

## REFERENCES

Albelda, R., & Withorn, A. (2002). *Lost ground: Welfare reform, poverty and beyond.* Boston: South End Press.

Allard, M. A., et al. (1997). *In harm's way? Domestic violence, AFDC receipt and welfare reform in Massachusetts.* Boston: McCormack Institute, University of Massachusetts.

American Cancer Society. (2007). *Breast Cancer Facts and Figures, 2007.* http://www.cancer.org/docroot/STT/content/STT_1_Cancer_Facts_Figures_2007.asp

Boonstra, H. (2007, Spring). The case for a new approach to sex education mounts; will policymakers heed the message? *Guttmacher Policy Review, 10,* 2.

Brandwein, R. (Ed.). (1999). *Battered women, children and welfare reform: The ties that bind.* Thousand Oaks, CA: Sage.

Center for American Women and Politics. (2006). *Facts and findings: Women serving in the 110th Congress 2007–2009.* New Brunswick, NJ: Eagleton Institute of Politics, Rutgers, The State University of New Jersey.

Center for Budget and Policy Priorities. (2005, August 30). *The number of uninsured Americans continued to rise in 2004.* Washington, DC: Author.

Center for Workforce Studies. (2006). *Licensed social workers in the United States, 2004.* Washington, DC: National Association of Social Workers.

Coco, M. (2007, Winter). This is what a speaker looks like. *Ms. Magazine,* 34–37.

Curcio, W. (1997). *The Passaic County study of AFDC recipients in a welfare-to-work program: A preliminary analysis.* Paterson, NJ: Passaic County Board of Social Services.

Hartmann, H., & Lee, S. (2003, April). *Social security: The largest source of income for both women and men in retirement.* Briefing paper no. D455. Washington, DC: Institute for Women's Policy Research.

Institute for Women's Policy Research News. (2006, December 20). *Running faster to stay in place?* Washington, DC: Author.

Jagger, A., & Struhl, P. (1978). *Feminist frameworks.* NY: McGraw Hill.

Kaiser Family Foundation. (2006, May). *Issue brief: An update on women's health policy.* Menlo Park, CA: The Henry J. Kaiser Family Foundation.

Kaufman, L. (2003, November 3). Abused mothers keep children in a test of rights and safety. *New York Times.* http://query.nytimes.comgst/fullpage.html

Lovell, V. (2003, June). *40-Hour work proposal significantly raises mothers' employment standard.* Research in Brief Publication No. D457. Washington, DC: IWPR.

National Association of Social Workers. [NASW]. (2007). NASW political action for candidate election (PACE): Social workers in state and local office, 2005. Available at http//:www.naswdc.org/pace/state.asp

Pearce, D., & McAdoo, H. (1981). *Women and children: Alone and in poverty.* Washington, DC: National Advisory Council on Economic Opportunity.

Peterson, J., Song, X., & Jones-DeWeaver, A. (2002). *Life after welfare reform: Low-income single parent families, pre- and post-TANF.* Washington, DC: Institute for Women's Policy Research.

Raphael, J. (1996). *Prisoners of abuse: Domestic violence and welfare receipt.* Chicago: Taylor Institute.

Raphael, J., & Tolman, R. (1997). *Trapped by poverty, trapped by abuse: New evidence documenting the relationship between domestic violence and welfare.* Chicago: Taylor Institute.

Seager, J. (2003). *The Penguin atlas of women in the world* (Rev. ed.). New York: Penguin Books.

U.S. Department of Commerce, Bureau of the Census. (2000). *Male-female ratio by race alone or in combination and Hispanic or Latino origin for the United States: 2000* (PHC-T-11). Washington, DC. http://www.census.gov

U.S. Department of Commerce, Bureau of the Census. (2005a). *S0101: Age and sex.* 2005 American community survey. Washington, DC. http://factfinder.census.gov

U.S. Department of Commerce, Bureau of the Census. (2005b). *S1101: Households and families.* American community survey. Washington, DC. http://factfinder.census.gov

U.S. Department of Commerce, Bureau of the Census. (2005c). *S1702: Poverty status in the last 12 months of families.* 2005 American community survey. Washington, DC. http://factfinder.census.gov

U.S. Department of Commerce, Bureau of the Census. (2005d). *B2004: Median earning in the past 12 months (in 2005 inflation-adjusted dollars) by sex and educational attainment for the population 25 years and over.* Washington, DC. http://factfinder.census.gov

U.S. Department of Health and Human Services, Administration for Children and Families, Office of Child Support Enforcement. (2006). *Washington, DC. Table 2, Statistical overview, fv 2004–2005.* http://www/acf.hhs.gov/

U.S. Department of Health and Human Services, Centers for Disease Control. (2000). *HIV/AIDS surveillance and epidemiology, 2000.* Washington, DC. http://cdc/gov/hiv/topics/surveillance/index.htm.

U.S. Department of Justice. (2001). *Sourcebook of criminal justice statistics.* Washington, DC. Retrieved from www.endvaw.org

U.S. Department of Justice, Bureau of Justice Statistics. (2003). *Crime victimization in the U.S. Table 1: Number, % distribution and rate of victimization by type of crime.* http://www.ojp.usdoj.gov/bjs/pub/pdf/dvus0501.pdf

Van Den Bergh, N. (Ed.). (1995). *Feminist practice in the 21st century.* Washington, DC: NASW Press.

Wallace, H. (2005). *Family violence: Legal, medical and social perspectives* (4th ed.). Boston: Pearson Education.

Werschkul, M. (2005, Winter/Spring). Earnings inequality for women continues, despite improvements in educational attainment. *IWPR Quarterly Newsletter*, p. 4. Washington, DC. IWPR.

## FURTHER READING

Brandwein, R., & Filiano, D. (2000). Toward real welfare reform: Voices of battered women. *Affilia: Journal of Women and Social Work, 15,* 224–243.

Browne, A., & Bassuk, S. (1997). Intimate violence in the lives of homeless and poorly housed women. *American Journal of Orthopsychiatry, 6,* 261–278.

Collins, P. H. (1990). Defining black feminist thought. In P. Collins (Ed.), *Black feminist thought: Knowledge, consciousness and the politics of empowerment* (pp. 19–40). New York: Routledge. Retrieved October 19, 2006, from http://www/hsph.harvard,edu/organizations/healthnet/woc/feminisms/collins2.html.

Danziger, S. (2003). Employment and earnings. In R. English (Ed.), *Encyclopedia of social work, 2003 supplement* (19th ed., pp. 29–38). Washington, DC: NASW Press.

Davis, D.-A. (2006). *Battered black women and welfare reform.* Albany: SUNY.

Feminist Ethics. (n.d.). *Stanford encyclopedia of philosophy.* Retrieved February 25, 2006, from http://www.seop.leeds.ac.ok/archives/sum1999/entries/feminismethics/

Goodan, S. (1998). *All things not being equal: Differences in caseworker support toward black and white welfare clients.* Harvard journal of African-American Public Policy, 4, 22–23.

Hays, S. (2003). *Flat broke with children.* New York: Oxford University Press.

Kenney, C., & Browne, K. (1996). *Report from the front lines: The impact of violence on poor women.* New York: NOW Legal Defense and Education Fund.

Miller, J. (1976). *Toward a new psychology of women.* Boston: Beacon.

Rose, S., & Hartmann, H. (2004). *Still a man's labor market: The long-term earnings gap.* Washington, DC: IWPR.

Scheyett, A. M., & McCarthy, E. (2006). Women and men with mental illnesses: Voicing different service needs. *Affilia: Journal of Women and Social Work, 21,* 407–418.

U.S. Department of Labor, Bureau of Labor Statistics. (2006, May). *Profile of the working poor* (Report no. 994). http://www.bls.gov

SUGGESTED LINKS

Center for American Women and Politics, Eagleton Institute of Politics, Rutgers, The State University of NJ.
   *www.cawp.rutgers.edu*
Center for Budget and Policy Priorities.
   *www.cbpp.org*
Center for Women Policy Studies.
   *www.centerwomenpolicy.org*
Center for Law and Social Policy.
   *www.clasp.org*
End Violence Against Women.
   *www.endvaw.org*
Institute for Women's Policy Research.
   *www.iwpr.org*
National Coalition Against Domestic Violence.
   *www.ncadv.org*
U.S. Department of Justice, Office of Justice Programs, Bureau of Justice Statistics.
   *www.ojp.usdoj.gov*

—RUTH A. BRANDWEIN

## PRACTICE INTERVENTIONS

**ABSTRACT:** Gender hierarchy is the most pervasive source of inequality in the world. In view of the commitment of social work to the goal of justice, redressing the consequences of inequality among the most disenfranchised should be at the core of professional intervention. Rather than discussing the merits of specific types of practice intervention adopted by social workers, I focus on strategies and knowledge-gathering techniques relevant to empowering women, with an emphasis on five social work methods.

**KEY WORDS:** gender hierarchy; women inequality; class, race, and gender oppression; social justice professional goal; psychological and social empowerment strategies

### The Professional Commitment to Social Justice for Women

Issues of women's social and economic oppression are at the core of the professional goal of social justice (for example, Gil, 1998; Jordan, 1990; Piven & Cloward, 1997; Wakefield, 1988). The codes and standards of the National Association of Social Workers lay out the goal:

- Promote the general welfare of society, from local to global levels, and the development of people, their communities, and environments. Social workers should advocate for living conditions conducive to the fulfillment of basic human needs

and should promote social, economic, political, and cultural values and institutions that are compatible with the realization of social justice.
- Facilitate informed participation by the public in shaping social policies and institutions.
- Engage in social and political actions that seek to ensure that all people have equal access to resources, employment, services, and opportunities they require to meet their basic human needs and to develop fully. Social workers should be aware of the impact of the political arena on practice and should advocate for changes in policy and legislation to improve social conditions in order to meet basic human needs and promote social justice (2003, pp. 394–395).

Wakefield's (1988) argument that professional goals are much more crucial to the legitimacy of a profession than are methods of intervention is crucial in this context. The effectiveness of strategies of intervention evolves over time with knowledge expansion and in response to social change. The social justice goal, on the other hand, defines permanently the profession of social work guiding all its activities and definitively practice with women.

### Societal Issues Impacting Practice with Women

Nussbaum (1999) argues that forces of social and economic inequalities impinging on women form the major social justice issue in any society. A culture that has justified, over centuries, the assignment of roles on the basis of sexual characteristics remains resistant to societal change because of the nature of the gendered culture (Fausto-Sterling, 2000). The interaction of class, race, and gender exacerbates the level of disadvantage (Arrighi, 2001; McAdoo, 2002). Despite real progress of women in economic autonomy, educational access, and legal statutes, the fact remains that the Equal Rights Amendment, which would have granted full social citizenship to women, failed to pass into law. Equity legislation resulting from the pressure of women's groups deals with discrete issues on a case-by-case basis.

The weakness of this one-step-at-a-time approach to helping women improve their status in a gendered society shows up in the prolonged fight for equal pay for equal work since the 1970s. The female–male wage gaps hover at 80%, with progress at less than 5% since the mid-1990s (Leonhardt, 2006). What is more, new freedoms in the economic and family spheres are ambiguous. The double burden of women in the work force is a direct result of the care responsibilities assigned to them. The United States is the only developed country in the West without public childcare (Figueira-McDonough, 2007).

A few facts portray the magnitude of the economic gaps and economic and social stressors that face women. About 2 million poor women live 50% below the poverty level, and among homeless single parents with children the overwhelming majority are women, many of whom are running away from abusive homes (Jones-DeWeever, Peterson, & Song, 2002; National Law Center of Homeless and Poverty, 2002); 60% of women on welfare have experienced physical violence (Davis, 1999); women prisoners have been sexually abused by their guards in state prisons (Geer, 2000; Human Rights Watch, 1996; 1 in every 3 girls below the age of 18, 34% before the age of 12, have been sexually abused (KidSafe Project, 2001).

### Choosing Appropriate Practices for Women

Since society may be biased against women's rights, social workers need to review models of intervention with a skeptical mind. Theories developed mainly by men, for example, interpret the world from their point of view. Training in critical thinking is indispensable for social workers, since most institutions with power over women (poor and non-Whites) often uphold biased assumptions.

Critical thought involves a two-track process: (a) inquiry into the authorship of the theories and their historical and cultural contexts, focusing on the dangers of partial and context-dependent knowledge, and (b) careful analysis of the internal logical coherence of the theories and the empirical evidence for alternative theories (Calhoun, 1995; Talaska, 1990). Applied to gender theories, the skeptical procedure has two foci: (a) the extent to which theories were developed by men, on the basis of limited experience and research, nonetheless claiming universal application, and (b) the exploration of alternative theories geared to women's experiences, together with examination of the evidence behind them and the alternatives they offer for practice. Each type of intervention has its own conceptual requirement for contributing to social justice.

### Different Methods of Social Work Practice and Applied Empowering Knowledge

INDIVIDUAL PRACTICE: MUTUALITY, RESPECT, AND COLLABORATION The relationship between the social worker and the client is the core of individual practice that can inform and transform the meaning of experiences. For women, especially marginalized women, personal experience is the lived version of socioeconomic reality. Difficulties undergone by marginalized women should not be dissected in terms of what is wrong, deficient, or missing according to the dominant culture but as signs of survival in the face of oppression and as potentially healthy protest against patriarchal norms. The canon of knowledge from which the therapist derives her understanding of behavior must be reshaped to include subjugated knowledge from the margins.

Feminist psychotherapies may heighten awareness of women's repression and the reactions to it, speeding the evolution of coping mechanisms. Cognitive and behavior therapies may develop habits and behaviors—assertiveness, pursuit of success—that make women better able to compete and hold their own in a man's world. Therapies inspired by essentialist theories may contribute to the valuation of women's culture and solidarity. Such approaches can strengthen women, but they do not necessarily deprivatize what has been silenced and kept secret in the lives of women.

Basic to the therapeutic relationship is recognition of the distance between a professional, usually from a higher socioeconomic background and invested with institutional authority, and the client. This gap puts the social worker at a disadvantage inasmuch as a full comprehension of the meaning attached to the client's issues is a precondition for authentic communication and development of the therapeutic relationship.

Principles of qualitative research, often applied in anthropology, offer valuable guidelines to bridge this distance. They are characterized by acceptance of the lack of knowledge about cultures outside one's experience, a nonjudgmental inquiry about patterns of behavior, and dependence on insiders to explain the meanings of observed patterns and desired outcomes. The strength of this approach is the maximization of knowledge when prior knowledge is low (Runkel & McGrath, 1972).

Transferred to socioclinical intervention, the strategy encompasses respect for the client, interpretation of her problem and its meaning as understood from her perspective, and its desired resolution. The following procedures, derived in part from critical and structural theories in social work, have the potential to increase trust and honest collaboration in the therapeutic relationship (Gambrill, 2006, pp. 385–394; Jackson & Servaes, 1999; Mullaly, 2007; Wood, 2006):

- Maintain interaction as a process of mutual learning, avoiding the professional–client hierarchy.
- Accept the experiential knowledge of clients and their analysis of the problem.
- Validate the client's resilience and the range of possibilities the client sees as appropriate to respond to her needs.
- Discuss contextual causes of the problem, highlighting social structural constraints.
- Share client files with them and open the files to corrections and explanations.

For oppressed clients, such as refugees, African Americans, immigrants, lesbians living in poverty and exposed to violence, these principles foster a validation of their worth that is a precondition to psychological empowerment.

## Group Work: Communication, Relationship, and Mutual Support

Group work gained prominence after World War II and for a couple of decades was an important action method of intervention (Toseland, 1995). Eventually, however, it was transformed into group therapy (Middleman & Goldman, 1987). Feminist theory renewed interest in this method and introduced innovations in group work. Comparative group studies, popular in social work research, have contributed to greater specification in interventions. When focusing on gender group composition, they have allowed researchers to estimate the effects of the same intervention on mixed groups, male only, and female only groups (Bride, 2001; Zelvin, 1999).

However, the greatest contribution to the theory and practice of group work with women came from research done at the Stone Center at Wellesley and Harvard (Gilligan, 1996; Miller & Silver, 1991). This decades-long program of research revealed the centrality of relational context and communication on the development of women. Social workers added new questions about the impact of gender identity and location to group intervention (Gutiérrez et al., 1998; Maxine & Nisivoccia, 2005). Group work is a method that can address issues of powerlessness through consciousness-raising and self-identification; it can concentrate on repressed socialization and experiences of oppression.

Insights derived form these studies underscore the major advantages of this type of intervention:

- Women respond better in relational settings that support communication
- Group membership can give a sense of protection and empowerment to powerless individuals (Gitterman & Shulman, 2005)

The professional literature is rich in examples suggesting different strategies that assess the consequences of the gender composition of groups, often crucial to the success of interventions. Although all the elements of group practice have to be adjusted to the relational imperative in women's development, the process of member selection is very important to this adjustment.

Many groups are formed out of a common trauma or by the referral of practitioners knowledgeable about clients' needs. In such cases the group worker can follow a clearer pattern of intervention, as exemplified in the work of Schiller and Zimmer (2005) with sexual abuse survivors.

Working with natural groups requires both a longer period of acceptance of the leader and agreement on goals of immediate interest to the group. Lee's work (2005) with homeless young women illustrates this process.

To evaluate the impact of recent changes on disenfranchised women, the use of focus groups is a useful type of practice. The selection of members is more open, and group duration is shorter, than is typically the case with types of groups. An example of this is an assessment of the consequences of the implementation of Temporary Assistance for Needy Families (TANF) in an extremely antiwelfare state (Luna, 2005; Luna & Figueira-McDonough, 2002). Women from poor neighborhoods with high rates of welfare recipients were invited to attend these groups and express their reaction to the welfare reform. The advantage of focus groups over techniques such as surveys is that they encourage interaction that stimulates the expression of feelings, reactions, and desired outcomes. They represent an important strategy for reaching out into new areas of women's oppression.

## Community Practice: Women's Grass Roots Strength

The method of community organization takes in a variety of strategies. As with all social work practice, an assessment of the client's strengths is essential prior to intervention. In the case of communities this means gauging the resources that can be mobilized collectively for dealing with local problems. Relevant community resources include local grassroots and formal organizations and the links they may have with influential external allies (Figueira-McDonough, 2001). Such stocktaking is particularly important when working in low-income communities that may have hidden strengths.

As with other social work macro methods, there has been a male bias in reporting on community achievements. The bias derives less from intentional dismissal of women's contributions than from the tendency of formal leadership, planning processes, organizational deals, and political agreements—functions habitually carried out by men—to get the limelight (Smith, 1990). The consensus has been that women's activity goes on primarily at the grassroots level (Weil, Gable, & Williams, 1998); a team of women studying and analyzing community projects brought to the forefront the breadth of women's grassroots activism.

Historical research on protests unearthed by Abramovitz (1996) has challenged the stereotype of the passive nature of poor women. Abramovitz found that women were at the forefront of protests, both as leaders and followers, concerning food prices, crime, dilapidated housing, and cuts in social benefits. Nancy

Naples has devoted much of her work to examining the activism of poor women during and after the War on Poverty (Naples, 1991, 1998). These "grassroots warriors" fought for federal grants that supported community activities, and they planned and staffed the programs supported by these grants. As the War on Poverty was dismantled, groups of women kept donating their time and searched for alternative funds to keep the services going. Naples found that this communitarian activism was often transmitted to their daughters.

Stoutland (1997) discovered a similar pattern in a study of the Community Development Corporation in Boston. Women were at the center of collective action. They were overwhelmingly the tenants' organization activists, a fact confirmed by other Community Development Corporations (Heskin, 1991, Leavitt & Saeger, 1990). Seitz's analysis (1995) of the local strike of the United Mine Workers in southwest Virginia uncovered the pivotal role of miners' wives in a part of the country known for its patriarchal culture. As the strike heated up, the women shifted from cooking meals and doing sewing for extra income to less traditional activities: they picketed the houses of mine owners and managers, boycotted businesses opposed to the strike, barred police access to the strikers, and dampened internal violence among the despairing miners. Finally, when the miners' demands were not met, the women took over the mine headquarters, and the conflict was settled at last.

Feldman (2004) also reported women's active resistance in Chicago's public housing controversies, and Finn (2002) has explored the resilience of women's groups in community building in a dangerous and unstable setting. The literature is in accord that women's activism is triggered by concern over the welfare of family and children. Women are the foot soldiers of community activism, and their indispensable contributions often go unnoticed. Greater attention is paid to grant-making, deals with business, government and religious organizations—all activities frequently dominated by men (Schorr, 1997).

Social workers cannot neglect the grassroots dimension of community practice. Some preliminary strategies suggest themselves:

- Analyze demographic data about the stability of the resident population (often associated with community attachment) and of local plants, indicating the geographical proximity of housing units (a predictor of interaction). Both indicators, stability and proximity, are pertinent to the formation of grassroots ties.
- Interview community leaders to find out about informal organizations that address women-related issues.
- Identify localities where women congregate (stores, churches, parks, welfare offices, and so forth) and gather information about their pressing concerns (Naples, 2003).

### Organizational Practice: Commitment to Social Work Values and Women's Rights

Howe (1980) criticized the liberal professional organizational practice model that pervaded the training of social workers. She argued that while social workers operated mainly in organizational settings, in such contexts the assumptions of traditional, free-standing liberal professions were not met. Hence, an organizational professional model should be adopted. Despite the popularity of private practice and the increase of organizational courses in many schools of social work, Howe's observations remain valid.

Organizational theory and research have expanded considerably, and students are offered a huge variety of models of analysis. In a review of this development, Netting and Rokwell (1998) note that the variety of the structural models has metamorphosed from their origins in the first half of the 20th century. Weber's ideal model was a response to the industrial expansion and the optimization of efficient production. The rational factory required a centralized hierarchy of decisions, implemented by strict rules for mass workers. Preexisting organizations such as the military and the church inspired this design, and the male imprint was undisputable. Recent innovations in organizational theory, influenced by open system, power dynamics, and organizational culture approaches, have been more responsive to the variety of goals of contemporary organizations, and more inclusive of women.

The relevance of organizational practice for women social workers stems directly from two facts. Women social workers in service organizations make up the majority of the rank and file staff, and many of these organizations, especially in the public sector, serve mostly poor women.

The role and power of women in nonprofit organizations are well documented (Oddental & O'Neil, 1994). Recent research on women has turned up important clues about leveraging women's organizational leadership and participatory management styles in order to enhance both communication and creative outcomes (Barrett & Davidson, 2006; Buzzanell, 2006). This holds promise for greater gender equality in organizational life. Kravetz's account (2004) of the evolution of feminist service organizations is an inspiring example. In addition, proposals for sharing organizational tasks with informal groups, as well as for capitalizing on the complementary strengths of primary and secondary groups, have been advanced as breakthroughs for human service organizations (Mulroy & Shay, 1997; Specht & Courtney, 1994).

Because they exemplify tremendous obstacles to progress in this type of practice with women, public service organizations are worth considering in detail. These organizations are likely to be structured by hierarchical decision-making and strict rules of implementation. Upholding professional values and working effectively with disempowered women clients will almost certainly necessitate major changes.

Jordan (1998) suggests that social workers have more power in the implementation of policies than they realize. Public services are in charge of implementing goals that are general and standardized; yet the specific circumstances they are supposed to address are complex and often idiosyncratic. The on-site skills of social workers can help render publicly endorsed goals workable.

From this perspective, social workers have both power and responsibility for policy outcomes (Jordan & Jordan, 2000; Mullaly, 2007). With power comes a degree of discretion. For example, a social worker in a youth program may or may not send a teenager back to an institution when a child violates curfew, as mandated by current statutes. The professional may decide that the spirit of the law does not apply in light of the particular circumstances that led to the breaking of the curfew. The social worker must of course justify such decisions on a case-by-case basis. In some public service organizations no discretion may be allowed. Routine enforcement of rigid rules of intervention will clash with social work values and the rights of clients. Under these conditions, the social worker has three options: submit, quit, or assert her professional role.

The first two responses may be the easiest and the most frequent. Submissive social workers or untrained case workers replacing them are known to contribute to the alienation of clients. In both cases, poor women in programs are shortchanged (Gray, 2005; Thretheway, 1997; Whitley & Dressel, 2002). Although difficult, the third option can have a positive impact on social services, as well as for the social work rank-and-file and service recipients. Asserting professional roles may involve,

- organizing professional groups within the agency to resist unprofessional regulation. Group resistance is stronger than individual resistance and is more disruptive for the organization.
- establishing links with other organizations or groups that face similar obstacles to their commitment to clients' rights.
- proving that the regulations in place subvert or contradict the public service goal.

Promoting solidarity among the social work rank-and-file with the support of professional associations is a vital step toward the first strategy. Gray (2005) argues that the National Association of Social Workers should recommend practice standards for social workers in public services. Infractions of these standards could legitimize resistance to poorly designed regulations. Consulting with other human service professions with experience in labor resistance strategies is also valuable. Interorganizational know-how and experience about the interdependence of services could facilitate the identification of potential external allies.

Opportunities for public service reform increase when the institutions are found to be deficient in fulfilling their mandate (Jordan & Jordan, 2000). So, while the third strategy could probably be the most effective, it is also hard to pull off. It requires an in-depth analysis of the policy under which the service was established in order to clarify its goals. It also requires a thorough examination of service outcomes. This could include analysis of administrative data, a survey of recipients regarding expectations and outcomes, and the use of case vignettes (McMillen et al., 2005).

### Policy Practice: Top-Down and Bottom-Up Influence

Two sets of deficiencies prevail in the sources of injustice that social workers have been increasingly concerned about since the mid-nineties: economic inequality and poverty and the policies that reinforce them (Hopps & Morris, 2000; Reisch & Gambrill, 1998; Van Wormer, 2004). Intertwined with these are the negative ideologies popularized by powerful groups about the poor (Gramsci, 1971; Lakoff, 2002) and their political marginality. This combination of factors underpins the enactment of policies with heavy burdens and few benefits for the poor (Schneider & Ingram, 1993).

The goal of policy practice in social work is to prevent or alter policies that have damaging consequences for powerless groups and to promote those that benefit them. In a gender hierarchical society, attention to policy impacts on poor women is central to this practice (Arrighi, 2001). Examining the effects of the 1996 Welfare Reform Act covering poor parents, 87% of whom are poor single mothers, serves as a template for other policies that affect negatively women in poverty.

Legislative practice, a type of top-down influence, has improved greatly since the last two decades of the past century, and carefully designed strategies have been developed recently for social workers (for example, Jansson, 2003). They include careful study of the legislation under review, research on the positions of decision-makers regarding past human service issues and legislation, reaching out for influential allies, matching lobbyists' skills to legislators' characteristics, the ability to cooperate with groups with partial over-lapping interests, and so on. The National Association of Social Workers and its state chapters help in this process, especially through their political action committees.

Schneider (2002) has argued convincingly that so-cial work legislative policy should focus on state legis-latures. Schneider's position is particularly relevant in the case of the 1996 Welfare Reform Act that trans-ferred many responsibilities to the states. It is signifi-cant for the topic at hand that nearly 90% of the recipients of this program are women (Jones De Weever et al., 2003).

Studies comparing the welfare of recipients before and after the reform with regard to levels of poverty, employment stability, and quality of childcare show marginal improvement after the reform or even dete-rioration (Jones-DeWeever, Peterson, & Song, 2002; Weil & Finegold, 2001). However, some states showed creativity and strategic coherence by evaluating the outcome of their interventions (Nox, 2002). This evi-dence corroborates Greenberg's conclusion (2001) that the lack of systematic evaluation of programs and shar-ing of successful interventions is the greatest weakness of the new welfare regime. Improvement in these areas is a must for improving the well-being of recipients.

Judicial intervention, another type of top-down in-fluence, has been successful in protecting the rights of clients. For example, in some states, settlements opened up access to services for non-English speakers. Injunc-tions lifted the requirement, set by private contrac-tors, of drug testing for prospective workers. The discontinuation of Medicaid coverage for individuals caring for children receiving government assistance was stopped. Finally, legislative decisions to lower the income cap for certain benefits were declared uncon-stitutional (Welfare Information Network, 2004).

Records of the hearings on the Temporary Assis-tance for Needed Families Act confirm that the nega-tive image of women in poverty is widespread. Legislators routinely defined poor single mothers as deviants, attributing their problems to laziness and sex-ual intemperance. These views, in turn, justified puni-tive features of the policy (for example, Segal & Kitty, 2003). The added burdens and decreased benefits decreed by TANF can be attributed in part to this sort of stereotyping.

This suggests the importance, for top-down policy practice, of evaluating outcomes for TANF programs. It also highlights the need to correct misinformed and discriminatory views about single mothers in poverty.

For social workers in policy practice committed to improve TANF at the sate level, three strategies may be relevant.

1.  Involvement in program outcome evaluations and identification of strategies for empowering women and enhancing their welfare. This entails a search of findings that relate concrete types of interven-tions to the goals of work stability and income above poverty. Examples of such evidence in Minneapolis, Wisconsin, and Michigan are promis-ing (Solomon, 2006; Welfare Information Network, 2001), as is the implementation of a TANF-like policy in Britain (Nelson & Whales, 2006).

2.  Review of evidence about policy implementations that infringe on human and civil rights granted by state constitutions. Information along these lines can contribute to effective judicial practice (Figueira-McDonough, 2006, pp. 369–372).

3.  Collection and distribution of statistics can counter the distorted image of single mothers in poverty. Media coverage that conveys the lived experience of these mothers is crucial. Prime examples are articles with pictures likely to attract readers, such as those used by the *New York Times* in reporting on "the neediest cases." Theatrical adaptations—for example, of Ehrenreich's *Nickel and Dimed* (2001) or of Nia Orm's *Please Take A Number* (2007)—also reach the public. They help ordinary citizens to participate in the experiences of women in poverty and foster understanding of the problems they face.

Social movements represent a type of bottom-up policy influence. The civil rights movement, the women's movement, and their impact on extending rights to marginalized populations are classic examples. The ingredients of success are clearly established: (a) widely known incidents recognized as cases of social injustice, (b) close interaction among the population suffering the injustice, (c) the emergence of leaders respected by the group, and (d) proposals to address the source of injustice (Gamson, 1995).

The women's movement pressed for the creation of volunteer services to deal with the neglected needs of women: rape crisis centers, women's health clinics, women's substance abuse and domestic abuse programs. Today such programs are institutionalized and they have affected policies across many states for the better (Kravetz, 2004). Another successful example is Mothers Against Drunk Driving (MADD). With chapters all over the country, Mothers Against Drunk Driving has become a major force in legislation on drunk driving and regula-tions on the sale of alcohol.

Social workers have a long history of participating in movements for social justice. Their involvement has been individual or through groups committed to the goals of the movement (Reisch & Andrews, 2001). To what extent can the practice skills of social workers contribute to movements that influence policies affecting women in poverty? Fine-tuning the two interventions just outlined may be a viable direction.

Organizational practice that focuses on improving the delivery of services in social service programs can go beyond the mismatch between policy goals and program implementation to question the justice of the policy itself. Diane Pearce (who coined the phrase *feminization of poverty*) has devised a creative strategy for improving TANF. Unlike others, she does not attack the work requirement of the program. She focuses instead on the goal, proclaimed by the policy, of achieving self-sufficiency for welfare recipients. She has developed an operational definition of the economic requirements for self-sufficiency (food, health, housing, transportation, and so forth). Since the cost of these basic resources varies significantly across states, she contends that the requirements for self-sufficiency have to be calculated locally. Groups committed to the improvement of TANF have adopted her strategy in many states (Pearce, 2002).

Similarly, community practice can contribute to social movements that matter to the well-being of women. Informal grassroots associations among women have proven their power in addressing issues that matter to them. Connecting these groups across communities around a shared concern is a catalytic strategy for women's movements. Analysts of the demise of the War on Poverty claim that the rapid dismantling of programs could have been prevented if affected communities had joined in concerted resistance (Halpern, 1995).

A contemporary example is the creation and development of a Montana-based grassroots advocacy and educational organization that emerged to respond to inequities in the state implementation of TANF (Finn, Castellanos, McOmber, & Kahan, 2000). Founded by two managers of the Job Opportunities and Basic Skills (JOBS) and with a board made up of single mothers living on below-poverty incomes, membership grew steadily, and so did the development of programs. The account of the learning process in dealing with the legislature affecting TANF recipients is impressive. The women often testified in favor of legislation on a number of bills that could affect favorably low-income mothers.

## The Continuum of Empowerment Interventions for Women

The empowerment of women, especially of socioeconomically marginalized women, is an expected outcome of social work interventions, founded on the professional principle of social justice. The ultimate goal, Gil (1998) argues, is to eliminate the structure of oppression. Linkages among the macrointerventions toward this end goal can be discerned in the foregoing proposals. But interventions targeted to individual empowerment often lack explicit links to social empowerment.

Dietz (2000) notes that women's traumas are often internalizations of external structures of domination. Lee's account (2005) of her practice with women in extreme poverty demonstrates how group success has to be accompanied by contextual changes in programs and policies. Thus, individual interventions should include features designed to promote the connection between psychological and social empowerment. In their intervention with individuals, social workers may encourage and facilitate contacts with groups facing similar problems. Easing the transition toward self-support groups would also become a step in the direction of social empowerment in the group work process. In both instances, information about and access to local activist groups engaged in changing structures at the root of individual problems would advance the connection between psychological and social empowerment.

## REFERENCES

Abramovitz, M. (1996). *Under Attack, Fighting Back: Women and welfare in the United States.* New York: Monthly Review Press.

Arrighi, B. (2001). *Understanding inequality: The intersection of race/ethnicity, class, and gender.* Lanham, MD: Rowman & Littlefield.

Barrett, M., & Davidson, M. J. (2006). *Gender and communication at work.* Burlington, VT: Ashgate.

Bride, B. E. (2001). Single gender treatment of substance abuse: Effects on treatment retention and completion. *Social Work Research, 25*(4), 223–232.

Buzzanell, P. M. (2006). *Rethinking organizational and managerial communication from feminist perspectives.* Thousand Oaks, CA: Sage.

Calhoun, C. (1995). *Critical social theory.* Oxford: Blackwell.

Davis, E. (1999). The economics of abuse: How violence perpetuates women's poverty. In R. A. Brandwein (Ed.), *Battered women, children and the welfare reform: The ties that bind* (pp. 17–30). Thousand Oaks, CA: Sage.

Dietz, C. A. (2000). Responding to oppression and abuse: A feminist challenge to clinical social work. *Affilia, 15*(3), 369–389.

Ehrenreich, B. (2001). *Nickel and dime: On (not) getting by in America.* New York: Holt.

Fausto-Sterling, A. (2000). *Sexing the body: Gender politics and construction of sexuality.* New York: Basic Books.

Feldman, R. M. (2004). *The dignity of resistance: Women residents' activism in Chicago public housing.* New York: Cambridge University Press.

Figueira-McDonough, J. (2001). *Community analysis and praxis: Towards a grounded civil society.* New York: Taylor & Francis.

Figueira-McDonough, J. (2006). *The welfare state and social work: Pursuing social justice*. Thousand Oaks, CA: Sage.

Figueira-McDonough, J. (2007). Childcare and the potential of breaking intergenerational poverty. In B. A. Arrighi & D. J. Maume (Eds.), *Child poverty in America today* (Vol. 1, pp. 171–187). Westport, CT: Praeger.

Finn, J., Castellanos R., McOmber, T., & Kahan K. (2000). Working for equality and economic liberation: Advocacy and education for welfare reform. *Affilia, 15*(2), 294–310.

Finn, J. L. (2002). Raíces: Gender-conscious community building in Santiago, Chile. *Affilia, 25*(4), 448–470.

Gambrill, E. (2006). *Social work practice: A critical thinker's guide*. New York: Oxford University Press.

Gamson, W. A. (1995). Constructing social protest. In H. Johnson & B. Kladermans (Eds.), *Social movements and culture* (pp. 85–106). Minneapolis: University of Minneapolis Press.

Geer, M. A. (2000, Spring). Human rights and wrongs in our backyard: Incorporating international human rights protections under domestic civil rights law—A case study of women in the United States prisons. *Harvard Human Rights Journal, 13*, 71–140.

Gil, D. (1998). *Confronting injustice and oppression: Concepts and strategies for social workers*. New York: Columbia University Press.

Gilligan, C. (1996). The centrality of relationships in human development: A puzzle, some evidence and a theory. In G. G. Noam & K. W. Fisher (Eds.), *Development and vulnerability in close relationships* (pp. 237–261). Mahwey, NJ: Erlbaum.

Gitterman, A., & Shulman L. (2005). The life model, oppression, vulnerability and resilience, mutual aid and the mediating function. In A. Gitterman & L. Shulman (Eds.), *Mutual aid groups, vulnerable and resilient populations and the life cycle* (pp. 139–165). New York: Columbia University Press.

Gramsci, A. (1971). *Selections from the prison notebooks of Antonio Gramsci* In (Q. Hoare & G. N. Smith, Trans.). (Eds.) New York: International Press.

Gray, K. A. (2005). Pride, prejudice, and a dose of shame: The meaning of public assistance. *Affilia, 20*(3), 329–345.

Greenberg, M. (2001). Welfare reform and devolution: Looking forward and backward. *Brookings Review, 19*(3), 20–24.

Gutiérrez, L., Reed B. G., Ortega R., & Lewis E. et al. (1998). Teaching about groups in a gendered world. In J. Figueira-McDonough, F. E. Netting, & A. Nichols-Casebolt (Eds.), *The role of knowledge in practice knowledge: Claiming half of the human experience* (pp. 169–200). New York: Garland.

Halpern, R. (1995). *Rebuilding the inner city*. New York: Columbia University Press.

Heskin, A. D. (1991). *The struggle for community*. Boulder, CO: Westview.

Hopps, J. G., & Morris R. (2000). *Social work at the millennium*. New York: Free Press.

Howe, E. (1980). Public professions and the private model of professionalism. *Social Work, 25*(2), 179–191.

Human Rights Watch. (1996). *All too familiar, sexual abuse of women prisoners in U.S. state prisons*. New York: Author, Women Rights Project.

Jackson, T. L., & Servaes J. (1999). *Theoretical approaches to participatory communication*. Cresskill, NJ: Hampton.

Jansson, B. S. (2003). *Becoming an effective policy advocate: From policy practice to social justice*. Pacific Grove, CA: Brooks/Cole.

Jones-DeWeever, A., Peterson J., & Song X. (2002). *Before and after welfare reform: The work and well-being of low-income single parent families*. Report series on low income families and children. Washington, DC: Institute for Women' Policy Research. www.iwpr.org

Jordan, B. (1990). *Social work in an unjust society*. London: Harvester Wheatsheaf.

Jordan, B. (1998). *The new politics of welfare: Social justice in a global context*. Thousand Oaks, CA: Sage.

Jordan, B., & Jordan C. (2000). *Social work and the third way: Tough love as social policy*. Thousand Oaks, CA: Sage

KidSafe Project. (1997–2001). *Child sexual abuse statistics*. Washington, DC: National Institute of Justice. http://republican.ses.ca.gov/web/36/projectkidsafe/stats.asp

Kravetz, D. (2004). *Tales from the trenches: Politics and the practice in feminist service organizations*. Lanham, MD: University Press of America.

Lakoff, G. (2002). *Moral politics: How liberals and conservatives think*. Chicago: University of Chicago Press.

Leavitt, J., & Saeger S. (1990). *From abandonment to hope: Community households in Harlem*. New York: Columbia University Press.

Lee, J. (2005). No place to go: Women and children. In A. Gitterman & L. Shulman (Eds.), *Mutual aid groups, vulnerable and resilient populations and the life cycle* (pp. 373–399). New York: Columbia University Press.

Leonhardt, D. (2006, December 24). Scant progress on closing gap in women's pay. *New York Times*, pp. 1, 18.

Luna, Y. (2005). *Social constructions, social control, and resistance: An analysis of welfare reform as a hegemonic process*. Unpublished doctoral dissertation, Arizona State University, Tempe.

Luna, Y. , & Figueira-McDonough, J. (2002). Charity, ideology and exclusion: Continuities and resistance in U.S. welfare reform. In J. Figueira-McDonough & R. C. Sarri (Eds.), *Women at the margins: Neglect, punishment and resistance* (pp. 321–345). New York: Haworth.

Maxine, L., & Nisivoccia D. (2005). When the world no longer feels safe. In A. Gitterman & L. Shulman (Eds.), *Mutual aid groups, vulnerable and resilient populations and the life cycle* (pp. 139–165). New York: Columbia University Press.

McAdoo, H. P. (2002). The storm is passing over: Marginalized African American women. In J. Figueira-McDonough & R. C. Sarri (Eds.), *Women at the margins: Neglect, punishment and resistance* (pp. 87–99). New York: Haworth.

McMillen, J. C., Proctor E. K., Megivern D., Striley C. W., Cabassa L. J., Munson M. R., et al. (2005). Quality care in the social services: Research agenda and methods. *Social Work Research, 19*(3), 181–191.

Middleman, R., & Goldberg G. (1987). Social practice with groups. In A. Middleman (Ed.), *Encyclopedia of social work* (18th ed., pp. 714–729). Silver Springs, MD: NASW Press.

Miller, J. B., & Silver I. P. (1991). A relational reframing of therapy. *Work in progress*, No. 52. Wellesley, MA: Stone Center Working Paper Series.

Mullaly, R. (2007). *New structural social work*. New York: Oxford University Press.

Mulroy, E. A., & Shay S. (1997). Nonprofit organizations and innovation. A model of neighborhood-based collaboration to prevent child maltreatment. *Social Work, 42*, 515–524.

Naples, N. (1991). Just what needed to be done: Political practice of women community workers in low-income neighborhoods. *Gender and Society, 5*(9), 478–496.

Naples, N. (1998) *Grassroots warriors: Activist mothers, community work and the war on poverty*. New York: Routledge.

Naples, N. (2003). *Feminism and method: Ethnography, discourse analysis, and activist research*. New York: Routledge.

National Association of Social Workers. (2003). Social workers ethical responsibilities to the broader society. In *Social work speaks: Policy statements* (pp. 381–395). Washington, DC: NASW Press.

National Law Center of Homeless and Poverty. (2002). *Homeless poverty in America*. www.nlchp.org/FA-HPLA

Nelson, E., & Whales J. (2006, December). With U.S. methods, Britain posts gains in fighting poverty. *The Wall Street Journal, 22*, pp. 1, 10.

Netting, F. E., & Rokwell M. K. (1998). Integrating gender into human service organization, administration and planning curricula. In J. Figueira-McDonough, F. E. Netting, & A. Nicchols-Casebolt (Eds.), *The role of gender in practice knowledge: Claiming half of the human experience* (pp. 287–321). New York: Garland.

Nox, V. (2002, Summer). Money also matters. *American Prospect*, A26–A31.

Nussbaum, M. C. (1999). *Sex and social justice*. New York: Oxford University Press.

Oddental, T., & O'Neil, M. (1994). *Women and power in the nonprofit sector*. San Francisco, CA: Jossey Bass.

Orm, N. (2007). *Please take a number*. www.niaorms.com

Pearce, D. M. (2002). Welfare reform now that we know it: Enforcing women's poverty and preventing self sufficiencyc. In J. Figueira-McDonough & R. C. Sarri (Eds.), *Women at the margins: Neglect, punishment and resistance* New York: Haworth.

Piven, F. F., & Cloward R. A. (1997). *The breaking of the American social compact*. New York: Free Press.

Reisch, M., & Gambrill E. (1998). *Social work in the 21st century*. Thousand Oaks, CA: Pine Forge.

Reisch, M., & Andrews J. (2001). *The road not taken: A history of radical social work in the United States*. New York: Brunner-Routledge.

Runkel, P. J., & McGrath, J. E. (1972). *Research on human behavior*. New York: Holt, Rinehart and Winston.

Schiller, L. Y., & Zimmer B. (2005). Sharing secrets. The power of women's groups for sexual abuse survivors. In A. Gitterman & L. Shulman (Eds.), *Mutual aid groups, vulnerable and resilient populations and the life cycle* (pp. 290–319). New York: Columbia University Press.

Schneider, A., & Ingram H. (1993). Social construction of target populations: Implications for politics and policy. *American Political Science Review, 87*(2), 334–346.

Schneider, R. (2002). Influencing "state" policy: Social arena for the 21st century. *Social Policy Journal, 1*(1), 113–116.

Schorr, L. B. (1997). *Common purpose: Strengthening families and neighborhoods to rebuild America*. New York: Doubleday.

Segal, E., & Kitty K. M. (2003). Political promises for welfare reform. *Journal of Poverty, 7*(1/2), 51–67.

Seitz, V. R. (1995). *Women, development and communities for empowerment in Appalachia*. Albany: State University of New York Press.

Smith, D. F. (1990). *The conceptual practice of power: A feminist sociology of knowledge*. Boston, MA: Northeastern University Press.

Solomon, D. (2006, December 15). The interim solution: For welfare clients, temporary jobs can be a roadblock. *The Wall Street Journal*, pp. 1, 16.

Specht, H., & Courtney M. (1994). *Unfaithful angels: How social work abandoned its mission*. New York: Free Press.

Stoutland, S. E. (1997). *Neither urban jungle nor urban village: Women, families and urban development*. New York: Garland.

Talaska, R. (1990). *Critical reasoning in contemporary culture*. Albany: State University of New York Press.

Thretheway, A. (1997). Resistance, identity, and empowerment: A postmodern feminist analysis of human service organization. *Communication Monographs, 64*, 281–301.

Toseland, R. (1995). *An introduction to group work*. Boston, MA: Allyn & Bacon.

Van Wormer, K. (2004). *Confronting oppression, restoring justice: From policy analysis to social action*. Alexandria, VA: Council on Social Work Education.

Wakefield, J. C. (1988). Psychotherapy, distributive justice and social work: Distributive justice as a conceptual framework for social work (Part I). *Social Service Review, 62*, 187–210.

Weil, A., & Finegold K. (2001). *Welfare reform: The next act*. Washington, DC: The Urban Institute Press.

Weil, M., Gable D. N., & Williams E. S. (1998). Women, communities and development. In J. Figueira-McDonough, F. E. Netting, & A. Nichols-Casebolt (Eds.), *The role of gender in practice knowledge: Claiming half of the human experience* (pp. 242–286). New York: Garland.

Welfare Information Network. (2004). The effect of litigation on the design and administration of welfare policies and programs. *Resources for Welfare Decision Making, 8, 3*. http://financeprogectinfo.org

Welfare Information Network. (2001). Earnings supplements and income disregards can ease transition from welfare to work. *Resources for Welfare Decision Making, 5*(12). http://financeproject.org

Whitley, D. M., & Dressel P. M. (2002). The controllers and the controlled. In J. Figueira-McDonough & R. C. Sarri (Eds.), *Women at the margins: Neglect, punishment and resistance* (pp. 103–123). New York: Haworth.

Wood, G. (2006). *The structural approach to direct practice: A social constructionist approach*. New York: Columbia University Press.

Zelvin, E. (1999). Applying relational theory to the treatment of women's addictions. *Affilia, 14*(1), 1–23.

—JOSEFINA FIGUEIRA-MCDONOUGH

## HEALTH CARE

ABSTRACT: This entry provides an abbreviated version of the status of women's health in the United States, highlighting health care utilization, health care expenditures, policy issues, barriers to health care, and the impact on populations at risk. The findings accentuate the importance of moving the women's health care agenda forward because of the persistence of health disparities not just among women of color but among women with disabilities, adolescents, women in violent relationships, women with AIDS, women who are incarcerated, women who are homeless, older low-income women, women on welfare, and lesbian women.

KEY WORDS: women's health; women of color and health; health care expenditures; barriers to access; women's policy issues

Although the early sociopolitical history of women's health care services has documented many disparities and deficits in how women were treated by the health care system, since mid-1950s progress had been made in improving women's health and in recognizing their contribution to the health care system. The efforts of the women themselves toward the promotion of health services for children are impressive.

### Women as Health Care Leaders
The women at Hull House promoted and developed the early legislation on women and children's health and simultaneously worked to ensure the professionalization of social work by placing the program under the auspices of the University of Chicago, where Sophonisba Breckinridge a Hull House resident became its first director (Costin, 1983b).

The political, cultural, social, and economic context that brought women's health to the forefront occurred during the early 1900s along with a surge of issues including woman's suffrage, child labor, the rights of women in industry, and the problems of immigrants (Costin, 1983a, p. 41). The seeds of reform planted in the 1900s led to the reforms of the 1930s and social programs were expanded and maintained. The appointment of Julia Lathrop as the first chief of the Children's Bureau marked the commencement of a life-long collaboration of social work pioneers such as Jane Addams, Florence Kelley, Edward T. Devine, Grace, and Edith Abbott in fighting for the causes of children and women.

### Maternal and Child Health
The passage of the Sheppard-Towner Act in 1921, whose goal was to reduce the incidence maternal and infant mortality and to promote maternal and child health, signaled the beginning of a federal-state matching program modeled after the Smith-Lever Act of 1914 for agricultural collaborative (Costin, Bell, & Downs, 1991 p. 502).

When the Sheppard-Towner Act was allowed to lapse, some physicians, led by Robert L. De Normandies of Harvard Medical School and the Children's Bureau Obstetric Advisory Committee along with Grace Abbott, designed a comprehensive study of maternal mortality that investigated the deaths of 7,537 women. The study revealed that a serious lack of adequate prenatal care and the incidence of puerperal septicemia resulted in enormous loss of life. The study further noted that the surgical techniques performed by untrained physicians and the use of pituitrin were associated with sepsis, hemorrhage, and ruptured uterus leading to death. There were many stillbirths, infant deaths, and physical or mentally disabled infant survivors. At least a quarter of the maternal deaths were a result of illegal abortions (Costin, 1983a).

Social workers were involved in the passage of the Federal Social Security Act of 1935 that included the Maternal and Child Health program (Title V) and Crippled Children's program (Title V). Amendments authorized grants to states to enable them to improve the health of mothers and children especially in rural or underserved or economically strained areas. The appropriations further provided for the development of a central medical social work section at the federal level (Davis & Schoen, 1978). Social workers served as consultants and their efforts on behalf of maternal and child health was widely recognized. Funds were expanded for the preservation and promotion of maternal health throughout the woman's reproductive cycle. In 1963, the Maternal and Child Health Act provided for prenatal care for high-risk women. The maternal and infancy projects reached large numbers of minority women. Some support for family planning services was provided under the Social Security Act of 1967 and expanded under the 1970 Family Planning and Population Research Act (Davis & Schoen, 1978). With the passage of Medicaid and Medicare in 1965, comprehensive health care was made available for the first time to poor women and to elderly women (Davis & Schoen, 1978), who were a majority of its recipients.

### Guiding Philosophical Perspectives
Social policies to improve women's work lives and maintain their health have been historically interrelated with the preservation of both the family and the woman's place within the family. As expressed by Abramovitz (1991, p. 37) "... the ideology of women's

roles represents dominant interests and explains reality in ways that create social cohesion and maintain the status quo." Dr. Holbrook summarized this pervasive attitude in the following statement "the Almighty, in creating the female sex, had taken the uterus and built up a woman around it" (Mahowald, 1993). Childbearing was considered a woman's contribution to society.

Women had a distinct perspective about medicine, but this perspective had gone largely unrecognized by the medical community (Broom, 1991). As women become visible in the work place, the sole association of women's health with reproductive health began to diminish. The absence of women in clinical trials led to the creation of the Office of Research on Women's Health at the National Institutes of Health.

However there are still remnants of this pervasive attitude. According to Inlander (1992), women are the "cash cows of medicine" because they generate billions of dollars for the medical system. According to De Buono, a Senior Medical Director of Pfizer Public Health Group women are critical health care decision makers because they control 69% of the amount paid for health care and in 1995 that amount was $1.1 Trillion. They also make health care decisions for 75% of households and account for 60% of all physician visits (The Women's Network for a Sustainable Future, 2003).

## Health Care Expenditures
In 2002 ninety percent of females had at least one health care expenditure. One third of expenses were covered by either Medicaid or Medicare and a little over 40% were covered by private insurance. The average expenditure was lower for males ($3,116) than for females ($3, 461). However, inpatient expenditures were higher for males than for females ($14,221 to $10,371) (Women's Health USA, 2005). Males exceeded females in expenditures for home health services and hospital outpatient services, while women exceeded men's in physician visits, services and prescription drugs.

A study on health care costs and expenditures found that males were more likely to have employer coverage and Medicare and women were more likely to have Medicaid and private nongroup coverage (Brennan, 2000). Table 1 demonstrates differences in coverage between males and females ages 18–64.

A report issued by the Kaiser Family Foundation/ Urban Institute (Salganicoff, Ranji, & Wyn, 2005) found that 38% of women had job-based insurance coverage, 25% were dependent on someone else for coverage, 6% had individual or private coverage, 3% had other, 19% were uninsured, and 9% were on Medicaid. Women of color were disproportionately

TABLE 1
*Comparison of Medicaid, Medicare and Insurance Coverage of Males and Females (1997)*

|  | FEMALE | MALE |
|---|---|---|
| Total (in millions) | 11.1 | 12.2 |
| Medicaid | 6.5% | 3.4% |
| Medicare | 4.3% | 3.5% |
| Uninsured | 10.8% | 8.1% |
| Employer | 69.2% | 76.6% |
| Nongroup | 10.7% | 7.6% |

From *Health insurance coverage of the near elderly.* Series B No. B-21, by N. Brennan, 2000, Washington, DC: The Urban Institute.

represented among the uninsured. Although they represented 32% of the U.S. female population, they constituted 51% of the uninsured.

## Health Care Utilization
The health care industry is heavily dependent on women. Women constitute the majority of health care consumers or patients, as well as health providers According to the US Equal Employment Opportunity Commission's aggregate report on health care and social assistance (2003), the percentage of women in the Health Care Industry is 79.1%.

Studies reveal that a number of variables contribute to the utilization and type of utilization of health care services. The average physician number of ambulatory visits by women in 2000 was 8.4. Eighty-two percent of women reported making an ambulatory care visit and 11% reported a hospital stay with and average length of 6.3 days. Over 90% of women made at least one preventive care visit and 75% filled a least one prescription. A few (3%) received home health services (Taylor, Larson, & Correa-de-Araujo, 2006).

Environmental factors, age, race, income, education, marital status, and residence, as well as the personal life style habits and health behavior, including diet, exercise, eating habits, smoking, drinking, and type of work, are factors that impact health status. Lack of insurance and access continue to contribute to disparities in health conditions of poor women and minorities (Galambos, 2006).

Almost one out of every four women reported having been diagnosed with anxiety or depression, according to the Kaiser Women's Health Survey (2005). Women delay reporting alcoholism and might not report attempted suicide, venereal disease, rape, or abortion, making the establishment of morbidity rates difficult (Clancy & Massion, 1992; Pinn, 1992).

Older women have limited income and access to health care is determined by whether they have insurance, Medicaid or Medicare. As women age they develop multiple chronic conditions such as diabetes, vision loss, incontinence, arthritis, and osteoporosis. They also suffer from unintentional injuries. Twice as many women as men experience depression triggered by loss, diabetes, stroke, heart disease, cancer, Alzheimer's disease Parkinson's disease, or arthritis (http://www.womancando.org/over65/olderwomenconditions.htm 2006).

For women of color, especially, quality of care and health outcomes is shaped by the physical and social environment, racism, and linguistic isolation (Women of Color Health Data Book, 2005). Although women of color experience many of the same health conditions as White women, they are often in poorer health, receive fewer health services, and suffer disproportionately from chronic diseases, disabilities, and premature death (Satcherl, 2001; Women's health care in the United States, 2004).

The *Women's Health USA 2005 report* found that 63% of non-Hispanic White women and to a lesser extent 53% of Hispanic women and 51% of non-Hispanic Black women reported excellent or very good health. Minority women appeared to be disproportionately affected by such chronic conditions as diabetes, hypertension, obesity, and AIDS. About two-thirds of women of color were over weight in 2001 (Women of Color Health Data Book, 2006).

According to the *Women of color health data book* (2006), heart disease was the leading cause of death for all females except Asian and Pacific Islander and American Indian females. Cancer was the leading cause of death for American Indians and Asian and Pacific Islander women of all ages. It was the second leading cause of death for Black, Hispanic, and White women of all ages. Lung cancer was the top cancer killer and breast cancer ranked number two. Among the causes of death for women of color were cerebrovascular diseases, diabetes, and unintentional injuries. The tenth leading cause of death for Black women between the ages of 25 and 44 was immunodeficiency virus. Table 2 highlights the differences in the causes of death among women. Over 70% of women infected with AIDS are women of color. (Morbidity and Mortality Weekly Report, 2005).

**AGE AND RACE OR ETHNICITY** According to Roberts (2002), Hispanic (33.2%) and Non-Hispanic Asian (31.4%) women between the ages of 18 and 64 were least likely to have a usual source of care. Almost three-fourths of Non-Hispanic White women received their usual health care service in an office setting. Non-Hispanic Blacks, Hispanics, and other single or multiple race non-Hispanics were more likely to have a hospital-based source of care (Roberts, 2006). Native Americans were least likely to be receiving prenatal care during the first trimester and least likely to have had a Pap test or mammogram (National Law Center, 2005).

Disparities in lack of safety in postoperative complications are reflected in higher rates for women

TABLE 2

*Leading Causes of Death for Women (per 100,000 women)*

|  | WHITE | BLACK | HISPANIC | ASIAN/PACIFIC ISLANDER | AMERICAN INDIAN/ALASKAN NATIVE |
|---|---|---|---|---|---|
| Coronary heart disease | 151.0 | 203.9 | 134.4 | 91.8 | 102.6 |
| Stroke | 56.7 | 75.6 | 42.6 | 49.3 | 44.4 |
| Lung cancer | 41.9 | 39.6 | 14,7 | 19.4 | 26.8 |
| Chronic lower respiratory diseases | 39.7 | 22.9 |  | 11.7 | 27.8 |
| Breast cancer | 26.0 | 34.8 | 16.7 | 12.7 | 13.5 |
| Unintentional injuries | 27.5 | 22.2 | 16.4 |  | 35.0 |
| Diabetes (underlying cause) | 20.4 | 49.2 | 35.9 | 16.3 | 45.6 |
| Influenza and pneumonia | 20.2 |  | 17.3 | 15.0 | 20.7 |
| Alzheimer's disease | 19.9 |  | 11.0 |  |  |
| Colorectal | 17.1 | 24.3 | 11.8 | 10.7 |  |
| Nephritis, nephrosis |  | 26.3 |  | 7.9 | 15,1 |
| Septicemia |  | 22.0 |  |  |  |
| Essential (primary) hypertension and hypertensive renal disease |  |  |  | 5.9 |  |
| Cirrhosis |  |  |  |  | 19.8 |

From *Healthy women: State trends in health and mortality*, by National Center for Health Statistics, 2004, Retrieved from http//www.cdc.gov/nchs/healthy-women.htm

especially for Black and Hispanic women (*Women's Health Care in the United States*, 2004).

Around 70.1 million women used alcohol during the year and 12.5 million used an illicit drug. Close to 6% actually met the criteria for abuse or dependence of alcohol or illicit drug, 5.2 million were alcohol dependent and two million drug dependent. Drug dependence was highest among American Indians or Alaska Natives as were smoking, cirrhosis deaths, and spousal abuse rates followed by Whites, Blacks, Hispanics, and Asians (The NSDUH Report, 2005). Women were the most frequent users of prescribed drugs and the primary abusers of therapeutic drugs whether prescribed or over-the-counter.

High income is associated with physician's office as the usual source of health care. In 2004 lack of affordability forced 27% of woman to delay or forgo need health care. Of those who were uninsured, 67% indicated that they delayed or went without care because of costs. Even insured women who had private coverage (17%) delayed or did not get needed care (Salganicoff, Ranji, & Wyn, 2005).

GEOGRAPHY Women residing in rural areas were less likely to have used any health services, have an ambulatory visit, or obtained prescriptions drugs than near rural women. Women in rural areas were less likely to obtain preventive health services and to be under or uninsured (Waxman, Cohen, Patchias, & Greenberger, 2004).

They were also less likely to access preventive health services and have higher rates of limited activity due to chronic health conditions (Waxman, J., Cohen, E., Patchias, E., & Greenberger, 2004). Women from the South and West were less likely to report use of any health services compared with those of the Midwest. Women in the West were less likely than those in the Northeast and Midwest to have an ambulatory visit (Taylor, Larson, & Correa-de-Araujo, 2006).

### Sexual Orientation

Studies indicate that lesbians seek care only when they have a problem, although most can identify a source of health care. Lesbians prefer female physicians and therapists. Discrimination based on their sexual orientation is very real. There is some indication that emotional and mental health problems may be more pervasive than health problems. The Gay Lesbian Medical Association (2006) suggested 10 things lesbians should discuss with health care providers: breast cancer, depression or anxiety, heart health, gynecological cancer, fitness, tobacco, alcohol, substance use, domestic violence, and osteoporosis.

There is an urgent need for research on Lesbian health according to the Institute of Medicine (National Women's Law Center, 2005). Current research fails to identify and address the health concerns experienced by lesbians, taking into account age, race, and ethnicity (Waxman et al., 2004) There are a range of special health needs for particular groups of women, including immigrant women, women veterans, incarcerated women, women with disabilities, women on welfare, adolescents, homeless women, and women with HIV/AIDS (Women's Health USA 2004; Women's Health USA 2005; Women's Health USA 2006; National Women's Law Center, 2005). They all have unique health problems and barriers to access and quality to overcome. Too many women lack health insurance and lack access to health and to health care providers. Psychosocial issues that are outside the scope of medical specialties cannot be ignored.

- The role of social workers is critical to facilitate, advocate, and broker the health care system. Because of the redirecting of funds from domestic spending to spending on the war effort, both health and human services have been reduced. There will be a need for social workers to be creative in the garnering and provision of services.
- Social workers in the public health arena need to focus attention on health lifestyles and preventive measures such as smoking cessation, screening for diseases and conditions, nutrition, and physical activity.
- Reproductive and maternal health, mental health, interpersonal violence, and cardiovascular disease are issues that need to be addressed continuously.
- There is a growing trend to recognize the participation of women in conducting gender-specific biomedical research and in promoting policy decisions that reflect the intent of the Women's Health Equity Act of 1991. The same preventive treatment afforded men during a crisis should be extended to women.
- Social workers need to lead efforts to eliminate sexism that result in discrepancies in women's health care and to reduce the fragmentation of women's care that result from the lack of integration of women's social, mental, and physical health need to continue.
- Finally, all social workers in medical and mental health settings need to join the national movement toward health care reform to provide basic health care, including psychosocial services, for all Americans including psychosocial services. Social workers need to join with women in creating a model of heath care services.

## REFERENCES

Abramovitz, M. (1991). *Regulating the lives of women*. Boston: South End Press, p. 37.

Brennan, N. (2000). *Health insurance coverage of the near elderly*. Series B No.B-21. Washington, DC: The Urban Institute.

Broom, D. (1991). *Damned if we do. Contradictions in Women's Health Care*. Sydney, Australia: Allen & Unwin Pty.

Clancy, C., & Massion, C. (1992). American women's health care: A patchwork quilt with gaps. *JAMA, 268*, 1918–1920.

Costin, L. (1983a). *Two sisters for social justice*. Urbana: University of Illinois Press.

Costin, L. (1983b). Women and physicians: The 1930 white house conference on children. *Social Work, 28*(2), 108–115.

Costin, L., Bell, C., & Downs, S. (1991). *Child welfare: Policies and practice*. United Kingdom: Longman Group.

Davis, K., & Schoen, K. (1978). Health and the war on poverty: A ten year appraisal. Washington, DC: Brookings Institution.

Galambos, C. (2006). Health care coverage for poor women: Dwindling support. *Health and Social Work, 31*, 3–6. Retrieved August 23, 2006, from http://plinks.ebscohost.com

Inlander, C. (1992). Making women a disease. *Nursing Economics, 10*, 146.

Mahowald, M. (1993). *Women and children in health care*. New York: Oxford University Press.

Gay Lesbian Medical Association. (2006). Ten things lesbians should discuss with health care providers. Retrieved August 14, 2006, from http://glma.org/indes.cfm?fuseaction = Page.viewPage&pageID = 691

Pinn, V. (1992). Women's health research. *JAMA, 268*, 1921–1922.

Roberts, M. (2006). Racial and ethnic difference in health insurance coverage and usual source of health care, 2000. Agency for Healthcare Research and Quality, *MEPS Chartbook* No.14 AHRQ Pub.No. 06–0004, Rockville. Retrieved September 21, 2006, from www.meps.ah

Salganicoff, A., Ranji, U., & Wyn, R. (2005, July). Women and health care: A national profile. Key findings from the Kaiser Women's Health Survey. Kaiser Family Foundation Publication No. 7336. Retrieved September 21, 2006, from http://www.kff.org/womenshealth/733

Satcherl, D. (2001). American women and health disparities. *Journal of American Medical Women's Association, 56*, 199–205. Retrieved November 1, 2006, from http://www.globalaging.org/health/usAmericanwomenandhealthdisparities.htm

Taylor, A., Larson, S., & Correa-de-Araujo, R. (2006). Women's health care utilization and expenditures. *Women's health issues, 16*, 66–79.

U.S. Department of Health and Human Services, Health Resources and Services Administration. *Women's Health USA 2005*. Rockville, Maryland: U.S. Department of Health and Human Services, 2005. Retrieved October 7, 2006, from http://mchb.hrsa.gov/whusa_05/pages/toc.htm

Waxman, J., Cohen, E., Patchias, E., & Greenberger, M. (2004). Making the grade on women's health. National Women's Law Center—Oregon Health & Science University. Retrieved September 21, 2006, from http://www.nwlc.org/details.cfm?id=1861&section=health

*Women's Health Care in the United States: Selected Findings from the 2004 National Healthcare Quality and Disparities Reports*. Fact Sheet. AHRQ Publication No. 05-P021. May 2005. Agency for Healthcare Research and Quality, Rockville, MD. Retrieved August 31, 2006 from http://www.ahrq.gov/qual/nhqrwomen/nhqrwomen.htm

*The Women's Network for a Sustainable Future*. Public health, women, and corporate responsibility. WNSF Net Notes, 2003, *1*(3), 1–3. Retrieved on November 19, 2007, from http://www.wnsf.org/index.php?com=static_content&view&do=view&id=216

## FURTHER READING

*AHRQ Women's Health Highlights: Recent Findings*. Program Brief. AHRQ Publication No. 06-P008, January 2006. Agency for Healthcare Research and Quality, Rockville, MD. Retrieved on August 31, 2006, from http://www.ahrq.gov/research/womenh1.htm

Disease and conditions that affect older women. Retrieved on August 14, 2006, from http://www.womancando.org/over65/olderwomenconditions.htm

Estronaut A Forum for Women's Health. *Women and substance abuse*. Retrieved on August 11, 2006, from http://www.estronaut.com/a/women_substance_abuse_drugs_alcohol.htm

Kaiser Family Foundation (2006, February). Women and HIV/AIDS in the United States. *HIV/AIDS Policy Fact Sheet* #6092–03. Retrieved on August 31, 2006, from www.kff.org

Kumabe, K., Nishida, C., O'Hara, D., & Woodruff, C. (1986). *A handbook for social work education and practice in community health settings*. Hawaii: University of Hawaii School of Social Work.

Office of Applied Studies, Substance Abuse and Mental Health Services Administration. (August 5, 2005). Substance abuse and dependence among women. *The NSDUH Report*. Retrieved August 5, 2006, from http://www.oas.samhsa.gov

Office of Applied Studies, SAMHSA. (2006). Women in substance abuse treatment. The DASIS Report. Retrieved on August 31, 2006, from http://www.drugabusestatistics.samhsa.gov/2k1/FemTX/FemTX.htm

Office of Research on Women's Health, National Institutes of Health. (2006). Women of color health data book adolescents to seniors. Retrieved September 21, 2006, from http://orwh.od.nih.gov/pubs/WomenofColor2006.pdf

Society for Women's Health Research. What do women suffer from? Retrieved on August 14, 2006, from http://www.womenshealthresearch.org/site/PageServer?pagename=hs_sbb_suffer

Health Resources and Services Administration, U.S. Department of Health and Human Services. (2005). *Women's Health USA 2005*. Rockville, MD: U.S. Department of Health and Human Services. Retrieved October 7, 2006, from http://mchb.hrsa.gov/whusa_05/pages/toc.htm

*Women's Health Care in the United States: Selected Findings From the 2004 National Healthcare Quality and Disparities Reports*.

Fact Sheet. AHRQ Publication No. 05-P021. (2005, May). Agency for Healthcare Research and Quality, Rockville, MD. Retrieved August 31, 2006, from http://www.ahrq. gov/qual/nhqrwomen/nhqrwomen.htm

### OTHER SOURCES

AHRQ Women's Health Highlights: Recent Findings. Program Brief. AHRQ Publication No. 06-P008, January 2006. Agency for Healthcare Research and Quality, Rockville, MD. Retrieved on August 31, 2006, from http://www.ahrq. gov/research/womenh1.htm

Disease and conditions that affect older women. Retrieved on August 14, 2006, from http://www.womancando.org/ over65/olderwomenconditions.htm

Estronaut A Forum for Women's Health. *Women and substance abuse*. Retrieved on August 11, 2006, from http://www.estro-naut.com/a/women_substance_abuse_drugs_alcohol.htm

Office of Applied Studies, SAMHSA (2006). Women in substance abuse treatment. The DASIS Report. Retrieved on August 31, 2006, from http://www.drugabusestatistics. samhsa.gov/2k1/FemTX/FemTX.htm

Society for Women's Health Research. What do women suffer from? Retrieved on August 14, 2006, from http:// www.womenshealthresearch.org/site/PageServer?pagename = hs_sbb_suffer

—MARIAN A. AGUILAR

**WOMEN IN SOCIAL POLICY.** *See* Social Policy; Women: Overview.

# WORKERS' COMPENSATION

ABSTRACT: Workers' Compensation is a form of social insurance financed and administered by each of the 50 states, the federal government (for federal workers), and the District of Columbia that protects workers and their families from some of the economic consequences of workplace-related accidents and illnesses.

KEY WORDS: social insurance; unemployment insurance; income support and maintenance; disability insurance; social security

Workers' Compensation (formerly known as Workman's Compensation), the earliest social insurance program enacted in the United States, protects workers who are injured on the job or who suffer job-related illnesses. The federal government established a Workers' Compensation program for its own employees in 1908. Starting in 1911, the individual states, with Wisconsin in the lead, inaugurated their own programs.

Workers' Compensation spread broadly during the Progressive Era, with relatively little opposition since it served both business and labor interests. Employer support was widespread because the program standardized their illness and injury obligations. Instead of an unpredictable court system, in which a worker's claim and a sympathetic jury might elicit exceedingly large financial awards, Workers' Compensation created predictable costs, procedures, and awards. For employees, Workers' Compensation provided guaranteed protection—automatic help when one could not continue on the job because of injury or illness.

### Work Injury and Illness

While workplace safety has improved considerably in the century since Workers' Compensation was initiated, a significant number of American worker's are still injured on the job annually; an additional number suffer work-related illnesses. These injuries run the gamut from lethal industrial accidents to injuries causing permanent disability (such as spinal cord injury) to chronic stress-related disorders (such as carpel tunnel syndrome) to minor scrapes and burns. Workers' Compensation covers the injury spectrum, modest or severe, temporary or permanent.

At one end of the continuum, Workers' Compensation—and other programs—provides monetary help to the spouses and dependent children of individuals who die on the job. About 6,000 workers are killed on the job annually and claims for compensation are filed for most. After 9/11/2001 for example, over 2,200 claims were made on behalf of surviving family members with an additional 3,400 claims from injured workers themselves. In addition to fatal accidents, nearly 60,000 workers, and former workers, die annually as a result of job-related diseases such as asbestosis and black lung disease.

Most Workers' Compensation claims, however, result from workplace accidents, the number of which has significantly declined since 1990 as a result of changing workplace conditions and greater employer and employee attention to safety. The leading cause of injuries—sprains and strains—account for 44% of all accidents. The remaining injuries—cuts, bruises, puncture and the like—are generally minor, usually requiring no time or just a few days off work. All told, 4.4 million injuries were reported in 2003, the equivalent of 5 cases per 100 workers.

### Eligibility, Coverage and Benefits

Workers' Compensation provides automatic, non-means tested protection to over 127 million workers —90% of the workforce—annually. The 10% or so of the workforce excluded work in states that do not cover employees in agriculture, domestic service, firms with fewer than 5 employees, and nonprofit organizations. Three types of compensation are provided—cash benefits, medical benefits, and rehabilitation services. In 2003, $54.9 billion was provided in benefits. Although most claims were for medical expenses, the bulk of program spending is in the form of income-replacement payments.

From the start, the primary objective of Workers' Compensation was to fairly compensate workers for lost wages. While benefit "adequacy" is the ostensible goal, actual wage replacement formulas vary considerably from state to state, and typically vary according to whether payments are for temporary or permanent disability. In the case of temporary disability, payments average about two-thirds of pretax wages, a level that policymakers in most states have come to see as fair to workers without providing a disincentive to returning to work. Most states also set "floors" and "ceilings" on compensation, so state-by-state variations are significant. In 2006, for example, the maximum weekly benefit in Iowa was $1133, and just $351 in Mississippi.

### Administration and Finance

Workers' Compensation is designed and operated by the states and, like other state programs, vary significantly by jurisdiction. They vary, for example, in terms of benefit levels, especially wage-replacement levels, the contingencies covered, the remedies for employer or employee appeals, and the balance between private and public involvement.

In all cases, however, Workers' Compensation is employer-funded. Most states require employers to purchase Workers' Compensation insurance policies, either from commercial firms or from a state Workers' Compensation fund. As with other forms of business insurance, premiums vary with industry classifications—the basis for assessing the degree of employee risk and the associated premium costs. In some states, individual employers are also "experience rated," meaning that their premiums reflect the number and types of claims made against them in the past. Some companies, particularly large firms, do "self insure," which means they forego insurance and pay any verified employee claims directly.

Workers' Compensation is an essential element in an extensive and complicated disability compensation system, a system that includes income support, health insurance, and social service components. In medical coverage, Workers' Compensation usually pays the medical costs for initial work-related injuries. Since Medicare does not come into effect until 29 months after the onset of a disabling condition, the "day one" coverage of Workers' Compensation is critical.

Workers' Compensation starts replacing lost income after a short wait period, 3–7 days for temporary disabilities, with employer-provided sick leave, where available, covering the first postaccident days. Temporary disability benefits are critical since Social Security disability insurance is restricted to individuals who have *long*-term impairments. For those workers who *don't* qualify for Social Security, Workers' Compensation long-term wage-replacement is available, providing critical safety set benefits. Finally, Workers' Compensation pays benefits to the survivors of workers who die on the job, in conjunction with Social Security survivor insurance. In helping injured workers get back on the job, Workers' Compensation coordinates with vocational rehabilitation programs.

### Policy Debates and Trends

While compensation is "no-fault," with benefits available whether the primary cause of the injury is employee or employer negligence, disagreements about the appropriate remedy for a worker's claim for compensation often occur. One area of contention is whether an injury is, in fact, work related. Psychiatric and substance abuse conditions, for example, create dilemmas—they are covered in some states, but not in others. Controversy also surrounds carpel tunnel syndrome; some argue this as a disability that is more an "ordinary disease of life" than one strictly work related. In situations where an injury claim reflects workplace conditions in combination with other circumstances, an administrative law judge typically resolves the issues in dispute.

The contentious issues surrounding Workers' Compensation reflect the perspectives and interests of the program's primary stakeholders such as unions, insurance carriers, employer organizations, and state regulatory and administrative agencies. In recent years, much of the debate has concerned costs, which rapidly rose in the 1990s. Reflecting what many in the business community interpreted as workers "gaming the system," many states enacted significant program changes in the decade from 1996 to 2006. Several experimented with cost containment reforms, such as deregulating insurance markets, encouraging competition, and giving carriers greater leeway in rate setting and procedures. A few states created public insurance funds to compete with private insurance firms, while others facilitated self-insurance by individual firms, or groups of firms. In California, the Republican Governor, Arnold Schwarzenegger, reduced program costs substantially by placing a cap on temporary disability payments and the use of chiropractors and physical therapists, requiring workers to choose their health care from a restricted HMO-type panel of providers, and requiring the use of generic drugs.

Unions have their own concerns. A long-term complaint has addressed dangerous work conditions, lax safety regulation, and business-friendly Workers' Compensation procedures that often shortchange or delay or inappropriately deny employee benefits. And given the fact that the value of worker benefits have been cut by nearly a third in recent years, unions have been demanding automatic cost-of-living adjustments in cash benefit levels as well as more clearly identified rights for injured workers.

### REFERENCES

Clayton, A. (2003–2004). Workers' compensation: A background for social security professionals. *Social Security Bulletin, 65*(4), 7–15.

National Academy of Social Insurance. (2005, July). *Workers' compensation: Benefits, coverage, and costs, 2003.* Washington, DC: Author.

National Academy of Social Insurance. (n.d.). *Fact sheet: Workers' compensation pays benefits in wake of september 11th attacks.* Washington, DC: Author.

Reno, V., Williams, C. T., & Sengupta, I. (2003–2004). Workers' compensation, social security disability insurance, and the offset: A fact sheet. *Social Security Bulletin, 65*(4), 3–6.

Thomason, T., Schmidle, T. P., & Burton, J. F., Jr. (2000). *Workers' compensation—Benefits, costs, and safety under alternative insurance arrangements.* Kalamazoo, MI: W.E. Upjohn Institute for Employment Research.

—PAUL TERRELL

**WORLD SOCIAL SITUATION.** *See* Globalization.

**WORLD WIDE WEB.** *See* Social Work Education: Electronic Technologies.

# Y

## YOUTH AT RISK

**ABSTRACT:** Runaways, throwaways, and homeless youths have always been present in the United States. In recent decades, however, society has become more aware of the problems they face as the problems have become more severe. The effectiveness of new approaches to helping these youths is yet to be determined.

**KEY WORDS:** runaway youth; homelessness; throwaways; foster care; substance abuse; youth suicide; juvenile justice; child welfare

### History

Since settlers arrived in the United States, youth have left home without their parents' permission. In colonial times, many immigrants were teenagers placed by poor families as indentured servants. During the 18th and 19th centuries, teenagers fled slavery in the South and tyranny in their native countries. Adolescents left home during the Great Depression of the 1930s to help with their families' economic burdens.

In the 1960s and 1970s, society recognized that runaways, who were often hungry and homeless, had to resort to stealing or selling drugs or their bodies to survive. Still viewed as delinquents, they were often arrested (Posner, 1991). Also in the 1970s, clinicians divided these youths into those who left home (a) because of their own psychological problems, and (b) to escape dysfunctional family environments.

The Juvenile Justice and Delinquency Prevention Act of 1974 (Pub. L No. 93-415) prohibited states from jailing youth for behavior that is not criminal if committed by adults. Congress recognized the need for short-term shelter and services for those who are forced from their homes (throwaways); those who run from residential facilities and foster homes; and those who run from their own homes to escape (a) abuse, neglect, or other family problems; or (b) parental control (Bass, 1992).

In the late 1980s, professionals realized that severe problems precluded some youths from returning home. Longer residential care was authorized (Pub. L No. 106-71). Congress also began to address problems that required more intensive intervention. It created programs to address substance abuse problems (Pub. L

No. 100-690) and street outreach to reduce sexual victimization of youths (Pub. L No. 103-322).

With the mid-1990s came a new focus on positive youth development. This approach focuses on building youths' skills and self-esteem while offering safe, stable housing and support services so that they can become healthy, successful, and independent adults.

### Definitions

A *runaway* has left home without permission and was away from home at least one night; or who was away from home, did not return home as expected, and chose to stay away overnight. (U.S. Department of Justice, 2002).

A *throwaway* was asked or told to leave home by a parent or other adult in the household for at least one night or was away from home and prevented from returning. The adult did not make arrangements for alternative care (U.S. Department of Justice, 2002).

*Homeless youth* are unaccompanied youth between the ages of 16 and 21 who cannot safely live with a relative and have no safe alternative living situation (Missing, Exploited and Runaway Children Protection Act, Pub. L No. 106-71, 2000).

These definitions are not mutually exclusive. Many youths experience both runaway and throwaway episodes. Both runaways and throwaways may become homeless.

### Latest Research

Most research has focused on identifying the scope of the problem, who is affected, and the problems facing those affected.

**SCOPE OF THE PROBLEM** Data on the problem is limited by several factors. Not all runaway episodes are reported, and it is difficult to locate all homeless youths. Efforts to count homeless youths often do not include those older than 18 years (Levin-Epstein & Greenberg, 2003). Data reported by programs are based on youth who choose to seek help. And, youths often are embarrassed to report some problems.

The Second National Incidence Studies of Missing, Abducted, Runaway, and Throwaway Children (NIS-MART-2) estimated that in 1999, 1,682,900 youths had a runaway or throwaway episode (Sedlak, Finkelhor, Hammer, & Schultz, 2002). An earlier study, conducted by the Research Triangle Institute (RTI) estimated that as many as 2.8 million youth reported a runaway episode (Research Triangle Institute [RTI], 1995). An estimated 500,000 to 1.3 million runaway and throwaway youths become homeless each year (National Alliance to End Homelessness, 2006).

DEMOGRAPHICS Runaways and homeless youths aged 12–17 are more likely to be female, over 50–68% (RTI, 1995; Administration for Children and Families [ACF], 2005). Those who enter shelters directly from the street are also more likely to be female. Fifty-four percent of throwaways entering programs from the street, however, are more likely to be male), as are street youths aged 18–21 (ACF, 2005).

A disproportionate percentage of these youths are Black. The percentage of Black youths ranged from 28% of homeless youths and 17% of runaways using federally funded shelters between 1985 and 1988 (U.S. General Accountability Office [GAO], 1989) to 40.7% of the youths in shelters in the RTI study. Runaway and Homeless Youth Management Information System (RHYMIS) data from FY 1997 identified 24% of youths in federally funded shelters (Thompson, Safyer, & Pollio, 2001), and from FY 2004 the data identified 27% of the youth who used shelter and transitional living programs as Black (ACF, FY 2005). The National Runaway Switchboard reported that, in FY 2004 and 2005, 27 and 29% of the youth callers, respectively, were Black (U.S. Department of Health and Human Services [HHS], 2006).

Youth of Hispanic ethnicity range from 13 to 19.7% of youths in shelters (RTI, 1995; Thompson et al., 2001). Approximately 17.7% of those in the RTI street component were Hispanic.

### Problems Faced by At-Risk Youth

Youths face problems that result from interpersonal issues, personal behavior, family behavior, societal attitudes and resources, and community environmental conditions.

Youths most frequently leave home due to severe interpersonal problems with parents or other family members. Experts estimate that 60% of females and 25% of males who runaway were sexually assaulted prior to leaving home (Anderson, 2004). NISMART-2 found that 21% of runaway or throwaway youths had been sexually or physically abused prior to leaving home, or were afraid they would be abused if they returned (Hammer, Finkelhor, & Sedlak, 2002).

RTI also found that youths most frequently run away because of family problems, with 63% of youth in the shelter sample and 61% of youth in the street sample

reporting emotional abuse. A household member had threatened to throw the youth out in 63% of the shelter sample and 70% of the street sample. Forty-six percent of runaway and homeless youth had been physically abused and 17% sexually abused (HHS, 1997).

An exploratory study found discrepancies between the views of youths and their parents regarding the cause of family dynamic problems. Unlike youths, none of parents believed that they contributed to their child's departure from home (Safyer et al., 2004).

Society and systems failures sometimes increase youths' problems. Youths who reside in substitute care facilities are more likely to runaway than those who live at home. They are likely to stay away longer and run farther. The longer they are away, the more likely it is that they will lack health-care and educational services, be victimized, and succumb to substance abuse or prostitution to survive. They may also turn to shoplifting, panhandling, stealing, or violence to survive. If they do return to care, they are more likely to run away repeatedly (Dedel, 2006; Sedlak, Finkelhor, Hammer, & Schultz, 2002).

Each year, between 20,000 and 25,000 youths aged 16 and older leave foster care through emancipation or because they "age out" of the system (National Alliance to End Homelessness, 2006). Anywhere from 12 to 36% of these youth experience homelessness (Child Welfare League of America, n.d.). Besides youths who become homeless after leaving foster care, youths released from a juvenile detention facility or other residential facility (for example, mental health) may become homeless if adequate resources are not available. A study of homelessness among young people in Minnesota revealed that one fourth of those who left foster care or a correctional facility within the past year had no stable housing when they left (Wilder Research, 2005). These youths have many personal issues. They are generally disconnected from caregivers and permanent, safe living situations. They suffer from higher than average rates of depression, mental health problems, alcohol and drug problems, and delinquency.

NISMART-2 found that 19% of the runaway and homeless youths were dependent upon substances, 18% were in the company of a substance abuser, and 17% were using hard drugs. Eleven percent were engaged in criminal activity during the runaway or throwaway episode. A summary of current research concluded that about 75% of homeless youth use drugs (The National Child Traumatic Stress Network, 2007).

RTI reported that 41% of females in the shelter component and 50% of females in the street component had ever been pregnant. Twelve percent of females in both components were pregnant at the time of the study. Studies from the mid-1990s suggest that 3–10% of homeless youths are gay, lesbian, bisexual, or transgender. More recent studies suggest that the percentage may range from 35 to 50%. Their sexual orientation often plays a role in the runaway or throwaway episode and they are more likely to be victimized than are other homeless youths (Ray, 2006).

Health and mental health problems are rampant. Over 50% of the adolescents entering the juvenile justice system have health problems and learning disabilities that were not diagnosed prior to entrance. Often these problems are not adequately addressed during confinement and youth leave without any help in obtaining needed services.

Almost half of the youth in foster care have chronic health problems. Sixty to 80% have severe mental health issues. Nearly 44% of those aging out of care have trouble accessing needed services. Only 21% of those leaving care were able to continue receiving mental health services (National Association of Social Workers, 2001). These youths are at increased risk for considering and attempting suicide (RTI, 1995). The longer they are homeless, the greater the risk for suicide (Centre for Suicide Prevention, 2004).

Youths face challenges in continuing their education. This affects their employability and self-sufficiency after exiting residential environments. In one study, 46% of youth had not finished high school 2 ½ to 4 years after leaving care. In another study of 133 former foster youth who exited care 12–18 months prior to the study, 37% had not finished high school (GAO, 1999).

The problems faced by these youths mirror those faced by disconnected adults in American Society. Those with little or no education are more likely to be unemployed and impoverished, and more likely to lack housing and health care. They are also more likely to suffer from serious health problems, including HIV and AIDS.

### Efforts to Address Youth Problems

The first three programs discussed here are administered by the Family and Youth Services Bureau (FYSB) in HHS. FYSB expects agencies that receive grants through these programs to promote positive youth development (PYD). As defined by FYSB, PYD must inform youths about healthy behaviors and interactions; provide safe, structured places for study and socializing or recreational activities; promote better relationships with adult role models; help youths develop skills (for example, literacy, competence, work readiness, social interaction); and help youths build self-esteem (ACF, 2006a, 2006b).

PYD is a promising practice that is increasingly used by nonprofit organizations and foundations in addition to government agencies. The effectiveness of PYD is still being assessed.

BASIC CENTER PROGRAM The Basic Center program, established by Pub. L No. 93-415 for runaways and later amended to include homeless youth, was designed to meet the immediate needs of adolescents who left home and remained away from home without parental permission. Local community-based grantees provide services outside of other service delivery systems (for example, juvenile justice, child welfare, mental health). Grantees provide outreach, short-term emergency shelter (up to 15 days), counseling (individual, group, and family), food, clothing, aftercare, and referrals for other services, as needed. Shelters must be located in areas frequented or easily reached by runaway and homeless youth, and must offer services 24 hours a day. Basic Center programs served 121,356 youths between FY 2004–2005, while 23,991 youths were turned away (HHS, 2006).

A key program goal is to reunite youth with their families. Without alternate state requirements, staff must contact a parent or guardian within 72 hours. For youths who cannot return home, staff try to find alternative living situations (ACF, 2006a).

TRANSITIONAL LIVING PROGRAM Recognizing the need of older homeless youths (aged 16–21) for longer term residential care, Congress amended P. L. 93–415 in 1988 to include the Transitional Living Program (TLP) for homeless youths. TLP provides residential care and intensive services for up to 18 months to help youths aged 16–21 who cannot return to their families, but are not prepared to live independently, and an additional 180 days for those not yet 18 years old. Besides housing, TLP programs provide independent living skills training; substance abuse education and prevention; referrals or access to mental health and medical treatment; services or referrals for education (secondary, postsecondary where possible, and vocational); and services or referrals to help pregnant and parenting homeless youths become effective parents. In FY 2004–2005, TLP programs served 8,202 youths, while 16,759 youths were turned away.

The Runaway, Homeless and Missing Children Protection Act of 2003 (Pub. L No. 108-96) expanded eligibility for TLP to include maternity group homes—but without separate funding. These facilities address the needs of pregnant homeless young women whose babies are at high risk for low birth weight and infant mortality.

STREET OUTREACH PROGRAM  The Street Outreach Program (SOP) is authorized by the Education and Prevention Services to Reduce Sexual Abuse of Runaway, Homeless, and Street Youth Program. SOP is designed to help street youth who are at risk of or have been subjected to sexual exploitation or abuse.

SOP staff builds relationships with young people living on the street and encourages them to move and adjust to appropriate living situations. Services must include treatment, counseling, and information and referral. Staff must have access to local emergency shelters appropriate for and available to young people and must be allowed to maintain their interactions with youth placed in these shelters. Staff must offer services during the hours youth tend to be on the streets, including nights and weekends. Staff includes people with gender, ethnicity, and experiences similar to those of the youth they serve. They must receive training and street-based supervision. In FY 2005, staff made 643,598 contacts with street youths (HHS, 2006).

OTHER PROGRAMS  In 1998, Congress amended Pub. L No. 93-415 to authorize the Drug Abuse Education and Prevention Program. Between FY1989 and 1995, this program funded demonstration and service delivery projects for runaways and homeless youths. Considered duplicative of other programs, it was discontinued. This program was an integrated part of the Runaway and Homeless Youth Network. Providers serving these youths must now coordinate with other service delivery systems to help youths obtain needed services. One study suggested that the unmet need for substance abuse services is growing (Sedlak, Schultz, Wiener, & Cohen, 1997).

Programs administered by the HHS Children's Bureau include the 1999 John H. Chafee Foster Care Independence Program (ILP) (Pub. L No. 106-169). Similar to the TLP, ILP funds may be used to provide room and board until age 21 for youths who have aged out of foster care (up to 30% of the state's allotment). FYSB and the Children's Bureau have been working to assure coordination between these programs. The Promoting Safe and Stable Families Amendments of 2001 (Pub. L No. 107-133) authorized vouchers for education and training, including post secondary learning and education, for youth who have aged out of foster care. These amendments also give states the option of allowing these young people to remain eligible for Medicaid up to age 21.

Other federally funded programs providing resources specifically for these youths include the Education for Homeless Children and Youth and the No Child Left Behind Programs administered by the U.S. Department of Education. Programs that may target these youth, among others, include the Health Care for the Homeless Program and the Projects for Assistance in Transition from Homelessness administered by HHS. The U.S. Department of Housing and Urban Development administers Shelter + Care and the Family Unification Program, which provides Section 8 vouchers for young people aging out of foster care.

## A Promising Community-Wide Approach

A community-wide program offering a continuum of support for runaway, throwaway, and homeless youths may result in successful outcomes. One example is Urban Peak Denver. This program collaborates with numerous federal, state, and local programs to obtain referrals and provide the following: street outreach and testing for sexually transmitted diseases; staff for a medical clinic, HIV testing, and an on-site pharmacy; educational services for General Equivalency Degree and post secondary education; employment services; substance abuse treatment; transitional and supportive housing; assessments and psychological evaluations; pregnancy prevention services; and recreation services. In 2004, 63% of the youths served by Urban Peak had a successful housing outcome (Burt, Pearson, & Montgomery, 2005).

## Key Roles for Social Workers and Future Trends

At the community level, social workers work with youths in foster care and ILP programs. They also work with youths in shelters, TLP programs, and other youth-serving agencies. Social workers must develop collaborative approaches to address the needs of youths. They must also work with youths where they feel comfortable, including on the street. Social workers need to serve youths through a continuum of care, including outreach, intake and assessment, case management, and aftercare. Equally important, they must be willing to conduct research on successful approaches to use in advocating for youths and the services or supports youths need.

National Association of Social Workers has developed standards for the practice of social work with adolescents. State and national continuing education is available to help social workers meet youths' needs. Social workers need to take advantage of training as new approaches, resources, and services become available for youths.

### REFERENCES

Administration for Children and Families [ACF]. (FY 2005). *NEO-RHYMIS.* Washington, DC: U.S. Department of Health and Human Services, Administration for Children and Families, Administration on Children, Youth and Families, Family and Youth Services Bureau. Reports retrieved December 14, 2006, from https://extranet.acf.hhs.gov/rhymis/custom_reports.html

Administration for Children and Families [ACF]. (2006a). *Funding opportunity title: Basic Center Program.* Retrieved December 14, 2006, from http://www.acf.hhs.gov/grants/open/HHS-2006-ACF-ACYF-CY-0063.html

Anderson, J. (Ed.). (2004). Research & advocacy digest. *Homeless, runaway & throwaway youth: Sexual victimization and the consequences of life on the streets.* Olympia, WA: The Washington Coalition on Sexual Assault Programs. Retrieved December 14, 2006, from http://www.wcsap.org/pdf/RAD%207-1.pdf

Bass, D. (1992). *Helping vulnerable youths: Runaway and homeless adolescents in the United States.* Washington, DC: NASW Press.

Burt, M. R., Pearson, C. L., & Montgomery, A. M. (2005). *Strategies for preventing homelessness.* Washington, DC: Prepared for the U.S. Department of Housing and Urban Development, Office of Policy Development and Research, by Walter R. McDonald & Associates, Inc., and The Urban Institute. Retrieved January 30, 2007, from http://www.urban.org/uploadedPDF/1000874_preventing_homelessness.pdf

Centre for Suicide Prevention. (2004). *Suicide among the homeless.* Retrieved January 5, 2007, from http://www.suicideinfo.ca/csp/assets/alert56.pdf

Child Welfare League of America. (n.d.). *Programs and resources for youth aging out of foster care.* Retrieved January 30, 2007, from http://www.cwla.org/programs/fostercare/agingoutresoruces.htm

Dedel, K. (2006). *Juvenile runaways.* Problem-oriented guides for police. Problem-specific guides series no. 37. Washington, DC: U.S. Department of Justice, Office of Community Oriented Policing Services. Retrieved January 30, 2007, from http://www.cops.usdoj.gov/mime/open.pdf?Item = 1694

Levin-Epstein, J., & Greenberg, M. H. (Eds.). (2003). *Leave no youth behind: Opportunities for Congress to reach disconnected youth.* Washington, DC: Center for Law and Social Policy. Retrieved December 5, 2006, from http://www.clasp.org/publications/Disconnected_Youth.pdf

U.S. General Accountability Office. (1989). *Homelessness: Homeless and runaway youth receiving services at federally funded shelters.* Washington, DC: Author

Wilder Research. (2005). *Homeless in Minnesota: A closer look—Youth and young adults on their own.* Retrieved January 25, 2007, from http://www.wilder.org/download.o.htm?report = 410&summary = 1

U.S. General Accountability Office. [GAO]. (1999). *Foster care challenges in helping youths live independently.* Washington, DC: Statement of Cynthia M. Fagnoni, Director, Education, Workforce, and Income Security Issues, Health, Education, and Human Services Division.

U.S. Department of Health and Human Services [HHS]. (1997). *Youth with runaway, throwaway, and homeless experiences: Prevalence, drug-use, and other at-risk behaviors.* Washington, DC: U.S. Department of Health and Human

Services, Administration for Children and Families, Administration on Children, Youth and Families; Family and Youth Services Bureau. Available from the National Clearinghouse on Families and Youth (301) 608–8098.

U.S. Department of Health and Human Services [HHS]. (2006). *Report to congress on the youth programs of the Family and Youth Services Bureau for fiscal years 2004 and 2005.* Washington, DC: U.S. Department of Health and Human Services, Administration for Children and Families, Administration on Children, Youth and Families, Family and Youth Services Bureau.

The National Child Traumatic Stress Network. (2007). *Culture and trauma brief* (V2 n1 2007). Retrieved February 5, 2007, from http://www.nctsnct.org/nctsn.assets/pdfs/culture_and_trauma_brief_v2n1_Homeless Youth.pdf

National Alliance to End Homelessness. (2006). *Fundamental issues to prevent and end youth homelessness (Youth homelessness series, brief no. 1).* Washington, DC: Author. Retrieved February 5, 2007, from http://www.fcadv.org/resources/pdfs/Fundamental%20Issues%20to%20Prevent%20and%20End%20Youth%20Homelessness.pdf

National Association of Social Workers. (2001). What social workers should know about the social context of adolescent health. In *Practice update from the National Association of Social Workers, Vol. 2, No. 1.* Washington, DC: Author. Retrieved January 30, 2007, from http://www.socialworkers.org/practice/adolescent.health/ah0201.asp

Posner, M. (1991). *Runaway youth and interagency collaboration: A review of the literature.* (Submitted to U.S. Department of Health and Human Services, Administration for Children and Families, Administration for Children, Youth and Families, Family and Youth Services Bureau.) Newton, MA: Project PROTECT, Education Development Center.

Ray, N. (2006). *Lesbian, gay, bisexual and transgender youth: An epidemic of homelessness.* New York: National Gay and Lesbian Task Force Policy Institute and the National Coalition for the Homeless.

Research Triangle Institute [RTI]. (1995). *Youth with runaway, throwaway, and homeless experiences: Prevalence, drug use, and other at-risk behaviors.* Washington, DC: Prepared for the U.S. Department of Health and Human Services, Administration for Children and Families, Administration on Children, Youth and Families by RTI.

Safyer, A. W., Thompson, S. J., Maccio, E. M., Zittel-Palamara, & Forehand, G. (2004). Adolescents' and parent's perceptions of runaway behavior: Problems and solutions. *Child and Adolescent Social Work Journal, 21*(8), 495–512.

Sedlak, A. J., Finkelhor, D., Hammer, H., & Schultz, D. J. (2002). *NISMART: National estimates of missing children: An overview.* Washington, DC: U.S. Department of Justice, Office of Justice Programs, Office of Juvenile Justice and Delinquency Prevention. Retrieved December 5, 2006, from http://www.ncjrs.gov/pdffiles1/ojjdp/196465.pdf

Sedlak, A. J., Schultz, D. J., Wiener, S., & Cohen, B. (1997). *National evaluation of runaway and homeless youth [Final report].* Washington, DC: Prepared by Westat, Inc., and the Urban Institute for HHS, Administration for Children and Families, Administration on Children, Youth and Families.

Thompson, S. J., Safyer, A. W., & Pollio, D. E. (2001). Differences and predictors of family reunification among subgroups of runaway youths using shelter services. *Social Work Research*, 25(3), 163–172. Washington, DC: National Association of Social Workers.

Hammer, H., Finkelhor, D., & Sedlak, A. J. (2002). *Runaway/thrownaway children: National estimates and characteristics*. Washington, DC: U.S. Department of Justice, Office of Justice Programs, Office of Juvenile Justice and Delinquency Prevention.

## FURTHER READING

Congressional Research Service Received through the CRS Web. (2005). *CRS Report for Congress homelessness: Recent statistics, targeted federal programs, and recent legislation*. Washington, DC: The Library of Congress, Congressional Research Service. Retrieved December 5, 2006, from http://www.fas.org/sgp/crs/misc/RL30442.pdf

Family and Youth Services Bureau. (2006). *Family and Youth Services Bureau Information memorandum runaway and homeless youth (RHY) program coordination with the McKinney-Vento School Act (Subtitle B or title VII; 42 U.S.C. 11432 et seq.)*. Washington, DC: U.S. Department of Health and Human Services. Retrieved January 30, 2007, from http://www.acf.hhs.gov/programs/fysb/content/aboutfysb/McKinney-Vento_IM.pdf

Greene, J. M., Sanchez, R., Harris, J., et al. (2003). *Incidence and Prevalence of Homeless and Runaway Youth Final Report*. Prepared for U.S. Department of Health and Human Services, Office of the Assistant Secretary for Planning and Evaluation, Office of Planning, Research and Evaluation, Administration for Children and Families.

Morton, M. (2007) *Written statement for a national academies national community forum on adolescent health care*. Washington, DC: National Network for Youth. Retrieved December 5, 2006, from http://www.nn4youth.org/site/DocServer/Adol_Health_Care.doc?docID = 1221

McNaught, K., & Onkeles, L. (2004). *Improving outcomes for older youth: What judges and attorneys need to know*. Tulsa, OK: National Resource Center for Youth Development. Retrieved December 30, 2006, from http://www.nrcys.ou.edu/yd/resources/publications/pdfs/improveoutcomes.pdf

National Academies of Sciences. (2004). Report brief. *Community programs to promote youth development*. Washington: National Academies of Sciences, Institute of Medicine, National Research Council. Retrieved December 30, 2006, from http://www.bocyf.org/youth_development_brief.pdf

National Clearinghouse on Families & Youth. (March 2006). *The exchange: Transitional living programs move homeless youth closer to independence*. Retrieved January 12, 2007, from http://www.ncfy.com/publications/exchange/0603_tlp.htm

National Clearinghouse on Families & Youth. (May 2006). *FYSB update. A research summary collaborating to promote positive youth development at the state and local levels*. Retrieved January 12, 2007, from http://www.ncfy.com/publications/pdf/update_0605.pdf

National Clearinghouse on Families & Youth. (July 2006). *The exchange aftercare staying in touch with youth after they have left the system*. Retrieved January 12, 2007, from http://www.ncfy.com/publications/exchange/0607_after.htm

Pollio, D. E., Thompson, S. J., Tobias, L., et. al. (2006). Longitudinal outcomes for youth receiving runaway/homelessness shelter services. *Journal of Youth Adolescence*, 35, 859–866. Springer Science + Business Media, Inc., published online at http://www.springerlink.com/content/07n04n555096t5v1/

Robertson, J. J., & Toro, P. A. (1998). *Homeless youth: Research, intervention, and policy from the 1998 national symposium on homelessness research*. Retrieved January 12, 2007, from http://aspe.hhs.gov/progsys/homeless/symposium/3-Youth.htm

U.S. Department of Health and Human Services. (1994). *Drug abuse prevention program for runaway and homeless youth promising practices from the field*. Washington, DC: U.S. Department of Health and Human Services, Administration for children and Families, Administration on Children, Youth and Families, Family and Youth Services Bureau. Available from the National Clearinghouse on Families and Youth (301) 608–8098.

U.S. Department of Labor. (2006). *Training and employment notice providing employment and training services to homeless and runaway youth*. Washington, DC: Author. Retrieved January 30, 2007, from http://wdr.doleta.gov/directives/corr_doc.cfm?DOCN = 2176

—DEBORAH BASS-RUBENSTEIN

## YOUTH SERVICES

**ABSTRACT:** Youth services are programs, activities, and services aimed at providing a range of opportunities for school-aged children, including mentoring, recreation, education, training, community service, or supervision in a safe environment. The current thrust of youth services is an emphasis on positive youth development. Best practices in youth services include the provision of safety, appropriate supervision, supportive relationships, opportunities to belong, positive social norms, support for efficacy and skill building, and integration of community, school, and family efforts.

**KEY WORDS:** out-of-school time; positive youth development; youth civic engagement

Youth services is an umbrella term for a wide range of programs, activities, and services aimed at youth, typically defined as school-aged children ages 6 to 18 years. Youth services can be targeted to particular populations, defined by neighborhoods or other characteristics, or available to all youth. The goals of youth services may be skill building, networking and support building, character development, physical health, community service, civic engagement, and prevention of at-risk behavior. Services can be delivered through local community centers of national organizations (for example, YMCAs), local groups of national organizations staffed primarily by volunteers (for example, Camp Fire), community-based cultural organizations, religious- or spiritual-based organizations, or even schools.

Service delivery models include mentoring programs, team sports and recreation, education and training, community service, or just a safe place for the after-school hours. Mahoney, Harris, and Eccles (2006) have identified five main reasons youth give for participating in youth services and activities, namely they (a) are enjoyable and exciting, (b) offer encouragement and support, (c) afford opportunities to build skills and to foster self-worth, (d) facilitate interactions with mentors and peers, and (e) provide youth a safe place to congregate.

## History

The first example of a youth services agency is the YMCA, whose full title (Young Men's Christian Association) indicates its original focus as a religiously based community organization for the young men populating major cities in the United Kingdom and the United States during the Industrial Revolution. The first YMCAs were established in London in 1844, but they were quickly exported to Canada and the United States. A parallel organization for young women, the Young Women's Christian Association (YWCA) was founded in 1855 in the United Kingdom to serve similar purposes for young women moving to cities for employment. Although begun as Christian organizations for young adults, they quickly evolved into ecumenical programs serving the health, social, and physical needs of all members of the communities they served.

The settlement house movement in the United States gave rise to organizations such as Hull House in Chicago, founded by Jane Addams and Ellen Gates Starr in 1889, and the Henry Street Settlement in New York, founded by Lillian Wald in 1893. Youth services at such organizations included educational programs, recreational facilities including gymnasiums and swimming pools, music and drama programs, and summer camps, among many other programs. In the early part of the 20th century, several national organizations were established largely around the goals of fostering leadership, citizenship, and life skills among youth, including the Boy Scouts of America (1910), the Camp Fire Girls (1910; expanded in 1975 to include boys and changed to Camp Fire USA), and the Girl Scouts of America (1912). Passage by the U.S. Congress of the Smith-Lever Act of 1914 established the Cooperative Extension Service to promote youth skill development in agriculture and homemaking through such programs as the 4-H program (Head, Heart, Hands, and Health). As part of his New Deal, President Franklin D. Roosevelt expanded youth services in the 1930s through the National Youth Administration and the Civilian Conservation Corps. Such programs were primarily aimed at providing opportunities for employment or vocational training.

The post-war period of the 1950s saw a change in attitudes about youth, when public concerns about increases in juvenile delinquency led to federal funding for programs aimed at addressing youth in crisis, including runaway and homeless youth, school dropouts, and teen parents. Over time, the emphasis switched to an appreciation of the importance of prevention of youth problem behavior.

Thus, the Juvenile Delinquency and Youth Offenses Control Act of 1961 promoted the development of youth programs aimed specifically at delinquency prevention and that included emphases on potential root causes of delinquency, such as poverty, unemployment, family breakdown, and discrimination based on race and class. Two acts in 1974, namely the Juvenile Justice and Delinquency Prevention Act and the Runaway Youth Act, continued funding for such prevention programs but also expanded to a new focus, namely encouraging youth civic engagement. The Runaway Youth Act in particular paved the way for the Family and Youth Services Bureau of the Department of Health and Human Services which was targeted to at-risk youth including runaway and homeless youth. Continuing through the 1980s, the majority of public funding for youth services was targeted at the prevention and control of juvenile delinquency and youth crime.

## Trends and Directions

From the mid-1990s to now, the thrust of youth services has changed from an emphasis on prevention of negative youth behaviors to the promotion of positive youth behaviors and development. This new lens for viewing and developing youth services is known as the positive youth development approach. The positive youth development approach is characterized by attention to youths' strengths and assets rather than their risks and deficits. These strengths can be at the individual level, such as self-esteem, leadership skills, motivation, or religiosity, the interpersonal level, such as relationships with parents or peers, or the community level, such as supportive youth-serving organizations, schools, and neighborhoods. The positive youth development approach recognizes that successful development requires supportive elements in youths' social and environmental contexts. This approach is also distinguished by its emphasis on the potential of *all* youth for positive development (Family and Youth Services Bureau, 2007).

According to Lerner (2004), youth services will be effective in promoting positive youth development if they (a) provide opportunities for youth participation and leadership, (b) emphasize the development of life skills, and (c) involve adult-youth relationships that are both caring and sustained. Traditional programs, such as 4-H and the Boy Scouts and Girl Scouts, are now subsumed under the positive youth development umbrella. Indeed, Lerner (2004) singles out 4-H as an exemplary program, in that it is built upon the contributions of youth to their families and communities and it is concerned with the development of both life skills and leadership skills.

One of the thrusts of the positive youth development approach has been an emphasis on facilitating youth civic engagement. Programs and services that promote youth civic engagement do so by enabling youth to become involved in their communities and encouraging them to envision and work toward tangible improvements in their communities (Family and Youth Services Bureau, 2007). Youth services agencies can promote civic engagement by creating opportunities to be involved in public policy discussions, community coalitions, boards of organizations, social movements, and service-learning projects.

Another recent trend (Bodilly & Beckett, 2005) in youth services has been increased attention to how youth spend their after-school time (also called out-of-school-time). As the number of mothers of school-age children working outside the home has increased over the last several decades, so has the demand for after-school arrangements for their children (Bodilly & Beckett, 2005). Yet after-school programs are not exclusively used by children with working mothers; while 17% of 5–14 year old children with working mothers participate in such organized activities, 11% of children whose mothers do not work outside the home participate in such programs. (Blau & Currie, 2004). The federal and state governments have also increased their support for after-school programs in the last several years. Some of these programs provide mere supervision and recreation, but there is a growing movement to have these programs focus on the promotion of academic achievement and the attainment of life skills through mentoring or other such programs included in the positive youth development approach to youth services. Programs that use evidence-based skill

training approaches have consistently been found to yield positive benefits for youth across academic, emotional, and behavioral domains (Durlak & Weissberg, 2007). Despite recent public and media concern that children are being "over-scheduled," Mahoney, Harris, and Eccles (2006) found no support for this notion and instead found that participation in organized activities was associated with a host of positive outcomes for youth, including better psychological adjustment, higher rates of school completion, and lower rates of risk behaviors.

### Best Practices

A recent review of available evaluation research on youth services programs convened by the National Academy of Sciences and the Institute of Medicine (Eccles & Appleton Gootman, 2002) concluded that there is consistent evidence that programs that successfully promote positive youth development tend to share eight key features:

(1) Physical and psychological safety
(2) Clear and consistent structure and appropriate adult supervision
(3) Supportive relationships
(4) Opportunities to belong
(5) Positive social norms
(6) Support for efficacy and mattering
(7) Opportunities for skill building
(8) Integration of family, school, and community efforts.

The report cited as exemplary programs the Teen Outreach Program, Big Brothers/Big Sisters, and Quantum Opportunities. Despite these findings, the report notes a specific need for more high-quality, theory-based, experimental evaluations of youth services programs.

### Roles or Implications for Social Work

Youth services agencies, particularly those working from the positive youth development framework, epitomize the core values of the social work profession as outlined by the National Association of Social Workers' Code of Ethics. Specifically, these programs encourage youth *service* to the community, promote youth involvement in social change to affect *social justice*, assume the *dignity and worth* of all youth, and emphasize and build upon the *importance of human relationships*. Social workers and youth services professionals should strive to promote these values by facilitating youth participation in all levels of their agencies and by actively seeking out and acting upon youths' own opinions, needs assessments, and strategies for positive change.

## REFERENCES

Blau, D., & Currie, J. (2004). *Preschool, day care, and after school care: Who's minding the kids? (Working paper 10670)*. Cambridge, MA: National Bureau of Economic Research.

Bodilly, S., & Beckett, M. K. (2005). *Making out-of-school time matter: Evidence for an action agenda*. Santa Monica, CA: RAND Corporation.

Durlak, J. A., & Weissberg, R. P. (2007). *The impact of after-school programs that promote personal and social skills*. Chicago, IL: Collaborative for Academic, Social and Emotional Learning.

Eccles, J., & Appleton Gootman, J. (Eds.). (2002). *Community programs to promote youth development*. Washington, DC: National Research Council and Institute of Medicine, National Academy Press.

Family and Youth Services Bureau. (2007). *Putting positive youth development into practice: A resource guide*. Washington, DC: Administration on Children, Youth and Families, Administration for Children and Families, U.S. Department of Health and Human Services.

Lerner, R. M. (2004). *Liberty: Thriving and civic engagement among America's youth*. Mahwah, NJ: Sage.

Mahoney, J. L., Harris, A. L., & Eccles, J. S. (2006). Organized activity participation, positive youth development, and the over-scheduling hypothesis. *Social Policy Report, 20*(4), 3–31.

## FURTHER READING

Camino, L., & Shepherd, Z. (2002). From periphery to center: Pathways for youth civic engagement in the day-to-day lives of communities. *Applied Developmental Science, 6*(4), 213–220.

Catalano, R. F., Berglund, M. L., Ryan, J. M., Lonczak, H. S., & Hawkins, J. D. (2004). Positive youth development in the United States: Research findings on evaluations of positive youth development programs. *Annals of the American Academy of Political and Social Science, 591*, 98–124.

Checkoway, B., Katie, R. S., Shakira, A., Margarita, A., Evelyn, F., Lisa, F., et al. (2003). Young people as competent citizens. *Community Development Journal, 38*(4), 298–309.

## SUGGESTED LINKS

Big Brothers Big Sisters
*http://www.bbbs.org/*
Teen Outreach Program
*http://www.wymanteens.org/teenoutreach.htm*
Promising Practices Network
*http://www.promisingpractices.net/default.asp*
ChildTrends, What Works A Guide to Effective Programs: Five Comprehensive Tools For Improving Outcomes For Children And Youth
*http://www.childtrends.org/_catdisp_page.cfm? LID=CD56B3D7-2F05-4F8E-BCC99B05A4CAEA04*

—ELIZABETH T. GERSHOFF

# Biographies

The editors in chief and the editorial board elected to continue the tradition of publishing biographical sketches, which was begun when NASW published the 15th edition of the *Encyclopedia of Social Work* in 1957. In selecting names for this section, the board sought to identify those people who had made important and outstanding contributions to the profession through their leadership, inspiration, focus, and courage. After reviewing the biographies in the 19th edition and supplement, the editors in chief sought nominations from the editorial board, contributors, from the NASW membership, and requested the following criteria for inclusion:

- The person must be deceased.
- The person must have contributed significantly to the general social welfare in the United States.
- Priority was given to people who made lasting contributions in social work practice and practice theory, advancement of social work, advancement of special populations, and development or implementation of programs of national importance.

The editors in chief and editorial board members nominated and selected contributors to write the forty new biographical sketches on the basis of their familiarity with the person being sketched. In addition, as much as possible, we selected social workers as authors, following our general criteria for authorship of the main entries. We also decided to continue the precedent set in the 18th edition of separating the biographies from the other entries, instead of interspersing them as had been done in the 15th, 16th, and 17th editions.

The people in the following biographical sketches represent much of the greatness of the profession: the heroes, both sung and unsung, the giants upon whose shoulders we stand.

*Fredrick Seidl*

## Abbott, Edith (1876–1957)

Edith Abbott, Dean of the School of Social Service Administration at the University of Chicago from 1924 to 1942, was one of the chief architects of the new model of social work education. Abbott was born in Grand Island, Nebraska, the daughter of Elizabeth Griffin Abbott, a high school principal and a women's suffrage leader, and Othman Abbott, first Lieutenant governor of Nebraska. Her sister, Grace Abbott, was born two years later. Edith Abbott graduated from the University of Nebraska in 1901, received her PhD in economics from the University of Chicago in 1905, and studied at the London School of Economics. In 1908, after teaching economics at Wellesley, she became assistant director of the research department of the Chicago School of Civics and Philanthropy (later incorporated as part of the University of Chicago).

Abbott emphasized the state's responsibility in social problems, the importance of public welfare administration, the social aspects of legislation, and the need for a more humane social welfare system. She was president of the National Conference of Social Work and the American Association of Schools of Social Work and was a founder of and frequent contributor to the *Social Service Review*. Abbott helped in establishing the Cook County Bureau of Public Welfare in 1926 and in drafting the Social Security Act of 1935. At the 1951 National Conference of Social Work, accepting an award for her contributions to social work, she gave a fiery speech demanding abolishment of means tests and establishment of children's allowances. Her books include *Immigration: Selected Documents and Case Records* (1924), *The Tenements of Chicago, 1908–1935* (1936), *Public Assistance* (1941), and *Social Welfare and Professional Education* (1942). See also *Two Sisters for Social Justice: A Biography of Grace and Edith Abbott* (1983), by Lela B. Costin.

*Jean K. Quam*

## Abbott, Grace (1878–1939)

Grace Abbott, dynamic Director of the U.S. Children's Bureau, was most influential in her work with child labor legislation, immigrants, and social security. Born in Grand Island, Nebraska, two years after her sister, Edith Abbott, she graduated from Grand Island College in 1898 and became a teacher. From 1908 to 1917, she was Director of the Immigrants Protective League of Chicago and a resident of Hull-House. Julia Lathrop, first Director of the U.S. Children's Bureau and a former resident of Hull-House, encouraged Abbott to become interested in child labor problems. In 1917, at President Wilson's invitation, Abbott moved to Washington to administer the child labor law. She helped to organize the 1919 White House Conference on Children, succeeded Lathrop as Director of the U.S. Children's Bureau in 1921, and edited numerous U.S. Children's Bureau publications on infant and child care and training. Abbott served as president of the National Conference of Social Work in 1924.

In 1934 she returned to Chicago as professor of public welfare at the University of Chicago's School of Social Service Administration. Abbott was also a member of the Advisory Council (1934–1935) that contributed to the establishment of the Social Security Act. Grace Abbott's writings, which reflect her professional experiences, include *The Immigrant and the Community* (1917); *From Relief to Social Security* (1941); and the two-volume classic, *The Child and the State* (1945). See also *Two Sisters for Social Justice: A Biography of Grace and Edith Abbott* (1983), by Lela B. Costin.

*Jean K. Quam*

### Abernathy, Ralph David (1926–1980)

Ralph David Abernathy, second only to his co-worker, Dr. Martin Luther King, Jr., as champion of the civil rights movement, was born in Linden, Alabama. The grandson of slaves, he was the tenth of 12 children. He was drafted into the U.S. Army and completed the general equivalency diploma on discharge. Dr. Abernathy was a graduate of Alabama State University, where he majored in mathematics. He completed one year of course work at Atlanta University and returned to Alabama State University, where he served as director of personnel, dean of men, and professor of social studies.

Dr. Abernathy was raised in the Baptist Church and announced his call to the ministry at the age of 22. He pastored two churches in Alabama. Dr. Abernathy met Dr. King in 1955 and helped to found the Southern Christian Leadership Conference (SCLC) in 1957 after the arrest of Rosa Parks. He and Dr. King led the Montgomery Bus Boycott for 381 days during which time his church and his home were bombed, he was wrongfully sued for $3 million, and he was severely beaten. Dr. Abernathy and Dr. King were jailed 44 times as a result of their civil rights activities, and they shared the victories (the passage of the Civil Rights Act of 1964, the Voting Rights Act of 1965, and the Fair Housing Act of 1968). It was King and Abernathy, through the SCLC, who ended de jure segregation in the South, thereby changing the course of history.

Having completed a master's degree in sociology at Atlanta University in 1958, Dr. Abernathy assumed the pastorate of the historic West Hunter Street Baptist Church in Atlanta. In 1961 he intensified his efforts in the civil rights movement. Dr. Abernathy was at Dr. King's side when the latter was assassinated on April 4, 1968. He succeeded Dr. King as president of the SCLC and was diligent in working to help poor and downtrodden people. He was responsible for the Poor People's Campaign that culminated in Resurrection City, addressed the United Nations in 1971, and was granted many awards and accolades, including 27 honorary doctoral degrees from some of the nation's most prestigious colleges and universities. In 1989 Harper & Row published Dr. Abernathy's autobiography, *And the Walls Came Tumbling Down*, a detailed account of his life and the nonviolent human and civil rights movement.

*Lou M. Beasley*

### Adams, Frankie Victoria (1902–1979)

Frankie Victoria Adams, prominent social worker, author, educator, and community organizer in social work, was born in Danville, Kentucky. She attended Knoxville College and earned her master's degree from the New York School of Social Research. After she left graduate school, she worked for the YWCA in Chicago.

In 1931 Adams joined the faculty of the Atlanta University School of Social Work, where she was assigned to teach community organization and develop courses in group work. She developed the Group Work and Community Organization concentrations at Atlanta University, served as administrative advisor to three deans, and performed as acting dean during two interims. Although she retired from Atlanta University in 1964, she continued to serve as a consultant to the school until three weeks before her death in 1979.

Adams wrote *A History of the Atlanta University School of Social Work: Reflections*. In addition, she was the author of *The Negro Woman in Industry: Sketches on Race Relations*, and she published in many scholarly social work journals on the topics of social work education and juvenile delinquency as well as group work. She also published in general interest publications such as *Phylon* and the *YMCA Magazine*. She was a member of the Committee on Group Work of the American Association of Social Workers and influenced curriculum development in group work at the national level.

During her tenure at Atlanta University, she influenced the lives of over 2,500 students. Each year the Georgia chapter of NASW presents the Frankie V. Adams Award to outstanding social workers in community organization as a lasting memorial to an outstanding Black social worker who influenced the development of social work education and of professional social work in the South.

*Lou M. Beasley*

### Addams, Jane (1860–1935)

Jane Addams—organizer, settlement house leader, and peace activist—is probably best remembered as the founder of Hull-House and the winner of the 1931 Nobel Peace Prize. Addams was the youngest of eight children, born to John Huy Addams, an Illinois state senator from 1854 to 1870. Senator Addams, a Quaker and an abolitionist, influenced his daughter's political views.

Addams was educated at Rockford Female Seminary and Women's Medical College, in Philadelphia and in Europe. In London she visited Toynbee Hall, the first settlement house, and was inspired to open Hull-House in Chicago with Ellen Gates Starr, an art teacher. Programs at Hull-House, which became models for other settlements, included children's clubs; nurseries; an art gallery; a circulating library; an employment bureau; a lunchroom; and classes in history, music, languages, painting, dancing, and mathematics. Addams fought corrupt aldermen and was appointed neighborhood sanitation inspector, seeking to gain more services. Francis Hackett, William Lyon Mackenzie King (later prime minister of Canada), John Dewey, Julia Lathrop, Florence Kelley, Alice Hamilton, Edith and Grace Abbott, Sophonisba Breckinridge, Jessie Binford, and many others came to live and work at Hull-House to learn more about social welfare.

Addams's efforts to advocate nationally for improved social conditions led her to the presidency of the National Conference of Charities and Correction and memberships in the National Child Labor Committee, the National Recreation Association, the National Association for the Promotion of Industrial Education, and the National Conference of Social Work.

Concerned about the effects of war on social progress, Addams played a prominent part in the formation of both the National Progressive Party in 1912, and the Women's Peace Party, of which she became president in 1915. She was also elected president of the Women's International Peace Congress at The Hague (later named the Women's International League for Peace and Freedom) in 1915. She was a delegate to similar congresses in Zurich (1919), Vienna (1921), The Hague (1922), Washington, DC (1924), Dublin (1926), and Prague (1929). Despite public opposition to her pacifist views, she continued in her efforts to condemn war and later urged the United States to join the League of Nations and the World Court. She won the Nobel Peace Prize in 1931, sharing the award with the American educator Nicholas Murray Butler. Among her books are *Democracy and Social Ethics* (1902), *Newer Ideals of Peace* (1907), *The Long Road of Woman's Memory* (1916), *Peace and Bread in Time of War* (1922), and two autobiographical pieces, *Twenty Years at Hull-House* (1910) *and The Second Twenty Years at Hull-House: September 1909 to September 1929* (1930). The many biographies of Jane Addams include *American Heroine* (1973), by Allen F. Davis; *Jane Addams: A Biography* (1937), by James Weber Linn; and *Jane Addams of Hull-House, 1860–1935* (1961), by Margaret Tims.

*Jean K. Quam*

## Alexander, Chauncey A. (1916–2005)

Chauncey Alexander served for fifteen years as Executive Director of the National Association of Social Workers (1967–1982), bringing to that organization creative, dedicated, activist and democratic management, which led to its growth and influence as a major social work organization. As director, he developed licensing and insurance programs for members, and worked for social change promoting ELAN (Education League Action Network, and PACE (Political Action for Candidate Election). He modeled activist social work leadership on local, national, and international landscapes, for a time serving as president of the International Federation of Social Workers. He was instrumental in developing an International Code of Ethics

Following graduation from the University of Southern California School of Social Work in 1943, his career included positions with the L.A. State Relief Administration, psychiatric social work at a state mental hospital, and work with returning GIs following World War II, at the Veterans Service Center. He became director of the Southern California Society of Mental Hygiene (1950–1954). He directed the Los Angeles Heart Association, building an organization with 60,000 volunteers (1955–1967). From his next position as Associate Director of the Regional Medical Programs at UCLA, he went to NASW.

His community service contributions are legion and have been recognized by many organizations. His work for civil rights was highlighted by his founding and presidency of the First Amendment Foundation, and founding and chairing the Health Care Council of Orange County, California. His numerous honors included being named "A Social Work Icon" by the California Social Work Hall of Distinction. He wrote numerous social work and management articles and co-authored a book with his wife Sally.

Following his retirement from NASW, Alexander taught in the Department of Social Work at California State University in Long Beach until shortly before his death.

*Paul A. Abels*

## Altmeyer, Arthur J. (1891–1972)

A recognized leader of social welfare policy, Arthur J. Altmeyer helped design and implement the most far-reaching social reform in American history, the Social Security Act of 1935. Born and educated in Wisconsin, Altmeyer taught briefly, became a school principal, and then took a position in Wisconsin state government. In 1931 he earned a PhD in economics at the University of Wisconsin, studying under Professor John R. Commons, a pioneer in the development of workers' compensation, unemployment insurance, health insurance, and other social legislation. As an administrator in Washington, DC (1934–1953), he helped put into practice the merit system for federal and state personnel programs (1939), survivor's insurance (1939), variable federal grants in relation to state per capita income (1939–1946), disability insurance (1939–1953), and federal financing of social work education (1939–1953). He also initiated and encouraged the movement for national health insurance from 1935 to 1953.

Altmeyer designed the social security program to be responsive to changes over time, making the Social Security Board one of the outstanding research units in the federal government. His appointment as social security commissioner was terminated by the Republicans in 1953. In *The Formative Years of Social Security: A Chronicle of Social Security Legislation and Administration, 1934–1954* (1966), Altmeyer described the early years of the Social Security program.

*Jean K. Quam*

### Anderson, Delwin M. (1916–2007)

Delwin M. (Del) Anderson was director of the Social Work Service, the largest program of social service in the United States at the time, in the Veteran's Administration from 1964 to 1974. He directed 2,600 social workers employed in 171 hospitals, 18 domiciliaries, and 206 outpatient clinics, the largest program of organized social service in the United States.

Anderson's work in the Veterans Administration focused on the importance of social work's commitment to treatment and rehabilitation in the context of the individual's medical and social environment. He laid stress on recognizing the social components of illness and physical injury, and upon planning with the person and utilizing the assets rather than focusing on the disability. Through his leadership, social services received representation within Veterans Administration policy-making groups, where attention was given to preserving the family ties of the veteran patient, and to providing the required resources and opportunities to advance the successful return to family and community life. Anderson also encouraged the appointment of social workers as consultants and administrators in other programs of the complex Veterans Administration.

Anderson received his master's in social work from the University of Minnesota in 1946 and started his career with the Veterans Administration in 1947 as a field social worker in Duluth, Minnesota. He worked his way through the positions of supervisor, chief social worker, and area chief before becoming the director of the Central office. Before his employment with the VA, he taught in the Graduate School of Social Work at the University of Minnesota and also worked as a program director in the Goodrich Social Settlement in Cleveland, Ohio.

Anderson served on the committees and boards of a number of social work organizations, including NASW, CSWE, the National Conference on Social Welfare, the American Hospitals Association, Society for Hospital Social Work Directors, and the National Council on Aging. He also published numerous articles including the section on "Veterans' Service" for the 1971 *Encyclopedia of Social Work* and served on the editorial board from 1965 to 1971, and was chairman of the editorial committee for Proceedings of the Annual Forum of the National Conference on Social Welfare in 1972. The Veterans Administration honored Anderson by selecting him to attend several Executive Seminars organized by the Civil Service Commission and the Brookings Institution. He received an award from the University of Minnesota for outstanding achievement at the 5th annual meeting of the School of Social Work Alumni Association in 1969 and the Veterans Administration's Distinguished Service Award in 1974.

After his retirement, Anderson, who lived in Arlington, Virginia, served on the Board of Trustees for the School of Social Work at Virginia Commonwealth University and was active in community groups.

*Kenneth S. Carpenter*

### Baldwin, Roger Nash (1884–1981)

Roger Baldwin, the founder of the American Civil Liberties Union (ACLU), began his career as a social worker and progressive reformer in St. Louis, Missouri. Although Roger Baldwin, as he put it, "graduated" from social work to become a political reformer, he urged social workers to take a more political stance in presentations to the National Conference of Social Work during the 1910s and 1920s.

Born in Massachusetts, Baldwin earned undergraduate and master's degrees from Harvard. In 1906, he took a job at a St. Louis settlement house. Baldwin initiated sociology courses at all-White Washington University and taught at the St. Louis School of Social Economy, where he proposed a program to educate African American social workers. Appointed chief probation officer for the St. Louis Juvenile Court, he co-authored with Bernard Flexner *Juvenile Courts and Probation* (1914), the first juvenile justice textbook. In 1910, Baldwin became secretary of the St. Louis Civic League, a government reform organization, and in 1915, he was appointed to the Missouri Children's Code Commission.

In 1917, fearing that the United States would soon enter World War I, Baldwin moved to New York City to work for the American Union Against Militarism (AUAM), which had been organized by Lillian Wald and other social workers to oppose the war. In response to government attempts to suppress the anti-war movement, Baldwin organized the Civil Liberties Bureau of the AUAM, a precursor to the ACLU. Jailed in 1918 for refusing to register for the draft, Baldwin founded the ACLU in 1920. He remained active in the ACLU until his death, serving as director until 1950. Roger Baldwin died in Ridgewood, New Jersey, in 1981. See Robert C. Cottrell, *Roger Nash Baldwin and the American Civil Liberties Union.* (2000). New York: Columbia University Press.

*Paul H. Stuart*

### Barrett, Janie Porter (1865–1948)

Janie Porter Barrett was a social welfare leader who founded the first social settlement in Virginia. She was born to emancipated slaves in Athens, Georgia. In 1894 Barrett began teaching after graduating from Hampton Institute in Virginia. She taught for five years before becoming involved in social welfare activities. In 1902, with the help of northern philanthropists, Barrett founded the Locust Street Social Settlement. This settlement was the first of its kind in Virginia and one of the first settlements for Black people in the United States. In 1908 she helped organize the Virginia State Federation of Colored Women's Clubs. As first president of the organization, she led the federation in the establishment of the Virginia Industrial School for Colored Girls, a rehabilitation facility. Barrett later became the superintendent of the school. By 1920, with help from child welfare leaders such as Hastings Hart, the institution had achieved national recognition. The William E. Harman Award for Distinguished Achievement Among Negroes was presented to her in 1929. In 1950 the Virginia Industrial School was renamed the Janie Porter Barrett School for Girls. See *Notable American Women* (1971), by Edward T. Jones, Janet W. James, and Paul S. Bayer, and *Dictionary of American Negro Biography* (1982), by Rayford W. Logan and Michael Winston.

*Wilma Peebles-Wilkins*

### Bartlett, Harriett M. (1897–1987)

Harriett Bartlett acted as the social work profession's theoretician, an intellectual giant despite being inarticulate, rigid, and inexperienced in the rigors of life. Educated at Vassar College, the London School of Economics, and the University of Chicago, she took what she called an unorthodox route to social work. Physically she was very tall, very thin, and very ascetic. As a social worker, she was compassionate, loving, and concerned about clients and their welfare. Through

early acquaintance with Dr. Richard Cabot, and later with his protégée Ida Cannon, she became a caseworker at Massachusetts General Hospital. She became heavily involved with the American Association of Medical Social Workers (AAMSW, formerly the American Association of Hospital Social Workers, the earliest association of professional social workers, organized in 1918). She wrote often for the association, acted as its president from 1942 to 1944, and was a spokesperson for medical social workers.

Bartlett's work appears in 20 journal articles and particularly in two monographs: *Some Aspects of Social Casework in a Medical Setting* and *Fifty Years of Social Work in the Medical Setting.* She described minutely what medical social workers do in NASW's *Social Work Practice in the Health Field.* As a caseworker at Massachusetts General Hospital and a writer and active member of AAMSW, Bartlett sought to apply what she had learned to what she called "the whole profession." Her objective was to identify the distinguishing characteristics of social work, an endeavor that was captured in *Analyzing Social Work Practice by Fields* and eventually in *The Common Base of Social Work Practice,* in which she highlighted social functioning as a central focus of social work practice. She believed in *all* social workers using shared values and knowledge and the same range of interventive measures. Her work as chair of the first Commission on Practice of NASW and its subcommittee on the Working Definition of Social Work led to the article titled "Toward Clarification and Improvement of Social Work Practice" (*Social Work,* April 1958) and led her to think about social work as a whole.

Bartlett's feelings about her contribution to social work are revealed in her oral history, part of a project of the NASW Publications Department. The history, available to qualified researchers at the Social Work Archives of the University of Minnesota, Twin Cities, contains a list of her seven monographs and 40 journal articles as well other biographical data. Besides her work at Massachusetts General Hospital, Bartlett was a consultant at the Children's Bureau and a member of the faculty at Simmons College for 10 years. She said, "As social work grew and changed from 1934 to 1970, during these 36 years my own thinking and writing moved and expanded with it, from the beginning in the hospital to the perspective of the whole profession."

*Beatrice N. Sounders*

### Barton, Clarissa (Clara) Harlowe (1821–1912)

Founder of the American Red Cross and its president from 1881 to 1904, Clara Harlowe Barton worked nationally and internationally to aid disaster victims. Born in Oxford, Massachusetts, she was educated at home. She began teaching in 1839 and established many free schools in New Jersey. After several years as a clerk in the Patent Office in Washington, DC, she became a volunteer nurse during the Civil War, distributing supplies to wounded soldiers. Appointed by President Lincoln, she supervised a systematic postwar search for missing prisoners.

In 1870 Barton worked at the front with the German Red Cross during the Franco-Prussian War and was awarded the Iron Cross. Returning to the United States, she organized the American National Committee of the Red Cross (later the American National Red Cross) and became its president. In 1884, as U.S. delegate to the Red Cross Conference in Geneva, she introduced the "American Amendment," ensuring that the Red Cross would provide relief in peacetime as well as in war.

She supervised relief work after the yellow fever epidemic in Florida (1887), the Johnstown flood (1889), the Russian famine (1891), the Armenian massacres in Turkey (1896), the Spanish-American War (1898), the Boer War (1899–1902), and the Galveston, Texas, flood in 1900. Barton retired in 1904 after colleagues criticized her leadership. Her books include *The Red Cross in Peace and War* (1899), *A Story of the Red Cross: Glimpses of Field Work* (1904), and *The Story of My Childhood* (1907). See also *Life of Clara Barton, Founder of the American Red Cross* (1922), by William E. Barton, and *Angel of the Battlefield: The Life of Clara Barton* (1956), by Ishbel Ross.

*Jean K. Quam*

### Bechill, William D. (1928–2007)

William D. (Bill) Bechill, one of the architects of the system of public social welfare service for aging Americans which was developed during the 20th century, is known primarily for his understanding of the needs of older Americans and their families. His identification with the social work profession was deep and broad. He delighted in reminding students and colleagues that his early career included work as a county welfare commissioner and that he had an ongoing concern with citizen rights and social justice. This concern led him to participate actively in sit-ins to protest segregation in lunch counters in Michigan and to surprise audiences with his keen awareness of unmet needs of children and adolescents, in addition to his identity with older people.

Bechill was born in Grosse Pointe, Michigan, and his keen sense of humor, honed over the course of a lifetime of eloquent and persuasive public speaking and testimony before many legislative bodies and citizens

groups, led him to delight in pointing out that his family lived just two house lots into that affluent suburb. He received his undergraduate degree from Beloit College in Wisconsin and his master's degree in Social Work from the University of Michigan in 1951.

He was a pioneer both in raising public and governmental consciousness about the needs of older Americans and their families, and skilled and effective in organizing and developing both public and voluntary organizations into advocacy systems to bring about policy and programmatic innovations to meet the needs of older Americans. His accomplishments included program development for the United Auto Workers, AFL-CIO and the State of California, under Governor Edmund G. Brown, Sr.

The original design of the Medi-Cal legislation in California, which anticipated much of the Federal Medicare was the product of Mr. Bechill's mind, pen, and yellow pad. In 1965, President Lyndon Baines Johnson appointed Mr. Bechill as the nations' first Commissioner on Aging. He moved his family, including his wife, Lucy Ann Bechill, and three sons, John D., Richard and Robert, to Kensington, MD. Mr. Bechill joined the faculty of the University of Maryland School of Social Work in 1969 and remained in that position until 1991. In addition, he was an active and articulate advocate for the needs of older Americans, and few of his former colleagues were surprised when he accepted appointment as Chair of the State of Maryland's Commission on Aging, by appointment of Governor Parris Glendening.

William D. Bechill was an outstanding example of effectiveness in uniting passionate belief and disciplined professionalism, the ability to pay attention to detail and reach eloquence in speaking. His belief in social justice and the values which underlie social work never wavered and his legacies to the profession and to the structure of American social welfare are extensive.

*Paul H. Ephross*

### Beck, Bertram (1918–2000)

In addition to his work at Fordham University, Bertram M. Beck was known for his leadership of the Henry Street Settlement, his contributions to preventing juvenile delinquency, and his many leadership positions in national, community, and social work organizations.

Bertram Beck received a master's in Social Work in 1942 from the University of Chicago. He later joined the faculty of the Fordham University School of Social Work, where he was appointed associate dean in 1987. In 1996, he became special assistant to the Dean, a position he held until the time of his death. At Fordham, he was instrumental in creating the managed care institute and the religion and poverty institute, which was named in his honor prior to his death.

He worked as a psychiatric social worker for the United States Air Force from 1942 to 1946. He held a number of positions during his outstanding social work career. He worked for the Community Service Society of New York as a family caseworker, public relations associate; and associate director of the Bureau of Public Affairs. He was director of the Special Juvenile Delinquency Project of the United States Children's Bureau; a lecturer at Smith College, School of Social Work; executive director of Mobilization for Youth, Inc.; and executive director of the Henry Street Settlement Urban Life Center.

Elected to the original board of NASW, he resigned this office to become its first Deputy Director of the Association, a position that he held until the early 1960s. Throughout his life he continued to be active in various association endeavors.

Mr. Beck was a consultant for the Foundation for Child Development; the Senate Committee on Juvenile Delinquency; the White House Conference on Children & Youth; the Office of Economic Opportunity; and the Ford Foundation.

Over the years, Mr. Beck was active in community services. Such areas were: Vice President, Board of Directors, Citizens' Committee for Children; Vice President, American Parents' Committee, Inc.; Member, Demonstration Project Panel; President's Committee on Juvenile Delinquency and Youth Development; Co-Chairman, Inner City Task Force, Department of Health, Education and Welfare Youth Development Administration; Member, Board of Directors, National Federation of Settlements and Neighborhood Centers; and Member, Advisory Council to the New York State Commission of Welfare.

Mr. Beck was awarded the *Parents' Magazine* Medal for Services to Children in 1954. He was the author of two books and numerous articles in books and journals, including *Encyclopaedia Britannica, Social Work Book, Saturday Review, Commonweal, Parents' Magazine, Ladies Home Journal, Social Work, Journal of the American Medical Association*, and *American Journal of Sociology*.

*Kenneth S. Carpenter*

## Beers, Clifford Whittingham (1876–1943)

Clifford Whittingham Beers devoted his life to the study and advancement of mental hygiene. Born in New Haven, Connecticut, Beers graduated from Yale in 1897. After a mental breakdown, he spent three years in mental institutions: a private asylum run for profit, a private nonprofit asylum, and a state hospital. In *A Mind That Found Itself* (1908), Beers described the inhumane treatment he received from untrained staff and his efforts to persuade the governor of Connecticut to investigate conditions in the state hospital. William James wrote the introduction for the book, which aroused intense public interest and the attention of psychiatrists and psychologists.

Beers founded the Connecticut Society for Mental Hygiene (1908), served as the first secretary of the National Committee for Mental Hygiene (1909), helped establish the American Foundation for Mental Hygiene (1928) and the International Foundation for Mental Hygiene (1931), and was the first secretary of the International Congress on Mental Health (1931), which he organized. For his work in broadening knowledge of the causes, treatment, and prevention of mental illness, Beers received the Legion of Honor from the French government and the gold medal of the National Institute of Social Sciences in 1933.

*Jean K. Quam*

## Berry, Margaret (1915–2002)

Margaret Berry was well known throughout the world of social work, nationally and internationally, both because of her work in the field of group work for more than 50 years, and her work with the National Conference on Social Welfare, of which she was President in 1970–1971 and then Executive Director from 1972 to 1979.

Margaret began working in the field of group work in 1941 in Pittsburgh, PA, at the Soho community house. Before becoming Executive Director of the National Federation of Settlements and Neighborhood Centers in 1952, she worked with the YWCA in Cleveland, Ohio, and the National Social Welfare Assembly, for which she worked with the German Youth Leadership Project under a Rockefeller Foundation grant. She continued her work with the National Federation of Settlements and Neighborhood Centers until 1971, for nearly 20 years.

Her contributions as a pioneer can be found in this period of almost 20 years, during which time many changes were seen in this area of group work. New affiliates were established in many communities, until she was responsible for 51 cities. Standard-setting became a part of the day to day business; training programs were developed for volunteers and those involved in operating programs; publications became necessary for the professionalism of group work; and it was necessary to address greater Congressional and legislative intervention in programs of a group work nature. She was actively involved in developing group work activities on an international basis.

These pioneering interests and activities required a person like Margaret Berry, with a good professional background, a vision and concern for those children and adults involved in group work programs, and a great deal of energy and dedication.

Margaret Berry was honored on several occasions for the contributions she made to the field of social work, particularly that of social group work. She received a Distinguished Alumni Award from Albion College and the School of Applied Social Sciences, Case-Reserve University, the Jane Addams Award from the National Federation of Settlements, the Grace Coyle Award for her International Contributions, and Special Citations from both the National Conference on Social Welfare and the National Committee on the Advancement of Social Work with Groups.

*Kenneth S. Carpenter*

### Bethune, Mary McLeod (1875–1955)

Mary McLeod Bethune was influential for 30 years in encouraging Black women to develop pride, self-respect, and self-control. She was born to emancipated slaves in Maysville, South Carolina. In 1894 she graduated from Scotia Seminary (now BarberScotia College), a religious and industrial school with an interracial faculty. Her courses there prepared her for teaching. For two years, she trained for missionary work at the Moody Bible Institute in Chicago, but because Black people were not accepted for missionary positions, she began a teaching career. The education and development of Black women was one of her deepest commitments. In 1904 Bethune founded the Daytona Normal and Industrial Institute for Women (now Bethune-Cookman College) in Florida. Her role as president of the National Association of Colored Women led to the founding of the National Council of Negro Women in 1935. In 1936 she became head of Negro Affairs in the National Youth Administration. During the New Deal, Bethune influenced policies that led to a more equitable distribution of resources within the Black community. Her leadership style of negotiation and interracial cooperation gave her national recognition among both Black and White people. When the Daytona Institute merged with the Cookman Institute for Boys, Bethune was named president of the college. She held this position until 1942. See *Mary McLeod Bethune: A Biography* (1964), by R. Holt; *Mary McLeod Bethune* (1951), by C. O. Peare; and *Mary McLeod Bethune* (1959), by E. M. Sterne.

*Wilma Peebles-Wilkins*

### Beveridge, Lord William (1879–1963)

William Beveridge was one of the founders of the British welfare state. During World War II, he chaired an important committee responsible for planning the reorganization of government social programs. The committee's recommendations facilitated a massive expansion of social services in Britain when the war ended, and Beveridge earned an international reputation for his advocacy of the welfare state.

Educated in law at Oxford University, he abandoned his legal studies and went to work at Toynbee Hall, the famous settlement house in the East End of London. In 1905 he joined the *Morning Post* as a journalist, and his articles on social conditions attracted widespread attention. Beveridge, who was particularly concerned about unemployment, recommended the creation of employment exchanges to help unemployed workers find jobs. In 1909, when his ideas were accepted by the British government, Beveridge was put in charge of establishing employment exchanges.

Beveridge's reputation grew, and he became widely recognized as an authority on social problems. During World War I he helped plan a system of food rationing. In 1919 he was appointed director of the London School of Economics, a position he held until 1937. Although he was a friend of the Webbs and other Fabians, he did not join the Fabian Society and identified himself as a liberal rather than a socialist.

When Prime Minister Winston Churchill named a committee in 1941 to plan the reorganization of Britain's social programs, he appointed Beveridge as the chairperson. The committee's report, *Social Insurance and Allied Services: A Report by Sir William Beveridge*, was published at the end of 1942 and soon became a bestseller. The report formed the basis for the Labour Government's social policies between 1945 and 1950 and fostered the creation of Britain's national health services; the introduction of comprehensive social security; and the expansion of public education, housing, and other social programs.

Beveridge, who earned an international reputation for his contribution to the postwar expansion of social services in Britain, was knighted in 1919; he became a peer, entitled to a seat in the House of Lords, in 1946. He wrote numerous books, including *Unemployment: A Problem of Industry* (1909), *Pillars of Security and Other Wartime Essays and Addresses* (1943), *Full Employment in a Free Society* (1944), *Why I Am a Liberal* (1945), *Voluntary Action: A Report on Methods of Social Advance* (1948), and *Power and Influence* (1953). See also *William Beveridge: A Biography* (1977), by Jose Harris.

*James Midgley*

### Blackey, Eileen (1902–1979)

Eileen Blackey made a significant contribution to the field of social work as a practitioner, an educator, an administrator, and a consultant. Born of Irish parents in

Blackpool, England, as the family was on its way to the United States, Blackey grew up in the Midwest and received a bachelor's degree from the University of Wisconsin in 1925. In 1930 she returned to school and received a master's degree from the Smith College School for Social Work. After the war Blackey entered the doctoral program at Case Western Reserve University. Her dissertation, "Group Leadership in Staff Training," was published by the U.S. Department of Health, Education, and Welfare and is considered a classic.

Blackey's professional career coincided with national and international events that offered her the opportunity to use her considerable talents. During the Great Depression, when emergency relief programs across the country were desperate for trained professionals, she established programs for inservice staff development in West Virginia and Florida. After World War I Blackey became director of staff development for social work service in the Veterans Administration, charged with training staff for positions in the administration's hospitals and clinics across the United States.

Blackey also made an important contribution to social work education in the United States and abroad. Before the war she taught at the Smith School and helped lay the groundwork for a school of social work in Hawaii. After the war she was asked to establish a school of social work at Hebrew University in Israel, and her reputation earned her consulting assignments throughout the Middle East. When she returned to the United States, she became Dean of the School of Social Work at the University of California, Los Angeles. After her retirement, she continued to consult with national and international schools of social work.

Blackey's death made impossible her plans to publish her experience with the United Nations Relief and Rehabilitation Agency as director of the Child Search and Repatriation Program in Germany. Her many articles on social work appeared in national and international journals, and her unpublished papers are in the Social Welfare History Archives Center of the University of Minnesota's Walter Library.

*Margaret Daniel*

### Bogardus, Emory (1882–1973)

Emory Bogardus came to know well the migrant farm laborers who gathered every year to bring in the harvest while he was a child in Indiana. This experience sharpened his interest in cultural and ethnic attitudes in the United States. While earning his MA from Northwestern University and his PhD from the University of Chicago, both in sociology, he lived in a settlement house in a crime-ridden slum district. There, he worked with immigrant laborers employed in steel mills and

directed a boys' club with a high proportion of delinquent youth. He then joined the economics faculty of the University of Southern California, where in 1915, he established the first Sociology Department in the West, and in 1920 the first school of social work in the West. He later became the Dean of the USC Graduate School.

Bogardus arrived in California just as Hiram Johnson's and the Municipal League's ambitious Progressive reform program emerged in 1911, reshaping the political and economic life of the state. It not only instituted enfranchisement of women and recall of the judiciary, but a distinctive form of government: the state, local or municipal commission, usually run by unpaid appointed professionals for reform and regulatory purposes. Bogardus's appointment to two such Commissions gave him valuable insight into the working of government politics as these bore on the provision of public social services, and this service enabled him to introduce widespread reforms. He served on the housing Commission, the focus of which was housing and health, especially of the poor and the immigrants. He chaired the Los Angeles Commission on Public Welfare that established standards and procedures, some still existing, which were emulated by similar commissions elsewhere in the state. For many years, he served on a number of voluntary social agency boards as a very active member. To stimulate scholarship and promote scientific study of society, in 1920 he founded Alpha Kappa Delta, the sociology honor society, which currently has nearly 500 chapters around the world.

His famous study on "social distance" is still used the world over to examine cultural, ethnic, and religious attitudes. Concurrently, he encouraged masters and doctoral students to examine a variety of issues and experiences that provided insight into social problems and the means developed to deal with them. These still constitute a primary source for examining and coping with major social issues in the arena of health, economic need, labor and industry, race relations, social control, community organization, and the refinement of professional social work education and services.

Bogardus authored over 250 articles and 24 books, a number of which have been translated into other languages. He was also the founder of *The Journal of Sociology and Social Research*, which he edited for 45 years. His influence on California social welfare and on the beginnings of social work education is incalculable.

*Frances Feldman and Haluk Soydan*

### Brace, Charles Loring (1826–1890)

Writer, minister, and social reformer, Charles Loring Brace was one of the organizers of the Children's Aid

Society of New York City. As its executive director for almost 40 years, Brace chronicled the problems of destitute, vagrant, and homeless children and initiated many child welfare services. After graduating from Yale University in 1846, Brace taught briefly and then entered Yale Divinity School. As a minister he preached to prisoners at Blackwell's Island in New York City. Frequently described as an independent thinker, Brace was an abolitionist and accepted Darwin's theory of evolution.

After traveling through Europe, Brace served as a city missionary in New York, becoming aware of the many homeless children roaming the streets. In 1853, when a group of influential citizens encouraged him to establish a mission for children, he founded the Children's Aid Society. Among its programs were industrial schools, reading rooms, newsboys' lodging houses, night schools, summer camps, sanatoriums, children's shelters, special classes for children with disabilities, and dental clinics. Brace's most controversial program was sending some 50,000 to 100,000 homeless children on "orphan trains" to be adopted by farmers in the West. Although placements were made with little investigation, most children successfully adjusted to their new homes. Brace's writings, especially his popular book *The Dangerous Classes of New York and Twenty Years' Work among Them* (1872), crystallized public sentiment on behalf of the needs of children. *Hungary in 1851* (1852) is Brace's account of a trip to that country, where he was imprisoned for criticizing the country's autocratic regime. His accomplishments are reviewed in *The Life of Charles Loring Brace Chiefly Told in His Own Letters* (1894), edited by Emma Brace.

*Jean K. Quam*

### Brager, George (1922–2003)

George Brager was a nationally recognized social work educator, practice scholar, social activist and administrator. Trained in group work at the University of Pennsylvania School of Social Work, during the 1950s Brager served as Executive Director of the Mount Vernon YM and YWHA, an agency particularly respected for its social activism and progressive programming. In 1960 Brager became a founding director of Mobilization for Youth (MFY) on Manhattan's Lower East Side. Under Brager's leadership MFY emerged as the conceptual prototype for the programs, which would constitute the War on Poverty in the late 1960s and early 1970s. The program concept—programs which created social and economic opportunity for clients—represented a radical departure from earlier social program models. Brager's scholarship focused on community and organizational practice including

*Community Action Against Poverty: Readings from the Mobilization Experience* (with Francis Purcell), *Community Organizing* (with Harry Spect), and *Changing Human Service Organizations* and *Supervising in the Human Services* (both with Stephen Holloway).

In the late 1960s Brager joined the faculty of the Columbia University School of Social Work and from 1981 to 1986 served as its Dean. His vision and leadership in that role, balancing as it did the competing interests in a dynamic school of social work, significantly elevated Columbia among the nation's top schools of social work. During that time Brager adapted the "teaching hospital" model of professional education to social work, founding Columbia University Community Services, later to evolve as Center for Urban Community Services—a homelessness serving agency—which served as a model training site for Columbia students. Brager's leadership in program design and conceptualizing innovative approaches to community and organizational practice had significant national impact from the 1960s through the 1990s.

*Stephen Holloway*

### Breckinridge, Sophonisba Preston (1866–1948)

Sophonisba Preston Breckinridge was an educator and social activist who taught the first course of public welfare administration and strongly advocated for a rigorous postgraduate curriculum in social work education. Born in Lexington, Kentucky, into a family noted for public service, she was a brilliant student. A graduate of Wellesley College in 1888, she became the first woman to graduate from the University of Chicago Law School, to be admitted to the bar in Kentucky, and to earn a PhD in political science and economics from the University of Chicago (1901). In 1902 she joined the faculty of the University of Chicago and helped develop the Chicago School of Civics and Philanthropy. As its Dean from 1908 to 1920, she convinced the university to accept the pioneering school of social work as a graduate professional school and designed two unique courses, "Social Work and the Courts" and "The Family and the State." She introduced the case method as the mode of instruction, publishing the first volume of edited case records for the use of students. She remained at the university until 1933.

Breckinridge was a charter member of the American Association of Social Workers and president of its Chicago chapter, twice president of the Illinois Conference on Social Welfare, and one of the organizers and the president (1933–1935) of the American Association of Schools of Social Work. For 14 years she was a resident of Hull-House during her annual vacation quarter from the university. She also championed unions, collective bargaining, better working conditions for women, and fair treatment for immigrants and Black people, and she was one of the first members of the Chicago branch of the National Association for the Advancement of Colored People. A managing editor of and contributor to the *Social Service Review*, she wrote a number of books, including *Women in the Twentieth Century* (1933), *Social Work and the Courts* (1934), and *Public Welfare Administration in the United States* (1938).

*Jean K. Quam*

### Briar, Scott (1926–1998)

Scott Briar, practitioner, researcher, scholar, and leader, has been hailed by some as one of the shapers of modern casework. A champion for empirically based practice, Briar posited that the "crucial questions to be asked of an intervention method are not 'Does it sound good?' or 'Is it fascinating?' but 'Does it work?' and 'Is it more effective than other methods?'" ("The Current Crisis in Social Casework," *Social Work Practice*, 1967). In his book, *Problems and Issues in Social Casework*, Briar and co-author Henry Miller laid out the pitfalls of practice methods that derive from insufficient evidence.

Briar received a BA from Washburn University in 1950, an MSW from Washington University in 1952, and worked as a psychiatric social worker and supervisor at the Menninger Foundation until completing his DSW at Columbia in 1961.

From 1959 to 1971, Briar was a faculty member at the University of California at Berkeley. While there, he co-authored the landmark study, *Police Encounters with Juveniles*, which documented routine racial profiling among law enforcement officers. From 1966 to 1969, Briar was a consultant to the Office of the Secretary of Health, Education, and Welfare.

In 1971, Briar became Dean at the University of Washington School of Social Work and, in 1975, oversaw the creation of its PhD program. He remained Dean until 1988 and taught until 1990.

When he was editor for *Social Work* from 1972 to 1976, his editorials reflected his penchant for raising questions about research-informed practice. Briar also served as a reviewer for NIMH, participated on several NIMH Task Forces, and was appointed to the U.S. President Commission on Mental Health Task Panel on Manpower and Personnel.

In the mid 1980s he served as the leader of the Deans and Directors (at the Conference of Deans and Directors, which later became the American Association of Schools of Social Work Records and, in 1987, was renamed the National Association of Deans and Directors of Schools of Social Work). From 1990 to

1994, Briar was the Director of Social Work at Florida International University where he launched the PhD program.

*Jennifer Briar-Bonpane* and *Katharine Briar-Lawson*

### Brockway, Zebulon Reed (1827–1920)

Zebulon Reed Brockway, whose lifelong work in prison service included 25 years as superintendent of the New York State Reformatory in Elmira, was a reformer who believed in rehabilitation rather than punishment. Born in Lyme, Connecticut, Brockway began his career as a clerk at the Connecticut State Prison in Wethersfield, where his father had been a director. His early positions included deputy to the warden at the Albany County Penitentiary (1851–1853), director of the Albany Municipal and County Almshouse (1853–1861), head of the Monroe County Penitentiary at Rochester (1861–1864), and superintendent of the Detroit House of Correction. He resigned in 1872 when his reforms were not fully accepted.

In 1875 Brockway became warden at the New York State Reformatory of Elmira, establishing reforms that applied advanced principles of penology. He initiated a program of physical and manual training for prisoners to prepare them for release and advocated the inclusion of indeterminate sentencing and parole in state statutes. Although the New York State Board of Charities, concerned about his innovations, recommended his dismissal in 1894, he was retained. During this period he also served as president of the National Prison Association (1897–1898). In 1905 he was elected mayor of Elmira, serving for two years. Brockway's history of the changes he observed in penal reform during his work in the field, *Fifty Years of Prison Service*, was published in 1912.

*Jean K. Quam*

### Bruno, Frank John (1874–1955)

Frank John Bruno was an administrator and educator whose expertise and leadership influenced American social work. After graduating from Williams College (1899) and Yale Divinity School (1902), he spent five years as a Congregational minister. In 1907 he became a general agent of the Associated Charities in Colorado, moving to the staff of the New York Charity Organization Society in 1911. In New York he studied at the New York School of Philanthropy (now the Columbia University School of Social Work), where he was greatly influenced by Mary Richmond. From 1914 to 1925, Bruno was general secretary of the Associated Charities of Minneapolis (later the Family Welfare Association).

Bruno was acting chair of the Department of Sociology and Social Work at the University of Minnesota

(1912–1922) and professor of applied sociology and head of the Social Work Department (later the George Warren Brown School of Social Work) at Washington University in St. Louis. As a civil rights advocate, Bruno created opportunities for Black students to receive social work training. As president of the National Conference of Social Work from 1932 to 1933 and president of the American Association of Social Workers from 1928 to 1930 and again during a period of turmoil in the organization in 1942, Bruno promoted the expansion of the profession. Bruno wrote *The Theory of Social Work* (1936) and *Trends in Social Work, 1874–1956* (1957). In 1955 the George Warren Brown School of Social Work published a monograph on Bruno, *Frank John Bruno, 1874–1955*.

*Jean K. Quam*

### Buell, Bradley (1893–1976)

Bradley Buell, community organizer and planner, consulted on and conducted research projects in 156 communities in the United States. Born in Chicago, Buell was educated at Oberlin College and the New York School of Philanthropy (now the Columbia University School of Social Work). As a result of work by Buell and others on the problems of the National Social Workers Exchange, the American Association of Social Workers evolved as the major professional social work association. Until 1923 Buell served the organization, first as its secretary and then as its associate executive.

His community organization activities included service as director of the New Orleans Community Chest and Council; field director of Community Chests and Councils, Inc.; and founder and executive director of Community Research Associates. From 1943 to 1947 Buell edited *Survey Midmonthly*, writing extensively on community planning. In 1952 he published *Community Planning for Human Services*, in which he analyzed the work of more than 100 agencies in St. Paul, Minnesota, during a one-year period, finding that multiproblem families used almost 50 percent of all services. Another book, *Solving Community Problems*, was published in 1973.

*Jean K. Quam*

### Burns, Eveline Mabel (1900–1985)

Eveline M. Burns was a social economist and educator who helped formulate the original Social Security Act. Born in London, she was educated at the London School of Economics. She moved to the United States in 1926 and joined the faculty of Columbia University in 1928, where she taught until her retirement in 1967. She served as a consultant to many government and private agencies; it was as a member of the President's

Committee on Economic Security in 1934 that she helped develop the specifics of the Social Security Act. She later became director of research for the Committee on Long-Range Work and Relief Policies of the National Resources Planning Board, which shaped public assistance and work programs through the 1940s. In addition to more than 100 articles, Burns wrote nine books, including *Social Security and Public Policy* (1956), which is the basic textbook on analysis of the social security program, and *Social Welfare in the Nineteen Eighties and Beyond* (1978). See also *Social Security in International Perspective: Essays in Honor of Eveline M. Burns* (1969), edited by Shirley Jenkins.

*John F. Longres*

### Cabot, Richard Clarke (1865–1939)

A well-known physician and educator, Richard Clarke Cabot initiated the first medical social work department in the United States at Massachusetts General Hospital in 1905. Born in Brookline, Massachusetts, Cabot graduated from Harvard University (1889) and Harvard Medical School (1892). His association with Harvard continued as a member of the medical school faculty from 1899 to 1933 and as a professor of social ethics from 1920 to 1934. He began as a physician at Massachusetts General Hospital in 1898 and became chief of staff in 1912.

As director of the Boston Children's Aid Society, Cabot saw the need to understand family relationships and environmental factors in diagnosing problems in children more effectively. The use of home visits by social workers to gain more information about patients became a model for social work practice in other hospitals. In 1930 he served as president of the National Conference on Social Work and received the National Institute of Social Science gold medal in 1931. An outspoken critic of the expense and inefficiency of medicine and an advocate for social work services, Cabot wrote extensively; his works include *Social Service and the Art of Healing* (1915), *Social Work: Essays on the Meeting Ground of Doctor and Social Worker* (1919), and *The Meaning of Right and Wrong* (1936).

*Jean K. Quam*

### Cannon, Ida Maud (1877–1960)

As director of the Social Service Department at Massachusetts General Hospital in Boston (1906–1946), Ida Maud Cannon defined and developed medical social work. Cannon attended the City and County Hospital Training School for Nurses in St. Paul, Minnesota, and the Boston School for Social Workers (now Simmons College School for Social Work).

Although medical social work was growing as a field of practice in New York and Baltimore, Cannon became its nationally recognized symbol through her activities at Massachusetts General Hospital in the department created by Dr. Richard Cabot.

Cannon's conception of medical social work involved moving beyond the hospital into community health and welfare agencies. She also advocated for the establishment of psychiatric clinics staffed by social workers in general hospitals. She held that social workers needed specialized medical knowledge and that a strong social work base and knowledge of casework techniques were the foundation of medical social work. A founder of the American Association of Hospital Social Workers (later the American Association of Medical Social Workers), Cannon served as its president and vice president. She also led the first committee on social work in a medical school. In 1923 she wrote *Social Work in Hospitals*, and in 1952 she published *On the Social Frontiers of Medicine: Pioneering in Medical Social Service*.

*Jean K. Quam*

### Cannon, Mary Antoinette (1884–1962)

During her long career as a social worker and educator, Mary Antoinette Cannon helped develop medical social work. She graduated from Bryn Mawr in 1907 and joined Dr. Richard Cabot's pioneering medical social work department at Massachusetts General Hospital. Continuing her career at the Boston Consumptives Hospital (1909–1910) and teaching high school, she received an MA from Columbia University in 1916. As director of social work at the University Hospital of Philadelphia (1916–1921), she became the first secretary of the American Association of Medical Social Workers.

Cannon's experiences led her to see the value of courses in psychiatry and medicine in schools of social work, an idea she put into practice at the New York School of Social Work, where she taught from 1921 to 1945. During this period she helped establish the Social Services Employees Union and served on its board of directors. She served as director of social work at the University of Puerto Rico (1941–1942), consultant to the New York office of the Commonwealth of Puerto Rico Department of Labor (1948–1952), and organizer of the first social workers' workshop in Puerto Rico in 1953. At the time of her death, she was volunteer director at the James Weldon Johnson Community Center in Harlem. Her writings include *Outline for a Course in Planned Parenthood* (1944) and *Social Casework: An Outline for Teaching* (1933), edited with Philip Klein.

*Jean K. Quam*

### Carlton, Thomas Owen (1937–1992)

Thomas Owen Carlton was an expert in curriculum development in social work education as well as an author, an editor, and a scholar in health social work and social policy. Born in Quincy, Illinois, he received a PhD in social work from the University of Pennsylvania, a master's degree in social work from the University of Southern California, a master's degree in government from California State University, and a bachelor's degree in international relations from the University of California, Los Angeles. From 1961 to 1963 he served in the U.S. Peace Corps in the Philippines, where he met his future wife.

Carlton left early employment in banking to become a social worker. His first love was teaching and writing in social policy, especially as it affected health social work. Carlton's approach to policy had a strong historical bent. He believed that profound and powerful themes in American history worked their way into social welfare and social welfare planning in the colonial period and well into the 20th century. He expressed his views during his long teaching and scholarly tenure at the School of Social Work of Virginia Commonwealth University, where he began in 1973 as an assistant professor and then became full professor, associate dean, and for 18 months in 1990–1991, acting dean. The founding chair of the school's health specialization program, Carlton wrote extensively on the school's history as the oldest school of social work in the South.

Carlton's writings were central to his career. He believed that scholarship in social work education should be a central characteristic of the professional. In 1984 he published *Clinical Social Work in Health Settings: A Guide to Professional Practice with Exemplars*, in which he demonstrated the application of Falck's membership theory to health social work. He served as editor in chief of *Health & Social Work* from 1986 to 1990. His editorials, which were enthusiastic, pointed, and thoroughly researched, became the subject of much discussion in the health social work field.

In 1990 Carlton was recognized by the Society of Hospital Social Work Directors of the American Hospital Association, which gave him the Hyman J. Weiner award for "leadership, scholarship, teaching ability, compassion, and commitment to values." In the final years of his career, Carlton often served as an educational consultant to hospitals and agencies. As part of one such assignment, he taught in Cyprus at a training program in rehabilitation sponsored by the World Rehabilitation Fund.

*Plans S. Falck*

## Carter, Genevieve (1907–1999)

Dr. Genevieve Carter was a distinguished social welfare researcher, social work administrator, and educator. She earned a doctorate degree in social research from the University of California, Berkeley, and enjoyed a dedicated and inspirational career. Her key work was in the areas of research methods and in the defining era of case management for the elderly.

Her social work career began during WWII when she lived for three years in Manzanar, serving as director of education and social welfare. She worked with the Japanese children and their families at the internment camp and assisted in their relocation after the war.

Later she took a position as director of the Research Division and then as director of the Welfare Planning Council in Los Angeles. Dr. Carter conducted important research that affected policy throughout California. Her findings became the basis of community planning and program development for youth services.

Her extensive research work then led her to a position in Washington, DC, as head of intra-mural research in the Department of Health, Education and Welfare (HEW). There she conducted social research that led to policy formulation that was implemented by California as well as other states.

Back in Los Angeles, Dr. Carter directed the newly created Regional Research Institute in Social Welfare, a federally funded facility in the University of Southern California School of Social Work. At USC, she not only provided research consultation to faculty and others in and outside the University, but was also involved in a wide range of research activities within the field of social work.

She was also involved with the founding of the National Association for Community Organization Social Workers—an organization that was the predecessor of NASW. When Dr. Carter retired from this activity in 1976, she continued with several research activities that she had initiated earlier with the Andrus Gerontology Center at USC, including studies of the aging process, of nursing home practices and others.

Dr. Carter's interest in the matters of aging and services for the elderly continued for the rest of her life. She even wrote a book on aging and humor.

*Haluk Soydan* and *Frances Feldman*

## Cassidy, Harry (1900–1951)

Harry Cassidy was a prominent Canadian social scientist, social welfare reformer, and social work educator during the 1930s and 1940s. He was a tireless crusader for public social welfare services in Canada and the United States. In 1926 he obtained a PhD in economics from the Robert Brookings Graduate School of Economics and Government, where the basis was laid for his lifelong interest in problems of poverty, living standards, industrial relations, and social legislation. Cassidy's social welfare studies of the early 1930s were among the first Canadian reports on unemployment, housing needs, and labor conditions. His two books, *Social Security and Reconstruction in Canada* (1943) and *Public Health and Welfare Reorganization* (1945), were the first to examine in detail Canadian social welfare programs at both the federal and provincial levels.

Cassidy taught social welfare at the University of Toronto from 1929 to 1934 and was director of social welfare for the province of British Columbia from 1934 to 1939. In this position he was instrumental in developing the province's public social services and in preparing a comprehensive scheme of public state health insurance. Had Cassidy's scheme been implemented, it would have been the first such insurance program in Canada. As a social scientist, Cassidy viewed his task as director of social welfare for British Columbia as being largely one of social engineering. He saw himself as a technical expert who would restructure the province's social services according to modern methods of management. He favored practical, efficient solutions to social problems, in accordance with the best tenets of social science, and he displayed an enormous interest in collecting social facts that were largely detached from theoretical considerations. Social progress for Cassidy depended on technology and bureaucracy.

Cassidy developed important schools of social work at the University of California, Berkeley, and at the University of Toronto, both of which are leading schools today largely as a result of his work. His plans for both schools were tremendously ambitious. He wanted to broaden the base of university education for social workers by placing much greater emphasis on the social sciences, social research, and the legal and administrative features of social welfare. Only then, he believed, could high standards be demanded, which would attract the best students and ultimately result in an increased status for professional social work. Even more important for Cassidy was that graduates of these improved educational programs would be able to assume leadership roles to ensure that public welfare was administered more efficiently and humanely.

*Allan Irving*

## Cassidy, Helen (1918–1994)

Helen Cassidy—social work educator, administrator, practitioner—received her MSW from Tulane University in 1939 and began an active career spanning 55 years until her death in 1994. The early years of her career were spent as a medical social worker, first in

Louisiana and then in Washington, DC, where she was the field director for the American National Red Cross, serving in three naval hospitals providing care to the armed forces. She then assumed overall administrative responsibility for social services programs and developed innovative approaches to offering coordinated casework/ group work services.

Cassidy joined Tulane University's social work faculty in 1950 as a field instructor coordinating the maternal and child health grants. In 1959 she became the coordinator of field instruction. She taught a variety of human behavior, methods, and health courses, culminating in the design of and teaching in the gerontology certificate program. Her career at Tulane was a distinguished one, including a Fulbright scholarship to conduct research in the United Kingdom; service in Spain for the United Nations as an expert in social casework, which resulted in national and international prominence; the development of a field instruction model that has been widely copied in the United States; election as the first female president of NASW in 1966; establishment and co-founding of the hospice movement in New Orleans; and appointment as acting dean of the School of Social Work.

Throughout Cassidy's long career she demonstrated a continuing concern for the welfare and well-being of all her students and fellow social work practitioners. In 1987 she chaired the first national NASW symposium in New Orleans, and in 1988 she was named Alumna of the Year by the Tulane University School of Social Work.

*Ronald Marks*

### Chavez, Cesar (1927–1993)

Cesar Chavez was born in the North Gila Valley of Arizona, 20 miles outside Yuma. His family owned a ranch and a grocery store, which it lost during the Great Depression. His father's search for work led them to the Central Valley of California, where his parents became migrant farm-workers. Chavez left school after finishing the eighth grade and joined the Marines at the age of 16. In 1948 he married Helen Fabela, and they worked together in the fields of the large ranches.

In 1952 Chavez was hired to chair a voter registration drive for Saul Alinsky's Community Service Organization. He registered more than 4,000 people in two months and became the general director of the national organization in 1958. In 1962 Chavez returned to the work that he loved: organizing farm-workers. Chavez began a different kind of social movement, fighting to establish farm-workers' rights and access to services. He established cooperative organizations whose membership benefits were paid for by dues and contributions.

The nonprofit corporations he established began with a burial fund, followed by a credit union, and then a health care system, which today covers the Central and Imperial valleys in California. Delano was the site of Chavez's greatest victories in his efforts to gain respect and better working conditions for farm workers. The Delano area was the headquarters of the union's strike of growers begun in 1965. A group of 67 "pilgrim" strikers left Delano on March 17, 1966, with the theme of "penitence, pilgrimage, and revolution." By the time the strikers arrived at the state capitol of Sacramento, they had been joined by 10,000 supporters. The strike and the five-year boycott of California table grapes brought international prominence to the United Farm Workers and Chavez and led Delano area growers to agree to a contract in 1970.

Chavez's advocacy went beyond social work in the conventional sense, finally focusing on the issue of birth defects and diseases caused by the application of fumigants, insecticides, and defoliants by agribusiness corporations. Before the U.S. government succeeded in banning the use of the insecticide DDT, the United Farm Workers won this ban in its first labor contracts with Californian agribusinesses. To achieve his successes, Chavez emulated his hero, Mahatma Gandhi, by relying on nonviolent methods and hunger strikes. See *Cesar Chavez: Autobiography of La Causa* (1975), by Jacques Levy and *Sal Si Puedes* (1969), by Peter Matthiessen.

*Juan Paz*

### Cloward, Richard (1926–2005)

Richard Cloward was an internationally renowned scholar, social activist, and master teacher. Professor Cloward's books, (many co-authored with his wife, Professor Frances Fox Piven), are found in commercial and college bookstores as well as in libraries throughout the world. His contributions to contemporary issues in the United States include: *Why Americans Don't Vote: and Why Politicians Want It That Way; The Mean Season; The New Class War; Reagan's Attack on the Welfare State and Its Consequence; Poor People's Movement: Why They Succeed; How They Fail; The Politics of Turmoil; Essays on Poverty, Race, and the Urban Crisis;* and *Regulating the Poor: The Functions of Public Welfare.* Professor Cloward's scholarship shaped sociological political science, and social welfare inquiry, debate, and public policy. *Regulating the Poor,* for example, was first published in 1971, translated into Italian and German, received the C. Wright Mills Award, and was listed among the 40 Most Notable Books by the American Library Association.

What distinguished Professor Cloward from most scholars was his social activism and his unflinching commitment to the poor and the oppressed. His scholarship was informed by and informed his experiences on the front lines, whether organizing welfare rights (in 1966, as co-founder of the National Welfare Rights Organization) or voter registration (in 1982, as co-founder of Human SERVE—Service Employees Registration and Voter Education). In recognition of his efforts to have human service employees register prospective voters, President Clinton invited Professor Cloward to participate in the White House signing of the Voter Motor Bill.

Professor Cloward was a member of Columbia University School of Social Work's faculty for 47 years. In the classroom, he inspired four generations of students to broaden their social-cultural-political perspectives. For his teaching brilliance, he received the Herman Stein Award for Excellence. Professor Cloward also received the NASW's and CSWE's lifetime achievement awards.

*Alex Gitterman*

### Cohen, Wilbur (1913–1987)

Wilbur Cohen, a leading figure in the history of social security and secretary of the U.S. Department of Health, Education, and Welfare (DHEW) under Lyndon B. Johnson, was born in Milwaukee, Wisconsin. After attending Alexander Meiklejohn's Experimental College at the University of Wisconsin, he accompanied Edwin E. Witte to Washington, DC, in 1934 and helped draft the original Social Security Act. As a staff member in the Social Security Administration (1935–1956), Cohen developed legislative proposals and successfully promoted amendments to broaden coverage and increase benefits. In 1956 Cohen became Professor of Public Welfare Administration at the University of Michigan and chaired the governor's Public Health Advisory Committee when Michigan became the first state to establish medical assistance for the elderly. In 1960 he led President John F. Kennedy's Task Force on Health and Social Security and in 1961 became DHEW's assistant secretary for legislation. Cohen was the chief architect of the 1965 amendments that inaugurated Medicare and Medicaid. Following passage of this legislation, President Johnson named Cohen undersecretary and, in 1968, secretary of DHEW.

Cohen became dean of the School of Education at the University of Michigan in 1969 and 10 years later the Sid W. Richardson professor of public affairs at the Lyndon Baines Johnson School of Public Affairs in Austin, Texas. In 1979 Cohen founded Save Our Security (SOS), an umbrella organization representing more than 100 groups, to oppose reductions in disability and welfare programs. During the 1980s Cohen energetically defended social security against cutbacks proposed by the Reagan administration.

A visionary as well as a legislative technician, Cohen wrote and lectured widely on public welfare policy issues. He received more than 30 awards and honorary degrees. Cohen's career is detailed in the Wilbur J. Cohen papers at the State Historical Society of Wisconsin.

*Roland L. Guyotte*

### Coyle, Grace Longwell (1892–1962)

Grace Longwell Coyle was the first social work educator to develop a scientific approach to group work practice. Born in North Adams, Massachusetts, Coyle received a BA from Wellesley College (1914), a certificate from the New York School of Philanthropy (1915), and an MA in economics (1928) and a doctorate in sociology from Columbia University (1931). Her early activities included work in settlement houses and the YWCA. From 1934 to 1962, she taught at the School of Applied Social Sciences at Western Reserve University in Cleveland, developing the first group work course to be taught at that university.

Coyle was president of the National Conference of Social Work (1940), the American Association of Social Workers (1942–1944), and the Council on Social Work Education (1958–1960). Her many writings—such as *Social Process in Organized Groups* (1930), *Studies in Group Behavior* (1937), *Group Experiences and Democratic Values* (1947), *Group Work with American Youth* (1948), and *Social Science in the Professional Education of Social Workers* (1958)—contributed to the acceptance of group work as a social work method.

*Jean K. Quam*

### Davis, Liane V. (1942–1995)

Liane Davis left a legacy as an advocate, scholar, and teacher whose commitment to social justice was lived out in every area of her life. As the child of social activists, she learned early lessons about justice and nonviolence. After receiving her BA degree from Antioch College, she became a child welfare caseworker in New York City. After completing her MSW degree at Adelphi University, she worked in a city health clinic in the Lower East Side of New York City. A second master's degree in psychology became the stepping-stone to her PhD in social psychology from the University of North Carolina at Chapel Hill.

In 1978 she became a lecturer and, later, a faculty member of the School of Social Welfare at the University at Albany, State University of New York. In 1989 she joined the faculty of the University of Kansas

School of Social Welfare and became associate dean of academic programs in 1992.

As a teacher, she inspired students to go beyond conventional boundaries and to creatively challenge systems that keep women "in their place." As an administrator, she provided leadership within the school and served as the school's representative on major university committees. She chaired NASW's National Committee on Women's Issues, was a member of the board of the Kansas chapter of NASW, and consulted for services to battered women. In 1995 the Council on Social Work Education honored her for distinguished recent contributions.

As a key figure in the renaissance of women's issues in social work, Davis taught and wrote about women's victimization, leaving a legacy of literature on women made vulnerable by abuse and poverty and on the services needed to support their strengths. Among her many publications, her classic article, "Female and Male Voices in Social Work" (*Social Work*, 1985), was among the first to critique the division between clinical social work practice and social work research from a feminist perspective. Her edited book, *Building on Women's Strengths* (1994), moved beyond analysis of the problems to an exploration of the transformational capacity inherent in the strengths of women. In a career cut short by death from cancer, Davis reflected a commitment to social work that is a beacon for the profession.

*Ann Weick*

### Day, Dorothy (1897–1980)

Dorothy Day, social activist, journalist, and publisher, was co-founder of the Catholic Worker Movement and edited the *Catholic Worker* for more than 40 years. Born in Brooklyn, Day attended the University of Illinois (1914–1916), leaving to begin writing for *Socialist Call*, *The Masses*, the *Liberator*, and Pathe Films. In 1928, seeing the Catholic Church as a church of immigrants and the laboring class, she converted to Catholicism. With Peter Maurin, a teacher, she began publishing the *Catholic Worker* in 1933. Her column "Day after Day" (later "On Pilgrimage") expressed pro-union and pacifist views and opposition to racism. In 1934 she and Maurin opened St. Joseph's House of Hospitality in New York City. Many other farms and houses of hospitality for poor and homeless people were based on their model.

A lifelong activist, Day traveled extensively on public speaking engagements. She was first arrested in 1917 during a Washington, DC, march for women's suffrage. At age 76 she was arrested for demonstrating in support of Cesar Chavez's United Farm Workers. Her books include *The Eleventh Virgin* (1924), *House of Hospitality* (1939), *On Pilgrimage* (1948), *Therese* (1960), and *On Pilgrimage: The Sixties* (1972). See also *Dorothy Day: A Biography* (1982), by William D. Miller.

*Jean K. Quam*

### De Forest, Robert Weeks (1848–1931)

Robert Weeks De Forest, president of the New York Charity Organization Society from 1888 to 1931, was a lawyer, philanthropist, and social reformer. A native New Yorker, he was often referred to as "New York's first citizen" because of his efforts on the city's behalf. He received an LLB from Columbia University Law School in 1872 and an MA from Yale University in 1873. For more than 50 years he served as general counsel of the Central Railroad of New Jersey. He helped draft New York's first tenement house law in 1901, fought the activities of loan sharks who took advantage of poor people, and helped found a national association to combat tuberculosis.

De Forest is credited with developing the New York School of Philanthropy, the first training school for social workers, and the Russell Sage Foundation, a model for other philanthropic foundations. He supported such projects as the Metropolitan Museum of Art, Survey Associates, the National Housing Association, the Prison Association of New York, and the State Charities Aid Association. De Forest also helped establish the disaster relief program of the American Red Cross and the Welfare Council of New York. His writings include *The Tenement-House Problem* (1903).

*Jean K. Quam*

### Devine, Edward Thomas (1867–1948)

Edward T. Devine, trained as an economist, was an outstanding educator, writer, and administrator. Born near Union, Iowa, Devine graduated in 1887 from Cornell College in Iowa. He studied economics at the University of Halle-Wittenberg in Germany and received his PhD from the University of Pennsylvania in 1895. During this period he lectured for the American Society for the Expansion of University Teaching, a pioneer adult education project, and at Oxford and Edinburgh. In 1896 he became general secretary of the New York Charity Organization Society. During his 20-year leadership, he formed the Wayfarer's Lodge and the Tenement House Committee (later the Committee on Housing), and he expanded the in-house magazine *Charities* to produce the leading social work journal of its day, *Survey*.

Devine helped found the National Association for the Study and Prevention of Tuberculosis and the National Child Labor Committee in 1904. That same year, he was named director of the New York School of Philanthropy, which he had helped found in 1898. As director (1904–1907, 1912–1917), he worked to establish a strong relationship between the school and Columbia University, where he was a professor of social economy. He was American Red Cross special representative in San Francisco in 1906 after the earthquake and was in charge of flood relief in Dayton, Ohio, in 1913. During World War 1, he headed American Red Cross relief work in France. He also directed the Graduate School of American University in Washington, DC, the Bellevue-Yorkville Health Demonstration in New York City, and the Nassau County Emergency Work and Emergency Relief Bureau in New York. His writings documenting the history of the profession include *Misery and Its Causes* (1909), *Social Work* (1928), *Progressive Social Action* (1933), and *When Social Work Was Young* (1939).

*Jean K. Quam*

### Dix, Dorothea Lynde (1802–1887)

Dorothea Lynde Dix, whose reporting of the neglect, suffering, and abuse of the insane prepared the way for the mental health movement, was born in Hampden, Maine. In 1841, after working as a schoolteacher, she became concerned about the conditions in prisons and almshouses for the insane. Despite her recurring bouts of tuberculosis and malaria, she encouraged state legislatures to support better institutions and finally persuaded Congress to appropriate public land for hospitals for the deaf and the insane. Although President Franklin Pierce vetoed this bill in 1854 and federal assistance was not given to state welfare programs until the 1930s, Dix lobbied nationally and internationally on behalf of the mentally ill and was personally responsible for the establishment of 32 public and private institutions. During the Civil War she served the Union as superintendent of army nurses. Her writings include an encyclopedia, a number of hymns and moral stories for children, *Remarks on Prisons and Prison Discipline in the United States* (1845), and *The Garland of Flora* (1829). See also *Dorothea Dix, Forgotten Samaritan* (1937), by Helen E. Marshall; *Life of Dorothea L. Dix* (1892), by Francis Tiffany; and *Stranger and Traveler: The Story of Dorothea Dix, American Reformer* (1975), by Dorothy Clarke Wilson.

*Jean K. Quam*

### Du Bois, William Edward Burghardt (1868–1963)

W. E. B. Du Bois was an outstanding Black scholar and militant civil rights activist for five decades. He was born of African, Dutch, and French ancestry in Great Barrington, Massachusetts. Du Bois earned two bachelor's degrees, one from Fisk University in 1888 and another from Harvard University in 1890. Prior to earning a doctorate from Harvard University in 1896, he studied at the University of Berlin. Du Bois began a career in university teaching and spent three years as professor in the Department of History and Economics at Atlanta University. He headed the University's Department of Sociology from 1932 to 1944. There, he organized efforts to begin a scientific study of the problems of the Black community. Du Bois promoted higher education for the "talented tenth," or leadership class, within the Black population. Actively fighting discrimination in all aspects of American life, Du Bois organized the Niagara Movement in 1905. This group was absorbed into the organization of the National Association for the Advancement of Colored People in 1909. Du Bois served on the NAACP Board of Directors from 1910 to 1934 and edited *The Crisis*, the organizational magazine he founded in 1910. A prolific writer, Du Bois wrote numerous articles and books on Black people in America and Africa. Notable among his works are *The Philadelphia Negro, A Social Study* (1899), *The Souls of Black Folk* (1903), and *The Autobiography of W. E. B. Du Bois* (1968). See also *W. E. B. Du Bois, Negro Leader in a Time of Crisis* (1959), by Francis L. Broderick.

*Wilma Peebles-Wilkins*

### Dunham, Arthur (1893–1980)

Arthur Dunham, pacifist and social work educator, wrote extensively about community development and social welfare administration. Born in St. Louis, Missouri, Dunham earned an AB from Washington University in St. Louis (1914) and an MA in political science from the University of Illinois (1917). He began his social work career as assistant director of a neighborhood center and as a family caseworker. A member of the Society of Friends (Quakers), Dunham refused to enter the service during World War I and was sentenced to 25 years' hard labor. However, in 1919, his sentence was overturned after only a few months.

Dunham was secretary of the Philadelphia Social Service Exchange (1919–1923), secretary of the Newton, Massachusetts, Central Council (1923–1925), and secretary of the Child Welfare Division of the Public Charities Association of Pennsylvania (1925–1935). In 1935 he became professor at the University of Michigan's Institute of Health and Social Sciences (later the School of Social Work), serving as its acting director from 1949 to 1951. During his retirement he held various visiting professorships; studied community development programs in India in 1956; and wrote a history of the Quakers, *The Ann Arbor*

*Friends Meeting 1935–1975: A History of Its First Forty Years* (1976). His other books, such as *Community Welfare Organization: Principles and Practice* (1958) and *Community Organization in Action* (1959), edited with Ernest B. Harper, contributed to the evolution of community organization as a social work method.

*Jean K. Quam*

### Dybwad, Rosemary Ferguson (1910–1992)

Rosemary Ferguson Dybwad, born in Howe, Indiana, gained international recognition for her pioneering efforts in bringing together nationally organized groups of parents of children with intellectual limitations into a worldwide movement. Following her graduation from Western College for Women, she received from the Institute of International Education a two-year exchange fellowship in sociology at the University of Leipzig and later returned to Germany to complete her PhD in sociology at the University of Hamburg. Her dissertation topic was "Social Work in American Reformatories for Women." She worked in correctional institutions in New Jersey and New York, resigning in 1939 prior to the birth of her first child.

In 1958 Dybwad was asked by her husband, Dr. Gunnar Dybwad, then executive director of the National Association for Retarded Children, to assist with a rapidly growing correspondence from parents around the world. She soon developed and edited an international newsletter that connected parent groups in Europe, North and South America, Asia, and the Pacific Rim. This effort led to the founding of the International League of Societies for Persons with Mental Handicap and the development of her most outstanding achievement, the *International Directory of Mental Retardation Resources*. The third edition of this compendium was published in 1989 by the President's Committee on Mental Retardation. A year later, on the occasion of Dybwad's 80th birthday, Brookline Press published a collection of her presentations at national and international conferences under the title *Perspectives on a Parent Movement: The Revolt of Parents of Children with Intellectual Limitations*. An early supporter of the self-advocacy movement, she participated actively in the first International People First Conference in Tacoma, Washington, in 1984.

*Constance W. Williams*

### Egypt, Ophelia Settle (1903–1984)

Ophelia Settle Egypt, a pioneer in family planning among economically disadvantaged African Americans, also made significant contributions in the areas of historical social research and social work education. Born in a small town near Clarksville, Texas, Egypt received a BA degree from Howard University in 1925 and obtained an MA in sociology from the University of Pennsylvania in 1928. In 1944 she was awarded an MS from the New York School of Social Work. She later received an advanced certificate for work toward a PhD at the Pennsylvania School of Social Work.

In 1929, while serving as a research assistant to Dr. Charles S. Johnson, director of the Social Science Department at Fisk University in Nashville, Tennessee, Egypt conducted original research on the conditions of slavery among African Americans. Her personal interviews with more than 100 former slaves in Tennessee and Kentucky are contained in *Unwritten History of Slavery: Autobiographical Accounts of Negro Ex-Slaves*, which was published by Fisk University in 1968. The original, historical research conducted by Johnson and Egypt was one of the earliest uses of oral history documentation in the United States, predating the Works Progress Administration 1936–1938 study, the largest collection of ex-slave interviews available in this country.

Egypt served as director of the medical social work program of Flint Goodridge Hospital in New Orleans (1935–1939) and assisted in the development of the program of studies at the Howard University School of Social Work (1939–1951). In 1952 Egypt became executive director of the Ionia R. Whipper Home, one of the few homes for unwed African American teenage mothers in the Washington, DC, area. Egypt is best known for her pioneering work in the area of planned parenthood through her efforts at the Parklands Planned Parenthood Clinic in Washington, DC, from 1956 to 1968. On October 15, 1981, the clinic was renamed the Ophelia Egypt Clinic, and Mayor Marion Barry proclaimed October 17, 1981, as Ophelia Settle Egypt day.

*Carrie J. Smith*

### Eliot, Martha May (1891–1978)

Martha May Eliot, educator and public health official, was associated for more than 30 years with the U.S. Children's Bureau. Born in Dorchester, Massachusetts, Eliot graduated from Radcliffe College in 1913 and received her MD in 1918 from Johns Hopkins University. She began her work with the Children's Bureau as director of the Division of Maternal and Child Health (1924–1934), becoming assistant chief (1934–1941), associate chief (1941 – 1949), and chief (1951). As administrator of the federal grants-in-aid program to help states develop health services for mothers and children, she introduced the idea of allotting some money for innovative programs designed by individual states. Eliot also introduced the use of social workers in public health programs and drew attention to the problems of juvenile delinquency and high infant mortality resulting from fetal damage and genetic defects. In 1946 she was vice chair of the U.S. delegation to the international health conference that drafted the constitution of the World Health Organization (WHO), and she was the only woman to sign the document. She was named chief medical consultant to the United Nations International Children's Emergency Fund (UNICEF) in 1947. From 1949 to 1951, she was assistant director general of WHO, and from 1952 to 1957 she was the U.S. representative to the executive board of UNICEF. Eliot taught at Yale University School of Medicine (1921–1949) and was professor of maternal and child health at the Harvard School of Public Health, chairing the department from 1957 to 1960. She served as president of the National Conference of Social Work in 1949 and became the first woman president of the American Public Health Association in 1947. Her writings include articles on her studies of rickets and on maternal and child health care.

*Jean K. Quam*

### Epstein, Abraham (1892–1942)

Abraham Epstein, a Russian immigrant who came to the United States in 1910, was a leader in the post–World War I movement for passage of social security legislation. A graduate of the University of Pittsburgh, Epstein was research director of the Pennsylvania Commission on Old Age Pensions (1918–1927) and helped draft Pennsylvania's first old age pension bill. During this time he also organized and served as secretary-treasurer of the Workers Education Bureau of America. In 1927 he founded the American Association for Old Age Security (later the American Association for Social Security). As its executive secretary, he was instrumental in building public support for the subsequent passage of social security legislation.

Epstein served as U.S. representative to the Social Insurance Commission of the International Labour Office (1934–1937), as a consulting economist to the Social Security Board, and as executive board member of the New York City Affairs Committee. He lectured on social insurance at New York University and Brooklyn College and edited the official publication of the American Association of Social Security, *Social Security*. Epstein wrote *Facing Old Age* (1922); *The Challenge of the Aged* (1928); and *Insecurity: A Challenge to America* (1938), a primary sourcebook in the field of social insurance.

*Maryann Syers*

### Epstein, Laura (1914–1996)

Laura Epstein developed one of the earliest and most fully developed methods of social work intervention,

task-centered treatment. This approach to practice was influential in the development of brief treatment approaches to psychotherapy. Her research is commonly used in graduate schools as a model of how a social intervention method is tested and refined during the initial years of implementation. Later in her career, she examined the influence of social structures and institutions on clinical social work practice in the 20th century.

Epstein was born in the Hyde Park neighborhood of Chicago and lived there most of her life. She earned a BA in psychology from the University of Chicago, as well as an MA from the University of Chicago School of Social Service Administration. Early in her career, she was active in union organizing. At a time when the Communist Party formed unions, Epstein's activities came under the scrutiny of the Federal Bureau of Investigation, and she was prevented from finding a job in social work. During World War II she worked at the war labor board in Chicago and completed statistical studies and assisted in mediating conflicts between labor and management. After the war she took a job at Traveler's Aid of Chicago that launched a career in social work, resulting in numerous books, articles, and national and international presentations. Her book *Brief Treatment* (1993) is used as a primary text for students of social work and other helping professions. She also wrote *Helping People: The Task-Centered Approach* (1988) and *Post Modernism and Social Work* (1995). Epstein's search for more humane and effective therapies influenced many students, practitioners, and clients. She received the University of Chicago School of Social Service Administration Charlotte Towle Medal for Lifetime Achievement in Social Work in June 1996.

*Jeanne C. Marsh*

### Fauri, Fedele Frederick (1909–1981)

Fedele Frederick Fauri, dean of the University of Michigan School of Social Work for almost 20 years, was one of the foremost experts on public welfare in the United States. Trained as an attorney, Fauri received his BA in 1930 and his JD in 1933 from the University of Michigan. His interest in public welfare began in 1934, when he became adviser and general assistant to a county relief administration in his home state.

Fauri served as legal adviser to the Old Age Assistance Bureau in Lansing (1937) and supervisor of the Michigan Bureau of Social Security (1941). In 1943 he became director of the Michigan Department of Social Welfare, and from 1947 to 1951, he worked in Washington, DC, as a senior specialist in social legislation for the Library of Congress as social security adviser to the House Ways and Means Committee.

Invited to be dean of the newly established School of Social Work at the University of Michigan in 1951, Fauri was instrumental in the establishment of the school's innovative doctoral program, combining social work and the social sciences. Fauri continued to act as a consultant on public welfare to various congressional committees, study commissions, and panels. After leaving the deanship in 1970, he became vice president for State Relations and Planning at the University of Michigan. After his retirement in 1975, he was Michigan state racing commissioner from 1975 to 1980. Fauri wrote many articles on public welfare and served as president of the Council on Social Work Education (1954–1956), the American Public Welfare Association (1967), and the National Conference on Social Welfare (1961–1962).

*Maryann Syers*

### Federico, Ronald Charles (1941–1992)

Ronald Federico was a leader in the development of undergraduate social work education. As a teacher, program administrator, and scholar, he helped shape social work education at the baccalaureate level. A native of the Bronx, New York, he received an undergraduate degree from Yale University, an MSW from the University of Michigan, and a PhD from Northwestern University.

Federico served as director of three undergraduate social work programs. He also served on the board of directors of the Council on Social Work Education, was instrumental in the development of the Association of Baccalaureate Social Work Program Directors, and was a member of the BSW Task Force of NASW. Federico provided curriculum consultation to countless social work education programs and served as mentor to a generation of undergraduate social work educators. He is co-author of *Educating the Baccalaureate Social Worker* (Vols. 1 and 2; 1978 and 1979) and *Human Behavior: A Perspective for the Helping Professions* (1982; revised 1985 and 1991) and author of many other books, including *Social Welfare in Today's World* (1990).

*Dean Pierce*

### Fernandis, Sarah A. Collins (1863–1951)

Sarah Fernandis was a civic leader and founder of the first black social settlement in the United States. She was born in Port Deposit, Maryland. Her undergraduate degree was from Hampton Institute in Virginia, and her master's degree in social work was from New York University. After three years of teaching in the Baltimore public schools, she began a lifelong career of organizing social welfare and public health activities in Black communities. Fernandis established the first

American settlement for Blacks in the District of Columbia and a second settlement in Rhode Island. Between 1913 and 1917 she organized the Women's Cooperative Civic League and became its first president. The league worked for improved sanitation and health conditions in Black neighborhoods. During World War I she moved to Pennsylvania and organized a War Camp Community Center. In 1920 Fernandis became the first Black social worker employed in the City Venereal Disease Clinic of the Baltimore Health Department. In this position she continued to work for improved health conditions in the Black community. See *Notable Maryland Women* (1977), edited by Winifred G. Helmes.

*Wilma Peebles-Wilkins*

### Fizdale, Ruth (1908–1994)

Ruth Fizdale, a caseworker and administrator in health care, was a pioneer in professionalizing social work. Early in her career, she was a psychiatric caseworker at the Mandel Clinic of the Michael Reese Hospital in Chicago. She later worked at Jewish Family Services in Brooklyn and at the New York Association for New Americans, where she used counseling and job training to help immigrants become self-sustaining within a year of arriving in the United States.

As chief of social services staff development for the Veterans Administration following World War II, she created an innovative structure for staff and student training, which later served as the basis for continuing the education of social workers in other health settings. Her work resulted in enhanced curricula in the schools of social work and had a positive impact on the quality of social work services in health care. In addition, she developed competitive stipends for students who entered Veterans Administration and other health care services.

For 19 years Fizdale was executive director of the Arthur Lehman Counseling Service (ALCS), where she developed the fee-for-services system in for-profit agencies. ALCS, which had been established to serve middle-class and upper-income clients, was known for charging reasonable fees and paying attractive salaries. Fizdale's work helped remove the "charitable institution" label from voluntary organizations and influenced the acceptance of work with people from all socioeconomic groups. Her book *Social Agency Structure and Accountability* (Burdick, 1974) was used in graduate schools, agencies, and private practice to standardize quality, fee-paid, social work services.

Fizdale actively worked with many professional social work organizations to improve the professional standing of social work, including the American Association of

Psychiatric Social Workers, NASW, and the National Conference on Social Welfare. She was a founding member of NASW's Competence Certification Board, which was responsible for overseeing the Academy of Certified Social Workers, the profession's first national credential.

She received her professional education at the University of Chicago, the Smith College School for Social Work, and the University of Pennsylvania. She served as adjunct associate professor emerita at the Mount Sinai School of Medicine. She was named a fellow of the Brookdale Center on Aging of Hunter College for her service to elderly people, and in 1994 Columbia University established the Helen Rehr and Ruth Fizdale Professorship of Health and Mental Health.

*Linda Beebe*

### Flexner, Abraham (1866–1959)

Abraham Flexner was an educator and educational reformer who influenced social work through his challenge to the professional status of the field. Of immigrant background, Flexner graduated from Johns Hopkins University in 1886 and spent his early career in secondary education as a teacher and a school principal. After a period of study at Harvard University and in Berlin, Flexner began his work in educational reform. His 1910 report to the Carnegie Foundation for the Advancement of Teaching, *Medical Education in the United States and Canada*, had tremendous impact on the development of medical education. He was a member and secretary of the General Education Board of the Rockefeller Foundation (1917–1925) and later became director of the Institute for Advanced Study at Princeton University (1930–1939).

At the 1915 National Conference of Charities and Correction, Flexner raised the question, "Is social work a profession?", listing six essential criteria for a profession. Although social work met four of them, a learned character, practicality, a tendency toward self-organization, and altruistic motivation, Flexner concluded that social work did not qualify as a profession because it lacked individual responsibility and educationally communicable techniques. His writings include *Abraham Flexner: An Autobiography* (1960).

*Maryann Syers*

### Folks, Homer (1867–1963)

Homer Folks was a pioneer during the early years of the social work profession, whose views were sought, respected, and acted on by legislators, governors, presidents, and foreign governments. Born in Hanover, Michigan, he graduated from Albion College in 1889 and from Harvard University in 1890. Folks served as general superintendent of the Children's Aid Society of Pennsylvania (1890–1893), executive director of the State Charities Aid Association of New York (1893–1947), commissioner of Public Charities of New York City (1902–1903), president of the National Conference on Social Welfare (1911 and 1923), and president of the board of directors of the National Tuberculosis Association (1912–1913). Folks also worked abroad with the American Red Cross from 1917 to 1919.

Folks was among the first to recognize illness as a major cause of poverty and to emphasize the importance of preventive public health measures. He played a leading role in the organization and administration of movements for the improvement of health and welfare. Both the New York State Public Health Law and the Public Welfare Act are credited to Folk's skill as a bill drafter. His public service activities included the care of dependent children, mental hygiene, tuberculosis control, public assistance programs, social research, and corrections and parole. In 1940 Folks was awarded the Distinguished Services Medal by the Theodore Roosevelt Memorial Association for his promotion of social justice, and in 1952 he became the first recipient of the National Tuberculosis Association's Will Ross Medal for his outstanding contributions toward the control of tuberculosis.

Folks is the author of *The Care of Destitute, Neglected and Delinquent Children* (1902) and *The Human Costs of the War* (1920). See also *Public Health and Welfare: The Citizen's Responsibility* (1958).

*Sara Harmon*

### Follett, Mary Parker (1868–1933)

Mary Parker Follett, a native of Quincy, Massachusetts, and an 1898 graduate of Radcliffe College, was active in vocational guidance, industrial relations, civic education, and settlement work. As a vocational counselor for Boston's Roxbury Neighborhood House, Follett became aware that poor working families needed social, recreational, and educational facilities. In 1909 her lobbying resulted in legislation that allowed her to open the Boston School Centers for after-school recreation and education programs.

As a member of the vocational guidance board of the Boston School Board and the Minimum Wage Board of the Women's Municipal League, Follett was active in the business community and addressed groups of businesspeople. She continued her interest in industrial relations after moving to England in 1924, serving as vice president of the National Community Center Association and as a member of the Taylor Society, an organization concerned with scientific management and efficiency in industry.

Follett's interest in the concept of "psychological interpenetration"—that is, a plan to get people of different socioeconomic and occupational backgrounds to understand one another's viewpoints—is described in her 1924 book, *Creative Experience*. See also *Dynamic Administration: The Collected Papers of Mary Parker Follett* (1941), edited by Henry C. Metcalf and L. Urick.

*Maryann Syers*

### Frankel, Lee Kaufer (1867–1931)

Lee Kaufer Frankel, originally trained as a chemist, is best known for his contributions to health insurance, family services, and Jewish welfare. Frankel received a BS (1887) and PhD (1888) from the University of Pennsylvania and taught chemistry there until 1893. After six years as a consulting chemist in Philadelphia, Frankel became manager of the United Hebrew Charities in New York City. An outstanding leader in the family service field and one of the early developers of family casework practice, he was also one of the first instructors at the New York School of Philanthropy and was instrumental in establishing the Training School for Jewish Social Work.

As president of the National Conference of Jewish Charities in 1912, Frankel was active in Jewish relief efforts during and after World War I. With a grant from the Russell Sage Foundation he conducted a two-year study of various forms of health insurance. This led to a position as manager of the Metropolitan Life Insurance Company's industrial department and then as second vice president. Frankel continued his interest in social welfare, initiating social programs within the company. Frankel served as director and vice president of the National Association for the Study and Prevention of Tuberculosis (1914), treasurer of the American Public Health Association (1919), president of the New York State Conference of Charities and Correction (1917), welfare director of the Post Office Department (1921–1922), chairperson of the National Health Council (1923–1925), and vice president of the National Conference of Social Work (1923–1924). His books include *Cost of Medical Care* (1929) and *The Health of the Worker* (1924). See also *Half a Century in Community Service* (1948), by Charles Bernheimer.

*Maryann Syers*

### Frazier, Edward Franklin (1894–1962)

E. Franklin Frazier is noted for his studies of the Black family and the Black middle class. He was born in Baltimore, Maryland. Frazier received a bachelor of arts degree from Howard University in 1916. He studied sociology at Clark University where he earned a master's degree in 1920 and a doctorate in 1931. In 1922 Frazier became director of the Atlanta University School of Social Work. He remained in this position

for five years before leaving Atlanta as a result of controversy created in the White community by his article in *Forum Magazine* on racial prejudice. For three years Frazier served as a research sociologist at Fisk University. In 1934 he became head of the Department of Sociology at Howard University and remained in this position until his retirement in 1959. Prior to the establishment of a separate School of Social Work at Howard, Frazier directed a social work program there for eight years. Frazier's career as an educator included precollegiate teaching as well as national and international university teaching. As a sociologist Frazier contributed widely to the knowledge of Black families through his research studies and publications. His works include *The Negro Family in Chicago* (1932), *The Negro Family in the United States* (1939), *Black Bourgeoisie* (1955), and *Race and Culture Contacts in the Modern World* (1957). See also R. W. Logan and M. Winston, *Dictionary of American Negro Biography* (1982).

*Wilma Peebles-Wilkins*

### Galarza, Ernesto (1905–1984)

Ernesto Galarza was a pioneer, an advocate, and a scholar, whose commitment to social justice, especially through the power of his convictions conveyed by the written word, triggered a number of significant policies on behalf of individuals and families without power in American democracy. His report, which was later published in a book titled *Merchants of Labor*, is credited with ending the Bracero program and its exploitative characteristics. His careful documentation of unjust treatment of farm workers in the Southwest and the deep South directly contributed to major policy changes. His report "Tragedy at Chualar," which was published as a book, led to the uncovering of unsafe conditions for farm workers and specifically the death of 32 farm workers as the result of unsafe practices in the transportation of farm workers, resulting in compensation for the families of the 32 men who were killed. Overall he directly contributed to policy changes in the health and safety of farm workers.

Social workers, and especially the School of Social Work at San Jose State University, benefited tremendously from Dr. Galarza's dispassionate analysis of social injustice, his advocacy and scholarly approach to controversial social policy issues and his careful and thorough documentation of celebrated cases that led to much-needed policy changes. A social worker close to Dr. Galarza characterized him as "Don Quixote with a pen." The School of Social Work honors him annually through a symposium and the Ernesto Galarza Scholarship Fund. In addition, the School of Social Work and a high school district created the Ernesto Galarza

Institute for Community Development and established it in the Eastside Union High School District in San Jose, California. His delightful and thought-provoking stories for children in both English and Spanish are a testimony to the importance that he and his family placed on education, which led Galarza to earn a PhD in history from Columbia University. His contribution to social work and social work education was through the power of his ideas, which he committed to writing and developed therein. The products of his labor are built into the various annual and established activities in social work education and social work services and remain a testimony to a man who devoted his life to the cause of social justice. Thus, social work honors him and is honored by his lifetime of achievements and the power of his ideas, which live on.

*Juan Ramos*

### Gallaudet, Edward Miner (1837–1917)

Like his father and elder brother, Edward Miner Gallaudet devoted his life to working with deaf people. Born in Hartford, Connecticut, near his father's school, he attended Trinity College. After graduating in 1856, he taught at the Gallaudet School for a period of time and then moved to Washington, DC, where he founded the Columbia Institute for the Deaf and Dumb. This school (renamed Gallaudet College in 1893 in honor of his father) was the first institution to provide college-level education for deaf people. In addition to his work with deaf people, Gallaudet wrote extensively on methods of education for deaf people and was president of the Convention of American Instructors of the Deaf from 1895 until 1917.

*Maryann Syers*

### Gallaudet, Thomas (1822–1902)

Thomas Gallaudet was the eldest son of Thomas Hopkins Gallaudet and Sophia Fowler, a deaf woman who had been a pupil at the Gallaudet School. Growing up near the school founded by his father, he learned sign language at an early age and eventually devoted his life to ministering to deaf people. Gallaudet graduated from Washington College in 1842 and began his career teaching at the New York Institution for the Deaf. Later he converted to the Episcopal Church and was ordained a priest in 1851. In 1850, while studying for the priesthood, he began a Bible class for deaf people at St. Stephen's Church in New York City, and in 1852 he established St. Ann's Church for Deaf Mutes, conducting regular services in sign language. In addition to his parish duties, Gallaudet founded the Gallaudet Home for aged and infirm deaf-mutes near Poughkeepsie, New York.

*Maryann Syers*

### Gallaudet, Thomas Hopkins (1787–1851)

Thomas Hopkins Gallaudet and his two sons, Thomas and Edward Miner, are renowned for their commitment to the education of deaf people. Born in Philadelphia, Gallaudet moved to Hartford, Connecticut, at the age of 13. After graduation from Yale University, poor health forced him to give up law school. Subsequently, he worked as a traveling salesperson and entered Andover Theological Seminary, graduating in 1814. During this time, the father of a deaf girl who was impressed with Gallaudet's ability to communicate with his daughter, raised money to send him to Europe to study methods for educating deaf people. In 1816 Gallaudet returned to the United States accompanied by Laurent Franc, one of the outstanding teachers at the Institute Royal des Sourds-Muets in Paris. In 1817 Gallaudet established the first free American school for the deaf in Hartford. The school taught deaf students and trained teachers of the deaf; Gallaudet remained its principal until 1830.

Gallaudet was instrumental in the establishment of public normal schools in Connecticut and worked to promote manual training programs in the schools. He was also interested in the education of black people and advocated for higher education for women. See *Gallaudet: Friend of the Deaf* (1964), by Etta Degering.

*Maryann Syers*

### Garrett, Annette Marie (1898–1957)

Annette Marie Garrett was a social worker and social work educator whose main contribution was in the development of casework practice. A native of Kansas, Garrett received her BA from the University of Kansas, did graduate work at the University of Chicago, and received an MSS from Smith College School for Social Work in 1928. After several years in casework practice, she was appointed chief of social service at the Judge Baker Guidance Center in Boston. In 1935 she became associate director of Smith College School for Social Work, remaining there until her death.

As an instructor and director of field operations, Garrett believed that students should have a wide range of firsthand field experience. Out of just such an experience, working with a troubled child in foster placement, she wrote *Casework Treatment of a Child* (1942). Her contributions to social work education include *Learning through Supervision* (1954). Garrett's influential book, *Interviewing, Its Principles and Methods* (1942), was translated into 12 languages, and her *Counseling Methods for Personnel Workers* (1945) helped to extend the use of casework principles to the new field of industrial counseling.

*Maryann Syers*

### Germain, Carel Bailey (1916–1995)

Carel Bailey Germain, scholar, teacher, writer, and theoretician, profoundly altered the shape of social work practice. A native of San Francisco, Germain was a devoted naturalist and was active in the Campfire Girls throughout her girlhood. Her love of and interest in nature had major significance for the future development of social work practice theory. She began her career in social work upon completing her BA degree at the University of California at Berkeley. Eventually, she and her family moved to the East Coast, and she returned to school, receiving her MSW from Columbia University in 1961.

Her outstanding abilities were immediately recognized, and she quickly assumed a leadership role, becoming assistant director of social work in the Department of Psychiatry at the University of Maryland School of Medicine and teaching at the School of Social Work. At age 49, she entered the doctoral program at Columbia University, completing her degree in 1971.

From that time until her death, Germain occupied a major position in the intellectual life of the profession. She was professor of social work at the University of Connecticut and at Columbia University. Her softspoken, elegant, and reflective presentation and her warm and generous relationships enchanted students and colleagues at these institutions and at many others across the country where she was visiting professor, lecturer, consultant, and workshop leader.

A prolific writer, she published her first juried article while still a doctoral student and went on to publish more than 50 subsequent articles and book chapters, as well as to author seven books. Her thinking and writing always reflected her erudition; her extensive knowledge of social work, the social and biological sciences, literature, and the arts; and her originality, creativity, and willingness to challenge cherished notions.

Germain's first publications, the classic "Social Study: Past and Future," which appeared in 1968, and her 1970 "Casework and Science: An Historical Encounter," challenged the 19th century scientism implicit in linear notions of "study—diagnosis—treatment," laying the groundwork for her future contributions. Germain introduced an ecological metaphor for social work theory and practice in her 1973 "An Ecological Perspective in Social Casework." This was followed by a series of articles exploring the person and environment relationship from an ecological perspective, a theme continued in an edited volume, *Social Work Practice: People and Environments* (1979).

In 1989, with Alex Gitterman, she published the widely used text, *The Life Model of Social Work*, a work that focused on the natural human processes of growth, coping, adaptation, and change. A book applying the ecological perspective to practice in health care followed, and her comprehensive text, *Human Behavior and the Social Environment: An Ecological View*, was published in 1991. *The Life Model of Social Work: Advances in Theory and Practice*, a major revision of Germain and Gitterman's practice text, appeared in 1996, shortly after her death.

Germain received many honors, including an honorary doctorate in humane letters from Smith College, The Lucille Austin Fellowship at Columbia University, and the Richard Lodge Memorial Prize at Adelphi University. Her papers have been deposited in the social work collection of the Sophia Smith Archives at Smith College, Northampton, Massachusetts, where they are available to scholars.

*Ann Hartman*

### Gibelman, Margaret (1947–2005)

Margaret Gibelman, a native New Yorker, was a cutting-edge scholar of the social work profession, the social service delivery system, and social work education. Gibelman published over 125 articles and eight books which identified the scope of social work practice and the challenges facing the delivery of services. She highlighted the influence of new trends on the profession, social workers, and clients, such as the purchase of social work services. Gibelman examined the professional environment of social workers in relation to volunteerism, advancement, and compensation. Recent work included a study of the glass ceiling in social work that made national news reminding this profession of the nature of sex discrimination. She was extraordinarily generous as mentor and editor to her students and colleagues.

Gibelman served as administrator, executive, and consultant at a range of not-for-profit agencies, professional organizations, and accrediting bodies. She was the Associate Executive Director of the Council on Social Work Education and Executive Director of both the National Association of School Psychologists and The Lupus Foundation of America. She consulted with NASW on a variety of task forces focusing on managed health care; social work response to homelessness; NASW Insurance Trust on risk management; legal vulnerability of social workers; data collection by NASW; revising the management information system; implementation materials for the new Code of Ethics; and exploring salaries of social workers. Other consultations were provided to The Department of Human Services, District of Columbia; Asthma and Allergy Foundation of America, Inc.; the Institute of Child Mental Health of Adelphi University; the American

Bar Association; the Council on Accreditation of Services for Families and Children; the American Public Welfare Association; and many other local and national organizations.

Gibelman was a faculty member at: Rutgers University, Catholic University, and Yeshiva University (the latter as tenured full professor, Director of the Doctoral Program). She held a DSW from Adelphi University; an MA in political science and MSW, both from Rutgers University; and a BA in political science from Ohio University.

*Miriam Dinerman, Kim Lorber, and Adele Weiner*

### Ginsberg, Mitchell I. (1915–1996)

Mitchell Ginsberg's contribution to social work was formidable, particularly his concern for disadvantaged people who looked to the government for assistance and his interest in the education of future social workers.

Ginsberg helped shape the "War on Poverty" in the 1960s. He headed New York City's public welfare program. He combined employment training, child welfare, family counseling, services to the aging, and economic assistance into a single public department. He headed that program from its inception until 1970. Meanwhile he consulted to numerous congressional committees and the U.S. Department of Health, Education, and Welfare.

In 1953 he joined the faculty of the Columbia University School of Social Work, serving as dean of the school from 1971 to 1981. Also, he assisted the university in discharging its social responsibilities through a program of neighborhood services and as co-director of the Center for the Study of Human Rights.

Ginsberg received many awards and four honorary doctoral degrees from leading universities. He served as president of NASW and as both chair and member of numerous national, state, and city commissions and committees.

*Bertram M. Beck*

### Gonzalez Molina de la Caro, Dolores (1910–1979)

Dolores Gonzalez Molina de la Caro was a pioneer in mental health training, public welfare, public health, school health, and university counseling in Puerto Rico. Born in a rural community where her father was a leader in local politics, she received social work training at the age of 19. At the rural vocational school to which she was assigned, her leadership abilities quickly emerged. She also studied at the New York School of Social Work and earned her master's degree in medical social work at the University of Chicago.

Caro's long career in public service included appointments as director of the Bureau of Medical Social Work and director of the Mental Health Program, both in the Department of Health in Puerto Rico. In her work she gave special emphasis to the development of training programs and to the integration of state and local services. She was also dean of students at Lesley College in Massachusetts and associate dean of students at the University of Puerto Rico, where she developed innovative support programs incorporating mental health and group dynamics. Her published works include *Human Relations in the Public Service* (1956) and the two-volume *Manual in Human Relations Training for Student Orientors* (1970).

*John F. Longres*

### Gottlieb, Naomi R. (1925–1995)

Naomi Gottlieb pioneered the development of new approaches to counteract inequities and stereotyped views of both men and women. After earning her DSW from the University of California at Berkeley in 1970, she joined the faculty of the University of Washington School of Social Work, where she became extensively involved in three major areas: gender issues in the social work curriculum, evaluation of social work practice, and the PhD program in social welfare. She also served as associate dean with responsibilities for curriculum and faculty matters from 1977 to 1985.

In the mid-1970s she co-authored a grant proposal that led to the creation of the first social work program in feminist practice in the country. She once said of this work: "Becoming a feminist and acting on my commitment to educate students to a feminist approach was one of the most important parts of my professional development—it was not just work, but something I did out of real love and conviction."

In addition, Gottlieb helped initiate and develop the University of Washington School of Social Work's doctoral program and coordinated the program for several years. The educational needs of students were at the forefront of all her actions, and she had a profound commitment to students, particularly to those from disadvantaged backgrounds.

She wrote numerous articles on women's issues and feminist practice, including the book *The Welfare Bind* (1974), and served as editor of *Alternative Social Services for Women* (1980) and *The Woman Client* (1987). She also co-founded *Affilia*, a journal on women and social work, and served as its book review editor.

In recognition of her leadership on women's issues, she was the first recipient of the Belle Spafford Endowed Chair in Women's Studies at the University of Utah Graduate School of Social Work in 1987.

At the time of her death, as a tribute to her profound commitment to students' learning, the University of Washington established the Naomi R. Gottlieb Endowed Fund to provide support for those seeking a PhD in social welfare.

*Nancy R. Hooyman*

### Granger, Lester Blackwell (1896–1976)

Lester Blackwell Granger, an outspoken advocate for interracial cooperation and equal opportunity for Black people, was best known for his leadership of the Urban League and for his efforts to desegregate the U.S. armed forces after World War 11. Born in Newport News, Virginia, Granger was the son of a physician and a schoolteacher. After graduating from Dartmouth College in 1917, Granger served for two years in France during World War I. Returning to civilian life, he worked for the New Jersey Urban League but soon left to teach at Winston-Salem State University and St. Augustine's College in Raleigh, North Carolina. In 1922 he became an extension worker at the Manual Training School for Colored Youth in Bordentown, New Jersey. He reorganized the Los Angeles affiliate of the Urban League in 1930, worked briefly at Bordentown, and returned to the Urban League in 1934.

Thus began Granger's 27-year association with the agency, uninterrupted except for the period from 1938 to 1940, when he established the Standing Committee on Negro Welfare of the Welfare Council of New York City, which attempted to obtain equality of social and welfare services for Black people. As leader of the Urban League (1940–1961), Granger worked to gain employment for Blacks and garner support for equal opportunity from industrial and community leaders. At the end of World War II—when the return of White veterans threatened the advances made by Black people—Granger initiated a community relations project aimed at abating racial tensions.

In 1945, after Granger was commissioned by the secretary of the U.S. Navy to study the serious racial tensions plaguing the Navy, his recommendations were implemented throughout the armed services. He also served as president of the National Conference of Social Work (1951– 1952) and as president of the International Conference on Social Welfare (1961).

*Maryann Syers*

### Gurin, Arnold (1917–1991)

Arnold Gurin was a leader in advancing community organization, social work policies and practices, planning and research, education, and administration in voluntary, government, and Jewish services. He served as caseworker in the Chicago Relief Administration; as a caseworker, employment interviewer, and migration worker to resettle victims of Nazi persecution in the National Refugee Service; and as director of budget research and director of field services for the Council of Jewish Federation. In the last capacity he was involved in a broad spectrum of social, health, and educational services of Jewish communities across the United States and Canada and in other countries. He then turned to social work education, teaching at Michigan State, Columbia, and Brandeis universities. At Brandeis he became professor and dean of the Florence Heller Graduate School for Advanced Studies in Social Welfare.

Gurin's guidance was sought by many organizations. He directed a landmark study of teaching community organization for the Council on Social Work Education as well as the evaluation of Project Renewal in Israel, an innovative program to help lift scores of deprived neighborhoods out of poverty. Gurin advised Israel on the development of social work education and the Jewish community of France on the professional education of the staff of communal agencies. He also assisted state and federal government agencies in addressing public–private agency relationships, the organization of social services, and other critical issues.

Those who sought Gurin's advice and assistance relied on the excellence of his standards, his balance of vision and realism, the depth and clarity of his thinking, his objectivity, and his skill in resolving conflicts and achieving consensus. He was an officer of NASW and was honored by the Massachusetts chapter as its Man of the Year. His books include *Community Organizations and Social Planning* (with Robert Penman, 1972) and *Community Organization Curriculum in Graduate Social Work Education* (1970). His other works include numerous articles, monographs, chapters in books, and papers.

*Philip Bernstein*

### Gurin, Helen (1918–1991)

Helen Gurin was a leading teacher, supervisor, and guide for a generation of professionals in social work and other fields and an outstanding therapist, planner, clinician, and administrator. After graduating from Hunter College, she earned a master's degree in educational psychology at City College, New York, and an MSW at the Columbia School of Social Work.

In addition to teaching social work students at the master's and doctoral levels, Gurin trained psychiatrists, psychiatric nurses, psychologists, and child care workers. Many in other professions sought her for training because of her depth of knowledge and insights in social work, coupled with her background in psychological thought and practice. Committed to ensuring that disadvantaged children would have the same quality of service that other children received, she was at the forefront of planning and establishing clinical programs to serve the child welfare system. Clinicians referred parents and children to her for therapy because of her exceptional skill in analyzing and treating complex social problems of families, especially children.

Gurin had a keen commitment to the institutional setting in which she worked and was a constructive institution builder. She practiced at the New York City Department of Social Welfare, the United Service for New Americans, the South Shore Children Guidance Service, the South Shore Planned Parenthood Center, the Lansing Child Guidance Clinic, and the Tavistock Clinic (London). Gurin also taught at the schools of social work of Simmons College, Michigan and Michigan State universities, and Smith College. In recognition of her unique leadership and service, the Massachusetts chapter of NASW named her Social Worker of the Year in 1983.

*Philip Bernstein*

### Gurteen, Stephen Humphreys (1836–1898)

Stephen Humphreys Gurteen, founder of the first Charity Organization Society in the United States, was born near Canterbury, England. After graduating from Cambridge University in 1863, he emigrated to the United States and worked as a lawyer and a teacher of Latin. In 1875 he was ordained as an Episcopal priest and appointed assistant minister of St. Paul's Church, Buffalo, New York. Buffalo was in the midst of the depression of 1873–1878, and Gurteen was put in charge of the church's relief work. He spent the summer of 1877 in England observing efforts to assist the poor, including the London Charity Organisation Society, and on his return proposed a Charity Organization Society (COS) for Buffalo that would involve prominent businessmen representing a variety of religious faiths. The Buffalo COS, launched in December 1877, differed little from the English model except for its policy of strict nonsectarianism, on which Gurteen had insisted.

Following a congregational rift, Gurteen left St. Paul's in 1880. He wrote about the COS movement and served for a year as director of the Chicago COS. From 1884 to 1886 he served as rector of a church in Springfield, Illinois. In 1886 he retired to New York City, where he pursued an interest in early English literature. Gurteen wrote *A Handbook of Charity Organization* (1882) and "Beginning of Charity Organizations in America" in *Lend a Hand* (1894). See also "Stephen Humphreys Gurteen and the American Origins of Charity Organization," *Social Service Review* (1966), by Verl S. Lewis.

*Paul H. Stuart*

### Hale, Clara (1905–1992)

Clara Hale was the first proprietor of a not-for-profit child care agency serving children born addicted to drugs or alcohol or with acquired immune deficiency syndrome (AIDS). Born in Philadelphia, Hale migrated to New York City after her marriage to Thomas Hale, who died prematurely. From 1941 to 1968, to care for her three young children as a young, single parent, she became a foster parent for more than 40 children. She was praised for her parenting skills, which she credited to her strict Black Baptist code of discipline.

"Mother," as she was called, started Hale House in her home in 1969 to care for addicted babies. In 1975 Hale House, now a licensed child care facility, became a residential center for children exposed in utero to addictive drugs and whose parents were temporarily unable to care for them.

Hale's work attracted national attention. In his 1985 State of the Union address, President Reagan called her an "American heroine." In the same year, at the age of 80, she was appointed to President Reagan's American Commission on Drug-Free Schools and was made an honorary "soror" of Delta Sigma Theta Sorority. Hale's unfinished dream was to develop a hospice for terminally ill children. A biography of her life and work—written by her daughter, Dr. Lorraine Hale, the current proprietor of Hale House—is in progress.

*Yuonne Asamoah*

### Hall, Helen (1892–1982)

Helen Hall was a Henry Street settlement house leader, social reformer, and consumer advocate. She directed the University Settlement in Philadelphia from 1922 to 1933, before succeeding Lillian Wald as director of the Henry Street Settlement in New York, in 1933. She remained in that position until her retirement in 1967. She served with the American Red Cross in France during and after World War I and in the Far East during World War II. She was an influential leader in the settlement house and consumer movements, directed numerous national and local studies on socioeconomic conditions, and actively campaigned to improve community conditions on New York's lower east side.

*Edith Olmsted*

### Hamilton, Gordon (1892–1967)

Gordon Hamilton was a practitioner, an educator, a consultant, and a writer whose works profoundly influenced the development of casework theory. Born into an upper-class family, she received her early education at home and obtained a BA from Bryn Mawr in 1914.

During World War 1 she did war work in England. Later she worked in Denver, Colorado, for the American Red Cross, meeting Mary Richmond, who recommended her to the New York City Charity Organization Society. After three years as a caseworker and a research secretary for the society, in 1923 she began her career with the New York School of Social Work. As an educator, Hamilton was closely involved with consultation and administration in various fields of practice. She worked with the Social Service Department of the Presbyterian Hospital in New York City (1925–1932) and served as director of Social Service in the Temporary Emergency Relief Administration (1935–1936), research consultant to the Committee on Social Issues of the Group for the Advancement of Psychiatry (1949–1953), and consultant for such international organizations as Church World Service and UNRRA (1944–1952).

Perhaps Hamilton's greatest contributions were as a teacher and a writer. A leading expression of the "diagnostic" school of thought, her enormously influential *Theory and Practice of Social Casework* (1940/1951) was widely translated and used as a training text for at least two decades. The book dealt with the philosophy and values underlying service provision and with such considerations as professional relationship, the use of community resources, and the relationship among social agencies, problem diagnosis, and casework intervention. Hamilton also argued that social workers should be interested in work with poor people and in the economic hardships that disrupt family life.

As a teacher she believed that knowledge of and ability to organize content were the keys to precise yet imaginative thinking in students. She worked with Eveline Burns and Philip Klein to develop a doctoral program in social work at Columbia University—efforts that led to the development of doctoral programs in other universities.

After her retirement from Columbia she served as editor in chief of *Social Work* (1956–1962), putting forth ideas about specialization method and the unity of social work goals and values. In a famous 1962 editorial, she proposed that the administration of income maintenance grants be separated from social service programs. Her works include *Principles of Social Case Recording, Psycho-therapy in Child Guidance*, and *Theory and Practice of Social Case Work*.

*John F. Longres*

### Haynes, Elizabeth Ross (1883–1953)

Elizabeth Ross Haynes (wife of George Edmund Haynes) is noted for her organizational work to improve the quality of life in the Black community. She was born in Mount Willing, Alabama. In 1903 Haynes received a bachelor of arts degree from Fisk University and 20 years later she earned a master's degree in sociology from Columbia University. She taught for four years, then turned to volunteer work and paid employment in social services. In 1918 Haynes became the assistant director of the Negro Economics Division in the U.S. Department of Labor (George E. Haynes was director). She spent two years as a consultant with the Domestic Service Section of the U.S. Employment Service. During her 10 years with the national board of the Young Women's Christian Association, she helped develop the association's Industrial Division. Her efforts to better the economic circumstances of Black people continued as she worked to improve state employment policies while serving on the New York State Temporary Commission of the Urban Colored Population. Her philosophy of Black upward mobility is communicated in her publications *Unsung Heroes* (1921) and *The Black Boy of Atlanta* (1952). See also *Notable American Women: The Modern Period* (1980), by B. Sicherman et al.

*Wilma Peebles-Wilkins*

### Haynes, George Edmund (1880–1960)

George Haynes (husband of Elizabeth Ross Haynes) was a social scientist who was recognized as co-founder of the National Urban League. Born in Pine Bluff, Arkansas, he received a bachelor's degree from Fisk University and a master's degree from Yale University. In 1910 Haynes became the first Black graduate of the New York School of Philanthropy. He received a PhD in economics in 1912 and was the first Black person to earn a doctorate from Columbia University. He was the director of Negro Economics for the U.S. Department of Labor and director of the Department of Social Sciences at Fisk University. Haynes was a social activist during a period of great concern over the living conditions of Black people migrating to urban centers. While serving as a research fellow for the Bureau of Social Research of the Charity Organization Societies, he began doing research on migration. His research activities generated active involvement in associations to improve the working conditions of Black people. These reform efforts led to the 1911 founding, with Ruth Standish Baldwin, of the Committee on Urban Conditions Among Negroes. In 1920 this committee became the National Urban League. He published many articles in addition to his research on the effects of migration on black people, *The Negro at Work in New York City* (1912). See also "Notes on a Forgotten Black Social Worker and Sociologist: George Edmund Haynes," *Journal of Sociology and Social Welfare* (1983), by

I. Carlton LaNey, and *Dictionary of American Negro Biography* (1982), by R. W Logan and M. Winston.

*Wilma Peebles-Wilkins*

### Hearn, Gordon (1914–1979)

Gordon Hearn was an influential theoretician and group worker who introduced general systems theory into social work. Born in Canada, where his father was an educator, he received his early education and professional experience there, working with boys in the Young Men's Christian Association. He earned a master's degree from George Williams College in Chicago in 1939 and was a member of the first doctoral class in group psychology organized and directed by Kurt Lewin at the Massachusetts Institute of Technology.

As a professor at Berkeley and as the first dean of the School of Social Work at Portland State University, Hearn taught and wrote in the field of human relations training. For many years, too, he was a staff associate of the National Training Laboratories. Gordon Hearn will also be remembered as a humanist who, in addition to his interests in group theory, was an accomplished painter. Among his published works are *Theory Building in Social Work* (1958) and *The General Systems Approach to the Understanding of Groups* (1962).

*John F. Longres*

### Hoey, Jane M. (1892–1968)

Jane M. Hoey's major contribution to social work was in the establishment and enforcement of standards in public welfare administration. The daughter of Irish immigrants, she was born in Greeley County, Nebraska. After receiving an MA in political science from Columbia University and a diploma from the New York School of Philanthropy in 1916, she began working for Harry Hopkins at the New York Board of Child Welfare. Employed by the American Red Cross, she later became secretary of the Bronx Committee of the New York Tuberculosis and Health Association. She helped organize the Health Division of the New York Welfare Council and became its assistant director in 1926. A combination of family and administrative experiences helped acquaint her with the political world. Her political skills were helpful in negotiations with government officials and in program interpretation when she served as a delegate to the United Nations.

Hoey later became director of social research for the National Tuberculosis Association and served as president of the National Conference of Social Work, the Council on Social Work Education, and the William J. Kerby Foundation. The Jane M. Hoey Chair in Social Policy was established by the Columbia University School of Social Work in 1962. Between 1931 and 1953, Hoey published a number of articles related to government policy and welfare.

*Larraine M. Edwards*

### Hopkins, Harry Lloyd (1890–1946)

Harry Hopkins became a national leader during the Great Depression as the administrator of the Federal Emergency Relief Administration (FERA), the country's first federal relief program. Born in Sioux City, Iowa, he graduated from Iowa's Grinnell College in 1912. He began his social work career as director of a boys' camp run by New York's Christodora House Settlement. While living at the house, Hopkins joined the staff of the Association for Improving the Condition of the Poor and served two years as an agent for its Bureau of Family Rehabilitation and Relief. In 1924 he was appointed executive director of New York's Temporary Emergency Relief Administration by Governor Franklin D. Roosevelt. Under Roosevelt's presidential administration, Hopkins headed the federal relief program for two years. He then became administrator of the Works Progress Administration, which replaced FERA, and he became secretary of commerce in 1938. Hopkins wrote *Spending to Save: The Complete Story of Relief* (1936). See also *Minister of Relief: Harry Hopkins and the Depression* (1963), by Searle E. Charles; *Harry Hopkins and the New Deal* (1974), by Paul A. Kurzman; and *Roosevelt and Hopkins* (1948), by Robert E. Sherwood.

*John F. Longres*

### Howard, Donald S. (1902–1982)

Donald S. Howard, an eminent social work educator and administrator, was born in Tokyo, the son of missionaries. A 1925 graduate of Otterbein College, he earned his PhD in 1971 from the School of Social Service Administration at the University of Chicago. He was director of research and statistics for the Colorado Emergency Relief Administration and Works Progress Administration (1934–1936) and then became research assistant and director of the Department of Social Work Administration of the Russell Sage Foundation, where he remained until 1948. During this time he also taught part time at Hunter College, Rutgers University, and Columbia University. In 1948 Howard was appointed first dean of the School of Social Welfare at the University of California, Los Angeles. He remained in that position until 1960 and remained on the faculty until his retirement in 1970. Howard believed deeply in the goal of improving the world for all people. As an educator, he emphasized the importance of social work's underlying values.

After his retirement he became chairperson of the Los Angeles County Mental Health Board, on which he had served since 1958. Active in many professional organizations, he served as president of the American Association of Social Workers. The author of numerous articles, Howard also wrote *The WPA and Federal Relief Policy* (1942) and *Social Welfare: Values, Means and Ends* (1969).

*Maryann Syers*

### Howard, Oliver Otis (1830–1904)

A native of Kennebec County, Maine, Oliver Otis Howard is an unknown entity in social welfare history and atypical of social welfare reformers in the 1800s. Guided by strong Christian beliefs, he was decorated for his heroics in the Civil War and served as the first commissioner for the Bureau of Refugees, Freedmen and Abandoned Lands. He founded Howard University, served as President Ulysses S. Grant's "Peace Commissioner" with Native Americans, was sent to the Northwest during the Indian Wars, was appointed superintendent of West Point Military Academy to help dispel race problems at the academy during the 1870s, and was an active member of numerous tract societies.

At age 20 Howard graduated from Bowdoin College and four years later from West Point. In 1861 he became a colonel in the Third Regiment of Maine Volunteers and rose to the rank of general. He fought in numerous battles and played a central role in General William T. Sherman's Atlanta campaign. Following the 1862 Battle of Fair Oaks, in which he lost his right arm, Howard always carried a Bible, tucked underneath the jacket of his right arm, into battle, earning him the nickname "the Christian General."

In 1865 President Andrew Johnson appointed Howard the first commissioner of the Freedmen's Bureau, which in effect, became the nation's first large-scale social welfare effort to cross geographic boundaries. Although President Franklin Pierce's veto of mental health legislation in 1854 deemed social welfare to be the province of the states, the bureau's educational, legal, and health services marked the first significant coordinated welfare effort by the national government. Under Howard's leadership and persistence, the bureau's efforts reached their pinnacle in 1867, but these early gains were short lived, as Howard faced tremendous opposition from southerners and northerners. Responding to these pressures, Congress continually narrowed the bureau's mission and limited its overall effectiveness as a change agent.

Supporters of Howard encouraged his candidacy in the 1868 presidential election, although charges of political corruption and mismanagement of the Freedmen's Bureau were levied against him by his political enemies. Two congressional investigations vindicated him of wrongdoing, but any possibility of national elected office was derailed.

From 1869 to 1874 he served as the third president of Howard University, and from 1881 to 1884 as superintendent of West Point. On his death, a *New York Times* editorial chronicled his military contributions, but no reference was made to his work with and on behalf of southern freedmen.

*Ira C. Colby*

### Howe, Samuel Gridley (1801–1876)

Samuel Gridley Howe was a noted philanthropist, educator, and advocate for the physically and mentally handicapped. A native Bostonian, Howe graduated from Brown University in 1821 and from Harvard Medical School in 1824. In 1831 he became director of the New England Asylum for the Blind (later renamed the Perkins Institute), which became internationally known under his leadership. In addition to his pioneering educational efforts for blind, deaf, and retarded people, Howe supported reform for mentally ill people, prisoners, and juvenile offenders. He encouraged investigation and supervision of state charitable and correctional systems. As a result the Massachusetts State Board of Charities was established in 1863. Under Howe's 10-year term as chairperson of the board, conditions in state institutions were studied and reforms were initiated to improve the quality of life for poor children, people with disabilities, and prison inmates.

Howe's writings include *Insanity in Massachusetts* (1843), *An Essay on Separate and Congregate Systems of Prison Discipline* (1846), and *The Refugee from Slavery in Canada West* (1864). See also *Samuel Gridley Howe* (1935), by Laura E. Richards, and *Samuel Gridley Howe, Social Reformer, 1801–1876* (1956), by Harold Schwartz.

*Larraine M. Edwards*

### Huantes, Margarita R. (1914–1994)

Margarita R. Huantes was a social worker and an adult educator. She was a pioneer in the adult literacy movement. As founder and first executive director of the San Antonio Literacy Council, she worked tirelessly to combat adult illiteracy for more than three decades. Since its founding in 1960, the San Antonio Literacy Council has taught more than 60,000 adults to read and write.

Born in Nueva Rosita, Coahuila, Mexico, Huantes immigrated with her family to San Antonio, Texas, when she was three months old. She received a bachelor of arts degree from the University of Texas in 1939 and a master of social work degree from Case Western Reserve University in 1948.

In her early career Huantes was a schoolteacher and later a social group worker in youth programs and community center settings. In the early 1970s she served on the faculty of the Worden School of Social Service at Our Lady of the Lake University. It was during her work in the community center that Huantes recognized the high rate of functional illiteracy, particularly among Mexican Americans, and worked to establish literacy programs and subsequently the San Antonio Literacy Council. She saw the council grow from a single class with a handful of students in a community center to more than 1,500 students in 20 centers.

Huantes received numerous local, state, and national honors and recognitions for her work in promoting literacy. She was a member of the Academy of Certified Social Workers, NASW, the National Association of Public School Educators, and the Adult Education Association among others.

Huantes published *Manual de Ciudadania* (1963, 1987), *First Lessons in English, Books I and II* (1965, 1980), *I Want to Learn English and Spanish* (1980), and several articles on adult basic education and women. She is one of 23 Hispanic people featured in *Spanish-Speaking Heroes* (1973) by Roger W. Axford, where she is described as "San Antonio's fighter against illiteracy."

*Santos H. Hernandez*

### Hudson, Walter W. (1934–1999)

Walter W. Hudson (April 17, 1934–August 5, 1999) was internationally recognized as a leader in measurement theory, development and testing of assessment and outcome evaluation tools, applied statistics, evidence-based practice methodology, and computer applications for practice. Dr. Hudson was prodigiously productive, developing and validating more than 35 different outcome measures for use in the human services. He maintained an active scholarly career, begun in the late 1960s, that included scores of articles, books *The Clinical Measurement Package: A Field Manual* (1982) and *Human Services Practice, Evaluation, & Computers* (1993), and computerized systems for professional use including *The Clinical Measurement Package*, the *WALMYR Assessment Scale Scoring Program* (WASSP), the *WALMYR Assessment Scale Training Package* (WASTP), and the *Multi-Problem Screening Inventory* (MPSI). Dr. Hudson also extensively engaged in professional consultation on assessment, evaluation, and the use of integrated information systems in human service agencies, as well as training human service professionals.

Walter Hudson's contributions to the field were recognized through multiple venues: he was the first recipient of the Lifetime Achievement Award from the Society for Social Work and Research, had a professorship endowed in his name at Florida State University, and had a special issue of the journal *Research on Social Work Practice* dedicated to his legacy and the impact that he had on so many. His academic career began at the George Warren Brown School of Social Work, and was followed by academic positions in the University of Hawaii, Arizona State University, and Florida State University. Dr. Walter Hudson was the foremost contributor of his time to the development, application, and training of empirical tools for assessment and evaluation in human service practice. In addition to his productivity and impact, Dr. Hudson was well known as an encouraging teacher, generous mentor, warm colleague, and humorous tale spinner.

*Paula S. Nurius*

### Jarrett, Mary Cromwell (1876–1961)

Mary Cromwell Jarrett delineated the specialty of psychiatric social work in mental hospitals. After graduating from Goucher College in 1900, she worked for the Boston Children's Aid Society. In 1913 Jarrett organized and headed the social services department of the Boston Psychopathic Hospital, and in 1918 she developed an eight-week course to help prepare social workers to meet the emergency psychiatric needs of patients. The Smith College School for Social Work was an outgrowth of this training course, and Jarrett was associate director there for five years. In 1923 she founded the Psychiatric Social Workers' Club (later the American Association of Psychiatric Social Workers).

As a staff member of the Welfare Council of New York City, Jarrett worked to alleviate the problems associated with chronic illness. From 1927 to 1943 she supported efforts to increase public awareness of chronic illness. Her books include *The Kingdom of Evils* (1922), with Elmer E. Southard; *Chronic Illness in New York City* (1933); and *Housekeeping Service for Home Care of Chronic Patients* (1938).

*Larraine M. Edwards*

### Johnson, Campbell Carrington (1895–1968)

Johnson spent most of his life working to improve military services and social conditions for the Black population. A native of Washington, DC, he was educated at Howard University, where he earned a bachelor's degree in 1920 and a law degree in 1922. Johnson spent 17 years as executive secretary of the Twelfth Street Branch of the Washington Young Men's Christian Association, a position he assumed in 1923. Camp

Lichtman, which he helped establish in 1932 for the recreation of Black youths, was one of his many community contributions. Beginning in 1932 Johnson taught social science at the Howard University School of Religion for 15 years. During this time he helped organize the Washington Housing Association. In 1940 he was appointed executive assistant to the director of the national Selective Services by President Franklin D. Roosevelt. Recalled to duty from the Army Reserve, Johnson remained with the Selective Service system for 28 years, attaining the rank of full colonel. He worked actively for the equitable treatment of Black men and women in the services. In 1946 Johnson was awarded the Army Commendation Ribbon and the Army Distinguished Service Medal. A posthumous award of the Legion of Merit and the Distinguished Service Award were made to his family in 1968. See *Dictionary of American Negro Biography* (1982), by R. W. Logan and M. Winston.

*Wilma Peebles-Wilkins*

### Jones, Mary Harris "Mother" (1830–1930)

Mary Harris "Mother" Jones, known as the "white-haired miner's angel" to those who loved her and "the most dangerous woman in America" to those who feared her, was a union organizer for the United Mine Workers of America and was known for her tireless efforts to improve the lives of working people; her courage in facing armed guards, angry mine owners, U.S. senators, or union presidents if they stood in her way; her willingness to go to jail for her beliefs; and her dramatic flair.

Jones was born on May 1, 1830, in Ireland and emigrated to the United States at age seven, according to her autobiography, which was published in 1925, when she was 95 years old. Her "Irish agitator" father, Richard Harris, worked as a laborer on railroad construction and ended up in Toronto where Mary Harris studied elementary education and dressmaking. As a young woman she taught at a convent school in Michigan and worked as a seamstress in Chicago. In 1861 she took a teaching job in Memphis, Tennessee, and married George Jones, a member of the Iron Moulders' Union and an organizer for the Knights of Labor. In 1867 a yellow fever epidemic hit Memphis, and in one week she lost her husband and their four children. In 1871 her dressmaking shop burned to the ground in the Chicago fire. She was in her late forties when she joined the Knights of Labor. In the early 1890s she began organizing coal miners.

With her motto, "Pray for the dead, and fight like hell for the living," Mother Jones participated in the 1892 Homestead strike against Carnegie Steel; the

1894 railman's strike; the anthracite strike of 1900; the Paint and Cabin Creek strike of 1913 in West Virginia; and the Colorado Fuel and Iron strike of 1913–1914, in which seven men, two women, and 11 children died in one of the most brutal attacks on workers in American history, known as the Ludlow Massacre.

Understanding that "no strike was ever won that did not have the support of the womenfolk," one of Mother Jones's successful strike tactics was the invention of the "bucket and broom brigade." In this show of protest, wives of striking miners would march with pots, pans, mops, and brooms to mine entrances, dressed in a wild assortment of rags with "loose-flying hair," scaring strikebreakers, mules, and mine owners and confusing company gunmen by banging loudly on pots and pans.

In 1903 Mother Jones sought to dramatize the evils of child labor by leading a march of small children from the striking textile mills of Philadelphia to Oyster Bay, Long Island, where President Theodore Roosevelt lived. When her band of child laborers, many of whom were victims of industrial accidents, reached the president's home, he declined to meet with them. The incident brought much-needed public attention to the issue, although it would be another 13 years before child labor was abolished legally.

Her successful tactics engaged the foes of labor. In 1902, when she was called into a West Virginia courtroom after being arrested for ignoring an injunction banning meetings of striking miners, a prosecuting attorney turned to Mother Jones and stated, "There sits the most dangerous woman in America. She comes into a state where peace and prosperity reign. She crooks her finger—20,000 contented men lay down their tools and walk out."

Coal companies hired the Pinkerton Detective Agency to discredit her, calling her a "vulgar, heartless, vicious creature with a fiery temper and a cold-blooded brutality rare even in the slums."

A U.S. senator trying to denigrate her efforts on behalf of working people, asked her, "Do you think the things you do are ladylike?" "It's the last thing on earth I want to be," she replied.

Mother Jones was a strong critic of the capitalist system: "I asked a man in prison once how he happened to be there and he said he had stolen a pair of shoes. I told him if he had stolen a railroad he would be a United States senator." She also agitated for the release of Mexican revolutionaries jailed in U.S. prisons. Although she held many old-fashioned views on the roles of women, she herself lived nontraditionally and was fond of saying, "No matter what your fight, don't be ladylike!" and "God almighty made women, and the

Rockefeller gang of thieves made the ladies." Mary Harris Jones died on November 30, 1930, and was buried in the miners' cemetery in Mount Olive, Illinois.

*Joanne "Rocky" Delaplaine*

### Keith-Lucas, Alan (1910–1995)

Alan Keith-Lucas was a noted writer, historian, storyteller, and social work educator for more than 50 years. Born in Cambridge, England, he received his BA with honors from Trinity College, Cambridge, an MS in social administration from Case Western Reserve University, a PhD in political science from Duke University, and a DLit from Campbell University. His interests included group care of children, the history of social work, and the integration of religious faith and social work practice.

Keith-Lucas wrote more than 30 books, including *Giving and Taking Help* (1972), *The Church Children's Home in a Changing World* (1962), *Decisions about People in Need* (1957), *The Poor You Have with You Always* (1989), and *Essays from More than Fifty Years in Social Work* (1989). He also wrote more than 150 professional articles or book chapters. He served on the faculty at the University of North Carolina at Chapel Hill's School of Social Work from 1950 to 1975, where he founded the Group Child Care Consultant Services and twice served as interim dean. He established the School of Social Work's off-campus programs that assist professionals in the field to obtain their degrees while working.

Keith-Lucas was internationally known for his unique insights into the needs of children and his persuasive style of teaching. He consulted to more than 100 youth-serving agencies, helping to shape a generation of professionals, particularly in religious-based residential homes. He held strong, often controversial opinions about the positive effects of group child care and advocated for their use throughout his life. Keith-Lucas retired from the University of North Carolina at Chapel Hill in 1975 as an Alumni Distinguished Professor Emeritus of Social Work. For 20 years after his retirement he continued to teach, consult, and write.

*Daniel Lebold*

### Kelley, Florence (1859–1932)

Florence Kelley was a lifelong advocate for government protection of women and children in the labor force. Born in Philadelphia, where her father was in politics, she earned her undergraduate degree from Cornell University. With credit for graduate studies at the University of Zurich, she obtained a law degree from Northwestern University. As an agent of the U.S. Bureau of Labor Statistics, Kelley investigated sweatshops before being appointed head of the Factory Inspection Department in 1892. In 1899 her work enforcing labor laws earned her the directorate of the National Consumer League, an organization founded by Josephine Shaw Lowell.

As a member of the New York Child Labor Committee in 1902 and of the National Child Labor Committee in 1904, Kelley crusaded against child labor. She and Lillian Wald advocated for government protection of children, leading to the establishment of the U.S. Children's Bureau in 1912. Her published works include *Some Ethical Gains through Legislation* (1905) and *Modern Industry in Relation to the Family, Health, Education, Morality* (1914). See also *Florence Kelley: The Making of a Social Pioneer* (1966), by Dorothy Blumberg, and *Impatient Crusader: Florence Kelley's Life Story* (1953), by Josephine Goldmark.

*Larraine M. Edwards*

### Kellogg, Paul Underwood (1879–1958)

Paul Underwood Kellogg's career as a journalist led him to actively support social welfare projects. Born in Kalamazoo, Michigan, Kellogg took special courses at Columbia University from 1901 to 1906 in addition to attending the New York School of Philanthropy in 1902. He received a PhD from Wesleyan University in 1937. Kellogg worked as a reporter in Michigan for two years before becoming editor of the New York magazine *Charities*. In 1901 he went to Pittsburgh and conducted the first social survey of labor conditions in the steel industry. The findings of his study were published in *The Pittsburgh Survey*, and as a result this approach was used in other cities. From 1912 until his retirement in 1952, Kellogg served as editor of *Survey*. His support for controversial causes earned him a medal for "courageous journalism" from the New York *Evening Post*.

In 1934 Kellogg was appointed vice chairman of the President's Committee on Economic Security by President Franklin D. Roosevelt. In the mid 1930s, Kellogg also served on the Federal Action Committee of the American Association of Social Workers. He was president of the National Conference of Social Work in 1939. With Arthur Gleason, he coauthored *British Labor and the War* (1919). See also *The Pittsburgh Survey* (1909–1914), edited by Paul Underwood Kellogg.

*Larraine M. Edwards*

### Kenworthy, Marion Edwena (1891–1980)

Marion Edwena Kenworthy was a pioneer in introducing psychoanalytic concepts into a social work curriculum. She was influential in the professionalization of social work, playing a role in heightening the profile of social workers both in the World War II military and in the juvenile justice system in New York City. A nationally renowned psychiatrist, Kenworthy increased the recognition of the value of the social work profession within her own discipline as she helped define roles for both professions and fostered interdisciplinary teamwork in various mental health forums throughout her career.

Born in Hampden, Massachusetts, Kenworthy graduated from Tufts University School of Medicine in 1913. After working in the Massachusetts state hospital system and at the Boston Psychopathic Hospital, she moved to New York City in 1919 and taught mental hygiene at the Central School of Hygiene at the Young Women's Christian Association. Through her work at the Vanderbilt Clinic, she met Dr. Bernard Glueck, who invited her to lecture at the New York School of Social Work in 1920. Kenworthy succeeded Dr. Glueck as medical director of the Bureau of Children's Guidance in 1924. After her own analysis by Otto Rank in 1921, Kenworthy began her psychoanalytic practice, which she maintained long after her retirement from teaching. One of the first psychiatrists in New York City to specialize in child psychiatry, she was an active participant in the child guidance movement.

Kenworthy taught full time at the New York School of Social Work from 1921 until her retirement in 1956. She developed a conceptual framework, the "ego-libido method," which she used to help students understand psychodynamic concepts and apply their understanding to work with individuals and families. On her retirement from the Columbia University School of Social Work, a chair in psychiatry was established in her name.

As a consultant, Kenworthy was instrumental in focusing attention on mental health services in the armed forces in the early 1940s. She advocated for the establishment of mental hygiene units in basic training camps and supported the creation of a distinct status for social workers in the service. In 1944 Kenworthy was appointed to the National Civilian Advisory Committee to the Women's Army Corps. Among her many elected positions, Kenworthy was the first woman president of the American Psychoanalytic Association (1958–1959), the American Academy of Child Psychiatry (1959–1961), and The Group for the Advancement of Psychiatry (GAP) (1959–1961). She was also the first chairperson of GAP's Committee on Psychiatric Social Work (1943–1949). Her many published works on mental hygiene, and children's mental health, include her coauthored (with Porter Lee) *Mental Hygiene and Social Work*, a summary of the work of the Bureau of Children's Guidance.

*Rebecca L. Sperling*

## King, Martin Luther, Jr. (1929–1968)

Martin Luther King, Jr., was a civil rights leader, an author, a minister, and an orator. Born in Atlanta, Georgia, to a middle-class family, King spent most of his career advocating for civil rights and protesting American social injustices. King entered Morehouse College at the age of 15 and graduated with a BA degree in sociology in 1948. Ordained as a minister, King graduated from Crozer Theological Seminary in Pennsylvania in 1951 with a BD degree. In 1955 he received a PhD from Boston University's School of Theology.

King's involvement with the Montgomery Bus Boycott helped to catapult him to national and international prominence. He soon became the voice of the nonviolent civil rights movement. King helped organize the Southern Christian Leadership Conference in 1957, and within a month he was elected president of the organization. King also gave moral and financial support to the Student Nonviolent Coordinating Committee, which was also headquartered in Atlanta. King's "Letter from the Birmingham Jail" has become a classic statement about African American-organized demand for equal access to opportunity. While King systematically confronted social injustices, he was constantly harassed by the FBI and a target of personal and professional attacks.

King's "I Have a Dream" speech was the highlight of the 1963 March on Washington, where he spoke to the crowd of more than 200,000 people of his dream of justice and peace for all Americans. King was invited to Sweden in 1963 to receive the Nobel Peace Prize, and in 1964 he was selected by *Time* magazine as Man of the Year, the first African American to be so honored. King was assassinated in Memphis, Tennessee, in 1968. In 1977 President Jimmy Carter posthumously awarded him the Medal of Freedom. King wrote numerous articles and several books, including *Stride Toward Freedom* (1958), *Why We Can't Wait* (1964), and *Where Do We Go from Here?* (1967).

*Iris Carlton-L&Vey*

## Kingsbury, Susan Myra (1870–1949)

Susan Myra Kingsbury, PhD, a pioneer in the field of social research, dedicated her career to the investigation and improvement of social and working conditions for women. She made a major contribution to social work education and the professionalization of social work in her role as director of the Carola Woerishoffer Graduate Department of Social Economy and Social Research at Bryn Mawr College from 1915 to 1936 (today, Bryn Mawr Graduate School of Social Work and Social Research).

Kingsbury's prior experience as an economics professor at Simmons College and director of research for the Women's Educational and Industrial Union in Boston from 1907 to 1915, prepared her for the challenges of designing a graduate program in social work, which at that time lacked the scholarly research and scientific methods necessary to be regarded as a true profession. The application of research to policy and social reform was central to the program Kingsbury created at Bryn Mawr with M. Carey Thomas, college president.

Kingsbury, who had directed a national study into the opportunities for women in social service in 1911–1913, recognized the necessity of graduate education in social work to prepare women for entrance and success in an expanding field of employment. The courses she and colleagues designed for three degree-granting programs (doctoral, master's, certificate) offered theoretical teaching with research and investigation and in time produced a number of new female researchers, administrators, and social work educators—all essential to the professionalization of social work.

The Woerishoffer Graduate Department programs were precursors to the current social work groupings of direct or clinical social work practice, community organization, social change and social policy, and research methods. The practicum instituted by Kingsbury, a distinguishing feature in preparing social workers for the profession, remains an integral part of graduate programs today known as field work.

*Mollie T. Marchione*

### Kitano, Harry H. L. (1926–2006)

Professor Emeritus Harry H. L. Kitano, the son of Japanese immigrants, was born in San Francisco, California. During World War II, he and his family were sent to Topaz "Relocation" Camp in Utah in accordance with Executive Order 9066. After the war, he entered U.C. Berkeley and by 1958 had completed his BA, MSW, and PhD degrees. He then joined the UCLA faculty with joint appointments in the Departments of Social Welfare and Sociology. During this time, he also was acting director of the Asian American Study Center, academic affirmative action officer, acting chair of the Department of Social Welfare, and a visiting professor at universities in Japan, England, and Hawaii. In 1990, he was appointed as the first incumbent of the Endowed Chair in Japanese American Studies at UCLA, the only academic Chair of its kind in an American university. Other honors include Nisei of the Biennium and Nikkei of the Year from the Japanese American Citizens League and Outstanding Volunteer from the Los Angeles County Human Relations Commission. He served on

the U.S. Department of Defense's Equal Opportunity Management Institute Board of Visitors (Chair), the Advisory Committee for Columbia University's Minority Leadership Project, the Los Angeles Police Department Advisory Committee, and the Japanese American National Museum.

Professor Kitano's scholarship centered on the application of social science theories and methods to the understanding of patterns of racial and ethnic conflict, cooperation, and interactions, particularly as these illuminated the contemporary Japanese American population's experiences. He authored and co-authored over 150 books and articles, including: *Japanese Americans: The Evolution of a Subculture; Race Relations* (through five editions), *Japanese Americans: From Relocation to Redress; Achieving the Impossible Dream.* Numerous other publications were based on his research on interracial marriages, juvenile delinquency, and mental health and alcohol abuse among Asian/Pacific Islander populations.

*Jeanne M. Giovannoni*

### Konopka, Gisela (1910–2003)

Gisela Konopka was a social justice advocate and humanitarian who became nationally and internationally famous as an expert in group work—particularly work targeted to troubled youth—and in research on delinquent adolescent girls. Born in Berlin, Germany, in 1910, she joined the resistance movement when the Nazis came to power and in 1936 was imprisoned in a concentration camp for six weeks. She earned her master's degree in social work at the University of Pittsburgh and in 1957 received her doctorate in social work at Columbia University. She served as a member of the University of Minnesota School of Social Work faculty from 1947 to 1978. Inspired by her roots in the resistance and her experiences during WWII, particularly the Holocaust, Gisela was foremost a humanitarian who brought a philosophy of love and practice that integrates work with the individual and the group with political action. In much of her later writing she emphasized the importance of philosophy over technique and method. She published hundreds of articles and several books. One work of particular importance was *Therapeutic Group Work with Children*, published in 1949. Another important book that had great influence on practice was *Social Group Work: A Helping Process* (1963).

Appointments held by Dr. Konopka included Coordinator of the Center for Urban Affairs (1968–1970) and Director of the Center for Youth Development and Research (1970–1978), both at the University of Minnesota. She served on the Board of Directors for NASW, as President of the Association of Ortho-psychiatry, and Director of the National Conference on Social Welfare. She received many awards, including the highest merit award of the Federal Republic of Germany for her work with German social services following the war. She died at 93 in 2003.

*James R. Reinardy*

### Kuralt, Wallace H., Sr. (1908–1994)

Wallace H. Kuralt, Sr., father of noted journalist Charles Kuralt, was a lifelong social work practitioner and administrator. Throughout his career, Kuralt was distinguished by his innovative spirit and deeply held convictions about helping children and families. From 1945 until his retirement in 1972, Kuralt directed the Mecklenburg County Department of Social Services (Charlotte, North Carolina). He pioneered efforts to implement child care and child development centers and is credited with instituting family planning services long before such programs were nationally accepted. Many of his innovative ideas served as models for public welfare programs throughout North Carolina and the nation. Kuralt was highly regarded as an imaginative administrator who was at the forefront of efforts to implement programs to enable welfare recipients to escape poverty and dependence. He was also a strong advocate of the value of early childhood education and stressed the importance of giving children a sense of their own worth and ability even before their kinder-garten years. Kuralt's advocacy efforts to improve public welfare programs included frequent testimony before government bodies, including the North Carolina general assembly, the U.S. Congress, and the United Nations. Numerous foreign countries sent social services officials from the public and private sectors to visit Mecklenburg County to learn about innovative pro-grams implemented by Kuralt. Kuralt was a skilled teacher and mentor, and many of those he influenced became successful directors of social service agencies throughout North Carolina. Kuralt was a 1931 graduate of the University of North Carolina at Chapel Hill and attended the university's School of Social Work from 1937 to 1938. In 1991 the Wallace H. Kuralt, Sr., Professorship in Public Welfare Policy and Adminis-tration was established at the University of North Carolina at Chapel Hill School of Social Work. In 1994 the Department of Social Services building in Charlotte was named in his honor.

*Elizabeth A. S. Benefield*

### Lassalle, Beatriz (1882–1965)

Beatriz Lassalle is recognized as the most important pio-neer of social work practice in Puerto Rico. Beginning her career at the age of 17, she dedicated herself to the needs of children and families, especially those affected by blindness and other disabilities. She studied at the New York School of Social Work from 1920 to 1921 and shortly afterward was named executive secretary of the Juvenile Red Cross of Puerto Rico, for which she established the first Department of Social Work. In 1922 she coordinated the first Child Congress ever held in Puerto Rico. During the Great Depression she headed programs in the Puerto Rico Emergency Reconstruction Administration, making social services an integral com-ponent of the Department of Health. She was a leader in the development of the first laws regulating social work practice in Puerto Rico.

Both before and after retirement Lassalle promoted social action and participated actively in civic affairs. She was president of the first suffragist organization in Puerto Rico, established the Home for Tubercular Chil-dren, and co-founded the Society for the Welfare of the Blind. In 1946 the College of Social Workers of Puerto Rico named her its honorary president and dedicated its sixth annual meeting to her as "testimony of profound admiration." After her death the Graduate School of Social Work at the University of Puerto Rico was named in her honor. See "Semblanza de la Srta. Beatriz Lassalle: Servia, Devisa de Una Vida," *Revista de Servicio Social* (1946), by Julia Denoyers.

*John F. Longres*

### Lathrop, Julia Clifford (1858–1932)

Julia Clifford Lathrop was a well-known advocate of the welfare of children and mentally ill people. The daugh-ter of abolitionists, she was born in Rockford, Illinois. Her social work career began at Hull-House after she graduated from Vassar College in 1880. As a resident of Hull-House, Lathrop was involved in the establishment of the Chicago United Charities and other activities to help poor people. In 1899 the establishment of the first juvenile court in the United States resulted from her work with Illinois law. After a European study tour of methods of caring for mentally ill people, Lathrop be-came involved in the founding efforts of the national mental hygiene movement. In addition, she helped found the country's first mental hygiene clinic for chil-dren, the Juvenile Psychopathic Institute, in 1909.

In 1912, Lathrop, an activist in the mothers' pension movement, became the first director of the U.S. Chil-dren's Bureau. During her 12 years as director, maternal and infant problems as well as the social, economic, and health problems of children were studied, investigated, and analyzed. After leaving the bureau, she became active in the women's suffrage movement. From 1925 to 1931 she served as an advisor to the Child Welfare

Committee of the League of Nations. See *My Friend, Julia Lathrop* (1935), by Jane Addams; and *Unto the Least of These: Social Services for Children* (1947), by Emma O. Lundberg.

*Larraine M. Edwards*

### Leashore, Bogart (1947–2007)

Bogart Leashore received his PhD in Social Work and Sociology from the University of Michigan in 1979 and joined the faculty of Howard University teaching initially in the School of Social Work. From 1979 to 1985 he was faculty member, Research Associate and Chair (1983–1985) in the Department of Urban Studies at Howard University. In 1985 he became the Associate Dean for the School of Social Work at Howard University where he served until the call to the deanship at Hunter College School of Social Work in 1991. In his 12 years as dean of Hunter College School of Social Work (HCSSW), he led the school through budget reductions, administrative cutbacks, accreditation challenges and enrollment increases. In so doing, he took HCSSW to new places—a Distance Learning Center, a Center for Permanency in Child Welfare, an Advanced Standing Master's Degree Program and a PhD Program.

Dean Leashore was a prominent actor in social work education. He served on the Commission on Accreditation of the Council on Social Work Education and served his social work education colleagues as president of the National Association of Deans and Directors of Schools of Social Work (2000–2002).

Dr. Leashore dedicated his life to high standards of professional education, to social justice and cultural diversity, to sound social work practice, and, above all, to the welfare of children. Within each of these contexts, his vision was informed by the proud inspiration of his mother, an early and active participant in the Civil Right's Movement. His favorite expression was "Stay the course."

Although he retired from Hunter College School of Social Work in 2003, his service and expertise were extended to Clark Atlanta University, Jackson State University, Delaware State University, and University of Akron and Cleveland State University Schools of Social Work.

*Willie Tolliver*

### Lee, Porter Raymond (1879–1939)

Porter Raymond Lee was a pioneer in the development of social work education. Born in Buffalo, New York, he graduated from Cornell University in 1903. He developed an interest in social work as an undergraduate student and later attended the summer institute of the New York School of Philanthropy. In 1909, after serving as assistant secretary of the Charity Organization Society of Buffalo, he succeeded Mary Richmond as general secretary of the Philadelphia Society for Organizing Charity. Lee joined the faculty of the New York School of Philanthropy as a social casework instructor in 1912. Recognizing the need for differential training in social work, he became instrumental in organizing the American Association of Schools of Social Work in 1919.

As a teacher and philosopher, Lee integrated ideas from other fields such as psychiatry, economics, and political science to help formulate a generic social casework theory. He served on a number of professional boards and was elected president of the National Conference of Social Work in 1929. Lee's published works include *Social Salvage* (1924), co-authored with Walter Pettit; *Mental Hygiene and Social Work* (1929), co-authored with Marion Kenworthy; and *Social Work: Cause and Function* (1937).

*Larraine M. Edwards*

### Lenroot, Katharine Fredrica (1891–1982)

Associated with the U.S. Children's Bureau for 37 years, Katharine Fredrica Lenroot became its chief in 1934. Lenroot was born and raised in Superior, Wisconsin, the daughter of Swedish immigrants. Influenced by her father, who was a congressional representative, senator, and a judge of the U.S. Court of Customs and Patent Appeals, Lenroot's interest in public affairs began early. In 1911, just two years out of high school, she spoke before a committee of the state legislature for a minimum wage law. Lenroot graduated from the University of Wisconsin in 1912 and in 1913 became a deputy of the Wisconsin Industrial Commission.

Lenroot's career with the Children's Bureau began in 1914 when she became a special agent. In 1915 she attended the New York School of Social Work and also became assistant director of the Social Service Division of the Children's Bureau. In 1922 she was made assistant chief, and in 1934 President Roosevelt appointed her chief. As the bureau's third chief, Lenroot represented the United States on the executive board of UNICEF, served as secretary of the 1950 White House Conference on Children and Youth, and testified frequently before Senate and House committees on juvenile delinquency, child labor laws, and federal aid for maternal and child welfare and school health services. Widely praised for her contributions to child welfare and for her skillful administration, Lenroot was also president of the National Conference of Social Work (1935) and a member of the board of the Child Welfare League of America. Her writings include

*Juvenile Delinquency, a Summary of Available Material on Extent, Causes, Treatment, and Prevention* (1929).

*Maryann Syers*

### Levy, Charles Samuel (1919–2006)

Charles "Chuck" Levy—professor, ethicist, Jewish communal professional—was born in New York City to immigrant parents. He left the Jewish communal service field in 1956/57 to join three colleagues as the founding faculty of a new school of social work at Yeshiva University in New York City. He served in the professorial ranks and as associate dean and acting dean of the Wurzweiler School of Social Work until his retirement as professor emeritus in 1982. He received his BS from City College, his MSW from Wayne State University, and his DSW from Columbia University School of Social Work. The author of dozens of articles on social group work, community work, Jewish communal service, social change, and the social work profession, his interest in the values and ethics of the social work profession crystallized during the 1970s. His thoughts and observations were articulated in a series of articles that appeared in major social work journals: "The Value Base of Social Work" (*Journal of Education for Social Work*, 1972), "Values and Planned Change" (*Social Casework*, 1972), "Ethics of Supervision" (*Social Work*, 1973), "On the Development of a Code of Ethics" (*Social Work*, 1974), and "Personal versus Professional Values: The Practitioner's Dilemma" (*Clinical Social Work*, 1976). He chaired the NASW Task Force on Ethics that produced the first code of ethics for the association which was adopted in 1979. His books *Social Work Ethics* (1976), *Guide to Ethical Decisions and Action for Social Service Administrators* (1982) and *Social Work Ethics on the Line* (1993) are considered classics in the field. He served as a mentor to generations of students, created an environment for the study and teaching of ethics, and influenced today's leading social work ethicists.

*Sheldon R. Gelman*

### Lewis, Harold (1920–2003)

Harold Lewis made major contributions to social work as a scholar, activist, and educator. After graduating from Brooklyn College in 1941, he served in U.S. Army intelligence in India during World War II, where his experiences influenced his decision to become a social worker. He earned his MSW from the University of Pittsburgh in 1948 and worked for two years as Research Director of United Community Services in Omaha, Nebraska, before joining the faculty at the University of Connecticut. In 1953, at the height of the McCarthy era, Lewis was forced to resign from the university because of his political activism.

Lewis received his DSW from the University of Pennsylvania where, upon his graduation in 1959, he was appointed Chair of its Research Sequence. In 1969–1970, prior to becoming Dean of the Hunter College School of Social Work, Lewis became the first social work fellow at the Center for the Advanced Study of the Behavioral and Social Sciences in Palo Alto, California. In the 1970s, he was the first social worker named to proposal review panels by the National Institute of Mental Health. While serving as Dean at Hunter for twenty years, he held leadership positions in virtually every major U.S. social welfare organization.

In his half-century career, Lewis published widely on social work values and ethics, the epistemology of practice, child welfare, social welfare administration, and social work education. He drew on diverse sources, including the philosopher John Rawls, the Latin American conscientization movement, and his personal contacts with social work leaders like Bertha Reynolds, Jessie Taft, Marion Hathway, and Kenneth Pray. Many of his articles and his seminal book, *The Intellectual Base of Social Work Practice* (1982), are considered classics. His work provides intellectual links between contemporary social workers and their professional ancestors.

*Michael Reisch*

### Lindeman, Eduard Christian (1885–1953)

Eduard Christian Lindeman's participation in community and professional organizations and his teachings and writings on social philosophy and group methods earned him the respect of the social work profession. One of 10 children of Danish immigrants, he studied on his own to qualify for college admission and graduated from Michigan Agricultural College in 1911. He edited an agricultural journal and became assistant to the minister of a Congregational church. A desire to combine teaching with religious activity resulted in his appointment to George Williams College in Chicago. In 1920 he became professor of sociology at North Carolina College for Women but was asked to resign because his opposition to segregation antagonized the local community.

Lindeman subsequently joined the faculty of the New York School of Social Work, where he remained until his retirement in 1950. In 1952 he became president of the National Conference of Social Work. His books include *Social Discovery: An Approach to the Study of Functional Groups* (1936) and *Wealth and Culture* (1936). See also *Eduard C. Lindeman and Social Work Philosophy* (1958), by Gisela Konopka.

*John F. Longres*

## Lindsay, Inabel Burns (1900–1983)

Inabel Lindsay was the first dean of the Howard University School of Social Work. Born in St. Joseph, Missouri, she prepared for a teaching career during her college education. After receiving her undergraduate degree, she entered the New York School of Social Work as an Urban League Fellow from 1920 to 1921. Sixteen years later she completed a master's degree at the University of Chicago, School of Social Service Administration. In 1952 Lindsay earned a doctorate in social work from the University of Pittsburgh. She taught a few years before beginning her social work experiences as a family welfare practitioner, agency administrator, and social researcher. In 1937 Lindsay joined the Department of Sociology at Howard University as an instructor and assistant in charge of social work under E. Franklin Frazier. In 1945 a School of Social Work was established at Howard University and Lindsay became dean. When she retired in 1967, Lindsay was the only female university academic dean in the Washington, DC, area. Committed to principles of social justice, she maintained a strong role in professional leadership while promoting the growth of the School of Social Work. Under Lindsay's leadership, the Howard University School of Social Work became the second accredited school in the country serving Black students. She published a number of survey papers and articles on community leadership, elderly people, and Black participation in social welfare. See "Portrait of a Dean: A Biography of Inabel Burns Lindsay, First Dean of the Howard University School of Social Work" (dissertation by LayMoyne Mason Matthews, University of Maryland, 1976).

*Wilma Peebles-Wilkins*

## Lodge, Richard (1921–1981)

A social work educator and administrator, Richard Lodge was a strong advocate for the essential role of theory in social work. Born in Ohio, Lodge graduated from the Carnegie Institute of Technology in 1943. He received his MSW from the University of Pittsburgh School of Social Work in 1950 and became a worker, supervisor, and administrator of group work agencies. In 1955 he joined the faculty of the University of Pennsylvania School of Social Work, receiving his DSW in 1958. In 1966 he was appointed dean of the School of Social Work at Virginia Commonwealth University, and in 1972 he became executive director of the Council on Social Work Education (CSWE).

As director of CSWE, Lodge implemented accreditation of baccalaureate social work programs, acted on proposals to bring practice and education into closer correspondence, and helped establish the Commission on the Role and Status of Women in Social Work Education and on Educational Planning. He was also active in maintaining threatened federal funding for social work education. Lodge left CSWE in 1978 to join the doctoral faculty at Adelphi University School of Social Work. At Adelphi, he taught courses in theory building in social work and co-founded a faculty study group researching new means of generating social work theory. Lodge was the author of numerous journal articles on social group work and social work education.

*Maryann Syers*

## Loeb, Martin B. (1913–1983)

Martin Loeb was a leader in both social work education and gerontology in higher education. Educated in Toronto, he received a PhD in human development from the University of Chicago in 1957. Loeb was director of the School of Social Work at the University of Wisconsin from 1965 to 1973 and director of the McBeath Institute on Aging and Adult Life, which he founded, from 1973 to 1980. Following his retirement in 1980, he remained active in university life, continuing to teach, conducting research, and participating in faculty governance. He presented his final paper, "Toward a Technology of Caring," just five days before his death.

Prior to joining the Wisconsin faculty, Loeb served on the faculties of the University of California, Los Angeles; the University of Kansas City; the University of Chicago; and the University of California, Berkeley. While on faculty, he directed several major research projects, including the Santa Monica Teen-Age Study and the Kansas City Study of Adult Life. His first book, co-authored with W. Lloyd Warner and Robert Havighurst, *Who Shall Be Educated? The Challenge of Unequal Opportunities* (1941), is regarded as a classic. He also wrote six other books, monographs, and some 30 articles and book chapters on a wide range of topics.

A member of many professional organizations, Loeb was a fellow of the Gerontological Society, the American Anthropological Society, the American Sociological Association, and the American Association for the Advancement of Science, as well as a member of NASW, CSWE, the Academy of Certified Social Workers, and the Society for the Study of Social Gerontology in Higher Education, for which he served as president in 1975–1976.

In addition to his professional academic career, Loeb was a professional dancer, a figure skater, an actor, a consulting editor for the *Toronto Star*, a sailor, an international traveler, and a maker of pewterware. Among the most important of his accomplishments was the contribution he made to the lives and careers of his students and colleagues. A dedicated mentor of many, he had the ability to identify talent and to find ways to develop that talent. Through Loeb's stimulation, vision, and leadership, the University of Wisconsin School of Social Work experienced significant growth and attained national prominence during his years as a faculty member and director.

*Mona Wasow*

### Love, Maria Maltby (1840–1931)

Maria Maltby Love, born in 1840 near Buffalo, New York, was a social architect and humanitarian who crusaded for education, health, and tenement reform. She pioneered two projects to help women and their families achieve better lives: the Fitch Creche (1881)—the first day nursery for the children of working women in the United States—and the Church District Plan (1896), a citywide, interdenominational program designed to provide neighborhood-based community services. Love was involved in the formation of the Charity Organization Society in Buffalo (1877) and organized its first Provident Scheme, the Fitch Creche. Besides being a day nursery, it offered health care programs and the city's first kindergarten to children of poor working women. An on-site nursemaids training school for young women was also the first in the nation. Creche staff provided family services outreach through home visitation, and a system of convalescent care boarding homes was created for ill women and children. The Creche and its innovative programs gained widespread national recognition at the Chicago World's Fair in 1893 and the Pan American Exposition in 1901. Internationally, Denmark and Siam adopted the Creche model.

Love was also the originator of the Church District Plan, which, by sectoring the entire city and placing each district in the care of a cooperating church, promoted the development of neighborhood outreach efforts within the community. The plan's first decade saw an enhancement of social work activities through the cooperative efforts of 122 interfaith congregations. The Church District Plan was presented at the National Conference on Charities and Correction in May 1896 and was copied in Brooklyn, New York; Seattle, Washington; and Cambridge, Massachusetts. Following her death, Love was honored in 1932 by the Charity Organization Society, which called her "a moving and guiding spirit in the development of social work."

*Renee Bowman Daniel* and *Karen Berner Little*

### Lowell, Josephine Shaw (1843–1905)

Josephine Shaw Lowell, a leader in the "scientific philanthropy movement"; helped to promote the reorganization of public and private charities in the United States. Born in West Roxbury, Massachusetts, she was educated in private schools around the country. Her volunteer service began at the start of the Civil War when she worked with a forerunner of the American Red Cross—the United States Sanitary Commission. She joined the New York State Charities Aid Association in 1873 and became the first female member of the New York State Board of Charities in 1876. Lowell spent 13 years with the board and succeeded in providing more institutions for mentally ill people and more correctional facilities for women. In 1882 she helped found the New York Charity Organization Society. Her concern for women in the labor force led her to become the first president of the Consumers League, an organization founded in 1891 to protect shop girls from exploitation in New York City. Lowell's published works include *Public Relief and Preventive Charity* (1884) and *Industrial Arbitration and Conciliation* (1893). See also *The Philanthropic Work of Josephine Shaw Lowel* (1911), by W. R. Stewart.

*Larraine M. Edwards*

### Lowy, Louis (1920–1991)

Louis Lowy was a scholar, a teacher, a leader in the fields of gerontology and social work education, and a pioneer in advancing international social work education. Born in Munich, Germany, he was studying philosophy at Charles University in Prague when World War II broke out. From 1941 to 1945, Lowy was imprisoned by the Nazis in concentration camps, and at the end of the war he was the sole survivor of his family. After working as a welfare worker in a displaced persons camp in Deggendorf, Bavaria, Lowy emigrated with his wife to Boston, Massachusetts, in 1946. While employed as a social group worker, he earned a BS from Boston University and an MSW from its Graduate School of Social Work. Following graduation he served at the Jewish Community Center in Bridgeport, Connecticut, as activities director for adults and elders, beginning a lifelong connection with the emerging field of gerontology. He returned to Boston in 1955 as assistant executive director of the Jewish Centers Association and in 1957 joined the faculty of the Boston University School of Social Work. He earned an EdD from the Harvard University Graduate School of Education in 1966.

In 1974 Lowy co-founded the Boston University Gerontology Center and became its co-director. His talent and skill as a great teacher and lecturer were recognized in 1979 when the trustees of Boston University awarded him the Metcalf Award for Excellence in Teaching. He retired from Boston University in 1985, having served as chair of the social welfare policy sequence for 16 years, associate dean for curriculum, and director of the joint doctoral program in sociology and social work. In 1988 Lowy was awarded an honorary doctoral degree by Wheelock College, and in 1990 he was honored with a Life Achievement Award by the Eastern Massachusetts chapter of NASW in recognition of his contributions to gerontology, social work education, and the profession of social work. Lowy's published works include *The Challenge and Promise of the Later Years: Social Work with the Aging* (1985), *Social Policies and Programs on Aging: What Is and What Should Be in the Later Years* (1986), and *Why Education in the Later Years* (co-authored with Darlene O'Connor, 1986). He also contributed chapters to numerous books, wrote many monographs, and authored more than 40 journal articles.

*Leonard Bloksberg*

### Lucas, Elizabeth Jessemine Kauikeolani Low (1895–1986)

Elizabeth (also known as Clorinda) Low Lucas was an advocate for children and the first Hawaiian woman to receive a professional education in social work. Lucas was the daughter of Elizabeth Napoleon, a descendant of Hawaiian and Tahitian royalty, and Ebenezer Parker Low, great grandson of John Palmer Parker, owner of the Parker Ranch and a direct descendant of King Kamehameha I. She married Charles W. Lucas. They had a daughter, Laura.

Lucas was born just after the Hawaiian monarchy was overthrown and three years before Hawaii was annexed by the United States. The Caucasians formed their own government and their own society. Socially ostracized, deprived of their language, their land, their government, their culture, and their religion, the Hawaiian people had been taught by the Christian missionaries to feel shame for what they were and what their parents and heroic ancestors were. By the time of annexation, they had lost their sense of worth and self-respect, in effect, their identity.

Lucas learned early the meaning, to children and adults, of the fundamental difference between basic values of her Hawaiian heritage—caring, sharing, trusting relationships, and co-operation in work and in play—and the values of competition and achievement as the measure of success held by the Caucasians. Guiding her wide-ranging professional activity was the long-term goal of a community, a society that would value and respect its people and would be socially just for all—a philosophy that is critical for humanity's survival today. Permeating all that she did was the concern that all children have the opportunity to develop understanding, attitudes, and strengths within themselves for daily living and problem solving that would enable them to take social responsibility as citizens for maintaining a humane and just society in the future. Lucas was accepted and respected in her own right in both Hawaiian and Caucasian cultures.

She became involved in community activity during her high school years when she worked as a volunteer with children in an impoverished neighborhood. Guiding her in this early community involvement and in her later professional efforts was a concern that all children have the opportunity to develop the necessary skills and attitudes for daily living and problem solving to become responsible citizens. Following her graduation from Smith College in 1917, Lucas worked in New York City for the national board of the Young Women's Christian Association in the Division of Education for Foreign-Born Women. On her return to Hawaii in 1921, she served as assistant director of the Strong Foundation Dental Clinic for underprivileged children and as executive secretary of the Hawaiian Humane Society, which then was concerned about abused children as well as abused animals.

Lucas received a diploma, the equivalent of an MSW degree, from the New York School (now Columbia University School of Social Work) in 1937 and returned to Hawaii to be the Oahu County chief of the Department of Social Welfare. She was later director of the Division of Child Welfare. In 1943 Lucas accepted the position of director of pupil guidance in the Department of Public Instruction, which she held until retirement in 1960. Lucas believed that the schools offered a natural opportunity for a team approach to the problems experienced by children. A team approach could bring the teacher, pupil, parent, community, and school into a trusting relationship that could create a better environment as well as new attitudes of acceptance and respect.

Lucas was the first woman to be selected as a member and rotating chair of the board of trustees of the Queen Liliuokalani Trust, which served orphaned and destitute Hawaiian children. Under her leadership, units of the Queen Liliuokalani Children's Center were established on the main islands. Lucas also served as president of the board of directors of the Kapiolani Children's and Maternity Hospital, chair of the State Commission on Children and Youth and in 1970 its delegate to the White House Conference, chair of the Kamehameha Schools Advisory Council, president of the 4-H Foundation board of directors, and president of the Pan-Pacific and Southeast Asian Women's Association. The breadth of Lucas's contribution to the community is partly reflected by some of the many awards she received: the Smith College Distinguished Alumni

Award; the David Malo Award of the West Honolulu Rotary Club; the Distinguished Service Award for Home, School, and Community Services of the Hawaiian Congress of the PTA; and the Francis E. Clark Award of the Hawaii Personnel and Guidance Association. In 1979 she was named a Living Trustee of Hawaii by the Buddhist Honpa Hongwanji Mission in Hawaii.

*Patricia L. Ewalt*

### Lurie, Harry Lawrence (1892–1973)

During his 60-year professional career, Harry Lawrence Lurie became a leader in the establishment and proliferation of Jewish charities. A native of Latvia, he earned both his bachelor's and master's degrees from the University of Michigan. His career began in 1913 as an agent for Buffalo's Federated Jewish Charities. Lurie held several leadership positions such as director of research for the Associated Jewish Charities of Detroit, superintendent of the Jewish Social Service Bureau of Chicago, and executive director of the National Bureau of Jewish Social Research. In 1932 Lurie became executive director of the newly created Council of Jewish Federations and Welfare Funds, remaining there until his retirement in 1954.

In addition to establishing several national and international Jewish philanthropic organizations, Lurie lectured at universities around the United States. He formulated basic curriculum guidelines for community organization for the Council on Social Work Education. Between 1937 and 1955, Lurie published a number of articles on social welfare, and in 1965 he became the first editor of the *Encyclopedia of Social Work*. He was the author of *A Heritage Affirmed: The Jewish Federation Movement in America* (1961).

*Larraine M. Edwards*

### Mahaffey, Maryann (1925–2006)

Maryann Mahaffey used her political influence to address the issues of poverty, women's rights, civil rights, and the peace movement. She served on the faculty of the School of Social Work at Wayne State University from 1965 until 1990, retiring with Emerita status. As a leading proponent of social workers becoming politically active, Mahaffey established some of the first internships in political settings in the late 1960s. This partnership between politics and social work was to become Mahaffey's life work, her legacy, and her hallmark. In 1974 Mahaffey was elected to Detroit City Council where she served until January, 2006. She was both President Pro Tem and President of the Council at different times throughout her eight-term political career. As a Detroit City Council member, Mahaffey was able to bring her social work training to bear as she

established a rape crisis center in the Detroit Police Department, improved housing opportunities for low-income people, and wrote the policy on homelessness for New Detroit, Inc. Mahaffey testified before the Michigan legislature, the U.S. House of Representatives and the U.S. Senate on many topics.

Mahaffey was born in Burlington, Iowa, and received her undergraduate degree from Cornell College, Iowa, in 1946. Her MSW was from the University of Southern California, awarded in 1951. Her writings include a book co-edited with John W. Hanks titled *Practical Politics, Social Work, and Political Responsibility*, (1982) NASW Press, Silver Spring, Maryland, "Lobbying and Social Work," published in the journal *Social Work* in 1972, and "Political Action in Social Work," in the *Encyclopedia of Social Work*, 18th Edition, in 1987. Among her many awards are the NASW Presidential Award for Exemplary Service to Social Work, YWCA Leadership Award, and the ACLU Civil Libertarian Award.

*Gary Mathews*

### Manning, Leah Katherine Hicks (1917–1979)

Leah Katherine Hicks Manning was instrumental in the development and passage of the Indian Child Welfare Act. Manning, a Shoshone-Paiute, was born in Reno, Nevada, and attended high school in Oklahoma. She was educated at Bacone Indian Junior College at Muskogee, Oklahoma, and Keuka College for Women in New York, becoming a fourth-grade teacher at an American Indian school. She studied social work at the University of Chicago, practiced in Los Angeles after World War II, and became a part-time social worker with the United Presbyterian Church.

In the early 1960s, Manning began working for the Bureau of Indian Affairs (BIA). In 1968 she earned an MSW from the University of Utah School of Social Work and was honored as the year's outstanding social work student. In 1971 she took a two-year leave of absence to set up and direct the first social services program for the Inter-Tribal Council of Nevada. This contracted program, run entirely by American Indian professionals, served the Indian population of member tribes. As a BIA staff development specialist, Manning promoted better understanding of Indian families and culture among social workers who worked with American Indians. She favored keeping Indian children on reservations or near their families to promote healthy development, a key component of the Indian Child Welfare Act. In 1974 the Nevada chapter of NASW named her Social Worker of the Year. She served on the National American Indian Graduate Scholarship Board, the executive board of the National

American Indian Women's Association, and the National Indian Presbyterian Advisory Committee and was a lifetime member of the National Congress of American Indians.

*Jean K. Quasi*

### Marin, Rosa C. (1912–1989)

Rosa C. Marin was a prominent social worker, educator, and research consultant. She was born in Arecibo, Puerto Rico, and received a bachelor of science degree from the University of Puerto Rico in 1933; she received a master of science degree in 1944 and a doctorate in social work in 1953, both from the University of Pittsburgh. She worked with the Puerto Rico Emergency Relief Administration from 1933 to 1940 as "town head," junior social worker, director, social supervisor, and chief researcher. From 1940 to 1944 she worked as supervisor of special projects and was chief of scientific research and statistics at the Health Department. From 1944 to 1974 she worked as professor, director of the research unit, and director of the School of Social Work of the University of Puerto Rico. In 1980 she received the professor emeritus distinction from the University of Puerto Rico. Dr. Marin founded *Revista Humanidad* in 1967, a social welfare journal well known in Latin America. She was a visiting professor of social work and social research in Colombia (1965), Peru (1965–1966), Bolivia (1966), Chile (1966), and Panama (1968) through the U.S. State Department. She was president of the Puerto Rican College of Social Work from 1943 to 1945 and president of the Puerto Rican chapter of NASW. She was a member of the Council on Human Resources, Association of Teachers of Puerto Rico, National Conference on Social Welfare, Social Newspaperwomen, American Academy of Politics and Social Sciences, American Association of Statisticians, and the Association of Research Centers Administration. She was a prolific researcher and writer and well known for studies on dependent multiproblem families in Puerto Rico, the female drug addict in Puerto Rico, and fraudulent medical prescriptions of controlled substances in Puerto Rico. Marin coauthored *Manpower Resources Projections* and was a key researcher for "La Vida." In 1987 she received the Bicentennial Medal of the University of Pittsburgh for lifetime achievement.

During the latter part of her career, Dr. Marin participated actively as a member of boards and as a researcher. Known as a humanist, she believed that "Compassion is the supreme value. Everything is subordinated to that." She made a strong impact among Puerto Rican social workers with her expertise as a social scientific researcher.

*Victor L. Garcia Toro*

### Marshall, Thurgood (1908–1993)

Thurgood Marshall, the first African American U.S. Supreme Court Justice, was born in Baltimore, Maryland, and is credited with ending American apartheid. Marshall was the great grandson of a former slave and of a Union soldier and was the son of a Pullman porter and schoolteacher. Marshall graduated from Howard University Law School after having been denied admission to the University of Maryland's law school because of his race.

Beginning in 1936, Marshall, as legal counsel for the National Association for the Advancement of Colored People, investigated lynchings, staged boycotts, won salary equalization for African American teachers, and obtained voting rights for African American southerners (*Smith v. Allwright*). Marshall also successfully challenged the legality of racially restrictive housing covenants (*Shelly v. Kraemer*). In 1954, Marshall successfully argued *Brown v. Board of Education of Topeka*, striking down segregation in public education in the United States.

President Kennedy appointed Marshall to the U.S. Court of Appeals in 1961. In 1965 President Johnson named Marshall the U.S. solicitor general. Marshall was the first African American to hold the post of solicitor general and in 1967 became the first African American Supreme Court Justice, a post he held until 1991. Although Marshall's career as an attorney included an array of "firsts," he was best known as a jurist who fought for the rights of the oppressed, civil and equal rights for ethnic minorities, women's rights, prisoners' rights, and rights of poor people. Marshall was well known for his opposition to the death penalty, believing it to be cruel and unusual punishment.

In 1992 NASW honored Justice Marshall with the first National Social Justice Award. NASW President Barbara White noted that NASW honors Marshall "because we recognize there are few individuals who can look back on a lifetime of work and know that the world is a different place because of their wisdom and courage."

*Karen D. Stout*

### Matthews, Victoria Earle (1861–1907)

Victoria Earle Matthews was a civic leader and activist in the Black women's club movement. She was born to a slave woman in Fort Valley, Georgia. Her formal education consisted of only brief public school attendance. She taught herself by using the library in a home in New York City, where she was a domestic worker. After writing for local literary publications, Matthews became involved in women's activities. In 1892 she became the first president of the Woman's Loyal Union of New York and Brooklyn. She participated with Josephine St. Pierre Ruffin in the founding of the National Federation of Afro-American Women. The federation was renamed the National Association of Colored Women after merging with the National Colored Women's League. Matthews worked as a national organizer for the league for two years and subsequently became concerned about young Black girls arriving in the city with no support. On tours of the South, Matthews investigated the circumstances related to prostitution among young black Girls. In 1897 she organized the White Rose Industrial Association for young Black women working in New York City. See *Notable American Women* (1971), by Edward T. James, Janet Wilson James, and Paul S. Boyer.

*Wilma Peebles-Wilkins*

## Mayo, Leonard Withington (1899–1993)

Leonard Mayo was born at the Berkshire Industrial Farm, in Canaan, New York, where his father was director. He graduated from Colby College in Maine and from 1922 to 1930 worked as an administrator in children's institutions. For the next five years, he did graduate work in sociology and social work at New York University and the New York School of Social Work, where he also was an instructor. From 1935 to 1941 Mayo was an administrator at the Welfare Council of New York City. He then served as dean of the School of Applied Social Sciences, Western Reserve University, Cleveland, from 1941 to 1948. He left Cleveland in 1949 to become director of the Association for the Aid of Crippled Children (later renamed the Foundation for Child Development) in New York City. He returned to Colby College as professor, from 1966 to 1971, developing a major that combined the social and natural sciences. In 1981 Mayo accepted a second post at Western Reserve University as vice president and development officer for the school he had formerly headed.

Mayo's influence spanned the areas of child welfare, mental retardation, and public health. In the course of a long career, he made an impact on social services for children and for disabled people in the United States and abroad. During World War II Mayo was chairperson of the Federal Commission on Children in Wartime. He served on four White House Conferences on Children and Youth and was an advisor to five presidents, from Truman to Ford. He also served as chairperson of President Kennedy's Committee on Mental Retardation, which produced recommendations that modernized care and services for mentally retarded people. Mayo served as president of the National Conference of Social Work, chairperson of the Social Welfare Department of the National Council of Churches,

and chairperson of the Board of the Child Welfare League of America. He was president of the International Union for Child Welfare from 1957 to 1973.

Mayo was awarded honorary doctorates by Colby College and Case Western Reserve University, the Albert Lasker Award in World Rehabilitation and a presidential citation for his work on employing people with disabilities. In 1978 a chair was established in his name at the school he had headed. He produced hundreds of speeches and published papers but only one book, *From Service to Research* (1965). In his last years, he worked on a book about children and families, which is unpublished.

Mayo's investment in children never flagged. When, in his 90s, Mayo read that a child had died in a county foster home, he sent the clipping to a friend with the message: "Do something about this!"

*Alvin L. Schorr*

## Meyer, Carol H. (1924–1996)

Carol Meyer, social work educator and prolific writer, occupied a leadership position in the continuing development and adaptation of social work practice to a changing world for more than three decades. In the tradition of Mary Richmond and Gordon Hamilton, her primary theoretical contribution was the expansion and enrichment of the individualizing or assessment process, a theme that is central in her first published article, "Quest for a Broader Base for Family Diagnosis" (1959), as well as in one of her last works, the widely used 1993 volume *Assessment in Social Work Practice*. A major theme in her teaching and writing was that client need as identified through the assessment process, not agency purpose, should determine the direction of practice.

Drawn to social work during her college years at the University of Pittsburgh by contact with social work pioneers Ruth Smalley and Gertrude Wilson, Meyer went on to earn her MSW at the New York School of Social Work (later Columbia University) and was among the first recipients of a doctoral degree from that institution. She worked to bring quality services to underserved and oppressed populations, paying particular attention to the needs of families and children. Throughout her career, she always set practice in the context of social policy, demonstrating and teaching that practitioners should be ready to tackle social and policy issues, as well as individual change.

A charismatic, engaging, and challenging teacher, lecturer, consultant, and workshop leader, she was a central figure on the Columbia University School of Social Work faculty for 34 years, providing a memorable experience to generations of students and traveling throughout the country to teach, train, and exhort, always with the purpose of advancing the practice of social work.

In her later years, she came to embrace feminist ideas and offered invaluable leadership in her term as editor of *Affilia*. Her influence was widely felt through her extensive publications and her editorship of *Social Work*. Her publications include dozens of articles, book chapters, and monographs appearing in major publications and six books, including *Staff Development in Public Welfare Agencies* (1966), *Social Work Practice: A Response to the Urban Crisis* (1970), *Assessment in Social Work Practice* (1993), and *The Foundations of Social Work Practice: A Graduate Text* (1995, co-edited with Mark A. Mattaini).

*Ann Hartman*

## Miller, Samuel O. (1931–1994)

Samuel O. Miller was a social work educator, scholar, and practitioner. Born in Panama, he earned a BA (cum laude) in sociology and education from Dakota Wesleyan University, an MSW (with honors) in casework from Boston University, and a PhD in social work practice from the University of Chicago School of Social Service Administration. From 1970 through 1973 he was an associate professor at the Western Michigan University School of Social Work. From 1973 until his death Miller was a faculty member at the Columbia University School of Social Work (associate professor, 1973–1989; professor, 1989–1994). Miller's teaching and scholarly contributions were complemented by an active private social work practice.

Miller was a member of the House of Delegates of the Council on Social Work Education (1982–1984) and a member of the board of directors of the Manhattan Country School, the James Weldon Johnson Counseling Center, and the New York City chapter of NASW. He was a recipient of a Career Teacher Award from the National Institute of Mental Health (NIMH), a Whitney Young Academic and Internship Award, and an NIMH National Research Service Award. Listed in *Who's Who among Blacks* and *Who's Who in the East,*

Miller had wide-ranging scholarly interests. Among the topics examined in his published articles and books are racial barriers in schools of social work, Hispanic social workers, clinical social work in cross-cultural contexts, primary prevention for ethnic minorities, maternity homes, long-term care facilities, and social work interventions for acquired immune deficiency syndrome (AIDS). With Barbara Dane, he co-authored *AIDS: Intervening with Hidden Grievers* (1993).

*Ronald A. Feldman*

## Minahan, Anne (1925–2005)

Anne Minahan, professor at the School of Social Work, University of Wisconsin-Madison from 1967 until her retirement in 1985, was a leader in social work education and social work practice. In 1973, with Professor Allen Pincus, Professor Minahan wrote *Social Work Practice, Model and Method*, which became the standard social work practice text in schools of social work throughout the U.S. and internationally. Discussing the importance of the book, the NASW News explained it "revolutionized the way social work practice was viewed...[It] introduced the ideas of systems theory, change agent, client system and action system and ... was used by social programs worldwide." Professor Minahan was very active in both the National Association of Social Workers and the Council on Social Work Education. She was editor in chief of *Social Work: The Journal of the National Association of Social Workers* from 1979–1982 and editor in chief of the *Encyclopedia of Social Work*, 18th Edition.

*Mel Morgenbesser*

## Morris, Robert (1910–2005)

Robert "Bob" Morris had a profound influence on long-term care policies and services available for the elderly, as well as on the awareness and understanding of social gerontological issues. His research and prolific writing had created a better understanding of the importance of social policy to the planning and delivering of social services and to the well being of people, particularly the elderly.

Morris was born in Akron, Ohio, and received his bachelor's degree from the University of Akron in 1931, his master's in social work from Western University in 1935, and his DSW from Columbia University, New York School of Social Work in 1959. He was a professor of social planning at Brandeis University and was a professor emeritus from 1959 to 1979.

In 1970 he became director of the Levinson Policy Institute at Brandeis and was thus very instrumental in the development of the university's role in social policy studies and research. Morris received research awards from the Ford Foundation, Veterans Administration, National Science Foundation, and the Department of Health, Education, and Welfare, and was a visiting lecturer/professor at several other schools of social work. He served on technical advisory committees of the National Institute of Mental Health, Veterans Administration, Social Security Administration, and the HEW Office of Human Development Services.

Morris's publications include several books and numerous articles in the fields of social planning, gerontology, and medical care. He was the recipient of special awards from the Hayes Fullbright Program for Italy, the Ford Foundation, the Max and Anna Levinson Family Trust, and the Treuhaft Fund.

Morris also found time to serve on a number of committees and editorial assignments for NASW. He was the editor of the *Encyclopedia of Social Work*, 16th Edition, 1971, the editor of the *Journal of Social Work* from 1960 to 1972, and was an advisor to other NASW publications.

*Edith Olmsted*

## Naparstek, Arthur J. (1939–2004)

Arthur Naparstek—community leader and partnership scholar—was born in 1939. He received his undergraduate degree from Illinois Wesleyan University, his MSW degree from New York University, and his PhD from the Florence Heller School for Advanced Studies at Brandeis University. As a community planning expert, he worked in neighborhood revitalization for over four decades. Naparstek headed the Poverty Commission in Cleveland, which not only established programs locally, but also created the multi-billion dollar federal Hope VI program that both conceptually as well as physically changed public housing in the United States. He also built partnerships internationally, particularly in Beit She'an and other cities in Israel, and he served as the Senior Vice President for United Jewish Communities. He served on the National Commission on Neighborhoods under appointment by President Carter, and on the Corporation for National Service under President Clinton. He also helped draft the Home Mortgage Disclosure Act, the Community Reinvestment Acts, and the Urban Revitalization Demonstration Acts (HOPE I–VI)

As Dean (1983–1988) and Grace Longwell Coyle Professor (1991–2004) at the Mandel School of Applied Social Sciences at Case Western Reserve University, he helped develop Social Work education by extending training to working professionals in the community, generating tuition support for students through partnerships with agencies and foundations, and working with Congressman Louis Stokes to create the Stokes Fellowship Program to bring promising students from across the United States to the Mandel School for master's degree training in community development. Naparstek authored over 100 articles, monographs, reports, and books, including *Community Building in Public Housing: Ties That Bind People and Their Communities* (1997), *Neighborhood Networks for Humane Mental Health Care* (1982), *Partnership Building in Mental Health and Human Services: A Community Support Systems Approach* (1979), and *Urban Disinvestment: New Implications for Community Organization, Research and Public Policy* (1975).

*Darlyne Bailey*

## Newstetter, Wilber I. (1896–1972)

Wilber I. Newstetter encouraged the development of specialized training for social workers in youth and group leadership. Born in Massillon, Ohio, he served in World War I and graduated from the University of Pennsylvania in 1919. Newstetter later received a master's degree in sociology from Western Reserve University. His career began with a position as head worker at the Woodland Center and directorship of Harkness Camp in Cleveland, Ohio. In 1926 he helped develop a two-year group work program at the School of Applied Social Sciences at Western Reserve University. During the 1930s, Newstetter established Cleveland's University Settlement—the first university-operated social work training center—which served families and youths and provided neighborhood outreach services. His recommendations helped establish a school of social work at the University of Pittsburgh, and he served as its first dean in 1938.

In the course of Newstetter's professional career, he served as an officer of the Cleveland Welfare Federation, the National Federation of Settlements, and the American Camping Association. He was also president of the American Association of Social Workers, the American Association of Schools of Social Work, and the National Conference on Social Welfare. With Marc Feldstein and Theodore Newcomb, he coauthored *Group Adjustment* (1938).

*Larraine M. Edwards*

## Northen, Helen (1912–2006)

Helen Northen, PhD, was an educator, scholar, and author of classic social work textbooks. Considered one of the foremost authorities on social work with groups, she also developed expertise and published extensively in the areas of clinical social work practice and health care. She was a prolific writer who continued to publish into her nineties and her books remain widely used in social work education.

Helen Northen was born in Butte, Montana, on June 5, 1912. She received her AB from the University of Washington in 1939, her MSW from the University of Pittsburgh in 1944, and her PhD from Bryn Mawr College in 1953. After two years (1951–1953) as an associate professor at the University of Hawaii School of Social Work, she joined the faculty at the University of Southern California School of Social Work, where she stayed for the remainder of her teaching career. She was a visiting senior scholar at the London School of Economics in 1961.

She spent her teaching career at the University of Southern California, where she taught courses at the master's and doctoral level, chaired doctoral dissertations, and held numerous leadership positions within the School of Social Work. She was a leader in formulating a generic model of social work that was adopted across social work education. She was known for her ability to identify and distill the essentials of social work practice into practical and teachable models. She was also a prolific writer.

Dr. Northen served in founding and leadership positions in professional organizations, including NASW, CSWE, the Association for the Advancement of Social Work with Groups (AASWG), Society for Clinical Social Workers, the National Academies of Practice, and the Group for the Advancement of Doctoral Education.

Her publications include: *Social Work with Groups, Clinical Social Work* (1982), *Child-Family-Neighborhood* (co-author) (1982), *Theories of Social Work with Groups* (co-editor) (1976), *Families and Health Care* (1990), and more than 50 articles, monographs, and book chapters. *Social Work with Groups*, first published in 1969, with later editions in 1988 and 2001 (with Roselle Kurland), was translated into Dutch, French, German, and Portuguese.

She also worked as a volunteer or consultant with numerous organizations, including: the American Red Cross, Camp Fire Girls, American Heart Association, the Veterans Administration, YWCA, City of Hope Medical Center, and Big Brothers of Greater Los Angeles.

Her honors include the 1998 Knee/Wittman Outstanding Achievement Award from NASW; the 1999 Faculty Lifetime Achievement Award from the University of Southern California; the University of Pittsburgh's Legacy Laureate Alumni Award; and NASW Social Work Pioneer. Dr. Northen died July 22, 2006 at the age of 94 in Seattle, Washington.

*Robert Carter Arnold*

### Pagan de Colon, Petroamerica (1911–1980)

Petroamerica Pagan de Colon championed the causes of employment, security, safe working conditions, and workers' rights throughout her public career. Born in the mountains of Puerto Rico, she studied social work at the University of Puerto Rico and human resources development at Columbia University. Her career began in rural vocational education, but her commitment to employment issues led to executive appointments with the Departments of Education and of Labor in Puerto Rico. In the course of her work, she introduced programs benefiting migrant workers, people with disabilities, and other disadvantaged groups. Her pioneering work in vocational rehabilitation continues to be the base around which these services are offered.

She helped draft original legislation for the protection and security of Puerto Rican migrant workers in the United States and developed employment services during Operation Bootstrap.

As increasing numbers of Puerto Ricans took industrial jobs in the United States, Pagan de Colon worked tirelessly, through program development and voter registration drives, to ensure that migration to the United States would not produce disillusionment. After 1960 she headed programs and departments in the U.S. Department of Labor and for the Organization of American States. She was honored as Woman of the Year by the Commonwealth of Puerto Rico in 1978, and in 1985, the Foundation for Workers' Homes named its home for retired workers in her honor. Similarly, the main meeting hall of the Puerto Rican Department of Labor was named in her honor. Her published speeches include "The Status of the Migrant: The Migrant and the Affluent Society" (1962) and "Migration: Dream or Disillusionment?" (1964).

*John F. Longres*

### Perkins, Frances (1882–1965)

Best known as the first woman member of a U.S. Cabinet, Frances Perkins was appointed secretary of labor in 1933 by President Franklin D. Roosevelt. Born in Boston, Perkins was raised in Worcester, Massachusetts, in a conservative Republican family. Trained as a chemist, she graduated from Mount Holyoke in 1902. She did social work for the Episcopal Church for two years, lived at Hull-House for six months to learn more about social work, and earned a master's degree from Columbia University in 1910. As secretary of the New York Consumer's League (1910–1912), executive secretary of the New York Committee on Safety (1912–1917), and director of investigations for the New York State Factory Commission (1912–1913), she earned a reputation as an authority on industrial conditions and hazards.

Perkins became executive director of the New York Council of Organizations for War Services (1919–1921), director of the Council on Immigrant Education (1921–1923), and member (1922–1926) and chair (1926–1929) of the New York State Industrial Board. There was criticism when Governor Roosevelt appointed her New York State Industrial Commissioner in 1929 and much greater outcry, when—as president—he appointed her secretary of labor.

As secretary, Perkins instituted a fact-finding system on employment and unemployment statistics, helped standardize state industrial legislation, and promoted the adoption of the social security system. Her social work background led her to advocate for improving workers' conditions, including minimum wages, maximum hours, child labor legislation, and unemployment compensation. In 1945 she resigned and was appointed to the U.S. Civil Service Commission, where she remained until 1953. She wrote a memoir of Roosevelt and many books and articles on labor issues. See also *Madam Secretary, Frances Perkins* (1976), by George Whitney Martin.

*Jean K. Quam*

### Perlman, Helen Harris (1905–2004)

Helen Harris Perlman, the Samuel Deutsch Distinguished Service Professor Emerita in the School of Social Service Administration, was a pioneering figure in social work who enriched the field of social work with many contributions spanning several decades. She graduated in 1926 from the University of Minnesota with a BA in English. Because her teachers advised it would be difficult for a female Jewish graduate to obtain a job in the humanities, she found a job working as a summer caseworker for the Chicago Jewish Service Bureau. She got a great deal of satisfaction helping people and continued in the field of social work until she received one of four Commonwealth Fund scholarships for students at the New York School of Social Work, now the Columbia University School of Social Work. She has said that "a whole world opened up to me," "I had no idea of the kinds of trouble people had. I got a great deal of satisfaction from being able to help people. I found that in many cases, families faced the same kind of problems and conflicts that one encountered in the great works of literature."

She joined the faculty of the School of Social Service Administration, University of Chicago, in 1945. She later became the Distinguished Service Professor Emerita. When she turned 90 the School of Social Service announced the establishment of the Helen Harris Perlman Visiting Professorship in the School. The chair was to be filled every two or three years and was endowed by several friends and an anonymous member of the SSA faculty in addition to Perlman and her late husband, Max Perlman.

Perlman was a sought-after speaker throughout her career, even when she was a student at the New York School of Social Work, and in later years universities in the United States, Europe, Asia, and elsewhere. She is probably best known for her work carrying forward and integrating concepts that emerged from diverging schools of psychoanalytic thought. Her most widely read work, which she began writing not long after she joined the faculty in Chicago was *Social Casework: A Problem Solving Process*, which is still used as a textbook in schools of social work. The book was published

in 1957 and has been translated into more than 10 languages. Her thinking diverged markedly from the then-current popularity of long-term psychotherapy. She didn't think that people always needed in-depth therapy. Today this concept of short-term therapy is a common form of help. She also wrote more than 75 articles and seven other books including *So You Want to Be a Social Worker, The Heart of Helping People,* and edited the book *Helping: Charlotte Towle on Social Casework.* She also wrote fiction, poetry, and stories, including the short story "Twelfth Summer," which was published in *The New Yorker* magazine in the 1950s.

She was active throughout her career in professional and educational organizations related to social work, and was honored by the National Association of Social Workers, the Association of Clinical Social Workers, and the Council of Social Work Education, and received honorary degrees from Boston University, the University of Southern Florida and the University of Minnesota.

*Kenneth S. Carpenter*

### Pernell, Ruby B. (1917–2001)

A scholar and leader in the development of social group work knowledge, values, and skills, Pernell earned her undergraduate (1939) and master's (1944) degrees from the University of Pittsburgh, and her doctorate in social administration (1959) from the University of London. Pernell's work touched many communities: she was a settlement house worker at the Soho Community House in Pittsburgh; a faculty member at the University of Minnesota School of Social Work; a social welfare attaché assigned to India for the State Department; a Visiting Professor at the Universities of Denver, Washington, and Atlanta; Grace Longwell Coyle Professor and professor emerita of Social Work at the School of Applied Social Sciences at Case Western Reserve University from 1968 to 2001 (now the Mandel School of Applied Social Sciences). Pernell also served as the Acting Dean of that institution from 1973 to 1974. She was a founding member of the Association for the Advancement of Social Work with Groups and a board member and advisor to many local and national organizations, including the Peace Corps. As part of her commitment to international social work and study-abroad programs, Pernell served as a consultant for many nations, including Britain, Egypt, the Sudan, Jamaica, Germany, Canada, Sri Lanka, and India. Dr. Pernell wrote over 35 articles and monographs, contributing regularly to journals such as *International Social Work, Journal of Education for Social Work,* and *Social Work,* and authoring chapters in *Fundamentals of Social Work Practice* (1982).

*Darlyne Bailey*

## Pray, Kenneth (1882–1948)

Kenneth Pray was a leader in social work education. A native of Whitewater, Wisconsin, he graduated from the University of Wisconsin and moved to Philadelphia where he worked as a reporter for the city's *Record*. Pray left journalism to become executive secretary of social planning and administration for the Public Charities Association. He was also interested in prison reform and served as a member of the boards of the Pennsylvania Prison Society, the Pennsylvania State Industrial School at Huntington, and the Pennsylvania State Industrial Home for Women at Muncy. Leadership roles in the American Association of Social Workers and the National Conference of Social Work were among his other professional activities. For 26 years, Pray served as director and professor of social planning and administration at the School of Social Work at the University of Pennsylvania.

During the latter part of his career, Pray chaired the National Council on Social Work Education committee that conducted the first major comprehensive study of social work education. He outlined the activities of the community organization social work method and was the author of *Social Work in a Revolutionary Age and Other Papers* (1949).

*Larraine M. Edwards*

## Rankin, Jeannette (1880–1973)

Jeannette Rankin, the first woman elected to the U.S. Congress and the only member of Congress to vote against U.S. participation in both world wars, was born near Missoula, Montana, and graduated from the University of Montana in 1902. After spending several years caring for her parents and younger siblings, she enrolled in 1908 at the New York School of Philanthropy, receiving her diploma the following year. After a brief career in social work, Rankin became active in successful campaigns for women's suffrage in Washington and Montana. In 1916 Rankin ran for Congress from her home state as a progressive Republican, favoring women's suffrage, protective legislation for children, Prohibition, and peace. Her election made her the first female member of the House of Representatives. She was one of 56 members of Congress who voted against President Wilson's declaration of war against Germany. During the remainder of her term, Rankin worked on legislation to aid women and children and on a women's suffrage amendment to the Constitution. In 1918 she was defeated in her bid for the Republican nomination for the Senate from Montana.

During the 1920s and 1930s, Rankin lobbied for social welfare legislation and peace. In 1940 she was again elected to the House of Representatives. She was the only member of Congress to vote against the declaration of war against Japan in 1941. Defeated for reelection, she spent the next decade in obscurity. During the late 1960s and early 1970s, she campaigned against the Vietnam War, again becoming nationally prominent. Rankin is the subject of two biographies: *Jeannette Rankin: First Lady in Congress* (1974), by Hannah Josephson, and *Flight of the Dove: The Story of Jeannette Rankin* (1980), by Kevin S. Giles. See also the biographical essay by Joan Hoff Wilson in *Notable American Women: The Modern Period* (1980).

*Paul H. Stuart*

## Rapoport, Lydia (1923–1971)

Lydia Rapoport, a prominent social work educator, theorist, and practitioner, was born in Vienna, Austria, and came to the United States with her parents in 1932. A graduate of Hunter College (1943), she received her MSS in psychiatric social work from Smith College School for Social Work in 1944 and became a psychiatric social worker in Chicago at the Michael Reese Hospital, University of Chicago hospitals, and the Jewish Children's Bureau. She also took a three-year training course in childhood psychoanalysis at the Chicago Institute for Psychoanalysis, becoming a specialist in treating emotionally disturbed children.

As a Fulbright scholar in the Social Sciences Department of the London School of Economics (1952–1954), Rapoport was instrumental in strengthening British training for social workers. In 1954 she joined the faculty of the School of Social Welfare at the University of California, Berkeley, directing its psychiatric social work programs and establishing an advanced training program in community mental health. On leave, Rapoport worked at Harvard University's Laboratory of Community Psychiatry, which led to her most important contribution to social work practice: crisis intervention and short-term therapy. Rapoport also served as the first United Nations interregional family welfare and family planning advisor in the Middle East.

Rapoport wrote numerous articles and two books, *Consultation in Social Work Practice* (1963) and *The Role of Supervision in Professional Education* (1963). See also *Creativity in Social Work: Selected Writings of Lydia Rapoport* (1975), edited by Sanford N. Katz.

*Maryann Syers*

## Reichert, Kurt (1916–2006) and Betty (1916–2004)

Dr. and Mrs. Reichert considered themselves a team throughout their lives and throughout their joint social work career. Their main contributions were in the health field as program and community planners, administrators, teachers, and writers.

The Reicherts developed a shared outlook on social work, explored in individual and joint papers, and acted on in their paid positions and in their many professional and community activities. Central to their ideas were holistic views of humankind and society and opposition to the fragmenting tendencies in the societal fabric and institutions, including social work.

Kurt was born in Austria and received his BA from Carleton College. Betty was born in Pennsylvania. They attended the master's program at the School of Social Service Administration, University of Chicago in the early 1940s and married during this time. Kurt later earned his PhD from the University of Minnesota School of Social Work.

The Reicherts were involved in civil rights throughout their careers. As President of NASW (1963–1965), Kurt helped to move the organization toward active participation in the civil rights movement and the adoption of affirmative action policies and procedures in elections, appointments and programs.

Betty was an early pioneer in family life education (1949–1952), offering this as a family agency service to a wide range of community groups and spearheading a network of family life education providers. The Reicherts collaborated on a broadcast interview series on family and social problems, *Let's Face It*, for which they received a national award in 1951.

The Reicherts emphasized the involvement of volunteers in all phases of health planning. Betty initiated the use of volunteers in her work with the mentally ill, retarded, and multi-handicapped children in several agencies. She also focused on the use of volunteers in new areas, including public service.

Kurt developed social work services in the Department of Psychiatry, University of Minnesota (1948–1952), and while directing the Office of Public Health Social Work of the New York State Department of Health (1954–1963) spearheaded the development of social work services and information and referral services in county health departments.

Much of the Reicherts' career was devoted to the education of social workers. Kurt joined the faculty of Bryn Mawr College School of Social Work (1964–1967) and became Secretary of the Commission on Accreditation of CSWE (1967–1970). He went on to San Diego State University, first as Dean, then as head of the Health Concentration. Betty served on the same faculty (1978–1981), developing instruction in school social work along field of practice lines. After their retirement in 1981, the Reicherts jointly received an award as Social Work Educators of the Year by the California Chapter of NASW.

The Reicherts were part of the movement from separate membership organizations to the formation of NASW, then from methods specializations to comprehensive fields of practice. Throughout their lives, each held many leadership positions in professional and community organizations. In his later years, Kurt rediscovered his Jewish heritage and renewed his involvement as an actor in community theater. They were proud that each had been individually elected an NASW Social Work Pioneer.

*Kenneth A. Carpenter*

## Reid, Bill (1928–2003)

William J. Reid of the School of Social Welfare was a Distinguished Professor at the State University of New York at Plattsburgh. He was nationally and internationally acclaimed as one of the most influential leaders, educators, practitioners, theorists, researchers, and scholars in the field of social welfare for his work in the implementation of empirical methods in the development and testing of new intervention strategies in social work, which was instrumental in bringing systematic knowledge to bear on practice and education in the field.

His research and methodology were at the forefront of the field of social welfare, and his task-centered model involved his students in an ideally symbiotic relationship between theoretical understanding and practical application.

Reid's persistence regarding the need to integrate research and practice was the impetus that led the Council on Social Work Education to require that accredited social work education programs incorporate this goal in their curricula. He was principally known as the inventor of the task-centered approach, widely recognized as pioneering a new method and philosophy of practice for social work.

The task-centered practice model brought about a significant shift in the way that work with individuals and families was done. He taught the value of short-term interventions and the importance of focusing on achievable tasks. He also stressed extending the task-centered model to work with families of children at risk of school failure.

The influence of Reid's work has been wide-ranging. His casework model is now widely used as the basis for delivering and managing private and public social work services both here and abroad. As a result of this contribution, the report of the special National Institute of Mental Health Social Work Research Task Force named Reid as one of the two most influential social work researchers in the field.

Reid, a prodigious scholar, authored or co-authored 14 books and more than 120 articles and chapters in books and professional journals. The extent of his work is very broad; it has been translated into seven languages, and has contributed to psychology and education as well as to social work and social welfare fields. His contribution to the profession included service on numerous editorial boards and a variety of consultancies. Reid was also the first editor of *Social Work Research and Abstracts*.

Reid was the recipient of several awards, including the National Association of Social Workers' Excellence in Research Award and was named George Herbert Jones Professor at the University of Chicago's School of Social Service Administration.

*Robert Carter Arnold*

### Reynolds, Bertha Capen (1885–1978)

Bertha Capen Reynolds, social worker, educator, and activist, advocated for the working class and oppressed groups and stressed the importance of working together for a more humane world. Born and raised in Stoughton, Massachusetts, she graduated from the Boston School of Social Work in 1914. She participated in the first course in psychiatry ever offered to social workers at Smith College in 1918 and in the historic Milford Conference in 1923. In 1925 she was appointed associate director of Smith College School for Social Work. She remained there until 1938 when she was asked to leave because she wanted rank-and-file workers to unionize to improve their working conditions and the lives of their clients. An acknowledged Marxist, she wrote extensively in *Social Work Today* (the journal of the rank-and-file movement) on the need for social workers to become more politically active and concerned about the civil rights of their clients.

Finding it difficult to obtain employment in schools of social work or social agencies, she believed she had been blacklisted for her union activities but in 1943 she was hired by the National Maritime Union, where she stayed until 1948. She taught and wrote, publishing *Between Client and Community* (1934), *Learning and Teaching in the Practice of Social Work* (1942), *Social Work and Social Living* (1951), *McCarthyism versus Social Work* (1954), and an autobiography, *An Uncharted Journey* (1963).

*Jean K. Quam*

### Richmond, Mary Ellen (1861–1928)

Mary Richmond was an outstanding practitioner, teacher, and theoretician who formulated the first comprehensive statement of principles of direct social work practice. Born in Belleville, Illinois, she joined the

Baltimore Charity Organization as an assistant treasurer at the age of 28. In 1891 her administrative abilities led to her appointment as general secretary. In addition to her assigned duties, she volunteered as a friendly visitor.

Concerned about the frequent failures of cases to respond to service, in 1897 she delivered her historic speech at the National Conference of Charities and Correction, calling for schools to train professional social workers. In 1899 she published the first comprehensive presentation of practical suggestions, *Friendly Visiting Among the Poor*.

In 1900 Richmond became general secretary of the Philadelphia Society for Organizing Charity. During her tenure she emphasized the need for volunteer effort. She also fought to obtain legislation for deserted wives and founded the Pennsylvania Child Labor Committee, the Public Charities Association, the juvenile court, and the Housing Association.

Between 1905 and 1909, Richmond was associated with *Charities*, which developed teaching materials for Charity Organization Societies nationwide. She then became director of the Russell Sage Foundation's Charity Organization Department in New York City. She also taught and did research at the New York School of Philanthropy.

From 1910 through 1922 she developed and headed summer institutes attended by secretaries of charity organization societies from all parts of the country. Her most celebrated book, *Social Diagnosis*, was based on her lectures and on her wide readings in history, law, logic, medical social work, psychology, and psychiatry. Widely hailed as evidence of the professionalization of social work, it was the first formulation of theory and method in identifying the problems of clients. In 1922 she defined social casework as "those processes which develop personality through adjustments consciously effected, individual by individual, between men and their social environment."

Richmond's other publications include *The Good Neighbor in the Modern City* (1907) and *What Is Social Case Work? An Introductory Description* (1922).

*John E. Longres*

### Riis, Jacob August (1848–1914)

The writings and lectures of Jacob August Riis on slum conditions had a profound effect on social reform for poor people at the turn of the century. Educated in Denmark by his father before coming to America in 1870, Riis worked as a police reporter in New York City for 22 years, first at the *Tribune* and then at the *Evening Sun*. In addition to his realistic descriptions of slum conditions, Riis recommended health, educational, and environmental reform. His work inspired other writers to give humanistic accounts of the harsh realities of slum life. As a result of the influence of Riis's writings, he developed a personal relationship with Theodore Roosevelt. To Riis's satisfaction, during Roosevelt's term as police commissioner, police lodging houses and the Mulberry Bend tenements were eliminated. Riis also worked to establish parks, playgrounds, and school facilities for children's clubs. In 1889 a settlement house in Mulberry Bend Park was renamed for him. His works include *How the Other Half Lives* (1890), *The Children of the Poor* (1892), *The Making of an American* (1901), and *The Battle with the Slum* (1902). See also *Jacob A. Riis, Police Reporter, Reformer, Useful Citizen* (1938), by Louise Ware.

*Larraine M. Edwards*

### Ripple, Lillian (1911–1993)

Lillian Ripple, recognized throughout the United States as a social work educator, scholar, and research specialist, was an esteemed graduate of the University of Chicago, where she earned her bachelor's, master's, and doctoral degrees at the School of Social-Service Administration. Her career began with volunteer work at Hull-House and proceeded through direct practice as a caseworker to specialization in research. After distinguished service as the director of research for the Welfare Council of Metropolitan Chicago, Ripple joined the faculty of the School of Social Service Administration at the University of Chicago. As a researcher who knew practice and as a practitioner who valued research, she was especially effective as an educator. When the School of Social Service Administration established a research center, Ripple, now a full professor, was the obvious choice to serve as its first director. It was in this capacity in 1964 that she produced her pioneering study of continuance and discontinuance in social treatment, *Motivation, Capacity and Opportunity: Studies in Casework Theory and Practice*. At the time, this study was regarded as the definitive work in the field of casework research and was widely used by educators and practitioners.

In 1968 Ripple ended her long association with the University of Chicago and its School of Social Service Administration to become associate director of the Council on Social Work Education (CSWE). Although she gave her attention in this position to all aspects of social work education, she again brought her scholarly and research talents to bear on the special problem of the structure and quality of social work preparation for professional practice. A task force under her leadership produced a report that generated a great deal of discussion within CSWE and NASW. At issue was the

concept of a BSW–MSW–DSW continuum. Although no consensus was reached within the educational system, experimentation was encouraged.

After her retirement in 1975, Ripple accepted an appointment as a consultant and trainer for the Central Council for Education and Training in London. Her experience with this organization, which serves in the United Kingdom as the accrediting body for social work education, was mutually rewarding. Her British colleagues enthusiastically concurred with the resolution passed earlier by the CSWE board of directors extolling her talents and expressing their profound respect for her contributions to social work education, practice, and research.

*Katherine A. Kendall*

### Rivera de Alvarado, Carmen (1910–1973)

Carmen Rivera de Alvarado had a distinguished career as a pioneer in social work practice and education in Puerto Rico and the United States. She graduated magna cum laude and received an award for excellence from the University of Puerto Rico. In 1935 she founded the first professional association of Puerto Rican social workers—the Insular Society of Social Workers—and served two terms as its president. One of the founders of the College of Social Workers of Puerto Rico (1940), which remains the island's foremost association of social workers, she also served as its first president. She received a social work master's degree from Washington University and a doctorate from the University of Pennsylvania.

Rivera de Alvarado's career included administrative and consultative positions in research, in-service training, maternal health, and medical and psychiatric social work. She served as a member of, consultant to, and principal speaker for numerous Latin American bodies, commissions, and congresses and was an outspoken champion of Puerto Rican independence. She was a revered professor at the Universities of Puerto Rico and Pennsylvania and at Hunter College, where she was named distinguished visiting professor. Among her writings are *The Social Worker Confronting the Dilemma of the Times* (1951), *Changing Values of the Puerto Rican Culture* (1967), and *Social Work at the Crossroads* (1973).

*John F. Longres*

### Robinson, Virginia Pollard (1883–1977)

Virginia Pollard Robinson was a native of Kentucky, who, after earning two degrees at Bryn Mawr College, taught high school English for four years and then, from 1911 to 1918, worked at a series of social work agencies in New York City. After 17 years at the Pennsylvania School of Social Work, she became Professor of Social Case Work at the University of Pennsylvania, where she continued until her retirement in 1952. Over 35 years of academic work, Virginia Robinson, who twice served as acting head of the School, gradually came to personify the School's very identity. She was the leading force and major theoretician behind the functional approach to social work that was the trademark of the Pennsylvania School of Social Work for over six decades.

Along with Kenneth L. M. Pray she pursued an affiliation between the Pennsylvania School of Social Work and the University of Pennsylvania. Toward that end they strengthened the school academic foundations and by the fall of 1927 they had supplemented the one-year General Certificate in Social Work with a Vocational Certificate in Social Work, which required a second year of study and field work. These two additions revolutionized social work education and laid the foundation for the current MSW program structure.

Under Robinson's leadership the School started the *Journal of Social Work Process* and Volume I, Number 1 was published in November 1937. Titled *The Relation of Function to Process in Social Case Work*, the volume was edited by Robinson's life-long companion Professor Jessie Taft. The functional approach advocated numerous novel elements of casework that today are the hallmark of any social work practice. It put the client at the center, focused on the problem that the client presented, used the client's will and abilities, made the social worker a tool of aid, made the process of help central, and it set boundaries, including the beginning and end of helping relationships. It is up to the client to choose the agency that offered the best services and it was the social worker's responsibility to enable the client to make that choice wisely and to use the agency effectively. The social worker is thus an agent on behalf of an empowered client. Heavily influenced by the work of Otto Rank, Virginia Robinson helped social work disengage from the influence of psychotherapy and focus on solving clients' problems.

Virginia Robinson was a social work theorist, who authored a significant number of influential works. They began with her PhD dissertation at Penn, published in the same year with the same title: *A Changing Psychology in Social Case Work* (Chapel Hill, North Carolina: The University of North Carolina Press, 1930) and concluded with an anthology, *The Development of a Professional Self: Teaching and Learning in Professional Helping Processes, Selected Writings, 1930–1968* (New York: AMS Press, 1978).

*Mark Frazier Lloyd*

### Robison, Sophie Moses (1888–1969)

Sophie Moses Robison's multifaceted roles of social worker, educator, and researcher helped create social policy changes for juvenile delinquents. A Phi Beta Kappa graduate of Wellesley College in 1909, she received a master's degree in German literature from Columbia University in 1913 and a graduate certificate from the New York School of Social Work in 1928. In 1936 she earned a PhD in sociology from Columbia University.

Believing that research methods were slanted against minorities and poor people, Robison challenged the differential treatment and outcomes for youths based on sociocultural factors. Her research efforts and recommendations resulted in urban educational reform. Robison held that research should be socially relevant and serve human needs. As an educator, she attempted to integrate theory and practice. Throughout her life, Robison was an activist in the civil rights and women's movements. In 1963 the Leah Rudas Memorial Fund was established in her daughter's memory at the Columbia University School of Social Work. Her works include *Can Delinquency Be Measured?* (1936), *Juvenile Delinquency: Its Nature and Control* (1936), and *Refugees at Work* (1942).

*Larraine M. Edwards*

### Rodriguez Pastor, Soledad (1897–1958)

Soledad Rodriguez Pastor was a pioneer in services for deaf and blind people, an active social reformer, and a leader in the development of professional social work in Puerto Rico. She was raised in a family of modest means by her father after the death of her mother. At the age of 17 she became a rural teacher, later working with the Insular Home for Girls and doing volunteer work with blind children. She studied at the Perkins Institute and became director of the Institute for Blind Children in 1936. In 1943 she organized and directed the Office of Services for the Handicapped for the Department of Health of Puerto Rico. She received a certificate in social work in 1946 from the University of Puerto Rico. Her wide range of activities included the organization of the first island-wide survey of the "feebleminded" and the creation of the first home-based classes for blind adults.

A leader in professional activities, she also served as editor of the *Journal of Public Welfare* of the Department of Health of Puerto Rico from 1945 to 1952. Poor health forced her to retire in 1950, but she continued to do volunteer work with tuberculosis patients and to hold conferences on the prevention of blindness and deafness. She was posthumously awarded the Citizen of the Year Award by the governor of Puerto Rico.

*John F. Longres*

### Roosevelt, Eleanor (1884–1962)

Sometimes called "First Lady of the World," Eleanor Roosevelt broke the mold for the role of the modern presidential spouse. She brought her own strong political and professional identity to the public life she shared with her husband, Franklin Delano Roosevelt. Though born into a family of wealth and privilege, she consciously sought to broaden her outlook. Eventually, she became a strong advocate for women, workers, minority groups, children, and poor people. Working in settlement houses on New York's Lower East Side brought her, as it did so many other women of her class, a first awareness of the reality of the lives of people living in poverty. She joined Florence Kelley's National Consumers League, and later the Women's Trade Union League, to improve the wages and working conditions of women workers.

As First Lady, Roosevelt represented the president in a variety of capacities. As his health deteriorated, she increasingly served as his eyes and ears. Her own independent work continued as she investigated social conditions and the effectiveness of programs to address them. Her investigations influenced many of the New Deal programs of her husband's administration. It was she who became the embodiment of the president's sympathy for the masses of the American people. After her husband's death, Roosevelt served as the U.S. representative to the General Assembly of the newly formed United Nations. She chaired the Commission on Human Rights and crafted its ambitious Universal Declaration of Human Rights, which the full body ratified in 1948. Roosevelt earned the respect and admiration of millions of common people worldwide through her work for civil rights and world peace. Upon her death, she was compared to Jane Addams, an acknowledgment of the range of her interests and commitments, her many talents, and the depth of her compassion.

*Fred Newdom*

### Rothenberg, Elaine Zipes (1921–1994)

Elaine Zipes Rothenberg, a nationally renowned social work educator, was consistent in her commitment to setting educational and professional standards for social work and to ensuring diversity in faculty and student populations. A New York native, she graduated from Queens College in New York in 1941. Two years later, she received a master of social science degree from the Smith College School for Social Work. In 1960 she joined the faculty of the School of Social Work at the Richmond Professional Institute, which became Virginia Commonwealth University (VCU) in 1968.

After 12 years of service at the School of Social Work, Rothenberg was appointed dean in 1972. During the years of her deanship, she built VCU's School of Social Work into one of national renown. Under her direction, the school developed a PhD program, off-campus programs, a part-time social work education program, and a highly regarded continuing education program. She insisted on, and was successful in, recruiting women and people of color to the faculty and student body long before it was an institutional priority. In 1982, Rothenberg resigned as dean and was asked to serve as the director of the university's self-study. Once the self-study had been compiled and VCU had been awarded accreditation, she was appointed acting vice president for academic affairs and occupied that position until she retired in 1988.

Her role as a leader in the accreditation process of schools of social work from 1974 until 1982 resulted in increasing professionalization and accountability in social work education. Rothenberg's advice and assistance were sought by many schools of social work because of the clarity of her thinking, her vision, and her commitment to social work values.

*Florence Z. Segal*

### Rothman, Beulah (1924–1990)

Beulah Rothman dedicated most of her life to the education, research, practice, and expansion of social work with groups. A native of New York City, she graduated from Long Island University (1945) and received MSW and DSW degrees from Columbia University School of Social Work (1947 and 1963, respectively). In 1957 Adelphi University School of Social Work employed Rothman as the first chairperson of its group work sequence. She subsequently became associate dean and director of the doctoral program until her retirement in 1981. Moving to Florida in 1981, she became Distinguished Professor at Barry University School of Social Work where she developed the PhD program and served as director. One of the three founders of the Association for the Advancement of Social Work with Groups (AASWG), Rothman served on its board. In 1983 she founded the Center for Group Work Studies, which became the Florida chapter of AASWG in 1988. Rothman served as its executive director and co-chaired AASWG's 12th Annual Symposium in Miami.

With Catherine Papell, Rothman co-edited the quarterly publication *Social Work with Groups: A Journal of Community and Clinical Practice* from 1978 to 1990. Two of her numerous articles have become basic readings in group work education: "Social Group Work Models—Possession and Heritage" (1966) and "Group Work's Contribution to a Common Method" (1966). A respected leader in the field of group work, she was curriculum consultant to many national and international schools of social work and received numerous honors, including Master Teacher by the Council of Social Work Education, the Distinguished Leadership Award of the National Committee for the Advancement of Group Work, and Outstanding Editor of the *Journal of Teaching in Social Work*. Her greatest achievement was her generous gift of time and energy and her dedication to her students, whom she encouraged and supported in their growth and development as social group workers.

*Linda Adler*

### Rubinow, Isaac Max (1875–1936)

Isaac Max Rubinow used his knowledge of medicine, economics, and social work to lead the American social insurance movement and to contribute to Jewish American welfare programs. Born in Russia, Rubinow came to America in 1893 and graduated from Columbia University in 1895. He received a medical degree from New York University in 1898 and a PhD in political science from Columbia University in 1914. Between 1904 and 1911, Rubinow's major activities were in the field of economics. He worked with the Bureau of Statistics of the U.S. Department of Agriculture, the U.S. Bureau of Labor, and the Bureau of Statistics of the U.S. Department of Commerce and Labor. From 1912 to 1915, he lectured on social insurance at the New York School of Philanthropy. As one of the nation's experts on social insurance, Rubinow often testified at congressional hearings on unemployment.

Rubinow was a consultant to the President's Committee on Economic Security, which drafted federal social security legislation. From 1923 to 1928, he directed the Jewish Welfare Society of Philadelphia, and from 1925 to 1929 he edited the *Jewish Social Service Quarterly*. He was instrumental in the founding of the Anti-Defamation League of B'nai B'rith in 1934. Rubinow was the author of *Social Insurance* (1913), *The Care of the Aged* (1931), and *The Quest for Social Security* (1934).

*Larraine M. Edwards*

### Rush, Benjamin (1746–1813)

Benjamin Rush was a political activist who worked to improve the quality of life in colonial America. Born in Byberry, Pennsylvania, he received a bachelor's degree from the College of New Jersey (later Princeton University) and a medical degree in 1768 from the University of Edinburgh in Scotland. He was a member of the Continental Congress and a signatory to the Declaration of Independence. Throughout his career he was an advocate for free public education, adequate

sanitation laws, prison reform, and abolition of slavery. Rush became a teaching physician at the University of Pennsylvania in 1780 and three years later was appointed to the staff at Pennsylvania Hospital. As a result of his concern, better accommodation was built for mentally ill people. In addition, he insisted that mentally ill people be treated with dignity and respect.

Rush's book *Medical Inquiries and Observations upon Diseases of the Mind* (1812) greatly influenced the development of psychiatric treatment. His works include *The Autobiography of Benjamin Rush* (1948), edited by G. W. Corner, and *Letters* (1951), edited by L. H. Butterfield. See also *Benjamin Rush* (1934), by Nathan Goodman, and *The Selected Writings of Benjamin Rush*, edited by Dagobert Runes.

*Larraine M. Edwards*

### Salomon, Alice (1872–1948)

Alice Salomon of Germany, leader in international movements for social work education, women's rights and peace, was the first president of the International Association of Schools of Social Work. Salomon began a social work course for women in 1899 and opened the first school of social work in Germany in 1908. One of the first women admitted to the University of Berlin, she earned a doctorate in 1906 for her dissertation on "unequal payment of men's and women's work." She worked closely with Jane Addams in the international peace and women's movements in the early 20th century, and arranged a peace visit for Addams to the German Chancellor in 1915. As Salomon wrote, "war annihilates everything social work tries to accomplish."

In 1928, Salomon chaired the Social Work Education section of the First International Conference of Social Work held in Paris. At the meeting, the International Association of Schools of Social Work (then called the International Committee) was founded and Salomon became president, a post she held until the end of World War II. In this role, she expanded international awareness and the structure for social work education. She conducted the first worldwide survey of social work education in 1937 under a grant from the Russell Sage Foundation. In 1932, Salomon was honored for her work. The school of social work she founded was named after her and she received the highest national honor from the Prussian cabinet. Under Nazi rule, Salomon was increasingly targeted because of her Jewish roots, pacifism, and humanitarianism. Her honors were revoked and in 1937, after returning from a speaking tour in the United States, she was interrogated and sent into permanent exile in the United States. She died in 1948 in New York. Salomon wrote more than

250 articles and 28 books, including her autobiography, *Character Is Destiny*. The school she founded in Berlin is once again the Alice Salomon School of Social Work.

*Lynne M. Healy*

## Samora, Julian (1920–1996)

Julian Samora was born in Pagosa Springs, Colorado, on March 29,1920. Until age 27, he lived in Colorado, where he attended Adams State College on a Boniles Foundation grant, receiving a BA degree in 1942. He returned there to begin his teaching career, serving from 1944 to 1955. Scholarships enabled him to continue his education toward an advanced degree in sociology, which he earned in 1947. By then he had firmly established himself in his field of study, pioneering the way as the first Mexican American in sociology and anthropology. He earned his doctorate in sociology and anthropology in 1953 at Washington University. After teaching preventive medicine and public health for two years at the University of Colorado School of Medicine, he accepted a position at Michigan State University teaching sociology and anthropology. His teaching career culminated at the University of Notre Dame, where he was professor of sociology (1959), the head of the department (1963–1966), director of the Mexican-American Graduate Studies Program (1971–1985), and director of the Graduate Studies Program (1981–1984). He retired from Notre Dame in 1985, having distinguished himself as a researcher and scholar in sociology and Mexican American studies and having left a legacy of scholarship, research, and leadership in his discipline.

Samora was a distinguished teacher who was deeply committed to education and to students. As a mentor to hundreds of students in sociology, anthropology, history, law, and Mexican studies, he was revered and given acknowledgment of the place of honor he held in the academic and the Mexican American communities. He co-founded the National Council of La Raza, an organization working on behalf of national issues affecting Mexican Americans.

Samora authored about 30 journal articles and numerous books. His books reflected the critical issues of the era and were the first of their kind, paving the way for the many studies and writers/researchers who followed. Some of his most well-known publications are *La Raza: Forgotten Americans* (1966), *Los Mojados: The Wetback Story* (1971), A *History of the Mexican American People* (with P. V. Simon) (1977), and *National Study of the Spanish-Speaking People* (1979).

Samora was an outstanding scholar who also served as an editor for *International Migrant Review*, *Maestro*, and other journals. He served on the President's Commission on Rural Poverty, the Commission on Civil Rights, the Ford Foundation, the National Endowment for the Humanities, the Bureau of the Census, the National Institute of Mental Health, the President's Commission on Income Maintenance Programs, and the American Association for the Advancement of Science. He was honored with many awards during his lifetime. As his final tribute to research, the establishment of the Julian Samora Research Institute at Michigan State University bears his name, providing lasting visibility to his distinguished career.

*Juliette Silva*

## Sanders, Daniel (1928–1989)

Daniel Sanders was an educator and leader in the field of international social work and social welfare. Sanders spent the first part of his life and career in Sri Lanka, where he served first as associate director of the Ceylon Institute of Social Work (1955–1961) and then as executive director and research associate at the Institute of Social Studies (1961–1965). A graduate of the University of Ceylon, he also received a diploma in social welfare from the University of Wales, Swansea. He continued his education in the United States, receiving both an MSW and a PhD in social work from the University of Minnesota. Sanders held the positions of associate professor (1971–1974) and then dean and professor (1974–1986). In both universities he developed a program with an emphasis on international social work. He was responsible for the establishment of the Center for the Study of International Social Welfare Policies and Services in Illinois. He was also a founder of the Inter-University Consortium for International Social Development and served as the organization's first president.

Sanders was the author or editor of six books, including *The Development Perspective in Social Work* (1982), *Education for International Social Welfare* (1983), *Visions of the Future: Social and Pacific Asian Perspectives* (1988), and *Peace and Development: An Interdisciplinary Perspective* (1989). He also authored numerous articles, monographs, and book chapters and served on several editorial boards. He wrote widely on the themes of peace, social development, and the international context of social work practice and education.

*M. C. Hokenstad*

## Satir, Virginia (1916–1988)

Virginia Satir, pioneer family therapist, author, consultant, and teacher, was born Virginia Mildred Pagenkopf on June 26, 1916, on a farm in Neillsville, Wisconsin, the eldest of five children. After earning a degree in education and teaching for several years, she entered the School of Social Service Administration at the University of Chicago, where she received her master's degree in social work in 1948. In recognition of her distinguished career, she was awarded an honorary Doctor of Social Sciences degree from the University of Wisconsin in 1973, and in 1976 she received a special alumni medal from the University of Chicago for her outstanding work in family therapy and human relationships.

Her early agency work included working with families at the Dallas Child Guidance Center (1949–1950). Returning to the Chicago area, she consulted for various social services agencies, conducted a private practice, and taught at the Illinois State Psychiatric Institute. In 1959 she moved to California, joining with Gregory Bateson, Don Jackson, and Jules Riskin in developing basic principles of human interaction and communication that have continued to serve as the theoretical foundation guiding the practice of family therapy. That collaboration led to the creation of one of the first and foremost formal training programs in family therapy at the Mental Research Institute in Palo Alto, California. As her vision broadened, she became a leading force in the human growth potential movement, serving as director of training at the Esalen Institute in the mid-1960s.

Satir's book *Conjoint Family Therapy*, published in 1964, remains a classic in the field and has been translated into a number of foreign languages. She published 11 other books in her lifetime, among them *Peoplemaking*, in 1972, and *New Peoplemaking*, in 1988, reaching a large international audience. She received many honors, such as Fellow of the American Association of Marriage and Family Therapy in 1973, was elected President of the Association for Humanistic Psychology, 1982–1983, and in 1983 was named one of the 100 most influential women in America by the *Ladies Home Journal*. From 1986 to 1988 she was a member of the California Task Force to Promote Self-Esteem and Personal and Social Responsibility. During her lifetime she conducted hundreds of workshops around the world, presenting her "human validation process model." Creator of a number of innovative experiential techniques, such as "family sculpting" and "family reconstruction," she emphasized health rather than pathology and focused on coping rather than problems, thereby enabling people to experience personal growth through self-affirmation and direct relationship change. Research studies have found her work to have greatly influenced the clinical practice of many social workers and other mental health professionals.

*Michele Baldwin Froma Walsh*

## Saunders, Cicely (1918–2005)

Dame Cicely Mary Strode Saunders is credited as the founder of the modern hospice and palliative care movement. She began her career as a ward nurse in London in 1941. There she cared for dying patients until a back injury in 1944 caused her to return to Oxford, where she became a hospital almoner (a medical social worker). By listening to patients' narratives she realized the dehumanizing impact of unrelieved suffering and envisioned opportunities for improved practice. This awakened in Saunders an awareness of dying as a uniquely personal journey, and inspired a dream to offer holistic care in a more home-like environment.

Colleagues advised Saunders to become a physician to increase her influence in changing medical practice. In 1958, Dr. Saunders developed a systematic approach to studying the symptom management needs of the terminally ill. Saunders's conceptualization of "total pain" as the complex interaction of physical, social, psychological, and spiritual concerns of each patient/family system revolutionized the delivery of care. Saunders's work in the early 1960s on the fundamentals of managing intractable pain became the cornerstone of a worldwide movement to improve care of the dying.

In London in 1967, Saunders opened St. Christopher's Hospice, the world's first dedicated hospice, where she pioneered a multi-professional team approach to patient care. Her willingness to provide strong analgesia in anticipation of patient discomfort instead of only in response to escalating pain challenged traditional assumptions regarding opiate use and rigid dosing schedules.

Saunders's multidisciplinary education and deep spiritual beliefs provided a unique perspective from which to respond to patient and family concerns. She conceptualized suffering as multifaceted and created novel approaches to address patient needs while enhancing their dignity and supporting their continued exploration of meaning. Success was measured as the relief of symptoms coupled with the patient's ability to interact with others in personally meaningful ways.

As a nurse, social worker and eventually a physician, Saunders was instrumental in changing the delivery of patient care at the end of life. In recognition of her tremendous international influence, Saunders received numerous honors and awards, including being made a Dame Commander of the British Empire in 1980 and becoming a Member of the Order of Merit in 1989. In 1981, she won a Templeton Prize and in 2001 her work at St. Christopher's received the Conrad N. Hilton Humanitarian Prize (the world's largest humanitarian award). Saunders was a prolific author; her works include "Social Work and Palliative Care—the Early History" published in the *British Journal of Social Work* (2001); *The Evolution of Palliative Care* (2003); *Beyond the Horizon: A Search for Meaning in Suffering* (1990); *Hospice Care on the International Scene* (1997); and *Watch with Me: Inspiration for a Life in Hospice Care* (2003).

*Shirley Otis-Green*

### Schottland, Charles Irwin (1906–1994)

Charles Schottland was a leader in social welfare policy making and administration in state, national, and international agencies and the founder of an innovative school of advanced studies in social welfare at Brandeis University. As an educator he brought a wealth of practical and political experience, mostly in government organizations, to academia.

During the Great Depression Schottland headed California's State Relief Administration and later worked in the Children's Bureau in Washington, DC. In World War II he served as General Dwight D. Eisenhower's chief of a section dealing with displaced people in Europe. He was decorated by five nations for his work in repatriating 5.5 million people. President Eisenhower appointed Schottland Commissioner of Social Security; in that position he initiated significant changes in the social security law. He was active in social welfare organizations at the national level, served as an adviser to several United Nations bodies, and was president of the International Council on Social Welfare.

In 1959 Schottland became the founding dean of the Florence Heller Graduate School for Advanced Studies in Social Welfare at Brandeis University. He brought health and welfare administrators and planners together with social scientists to train policymakers and researchers at the doctoral level. At a time of major changes in social work and social welfare, Schottland emphasized the fast-growing public sector. His accessible, calm style of leadership was a vital ingredient in the school's development. He devoted two of his 20 years at Brandeis to serving as the university's third president.

Schottland had a vast network of professional and personal relationships from his work in the federal government and on the international scene. He brought leading figures from every field of social welfare to teach and lecture at the Heller School. Those who knew him as a dean, teacher, or colleague admired the skillful ways in which he combined his many years of first-hand experience as a policymaker and administrator with an incisive grasp of social problems and programs.

*Robert Perlman*

### Schwartz, William (1916–1982)

William Schwartz, social work educator and theorist, played a major role in improving the standards of practice, supervision, and teaching and contributed to the theory and practice of group social work. Born and raised in New York City, Schwartz was active in youth group work throughout his early career. After graduating from Brooklyn College in 1939, Schwartz served as youth director at the Young Men's Hebrew Association (YMHA) Community Center in Lynn, Massachusetts (1943–1944); director of activities for the Jewish Community Center in Bridgeport, Connecticut (1944–1945); and supervisor of the senior division of Bronx House.

Schwartz earned an MS in 1948 from the New York School of Social Work at Columbia University and was employed as director of the Horace Mann Lincoln Neighborhood Center (1946–1947) and assistant director of the Manhattanville Neighborhood Center, an interracial settlement house in New York. He spent the summertime (1938–1957) directing summer camping programs for the YMHA, Educational Alliance of New York City, the Jewish Community Center, and other organizations. Schwartz was on the faculty of the School of Social Administration at Ohio State University (1950–1955), the School of Social Work at the University of Illinois in Chicago (1955–1962), and the New York School of Social Work at Columbia University (1962–1977); he was a distinguished visiting professor at Fordham University (1977–1982). Schwartz wrote on group work as a developmental and rehabilitative force for mutual aid, and his text, *The Practice of Group Work* (1971), co-edited with Serapio Zalba, became required reading in many graduate schools of social work.

*Maryann Syers*

### Scott, Carl A. (1928–1986)

Carl A. Scott, a champion of equity and social justice in social work education, was born in Battle Creek, Michigan. He received a BA in psychology (1950) and an MSW (1954) from Howard University. Early in his career, Scott held practice and administrative positions in children and family services agencies and was director of admissions and assistant professor at the New York University School of Social Work. In 1968 he joined the staff of the Council on Social Work Education (CSWE) as a senior consultant on minority groups. Scott was at the helm of CSWE's early efforts to foster diversity in social work education. He secured funding from government and private sources to recruit students and faculty from minority groups to schools of social work and guided five minority task forces in developing programs directed toward enhancing minority presence in curricula. He also designed minority fellowship programs to prepare mental health researchers and clinicians. Through these programs, which are among CSWE's most highly regarded activities, African Americans, Asian Americans, Native Americans, Mexican Americans, and Puerto Ricans have received stipend support for doctoral study.

Scott wrote or edited a number of CSWE publications, including *Ethnic Minorities in Social Work Education* (1970), *The Current Scene in Social Work Education* (with Arnulf Pins, Frank Loewenberg, and Alfred Stamm, (1971)), and *Primary Prevention Approaches to the Development of Mental Health Services for Ethnic Minorities* (with Samuel O. Miller and G. M. Styles O'Neal, (1982)). See also *Perspective on Equity and Justice in Social Work: The Carl A. Scott Memorial Lecture Series, 1988–1992*, edited by Dorothy M. Pearson.

*Dorothy M. Pearson*

### Seton, Elizabeth Ann Bayley (Mother Seton) (1774–1821)

Elizabeth Ann Bayley Seton founded the religious order of the Sisters of Charity and was among the first leaders in parochial education and Catholic social services in the United States. Early in her married life she was one of the founders of the Society for the Relief of Poor Widows with Small Children. After the death of her husband in 1803, she converted to Catholicism. In 1809 she became a nun and took the name of Mother Seton. A few years later she was selected to head a new, girls' academy near Baltimore. In 1812 she was joined by a community of religious women who became known as the American Sisters of Charity of St. Joseph. Mother Seton later established free schools for poor children in Philadelphia, forming the core of the parochial school system. The first Catholic orphanage, the first Catholic hospital, and the first Catholic maternity hospital were operated by Mother Seton and the Sisters of Charity. On September 14, 1975, she became the first American to be canonized by the Church. See *Mother Seton and American Women* (1947), by L. Feeney, and *Elizabeth Bayley Seton: 1774–1821* (1951), by A. Melville.

*Larraine M. Edwards*

### Shyne, Ann Wentworth (1914–1995)

Ann Shyne, a leader in the development of contemporary social work research, was born in Troy, New York. She graduated from Vassar College in 1935, obtained her MSW from Smith College School for Social Work in 1937, and received a PhD in social work

and social research from Bryn Mawr College in 1943. She was first employed as a social worker for the Austin Riggs Psychiatric Center in Massachusetts. She began her research career in 1945 at the Family Service Association of America, and from 1955 to 1968 she directed research projects at the Community Service Society of New York. She then served as Director of Research of the Child Welfare Association of America until her retirement in 1976.

Shyne was a founding member, officer, and the only female member of the highly influential Social Work Research Group in the 1950s and 1960s. The Social Work Research Group was an NASW-sponsored organization of leaders in U.S. social work research. The group was successful in promoting research on social work practice and on social programs and policies and in the development of research activities and curricula in schools of social work.

Shyne designed and directed numerous foundation and federally funded research projects. Her articles, reports, and monographs based on these projects, as well as her writings on research and practice methods, had considerable impact on family and child welfare services and on social work research. She co-authored such influential publications as *Brief and Extended Casework* (1969, with William J. Reid), *Children Adrift in Foster Care* (1973, with Edmund Sherman and Renee Neuman), and *A Second Chance for Families* (1976, with Mary Ann Jones). These works were instrumental in promoting new approaches to foster care and the development of brief treatment in social work and related fields. In 1988 she received NASW's first Lifetime Achievement Award in recognition of her accomplishments in social work research.

*Edmund Sherman* and *William J. Reid*

### Sieder, Violet M. (1909–1988)

Violet Sieder was a distinguished social welfare educator and leader. Her major professional interests and contributions were in community organization, rehabilitation, and volunteerism. She received her undergraduate education at Douglass College, Rutgers University; a master's degree from the University of Chicago School of Social Service Administration; and a PhD from the Florence Heller Graduate School for Advanced Studies in Social Welfare, Brandeis University. Sieder's career in social services began during the Great Depression. From 1931 to 1944 she held positions as investigator for the New Jersey Department of Labor; supervisor for the New Jersey Emergency Relief Administration; executive secretary for the Allegany County, Maryland, Welfare Board; research assistant for the Maryland Board of State Aid and Charities; consultant to the U.S. Children's Bureau; and executive secretary of the Bronx, New York, Council for Social Welfare. From 1944 to 1954 she served as associate director, Health and Welfare Planning Department, Community Chest and Councils of America. In 1954 she was appointed professor and chair of community organization at the New York School of Social Work, Columbia University.

In 1959 Sieder enrolled in the first class of the newly established doctoral program in social policy at the Florence Heller Graduate School, Brandeis University. Within two years she was invited to join that school's faculty to teach social planning, community organization, and rehabilitation. After her retirement from Brandeis in 1974, she remained active as a volunteer organizer. Her major achievement during the final phase of her career was organizing the Massachusetts Human Services Coalition, a statewide advocacy agency and serving as its first president from 1975 to 1981. Sieder served NASW as a member of the Commission on Social Work Practice, the Committee on Community Organization, and the Central Review Committee. She also chaired the Committee on Community Organization of the Council on Social Work Education and served on the Executive and Nominating Committees of the National Conference on Social Welfare.

Sieder was also active on the international scene. After World War II, she served as a consultant on community organization to the U.S. State Department High Commission on Germany and to the London and National Councils of Social Services in England. She later was chair of the NASW Committee on International Social Work, a member of the Executive Committee of the International Federation of Social Workers, and secretary of the Editorial Committee of the International Conference of Social Work. She traveled widely to maintain contacts with social workers and their professional schools and organizations and undertook teaching assignments for schools of social work in Zagreb, Yugoslavia, and Rio de Janeiro, Brazil. Sieder was named Social Worker of the Year by NASW's Massachusetts chapter in 1976 and was honored by the national organization with a citation for service.

*David G. Gil*

### Simkhovitch, Mary Kingsbury (1867–1951)

Mary Kingsbury Simkhovitch achieved international recognition as the founder of the Greenwich House social settlement in New York City. A native of Chestnut Hill, Massachusetts, she received an undergraduate degree from Boston University in 1890. Later she did graduate work at Radcliffe College and the University of Berlin. Simkhovitch began her social work career working with immigrants at the College Settlement and Friendly Aid House in New York. In 1902 she founded Greenwich House, remaining there until her retirement in 1946. The settlement met the needs of the community by providing such services as a day care center, a family counseling service, and cultural activities. In addition to her pioneering work in public housing, Simkhovitch was a professor of social economy at Barnard College for three years and an associate professor in social economy at Teachers College of Columbia University for three years.

Simkhovitch's other professional activities included membership in the New York City Housing Authority, the New York State Board of Social Welfare, and the National Public Housing Conference. Simkhovitch wrote *The City Worker's World in America* (1917), *Neighborhood: My Story of Greenwich House* (1938), *Group Life* (1940), and *Here Is God's Plenty: Reflections on American Social Advance* (1949).

*Larraine M. Edwards*

### Smalley, Ruth Elizabeth (1903–1979)

Ruth Elizabeth Smalley was born in Chicago and received her bachelor's degree in 1924 from the University of Minnesota, her Master of Social Work degree in 1929 from Smith College, and her Doctor of Social Work degree in 1949 from the University of Pittsburgh. She practiced first in the Bureau of Child Guidance in New York from 1929 to 1932 and was then on the faculties of the University of Chicago, Smith College, and the University of Pittsburgh before coming to the School of Social Work at the University of Pennsylvania in 1950 as Professor of Social Casework. Ruth E. Smalley was a nationally prominent advocate of the functional approach to social work.

In 1958, the University appointed Ruth Elizabeth Smalley the Dean of the School of Social Work. She was the first woman to be appointed Dean of the School and the second woman to be named an academic dean at Penn. She held closely to the school's functional theory and practice, making it a brand name for the Pennsylvania School of Social Work. Under her leadership, admission grew by over 40 percent and faculty from 17 in 1958 to 24 in 1966.

Dean Smalley established, in 1960, a new NIMH-funded research center at the School. This set the foundation for research-based social work in many schools of social work nationwide. She negotiated, over several years, a new building for the School, which was constructed at 3701 Locust Walk—the heart of Penn's campus—which housed her office and the School's faculty in June 1966.

She celebrated, in 1959, the 50th anniversary of the School's founding. She delayed the first event in the celebration until January 1959, so that it would coincide with the annual meeting of the Council on Social Work Education (CSWE), which met in Philadelphia that year. Feeling that she had achieved her administrative goals, she resigned in 1966. In addition to her most successful tenure as Dean, Ruth E. Smalley also served as President of the Council on Social Work Education from 1960 to 1963 and on the Temporary Interassociation Committee, which established the National Association of Social Workers (NASW).

Ruth Smalley was active in attempting to improve and invigorate the functional approach to social work and her academic efforts culminated in her 1967 seminal book, *Theory for Social Work Practice* (New York: Columbia University Press). She also published many chapters such as "The Functional Approach to Casework Practice," in R. W. Roberts. &. R. H. Nee. (Eds.), *Theories of Social Casework* (1970) (pp. 77–128), Chicago: University of. Chicago Press.

*Ram A. Cnaan*

### Smith, Zilpha Drew (1852–1926)

Zilpha Drew Smith developed the method of friendly visiting in the charity organization movement. Born in Pembroke, Massachusetts, she was trained as a telegraph operator at Boston Normal School. She began her career as head of office staff with Associated Charities of Boston in 1879, and in 1886 was appointed general secretary. Smith devised a systematic approach to screening and investigating relief applications by using friendly visitors. She later helped Mary Richmond develop a similar program in Baltimore. In 1888 Smith founded the Monday Evening Club, the country's first social workers' discussion group. A strong advocate of trained charity workers, she left direct service to help develop a school of social work. Smith became associate director of the Boston School of Social Work in 1904 and remained there until her retirement in 1918. In later years, she became convinced of the necessity for public assistance and helped shape the legislation for mothers' aid in Massachusetts. She wrote *Deserted Wives and Deserting Husbands* (1901).

*Larraine M. Edwards*

### Snyder, Mitchell "Mitch" (1943–1990)

Mitch Snyder left the comforts of a well-paying job as a management consultant at the age of 26 because he believed that there was something more meaningful in life to accomplish. He took to the streets and eventually was arrested for car theft. He was sentenced to Danbury Prison where he spent three years with Daniel and Philip Berrigan, radical Catholic antiwar protestors. While in prison Snyder organized a work strike that shut down the prison for eight days because inexpensive inmate labor was being used to make parts for the Polaris submarine. It was in prison that Snyder found the value of working together in a community for social change.

After leaving prison in 1972, he helped form the Prisoners Strike for Peace in New York. Later, in 1973, he relocated to Washington, DC, and joined the Creative Community for Non-Violence (CCNV), a non-hierarchical religious community of 50 to 60 people who provide food, shelter, medical care, and clothing to approximately 2,000 people each day. CCNV is also deeply involved in political activities intended to change violent and unjust programs, policies, and values. Snyder committed numerous acts of nonviolent civil disobedience. He fasted, lived on the streets for extended periods, and demonstrated in a variety of ways. Snyder received no salary. He lived in the CCNV-operated 1,400-bed Second Street Shelter for the homeless, the largest and most-comprehensive facility of its kind in the nation. The Second Street Shelter was the object of a two-year struggle with the Reagan administration. For example, in November 1984 Snyder completed a 51-day hunger strike that almost cost him his life. He was successful in getting President Reagan to agree to provide funds for repair to the shelter run by CCNV. The struggle has been documented in a made-for-television movie, "Samaritan: The Mitch Snyder Story"; an Academy Award-nominated documentary, "Promises to Keep"; and a book, *Signal through the Flames: Mitch Snyder and America's Homeless* (1986). Snyder recorded his ideas about homelessness in a book with co-author Mary Ellen Holmes titled *Homelessness in America: A Forced March to Nowhere* (1983).

Snyder spent considerable time traveling around the country and speaking to a variety of organizations about poverty and homelessness. He and other CCNV members also provided support to cities that needed help in creating emergency facilities for poor and homeless people or in combating local efforts against them.

*Frederick A. DiBlasio* and *John R. Belcher*

### Specht, Harry (1929–1995)

Harry Specht, nationally and internationally renowned for his scholarship, leadership, and advocacy in social welfare, was one of the most prominent and powerful intellectual voices in his generation of social work educators. A child of the Great Depression, his professional life was marked by an abiding compassion for underprivileged people, which stemmed in part from

Specht's early life experiences; the first social workers he had contact with placed Specht and his siblings in foster care. On his own at an early age, Specht worked his way through high school and then through City College of New York, earning an AB in 1951. He obtained his MSW in 1953 from Case Western Reserve University.

Specht began his professional career in New York's settlement houses—Bronx House, Lenox Hill, and the Mt. Vernon Young Men's-Women's Hebrew Association—where he worked with street gangs and other groups. Returning to graduate school in the early 1960s, Specht received his PhD from Brandeis University. He then worked for Mobilization for Youth on the Lower East Side of New York City. In 1964 he moved to California to become the associate director of the Contra Costa Council of Community Services, and several years later he joined the social work faculty at San Francisco State University. In 1967 he was recruited to the faculty at the School of Social Welfare, University of California at Berkeley, where he rose through the professorial ranks; in 1977 Specht was appointed dean of the school, a position he held for 17 years.

Specht wrote more than a dozen books and 50 articles, which were translated into Japanese, Chinese, and German. His book *Community Organizing* (1973, with George Brager and, later, James Torczyner) remains one of the basic texts in its field. Specht's last and most controversial book, *Unfaithful Angels: How Social Work Has Abandoned Its Mission* (1995, with Mark Courtney), takes the profession to task for abdicating its historical mission of service to poor people.

Specht was a senior Fulbright Scholar in 1973 and the recipient of numerous honors, including the 1991 Daniel S. Koshland Award; the 1992 NASW Presidential Award for Outstanding Leadership in Social Work Education; and the Berkeley Citation, the highest honor awarded by the University of California at Berkeley.

*Neil Gilbert*

### Spellman, Dorothea C. (1907–1979)

A distinguished social work educator and practitioner, Dorothea C. Spellman made her primary contributions in group work and as an advocate for a unified profession during the years before the formation of the National Association of Social Workers. Born in St. Louis, Missouri, Spellman received a BA in 1928 from Washington University. After teaching for a year, she entered the School of Applied Social Sciences of Western Reserve University to study group work and subsequently worked for Young Women's Christian Associations (YWCAs) in Cleveland and Honolulu

and at the Brashear Settlement in Pittsburgh. In 1944 she joined the faculty of the Graduate School of Social Work at the University of Denver, heading the group work specialization until 1977.

As a member of the Temporary Inter-Association Council of Social Work Membership Organization and an early board member of NASW, Spellman fought to unite the many specializations in the field of social work. She also demonstrated the important role of group work. In the profession and the community, she was a strong advocate of social change to achieve social justice, helping to establish the Social Services Employees Union and the American Civil Liberties Union in the 1930s and 1940s and later joining the civil rights movement. Spellman was a long time member of the National Board of the YWCA and consultant to the Southern Ute Tribal Council and the Navajo Tribal Council.

*Maryann Syers*

### Starr, Ellen Gates (1859–1940)

Ellen Gates Starr is best known for co-founding Hull-House with Jane Addams. Born on a farm in rural Illinois, she attended Rockford Seminary for Women, where she met Jane Addams and the two began a lifetime relationship. After Starr taught at a prominent girls' school in Chicago, and following a long and intense correspondence with Jane Addams, Starr and Addams traveled together in Europe. It was during this trip that they shared with each other their concern with the lack of meaningful options for women, particularly educated women. Although they were influenced by the social and cultural goals of Toynbee Hall in England, the goal of both women in starting Hull-House was to provide for themselves and for other women a new avenue for living independently and giving meaning to life.

Hull-House opened in 1889. Aesthetic, artistic, and eventually religious values were for Starr the key to human liberation. This belief system shaped almost all the contributions she made to Hull-House. It was she who established reading clubs, cultural and language classes, and skilled crafts at Hull-House. She learned the craft of bookbinding in England and established a bookbindery in Hull-House, though it proved quite impractical.

The condition of the poor population, particularly the immigrant poor people who lived in the neighborhood around Hull-House, led Starr to become active in the labor movement in Chicago. Industrial society offended her not only because of the social conditions it spawned but also because she saw it dampening the aesthetic and spiritual lives of its participants. A frequent figure on the picket lines during the strikes of the garment and textile workers, Starr often used her influence to complain about the brutal treatment of strikers by the police force. While at Hull-House, she also helped organize against child labor, was a charter member of the Illinois branch of the National Women's Trade Union, and ran in local elections as a socialist.

Starr's life at Hull-House took a somewhat different direction than that followed by many of the women who came to live there and who became prominent social reformers. She had an intense personality and was prone to sudden outbursts of temper. Moreover, she was set apart by her growing interest in religion, and as an older woman she devoted more and more time to her own spiritual quest. Although born a Unitarian, Starr converted to Catholicism later in life. Starr's active association with Hull-House ended in 1929 when she became paralyzed below the waist, following an operation for a tubercular tumor. Until her death at age 80, she lived at the Convent of the Holy Child in Suffern, New York, and at the time of her death was an obviate of the Third Order of St. Bernadet.

Starr wrote editorials and newspaper and magazine articles, dealing primarily with labor issues, her reasons for becoming a socialist, and eventually her religious conversion. Among these are "The Chicago Clothing Strike," *New Review*, March 1916; "Hull-House Bookbinding," *Commons*, June 30, 1900; and "A Bypath into the Great Roadway," *Catholic World*, May/June 1924. Her papers and letters are in the Sophia Smith Collection at Smith College.

*Susan Donner*

### Switzer, Mary Elizabeth (1900–1971)

Mary Elizabeth Switzer's 20-year administration of major federal social agencies influenced the evolution and expansion of federally funded services to those in need. Born in Newton, Massachusetts, she graduated from Radcliffe College in 1921. Her federal career began as an assistant secretary with the Minimum Wage Board in Washington, DC. In 1934 she worked with the assistant secretary of the treasury, who supervised the U.S. Public Health Service. Here Switzer developed a concern for the delivery of health, medical, and social services and served in several administrative positions over a 16-year period. In 1950 she was named director of the Office of Vocational Rehabilitation (OVR) in the Federal Security Agency (later the U.S. Department of Health, Education, and Welfare). For the next few years she was successful in increasing and improving services to people with disabilities.

When she became head of the new Social and Rehabilitation Service in 1967, Switzer acquired the greatest administrative responsibility of any woman in U.S. government history. The budget of this service for disabled people, elderly people, and mothers and children exceeded $8 billion. After Switzer's federal career ended in 1970, she continued to support efforts to enhance the quality of life for those in need. Between 1955 and 1969, she published several articles on disability and rehabilitation.

*Larraine M. Edwards*

### Taft, Julia Jessie (1882–1960)

Julia Jessie Taft founded the "functional" school of social casework practice, which was based on the psychoanalytic approach of Otto Rank. She received a master's degree from Drake University in 1904 and a doctorate in psychology from the University of Chicago in 1913. After practicing psychology for four years, she became director of the Child Study Department of the Children's Aid Society in Pennsylvania. In addition to gaining recognition as a therapist and mental health consultant, Taft became a social work instructor. With the help of Virginia Robinson, she developed a psychologically oriented curriculum at the Pennsylvania School of Social Work, where she taught until her retirement in 1952. In 1959 the school awarded her a citation for her contributions to social work. Taft was the author of *The Dynamics of Therapy in a Controlled Relationship* (1933) and the editor of *A Functional Approach to Family Casework* (1944). See also *Jessie Taft, Therapist and Social Work Educator.(1962)*, by Virginia Robinson.

*Larraine M. Edwards*

### Taylor, Graham (1851–1938)

The Chicago Commons settlement house founded by Graham Taylor in 1894 helped to improve slum conditions in Chicago. Born in Schenectady, New York, Taylor was educated at Rutgers College and at the Theological Seminary of the Reformed Church at New Brunswick, New Jersey. Ordained a minister in 1873, Taylor became interested in applied religion. In 1892 he began teaching social economics at the Chicago Theological Seminary and while there encouraged his students to assume responsibility for solving social problems. Modeling his activities at Chicago Commons on the work of Jane Addams, Taylor initiated such projects as drafting protective labor legislation, promoting better housing conditions, developing playground facilities, and publishing the charity periodical *Commons* (later *Survey*).

Among Taylor's other contributions were the 12-week training courses he established for social workers. These courses were incorporated as the Chicago School of Civics and Philanthropy in 1908, with Taylor serving as president of the Board of Trustees. Taylor's published works include *Religion in Social Action* (1913), *Pioneering on Social Frontiers* (1930), and *Chicago Commons through Forty Years* (1936). See also *Graham Taylor, Pioneer for Political Justice, 1851–1938* (1964), by Louise Wade.

*Larraine M. Edwards*

### Terrell, Mary Eliza Church (1863–1954)

Mary Church Terrell was a leading educator, social reformer, and participant in the international women's movement. Born in Memphis, Tennessee, she was educated in classical studies at Oberlin College. She received her BA in 1884 and her MA in 1888. Her mastery of foreign languages was achieved through a study tour of France, Germany, and Italy. A lecturer at Wilberforce University for two years, she later taught Latin in the District of Columbia secondary schools.

Terrell is best known for her professional lecture tours and writings on race relations and women's rights. In 1904 she represented black women at the International Congress of Women in Berlin, delivering her address in three languages. She participated in the 1919 International League for Peace and Freedom in Zurich, under the presidency of Jane Addams. A lifelong social activist, Terrell was also involved in organizing meetings of the National Association for the Advancement of Colored People, was a member of the National American Women's Suffrage Association, and demonstrated actively against segregation until the time of her death. Her ideals and activities are expressed in her autobiography, *A Colored Woman in a White World* (1940). See also *Mary Church Terrell: Respectable Person* (1959), by Gladys B. Shepperd.

*Wilma Peebles-Wilkins*

### Thomas, Jesse O. (1883–1972)

Jesse O. Thomas was one of the founders of the Atlanta University School of Social Work. Born in McComb, Mississippi, Thomas studied at Tuskegee Institute in Alabama, the New York School, and the Chicago School of Research. Before joining the Urban League in 1919 as field secretary for the southern states, he held leadership positions in industrial education. In 1928 he served on the Mississippi Flood Relief Committee.

During his term as Urban League field secretary, in Atlanta, Thomas substituted for the national executive secretary, Eugene Kinckle Jones, at the 1920 National Conference of Social Work in New Orleans. It was at this meeting that he called attention to the shortage of trained black social workers—a call that brought recognition of the need for a school to educate Black

professionals. With the help of Robert Cloutman Dexter, Thomas subsequently organized a group that led to the founding in 1920 of the Atlanta University School of Social Services (later the School of Social Work). Details of these organizing efforts appear in Thomas's autobiography *My Story in Black and White* (1967). See also *Black Heritage in Social Welfare, 1860–1930* (1978), by E. L. Ross.

*Wilma Peebles-Wilkins*

### Titmuss, Richard Morris (1907–1973)

Richard Morris Titmuss, scholar, author, and educator, made great contributions to social policy and administration. The son of a farmer in Great Britain, Titmuss left school at 15. After a few years as an office boy, he began work at the county fire insurance office, achieving success rapidly. As family breadwinner, he had first-hand experience of dependency, and as a company inspector, he learned more from company statistics and client records.

In the late 1930s, Titmuss began to write on such questions as poverty, migration, social class, and public health. His early books, such as *Poverty and Population* (1938) and *Birth, Poverty and Wealth* (1943), reflected his growing interest in the socioeconomic origins of poverty and the relationship between inequality and dependency and are examples of well-conceived, impartial scientific investigation. During these years Titmuss also became a fellow of the Royal Statistical Society and the Royal Economic Society.

In 1950 his widely acclaimed book, *Problems of Social Policy*, a study of the British social services during World War II, led to his appointment as chair of Social Administration at the London School of Economics, although he had no university degree or even a secondary school equivalency certificate. As an educator and administrator, Titmuss developed the new subject area of social policy and administration as a legitimate, intellectually respectable field of inquiry and demonstrated a strong commitment to vocational social work education. Through his writings, Titmuss had worldwide influence on issues of social welfare and its underlying philosophy. His other works include *The Irresponsible Society* (1960), *Income Distribution and Social Change* (1962), *Commitment to Welfare* (1968), and *The Gift Relationship* (1973). See also *Richard Titmuss: Welfare and Society*, by David A. Reisman.

*Maryann Syers*

### Towle, Charlotte (1896–1966)

Charlotte Towle was born and grew up in Butte, Montana. She graduated from Goucher College in Maryland in 1919 with a BA in education. After graduation she did volunteer work with the American Red Cross and worked for the Veterans Bureau in San Francisco and as a psychiatric caseworker in Tacoma, Washington. She attended the New York School of Social Work on a Commonwealth Fellowship and completed her degree in 1926. Following this, she served as director of the Home Finding Department of the Children's Aid Society in Philadelphia, where she was influenced by the "functional" approach to casework. From 1928 to 1932 she was a field work supervisor at the Institute for Child Guidance in New York. She joined the School of Social Service Administration at the University of Chicago in 1932 and remained there until her retirement.

Towle's major accomplishments include her work in creating a generic casework curriculum, her study of the educational process of training social workers, and her attempts to link the understanding of human behavior and needs with the administration of public assistance programs. Among her works are *Common Human Needs* (1965), *The Learner in Education for the Professions* (1954), and *Social Case Records from Psychiatric Clinics* (1941). See also *Helping: Charlotte Towle on Social Work and Social Casework* (1969), by Helen Harris Perlman.

*John F. Longres*

### Truth, Sojourner (1797–1883)

Sojourner Truth was a reformer and evangelist before and during the Civil War. Born into slavery in Ulster County, New York, she was named Isabella (Bell) Baumfree by her Dutch owner. As a fugitive slave in 1826, she was given refuge in New York City by the Van Wagener family and later took that surname. Influenced by the negative experiences of slavery and inspired by religious enthusiasts, she became an evangelist. In 1843 she took the name Sojourner Truth and began speaking tours to advocate for the abolition of slavery and for women's suffrage. With men, such as Frederick Douglass, and with suffrage leaders Elizabeth Cady Stanton and others, she was active in the abolitionist movement.

During the Civil War, Truth helped Union soldiers, and in 1864 she served as "counselor to the freed people" at the National Freedmen's Relief Association. Truth supported herself by selling an autobiography written for her by Olive Gilbert, *The Narrative of Sojourner Truth, A Northern Slave* (1850). See also *Journey Toward Freedom: The Story of Sojourner Truth* (1967), by Jacqueline Bernard; *Sojourner Truth: God's Faithful Pilgrim* (1938), by Arthur H. Fauset; and *Her Name Was Sojourner Truth* (1962), by Hertha Pauli.

*Wilma Peebles-Wilkins*

### Tubman, Harriet (1820–1913)

Harriet Tubman became known as the Moses of Black people for her leadership in the Underground Railroad movement. Born a slave in Dorchester County, Maryland, she was given the name Araminta Ross. She later took her mother's first name, Harriet. Escaping from bondage in 1849, Tubman fled to Philadelphia. She returned to Maryland some 19 times to rescue her family and the other slaves she had left behind and is thought to have rescued as many as 300 slaves before the Civil War. She worked with such individuals as the Quaker Thomas Garrett and the Black Philadelphia leader William Still. During the Civil War, Tubman served three years as a cook, nurse, spy, and scout. After the war, she set up the Harriet Tubman Home for Indigent Aged Negroes. After years of struggling with red tape, Tubman was given a $20 per-month government pension for her military service, which she used to help support her Harriet Tubman Home. Near the end of her life, she supported education for freedmen in the South and women's suffrage. Tubman was also involved in the organization of the National Federation of Afro-American Women. See *Harriet Tubman: The Moses of Her People* (1886), by S. H. Bradford; *Harriet Tubman: Negro Soldier and Abolitionist* (1943), by E. Conrad; *Harriet Tubman* (1955), by A. Petry; and *Freedom Train, The Story of Harriet Tubman* (1954), by D. Sterling.

*Wilma Peebles-Wilkins*

### Van Kleeck, Mary Ann (1883–1972)

Mary Ann van Kleeck began her career as a settlement worker and became a noted labor researcher and strong advocate for workers rights, especially the rights of women workers. Following graduation from Smith College, van Kleeck worked for the College Settlement Association on New York's Lower East Side. After she studied at Columbia, the Russell Sage Foundation hired her to head the committee on Women Work. In 1916, she was named director of the newly created Department of Industrial Studies at Russell Sage, a position she held for over 40 years. Her early labor research led to legislation protecting women workers. Later, van Kleeck examined numerous aspects of labor and the workplace. Her study of the role of employee representation led to the conclusion that labor is more productive and efficient when workers participate in the management of organizations. One of the first to study the effect of technology on employment and standards of living, her findings indicated that introduction of technology often led to unemployment.

Van Kleeck lectured at the New York School of Philanthropy and Smith College School for Social

Work; served on the board of the American Civil Liberties Union; and was a leader in the Hospites, a refugee organization that aided social workers fleeing Nazi Germany. She served on many government commissions. She was appointed to President Harding's Conference on Unemployment in 1921, to Hoover's Law Enforcement and Observance Commission in 1929 that investigated the relationship between unemployment and urban poverty, and others. Many of her positions were controversial. Van Kleeck opposed a proposed Equal Rights Amendment in the 1920s as she believed this would undo the protections for women workers that had just been won. She also supported centralized economic planning and Soviet-style socialism and opposed oaths of allegiance for teachers. It is not surprising that she was subpoenaed by Senator McCarthy's Committee and denied visas in the 1950s. Her extensive papers are in the Smith College Archives.

*Lynne M. Healy*

## Vasey, Wayne (1910–1992)

Wayne Vasey was a gifted educator and prominent leader in the fields of social policy and social welfare. A native of Iowa, he was educated at William Penn College and the University of Denver. He served as director or dean of social work schools at the University of Iowa (1948–1952), Rutgers University (1954–1962), and Washington University (1962–1968) and founding executive of the first two. In subsequent years he was a professor at the University of Michigan School of Social Work (1968–1975), co-director of the University of Michigan-Wayne State University Institute of Gerontology, and visiting distinguished professor at San Diego State University and the University of South Florida. His many board memberships and offices included the presidencies of the National Conference on Social Welfare and the Association for Gerontology in Higher Education.

At a time when social work's dominant perspective in practice as well as education was shifting from the social to the clinical, Vasey was an influential voice in charting a course toward a more balanced emphasis. His book, *Government and Social Welfare* (1958), spelled out the tasks and goals of the profession in the context of multilevel welfare systems and a changing philosophy of government responsibility. He stressed the need for social work involvement in the social and political arena and, during the latter part of his career, addressed the problems of elderly people and the need for communitywide planning on their behalf through his teaching, administrative work, and writing.

Vasey's professional perspective, as reflected in some 30 published writings, visualized the developments of fields such as public welfare, gerontology, and the social work profession as intricately bound up with the functioning of the basic societal institutions and the process of social change. This orientation furnished him with a useful platform for his consultations to the secretary of health, education, and welfare and to other key organizations involved in American social welfare.

*Ludwig L. Geismar*

## Vigilante, Joseph (1925–2005)

Joseph Vigilante was a leader of social work education for over four decades who made major contributions to the field of international social work, neighborhood-based social services, and social services to the aged and the disabled. A native of New York City, Vigilante received his MSW and DSW from Columbia University. Upon graduation, he worked as a caseworker and child welfare worker in New York and Wisconsin and joined the faculty of Adelphi University in 1954.

In 1960, he published a major study of social policy and social action activities of selected national welfare organizations. Two years later, he became Dean of Adelphi's School of Social Work, a position he held for twenty-five years. During this period, he served as a consultant to numerous state and federal agencies in the United States and held major leadership positions in state and national social welfare organizations, such as the New York State Association of Deans of Social Work Schools, the National Association of Social Workers, and the Council on Social Work Education.

At the national policy level, Vigilante played a pivotal role in promoting the rights of people with developmental and learning disabilities. His major works included *Response to Change: The Educational Alliance and Its Future* (1970), *Meeting Human Needs* (1975), *Reaching People: The Structure of Neighborhood Services* (1978), and *Reaching the Aged: Social Services in Forty-Four Countries* (1979). The latter three books were among the first published by U.S. scholars which engaged in a cross-national comparison of social service delivery systems. Vigilante was also an innovative and entrepreneurial educator who promoted the development of part-time, satellite, and distance education for social workers and taught a phenomenological approach to social work theory and practice.

*Michael Reisch*

## Vinter, Robert (1921–2006)

Robert Vinter was with the University of Michigan School of Social Work for 31 years. He joined the faculty in 1954 after earning his MSW degree in psychology and his PhD degree from Columbia

University. While at the Michigan School of Social Work he taught masters- and doctoral-level courses and conducted research studies. He served as associate dean from 1964 to 1970 and as acting dean from 1970 to 1971. He served as the Arthur Dunham Professor of Social Work prior to his retirement in 1985.

He was well known for his work in the field of juvenile delinquency and was a consultant for several federal agencies dealing with the field of juvenile delinquency including the Division of Juvenile Delinquency, the Children's Bureau, Department of Health, Education and Welfare; the President's Committee on Juvenile Delinquency, U.S. Department of Health, Education and Welfare; and the Department of Justice. His colleague Dr. Rosemary Sam, professor emerita of social work at the Michigan School of Social Work, commented at the time of his death that he had a lasting impact on programs and policies relative to juvenile delinquency throughout the United States. He also served as a consultant and was a member of several national and state mental health committees.

He was also well known in group work circles, helping to develop the theory and practice of group work. He was responsible for attracting a number of outstanding group workers to the faculty of the Michigan School of Social Work. He was recognized as an excellent teacher by his students as well as a mentor.

He was a founding member of the National Association of Social Workers and served on numerous committees of the Association as well as committees and organizations dealing with the field of social group work. Both he and his wife, Sally Vinter, were active in local and state social welfare committees and organizations.

*Kenneth S. Carpenter*

### Wald, Lillian (1867–1940)

Lillian Wald was a pioneer in public health nursing. A native of Cincinnati, Ohio, she enrolled at New York Hospital for nurses' training, graduating in 1891. Wald decided to live among New York City's poor immigrants to provide them with nursing care. In 1893 she and a colleague, Mary Brewster, founded the Henry Street Settlement (originally called the Nurses Settlement). During her 40 years as its director, professional nursing care and visiting nurse services were provided to poor people at little or no cost. In addition to nursing, Wald had a strong interest in child welfare problems and was one of the founders of the New York Child Labor Committee. In association with Florence Kelley, Wald is credited with the proposal that led to the establishment of the Children's Bureau in 1912. Her works include *The House on Henry Street* (1915) and *Windows on Henry Street* (1934). See also *Lillian*

*Wald, Neighbor and Crusader* (1938), by R. L. Duffus, and *Lillian Wald, Angel of Henry Street* (1948), by Beryl Williams.

*Larraine M. Edwards*

### Washington, Booker Taliaferro (1856–1915)

Booker T. Washington, an outstanding proponent of industrial education for Blacks, was also known for his accommodationist approach to race relations in the segregated South. Born into slavery on a plantation in Franklin County, Virginia, Washington graduated from Hampton Normal and Agricultural Institute in Virginia in 1875 and began a teaching career. He became head of Tuskegee Normal and Industrial Institute in 1881 where he remained for more than 20 years. Under Washington's leadership, Tuskegee developed into an endowed institution with expanded faculty and facilities. With support from fellow Blacks and concerned Whites, Washington promoted economic advancement through racial pride and individual industry. This approach to racial inequality was expressed in an address at the Atlanta Cotton States and International Exposition in 1895. Also known as the Atlanta Compromise, the speech drew criticism from more politically active Black intellectuals. Washington's many accomplishments in the Black community included the founding of the Negro Business League. Among his writings are publications on industrial education and economic development and the autobiographical works *The Story of My Life and Work* (1900), *Up from Slavery* (1901), and *My Larger Education* (1911). See also *Booker T. Washington Papers* (Vols. 1–4, 1972–1975), edited by Louis R. Harlan; and *Booker T. Washington Papers* (Vols. 5–13, 1976–1984), edited by L. R. Harlan and R. W Smock.

*Wilma Peebles-Wilkins*

### Washington, Forrester Blanchard (1887–1963)

Forrester B. Washington, an Urban League Fellow and director of the Atlanta University School of Social Work for 27 years, was born in Salem, Massachusetts. Washington graduated from Tufts College in 1909 and received a master's degree from Columbia University in 1917. Before becoming a social work educator, he served in leadership positions with such Black social welfare agencies as the Armstrong Association in Philadelphia (forerunner of the Urban League) and the Urban League in Detroit and at the national level.

A strong proponent of the scientific method for professional training of social workers, Washington used his knowledge and understanding of the needs of Black people to broaden the curriculum at the Atlanta University School of Social Work. Under

Washington's leadership (1927–1954), the school underwent tremendous growth, faculty size increased, and the school was accredited and gained national recognition. Social research and community projects sponsored by the Atlanta University School of Social Work supported social work in the Black community. See *The Legacy of Forrester B. Washington: Black Social Work Educator and Nation Builder* (1970), by the Atlanta University School of Social Work, and *Black Heritage in Social Welfare* (1978), by E. L. Ross.

*Wilma Peebles-Wilkins*

### Weiner, Hyman J. (1926–1980)

Professor Weiner was a nationally recognized program innovator, administrator, and educator. He was a pioneer in the conceptualization and implementation of group services in the health field. Following receipt of his MSW in 1951, Professor Weiner innovated group work services in hospitals, and subsequently instructed social work students at a chronic disease hospital. From 1961 to 1967, Professor Weiner was the director of the Sidney Hillman Health Center of the Amalgamated Clothing Workers, a mental health clinic in a labor-managed health facility. In this setting, Professor Weiner designed and field-tested techniques of short-term mental health services delivered by an interdisciplinary team.

Upon completing his doctorate in 1964, Professor Weiner used these employment experiences to publish imaginative and bold articles: "The Hospital, The Ward and the Patient as Client—Use of Group Methods"; "Toward Techniques of Social Change"; "Labor and Community Rehabilitation Effort"; "The Impact of Chronic Illness on a Union Population"; "Social Change and Social Group Work Practice"; "Involving a Labor Union in the Rehabilitation of the Mentally Ill"; "Implications of the Ward Culture for Group Work Services"; and "A Group Approach to Link Labor with Community Mental Health." He also co-authored a ground-breaking book, *Mental Health in the World of Work*.

In 1967, Professor Weiner joined the Columbia University School of Social work faculty as Professor and Director of the Social Welfare Research Institute. He also pioneered an Industrial Social Welfare Center and contributed to the building of industrial welfare curricula throughout the United States. Subsequently, he developed the Maternal and Child Health specialization. For a brief period of time, from 1975 to 1977, he served as Dean of the New York University School of Social Work.

Professor Weiner had a zest for life and a magnificent sense of humor. His tragic, accidental death left a significant void in the profession and in many people's lives.

*Alex Gitterman*

### Wells-Barnett, Ida Bell (1862–1931)

Ida Wells-Barnett was a journalist, civil rights spokeswoman, and civic organizer. Born to slave parents in Holly Springs, Mississippi, she received a high school education at Rust College—a freedmen's school—and studied at Fisk University in 1884. After seven years as a teacher, Barnett was fired for giving newspaper exposure to the poor educational provisions for Black children in Memphis, Tennessee. Her journalistic career began in 1892, and she was co-owner of the Memphis *Free Speech* until the offices were destroyed by a mob in 1892. Despite this, she continued to write and lecture about the plight of Blacks in the South, particularly the lynching of Black men. Barnett's activity in the women's club movement led to the organization of a Black women's club in Chicago. A settlement house was maintained by the Negro Fellowship League—another organization that she founded in Chicago in 1908. As chairperson of the Anti-Lynching Bureau of the National Afro-American Council—a forerunner of the National Association for the Advancement of Colored People (NAACP)—she participated in the founding meeting of the NAACP. Another of her great concerns was women's suffrage, and Barnett founded the Alpha Suffrage Club of Chicago, the first Black women's organization of its kind. Barnett's *A Red Record* (1895) includes autobiographical material and data on lynching. See also *Crusade for Justice: The Autobiography of Ida B. Wells* (1970), edited by Alfreda Wells Duster.

*Wilma Peebles-Wilkins*

### White, Eartha Mary Magdalene (1876–1974)

Eartha White, a civic-minded Black businesswoman, organized health and welfare services for the Black community in Jacksonville, Florida, the place of her birth. After studying at Madame Thurber's National Conservatory of Music in New York, she spent a year on tour with an opera company. White returned to Jacksonville to study and teach before initiating her lifelong community service activities, which were supported by profits from buying and selling small businesses and other real estate. Before World War I, White was involved in organizing and fund-raising activities for elderly people and children, and during the war she coordinated war camp services. In 1928 she founded the Clara White Mission for the homeless, named in honor of her mother. This mission, which served as a relief center for Black people during the Great Depression, expanded after World War II to include other services, such as care for dependent children and unwed mothers. While serving in the Women's National Defense Program during World War II, White donated a building and provided American Red Cross services to enlisted men, and in 1967 she established a 120-bed facility for welfare patients, the Eartha M. M. White Nursing Home. Among the honors she received for her public service contributions were the Better Life Award of the American Nursing Home Association and the Booker T. Washington Symbol of Service Award from the National Negro Business League. See *Notable American Women: The Modern Period* (1980), by B. Sicherman et al.

*Wilma Peebles-Wilkins*

### Wickenden, Elizabeth (1909–2001)

Shortly after graduating from Vassar College in 1931, Elizabeth Wickenden, also known as "Wicky," began an exemplary career as social welfare administrator, advisor to public and nonprofit organizations, policy writer, and advocate, continuing until shortly before her death in 2001. One of those rare individuals whose vision and commitment gave shape to contemporary social welfare institutions, her expertise spanned child welfare, social security, health, public assistance, unemployment, and legal services policies and programs.

Moving to Washington, DC, in 1933, she held administrative positions through 1941 in the Federal Emergency Relief Administration (FERA), Works Progress Administration (WPA), National Youth Administration, and the Federal Security Agency's Office of Defense, Health and Welfare Services. The legislative director for the American Public Welfare Association through 1951, she later consulted with and advised numerous nonprofit and government organizations. These include the National Assembly of Social Workers, Family Service Association, National Urban League, YMCA, Child Welfare League of America, National Assembly for Social Policy and Development, Children's Defense Fund, Field Foundation, Federal Advisory Council on Public Welfare, the Kennedy administration's Task Force on Health and Social Security Legislation and the Office of Economic Opportunity's Legal Services Advisory Committee (see http://www.ssa.gov/history/archives/wickyguide.htm).

Her organizational and analytic skills launched an effective coalition of social welfare and labor organizations, known as the "Wicky Lobby," giving shape and support to social welfare policies during the 1950s. A pioneering legal rights advocate, she advanced legal services and class action strategies on behalf of public assistance and child welfare clients. Having moved to New York City in 1951, she was also active in state and local social welfare issues and conducted seminars on social policy as faculty at City University of New York (1965–1974), Hunter College School

of Social Work (1979–1983), and Fordham University Graduate School of Social Service (1979–1983).

In the late 1970s and 1980s, as the nation's politics became less favorable to the policies her generation of leaders helped establish, she devoted much time to writing and advocacy on behalf of social security and related policies. She published an influential newsletter for the Study Group on Social Security, helped organize the Save Our Security Coalition and later served as a founding board member of the National Academy on Social Insurance.

*Eric R. Kingson*

### Wiley, George (1931–1973)

George Wiley is credited with organizing poor people into a significant political force in the United States during the late 1960s and early 1970s. Educated as a chemist, he graduated from the University of Rhode Island in 1953 and received his PhD from Cornell University. In 1960, he became associate professor of chemistry at Syracuse University and also began his work as a reformer, organizer, and social activist, founding a local chapter of the Congress of Racial Equality (CORE) at Syracuse and serving on the National Action Council of CORE.

Wiley left Syracuse in 1966 to found the Poverty/Rights Action Center in Washington, DC, a central communications link for groups of poor people trying to work together. Representatives of the groups involved established the National Welfare Rights Organization (NWRO) in 1967 and appointed Wiley its first executive director. NWRO, the largest poor people's membership organization in the United States, lobbied for a guaranteed adequate income for all and for improved welfare services at the state and local levels. Wiley resigned in 1973 to organize a broader-based organization devoted to tax reform and national health insurance.

A brilliant community organizer, Wiley had begun to found the Movement for Economic Justice when he drowned in a boating accident at age 42. See *A Passion for Equality: George A. Wiley and the Movement* (1977), by Nick Kratz.

*Jean K. Quam*

### Wilkins, Roy (1901–1981)

Roy Wilkins became a national civil rights spokesperson during his 46 years of leadership of the National Association for the Advancement of Colored People (NAACP). He was born in St. Louis, Missouri, and earned a BA degree from the University of Minnesota in 1923. Wilkins subsequently took a job in journalism at the *Kansas City Call*. His concern about segregation caused him to resume activities he had begun in college with the NAACP. In 1931, Wilkins became the assistant executive secretary of the NAACP. From 1934 to 1949, he served as editor of *Crisis* magazine, succeeding W. E. B. Du Bois. As chairperson of the National Emergency Civil Rights Mobilization in 1949, he worked for fair employment and other civil rights legislation.

In 1955 Wilkins was named executive director of the NAACP and during his 22 years in that position he struggled for justice and civil rights in all aspects of American life. Among the numerous awards he received were the Roosevelt Distinguished Service Medal in 1968 and the presidential Medal of Freedom in 1969. His books include an autobiography (with Tom Mathews), *Standing Fast* (1982), and a book of public speeches compiled by Helen Solomon and Aminda Wilkins, *Talking It Over* (1977).

*Wilma Peebles-Wilkins*

### Williams, Anita Rose (1891–1983)

Anita Rose Williams was the first Black Catholic social worker in the United States and the first Black supervisor employed by a Baltimore, Maryland, agency. Born in Baltimore, she had no formal education beyond high school, although she attended sociology lectures at Johns Hopkins University. During the early 1900s, she did volunteer work in family and child welfare agencies. In 1921 she restructured the city's four Black parishes as the Bernard Atkins Organization, which promoted economic and social assistance to Catholic youths. In 1923, after a year of employment with the Vincent de Paul Society, she began working for the Bureau of Catholic Charities of Baltimore. With the help of four other social workers, she organized District Eleven of the Baltimore Emergency Relief Commission. Before returning to Catholic Charities in 1936, she worked as a supervisor for the commission for three years. She retired from Catholic Charities in 1958. Williams also served on a number of health, welfare, and human relations boards. A building at the Barrett School for Girls in Glen Burnie, Maryland, was named in her honor. See *Notable Maryland Women* (1977), edited by Winifred G. Helmes.

*Wilma Peebles-Wilkins*

### Witte, Ernest Frederic (1904–1986)

Ernest Frederic Witte was an educator and administrator whose work in the social welfare field was influential both in the United States and internationally. Born in Swanton, Nebraska, he graduated from the University of Nebraska, received his PhD from the University of Chicago in 1932, and taught economics at Ohio Wesleyan University. During the Great Depression,

Witte served on various federal relief commissions and as a field representative of the Social Security Board. From 1937 to 1939, he was director of the University of Nebraska Graduate School of Social Work and, for the next four years, of the Graduate School of Social Work at the University of Washington.

During World War II, Witte co-ordinated welfare services in Allied-occupied Italy and was subsequently in charge of the welfare section of Supreme Headquarters in France. He continued his work with refugees and displaced persons in occupied Germany, where he was among the first to deal with survivors of the Nazi death camps.

Decorated by the French, Dutch, and U.S. governments for his war efforts, Witte returned to the United States to head the social services division of the Veterans Administration. In 1963, after 10 years as executive director of the Council on Social Work Education (CSWE), Witte was appointed by the State of California to set up graduate schools of social work at California State University at Fresno, California State University at Sacramento, and San Diego State University, where he served as dean until 1968. He held the deanship of the University of Kentucky's School of Social Professions from 1969 to 1974 and then headed the Institute for Graduate Social Work at the University of Trondheim in Norway. He returned to the United States in 1979. Although retired, Witte remained active as a consultant, continuing his work in such organizations as CSWE, NASW, and the Unitarian Universalist Church and maintaining his lifelong commitment to improve conditions for those groups most at risk in society. Witte contributed articles to numerous professional journals and reference books, including the 16th edition of *the Encyclopedia of Social Work*.

*John F. Longres*

### Wittman, Milton (1915–1994)

Milton Wittman played a key role in the expansion of opportunities for social work education and for the involvement of social workers in the provision of mental health services. Born in New York City, his social work education and career began in the Midwest. He received a BA degree from the University of Nebraska and an MA degree from the University of Chicago School of Social Service Administration. He later received a doctorate in social work from the Columbia University School of Social Work, where he taught for a year after his retirement, and completed a year of postdoctoral study at the London School of Economics.

After holding caseworker positions in Lincoln, Nebraska; Chicago; and St. Louis, Wittman spent four years in the U.S. Army during World War II, rising to the rank of major as chief of rehabilitation programs at a base in New Guinea. He was chief social worker for the Veterans Administration facility in Milwaukee before joining the newly formed National Institute of Mental Health (NIMH) in 1947. At NIMH Wittman administered a unique social work training grant program and also worked to find ways of meeting the social work manpower requirements of the national community mental health program. During his 32-year career at NIMH, Wittman worked on these objectives with schools of social work; the Council on Social Work Education, NASW, and other professional organizations; and federal, state, and local mental health, public health, and social welfare programs. An effective administrator, he succeeded in broadening the scope, priorities, and funding of the NIMH social work training grant program. His efforts contributed to the incorporation of mental health content as an integral part of the education of all social workers and to the emergence of new roles for social workers in mental health. He also helped to support curriculum revisions, scholarship aid, and practice innovations that reflected cultural and racial diversities and balanced inequities and promoted public health principles and the importance of prevention in social work practice and education.

In the 1960s he was appointed chairperson of the Federal Task Force on Social Work Education and Manpower. The task force report, "Closing the Gap in Social Work Manpower," resulted in the funding of social work education for welfare pro grams. In 1977 Wittman was named social work's first Professional Liaison Officer in the Public Health Service Commissioned Corps. His appointment gave a new level of visibility to social work in the public health service and provided an opportunity to coordinate standards across health programs.

A leader in social work as well as public health and mental health organizations, Wittman served on numerous national, state, and local boards and committees. He was a frequent speaker at conferences and seminars and a prolific writer who published more than 30 articles and chapters in books and monographs. His optimism and courage in coping with multiple disabilities during the last decade of his life, as well as his interest in and dedication to the field of social work, were a great source of inspiration for many.

*Ruth Irelan Knee*

### Young, Whitney Moore, Jr. (1921–1971)

Whitney Moore Young, Jr., was the son of a Kentucky educator. He graduated from Kentucky State College at 18 and became a high school teacher and coach. From 1942 to 1944, while in the U.S. Army, he studied engineering at the Massachusetts Institute of Technology. After his discharge, he received an MSW from the University of Minnesota (1947) and began to work with the Urban League in Minnesota. He became executive secretary of the Urban League in Omaha, Nebraska (1950), taught social work at the University of Nebraska and Creighton University, and became dean of the Atlanta University School of Social Work (1954).

In 1961 Young was appointed executive director of the National Urban League, remaining there until his death. (He drowned during a visit to Nigeria.) He became president of the National Conference on Social Welfare in 1965 and president of NASW in 1966. A noted civil rights leader and statesman, he worked to eradicate discrimination against Blacks and poor people. He served on numerous national boards and advisory committees and received many honorary degrees and awards, including the Medal of Freedom (1969), presented by President Lyndon Johnson, for his outstanding civil rights accomplishments. Young's books include *Beyond Racism: Building an Open Society* (1969).

*Wilma Peebles-Wilkins*

### Youngdahl, Benjamin Emanuel (1897–1970)

Benjamin Emanuel Youngdahl, public welfare administrator, educator, and lecturer, influenced the social work profession as president of the American Association of Schools of Social Work (1947–1948), the American Association of Social Workers (1951–1953), and the National Conference on Social Welfare (1955–1956). Born in Minneapolis, Minnesota, Youngdahl grew up in a prominent Swedish Lutheran family. He graduated from Gustavus Adolphus College in 1920, earned an MA from Columbia University, and returned to Gustavus Adolphus as a professor of sociology and economics. A passionate New Dealer, during the Great Depression Youngdahl worked in various Minnesota welfare programs, becoming director of social services for the State Emergency Relief Administration (1933) and director of public assistance under the State Board of Control (1937).

In 1939 Youngdahl joined the faculty of Washington University's George Warren Brown School of Social Work, St. Louis, Missouri. As dean of the school (1945–1962), Youngdahl upgraded training standards, developed a more integrated curriculum, doubled the school's enrollment, and established a doctoral program. In 1947 the school was the first division of Washington University to admit Black students. For his concern for civil liberties, he received the Florina

Lasker Award in Social Work in 1963. Youngdahl's writings on social action and social work education appear in his book *Social Action and Social Work* (1966).

*Jean K. Quam*

### Younghusband, Dame Eileen (1902–1981)

Dame Eileen Younghusband, international educator and scholar, influenced the development of social work education around the world. Born in London, she was the daughter of mountaineer and explorer Sir Francis Younghusband. She earned a certificate in social studies and a diploma in sociology at the London School of Economics and then joined the faculty (1929–1957). During World War II she set up one of the first Citizen's Advice Bureaus, worked with the Service of Youth Program and the United Nations Relief and Rehabilitation Administration, and conducted a national survey of welfare functions.

Younghusband taught the first generic casework courses in Great Britain and advocated the expansion of university-based training for social workers. After several years as presiding magistrate of the Hammersmith Juvenile Court in London, she was recruited by the Council on Social Work Education in 1960 to design a project to strengthen American social work education in the field of corrections. She helped transform the International Association of Schools of Social Work from a predominantly Western organization into a worldwide, United Nations-linked body to establish schools of social work in developing countries. She served on the executive board (1950), as vice president (1954–1961), and as president (1961–1968) and was named honorary president for life.

Younghusband chaired the British Committee on Social Workers of the Local Authority Health and Welfare Services, which organized and developed extra university social work training, and helped initiate the Council for Training in Social Work and the National Institute of Social Work. She received many honorary degrees and honors, and in 1964 Queen Elizabeth II conferred on her the Order of Dame Commander of the British Empire. Her writings include *Third International Survey of Training for Social Work* (1959), *Social Work and Social Change* (1964), *Casework with Families and Children* (1965), *Social Work and Social Values* (1967), *Education for Social Work* (1968), and *Social Work in Britain, 1950–1975* (1978).

*Jean K. Quam*

# Appendix 1

## ETHICAL STANDARDS IN SOCIAL WORK: THE NASW CODE OF ETHICS

**ABSTRACT:** Ethical standards in social work have matured significantly in recent years. As in most professions, social work's principal code of ethics has evolved from a brief, broadly worded document to a detailed, comprehensive guide to ethical practice. This article summarizes the diverse purposes and functions of professional codes of ethics and the historical trends and changes in social work's codes of ethics. The key components of the NASW Code of Ethics—the code's preamble, broad ethical principles, and more specific ethical standards—are described.

**KEY WORDS:** Code of Ethics; ethical principles; ethical standards; social work ethics; social work values

One of the hallmarks of a profession is its willingness to establish ethical standards to guide practitioners' conduct (Greenwood, 1957; Hall, 1968; Lindeman, 1947). Ethical standards are created to address ethical issues in practice and to provide guidelines for determining what ethically acceptable or unacceptable behavior is.

Professions typically publicize their ethical standards in the forms of codes of ethics (Bayles, 1986; Kultgen, 1982). According to Jamal and Bowie (1995), codes of ethics are designed to address three major issues. First, codes address problems of moral hazard, or instances when a profession's self-interest may conflict with the public's interest (for example, whether accountants should be obligated to disclose confidential information concerning serious financial crimes that their clients have committed, or whether dentists should be permitted to refuse to treat people who have a serious immune disease, such as HIV-AIDS). Second, codes address issues of professional courtesy—that is, rules that govern how professionals should behave to enhance and maintain a profession's integrity (for example, whether lawyers should be permitted to advertise and solicit clients, whether physicians should accept gifts from pharmaceutical company representatives, or whether psychologists should be permitted to engage in sexual relationships with former patients). Finally, codes address issues that concern professionals' duty to serve the public interest (for example, the extent of nurses' or social workers' obligation to assist when faced with a public emergency or to provide low-income people with pro bono services).

Like other professions such as medicine, nursing, law, psychology, journalism, and engineering, social work has developed a comprehensive set of ethical standards. These standards have evolved over time, reflecting significant changes in the broader culture and in social work's mission, methods, and priorities. They address a wide range of issues, including, for example, social workers' handling of confidential information and electronic communications, dual relationships and boundary issues, conflicts of interest, informed consent, termination of services, administration, supervision, education and training, research, and political action.

Ethical standards in social work appear in various forms. The *NASW Code of Ethics* (NASW, 1999) is the most visible compilation of the profession's ethical standards. Ethical standards can also be found in codes of ethics developed by other social work organizations (for example, the National Association of Black Social Workers [NABSW] and the Clinical Social Work Association [CSWA]), regulations promulgated by state legislatures and licensing boards, and codes of conduct adopted by social service organizations and other employers. In addition, social work literature contains many discussions on ethical norms in the profession (Congress, 1999; Loewenberg, Dolgoff, & Harrington, 2005; Reamer, 2006a, 2006b).

### The Profession's Early Years

During the earliest years of social work's history, few formal ethical standards existed. The earliest known attempt to formulate a code was an experimental draft code of ethics printed in the 1920s and attributed to Mary Richmond (Pumphrey, 1959). Although several other social work organizations formulated draft codes during the profession's early years (for example, the American Association for Organizing Family Social Work and several chapters of the American Association of Social Workers [AASW]), it was not until 1947 that the AASW, the largest organization of social workers of that era, adopted a formal code (Johnson, 1955). In 1960 NASW adopted its first code of ethics, five years after the association was formed. Over time, the *NASW Code of Ethics* has been recognized as the most visible and influential code of ethics in the United States.

In 1960 the *NASW Code of Ethics* consisted of 14 proclamations concerning, for example, every social worker's duty to give precedence to professional responsibility over personal interests; to respect the privacy of clients; to give appropriate professional service in public emergencies; and to contribute knowledge, skills, and support to human welfare programs. First-person statements (that is, "I give precedence to my professional responsibility over my professional interests" and "I respect the privacy of the people I serve" [p. 1]) were preceded by a preamble that set forth social workers' responsibility to uphold humanitarian ideals, maintain and improve social work service, and develop the philosophy and skills of the profession. In 1967 a 15th principle pledging nondiscrimination was added to the proclamations.

Soon after the adoption of the code, however, NASW members began to express concern about its level of abstraction, its scope and usefulness for resolving ethical conflicts, and its provisions for handling ethics complaints about practitioners and agencies (McCann & Cutler, 1979). In 1977 NASW established a task force to revise the code and enhance its relevance to practice; the result was a new code adopted by NASW in 1979.

The 1979 code included six sections of brief, unannotated principles with a preamble setting forth the code's general purpose and stating that the code's principles provided standards for the enforcement of ethical practices among social workers. The code included major sections concerning social workers' general conduct and comportment and ethical responsibilities to clients, colleagues, employers, employing organizations, the social work profession, and society. The code's principles were both prescriptive ("The social worker should act to prevent the unauthorized and unqualified practice of social work" [principle V.M.3]) and proscriptive ("The social worker should not exploit relationships with clients for personal advantage" [principle II.F.2]). Several of the code's principles were concrete and specific ("The social worker should under no circumstances engage in sexual activities with clients" and "The social worker should respect confidences shared by colleagues in the course of their professional relationships and transactions" [principle III.J.2]), whereas others were more abstract, asserting ethical ideals ("The social worker should promote the general welfare of society" [principle VI.P] and "The social worker should uphold and advance the values, ethics, knowledge, and mission of the profession" [principle V.M]).

The 1979 code was revised twice (NASW 1990, 1993), eventually including 70 principles. In 1990 several principles related to solicitation of clients and fee splitting were modified following an inquiry into NASW policies by the U.S. Federal Trade Commission (FTC), begun in 1986, concerning possible restraint of trade. As a result of the FTC inquiry, principles in the code were revised to remove prohibitions concerning solicitation of clients from colleagues of one's agency and to modify wording related to accepting compensation for making a referral. NASW also entered into a consent agreement with the FTC concerning issues raised by the inquiry.

In 1993 the NASW Delegate Assembly voted to further amend the code of ethics to include five new principles, three related to the problem of social worker impairment and two related to the challenge of dual and multiple relationships. The first three principles addressed instances when social workers' own problems and impairment interfere with their professional functioning, and the latter two addressed the need to avoid social, business, and other nonprofessional relationships with clients because of the possibility of conflicts of interest (NASW, 1993).

The 1993 Delegate Assembly also passed a resolution to establish a task force to draft an entirely new code of ethics for submission to the 1996 Delegate Assembly. The task force was established in an effort to develop a new code of ethics that would be far more comprehensive in scope and relevant to contemporary practice. Since the adoption of the 1979 code, social workers had developed a keener grasp of a wide range of ethical issues facing practitioners, many of which were not addressed in the NASW code. The broader field of professional ethics (also called practical ethics), which had emerged in the early 1970s, had matured considerably, resulting in the identification and greater understanding of novel and challenging ethical issues not addressed in the 1979 code. Especially during the 1980s, scholarly analyses of ethical issues in the professions generally, and social work in particular, burgeoned. (For discussion of this development and the factors that accounted for it, see the entry "Ethics and Values" elsewhere in this encyclopedia).

### The Current NASW Code of Ethics

The Code of Ethics Revision Committee was appointed in 1994 and spent two years drafting a new code. The committee, which was chaired by this author and included a professional ethicist and social workers from a variety of practice and educational settings, carried out its work in three phases. The committee first reviewed literature on social work ethics and professional ethics generally to identify key concepts and issues that might be addressed in the new code. The committee also reviewed the 1979 code to identify content that should be retained or deleted and areas where content might be added. The committee then discussed possible ways of organizing the new code to enhance its relevance and use in practice.

During the second phase, which overlapped with phase one activities, the committee issued formal invitations to all NASW members and to members of various social work organizations to suggest issues that might be addressed in the new code. The committee then reviewed its list of relevant content areas drawn from the literature and from public comment and developed a number of rough drafts, the last of which was shared with a small group of ethics experts in social work and other professions for their comments.

In the third phase, the committee made a number of revisions based on the feedback it received from the experts who reviewed the document, published a copy of the draft code in the January 1996 issue of the *NASW News*, and invited NASW members to submit comments to be considered by the committee as it prepared the final draft for submission to the 1996 Delegate Assembly. In addition, during this last phase, members of the committee met with each of the NASW Delegate Assembly regional coalitions to discuss the code's development and receive delegates' comments and feedback. The code was then presented to and ratified by the Delegate Assembly in August 1996 and implemented in January 1997.

Only one change has been made to the current code since its ratification. In 1999 a clause was deleted from one standard (1.07[c]) because of concern about possible misinterpretation and risk to clients. The problematic clause stated that social workers are obligated to disclose confidential information without clients' permission when laws or regulations require disclosure. Some social workers were concerned that this statement might require members of the profession to disclose the identity of, and sensitive information about, undocumented immigrants, contrary to social workers' commitment to clients.

In 2006, NASW sponsored a social work ethics summit, the principal purpose of which was to examine the status and relevance of the NASW code. Summit participants closely examined and discussed the strengths and limitations of the code and the ways in which it is used in the profession. Summit participants also considered whether revision of the code was warranted. Participants agreed unanimously that the current code serves the profession well and did not warrant revision.

The code, which contains the most comprehensive statement of ethical standards in social work, includes four major sections. (The complete text of the code is included in the Appendix.) The first section, "Preamble," summarizes social work's mission and core values. This is the first time in NASW's history that its code of ethics has contained a formally sanctioned mission statement and an explicit summary of the profession's core values. The mission statement emphasizes social work's historic and enduring commitment to enhancing human well-being and helping meet the basic needs of all people, with particular attention to the needs and empowerment of people who are vulnerable, oppressed, and living in poverty. The mission statement clearly reflects social work's unique concern about vulnerable populations and the profession's simultaneous focus on individual well-being and the environmental forces that create, contribute to, and address problems in living. The preamble also highlights social workers' determination to promote social justice and social change with and on behalf of clients.

The preamble also identifies six core values on which social work's mission is based: service, social justice, dignity and worth of the person, importance of human relationships, integrity, and competence. The Code of Ethics Revision Committee settled on these core values after systematically reviewing the literature on the subject.

The second section, "Purpose of the NASW Code of Ethics," provides an overview of the code's main functions and a brief guide for dealing with ethical issues or dilemmas in social work practice. This section alerts social workers to the code's various purposes:

- to set forth broad ethical principles that reflect the profession's core values and establish ethical standards to guide social work practice;
- to help social workers identify relevant considerations when professional obligations, conflicts, or ethical uncertainties arise;
- to familiarize practitioners new to the field to social work's mission, values, and ethical standards;
- to provide ethical standards to which the general public can hold the social work profession accountable, and
- to articulate standards that the profession itself (and other bodies that choose to adopt the code, such as licensing and regulatory boards, professional liability insurance providers, courts of law, agency boards of directors, and government agencies) can use to assess whether social workers have engaged in unethical conduct.

This section's brief guide for dealing with ethical issues highlights various resources social workers should consider when faced with difficult ethical decisions. Such resources include ethical theory and decision making, social work practice theory and research, laws, regulations, agency policies, and other relevant codes of ethics. Social workers are encouraged to obtain ethics consultation when appropriate, perhaps from an agency-based or social work organization's ethics committee, regulatory bodies (for example, a state licensing board), knowledgeable colleagues, supervisors, or legal counsel.

One of the key features of this section of the code is its explicit acknowledgement that instances sometimes arise in social work in which the code's values, principles, and standards conflict. The code does not provide a formula for resolving such conflicts and "does not specify which values, principles, and standards are most important and ought to outweigh others in instances when they conflict" (NASW, 1999, p. 3). The code states that "reasonable differences of opinion can and do exist among social workers with respect to the ways in which values, ethical principles, and ethical standards should be rank-ordered when they conflict. Ethical decision making in a given situation must apply the informed judgment of the individual social worker and should also consider how the issues would be judged in a peer review process where the ethical standards of the profession would be applied. . . . Social workers' decisions and actions should be consistent with the spirit as well as the letter of this Code" (NASW, 1999, p. 3).

The code's third section, "Ethical Principles," presents six broad ethical principles that inform social work practice, one for each of the six core values cited in the preamble. The principles are presented at a fairly high level of abstraction to provide a conceptual base for the profession's more specific ethical standards. The code also includes a brief annotation for each of the principles. For example, the ethical principle associated with the value "importance of human relationships" states that "social workers recognize the central importance of human relationships" (p. 6). The annotation states that "social workers understand that relationships between and among people are an important vehicle for change. Social workers engage people as partners in the helping process. Social workers seek to strengthen relationships among people in a purposeful effort to promote, restore, maintain, and enhance the well-being of individuals, families, social groups, organizations, and communities" (p. 6).

The code's final section, "Ethical Standards," includes 155 specific ethical standards to guide social workers' conduct and provide a basis for adjudication of ethics complaints filed against NASW members. The standards fall into six categories concerning social workers' ethical responsibilities to clients, to colleagues, in practice settings, as professionals, to the profession, and to society at large. The introduction to this section of the code states explicitly that some of the standards are enforceable guidelines for professional conduct and some are standards to which social workers should aspire. Furthermore, the code states, "the extent to which each standard is enforceable is a matter of professional judgment to be exercised by those responsible for reviewing alleged violations of ethical standards" (p. 7).

In general, the code's standards concern three kinds of issues (Reamer, 2003, 2006b). The first includes what

can be described as "mistakes" social workers might make that have ethical implications. Examples include leaving confidential documents displayed in public areas in such a way that they can be read by unauthorized persons or forgetting to include important details in a client's informed consent document. The second category includes issues associated with difficult ethical decisions—for example, whether to disclose confidential information to protect a third party from harm, barter with low-income clients who want to exchange goods for social work services, or terminate services to a noncompliant client. The final category includes issues pertaining to social worker misconduct, such as exploitation of clients, boundary violations, or fraudulent billing for services rendered.

### Ethical Responsibilities to Clients

The first section of the code's ethical standards is the most detailed. It addresses a wide range of issues involved in the delivery of services to individuals, families, couples, and small groups of clients. In particular, this section focuses on social workers' commitment to clients, clients' right to self-determination, informed consent, professional competence, cultural competence and social diversity, conflicts of interest, privacy and confidentiality, client access to records, sexual relationships and physical contact with clients, sexual harassment, the use of derogatory language, payment for services, clients who lack decision-making capacity, interruption of services, and termination of services.

1960 and 1979 codes, the current NASW Code of Ethics acknowledges that although social workers' primary responsibility is to clients, instances can arise when "social workers responsibility to the larger society or specific legal obligations may on limited occasions supersede the loyalty owed clients" (standard 1.01, p. 7). Examples include when a social worker is required by law to report that a client has abused a child or has threatened to harm self or others. In a similar vein, the code also acknowledges that clients' right to self-determination, which social workers ordinarily respect, may be limited when clients' actions or potential actions pose a serious, foreseeable, and imminent risk to themselves or others.

Standards on informed consent were added to the current code specifying the elements that should be included when social workers obtain consent from clients or potential clients for the delivery of services; the use of electronic media such as computers, telephone, radio, and television, to provide services; audio- or videotaping of clients; third-party observation of clients who are receiving services; and release of information.

Another section added to the current code pertains to the subject of cultural competence and social diversity. In recent years social workers have enhanced their understanding of the relevance of cultural and social diversity in their work with clients, in communities, and in organizations. The code requires that social workers take reasonable steps to understand and be sensitive to clients' cultures and social diversity with respect to race, ethnicity, national origin, color, sex, sexual orientation, age, marital status, political belief, religion, and mental or physical disability.

Unlike earlier versions of the code of ethics, the current code pays substantial attention to the topics of conflicts of interest and problematic dual or multiple relationships, for example, involving social workers' social relationships with former clients or when social workers provide services to two or more persons who have a relationship with each other.

The current code substantially expands the profession's standards on privacy and confidentiality. Noteworthy are details concerning social workers' obligation to disclose confidential information to protect third parties from serious harm; confidentiality guidelines when working with families, couples, or groups; disclosure of confidential information to third-party payers; discussion of confidential information in public and semipublic areas; disclosure of confidential information during legal proceedings (privileged information); protection of clients' written and electronic records; the use of case material in teaching and training; and protection of the confidentiality of deceased clients. The code requires social workers to discuss confidentiality policies and guidelines as soon as possible in the social worker–client relationship and as needed throughout the course of the relationship.

The current code has also expanded standards related to social workers' sexual relationships with current and former clients, clients' relatives, and other individuals with whom clients maintain a close, personal relationship. Also included is a standard concerning appropriate and inappropriate physical contact with clients.

An unprecedented section of the code focuses on social workers' use of barter—that is, accepting goods or services from clients as payment for professional service. After considerable discussion, the Code of Ethics Revision Committee decided to stop short of banning bartering outright, recognizing that in some communities bartering is a widely accepted form of payment. However, the code advises social workers to avoid bartering because of the potential for conflicts of interest, exploitation, and inappropriate boundaries in social workers' relationships with clients.

The code also includes extensive guidelines concerning social workers' termination of services to clients. The code focuses primarily on termination of services when clients no longer need services, when clients have not paid an overdue balance, and when social workers leave an employment setting.

## Ethical Responsibilities to Colleagues

This section of the code addresses issues concerning social workers' relationships with professional colleagues. These include respect for colleagues; proper treatment of confidential information shared by colleagues; interdisciplinary collaboration and disputes among colleagues; consultation with colleagues; referral for services; and sexual relationships with and sexual harassment of colleagues.

The current code particularly strengthens ethical standards pertaining to impaired, incompetent, and unethical colleagues. Social workers who have direct knowledge of a social work colleague's impairment (which may be caused by personal problems, psychosocial distress, substance abuse, or mental health difficulties, and which interferes with practice effectiveness), incompetence, or unethical conduct, are required to consult with that colleague when feasible; assist the colleague in taking remedial action; and if these measures do not address the problem satisfactorily, take action through appropriate channels established by employers, agencies, NASW, licensing bodies, and other professional organizations.

## Ethical Responsibilities in Practice Settings

This section of the code addresses a wide range of issues pertaining to social work supervision; consultation; education and training; performance evaluation; client records; billing for services; client transfer; agency administration; continuing education and staff development; commitments to employers; and labor-management disputes. Standards in this section state that social work supervisors, consultants, educators, and trainers should avoid engaging in any dual or multiple relationships when there is a risk of exploitation or potential harm. Another standard requires that social workers who function as educators or field instructors for students should take reasonable steps to ensure that clients are routinely informed when services are being provided by students.

Several standards pertain to client records. The current code enhances documentation standards to which social workers are held. In particular, the code requires that records include sufficient, accurate, and timely documentation to facilitate the delivery of services and ensure continuity of services provided to clients in the future. Documentation should avoid gratuitous detail and include only information that is directly relevant to the delivery of services. The code also spells out expectations concerning protection of clients' privacy, record storage and retention, and accurate billing for services.

The code urges social workers to be particularly careful when an individual who is receiving services from another agency or colleague contacts a social worker for services. Several standards are designed to protect clients from exploitation and to avoid conflicts of interest. The code requires social workers to discuss with potential clients the nature of their current relationship with other service providers and the implications, including possible benefits and risks, of entering into a relationship with a new service provider. If a new client has been served by another agency or colleague, social workers should discuss with the client whether consultation with the previous service provider is in the client's best interest.

The code greatly expands coverage of ethical standards related to agency administration. Key issues involve social work administrators' obligation to advocate for resources to meet clients' needs; provide adequate staff supervision; allocate resources fairly; ensure a working environment consistent with code standards; and arrange for appropriate continuing education and staff development.

The code also includes a number of ethical standards for social work employees, for example, related to unethical personnel practices and misappropriation of agency funds. Especially important are standards concerning social workers' obligation to address employing organizations' policies, procedures, regulation, or administrative orders that interfere with the ethical practice of social work.

A novel feature of the code is the acknowledgement of ethical issues social workers sometimes face as a result of labor–management disputes. Although the code does not prescribe how social workers should handle dilemmas related to going on strike, it does permit social workers to engage in organized labor-related actions to improve services to clients and working conditions.

### Ethical Responsibilities as Professionals

This section of the code focuses on issues primarily related to social workers' professional integrity. In addition to emphasizing social workers' obligation to be proficient, the code exhorts social workers to routinely review and critique the professional literature; participate in continuing education; and base their work on recognized knowledge, including empirically based knowledge, relevant to social work practice and ethics.

Several standards address social workers' values and personal conduct. The code states that social workers should not practice, condone, facilitate, or collaborate with any form of discrimination and should not permit their private conduct to interfere with their ability to fulfill their professional responsibilities. The code further obligates social workers to make clear distinctions between statements and actions engaged in as a private individual and those engaged in as a social worker.

A prominent theme in the code concerns social workers' obligation to be honest in their relationships with all parties, including accurately representing their professional qualifications, credentials, education, competence, and affiliations. Also, social workers are obligated to take responsibility and credit, including authorship credit, only for work they have actually performed and to which they have contributed. In addition, the code requires that social workers not engage in uninvited solicitation of potential clients who, because of their circumstances, are vulnerable to undue influence, manipulation, or coercion.

One of the most important standards in the code concerns social workers' personal impairment. The code mandates that social workers must not allow their personal problems, psychosocial distress, legal problems, substance abuse, or mental health difficulties to interfere with their professional judgment and performance or jeopardize others for whom they have a professional responsibility. In instances where social workers find that their personal difficulties interfere with their professional judgment and performance, they are obligated to seek professional help, make adjustments in their workload, terminate their practice, or take other steps necessary to protect clients and others.

### Ethical Responsibilities to the Profession

Social workers' ethical responsibilities are not limited to clients, colleagues, and the public at large; they also include the social work profession itself. Standards in this section of the code focus on the profession's integrity and social work evaluation and research. The principal theme concerning the profession's integrity pertains to social workers' obligation to maintain and promote high standards of practice by engaging in appropriate study and research, teaching, publication, presentations at professional conferences, consultation, service to the community and professional organizations, and legislative testimony.

The code also includes a substantial series of standards concerning evaluation and research. The standards emphasize social workers' obligation to monitor and evaluate policies, implementation of programs, and practice interventions. In addition, the code requires social workers to critically examine and keep current with emerging knowledge and to use evaluation and research evidence in their professional practice.

The code requires social workers involved in evaluation and research to follow widely accepted guidelines concerning the protection of evaluation and research participants. Standards focus specifically on the role of informed consent procedures in evaluation and research; the need to ensure that evaluation and research participants have access to appropriate supportive services; the confidentiality and anonymity of information obtained during the course of evaluation and research; the obligation to report results accurately; and the handling of potential or real conflicts of interest and dual relationships involving evaluation and research participants.

### Ethical Responsibilities to Society at Large

The social work profession has always been committed to social justice. This commitment is clearly reflected in the code's preamble and in the final section of the code's standards. The standards explicitly highlight social workers' obligation to engage in activities that promote social justice and the general welfare of society, including local, national, and international efforts. These activities may include facilitating public discussion of social policy issues; providing professional services in public emergencies; engaging in social and political action (for example, lobbying and legislative advocacy) to address basic human needs; promoting conditions that encourage respect for the diversity of cultures and socieeties; and acting to prevent and eliminate domination, exploitation, and discrimination against any person, group, or class of people.

### Conclusion

Ethical standards in social work, particularly as reflected in the *NASW Code of Ethics*, have changed dramatically during the profession's history. Along with all other professions, and largely as a result of the emergence of the professional ethics field beginning in the 1970s, social work's ethical standards have matured considerably. The current *NASW Code of Ethics* reflects social workers' increased understanding of ethical issues in the profession and the need for comprehensive ethical standards.

By themselves, ethical standards in social work cannot guarantee ethical behavior. Ethical standards can certainly guide practitioners who encounter ethical challenges and establish norms by which social workers' actions can be judged. However, in the final analysis, ethical standards in general, and codes of ethics in particular, are only one tool in social workers' ethical arsenal. In addition to specific ethical standards, social workers must draw on ethical theory, concepts, and decision-making guidelines; social work theory and practice principles; and relevant laws, regulations, and agency policies. Most of all, social workers must consider ethical standards within the context of their own values and ethics. As the *NASW Code of Ethics* states, ethical principles and standards "must be applied by individuals of good character who discern moral questions and, in good faith, seek to make reliable ethical judgments" (p. 4).

### REFERENCES

Bayles, M. (1986). Professional power and self-regulation. *Business and Professional Ethics Journal, 5*, 26–46.

Congress, E. (1999). *Social work values and ethics.* Belmont, CA: Wadsworth.

Greenwood, E. (1957). Attributes of a profession. *Social Work, 2*, 44–55.

Hall, R. H. (1968). Professionalization and bureaucratization. *American Sociological Review, 33*, 92–104.

Jamal, K., & Bowie, N. (1995). Theoretical considerations for a meaningful code of ethics. *Journal of Business Ethics, 14*, 703–714.

Johnson, A. (1955). Educating professional social workers for ethical practice. *Social Service Review, 29*, 125–136.

Kultgen, J. (1982). The ideological use of professional codes. *Business and Professional Ethics Journal, 1*, 53–69.

Lindeman, E. (1947). *Social work matures in a confused world.* Albany, NY: State Conference on Social Workers.

Loewenberg, F., Dolgoff, R., & Harrington, D. (2005). *Ethical decisions for social work practice* (7th ed.). Belmont, CA: Brooks/Cole.

McCann, C. W., & Cutler, J. P. (1979). Ethics and the alleged unethical. *Social Work, 24*, 5–8.

National Association of Social Workers. (1960). *NASW code of ethics.* Washington, DC: Author.

National Association of Social Workers. (1979). *NASW code of ethics.* Silver Spring, MD: Author.

National Association of Social Workers. (1990). *NASW code of ethics.* Washington, DC: Author.

National Association of Social Workers. (1993). *NASW code of ethics.* Washington, DC: Author.

National Association of Social Workers. (1996). *NASW code of ethics.* Washington, DC: Author.

National Association of Social Workers. (1999). *NASW code of ethics.* Washington, DC: Author.

Pumphrey, M. W. (1959). *The teaching of values and ethics in social work education.* New York: Council on Social Work Education.

Reamer, F. G. (2003). *Social work malpractice and liability: Strategies for prevention* (2nd ed.). New York: Columbia University Press.

Reamer, F. G. (2006a). *Ethical standards in social work: A review of the NASW code of ethics* (2nd ed.). Washington, DC: NASW Press.

Reamer, F. G. (2006b). *Social work values and ethics* (3rd ed.). New York: Columbia University Press.

—FREDERIC G. REAMER

# Appendix 2

## EVOLUTION OF SELECTED ORGANIZATIONS

| Pre–1900 | 1901–1910 | 1911–1920 | 1921–1930 | 1931–1940 | 1941–1950 |
|---|---|---|---|---|---|
| **CHILDREN** | | | | | |
| | | Child Welfare League of America (CWLA)–1920 | | | |
| National Federation of Day Nurseries–1898 | | | National Committee on Nursery Schools–1926 | National Assn of Day Nurseries–1938 | National Assn for Nursery Education–1946 |
| **FAMILIES** | | | | | |
| | | American Assn for Organizing Family Social Work–1911 | Family Welfare Assn of America–1930 | | Family Service Assn of America–1946 |
| **AGING** | | | | | |
| | | | | | Gerontological Society of America–1945 |
| | | | | | National Council on Aging–1950 |
| **SOCIAL WELFARE** | | | | | |
| Conference of Boards of Public Charities–1875–1879 | | National Conference of Charities and Correction–1882–1916 | | | |
| Conference of Charities–1875–1879 | | | | | |
| Conference of Charities and Correction–1880–1881 | | | | | |
| **PUBLIC WELFARE** | | | | | |
| | | | American Association of Public Welfare Officials (AAPWO)–1930 | AAPWO changed its name to the American Public Welfare Association (APWA)–1932 | |
| **SOCIAL WORK EDUCATION** | | | | | |
| | | Assn of Training Schools for Professional Social Work–1919 | International Permanent Secretariat of Social Workers–1928 | American Assn of Schools of Professional Social Work–1931 | National Assn of Schools of Social Administration–1942 |
| | | | International Committee of Schools of Social Work–1929 | | |
| | | | | American Assn of Schools of Social Work–1933 | National Council on Social Work Education–1946 |
| | | | | | |

| 1951–1960 | 1961–1970 | 1971–1980 | 1981–1990 | 1991–2000 | 2001–2007 |
|---|---|---|---|---|---|
| | | Florence Crittenton Assn of America merges with CWLA–1976 | | American Assn of Psychiatric Services for Children merges with CWLA–1997 | |
| | National Assn for the Education of Young Children–1964 | | | Alliance for Children and Families–1998 | |
| | | | Family Service America–1983 | Families International, Inc.–1993 | |
| American Society on Aging–1954 | | | | | |
| | | | | | |
| National Conference of Social Work–1917–1956 | | | | | |
| National Conference on Social Welfare–1957 | | | | | |
| | | | | | |
| | | | | APWA changed its name to American Public Human Services Association–1998 | |
| American Assn of Schools of Social Work & National Council on Social Work Education merged into Council on Social Work Education–1952 | | | Association for Gerontology Education in Social Work–1981 | St. Louis Group–1999 | |
| | | | Assn of Baccalaureate Social Work Program Directors–1982 | | |
| | | | Group for the Advancement of Doctoral Education–1982 | | |
| | | | National Assn of Deans and Directors of Schools of Social Work–1982 | | |

| Pre–1900 | 1901–1910 | 1911–1920 | 1921–1930 | 1931–1940 | 1941–1950 |
|---|---|---|---|---|---|
| **NASW PREDECESSORS** | | | | | |
| | | American Assn of Hospital Social Workers–1918 | | American Assn of Medical Social Workers–1934 | |
| | | National Social Workers' Exchange–1919 | American Assn of Social Workers–1921 | | |
| | | National Assn of Visiting Teachers–1919 | | | National Assn of School Social Workers–1945 |
| | | | American Assn of Psychiatric Social Workers–1926 | | |
| | | | | American Assn for the Study of Group Work–1936 | American Assn of Group Workers–1946 |
| | | | | | Assn for the Study of Community Organization–1946 |
| | | | | | Social Work Research Group–1949 |
| **SOCIAL WORK ORGANIZATIONS** | | | | | |
| | | | | | |
| | | | | | |
| | | | | | |
| | | | | | |
| | | | | | |
| | | | | | |
| **SOCIAL WORK REGULATION** | | | | | |
| | | | | | |
| **SOCIAL WORK RESEARCH** | | | | | |
| | | | | | |
| | | | | | |

| 1951–1960 | 1961–1970 | 1971–1980 | 1981–1990 | 1991–2000 | 2001–2007 |
|---|---|---|---|---|---|
| | | | | | |
| American Assn of Medical Social Workers merged into NASW–1955 | | | | | |
| American Assn of Social Workers merged into NASW–1955 | | | | | |
| National Assn of School Social Workers merged into NASW–1955 | | | | | |
| American Assn of Psychiatric Social Workers merged into NASW–1955 | | | | | |
| Assn of Group Workers merged into NASW–1955 | | | | | |
| Assn for the Study of Community Organization merged into NASW–1955 | | | | | |
| Social Work Research Group merged into NASW–1955 | | | | | |
| | | | | | |
| International Federation of Social Workers (IFSW)–1956 | National Assn of Black Social Workers–1968 | Clinical Social Work Assn (formerly Clinical Social Work Federation)–1973 | | | |
| | Society for Social Work Leaders in Healthcare–1966 | | | | |
| | | | Assn of Oncology Social Work–1984 | School Social Work Assn of America–1994 | |
| | | | National NETWORK for Social Work Managers–1985 | Latino Social Workers Organization–1997 | |
| | | | Assn for Community Organization and Social Administration–1987 | | |
| | | | American Board of Examiners in Clinical Social Work–1987 | | |
| | | | | | |
| | | Assn of Social Work Boards–1979 | | | |
| | | | | | |
| | | | | Institute for the Advancement of Social Work Research–1993 | |
| | | | | Society for Social Work and Research–1993 | |

# Appendix 3

## DISTINCTIVE DATES IN SOCIAL WELFARE HISTORY

### 17th Century

*1601.* The Elizabethan Poor Law is enacted by the English parliament, establishing three categories of people eligible for relief: (a) able-bodied poor people; (b) "impotent poor" people (that is, "unemployables"—aged, blind, and disabled people); and (c) dependent children. This law, on which colonial poor laws were based, became a fundamental concept in U.S. public welfare.

*1624.* Virginia colony passes the first legislation recognizing services and needs of disabled soldiers and sailors based on "special work" contributions to society.

*1642.* Plymouth colony enacts a poor law that directs relief cases be discussed at town meetings.

*1647.* The first colonial Poor Law enacted by Rhode Island emphasizes public responsibility for "relief of the poor, to maintain the impotent, and to employ the able, and shall appoint an overseer for the same purpose. Sec. 43 Eliz. 2."

*1657.* Scots' Charitable Society, the first American "friendly society," founded in Boston, represents the starts of voluntary societies to meet special welfare needs.

The first almshouse is established in Rensselaerswyck, New York, followed by one in Plymouth in 1658, and another in Boston in 1660.

*1662.* The Settlement Act (Law of Settlement and Removal) is passed by the English parliament to prevent movement of indigent groups from parish to parish in search of relief. The law makes residence a requirement for assistance, thus influencing American colonies.

*1692.* The Province of Massachusetts Bay Acts establish indenture contracting or "binding out" for poor children so they will live "under some orderly family government."

*1697.* The Workhouse Test Act is passed by the English parliament as a means of forcing unemployed people to work for relief; the act is copied by the colonies.

### 18th Century

*1703.* The New Plymouth Colony Acts establish systems of indenture and apprenticeships for children.

*1729.* The Ursuline Sisters of New Orleans establish a private home to care for mothers and children who are survivors of Indian massacres and a smallpox epidemic.

*1773.* The first public mental hospital, Williamsburg Asylum, is established in Williamsburg, Virginia. It is later renamed Eastern Hospital.

*1776.* The Declaration of Independence is adopted on July 4 by action of the Second Continental Congress.

*1777.* John Howard completes his study of English prison life and inhumane treatment of prisoners; his study influences reform efforts in the United States.

*1782.* The Gilbert Act is passed. Assistance in the home is established.

*1787.* The U.S. Constitution is completed in convention on September 17.

*1790.* The first state public orphanage is founded in Charleston, South Carolina.

*1791.* The Bill of Rights is ratified on December 15 by Virginia; 10 of the 12 proposed amendments became part of the U.S. Constitution.

*1795.* The Speemhamland system, establishing a "poverty line," is created to enable wage supplementation.

*1797.* Massachusetts enacts the first law regarding insane people as a special group of dependents.

*1798.* The United States Public Health Service is established following severe epidemics in Eastern Seaboard cities, which were caused by diseases brought into the country as a result of increased shipping and immigration.

### 19th Century

*1812.* The first American textbook on psychiatry, *Medical Inquiries and Observations upon the Diseases of the Mind,* by Dr. Benjamin Rush, is published.

*1813.* Connecticut enacts the first labor legislation to require mill owners to have children in factories taught reading, writing, and arithmetic.

*1817.* The first free U.S. school for the deaf—the Gallaudet School—is founded in Hartford, Connecticut.

*1818.* New York, Baltimore, and Philadelphia Societies for the Prevention of Pauperism are established to help victims of the depression following the War of 1812.

*1819.* The U.S. House of Representatives passes a bill that grants the Connecticut Asylum for the deaf and dumb six sections of public land.

*1822.* The first state institution for deaf people is established in Kentucky.

*1824.* The House of Refuge, the first state-funded institution for juvenile delinquents, is founded in New York.

The Bureau of Indian Affairs is organized in the War Department. It is later (1849) moved to the Department of the Interior.

*1829.* The New England Asylum for the Blind (later the Perkins Institution), the first such private institution, is founded.

*1834.* The Poor Law Reform Act, the first major poor law legislation in England since the Elizabethan Poor Law of 1601, influences American social welfare with its emphasis on complete assumption by able-bodied people of responsibility for their own economic security.

*1836.* The first restrictive child labor law is enacted in Massachusetts (at the time, two-fifths of all employees in New England factories were aged 7–16).

*1837.* The first state institution for blind people is established in Ohio.

*1841.* Dorothea Dix investigates the care provided to insane people. She ultimately is responsible for establishing 41 state hospitals and the federal St. Elizabeth's Hospital in Washington, DC.

*1843.* Robert Hartley and associates organize the New York Association for Improving the Condition of the Poor, which later merges with the Charity Organization Society of New York to form the present Community Service Society.

*1844.* Drapery clerk George Williams organizes the first Young Men's Christian Association (YMCA) in London.

*1846.* John Augustus, a shoemaker in Boston, gives up his work as a shoemaker to devote time to taking people on probation from the courts; from 1841 to 1858, Augustus took 1,152 men and 794 women on probation.

*1848.* Pennsylvania establishes the first minimum wage law in the United States.

*The Communist Manifesto,* published by Karl Marx and Friedrich Engels, influences worker demands in the United States for labor and social welfare reforms.

*1850.* The first school for "idiotic and feeble-minded" youths is incorporated in Massachusetts.

*1851.* The YMCA is founded in North America (Montreal). Traveler's Aid (now Traveler's Aid International) is founded by Bryan Mullanphy in St. Louis, Missouri.

*1853.* The Children's Aid Society of New York— the first child placement agency separate from an institutional program—is founded by the Reverend Charles Loring Brace.

*1854.* A bill that authorized grants of public land to establish hospitals for insane people and that was initiated by Dorothea Dix and passed unanimously by Congress is vetoed by President Franklin Pierce.

The rationale for the veto was that the general welfare clause in the U.S. Constitution reserves such care to the states, not to the federal government, an interpretation that establishes federal welfare policy until the Social Security Act of 1935.

The first day nursery in the United States opens in New York City.

*1855.* The first Young Men's Hebrew Association is organized in Baltimore.

The YMCA is organized in Boston by retired sea captain Thomas C. Sullivan.

*1859. The Origin of Species,* published by Charles Darwin, sets forth the theory of evolution, which provides a scientific approach to the understanding of plant and animal development.

*1861.* The United States Sanitary Commission, a forerunner of the American Red Cross, is established by the Secretary of War to encourage women's volunteer service during the Civil War.

*1862.* The Freedmen's Aid Societies are established in the North to send teachers and relief supplies to former slaves in the South.

The Port Royal Experiment, a precursor to the Freedmen's Bureau, is begun. It is a presidentially authorized but voluntarily funded relief and rehabilitation program to relieve the destitution of 10,000 slaves who have been abandoned on island plantations.

*1863.* The New York Catholic Protectory is established. It eventually becomes the largest single institution for children in the country.

The first State Board of Charities is established in Massachusetts to supervise the administration of state charitable, medical, and penal institutions.

*1865.* President Lincoln issues the Emancipation Proclamation.

The Freedmen's Bureau (Bureau of Refugees, Freedmen and Abandoned Lands) is founded as a joint effort of the federal government with private and philanthropic organizations. The bureau provides food, clothing, and shelter for freedmen and refugees; administers justice to protect the rights of Black men; protects freedmen and refugees from physical violence and fraud; and provides education.

Slavery is abolished by the 13th amendment, which is ratified on December 6.

*1866.* The first municipal Board of Health is created by the New York Metropolitan Health Law.

The Young Women's Christian Association (YWCA), which originated in England in 1855, is founded in Boston by Grace Dodge. The YWCA establishes the first boardinghouse for female students, teachers, and factory workers in 1860 and the first child care facility in 1864. It initiates a history of "firsts" for helping women.

*1867.* The state of Ohio authorizes county homes for children.

*1868.* The Massachusetts Board of State Charities begins payments for orphans to board in private family homes.

The 14th amendment is ratified on July 9; it provides that all people born or naturalized in the United States are U.S. citizens and have rights no state can abridge or deny.

*1869.* The first permanent state board of health and vital statistics is founded in Massachusetts.

The first Charity Organization Society (COS) is established in London.

*1870.* The Massachusetts Board of State Charities appoints the first "agent" to visit children in foster homes.

The National Prison Association is founded in Cincinnati; it is renamed American Prison Association in 1954 and is now called the American Correctional Association.

The Home for Aged and Infirm Hebrews of New York City opens; it is the first Jewish institutional home in the United States.

Ratification on February 3 of the 15th amendment to the U.S. Constitution establishes the right of citizens (except women) to vote, regardless of race, color, or previous servitude.

*1871. The Descent of Man,* published by Charles Darwin, applies the theory of evolution to the human species, thus breaking the authority of theologians in the life sciences and providing a basis for a scientific approach to humans and their social relationships.

*1872.* The American Public Health Association is founded (the Social Work Section is later formed in 1976).

*The Dangerous Classes of New York and Twenty Years' Work among Them,* by Charles Loring Brace, exposes the conditions of immigrants and children and helps initiate the adoption movement in the United States.

*1874.* Representatives of the State Boards of Charities of Massachusetts, Connecticut, New York, and Wisconsin organize the Conference of Boards of Public Charities within the American Social Science Association on May 20. Being an annual conference, it became the National Conference of Charities and Correction in 1879 in a takeover by the voluntary agencies. It was a precursor to the National Conference of Social Work, renamed in 1917. The organization became the National Council on Social Welfare in July 1956.

*1875.* New York State grants per capita subsidies to the New York Catholic Protectory for the care of children who would otherwise be public charges.

The New York Society for the Prevention of Cruelty to Children is incorporated.

*1876.* The New York State Reformatory at Elmira is founded; it is a model penal institution for children. Zebulon K. Brockway, a noted corrections reformer and founder of the National Prison Association, is appointed as the first warden.

The American Association for the Study of the Feeble-Minded is organized. (The name is changed to the American Association on Mental Deficiency in 1933 and to the American Association on Mental Retardation in 1987.)

*1877.* The first Charity Organization Society in the United States is founded in December in Buffalo by the Reverend S. Humphreys Gurteen. The society operates on four principles: (a) detailed investigation of applicants, (b) a central system of registration to avoid duplication, (c) cooperation between the various relief agencies, and (d) extensive use of the volunteers in the role of "friendly visitors."

The Society for Prevention of Cruelty to Children is established in New York.

*1879.* Franklin B. Sanborn, chair of the Massachusetts State Board of Charities, advocates use of foster homes for delinquent and dependent children.

The Conference of Boards of Public Charities is renamed the National Conference of Charities and Correction in the first session, independent of the American Social Science Association (1865).

*1880.* The Salvation Army is founded in the United States after William Booth established it in London in 1878.

*1881.* Clara Barton organizes the American Association of the Red Cross, which is renamed the American National Red Cross in 1893, and the American Red Cross in 1978.

Booker T. Washington founds the Tuskegee Normal and Industrial Institute, a leading Black educational institution that emphasizes industrial training as a means to self-respect and economic independence for African Americans.

*1883.* The Federal Civil Service Commission is established.

*1884.* Germany, under Bismarck, inaugurates accident, sickness, and old age insurance for workers, influencing future U.S. worker demands for social welfare measures.

Toynbee Hall, the first social settlement, is opened in East London by Samuel A. Barnett, vicar of St. Jude's Parish. It was visited by many Americans, and became a model for American settlement houses.

*1885.* The first course on social reform is initiated by Dr. Francis G. Peabody at Harvard University.

It is Philosophy II, described as "The Ethics of Social Reform: The Questions of Charity, Divorce, the Indians, Labor, Prisons, Temperance, Etc., as Problems of Practical Ethics-Lectures, Essays and Practical Observations."

1886. The first settlement house in the United States, the Neighborhood Guild (now the University Settlement), is founded on New York City's Lower East Side.

1887. The only 19th-century National Conference of Charities and Correction "Dealing with Indians and Negroes" is organized in 1887 and 1892 by Phillip C. Garrett, who states that the society had a special responsibility toward "the Indian because of being displaced and toward the Negro because of being here through no wish of their own."

The first attempt at cooperative financing is made in Denver.

1889. Hull-House, the most famous settlement house, is opened on September 14 by Jane Addams and Ellen Gates Starr on Chicago's West Side.

1890. *How the Other Half Lives*, by Jacob A. Riis, is published. A documentary and photographic account of housing conditions in New York City slums, it helps initiate the U.S. public housing movement.

1893. In September, Lillian Wald and Mary Brewster found the Nurses Settlement, a private non-sectarian home nursing service. In 1895, it moved to become the famous Henry Street Settlement.

1894. *American Charities*, by Amos G. Warner, is published. A social work classic, it is the first systematic attempt to describe the field of charities in the United States and to formulate the principles of relief.

1895. The first Federation of Jewish Charities is established in Boston.

1896. The first special class for "mentally deficient" people in an American public school is established in Providence, Rhode Island.

Volunteers of America is founded.

1897. The first state hospital for crippled children is founded in Minnesota.

1898. The first social work training school is established as an annual summer course for agency workers by the New York Charity Organization Society, which in 1904 becomes the New York School of Philanthropy (and later the Columbia University School of Social Work).

The National Federation of Day Nurseries is organized.

1899. The first U.S. juvenile court is established in June as part of the Circuit Court of Chicago.

Florence Kelley, who initiated fact-finding as a basic approach to social action, organizes the National Consumers League in New York City. The League is a combination of several local leagues, the earliest of which was formed in New York by Josephine Shaw Lowell to campaign against sweatshops and to obtain limits on hours of work for girls.

*Friendly Visiting among the Poor* by Mary E. Richmond, is published in January as "A Handbook of Charity Workers."

The National Conference of Jewish Charities is established in New York to coordinate the developing network of private Jewish social services.

The first juvenile court in America is established in Chicago.

## 20th Century

1902. Maryland enacts the first U.S. worker's compensation law, which is declared unconstitutional in 1904.

*Care of Destitute, Neglected and Delinquent Children*, by Homer Folks, founder of the New York State Charities Aid Association, is a major influence on service directions in child welfare.

Goodwill Industries of America is founded.

1903. The Chicago School of Civics and Philanthropy (now the University of Chicago School of Social Service Administration) is founded by Graham Taylor.

1904. The National Child Labor Committee, which is organized by a combination of New York and Chicago settlement groups, becomes primarily responsible for the 1909 White House Conference on Children.

The New York School of Philanthropy (now the Columbia University School of Social Work) is founded, with a one-year educational program.

The National Association for the Study and Prevention of Tuberculosis (later the National Tuberculosis Association and now the American Lung Association) is founded on March 28.

*Poverty*, the classic work by Robert Hunter, is published; it states that at least 10 million Americans, or one out of every eight, are poor.

A young New York City court clerk named Ernest Coulter recognized that caring adults could help many of the kids coming through his courtroom stay out of trouble, and he set out to find volunteers. That marked the beginning of the Big Brothers movement. By 1916, Big Brothers had spread to 96 cities across the country. At around the same time, the members of a group called Ladies of Charity were befriending girls who had come through the New York Children's Court. That group would later become Catholic Big Sisters. Both groups continued to work independently until 1977, when Big Brothers of America and Big Sisters International joined forces and became Big Brothers Big Sisters of America.

*1905*. Medical social work is initiated with the employment of Garnet I. Pelton by Richard L. Cabot, MD, at Massachusetts General Hospital in Boston.

Although not a government agency, the American Red Cross was chartered by Congress to "carry on a system of national and international relief in time of peace and apply the same in mitigating the sufferings caused by pestilence, famine, fire, floods, and other great national calamities, and to devise and carry on measures for preventing the same."

*1906*. The National Recreation Association is organized, later becoming the National Recreation and Park Association following a 1965 merger of the American Institute of Park Executives, American Recreation Society, National Conference on State Parks, and National Recreation Association.

Boys & Girls Clubs of America had its beginnings in 1860. In 1906 several Boys Clubs decided to affiliate and the Federated Boys Clubs in Boston was formed with 53 member organizations—this marked the start of a nationwide movement.

The first school social workers' programs are introduced in Boston, Hartford, and New York under private agencies.

*1907*. The Russell Sage Foundation is incorporated "to improve the social and living conditions in the U.S."; it later financed publication of the *Social Work Year Book* (now the *Encyclopedia of Social Work*, published by the NASW Press).

Psychiatric social work is initiated with the employment of Edith Burleigh and M. Antoinette Cannon by James J. Putnam, MD, to work with mental patients in the neurological clinic of Massachusetts General Hospital in Boston.

The National Probation Association is founded (renamed the National Probation and Parole Association in 1947, and the National Council on Crime and Delinquency in 1960).

*1908*. The first community welfare council is organized in Pittsburgh as the Pittsburgh Associated Charities.

*A Mind that Found Itself*, by Clifford Beers, is published. It is an exposé of the inadequacies of mental hospitals; it initiates the mental health movement.

The Federal Council of Churches of Christ in America begins to coordinate its network of social services.

Workers' compensation is enacted by the federal government; it represents the earliest form of social insurance in the United States.

*1909*. The National Committee for Mental Hygiene (now the National Mental Health Association) is founded by Clifford Beers.

Jane Addams is elected as the first woman president of the National Conference of Charities and Correction (later the National Council on Social Welfare).

England's Royal Poor Law Commission majority report seeks to modify the Poor Law as "the principle of 1834," defining the relationship of private, voluntary welfare organizations to the public assistance system. The minority recommends breaking up the Poor Law and transferring responsibility to divisions of local government, implying the creation of universal services and anticipating features of a 20th-century welfare state.

The Juvenile Psychopathic Institute is established in Chicago by Dr. William Healy, on the initiative of Julia Lathrop, to study offenders brought to the juvenile court. The institute initiates delinquency research and examination of children by a professional team.

Sigmund Freud delivers six lectures of "An Outline of Psychoanalysis" at Clark University, Worcester, Massachusetts.

The first White House Conference on Children (concerned with the care of dependent children) is initiated under the sponsorship of President Theodore Roosevelt on the suggestion of James E. West, who later heads the Boy Scouts of America.

The Pittsburgh Survey, the first exhaustive description and analysis of a substantial modem city, is begun.

The Niagara Movement stimulates the formation of the National Association for the Advancement of Colored People (NAACP) in May. The NAACP is a broad-based organization with interracial membership.

*1910*. The Boy Scouts of America is founded by William D. Boyce. It originally was started in England by Lord Baden-Powell.

The American Camping Association is founded to research, develop, and implement a program of inspection and accreditation of camps.

Camp Fire Girls (now Camp Fire USA) is founded.

Catholic Charities is founded.

The first social work training program for Black workers is started by Dr. George Edmund Haynes at Fisk University in Nashville. The National League on Urban Conditions Among Negroes (now the National Urban League) is organized by Dr. George E. Haynes and Eugene Kinckle Jones through a union of the Committee for Improving the Industrial Conditions of Negroes in New York (formed in 1907); the National League for the Protection of Colored Women (formed in 1906); and the Committee on Urban Conditions Among Negroes (formed in 1910).

*1911*. The First Mother's Aid Law is enacted in Illinois.

The first state workers' compensation law that was not later declared unconstitutional is enacted by the state of Washington.

The American Association for Organizing Family Social Work is formed to promote the development of family social work. (In 1930 the organization becomes the Family Welfare Association of America and in 1946 the Family Service Association of America. In 1983 the name is changed to Family Service America; in 1995 it is Families International, Inc.)

Social workers are placed on payrolls of New York's mental hospitals. Aftercare work soon becomes an integral part of the services of such institutions throughout the United States.

The National Federation of Settlements is founded (it became the National Federation of Settlements & Neighborhood Centers in 1959, and the United Neighborhood Centers of America in 1979).

The New York Psychoanalytic Society and Institute is founded.

*1912.* The Children's Bureau Act (ch. 73, 37 Stat. 79) is passed on April 9. It establishes the U.S. Children's Bureau as a separate government agency, based on an idea initiated by Florence Kelley and Lillian Wald, Julia C. Lathrop is appointed the first chief.

Girl Scouts of the United States of America is founded.

Survey Associates, Inc., a membership society combining research and journalism methods for the advancement of general welfare, is founded. Publications are used as "shuttles of understanding"; Paul Kellogg is editor. *Survey Midmonthly* spans the fields of social work, and *Survey Graphic*, which is addressed to lay readers, swings wider arcs of social and economic concern.

*1913. Social Insurance*, by I. M. Rubinow, advocates a comprehensive social insurance system to protect against sickness, old age, industrial accidents, invalidism, death, and unemployment.

The Modern Community Chest movement is begun with the organization of the Cleveland Federation for Charity and Philanthropy as an experiment in federated financing, after a first trial in Denver in 1888. The Community Chests and Councils of America is organized in 1918.

The U.S. Department of Labor and Department of Commerce, established in 1903, are separated into two departments on March 4.

The Anti-Defamation League (ADL) was launched in response to rampant anti-Semitism and discrimination against Jews. The mission of ADL is to expose and combat the purveyors of hatred in our midst, responding to whatever new challenges may arise.

*1914.* National Negro Health Week, the first health program for Blacks inaugurated by a Black, is begun by Booker T. Washington.

The Joint Distribution Committee for Relief of Jewish War Sufferers (now American Jewish Joint Distribution Committee) is founded.

*1915.* The Bureau for the Exchange of Information Among Child-Helping Organizations is founded.

Abraham Flexner in his address to the National Conference of Charities and Correction on "Is Social Work a Profession?" states social work does not qualify as a bona fide profession, consequently stimulating continual definition efforts by social workers.

*1916.* National health insurance is advocated by I. M. Rubinow, executive secretary of the American Medical Association Social Insurance Commission.

The American Birth Control League is founded (becoming the Planned Parenthood Federation of America in 1939).

The first birth control clinic is opened by Margaret Sanger in Brooklyn, New York.

Social worker Jeannette Rankin is the first woman elected to Congress (and cast the only vote opposed to our entering World War I).

The Child Labor Act (ch. 676, 520 Stat. 1060) is passed by Congress on June 25; the act forbids interstate commerce of goods manufactured by child labor and is declared unconstitutional by the Supreme Court in 1918.

*1917. Social Diagnosis*, by Mary Richmond, is published in May. It is the first textbook on social casework, marking the development of a body of social work knowledge and techniques.

The first state department of public welfare is established in Illinois.

The National Conference of Charities and Correction becomes the National Conference of Social Work.

The National Social Workers Exchange (becoming, in 1921, the American Association of Social Workers and merging with other organizations to form NASW in 1955) is organized as "the only social work organization with specific concern for matters of personnel [and] additional functions pertaining to professional standards."

The National Jewish Welfare Board is established (becoming the Jewish Welfare Board in 1977, and the Jewish Community Centers Association of North America in 1990).

*1918.* The American Association of Hospital Social Workers is organized (it becomes the American Association of Medical Social Workers in 1934, and merges with other organizations to form NASW in 1955).

The National Association of Jewish Center Workers is organized (in 1970 it becomes the Association of Jewish Center Workers, and in 1989, the Association of Jewish Center Professionals).

The first formal training program for psychiatric social workers is instituted at Smith College in Northampton, Massachusetts.

The Vocational Rehabilitation Act of 1918 (ch. 107, 40 Stat. 617) is passed on June 27. It establishes the first national program that provides physically handicapped veterans with occupational training and prostheses and, in 1920, is extended to provide rehabilitation in civilian life.

The Women's Bureau helps establish the U.S. Department of Labor.

The Community Chests and Councils of America is founded (in 1956 it becomes the United Community Funds and Councils of America and in 1970 the United Way).

*1919.* The National Association of Visiting Teachers is formed (it later becomes the National Association of School Social Workers, which subsequently merges with other organizations to form NASW in 1955).

The Association of Training Schools for Professional Social Work (a forerunner of the American Association of Schools of Social Work, now the Council on Social Work Education) is formed by leaders of 15 schools of social work. It is the first organization concerned exclusively with social work education and educational standards in Canada and the United States.

*1920.* The Chicago School of Civics and Philanthropy becomes the Graduate School of Social Service Administration, University of Chicago.

The Atlanta School of Social Service (now the Atlanta School of Social Work) opens in September, originating from Institutes of Social Service sponsored by the Neighborhood Union of Morehouse College from 1919 to 1920. Complete professionalization comes under the directorship of E. Franklin Frazier in 1922. The school is incorporated and chartered on March 22, 1924.

The National Conference of Catholic Charities is founded to coordinate a network of sectarian social services.

The right of women to vote is passed on August 18 as the 19th amendment.

The Child Welfare League of America (CWLA) is founded (in 1976 CWLA absorbs the Florence Crittenton Association).

The American Civil Liberties Union (ACLU) is founded and maintains the position that civil liberties must be respected, even in times of national emergency.

*1921.* The National Social Workers Exchange becomes the American Association of Social Workers (which later merges into NASW), the first national professional association of all social workers.

The Social Work Publicity Council is founded as the primary agency for interpreting social problems and social work. The Council served as a clearinghouse for ideas and materials on public relations and published *Channels* periodical and special bulletins.

The Maternity and Infancy Hygiene Act (Sheppard-Towner Act) (ch. 135, 42 Stat. 224), which provides for the first national maternal and child health program, is passed by Congress on November 23. The Commonwealth Fund establishes demonstration clinics for child guidance, initiating the child guidance clinic movement and establishing the essential role of social workers.

The Association of Junior Leagues of America is founded (it becomes the Association of Junior Leagues in 1971 and the Association of Junior Leagues International in 1990).

The Snyder Act of 1921 (P.L. 67-85), the principal legislation authorizing federal funds for health services to recognized Indian Tribes, is passed.

*1923.* The Jewish Welfare Society of Philadelphia establishes the first organized homemaker service.

The first course in group work in a school of social work is introduced at Western Reserve University in Cleveland, Ohio, by Clara Kaiser.

*Education and Training for Social Work* is published, detailing the first major study of social work education conducted by James H. Tufts, professor of philosophy at the University of Chicago.

*1924.* The Atlanta School of Social Work is incorporated on March 22 as the first Black school.

*1926.* The American Association of Psychiatric Social Workers, originally a section of the American Association of Hospital Social Workers, is organized. (It later merges into NASW.)

The Veteran's Administration establishes the social work program under the Veteran's Bureau.

The first union for social workers, the American Federation of Workers (AFW), is formed in New York.

*1927.* The first school of social work is professionally certified by the American Association of Schools of Social Work.

The American Association for Old Age Security is organized to further national interest in legislation for aged people; Abraham Epstein is appointed as the director.

*1928.* The Milford Conference on November 9 and 10 accepts a committee report defining generic social casework and promulgating the principle that process in social casework and the equipment of the social worker should be basically the same for all fields of practice, and that social work is one profession.

The International Conference of Social Work (ICSW) is formed during the first international conference of philanthropists, charity organizers, social workers, government officials, and others in Paris. The organization later became the International Council on Social Welfare.

*1929. The Social Work Year Book* (now the *Encyclopedia of Social Work*) is initiated under the auspices of the Russell Sage Foundation. (Publication is transferred to AASW in 1951, and to NASW in 1955.)

The International Association of Schools of Social Work (IASSW) is formed by 46 schools in 10 countries. The impetus for the new organization came from the 1928 international conference, in which participants called for social work education as a means of professionalizing social work and improving services. (ICSSW later became the IASSW.)

*1930.* The American Public Welfare Association is founded.

Grace Coyle published the first group work text entitled *Special Process in Organized Groups.*

*1931.* The Nobel Peace Prize is awarded to renowned social worker Jane Addams.

The Temporary Emergency Relief Administration is established in New York State by Governor Franklin Delano Roosevelt as a prototype of federal public relief to unemployed people. Social worker Harry Hopkins is named Director.

The Boys Club Federation of America becomes Boys Clubs of America.

*1932.* President Herbert Hoover signs the Emergency Relief and Construction Act (ch. 520, 47 Stat. 709) into law on July 21; a provision of the act enables the Reconstruction Finance Corporation to lend money to states for relief purposes, moving federal government into the field of public relief.

Formal accreditation is initiated by the American Association of Schools of Social Work with development of a minimum curriculum requiring at least one academic year of professional education encompassing both classroom and field instruction.

The Council of Jewish Federations and Welfare Funds is founded (in 1978 it becomes the Council of Jewish Federations).

*1933.* The Civilian Conservation Corps Act (ch. 17, 48 Stat. 22) is passed by Congress on March 31. The act is established to meet part of the need caused by the Great Depression by providing work and education programs for unemployed and unmarried young men aged 17–23.

The Federal Emergency Relief Act (ch. 30, 48 Stat. 55) is passed on May 12. It creates the Federal Emergency Relief Administration (FERA), which provides 25% matching and direct grants to states for public distribution for relief. Social worker Harry Hopkins becomes the director on May 22. (On April 8, 1935, the Federal Emergency Relief Administration is superseded by the Works Progress Administration, which is phased out in 1943.)

European psychoanalysts begin to flee the Nazi regime for the United States and influence the child guidance movement.

*1934.* The first licensing law for social workers is passed in Puerto Rico and is a precursor to later state laws.

The National Housing Act (ch. 847, 48 Stat. 1246) is enacted by Congress on June 27. It is the first law in U.S. history designed to promote housing construction.

The National Foundation for Infantile Paralysis is initiated by President Franklin D. Roosevelt to raise funds for a Warm Springs Foundation, Georgia, treatment center. It becomes the successful Annual March of Dimes under Basil O'Connor.

*Social Work Today*, progressive publication of 1930s depression period, is begun by Social Work Today, Inc. This individual and organizational membership group also published professional pamphlets and conducted educational activities; it was discontinued in 1942.

*1935.* The Health, Education and Welfare Act (Social Security Act; ch. 531, 49 Stat. 620) is passed by Congress on August 14, providing old age assistance benefits, a Social Security Board, grants to states for unemployment compensation administration, aid to dependent children, maternal and child welfare, public health work, and aid to blind people. Social worker Jane M. Hoey is appointed as the first director of the Federal Bureau of Public Assistance, which administers federal-state aid to aged people, blind people, and dependent children under the provisions of the act.

The National Conference on Social Work, in its reorganization, recognizes group work as a major function of social work along with social casework, community organization, and social action.

The Works Progress Administration is created by presidential executive order on May 6—and the Federal Emergency Relief Administration is terminated—to shift the federal government from home relief to work relief. The administration is committed to provide work "for able-bodied but destitute workers."

The National Youth Administration is created by presidential executive order on June 26 as a division of the Works Progress Administration to provide work and school aid under direction of social worker Aubrey Williams.

The National Labor Relations Act, also known as the Wagner Act, is signed into law by Franklin D. Roosevelt, on July 5. It establishes the National Labor Relations Board and addresses relations between unions and employers in the private sector.

*1936.* The American Association for the Study of Group Work is organized (in 1946 it becomes the American Association of Group Workers, and merges into NASW in 1955).

*1937.* A state-administered program in North Carolina pioneers the development of family planning as part of maternal and child health services.

The Housing Act (ch. 896, 50 Stat. 885) is passed by Congress on September 1 to provide subsidies and credit to states and local governments. It is the first attempt to finance residential accommodations for tenants not exclusively federal employees.

*1938.* The Works Progress Administration Act (ch. 554, 52 Stat. 809) is passed by Congress on June 21.

The National Association of Day Nurseries, formerly the National Federation of Day Nurseries founded in 1898, is established. (The organization becomes the National Association for the Education of Young Children in 1964.)

Fair Labor Standards Act (sections 201–219 of title 29) originally enacted in 1938 and amended periodically is administered by the U.S. Department of Labor. It sets minimum wages, payment of time-and-a-half for work beyond 40 h in a week, provisions of equal pay for equal work, and child labor standards.

*1939.* A food stamp plan to dispose of agricultural commodities is begun in Rochester, New York.

*1941.* The United Service Organization is incorporated in February to coordinate services provided to armed forces and defense workers by six voluntary agencies: (a) National Jewish Welfare Board, (b) National Catholic Community Service, (c) National Traveler's Aid Association, (d) Salvation Army, (e) YMCA, and (f) YWCA.

*1942.* The first U.S. responsibility to provide day care for children of working mothers is initiated through the Lanham Act (ch. 260, 55 Stat. 361), providing 50% matching grants to local communities for use in operation of day care centers and family day care homes.

The United Seaman's Service is established in the National Maritime Union in September to provide medical, social work, and other services to merchant seamen; Bertha C. Reynolds is named the director.

The National Association of Schools of Social Administration (now the Council on Social Work Education) is formed by 34 land grant college undergraduate social work programs.

The Congress of Racial Equality (CORE) is established.

*1943.* The United Nations Relief and Rehabilitation Administration is established by 44 nations for post–war relief and refugee settlement.

The American Council of Voluntary Agencies for Foreign Service is established "to promote joint program planning and coordination of national voluntary agency activities on foreign relief and rehabilitation."

*1944.* The Servicemen's Readjustment Act (ch. 268, 58 Stat. 284), the "G.I. Bill of Rights," provides education and training through state-administered payments to educational units; subsistence allowance; loans for purchase or construction of homes, farms, or business property; job counseling and employment placement; and 52 weeks of adjustment allowances. It is liberalized by Amendment 12/21A5 (ch. 588, P.L. 268) and initiated many men into the social work profession.

*1945.* The National Social Welfare Assembly, formerly the National Social Work Council formed in 1923, is organized (it is now the National Assembly of National Voluntary Health and Social Welfare Organizations).

The United Nations is chartered in April, including the Economic and Social Council, to provide "international machinery for the promotion and social advancement of all peoples" and coordinate agencies dealing with social welfare problems, such as the World Health Organization, United Nations International Children's Emergency Fund, International Labor Office, and International Refugee Organization.

*Common Human Needs*, by Charlotte Towle and published by the Federal Security Agency, reaffirms the principle of public assistance services as a right and the need for public assistance staffs to understand psychological needs and forces and their relationship to social forces and experiences. (Banned by the federal government in 1951, it is then distributed by the American Association of Social Workers.)

The Girls Clubs of America is founded. (The organization becomes Girls, Inc., in 1990.)

*1946.* The Hospital Survey and Construction Act (ch. 958, 60 Stat. 1040), or Hill-Burton Act (P.L. 79-725), is passed by Congress, initiating massive construction and expansion of inpatient hospital facilities with significant standards requirements for community participation.

Pioneer House, a group home for troubled adolescents, opens in Detroit.

The National Mental Health Act (ch. 538, 60 Stat. 421), passed on July 3, recognizes mental illness as a national public health problem.

The Association for the Study of Community Organization is formed (it merges into NASW in 1955).

The Full Employment Act (ch. 33, 60 Stat. 23) is passed by Congress on February 20. It establishes a policy of federal responsibility for employment.

Big Brothers of America is founded (in 1977 it merges with Big Sisters to form Big Brothers/Big Sisters of America).

Military social work begins under the Office of the Surgeon General of the United States Army, as MSWs now become commissioned officers, and a new field of practice is born.

*1948.* The American Association of Social Workers and School of Applied Social Sciences of Western Reserve University (now Case Western Reserve University) sponsors a conference that helps define the identity and function of research in social work as distinguished from social research.

*1949.* The Social Work Research Group is organized (it merges into NASW in 1955).

*1950. Social Workers in 1950,* published by the Bureau of Labor Statistics, is the first survey of 75,000 social workers, with 50,000 replies.

The Social Security Act Amendments (ch. 809, 64 Stat. 477) are passed on August 28. The amendments establish a program of aid to permanently and totally disabled people and broaden Aid to Dependent Children (later Aid to Families with Dependent Children) to include relatives with whom a child is living. The amendments extend Old-Age and Survivors' Insurance and liberalize other programs.

The National Council on Aging is founded.

The Mattachine Society and ONE, Inc., are founded as the first gay rights organizations.

*1951. Social Work Education in the United States,* by Ernest V. Hollis and Alice L. Taylor, is published. Generally known as the Hollis-Taylor Report, it is a comprehensive study of social work education "in relation to the responsibility of social work in the broad field of social welfare."

The American Association of Social Workers reissues *Common Human Needs* after the federal government burns its stock in response to pressure from the American Medical Association.

The American Association of Social Workers publishes the 11th edition of the *Social Work Year Book,* following 10 editions published by the Russell Sage Foundation.

*1952.* The U.S. Children's Bureau grants funds for special projects to develop and coordinate statewide programs for medical and social services to unwed mothers.

The Council on Social Work Education is created from temporary study and a coordinating body, the National Council on Social Work Education (in 1946), to unite the school accrediting responsibility of the National Association of Schools of Social Administration and the American Association of Schools of Social Work. The Council includes board representatives of schools, faculty, agencies, and the public for educational policy and decisions.

The U.S. Committee of the International Conference on Social Welfare is formed.

*1953.* The U.S. Department of Health, Education and Welfare is established on April 11.

*1954.* Rutland Corner House in Brookline, Massachusetts, is established as the first urban transitional residence (halfway house) for mental patients.

*Brown v. Board of Education of Topeka,* Shawnee County, Kansas, (347 U.S. 483) eliminates the "separate but equal" doctrine in educational facilities.

*1955.* NASW commences operation on October 1 through a merger of five professional membership associations: (a) American Association of Group Workers, (b) American Association of Medical Social Workers, (c) American Association of Psychiatric Social Workers, (d) American Association of Social Workers, and (e) National Association of School Social Workers and two study groups (i) Association for the Study of Community Organization and (ii) Social Work Research Group.

The National Association of Puerto Rican Hispanic Social Workers is organized.

Daughters of Bilitis, the first major lesbian organization, is founded.

*1956.* The International Federation of Social Workers (IFSW) is established.

*1957.* The Civil Rights Act (P.L. 85-315, 71 Stat. 634) is passed by Congress on September 9. It is the first such act since 1875; it establishes the Commission on Civil Rights and strengthens federal enforcement powers.

NASW publishes the 13th edition of the *Social Work Year Book.*

*1958. A Working Definition of Social Work Practice,* developed by the National Commission on Practice headed by Harriett Bartlett, is published by NASW. It establishes the basic constellation of elements of social work practice: values, purpose, sanction, knowledge, and method.

The American Association of Retired Persons (AARP) is founded by Ethel Percy Andrus, a retired high school principal. AARP evolved from Dr. Andrus's establishment of the National Retired Teachers Association in 1947 to promote her philosophy of productive aging, and in response to the need of retired teachers for health insurance. The organization officially changes its name in 1999.

*1959. The Social Work Curriculum Study,* by Werner W. Boehm, director and coordinator, is published by the Council on Social Work Education. The 13-volume study is a "milestone in the development of effective educational programs for professions."

*1960.* The National Committee for Day Care is established to promote day care as an essential part of child welfare services and to develop standards of care.

Newburgh, New York, legislates 13 restrictive work requirements for welfare recipients, precipitating a nationwide retrogression in public welfare.

*1961.* The Juvenile Delinquency and Youth Offenses Control Act (P.L. 87-274, 75 Stat. 572), which recognizes economic and social factors leading to crime, is passed by Congress. The act authorizes grant funds for demonstration projects for comprehensive delinquency programs in ghettos.

The Academy of Certified Social Workers is incorporated by NASW to promote standards for professional social work practice and the protection of social welfare clients. It requires a master of social work degree and two years of supervised practice by an Academy of Certified Social Workers member.

*1962. The Other America,* by Michael Harrington, is published, awakening the United States to the problem of poverty.

The Manpower Development and Training Act (P.L. 87-415) is passed by Congress to provide government financing of training to move unemployed and displaced workers into new fields.

CSWE recognizes C.O. as a legitimate professional specialization.

*1963.* The Mental Retardation Facilities and Community Mental Health Centers Construction Act (P.L. 88-164) is passed on October 31, authorizing appropriations to states that started significant development of community health and retardation services with single state agency administration and advisory committees with consumer representation.

The Civil Rights March on Washington is held at the peak of the civil rights coalition movement.

*1964.* The Civil Rights Act (P.L. 88-352) is passed by Congress on July 2, and results in significant changes for racial and ethnic groups in institutional health care programs and procedures to ensure equal treatment, in policies to eliminate discrimination in employment and pre-employment, and in policies to open entry opportunities in particular occupations.

The Food Stamp Act (P.L. 88-525) is passed on August 31 to provide cooperative federal-state food assistance programs for improved levels of nutrition in low-income households.

The Economic Opportunity Act (P.L. 88-452) is passed by Congress on August 20, establishing the Office of Economic Opportunity and calling for the creation of Volunteers in Service to America, Job Corps, Upward Bound, Neighborhood Youth Corps, Operation Head Start, and Community Action programs.

*1965.* The Elementary and Secondary Education Act (P.L. 89-10) is passed on April 11, initiating the first major infusion of federal funds into the U.S. educational system. The Act provides aid to economically disadvantaged children, counseling and guidance services, community education, and planning.

The Older Americans Act (P.L. 89-73) is passed by Congress on July 14, creating the Administration on Aging, the first central body within the federal government dealing with aging.

The Social Security Amendments ("Medicare Act;" P.L. 89-97) are enacted on July 30 as Title XVIII of the Security Act. The amendments provide federal health insurance benefits for the aged (above 65 years) and entitled people to benefits under Title II. The amendments establish a compulsory hospital-based program for aged people; a voluntary supplemental plan to provide physicians and other health services; and an expanded medical assistance program (Medicaid) for needy and medically needy aged, blind, and disabled people and their families.

Medicaid, enacted on July 30 as Title XIX of the Social Security Act, provides federal grants to match state programs of hospital and medical services for welfare recipients and medically indigent populations.

*Abstracts for Social Workers* is initiated by NASW under contract with the National Institute for Mental Health. (The journal is subsequently titled *Social Work Research & Abstracts* when a primary research journal is added in 1977 and retitled *Social Work Abstracts* when the two journals are separated in 1994.)

Heart Disease, Cancer and Stroke Amendments (P.L. 89-239), or Regional Medical Programs, provide grants for planning to establish regular cooperative arrangements among medical schools, research institutions, and hospitals to meet local health needs. The amendments require broadly representative advisory committees and involve key social worker leadership.

The Academy of Certified Social Workers is promoted by NASW as a national standard-setting body for social work practice.

*Closing the Gap in Social Work Manpower* is published by the U.S. Department of Health, Education, and Welfare, in November; it projects escalating demands for social workers and delineates the master of social work and bachelor of social work classifications. It also plays an exceptional role in focusing labor force problems and advocating for the bachelor of social work as an entry professional classification.

*Griswold v. State of Connecticut* (381 U.S. 479) holds against state fine of Planned Parenthood for providing contraceptive information to married people. It initiates a constitutional concept of privacy formulated by Thomas I. Emerson, which later leads to the *Roe v. Wade* decision in 1973.

NASW publishes the 15th edition of the *Encyclopedia of Social Work*, as a follow-on to the 14 editions of the *Social Work Year Book*.

*1966*. The Narcotic Addict Rehabilitation Act (P.L. 89-793), passed by Congress on November 8, emphasizes total treatment and aftercare rather than criminal prosecution and fragmented efforts, providing pretrial civil commitment in the custody of the Surgeon General for treatment.

The Comprehensive Health Planning and Public Health Services Amendments of 1966 (P.L. 89-749), passed by Congress on November 3, authorizes grants to support comprehensive state planning for health services, labor, and facilities. The Veteran's Readjustment Benefits Act (P.L. 89-358) enhances service in the armed forces, extending higher education and providing vocational readjustment. It also emphasizes programs requiring veterans to make contributions to their own educational programs.

The Society for Hospital Social Work Directors is formed under the auspices of the American Hospital Association (in 1993 the society changes its name to the Society for Social Work Administrators in Health Care to reflect changes in health care).

*1967*. In May, the U.S. Supreme Court in the *In re Gault* decision rules that timely notice of all charges against a juvenile must be given and that a child has the right to be represented by legal counsel, to confront and cross-examine complainants, and to be protected against self-incrimination in juvenile delinquency proceedings.

The Child Health Act (P.L. 90-248), passed by Congress on January 2, adds three new types of medical care project grants (a) infant care, (b) family planning, and (c) dental care to social security.

Age Discrimination in Employment Act is passed.

*1968*. The National Association of Black Social Workers, the National Association of Puerto Rican Social Service Workers, and the Asian American Social Workers are established.

The Southwest Council of La Raza is organized (in 1973 it becomes the National Council of La Raza, a major national coalition).

The Center for Law and Social Policy (CLASP) was founded as a public interest law firm by Charles Halpern and three other young lawyers, with the assistance of Justice Arthur Goldberg. For 14 years, CLASP helped develop new areas of legal work on women's rights, mental health, environmental protection, international human rights, health care for the poor, international trade, employment rights, and mine health and safety. Several prominent organizations, including the National Women's Law Center and the Bazelon Center on Mental Health Law, began their work as part of CLASP.

Juvenile Delinquency Prevention and Control Act (JDPCA) is enacted. This act assigned to HEW responsibility for developing a national approach to the problem of Juvenile Delinquency. States were to prepare and implement comprehensive juvenile delinquency plans and, upon approval, receive federal funds to carry out prevention, rehabilitation, training, and research programs. (The Juvenile Justice and Delinquency Prevention Act (JJDPA) of 1974 replaced JDPCA and provides the major source of federal funding to improve states' juvenile justice systems.)

*1969*. Richard M. Nixon proposes the Family Assistance Plan in a historic message to Congress. He asserts the welfare system has failed and recommends a federal welfare system with a virtually guaranteed annual income. The House, but not the Senate, passes the plan, which is subsequently reintroduced in 1971. After two years of negotiation with welfare groups, the plan is withdrawn.

The bachelor of social work degree is recognized for NASW membership as a result of a national membership referendum and is implemented in 1970.

The Social Worker's Professional Liability Insurance program is started by the NASW; it is transferred to the NASW Insurance Trust in 1985.

The Association of American Indian Social Workers is founded (in 1981 it becomes the Association of Indian and Alaskan Native Social Workers, and in 1984, the National Indian Social Workers Association).

*1970*. Racketeer Influences and Corrupt Organizations Act ("RICO;" P.L. 91-452) is passed to combat organized crime and illegal conspiracies. RICO gives law enforcement authorities greater leeway in investigating and prosecuting crimes. The act permits more leniency in obtaining wiretaps, protecting witnesses, granting immunity, and plea bargaining.

Occupational Safety and Health Act (OSHA) is passed.

*1971*. The ACTION agency is formed through President Nixon's reorganization plan, centralizing direction of volunteer agencies, including Volunteers in Service to America, Peace Corps, and others, and beginning a pattern of reductions.

Congress passes the Comprehensive Child Development Act to provide comprehensive high quality day care and support services to all children. President Nixon vetoes the act.

The Educational Legislative Action Network (ELAN) is initiated by NASW as a national congressional district legislative structure; ELAN commits the social work profession to legislative advocacy as a professional responsibility.

NASW initiates the objective examination, the first national testing of social work knowledge and practice, for the Academy of Certified Social Workers.

The National Federation of Clinical Social Workers is established (in 2006 it becomes the Clinical Social Work Association).

*1972.* Community-based work and education programs for juvenile delinquents are established by the Massachusetts Youth Services Department to replace juvenile reformatories.

Supplemental Security Income (P.L. 92-603) establishes a separate program administration for aged, blind, and disabled populations in the Social Security Amendments of 1972 (P.L. 92-603), which are passed on October 30 and become effective on January 1, 1974.

The State and Local Fiscal Act (P.L. 92-512), "Revenue Sharing," becomes a landmark in the federal-state-local relationship, providing states and localities with specified portions of federal individual income tax collections to be used for nine specific priority expenditures.

The Equal Employment Opportunity Act (P.L. 92-261) is passed to grant the Equal Employment Opportunity Commission authority to issue judicially enforceable cease-and-desist orders. The act establishes a quasi-judicial agency to implement national policy of employment opportunity without discrimination of race, color, religion, national origin, or gender.

The landmark legal principle of "right to treatment" is established in *Wyatt v. Stickney* (344 F Supp. 387, M.D. Ala., N.D. 1972) by Frank M. Johnson, Jr., chief judge of the U.S. Middle District Court in Montgomery, Alabama. The ruling sets forth minimal constitutional standards of care, treatment, and habilitation for patients involuntarily confined to public mental hospitals in Alabama.

The National Institute on Drug Abuse is established on March 21 by the Drug Abuse Office and Treatment Act (P.L. 92-255) to provide leadership, policies, and goals for the total federal effort to prevent, control, and treat narcotic addiction and drug abuse.

Professional Standards Review Organizations are initiated on October 30 as part of the Social Security Amendments. This national program of local and state organizations establishes service standards and reviews quality and costs of health services provided to beneficiaries of Medicare, Medicaid, and maternal and child health programs. Through NASW intervention, the program includes social workers in all phases.

*1973.* The Health Maintenance Organization Act ("HMO Act;" P.L. 93-222) is enacted on December 29, and solidifies the term *HMO* and gives HMOs greater access to the employer-based market, providing for the rapid expansion of HMOs in later years.

Through NASW intervention, the act includes social services components and standards.

*Roe v. Wade* (410 U.S. 179) determines that a Texas statute prohibiting abortion violates the due process clause of the 14th amendment. The decision establishes that trimester stages of pregnancy determine state's limits on regulation of abortions. It also affirms the right of privacy.

The Children's Defense Fund is founded by Marian Wright Edelman to "provide long-range advocacy on behalf of nation's children."

*1974.* The Council on Social Work Education offers accreditation to bachelor of social work programs.

The Child Abuse Prevention and Treatment Act (P.L. 93-247), passed by Congress on January 31, initiates financial assistance for demonstration programs for prevention, identification, and treatment of child abuse and neglect and establishes the National Center on Child Abuse and Neglect.

The Comprehensive Employment and Training Act (CETA; P.L. 92-603) initiates extensive job education and experience opportunities for unemployed people.

Employee Retirement Income Security Act (ERISA) sets minimum standards for pension plans in private industry.

Equal Credit Opportunity Act (P.L. 93-495) requires retail firms and lending institutions to use the same criteria for everyone in deciding whether to grant credit regardless of gender, marital status, or racial or ethnic group.

*1975.* The National Health Planning and Resources Development Act of 1974 (P.L. 93-641) is enacted on January 4, combining regional medical programs, comprehensive health planning, and Hill-Burton programs to establish an integrated system of national, state, and area planning agencies with consumer majorities on policy bodies.

The Social Service Amendments of 1974 (P.L. 93-647), Title XX of the Social Security Act, are enacted on January 3, initiating comprehensive social services programs directed toward achieving economic self-support and preventing dependence. Five levels of services, meeting federal standards, are implemented by states with 75% federal subsidy. The amendments were initiated and planned as a result of NASW opposition and coalition-building against the Nixon administration's attempt to misuse regulations to reduce social services expenditures.

The Education for All Handicapped Children Act (P.L. 94-142), enacted on November 29, extends national public education policy to mandate free public education for all handicapped people. The provision for social work services in the public schools by 1978 is included through NASW intervention.

The Indian Self-Determination and Education Assistance Act (P.L. 93-638) removed most of the direct social services and educational functions from the Bureau of Indian Affairs (BIA) and permitted certain Native American organizations, commonly known as 638s, to provide such services or contract with the Federal government. This legislation was extended in 1988.

*1976.* The Political Action for Candidate Election is initiated as a political action committee of NASW, committing the social work profession to political action as a professional responsibility.

In a class action suit, Judge Frank M. Johnson, Jr., of the U.S. Middle District Court in Montgomery Alabama, rules on January 13 that conditions of confinement is the Alabama penal system constitute cruel and unusual punishment where they bear no reasonable relationship to legitimate institutional goals.

The Health Professional Educational Assistance Act (P.L. 94-484), enacted on October 12, applies to all health professions and authorizes funding to train social workers in health care, including administration, policy analysis, and social work. This is the first mention of schools of social work in national health legislation.

The *International Code of Ethics for Professional Social Workers*, written by Chauncey A. Alexander, is adopted at the Puerto Rico Assembly by the International Federation of Social Workers, which consists of 52 national professional social worker organizations.

NASW endorses Carter and Mondale, the Democratic Party candidates for president and vice president, initiating the NASW Political Action for Candidate Election program to raise funds for political action, the first such political effort for a professional social work organization.

The Rural Social Work Caucus is initiated to aid rural social workers.

*Health & Social Work*, the first health specialty journal, is published by NASW.

Indian Health Care Improvement Act of 1976 (P.L. 94-437) is enacted to implement the federal responsibility for the care and education of the Indian people by improving the services and facilities of federal Indian health programs and encouraging maximum participation of Indians in such programs.

*1977.* NASWs journal *Abstracts for Social Workers* is expanded to *Social Work Research & Abstracts*.

In 1977, the Health Care Financing Administration (HCFA) is established under the Department of Health, Education, and Welfare for the coordination of Medicare and Medicaid. The responsibility for enrolling beneficiaries into Medicare and processing premium payments remained with Social Security Administration.

The Group for the Advancement of Doctoral Education in Social Work is formed.

*1978.* The Child Abuse Prevention and Treatment and Adoption Reform Act (P.L. 95-266) is passed on April 24, extending the 1974 act and initiating new programs to encourage and improve adoptions.

The Full Employment and Balanced Growth Act (P.L. 95-523) is passed on October 27 by Congress through the tenacity of Congressman Augustus Hawkins (D-CA). The act reaffirms the right of all Americans to employment and asserts the federal government responsibility to promote full employment, production and real income, balanced growth, and better economic policy planning and coordination.

*Social Work in Education*, a journal for school social workers, is published by NASW.

Indian Child Welfare Act (P.L. 95-608) is enacted to promote the best interests of Native American children and the stability and security of Native American tribes and families. Key provisions include the right of the child's parents or the tribe to be notified of and to intervene in child custody proceedings, higher standards of proof in termination of parental rights proceedings, and certain preferences when a Native American child is placed in foster care.

The National Hospice Organization is founded (it changes its name to the National Hospice and Palliative Care Organization in 2000).

The first "Conference on Social Work Practice in Labor and Industrial Settings" is held in New York, launching the new field of occupational social work practice.

*1979.* The American Association of State Social Work Boards is initiated; the association consists of state boards and authorities empowered to regulate the practice of social work within their own jurisdictions.

*1980.* The Adoption Assistance and Child Welfare Act (P.L. 96-272) restructures child welfare services, mandating reasonable efforts to prevent out-of-home placement.

The Department of Health and Human Services (HHS) is created when the Department of Health, Education, and Welfare is divided into two agencies: the Department of Education and HHS. The Health Care Financing Administration becomes an agency under HHS.

The National Association of Perinatal Social Workers is incorporated.

*1981.* The Omnibus Budget Reconciliation Act (P.L. 97-35), passed by Congress on August 13, initiates a federal policy reversal of "general welfare" responsibility for human services, reducing federal programs (including food stamps, child nutrition, comprehensive employment and training, mental health, and community development) by means of block grants under the guise of decentralization to states.

The Social Service Block Grant Act (P.L. 97-35), passed by Congress on August 13, and part of the Omnibus Budget Reconciliation Act of 1981, amends Title XX of the Social Security Act to consolidate social services programs and to decentralize responsibility to the states.

Human immunodeficiency virus (HIV) and acquired immune deficiency syndrome (AIDS) are first identified in the United States and soon are defined as an epidemic. New requirements of social workers are initiated: They must further their knowledge of transmission and prevention of the virus, adapt practice techniques, and act on civil rights and service policies.

*1982.* The Tax Equity and Fiscal Responsibility Act (P.L. 97-248), passed by Congress on September 3, initiates severe reductions in service provisions of Medicare, Medicaid, Utilization and Quality Control Peer Review, Aid to Families with Dependent Children, child support enforcement, supplemental security income, and unemployment compensation. The legislation provides the "largest tax increase ever recommended in a single piece of legislation." It gives Medicare beneficiaries the option to enroll in health maintenance organizations.

The Group for the Advancement of Social Work Groups and the Group for the Advancement of Doctoral Education (GADE) is established.

*1983.* The Social Security Amendments (P.L. 98-81), passed on April 20, secures the program, providing mandatory coverage of federal employees and employees of nonprofit organizations, withdrawing and reducing benefits such as cost of living delay to calendar year, increasing retirement age, and reducing initial benefits.

The Hospital Prospective Payment System replaces Medicare cost reimbursement systems with predetermined payment rates for 468 diagnosis related groups, initiating significant role changes for social workers in discharge planning and increased service coordination requirements.

The Migrant and Seasonal Agricultural Worker Protection Act (P.L. 97-470) is enacted to protect migrant farm workers from unfair labor practices or working, living, or housing conditions that are unhealthy or unsafe. The law also requires employers to inform workers, in writing, of their rights, their wages and benefits, and the length and terms of their employment.

*1984.* In recognition of the many contributions of the social work profession to the welfare of our society, the Congress, by Senate Joint Resolution 112, authorizes and requests President Ronald Reagan to proclaim the month of March 1984, as "National Social Work Month."

The Association of Oncology Social Work (AOSW) is founded.

*1985.* The Consolidated Omnibus Budget Reconciliation Act (COBRA) encourages states to provide case management as an optional Medicaid service.

The National NETWORK for Social Work Managers is formed as a professional society by Robert Maslyn to advance knowledge, theory, and practice of management and administration in social services and the social work profession and to obtain recognition of social work managers.

*1986.* The Immigration Reform and Control Act (P.L. 99-603) provides temporary resident status for undocumented workers who have continuously resided in the United States since before January 1, 1982. The act allows them to become permanent residents after an additional 18-month period. Provisions make it unlawful for any person to knowingly employ undocumented workers. The objectives of the act are to decrease the number of illegal aliens as current residents, regain control of U.S. borders, and increase the number of legal migrant workers.

The Tax Reform Act (P.L. 99-514) reduces and consolidates tax brackets into two basic rates: (a) 15% and (b) 28%. The law increases the standard deduction for all taxpayers, with the largest increases for heads of households, single parents, and others who maintain households for dependent children. The Earned Income Tax Credit provision significantly increases the credit and raises the income levels at which the credit begins to be reduced and eliminated.

NASW establishes the National Center for Social Policy and Practice to analyze practice data and make recommendations on social policy, including information, policy, and education services.

The Anti-Drug Abuse Act (P.L. 99-570) creates the Office for Substance Abuse Prevention in the Alcohol, Drug Abuse, and Mental Health Administration. It also includes funding for a White House Conference for a Drug-Free America in fiscal year 1988 and authorizes funding of $450 million over three years to develop drug education and prevention programs through a new Drug-Free Schools and Communities Act.

The Education of the Handicapped Act Amendments (P.L. 99-457) establishes a new federal discretionary program to assist states to develop and implement early intervention services for handicapped infants and toddlers (birth through age 2) and their families. Seven criteria for 11 early intervention services" include provisions for qualified personnel, including social workers, and individualized family service plans; the states must serve all children.

The Office of Minority Health is established by the Department of Health and Human Services. It advises the Secretary and the Office of Public Health and Science on public health program activities affecting American Indians and Alaska Natives, Asian Americans, Blacks or African Americans, Hispanics or Latinos, Native Hawaiians and other Pacific Islanders.

Barbara Mikulski, a professional social worker, becomes the first female U.S. Senator elected with an MSW degree. Re-elected in 1992, 1998, and 2004, she is the senior woman in the Senate today.

1987. *The Social Work Dictionary* (1st edition), the first compilation of terms related to social work, is published by NASW.

The Stewart B. McKinney Homeless Assistance Act (P.L. 100-77) establishes the Interagency Council on Homeless to use public resources and programs in a more coordinated manner and to provide funds to assist homeless people, especially elderly people, people with disabilities, families with children, Native Americans, and veterans.

1988. The Family Support Act (P.L. 100-485) alters welfare provisions in critical ways. The act includes provisions for improved child support enforcement; state-run education, training, and employment programs for recipients of Aid to Families with Dependent Children; and supportive services for families during and after participation in employment and training. The act also establishes the Job Opportunities in the Business Sector program. Other provisions include guaranteed child care, transitional benefits, and reimbursement for work-related expenses.

The Hunger Prevention Act (P.L. 100-435) expands the federal food stamp program and initiates state outreach, employment, and training programs.

The Adoption Assistance and Child Welfare Act (P.L. 96-272) requires states to offer prevention services before removing a child from a home.

The NASW Communications Network is established by Suzanne Dworak-Peck as an affiliate group to encourage socially conscious media programming and accurate portrayal of social issues and professional social work. The Network uses a computerized network of several hundred social workers for technical medial assistance.

The Medicare Catastrophic Coverage Act (P.L. 100-360) limits yearly out-of-pocket expenses for beneficiaries; adds a prescription drug benefit; extends hospice, respite, and home health benefits; adds a Medicaid buy-in provision; and offers some protection of a couple's assets for nursing home care. The act later is rescinded by Congress as a result of senior citizen protests about added premium requirements.

The Augustus F. Hawkins/Robert T. Stafford Elementary and Secondary School Improvement Amendments (P.L. 100-297) authorize funding for elementary and secondary education, including Chapter I, Financial Assistance; Chapter II, Federal; State & Local Partnership for Educational Improvement; dropout prevention; suicide prevention; and other programs. For the first time, use of pupil service personnel (including social workers and other professionals) is promoted and, in some cases, required.

The Civil Rights Restoration Act (P.L. 100-259) overturns the 1984 Supreme Court *Grove City College v. Bell* decision and clarifies that four major civil rights laws pertaining to gender, disability age, and race must be interpreted to prohibit discrimination throughout entire organizations if any program received federal funds.

*Social Work Speaks* is developed by NASW in order to pragmatically use the Delegate Assembly's social policy statements with legislators (elected, appointed officials, and staff) and the media.

1989. Appropriations legislation for fiscal year 1990 for the departments of Labor, Health and Human Services, and Education (P.L. 101-166) include requirements that the National Institute of Mental Health (NIMH) distribute clinical training funds equitably among five core mental health professions, increasing social work's share. Other provisions include encouraging scholarships for people with master of social work degrees to provide case management to people with AIDS, commending the NIMH Task Force on Social Work Research and Support for "services research" and providing appropriations for research on rural mental health.

*1990.* The social work profession is legally regulated in 50 states and jurisdictions as of January 1, 1990.

The Americans with Disabilities Act (42 U.S.C. 1210) is signed into law July 26 and becomes effective in 1992. This comprehensive civil rights law for people with disabilities prohibits employment discrimination (Title 1); discrimination in state and local government services (Title II); and discrimination in public accommodations and commercial facilities (Title III).

Individuals with Disabilities Education Act (IDEA) (P.L. 101-476) was enacted in 1990 and expanded in 1997 to ensure appropriate services and a public education to children with disabilities from ages 3 to 21. IDEA replaced the Education for All Handicapped Children Act of 1975.

The Ryan White Comprehensive AIDS Resources Emergency Act (P.L. 101-381) authorizes $880 million annually to provide emergency relief to metropolitan areas hardest hit by the AIDS epidemic. Other provisions address comprehensive planning, early intervention, treatment of children, and AIDS in rural areas.

The NASW School Social Work Specialist Credential is created.

NASW transforms its publications department into the NASW Press.

The Office of Research on Minority Health is established by Congress. (The Health Revitalization Act of 1993 (P.L. 103-43) establishes the Office of Research on Minority Health in the Office of the Director, National Institutes of Health (NIH).

To recognize the fact that girls are a part of Boys Clubs of America, the national organization's name is changed to Boys & Girls Clubs of America.

*1991.* The NASW Academy of Certified Baccalaureate Social Workers is established.

The Civil Rights Act (P.L. 102-166) amends the Civil Rights Act of 1964 to reverse a set of Supreme Court decisions that eroded protection of women and people of color in the workplace. Victims of intentional discrimination based on gender, disability, or religion, but not age, can obtain monetary damages.

*1992.* The Alcohol, Drug Abuse, and Mental Health Administration (ADAMHA) Reorganization Act (P.L. 102-321) transfers the research function in mental health, alcohol, and other substance abuse to the National Institutes of Health and establishes separate state block grants for mental health and substance abuse services. The National Institute of Mental Health, the National Institute of Drug Abuse, and the National Institute on Alcohol Abuse and Alcoholism are moved from ADAMHA to the National Institutes of Health. ADAMHA, renamed the Substance Abuse and Mental Health Services Administration (SAMSHA), includes the Center for Substance Abuse Treatment, the Center for Substance Abuse Prevention, and the Center for Mental Health Services.

On June 9, Senator Daniel K. Inouye (D-HI) introduces the NASW National Health Care Proposal as S. 2817, the National Health Care Act. Based on NASW universal health care policies, it is the only bill to price out the costs of a new health care system.

The Preventive Health Amendments (P.L. 102-531) include a new Office of Adolescent Health in the Department of Health and Human Services. Among the responsibilities of the new office is the coordination of training for health providers, including social workers, who work with adolescents.

The Older Americans Act Amendments (P.L. 102-375) reauthorize Older American Act programs for four years and include provisions for long-term care ombudsmen, legal assistance, outreach, counseling, and abuse and neglect prevention programs. The amendments authorize a White House Conference on Aging by the end of 1994; grants for training in gerontology in schools of social work; and counseling, training, and support services for caregivers.

The Higher Education Amendments (P.L. 102-325) create new opportunities for reduction and cancellation of federal Perkins loan indebtedness for social work students who seek employment in child welfare, mental health, juvenile justice, or other agencies serving high-risk children and families from low-income communities, as well as those who provide early intervention services to infants and toddlers with disabilities.

The NASW Press publishes the *Social Work Almanac,* the first stand-alone compilation of statistics related to social work content.

*1993.* The National and Community Service Trust Act (P.L. 103-82) provides funds for community services, further institutionalizing the federal responsibility for meeting unmet social needs, including educational awards and living allowances for full-time community service.

The Family and Medical Leave Act (P.L. 103-3), passed on February 5, balances demands of workplace and family needs by requiring that employers of 50 or more employees allow up to 12 weeks of unpaid leave annually for a child's birth or adoption, the care of a spouse or immediate family member, or the employee's "serious health condition"—one requiring either inpatient care or ongoing treatment by a health provider.

The Family Preservation and Support Services Provisions (P.L. 103-66), part of the Omnibus Budget Reconciliation Act, provides $1 billion for a comprehensive approach to improving the child welfare system, emphasizing prevention and early intervention to maintain a natural care system.

The Brady Handgun Violence Prevention Act (P.L. 103-159) is signed by President Clinton on November 24. The bill institutes a five-day waiting period for handgun purchase, to be replaced in five years by a nationwide "instant check" system to ensure that guns are not being sold to criminals.

National Voter Registration Act ("Motor Voter Law;" P.L. 103-31) gives U.S. citizens the opportunity to register to vote when applying for driver's licenses, welfare assistance, and government services. The legislation was initiated by HumanSERVE and social worker Richard Cloward.

The Institute for Advancement of Social Work Research (IASWR) is founded by five national professional organizations that represent social work practice and education communities, to fulfill recommendations from a 1991 report adopted by National Institute of Mental Health's advisory council, which highlight the need to strengthen social work research resources.

The Society for Social Work and Research (SSWR) is a nonprofit, professional society incorporated in the State of New York in 1993. The Society is devoted to the involvement of social workers, other social work faculty, and social work students in research and to promotion of human welfare through research and research applications.

*1994.* The Improving America's Schools Act (P.L. 103-382) reauthorizes the Elementary and Secondary Education Act for five years. Provisions include the Elementary School Counseling Demonstration Act; Title I, Helping Disadvantaged Children Meet High Standards; Title II, the Dwight D. Eisenhower Professional Development Program; Title IV, Safe and Drug-Free Schools and Communities; Families of Children with Disabilities Support Act; Urban and Rural Education Assistance; MultiEthnic Placement Act; and many others.

The Violent Crime Control and Law Enforcement Act (P.L. 103-322) is signed by President Clinton on September 13. In addition to authorizing new prisons and other punishment provisions, the law includes 16 prevention programs, among them grants to combat violence against women, drug treatment programs, and a local crime prevention block grant program. The Violence Against Women Act of 1993, which increases penalties for offenders, authorizes funding for prevention and training, and provides protection for victims, is incorporated into P.L. 103-322.

The Freedom of Access to Clinic Entrances Act (P.L. 103-259) is enacted on May 26 to combat violence against "abortion clinics." The act makes it a federal offense to restrict access to reproductive health services or to destroy the property of reproductive health services facilities.

The NASW Press separates *Social Work Research & Abstracts* and creates *Social Work Abstracts,* which publishes abstracts of previously published materials, and *Social Work Research,* which publishes primary research articles.

Person-in-Environment (PIE) System is published by the NASW Press to enable social workers to describe, classify, and code the problems of adult clients.

The Multi-Ethnic Placement Act (P.L. 103-382) prohibits the delay or denial of any adoption or placement in foster care due to the race, color, or national origin of the child or of the foster or adoptive parents, and requires states to provide for diligent recruitment of potential foster and adoptive families who reflect the ethnic and racial diversity of children for whom homes are needed. The 1996 amendment to the Act (S. 1808 of P.L. 104-188) is known as the Removal of Barriers to Interethnic Adoption Act, and further affirms the prohibition against delaying or denying the placement of a child for adoption or foster care on the basis of race, color, or national origin of the foster or adoptive parents or of the child involved.

The School Social Work Association of America is formed in July.

AmeriCorps is established to facilitate volunteer human services efforts in American communities.

The International Convention on the Elimination of All Forms of Racial Discrimination is ratified by the Untied States and many other nations.

The American Medical Association rejects "reparative therapies" designed to change homosexuals into heterosexuals and calls for a "nonjudgmental recognition of sexual orientation" by physicians.

*1995.* On April 19, the Alfred P. Murrah Federal Building in Oklahoma City is bombed. The attack claimed 168 lives and injured 800. Until the September 11, 2001, attacks, it was the deadliest act of terrorism on U.S. soil.

The U.S. National Voter Registration Act of 1993 (P.L. 103-31) goes into effect, giving U.S. citizens easier access to voter registration while applying for government services.

The U.S. government signs the International Convention on the Right of the Child treaty.

A saliva test for the AIDS virus is approved by the Food and Drug Administration. The new test, which in trials showed a 2% error rate (for positive and negative results), is less accurate than the Western Blot blood test.

The final Family Medical Leave Act regulations (signed by President Clinton in 1993) recognizes clinical social workers who are authorized to practice without supervision under state law and are performing within the scope of their practice.

NASW's *Encyclopedia of Social Work*, 19th edition, and its CD-ROM version unveiled in April with a reception at the Library of Congress. The CD-ROM version is NASW's first full-text electronic information product.

The Action Network for Social Work Education and Research (ANSWER) coalition is formed.

1996. President Bill Clinton signs into law the Personal Responsibility and Work Opportunity Reconciliation Act of 1996 (P.L. 104-193), a reform that restricts or eliminates many entitlement programs for the poor, including Aid to Families with Dependent Children (AFDC), to be replaced by the Temporary Assistance for Needy Families (TANF) programs, and severely restricts many other programs such as Supplemental Security Income (SSI) and nutrition programs.

The NASW *Code of Ethics*, which originated in 1960, is revised.

In *Jaffee v. Redmond*, the U.S. Supreme Court decides social workers, in federal courts, have rights of privileged communication with clients.

The Health Insurance Portability and Accountability Act (HIPPA; P.L. 104-191) is passed: Title I deals with protecting health insurance coverage for people who lose or change jobs. HIPAA Title II includes an administrative simplification section, which deals with the standardization of healthcare-related information systems.

The Institute for the Advancement of Political Social Work Practice at the University of Connecticut is established. The Institute works to increase the number of social workers who pursue careers in electoral politics and works to investigate ways in which social workers can facilitate the political empowerment of clients.

The Defense of Marriage Act (DOMA; P.L. 104-199) is passed by Congress and signed by President Bill Clinton on September 21. The law has two effects: No state or other political subdivision with the United States may recognize a marriage between persons of the same sex, even if the marriage was concluded or recognized in another state, and the federal government may not recognize same-sex or polygamous marriages for any purpose, even if concluded or recognized by one of the states.

Mental Health Employment Parity Act is passed.

1997. In December, the American Association of State Social Work Boards (ASWB) unveils a comprehensive model law to regulate the practice of social work. It is a useful tool for states drafting legislation.

The Omnibus Consolidation Appropriations Act (P.L. 104-208) restores some of the social service funding eliminated by the Personal Responsibility and Work Opportunity Reconciliation Act of 1996.

Medicare C is the Medicare + Choice program established by P.L. 105-33. The program is provided through the private sector and has a variety of plan options.

Balanced Budget Act authorized Title XXI Social Security Act. Title XXI, known as the State Children's Health Insurance Program (SCHIP), expanded Medicaid eligibility to include low-income children whose family's income exceeds Medicaid eligibility. SCHIP is currently under legislation review.

Congress reauthorizes the Child Abuse Prevention and Treatment Act through 2001 and made changes in the landmark protection law, among them the elimination of the National Center on Abuse and Neglect. It grants the Department of Health and Human Services the power to establish an Office on Child Abuse to replace the center.

The Adoptions and Safe Families Act (P.L. 105-89) is signed by President Clinton on November 19. The law amends the 1980 Child Welfare Act (P.L. 96-272), clarifies that the health and safety of children served by child welfare agencies must be their paramount concern and aims to move children in foster care more quickly into permanent homes.

At the suggestion of a presidentially appointed advisory commission on managed health care and quality issues, President Clinton endorses a consumer bill of rights for health care. The Managed Care Consumer Bill of Rights became fully effective on April 1. The Executive Law and General Business Law authorize the Attorney General to bring a lawsuit against any business entity, in this case health plans, which repeatedly engages in fraudulent, deceptive, or illegal business activity.

1998. Social work in the United States celebrates the centennial of professional social work education, recognizing more than 100 years of social work's contribution to the well-being of individuals, families, communities, society, and the natural environment.

The July Supreme Court decision in *Swidler & Berlin v. United States* reaffirms the high court's 1996 extension of psychotherapist–client privilege to social workers involved in federal court cases.

The Mental Health Parity Act of 1996 (P.L. 104-274) takes effect on January 1. The Act requires health insurance companies to reimburse for mental health care as they would for physical health care. Mental illnesses are covered; however, neither substance abuse nor chemical dependency treatments are covered and it excludes companies with fewer than 50 employees.

The Health Professions Partnerships Act (P.L. 105-392) amends the Public Health Service Act to consolidate and reauthorize health professions and minority and disadvantaged health education programs. Title I concerns health professions education and financial assistance programs. Title II revises and extends programs of the Office of Minority Health. Title III includes selected initiatives concerned with state offices of rural health, demonstration projects regarding Alzheimer's disease, and project grants for immunization services. Title IV offers miscellaneous provisions.

The Children's Online Privacy Protection Act takes effect April 21, and applies to the online collection of personal information from children below 13.

*1999.* The NASW *Code of Ethics*, which originated in 1960, and revised in 1996, incorporates minor revisions, emphasizing the parameters of sexual misconduct.

The Medicare provisions in the 1996 Balanced-Budget Law takes effect in January, and establishes reimbursement for social workers who provide "professional consultation via telecommunications systems."

The Ticket to Work Act (P.L. 106-170) makes it possible for Americans with disabilities to join the workforce without losing Medicaid and Medicare eligibility.

The first Social Work Summit is convened in Washington, DC; 44 social work organizations come together to reflect on the importance of—and to facilitate the process of—unifying the profession. This was the first meeting of the leaders of the many diverse organizations whose members are professional social workers.

*2000.* The Millennium Declaration and the Millennium Development Goals (MDG) are adopted by the United Nations Member States in 2000.

Healthy People 2010, a set of national goals developed by the U.S. Department of Health and Human Services, builds on the 1979 Surgeon General's Report, *Healthy People* and *Healthy People* 2000: *National Health Promotion and Disease Prevention Objectives*. Like its predecessors, Healthy People 2010 provides a framework for prevention for the nation.

The Human Genome Project announces and publishes the first complete sequencing of the genetic blueprint for human beings.

Office of Surgeon General names five public health priorities: disease prevention, eliminating health disparities, public health preparedness, improving health literacy, and organ donation.

President Clinton on November 22 signs the Minority Health and Health Disparities Research and Education Act (P.L. 106-525), legislation that focuses on the disparities in the incidence of disease and health care outcomes among racial minority groups compared with the overall population. The National Center on Minority Health and Health Disparities was established by the passage of the Act.

The American Association of State Social Work Boards shortens its name to the Association of Social Work Boards.

The Veterans Millennium Health Care and Benefits Act (P.L. 106-117) enhances adult health, day care, in-home services, and long-term care in the Department of Veterans Affairs, and enhances the role of social work.

Affirmative action in university admissions is challenged in the University of Michigan College of Literature, Science and the Arts and the Law School.

The Million Mom March is held on the National Mall on May 14, drawing 750,000 mothers, relatives, and friends to Washington, DC, to call on Congress to pass definitive gun legislation.

Debbie Stabenow, a professional social worker, is the second social worker to be elected to the U.S. Senate. She was re-elected in 2006 and serves on the Senate Finance Committee.

*2001.* The Health Care Financing Administration is renamed the Centers for Medicare & Medicaid Services (CMS).

On the morning of September 11, 2001, 19 terrorists hijacked four commercial passenger jet airliners and crashed two of the airliners in the World Trade Center towers (I and II) in New York City, and another plane into the Pentagon. Passengers and members of the flight crew of the fourth plane attempted to take control of their plane from the hijackers and crashed into a field near the town of Shanksville in rural Pennsylvania.

No Child Left Behind Act (P.L. 107-110), the education reform legislation, is signed into law to help children and schools that are not meeting specified standards, and requires annual state tests in reading and mathematics in Grades 3–8.

The National Association of Social Workers Foundation is founded as a charitable organization created to enhance the well-being of individuals, families, and communities through the advancement of social work practice. The Foundation is an expansion of the Research and Education Fund.

By executive order, President Bush established the White House Office of Faith-Based and Community Initiatives.

NASW and the Council on Social Work Education releases the history video, *Legacies of Social Change: 100 Years of Professional Social Work in the United States.*

Actions by Congress and the Health Care Financing Administration (HCFA) provide relief for problems and potential obstacles that social workers have faced in providing mental health services to residents of skilled nursing facilities (SNFs) and independently billing Medicare Part B. As part of a major spending bill, Congress eliminates "consolidated billing," which for social workers means they will be able to provide psychotherapy services to nursing home patients and directly bill Medicare Part B for services provided.

*2002.* The U.S. Department of Homeland Security is created by the Homeland Security Act of 2002 (P.L. 107-296), primarily to prevent terrorist attacks within the United States and to minimize the damage from potential attacks and natural disasters.

On May 15 Congress enacts the Notification and Federal Employee Antidiscrimination and Retaliation Act ("No FEAR Act;" P.L. 107-174) to require that federal agencies be accountable for violations of antidiscrimination and whistleblower protection laws.

Sarbanes-Oxley Act and the Corporate and Criminal Fraud Accountability Act (P.L. 107-204) are signed on July 30. The Act provides protection for employees of publicly traded companies who provide evidence of fraud.

The second Social Work Summit is convened in Washington, DC, with 45 national social work organizations, representing a variety of fields of practice and practice setting, minority and ethnic groups, political and religious ideologies, practice methods, functions, and agencies.

*2003.* The Immigration and Naturalization Service (INS) is dissolved and replaced by two distinct agencies, the Bureau of Citizenship and Immigration Services and the Border and Transportation Security Directorate. Both agencies are part of the U.S. Department of Homeland Security.

On June 29 President Bush signs H.R. 1812, the Patient Navigator Outreach and Chronic Disease Prevention Act of 2005, which authorizes appropriations through FY 2010 for the Department of Health and Human Services to establish a competitive grant program designed to help patients access health care services.

In *Grutter v. Bollinger,* the U.S. Supreme Court stated that race could be used as one factor for the University of Michigan's admissions, but in *Gratz v. Bollinger,* the Court indicated that points given to perspective student based solely on race were unconstitutional because the process violated the Equal Protection Clause.

*2004.* The NASW Center for Workforce Studies in the NASW Foundation is established to conduct studies of the current social work labor force; enhance professional development, and disseminate information and resources on evidence-based practices.

On April 25 NASW is a co-sponsoring partner for the March for Women's Lives, one of the largest demonstrations at the National Mall in Washington, DC (an estimated 1,000,000 people attended).

The U.S. Patent and Trademark Office approves the Certificate of Registration of the trademark, "NASW Social Work Pioneers."

*2005.* In March, the National Association of Social Workers (NASW) convened the first-ever Social Work Congress, with 400 social work leaders from various organizations and practice areas to frame the social work agenda for the next decade. The Congress adopted 12 imperatives for the profession's future.

At its 50th Anniversary Gala, coinciding with the Social Work Congress, NASW launches a National Social Work Public Education Campaign to reintroduce social work to the American public. The multiyear campaign's purpose is to educate citizens about the services social workers provide and to help them find those services in their communities. The cornerstone of the campaign is the launch of a consumer Web site, http://www.HelpStartsHere.org.

The U.S. Supreme Court strikes down the Texas sodomy statute in *Lawrence and Garner v. Texas.*

The U.S. Supreme Court rules in favor of the defendant in the death-penalty case of *Wiggins v. Smith,* in which the defendant's attorneys failed to obtain a psychosocial assessment by a social worker before his sentencing hearing. They denied the jury of evidence of the defendant's history of sexual and physical abuse, circumstances that might have influenced a jury not to impose the death penalty. This case established a standard for capital murder cases that highlights the importance of social work evaluations.

On July 1 social work becomes a licensed profession in the state of Michigan, establishing licensing for social workers in all 50 states in the United States.

The fifth White House Conference on Aging is held December 11–14, in Washington, DC.

*2006.* Medicare Part D goes into effect on January 1. It is the new, voluntary prescription drug plan, authorized by the Medicare Prescription Drug Improvement and Modernization Act of 2003 (P.L. 108-173).

Voting Rights Act (also referred to as the Rosa Parks Voting Rights Act of 2006) is signed by President Bush on July 27 for a 25-year extension of the National Voting Rights Act of 1965 (P.L. 88-352), the landmark legislation that outlawed segregation in the U.S. schools and public places.

Older Americans Act Amendments of 2006 (P.L. 109-365) are passed that amend the Older Americans Act of 1965 to authorize appropriations for fiscal years 2007–2011.

President Bush signs the Lifespan Respite Care Act (HR 3248) and authorizes nearly $290 million in competitive grants to help fund state-based respite care programs.

Ryan White HIV/AIDS Treatment Modernization Act provides the Federal HIV/AIDS programs in the Public Health Service Act under Title XXVI flexibility to respond effectively to the changing epidemic. The new law changes how Ryan White funds can be used, with an emphasis on providing life-saving and life-extending services for people living with HIV or AIDS across the United States.

NASW Center for Workforce Studies conducts a benchmark national survey of licensed social workers in the fall of 2004, and releases the final report, *Assuring the Sufficient of a Frontline Workforce: A National Study of Licensed Social Workers* in March.

The Social Work Reinvestment Initiative is designed to unify and advance the social work profession through legislative, policy, and regulatory work that recognizes the role of professional social workers in the delivery of health and human services.

*2007.* The Fair Minimum Wage Act (P.L. 110-28, Title VIII) amends the Fair Labor Standards Act of 1938 and gradually raises the federal minimum wage from $5.15 per hour to $7.25 per hour. It was signed into law on May 25.

In June, the NASW Insurance Trust becomes NASW Assurance Services, Inc., a wholly owned subcorporation of NASW.

President Bush signs the First Higher Education Extension Act (S. 1704) to provide for an extension of the Higher Education Act of 1965 through July 31, 2007.

The 20th edition of the *Encyclopedia of Social Work* is co-published with NASW and Oxford University Press.

### FURTHER READING

Alexander, C. A. (1995). Appendix 2: Distinctive dates in social welfare history. In R. L. Edwards (Ed. in Chief), *The encyclopedia of social work* (19th ed., vol. 3, pp. 2631–2647). Washington, DC: NASW Press.

Barker, R. L. (2003). *The social work dictionary* (5th ed.). Washington, DC: NASW Press.

*NASW News.* (1995–2006).

National Association of Social Workers. (2006). *Social work speaks: NASW policy statements 2006–2009* (7th ed.). Washington, DC: Author.

### SUGGESTED LINKS

NASW Foundation
  *http://www.naswfoundation.org*
Social Work Portal
  *http://www.socialworkers.org/swportal/*

—BECKY S. CORBETT

# Appendix 4

## INDICATORS FOR THE ACHIEVEMENT OF THE NASW STANDARDS FOR CULTURAL COMPETENCE IN SOCIAL WORK PRACTICE

### Standard 1. Ethics and Values
Social workers shall function in accordance with the values, ethics, and standards of the profession, recognizing how personal and professional values may conflict with or accommodate the needs of diverse clients.

### Standard 2. Self-Awareness
Social workers shall seek to develop an understanding of their own personal and cultural values and beliefs, as one way of appreciating the importance of multicultural identities in the lives of people.

### Standard 3. Cross-Cultural Knowledge
Social workers shall have and continue to develop specialized knowledge and understanding of the history, traditions, values, family systems, and artistic expressions of the major client groups that they serve.

### Standard 4. Cross-Cultural Skills
Social workers shall use appropriate methodological approaches, skills, and techniques that reflect the workers' understanding of the role of culture in the helping process.

### Standard 5. Service Delivery
Social workers shall be knowledgeable about and skillful in the use of services available in the community and broader society and be able to make appropriate referrals for their diverse clients.

### Standard 6. Empowerment and Advocacy
Social workers shall be aware of the effect of social policies and programs on diverse client populations, advocating for and with clients whenever appropriate.

### Standard 7. Diverse Workforce
Social workers shall support and advocate for recruitment, admissions and hiring, and retention efforts in social work programs and agencies that ensure diversity within the profession.

### Standard 8. Professional Education
Social workers shall advocate for and participate in educational and training programs that help advance cultural competence within the profession.

### Standard 9. Language Diversity
Social workers shall seek to provide or advocate for the provision of information, referrals, and services in the language appropriate to the client, which may include use of interpreters.

### Standard 10. Cross-Cultural Leadership
Social workers shall be able to communicate information about diverse client groups to other professionals.

Prepared by the NASW National Committee on Racial and Ethnic Diversity. Submitted to the NASW Board of Directors for review and approval June 16, 2006.

### Introduction
The *Standards for Cultural Competence in Social Work Practice* are based on the policy statement "Cultural Competence in the Social Work Profession" published in *Social Work Speaks: NASW Policy Statements* (2000b) and the NASW *Code of Ethics* (2000a), which charges social workers with the ethical responsibility of being culturally competent. Both were originally adopted by the 1996 NASW Delegate Assembly. The Indicators for the Achievement of the NASW Standards for Cultural Competence in the Social Work Profession are designed as an extension of the Standards to provide additional guidance on the implementation and realization of culturally competent practice.

NASW "supports and encourages the development of standards for culturally competent social work practice, a definition of expertise, and the advancement of practice models that have relevance for the range of needs and services represented by diverse client populations" (NASW, 2000b, p. 61). The material that follows is the first attempt by the profession to delineate standards for culturally competent social work practice.

The United States is constantly undergoing major demographic changes. The 1990 to 2000 population growth was the largest in American history with a dramatic increase in people of color from 20 percent to 25 percent (Perry & Mackum, 2001). Those changes alter and increase the diversity confronting social workers daily in their agencies. The complexities associated with cultural diversity in the United States affect all aspects of professional social work practice, requiring social workers to strive to deliver culturally competent services to an ever-increasing broad range of clients. The social work profession traditionally has emphasized the importance of the person-in-environment and the dual perspective, the concept that all people are part of two systems: the larger societal system and their immediate environments (Norton, 1978). Social workers using a person-in-environment framework for assessment need to include to varying degrees important cultural factors that have meaning for clients and reflect the culture of the world around them.

In the United States, cultural diversity in social work has primarily been associated with race and ethnicity, but diversity is taking on a broader meaning to include the socio-cultural experiences of people of different genders, social classes, religious and spiritual beliefs, sexual orientations, ages, and physical and mental abilities. A brief review of the social work literature in the past few years points to the range of potential content areas that require culturally sensitive and culturally competent interventions. These include addressing racial identity formation for people of color as well as for white people; the interrelationship among class, race, ethnicity, and gender; working with low-income families; working with older adults; the importance of religion and spirituality in the lives of clients; the development of gender identity and sexual orientation; immigration, acculturation, and assimilation stresses; biculturalism; working with people with disabilities; empowerment skills; community building; reaching out to new populations of color; and how to train for culturally competent models of practice.

Therefore, cultural competence in social work practice implies a heightened consciousness of how clients experience their uniqueness and deal with their differences and similarities within a larger social context. The achievement of cultural competence is an ongoing process. Although these indicators describe an ideal state, the National Committee on Racial and Ethnic Diversity (NCORED) encourages social work practitioners and agency leaders to put forth good faith efforts to use them.

## Definitions

The NASW Board of Directors, at its June 2001 meeting, accepted the following definitions of *culture, competence,* and *cultural competence* in the practice of social work. These definitions are drawn from the NASW *Code of Ethics* and *Social Work Speaks.*

### Areas of Practice

"These activities may be in the form of direct practice, community organizing, supervision, consultation, administration, advocacy, social and political action, policy development and implementation, education, and research and evaluation" (NASW, 1999, p. 1).

### Clients

"Clients' is used inclusively to refer to individuals, families, groups, organizations, and communities" (NASW, 1999, p. 1).

### Culture

"The word 'culture' is used because it implies the integrated pattern of human behavior that includes thoughts, communications, actions, customs, beliefs, values, and institutions of a racial, ethnic, religious, or social group" (NASW, 2000b, p. 61). Culture often is referred to as the totality of ways being passed on from generation to generation. The term culture includes ways in which people with disabilities or people from various religious backgrounds or people who are gay, lesbian, or transgender experience the world around them.

The Preamble to the NASW *Code of Ethics* begins by stating:

The primary mission of the social work profession is to enhance human well-being and help meet the basic human needs of all people, with particular attention to the needs and empowerment of people who are vulnerable, oppressed, and living in poverty. It goes on to say, "Social workers are sensitive to cultural and ethnic diversity and strive to end discrimination, oppression, poverty, and other forms of social injustice" (NASW, 2000a, p. 1). Second, culture is mentioned in two ethical standards:

Value: *Social Justice* and the Ethical Principle: *Social workers challenge social injustice.* This means that social workers' efforts at social change seek to promote sensitivity to and knowledge of oppression and cultural and ethnic diversity.

Value: *Dignity and Worth of the Person* and the Ethical Principle: *Social workers respect the inherent dignity and worth of the person.* This value states that social workers treat each person in a caring and respectful fashion, mindful of individual differences and cultural and ethnic diversity.

### Competence

The word "competence" is used because it implies having the capacity to function effectively within the context of culturally integrated patterns of human behavior defined by the group. In the *Code of Ethics* competence is discussed in several ways. First, it is discussed as a value of the profession. Value: *Competence* and the Ethical Principle: *Social workers practice within their areas of competence and develop and enhance their professional expertise.* This value encourages social workers to continually strive to increase their professional knowledge and skills and to apply them in practice. Social workers should aspire to contribute to the knowledge base of the profession. Second, competence is discussed as an ethical standard.

## 1.04 COMPETENCE

- Social workers should provide services and represent themselves as competent only within the boundaries of their education, training, license, certification, consultation received, supervised experience, or other relevant professional experience.
- Social workers should provide services in substantive areas or use intervention techniques or approaches that are new to them only after engaging in appropriate study, training, consultation, and supervision from people who are competent in those interventions or techniques.
- When generally recognized standards do not exist with respect to an emerging area of practice, social workers should exercise careful judgment and take responsible steps (including appropriate education, research, training, consultation, and supervision) to ensure the competence of their work and to protect clients from harm.

Cultural competence is never fully realized, achieved, or completed, but rather cultural competence is a lifelong process for social workers, who will always encounter diverse clients and new situations in their practice. Supervisors and workers should have the expectation that cultural competence is an ongoing learning process, integral and central to daily supervision.

### Cultural Competence

*Cultural competence* refers to the process by which individuals and systems respond respectfully and effectively to people of all cultures, languages, classes, races, ethnic backgrounds, religions, and other diversity factors in a manner that recognizes, affirms, and values the worth of individuals, families, and communities, and protects and preserves the dignity of each.

"Cultural competence is a set of congruent behaviors, attitudes, and policies that come together in a system or agency or among professionals and enable the system, agency, or professionals to work effectively in cross-cultural situations" (NASW, 2000b, p. 61).

Operationally defined, *cultural competence* is the integration and transformation of knowledge about individuals and groups of people into specific standards, policies, practices, and attitudes used in appropriate cultural settings to increase the quality of services, thereby producing better outcomes (Davis & Donald, 1997). Competence in cross-cultural functioning means learning new patterns of behavior and effectively applying them in appropriate settings.

Gallegos (1982) provided one of the first conceptualizations of ethnic competence as "a set of procedures and activities to be used in acquiring culturally relevant insights into the problems of minority clients and the means of applying such insights to the development of intervention strategies that are culturally appropriate for these clients" (p. 4). This kind of sophisticated cultural competence does not come naturally to any social worker and requires a high level of professionalism and knowledge. There are five essential elements that contribute to a system's ability to become more culturally competent. The system should (1) value diversity, (2) have the capacity for cultural self-assessment, (3) be conscious of the dynamics inherent when cultures interact, (4) institutionalize cultural knowledge, and (5) develop programs and services that reflect an understanding of diversity between and within cultures. These five elements must be manifested in every level of the service delivery system. They should be reflected in attitudes, structures, policies, and services.

The specific Ethical Standard for culturally competent social work practice is contained under *Section 1. Social Workers' Ethical Responsibilities to Clients.*

### 1.05 CULTURAL COMPETENCE AND SOCIAL DIVERSITY

Social workers should understand culture and its functions in human behavior and society, recognizing the strengths that exist in all cultures.

Social workers should have a knowledge base of their clients' cultures and be able to demonstrate competence in the provision of services that are sensitive to clients' cultures and to differences among people and cultural groups.

Social workers should obtain education about and seek to understand the nature of social diversity and oppression with respect to race, ethnicity, national origin, color, sex, sexual orientation, age, marital status, political belief, religion, and mental or physical disability. Finally, the Code re-emphasizes the importance of cultural competence in the last section of the Code, *Section 6. Social Workers Ethical Responsibilities to the Broader Society.*

**6.04 SOCIAL AND POLITICAL ACTION** Social workers should act to expand choice and opportunity for all people, with special regard for vulnerable, disadvantaged, oppressed, and exploited people and groups. Social workers should promote conditions that encourage respect for cultural and social diversity within the United States and globally. Social workers should promote policies and practices that demonstrate respect for difference, support the expansion of cultural knowledge and resources, advocate for programs and institutions that demonstrate cultural competence, and promote policies that safeguard the rights of and confirm equity and social justice for all people.

Social workers should act to prevent and eliminate domination of, exploitation of, and discrimination against any person, group, or class on the basis of race, ethnicity, national origin, color, sex, sexual orientation, age, marital status, political belief, religion, or mental or physical disability.

### Goals and Objectives of the Standards

These standards address the need for definition, support, and encouragement of the development of a high level of social work practice that encourages cultural competence among all social workers so that they can respond effectively, knowledgeably, sensitively, and skillfully to the diversity inherent in the agencies in which they work and with the clients and communities they serve.

These standards intend to move the discussion of cultural competence within social work practice toward the development of clearer guidelines, goals, and objectives for the future of social work practice.

The specific goals of the standards are:

* to maintain and improve the quality of culturally competent services provided by social workers and programs delivered by social service agencies
* to establish professional expectations so that social workers can monitor and evaluate their culturally competent practice;
* to provide a framework for social workers to assess culturally competent practice;
* to inform consumers, governmental regulatory bodies, and others, such as insurance carriers, about the profession's standards for culturally competent practice;
* to establish specific ethical guidelines for culturally competent social work practice in agency or private practice settings;
* to provide documentation of professional expectations for agencies, peer review committees, state regulatory bodies, insurance carriers, and others, and interact with each other.

### Standards for Cultural Competence in Social Work Practice

**STANDARD 1. ETHICS AND VALUES** Social workers shall function in accordance with the values, ethics, and standards of the profession, recognizing how personal and professional values may conflict with or accommodate the needs of diverse clients.

**INTERPRETATION** A major characteristic of a profession is its ability to establish ethical standards to help professionals identify ethical issues in practice and to guide them in determining what is ethically acceptable and unacceptable behavior (Reamer, 1998). Social work has developed a comprehensive set of ethical standards embodied in the NASW *Code of Ethics* that "address a wide range of issues, including, for example, social workers' handling of confidential information, sexual contact between social workers and their clients, conflicts of interest, supervision, education and training, and social and political action" (Reamer, 1998, p. 2). The Code includes a mission statement, which sets forth several key elements in social work practice, mainly the social workers' commitment to enhancing human well-being and helping meet basic human needs of all people; client empowerment; service to people who are vulnerable and oppressed; focus on individual well-being in a social context; promotion of social justice and social change; and sensitivity to cultural and ethnic diversity. Social workers clearly have an ethical responsibility to be culturally competent practitioners.

The Code recognizes that culture and ethnicity may influence how individuals cope with problems and interact with each other. What is behaviorally appropriate in one culture may seem abnormal in another. Accepted practice in one culture may be prohibited in another. To fully understand and appreciate these differences, social workers must be familiar with varying cultural traditions and norms. Clients' cultural backgrounds may affect their help-seeking behaviors as well. The ways in which social services are planned and implemented need to be culturally sensitive to be culturally effective. Cultural competence builds on the profession's valued stance on self-determination and individual dignity and worth, adding inclusion, tolerance, and respect for diversity in all its forms. It requires social workers to struggle with ethical dilemmas arising from value conflicts or special needs of diverse clients such as helping clients enroll in mandated training or mental health services that are culturally insensitive. Cultural competence requires social workers to recognize the strengths that exist in all cultures. This does not imply a universal nor automatic acceptance of all practices of all cultures. For example, some cultures subjugate women, oppress persons based on sexual orientation, and value the use of corporal punishment and the death penalty. Cultural competence in social work practice must be informed by and applied within the context of NASW's *Code of Ethics* and the United Nations Declaration of Human Rights.

### Indicators

CULTURALLY COMPETENT SOCIAL WORKERS WILL DEMONSTRATE

1. knowledge of the NASW *Code of Ethics*
2. knowledge of social justice and human rights principles
3. ability to describe areas of conflict and accommodation between personal values, professional values, and those of other cultures
4. ability to recognize the convergence and disparity between the values of the dominant society and the values of the historically oppressed, under-represented, and underserved populations
5. appreciation and respect for cultural differences and strengths
6. awareness of the ethical dilemmas they may encounter when they work with diverse clients in relationship to:
   • boundaries
   • norms of behavior
   • styles of advocacy
   • diverse values and beliefs
   • dual relationships
   • styles of conflict management.

STANDARD 2. SELF-AWARENESS Social workers shall develop an understanding of their own personal and cultural values and beliefs as the first step in appreciating the importance of multicultural identities in the lives of people.

INTERPRETATION Cultural competence requires social workers to examine their own cultural backgrounds and identities to increase their awareness of personal assumptions, values, and biases. The workers' self-awareness of their own cultural identities is as fundamental to practice as the informed assumptions about clients' cultural backgrounds and experiences in the United States. This awareness of personal values, beliefs, and biases informs their practice and influence relationships with clients. Cultural competence includes knowing and acknowledging how fears, ignorance, and the "isms" (racism, sexism, ethnocentrism, heterosexism, ageism, classism, etc.) have influenced their attitudes, beliefs, and feelings.

Social workers need to be able to move from being culturally aware of their own heritage to becoming culturally aware of the heritage of others. They can value and celebrate differences in others rather than maintain an ethnocentric stance and can demonstrate comfort with differences between themselves and others. They have an awareness of personal and professional limitations that may warrant the referral of a client to another social worker or agency that can best meet the clients' needs. Self-awareness also helps in understanding the process of cultural identity formation and helps guard against stereotyping. As one develops the diversity within one's own group, one can be more open to the diversity within other groups.

Cultural competence also requires social workers to appreciate how workers need to move from cultural awareness to cultural sensitivity before achieving cultural competence and to evaluate growth and development throughout these different levels of cultural competence in practice.

Self-awareness becomes the basis for professional development and should be supported by supervision and agency administration. Agency administrators and public policy advocates also need to develop strategies to reduce their own biases and expand their self-awareness.

### Indicators

CULTURALLY COMPETENT SOCIAL WORKERS WILL

1. examine and describe their cultural background, social identities, and cultural heritage to increase awareness of assumptions, values, beliefs, and biases and recognize how these affect services and influence relationships and interactions with clients.
2. identify how absence of knowledge, fears, and "isms" (racism, sexism, ethnocentrism, heterosexism, ageism, classism) have influenced their attitudes, beliefs, and feelings.
3. develop and apply strategies to inform and change their detrimental attitudes, beliefs, and feelings.
4. demonstrate an awareness of personal or professional limitations that may warrant the referral of a client or organization to another resource that can better meet their needs and the skills to do this effectively.
5. demonstrate increased comfort with self- and other-awareness about different cultural customs and views of the world.
6. use relationships with supervisors, mentors, and colleagues to enrich self-awareness.

STANDARD 3. CROSS-CULTURAL KNOWLEDGE Social workers shall have and continue to develop specialized knowledge and understanding about the history, traditions, values, family systems, and artistic expressions of major client groups served.

INTERPRETATION Cultural competence is not static and requires frequent relearning and unlearning about diversity. Social workers need to take every opportunity to expand their cultural knowledge and expertise by expanding their understanding of the following areas: "the impact of culture on behavior, attitudes, and values; the help-seeking behaviors of diverse client groups; the role of language, speech patterns, and communication styles of various client groups in the communities served; the impact of social service policies on various client groups; the resources (agencies, people, informal helping networks, and research) that can be used on behalf of diverse client groups; the ways that professional values may conflict with or accommodate the needs of diverse client groups; and the power relationships in the community, agencies, or institutions and their impact on diverse client groups" (Gallegos, 1982, pp. 7–8).

Social workers need to possess specific knowledge about the particular providers and client groups they work with, including the range of historical experiences, resettlement patterns, individual and group oppression, adjustment styles, socioeconomic backgrounds, life processes, learning styles, cognitive skills, worldviews and specific cultural customs and practices, their definition of and beliefs about the causation of wellness and illness or normality and abnormality, and how care and services should be delivered. They also must seek specialized knowledge about U.S. social, cultural, and political systems, how they operate, and how they serve or fail to serve specific client groups. This includes knowledge of institutional, class, cultural, and language barriers that prevent diverse client group members from using services.

Cultural competence requires explicit knowledge of traditional theories and principles concerning such areas as human behavior, life cycle development, problem-solving skills, prevention, and rehabilitation. Social workers need the critical skill of asking the right questions, being comfortable with discussing cultural differences, and asking clients about what works for them and what is comfortable for them in these discussions. Furthermore, culturally competent social workers need to know the limitations and strengths of current theories, processes and practice models, and which have specific applicability and relevance to the service needs of culturally diverse client groups.

### Indicators

CULTURALLY COMPETENT SOCIAL WORKERS WILL

1. expand their cultural knowledge and expertise by studying
   - the help-seeking behaviors and pathways of diverse client groups;
   - the historical context of diverse communities;
   - the role of language, speech patterns, and communication styles of diverse client groups;
   - the impact of social service policies on diverse groups served;
   - the resources such as agencies, people, informal helping networks, and research that can be mobilized on behalf of diverse clients.
2. possess specific knowledge about traditional and nontraditional providers and client groups that they serve, including
   - historical experiences, immigration, resettlement patterns, individual and group oppression, adjustment styles, socioeconomic backgrounds, and life processes;
   - learning styles, cognitive skills, worldviews, and specific cultural concerns and practices;
   - definitions of and beliefs about service-related concepts such as the causation of wellness and illness, physical and psychological disorders, normality and abnormality, family roles and responsibilities, child rearing practices, birth, marriage, death and dying, and so forth;
   - beliefs and practices related to how care and services should be delivered, including diverse approaches to service delivery and alternative healing options;
   - factors associated with acculturation and assimilation.
3. demonstrate knowledge of the power relationships in the community and in institutions, and how these affect diverse groups.
4. possess specific knowledge about U.S., global, social, cultural, and political systems—how they operate and how they serve or fail to serve client groups, including knowledge about institutional, class, cultural, and language barriers to service.
5. identify the limitations and strengths of contemporary theories and practice models and identify those that have applicability and relevance to their specific client population.
6. recognize the heterogeneity within cultural groups and similarity across cultural groups.
7. describe how privilege is manifested by people within different groups.
8. describe the effects that dominant and non-dominant status has on interpersonal relations and group dynamics in the workplace.
9. distinguish between intentional and unintentional assertion of race and class privilege.
10. recognize the intersection of "isms" (for example, racism with classism) and the institutionalization of "isms."

11. acknowledge the ways in which their membership in various social groups influences their world view and contributes to their own patterns of privileged behavior or internalized oppression.
12. understand the interaction of the cultural systems of the social worker, client, the particular service setting, and the broader immediate community.

STANDARD 4. CROSS-CULTURAL SKILLS Social workers shall use appropriate methodological approaches, skills, and techniques that reflect the workers' understanding of the role of culture in the helping process.

INTERPRETATION The personal attributes of a culturally competent social worker include qualities that reflect genuineness, empathy, and warmth; the capacity to respond flexibly to a range of possible solutions; an acceptance of and openness to differences among people; a willingness to learn to work with clients of different backgrounds; an articulation and clarification of stereotypes and biases and how these may accommodate or conflict with the needs of diverse client groups; and personal commitment to alleviate racism, sexism, homophobia, ageism, and poverty. These attributes are important to the direct practitioner and to the agency administrator.

More specifically, social workers should have the skills to

- work with a wide range of people who are culturally different or similar to themselves, and establish avenues for learning about the cultures of these clients
- assess the meaning of culture for individual clients and client groups, encourage open discussion of differences, and respond to culturally biased cues
- master interviewing techniques that reflect an understanding of the role of language in the client's culture
- conduct a comprehensive assessment of client systems in which cultural norms and behaviors are evaluated as strengths and differentiated from problematic or symptomatic behaviors
- integrate the information gained from a culturally competent assessment into culturally appropriate intervention plans and involve clients and respect their choices in developing goals for service
- select and develop appropriate methods, skills, and techniques that are attuned to their clients' cultural, bicultural, or marginal experiences in their environments
- generate a wide variety of verbal and nonverbal communication skills in response to direct and indirect communication styles of diverse clients

- understand the interaction of the cultural systems of the social worker, the client, the particular agency setting, and the broader immediate community
- effectively use the clients' natural support system in resolving problems—for example, folk healers, storefronts, religious and spiritual leaders, families of creation, and other community resources;
- demonstrate advocacy and empowerment skills in work with clients, recognizing and combating the "isms," stereotypes, and myths held by individuals and institutions;
- identify service delivery systems or models that are appropriate to the targeted client population and make appropriate referrals when indicated;
- consult with supervisors and colleagues for feedback and monitoring of performance and identify features of their own professional style that impede or enhance their culturally competent practice;
- evaluate the validity and applicability of new techniques, research, and knowledge for work with diverse client groups.

### Indicators
#### CULTURALLY COMPETENT SOCIAL WORKERS WILL

1. interact with persons from a wide range of cultures;
2. display proficiency in discussing cultural differences with colleagues and clients;
3. develop and implement a comprehensive assessment of clients in which culturally normative behavior is differentiated from problem or symptomatic behavior;
4. assess cultural strengths and limitations/challenges and their impact on individual and group functioning, and integrate this understanding into intervention plans;
5. select and develop appropriate methods, skills, and techniques that are attuned to their clients' cultural, multicultural, or marginal experiences in their environments;
6. adapt and use a variety of culturally proficient models;
7. communicate effectively with culturally and linguistically different clients through language acquisition, proper use of interpreters, verbal and nonverbal skills, and culturally appropriate protocols;
8. advocate for the use of interpreters who are both linguistically and culturally competent and prepared to work in the social services environment;
9. effectively employ the clients' natural support system in resolving problems, for example, folk

healers, indigenous remedies, religious leaders, friends, family, and other community residents and organizations;

10. advocate, negotiate, and employ empowerment skills in their work with clients;

11. consult with supervisors and colleagues for feedback and monitoring of performance and identify features of their own professional style that impede or enhance their culturally competent practice.

**STANDARD 5. SERVICE DELIVERY** Social workers shall be knowledgeable about and skillful in the use of services available in the community and broader society and be able to make appropriate referrals for their diverse clients.

**INTERPRETATION** Agencies and professional social work organizations need to promote cultural competence by supporting the evaluation of culturally competent service delivery models and setting standards for cultural competence within these settings. Culturally competent social workers need to be aware of and vigilant about the dynamics that result from cultural differences and similarities between workers and clients. This includes monitoring cultural competence among social workers (agency evaluations, supervision, in-service training, and feedback from clients).

Social workers need to detect and prevent exclusion of diverse clients from service opportunities and seek to create opportunities for clients, matching their needs with culturally competent service delivery systems or adapting services to better meet the culturally unique needs of clients. Furthermore, they need to foster policies and procedures that help ensure access to care that accommodates varying cultural beliefs.

For direct practitioners, policymakers, or administrators, this specifically involves

- actively recruiting multiethnic staff and including cultural competence requirements in job descriptions and performance and promotion measures;
- reviewing the current and emergent demographic trends for the geographic area served by the agency to determine service needs for the provision of interpretation and translation services;
- creating service delivery systems or models that are more appropriate to the targeted client populations or advocating for the creation of such services;
- including participation by clients as major stakeholders in the development of service delivery systems;

- ensuring that program decor and design is reflective of the cultural heritage of clients and families using the service;
- attending to social issues (for example, housing, education, police, and social justice) that concern clients of diverse backgrounds;
- not accepting staff remarks that insult or demean clients and their culture;
- supporting the inclusion of cultural competence standards in accreditation bodies and organizational policies as well as in licensing and certification examinations;
- developing staffing plans that reflect the organization and the targeted client population (for example, hiring, position descriptions, performance evaluations, training);
- developing performance measures to assess culturally competent practice;
- including participation of client groups in the development of research and treatment protocols.

**Indicators**

**CULTURALLY COMPETENT SOCIAL WORKERS WILL**

1. identify the formal and informal resources in the community, describe their strengths and weaknesses, and facilitate referrals as indicated, tailored to the culturally relevant needs of the client;

2. actively advocate for and co-operate with efforts to create culturally competent services and programs by:
   - recruiting multiethnic/multicultural staff and including cultural competence requirements in job descriptions and performance and promotion measures;
   - reviewing the current and emergent demographic trends for the geographic area served by the agency to determine needs for the provision of interpretation and translation services;
   - creating service delivery systems or models that are more appropriate to the targeted client populations or advocating for the development and implementation of such services;
   - including clients as major stakeholders in the participation, decision making, and evaluation of service delivery systems;
   - ensuring that program decor and design is reflective of the cultural heritage of clients and families using the service;
   - attending to social issues (for example, housing, education, police, and social justice) that concern clients of diverse backgrounds;

- finding effective strategies for confronting staff remarks that insult or demean clients and their culture;
- supporting the inclusion of cultural competence standards in accreditation bodies and organizational policies as well as in licensing and certification examinations;
- developing staffing plans that reflect the targeted client population (for example, hiring, position descriptions, performance evaluations, training);
- developing performance measures to assess culturally competent practice;
- supporting participation of client groups in the development of research, treatment, and intervention protocols.

3. build culturally competent organizations through the following policies and practices:
- an administrative mission and purpose that embodies cultural competency/proficiency in values, goals, and practices;
- effective recruitment of multilingual and multicultural staff;
- staff composition reflecting the diversity of the client population;
- service planning strategy that includes an assessment/analysis of the client demographics compared to the demographic trends of the service community;
- expanded service capacity to improve the breadth and depth of services to a greater variety of cultural groups;
- meaningful inclusion of clients and community members representing relevant cultural groups in decision-making and advisory governance entities, program planning, program evaluation, and research endeavors; physical plant designed and decorated in a manner that is welcoming to the diverse cultural groups served;
- engagement in advocacy to improve social issues relevant to client group;
- work climate, through formal and informal means, that addresses workforce diversity and challenges and promotes respect for clients and colleagues of different backgrounds;
- documented advocacy for culturally competent policies and procedures of accrediting, licensing, certification bodies, contracting agencies, and so forth;
- inclusion of cultural competency as a component of human resource management in job descriptions, performance evaluations, promotions, training, and other areas.

## STANDARD 6. EMPOWERMENT AND ADVOCACY

Social workers shall be aware of the effect of social policies and programs on diverse client populations, advocating for and with clients whenever appropriate.

### Interpretation

Culturally competent social workers are keenly aware of the deleterious effects of racism, sexism, ageism, heterosexism or homophobia, anti-Semitism, ethnocentrism, classism, and xenophobia on clients' lives and the need for social advocacy and social action to better empower diverse clients and communities.

As first defined by Solomon (1976), *empowerment* involves facilitating the clients' connection with their own power and, in turn, being empowered by the very act of reaching across cultural barriers. Empowerment refers to the clients' ability to do for themselves, while advocacy implies doing for the client. Even in the act of advocacy, social workers must be careful not to impose their values on clients and must seek to understand what clients mean by advocacy. Respectful collaboration needs to take place to promote mutually agreed-on goals for change.

Social workers need a range of skills and abilities to advocate for and with clients against the underlying devaluation of cultural experiences related to difference and oppression and power and privilege in the United States. The empowerment tradition in social work practice suggests a promotion of the combined goals of consciousness raising and developing a sense of personal power and skills while working toward social change. Best practice views this as a process and outcome of the empowerment perspective (Gutiérrez, 1990; Simon, 1994). Social workers using this standard will apply an ecosystems perspective and a strengths orientation in practice. This means that workers consider client situations as they describe needs in terms of transitory challenges rather than fixed problems. According to Gutiérrez and Lewis (1999), empowerment is a model for practice, a perspective and a set of skills and techniques. The expectation is that culturally competent social workers reflect these values in their practice.

### Indicators

CULTURALLY COMPETENT SOCIAL WORKERS WILL

1. advocate for public policies that respect the cultural values, norms, and behaviors of diverse groups and communities.
2. select appropriate intervention strategies to help colleagues, collaborating partners, and institutional representatives examine their own

awareness and lack of awareness and behavioral consequences of the "isms," such as exclusionary behaviors, or oppressive policies by

- assessing the level of readiness for feedback and intervention of the dominant group member;
- selecting either education, dialogue, increased intergroup contact, social advocacy, or social action as a strategy;
- participating in social advocacy and social action to better empower diverse clients and communities at the local, state, and/or national level.

3. use practice methods and approaches that help the client facilitate a connection with their own power in a manner that is appropriate for their cultural context.
4. provide support to diverse cultural groups who are advocating on their own behalf.
5. partner, collaborate, and ally with client groups in advocacy efforts.
6. work to increase the client group's skills and sense of self-efficacy as social change agents.
7. demonstrate appropriate thoughtfulness regarding the role of their own personal values, particularly in terms of when to assert personal values during advocacy work and when to avoid imposing personal values during empowerment work.
8. demonstrate intentional effort to assure that one does not impose one's own personal values in practice.

**STANDARD 7. DIVERSE WORKFORCE** Social workers shall support and advocate for recruitment, admissions and hiring, and retention efforts in social work programs and agencies that ensure diversity within the profession.

**INTERPRETATION** Increasing cultural competence within the profession requires demonstrated efforts to recruit and retain a diverse cadre of social workers, many of whom would bring some "indigenous" cultural competence to the profession, as well as demonstrated efforts to increase avenues for the acquisition of culturally competent skills by all social workers. Diversity should be represented at all levels of the organization, and not just among direct practitioners.

The social work profession has espoused a commitment to diversity, inclusion, and affirmative action. However, available statistics indicate that in the United States social workers are predominantly White (88.5 percent) and female (78.0 percent). The proportion of people of color has remained relatively stable in the social work membership of the National

Association of Social Workers over a period of several years: 5.3% identify themselves as African American; Hispanics, including Mexican Americans, Puerto Ricans, and other Hispanic groups constitute about 2.8% of the membership; Asians and Pacific Islanders 1.7%; and American Indians/First Nations People 0.5% (Gibelman & Schervish, 1997). Social work client populations are more diverse than the social work profession itself. In many instances, service to clients is targeted to marginalized communities and special populations, groups that typically include disproportionately high numbers of people of color, elderly people, people with disabilities, and clients of lower socioeconomic status.

Matching workforce to client populations can be an effective strategy for bridging cultural differences between social worker and client, although it cannot be the only strategy. The assumption is that individuals of similar backgrounds can understand each other better and communicate more effectively (Jackson & López, 1999). Yet an equally compelling fact is that "the majority of clinicians from the mainstream dominant culture will routinely provide care for large numbers of patients of diverse ethnic and/or cultural backgrounds. Clearly increasing the numbers of culturally diverse social workers is not sufficient. Even these professionals will need to be able to provide care for patients who are not like themselves" (Jackson & López, 1999, p. 4). In addition, culturally competent social workers who bring a special skill or knowledge to the profession, like bicultural and bilingual skills, or American Sign Language (ASL) skills, are entitled to professional equity and should not be exploited for their expertise but should be appropriately compensated for skills that enhance the delivery of services to clients.

### Indicators
**CULTURALLY COMPETENT SOCIAL WORKERS WILL**

1. advocate for and support human resource policies and procedures that ensure diversity and inclusion within their organization;
2. work to achieve a workforce and organization that reflect the demographics of the population throughout all levels of the organization;
3. advocate for and support policies that assure equity and appropriate compensations for social workers who bring special skills or knowledge to the profession, such as bicultural and bilingual skills or American Sign Language skills;
4. advocate for and support recruitment and retention strategies that increase the diversity within the profession through social work programs and schools of social work;

5. promote and maintain the expectation that all staff, regardless of cultural membership, continuously engage in the process of improving cultural proficiency and capacity to serve a variety of populations.

## CULTURALLY COMPETENT ORGANIZATIONS WILL

1. develop and implement human resource and other organizational policies, procedures, and practices that support staff diversity.
2. develop and implement policies, procedures, and practices that effectively address the dynamics of a diverse workforce.
3. regularly monitor the extent to which their management and staff composition reflect the diversity of the client population.
4. take corrective action as appropriate and refocus recruitment efforts; review their selection policies for inadvertent exclusion of the underrepresented, underserved, and oppressed cultural group.
5. regularly monitor and take remedial action as needed to ensure that client groups may receive services in their native or preferred language by actively recruiting and seeking to retain multilingual staff
   • providing "second language" courses to existing staff.
   • providing appropriate compensations for social workers who bring special language skill or knowledge to the profession, such as bicultural and bilingual skills or American Sign Language skills.
6. include cultural competence as a requirement for job performance by including these requirements in job descriptions, performance evaluations, promotions, and training;
7. foster a work climate, through formal and informal means, that addresses workforce diversity challenges and promotes respect for clients and colleagues of different backgrounds;
8. establish cultural norms of openness and respect for discussing situations in which insensitive or exclusionary behaviors were experienced.

**STANDARD 8. PROFESSIONAL EDUCATION** Social workers shall advocate for and participate in educational and training programs that help advance cultural competence within the profession.

**INTERPRETATION** Cultural competence is a vital link between the theoretical and practical knowledge base that defines social work expertise. Social work is a practice-oriented profession, and social work education and training need to keep up with and stay ahead of changes in professional practice, which include the changing needs of diverse client populations. Diversity needs to be addressed in social work curricula and needs to be viewed as central to faculty and staff appointments and research agendas.

The social work profession should be encouraged to take steps to ensure cultural competence as an integral part of social work education, training and practice, and to increase research and scholarship on culturally competent practice among social work professionals. This includes undergraduate, master's and doctoral programs in social work as well as post-master's training, continuing education, and meetings of the profession. Social agencies should be encouraged to provide culturally competent in-service training and opportunities for continuing education for agency-based workers. NASW should contribute to the ongoing education and training needs of all social workers, with particular emphasis on promoting culturally competent practice in continuing education in terms of content, faculty, and auspice.

In addition, the NASW Code of Ethics clearly states, "Social workers who provide supervision and consultation are responsible for setting clear, appropriate, and culturally sensitive boundaries" (p. 14). This highlights the importance of providing culturally sensitive supervision and field instruction, as well as the pivotal role of supervisors and field instructors, in promoting culturally competent practice among workers and students.

## Indicators

## CULTURALLY COMPETENT SOCIAL WORKERS WILL

1. promote professional education that advances cultural competency within the profession;
2. advocate for the infusion and integration of cultural competency standards in social work curricula and research at the BSW, MSW, and PhD levels;
3. promote and enhance culturally competent knowledge by encouraging and conducting research that develops conceptual, theoretical, and practice skills that can guide practice;
4. advocate for state-of-the-art professional education on diversity and working with diverse populations;
5. train staff in cross-cultural communication, culturally diverse customs, and techniques for resolving racial, ethnic, or cultural conflicts between staff and the clients served.

## CULTURALLY COMPETENT ORGANIZATIONS WILL

1. provide ongoing training, leadership, and support for improving cultural competency skills to all employees, including top management, middle management, frontline supervisors, frontline staff, and administrative/custodial staff;
2. resolve racial, ethnic, or cultural conflicts between staff and the clients served and among employees within the organization itself;
3. conduct evaluation research to determine their effectiveness in serving or interacting with culturally diverse client groups.

## STANDARD 9. LANGUAGE DIVERSITY Social workers shall seek to provide and advocate for the provision of information, referrals, and services in the language appropriate to the client, which may include the use of interpreters.

**INTERPRETATION** Social workers should accept the individual person in his or her totality and ensure access to needed services. Language is a source and an extension of personal identity and culture and is, therefore, one way individuals interact with others in their families and communities and across different cultural groups. Individuals and groups have a right to use their language in their individual and communal life.

Language diversity is a resource for society, and linguistic diversity should be preserved and promoted. The essence of the social work profession is to promote social justice and eliminate discrimination and oppression based on linguistic or other diversities. Title VI of the Civil Rights Act clarifies the obligation of agencies and service providers to not discriminate or have methods of administering services that may subject individuals to discrimination.

Agencies and providers of services are expected to take reasonable steps to provide services and information in an appropriate language other than English to ensure that people with limited English proficiency are effectively informed and can effectively participate in and benefit from its programs.

It is the responsibility of social services agencies and social workers to provide clients services in the language of their choice or to seek the assistance of qualified language interpreters. Social workers need to communicate respectfully and effectively with clients from different ethnic, cultural, and linguistic backgrounds; this might include knowing the client's language. Language translation should be done by trained professional interpreters (for example, certified or registered sign language interpreters). Interpreters generally need proficiency in both English and the other language, as well as orientation and training.

Social agencies and social workers have a responsibility to use language interpreters when necessary, and to make certain that interpreters do not breach confidentiality, create barriers to clients when revealing personal information that is critical to their situation, are properly trained and oriented to the ethics of interpreting in a helping situation, and have fundamental knowledge of specialized terms and concepts specific to the agency's programs or activities.

### Indicators
## CULTURALLY COMPETENT SOCIAL WORKERS WILL

1. demonstrate an understanding that language is part of the social identity of a client;
2. advocate for rights of individuals and groups to receive resources in their own language;
3. provide and advocate for information, referrals, and services in an appropriate language for the client;
4. provide jargon-free, easy-to-read material;
5. use descriptive and graphic representations (for example, pictures, symbol formats) for individuals with limited proficiency in the dominant language or with limited literacy in their own language;
6. advocate for the preservation and appreciation of language diversity among clients;
7. advocate for reasonable accommodations of the client's language needs, including the provision of professional sign language interpreters and translators;
8. improve their own ability to speak, read, write and understand the languages and dialects of their clients without attempting to engage in dialogue that is beyond their own skill level;
9. check to ensure accurate communication, realizing that there can be significant variations of word usage and colloquialisms within the same language family based on nationality or region;
10. prepare themselves to work effectively with interpreters and translators (for example, attend workshops, seek consultation from interpretation and translation services, become familiar with standards of professional interpretation and techniques of translation and back-translation) and advocate for appropriate agency policies to support the effective use of and orientation for interpreters and translators.

## STANDARD 10. CROSS-CULTURAL LEADERSHIP

Social workers shall be able to communicate information about diverse client groups to other professionals.

INTERPRETATION Social work is the appropriate profession to take a leadership role not only in disseminating knowledge about diverse client groups, but also in actively advocating for fair and equitable treatment of all clients served. This role should extend within and outside the profession.

Guided by the NASW *Code of Ethics*, social work leadership is the communication of vision to create proactive processes that empower individuals, families, groups, organizations, and communities. Diversity skills, defined as sensitivity to diversity, multicultural leadership, acceptance and tolerance, cultural competence, and tolerance of ambiguity, constitute one of the core leadership skills for successful leadership (Rank & Hutchison, 2000). Social workers should come forth to assume leadership in empowering diverse client populations, to share information about diverse populations to the general public, and to advocate for their clients' concerns at interpersonal and institutional levels, locally, nationally, and internationally.

With the establishment of standards for cultural competence in social work practice, there is an equally important need for the profession to provide ongoing training in cultural competence and to establish mechanisms for the evaluation of competence-based practice. As the social work profession develops cultural competencies, it must have the ability to measure those competencies. The development of outcome measures needs to go hand in hand with the development of these standards.

### Indicators

#### CULTURALLY COMPETENT SOCIAL WORKERS WILL

1. take leadership roles and take responsibility to promote cultural competence within the social work profession;
2. take leadership roles in communicating and disseminating information on cultural competency and client diversity to other professions through activities such as serving on committees, making presentations, writing articles, developing guidelines, and conducting research;
3. take leadership roles in empowering diverse clients to assume advocacy roles within one's own organization and in the community;
4. advocate for fair and equitable treatment for diverse groups in and outside the profession;

5. create a proactive process that empowers individuals, families, groups, organizations, and communities;
6. establish strategies for people and organizations within the profession to share information and learning with one another on how to engage in culturally competent behavior and promote culturally competent practices and policies;
7. model culturally competent behavior in their interactions with client groups, other professionals, and each other.

Note: These standards build on and adhere to other standards of social work practice established by NASW, including, but not limited to, NASW Standards for the Classification of Social Work Practice, Standards for the Practice of Clinical Social Work, Standards for Social Work Case Management, Standards for Social Work Practice in Child Protection, Standards for School Social Work Services, Standards for Social Work in Health Care Settings, Standards for Social Work Personnel Practices, and Standards for Social Work Services in Long-Term Care Facilities.

Free information on the Standards is located on the NASW Web site:

http://www.socialworkers.org.

### REFERENCES

Davis, P., & Donald, B. (1997). *Multicultural counseling competencies: Assessment, evaluation, education and training, and supervision.* Thousand Oaks, CA: Sage Publications.

Gallegos, J. S. (1982). The ethnic competence model for social work education. In B. W. White (Ed.), *Color in a white society* (pp. 1–9). Silver Spring, MD: National Association of Social Workers.

Gibelman, M., & Schervish, P. H. (1997). *Who we are: A second look.* Washington, DC: NASW Press.

Gutiérrez, L. M. (1990). Working with women of color: An empowerment perspective. *Social Work, 35*, 149–153.

Gutiérrez, L. M., & Lewis, E. A. (1999). *Empowering women of color.* New York: Columbia University Press.

Jackson, V., & López, L. (Eds.). (1999). *Cultural competency in managed behavioral healthcare.* Dover, NH: Odyssey Press.

National Association of Social Workers. (2000a). NASW code of ethics. Washington, DC: NASW.

National Association of Social Workers. (2000b). Cultural competence in the social work profession. In *Social work speaks: NASW policy statements 2000–2003* (5th ed.). Washington, DC: Author.

National Association of Social Workers. (2001). NASW standards for cultural competence in social work practice. Washington, DC: NASW Press.

Norton, D. G. (1978). *The dual perspective*. New York: Council on Social Work Education.

Perry, M. J., & Mackum, P. J. (2001). *Population change and distribution: 1990–2000*. United States 2000 Brief Series, April 2, 2001. Retrieved June 28, 2001, from http://www.census.gov/prod/2001pubs/c2kbr0 1-2.pdf

Rank, M. G., & Hutchison, W. S. (2000). An analysis of leadership within the social work profession. *Journal of Social Work Education, 36,* 487–503.

Reamer, F. G. (1998). *Ethical standards in social work: A critical review of the NASW code of ethics*. Washington, DC: NASW Press.

Simon, B. (1994). *The empowerment tradition in American social work*. New York: Columbia University Press.

Solomon, B. (1976). *Black empowerment*. New York: Columbia University Press.

# Topical Outline of Entries

This topical outline presents an overview of the Encyclopedia, with entries listed under the following subject categories:

## HUMAN BEHAVIOR

## THE PROFESSION

## SOCIAL CONDITIONS AND CHALLENGES

Voluntarism
Women
    Health Care
Youth at Risk
Youth Services

## SOCIAL ENVIRONMENTS

Asset Building
Charitable Foundations
Citizen Participation
Community Economic Development
Community
    Overview
Crime and Criminal Behavior
Criminal Justice
    Overview
    Corrections
    Criminal Courts
Dual Degree Programs
Economics and Social Welfare
Education Policy
Environment
Globalization
Health Care Financing
Health Care
    Overview
International Association of Schools of Social Work
    (IASSW)
International Federation of Social Workers
    (IFSW)
International Social Welfare
    Overview
    Organizations and Activities
International Social Work
    Overview
    Education
International Social Work and Social Welfare
    Africa (Sub-Sahara)
    Asia
    Australia and Pacific Islands
    Caribbean
    Central America
    Europe
    Middle East and North Africa
    North America
    South America
Juvenile Justice
    Overview
    Juvenile and Family Courts
Leadership
Managed Care

Media Campaigns
Political Ideology and Social Welfare
Probation and Parole
Reproductive Health
Retirement
Social Policy
    Overview
    History (Colonial Times to 1900)
    History (1900–1950)
    History (1950–1980)
    History (1980 to Present)
Unemployment Insurance
Unions
Workers' Compensation

## SOCIAL JUSTICE

Advocacy
Children's Rights
Civil Liberties
Civil Rights
Consumer Rights
Disparities and Inequalities
Environmental Justice
Health Care Reform
Human Rights
Income Distribution
Oppression
Peace
Political Process
Restorative Justice
Social Justice
Social Movements
Voter Education

## BIOGRAPHIES

Abbott, Edith
Abbott, Grace
Abernathy, Ralph David
Adams, Frankie Victoria
Addams, Jane
Alexander, Chauncey A.
Altmeyer, Arthur J.
Anderson, Delwin
Baldwin, Roger Nash
Barrett, Janie Porter
Bartlett, Harriett M.
Barton, Clarissa (Clara) Harlowe
Bechill, William
Beck, Bertram

# Directory of Contributors

ANN A. ABBOTT
*West Chester University, West Chester, PA*
  Professional Conduct

PAUL A. ABELS
*California State University, Long Beach, CA*
  Alexander, Chauncey A.

MIMI ABRAMOVITZ
*Hunter College, City University of New York*
  Political Ideology and Social Welfare

LAURA S. ABRAMS
*University of California, Los Angeles*
  Bisexuality

JULIE ABRAMSON
*University at Albany, State University of New York*
  Teams

JAMES "IKE" ADAMS
*University of Alabama*
  Men: Overveiw

LINDA ADLER
*Independent Scholar, Bellingham, WA*
  Rothman, Beulah

KYLIE AGLLIAS
*University of Newcastle, New South Wales, Australia*
  International Social Work and Social Welfare:
    Australia and the Pacific Islands

MARIAN A. AGUILAR
*Texas A & M International University*
  Women: Health Care

FREDERICK L. AHEARN
*Catholic University of America*
  Displaced People

EUGENE AISENBERG
*University of Washington*
  Latinos and Latinas: Overview

KRISTINE J. AJROUCH
*Eastern Michigan University*
  Arab Americans

SHEILA H. AKABAS
*Columbia University*
  Employee Assistance Programs

ALEAN AL-KRENAWI
*Ben-Gurion University of the Negev, Israel*
  International Social Work and Social Welfare:
    Middle East and North Africa

KATHRYN P. ALESSANDRIA
*West Chester University, West Chester, PA*
  White Ethnic Groups

RUDOLPH ALEXANDER, JR.
*Ohio State University*
  Criminal Justice Overview

PAULA ALLEN-MEARES
*University of Michigan*
  School Social Work

GUNNAR ALMGREN
*University of Washington*
  Demographics

CATHERINE ALTER
*University of Denver, Emerita*
  Interorganizational Practice Interventions

TERRY ALTILIO
*Beth Israel Medical Center, New York*
  Pain

MARYANN AMODEO
*Boston University*
  Alcohol and Drug Problems: Practice Interventions

JEANE W. ANASTAS
*New York University*
  Ethics in Research

SAUL ANDRON
*Yeshiva University, New York*
  Jewish Communal Services

BETH ANGELL
*University of Chicago*
  Behavioral Theory

HELMUT ANHEIER
*University of California, Los Angeles, and University of*
*Heidelberg, Germany*
    Charitable Foundations

ROBERT C. ARNOLD
*National Association of Social Workers, Washington, DC*
    Northen, Helen
    Reid, Bill

NINA L. ARONOFF
*Wheelock College, Boston, MA*
    Interprofessional and Partnered Practice

ADRIENNE ASCH
*Yeshiva University, New York*
    Blindness and Visual Impairment

REBECCA S. ASHERY
*Independent Scholar, Potomac, MD*
    Primary Health Care

YVONNE ASAMOAH
*Hunter College, City University of New York, Emerita*
    Hale, Clara

RON AVI ASTOR
*University of Southern California*
    School Violence

DARLYNE BAILEY
*University of Minnesota*
    Leadership
    Naparstek, Arthur J.
    Pernell, Ruby B.

W. DWIGHT BAILEY
*National Association of Social Workers,*
*Washington, DC*
    Confidentiality and Privileged Communication

PETA-ANNE BAKER
*University of the West Indies, Mona, Kingston, Jamaica*
    International Social Work and Social Welfare:
      Caribbean

MICHELE BALDWIN
*Northwestern University*
    Satir, Virginia

PALLASSANA R. BALGOPAL
*University of Illinois Urbana–Champaign, Emeritus*
    Asian Americans: Overview

MICHELLE S. BALLAN
*Columbia University*
    Termination

GISOO BARNES
*Temple University*
    HIV/AIDS: Children

RICHARD P. BARTH
*University of Maryland*
    Adoption

DEBORAH BASS-RUBENSTEIN
*Independent Health and Human Services Consultant,*
*Manassas, VA*
    Youth at Risk

LAINA Y. BAY-CHENG
*University at Buffalo, State University of New York*
    Human Sexuality

MARCIA BAYNE-SMITH
*Queens College, City University of New York*
    Caribbean Americans

MIRIAM L. BEARSE
*National Indian Child Welfare Association, Portland, OR*
    Native Americans: Practice Interventions

LOU M. BEASLEY
*Clark Atlanta University*
    Abernathy, Ralph David

DAVID BECERRA
*Arizona State University*
    Alcohol and Drug Problems: Prevention

BERTRAM M. BECK (*deceased*)
*Henry Street Settlement Urban Life Center*
    Ginsberg, Mitchell I.

LINDA BEEBE
*American Psychological Association and NASW Press,*
*Washington, DC*
    Fizdale, Ruth

JOHN R. BELCHER
*University of Maryland, Baltimore*
    Snyder, Mitchell "Mitch"

JENNIFER L. BELLAMY
*Washington University in St. Louis*
    Best Practices

RAMI BENBENISHTY
*Hebrew University of Jerusalem*
   School Violence

ELIZABETH A. S. BENEFIELD
*University of North Carolina at Chapel Hill*
   Kuralt, Wallace H., Sr.

KIA J. BENTLEY
*Virginia Commonwealth University*
   Psychotropic Medications

INSOO KIM BERG (*deceased*)
*Brief Family Therapy Center, Milwaukee, WI*
   Authoritative Settings and Involuntary Clients

CANDYCE S. BERGER
*Stony Brook University, State University of
New York*
   Health Care Financing

KAREN BERNER LITTLE
*Daemon College, Amherst, NY*
   Love, Maria Maltby

PHILIP BERNSTEIN
*Council of Jewish Federations, New York*
   Gurin, Arnold
   Gurin, Helen

MARIANNE BERRY
*University of Kansas*
   Home-Based Interventions

FRED H. BESTHORN
*University of Northern Iowa*
   Environment

SONDRA G. BEVERLY
*Independent Scholar, Lawrence, KS*
   Earned Income Tax Credit

DAVID E. BIEGEL
*Case Western Reserve University*
   Social Work Education Research

JOEL BLAU
*Stony Brook University, State University of New York*
   Income Distribution

SARAH E. BLEDSOE
*University of North Carolina at Chapel Hill*
   Best Practices

LEONARD BLOKSBERG
*Boston University*
   Lowy, Louis

MARTIN BLOOM
*University of Connecticut, Emeritus*
   Prevention

ROBERT BLUNDO
*University of North Carolina at Wilmington*
   Men: Practice Interventions
   Strengths-Based Framework

STEPHANIE CLINTONIA BODDIE
*Washington University in St. Louis*
   Faith-Based Agencies and Social Work

RENEÉ BOWMAN DANIEL
*Daemon College, Amherst, NY*
   Love, Maria Maltby

RUTH A. BRANDWEIN
*University of Tennessee*
   Women: Overview

JENNIFER BRIAR-BONPANE
*Independent Scholar, Seattle, WA*
   Briar, Scott

KATHARINE BRIAR-LAWSON
*University at Albany, State University of New York*
   Briar, Scott
   Family Services

MARY BRICKER-JENKINS
*Temple University, Emerita*
   Progressive Social Work

ELEANOR L. BRILLIANT
*Rutgers University, Emeritus*
   Management: Volunteers

LAURA R. BRONSTEIN
*Binghamton University, State University of New York*
   Teams

PATRICIA BROWNELL
*Fordham University*
   Adult Protective Services

POLLY Y. BROWNING
*University of Texas at Austin*
   Eating Disorders

ANNA CELESTE BURKE
*Ohio State University*
    Alcohol and Drug Problems: Law Enforcement and
        Legal Policy

JEFFREY A. BUTTS
*University of Chicago*
    Probation and Parole

ANGEL P. CAMPOS
*Stony Brook University, State University of
New York*
    Latinos and Latinas: Puerto Ricans

EDWARD R. CANDA
*University of Kansas*
    Human Needs: Religion and Spirituality

BONNIE E. CARLSON
*University at Albany, State University of
New York*
    Intimate Partner Violence

IRIS CARLTON-LANEY
*University of North Carolina at Chapel Hill*
    King, Martin Luther, Jr.
    Social Policy: History (1900–1950)

KENNETH S. CARPENTER
*NASW Foundation, Washington, DC*
    Anderson, Delwin M.
    Beck, Bertram
    Berry, Margaret
    Perlman, Helen Harris
    Reichert, Kurt and Betty
    Vinter, Robert

VALIRE CARR COPELAND
*University of Pittsburgh*
    Maternal and Child Health

KATHLEEN A. CASEY
*University of Texas at Austin*
    Rehabilitation

SHAWN A. CASSIMAN
*University of Dayton*
    Supplemental Security Income

KAREN CASTELLANOS-BROWN
*University of Maryland, Baltimore*
    Life Span: Early Childhood and Pre-School

LETHA A. CHADIHA
*University of Michigan*
    Family Caregiving

YVONNE CHASE
*University of Alaska–Anchorage*
    Professional Liability and Malpractice

PRANAB CHATTERJEE
*Case Western Reserve University*
    Technology Transfer

BENSON CHISANGA
*University of Montana*
    Community Development

NAMKEE G. CHOI
*University of Texas at Austin*
    Adult Day Care

YOONSUN CHOI
*University of Chicago*
    Asian Americans: Koreans

GRACE CHRIST
*Columbia University*
    Terminal Illness

ELIZABETH J. CLARK
*Executive Director, National Association of Social
Workers, Washington, DC*
    National Association of Social Workers

MARY ANN CLUTE
*Eastern Washington University*
    Disability: Physical Disabilities

RAM A. CNAAN
*University of Pennsylvania*
    Contexts/Settings: Faith-Based Settings
    Smalley, Ruth Elizabeth

JO ANN R. COE REGAN
*University of Hawai'i at Manoa*
    Technology: Technology in Social Work
        Education

IRA C. COLBY
*University of Houston*
    Howard, Oliver Otis
    Social Work Education: Social Welfare
        Policy

ALLAN HUGH COLE, JR.
*Austin Presbyterian Theological Seminary*
   Epistemology

ELAINE CONGRESS
*Fordham University*
   Code of Ethics

PATRICIA COOK-CRAIG
*University of Kentucky*
   Organizational Learning

BECKY S. CORBETT
*BSCorbett Consulting, LLC, Washington, DC*
   Appendix: Distinctive Dates in Social Welfare
      History
   Appendix: Evolution of Selected
      Organizations

JACQUELINE CORCORAN
*Virginia Commonwealth University*
   Direct Practice

KEVIN CORCORAN
*Portland State University*
   Scales and Indices

TERRI COMBS ORME
*University of Tennessee*
   Life Span: Parenting

MARK E. COURTNEY
*University of Washington*
   Child Welfare: History and Policy
      Framework

CHARLES D. COWGER
*University of Missouri–Columbia, Emeritus*
   Peace

LOIS ANNE COWLES
*Idaho State University, Emerita, and St. Thomas Clinic,
Franklin, IN*
   Health Care: Practice Interventions

CAROLE B. COX
*Fordham University*
   Alzheimer's Disease and Other Dimentias

MARK CREEKMORE
*University of Michigan*
   Cultural Institutions and the Arts

TERRY L. CROSS
*National Indian Child Welfare Association,
Portland, OR*
   Cultural Competence

ELLEN L. CSIKAI
*University of Alabama*
   End-of-Life Decisions

HERMAN CURIEL
*University of Oklahoma*
   Latinos and Latinas: Mexicans

MARGARET DANIEL (*deceased*)
*National Institute of Mental Health, Bethesda, MD*
   Blackey, Eileen

ELIZABETH ANN DANTO
*Hunter College, City University of New York*
   Psychoanalysis

SANDRA K. DANZIGER
*University of Michigan*
   Social Problems

JEREMY DARMAN
*Social Science Associates, Utica NY*
   Juvenile Delinquency

JOSEPH DAVENPORT, III
*Independent Scholar, Columbia, MO*
   Rural Practice

JUDITH A. DAVENPORT
*University of Missouri–Columbia, Emerita*
   Rural Practice

DIANE RAE DAVIS
*Eastern Washington University*
   Harm Reduction

KING DAVIS
*University of Texas at Austin*
   Disparities and Inequalities

LARRY E. DAVIS
*University of Pittsburgh*
   African Americans: Overview

PHYLLIS J. DAY
*Independent Scholar, West Lafayette, IN*
   Social Policy: History (Colonial Times to 1900)

DIANE DE ANDA
*University of California, Los Angeles, Emerita*
    Adolescents: Overview
    Adolescents: Demographics and Social Issues

DONNA DEANGELIS
*Association of Social Work Boards, Culpepper, VA*
    Licensing

PETER DEJONG
*Calvin College, Grand Rapids, MI*
    Interviewing

MELVIN DELGADO
*Boston University*
    Urban Practice

JOANNE "ROCKY" DELAPLAINE
*Labor Heritage Foundation, Washington, DC*
    Jones, Mary Harris "Mother"

KEVIN L. DEWEAVER
*University of Georgia*
    Disability: Neurocognitive Disabilities

ELLEN R. DEVOE
*Boston University*
    Human Needs, Family

FREDERICK A. DIBLASIO
*University of Maryland, Baltimore*
    Snyder, Mitchell "Mitch"

MIRIAM DINERMAN
*Rutgers University, Emerita*
    Gibelman, Margaret

DIANA M. DINITTO
*University of Texas at Austin*
    Comorbidity

ANDREW DOBELSTEIN
*University of North Carolina at Chapel Hill, Emeritus*
    Privatization

KAREN DODGE
*University of Miami and Palm Beach County Health Department*
    Migrant Workers

SILVIA DOMÍNGUEZ
*Northeastern University*
    Social Capital

SUSAN DONNER
*Smith College*
    Starr, Ellen Gates

MICHAEL A. DOVER
*Cleveland State University*
    Human Needs: Overview

AMANDA DUFFY RANDALL
*University of Nebraska at Omaha*
    Licensing

PAUL DUONGTRAN
*University of Wyoming*
    Asian Americans: Southeast Asians

CATHERINE N. DULMUS
*University at Buffalo*
    Mental Illness: Adults

LARRAINE M. EDWARDS
*Practitioner, Winston–Salem, NC*
    Hoey, Jane M.
    Howe, Samuel Gridley
    Jarrett, Mary Cromwell
    Kelley, Florence
    Kellogg, Paul Underwood
    Lathrop, Julia Clifford
    Lee, Porter Raymond
    Lowell, Josephine Shaw
    Lurie, Harry Lawrence
    Newstetter, Wilber I.
    Pray, Kenneth
    Riis, Jacob August
    Robison, Sophie Moses
    Rubinow, Isaac Max
    Rush, Benjamin
    Seton, Elizabeth Ann Bayley (Mother Seton)
    Simkhovitch, Mary Kingsbury
    Smith, Zilpha Drew
    Switzer, Mary Elizabeth
    Taft, Julia Jessie
    Taylor, Graham
    Wald, Lillian

NABILA EL-BASSEL
*Columbia University*
    Practice Interventions and Research

DOREEN ELLIOTT
*University of Texas at Arlington*
    International Social Welfare: Organizations and
        Activities

PAUL H. EPHROSS
*University of Maryland*
 Bechill, William D.

IRWIN EPSTEIN
*Hunter College, City University of New York*
 Agency-Based Research

JOYCE E. EVERETT
*Smith College*
 Foster Care

PATRICIA L. EWALT
*University of Hawai'i at Manoa*
 Lucas, Elizabeth Jessemine Kauikeolani Low

MARK EZELL
*University of Kansas*
 Juvenile Justice: Juvenile and Family Courts

MIKE FABRICANT
*Hunter College, City University of New York*
 Settlements and Neighborhood Centers

HANS S. FALCK
*Virginia Commonwealth University*
 Carlton, Thomas Owen

FRANCES FELDMAN
*University of Southern California, Emerita*
 Bogardus, Emory
 Carter, Genevieve

RONALD A. FELDMAN
*Columbia University*
 Miller, Samuel O.

PATRICIA A. FENNELL
*Albany Health Management Associates, Inc.*
 Chronic Illness

KRISTIN M. FERGUSON
*University of Southern California*
 Civil Society

LISA A. FERRETTI
*University at Albany, State University of New York*
 Retirement

JOSEFINA FIGUEIRA-MCDONOUGH
*Arizona State University, Emerita*
 Women: Practice Interventions

JERRY FINN
*University of Washington, Tacoma*
 Technology: Technology in Micro Practice

JANET L. FINN
*University of Montana*
 Social Justice

JOEL FISCHER
*University of Hawai'i*
 Single-System Designs

ROBERT FISHER
*University of Connecticut*
 Settlements and Neighborhood Centers

JERRY FLOERSCH
*Case Western Reserve University*
 Social Work Practice: Theoretical Base

SONDRA J. FOGEL
*University of South Florida*
 Sexual Harassment

ROWENA FONG
*University of Texas at Austin*
 Asian Americans: Practice Interventions

LARRY W. FOSTER
*Cleveland State University*
 Bioethics

FRANCES FOX-PIVEN
*Graduate Center, City University of New York*
 Voter Education

LYDIA M. FRANCO
*Mount Sinai School of Medicine, New York*
 HIV/AIDS: Practice Interventions

TODD MICHAEL FRANKE
*University of California, Los Angeles*
 Adolescents: Overview
 Adolescents: Demographics and
 Social Issues

CYNTHIA FRANKLIN
*University of Texas at Austin*
 Family Therapy

CHERYL L. FRANKS
*Columbia University*
 Privilege

STACEY FREEDENTHAL
*University of Denver*
Suicide

EDITH M. FREEMAN
*University of Kansas, Emerita*
Methods of Practice Interventions

PETER GABOR
*University of Calgary*
Program Evaluation

COLLEEN GALAMBOS
*University of Missouri–Columbia*
Health Care: Overview

MAEDA J. GALINSKY
*University of North Carolina at Chapel Hill*
Groups

DOROTHY N. GAMBLE
*University of North Carolina at Chapel Hill,
Emerita*
Community: Practice Interventions

VICTOR L GARCIA TORO
*University of Puerto Rico*
Marin, Rosa C.

DANIEL S. GARDNER
*New York University*
Aging: Racial and Ethnic Groups

DIANA R. GARLAND
*Baylor University, Waco, TX*
Christian Social Services

CHARLES D. GARVIN
*University of Michigan*
Groups

LAUREN B. GATES
*Columbia University*
Vocational Services

LUDWIG L. GEISMAR
*Rutgers University, Emeritus*
Vasey, Wayne

SHELDON R. GELMAN
*Yeshiva University, New York*
Jewish Communal Services
Levy, Charles Samuel

CAREL B. GERMAIN (*deceased*)
*University of Connecticut*
Ecological Framework

ELIZABETH T. GERSHOFF
*University of Michigan*
Youth Services

JACOB GERSHONI
*Columbia Presbyterian Medical Center, New York*
Psychodrama

DAVID G. GIL
*Brandeis University*
Sieder, Violet M.

MJ GILBERT
*University of Minnesota*
Transgender People

NEIL GILBERT
*University of California, Berkeley*
Specht, Harry

DAVID F. GILLESPIE
*Washington University in St. Louis*
Disasters

JEANNE M. GIOVANNONI
*University of California, Los Angeles, Emerita*
Kitano, Harry H.L.

ALEX GITTERMAN
*University of Connecticut*
Cloward, Richard
Ecological Framework
Weiner, Hyman J.

EDA G. GOLDSTEIN
*New York University, Emerita*
Psychosocial Framework

JUDITH G. GONYEA
*Boston University*
Life Span: Oldest Senior/Aged-Late ("Old Old")

CAROL GORENBERG
*National Association of Social Workers, Washington, DC*
Confidentiality and Privileged Communication

STEPHEN H. GORIN
*Plymouth State University, Plymouth, NH*
Health Care Reform

CHRISTI GRANSTAFF
*National Association of Social Workers Political Action for Candidate Election, Washington, DC*
  Political Social Work

JOHN R. GRAHAM
*University of Calgary*
  International Social Work and Social Welfare: Middle East and North Africa

DARLENE GRANT
*University of Texas at Austin*
  Clinical Social Work

MEL GRAY
*University of Newcastle, New South Wales, Australia*
  International Social Work and Social Welfare: Australia and Pacific Islands

GILBERT J. GREENE
*Ohio State University*
  Brief Therapies

ROBERTA R. GREENE
*University of Texas at Austin*
  Resilience

CATHERINE G. GREENO
*University of Pittsburgh*
  Mental Health: Overview

RICHARD M. GRINNELL, JR.
*Western Michigan University*
  Program Evaluation

JESSICA GROGAN
*University of Texas at Austin*
  Humanistic Therapies

KIRSTEN A. GRØNBJERG
*Indiana University*
  Fundraising

THOMAS P. GULLOTTA
*Child & Family Agency, New London, CT*
  Prevention

SHENYANG GUO
*University of North Carolina at Chapel Hill*
  Quantitative Research

NEIL B. GUTERMAN
*University of Chicago*
  Community Violence

LORRAINE GUTIERREZ
*University of Michigan*
  Cultural Institutions and the Arts

ROLAND L. GUYOTTE
*University of Minnesota, Morris*
  Cohen, Wilbur

JAN L. HAGEN
*University at Albany, State University of New York*
  Temporary Assistance for Needy Families

MUHAMMAD HAJ-YAHIA
*Hebrew University of Jerusalem*
  Community Violence

NIGEL HALL
*Kingston University, Surrey, UK*
  International Federation of Social Workers (IFSW)

DONNA HARDINA
*California State University, Fresno*
  Citizen Participation

DANIEL HARKNESS
*Boise State University*
  Consultation

SARA HARMON
*State Communities AID Association, Albany, NY*
  Folks, Homer

SUSAN C. HARNDEN
*University of Texas at Austin*
  Couples

DONNA HARRINGTON
*University of Maryland, Baltimore*
  Life Span: Early Childhood and Pre-School

JESSE J. HARRIS, COL. USA RET.
*University of Maryland, Baltimore*
  Military Social Work

MARY BETH HARRIS
*University of Central Florida*
  Family Life Education

SUNNY HARRIS ROME
*George Mason University*
  Forensic Social Work

ANN HARTMAN
*Smith College*
    Germain, Carel Bailey
    Meyer, Carol H.

LESLIE HASCHE
*Washington University in St. Louis*
    Aging: Services

YEHESKEL "ZEKE" HASENFELD
*University of California, Los Angeles*
    Contracting Out of Social Services

KAREN S. HAYNES
*California State University, San Marcos*
    Political Process

LYNNE M. HEALY
*University of Connecticut*
    International Social Work: Overview
    Salomon, Alice van Kleeck, Mary Ann

BRENDA N. HENRY
    Maternal and Child Health

SANTOS H. HERNÁNDEZ
*University of Texas at Arlington*
    Huantes, Margarita R.
    Mutual Aid Societies

JOHN M. HERRICK
*Michigan State University*
    Social Policy: Overview

RICHARD HIBBERT
*Mount Sinai School of Medicine, New York*
    HIV/AIDS: Practice Interventions

SARAH HICKS
*Washington University in St. Louis*
    Alaska Natives

RICK HOEFER
*University of Texas at Arlington*
    Social Welfare Expenditures

KAY S. HOFFMAN
*University of Kentucky*
    Social Work Education: Overview

M. C. TERRY HOKENSTAD
*Case Western Reserve University*
    International Social Work: Education
    Sanders, Daniel

TOM HOLLAND
*University of Georgia*
    Organizations and Governance

STEPHEN HOLLOWAY
*Barry University, Miami Shores, FL, Emeritus*
    Brager, George

JESSICA HOLMES
*Council on Social Work Education, Alexandria, VA*
    Council on Social Work Education

LAURA HOPSON
*University of Texas at Austin*
    Family Therapy

NANCY R. HOOYMAN
*University of Washington*
    Aging: Overview
    Gottlieb, Naomi R.

JUNE GARY HOPPS
*University of Georgia*
    Social Work Profession: Overview

HEATHER HORTON
*University at Albany, State University of New York*
    Group Work

MATTHEW O. HOWARD
*University of North Carolina at Chapel Hill*
    Evidence-Based Practice

ROBERT B. HUDSON
*Boston University*
    Pension and Retirement Programs

NANCY A. HUMPHREYS
*University of Connecticut*
    Hate Crimes

SKI HUNTER
*University of Texas at Arlington*
    Adults: Overview

BARBARA HUNTER-RANDALL JOSEPH (*deceased*)
*College at Old Westbury, State University of New York*
    Human Need: Overview
    Progressive Social Work

DAVID L. HUSSEY
*Kent State University*
    Adolescents: Practice Interventions

ELIZABETH D. HUTCHISON
*Virginia Commonwealth University*
    Social Work Education: Human Behavior & Social
    Environment

CHERYL A. HYDE
*Temple University*
    Feminist Social Work Practice

DEMETRIUS S. IATRIDIS
*Boston College*
    Policy Practice

LARRY D. ICARD
*Temple University*
    HIV/AIDS: Children

RUTH IRELAN KNEE
*Consultant in Long-Term/Mental Health Care,
Fairfax, VA*
    Wittman, Milton

ALLAN IRVING
*Widener University*
    Cassidy, Harry

RICHARD ISRALOWITZ
*Ben-Gurion University, Beer Sheva, Israel*
    Alcohol and Drug Problems: Overview

D. LYNN JACKSON
*University of North Texas*
    Abortion

MAXINE JACOBSON
*University of Montana*
    Social Justice

KRISTINA JASKYTE
*University of Georgia*
    Management: Practice Interventions

SRINIKA JAYARATNE
*University of Michigan*
    Dual Degree Programs

JEFFREY M. JENSON
*University of Denver*
    Evidence-Based Practice

SEAN JOE
*University of Michigan*
    Life Span: Young Adulthood

ALICE K. JOHNSON BUTTERFIELD
*University of Illinois at Chicago*
    Community Development

JESSICA K. M. JOHNSON
*Boston College*
    Divorce

BARBARA L. JONES
*University of Texas at Austin*
    Children: Health Care

DAVID N. JONES
*International Federation of Social Workers,
Birmingham, UK*
    International Social Work and Social Welfare:
    Europe

DNIKA JONES TRAVIS
*University of Southern California*
    Management: Human Resources

LANI V. JONES
*University at Albany, State University of New York*
    Life Span: Overview

MELISSA JONSON-REID
*Washington University in St Louis*
    Education Policy

CATHELEEN JORDAN
*University of Texas at Arlington*
    Assessment

MILDRED C. JOYNER
*West Chester University, West Chester, PA*
    Baccalaureate Social Workers

MARIA JULIA
*Ohio State University*
    International Social Work and Social Welfare:
    Central America

JILL DONER KAGLE
*University of Illinois at Urbana–Champaign, Emerita*
    Recording

KOSTA N. KALOGEROGIANNIS
*Mount Sinai School of Medicine, New York*
    HIV/AIDS: Practice Interventions

ROSALIE A. KANE
*University of Minnesota*
    Long-Term Care

STEPHEN A. KAPP
*University of Kansas*
    Agency-Based Research

HOWARD KARGER
*University of Houston*
    Unions

LENARD W. KAYE
*University of Maine*
    Aging: Practice Interventions

KAREN KAYSER
*Boston College*
    Divorce

MICHAEL S. KELLY
*Loyola University, Oak Park, IL*
    Task-Centered Practice

PATRICIA J. KELLY
*University of Missouri–Kansas City*
    Reproductive Health

PATRICIA KELLEY
*University of Iowa, Emerita*
    Narratives

KATHERINE A. KENDALL
*Council on Social Work Education, Alexandria,*
*VA (Ret.)*
    Ripple, Lillian

SHANTI K. KHINDUKA
*Washington University in St. Louis*
    Globalization

JOHNNY S. KIM
*University of Kansas*
    Strengths Perspective

ERIC R. KINGSON
*Syracuse University*
    Social Security Program
    Wickenden, Elizabeth

KAREN S. KNOX
*Texas State University–San Marcos*
    Victim Services

CHRISTOPHER P. KOGUT
*Virginia Commonwealth University*
    Psychotropic Medications

NORMA KOLKO PHILLIPS
*Lehman College, City University of New York*
    Terrorism

MARY ELLEN KONDRAT
*University of Kansas*
    Person-in-Environment

JORDAN I. KOSBERG
*University of Alabama*
    Men: Overview

JOSEPH KOZAKIEWICZ
*Michigan State University*
    Child Support

BETTY J. KRAMER
*University of Wisconsin–Madison*
    Palliative Care

DERRICK KRANKE
*Case Western Reserve University*
    Technology Transfer

NANCY P. KROPF
*Georgia State University*
    Life Span: Older Adulthood/Seniors
    ("Young Old")

PAUL A. KURZMAN
*Hunter College, City University of New York*
    Occupational Social Work

MARINA LALAYANTS
*Hunter College, City University of New York*
    Research: Overview

SUSAN J. LAMBERT
*University of Chicago*
    Human Needs: Work and Development

SHANNON R. LANE
*University of Connecticut*
    Hate Crimes

HEATHER LARKIN
*University at Albany, State University of New York*
    Life Span: Childhood and Latency

MARIE M. LAURIA
*University of North Carolina at Chapel Hill*
    Oncology Social Work

CATHERINE K. LAWRENCE
*University at Albany, State University of New York*
Temporary Assistance for Needy Families

HAL A. LAWSON
*University at Albany, State University of New York*
Collaborative Practice

EUN-KYOUNG OTHELIA LEE
*Boston College*
Multiculturalism

LESLIE LEIGHNINGER
*Arizona State University*
Historiography

LAURA LEIN
*University of Texas at Austin*
Child Care Services

DANIEL LEBOLD
*University of North Carolina*
Keith-Lucas, Alan

LORI LESTER
*Independent Scholar, Ft. Walton Beach, FL*
Advocacy

CATHLEEN A. LEWANDOWSKI
*University at Albany, State University of New York*
Life Span: Development and Infancy
(Birth to Age Three)

MICHAEL ANTHONY LEWIS
*Stony Brook University, State University of New York*
Economics and Social Welfare

DONALD M. LINHORST
*Saint Louis University*
Consumer Rights

JULIA H. LITTELL
*Bryn Mawr College*
Meta-Analysis

MICHELLE LIVERMORE
*Louisiana State University*
Employment and Unemployment

JACQUELINE L. LLOYD
*Temple University*
HIV/AIDS: Children

MARK FRAZIER LLOYD
*University of Pennsylvania*
Robinson, Virginia Pollard

SADYE L. M. LOGAN
*University of South Carolina*
Family: Overview

NANCY LOHMANN
*West Virginia University*
Management: Financial

ROGER A. LOHMANN
*West Virginia University*
Management: Financial

JOHN F. LONGRES
*University of Washington, Emeritus*
Burns, Eveline Mabel
Gonzalez Molina de la Caro, Dolores
Hamilton, Gordon
Hearn, Gordon
Hopkins, Harry Lloyd
Lassalle, Beatriz
Latinos and Latinas: Overview
Lindeman, Eduard Christian
Pagan de Colon, Petroamerica
Richmond, Mary Ellen
Rivera de Alvarado, Carmen
Rodriguez Pastor, Soledad
Towle, Charlotte
Witte, Ernest Frederic

LUZ MARILIS LÓPEZ
*Boston University*
Alcohol and Drug Problems: Practice Interventions

SANDRA A. LOPEZ
*University of Houston*
Contexts/Settings: Private/Independent Practice
Settings

KIM LORBER
*Ramapo College of New Jersey*
Gibelman, Margaret

TONY B. LOWE
*University of Georgia*
Social Work Profession: Overview

YUHWA EVA LU
*New York University*
Asian Americans: Chinese

JAMES E. LUBBEN
*Boston College*
    Social Work Education: Doctoral

DOMAN LUM
*California State University, Sacramento, Emeritus*
    Culturally Competent Practice

ELAINE M. MACCIO
*Louisiana State University*
    Marriage and Domestic Partners

MARK J. MACGOWAN
*Florida International University*
    Group Dynamics

ROMEL W. MACKELPRANG
*Eastern Washington University*
    Disability: Overview

GORDON MACNEIL
*University of Alabama*
    Compulsive Behaviors

ROBERT G. MADDEN
*Saint Joseph College, West Hartford, CT*
    Legal System

SANDY MAGAÑA
*University of Wisconsin–Madison*
    Supplemental Security Income

ANNETTE M. MAHONEY
*Hunter College, City University of New York*
    Caribbean Americans

GERALD P. MALLON
*Hunter College, City University of New York*
    Gay Families and Parenting

ANTHONY N. MALUCCIO
*University of Connecticut, Emeritus*
    Children: Practice Interventions

JILL E. MANSKE
*United States Department of Veteran Affairs, Washington, DC*
    Veteran Services

MOLLIE T. MARCHIONE
*University of Texas at Austin*
    Kingsbury, Susan Myra

RONALD MARKS
*Tulane University*
    Cassidy, Helen

JOANNE MARLATT OTTO
*Independent Scholar, Boulder, CO*
    Adult Protective Services

JEANNE C. MARSH
*University of Chicago*
    Epstein, Laura

FLAVIO F. MARSIGLIA
*Arizona State University*
    Alcohol and Drug Problems: Prevention

JAMES I. MARTIN
*New York University*
    Gay Men: Overview

JERRY D. MARX
*University of New Hampshire*
    Philanthropy

JON KEI MATSUOKA
*University of Hawai'i*
    Social Impact Assessment

GARY MATHEWS
*Western Michigan University*
    Mahaffey, Maryann

BERNARD MAYER
*CDR Associates, Boulder, CO*
    Conflict Resolution

PHILLIP MCCALLION
*University at Albany, State University of New York*
    Retirement

MARY M. MCKAY
*Mount Sinai School of Medicine, New York*
    HIV/AIDS: Practice Interventions

J. CURTIS MCMILLEN
*Washington University in St. Louis*
    Quality of Care

KELLY MCNALLY KONEY
*Independent Scholar, Atlanta, GA*
    Contexts/Settings: Interorganizational
    Contexts

C. Aaron McNeece
*Florida State University*
    Criminal Justice: Corrections

John G. McNutt
*University of Delaware*
    Social Work Practice: History and Evolution
    Technology: Technology in Macro Practice

Ruth McRoy
*University of Texas at Austin*
    Multiculturalism

Maria S. Mera
*Fordham University*
    Termination

Taiwanna Messam
*Mount Sinai School of Medicine, New York*
    HIV/AIDS: Practice Interventions

Lori Messinger
*University of Kansas*
    Lesbians: Overview

Megan Meyer
*University of Maryland*
    Political Interventions

Mizan R. Miah
*Southern Illinois University, Carbondale*
    Social Development

James S. Mickelson
*Independent Scholar, Vista, CA*
    Political Process

James Midgley
*University of California, Berkeley*
    Beveridge, Lord William
    International Social Welfare: Overview

David B. Miller
*Case Western Reserve University*
    Life Span: Young Adulthood

Robert L. Miller, Jr.
*University at Albany, State University of New York*
    Gay Men: Practice Interventions

Sharon E. Milligan
*Case Western Reserve University*
    Community Building

Lorraine C. Minnite
*Barnard College*
    Voter Education

Terry Mizrahi
*Hunter College, City University of New York*
    Health Care Reform

Brij Mohan
*Louisiana State University*
    Asian Americans: South Asians

Noreen Mokuau
*University of Hawai'i at Manoa*
    Native Hawaiians and Pacific Islanders

Jacqueline Mondros
*Hunter College, City University of New York*
    Community Organization

Heehyul Moon
*Case Western Reserve University*
    Technology Transfer

Sharon E. Moore
*University of Louisville*
    African Americans: Practice Interventions

Amanda Moore McBride
*Washington University in St. Louis*
    Civic Engagement

Michàlle E. Mor Barak
*University of Southern California*
    Management: Human Resources

Paula T. T. Morelli
*University of Hawai'i at Manoa*
    Social Impact Assessment

Sherri Morgan
*National Association of Social Workers,
Washington, DC*
    Confidentiality and Privileged Communication

Mel Morgenbesser
*University of Wisconsin–Madison*
    Minahan, Anne

Deana F. Morrow
*Winthrop University, Rock Hill, South Carolina*
    Lesbians: Practice Interventions

NANCY MORROW-HOWELL
*Washington University in St. Louis*
   Aging: Services

JENNIFER E. MOSLEY
*University of Chicago*
   Contexts/Settings: Agency and Organization in
      Non-Profit Settings

TAMARAH MOSS-KNIGHT
*Howard University*
   African Americans: Immigrants of African Origin

DAVID P. MOXLEY
*University of Oklahoma*
   Interdisciplinarity

NANCY R. MUDRICK
*Syracuse University*
   Blindness and Visual Impairment

EDWARD J. MULLEN
*Columbia University*
   Best Practices

ELIZABETH A. MULROY
*University of Maryland, Baltimore*
   Community Needs Assessment

REBECCA S. MYERS
*National Association of Social Workers,
Washington, DC*
   Political Social Work

TONI NACCARATO
*University at Albany, State University of New York*
   Family Services

LARRY NACKERUD
*University of Georgia*
   Unemployment Insurance

PAMELA ANEESAH NADIR
*Arizona State University*
   Muslim Social Services

FLORENCE ELLEN NETTING
*Virginia Commonwealth University*
   Macro Social Work Practice

FRED NEWDOM
*ProAct Consulting Services, Albany, NY*
   Roosevelt, Eleanor

CHRISTINA E. NEWHILL
*University of Pittsburgh*
   Client Violence

PETER A. NEWMAN
*University of Toronto*
   HIV/AIDS: Overview

DORINDA N. NOBLE
*Texas State University–San Marcos*
   Children: Overview

BILL NUGENT
*University of Tennessee*
   Psychometrics

JOEY NUÑEZ ESTRADA
*University of Southern California*
   School Violence

PAULA S. NURIUS
*University of Washington*
   Cognition and Social Cognitive Theory
   Hudson, Walter W.

JULIA OCHIENG
*Virginia Commonwealth University*
   Advocacy

EDITH OLMSTED
*Independent Scholar, Brooklyn, NY*
   Hall, Helen
   Morris, Robert

JOHN G. ORME
*University of Tennessee*
   Single-System Designs

CARMEN ORTIZ HENDRICKS
*Yeshiva University, New York*
   Latinos and Latinas: Practice Interventions

KWAKU OSEI-HWEDIE
*University of Botswana*
   International Social Work and Social Welfare:
      Africa (Sub-Sahara)

SHIRLEY OTIS-GREEN
*City of Hope National Medical Center,
Duarte, CA*
   Health Care Social Work
   Saunders, Cicely

PHILIP M. OUELLETTE
*Indiana University*
   Social Work Education: Electronic Technologies

SANDRA OWENS-KANE
*University of Nevada, Las Vegas*
   Family Caregiving

MARTHA N. OZAWA
*Washington University in St. Louis*
   Income Security

THOMAS PACKARD
*San Diego State University*
   Organizational Development and Change

DEBORAH PADGETT
*New York University*
   Qualitative Research

RUTH PARIS
*Boston University*
   Human Needs: Family

YOOSUN PARK
*Smith College*
   Asian Americans: Japanese

RUTH J. PARSONS
*University of Denver*
   Empowerment Practice

LISA S. PATCHNER
*Ball State University*
   Disability: Neurocognitive Disabilities

DAVID A. PATTERSON
*University of Tennessee*
   Technology: Tools and Applications
      of Technology

GEORGE T. PATTERSON
*Hunter College, City University of New York*
   Police Social Work

RINO J. PATTI
*University of Southern California, Emeritus*
   Management: Overview

JUAN PAZ
*Arizona State University*
   Chavez, Cesar

DOROTHY M. PEARSON
*Howard University, Emerita*
   Scott, Carl A.

PETER J. PECORA
*University of Washington*
   Child Welfare: Overview

WILMA PEEBLES-WILKINS
*Boston University, Emerita*
   Barrett, Janie Porter
   Bethune, Mary McLeod
   Du Bois, William Edward Burghardt
   Fernandis, Sarah A. Collins
   Frazier, Edward Franklin
   Haynes, Elizabeth Ross
   Haynes, George Edmund
   Johnson, Campbell Carrington
   Lindsay, Inabel Burns
   Matthews, Victoria Earle
   Professional Impairment
   Terrell, Mary Eliza Church
   Thomas, Jesse O.
   Truth, Sojourner
   Tubman, Harriet
   Washington, Booker Taliaferro
   Washington, Forrester Blanchard
   Wells-Barnett, Ida Bell
   White, Eartha Mary Magdalene
   Wilkins, Roy
   Williams, Anita Rose
   Young, Whitney Moore, Jr.

KYLE L. PEHRSON, COL. USA RET.
*Brigham Young University*
   Military Social Work

ROBERT PERLMAN
*Brandeis University, Emeritus*
   Schottland, Charles Irwin

TRISTA D. PICCOLA
*Arlington County Human Services, Arlington, VA*
   Family Preservation and Home-Based Services

DEAN PIERCE
*University of Nevada, Reno*
   Federico, Ronald Charles

JOHN POERTNER
*University of Illinois at Urbana–Champaign, Emeritus*
   Management: Quality Assurance

WILLIAM L. POLLARD
*National Association of State Universities and Land-Grant Colleges (NASULGC), New York*
   Civil Rights

CAROLYN I. POLOWY
*National Association of Social Workers, Washington, DC*
   Confidentiality and Privileged Communication

ELIZABETH C. POMEROY
*University of Texas at Austin*
   Eating Disorders

DENNIS L. POOLE
*University of South Carolina*
   Voluntarism

DELANIE P. POPE
*Michigan State University*
   Child Support

PHILIP R. POPPLE
*University of Texas at Arlington*
   Social Services

JUDY L. POSTMUS
*Rutgers University*
   Sexual Assault

MIRIAM POTOCKY
*Florida International University*
   Immigrants and Refugees

ENOLA PROCTOR
*Washington University in St. Louis*
   Quality of Care

JEAN K. QUAM
*University of Minnesota*
   Abbott, Edith
   Abbott, Grace
   Addams, Jane
   Altmeyer, Arthur J.
   Barton, Clarissa (Clara) Harlowe
   Beers, Clifford Whittingham
   Brace, Charles Loring
   Breckinridge, Sophonisba Preston
   Brockway, Zebulon Reed
   Bruno, Frank John
   Buell, Bradley
   Cabot, Richard Clarke
   Cannon, Ida Maud
   Cannon, Mary Antoinette

   Coyle, Grace Longwell
   Day, Dorothy
   De Forest, Robert Weeks
   Devine, Edward Thomas
   Dix, Dorothea Lynde
   Dunham, Arthur
   Eliot, Martha May
   Manning, Leah Katherine Hicks
   Perkins, Frances
   Reynolds, Bertha Capen
   Wiley, George
   Youngdahl, Benjamin Emanuel
   Younghusband, Dame Eileen

IRENE QUEIRO-TAJALLI
*Indiana University*
   International Social Work and Social Welfare:
     South America

JUAN RAMOS
*National Institute of Mental Health, Rockville, MD*
   Galarza, Ernesto

MARK R. RANK
*Washington University in St. Louis*
   Poverty

JANICE M. RASHEED
*Loyola University Chicago*
   Family: Practice Interventions

MIKAL N. RASHEED
*Chicago State University*
   Family: Practice Interventions

ELOISE RATHBONE-McCUAN
*University of Missouri–Kansas City*
   Elder Abuse

MARY RAYMER
*Independent Scholar, Williamsburg, Michigan*
   Hospice

FREDERIC G. REAMER
*Rhode Island College*
   Ethics and Values
     Appendix: Ethical Standards in Social Work:
     The NASW Code of Ethics

DONA J. REESE
*Southern Illinois University*
   Hospice

WILLIAM J. REID (*deceased*)
*University at Albany, State University of New York*
Shyne, Ann Wentworth

P. NELSON REID
*University of North Carolina Wilmington*
Social Policy: History (1980 to Present)

JAMES R. REINARDY
*University of Minnesota, Twin Cities*
Konopka, Gisela

MICHAEL REISCH
*University of Michigan*
Lewis, Harold
Social Movements
Vigilante, Joseph

FRANK C. RICHARDSON
*University of Texas at Austin*
Humanistic Therapies

MARION REIDEL
*Columbia University*
Privilege

CHRISTINA RISLEY-CURTISS
*Arizona State University*
Human-Other Animal Bond

VICTORIA M. RIZZO
*Columbia University*
Medicaid and Medicare

CHARLES L. ROBBINS
*Stony Brook University, State University of New York*
Medical Illness

ALBERT R. ROBERTS
*Rutgers University*
Crisis Interventions
Mental Illness: Adults

MARIA ROBERTS-DeGENNARO
*San Diego State University*
Case Management

MARY E. ROGGE
*University of Tennessee*
Environmental Justice

VIRGINIA RONDERO HERNANDEZ
*California State University, Fresno*
Generalist and Advanced Generalist Practice

ANN ROSEGRANT ALVAREZ
*University of Hawai'i at Manoa*
Social Work Education: Multiculturalism

CATHERINE ROSENTHAL GELMAN
*New York University*
Aging: Racial and Ethnic Groups

FARIYAL ROSS-SHERIFF
*Howard University*
African Americans: Immigrants of
African Origin

KATHLEEN A. ROUNDS
*University of North Carolina at Chapel Hill*
Adolescents: Pregnancy

ALLEN RUBIN
*University of Texas at Austin*
Survey Research

BETTY J. RUTH
*Boston University*
Public Health

YEKUTIEL SABAH
*Israeli Ministry of Social Affairs and Hebrew University
of Jerusalem*
Organizational Learning

MARJORIE R. SABLE
*University of Missouri*
Reproductive Health

JON SIMON SAGER
*University of Southern California*
Social Planning

ROSEMARY C. SARRI
*University of Michigan, Emerita*
Juvenile Justice: Overview

BEATRICE N. SAUNDERS
*Fordham University, Emerita*
Bartlett, Harriett M.

HILLEL SCHMID
*Hebrew University of Jerusalem*
Contracting Out of Social Services

DAVID J. SCHNALL
*Yeshiva University, New York*
Jewish Communal Services

ROBERT L. SCHNEIDER
*Virginia Commonwealth University*
Advocacy

DICK SCHOECH
*University of Texas at Arlington*
Technology: Overview

ALVIN L. SCHORR
*Case Western Reserve University, Emeritus*
Mayo, Leonard Withington

TOBA SCHWABER KERSON
*Bryn Mawr College*
Human Needs: Health

FLORENCE Z. SEGAL
*Gateway Homes, Richmond VA*
Rothenberg, Elaine Zipes

STEVEN P. SEGAL
*University of California, Berkeley*
Deinstitutionalization
Self-Help Groups

UMA A. SEGAL
*University of Missouri–St. Louis*
Immigration Policy

FREDRICK SEIDL
*University at Buffalo, Emeritus*
Biographies: Introduction

MARGARET E. SEVERSON
*University of Kansas*
Crime and Criminal Behavior

GARY L. SHAFFER
*University of North Carolina at Chapel Hill*
Social Work Education: Field Work

BRADFORD W. SHEAFOR
*Colorado State University*
Organizations and Associations

WES SHERA
*University of Toronto, Emeritus*
International Social Work and Social Welfare:
North America

MARTHA A. SHERIDAN
*Gallaudet University*
Deafness and Hardness of Hearing

EDMUND SHERMAN
*University at Albany, State University of New York*
Shyne, Ann Wentworth

MICHAEL SHERRADEN
*Washington University in St. Louis*
Asset Building

MARGARET SHERRARD SHERRADEN
*University of Missouri–St. Louis*
Community Economic Development

CLAYTON T. SHORKEY
*University of Texas at Austin*
Gestalt Therapy

LAWRENCE SHULMAN
*University of Buffalo, State University of New York*
Supervision

KRISTINE SIEFERT
*University of Michigan*
Hunger, Nutrition, and Food Programs

JULIETTE SILVA
*San Jose State University*
Samora, Julian

SARAH SISCO
*New York City Department of Health and
Mental Hygiene*
Public Health

CAROLYN SMITH
*University at Albany, State University of New York*
Juvenile Delinquency

CARRIE J. SMITH
*Howard University*
Egypt, Ophelia Settle

NANCY J. SMYTH
*University at Buffalo*
Trauma

LONNIE R. SNOWDEN
*University of California, Berkeley*
Mental Illness: Service System

SUNG S. L. SOHNG
*University of Washington*
Community-Based Participatory Research

PHYLLIS SOLOMON
*University of Pennsylvania*
    Mental Health: Practice Interventions

MARY SORMANTI
*Columbia University*
    Bereavement Practice

TRACY M. SOSKA
*University of Pittsburgh*
    Housing

HALUK SOYDAN
*University of Southern California*
    Bogardus, Emory
    Carter, Genevieve
    Intervention Research

REBECCA L. SPERLING
*Marymount Manhattan College*
    Kenworthy, Marion Edwena

DAVID W. SPRINGER
*University of Texas at Austin*
    Rehabilitation

KAREN M. STALLER
*University of Michigan*
    Children's Rights
    Social Problems

LEE STAPLES
*Boston University*
    Community Organization

MARLYS STAUDT
*University of Tennessee*
    Mental Illness: Children

THEODORE J. STEIN
*University at Albany, State University of
New York*
    Civil Liberties

MARK J. STERN
*University of Pennsylvania*
    Social Policy: History (1950–1980)

DAVID STOESZ
*Virginia Commonwealth University and policyAmerica,
Alexandria, VA*
    Contexts/Settings: Corporate Settings

KAREN D. STOUT
*University of Houston*
    Marshall, Thurgood

VIRGINIA C. STRAND
*Fordham University*
    Single Parents

SHULAMITH LALA ASHENBERG STRAUSSNER
*New York University*
    Alcohol and Drug Problems: Overview

CALVIN L. STREETER
*University of Texas at Austin*
    Community: Overview

KIMBERLY STROM-GOTTFRIED
*University of North Carolina at Chapel Hill*
    Continuing Education

PAUL H. STUART
*Florida International University*
    Baldwin, Roger Nash
    Gurteen, Stephen Humphreys
    Rankin, Jeannette
    Social Work Profession: History

W. PATRICK SULLIVAN
*Indiana University*
    Disability: Psychiatric Disabilities

MARYANN SYERS
*Augsburg College, Minneapolis*
    Epstein, Abraham
    Fauri, Fedele Frederick
    Flexner, Abraham
    Follett, Mary Parker
    Frankel, Lee Kaufer
    Gallaudet, Edward Miner
    Gallaudet, Thomas
    Gallaudet, Thomas Hopkins
    Garrett, Annette Marie
    Granger, Lester Blackwell
    Howard, Donald S.
    Lenroot, Katharine Fredrica
    Lodge, Richard
    Rapoport, Lydia
    Schwartz, William
    Spellman, Dorothea C.
    Titmuss, Richard Morris

ZEBULON TAINTOR
*New York University*
    Psychosocial and Psychiatric Rehabilitation

JEANETTE C. TAKAMURA
*Columbia University*
  Aging: Public Policy

NGOH TIONG TAN
*Augsburg College, Minneapolis*
  International Social Work and
    Social Welfare: Asia

ABYE TASSE
*Addis Ababa University, Ethiopia*
  International Association of Schools of
    Social Work (IASSW)

PAUL TERRELL
*University of California, Berkeley, Emeritus*
  Workers' Compensation

WILLIE TOLLIVER
*Hunter College, City University of New York*
  Leashore, Bogart

RONALD W. TOSELAND
*University at Albany, State University of New York*
  Group Work

ELIZABETH M. TRACY
*Case Western Reserve University*
  Family Preservation and Home-Based Services

TONY TRIPODI
*Ohio State University, Emeritus*
  Research: Overview

MICHAEL UEBEL
*Independent Scholar, Austin, TX*
  Gestalt Therapy

KATRINA M. UHLY
*University of Minnesota*
  Leadership

YVONNE A. UNRAU
*Western Michigan University*
  Program Evaluation

CHARLES L. USHER
*University of North Carolina at Chapel Hill*
  Experimental and Quasi-Experimental Design

DOROTHY VAN SOEST
*University of Washington*
  Oppression

KATHERINE VAN WORMER
*University of Northern Iowa*
  Restorative Justice

VIKKI L. VANDIVER
*Portland State University and Oregon Health and Sciences University*
  Managed Care

MARIA VIDAL DE HAYMES
*Loyola University Chicago*
  Latinos and Latinas: Cubans

VERA VOGELSANG-COOMBS
*Cleveland State University*
  Strategic Planning

ERIC F. WAGNER
*Florida International University*
  Motivational Interviewing

JOHN M. WALLACE, JR.
*University if Pittsburgh*
  African Americans: Overview

JOSEPH WALSH
*Virginia Commonwealth University*
  Cognitive Therapy
  Psychoeducation

FROMA WALSH
*University of Chicago*
  Satir, Virginia

JUDITH A. WALTER
*Catholic University of America*
  Displaced People

KEITH WARREN
*Ohio State University*
  Chaos Theory and Complexity Theory

MONA WASOW
*University of Wisconsin–Madison, Emerita*
  Loeb, Martin B.

JULIA M. WATKINS
*Council on Social Work Education, Alexandria, VA*
  Council on Social Work Education

HILARY N. WEAVER
*University at Buffalo, State University of New York*
  Native Americans: Overview

ANN WEICK
*University of Kansas, Emeritus*
Davis, Liane V.

MARIE WEIL
*University of North Carolina at Chapel Hill*
Community: Practice Interventions

ADELE WEINER
*Metropolitan College of New York*
Gibelman, Margaret
Prostitution

TOBY WEISMILLER
*Independent Scholar, Silver Spring, MD*
Social Work Profession: Workforce

JOAN O. WEISS
*National Association of Social Workers,*
*Washington, DC*
Genetics

SUSAN J. WELLS
*University of Minnesota*
Child Abuse and Neglect

DAVID WESTHUIS
*Indiana University*
Social Work Education: Electronic Technologies

DARRELL P. WHEELER
*Hunter College, City University of New York*
Men: Health and Mental Health Care

JENNIFER WHEELER BROOKS
*University of Kansas*
Lesbians: Overview

TRACEY WHITAKER
*National Association of Social Workers, Washington, DC*
Social Work Profession: Workforce

BARBARA J. WHITE
*Gallaudet University*
Deafness and Hardness of Hearing

JAMES K. WHITTAKER
*University of Washington*
Children: Group Care

TRACI L. WIKE
*University of North Carolina at Chapel Hill*
Adolescents: Pregnancy

CONSTANCE W. WILLIAMS
*Brandeis University*
Dybwad, Rosemary Ferguson

JANET B. W. WILLIAMS
*Columbia University and MedAvante,*
*Hamilton, NJ*
Diagnostic and Statistical Manual of Mental
Disorders

SHEARA A. WILLIAMS
*University of Houston*
Violence

LARRY D. WILLIAMS
*West Chester University, West Chester, PA*
Baccalaureate Social Workers

TRINA R. WILLIAMS SHANKS
*University of Michigan*
African Americans: Overview

RICHARD WOLFF
*Independent Scholar, West Palm Beach, FL*
Migrant Workers

YIN-LING IRENE WONG
*University of Pennsylvania*
Homelessness

GAIL WOODS WALLER
*National Association of Social Workers,*
*Washington, DC*
Media Campaigns

JOSEPH M. WRONKA
*Springfield College, Springfield, MA, and*
*Universal Declaration of Human Rights Project,*
*Waltham, MA*
Human Rights

JOHN A. YANKEY
*Case Western Reserve University*
Strategic Planning

DIANE S. YOUNG
*Syracuse University*
Criminal Justice: Criminal Courts

FLORE ZÉPHIR
*University of Missouri–Columbia*
Haitian Americans

SHERYL ZIMMERMAN
*University of North Carolina at Chapel Hill*
   Adults: Group Care

JOAN LEVY ZLOTNIK
*Institute for the Advancement of Social Work Research, Washington, DC*
   Research: History of Research

# Index

Page numbers followed by an *f* or *t* indicate figures and tables. Page ranges in **bold** indicate main entries.

Asthma, 1:263
Astor, William Waldorf, 3:355
Asylum-seekers, 2:441, 2:448, 3:266
Asynchronous learning environments, 4:217
Atlanta Neighborhood Union, 4:72
At-risk youth. *See* Youth at risk
Attachment theory, 2:202, 3:95, 3:105, 3:118, 4:127
    in adolescent development, 1:8–9
    divorce and, 2:80
    human needs and, 2:407–408
Attempted suicide, 4:182
Attention deficit/hyperactivity disorder (ADHD),
        3:9, 3:469
Attributed needs, 2:400
Audism, 2:3
Audit trail, in qualitative research, 3:487
Augustus, John, 3:415, 4:68
Australia
    economic and political features, 2:500–501
    family preservation services in, 2:203
    progressive social work in, 3:435
    social conditions in, 2:501
    social policy and welfare services in, 2:501
    social welfare policy, 4:134
    social work education in, 2:490
    social work role in, 2:501–502
Australian Association of Social Workers, 1:326, 2:502
Australian Code of Ethics, 1:328
Austria, 2:512
Authenticity, as competency, 3:64–65
Authoritarian parents, 3:105, 3:118
Authoritative parents, 3:105, 3:118
Authoritative settings and involuntary clients,
        **1:182–184,** 1:251
Authorship, 2:155
Autism spectrum disorders, 2:45–46
Auto-ethnography, 3:486
Available Responsiveness and Continuity (ARC)
        model, 3:159
Average indexed monthly earnings, 2:465
*Avodah* (Jewish Service Corps), 3:7
Avon, 3:197
Ayllon, Teodoro, 1:189

### B

Baby, Think It Over program, 1:30
Baby Boomer retirement, 3:534
Baccalaureate Program Director's Association, 3:330
Baccalaureate social workers, **1:185–187**
    advance standing and, 1:187
    educational objectives, 1:185–186
    employment and profiles of, 1:186
    evolution of standards for, 1:185

    by gender and ethnicity, 1:186*t*
    licensing of, 1:186
Baccalaureate social work programs, 4:110–111
    accreditation of, 4:109
    advanced generalist practice and, 2:265
    faculty, 4:112
    field work requirements, 4:121
    licensure requirements, 3:89
    licensure structure, 3:88
    political intervention practica in, 3:375
    research education and, 4:131
Bachelet, Michelle, 2:523
Bacon, Francis, 2:37, 2:536
Badgett, M.V. Lee, 3:75
Baer, Donald, 1:189
Bahamas, 2:504
Bahrain, 2:514
Bailey-Dempsey, Cynthia, 4:198
Baitul Salaam Network, 3:284
Baker, Edith M., 3:193
Baker, Josephine, 3:192
Balanced and restorative justice programs, 3:15–16
Balanced Budget Act (1997), 2:320, 2:335, 3:145, 4:82
Balanced budgets, 3:168–169
Balch, Emily Greene, 1:61
Baldwin, Roger Nash, 4:320
Baldwin, Ruth, 4:72
Ball, Robert, 4:96
*Balsero* (rafters) crisis, 3:46–47
Banco del Sur, 2:523
Bancroft, Frank, 3:377
Bandura, Albert, 1:190
Bangladesh, 2:497
Banking, on Internet, 4:207
Baptist Orphanage, 2:169
Barbados, 2:503, 2:504, 2:505
Bardhill, Ray, 2:183
Barker, Roger, 2:38
Barnett, Samuel, 2:169
Barrett, Janie Porter, 4:72, 4:321
Bartlett, Harriet M., 2:261, 3:349, 4:321
Barton, Clarissa (Clara) Harlowe, 4:69, 4:321
Base, in budgeting, 3:169
Baseline
    in single-system design, 4:33
    in strategic planning, 4:170
Basic Center Program, for at-risk youth, 4:309
Basic needs model, 2:399
Bates, Arnold, 1:313
Batista, Fulgencio, 3:45
BATNA, 1:416
Battered husband syndrome, 3:206
Battering. *See* Domestic violence

mental health of, 4:285–286
physical maturation of, 1:4–5
policies and politics affecting, 4:286–287
poverty and inequality and, 4:282
practice interventions for, 4:290–296
retirement and, 3:535
sexual assault and, 4:284–285
Temporary Assistance for Needy Families and, 4:283–284
trends and challenges in, 4:287–288
victim services for, 4:257
women's status in the U.S., 2:217–218
Women, Infants and Children Supplemental Food program (WIC), 2:436, 2:437, 4:102
*Women and Madness* (Chesler), 3:224
Women as Resources Against Poverty, 4:20
*Women in Industry* (Abbott), 2:421
Women in Industry Service, 4:159
Women's Bureaus, 4:257
Women's Central Association of Relief on the Battlefield, 4:69
Women's clubs, 3:355, 3:376, 4:71
Women's health care, 4:299–302. *See also* Reproductive health
 age and ethnicity in, 4:301–302
 expenditures on, 4:300
 geography as factor in, 4:302
 guiding philosophy in, 4:299–300
 leaders in, 4:299
 leading causes of women's death, 4:301t
 maternal and child health, 4:299
 pregnancy and, 3:506–507
 in prison, 2:322
 sexual orientation as factor in, 4:302
 sources of care, 4:301
 utilization, 4:300–301
 women of color and, 4:301
Women's Health Equity Act (1991), 4:302
Women's International League for Peace and Freedom, 2:484, 3:341
Women's Peace Party, 2:484
Women's practice interventions
 appropriateness of, 4:291
 community approaches in, 4:292–293
 different methods of, 4:291
 group work, 4:292
 organizational approach in, 4:293–294
 societal issues impacting, 4:290–291
 therapeutic relationship in, 4:291
Women's Trade Union League, 4:54
Worden, William, 1:193
Word processing software, 4:219

Work. *See also* Employment
 as human need, 2:418–422
 interpersonal relationships and, 2:420–421
 low-level workers, job quality and, 2:421–422
 occupational social work, 3:311–319
 qualities of, affecting well-being, 2:419–421
 social work roles, 2:421
Work appraisals, 3:174–175
Worker protection, 2:121–122
Workers' compensation, **4:304–306**
Workers Protection Act, 3:266
Workfare, 2:520
Work first strategy, 3:317, 4:226
Workforce
 changes in, and occupational social work, 3:317
 defined, 4:164
 in social work profession, 4:164–168
Workforce Investment Act (1988), 2:109, 2:120
Workforce Investment Act (1998), 4:63, 4:264
Workforce preparation, 2:108–109
Workhouses, 4:67–68
Work Incentive Program, 2:120, 4:63, 4:100
Working memory, 1:333
Working mothers, 3:98
Working parents, 3:105–106
Work-life support, 2:421
Works Progress Administration, 2:121, 4:73
World Association for Psychosocial Rehabilitation, 3:459
World Bank, 2:480, 2:485, 2:508, 2:523, 4:36
World Congress of Gay, Lesbian, Bisexual and Transgender Jews, 3:77
World Health Organization, 2:411, 2:480
 disablement theory and, 3:500
 on disasters, 2:61
 on palliative care, 3:337–338
 on vision impairment, 1:207
World Medical Association, 2:151
World Social Forum, 3:439
World Vision International, 2:481
World War I
 military social work in, 3:270
 nativism during, 4:72
 pacifism and, 4:54
 social work during, 4:159
World War II
 gay identity formation during, 2:249
 Japanese internment during, 1:167, 1:300, 4:75
 military social work in, 3:270
 social work profession during, 4:160–161
Wright, Beatrice, 2:38
Wright, Frances, 3:72
Written contracts, 1:224